Directory of American Firms Operating in Foreign Countries

14th Edition

VOLUME 3

Alphabetical Distribution of American Corporations by Country

I-Z

A World Trade Academy Press Publication
Established in 1955 by Juvenal L. Angel

Uniworld Business Publications, Inc.
342 East 51st Street
New York, NY 10022

First Edition	1955
Second Edition	1957
Third Edition	1959
Fourth Edition	1961
Fifth Edition	1964
Sixth Edition	1966
Seventh Edition	1969
Eighth Edition	1975
Ninth Edition	1979
Tenth Edition	1984
Eleventh Edition	1987
Twelfth Edition	1991
Thirteenth Edition	1994
Fourteenth Edition	1996

Copyright © 1996 by
Uniworld Business Publications, Inc.

Published by
Uniworld Business Publications, Inc.
342 E. 51st St.
New York, N.Y.

ISBN: 0-8360-0041-2

Library of Congress Catalog Card Number: 55-39067

Manufactured in the United States of America

INTRODUCTION

Since it was first published in 1955, *Directory of American Firms Operating in Foreign Countries* has been an authoritative source of information on American firms which have subsidiaries or affiliates outside the United States. Designed to aid anyone interested in American business activities abroad, it is the only reference work of its kind. The directory has been used by public, university, business, government and special libraries, banks, accounting, brokerage and investment firms, manufacturers, transportation companies, advertising and personnel agencies, researchers, embassies and many governmental agencies dealing with commerce, trade and foreign relations.

This 14th edition contains more than 2,500 U.S. corporations with some 18,500 branches, subsidiaries and affiliates in 132 countries.

The Directory consists of three volumes:

Volume 1 lists, in alphabetical order, American firms which have operations abroad. Each entry contains the company's U.S. address and telephone number, fax number when provided, principal product or service, number of employees, and the foreign countries in which it has a subsidiary or affiliate. Some key personnel are noted. The titles President (P), Foreign Officer (FO) and Personnel Director (Per) used in this directory are meant to be generic and are assigned to the names given to us as the chief executive or operating officer, the person in charge of foreign operations, and the person in charge of human resources.

Volumes 2 and 3 contain listings by country–from Algeria to Zimbabwe–of the American firms' foreign operations. Each country listing includes, alphabetically, the name of the U.S. parent firm, its address, phone number and principal product or service, and the name and address of its subsidiary(ies) or affiliate(s) in that country. If a complete foreign mailing address is not given, inquiries should be directed to the U.S. address.

The overseas companies in this directory are those in which American firms have a substantial direct capital investment and which have been identified by the parent as a wholly or partially owned subsidiary, affiliate or branch. Franchises, representatives and non-commercial enterprises or institutions, such as hospitals, schools, etc., financed or operated by American philanthropic or religious organizations, are not included.

Source and Accuracy of Listings

In preparing this 14th edition, we have deleted firms which no longer maintain operations abroad or have been acquired by foreign companies, and we have added new listings. The primary sources of information were questionnaires mailed to and completed by the parent corporations, and/or annual reports provided by them. Direct telephone and telefax contact was used extensively for verification and clarification. Each firm in the last edition was sent an announcement of the new edition, along with a print-out of its previous entry, and asked to provide current data. It was stated that if we did not receive a response from a firm, and there was no evidence that it had gone out of business, the previous entry would be carried forward to this edition.

The aim of this directory is to provide accurate, up-to-date listings. However, the editor and publisher cannot guarantee that the information received from a company or other source as the basis for an entry is correct. In addition, the designations and listings are not to be considered definitive as to legal status or the relationship between the American and the foreign firms.

As extensive as this compilation may be, it does not claim to be all-inclusive. It contains only what has been disclosed to us. Also, in a directory of this scope some inaccuracies are inevitable. It would be appreciated if the reader noting such would inform us so corrections can be made in the next edition.

Acknowledgements

Our sincerest appreciation is extended to all the company representatives who cooperated so generously in providing information for this directory, and to everyone who assisted in its preparation.

Abbreviations Used in This Book

A/C . . . . Air Conditioning
Access . . . . Accessories
Adv . . . . Advertising
Affil . . . . Affiliate(d)
Agcy . . . . Agent/Agency
Agric . . . . Agriculture
Arch . . . . Architect(ural)
Assur . . . . Assurance
Auto . . . . Automotive
Aux . . . . Auxiliary
Bldg . . . . Building
Bus . . . . Business
Chem . . . . Chemical
Cir . . . . Circulation
Com. . . . . Components
Coml . . . . Commercial
Commun . . . . Communications
Conslt. . Consultant/Consulting
Constr . . . . Construction
Corp . . . Corporate/Corporation
Cust . . . . Customer
Dept. . . . . Department
Devel . . . . Development
Diag . . . . Diagnostic
Dist . . . . District
Distr . Distributor/Distribution
Divers . . . . Diversified
Dom . . . . Domestic
Econ . . . . Economics

Educ . . . . Education(al)
Elec . . . . Electric(al)
Electr . . . . Electronic(s)
Emp. . . . . Employee(s)
Engr . . . . Engineer(ing)
Envi . . . . Environmental
Equip. . . . . Equipment
Exch. . . . . Exchange
Exec. . . . . Executive
Exp. . . . . Export(er)
Explor . . . . Exploration
Fax . . . . Facsimile
Fin . . . . Financial/Finance
Fl. . . . . Floor
For. . . . . Foreign
Frt . . . . Freight
Furn . . . . Furniture
Fwdg. . . . . Forwarding
Gds . . . . Goods
Gen . . . . General
Hdwe. . . . . Hardware
Hos. . . . . Hospital
Hydr . . . . Hydraulic(s)
Imp. . . . . Import(er)
Ind . . . . . . Industrial/Industry
Inf . . . . Information
Ins . . . . Insurance
Inspec . . . . Inspect(ion)
Instru . . . . Instrument

Intl.	International	Prod.	Production
Invest	Investment	Prog	Programming
JV	Joint Venture	Pub(l)	Publisher/Publishing
Lab	Laboratory	R&D	Research & Development
Liq.	Liquid	Recre	Recreation(al)
Mach	Machine(ry)	Refrig.	Refrigeration
Maint	Maintenance	Reins	Reinsurance
Mat	Material	Rel	Relations
Mdse	Merchandise	Rep	Representative
Mdsng	Merchandising	Ret	Retail(er)
Meas	Measurement	Rfg	Refining
Med	Medical	Ry	Railway
Mfg	Manufacturing	Sci	Scientific
Mfr	Manufacture(r)	Serv	Service(s)
Mgmt	Management	Spec	Special(ty)/Specialized
Mgn	Managing	Sta	Station
Mkt	Market	Sub	Subsidiary
Mktg	Marketing	Super	Supervision
Nat	Natural	Svce	Service(s)
Oper	Operation	Sys	System
Orgn	Organization(al)	TV	Television
Pass	Passenger	Tech	Technical/Technology
Petrol	Petroleum	Tel	Telephone
Pharm	Pharmaceutical(s)	Telecom	Telecommunications
Plt	Plant	Temp	Temperature
Prdt	Product(s)	Trans.	Transmission
Prin	Principal	Transp	Transport(ation)
Print	Printing	Whl	Wholesale(r)
Proc	Process(ing)	Whse	Warehouse

Notes on Alphabetizing

Alphabetizing in this directory is by computer sort which places numerals before letters; and among names, places blanks, hyphens and ampersands before letters. Thus, 3D Co. precedes AZ Co., which precedes A-Z Co., which precedes A&Z Co., which precedes Abiz Co.

Names such as The Jones Corp., Charles Jones Inc., and L.M. Jones & Co. are alphabetized conventionally: all will be found under J.

Names which consist of initials only (e.g., LFM Co.) are in strict alphabetical order: Lewis Corp., LFM Co., Lintz Inc.

Mac/Mc names are found at the end of the M's: Mueller & Co., Myers Supply Inc., MacDougal Corp., McMurphy Electronics Co.

Table of Contents

ALPHABETICAL DISTRIBUTION OF AMERICAN CORPORATIONS
BY COUNTRY–"I" to "Z" 727-1412

INDIA

3M   3M Center, St Paul, MN 55144-1000, Tel: (612) 733-1110
(Mfr diversified prdts for industry, health care, imaging, commun, transport, safety, consumer, etc)
     Birla 3M Ltd., Jubilee Bldg., 45 Museum Rd., Bangalore 560 001, India

ADAMAS CARBIDE CORP   Market & Passaic St, Kenilworth, NJ 07033,
Tel: (201) 241-1000
(Metal prdts)
     Indicarb, 64 Palace Rd., Vasanatha Nagar, Bangalore 560 052, India

ALLEN-BRADLEY CO   PO Box 2086, Milwaukee, WI 53201, Tel: (414) 382-2000
(Mfr eletrical controls & info devices)
     Allen-Bradley India Ltd., C-11 Industrial Area, Site 4, Sahibabad,
       Dist. Ghaziabad 201 010, India

AMP INC   PO Box 3608, Harrisburg, PA 17105-3608, Tel: (717) 564-0100
(Devel/mfr electronic & electrical connection prdts & sys)
     AMP India Pvt. Ltd., Bangalore, India
     AMP Tools (India) Pvt. Ltd., Plot 44, Cochin Export Processing Zone, Kakkanad,
       Cochin 682 030, India

AMPHENOL PRODUCTS   1925A Ohio St, Lisle, IL 60532, Tel: (708) 960-1010
(Elect interconnect/penetrate sys & assemblies)
     Amphetronix Ltd., Plot 105, Bhosari Ind. Area, P.O. Box 1, Poona 411 026, India

ANALOG DEVICES INC   1 Technology Way, Box 9106, Norwood, MA 02062,
Tel: (617) 329-4700
(Mfr integrated circuits & related devices)
     Analog Devices Asian Sales Inc., 1A Church St., Bangalore 560 001, India

ARBOR ACRES FARM INC   439 Marlborough Rd, Glastonbury, CT 06033,
Tel: (860) 633-4681
(Producers of male & female broiler breeders, commercial egg layers)
     Arbor Acres Farm India Ltd., P.O. Box 73, Raipur Rd., Dehra Dun,
       Uttar Pradesh 248 001, India
     Getz Bros. & Co., 2 Brabourne Rd., Bombay 400 001, India

ARMSTRONG WORLD INDUSTRIES INC   PO Box 3001, Lancaster, PA 17604,
Tel: (717) 397-0611
(Mfr/mkt interior furnishings & spec prdts for bldg, auto & textile inds)
     Inarco Ltd., Bombay, India (all inquiries to U.S. address)

ASSOCIATED MERCHANDISING CORP   1440 Broadway, New York, NY 10018,
Tel: (212) 536-4000
(Retail service organization)

(cont)

Associated Merchandising Corp., 2/F World Trade Tower, Barakhamba Rd.,
New Delhi 110 001, India
Associated Merchandising Corp., 220 Backbay Reclamation, Nariman Point,
Bombay 400 021, India

ATWOOD OCEANICS INTL   PO Box 218350, Houston, TX 77218, Tel: (713) 492-2929
(Offshore drilling for gas/oil)
Atwood Oceanics Intl., P.O. Box 1511, Bombay 400 001, India

AUTOMATIC SWITCH CO   Hanover Rd, Florham Park, NJ 07932, Tel: (201) 966-2000
(Mfr solenoid valves, emergency power controls, pressure & temp switches)
ASCO (India) Ltd., 147 Karapakkan Village, Madras 600 096, India

BANDAG INC   2905 NW 61, Muscatine, IA 52761, Tel: (319) 262-1400
(Mfr/sale retread tires)
Indag Rubber Ltd., New Delhi, India

BANKAMERICA CORP   555 California St, San Francisco, CA 94104,
Tel: (415) 622-3456
(Financial services)
Bank of America NT & SA, DCM Bldg. 6/F, 15 Barakhamba Rd., New Delhi 110 001, India

BANKERS TRUST CO   280 Park Ave, New York, NY 10017, Tel: (212) 250-2500
(Banking)
Bankers Trust Co., 702 Dalamal House, Plot 206, Nariman Point, Jamnalal Bajaj Marg,
Bombay, 400 021, India
Bankers Trust Co., 202 Hotel President, Coffee Parade, Bombay 400 005, India

C R BARD INC   730 Central Ave, Murray Hill, NJ 07974, Tel: (908) 277-8000
(Mfr health care prdts)
Bard International, 53 Free Press House, 215 Nariman Point, Bombay 400 021, India

BENTLY NEVADA CORP   PO Box 157, Minden, NV 89423, Tel: (702) 782-3611
(Electronic monitoring system)
Sherman Intl. Pvt. Ltd., Himalaya House H-88, 23 Kasturba Gandhi Marg.,
New Delhi 110 001, India
Sherman Intl. Pvt. Ltd., 711 Maker Chamber V, 221 Nariman Pt., Bombay, 400 021,
India

BLACK CLAWSON CO   405 Lexington Ave, New York, NY 10174, Tel: (212) 916-8000
(Paper & pulp mill mach)
Black Clawson India Engineers Pvt. Ltd., 38/3 Mount Rd., Madras 600 006, India

THE BLACKSTONE GROUP INC   360 N Michigan Ave, Chicago, IL 60601,
Tel: (312) 419-0400
(Mktg research, business consult, engineering design & software)
The Blackstone Group of India, F-14 Upper Ground Floor, East of Kailash,
New Delhi 110 065, India
The Blackstone Group of India, AA 25 Anna Nagar, Madras 600 040, India
The Blackstone Group of India, 68/A, First Floor, Kunj Society, Alkapuri,
Baroda 390 005, India

BRANSON ULTRASONICS CORP   41 Eagle Rd, Danbury, CT 06813-1961,
Tel: (203) 796-0400
(Mfr plastics assembly equip, ultrasonic cleaning equip)
Nevik Sales & Services, P.O. Box 6840, Santa Cruz East, Bombay 400 055, India

BROWN & ROOT INC 4100 Clinton Dr, Houston, TX 77020-6299,
  Tel: (713) 676-3011
  (Engr, constr & maintenance)
    Brown & Root Intl. Inc., Taj Mahal Hotel, Apollo Bunder, Bombay 400 039, India
    Wharton Williams Taylor BV, 1111-B Raheja Chambers, Nariman Point, Bombay 400 021,
      India

BRY-AIR INC PO Box 269, Rte 37 W, Sunbury, OH 43074, Tel: (614) 965-2974
  (Mfr industrial dehumidifiers/auxiliary equip for plastics ind)
    Bry-Air India Pvt. Ltd., 20 Rajpur Rd., Civil Lines, Delhi, India

LEO BURNETT CO INC 35 West Wacker Dr, Chicago, IL 60601, Tel: (312) 220-5959
  (Advertising agency)
    Chaitra Advertising Pvt. Ltd., 9/11 N.S. Patkar Marg, Ardeshir B. Godrej Chowk,
      Bombay 400 036, India

CARL BYOIR & ASSOCIATES INC 420 Lexington Ave, New York, NY 10017,
  Tel: (212) 210-6000
  (Public relations, intl commun)
    Marketing Mix Group Ltd., 5 Lindsay St., Calcutta 700 016, India

CARBOLINE CO 350 Hanley Industrial Ct, St Louis, MO 63144,
  Tel: (314) 644-1000
  (Mfr coatings, sealants)
    CDC Carboline (India) Pvt. Ltd., 162 A Greams Rd., Madros 600 006, Tamil, Nadu,
      India

CARRIER CORP One Carrier Place, Farmington, CT 06034-4015,
  Tel: (203) 674-3000
  (Mfr/distr/svce A/C, heating & refrigeration equip)
    Carrier Aircon Ltd., Narsingpur, Kherki dhaula Post, Gurgaon, 12001 Haryana, India

CATERPILLAR INC 100 N E Adams St, Peoria, IL 61629, Tel: (309) 675-1000
  (Mfr earth/material-handling & constr mach & equip, engines, generators)
    Tractor Engineers Ltd., Saki-Vihar Rd., Powai, Bombay 400 072, India

CHASE MANHATTAN BANK N A 1 Chase Manhattan Plaza, New York, NY 10081,
  Tel: (212) 552-2222
  (Intl banking)
    Chase Manhattan Bank NA, New India Assurance Bldg., 87 Mahatma Gandhi Rd.,
      P.O.Box 1961, Bombay 400 023, India

CHEMICAL BANK 270 Park Ave, New York, NY 10017-2070, Tel: (212) 270-6000
  (Banking & financial services)
    Chemical Bank, 1008 Dalamal House 10/F, Nariman Point, Bombay 400 021, India

THE CHEMITHON CORP 5430 W Marginal Way, SW, Seattle, WA 98106,
  Tel: (206) 937-9954
  (Mfr/serv chem process equip for deterget, spec chem & power generation ind)
    Chemiton Engineers (P) Ltd., 317 Maker V, 221 Nariman Point, Bombay 400 021, India

CHEMTEX INTL INC 560 Lexington Ave, New York, NY 10022, Tel: (212) 752-5220
  (Mfr fibers & petrochemicals; engineering, procurement, contruction, construction
  mgmt)
    Chemtex Engineering of India Ltd., Chemtex House, Main St., Sector 12,
      Hiranandani Gardens, Powai, Bombay 400-076, India

(cont)

Thapar Chemtex Consultants Ltd., First Floor, B-1 Tower, Corporate Block,
   Golden Enclave, Airport Rd., Bangaloare 560 017, India

THE CHERRY CORP   3600 Sunset Ave, PO Box 718, Waukegan, IL   60087,
   Tel: (708) 662-9200
   (Mfr electrical switches, electronic keyboards, controls & displays, semiconductors)
      TVS Cherry Pvt. Ltd., 7B West Veli St., Madurai 625-001, India

CHESTERTON BINSWANGER INTL   Two Logan Sq, 4th fl, Philadelphia,
   PA 19103-2759, Tel: (215) 448-6000
   (Real estate & related svces)
      Chesterton Intl. plc, Bombay, India

CHEVRON CORP   225 Bush St, San Francisco, CA 94104, Tel: (415) 894-7700
   (Oil & gas exploration, production, refining, products; oilfield & financial services)
      Chevron Corp., all mail to U.S. address

CHICAGO PNEUMATIC TOOL CO   2200 Bleecker St, Utica, NY 13501,
   Tel: (315) 792-2600
   (Mfr air tools & equip)
      Chicago Pneumatic (India) Ltd., P.O. Box 7761, 201/302 L.B. Shastri Marg, Mulund,
      Bombay 400 080, India

CITICORP   399 Park Ave, New York, NY 10043, Tel: (212) 559-1000
   (Banking & financial services)
      Citbank NA, India

COLGATE-PALMOLIVE CO   300 Park Ave, New York, NY 10022, Tel: (212) 310-2000
   (Mfr pharms, cosmetics, toiletries, detergents)
      Colgate Palmolive (India) Pvt. Ltd., Steelcrete House, 3 Dinshaw Vacha Rd.,
      Bombay 400 020, India

COLUMBIA PICTURES INDUSTRIES INC   711 Fifth Ave, New York, NY 10022,
   Tel: (212) 751-4400
   (Producer & distributor of motion pictures)
      Columbia Films of India Ltd., 1/F Metro House, Mahatma Gandhi Rd., P.O. Box 390,
      Bombay 400 001, India

COMBUSTION ENGINEERING INC   900 Long Ridge Road, Stamford, CT 06902,
   Tel: (203) 329-8771
   (Tech constr)
      Combustion Engineering Overseas Inc., M-24 Greater Kailash 1, New Delhi 110 048,
      India

CORNING INC   One Riverfront Plaza, Corning, NY 14831, Tel: (607) 974-9000
   (Mfr glass & specialty materials, consumer prdts; communications, lab services)
      Samcor Glass Ltd., New Delhi, India

CPC INTERNATIONAL INC   PO Box 8000, Englewood Cliffs, NJ 07632,
   Tel: (201) 894-4000
   (Consumer foods, corn refining)
      Corn Products Co. (India) Ltd., Shree Niwas House, M. Somani Marg, P.O. Box 994,
      Bombay 400 001, India

CRAY RESEARCH INC   655 Lone Oak Dr, Eagan, MN 55121, Tel: (612) 452-6650
(Supercomputer systems & services)
  Cray Research (India) Ltd., c/o India/NCMRWF, Delhi Project Office,
    P.O. Box 3002 Lodi Rd., New Delhi, India

CUMMINS ENGINE CO INC   PO Box 3005, Columbus, IN 47202, Tel: (812) 377-5000
(Mfr diesel engines)
  Kirldskar Cummins Ltd., Kothrun, Pune 411 029, India

D'ARCY MASIUS BENTON & BOWLES INC (DMB&B)   1675 Broadway, New York,
NY 10019, Tel: (212) 468-3622
(Advertising & communications)
  Enterprise Advertising Pvt. Ltd., 4/F Pharma Search House, BG Kher Rd., Worli,
    Bombay 400 081, India

DANA CORP   PO Box 1000, Toledo, OH 43697, Tel: (419) 535-4500
(Engineer/mfr/mkt prdts & sys for vehicular, ind & mobile off-highway mkt & related
aftermarkets)
  Perfect Circle Victor Ltd., Magnet House, Narottan Morarjee Marg, Ballard Estate,
    Bombay 400 038, India

DATA CONVERSION INC   238 Main St, Cambridge, MA 02142, Tel: (617) 354-7424
(Software consult & contract programming serv)
  Patni Computer Systems Ltd., 303/304 Regent Chambers, Nariman Point,
    Bombay 400 021, India

DE ZURIK   250 Riverside Ave N, Sartell, MN 56377, Tel: (612) 259-2000
(Mfr manual, process & control valves)
  DeZurik-India Ltd., Plot 73, Industrial Estate, Perunguei, Madras 600 096, India

DEVLIEG MACHINE CO   Fair St, Royal Oak, MI 48073, Tel: (313) 549-1100
(Boring & milling machs)
  Alfred Herbert India Ltd., 13/3 Strand Road, Calcutta 700 001, India
  Precision Tooling Systems Ltd., P.O. Sattur, Dist. Dharwar, Karnataka 580 004, India

DIAMOND CHAIN CO   402 Kentucky Ave, Indianapolis, IN 46225,
Tel: (317) 638-6431
(Mfr roller chains)
  T.I. Diamond Chain Ltd., 11/12 North Beach Rd., Madras 600 001, India

THE DOW CHEMICAL CO   2030 Dow Center, Midland, MI 48674, Tel: (517) 636-1000
(Mfr chems, plastics, pharms, agric prdts, consumer prdts)
  Dow Chemical NV, P.O. Box 109, New Delhi 110 001, India
  IDL Chemicals Ltd., Kukatpally, Sanatnagar (I.E.), P.O. Box, Hyderabad 500 018,
    India
  Polychem Ltd., 7 Jamshedji Tata Rd., Churchgate Reclamation, Bombay 400 020, India

DURAMETALLIC CORP   2104 Factory St, Kalamazoo, MI 49001, Tel: (616) 382-8720
(Mfr mech seals, compression packings, auxiliaries)
  Durametallic India Ltd., 147 Karapakkam Village, Mahabalipuram Rd., Sholinganallur,
    P.O. Box, Madras 600 096, India

EASTMAN KODAK CO   343 State St, Rochester, NY 14650, Tel: (716) 724-4000
(Devel/mfr photo & chem prdts, info mgmt/video/copier sys, fibers/plastics for
various ind)
  India Photographic Co. Ltd., Kodak House, Dr. Dadabhai Naoroji Rd., P.O. Box 343,

(cont)

Bombay 400 001, India
India Photographic Co. Ltd., also in Bangalore, Calcutta, Madras & New Delhi, India

EG&G INC   45 William St, Wellesley, MA 02181-4078, Tel: (617) 237-5100
(Diversified R/D, mfg & services)
EG&G Sealol Hindustan Ltd., Bhupati Chambers 4/F, 13 Mathew Rd., Opera House,
Bombay 400 004, India
EG&G Sealol Hindustan Ltd., Survey 212/2, Sholapur Rd., Hadapsar, Pune 411 028,
India

ENERPAC   13000 W Silver Spring Dr, Butler, WI 53007, Tel: (414) 781-6600
(Mfr/sale high pressure hydraulic maint tools)
Enerpac Hydraulics (India) Pvt. Ltd., 203 Vardhaman Chamber, Vashi,
New Bombay 400-705, Maharashtra, India

ENTHONE INC   West Haven Industrial Park, PO Box 900, New Haven, CT 06516,
Tel: (203) 934-8611
(Metal finishing chems & equip)
Grauer & Well (India) Ltd., Sukh Sgar, Hughes Rd., Corner Chowpathy,
Bombay 400 007, India

EXPEDITORS INTL OF WASHINGTON INC   PO Box 69620, Seattle, WA 98168-9620,
Tel: (206) 246-3711
(Air/ocean freight forwarding, customs brokerage, intl logistics solutions)
Expeditors Intl. Service Center, Khasta 411, 50B Sainik Farms, Village Khirki,
Tehsil-Mehrauli, New Delhi 110 062, India

FIRST NATIONAL BANK OF BOSTON   100 Federal St, Boston, MA 02110,
Tel: (617) 434-2200
(Commercial banking)
Industrial Credit & Investment Corp of India Ltd., 163 Backbay Reclamation,
Bombay 400 020, India

GENERAL BINDING CORP   One GBC Plaza, Northbrook, IL 60062,
Tel: (708) 272-3700
(Binding & laminating equip & associated supplies)
GBC Hi-Tech (India) Ltd., A-216 Okhla Industrial Area Phase I, New Delhi 100 020,
India

GENERAL ELECTRIC CO   3135 Easton Tpk, Fairfield, CT 06431,
Tel: (203) 373-2211
(Diversified manufacturing, technology & services)
General Electric Co.,
all mail to U.S. address; phone (800) 626-2004 or (518) 438-6500

GETZ BROS & CO INC   150 Post St, #500, San Francisco, CA 94108,
Tel: (415) 772-5500
(Divers mfg, mktg/distr serv, travel serv)
Muller & Phipps (India) Ltd., Queen's Mansion, Amrit Keshav Naik Marg,
Fort Bombay 400 001, India

THE GILLETTE CO   Prudential Tower, Boston, MA 02199, Tel: (617) 421-7000
(Devel/mfr personal care/use prdts: blades & razors, toiletries, cosmetics,
stationery)
Indian Shaving Products Ltd., Rajasthan, India

THE GOODYEAR TIRE & RUBBER CO   1144 E Market St, Akron, OH 44316,
   Tel: (216) 796-2121
   (Mfr tires, automotive belts & hose, conveyor belts, chemicals; oil pipeline
   transmission)
      Goodyear India Ltd., 3/F Godreg Bhavan, Mathura Rd., New Delhi 110 065, India

W L GORE & ASSOCIATES INC   555 Paper Mill Road, Newark, DE 19711,
   Tel: (302) 738-4880
   (Mfr electr, ind filtration, med & fabric prdts)
      Garg Associates Pvt. Ltd., 5 Nai Abadi, Ghaziabad U.P., India

GREFCO INC   3435 W Lomita Blvd, Torrance, CA 90505, Tel: (213) 517-0700
   (Filter powders)
      Amoi Dicalite Ltd., Behind Haldervas Octroi Naka, Raknial Rd., Ahmedahad 380 023,
      India

GREY ADVERTISING INC   777 Third Ave, New York, NY 10017, Tel: (212) 546-2000
   (Advertising)
      Trikaya Grey, Phoenix Estate, Block 2-D, 3rd fl., 462 Tulsi Pipe Rd.,
      Bombay 400 013, India

GTE CORP   One Stamford Forum, Stamford, CT 06904, Tel: (203) 965-2000
   (Electr prdts, telecom sys, publ & commun)
      Sylvania & Laxman Ltd., 68/2 Najafgarh Rd., New Delhi 110 015, India

GUARDIAN PACKAGING CORP   6590 Central Ave, Newark, CA 94560,
   Tel: (415) 797-3710
   (Mfr flexible packaging materials)
      Guardian Plasticote Ltd., 12 Hochiminh Arni, Calcutta 700 016, India

HARIG MFG CORP   5757 W Howard St, Chicago, IL 60648, Tel: (312) 631-5050
   (Machine tools & dies)
      Harig India Pvt. Ltd., P.O. Mohan Nagar, G.T. Rd., Ghaziabad 201 007, India

THE HARPER GROUP   260 Townsend St, PO Box 77933, San Francisco,
   CA 94107-1719, Tel: (415) 978-0600
   (Ocean/air freight fwdg, customs brokerage, packing & whse, logistics mgt, ins)
      Circle Freight Intl. (India) Pvt. Ltd., Atlanta Tower, Sahar Rd., Sahar,
      Bombay 400 099, India
      Circle Freight Intl. (India) Pvt. Ltd., also in Ahmedabad, Bangalaore, Calcutta,
      Cochin, Delhi, Hyderabad, Madras & Pune, India

HECKETT   PO Box 1071, Butler, PA 16001-1071, Tel: (412) 283-5741
   (Metal reclamation, steel mill services)
      Ferro Scrap Nigam Ltd., P.O. Box 37, Bldgs. 54 & 56, Old BSP Admin. Office Complex,
      Bhilai, Madhya Pradesh 490 001, India

H J HEINZ CO   PO Box 57, Pittsburgh, PA 15230-0057, Tel: (412) 456-5700
   (Processed food prdts & nutritional services)
      Heinz India Pvt. Ltd., Bombay, India

HERCULES INC   Hercules Plaza, Wilmington, DE 19894-0001, Tel: (302) 594-5000
   (Mfr spec chems, plastics, film & fibers, coatings, resins, food ingredients)
      Herdillia Chemicals Ltd., Air India Bldg., Post Bag 9962, Nariman Point,
      Bombay 400 021, India

HEWLETT-PACKARD CO   3000 Hanover St, Palo Alto, CA 94304-0890,
  Tel: (415) 857-1501
  (Mfr computing, communications & measurement prdts & services)
     Hewlett-Packard India Ltd., Paharpur Business Centre, 21 Nehru Place,
        New Delhi 110 019, India

HOLIDAY INNS INC   3742 Lamar Ave, Memphis, TN 38195, Tel: (901) 362-4001
  (Hotels, restaurants, casinos)
     Holiday Inns Inc., Juhu Beach, Bombay 400 049, India
     Holiday Inns Inc. - India, Fatehabab Rd., Taj Ganj, Agra, India

HONEYWELL INC   PO Box 524, Minneapolis, MN 55440-0524, Tel: (612) 951-1000
  (Devel/mfr controls for home & building, industry, space & aviation)
     Tata Honeywell Ltd., 55-A/8 & 9, Hadapsar Industrial Estate, Pune 411 013, India

HORWATH INTL   415 Madison Ave, New York, NY 10017, Tel: (212) 838-5566
  (Public accountants & auditors)
     N.M. Raiji Co., Universal Insurance Bldg., Pherozeshaha Mehta Rd., Bombay 400 001,
        India
     P.K. Chopra & Co., N Block, Bombay Life Bldg., Above Post Office, Connaught Place,
        New Delhi 110 001, India

HOUGHTON INTL INC   PO Box 930, Valley Forge, PA 19482-0930,
  Tel: (610) 666-4000
  (Mfr spec chems, hydraulic fluids, lubricants)
     Houghton Hardcastle India Ltd., Brabourne Stadium, 87 Veer Nariman Rd.,
        Bombay 400 020, India

HYATT INTL CORP   200 West Madison, Chicago, IL 60606, Tel: (312) 750-1234
  (Intl hotel mgmt)
     Hyatt Intl. Hotels, New Delhi, India

IBM CORP   Old Orchard Rd, Armonk, NY 10504, Tel: (914) 765-1900
  (Information products, technology & services)
     TISL (JV), Golden Enclave, Airport Rd., Bangalore 560 017, India

INDUCTOTHERM CORP   10 Indel Ave, Rancocas, NJ 08073-0157, Tel: (609) 267-9000
  (Mfr induction melting furnaces)
     Inductotherm (India) Ltd., Ambli-Bopal Rd., Bopal, Ahmedabad 380 054, India

INGERSOLL-RAND CO   200 Chestnut Ridge Rd, Woodcliff Lake, NJ 07675,
  Tel: (201) 573-0123
  (Mfr compressors, rock drills, pumps, air tools, door hardware, ball bearings)
     Ingersoll-Rand India, Rhone-Poulenc House, S.K. Ahire Marg., P.O. Box 9138,
        Bombay 400 025, India
     Ingersoll-Rand India, 22/29 GIDC Estate, Naroda, Ahmedabad 382 330, India

INTERNATIONAL COMPONENTS CORP   420 N May St, Chicago, IL 60622,
  Tel: (312) 829-2525
  (Mfr/sale/svce portable DC battery chargers)
     International Components Corp. (India) Ltd., 3-A Kodambakkam High Rd.,
        Nungambakkam, Madras 600 034, India

INTERNATIONAL SYSTEMS & CONTROLS CORP   PO Box 2589wy, Houston, TX 77001,
Tel: (713) 526-5461
(Holding company)
 BS&B Safety Systems (India) Ltd., 147 Kara Pakakam Village, Madras 600 096, India

INTERRA TECHNOLOGIES INC   800 Tully St, #180, Houston, TX 77079-5420,
Tel: (713) 531-4040
(Geophysical & geographic info sys servs, software/dbase design & implementation)
 Interra Technologies (India) Pte. Ltd., Unit 32 SDFI, SEEPZ, Andheri East,
   Bombay 400 096, India

ITT CORP   1330 Ave of the Americas, New York, NY 10019-5490,
Tel: (212) 258-1000
(Design/mfr communications & electronic equip, hotels, insurance)
 ITT Far East & Pacific Inc., 17 Parliament St., New Delhi 110 001, India

ITT SHERATON CORP   60 State St, Boston, MA 02108, Tel: (617) 367-3600
(Hotel operations)
 Chola Sheraton, 10 Cathedral Rd., Madras 600 086, India
 Maurya Sheraton Hotel & Towers, Diplomatic Enclave, Sardar Patel Marg, 110 021,
   India
 Mughal Sheraton, Fatehabad Rd., Agra 282 001, India

JCPENNEY PURCHASING CORP   PO Box 10001, Dallas, TX 75301-0001,
Tel: (214) 431-5380
(Department stores)
 JCPenney Purchasing Corp., 139/T Juhu Rd., Santacruz W., Bombay 400 049, India

JOHNSON & JOHNSON   One Johnson & Johnson Plaza, New Brunswick, NJ 08933,
Tel: (908) 524-0400
(R&D/mfr/sale health care prdts)
 Johnson & Johnson Ltd., 30 Forjett St., Post Box 9301, Bombay 400 036, India

JOY ENVIRONMENTAL TECHNOLOGIES INC   10700 North Freeway, Houston, TX 77037,
Tel: (713) 878-1000
(Design/eng air pollution control & material handling sys)
 The Indure Pvt. Ltd., Indure House, Greater Kailash II, New Delhi 110 048, India

A T KEARNEY INC   222 West Adams St, Chicago, IL 60606, Tel: (312) 648-0111
(Mgmt consultants, executive search)
 A.T. Kearney Inc., all mail to U.S. address

KEYSTONE INTL INC   PO Box 40010, Houston, TX 77040, Tel: (713) 466-1176
(Mfr butterfly valves, actuators & control accessories)
 Keystone Valves, locations throughout India

KIRKWOOD INDUSTRIES INC   4855 W 130th St, Cleveland, OH 44135-5182,
Tel: (216) 267-6200
(Mfr elect components, commutators, mica insulation, slip rings, carbon brushes)
 Sahney Kirkwood Ltd., 27 Kirol, Vidyavihar West, P.O. Box 9222, Bombay 400 086,
   India

KROPP FORGE CO   5301 W Roosevelt Rd, Chicago, IL 60650, Tel: (312) 656-8558
(Carbon & alloy steel forgings)
 Shama Forge Co. Ltd., 14/F Connaught Place, New Delhi 110 001, India

THE KULJIAN CO   3624 Science Center, Philadelphia, PA 19104,
 Tel: (215) 243-1900
 (Studies, design, engineeering, constr mgmt, site supervision)
  Development Consultants Pvt. Ltd., 24-B Park St., Calcutta 700 016, India
  Development Consultants Pvt. Ltd., Nirimal, Nariman Point, Bombay 400 001, India
  Development Consultants Pvt. Ltd., Hamed Bldg., 193 Anna Salai, Madras 600 006,
   India
  The Kuljian Corp. India Pvt. Ltd., 307-309 Sahyog, 58 Nehru Place,
   New Delhi 110 019, India

LINTAS:WORLDWIDE   1 Dag Hammarskjold Plaza, New York, NY 10017,
 Tel: (212) 605-8000
 (Advertising agency)
  Lintas:India, Express Towers, Nariman Point, Bombay 400 021, India

ARTHUR D LITTLE INC   25 Acorn Park, Cambridge, MA 02140-2390,
 Tel: (617) 498-5000
 (Mgmt, environ, health & safety consulting; tech & prdt development)
  Arthur D. Little India Inc., Shelleys Estate, 30 P.J. Ramchandani Marg,
   Bombay 400 039, India

LOCKHEED MARTIN CORP   6801 Rockledge Dr, Bethesda, MD 20817,
 Tel: (301) 897-6000
 (Design/mfr/mgmt sys in fields of space, defense, energy, electronics, materials,
 info & tech svces)
  Lockheed Martin Intl. Ltd., 9 Jor Bagh, 1st fl., New Delhi 110 003, India

LOCTITE CORP   10 Columbus Blvd, Hartford, CT 06106, Tel: (203) 520-5000
 (Mfr/sale ind adhesives & sealants)
  Loctite India Pvt. Ltd., 38 Marol Co-op Ind. Estate, M.V. Rd., Saki Naka,
   Andheri (East), Bombay 400 059, India

THE LUBRIZOL CORP   29400 Lakeland Blvd, Wickliffe, OH 44092-2298,
 Tel: (216) 943-4200
 (Mfr chem additives for lubricants & fuels)
  Lubrizol India Ltd., Leo House, 4/F, 88-C Old Prabhadevi Rd., Bombay 400 025, India

MARATHON LE TOURNEAU CO   PO Box 2307, Longview, TX 75606, Tel: (903) 237-7000
 (Mfr heavy constr, mining mach & equip)
  General Marketing & Mfg. Co. Ltd., Birla Bldg. 14/F, 9/I R. N. Mukherjee Rd,
   Calcutta 700 001, India

MERCK SHARP & DOHME INTL   PO Box 2000, Rahway, NJ 07065, Tel: (201) 574-4000
 (Pharms, chems & biologicals)
  Merck, Sharp & Dohme of India Ltd., New India Centre, 17 Cooperage, Bombay 400 039,
   India

METAL-CLADDING INC   PO Box 630, 470 Niagara Way, North Tonawanda, NY 14120,
 Tel: (716) 693-6205
 (FRP tanks & custom constr, scrubbers, odor control equip)
  Fibreglass Mouldings Corp., 75C Park St., Calcutta 700 016, India

MICRO ABRASIVES CORP   720 Southampton Rd, Westfield, MA 01086-0517,
 Tel: (413) 562-3641
 (Abrasive powders,)
  Micro Abrasives (India) Ltd., 65 Jor Bagh, New Delhi 110 003, India

MICROSOFT CORP   One Microsoft Way, Redmond, WA 98052-6399,
  Tel: (206) 882-8080
  (Computer software, peripherals & services)
    Microsoft India, c/o Tata Unisys, Masjid Moth Com'l. Complex, Greater Kailash II,
    New Delhi 110 048, India

MILLIPORE CORP   Ashley Rd, Bedford, MA 01730, Tel: (617) 275-9205
  (Mfr precision filters, hi-performance liquid chromatography instru)
    Millipore (India) Pvt. Ltd., 50A, 2nd Phase Ring Rd., Peenya, Bangalore 560 058,
    India

MINE SAFETY APPLIANCES CO   PO Box 426, Pittsburgh, PA 15230,
  Tel: (421) 273 5000
  (Safety equip, ind filters)
    Mine Safety Appliances Ltd., P-25 Transport Depot Rd., Calcutta 700 088, India

MOLEX INC   2222 Wellington Ct, Lisle, IL 60532, Tel: (708) 969-4550
  (Mfr electronic, electrical & fiber optic interconnection prdts & sys, switches,
  application tooling)
    Molex Inc., Bangalore, India

MONMOUTH PLASTICS INC   PO Box 921, Asbury Park, NJ 07712, Tel: (201) 775-5100
  (Flame retardant concentrates, thermoplastic sys, spec formulations)
    Vanjundesbukira Enterprises, P.O. Box 6821, 21 Gundapath St., Bangalore 560 002,
    India

MOOG INC   East Aurora, NY 14052-0018, Tel: (716) 652-2000
  (Mfr precision control components & sys)
    Moog Controls (India) Pvt. Ltd., Plot 1, 2, 3 Electric City, Bangalore, India

MOORE PRODUCTS CO   Sumneytown Pike, Spring House, PA 19477,
  Tel: (215) 646-7400
  (Mfr process control instru)
    Moore Controls Pvt. Ltd., Bombay-Poona Rd., Kasarwadi, Poona 411 034, India

MOTION PICTURE EXPORT ASSN OF AMERICA   1133 Ave of the Americas, New York,
  NY 10036, Tel: (212) 840-6161
  (Motion picture trade association)
    MPEAA, 18D Rd., Maharani, New Delhi 110 065, India

MULLER & PHIPPS INTL CORP   Box 3994, San Francisco, CA 94119,
  Tel: (415) 772-5650
  (General merchandise)
    Muller & Phipps India Pvt. Ltd., Queens Mansion, Bation Rd., Bombay 400 001, India
    Muller & Phipps India Pvt. Ltd., P.O. Box 773, Bombay, India

McCANN-ERICKSON WORLDWIDE   750 Third Ave, New York, NY 10017,
  Tel: (212) 697-6000
  (Advertising)
    Tara Sinha Associates Pvt. Ltd., 15 Green Park Ext., New Delhi 110 016, India

THE McGRAW-HILL COS   1221 Ave of the Americas, New York, NY 10020,
  Tel: (212) 512-2000
  (Books, magazines, info sys, financial serv, broadcast operations)
    Tata McGraw Hill Publishing Co. Ltd., 12/4 Asaf Ali Rd., New Delhi 110 002, India

McNALLY PITTSBURG INC   100 N Pine, PO Box 651, Pittsburg, KS 66762,
Tel: (316) 231-3000
(Mfr/erection of coal processing plants & material handling sys)
   McNally Bharat Engineering Co. Ltd., Kumardhubi Dist. Dhanbad, Bihar, India

NALCO CHEMICAL CO   One Nalco Center, Naperville, IL 60563-1198,
Tel: (708) 305-1000
(Chems for water & waste water treatment, oil prod & refining, ind processes;
water/energy mgmt serv)
   Nalco Chemicals India Ltd., Suite 6, 20-A Park St., Calcutta 700 016, India

NATIONAL-STANDARD CO   1618 Terminal Rd, Niles, MI 49120, Tel: (616) 683-8100
(Mfr wire, wire related prdts, mach & med prdts)
   National-Standard Duncan Ltd., 19/F Commerce Centre 1, Cuffe Parade,
      Bombay 400 005, India

NORDSON CORP   28601 Clemens Rd, Westlake, OH 44145, Tel: (216) 892-1580
(Mfr ind application equip & packaging mach)
   Nordson Corp. South Asia Regional Office, #3 Ground Floor, Maya Apartments,
      Rd. #15, Chembur, Bombay 400 071, India

NORGREN   5400 S Delaware St, Littleton, CO 80120-1663, Tel: (303) 794-2611
(Mfr pneumatic filters, regulators, lubricators, valves, automation sys, dryers,
push-in fittings)
   Shavo Norgren India Pvt. Ltd., 78 Mittal Chambers, Nariman Point, Bombay 400 021,
      India

NORTON CO   1 New Bond St, Worcester, MA 01606, Tel: (508) 795-5000
(Abrasives, drill bits, constr & safety prdts, plastics)
   Grindwell Norton Ltd., Army & Navy Bldg., 148 Mahatma Gandhi Rd., Bombay 400 023,
      India
   Grindwell Norton Ltd., Devanahalli Rd., off Old Madras Rd., Bangalore, India

OCCIDENTAL PETROLEUM CORP   10889 Wilshire Blvd, Los Angeles, CA 90024,
Tel: (213) 879-1700
(Petroleum & petroleum prdts, chems, plastics)
   Intl. Ore & Fertilizer India Pvt. Ltd., 5/F 71 Nehru Place, Guru Angad Bhavan,
      New Delhi 110 019, India

OCEANEERING INTL INC   PO Box 218130, Houston, TX 77218-8130,
Tel: (713) 578-8868
(Underwater serv to offshore oil & gas ind)
   Oceaneering Intl. Inc., Operational base in Bombay

THE OILGEAR CO   2300 S 51st St, Milwaukee, WI 53219, Tel: (414) 327-1700
(Mfr hydraulic power transmission mach)
   Oilgear Towler Polyhydron Pvt. Ltd., Plot #4 R.S. #680/2,
      Belgaum Mfrs. Co-op Industrial Estate Ltd., Udyambag, Belgaum 590 008, India

OTIS ELEVATOR CO   10 Farm Springs, Farmington, CT 06032, Tel: (860) 676-6528
(Mfr elevators & escalators)
   Otis Elevator Co. (India) Ltd., Gateway Bldg., Apollo Bunder, Bombay 400 039, India
   Otis Elevator Co. (India) Ltd., Akurli Rd., Kandivli (East), Bombay 400 101, India

PFAUDLER CO   PO Box 1600, Rochester, NY 14692, Tel: (716) 235-1000
   (Mfr glass lined reactor vessels)
      Gujarat Machinery Manufacturers Ltd., Churchgate House, 32-34 Veer Nariman Rd.,
      Fort Bombay 400 001, India

PFIZER INC   235 E 42nd St, New York, NY 10017-5755, Tel: (212) 573-2323
   (Mfr healthcare products)
      Duchem Laboratories Ltd., India
      Dumex Ltd., India
      Pfizer Ltd., India

PHELPS DODGE CORP   2600 N Central Ave, Phoenix, AZ 85004-3014,
   Tel: (602) 234-8100
   (Copper, minerals, metals & spec engineered prdts for trans & elect mkts)
      Asian Cables Ltd., Great Mahal, 463 Dr. Annie Senant Rd., Worit, Bombay 400 025,
      India

PHILLIPS PETROLEUM CO   Phillips Bldg, Bartlesville, OK 74004,
   Tel: (918) 661-6600
   (Crude oil, natural gas, liquefied petroleum gas, gasoline & petro-chems)
      Cochin Refineries Ltd., Post Bag 2, P.O. Ambalamugal, Ernakulam District,
      Kerala 632 302, India
      Gujarat Carbon Ltd., Harikripa, Alkapuri, Baroda, Gujarat 390 005, India
      Phillips Carbon Black Ltd., Duncan House, 31 Netaji Subhas Rd., Calcutta 700 001,
      India
      Phillips Petroleum Intl. Corp., 1-A Vandhana Blvd., 11 Tolstov Marg,
      New Delhi 110 001, India

PILLAR INDUSTRIES   N92 W15800 Megal Dr, Menomonee Falls, WI 53051,
   Tel: (414) 255-6470
   (Mfr induction heating & melting equip)
      Pillar Induction (India) Pvt. Ltd., 2nd Ave., Block A-13, Anna Nagar,
      Madras 600 102, India

PNEUMO ABEX CORP   485 Frontage Rd, Burr Ridge, IL 60521, Tel: (708) 323-4446
   (Mfr aerospace & automotive friction materials & equip)
      Sundaram-Abex Ltd., 130 Mount Rd., Madras 600 060, India

PRECISION VALVE CORP   PO Box 309, Yonkers, NY 10702, Tel: (914) 969-6500
   (Mfr aerosol valves)
      Precision Valve (India) Pvt. Ltd., 228 Pragti (TODI) Ind. Estate, N.M. Joshi Marg,
      Lower Parel, Bombay 400 011, India

RADISSON HOTELS INTL   Carlson Pkwy, PO Box 59159, Minneapolis,
   MN 55459-8204, Tel: (612) 540-5526
   (Hotels)
      Radisson Hotels Intl., Bangalore, Goa, Kovalam, Mysore & New Delhi,
      India (inquiries to U.S. address)

RAYCHEM CORP   300 Constitution Dr, Menlo Park, CA 94025, Tel: (415) 361-3333
   (Devel/mfr/mkt materials science products for electronics, telecommunications &
   industry)
      Raychem Technologies (India) Pvt. Ltd., also in Madras & New Delhi, India
      Raychem (Delaware) Ltd., 2-C Jubilee Bldg., 45 Museum Rd., Bangalore 560 001, India
      Raychem Technologies (India) Pvt. Ltd., Ceat Mahal Annexe,
        463 Dr. Annie Basant Rd., Bombay 400 025, India

READING & BATES CORP   901 Threadneedle, #200, Houston, TX 77079,
  Tel: (713) 496-5000
  (Offshore contract drilling)
     Reading & Bates Exploration Co., Ashok Hall 2/F, S.V. Rd., Vile Parle (W),
        Bombay 400 056, India
     Reading & Bates Exploration Co., Bhavani Mansions 2/F, #3, 4th Lane,
        Nungambakkam High Rd., Madras 600 034, India

RMS GROUP INC   43-59 10th St, Long Island City, NY 11101, Tel: (212) 684-5470
  (Technology-transfer development & sales)
     RMS Projects Pvt. Ltd., 4 Arakash Rd., 1/F, Ramnagar, New Delhi, India

ROCKWELL INTL CORP   2201 Seal Beach Blvd, PO Box 4250, Seal Beach,
  CA 90740-8250, Tel: (310) 797-3311
  (Prdts & serv for aerospace, automotive, electronics, graphics & automation inds)
     Allen-Bradley India Ltd., C-11, Site IV, Industrial Area, Sahibabad 201 010,
        Dist. Ghaziabad, India
     Allen-Bradley.India Ltd., also in Bangalore, Bombay, Calcutta, Hyderabad,
        Jamshedpur, New Delhi & Pune, India

ROE INTL INC   217 River Ave, Patchogue, NY 11772, Tel: (516) 289-0500
  (Steel measuring tapes & tape rules, screwdrivers, nut drivers)
     Lal-Roe Measuring Tools Pvt. Ltd., 19 Church Bunder, P.O. Box 5075, Bombay 400 009,
        India

SALEM CORP   PO Box 2222, Pittsburgh, PA 15230, Tel: (412) 923-2200
  (Mfr ind furnaces, coal processing equip, metal finishing equip)
     Wesman Engineering Co. Pvt. Ltd., Calcutta, India

SCHENECTADY INTERNATIONAL INC   PO Box 1046, Schenectady, NY 12301,
  Tel: (518) 370-4200
  (Mfr elec insulating varnishes, enamels, phenolic resins, alkylphenols)
     Schenectady India Ltd., Plot 20, NS Road 9, Jvd. Scheme, Bombay 400 049, India

SCHERING INTL   PO Box 500, Kenilworth, NJ 07033, Tel: (201) 558-4000
  (Pharms, medicines, toiletries, cosmetics, human & animal health prdts)
     C.E. Fulford (India) Pvt. Ltd., Oxford House, Apollo Bunder, Bombay 400 039, India

SEA-LAND SERVICE INC   150 Allen Rd, Liberty Corner, NJ 07920,
  Tel: (201) 558-6000
  (Container transport)
     Sea-Land Services Inc., c/o Randip Shipping & Transport Co., Maker Tower East,
        Duffe Parade, Colaba, Bombay 400 005, India
     Sea-Land Services Inc., c/o Citibank NA, P.O. Box 175, Bombay 400 001, India

SEALOL INC   Warwick Industrial Park, PO Box 2158, Providence, RI 02905,
  Tel: (401) 781-4700
  (Mfr seals, joints, valves)
     Sealol Hindustan Ltd., Survey 212/2B, Shalapur Rd., Pune, Hadspsar, Poona 411 028,
        India

G D SEARLE & CO   5200 Old Orchard Rd, Skokie, IL 60077, Tel: (708) 982-7000
  (Mfr pharms, health care & optical prdts, specialty chems)
     Searle (India) Ltd., Ralli House, 21 Damodardas Sukhadvala Marg, P.O. Box 233,
        Bombay 400 001, India

SIGNODE PACKAGING SYSTEMS   3600 W Lake Ave, Glenview, IL 60025,
Tel: (708) 724-6100
(Mfr packaging systems)
   Signode India Ltd., Lulla Centre, 5 S.P. Rd., Begumpet, Hyderabad 500 016, India

SIMON & SCHUSTER INC   1230 Ave of the Americas, New York, NY 10020,
Tel: (212) 698-7000
(Publisher)
   Prentice-Hall of India Pvt. Ltd., 14-97 Connaught Circus, New Delhi 110 001, India

SPS TECHNOLOGIES INC   301 Highland Ave, Jenkintown, PA 19046-2630,
Tel: (215) 572-3000
(Mfr aerospace & ind fasteners, tightening sys, magnetic materials, superalloys)
   Precision Fasteners Ltd., New India Centre, 17 Cooperage Rd., Marahashtra,
     Bombay 400 039, India

SPSS INC   444 N Michigan Ave, Chicago, IL 60611, Tel: (312) 329-2400
(Mfr statistical software)
   SPSS UK Ltd., Ashok Hotel #223, 50B Chanakyapuri, New Delhi 110 021, India

STOKES DIV   5500 Tabor Rd, Philadelphia, PA 19120, Tel: (215) 289-5671
(Vacuum pumps & components, vacuum dryers, oil-upgrading equip)
   Pennwalt India Ltd., 507 Kakad Chambers, 132 Dr. Annie Besant Rd., Worli,
     Bombay 400 018, India

TEKTRONIX INC   26660 SW Parkway, Wilsonville, OR 97070, Tel: (503) 627-7111
(Mfr test & meas, visual sys & commun prdts)
   Hinditron Tektronix Instruments Ltd., Bangalore, Bombay, New Delhi, Calcutta,
     Madras, Pune, Ahmadabad & Secunderabad, India

TELLABS INC   4951 Indiana Ave, Lisle, IL 60532, Tel: (708) 969-8800
(Design/mfr/svce voice/data transport & network access sys)
   Tellabs Inc., Bangalore, India

THERMON   100 Thermon Dr, PO Box 609, San Marcos, TX 78667-0609,
Tel: (512) 396-5801
(Mfr steam & electric heat tracing sys, components & accessories)
   Thermon Heat Tracers Ltd., Thermon Bhavan, 30 Shivajinagar, Pune 411 005, India

TRANE CO   3600 Pammel Creek Rd, La Crosse, WI 54601, Tel: (608) 787-2000
(Mfr/distr/svce A/C sys & equip)
   Trane India Ltd., 604 Dalamal House, 206 Jamnal Bajaj Rd., Nariman Point,
     Bombay 400 021, India

TRINOVA CORP   3000 Strayer, PO Box 50, Maumee, OH 43537-0050,
Tel: (419) 867-2200
(Mfr engr components & sys for ind)
   Vickers Systems Intl., Unity Bldg. 8/F, Tower Block, J.C. Rd., Bangalore 560 002,
     India

U S WHEAT ASSOCIATES   1200 NW Front Ave, #600, Portland, OR 97209,
Tel: (503) 223-8123
(Market development for wheat prdts)
   U.S. Wheat Associates Inc., 902 New Delhi House, 27 Barakhamba Rd.,
     New Delhi 110 001, India

UNION CAMP CORP   1600 Valley Rd, Wayne, NJ 07470, Tel: (201) 628-2000
  (Mfr paper, packaging, chems, wood prdts)
    Bush Boake Allen Ltd., 1-5 Seven Wells St., St. Thomas Mount, Madras, India

UNITED CATALYSTS INC   1227 S 12th St, PO Box 32370, Louisville, KY 40232,
  Tel: (502) 634-7200
  (Mfr catalysts for petroleum, chem & food inds)
    United Catalysts India Ltd., 240 D Noroji Rd., Bombay, India

VANTON PUMP & EQUIPMENT CORP   Hillside, NJ 07205, Tel: (201) 926-2435
  (Mfr commercial & ind pumps, valves & accessories)
    Vanton Pumps (India) Pvt. Ltd., 1 Atco Colony Rd., Alandur, Madras 600 016, India

VARIAN ASSOCIATES INC   3100 Hansen Way, Palo Alto, CA 94304-1030,
  Tel: (415) 493-4000
  (Mfr microwave tubes & devices, analytical instru, semiconductor process & med equip,
  vacuum sys)
    Varian Intl. AG, 7 Community Centre, Basant Lok, Vasant Vihar, New Delhi 110 057,
    India

WACKENHUT CORP   1500 San Remo Ave, Coral Gables, FL 33146,
  Tel: (305) 666-5656
  (Security systems & services)
    Wackenhut (India) Pvt. Ltd., 45 Basant Lot, Vasant Vihar, New Delhi 110 057, India

WARNER-LAMBERT CO   201 Tabor Road, Morris Plains, NJ 07950,
  Tel: (201) 540-2000
  (Mfr ethical & proprietary pharms, confectionary & consumer prdts)
    Parke-Davis (India) Ltd., 254-B Nirlon House, Dr. Annie Besant Rd., Worli,
    Bombay 400 025, India

WEATHERFORD INTL INC   1360 Post Oak Blvd, PO Box 27608, Houston,
  TX 77227-7608, Tel: (713) 439-9400
  (Oilfield servs, prdts & equip; mfr marine cranes)
    Oilfield Eqmt. & Services Pvt. Ltd., Vaswani Mansions, Dinshaw Vachha Rd.,
    Bombay 400 020, India

JERVIS B WEBB CO   34375 W Twelve Mile Rd, Farmington Hills, MI 48331,
  Tel: (810) 553-1220
  (Mfr integrators of material handling sys)
    Webb India Ltd., Khaleel Plaza, 32/1 RV Rd., Basavanagudi, Bangalore 560 004, India

WHEATON INDUSTRIES   1101 Wheaton Ave, Milville, NJ 08332, Tel: (609) 825-1400
  (Mfr glass & plastic containers, plastic prdts)
    Vazir Glass Works Ltd., M. Vasenji Rd., Bombay 400 059, India

WHIRLPOOL CORP   2000 N M-63, Benton Harbor, MI 49022-2692,
  Tel: (616) 923-5000
  (Mfr/mkt home appliances)
    Kelvinator of India, New Delhi, India
    TVS Whirlpool Ltd., Madras, India

XEROX CORP   800 Long Ridge Rd, PO Box 1600, Stamford, CT 06904,
  Tel: (203) 968-3000
  (Mfr document processing equip, sys & supplies)

Modi Xerox Ltd., New Delhi, India
Xerox Corp., Rampur, India

INDONESIA

3COM CORP   5400 Bayfront Plaza, Santa Clara, CA 95052-8145,
  Tel: (408) 764-5000
  (Devel/mfr computer networking prdts & sys)
   3Com Asia Ltd., Indonesia

3M   3M Center, St Paul, MN 55144-1000, Tel: (612) 733-1110
  (Mfr diversified prdts for industry, health care, imaging, commun, transport, safety,
  consumer, etc)
   PT 3M Indonesia, Wisma Bank Dharmala 11/F, Jl. Jend. Sudirman Kav 28,
   Jakarta 12910, Indonesia

A L LABORATORIES INC   One Executive Drive, PO Box 1399, Fort Lee, NJ 07024,
  Tel: (201) 947-7774
  (Devel/mfr spec human pharms & animal health micronutrients)
   PT Dumex Indonesia, P.O. Box 1044/JAT, Jakarta 13010, Indonesia

A-Z INTL TOOL CO   PO Box 7108, Houston, TX 77248-7108, Tel: (713) 880-8888
  (Mfr oil field, milling & casing cutting tools)
   A-Z Intl. Tool Co, c/o P.T. Gema Supra Abadi, Bumi Daya Plaza,
   Jalan Iman Bonjol 61, Jakarta, Indonesia

AMWAY CORP   7575 E Fulton Rd, Ada, MI 49355, Tel: (616) 676-6000
  (Mfr/sale home care, personal care, nutrition & houseware prdts)
   PT Jasa Manajemen Amway, Wisma SSK, Jl. Daan Mogot KM 11, Jakarta Barat, Indonesia

ARBOR ACRES FARM INC   439 Marlborough Rd, Glastonbury, CT 06033,
  Tel: (860) 633-4681
  (Producers of male & female broiler breeders, commercial egg layers)
   PT Charoen Pokhpand Indonesia Animal Feedmill Co. Ltd., P.O. Box 83/JKT,
   Jakarta Kota, Indonesia

AVIS INC   900 Old Country Rd, Garden City, NY 11530, Tel: (516) 222-3000
  (Car rental serv)
   Avis Rent A Car System Inc., Jalan Diponegoro 25, Jakarta, Indonesia

BAKER OIL TOOLS   PO Box 40129, Houston, TX 77240-0129, Tel: (713) 466-1322
  (Mfr/serv oil/gas well completions equip)
   Baker Oil Tools, c/o PT Imeco Inter Sarang, 4/F, Jalan Ampera Raya Kav 10,
   Cilandak, Jakarta Selatan 12550, Indonesia

BANKAMERICA CORP   555 California St, San Francisco, CA 94104,
  Tel: (415) 622-3456
  (Financial services)
    Bank of America NT & SA, 17 Wisma Antara Bldg., Jl. Medan Merdeka Selatan,
    Jakarta 10011, Indonesia

BANKERS TRUST CO   280 Park Ave, New York, NY 10017, Tel: (212) 250-2500
  (Banking)
    Bankers Trust Co., Jl. M.H. Thamrin 59, Wisma Nusantara Bldg., 26th Fl., Jakarta,
    Indonesia

BECHTEL GROUP INC   50 Beale St, PO Box 3965, San Francisco, CA 94119,
  Tel: (415) 768-1234
  (Engineering & constr)
    Bechtel Inc., Jl. Thamrin, P.O. Box 460, Jakarta, Indonesia
    Pacific Bechtel Corp., Jl. Menteng Raya 8, P.O. Box 467, Jakarta, Indonesia

LOUIS BERGER INTL INC   100 Halsted St, East Orange, NJ 07019,
  Tel: (201) 678-1960
  (Consulting engineers, architects, economists & planners)
    Louis Berger Intl. Inc., P.O. Box 4312, Kelurahan Mampang, Jakarta 12043, Indonesia

SAMUEL BINGHAM CO   1555 N Mittel Blvd, #T, Wood Dale, IL 60191-1046,
  Tel: (708) 238-4000
  (Print & industrial rollers, inks)
    PT Kahardjaja, P.O. Box 2189, Jakarta, Indonesia

BRANSON ULTRASONICS CORP   41 Eagle Rd, Danbury, CT 06813-1961,
  Tel: (203) 796-0400
  (Mfr plastics assembly equip, ultrasonic cleaning equip)
    PT Ria Sarana Perdana Engineering, Jl. Bandengan Utara 83 L/M, Jakarta 14440,
    Indonesia

BROWN & ROOT INC   4100 Clinton Dr, Houston, TX 77020-6299,
  Tel: (713) 676-3011
  (Engr, constr & maintenance)
    PT Brown & Root Indonesia, P.O. Box 3030/JKT, Jakarta, Indonesia
    Sunda Straits Fabrication Yard, P.O. Box 3030/JKT, Jakarta, Indonesia

CARL BYOIR & ASSOCIATES INC   420 Lexington Ave, New York, NY 10017,
  Tel: (212) 210-6000
  (Public relations, intl commun)
    Travel Indonesia, P.O. Box 3651/JKT, Jakarta, Indonesia

CAMCO INC   7010 Ardmore St, Houston, TX 77021, Tel: (713) 747-4000
  (Oil field equip)
    Camco Services, 214 Melawai Raya 18, Keb. Baru, Indonesia

CARBOLINE CO   350 Hanley Industrial Ct, St Louis, MO 63144,
  Tel: (314) 644-1000
  (Mfr coatings, sealants)
    PT Pacific Paint, Jalan Gunung Sahari XI/291, Jakarta 10720, Indonesia
    PT Tirtajaya Segara, Jl. Hayam Wuruk 3T, P.O. Box 4228, Jakarta 10120, Indonesia

CARGILL   PO Box 9300, Minneapolis, MN 55440, Tel: (612) 475-7575
(Food prdts, feeds, animal prdts)
  Cargill Indonesia, P.O. Box 4345, Jakarta 1001, Indonesia

CBI INDUSTRIES INC   800 Jorie Blvd, Oak Brook, IL 60521, Tel: (708) 654-7000
(Holding co: metal plate fabricating, constr, oil & gas drilling)
  PT CBI Indonesia, Graha Puma Yudha Bldg., Rm. 1503, Jakarta, Indonesia

CENTRAL NATIONAL-GOTTESMAN INC   3 Manhattanville Rd, Purchase,
 NY 10577-2110, Tel: (914) 696-9000
(Worldwide sales pulp & paper prdts)
  PT Intersentral Nugraha, Wijaya Grand Centre Block H-18, Jl. Wijaya II,
    Kebayron Baru, Jakarta 12160, Indonesia

CHASE MANHATTAN BANK N A   1 Chase Manhattan Plaza, New York, NY 10081,
 Tel: (212) 552-2222
(Intl banking)
  Chase Manhattan Bank N.A., Jalan Medan Merdeka Barat 6, GPO Box 311, Jakarta,
    Indonesia

CHEMICAL BANK   270 Park Ave, New York, NY 10017-2070, Tel: (212) 270-6000
(Banking & financial services)
  Chemical Bank, Bumi Daya Plaza, 61 Jalan Imam Bonjol, Jakarta 10310, Indonesia

CHEMTEX INTL INC   560 Lexington Ave, New York, NY 10022, Tel: (212) 752-5220
(Mfr fibers & petrochemicals; engineering, procurement, contruction, construction
mgmt)
  Chemtex Overseas Inc., Level 12, Wism Bank Dharmala, Jl. Jenderal Sudiman Kav 28,
    Jakarta Selatan 12910, Indonesia

CHESTERTON BINSWANGER INTL   Two Logan Sq, 4th fl, Philadelphia,
 PA 19103-2759, Tel: (215) 448-6000
(Real estate & related svces)
  Pt. Chesterton Nusantara, Chase Plaza level 3, Jl. Jend. Sudirman, Kav. 21,
    Jakarta 12910, Indonesia

CHEVRON CORP   225 Bush St, San Francisco, CA 94104, Tel: (415) 894-7700
(Oil & gas exploration, production, refining, products; oilfield & financial services)
  Amoseas Indonesia Inc., all mail to U.S. address
  PT Caltex Pacific Indonesia, all mail to U.S. address

CIGNA CORP   One Liberty Place, Philadelphia, PA 19192, Tel: (215) 523-4000
(Ins, invest, health care & other fin servs)
  PT Asuransi Cigna Indonesia, The Landmark Centre 9/F-#901,
    Jalan Jen Sudirman Kav. 70-A, Jakarta 12910, Indonesia

CITICORP   399 Park Ave, New York, NY 10043, Tel: (212) 559-1000
(Banking & financial services)
  Citibank NA, Indonesia

THE COCA-COLA CO   PO Drawer 1734, Atlanta, GA 30301, Tel: (404) 676-2121
(Mfr/mkt/distr soft drinks, syrups & concentrates, juice & juice-drink prdts)
  Jakarta Coca-Cola Bottler, all mail to U.S. address

COMBUSTION ENGINEERING INC   900 Long Ridge Road, Stamford, CT 06902,
  Tel: (203) 329-8771
  (Tech constr)
    Gray Tool Intl., c/o P.D. Hasil Trading Co., P.O. Box 2135, Pasar Baru, Indonesia

CONOCO INC   600 N Dairy Ashford Rd, Houston, TX 77079, Tel: (713) 293-1000
  (Oil, gas, coal, chems, minerals)
    Conoco Irian Jaya Co., P.O. Box 367, Jakarta, Indonesia
    Continental Oil Co. of Indonesia, Five Pillars Office Park,
      Jalan Let. Jen. M.T. Haryono 58, Jakarta, Indonesia

CONTINENTAL CAN CO   PO Box 5410, Stamford, CT 06856, Tel: (203) 357-8110
  (Packaging prdts & mach, metal, plastic & paper containers)
    PT United Can Co. Ltd., Jalan Abdul Muis 12, Jakarta, Indonesia

CORE LABORATORIES   10205 Westheimer, Houston, TX 77042, Tel: (713) 972-6311
  (Petroleum testing/analysis, analytical chem, lab & octane analysis instrumentation)
    PT Corlab Indonesia, Bldg. 303 Cilandak Commercial Estate, JL Cilandak KKO,
      Jakarta, Selantan 12560, Indonesia

CORESTATES FINANCIAL CORP   1500 Market St, Philadelphia, PA 19101,
  Tel: (215) 973-3100
  (Banking)
    Corestates Bank, Bank Surya Bldg. #11-03, Jalan M.H. Thamrin Kav 9, Jakarta,
      Indonesia

CPC INTERNATIONAL INC   PO Box 8000, Englewood Cliffs, NJ 07632,
  Tel: (201) 894-4000
  (Consumer foods, corn refining)
    PT Knorr Indonesia, Wisma Bank Dharmala #1706, Jl. Jenderal Sudirman, Kav. 28,
      Jakarta 12920, Indonesia

CROWLEY MARITIME CORP   155 Grand Ave, Oakland, CA 94612, Tel: (510) 251-7500
  (Marine transp)
    PT Patra Drilling Contractor, Jalan Banka Raya 59, P.O. Box 12730, Jakarta Selatan,
      Indonesia

CROWN CORK & SEAL CO INC   9300 Ashton Rd, Philadelphia, PA 19136,
  Tel: (215) 698-5100
  (Mfr cans, bottle caps; filling & packaging mach)
    PT Crown Cork & Seal Indonesia, P.O. Box 3420/JKT, Jakarta, Indonesia

D'ARCY MASIUS BENTON & BOWLES INC (DMB&B)   1675 Broadway, New York,
  NY 10019, Tel: (212) 468-3622
  (Advertising & communications)
    PT Perwanal/DMB&B, Jl. Buncit Raya Penaten 28, Pasar Minggu, Jakarta 12510,
      Indonesia

DAMES & MOORE   911 Wilshire Blvd, Los Angeles, CA 90017, Tel: (213) 683-1560
  (Engineering, environmental & construction mgmt services)
    PT Environment Nusa Geotechnica, JL Tebet Barat IV #33, Jakarta 12810, Indonesia

THE DOW CHEMICAL CO   2030 Dow Center, Midland, MI 48674, Tel: (517) 636-1000
  (Mfr chems, plastics, pharms, agric prdts, consumer prdts)
    Pacific Chemicals Indonesia PT, Jl. M.H. Thamrin 59, Jakarta, Indonesia

DRAVO CORP   1 Oliver Plaza, Pittsburgh, PA 15222, Tel: (412) 777-5000
(Material handling equip, process plants)
    Dravo Pacific Inc., P.O. Box 3021/KBY, Jakarta Selatan, Indonesia

EXPEDITORS INTL OF WASHINGTON INC   PO Box 69620, Seattle, WA 98168-9620,
Tel: (206) 246-3711
(Air/ocean freight forwarding, customs brokerage, intl logistics solutions)
    Expeditors Cargo Management Systems, c/o PT Jangkar Pacific, Jl. Panggung 20,
    Suragaya, Indonesia
    Expeditors/PT Lancar Utama Tatanusa, Jalan Let. Jend. Soeprato 86A-B,
    Jakarta 10540, Indonesia

EXXON CORP   225 E John W Carpenter Freeway, Irving, TX 75062-2298,
Tel: (214) 444-1000
(Petroleum explor, prod, refining; mfr petrol & chem prdts; coal & minerals)
    PT Stanvac Indonesia, Jalan H.R. Rasuna Said, Sampoerna Plaza, Jakarta, Indonesia

FAIRCHILD CAMERA & INSTRUMENT CORP   PO Box 58090, Santa Clara,
CA 95052-8090, Tel: (408) 743-3355
(Mfr electr instru & controls)
    Fairchild Semiconductor Indonesia PT, Jl. Raya Bogor, P.O. Box 183/JKT, Jakarta,
    Indonesia

FELTON INTERNATIONAL INC   599 Johnson Ave, Brooklyn, NY 11237,
Tel: (212) 497-4664
(Essential oils & extracts, perfumes & flavor material, aromatic chems)
    C.V. Feltindo, 29A Jalan Kemuning, Jakarta, Indonesia

FIRST NATIONAL BANK IN DALLAS   PO Box 6031, Dallas, TX 75283,
Tel: (214) 744-8000
(Commercial banking)
    First Natl. Bank of Chicago, Jl. Lapangan Banteng Selatan, Jakarta, Indonesia

FLUOR DANIEL INC   3333 Michelson Dr, Irvine, CA 92730, Tel: (714) 975-2000
(Engineering, construction, maintenance & technical services)
    Fluor Daniel Eastern Inc., P.O. Box 4569, Jakarta 12045, Indonesia

FMC CORP   200 E Randolph Dr, Chicago, IL 60601, Tel: (312) 861-6000
(Produces chems & precious metals, mfr machinery, equip & sys for ind, agric & govt)
    PT Bina Guna Kimia, Indonesia
    PT FMC Santana Petroleum Equipment Indonesia, Indonesia

FREEPORT-McMORAN INC   1615 Poydras St, New Orleans, LA 70112,
Tel: (504) 582-4000
(Natural resources exploration & processing)
    PT Freeport Indonesia Co., Jl. Thamrin 59, P.O. Box 3148, Jakarta, Indonesia

FRITZ COMPANIES INC   706 Mission St, San Francisco, CA 94103,
Tel: (415) 904-8360
(Integrated transportation, sourcing, distribution & customs brokerage services)
    PT Fritz Ritra Intl. Transportation, Ritra Bldg. 3/F, J. Warung Buncit Raya 6,
    Jakarta 12740, Indonesia

GENERAL ELECTRIC CO   3135 Easton Tpk, Fairfield, CT 06431,
Tel: (203) 373-2211
(Diversified manufacturing, technology & services)

(cont)

General Electric Co.,
all mail to U.S. address; phone (800) 626-2004 or (518) 438-6500

GEORGIA-PACIFIC CORP   133 Peachtree St NE, Atlanta, GA 30303,
Tel: (404) 652-4000
(Lumber & paper prdts, metal prdts, chems & plastics)
Georgia-Pacific Indonesia PT, Jl. Prof. Kusuma Atmadja 83, Jakarta, Indonesia

THE GILLETTE CO   Prudential Tower, Boston, MA 02199, Tel: (617) 421-7000
(Devel/mfr personal care/use prdts: blades & razors, toiletries, cosmetics,
stationery)
PT Gillette Indonesia, Jakarta, Indonesia

GLOBAL INTERNATIONAL   1304 Willow St, Martinez, CA 94553, Tel: (510) 229-9330
(International moving & forwarding)
Global Transportation Services Group, Jl. Plaju 6, PO Box 3821/JKT, Jakarta,
Indonesia
PT Global Removindo Intl., Mampang Plaza, Jl. Mampang Prapatan Raya 100,
Jakarta 12760, Indonesia

GLOBAL MARINE INC   777 N Eldridge, Houston, TX 77079, Tel: (713) 596-5100
(Offshore contract drilling, turnkey drilling, oil & gas explor & prod)
Global Marine Inc., Jakarta, Indonesia

GOLDMAN SACHS & CO   85 Broad St, New York, NY 10004, Tel: (212) 902-1000
(Investment bankers/brokers)
Asian & Euro-American Capital Corp. Ltd. PT, Jl. Kebon Sirih 66-70,
P.O. Box 3259/JKT, Jakarta, Indonesia

THE GOODYEAR TIRE & RUBBER CO   1144 E Market St, Akron, OH 44316,
Tel: (216) 796-2121
(Mfr tires, automotive belts & hose, conveyor belts, chemicals; oil pipeline
transmission)
PT Goodyear Indonesia, P.O. Box 5, Jl. Pemuda 27, Bogor, West Java 16161, Indonesia

GREY ADVERTISING INC   777 Third Ave, New York, NY 10017, Tel: (212) 546-2000
(Advertising)
Rama & Grey Advertising, J. Sultan Hasanuddin 72, Jakarta 12160, Indonesia

GTE DIRECTORIES CORP   West Airport Dr, DFW Airport, TX 75261-9810,
Tel: (214) 453-7000
(Pub telephone directories)
PT Elnusa Yellow Pages, 77-81 Jl. R.S. Fatmawati, Jakarta 12150, Indonesia

FRANK B HALL & CO INC   549 Pleasantville Rd, Briarcliff Manor, NY 10510,
Tel: (914) 769-9200
(Insurance)
PT Bimantara Graha Insurance Brokers, Bimantara Bldg., Jl. Kebon Sirih 17-19,
P.O. Box 113/MT, Jakarta 1034, Indonesia

THE HARPER GROUP   260 Townsend St, PO Box 77933, San Francisco,
CA 94107-1719, Tel: (415) 978-0600
(Ocean/air freight fwdg, customs brokerage, packing & whse, logistics mgt, ins)
Circle Freight Intl., c/o Unipara Express, Jl. Kyai Caringin Blok A/6,
Jakarta 10150, Indonesia

HARVEST INTL INC   1155 Connecticut Ave NW, Washington, DC 20036,
  Tel: (202) 467-8595
  (Business consultants)
    PT Harvest Intl., Wisma Metropolitan I, 10/F, Jalan Jendral Sudisman KAV 29,
    Jakarta, Indonesia

HONEYWELL INC   PO Box 524, Minneapolis, MN 55440-0524, Tel: (612) 951-1000
  (Devel/mfr controls for home & building, industry, space & aviation)
    Honeywell Pte. Ltd., Wisma Abadi, Jalan Kyai Caringin 29-31, Room B4-b, 3rd fl.,
    Jakarta Pusat 10160, Indonesia

HORWATH INTL   415 Madison Ave, New York, NY 10017, Tel: (212) 838-5566
  (Public accountants & auditors)
    Drs. D.L. Pamintori S. & Rekan, Wisma Sejahtera, #1C & #1E,
    Jalan Let. Jend.S.Parman Kav.75, Jakarta Barat 11410, Indonesia

HYATT INTL CORP   200 West Madison, Chicago, IL 60606, Tel: (312) 750-1234
  (Intl hotel mgmt)
    Hyatt Intl. Hotels, Bali, Jakarta & Surabaya, Indonesia

IBM CORP   Old Orchard Rd, Armonk, NY 10504, Tel: (914) 765-1900
  (Information products, technology & services)
    IBM Indonesia PT, 5 Jim H. Thamrin, Jakarta, Indonesia

IMCO SERVICES   5950 N Course Dr, Houston, TX 70072, Tel: (713) 561-1300
  (Drilling fluids)
    IMCO Services Indonesia PT, Setiabudi Bldg. 1, H.R. Rasuma Said 62, P.O. Box 3033,
    Jakarta, Indonesia

INTERNATIONAL FLAVORS & FRAGRANCES INC   521 W 57th St, New York, NY 10019,
  Tel: (212) 765-5500
  (Create/mfr flavors, fragrances & aroma chems)
    Essence Indonesia PT, Jl. Oto Iskandardinata 74, P.O. Box 3008/DKT, Jakarta,
    Indonesia

ITT CORP   1330 Ave of the Americas, New York, NY 10019-5490,
  Tel: (212) 258-1000
  (Design/mfr communications & electronic equip, hotels, insurance)
    ITT Far East & Pacific Inc., Jl. Gondangdia Lama 26, Menteng, P.O. Box 2401,
    Jakarta, Indonesia

JOHNSON & HIGGINS   125 Broad St, New York, NY 10004-2424, Tel: (212) 574-7000
  (Ins brokerage, employee benefit conslt, risk mgmt, human resource conslt, ins/reins
  servs)
    PT ATAP INDAH, Jakarta, Indonesia

JOHNSON & JOHNSON   One Johnson & Johnson Plaza, New Brunswick, NJ 08933,
  Tel: (908) 524-0400
  (R&D/mfr/sale health care prdts)
    Janssen Pharmaceutica, Jakarta, Indonesia
    Johnson & Johnson Indonesia PT, P.O. Box 3200, Jakarta, Indonesia

S C JOHNSON & SON INC   1525 Howe St, Racine, WI 53403, Tel: (414) 631-2000
  (Home, auto, commercial & personal care prdts, specialty chems)
    PT S.C. Johnson & Son Indonesia Ltd., Jl. Pasar Minggu Km. 18, P.O. Box 41/JNG,
    Jakarta, Indonesia

A T KEARNEY INC   222 West Adams St, Chicago, IL 60606, Tel: (312) 648-0111
   (Mgmt consultants, executive search)
      A.T. Kearney Inc., all mail to U.S. address

THE M W KELLOGG CO   601 Jefferson Ave, Houston, TX 77002, Tel: (713) 753-2000
   (Design, engr, procurement & constr for process & energy ind)
      W. M. Kellogg Co., Wisma Kosgoro 15/F, 53 JL. M.H. Thamrin, Jakarta Pusat, Indonesia

KIMBERLY-CLARK CORP   PO Box 619100, Dallas, TX 75261, Tel: (214) 281-1200
   (Mfr fiber-based prdts for personal care, lumber & paper prdts)
      PT Kimsari Paper Indonesia, Medan, Indonesia

LINTAS:WORLDWIDE   1 Dag Hammarskjold Plaza, New York, NY 10017,
   Tel: (212) 605-8000
   (Advertising agency)
      PT Citra:Lintas Indonesia, Wisma Metropolitan II/15F, Jl. Jendr. Sudirman 31,
         Jakarta 12920, Indonesia

MARATHON OIL CO   539 S Main St, Findlay, OH 45840, Tel: (419) 422-2121
   (Petroleum explor & prod)
      Marathon Petroleum Indonesia Ltd., P.O. Box 3293, Jakarta, Indonesia

MILCHEM INC   3900 Essex Lane, PO Box 22111, Houston, TX 77027,
   Tel: (214) 439-8000
   (Gas & oil well drilling fluids & chem additives)
      PT Milchem Indonesia, D-5 Setiabudi Bldg., Jl. H.R. Rasuna Said 62, Kuningan,
         Jakarta Selatan, Indonesia

MORGAN GUARANTY TRUST CO   23 Wall St, New York, NY 10260, Tel: (212) 483-2323
   (Banking)
      Morgan Guaranty Trust Co., Wisma Stephens, 88 Jalan Raja Chulan (05-12), Jakarta,
         Indonesia

McCANN-ERICKSON WORLDWIDE   750 Third Ave, New York, NY 10017,
   Tel: (212) 697-6000
   (Advertising)
      Grafik Advertising, Jalan Riau 17, Jakarta, Indonesia

McDERMOTT INTL INC   1450 Poydras St, PO Box 60035, New Orleans,
   LA 70160-0035, Tel: (504) 587-5400
   (Engineering & construction)
      PT McDermott Indonesia, Landmark Tower, P.O. Box 14281/JKT, Jl. Jend,
         Sudirman Kav. 70A, Jakarta, Indonesia

NALCO CHEMICAL CO   One Nalco Center, Naperville, IL 60563-1198,
   Tel: (708) 305-1000
   (Chems for water & waste water treatment, oil prod & refining, ind processes;
   water/energy mgmt serv)
      PT Nalco Perkasa, c/o P.T. Astenia-Napan, Wisma Indocement,
         Jl. Jend Sudirman Kav. 70-71, Jakarta 12910, Indonesia

NATIONAL STARCH & CHEMICAL CO   10 Finderne Ave, Bridgewater, NJ 08807-3300,
   Tel: (908) 685-5000
   (Mfr adhesives & sealants, resins & spec chems, electr materials & adhesives, food
   prdts, ind starch)
      PT Danako Mitra Adhesives, Jakarta, Indonesia

NEWMONT GOLD CORP   1700 Lincoln St, Denver, CO 80203, Tel: (303) 863-7414
  (Gold mining)
    PT Newmont Minahasa Raya, Atria Square 14th fl., Jl. Jend. Sudirman Kav. 334,
      Jakarta 10220, Indonesia
    PT Newmont Nusa Tanggara, Atria Square 14th fl., Jl. Jend. Sudirman Kav. 334,
      Jakarta 10220, Indonesia

OCEANEERING INTL INC   PO Box 218130, Houston, TX 77218-8130,
  Tel: (713) 578-8868
  (Underwater serv to offshore oil & gas ind)
    Oceaneering Intl. Inc., Operational bases in Balikpapan & Jakarta

OSMONICS INC   5951 Clearwater Dr, Minnetonka, MN 55343-8995,
  Tel: (612) 933-2277
  (Mfr fluid filtration & separation equip & components)
    Osmonics Indonesia, c/o PT Sembada Perdana Insan, Jl. Taman Tanah Abang 111 #19,
      Jakarta 10160, Indonesia

OTIS ELEVATOR CO   10 Farm Springs, Farmington, CT 06032, Tel: (860) 676-6528
  (Mfr elevators & escalators)
    P.T. Citas Otis Elevator, Jalan Sultan Hasanuddin 56, Jakarta 12160, Indonesia

PARKER DRILLING CO   8 E Third St, Tulsa, OK 74103-3637, Tel: (918) 585-8221
  (Drilling contractor)
    Parker Drilling Co. of Indonesia-PT Dati, Jalan Sultan Hasanuddin 28,
      Kebayoran Bara, Jakarta 12160, Indonesia
    Parker Drilling Co. of Indonesia-PT Sebina, Griya Ampera Bldg., Jl. Ampera Raya 18,
      Kemang, Jakarta, Indonesia

PARSONS DE LEUW INC   1133 15th St NW, Washington, DC 20005,
  Tel: (202) 775-3300
  (Consulting engineers)
    De Leuw Cather Intl. Ltd., P.O. Box 36, Ujung Berung, Bandung, West Java, Indonesia

PARSONS ENGINEERING SCIENCE INC   100 W Walnut St, Pasadena, CA 91124,
  Tel: (818) 440-6000
  (Environmental engineering)
    Parsons Engineering Science Inc., Jl Prapen Indah II/F2, Surabaya 60299, Indonesia

PETROLITE CORP   369 Marshall Ave, St Louis, MO 63119-1897,
  Tel: (314) 961-3500
  (Mfr/prod spec chem treating programs, performance-enhancing additives & related
  equip & svces)
    PT Petrolite Indonesia Pratama, Batu Ampar, Pulua Batam, Indonesia

PFIZER INC   235 E 42nd St, New York, NY 10017-5755, Tel: (212) 573-2323
  (Mfr healthcare products)
    PT Pfizer Indonesia, Indonesia

PHILLIPS PETROLEUM CO   Phillips Bldg, Bartlesville, OK 74004,
  Tel: (918) 661-6600
  (Crude oil, natural gas, liquefied petroleum gas, gasoline & petro-chems)
    Phillips Petroleum Co. Indonesia, Jl. Melawai Raya No. 16, Keb. Baru, Jakarta,
      Indonesia

READING & BATES CORP   901 Threadneedle, #200, Houston, TX   77079,
  Tel: (713) 496-5000
  (Offshore contract drilling)
    Reading & Bates Exploration Co., Jalan Pupuk 44, Balikpapan, East Kalimantan 76114,
    Indonesia
    Reading & Bates Exploration Co., c/o PT Bosara Mulia, Tifa Bldg. #706,
    Jl. Kuningan Barat 26, Jakarta, Indonesia

THE RENDON GROUP INC   2000 S St. NW, Washington, DC   20009,
  Tel: (202) 745-4900
  (Public relations, print & video production, strategic communicaitons)
    PT TRG, Plaza 89, 4th fl., Suite 407, Jl. H.R. Rasuna Said 4-7, Jakarta 12940,
    Indonesia

THE ROCKPORT CO   220 Donald J Lynch Blvd, Marlboro, MA   01752,
  Tel: (508) 485-2090
  (Mfr/imp dress & casual footwear)
    Rockport Indonesia, Jl. Kapten Tendean 1, 4/F, Jakarta 12710, Indonesia

ROHM AND HAAS CO   100 Independence Mall West, Philadelphia, PA   19106,
  Tel: (215) 592-3000
  (Mfr ind & agric chems, plastics)
    Rohm and Haas Asia Inc., Summitmas Tower, 4th Fl., JL Jend. Sudirman Kav 61-62,
    Jakarta 12190, Indonesia

ROWAN COMPANIES INC   2800 Post Oak Blvd, Houston, TX   77056-6196,
  Tel: (713) 621-7800
  (Contract drilling & air charter service)
    Rowan Intl. Inc., Jl. Letjen M.T. Haryono 58, Pancoran, Jakarta, Indonesia

SONAT OFFSHORE DRILLING INC   PO Box 2765, Houston, TX   77252-2765,
  Tel: (713) 871-7500
  (Offshore oil well drilling)
    Sonat Offshore Drilling, P.T. Unimas Motor Wasta, 3F Wisma Metropolitan,
    Jl. Jeno. Sudirman Kav. 24, Jakarta 12920, Indonesia

STANDARD OIL CO OF CALIFORNIA   225 Bush St, San Francisco, CA   94104,
  Tel: (415) 894-7700
  (Oil explor & prod, petroleum prdts)
    Caltex Pacific Indonesia PT, Jl. Thamrin, P.O. Box 158, Jakarta, Indonesia

STONE & WEBSTER ENGINEERING CORP   245 Summer St, Boston, MA   02210-2288,
  Tel: (617) 589-5111
  (Engineering, constr & environmental & mgmt services)
    Stone & Webster Canada Ltd., Central Plaza Bldg. 16/F, 47 Jl Jenderal Sudirman,
    Jakarta 12190, Indonesia

STV GROUP   11 Robinson St, PO Box 459, Pottstown, PA   19464-0459,
  Tel: (215) 326-4600
  (Engineering, architectural, planning, environmental & construction mgmt services)
    STV Inc., Jl Mampang Propatan 15/#1, Jakarta 12790, Indonesia

TENNESSEE ASSOCIATES INTL   223 Associates Blvd, PO Box 710, Alcoa,
  TN 37701-0710, Tel: (423) 982-9514
  (Mgt consulting servs)

TAI Indonesia, Suite 4A, 21F Setiabudi Bldg. 1, Jl. H.R. Rasuna Said, Kuningan,
   12920 Jakarta Selatan, Indonesia

TEXACO INC   2000 Westchester Ave, White Plains, NY 10650, Tel: (914) 253-4000
   (Explor/mktg crude oil, mfr petro chems & prdts)
      PT Caltex Pacific Indonesia, Jl. Kebon Sirih 52, Jakarta, Java, Indonesia

TIDEWATER INC   Tidewater Place, 1440 Canal St, New Orleans, LA 70112,
   Tel: (504) 568-1010
   (Marine serv & equip to companies engaged in explor, development & prod of oil, gas &
   minerals)
      Tidex Intl. Inc., Jalan Mesjid I 32, Jakarta Seratan 12001, Indonesia

TRANE CO   3600 Pammel Creek Rd, La Crosse, WI 54601, Tel: (608) 787-2000
   (Mfr/distr/svce A/C sys & equip)
      PT Tatasol Pratama, Jalan Abdul Muis 24-26, Jakarta Pusat 10160, Indonesia
      PT Tatasol USI Pratama, 42-44 Jalan Kayoon, Surabaya 60270, Indonesia

UNION CARBIDE CORP   39 Old Ridgebury Rd, Danbury, CT 06817,
   Tel: (203) 794-2000
   (Mfr industrial chemicals, plastics, resins)
      PT Union Carbide Indonesia, Wisma Metropolitan II, Jl. Jendra Sudiman,
         P.O. Box 2677, Jakarta 12920, Indonesia

USX CORP   600 Grant St, Pittsburgh, PA 15219-4776, Tel: (412) 433-1121
   (Steel & related resources, oil & gas, engineering, real estate)
      Marathon Petroleum Indonesia Ltd., Jl. H.R. Rasuna Said, Kav. B-10,
         Lippo Life Bldg., Jakarta, Indonesia

VIRGINIA INTL CO   2815 N Augusta St, Staunton, VA 24401, Tel: (703) 886-3425
   (Oil & gas explor, development & sales)
      Virginia Intl. Co., Jl. M.H. Thamrin 5, P.O. Box 2941, Jakarta, Indonesia

WARNER-LAMBERT CO   201 Tabor Road, Morris Plains, NJ 07950,
   Tel: (201) 540-2000
   (Mfr ethical & proprietary pharms, confectionary & consumer prdts)
      PT Warner-Lambert Indonesia, Arthaloka Bldg., 9th Fl., P.O. Box 2414,
         Jl. Jendral Sudirman 2, Jakarta 10001, Indonesia

WEATHERFORD INTL INC   1360 Post Oak Blvd, PO Box 27608, Houston,
   TX 77227-7608, Tel: (713) 439-9400
   (Oilfield servs, prdts & equip; mfr marine cranes)
      Weatherford Oil Tool Pte. Ltd., P.T. Wira Insani, Cilandak Commercial Estate,
         Unit 406, P.O. Box 7587, Jakarta 12560, Indonesia

WESTERN ATLAS INTL INC   10205 Westheimer, PO Box 1407, Houston,
   TX 77251-1407, Tel: (713) 266-5700
   (Full service to the oil industry)
      Western Atlas Logging Services, Bldg. 404W, Cilandak Commercial Estate 1427,
         Jl. Cilandak KKO, Jakarta 12560, Indonesia
      Western Geophysical, c/o PT Talanavindo, Jl. Sultan Iskandar Muda F-25,
         Kebayoran Salatan, Jakarta 12240, Indonesia

WILBUR-ELLIS CO   320 California St, #200, San Francisco, CA 94104,
   Tel: (415) 772-4000
   (Intl merchants & distributors)

(cont)

Connell Bros. Co. Ltd., Lippo Centre 504, Jl. Gatot Subroto Kav. 35-36,
Jakarta 12950, Indonesia

WMX TECHNOLOGIES INC   3003 Butterfield Rd, Oak Brook, IL 60563,
Tel: (708) 572-8800
(Environmental services)
Waste Management Indonesia, Wisma Geha, Lantai 2, Jalan Timor 25, Jakarta 10350,
Indonesia

XEROX CORP   800 Long Ridge Rd, PO Box 1600, Stamford, CT 06904,
Tel: (203) 968-3000
(Mfr document processing equip, sys & supplies)
Xerox Corp., Jakarta, Indonesia

IRELAND

3COM CORP   5400 Bayfront Plaza, Santa Clara, CA 95052-8145,
Tel: (408) 764-5000
(Devel/mfr computer networking prdts & sys)
3Com, Ireland

3M   3M Center, St Paul, MN 55144-1000, Tel: (612) 733-1110
(Mfr diversified prdts for industry, health care, imaging, commun, transport, safety,
consumer, etc)
3M Ireland Ltd., 3M House, Adelphi Centre, Upper George St., Dun Laoghaire,
Co. Dublin, Ireland

A-Z INTL TOOL CO   PO Box 7108, Houston, TX 77248-7108, Tel: (713) 880-8888
(Mfr oil field, milling & casing cutting tools)
A-Z Intl. Tool Co., Cavan, Ireland

ABBOTT LABORATORIES   100 Abbott Park Rd, Abbott Park, IL 60064-3500,
Tel: (708) 937-6100
(Devel/mfr/sale diversified health care prdts & services)
Abbott Labs Ireland Ltd., Sligo/Donegal/Cootehill/Finisklin, Ireland

AIR PRODUCTS & CHEMICALS INC   7201 Hamilton Blvd, Allentown, PA 18195-1501,
Tel: (215) 481-4911
(Mfr ind gases & related equip, spec chems, environmental/energy sys)
Air Products Ireland Ltd., Unit 950, Western Industrial Estate 2, Killeen Rd.,
Naasroad, Dublin, Ireland

ALLERGAN INC   2525 Dupont Dr, PO Box 19534, Irvine, CA 92713-9534,
Tel: (714) 752-4500
(Mfr therapeutic eye care prdts, skin & neural care pharms)
Allergan Ireland Ltd., County Mayo, Ireland

ALLIEDSIGNAL INC   101 Columbia Rd, PO Box 2245, Morristown, NJ 07962-2245,
  Tel: (201) 455-2000
  (Mfr aerospace & automotive prdts, engineered materials)
    AlliedSignal Turbos Ltd., 411 Western Ext., Industrial Estate, Waterford, Ireland

AMDAHL CORP   1250 E Arques Ave, PO Box 3470, Sunnyvale, CA 94088-3470,
  Tel: (408) 746-6000
  (Devel/mfr large scale computers, software, data storage prdts, info-technology
  solutions & support)
    Amdahl (UK) Ltd., Balheary Industrial Park, Swords, County Dublin, Ireland

AMERICAN EXPRESS CO   World Financial Center, New York, NY 10285-4765,
  Tel: (212) 640-2000
  (Travel, travelers cheques, charge card & financial services)
    American Express Ireland Ltd., all inquiries to U.S. address

AMP INC   PO Box 3608, Harrisburg, PA 17105-3608, Tel: (717) 564-0100
  (Devel/mfr electronic & electrical connection prdts & sys)
    AMP Ireland Ltd., 65 Broomhill Rd., Tallaght Industrial Estate, Tallaght County,
      Dublin 24, Ireland

ANALOG DEVICES INC   1 Technology Way, Box 9106, Norwood, MA 02062,
  Tel: (617) 329-4700
  (Mfr integrated circuits & related devices)
    Analog Devices BV, Bay F-1, Raheen Industrial Estate, Limerick, Ireland

ANTI-HYDRO WATERPROOFING CO   265-277 Badger Ave, Newark, NJ 07108,
  Tel: (201) 242-8000
  (Bldg specialties)
    Anti Hydro of Ireland Ltd., Thormanby Rd., Howth, Dublin, Ireland

APPLE COMPUTER INC   1 Infinite Loop, Cupertino, CA 95014, Tel: (408) 996-1010
  (Personal computers, peripherals & software)
    Apple Computer Ltd., Holly Hill Ind. Estate, Holly Hill, Cork, Ireland

APPLIED MAGNETICS CORP   75 Robin Hill Rd, Goleta, CA 93117,
  Tel: (805) 683-5353
  (Mfr magnetic recording heads)
    Applied Magnetics Ireland Ltd., 10A Industrial Estate, Santry Ave., Dublin 9,
      Ireland

ARBOR ACRES FARM INC   439 Marlborough Rd, Glastonbury, CT 06033,
  Tel: (860) 633-4681
  (Producers of male & female broiler breeders, commercial egg layers)
    Arbor Acres Ireland, Walshestown, Mullingar, Westmeath, Ireland

AST RESEARCH INC   16215 Alton Parkway, PO Box 19658, Irvine, CA 92713-9658,
  Tel: (714) 727-4141
  (Design/devel/mfr hi-perf desktop, server & notebook computers)
    AST Ireland, National Technological Park, Plassey, Limerick, Ireland

AT&T INTERNATIONAL   412 Mt Kemble Ave, Morristown, NJ 07962-1995,
  Tel: (810) 262-6646
  (Telecommunications)
    AT&T Ireland, Corke Abbey, Bray, County Dublin, Dublin, Ireland

AVERY DENNISON CORP   150 N Orange Grove Blvd, Pasadena, CA 91103,
Tel: (818) 304-2000
(Mfr pressure-sensitive adhesives & materials, office prdts, labels, tags, retail sys, spec chems)
  Avery Label Ltd., Aalkinstown Ave., Long Mile Rd., P.O. Box 586, Dublin, Ireland
  Fasson Ireland Ltd., Dublin Indus. Estate Fing, 37B Barrow Rd., Dublin 11, Ireland

AVNET INC   80 Cutter Mill Rd, Great Neck, NY 11021, Tel: (516) 466-7000
(Distr electr components, computers & peripherals)
  Avnet Lyco Ltd., Chapel Lane, Swords, County Dublin, Ireland

AVON PRODUCTS INC   9 W 57th St, New York, NY 10019, Tel: (212) 546-6015
(Mfr/distr beauty & related prdts, fashion jewelry, gifts & collectibles)
  Arlington Ltd., Cooltedexry, Port Arlington, Co. Laois, Ireland

THE BANK OF NEW YORK   48 Wall St, New York, NY 10286, Tel: (212) 495-1784
(Banking)
  BNY Fund Management (Ireland) Ltd., AIB Investment House, Percy Place, Dublin 4, Ireland

BANKAMERICA CORP   555 California St, San Francisco, CA 94104,
Tel: (415) 622-3456
(Financial services)
  Bank of America NT & SA, Russell Ct., St. Stephen's Green, Dublin 2, Ireland

C R BARD INC   730 Central Ave, Murray Hill, NJ 07974, Tel: (908) 277-8000
(Mfr health care prdts)
  C.R. Bard Ireland Ltd., Parkmore Industrial Estate, Galway, Ireland

BAXTER HEALTHCARE CORP   1 Baxter Pky, Deerfield, IL 60015,
Tel: (708) 948-2000
(Mfr disposable medical prdts)
  Baxter Healthcare Ltd., Unit 7, Deansgrange Ind. Estate, Blackrock, Co. Dublin, Ireland
  Baxter Healthcare Ltd., also in Castlebar & Swinford, Ireland

BECKMAN INSTRUMENTS INC   2500 Harbor Blvd, Fullerton, CA 92634,
Tel: (714) 871-4848
(Devel/mfr/mkt automated systems & supplies for biological analysis)
  Beckman Instruments Ireland, Beckman Industrial Estate, Mervue, Galway, Ireland

BIJUR LUBRICATING CORP   50 Kocher Dr, Bennington, VT 05201-1994,
Tel: (802) 447-2174
(Design/mfr centralized lubrication equip)
  Bijur Ireland Ltd., Gort Rd., Ennis, County Clare, Ireland

BISSELL INC   2345 Walker Road, NW, Grand Rapids, MI 49504,
Tel: (616) 453-4451
(Mfr home care prdts)
  Bissell Inc., Drogheda, Ireland

BOOLE & BABBAGE INC   510 Oakmead Pkwy, Sunnyvale, CA 94086,
Tel: (408) 735-9550
(Devel/support enterprise automation & systems mgmt software)
  Boole & Babbage Europe, Unit 5, Leopardstown Office Park, Foxrock, Dublin 18, Ireland

BORDEN INC   180 E Broad St, Columbus, OH 43215-3799, Tel: (614) 225-4000
  (Mfr foods, snacks & beverages, adhesives)
    Borden Co. Ltd., all mail to U.S. address

BOSE CORP   The Mountain, Framingham, MA 01701-9168, Tel: (508) 879-7330
  (Mfr audio equip)
    Bose Ireland, Castleblayney Rd., Carrickmacross, Monaghan, Ireland

BOURNS INC   1200 Columbia Ave, Riverside, CA 92507, Tel: (909) 781-5500
  (Mfr resistive com & networks, precision potentiometers, panel controls, switches,
  transducers)
    Bourns Electronics (Ireland), Mahon Industrial Estate, Blackrock, Cork, Ireland

BROWN-FORMAN CORP   PO Box 1080, Louisville, KY 40201-1080,
  Tel: (502) 585-1100
  (Mfr/dist distilled spirits, china, crystal, silverware, luggage)
    Clintock Ltd., Fox & Geese, Robinhood Rd., Clondalkin, Dublin 22, Ireland

BUDGET RENT-A-CAR CORP OF AMERICA   4225 Napierville Rd, Lisle, IL 60532,
  Tel: (708) 955-1900
  (Self-drive car hire)
    Budget Rent-A-Car System, Pembroke Rd., Ballsbridge, Dublin 4, Ireland

CALIFORNIA PELLET MILL CO   221 Main St, #420, San Francisco, CA 94105,
  Tel: (415) 431-3800
  (Mfr mach for pelleting)
    CPM/Europe Ltd., Industrial Estate, Whitemill, Wexford, Ireland

CHASE MANHATTAN BANK N A   1 Chase Manhattan Plaza, New York, NY 10081,
  Tel: (212) 552-2222
  (Intl banking)
    The Chase Manhattan Bank of Ireland, Stephen Ct., 18-21 St. Stephen's Green,
      Dublin 2, Ireland

A W CHESTERTON CO   Middlesex Industrial Park, Stoneham, MA 02180,
  Tel: (617) 438-7000
  (Packing gaskets, sealing prdts sys, etc)
    Chesterton Industries BV, Dublin, Ireland

THE CHUBB CORP   15 Mountain View Rd, Warren, NJ 07060, Tel: (908) 580-2000
  (Holding co: property/casualty ins)
    Chubb Insurance Co. of Europe, Ireland

CITICORP   399 Park Ave, New York, NY 10043, Tel: (212) 559-1000
  (Banking & financial services)
    Citibank NA, Ireland

COLGATE-PALMOLIVE CO   300 Park Ave, New York, NY 10022, Tel: (212) 310-2000
  (Mfr pharms, cosmetics, toiletries, detergents)
    Colgate-Palmolive Ireland Ltd., Unit C, Airport Industrial Estate, Swords Rd.,
      Santry, Dublin 9, Ireland

COMBINED INSURANCE CO OF AMERICA   123 N Wacker Dr, Chicago, IL 60606,
  Tel: (312) 701-3000
  (Insurance)
    Combined Insurance Co. of Ireland, Merrion House, Merrion Rd., Dublin 4, Ireland

COMPUTER ASSOCIATES INTL INC　One Computer Associates Plaza, Islandia,
NY 11788, Tel: (516) 342-5224
(Devel/mkt/mgt info mgt & bus applications software)
　Computer Associates Plc, Europa House, Harcourt St., Dublin 2, Ireland

CONCURRENT COMPUTER CORP　2 Crescent Pl, Oceanport, NJ 07757,
Tel: (908) 870-4500
(Mfr computer systems & software)
　Concurrent Computers (Ireland) Ltd., 30 Green Mount Office Park, Harolds Cross,
　Dublin 6, Ireland

CONOCO INC　600 N Dairy Ashford Rd, Houston, TX 77079, Tel: (713) 293-1000
(Oil, gas, coal, chems, minerals)
　Conoco Ireland Ltd., Conoco House, Deansgrange, Blockrock, Dublin, Ireland

COOPER INDUSTRIES INC　1001 Fannin St, PO Box 4446, Houston, TX 77210-4446,
Tel: (713) 739-5400
(Mfr/distr electrical prdts, tools & hardware, automotive prdts)
　Cooper Automotive, Naas, Kildare, Ireland

CPC INTERNATIONAL INC　PO Box 8000, Englewood Cliffs, NJ 07632,
Tel: (201) 894-4000
(Consumer foods, corn refining)
　CPC Foods (Ireland) Ltd., Goldenbridge, Inchicore, Dublin 12, Ireland

A T CROSS CO　1 Albion Rd, Lincoln, RI 02865, Tel: (401) 333-1200
(Mfr writing instruments)
　A.T. Cross Co., 1 Cleaghmore, Ballinasloe, County Galway, Ireland

CROWN CORK & SEAL CO INC　9300 Ashton Rd, Philadelphia, PA 19136,
Tel: (215) 698-5100
(Mfr cans, bottle caps; filling & packaging mach)
　The Irish Crown Cork Co. Ltd., Church Field Industrial Estate, Cork, Ireland

CROWN EQUIPMENT CORP　40 S Washington St, New Bremen, OH 45869,
Tel: (419) 629-2311
(Mfr/sales/svce forklift trucks, stackers)
　Crown Equipment, Galway, Ireland

D'ARCY MASIUS BENTON & BOWLES INC (DMB&B)　1675 Broadway, New York,
NY 10019, Tel: (212) 468-3622
(Advertising & communications)
　DMB&B, Stephens House, 7/8 Upper Mount St., Dublin 2, Ireland

DAMES & MOORE　911 Wilshire Blvd, Los Angeles, CA 90017, Tel: (213) 683-1560
(Engineering, environmental & construction mgmt services)
　Dames & Moore, 2214 Richmond Business Campus, North Brunswick St., Dublin 7, Ireland

DANIEL INTERNATIONAL CORP　100 Fluor Daniel Dr, Greenville, SC 29607-2762,
Tel: (803) 281-4400
(Gen contractor, engr & constr)
　Daniel/McCarthy Ltd., Glandore House, Balgriffin, Raheny, Dublin 5, Ireland

DATA GENERAL CORP　4400 Computer Dr, Westboro, MA 01580, Tel: (617) 366-8911
(Design, mfr gen purpose computer sys & peripheral prdts & servs)
　Data General Ireland Ltd., Haddington Court, Haddington Rd., Dublin 4, Ireland

DATAPRODUCTS CORP   6200 Canada Ave, PO Box 746, Woodland Hills, CA 91365,
 Tel: (818) 887-8000
 (Mfr computer printers & supplies)
   Dataproducts (Dublin) Ltd., Clonshaugh Ind. Estate, Clonshaugh, Dublin 17, Ireland

DEVCON CORP   30 Endicott St, Danvers, MA 01923, Tel: (617) 777-1100
 (Mfr filled epoxies, urethanes, adhesives & metal treatment prdts)
   Devcon Ltd., Shannon Ind. Estate, Shannon Free Airport, County Clare, Ireland

DIDDE WEB PRESS CORP   1200 Graphic Arts St, Emporia, KS 66801,
 Tel: (316) 342-4740
 (Mfr printing presses & related equip)
   Didde Graphic Systems BV, 13 Annacotty Industrial Estate, County Limerick, Ireland

DIGITAL EQUIPMENT CORP   146 Main St, Maynard, MA 01754-2571,
 Tel: (508) 493-5111
 (Networked computer systems & services)
   Digital Equipment Ireland Ltd., Park House, Circular Rd. N, Dublin, Ireland

R R DONNELLEY & SONS CO   77 W Wacker Dr, Chicago, IL 60601-1696,
 Tel: (312) 326-8000
 (Coml printing, allied commun servs)
   Irish Printers (Holdings) Ltd., Clonshaugh Industrial Estate, Clonshaugh,
     Dublin 17, Ireland

DONNELLY CORP   414 E Fortieth St, Holland, MI 49423, Tel: (616) 786-7000
 (Mfr mirrors, interior lighting & modular window sys for transp & elec info display
 mkt)
   Donnelly Mirrors Ltd., Naas, County Kildare, Ireland

DRIVER-HARRIS CO   308 Middlesex St, Harrison, NJ 07029, Tel: (201) 483-4802
 (Mfr non-ferrous alloys)
   Irish Driver-Harris Co. Ltd., 5A Ballymount Trading Estate, Lower Ballymount Rd.,
     Walkinstown, Dublin 12, Ireland
   Irish Driver-Harris Co. Ltd., John Street, New Ross, Wexford, Ireland

E I DU PONT DE NEMOURS & CO   1007 Market St, Wilmington, DE 19898,
 Tel: (302) 774-1000
 (Mfr/sale diversified chems, plastics, specialty prdts & fibers)
   Conoco Ireland Ltd., Ireland

THE DURIRON CO INC   PO Box 8820, Dayton, OH 45401-8820, Tel: (513) 476-6100
 (Mfr chem equip, pumps, valves, filters, fans, heat exchangers)
   Durco Ireland, Shannon Town Center #2, Shannon, County Clare, Ireland

DYNATECH CORP   3 New England Executive Park, Burlington, MA 01803,
 Tel: (617) 272-6100
 (Devel/mfr communications equip)
   TTC (Ireland) Ltd., County Meath, Ireland

EASTMAN KODAK CO   343 State St, Rochester, NY 14650, Tel: (716) 724-4000
 (Devel/mfr photo & chem prdts, info mgmt/video/copier sys, fibers/plastics for
 various ind)
   Kodak Ireland Ltd., Kodak House, Pottery Rd., Dun Laoghaire, Co. Dublin, Ireland

ECOLOGY AND ENVIRONMENT INC   368 Pleasant View Dr, East Amherst,
  NY 14086-1397, Tel: (716) 684-8060
  (Environmental, scientific & engineering consulting)
      Ecology and Environment Ltd., Poulgorm, Maryboto 4,11, Douglas, Cork, Ireland

EFCO   1800 NE Broadway Ave, Des Moines, IA 50316-0386, Tel: (515) 266-1141
  (Mfr systems for concrete construction)
      EFCO, 2B Crofton Ct., Naas, Co. Kildare, Ireland

EG&G INC   45 William St, Wellesley, MA 02181-4078, Tel: (617) 237-5100
  (Diversified R/D, mfg & services)
      EG&G Intl./Sealol Div., Shannon Free Airport, County Clare, Ireland
      EG&G Ireland/Instruments Div., Blanchardstown Industrial Park, Blanchardstown,
      Dublin 15, Ireland

ELECTRONIC SPACE SYSTEMS CORP (ESSCO)   Old Powder Mill Rd, Concord,
  MA 01742, Tel: (508) 369-7200
  (Designs & mfr radomes, antennas, radar, range reflectors, & satellite commun)
      Essco Collins Ltd., Kilkishen, Clare, Ireland

FARAH INC   8889 Gateway Blvd W, El Paso, TX 79925, Tel: (915) 593-4000
  (Mfr wearing apparel)
      Farah (Exports) Ireland Ltd., Ashe Rd., Shantalla, Galway, Ireland
      Farah Mfg. Ireland Ltd., Ashe Rd., Shantalla, Galway, Ireland

FILENET CORP   3565 Harbor Blvd, Costa Mesa, CA 92626, Tel: (800) 345-3688
  (Provides software prdts & related svces for document imaging & workflow mgmt)
      FileNet Co. Ltd., St. John's Court, Swords Rd., Dublin 9, Ireland

FIRST NATIONAL BANK IN DALLAS   PO Box 6031, Dallas, TX 75283,
  Tel: (214) 744-8000
  (Commercial banking)
      First Natl. Bank of Chicago, 44/45 St. Stephen's Green, Dublin 2, Ireland

FMC CORP   200 E Randolph Dr, Chicago, IL 60601, Tel: (312) 861-6000
  (Produces chems & precious metals, mfr machinery, equip & sys for ind, agric & govt)
      FMC Intl. AG, Ireland
      FMC Manufacturing Ltd., Ireland
      Norfolk Investments Ltd., Ireland

FORD MOTOR CO   The American Road, Dearborn, MI 48121, Tel: (313) 322-3000
  (Mfr motor vehicles)
      Ford Motor Co., Marina, Cork, Ireland

GELMAN SCIENCES INC   600 S Wagner Rd, Ann Arbor, MI 48106-1448,
  Tel: (313) 665-0651
  (Mfr microporous membrane filters & devices)
      Gelman Sciences Ltd. Ireland, Ashgrove Park, Ashgrove Industrial Estate, Kill Ave.,
      Dun Laoire, Co. Dublin, Ireland

GENCORP INC   175 Ghent Rd, Fairlawn, OH 44333-3300, Tel: (216) 869-4200
  (Mfr aerospace/defense, automotive & polymer prdts)
      Henniges Vehicle Sealing Div., Crossmolina Rd., Ballina, County Mayo, Ireland
      Penn Racquet Sports Co (Ireland), Lynn Rd., Mullingar, County Westmeath, Ireland

GENERAL ELECTRIC CO   3135 Easton Tpk, Fairfield, CT 06431,
  Tel: (203) 373-2211
  (Diversified manufacturing, technology & services)
    General Electric Co.,
      all mail to U.S. address; phone (800) 626-2004 or (518) 438-6500

GENERAL FOODS CORP   250 North St, White Plains, NY 10625, Tel: (914) 335-2500
  (Processor, distributor & mfr of foods)
    Alfred Bird & Sons (Ireland) Ltd., Ninth Lock Rd., Clondalkin, Dublin 22, Ireland

GENERAL INSTRUMENT CORP   181 W Madison, Chicago, IL 60602,
  Tel: (312) 541-5000
  (Mfr broadband communications & power rectifying components)
    General Semiconductor Industries, IDA Industrial Estate, Macroom, Co. Cork, Ireland

GENERAL MOTORS CORP   3044 W Grand Blvd, Detroit, MI 48202-3091,
  Tel: (313) 556-5000
  (Mfr full line vehicles, automotive electronics, coml technologies, telecom, space,
  finance)
    General Motors Distribution Ireland Ltd., Belgard Rd., Tallaght, Dublin, Ireland
    Packard Electric Ireland Ltd., Airton Rd., Tallaght, Dublin, Ireland

THE GILLETTE CO   Prudential Tower, Boston, MA 02199, Tel: (617) 421-7000
  (Devel/mfr personal care/use prdts: blades & razors, toiletries, cosmetics,
  stationery)
    Braun Ireland Ltd., Carlow, Ireland
    Gillette Ireland Ltd., Carlow, Ireland
    Jafra Cosmetics Intl. Ltd., Foxrock, Dublin, Ireland
    Rethgil Properties Ltd., Dublin, Ireland

GOW-MAC INSTRUMENT CO   PO Box 32, Bound Brook, NJ 08805-0032,
  Tel: (908) 560-0600
  (Mfr analytical instru)
    Gow-Mac Instrument Co. Ireland, Shannon Airport, County Clare, Ireland

GREY ADVERTISING INC   777 Third Ave, New York, NY 10017, Tel: (212) 546-2000
  (Advertising)
    Campbell Grey & Associates, 6 Adelaide Ct., Adelaide Rd., Dublin 2, Ireland

FRANK B HALL & CO INC   549 Pleasantville Rd, Briarcliff Manor, NY 10510,
  Tel: (914) 769-9200
  (Insurance)
    Frank B. Hall (Ireland) Ltd., Macdonagh & Boland Group Ltd., 10/12 Lansdowne Rd.,
      Dublin 4, Ireland

HALLMARK CARDS INC   PO Box 419580, Kansas City, MO 64141, Tel: (816) 274-5100
  (Mfr greeting cards & related prdts)
    Hallmark Cards (Ireland) Ltd., Butterfield Ave., Rathfarnham, Dublin 14, Ireland

HARRIS CALORIFIC CO   2345 Murphy Blvd, Gainesville, GA 30501,
  Tel: (404) 536-8801
  (Mfr gas welding & cutting equip)
    Harris Calorific Ireland, Div. Emerson Electric Ireland Ltd., Harris House,
      Charvey Lane, Rathnew, Wicklow, Ireland

H J HEINZ CO   PO Box 57, Pittsburgh, PA 15230-0057, Tel: (412) 456-5700
(Processed food prdts & nutritional services)
   Custom Foods Ltd., Dundalk, Ireland
   H.J. Heinz Co. (Ireland) Ltd., Dublin, Ireland

HEWLETT-PACKARD CO   3000 Hanover St, Palo Alto, CA 94304-0890,
Tel: (415) 857-1501
(Mfr computing, communications & measurement prdts & services)
   Hewlett-Packard Ireland Ltd., Hewlett-Packard House, Stradbrook Rd., Black Rock,
   County Dublin, Ireland

HIGH VOLTAGE ENGINEERING CO   401 Edgewater Pl, Wakefield, MA 01880,
Tel: (617) 224-1001
(Holding co: industrial & scientific instruments)
   HIVEC-Ireland, Rathealy Rd., Fermoy, Co. Cork, Ireland

HOOD SAILMAKERS INC   200 High Point Ave, Portsmouth, RI 02871,
Tel: (401) 683-4660
(Mfr yacht sails)
   Hood Textiles Ltd., McCurtain Hill, Clonakilty, County Cork, Ireland

HORWATH INTL   415 Madison Ave, New York, NY 10017, Tel: (212) 838-5566
(Public accountants & auditors)
   Simpson Xavier, Simpson Xavier Court, Merchants Quay, Dublin 8, Ireland
   Simpson Xavier, 4 Michael St., Limerick, Ireland

HOSKINS MFG CO   10776 Hall Rd, PO Box 218, Hamburg, MI 48139-0218,
Tel: (810) 231-1900
(Mfr elec resistance & spec alloys)
   Hoskins Alloys Intl., Kildare Enterprise Centre, Melitta Rd., Kildare Town,
   Co. Kildare, Ireland

HUNT SCREW & MFG CO   4117 N Kilpatrick Ave, Chicago, IL 60641,
Tel: (312) 283-6900
(Machine parts & components)
   Hunt Associates Ltd., Leislip, Kildare, Ireland

IBM CORP   Old Orchard Rd, Armonk, NY 10504, Tel: (914) 765-1900
(Information products, technology & services)
   IBM Ireland Ltd., Ireland

IDEX CORP   630 Dundee Rd, #400, Northbrook, IL 60062, Tel: (708) 498-7070
(Mfr ind pumps, lubrication sys, metal fabrication equip, bending & clamping devices)
   Viking Pump (Europe) Ltd., R-79 Shannon Industrial Estate, Shannon, County Clare,
   Ireland

ILLINOIS TOOL WORKS INC   3600 W Lake Ave, Glenview, IL 60025,
Tel: (708) 724-7500
(Mfr gears, tools, fasteners, sealants, plastic & metal components for ind, med, etc.)
   Devcon Corp., Dublin, Ireland
   ITW Hi-Cone Ltd., Mallow, Ireland

INGERSOLL-RAND CO   200 Chestnut Ridge Rd, Woodcliff Lake, NJ 07675,
Tel: (201) 573-0123
(Mfr compressors, rock drills, pumps, air tools, door hardware, ball bearings)
   CPM Europe Ltd., Whitemill Industrial Estate, Wexford, Ireland

Ingersoll-Rand Co. Ireland, John F. Kennedy Dr., Bluebell, Dublin 12, Ireland
Ingersoll-Rand Co. Ireland Ltd., John F. Kennedy Dr., Bluebell, Dublin 12, Ireland

INTERGRAPH CORP   Huntsville, AL 35894-0001, Tel: (205) 730-2000
(Devel/mfr interactive computer graphic systems)
Intergraph Ireland, Stradbrook House, Stradbrook Rd., Blackrock, Co. Dublin, Ireland

INTERMEC CORP   6001 36th Ave West, PO Box 4280, Everett, WA 98203-9280,
Tel: (206) 348-2600
(Mfr/distr automated data collection sys)
Intermec Ireland Ltd., 19-20 York Rd., Dunlaoire, County Dublin, Ireland

INTERNATIONAL SYSTEMS & CONTROLS CORP   PO Box 2589wy, Houston, TX 77001,
Tel: (713) 526-5461
(Holding company)
BS&B Safety Systems Ltd., Kaheen Industrial Estate, Limerick, Ireland

FRANK IX & SONS INC   469 Seventh Ave, New York, NY 10018, Tel: (212) 239-4480
(Textiles)
Frank Ix & Sons NY Corp., Ennis, Ireland

JACOBS ENGINEERING GROUP INC   251 S Lake Ave, Pasadena, CA 91101,
Tel: (818) 449-2171
(Engineering, design & consulting; construction & construction mgmt; process plant maintenance)
Jacobs Engineering Inc., Merrion House, Merrion Rd., Dublin 4, Ireland
Jacobs Engineering Inc., Mahon Industrial Estate, Blackrock, County Cork, Ireland

JOHNSON & HIGGINS   125 Broad St, New York, NY 10004-2424, Tel: (212) 574-7000
(Ins brokerage, employee benefit conslt, risk mgmt, human resource conslt, ins/reins servs)
Johnson & Higgins UK Ltd., Dublin, Ireland

JOHNSON & JOHNSON   One Johnson & Johnson Plaza, New Brunswick, NJ 08933,
Tel: (908) 524-0400
(R&D/mfr/sale health care prdts)
Janssen Pharmaceutical Ltd., Little Island, Cork, Ireland
Johnson & Johnson Ireland Ltd., Belgard Rd., Tallaght, Dublin 24, Ireland

S C JOHNSON & SON INC   1525 Howe St, Racine, WI 53403, Tel: (414) 631-2000
(Home, auto, commercial & personal care prdts, specialty chems)
Johnson Wax Ireland Ltd., Robinhood Industrial Estate, Clon Dalkin Co., Dublin, Ireland

K-TEL INTL INC   2605 Fernbrook Lane N, Plymouth, MN 55447,
Tel: (612) 559-6800
(Sale/distr packaged consumer entertainment & convenience prdts)
K-Tel Ireland Ltd., 30/32 Sir John Rogersons Quay, Dublin 2, Ireland

KDI CORP   5721 Dragon Way, Cincinnati, OH 45227, Tel: (513) 272-1421
(Holding co: diversified mfg)
Vanguard Plastics (Ireland) Ltd., Millbrook Rd., Old Castle, County Meath, Ireland

KELLOGG CO   One Kellogg Sq, PO Box 3599, Battle Creek, MI 49016-3599,
Tel: (616) 961-2000
(Mfr ready-to-eat cereals, convenience foods)
Kellogg Co. of Ireland Ltd., Dublin, Ireland (all inquiries to U.S. address)

KELLY SERVICES   999 W Big Beaver Rd, Troy, MI   48084, Tel: (810) 244-4313
(Temporary help placement)
   Kelly Services (Ireland) Ltd., 21-22 Grafton, Dublin 2, Ireland

KEY TRONIC CORP   PO Box 14687, Spokane, WA   92214, Tel: (509) 928-8000
(Computers & peripherals)
   Key Tronic Europe Ltd., The Ramparts, Dundalk, Louth, Ireland

KOLLMORGEN CORP   1601 Trapelo Rd, Waltham, MA   02154, Tel: (617) 890-5655
(Mfr printed circuits, elec motors & controls, electro-optical instru)
   Kollmorgan (Ireland) Ltd., Gort Rd., Ennis, County Clare, Ireland

KRAFT INC   Kraft Court, Glenview, IL   60025, Tel: (708) 998-2000
(Dairy prdts, processed food, chems)
   Dowdall, O'Mahoney & Co. Ltd., 5/9 Union Quay, Cork, Ireland

KWIK LOK CORP   PO Box 9548, Yakima, WA   98909, Tel: (509) 248-4770
(Mfr bag closing mach)
   Kwik Lok Corp., Shannon, Ireland

LAWTER INTERNATIONAL INC   990 Skokie Blvd, Northbrook, IL   60062,
Tel: (708) 498-4700
(Resins, pigments, coatings)
   Lawter Products BV, Waterford, Ireland

LEEDS+NORTHRUP   795 Horsham Rd, PO Box 1010, Horsham, PA   19044-8010,
Tel: (215) 442-8000
(Mfr process control instrumentation, liquid & particle analysis)
   Leeds+Northrup Ireland, Clonshaugh Ind. Estate, Coolock, Dublin 17, Ireland

LOCTITE CORP   10 Columbus Blvd, Hartford, CT   06106, Tel: (203) 520-5000
(Mfr/sale ind adhesives & sealants)
   Loctite (Ireland) Ltd., Tallaght Business Park, Whitestown, Tallaght, Dublin 24,
      Ireland

LOUISIANA-PACIFIC CORP   111 SW Fifth Ave, Portland, OR   97204-3601,
Tel: (503) 221-0800
(Mfr lumber & building products)
   Louisiana-Pacific Coillte Ireland Ltd., 41-45 St. Stephen's Green, Dublin 2, Ireland

M/A COM INC   43 South Ave, Burlington, MA   01803, Tel: (617) 272-9600
(Mfr electronic components, communications equip)
   Adams-Russell, Kilbarry Industrial Estate, Dublin Hill, Cork, Ireland

R H MACY & CO INC   151 West 34th St, New York, NY   10001, Tel: (212) 695-4400
(Department stores, importers)
   R.H. Macy & Co. Inc., 51 Wellington Rd., Dublin 4, Ireland
   R.H. Macy & Co. Inc., Ballsbridge, Dublin 4, Ireland

MAIDENFORM INC   90 Park Ave, New York, NY   10016, Tel: (212) 953-1400
(Mfr intimate apparel)
   Maidenform Intl. Ltd., Shannon Industrial Estate, Shannon, Co. Clare, Ireland

MALLINCKRODT MEDICAL INC   675 McDonnell Blvd, PO Box 5840, St Louis,
MO   63134, Tel: (314) 895-2000
(Mfr specialty medical prdts)

Mallinckrodt Medical, Athlone, Ireland
Mallinckrodt Medical Imaging-Ireland, Dublin, Ireland

MANPOWER INTL INC   5301 N Ironwood Rd, PO Box 2053, Milwaukee,
 WI 53201-2053, Tel: (414) 961-1000
 (Temporary help service)
   Manpower Ireland Ltd., 54 Grafton St., Dublin, Ireland

MARATHON OIL CO   539 S Main St, Findlay, OH 45840, Tel: (419) 422-2121
 (Petroleum explor & prod)
   Marathon Petroleum Ireland Ltd., Mahon Industrial Estate, Blackrock, Cork, Ireland

MARSH & McLENNAN COS INC   1166 Ave of the Americas, New York, NY 10036-1011,
 Tel: (212) 345-5000
 (Insurance)
   Mathews, Mulcahy & Sutherland Ltd., 10-11 S. Leinster St, Dublin 2, Ireland

MASONITE CORP   1 S Wacker Dr, Chicago, IL 60606, Tel: (312) 750-0900
 (Mfr hardboard, softboard & molded prdts)
   Masonite Ireland, Dublin Rd., ICA Industrial Estate, Carrick-on-Shannon,
    Co. Leitrim, Ireland

MAXTOR CORP   211 River Oaks Pkwy, San Jose, CA 95134, Tel: (408) 432-1700
 (Design/mfr magnetic storage prdts)
   Maxtor Ireland Ltd., Bray, County Wicklow, Ireland

MEASUREX CORP   One Results Way, Cupertino, CA 95014-5991, Tel: (408) 255-1500
 (Mfr computer integrated mfg sys)
   Measurex Ireland Ltd., Industrial Estate, Waterford, Ireland

MEDITE CORP   PO Box 550, Medford, OR 97501, Tel: (503) 773-7491
 (Mfr medium density fiberboard)
   Medite of Europe, Box 32, Clonimel, Co. Tipperary, Ireland

MELLON BANK NA   One Mellon Bank Center, Pittsburgh, PA 15258,
 Tel: (412) 234-5000
 (Commercial & trade banking, foreign exchange)
   Premier Financial Services (Ireland) Ltd., 20-22 Lower Hatch St., Dublin 2, Ireland

MEMOREX CORP   San Thomas at Central Expressway, Santa Clara, CA 95052,
 Tel: (408) 987-1000
 (Magnetic recording tapes, etc)
   Memorex Ireland Ltd., Kestral House, Clanwilliam House, Clanwilliam Place,
    Lower Mount St., Dublin 2, Ireland

MERRILL LYNCH   World Financial Center, New York, NY 10281-1323,
 Tel: (212) 449-1000
 (Security brokers & dealers, investment & business services)
   Merrill Lynch & Co. Ltd., 69 St. Stephen's St., Dublin 2, Ireland

MICROSEMI CORP   2830 S Fairview St, Santa Ana, CA 92704, Tel: (714) 979-8220
 (Mfr seimconductors)
   Microsemi Corp. - Ireland, Gort Rd., Ennis, Co. Clare, Ireland

MICROSOFT CORP   One Microsoft Way, Redmond, WA 98052-6399,
  Tel: (206) 882-8080
  (Computer software, peripherals & services)
    Microsoft Ireland Ltd., Blackthorn Rd., Sandyford Ind. Estates, Dublin 18, Ireland

MILTON ROY CO   14845 W 64th Ave, PO Box FH, Arvada, CO 80004,
  Tel: (303) 425-0800
  (Med & ind equip, process control instru)
    LDC-Shannon, Shannon Industrial Estate, Bldg. 89, Clare, Ireland

MOLEX INC   2222 Wellington Ct, Lisle, IL 60532, Tel: (708) 969-4550
  (Mfr electronic, electrical & fiber optic interconnection prdts & sys, switches,
  application tooling)
    Molex Inc., Millstreet Town & Shannon, Ireland

MOOG INC   East Aurora, NY 14052-0018, Tel: (716) 652-2000
  (Mfr precision control components & sys)
    Moog Ltd. (Ireland), Ringeskiddy, Co. Cork, Ireland

MOTOROLA INC   1303 E Algonquin Rd, Schaumburg, IL 60196, Tel: (708) 576-5000
  (Mfr commun equip, semiconductors, cellular phones)
    Motorola Ireland Ltd., Unit 12, Santry Ind. Estate, Santry Hall, Dublin 9, Ireland

NATIONAL CAR RENTAL SYSTEM INC   7700 France Ave S, Minneapolis, MN 55435,
  Tel: (612) 830-2121
  (Car rental)
    Baggott Street Bridge, other locations in Ireland
    National Car Rental, Baggott St. Bridge, Dublin 4, Ireland

NATIONAL STARCH & CHEMICAL CO   10 Finderne Ave, Bridgewater, NJ 08807-3300,
  Tel: (908) 685-5000
  (Mfr adhesives & sealants, resins & spec chems, electr materials & adhesives, food
  prdts, ind starch)
    National Adhesives (Ireland) Ltd., Dublin, Ireland

NEWAY MANUFACTURING INC   1013 N Shiawassee St, PO Box 188, Corunna,
  MI 48817-0188, Tel: (517) 743-3458
  (Mfr valve seat cutters & refacers)
    Neway Manufacturing Ltd., Unit 2 IDA Cluster Devel., Spollanstown Tullamore,
    County Offaly, Ireland

A C NIELSEN CO   Nielsen Plaza, Northbrook, IL 60062-6288, Tel: (708) 498-6300
  (Market research)
    A.C. Nielsen of Ireland Ltd., 36 Merrion Sq., Dublin 2, Ireland

NORTHERN TELECOM SYSTEMS CORP   PO Box 1222, Minneapolis, MN 55440,
  Tel: (612) 932-8000
  (Remote information processing sys)
    Data 100 Europe BV, Ovens, Cork, Ireland

NORTON CO   1 New Bond St, Worcester, MA 01606, Tel: (508) 795-5000
  (Abrasives, drill bits, constr & safety prdts, plastics)
    Drill Tools Ireland Ltd., Shannon Industrial Estate, Shannon, County Clare, Ireland

C M OFFRAY & SON INC   Route #24, Box 601, Chester, NJ 07930-0601,
Tel: (908) 879-4700
(Mfr narrow fabrics)
  Offray Ribbon Ltd., Ashbury Rd., Roscrea, County Tipperary, Ireland

OLIN CORP   120 Long Ridge Rd, PO Box 1355, Stamford, CT 06904-1355,
Tel: (203) 356-2000
(Mfr chems, metals, applied physics in elect, defense, aerospace inds)
  Olin Chemicals BV, Swords, Dublin, Ireland

PANAMETRICS   220 Crescent, Waltham, MA 02154, Tel: (617) 899-2719
(Elec measuring devices)
  Panametrics, Shannon, Ireland

PEPSICO INC   700 Anderson Hill Rd, Purchase, NY 10577-1444,
Tel: (914) 253-2000
(Beverages, snack foods, restaurants)
  Pepsi-Cola Mfg. (Ireland), Ireland
  PepsiCo (Ireland) Ltd., Ireland
  Seven-Up Ireland Ltd., Ireland
  The Concentrate Mfg. Co. of Ireland, Ireland

PFIZER INC   235 E 42nd St, New York, NY 10017-5755, Tel: (212) 573-2323
(Mfr healthcare products)
  Pfizer International Bank Europe, Ireland
  Pfizer Pension Trustees (Ireland) Ltd., Ireland
  Pfizer Sales Co. Ltd., Ireland
  Pfizer Service Co. Ireland, Ireland

PHILLIPS PETROLEUM CO   Phillips Bldg, Bartlesville, OK 74004,
Tel: (918) 661-6600
(Crude oil, natural gas, liquefied petroleum gas, gasoline & petro-chems)
  O'Brien Plastics Ltd., Bishopstown, Cork, Ireland
  Star Plastics Co. Ltd., Ballyconnell, Cavan, Ireland

PULSE ENGINEERING INC   12220 World Trade Dr, PO 12235, San Diego, CA 92112,
Tel: (619) 674-8100
(Engineer/mfr OEM devices for local area network mkts & major voice/data transmission sys)
  Pulse Engineering Inc., Dunmore Rd., Tuam, County Galway, Ireland

PUROLATOR COURIER CORP   3240 Hillview Ave, Palo Alto, CA 94304,
Tel: (415) 494-2900
(Time-sensitive package delivery)
  Purolator Ireland Ltd., Glasnevin, Dublin 2, Ireland

QUIGLEY CO INC   235 E 42nd St, New York, NY 10017, Tel: (212) 573-3444
(Mfr refractory specs, application equip)
  Quigley Co. of Europe, Tivoli Industrial Estate, Cork, Ireland

RAND McNALLY   8255 N Central Park Ave, Skokie, IL 60076, Tel: (708) 329-8100
(Publishing & book services, docusystems, media services)
  Rand McNally-Media Services, D.1 Shannon Industrial Estate, Co. Claire, Ireland

RAYCHEM CORP   300 Constitution Dr, Menlo Park, CA 94025, Tel: (415) 361-3333
(Devel/mfr/mkt materials science products for electronics, telecommunications &
industry)
    Raychem International Ltd., 100/104 Industrial Estate, Shannon, Ireland

REVLON INC   625 Madison Ave, New York, NY 10022, Tel: (212) 527-4000
(Mfr cosmetics, fragrances, toiletries, beauty care prdts)
    Hydrocurve Ltd., Ireland
    Reheis Chemical Ltd., Ireland
    Roux Intl. Ltd., Ireland
    Technicon Ireland Ltd., Ireland

RHONE-POULENC RORER INC   PO Box 1200, Collegeville, PA 19426-0107,
Tel: (215) 454-8000
(R&D/mfr human pharmaceuticals)
    Rorer Ireland Ltd., Nenagh, Ireland

RIDGE TOOL CO   400 Clark St, Elyria, OH 44035, Tel: (216) 323-5581
(Hand & power tools for working pipe, drain cleaning equip, etc)
    The Ridge Tool Co., Div. of Emerson Electric Ireland Ltd., Cork, Ireland

ROCKWELL INTL CORP   2201 Seal Beach Blvd, PO Box 4250, Seal Beach,
CA 90740-8250, Tel: (310) 797-3311
(Prdts & serv for aerospace, automotive, electronics, graphics & automation inds)
    ROR Rockwell (Ireland) Ltd., Newhall, Naas, Co. Kildare, Ireland

ROUX LABORATORIES INC   PO Box 37557, Jacksonville, FL 32236,
Tel: (904) 693-1200
(Hair coloring prdts)
    Roux Intl. Ltd., Harmonstown Rd., Artane, Dublin 5, Ireland

SARA LEE CORP   3 First National Plaza, Chicago, IL 60602-4260,
Tel: (312) 726-2600
(Mfr/distr food & consumer packaged goods, tobacco prdts, intimate apparel & knitwear)
    Pretty Polly Ltd., Park Rd., Killarney, Co. Kerry, Ireland

SCHERING INTL   PO Box 500, Kenilworth, NJ 07033, Tel: (201) 558-4000
(Pharms, medicines, toiletries, cosmetics, human & animal health prdts)
    Schering Corp. USA, Dublin, Ireland

SCHLEGEL CORP   1555 Jefferson Rd, PO Box 23197, Rochester, NY 14692-3197,
Tel: (716) 427-7200
(Mfr engineered perimeter sealing systems for residential & commercial constr)
    Schlegel Ireland Ltd., Dublin Rd., Loughrea, Co. Galway, Ireland

SCI SYSTEMS INC   PO Box 1000, Huntsville, AL 35807, Tel: (205) 882-4800
(R/D & mfr electronics systems for commerce, industry, aerospace, etc)
    SCI Ireland Ltd., Rathealy Rd., Fermon, Cork, Ireland

SEA-LAND SERVICE INC   150 Allen Rd, Liberty Corner, NJ 07920,
Tel: (201) 558-6000
(Container transport)
    B & I International Ferryport, Alexander Rd., Dublin 1, Ireland

SHARED MEDICAL SYSTEMS CORP   51 Valley Stream Pkwy, Malvern, PA 19355,
  Tel: (215) 219-6300
  (Computer-based info processing for healthcare ind)
    SMS Ireland, SMS House, St. John's Business Centre, Swords Rd., Santry, Dublin,
    Ireland

A O SMITH CORP   11270 W Park Pl, Milwaukee, WI 53224, Tel: (414) 359-4000
  (Auto & truck frames, motors, water heaters, storage/handling sys, plastics, railroad
  prdts)
    A.O. Smith Electric Motors Ireland Ltd., Boghall Rd., Bray, Wicklow, Ireland

SPS TECHNOLOGIES INC   301 Highland Ave, Jenkintown, PA 19046-2630,
  Tel: (215) 572-3000
  (Mfr aerospace & ind fasteners, tightening sys, magnetic materials, superalloys)
    SPS Intl. Ltd., Shannon Airport Industrial Estate, Shannon, County Clare, Ireland
    SPS/Hi-Life Tool Div., Shannon Airport Industrial Estate, Shannon, County Clare,
    Ireland

STANDEX INTL CORP   6 Manor Pkwy, Salem, NH 03079, Tel: (603) 893-9701
  (Mfr diversified graphics, institutional, ind/electr & consumer prdts)
    Standex (Ireland) Ltd., Acragar Rd., Mountmellick, Co. Laois, Ireland

STIEFEL LABORATORIES INC   255 Alhambra Circle, Coral Gables, FL 33134,
  Tel: (305) 443-3807
  (Mfr pharmaceuticals, dermatological specialties)
    Stiefel Laboratories (Ireland) Ltd., Finisklin Industrial Estate, Sligo, Ireland
    Stiefel Laboratories (Ireland) Ltd., 15/16 Stillorgan Industrial Park, Blackrock,
    Co. Dublin, Ireland

SUMMIT TECHNOLOGY INC   21 Hickory Dr, Waltham, MA 02154, Tel: (617) 890-1234
  (Mfr medical lasers)
    Summit Technology Ireland, Model Farm Rd., Cork Business & Technology Centre, Cork,
    Ireland

TACONIC PLASTICS INC   PO Box 69, Petersburg, NY 12138, Tel: (518) 658-3202
  (Mfr teflon/silicone-coated fiberglass fabrics, tapes & belts; spec tapes, circuit
  board substrates)
    Taconic Plastics Inc., Mullingar, Ireland

TECHNICON INSTRUMENTS CORP   511 Benedict Ave, Tarrytown, NY 10591-5097,
  Tel: (914) 631-8000
  (Mfr/serv automated blook anal equip, reagents & diagnostics)
    Technicon (Ireland) Ltd., Church Lane, Swords, County Dublin, Ireland

TEKTRONIX INC   26660 SW Parkway, Wilsonville, OR 97070, Tel: (503) 627-7111
  (Mfr test & meas, visual sys & commun prdts)
    Tektronix Ireland Ltd., Dublin, Ireland

TELLABS INC   4951 Indiana Ave, Lisle, IL 60532, Tel: (708) 969-8800
  (Design/mfr/svce voice/data transport & network access sys)
    Tellabs Ltd., Shannon Industrial Estate, County Clare, Ireland

TEXACO INC   2000 Westchester Ave, White Plains, NY 10650, Tel: (914) 253-4000
  (Explor/mktg crude oil, mfr petro chems & prdts)
    Texaco Ireland Ltd., Texaco House, Ballsbridge, Dublin 4, Ireland

THERM-O-DISC INC   1320 S Main St, Mansfield, OH 44907-0538,
  Tel: (419) 525-8500
  (Mfr thermostats, controls, sensor & thermal cutoffs, switches)
    Therm-O-Disc/Ireland, Raheen Estate, Limerick, Ireland

THE TOPPS CO INC   1 Whitehall St, New York, NY 10004-2108,
  Tel: (212) 376-0300
  (Mfr chewing gum & confections)
    Topps Ireland Ltd., Inhishmore, Ballincollig, Cork, Ireland

TRANE CO   3600 Pammel Creek Rd, La Crosse, WI 54601, Tel: (608) 787-2000
  (Mfr/distr/svce A/C sys & equip)
    Trane (UK) Ltd., 8 The Mall, Lucan, Co. Dublin, Ireland

TRUE TEMPER CORP   465 Railroad Ave, Camp Hill, PA 17011, Tel: (717) 737-1500
  (Mfr hand & edge tools, farm & garden tools, wheelbarrows)
    True Temper (Ireland) Ltd., White's Cross, Ireland

U S SURGICAL CORP   150 Glover Ave, Norwalk, CT 06856, Tel: (203) 845-1000
  (Mfr/devel/mkt surgical staplers, laparoscopic instru & sutures)
    U.S. Surgical Corp (Ireland) Ltd., all mail to U.S. address

UNIFI INC   7201 W Friendly Ave, Greensboro, NC 27410-6237,
  Tel: (910) 294-4410
  (Yarn spinning mills, throwing/winding mills)
    Unifi Textured Yarns Europe Ltd., Ballyraine, Letterkenny, Donegal, Ireland

UNION CAMP CORP   1600 Valley Rd, Wayne, NJ 07470, Tel: (201) 628-2000
  (Mfr paper, packaging, chems, wood prdts)
    Union Camp Ireland Ltd., Cookstown, Ashbourne, Meath, Ireland

UNITRODE CORP   7 Continental Blvd, Merrimack, NH 03054, Tel: (603) 424-2410
  (Mfr electronic components)
    Unitrode Ireland Ltd., Industrial Estate, Shannon, County Clare, Ireland

UOP INC   Ten UOP Plaza, Des Plaines, IL 60016, Tel: (708) 391-2000
  (Diversified research, development & mfr of ind prdts & sys mgmt studies & serv)
    UOP Johnson Well Screens (Ireland) Ltd., Leixlip, Ireland

UPRIGHT INC   1775 Park St, Selma, CA 93662, Tel: (209) 891-5200
  (Mfr aluminum scaffolds & aerial lifts)
    UpRight Ireland Ltd., Industrial Estate, Pottery Rd., Dun Laoire, Dublin, Ireland

USX CORP   600 Grant St, Pittsburgh, PA 15219-4776, Tel: (412) 433-1121
  (Steel & related resources, oil & gas, engineering, real estate)
    Marathon Petroleum Ireland Ltd., Mahon Industrial Estate, Blackrock, Cork, Ireland

WARD HOWELL INTL INC   99 Park Ave, New York, NY 10016-1699,
  Tel: (212) 697-3730
  (Executive recruiting)
    Ward Howell Intl., 12 Richview Office Park, Clonskeagh, Dublin 14, Ireland

WARNER-LAMBERT CO   201 Tabor Road, Morris Plains, NJ 07950,
  Tel: (201) 540-2000
  (Mfr ethical & proprietary pharms, confectionary & consumer prdts)

Warner-Lambert Ireland Ltd., General Diagnostics Div., Pottery Rd., Dun Laoghaire,
  Dublin, Ireland

WELLMAN INC   1040 Broad St, #302, Shrewsbury, NJ 07702, Tel: (908) 542-7300
  (Plastic recycler; mfr polyester fibres & resins)
    Wellman Intl. Ltd., Mullagh, Kells, Meath, Ireland

WESTINGHOUSE ELECTRIC CORP   11 Stanwix St, Pittsburgh, PA 15222-1384,
  Tel: (412) 244-2000
  (TV/radio broadcasting, mfr electr sys for ind/defense, fin & environmental servs)
    Thermo King Europe, Monivea Rd., Mervue, Galway, Ireland

WEYENBERG SHOE MFG CO   234 E Reservoir Ave, PO Box 1188, Milwaukee,
  WI 53201-1188, Tel: (414) 263-8800
  (Mfr men's shoes)
    Weyenberg Shoe Mfg. Co. of Ireland Ltd., c/o Stokes Kennedy Crowley, 1 Stokes Pl.,
      St. Stephen's Green, Dublin 2, Ireland

HARRY WINSTON INC   718 Fifth Ave, New York, NY 10019, Tel: (212) 245-2000
  (Diamonds, lapidary work)
    Harry Winston Irish Rough Diamonds Ltd., Hermitage, Ennis, Clare, Ireland

XEROX CORP   800 Long Ridge Rd, PO Box 1600, Stamford, CT 06904,
  Tel: (203) 968-3000
  (Mfr document processing equip, sys & supplies)
    Xerox Corp., Dublin, Ireland

XILINX INC   2100 Logic Dr, San Jose, CA 95124-3400, Tel: (408) 559-7779
  (Programmable logic & related development sys software)
    Xilinx Ireland, Logic Dr., Citywest Business Campus, Saggart County, Dublin, Ireland

ISRAEL

3M   3M Center, St Paul, MN 55144-1000, Tel: (612) 733-1110
  (Mfr diversified prdts for industry, health care, imaging, commun, transport, safety,
  consumer, etc)
    3M Israel Ltd., c/o Monarch Consulting Co., 91 Medina Ha 'Yehudim St.,
      P.O. Box 2042, Herzilya 46120, Israel

AEROMARITIME INC   11240 Waples Mill Rd, Fairfax, VA 22030,
  Tel: (703) 359-6633
  (Military electronics)
    Elul Technologies Ltd., 35 Shaul Hamelech Blvd., Tel Aviv, Israel

AIR EXPRESS INTL CORP   120 Tokeneke Rd, PO Box 1231, Darien, CT 06820,
  Tel: (203) 655-7900
  (Air frt forwarder)

(cont)

Air Express Int., c/o Mayan Customs & Transport Services Ltd.,
    35 Shaul Hamelech Blvd., Tel Aviv, Israel

AMERICAN STANDARD INC   1 Centennial Ave, Piscataway, NJ 08855,
    Tel: (908) 980-3000
    (Mfr heating & sanitary equip)
       Solcoor Marketing & Purchasing Ltd., 74 Petach Tikva Rd., P.O. Box 20200, Tel Aviv,
       Israel

ANALOG DEVICES INC   1 Technology Way, Box 9106, Norwood, MA 02062,
    Tel: (617) 329-4700
    (Mfr integrated circuits & related devices)
       Analog Devices (Israel) Ltd., Giron Center, 3-5 Jabolinsky St.,
       Raananna Central 43363, Israel

APPLIANCES OVERSEAS INC   276 Fifth Ave, #407, New York, NY 10001-4509,
    Tel: (212) 545-8001
    (Distr/sale appliances & electronics)
       Appliances Overseas, 120 Ben Yahuda St., Tel Aviv T14614DT, Israel

ASSOCIATED MERCHANDISING CORP   1440 Broadway, New York, NY 10018,
    Tel: (212) 536-4000
    (Retail service organization)
       Associated Merchandising Corp., Textile Center Bldg. 14/F, 2 Koifman St.,
       Tel Aviv 61500, Israel

ASTRONAUTICS CORP OF AMERICA   PO Box 523, Milwaukee, WI 53201-0523,
    Tel: (414) 447-8200
    (Design/devel/mfr aircraft instru, avionic & electronics sys)
       Astronautics C.A. Ltd., 23 Hayarkon St., P.O. Box 882, Bnei-Brak, Israel

AUGAT INC   89 Forbes Blvd, Mansfield, MA 02048, Tel: (508) 543-4300
    (Interconnection prdts)
       Augat Ltd., Office 30, Sokolov St. 48A, Ramat Hasharon 47235, Israel

AVX CORP   750 Lexington Ave, New York, NY 10022-1208, Tel: (212) 935-6363
    (Mfr multilayer ceramic capacitors)
       AVX Israel Ltd., P.O. Box 3108, Jerusalem 91030, Israel

BARNWELL INDUSTRIES INC   1100 Alakea St, #2900, Honolulu, HI 96813,
    Tel: (808) 531-8400
    (Holding co: explor/devel gas & oil, drill water sys, farming/mktg papayas)
       Barnwell of Israel Ltd., P.O. Box 3005, Tel Aviv 61030, Israel

SAMUEL BINGHAM CO   1555 N Mittel Blvd, #T, Wood Dale, IL 60191-1046,
    Tel: (708) 238-4000
    (Print & industrial rollers, inks)
       Haglil Ltd., P.O. Box 862, Ashdod 77107, Israel

BIO-RAD LABORATORIES INC   1000 Alfred Nobel Dr, Hercules, CA 94547,
    Tel: (510) 724-7000
    (Mfr life science research prdts, clinical diagnostics, analytical instruments)
       Bio-Rad Laboratories Inc., Rehovot, Israel

BOGUE ELECTRIC MFG CO   100 Pennsylvania Ave, Paterson, NJ 07509,
  Tel: (201) 523-2200
  (Electrical equip)
    American Aviation, Udim 42905, Israel

BRANSON ULTRASONICS CORP   41 Eagle Rd, Danbury, CT 06813-1961,
  Tel: (203) 796-0400
  (Mfr plastics assembly equip, ultrasonic cleaning equip)
    Elina Ltd., P.O. Box 11439, Bet-Dagan 58001, Israel

BRINK'S INC   Thorndal Circle, Darien, CT 06820, Tel: (203) 655-8781
  (Security transportation)
    Brink's Israel Ltd., Migdal Shalom Mayer Bldg., 9 Ahad-Haam St., P.O. Box 29785,
    Tel Aviv, Israel

CARL BYOIR & ASSOCIATES INC   420 Lexington Ave, New York, NY 10017,
  Tel: (212) 210-6000
  (Public relations, intl commun)
    Gitam Image Promotion Ltd., 1 Zabotinsky, Ramat Gan, Israel

CHINET CO   101 Merritt 7, Norwalk, CT 06851, Tel: (203) 846-1499
  (Mfr molded containers)
    Mai Israel Packing Works Ltd., P.O. Box 162, Nathanya, Israel

CHIPCOM CORP   118 Turnpike Rd, Southborough, MA 01772, Tel: (508) 460-8900
  (R&D/mfr local area network components)
    Chipcom Ltd., Kiryat Weizmann, Multipurpose Bldg. 3, P.O. Box 2014, Rihovot 76120,
    Israel

THE CHRISTIAN SCIENCE PUBLISHING SOCIETY   1 Norway St, Boston, MA 02115,
  Tel: (617) 450-2000
  (Publishing, broadcasting)
    The Christian Science Monitor Publication, Beit Agron, Box 3, 37 Hillel St.,
    Jerusalem 93503, Israel

CIGNA CORP   One Liberty Place, Philadelphia, PA 19192, Tel: (215) 523-4000
  (Ins, invest, health care & other fin servs)
    Cigna Insurance Co., c/o Tocatly & Sons, Migdal Shalom Mayer, P.O. Box 1025,
    Tel Aviv, Israel
    Cigna Insurance Co. of Europe SA/NV (Securitas Ins. Ltd.), 38 Rothschild Bldg.,
    P.O. Box 1791, Tel Aviv, Israel

COLUMBIA PICTURES INDUSTRIES INC   711 Fifth Ave, New York, NY 10022,
  Tel: (212) 751-4400
  (Producer & distributor of motion pictures)
    Albert D. Matalon & Co. Ltd., 15 Hess St., Tel Aviv, Israel

COMBUSTION ENGINEERING INC   900 Long Ridge Road, Stamford, CT 06902,
  Tel: (203) 329-8771
  (Tech constr)
    Intl. Process Controls Ltd., 6 Druyanov St., P.O. Box 46052, Tel Aviv, Israel

COMMERCIAL CREDIT LOANS INC   300 St Paul Place, Baltimore, MD 21202,
  Tel: (301) 332-3000
  (Leasing of capital goods)
    Commercial Credit Service Israel Ltd., 43 Brodetsky St., P.O. Box 39023, Tel Aviv,
    Israel

COMPUTER ASSOCIATES INTL INC   One Computer Associates Plaza, Islandia,
NY 11788, Tel: (516) 342-5224
(Devel/mkt/mgt info mgt & bus applications software)
    C.A. Computer Associates Israel Ltd., Deborah Hanevia St., Neva Sharet, Atidim,
    P.O. Box 58160, Tel Aviv 61580, Israel

CONTAINER-STAPLING CORP   27th & ICC Tracks, Herrin, IL 62948,
Tel: (618) 942-2125
(Ind stapling machs & supplies)
    Packaging & Printing Systems (Dvikol) Ltd., 53 Petach Tikva Rd., P.O. Box 20122,
    Tel Aviv, Israel

CPC INTERNATIONAL INC   PO Box 8000, Englewood Cliffs, NJ 07632,
Tel: (201) 894-4000
(Consumer foods, corn refining)
    Israel Edible Products Ltc., 91 Medinat Hayehudim Str., Herzelia Pituach 46766,
    Israel

D-M-E COMPANY   29111 Stephenson Highway, Madison Heights, MI 48071,
Tel: (313) 398-6000
(Basic tooling for plastic molding & die casting)
    R. M. Industrial Services Ltd., 27 Schocken St., Tel Aviv 66532, Israel

DIGITAL EQUIPMENT CORP   146 Main St, Maynard, MA 01754-2571,
Tel: (508) 493-5111
(Networked computer systems & services)
    Digital Equipment (DEC) Ltd.,

DOW CORNING CORP   2220 W Salzburg Rd, PO Box 1767, Midland, MI 48640,
Tel: (517) 496-4000
(Silicones, silicon chems, solid lubricants)
    Shubim Ltd., 9 Bar Kochva St., P.O. Box 14191, Tel Aviv, Israel

EATON CORP   1111 Superior Ave, Cleveland, OH 44114, Tel: (216) 523-5000
(Advanced tech prdts for transp & ind mkts)
    Automotive Equipment Ltd., 74 Petach Tikva Rd., P.O. Box 20205, Tel Aviv, Israel

EPSTEIN ENGINEERING EXPORT LTD   600 W Fulton St, Chicago, IL 60606-1199,
Tel: (312) 454-9100
(Engr & constr)
    A. Epstein & Sons (UK) Ltd., The Industry House, 29 Hamered St., Tel Aviv 68125,
    Israel

FRITZ COMPANIES INC   706 Mission St, San Francisco, CA 94103,
Tel: (415) 904-8360
(Integrated transportation, sourcing, distribution & customs brokerage services)
    Fritz Companies Israel Ltd., 34 Beit Hillel St., Tel Aviv 67017, Israel

GENERAL DYNAMICS CORP   3190 Fairview Park Dr, Falls Church, VA 22042-4523,
Tel: (703) 876-3000
(Mfr aerospace equip, submarines, strategic sys, armored vehicles, defense support
sys)
    General Dynamics Corp., all mail to Embassy of the USA/Israel, Peace Marble,
    APO New York 09672-0008

GENERAL ELECTRIC CO   3135 Easton Tpk, Fairfield, CT 06431,
  Tel: (203) 373-2211
  (Diversified manufacturing, technology & services)
    General Electric Co.,
      all mail to U.S. address; phone (800) 626-2004 or (518) 438-6500

GLENOIT MILLS INTL CORP   111 West 40th St, New York, NY 10018,
  Tel: (212) 391-3915
  (Synthetic pile fabrics)
    Glenoit Intl., P.O. Box 68, Or Akiva-Caesarea, Israel

HORWATH INTL   415 Madison Ave, New York, NY 10017, Tel: (212) 838-5566
  (Public accountants & auditors)
    Horwath, Bawly, Millner & Co., P.O. Box 33777, 5 Habankim St., Haifa, Israel 31337
    Horwath, Bawly, Millner & Co., P.O. Box 50025, 27 Hamered St., Tel Aviv,
      Israel 68125

HOUGHTON INTL INC   PO Box 930, Valley Forge, PA 19482-0930,
  Tel: (610) 666-4000
  (Mfr spec chems, hydraulic fluids, lubricants)
    Delkol Ltd., P.O. Box 31, Lod 71100, Israel

HYATT INTL CORP   200 West Madison, Chicago, IL 60606, Tel: (312) 750-1234
  (Intl hotel mgmt)
    Hyatt Intl. Hotels, Jerusalem, Israel

IBM CORP   Old Orchard Rd, Armonk, NY 10504, Tel: (914) 765-1900
  (Information products, technology & services)
    IBM Israel Ltd., IBM House, 2 Weizmann St., P.O. Box 33666, Tel Aviv 61336, Israel

ICC INDUSTRIES INC   720 Fifth Ave, New York, NY 10019, Tel: (212) 397-3300
  (Chems & plastics)
    ICC (Israel) Chemicals Ltd., P.O. Box 11109, 94 Ben Gurion Rd., Tel Aviv, Israel

INTERGRAPH CORP   Huntsville, AL 35894-0001, Tel: (205) 730-2000
  (Devel/mfr interactive computer graphic systems)
    Intergraph Electronics Ltd., 20 Galgalei Haplada Industrial Area, P.O. Box 708,
      Herzlia 46106, Israel

INTERMEC CORP   6001 36th Ave West, PO Box 4280, Everett, WA 98203-9280,
  Tel: (206) 348-2600
  (Mfr/distr automated data collection sys)
    Intermec Bar Code Ltd., 8 Ma'aleh Hashoevah St., Ramat-Gan 52554, Israel

INTERNATIONAL DIESEL ELECTRIC CO INC   100 Midland Ave, Middletown, NY 10940,
  Tel: (914) 342-3994
  (Engine generating equip)
    Electra (Israel) Ltd., 19 Petach Tikva Rd., P.O. Box 2180, Tel Aviv, Israel

INTERNATIONAL PAPER   2 Manhattanville Rd, Purchase, NY 10577,
  Tel: (914) 397-1500
  (Mfr/distr container board, paper, wood prdts)
    International Paper USA Ltd., Starco Bldg., P.O. Box 34056, Haifa, Israel

INTERNATIONAL VITAMIN CORP OVERSEAS   500 Halls Mill Rd, Freehold, NJ 07728,
   Tel: (908) 308-3000
   (Mfr/distr vitamins & dietary supplements)
      American Vitamin-Israel, 32 Hazohar, Tel Aviv, Israel

ITEL CORP   2 N Riverside Plaza, Chicago, IL 60606, Tel: (312) 902-1515
   (Transport & equip leasing & serv)
      Itel Israel Ltd., 4 Weizmann St., Tel Aviv, Israel

ITT SHERATON CORP   60 State St, Boston, MA 02108, Tel: (617) 367-3600
   (Hotel operations)
      Sheraton Jerusalem Plaza, 47 King George St., Jerusalem 91076, Israel
      Tel Aviv Sheraton Hotel & Towers, 115 Hayarkon St., Tel Aviv, Israel

KOCH ENGINEERING CO INC   PO Box 8127, Wichita, KS 67208, Tel: (316) 832-5110
   (Mass transfer prdts, static mixers, mist eliminator sys)
      Koch Engineering Co. Ltd., 17 Modiin St., P.O. Box 6111, Bnei Brak, Israel

LOCKHEED MARTIN CORP   6801 Rockledge Dr, Bethesda, MD 20817,
   Tel: (301) 897-6000
   (Design/mfr/mgmt sys in fields of space, defense, energy, electronics, materials,
   info & tech svces)
      Lockheed Martin Intl. SA, Asia House, 4 Weizman St., Tel Aviv 64239, Israel

R H MACY & CO INC   151 West 34th St, New York, NY 10001, Tel: (212) 695-4400
   (Department stores, importers)
      R.H. Macy Inc., America House, 35 Shaul Hamelech Blvd., Tel Aviv, Israel

MANPOWER INTL INC   5301 N Ironwood Rd, PO Box 2053, Milwaukee,
   WI 53201-2053, Tel: (414) 961-1000
   (Temporary help service)
      Manpower Israel Ltd., 90-92 Igal Alon St., Tel Aviv 67891, Israel

MENNEN-MEDICAL INC   10123 Main St, Clarence, NY 14031, Tel: (716) 759-6921
   (Electronic med equip, physiological monitors)
      Mennen Medical Ltd., Kiryat Weizmann, P.O. Box 102, Rehovot, Israel

MICROSOFT CORP   One Microsoft Way, Redmond, WA 98052-6399,
   Tel: (206) 882-8080
   (Computer software, peripherals & services)
      Microsoft Israel, Tuval 34, Ramat-Gan 52522, Israel

MOTOROLA INC   1303 E Algonquin Rd, Schaumburg, IL 60196, Tel: (708) 576-5000
   (Mfr commun equip, semiconductors, cellular phones)
      Motorola Israel Ltd., 3 Kremenetski St., Tel Aviv, Israel

MacDERMID INC   245 Freight St, Waterbury, CT 06702, Tel: (203) 575-5700
   (Chem processing for metal ind, plastics, electronics cleaners, strippers)
      MacDermid Israel Ltd., P.O. Box 13011, Tel Aviv 61130, Israel

THE MacNEAL-SCHWENDLER CORP   815 Colorado Blvd, Los Angeles, CA 90041,
   Tel: (213) 258-9111
   (Devel/mfr computer-aided engineering software)
      MSC/EMAS European Product Marketing, P.O. Box 998, 29a Jerusalem Blvd.,
         Kiriat Yam 29011, Israel

NATIONAL CAR RENTAL SYSTEM INC   7700 France Ave S, Minneapolis, MN 55435,
  Tel: (612) 830-2121
  (Car rental)
    National Car Rental System, Box 26113, Tel Aviv, Israel

NETMANAGE INC   10725 N De Anza Blvd, Cupertino, CA 95014, Tel: (408) 973-7171
  (Devel/mfr computer software applications & tools)
    NetManage Inc., Haifa, Israel

RADISSON HOTELS INTL   Carlson Pkwy, PO Box 59159, Minneapolis,
  MN 55459-8204, Tel: (612) 540-5526
  (Hotels)
    Colony's Beach Resort, S. Bat Yam, Israel (inquiries to U.S. address)
    Colony's Mandarin Resort, N. Tel Aviv, Israel (inquiries to U.S. address)

REPUBLIC STEEL CORP   PO Box 6778, Cleveland, OH 44101, Tel: (216) 622-5000
  (Alloy, carbon & stainless steel, chems, electrical conduit, etc)
    Eitan Imported Buildings Ltd., Asia House, 4 Weizmann St., Tel Aviv, Israel
    Jacobson Agencies Ltd., 72 Heh Beiyar St., Tel Aviv, Israel

REVLON INC   625 Madison Ave, New York, NY 10022, Tel: (212) 527-4000
  (Mfr cosmetics, fragrances, toiletries, beauty care prdts)
    Revlon (Israel) Ltd., Industrial Zone, P.O. Box 131, Ashdod, Israel

ROBERT HALF INTL INC   2884 Sand Hill Rd, #200, Menlo Park, CA 94025,
  Tel: (415) 854-9700
  (Personnel servs)
    Robert Half Intl. Inc., Hatachana 4, Jerusalem, Israel

SBC COMMUNICATIONS INC   175 E Houston, San Antonio, TX 78205,
  Tel: (210) 821-4105
  (Telecommunications)
    SBC Communications Inc., Israel

SIGMA-ALDRICH CORP   3050 Spruce St, St Louis, MO 63103, Tel: (314) 771-5765
  (Chems & biochems, aluminum & structural steel components)
    Makor Chemical Ltd., P.O. Box 25469, Jerusalem 91060, Israel
    Sigma Israel Chemical Ltd., P.O. Box 37673, Tel Aviv, Israel

SILICONIX INC   2201 Laurelwood Dr, Santa Clara, CA 95054, Tel: (408) 988-8000
  (Semiconductor components)
    Talviton Electronics Ltd., 9 Biltmore St., P.O. Box 21104, Tel Aviv, Israel

SLANT/FIN CORP   100 Forest Dr at East Hills, Greenvale, NY 11548,
  Tel: (516) 484-2600
  (Mfr heating & A/C sys & comps)
    Slant/Fin Hidron Ltd., 7 Ben Zion St., Tel Aviv 61322, Israel

TELEDYNE INC   2049 Century Park East, Los Angeles, CA 90067-3101,
  Tel: (310) 277-3311
  (Divers mfg: aviation & electronics, specialty metals, industrial & consumer prdts)
    Teledyne Israel, America House, 35 Shaul Hamelech Blvd., Tel Aviv 64927, Israel

TRACOR INC   6500 Tracor Lane, Austin, TX 78725-2000, Tel: (512) 926-2800
  (Time & frequency prdts, gas & liquid chromatographs, eng serv, ship repair)
    Rokar Intl., Science-based Industries Campus, Bldg. C, Har-Hotzvim,
    Jerusalem 91079, Israel

TRANS WORLD AIRLINES INC   505 N 6th St, St Louis, MO 63101,
Tel: (314) 589-3000
(Air transportation)
   Trans World Airlines, City Tower Bldg., 34 Ben Yehuda St., Jerusalem, Israel
   Trans World Airlines (TWA) Inc., 74-76 Hayarkon St., Tel Aviv, Israel

VISHAY INTERTECHNOLOGY INC   63 Lincoln Highway, Malvern, PA 19355,
Tel: (215) 644-1300
(Mfr resistors, strain gages, capacitors, inductors, printed circuit boards)
   Dale Israel Electronics Ltd., Industrial Park, P.O. Box 87, Dimona 86100, Israel
   Draloric Israel, Industrial Park, P.O. Box 87, Dimona 86100, Israel
   Vishay Israel Ltd., 2 Haofan St., Holon 58125, Israel

VOLT INFORMATION SCIENCES INC   1221 Sixth Ave, 47th fl, New York,
NY 10020-1001, Tel: (212) 704-2400
(Computerized publishing, telecommunications & computer systems & services)
   Volt Autologic Ltd., 6 Ahallay St., Ramat Gan 52522, Israel

WITCO CORP   1 American Lane, Greenwich, CT 06831-4236, Tel: (203) 552-2000
(Mfr chem & petroleum prdts)
   Witco Chemical Ltd., P.O. Box 975, Haifa 31000 Haifa,

WOLFE AXELROD ASSOCIATES   420 Lexington Ave, New York, NY 10170,
Tel: (212) 370-4500
(Financial public relations, investor relations)
   Wolfe Axelrod Associates, c/o Stephen J. Kohn, 42 Brenner St., Ranana, Israel

ITALY

3COM CORP   5400 Bayfront Plaza, Santa Clara, CA 95052-8145,
Tel: (408) 764-5000
(Devel/mfr computer networking prdts & sys)
   3Com Mediterraneo, Milan & Rome, Italy

3M   3M Center, St Paul, MN 55144-1000, Tel: (612) 733-1110
(Mfr diversified prdts for industry, health care, imaging, commun, transport, safety, consumer, etc)
   3M Italia SpA, Via San Bovio 3, 20090 Segrate (Milan), Italy

AAF-McQUAY INC   111 S Calvert St, #2800, Baltimore, MD 21202,
Tel: (410) 528-2755
(Mfr air quality control prdts: heating, ventilating, air-conditioning & filtration prdts & services)
   AAF SRL, Via Valassina 24, 20159 Milan, Italy
   McQuay Italia SpA, Via Piani di Santa Maria 72, 00040 Ariccia, Italy

ABBOTT LABORATORIES   100 Abbott Park Rd, Abbott Park, IL 60064-3500,
   Tel: (708) 937-6100
   (Devel/mfr/sale diversified health care prdts & services)
      Abbott SpA, Campoverde, Italy

ACUFF-ROSE PUBLICATION INC   65 Music Square W, Nashville, TN 37203,
   Tel: (615) 321-5000
   (Music publisher)
      Edizioni Acuff-Rose SRL, Via Quintiliano 40, 20138 Milan, Italy

ADAMAS CARBIDE CORP   Market & Passaic St, Kenilworth, NJ 07033,
   Tel: (201) 241-1000
   (Metal prdts)
      Adamas Carbide Corp., Via Bairo 6, 10081 Castellamonte, Italy

ADEMCO INTL   165 Eileen Way, Syosset, NY 11791, Tel: (516) 921-6704
   (Mfr security, fire & burglary sys & prdts)
      Ademco Italia SpA, Via Cristoforo Colombo 1, 20090 Corsico (Milan), Italy

AIR EXPRESS INTL CORP   120 Tokeneke Rd, PO Box 1231, Darien, CT 06820,
   Tel: (203) 655-7900
   (Air frt forwarder)
      Air Express Intl., c/o Coimexco S.p.A., Aeroporto Forlanini, 20090 Milan, Italy
      Air Express Intl., c/o Coimexco S.p.A., Alitalia Cargo Building, Rm. 219,
      Aeroporto Leonardo da Vinci, Rome, Italy

ALBANY INTL CORP   PO Box 1907, Albany, NY 12201, Tel: (518) 445-2200
   (Paper mach clothing, engineered fabrics, plastic prdts, filtration media)
      Albany Intl. Italiana SpA, Viale Lombardi 68, 20010 Inveruno, Italy

ALBERTO-CULVER CO   2525 Armitage Ave, Melrose Park, IL 60160,
   Tel: (708) 450-3000
   (Mfr/mktg personal care & beauty prdts, household & grocery prdts, institutional food
   prdts)
      Alberto-Culver Products SRL, Viale Brenta 18, 20139 Milan, Italy
      Indola SpA, Viale Brenta 18, 20139 Milan, Italy

ALLEN-BRADLEY CO   PO Box 2086, Milwaukee, WI 53201, Tel: (414) 382-2000
   (Mfr eletrical controls & info devices)
      Allen-Bradley Italia SRL, Via Tortona 33, 20144 Milan, Italy
      Nuova OSAI SRL, Allen-Bradley Motion Control Div., Stradale Torino 603,
      10015 Ivrea, Italy

ALLERGAN INC   2525 Dupont Dr, PO Box 19534, Irvine, CA 92713-9534,
   Tel: (714) 752-4500
   (Mfr therapeutic eye care prdts, skin & neural care pharms)
      Allergan Pharmaceuticals Inc., Via Costarica 20/22, 00040 Pomezia, Italy

ALLIEDSIGNAL INC   101 Columbia Rd, PO Box 2245, Morristown, NJ 07962-2245,
   Tel: (201) 455-2000
   (Mfr aerospace & automotive prdts, engineered materials)
      Airsupply Intl., Via S. Gregorio 6, 20124 Milan, Italy
      AlliedSignal Automotive Italia SA, Via Cavelli 53a, 26013 Crema, Italy
      AlliedSignal Freni SpA, Zona Industriale, Casella Postale 27, 70026 Modugno (Bari),
      Italy

AMDAHL CORP   1250 E Arques Ave, PO Box 3470, Sunnyvale, CA 94088-3470,
  Tel: (408) 746-6000
  (Devel/mfr large scale computers, software, data storage prdts, info-technology
  solutions & support)
    Amdahl Italia SpA, Via Elio Vittorini 129, 00144 Rome, Italy

AMERICAN AIRLINES INC   PO Box 619616, Dallas-Ft Worth Arpt, TX 75261-9616,
  Tel: (817) 355-1234
  (Air transp)
    American Airlines Inc., Via Sicilia 50, 00187 Rome, Italy

AMERICAN APPRAISAL ASSOCS INC   411 E Wisconsin Ave, Milwaukee, WI 53202,
  Tel: (414) 271-7240
  (Valuation consulting serv)
    American Appraisal Italia SRL, Centro Direzionale Colleoni, Viale Colleoni 21,
      Edificio Pegaso 1, 20041 Agrate, Milan, Italy

AMERICAN EXPRESS CO   World Financial Center, New York, NY 10285-4765,
  Tel: (212) 640-2000
  (Travel, travelers cheques, charge card & financial services)
    American Express Co. SpA
    American Express Factoring Ltda.
    American Express Locazioni Finanziarie SRL

AMERICAN STANDARD INC   1 Centennial Ave, Piscataway, NJ 08855,
  Tel: (908) 980-3000
  (Mfr heating & sanitary equip)
    WABCO Westinghouse Compagnia Freni SpA, Via Pier Carlo Boggio 20, 10138 Turin, Italy
    WABCO Westinghouse Compagnia Italiana Segnali SpA, Via Volvera 51,
      10045 Piossasco-Turin, Italy

AMERICAN UNIFORM CO   PO Box 2130, Cleveland, TN 37311, Tel: (615) 476-6561
  (Mfr work clothing, uniforms)
    Amuco Italiana SpA, Via Pina Odardine 29, 83100 Avellino, Italy

AMETEK INC   Station Sq, Paoli, PA 19301, Tel: (610) 647-2121
  (Mfr instru, elect motors, engineered materials)
    Ametek Italia SRL, Via de Barzi, 20087 Robecco Sul Naviglio, Milan, Italy

AMICON INC   72 Cherry Hill Dr, Beverly, MA 01915, Tel: (508) 777-3622
  (Mfr/sale/svce bioseparation, membrane ultrafiltration, chromatography)
    Grace Italiana SpA, Div. Amicon, Via Trento 7, 20017 Passirana di Rho, Italy

AMP INC   PO Box 3608, Harrisburg, PA 17105-3608, Tel: (717) 564-0100
  (Devel/mfr electronic & electrical connection prdts & sys)
    AMP Italia SpA, Via Fratelli Cervi 15, 10093 Collegno (Turin), Italy

AMPEX SYSTEMS CORP   401 Broadway, Redwood City, CA 94063-3199,
  Tel: (415) 367-2011
  (Mfr hi-perf helical scanning recording sys & associated tape media)
    Ampex Italiana SpA, Italy
    Ampex Italiana SpA, Via Cristoforo Colombo 40, 20090 Trezzano sul Naviglio, Milan,
      Italy

AMPHENOL PRODUCTS   1925A Ohio St, Lisle, IL 60532, Tel: (708) 960-1010
(Elect interconnect/penetrate sys & assemblies)
   Amphenol-Sicem Italia, Via Senato 6B, 20020 Arese, Milan, Italy

AMSTED INDUSTRIES INC   205 N Michigan, Chicago, IL 60601, Tel: (312) 645-1700
(Steel castings for railroad & ind use, wire prdts, refrig & heading equip)
   Baltimore Aircoil Italia SRL, Loc Giardini, 23030 Chiuro, Italy

AMWAY CORP   7575 E Fulton Rd, Ada, MI 49355, Tel: (616) 676-6000
(Mfr/sale home care, personal care, nutrition & houseware prdts)
   Amway Italia SRL, Via G. di Vittorio 10, 20094 Corsico (Milan), Italy

ANALOG DEVICES INC   1 Technology Way, Box 9106, Norwood, MA 02062,
Tel: (617) 329-4700
(Mfr integrated circuits & related devices)
   Analog Devices SRL, Via Galileo Galilei 2, 20091 Bresso, Italy

ANDREW CORP   10500 W 153rd St, Orlando Park, IL 60462, Tel: (708) 349-3300
(Mfr antenna sys, coaxial cable, electronic commun & network connectivity sys)
   Andrew SRL, Via Cellini 3, 20129 Milan, Italy

APPLE COMPUTER INC   1 Infinite Loop, Cupertino, CA 95014, Tel: (408) 996-1010
(Personal computers, peripherals & software)
   Apple Computer SpA, Via Bovio 5, Zona Ind. di Mancasale, 42100 Reggio, Emilia, Italy

APPLIED POWER INC   13000 W Silver Spring Dr, Butler, WI 53007,
Tel: (414) 781-6600
(Mfr hi-pressure tools, vibration control prdts, electrical tools & consumables, tech
furniture)
   Applied Power Italiana SpA, Via Canova 4, 20094 Corsico, Milan, Italy

ARBOR ACRES FARM INC   439 Marlborough Rd, Glastonbury, CT 06033,
Tel: (860) 633-4681
(Producers of male & female broiler breeders, commercial egg layers)
   Arbor Acres Italia SpA, Localita Mojentina, 20070 San Rocco Al Porto, Milan, Italy

ARGO INTL CORP   140 Franklin St, New York, NY 10013, Tel: (212) 431-1700
(Distr electrical spare parts)
   Argo Intl. Europe Ltd., Viale Dei Mille 74, Florence, Italy

ARMSTRONG WORLD INDUSTRIES INC   PO Box 3001, Lancaster, PA 17604,
Tel: (717) 397-0611
(Mfr/mkt interior furnishings & spec prdts for bldg, auto & textile inds)
   Armstrong World Industries Italia SRL, Trezzano Rosa,
   Italy (all inquiries to U.S. address)

ARROW ELECTRONICS INC   25 Hub Dr, Melville, NY 11747, Tel: (516) 391-1300
(Distr electronic components)
   Silverstar, Viale Fulvio Testi 280, 20126 Milan, Italy

ARTOS ENGINEERING CO INC   W228 N2792 Duplainville Rd, Waukesha, WI 53186,
Tel: (414) 524-6600
(Mfr metalworking machinery)
   Artos Italia SpA, Strada Nizza 48, La Loggia, 10040 Piemonte, Italy

ASARCO INC   180 Maiden Lane, New York, NY 10038, Tel: (212) 510-2000
  (Nonferrous metals, specialty chems, minerals, mfr industrial prdts, environmental
  services)
    Enthone-Omi Inc., Italy

ASGROW SEED CO   2605 E Kilgore Rd, Kalamazoo, MI 49002, Tel: (616) 384-5675
  (Research/mfr agronomic & vegetable seeds; seed technologies)
    Asgrow Italia, Via San Colombano 81/A, 20075 Lodi (Milan), Italy

ASHLAND OIL INC   1000 Ashland Dr, Russell, KY 41169, Tel: (606) 329-3333
    (Petroleum exploration, refining & transportation; mfr chemicals, oils & lubricants)
      Ashland Chemical Italiana SpA, Via Giacomo Watt 42, 20143 Milan, Italy

ASSOCIATED MERCHANDISING CORP   1440 Broadway, New York, NY 10018,
  Tel: (212) 536-4000
  (Retail service organization)
    Amcrest Corp., Piazza della Republica 32, 20124 Milan, Italy
    Amcrest Corp., Via Guicciardini 13, 50125 Florence, Italy

ASSOCIATED PRESS INC   50 Rockefeller Plaza, New York, NY 10020-1605,
  Tel: (212) 621-1500
  (News gathering agency)
    The Associated Press, Piazza Grazioli 5, Rome, Italy

AST RESEARCH INC   16215 Alton Parkway, PO Box 19658, Irvine, CA 92713-9658,
  Tel: (714) 727-4141
  (Design/devel/mfr hi-perf desktop, server & notebook computers)
    AST Italy, Via Cassanese 224, Palazzo Cimabue, Centro Direzionale Milano Citre,
      20090 Segrate, Milan, Italy

AT&T INTERNATIONAL   412 Mt Kemble Ave, Morristown, NJ 07962-1995,
  Tel: (810) 262-6646
  (Telecommunications)
    AT&T Italia SpA, 153 Via Cristoforo Colombo, 00147 Rome, Italy

AUGAT INC   89 Forbes Blvd, Mansfield, MA 02048, Tel: (508) 543-4300
  (Interconnection prdts)
    Augat SRL, Via Benedetto Marcello 36, 20124 Milan, Italy

AUTODESK INC   2320 Marinship Way, Sausalito, CA 94965, Tel: (415) 332-2344
  (Devel/mkt/support computer-aided design, engineering, scientific & multimedia
  software prdts)
    Autodesk SRL, Milanofiori, Strada 4, Palazzo A6, 20090 Assago (Milan), Italy

AVERY DENNISON CORP   150 N Orange Grove Blvd, Pasadena, CA 91103,
  Tel: (818) 304-2000
  (Mfr pressure-sensitive adhesives & materials, office prdts, labels, tags, retail
  sys, spec chems)
    Avery Etichette Italia SpA, Viale dell'Industrie 53, 20037 Paderno, Italy
    Fasson Italia SpA, Corso Italia 2, 21040 Origgio, Varese, Italy

AVNET INC   80 Cutter Mill Rd, Great Neck, NY 11021, Tel: (516) 466-7000
  (Distr electr components, computers & peripherals)
    Avnet EMG SRL, Via Novara 50, 20153 Milan, Italy

AVON PRODUCTS INC   9 W 57th St, New York, NY 10019, Tel: (212) 546-6015
(Mfr/distr beauty & related prdts, fashion jewelry, gifts & collectibles)
  Avon Cosmetics SpA, Via XXV Aprile 15, 22077 Olgiate, Comasco (Como), Italy

THE BADGER CO INC   One Broadway, Cambridge, MA 02142, Tel: (617) 494-7312
(Engr & const serv to process ind)
  Badger Intaliana SRL, Via Vincenzo Monti 51, 20123 Milan, Italy

BAILEY-FISCHER & PORTER CO   125 E County Line Rd, Warminster, PA 18974,
  Tel: (215) 674-6000
(Design/mfr meas, recording & control instru & sys; mfr ind glass prdts)
  Bailey-Fischer & Porter Italiana SpA, Casella Postale 44, Via Gorizia 16,
    20063 Cernusco sul Naviglio, Milan, Italy

BAIN & CO INC   2 Copley Place, Boston, MA 02117-0897, Tel: (617) 572-2000
(Strategic management consulting services)
  Bain, Cuneo e Associati, Via Crocefisso 10/12, 20122 Milan, Italy
  Bain, Cuneo e Associati, Via Lutezia 8, 00198 Rome, Italy

BAKER OIL TOOLS   PO Box 40129, Houston, TX 77240-0129, Tel: (713) 466-1322
(Mfr/serv oil/gas well completions equip)
  Baker Oil Tools (Italia) SRL, Strada Statale 602, Km. 5.170, Santa Teresa,
    65010 Spoltore (Pescara), Italy

BANKAMERICA CORP   555 California St, San Francisco, CA 94104,
  Tel: (415) 622-3456
(Financial services)
  Bank of America NT & SA, Corso Matteotti 10, 20121 Milan, Italy

BANKERS TRUST CO   280 Park Ave, New York, NY 10017, Tel: (212) 250-2500
(Banking)
  Bankers Trust Co., Italy

C R BARD INC   730 Central Ave, Murray Hill, NJ 07974, Tel: (908) 277-8000
(Mfr health care prdts)
  Bard SpA, Via Cina 444, 00144 Rome, Italy

BAUSCH & LOMB INC   1 Chase Square, Rochester, NY 14601, Tel: (716) 338-6000
(Mfr vision care prdts & accessories)
  Bausch & Lomb Italy SpA, Macherio, Italy

BAXTER HEALTHCARE CORP   1 Baxter Pky, Deerfield, IL 60015,
  Tel: (708) 948-2000
(Mfr disposable medical prdts)
  Baxter SpA, also in Sesto Fiorentino, Milan & Mirandola, Italy
  Baxter SpA, Viale Tiziano 25, 00196 Rome, Italy
  Laboratori Don Baxter SpA, Via Flavia 122, 34146 Trieste, Italy

BECKMAN INSTRUMENTS INC   2500 Harbor Blvd, Fullerton, CA 92634,
  Tel: (714) 871-4848
(Devel/mfr/mkt automated systems & supplies for biological analysis)
  Beckman-Analytical SpA, Centro Direzionale Lombardo, Palazzo F/1, Via Roma 108,
    20060 Cassina de Pecchi, Milan, Italy

BINKS MFG CO   9201 W Belmont Ave, Franklin Park, IL   60131,
  Tel: (708) 671-3000
  (Mfr of spray painting & finishing equip)
    Binks Intl. (Italia) SRL, Via Amsterdam 15, 24040 Zingonia Bergamo, Italy

BIO-RAD LABORATORIES INC   1000 Alfred Nobel Dr, Hercules, CA   94547,
  Tel: (510) 724-7000
  (Mfr life science research prdts, clinical diagnostics, analytical instruments)
    Bio-Rad Laboratories SRL, Milan, Italy

BLACK & DECKER CORP   701 E Joppa Road, Towson, MD   21286, Tel: (410) 716-3900
  (Mfr power tools & accessories, security hardware, small appliances, fasteners, info
  sys & servs)
    Black & Decker Corp., all mail to U.S. address

BLACK BOX CORP   1000 Park Dr, Lawrence, PA   15055, Tel: (412) 746-5500
  (Direct marketer & tech service provider of commun, networking & related computer
  connectivity prdts)
    Black Box Italia SpA, Viale Delle Industrie 11, 20090 Vimodrone, Milan, Italy

BOGUE ELECTRIC MFG CO   100 Pennsylvania Ave, Paterson, NJ   07509,
  Tel: (201) 523-2200
  (Electrical equip)
    Hobart Intl., Rome, Italy

BOOLE & BABBAGE INC   510 Oakmead Pkwy, Sunnyvale, CA   94086,
  Tel: (408) 735-9550
  (Devel/support enterprise automation & systems mgmt software)
    Boole & Babbage Europe, Via Venezia 59/15, c/Copgnifo, 35129 Padua, Italy
    Boole & Babbage Europe, Via R.R. Pereira 97, 00136 Rome, Italy
    Boole & Babbage Italia SRL, Via Cernaia 2, 20121 Milan, Italy

BOOZ ALLEN & HAMILTON INC   101 Park Ave, New York, NY   10178,
  Tel: (212) 697-1900
  (Mgmt consultants)
    Booz, Allen & Hamilton Italia Ltd., Via Baracchini 1, 20123 Milan, Italy

BORDEN INC   180 E Broad St, Columbus, OH   43215-3799, Tel: (614) 225-4000
  (Mfr foods, snacks & beverages, adhesives)
    Borden Inc., all mail to U.S. address
    FIAP SpA, Via Isonzo 26, 22078 Turate, Italy

BORG-WARNER AUTOMOTIVE INC   200 S Michigan Ave, Chicago, IL   60604,
  Tel: (312) 322-8500
  (Mfr automotive components; provider of security services)
    Regina-Warner SpA, Via Monza 90, 22052 Cernusco Lombardone, Italy

BOSE CORP   The Mountain, Framingham, MA   01701-9168, Tel: (508) 879-7330
  (Mfr audio equip)
    Bose SpA, Via Luigi Capucci 12, 00147 Rome, Italy

BOYDEN CONSULTING CORP   375 Park Ave, #1008, New York, NY   10152,
  Tel: (212) 980-6480
  (Executive search)
    Boyden Intl. SRL, Via Lazzaro Palazzi 2A, Milan, Italy

W H BRADY CO   6555 W Good Hope Rd, Milwaukee, WI 53223, Tel: (414) 358-6600
(Mfr ind ID for wire marking, circuit boards; facility ID & signage)
    Seton Italia SRL, Casella Postale 51, 20037 Paderno Dugnano (Milan), Italy
    W.H. Brady NV, Via Melzi d'Eril 29, 20154 Milan, Italy

BRANSON ULTRASONICS CORP   41 Eagle Rd, Danbury, CT 06813-1961,
Tel: (203) 796-0400
(Mfr plastics assembly equip, ultrasonic cleaning equip)
    Branson Ultrasuoni SpA, Via Dei Lavoratori 25, 20092 Cinisello Balsamo, Milan, Italy

W BRAUN CO   300 N Canal St, Chicago, IL 60606, Tel: (312) 346-6500
(Design/mfr/supply packaging)
    Filiale Italiana, Italy

BRINK'S INC   Thorndal Circle, Darien, CT 06820, Tel: (203) 655-8781
(Security transportation)
    Brink's Securmark SpA, Florence, Italy

BROWN GROUP INC   8300 Maryland Ave, St Louis, MO 63105, Tel: (314) 854-4000
(Mfr/sale footwear)
    Pagoda Italia, Via Garibaldi 8, 50123 Florence, Italy

BULAB HOLDINGS INC   1256 N McLean Blvd, Memphis, TN 38108,
Tel: (901) 278-0330
(Mfr microbicides, biocides, additives, corrosion inhibitors, chems)
    Buckman Laboratories Italiana SRL, Via Verdi 3, Zibido San Giacomo, 20080 Milan,
    Italy

LEO BURNETT CO INC   35 West Wacker Dr, Chicago, IL 60601, Tel: (312) 220-5959
(Advertising agency)
    Leo Burnett Co. SRL, Via Fatebenefratelli 14, 20121 Milan, Italy

BURR-BROWN RESEARCH CORP   PO Box 11400, Tucson, AZ 85734, Tel: (602) 746-1111
(Electronic components & sys modules)
    Burr-Brown Intl. SRL, Via Zante 14, 20138 Milan, Italy

BURSON-MARSTELLER   230 Park Ave, New York, NY 10003-1566, Tel: (212) 614-4000
(Public relations/public affairs consultants)
    Burson-Marsteller SRL, Piazza S. Alessandro 6, 20123 Milan, Italy

BUTTERICK CO INC   161 Ave of the Americas, New York, NY 10013,
Tel: (212) 620-2500
(Sewing patterns)
    Vla G.A. Boltraffio, Via Cola Montano 10, 20159 Milan, Italy

CARL BYOIR & ASSOCIATES INC   420 Lexington Ave, New York, NY 10017,
Tel: (212) 210-6000
(Public relations, intl commun)
    Chiappe Byoir Associati, Via Carducci 16, 20123 Milan, Italy

CABOT CORP   75 State St, Boston, MA 02109-1807, Tel: (617) 890-0200
(Mfr carbon blacks, plastics; oil & gas, info sys)
    Cabot Italiana SpA, Casella Postale 444, Via Senistra Canate Candiano,
    48100 Ravenna, Italy

CALCOMP INC   2411 W La Palma Ave, Anaheim, CA   92801, Tel: (714) 821-2000
(Mfr computer graphics peripherals)
   Calcomp SpA, Via dei Tulipani 5, 20090 Pieve Emanuele, Milan, Italy

CANBERRA INDUSTRIES INC   One State St, Meriden, CT   06450, Tel: (203) 238-2351
(Mfr instru for nuclear research)
   Canberra-Packard SRL, Via Vincenzo Monti 23, 20016 Pero Milan, Italy
   Canberra-Packard SRL, Via della Circonvallazione Nomentana 514, 00162 Rome, Italy

CARBOLINE CO   350 Hanley Industrial Ct, St Louis, MO   63144,
Tel: (314) 644-1000
(Mfr coatings, sealants)
   APSA SpA, Via Pirelli 30, 20124 Milan, Italy

CARPENTER TECHNOLOGY CORP   101 W Bern St, PO Box 14662, Reading,
PA 19612-4662, Tel: (610) 208-2000
(Mfr specialty steels & structural ceramics for casting ind)
   Carpenter Technology (Italy) SRL, Via Monte Rosa 60, 20149 Milan, Italy

CARRIER CORP   One Carrier Place, Farmington, CT   06034-4015,
Tel: (203) 674-3000
(Mfr/distr/svce A/C, heating & refrigeration equip)
   Delchi Carrier SpA, Via Raffaello Sanzio 9, 20058 Villasanta, Milan, Italy

CARTER-WALLACE INC   1345 Ave of the Americas, New York, NY   10105,
Tel: (212) 339-5000
(Mfr personal care prdts, pet prdts)
   Italia Laboratorio Bouty SpA, Via Vanvitelli 6, 20129 Milan, Italy

CELITE CORP   PO Box 519, Lompoc, CA   93438, Tel: (805) 735-7791
(Mining/process diatomaceous earth (diatomite))
   Celite Italiana SRL, Via Anfiteatro 5, 20121 Milan, Italy

CENTRAL NATIONAL-GOTTESMAN INC   3 Manhattanville Rd, Purchase,
NY   10577-2110, Tel: (914) 696-9000
(Worldwide sales pulp & paper prdts)
   Central National Italia SRL, Via Antonio da Recante 4, 20124 Milan, Italy

CHASE MANHATTAN BANK N A   1 Chase Manhattan Plaza, New York, NY   10081,
Tel: (212) 552-2222
(Intl banking)
   Chase Investimenti Mobiliari SPA, Piazza Meda 1, 20121 Milan, Italy
   Chasefin Chase Finanziaria SPA   ., Piazzale Accursio 18, 20156 Milan, Italy

CHEMICAL BANK   270 Park Ave, New York, NY   10017-2070, Tel: (212) 270-6000
(Banking & financial services)
   Chemical Bank, Via Brera 5, 20121 Milan, Italy
   Chemical Bank, Viale Leigi 10, 00198 Rome, Italy
   Chemical Finanziaria SpA, Via Brera 5, 20121 Milan, Italy

CHESTERTON BINSWANGER INTL   Two Logan Sq, 4th fl, Philadelphia,
PA 19103-2759, Tel: (215) 448-6000
(Real estate & related svces)
   Redilco SpA, Via dell' Arcivescovado 1, 20122 Milan, Italy

CHICAGO PNEUMATIC TOOL CO   2200 Bleecker St, Utica, NY 13501,
  Tel: (315) 792-2600
  (Mfr air tools & equip)
    Chicago Pneumatic Tool SpA, Via Bisceglie 91/7, 20152 Milan, Italy

CHINET CO   101 Merritt 7, Norwalk, CT 06851, Tel: (203) 846-1499
  (Mfr molded containers)
    Keyes Italiana SpA, Fuimefreddo di Sicilia (Catania), Italy

CHIQUITA BRANDS INTL INC   250 E Fifth St, Cincinnati, OH 45202,
  Tel: (513) 784-8000
  (Distribution food products)
    Chiquita Italia SpA, Via Tempio del Ciela 3, 00144 Rome, Italy

CHIRON CORP   4560 Horton St, Emeryville, CA 94608-2916, Tel: (510) 601-2412
  (Research/mfg/mktg therapeutics, vaccines, diagnostics, ophthalmics)
    Chiron Biocine SpA, Via Fiorentina 1, 53100 Siena, Italy
    Ciba Corning Diagnostics SpA, Via Roma 109, Palazzo E, 20060 Cassina de' Pecchi,
    Italy

THE CHUBB CORP   15 Mountain View Rd, Warren, NJ 07060, Tel: (908) 580-2000
  (Holding co: property/casualty ins)
    Chubb Insurance Co. of Europe, Italy

CIGNA CORP   One Liberty Place, Philadelphia, PA 19192, Tel: (215) 523-4000
  (Ins, invest, health care & other fin servs)
    Cigna Insurance Co. of Europe SA/NV, Viale Maresciallo Pilsudski 124, 00197 Rome,
    Italy
    Cigna Italy-Societa A Responsabilita Limitada, Viale Maresciallo Pilsudski 124,
    00197 Rome, Italy
    Esis Intl. Inc., Via della Moscova 3, 20120 Milan, Italy

CITICORP   399 Park Ave, New York, NY 10043, Tel: (212) 559-1000
  (Banking & financial services)
    Citibank NA, Italy

COBE LABORATORIES INC   1185 Oak St, Lakewood, CO 80215, Tel: (303) 232-6800
  (Mfr med equip & supplies)
    Kilab SRL, Medolla, Italy

THE COCA-COLA CO   PO Drawer 1734, Atlanta, GA 30301, Tel: (404) 676-2121
  (Mfr/mkt/distr soft drinks, syrups & concentrates, juice & juice-drink prdts)
    Coca-Cola Italy, all mail to U.S. address

THE COLEMAN CO INC   1526 Cole Blvd, #300, Golden, CO 80401,
  Tel: (303) 202-2470
  (Mfr/distr/sales camping & outdoor recreation prdts)
    Coleman SVB (Italy), Via Canova 11, 25010 Centenaro-Lonato (Brescia), Italy

COLGATE-PALMOLIVE CO   300 Park Ave, New York, NY 10022, Tel: (212) 310-2000
  (Mfr pharms, cosmetics, toiletries, detergents)
    Colgate-Palmolive SpA, Via Georgione 59/63, 00147 Rome, Italy

COLUMBIA PICTURES INDUSTRIES INC   711 Fifth Ave, New York, NY 10022,
  Tel: (212) 751-4400
  (Producer & distributor of motion pictures)
    Columbia Pictures SRL, Via Palestro 24 CAP, 00185 Rome, Italy

COMBUSTION ENGINEERING INC   900 Long Ridge Road, Stamford, CT 06902,
  Tel: (203) 329-8771
  (Tech constr)
    C-E Refractories, Sirma SpA, Via della Chimica 4, 30033 Malcontental/Venice, Italy
    C-E Vetco Service, Via della Betulle 16, 48023 Ravenna, Italy
    Vetco, Via dei Martinitt 7, 20146 Milan, Italy

COMMERCIAL INTERTECH CORP   1775 Logan Ave, PO Box 239, Youngstown,
  OH 44501-0239, Tel: (216) 746-8011
  (Mfr hydraulic com, fluid purification sys, pre-engineered bldgs, stamped metal prdts)
    Commercial Hydraulics SRL, Via dell' Agricoltura 1/A, 37012 Bussolengo, Verona,
      Italy

COMPUTER ASSOCIATES INTL INC   One Computer Associates Plaza, Islandia,
  NY 11788, Tel: (516) 342-5224
  (Devel/mkt/mgt info mgt & bus applications software)
    Computer Associates SpA, Palazzo Leonardo, Via Francesco Sforza 3,
      20080 Basiglio Milan, Italy

COMPUTERVISION CORP   100 Crosby Dr, Bedford, MA 01730-1480,
  Tel: (617) 275-1800
  (Supplier of mechanical design automation & prdt data mgmt software & services)
    Computervision Italia SpA, Via Modigliana 45, 20090 Segrate, Milan, Italy

CONOCO INC   600 N Dairy Ashford Rd, Houston, TX 77079, Tel: (713) 293-1000
  (Oil, gas, coal, chems, minerals)
    Conoco Idrocarburi SpA, Via Vittorio Veneto 116, 00187 Rome, Italy
    Continental Oil Co. of Italy, c/o Studio Dott. Rag. Sergio Pagani, Via G. Frua 24,
      20146 Milan, Italy

CONTEL FEDERAL SYSTEMS   15000 Conference Center Dr, Chantilly,
  VA 22021-3808, Tel: (703) 818-4000
  (Telecom sys)
    Contel Page Europa, Viale del Campo, 00153 Rome, Italy

CONTINENTAL BANK NA   231 S LaSalle St, Chicago, IL 60697, Tel: (312) 828-2345
  (Coml banking servs)
    Continental Bank Corp., Via Turati 18, 20121 Milan, Italy
    Continental Illinois Finanziaria SpA, Via Turati 18, 20121 Milan, Italy

COOPER INDUSTRIES INC   1001 Fannin St, PO Box 4446, Houston, TX 77210-4446,
  Tel: (713) 739-5400
  (Mfr/distr electrical prdts, tools & hardware, automotive prdts)
    Cooper Automotive, Carpi, Modena, Italy
    Cooper Automotive, Casarza Ligure, Genoa, Italy
    Cooper Automotive, Druento, Turin, Italy
    Kirsch Div., Milan, Italy

CORESTATES FINANCIAL CORP   1500 Market St, Philadelphia, PA 19101,
  Tel: (215) 973-3100
  (Banking)
    Corestates Bank, Corso Europa 14, 20122 Milan, Italy

CORNING INC   One Riverfront Plaza, Corning, NY 14831, Tel: (607) 974-9000
  (Mfr glass & specialty materials, consumer prdts; communications, lab services)
    CALP SpA, Sienna, Italy
    Corning SpA, Milan, Italy

COSTAR CORP   One Alewife Center, Cambridge, MA 02140, Tel: (617) 868-6200
  (Mfr disposable products for life science research labs)
    Costar Italia SRL, Via Don Luigi Sturzo 10, 20049 Concorezzo (Milan), Italy

COULTER CORP   PO Box 169015, Miami, FL 33116-9015, Tel: (305) 885-0131
  (Mfr blood analysis sys, flow cytometers, chem sys, scientific sys & reagents)
    Coulter Scientific SpA, Viale Monza 338, 20128 Milan, Italy

CPC INTERNATIONAL INC   PO Box 8000, Englewood Cliffs, NJ 07632,
  Tel: (201) 894-4000
  (Consumer foods, corn refining)
    CPC Italia SpA, Via G. Gozzano 14, 20092 Cinisello Balsamo (MI), Italy

CRAY RESEARCH INC   655 Lone Oak Dr, Eagan, MN 55121, Tel: (612) 452-6650
  (Supercomputer systems & services)
    Cray Research SRL, Via Vivaio 11, 20122 Milan, Italy

CROWN CORK & SEAL CO INC   9300 Ashton Rd, Philadelphia, PA 19136,
  Tel: (215) 698-5100
  (Mfr cans, bottle caps; filling & packaging mach)
    Crown Cork Co. Italy SpA, Italy

CULLIGAN INTL CO   One Culligan Parkway, Northbrook, IL 60062,
  Tel: (708) 205-6000
  (Water treatment prdts & serv)
    Culligan Italiana SpA, Via Gandolfi 6, Cadriano di Granarolo, Emilia,
      40136 Bologna, Italy

CUMMINS ENGINE CO INC   PO Box 3005, Columbus, IN 47202, Tel: (812) 377-5000
  (Mfr diesel engines)
    Cummins Diesel Italia SpA, Piazza Locatelli 8, Zona Industriale, 20098,
      San Guiliano, Milan, Italy

D'ARCY MASIUS BENTON & BOWLES INC (DMB&B)   1675 Broadway, New York,
  NY 10019, Tel: (212) 468-3622
  (Advertising & communications)
    DMB&B SpA, Via Correggio 18, 20149 Milan, Italy
    DMB&B SpA, other locations in Italy

D-M-E COMPANY   29111 Stephenson Highway, Madison Heights, MI 48071,
  Tel: (313) 398-6000
  (Basic tooling for plastic molding & die casting)
    COMAT-DME SpA, Via Desiderio 24, 20131 Milan, Italy

DAMES & MOORE   911 Wilshire Blvd, Los Angeles, CA 90017, Tel: (213) 683-1560
  (Engineering, environmental & construction mgmt services)
    Dames & Moore, Via Caldera 21, 20153 Milan, Italy

DANA CORP   PO Box 1000, Toledo, OH 43697, Tel: (419) 535-4500
  (Engineer/mfr/mkt prdts & sys for vehicular, ind & mobile off-highway mkt & related
  aftermarkets)

(cont)

Spicer Italia, Via Provinciale Lucchese 187/1, 50019 Osmannora, Italy
Warner Electric SpA, Via Bernardina Verro 90, 20141 Milan, Italy

DATA GENERAL CORP   4400 Computer Dr, Westboro, MA 01580, Tel: (617) 366-8911
(Design, mfr gen purpose computer sys & peripheral prdts & servs)
Data General SpA, Milan, Italy

DATA SWITCH CORP   1 Enterprise Dr, Shelton, CT 06484, Tel: (203) 926-1801
(Mfr computer switches, channel extenders, networking sys, fiber-optic data center
prdts)
Data Switch Italia SRL, Via Benedetto Croce 49, 00142 Rome, Italy

DATAEASE INTL INC   7 Cambridge Dr, Trumbull, CT 06611, Tel: (203) 374-8000
(Mfr applications devel software)
DataEase Italia, Italy

DATAPRODUCTS CORP   6200 Canada Ave, PO Box 746, Woodland Hills, CA 91365,
Tel: (818) 887-8000
(Mfr computer printers & supplies)
Dataproducts SRL, Milanofiori Palazzo F1, Assago 20094, Italy

DATAWARE TECHNOLOGIES INC   222 Third St, #3300, Cambridge, MA 02142,
Tel: (617) 621-0820
(Multi-platform, multi-lingual software solutions & services for electronic info
providers)
Dataware Technologies SRL, Via del Quirinale 26, 00187 Rome, Italy

DDB NEEDHAM WORLDWIDE INC   437 Madison Ave, New York, NY 10022,
Tel: (212) 415-2000
(Advertising)
Broucc/Verba DDB Needham SRL, Via Solari 11, 20144 Milan, Italy
Broucc/Verba DDB Needham SRL, Galleria Passarella 2, 20122 Milan, Italy

DECISION STRATEGIES INTL INC   801 Second Ave, New York, NY 10017-4706,
Tel: (212) 599-9400
(Business intelligence & investigative consulting)
Decision Strategies Intl. SRL, Via della Scrofa 57, 00186 Rome, Italy

DEERE & CO   John Deere Rd, Moline, IL 61265, Tel: (309) 765-8000
(Mfr/sale agri/constr/utility/forestry & lawn/grounds care equip)
John Deere Italiana, Via G. di Vittorio 1, 20060 Vignate (Milan), Italy

DEKALB PLANT GENETICS   3100 Sycamore Rd, DeKalb, IL 60115,
Tel: (815) 753-7333
(Devel/produce hybrid corn, sorghum, sunflowers, sudax, varietal soybeans, alfalfa)
DeKalb Italiana SpA, Corso del Popolo 58, 30172 Venice, Italy
Deris SRL, Via Toscanini 40, 30016 Jesolo (VE), Italy

DELL COMPUTER CORP   2214 W Braker Ln, Austin, TX 78758-4063,
Tel: (512) 338-4400
(Design/mfr personal computers)
Dell Computer SpA, Via Fermi 20, 20090 Assago, Italy

DELTA DRILLING CO   PO Box 2012, Tyler, TX 75710, Tel: (214) 595-1911
(Oil & gas explor & contract drilling)
Delta Overseas Drilling Co., Casella Postale 100, 00054 Fiumicino, Rome, Italy

DELTA US CORP   PO Box 2012, Tyler, TX 75710, Tel: (214) 595-7700
  (Contract oil/gas well drilling)
    Delta Overseas Drilling Co., Casella Postale 100, 00054 Fiumicino, Rome, Italy

DENTSPLY INTL INC   PO Box 872, York, PA 17405, Tel: (717) 845-7511
  (Mfr dental, medical & ind supplies & equip)
    De Art SRL, Via Rimini 22, 20142 Milan, Italy

THE DEXTER CORP   1 Elm Street, Windsor Locks, CT 06096, Tel: (203) 627-9051
  (Mfr nonwovens, polymer prdts, magnetic materials, biotechnology)
    Dexter Aerospace Materials, Via Della Industrie 22,
      31020 San Zenone Degli Ezzeline, Treviso, Italy
    Lexter SA, Via Bellinzona 289, 22100 Como Pontechiasso, Italy

DIGITAL EQUIPMENT CORP   146 Main St, Maynard, MA 01754-2571,
  Tel: (508) 493-5111
  (Networked computer systems & services)
    Digital Equipment SpA, Viale Fulvia Testi 280, 20126 Milan, Italy

DIONEX CORP   1228 Tital Way, PO Box 3603, Sunnyvale, CA 94088-3603,
  Tel: (408) 737-0700
  (Devel/mfr/mktg/svce chromatography sys & relted prdts)
    Dionex SRL, Vicolo del Casale di San Nicola 2, 00123 Rome, Italy

WALT DISNEY CO   500 S Buena Vista St, Burbank, CA 91521, Tel: (818) 560-1000
  (Film/TV prod, theme parks, resorts, publishing, recording, retail stores)
    Creazioni Walt Disney SpAI, Via Hoepli 3, 20121 Milan, Italy

DONALDSON CO INC   PO Box 1299, Minneapolis, MN 55440, Tel: (612) 887-3131
  (Mfr filtration prdts & sys)
    Donaldson Italia SRL, Z.I. Strada A 17, 46035 Ostiglia, Italy

DOW CORNING CORP   2220 W Salzburg Rd, PO Box 1767, Midland, MI 48640,
  Tel: (517) 496-4000
  (Silicones, silicon chems, solid lubricants)
    Dow Corning SpA, Via Colleoni 11, Palazzo Sirio, 20041 Agrate, Italy

DRAKE BEAM MORIN INC   100 Park Ave, New York, NY 10017, Tel: (212) 692-7700
  (Human resource mgmt consulting & training)
    DBM Italy, Via S. Gregorio 6, 20124 Milan, Italy
    DBM Italy, also in Modena, Padua, Rome & Treviso, Italy

DRESSER INDUSTRIES INC   PO Box 718, Dallas, TX 75221-0718,
  Tel: (214) 740-6000
  (Diversified supplier of equip & tech serv to energy & natural resource ind)
    Masoneilan SpA, Via del Cassano 47, 80020 Casavatore, Italy
    Worthington Pompe Italia SpA, Via Rossini 90, 20033 Desio, Italy
    Worthington SpA, Via Pirelli 19, 20124 Milan, Italy
    Worthington Turbodyne SpA, Strada Provinciale 161, Km. 8.5 Premenugo,
      20090 Settala, Italy

DREVER CO   PO Box 98, Huntington Valley, PA 19006-0098, Tel: (215) 947-3400
  (Mfr industrial furnaces)
    Ing. F. Ferre & C., Via Gialomo Watt 32, 20143 Milan, Italy

DRIVER-HARRIS CO   308 Middlesex St, Harrison, NJ 07029, Tel: (201) 483-4802
  (Mfr non-ferrous alloys)
    Driver-Harris Italiana SpA, Via Ospiate 51, 20017 Terrazzano di Rho, Milan, Italy

E I DU PONT DE NEMOURS & CO   1007 Market St, Wilmington, DE 19898,
  Tel: (302) 774-1000
  (Mfr/sale diversified chems, plastics, specialty prdts & fibers)
    Du Pont de Nemours Italiana SpA, Italy

THE DURIRON CO INC   PO Box 8820, Dayton, OH 45401-8820, Tel: (513) 476-6100
  (Mfr chem equip, pumps, valves, filters, fans, heat exchangers)
    Durco Europe SA, 3 Via Generale dalla Chiesa, 24060 Costa Di Meggate, Italy

DYNATECH CORP   3 New England Executive Park, Burlington, MA 01803,
  Tel: (617) 272-6100
  (Devel/mfr communications equip)
    Dynatech Communicatoins SRL, Rome, Italy

EASTMAN KODAK CO   343 State St, Rochester, NY 14650, Tel: (716) 724-4000
  (Devel/mfr photo & chem prdts, info mgmt/video/copier sys, fibers/plastics for
  various ind)
    Kodak SpA, Casella Postale 11057, 20110 Milan, Italy
    Kodak SpA, also in Marcianise, Naples, Padua & Rome, Italy

EATON CORP   1111 Superior Ave, Cleveland, OH 44114, Tel: (216) 523-5000
  (Advanced tech prdts for transp & ind mkts)
    Eaton SpA, Strada Lombardore, Km. 15.300, Leini 10040, Italy

EATON CORP/CUTLER HAMMER   4201 North 27th St, Milwaukee, WI 53216,
  Tel: (414) 449-6000
  (Electric control apparatus, mfr of advanced technologic prdts)
    Ghisalba SpA, Via Tevere 15, 10090 Cascine Vica, Rivoli, Italy

EBASCO SERVICES INC   2 World Trade Center, New York, NY 10048-0752,
  Tel: (212) 839-1000
  (Engineering, constr)
    Ebasco Italia SRL, Italy

EG&G INC   45 William St, Wellesley, MA 02181-4078, Tel: (617) 237-5100
  (Diversified R/D, mfg & services)
    EG&G SpA/Instruments Div., Via Bernardo Rucellai 23, 20126 Milan, Italy
    EG&G SpA/Sealol Div., Via Bernardo Rucellai 23, 20126 Milan, Italy

ENCYCLOPAEDIA BRITANNICA INC   310 S Michigan Ave, Chicago, IL 60604,
  Tel: (312) 321-7000
  (Publishing)
    Encyclopaedia Britannica (Italy) Ltd., Via Angelo Bargoni 28, 00153 Rome, Italy

ENGELHARD CORP   101 Wood Ave S, CN 770, Iselin, NJ 08830, Tel: (908) 205-5000
  (Mfr pigments, additives, catalysts, chemicals, engineered materials)
    Engelhard CLAL, Via Ronchi 17, 20134 Milan, Italy
    Engelhard SRL, Via di Salone 245 (Settecamini), 00131 Rome, Italy

ENTHONE INC   West Haven Industrial Park, PO Box 900, New Haven, CT 06516,
  Tel: (203) 934-8611
  (Metal finishing chems & equip)
    IMASA SpA, Viale Toscana 40, 20093 Cologno Monvese, Milan, Italy

ERICO PRODUCTS INC   34600 Solon Road, Cleveland, OH 44139,
  Tel: (216) 248-0100
  (Mfr electric welding apparatus & hardware, metal stampings, specialty fasteners)
    Erico Italia SpA, Via Mencci 16, 20019 Settimo, Milan, Italy

ESTERLINE TECHNOLOGIES   10800 NE 8th St, Bellevue, WA 98004,
  Tel: (206) 453-9400
  (Mfr equip & instru for ind automation, precision meas, data acquisition)
    W.A. Whitney Italia SpA, Strade del Francese 132/9, Turin 10156, Italy

EXPEDITORS INTL OF WASHINGTON INC   PO Box 69620, Seattle, WA 98168-9620,
  Tel: (206) 246-3711
  (Air/ocean freight forwarding, customs brokerage, intl logistics solutions)
    Expeditors Intl. Italia SRL, Via Leonardo da Vinci 13, 20090 Segrate, Milan, Italy

EXXON CORP   225 E John W Carpenter Freeway, Irving, TX 75062-2298,
  Tel: (214) 444-1000
  (Petroleum explor, prod, refining; mfr petrol & chem prdts; coal & minerals)
    Esso Italiana SpA, Viale Castello della Magliana, 00148 Rome, Italy

FEDERAL-MOGUL CORP   PO Box 1966, Detroit, MI 48235, Tel: (810) 354-7700
  (Mfr/distr precision parts for automobiles, trucks, & farm/constrution vehicles)
    Federal-Mogul SpA, Italy

FERRO CORPORATION   1000 Lakeside Ave, Cleveland, OH 44114,
  Tel: (216) 641-8580
  (Mfr chems, coatings, plastics, colors, refractories)
    Ferro Italia SRL, Via Radici in Piano 312, 41041 Casinalbo, Italy

FINNIGAN CORP   355 River Oaks Parkway, San Jose, CA 95134-1991,
  Tel: (408) 433-4800
  (Mfr mass spectrometers)
    Finnigan MAT SRL, Italy

FISHER CONTROLS INTL INC   8000 Maryland Ave, Clayton, MO 63105,
  Tel: (314) 746-9900
  (Mfr ind process control equip)
    Fisher Controls SpA, Via Pio La Torre 14/C, 20090 Vimodrone, Milan, Italy
    Fisher Controls SpA, Via Vittore Carpaccio 60, 00147 Rome, Italy

FLORASYNTH INC   300 North St, Teterboro, NJ 07608, Tel: (201) 288-3200
  (Mfr fragrances & flavors)
    ICSA-Florasynth, Via F.lli Roselli 5, 20090 Premenugo di Settala (Milan), Italy

FMC CORP   200 E Randolph Dr, Chicago, IL 60601, Tel: (312) 861-6000
  (Produces chems & precious metals, mfr machinery, equip & sys for ind, agric & govt)
    FMC Food Machinery Italy SpA, Italy
    FMC Packaging Machinery SpA, Italy

FOOTE CONE & BELDING COMMUNICATIONS INC   101 E Erie St, Chicago,
  IL 60611-2897, Tel: (312) 751-7000
  (Advertising agency)

(cont)

Euroadvertising, Viale Shakespeare 47, 00144 Rome, Italy
Euromac, Via della Loggia 2Y, 60121 Ancona, Italy
Park-Concept Advertising & Marketing, Via della Moscova 14/A, 20121 Milan, Italy
Publicis-FCB/MAC, Via della Moscova 14/A, 20121 Milan, Italy

FORD MOTOR CO   The American Road, Dearborn, MI 48121, Tel: (313) 322-3000
   (Mfr motor vehicles)
      Ford Italiana SpA, Viale Pasteur 8/10, Casella Postale 10058, 00144 Rome EUR, Italy

FOSTER WHEELER CORP   Perryville Corporate Park, Clinton, NJ 08809-4000,
   Tel: (908) 730-4000
   (Engr, constr, mfg)
      Foster Wheeler Italiana SpA, Via Sebastiano Caboto 1, 20094 Corsico (Milan), Italy

GAF CORP   1361 Alps Rd, Wayne, NJ 07470, Tel: (201) 628-3000
   (Chems, bldg materials, commun)
      ISP (Italia) SRL, Via Pipamonti 66, 20141 Milan, Italy

GENERAL BINDING CORP   One GBC Plaza, Northbrook, IL 60062,
   Tel: (708) 272-3700
   (Binding & laminating equip & associated supplies)
      General Binding Corp. Italia SpA, Viale Milanofiori Palazzo F10,
         20090 Assago (Milano), italy

GENERAL ELECTRIC CO   3135 Easton Tpk, Fairfield, CT 06431,
   Tel: (203) 373-2211
   (Diversified manufacturing, technology & services)
      General Electric Co.,
         all mail to U.S. address; phone (800) 626-2004 or (518) 438-6500

GENERAL FOODS CORP   250 North St, White Plains, NY 10625, Tel: (914) 335-2500
   (Processor, distributor & mfr of foods)
      Simmenthal SpA, Via Borgazzi 87, 20052 Monza, Milan, Italy

GENERAL INSTRUMENT CORP   181 W Madison, Chicago, IL 60602,
   Tel: (312) 541-5000
   (Mfr broadband communications & power rectifying components)
      General Instrument Italia SRL, Via Cantu 11, 20092 Cinisello, Balsamo, Milan, Italy

GENERAL MOTORS ACCEPTANCE CORP   3044 West Grand Blvd, Detroit, MI 48202,
   Tel: (313) 556-5000
   (Automobile financing)
      GMAC Italia SpA, Piazzale dell Industria 40, 00144 Rome, Italy
      GMAC Italia SpA, Via Rivoltana 13, Milano San Felice, 20090 Segrato, Italy

GENERAL MOTORS CORP   3044 W Grand Blvd, Detroit, MI 48202-3091,
   Tel: (313) 556-5000
   (Mfr full line vehicles, automotive electronics, coml technologies, telecom, space,
   finance)
      General Motors Italia SpA, Piazza dell' Industria, 00144 Rome 00144, Italy

GENICOM CORP   14800 Conference Center Dr, #400, Chantilly, VA 22021-3806,
   Tel: (703) 802-9200
   (Supplier of network sys, service & printer solutions)
      Genicom SpA, Via Achille Grandi 12, 20093 Cologno Monzese, Italy

GENRAD INC   300 Baker Ave, Concord, MA 01742, Tel: (508) 369-4400
  (Mfr automatic test equip)
    GenRad SpA, Via Fantoli 21/13, 20138 Milan, Italy

GEORGIA BONDED FIBERS INC   1040 W 29th St, PO Box 751, Buena Vista,
  VA 24416, Tel: (703) 261-2181
  (Mfr insole & luggage material)
    Bontex Italia SRL, Via del Commercio, 37066 Sommacampagna, Verona, Italy

THE GILLETTE CO   Prudential Tower, Boston, MA 02199, Tel: (617) 421-7000
  (Devel/mfr personal care/use prdts: blades & razors, toiletries, cosmetics,
  stationery)
    Braun Italia SRL, Milan, Italy
    Gillette Group Italy SpA, Milan, Italy
    Jafra Cosmetics SpA, Saronno, Italy

THE GLEASON WORKS   1000 University Ave, Rochester, NY 14692,
  Tel: (716) 473-1000
  (Mfr gear mfg machine tools; tooling & servs)
    Gleason Milano, Via Caldera 21/B3, 20153 Milan, Italy

GLITSCH INC   PO Box 660053, Dallas, TX 75266-0053, Tel: (214) 631-3841
  (Mfr/svce mass transfer/chem separation equip, process engr)
    Glitsch Italiana SpA, SS 148 Pontina Km 52, 04010 Campoverde di Aprilia, Italy

GLOBAL INTERNATIONAL   1304 Willow St, Martinez, CA 94553, Tel: (510) 229-9330
  (International moving & forwarding)
    Global International, Via T. Moneta 17, 20161 Milan, Italy

GNM & ASSOCIATES INC   8630 Fenton St, #820, Silver Spring, MD 20910,
  Tel: (301) 588-6110
  (Consulting engineers, architects & planners)
    GNM & Associates Inc., Via Graziano 6, 00165 Rome, Italy

THE GOODYEAR TIRE & RUBBER CO   1144 E Market St, Akron, OH 44316,
  Tel: (216) 796-2121
  (Mfr tires, automotive belts & hose, conveyor belts, chemicals; oil pipeline
  transmission)
    Goodyear Italiana SpA, Piazza G. Marconi 25, Casella Postale 10768, 10100 Rome,
    Italy

W R GRACE & CO   One Town Center Rd, Boca Raton, FL 33486-1010,
  Tel: (407) 362-2000
  (Mfr spec chems & materials: packaging, health care, catalysts, construction, water
  treatment/process)
    Grace Italiana SpA, Casella Postale 108, 20017 Rho (Milan), Italy

GRACO INC   4050 Olson Memorial Hwy, PO Box 1441, Minneapolis, MN 55440-1441,
  Tel: (612) 623-6000
  (Mfr/serv fluid handling equip & sys)
    Graco SRL, Via Serra 22, 40012 Lippo Calderarra di Reno, Bologna, Italy

GREAT LAKES CHEMICAL CORP   One Great Lakes Blvd, W Lafayette, IN 47906,
  Tel: (317) 497-6100
  (Mfr bromine & derivatives, furfural & derivatives)
    Great Lakes Chemical Italia SRL, Milan, Italy

GREY ADVERTISING INC   777 Third Ave, New York, NY 10017, Tel: (212) 546-2000
   (Advertising)
      Milano & Grey, Via Bertani 6, 20154 Milan, Italy

GROUNDWATER TECHNOLOGY INC   100 River Ridge Dr, Norwood, MA 02062,
   Tel: (617) 769-7600
   (Industrial site cleanup, mgmt & consulting)
      Groundwater Technology Italia SRL, Via Madonna 6/E, 22063 Cantu, Italy

GTE CORP   One Stamford Forum, Stamford, CT 06904, Tel: (203) 965-2000
   (Electr prdts, telecom sys, publ & commun)
      GTE SpA, Viale Europa 46, 20093 Colonia Monzesz, Milan, Italy

FRANK B HALL & CO INC   549 Pleasantville Rd, Briarcliff Manor, NY 10510,
   Tel: (914) 769-9200
   (Insurance)
      Frank B. Hall Italia SpA, Via Bruxelles 51, 00198 Rome, Italy
      Frank B. Hall Italia SpA, Via Olmetto 1, 20123 Milan, Italy
      Frank B. Hall Overseas Ltd., Via Borgonuovo 26, 20121 Milan, Italy

HARNISCHFEGER INDUSTRIES INC   PO Box 554, Milwaukee, WI 53201,
   Tel: (414) 671-4400
   (Mfr mining & material handling equip, papermaking mach, computer sys)
      Beloit Italia SpA, Via Martiri del XXI 76, 10064 Pinerolo (Turin), Italy

THE HARPER GROUP   260 Townsend St, PO Box 77933, San Francisco,
   CA 94107-1719, Tel: (415) 978-0600
   (Ocean/air freight fwdg, customs brokerage, packing & whse, logistics mgt, ins)
      Circle Freight Italia-Eurolevant SRL, Via F. Baracca 25/27,
         20090 Novegro di Segrate, Milan, Italy

HARRIS CALORIFIC CO   2345 Murphy Blvd, Gainesville, GA 30501,
   Tel: (404) 536-8801
   (Mfr gas welding & cutting equip)
      Harris Europa SpA, Via Nazionale 79, 40065 Pianoro, Bologna, Italy

HEIN-WERNER CORP   PO Box 1606, Waukesha, WI 53187-1606, Tel: (414) 542-6611
   (Mfr auto body repair equip, engine rebuilding & brake repair equip, hydraulic
   cylinders)
      Blackhawk Italia SRL, Via dell'Industria 5, 37066 Sommacampagna, Verona, Italy

H J HEINZ CO   PO Box 57, Pittsburgh, PA 15230-0057, Tel: (412) 456-5700
   (Processed food prdts & nutritional services)
      AIAL (Arimpex SRL Industrie Alimentari), Commessaggio, Italy
      Dega SRL, Mori, Italy
      Heinz Italia SpA, Milan, Italy
      PLADA SpA (Plasmon Dietetici Alimentari SpA), Milan, Italy

HERCULES INC   Hercules Plaza, Wilmington, DE 19894-0001, Tel: (302) 594-5000
   (Mfr spec chems, plastics, film & fibers, coatings, resins, food ingredients)
      Hercules Italia SpA, Via Rosellini 2, 20124 Milan, Italy

HERSHEY FOODS CORP   100 Crystal A Dr, Hershey, PA 17033, Tel: (717) 534-6799
   (Mfr chocolate, food & confectionery prdts)
      Sperlari SRL, Via Milano 16, 26100 Cremona, Italy

HEWLETT-PACKARD CO   3000 Hanover St, Palo Alto, CA 94304-0890,
  Tel: (415) 857-1501
  (Mfr computing, communications & measurement prdts & services)
    Hewlett-Packard Italiana SpA, Via Giuseppe di Vittorio 9,
      20063 Cernusco sul Naviglio, Milan, Italy

HOLIDAY INNS INC   3742 Lamar Ave, Memphis, TN 38195, Tel: (901) 362-4001
  (Hotels, restaurants, casinos)
    Holiday Inn, Viale Castello della Magliana 65, Casella Postale 10210,
      Parco dDei Medici, Rome, Italy

HONEYWELL INC   PO Box 524, Minneapolis, MN 55440-0524, Tel: (612) 951-1000
  (Devel/mfr controls for home & building, industry, space & aviation)
    Honeywell Intl. Management SpA, Via Vittor Pisani 13, 20124 Milan, Italy
    Honeywell SpA, Via Vittor Pisani 13, 20124 Milan, Italy

HORWATH INTL   415 Madison Ave, New York, NY 10017, Tel: (212) 838-5566
  (Public accountants & auditors)
    Horwath & Horwath Italia, Via Calabria 7, 00187 Rome, Italy
    Polandri Horwath, Piazza Navona 49, 00186 Rome, Italy

HOUGHTON INTL INC   PO Box 930, Valley Forge, PA 19482-0930,
  Tel: (610) 666-4000
  (Mfr spec chems, hydraulic fluids, lubricants)
    Houghton Italia SpA, Casella Postale 6069, 16100 Genoa, Italy

HOWMET CORP   475 Steamboat Rd, PO Box 1960, Greenwich, CT 06836-1960,
  Tel: (203) 661-4600
  (Mfr precision investment castings, alloys, engineering & refurbishment)
    Ciral IT, Via P.G.A. Filippino 119, 00144 Rome, Italy

HUBBARD FARMS INC   PO Box 415, Walpole, NH 03608, Tel: (603) 756-3311
  (Poultry breeding R&D, poultry foundation breeding stock)
    Hubbard Italia SRL, Via IV Novembre 89, 28060 Vicolungo, Italy

HUGHES AIRCRAFT CO   PO Box 80028, Los Angeles, CA 90080-0028,
  Tel: (310) 568-6904
  (Mfr electronics equip & sys)
    Hughes Aircraft Intl. Service Co., Lungotevere Mellini 44, 00193 Rome, Italy

IBM CORP   Old Orchard Rd, Armonk, NY 10504, Tel: (914) 765-1900
  (Information products, technology & services)
    IBM Italia SpA, Sesrate 20090, Italy

IL INTERNATIONAL INC   400 Long Beach Blvd, Stratford, CT 06497,
  Tel: (203) 378-4000
  (Dist residential & commercial lighting prdts)
    Italiana Luce SRL, Via Edison 18, 20019 Settimo Milanese, Italy

ILLINOIS TOOL WORKS INC   3600 W Lake Ave, Glenview, IL 60025,
  Tel: (708) 724-7500
  (Mfr gears, tools, fasteners, sealants, plastic & metal components for ind, med, etc.)
    ITW Fastex Italia SpA, Turin, Italy

IMO INDUSTRIES INC   1009 Lenox Dr, Bldg 4 West, Lawrenceville,
  NJ 08648-0550, Tel: (609) 896-7600
  (Mfr/support mech & electr controls, engineered power prdts)

(cont)

Imo Industries SRL, TransInstruments Div., Via Correggio 19, 20149 Milan, Italy
Roltra-Morse SpA, Via Albenga 9, 10090 Cascine Vica, Rivoli (Turin), Italy

IMS INTERNATIONAL INC   100 Campus Rd, Totowa, NJ 07512, Tel: (201) 790-0700
(Market research reports)
IMS Italiana SpA, Via Meravigli 12, 20123 Milan, Italy

INGERSOLL-RAND CO   200 Chestnut Ridge Rd, Woodcliff Lake, NJ 07675,
Tel: (201) 573-0123
(Mfr compressors, rock drills, pumps, air tools, door hardware, ball bearings)
Ingersoll-Rand Italiana SpA, Via Rivoltana 6, 20060 Vignate (Milan), Italy
Worthington SpA, Via Rossini 90-92, 20033 Desio (Milan), Italy

INSTRON CORP   100 Royall St, Canton, MA 02021-1089, Tel: (617) 828-2500
(Mfr material testing instruments)
Instron Intl. Ltd., Via del Cignoli, Milan, Italy

INSTRUMENTATION LABORATORY   113 Hartwell Ave, Lexington, MA 02173-3190,
Tel: (617) 861-0710
(Med & sci analyzers & meas instru)
Instrumentation Laboratory SpA, Via Socrate 41, 20128 Milan, Italy

INTERGRAPH CORP   Huntsville, AL 35894-0001, Tel: (205) 730-2000
(Devel/mfr interactive computer graphic systems)
Intergraph Italia LLC, Strada 7, Palazzo R, Milanofiori, 20089 Rozzano (Mi), Italy

INTERMEC CORP   6001 36th Ave West, PO Box 4280, Everett, WA 98203-9280,
Tel: (206) 348-2600
(Mfr/distr automated data collection sys)
BPS Intermec SRL, Via Cornaggia 58, Cinisello Balsamo, 20092 Milan, Italy

INTERNATIONAL FLAVORS & FRAGRANCES INC   521 W 57th St, New York, NY 10019,
Tel: (212) 765-5500
(Create/mfr flavors, fragrances & aroma chems)
Intl. Flavors & Fragrances, Via Fratelli Cervi, 20090 Trezzano sul Naviglio, Milan,
Italy

INTERNATIONAL PAPER   2 Manhattanville Rd, Purchase, NY 10577,
Tel: (914) 397-1500
(Mfr/distr container board, paper, wood prdts)
Anitec Image Italia SRL, S.S. 233 Km. 20.5, 21040 Origgio (Va), Italy
Aussedat Rey Italia SRL, Viale Milanofiori, Palazzo F1, 20090 Assago, Italy
Cartiera di Valtaggio SRL, Loc. Pian Maxina, 15060 Voltaggio, Italy
Horsell Italia Industrie Grafiche SRL, Viale del Lavoro,
37036 S. Martino Buon Albergo, Italy
Ilford Photo SpA, S.S. 233 Km. 20.5, 21040 Origgio, Italy
International Paper Italia SpA, Via Omago 55, 20040 Bellusco (Milan), Italy
International Paper Italia SpA, also in Catania, Felico sul Panaro, Magione,
Pedemonte di Serra & Rome, Italy

INTERNATIONAL RECTIFIER CORP   233 Kansas St, El Segundo, CA 90245,
Tel: (310) 322-3331
(Mfr semiconductor components)
Intl. Rectifier Corp. Italiana, Via Privata Liguria 49, 10071 Borgaro-Turin, Italy

INTRALOX INC   PO Box 50699, New Orleans, LA 70150, Tel: (504) 733-0463
  (Mfr plastic, modular conveyor belts & access)
    Intralox Italia, Italy

IONICS INC   65 Grove St, Watertown, MA 02172, Tel: (617) 926-2500
  (Mfr desalination equip)
    Ionics Italba, Via Livraghi 1/B, 21026 Milan, Italy

ITT SHERATON CORP   60 State St, Boston, MA 02108, Tel: (617) 367-3600
  (Hotel operations)
    Sheraton Sales Center, Via Vittor Pisani 7, 20124 Milan, Italy

JOHNSON & HIGGINS   125 Broad St, New York, NY 10004-2424, Tel: (212) 574-7000
  (Ins brokerage, employee benefit conslt, risk mgmt, human resource conslt, ins/reins
  servs)
    Johnson & Higgins SpA, Viale della Liberazione 18, 20124 Milan, Italy
    Johnson & Higgins SpA, also in Rome, Padua, Turin & Bologna, Italy

JOHNSON & JOHNSON   One Johnson & Johnson Plaza, New Brunswick, NJ 08933,
  Tel: (908) 524-0400
  (R&D/mfr/sale health care prdts)
    Ethicon SpA, Rome, Italy
    Janssen-Cilag SpA, Viale Castello della Magliana 38, 00148 Rome, Italy
    Johnson & Johnson SpA, Casella Postale 10742, 00144 Rome, Italy
    Ortho Diagnostic Systems SpA, Casella Postale 17171, 20170 Milan, Italy

S C JOHNSON & SON INC   1525 Howe St, Racine, WI 53403, Tel: (414) 631-2000
  (Home, auto, commercial & personal care prdts, specialty chems)
    Johnson Wax SpA, Casella Postale 18, 20020 Arese, Italy

JOHNSON CONTROLS INC   5757 N Green Bay Ave, PO Box 591, Milwaukee,
  WI 53201-0591, Tel: (414) 228-1200
  (Mfr facility mgmt & control sys, auto seating, batteries & plastics)
    Johnson Controls SpA, Vitale Fratelli Casiraghi 409/413, 20099 Sesto S. Giovanni,
      Milan, Italy
    Johnson Controls SpA, Via Piave 6, 22050 Lomagna (Como), Italy

THE JOURNAL OF COMMERCE   2 World Trade Center, New York, NY 10048,
  Tel: (212) 837-7000
  (Newspaper publisher)
    The Journal of Commerce, Piazza Fontane Marse 3, 16123 Genoa, Italy,

KAHLE ENGINEERING CO   50 S Center St, Bldg 1, Orange, NJ 07050,
  Tel: (201) 678-2020
  (Mfr automatic assembly mach, med/ind prdts)
    Kahle Europea SpA, Via Artigiani 1, 24043 Caravaggio (BG), Italy

A T KEARNEY INC   222 West Adams St, Chicago, IL 60606, Tel: (312) 648-0111
  (Mgmt consultants, executive search)
    A.T. Kearney SpA, Via Durini 18, 20122 Milan, Italy

KEITHLEY INSTRUMENTS INC   28775 Aurora Rd, Cleveland, OH 44139,
  Tel: (216) 248-0400
  (Mfr electr test/meas instru, PC-based data acquisition hdwe/software)
    Keithley Instruments SRL, Viale S. Gimignano 38, 20146 Milan, Italy

KELLOGG CO   One Kellogg Sq, PO Box 3599, Battle Creek, MI 49016-3599,
 Tel: (616) 961-2000
 (Mfr ready-to-eat cereals, convenience foods)
   Kellogg Italia SpA, Agrate Brianza (Milan), Italy (all inquiries to U.S. address)

KENNAMETAL INC   PO Box 231, Latrobe, PA 15650, Tel: (412) 539-5000
 (Tools, hard carbide & tungsten alloys)
   Nuova Cames SpA, Via Corrado 11 Salico 50, 20141 Milan, Italy

KENNEDY VAN SAUN CORP   PO Box 500, Danville, PA 17821, Tel: (717) 275-3050
 (Mineral processing & handling equip)
   Franco Tosi Industrial SpA, Piazzo Monumento 12, 20025 Legnano, Italy

KERR MANUFACTURING CO   28200 Wick Rd, Romulus, MI 48174, Tel: (313) 946-7800
 (Mfr dental supplies, jewelry mfg supplies & equip)
   Kerr Italia SpA, Casella Postale 46, Via Passanti 140, 84018 Scafati (Salerno),
     Italy
   Sybron Italia SpA, Casella Postale 46, Via Passanti 140, 84018 Scafati (Salerno),
     Italy

KEYSTONE INTL INC   PO Box 40010, Houston, TX 77040, Tel: (713) 466-1176
 (Mfr butterfly valves, actuators & control accessories)
   BIFFI Italia, Italy
   Keystone SRL, Italy
   Keystone Vanessa, Italy

KIDDER PEABODY GROUP INC   10 Hanover Sq, New York, NY 10005,
 Tel: (212) 510-3000
 (Investment banking)
   Kidder, Peabody Italia SRL, c/o SOPAF S.p.A, Largo Richini 6, 20122 Milan, Italy

KIMBERLY-CLARK CORP   PO Box 619100, Dallas, TX 75261, Tel: (214) 281-1200
 (Mfr fiber-based prdts for personal care, lumber & paper prdts)
   Kimberly-Clark SpA, Italy

KIRSCH   309 N Prospect St, Sturgis, MI 49091-0370, Tel: (616) 659-5228
 (Mfr drapery hardware & accessories, wood shelving, woven wood shades, etc)
   Cooper Industries Italia, Via Roma 108, Centro Direzional Lombardo, Palazo B/1,
     20060 Cassina de Pecchi, Milan, Italy

THE KNOLL GROUP   105 Wooster St, New York, NY 10021, Tel: (212) 343-4000
 (Mfr/sale office furnishings)
   Knoll Intl. Italy SpA, Via Jucker 33, 22025 Legnano (Milan), Italy

KOCH ENGINEERING CO INC   PO Box 8127, Wichita, KS 67208, Tel: (316) 832-5110
 (Mass transfer prdts, static mixers, mist eliminator sys)
   Koch Intl. SpA, Casella Postale 13, 24061 Albano S. Alessandro, Italy

KORN/FERRY INTL   1800 Century Park East, Los Angeles, CA 90067,
 Tel: (310) 552-1834
 (Executive search)
   Korn/Ferry Intl., Sala dei Longobardi 2, 20121 Milan, Italy
   Korn/Ferry Intl., Via Nicolo Tartaglia 11, 00197 Rome, Italy

KRAFT INC   Kraft Court, Glenview, IL 60025, Tel: (708) 998-2000
(Dairy prdts, processed food, chems)
  Kraft SpA, Via Pola 11, 20124 Milan, Italy

KURT SALMON ASSOCIATES INC   1355 Peachtree St NE, Atlanta, GA 30309,
  Tel: (404) 892-0321
(Management consulting: consumer products, retailing)
  Kurt Salmon Associates SRL, Via Sporting Mirasole 2, Noverasco di Opera,
    20090 Milan, Italy

LEARONAL INC   272 Buffalo Ave, Freeport, NY 11520, Tel: (516) 868-8800
(Mfr chem specialties)
  Elga Ronal SRL, Via della Merlata 8, 20014 Nerviano, Milan, Italy

LEEDS+NORTHRUP   795 Horsham Rd, PO Box 1010, Horsham, PA 19044-8010,
  Tel: (215) 442-8000
(Mfr process control instrumentation, liquid & particle analysis)
  Leeds+Northrup Italy SpA, Via dei Lavoratori 124, 20092 Cinisello Balsamo, Milan,
    Italy

LEVI STRAUSS & CO   1155 Battery, San Francisco, CA 94111, Tel: (415) 544-6000
(Mfr casual wearing apparel)
  Levi Strauss Italia SpA, Italy

ELI LILLY & CO   Lilly Corporate Center, Indianapolis, IN 46285,
  Tel: (317) 276-2000
(Mfr pharmaceuticals, animal health prdts)
  Eli Lilly Italia SpA, Via Gramsci 731-733, Sesto Fiorentino 50019, Florence, Italy

LINTAS:WORLDWIDE   1 Dag Hammarskjold Plaza, New York, NY 10017,
  Tel: (212) 605-8000
(Advertising agency)
  Lintas:Milano, Via Pantano 26, 20122 Milan, Italy

ARTHUR D LITTLE INC   25 Acorn Park, Cambridge, MA 02140-2390,
  Tel: (617) 498-5000
(Mgmt, environ, health & safety consulting; tech & prdt development)
  Arthur D. Little Intl. Inc., Via Serbelloni 4, 20122 Milan, Italy

LITTON INDUSTRIES INC   21240 Burbank Blvd, Woodland Hills, CA 91367,
  Tel: (818) 598-5000
(Elec sys, ind automation, resource explor)
  Veam, Via Statuto 2, 20020 Arese Milan, Italy

LOCKHEED MARTIN CORP   6801 Rockledge Dr, Bethesda, MD 20817,
  Tel: (301) 897-6000
(Design/mfr/mgmt sys in fields of space, defense, energy, electronics, materials,
  info & tech svces)
  Lockheed Martin Intl., Via Fillungo 107, 55100 Lucca, Italy

LOCTITE CORP   10 Columbus Blvd, Hartford, CT 06106, Tel: (203) 520-5000
(Mfr/sale ind adhesives & sealants)
  Loctite Europa E.E.I.G., Via Talete 56, 20047 Brugherio (Milan), Italy
  Loctite FAS SpA, Via Vigevano 27, 28065 Cerano, Italy
  Loctite Italia SpA, Via Talete 56, 20047 Brugherio (Milan), Italy

LSB INDUSTRIES INC   16 S Pennsylvania Ave, Oklahoma City, OK 73107,
Tel: (405) 235-4546
(Mfr acids, agricultural & industrial chemicals)
  LSB Europe Ltd., Via Vittor Pisani 14, 20124 Milan, Italy

LTX CORP   LTX Park, University Ave, Westwood, MA 02090, Tel: (617) 461-1000
(Design/mfr computer-controlled semiconductor test systems)
  LTX (Italia) SRL, Palazzo Cassiopea, Scale 1, 20041 Agrate Brianza, Italy

THE LUBRIZOL CORP   29400 Lakeland Blvd, Wickliffe, OH 44092-2298,
Tel: (216) 943-4200
(Mfr chem additives for lubricants & fuels)
  Lubrizol Italiana SpA, Italy

LYKES BROS STEAMSHIP CO INC   Lykes Center, 300 Poydras St, New Orleans,
LA 70130, Tel: (504) 523-6611
(Ocean frt trans)
  Lykes Lines Agency Inc., Casella Postale 1095, 16122 Genoa, Italy

R H MACY & CO INC   151 West 34th St, New York, NY 10001, Tel: (212) 695-4400
(Department stores, importers)
  R.H. Macy & Co. Intl., Piazza Independenza 21, 50129 Florence, Italy

MAGNETROL INTERNATIONAL   5300 Belmont Rd, Downers Grove, IL 60515-4499,
Tel: (708) 969-4000
(Mfr level & flow instrumentation)
  Magnetrol Intl. Italy, Via Abbadesse 44, 20124 Milan, Italy

MANPOWER INTL INC   5301 N Ironwood Rd, PO Box 2053, Milwaukee,
WI 53201-2053, Tel: (414) 961-1000
(Temporary help service)
  Manpower Italia SRL, Via Baracchini 9, 20123 Milan, Italy

MARCAM CORP   95 Wells Ave, Newton, MA 02159, Tel: (617) 965-0220
(Applications software & services)
  Marcam Italia SRL, Italy

MARKEM CORP   150 Congress St, Keene, NH 03431, Tel: (603) 352-1130
(Marking and printing mach; hot stamping foils)
  Markem SRL, Via Correggio 55, 20149 Milan, Italy

MARSH & McLENNAN COS INC   1166 Ave of the Americas, New York, NY 10036-1011,
Tel: (212) 345-5000
(Insurance)
  Marsh & McLennan Italia & Co. SpA, Via dei Giardini 7, 20121 Milan, Italy

MASCO CORP   21001 Van Born Rd, Taylor, MI 48180, Tel: (313) 274-7400
(Mfr home improvement, building & home furnishings prdts)
  Keoma SRL, Z.I. Sant' Andrea, 34170 Gorizia, Italy
  Rubinetterie Mariani SpA, Via Berlino 2/4, 24040 Zingonia (Bergamo), Italy

MATTEL INC   333 Continental Blvd, El Segundo, CA 90245, Tel: (310) 252-2000
(Mfr toys, dolls, games, crafts & hobbies)
  Fisher-Price SRL, Via Cassanese 224, 20090 Segrate, Italy
  Mattel Mfg. Europe SRL, Via Vittorio Veneto 119, 28040 Oleggio Castello,
    Piemonte Italy

GEORGE S MAY INTL CO   303 S Northwest Hwy, Park Ridge, IL 60068-4255,
Tel: (708) 825-8806
(Mgmt consulting)
  George S. May Intl. SpA, Centro Direzionale Colleoni, Palazzo Orio 1,
    20041 Agrate Brianza, Milan, Italy

MCI INTERNATIONAL   2 International Dr, Rye Brook, NY 10573,
Tel: (914) 937-3444
(Telecommunications)
  MCI Intl. Italy SRL, Via PO 2, Apt. 110, 00198 Rome, Italy

MEAD CORP   Courthouse Plaza, NE, Dayton, OH 45463, Tel: (513) 222-6323
(Mfr paper, packaging, pulp, lumber & other wood prdts, school & office prdts; electr
pub, distri)
  Avio Cart SpA, Via Campagnole 1, 38063 Avio, Italy

MEASUREX CORP   One Results Way, Cupertino, CA 95014-5991, Tel: (408) 255-1500
(Mfr computer integrated mfg sys)
  Measurex Italia SRL, Via San Vittore 45, 20123 Milan, Italy

MEDTRONIC INC   7000 Central Ave, NE, Minneapolis, MN 55432,
Tel: (612) 574-4000
(Mfr/sale/svce therapeutic medical devices)
  Medtronic Italia SpA, Piazza Duca d'Aosta 12, 20124 Milan, Italy

MERCK SHARP & DOHME INTL   PO Box 2000, Rahway, NJ 07065, Tel: (201) 574-4000
(Pharms, chems & biologicals)
  Merck, Sharp & Dohme Italia SpA, Via G. Fabbroni 6, 00191 Rome, Italy

MERGENTHALER LINOTYPE CO   201 Old Country Rd, Melville, NY 11747,
Tel: (516) 673-4197
(Photocomposition machs, sys & equip)
  Linotype Italia SpA, Via Sempione 2B, 20016 Pero, Milan, Italy

MERIDIAN DIAGNOSTICS INC   3471 River Hills Dr, Cincinnati, OH 45244,
Tel: (513) 271-3700
(Devel/mfr immunodiagnostic test kits, reagents, bacteria/parasite collection &
preservation sys)
  Meridian Diagnostics Europe SRL, Milan, Italy

METAL-CLADDING INC   PO Box 630, 470 Niagara Way, North Tonawanda, NY 14120,
Tel: (716) 693-6205
(FRP tanks & custom constr, scrubbers, odor control equip)
  Hurner Italia SRL, Via Spontini 4, 20124 Milan, Italy

METCO DIV OF PERKIN-ELMER   1101 Prospect Ave, PO Box 1006, Westbury,
NY 11590-0201, Tel: (516) 334-1300
(Mfr/serv thermal spray coating equip & supplies)
  Metco Italia SpA, Via Monte Suello 9, 20133 Milan, Italy

MICROMERITICS INSTRUMENT CORP   One Micromeritics Dr, Norcross,
GA 30093-1877, Tel: (404) 662-3620
(Mfr analytical instruments)
  Micromeritics SRL, Via W. Tibagi 26/7, 20068 Peschiera Borromeo, Milan, Italy

MICROSOFT CORP   One Microsoft Way, Redmond, WA 98052-6399,
  Tel: (206) 882-8080
  (Computer software, peripherals & services)
    Microsoft Italy SpA, Centro Direzionale, Milano Oltre, Palazzo Tiepolo,
      Via Cassanese 224, 20090 Segrate (M), Italy

MILLER ELECTRIC MFG CO   PO Box 1079, Appleton, WI 54912-1079,
  Tel: (414) 734-9821
  (Mfr arc welding machs)
    Miller Europe SpA, Via Privata ISEO, 20098 San Giuliano, Milan, Italy

MILLIPORE CORP   Ashley Rd, Bedford, MA 01730, Tel: (617) 275-9205
  (Mfr precision filters, hi-performance liquid chromatography instru)
    Millipore SpA, Via Achille Grandi 23, 20090 Vimodrone, Milan, Italy

MINE SAFETY APPLIANCES CO   PO Box 426, Pittsburgh, PA 15230,
  Tel: (421) 273 5000
  (Safety equip, ind filters)
    MSA Italiana SpA, Caselle Postale 1719, 20101 Milan, Italy

MOBIL CORP   3225 Gallows Rd, Fairfax, VA 22037-0001, Tel: (703) 846-3000
  (Petroleum explor & refining, mfr petrol prdts, chems, petrochems)
    Mobil Chimica Italiana SpA, Via Paleocapa 7, 20122 Milan, Italy
    Mobil Chimica Italiana SpA, Casella Postale 289, 80100 Naples, Italy
    Mobil Lube Italiana SpA, Via Vitalian Brancati 60, 00144 Rome, Italy
    Mobil Oil Italiana SpA, Piazzall dell' Agucoltura 24, 00144 Rome, Italy
    Mobil Plastics Italiana SpA, Strada Statale Passo del Giogo, 50038 Florence, Italy

MOLEX INC   2222 Wellington Ct, Lisle, IL 60532, Tel: (708) 969-4550
  (Mfr electronic, electrical & fiber optic interconnection prdts & sys, switches,
  application tooling)
    Molex Inc., Padova, Italy

MONTGOMERY WARD & CO INC   Montgomery Ward Plaza, Chicago, IL 60671,
  Tel: (312) 467-2000
  (Retail merchandisers)
    Montgomery Ward & Co. Inc., Borgognissanti 28, 50123 Florence, Italy

MOOG INC   East Aurora, NY 14052-0018, Tel: (716) 652-2000
  (Mfr precision control components & sys)
    Moog Italiana SRL, Via dei Tre Corsi, Zona Industriale Sud-D1, 21046 Malnate, Italy

MOORE PRODUCTS CO   Sumneytown Pike, Spring House, PA 19477,
  Tel: (215) 646-7400
  (Mfr process control instru)
    Moore Products Co. Italia SRL, Via Benedetto Marcello 5, 20124 Milan, Italy

MORGAN GUARANTY TRUST CO   23 Wall St, New York, NY 10260, Tel: (212) 483-2323
  (Banking)
    Morgan Guaranty Trust Co., Piazza del Carmine 4, 20121 Milan, Italy

MORTON INTERNATIONAL INC   100 N Riverside Plaza, Chicago, IL 60606-1596,
  Tel: (312) 807-2000
  (Mfr adhesives, coatings, finishes, spec chems, advanced & electr materials, salt,
  airbags)

Morton Intl. SpA, Via Trieste 23/25/27, 22076 Mozzate (Como), Italy
Morton Intl. SpA, Via Lombardia 52, 21040 Castronno/Varese, Italy

MOTION PICTURE EXPORT ASSN OF AMERICA   1133 Ave of the Americas, New York,
NY 10036, Tel: (212) 840-6161
(Motion picture trade association)
Motion Picture Export Assn. of Rome, Via del Tritone 12, 61 Rome, Italy

MOTOROLA INC   1303 E Algonquin Rd, Schaumburg, IL 60196, Tel: (708) 576-5000
(Mfr commun equip, semiconductors, cellular phones)
Motorola SpA, Viale Milanofiori C-2, 20094 Assago, Milan, Italy

MSI DATA CORP   340 Fischer Ave, Costa Mesa, CA 92626, Tel: (714) 549-6000
(Portable data entry terminals)
MSI Data Italiana SRL, Via Cerrone di San Martino 5, Milan, Italy
MSI Data Italiana SRL, Via Anfiteatro 15, 20121 Milan, Italy

MTS SYSTEMS CORP   14000 Technology Dr, Eden Prairie, MN 55344-2290,
Tel: (612) 937-4000
(Devel/mfr mechanical testing & simulation prdts & servs, ind meas & automation
instrumentation)
MTS Systems SRL, Via Tirreno 151, 10136 Turin, Italy

MacDERMID INC   245 Freight St, Waterbury, CT 06702, Tel: (203) 575-5700
(Chem processing for metal ind, plastics, electronics cleaners, strippers)
MacDermid Italiana SRL, Via Vercellone 54, 13042 Cavaglia (Vercelli), Italy

THE MacNEAL-SCHWENDLER CORP   815 Colorado Blvd, Los Angeles, CA 90041,
Tel: (213) 258-9111
(Devel/mfr computer-aided engineering software)
MacNeal-Schwendler Co. (Italia) SRL, Via Confienza 15, 10121 Turin, Italy
MacNeal-Schwendler Co. (Italia) SRL, Viale America 93, 00144 Rome, Italy

McCANN-ERICKSON WORLDWIDE   750 Third Ave, New York, NY 10017,
Tel: (212) 697-6000
(Advertising)
McCann-Erickson Italiana SpA, Via Meravegli 2, 20123 Milan, Italy
McCann-Erickson Italiana SpA, La Ferratella, Via Elio Vittorini 129, 00144 Rome,
Italy
Universal McCann SRL, Via Bassano Parrone 6, 20123 Milan, Italy

McKINSEY & CO INC   55 E 52nd St, New York, NY 10022, Tel: (212) 446-7000
(Mgmt consultants)
McKinsey & Co., Piazza del Duomo 22, 20122 Milan, Italy

NALCO CHEMICAL CO   One Nalco Center, Naperville, IL 60563-1198,
Tel: (708) 305-1000
(Chems for water & waste water treatment, oil prod & refining, ind processes;
water/energy mgmt serv)
Nalco Italiana SpA, Viale dell Esperanto 71, 00144 Rome, Italy

NATIONAL DATA CORP   National Data Plaza, Atlanta, GA 30329-2010,
Tel: (404) 728-2000
(Info sys & servs for retail, healthcare, govt & corporate mkts)
FIENCO, Italy

NATIONAL GYPSUM CO   2001 Rexford Rd., Charlotte, NC 28211,
  Tel: (704) 365-7300
  (Building prdts & servs)
    Austin Italia SpA, Milan, Italy

NATIONAL SERVICE INDUSTRIES INC   1420 Peachtree St NE, Atlanta, GA 30309,
  Tel: (404) 853-1000
  (Mfr lighting equip, spec chems; textile rental)
    Zep Europe, Rome, Italy

NATIONAL STARCH & CHEMICAL CO   10 Finderne Ave, Bridgewater, NJ 08807-3300,
  Tel: (908) 685-5000
  (Mfr adhesives & sealants, resins & spec chems, electr materials & adhesives, food
  prdts, ind starch)
    National Starch & Chemical SpA, Mezzago (Milan), Italy

NATIONAL UTILITY SERVICE INC   One Maynard Dr, PO Box 712, Park Ridge,
  NJ 07656, Tel: (201) 391-4300
  (Utility rate consulting)
    NUS Italia SRL, Via Deruta 20, 20132 Milan, Italy

THE NEW YORK TIMES CO   229 W 43rd St, New York, NY 10036, Tel: (212) 556-1234
  (Communications, newspaper & magazine publishing, broadcasting, forest prdts)
    The New York Times Rome Bureau SRL, Corso Victorio Emanuel 2, 00186 Rome, Italy

NICHOLSON FILE CO   PO Box 728, Apex, NC 27502, Tel: (919) 362-7500
  (Files, rasps, saws)
    Cooper Group SpA, Via Canova 19, 20090 Trezzanosul Naviglio, Milan, Italy

A C NIELSEN CO   Nielsen Plaza, Northbrook, IL 60062-6288, Tel: (708) 498-6300
  (Market research)
    D&B Marketing Information Services SpA, Via G. DiVittorio 10, 20094 Corsico, Minal,
    Italy

NORDSON CORP   28601 Clemens Rd, Westlake, OH 44145, Tel: (216) 892-1580
  (Mfr ind application equip & packaging mach)
    Nordson Italia SpA, Via Dei Gigli 3/b, 20090 Pieve Emanuele, Milan, Italy

NORTON CO   1 New Bond St, Worcester, MA 01606, Tel: (508) 795-5000
  (Abrasives, drill bits, constr & safety prdts, plastics)
    Christensen Diamond Product Co. SpA, Via Flaminia 160, 00196 Rome, Italy
    Norton SpA, Via per Cesano Boscone 4, 20094 Corsico, Milan, Italy

OAKITE PRODUCTS INC   50 Valley Rd, Berkeley Heights, NJ 07922,
  Tel: (908) 464-6900
  (Mfr chem prdts for ind cleaning & metal treating)
    Nuovo Masco SpA, Via Vigevano 61, 28069 San Martino di Trecate, Novara, Italy

ODI   25 Mall Rd, Burlington, MA 01803, Tel: (617) 272-8040
  (Mgt & consul serv)
    ODI Italia, Via T. Salvini 5, 20122 Milan, Italy

THE OILGEAR CO   2300 S 51st St, Milwaukee, WI 53219, Tel: (414) 327-1700
  (Mfr hydraulic power transmission mach)
    Oilgear Towler SRL, Via Artigianale 23, 25010 Montirone (Brescia), Italy

ON-LINE SOFTWARE INTL INC   2 Executive Dr, Fort Lee, NJ 07024,
  Tel: (201) 592-0009
  (Software & related servs; consult & educ servs)
    On-Line Software Italia SRL, Italy

OPTICAL COATING LAB INC (OCLI)   2789 Northpoint Pkwy, Santa Rosa,
  CA 95407-7397, Tel: (707) 545-6440
  (Mfr thin film precision coated optical devices)
    Optical Coating Laboratory SRL, Largo Corsia dei Servi 11, 20122 Milan, Italy

ORACLE CORP   500 Oracle Parkway, Redwood Shores, CA 94065,
  Tel: (415) 506-7000
  (Develop/mfr software)
    Oracle Italia/Datamat SpA, Via Laurentina 756, 00143 Rome, Italy

OTIS ELEVATOR CO   10 Farm Springs, Farmington, CT 06032, Tel: (860) 676-6528
  (Mfr elevators & escalators)
    Otis SpA, Via Firenze 11, 20063 Cernusco sul Naviglio, Milan, Italy

OWENS-CORNING FIBERGLAS CORP   Fiberglas Tower, Toledo, OH 43659,
  Tel: (419) 248-8000
  (Mfr insulation, building materials, glass fiber prdts)
    Owens-Corning Fiberglas (Italy) SRL, Italy

OWENS-ILLINOIS INC   1 Seagate, Toledo, OH 43666, Tel: (419) 247-5000
  (Glass & plastic containers, house- hold & ind prdts, packaging)
    Owens-Illinois Inc., Via Montelungo 4, Casella Postale 243, 56100 Pisa, Italy

PAINEWEBBER GROUP INC   1285 Ave of the Americas, New York, NY 10019,
  Tel: (212) 713-2000
  (Stock brokerage serv & invest)
    PaineWebber Intl., Via Borgonuovo 10, 20121 Milan, Italy

PANDUIT CORP   17301 Ridgeland Ave, Tinley Park, IL 60477-0981,
  Tel: (708) 532-1800
  (Mfr elec/electr wiring comps)
    Panduit SAS, Via Como 10, 20020 Lainate, Milan, Italy

PARKER HANNIFIN CORP   17325 Euclid Ave, Cleveland, OH 44112,
  Tel: (216) 531-3000
  (Mfr motion-control prdts)
    Parker Hannifin SpA, Viale Lombardia 87, 25031 Capriolo (BS), Italy
    Parker Hannifin SpA, Div. SCEM RCD, Via E. Fermi 5, 20060 Gessate (MI), Italy
    Parker-Hannifin SpA, Via Privata Archimede 1, 20094 Corsico, Milan, Italy
    Parker-Hannifin SpA, Cylinder & Pneumatics, Via Carducci 11, 21010 Arsago Seprio,
      Italy

PDA ENGINEERING   2975 Redhill Ave, Costa Mesa, CA 92626, Tel: (714) 540-8900
  (Computer-aided engineering software & services, advanced materials technology &
  training)
    PDA Engineering Intl. SRL, Via Confienza 15, 10121 Turin, Italy

THE PERKIN-ELMER CORP   761 Main Ave, Norwalk, CT 06859-0001,
  Tel: (203) 762-1000
  (Mfr analytical instrumentation sys, high performance thermal spray coatings)
    Perkin-Elmer Italia SpA, Via Venezia 59, 35129 Padua, Italy

PETROLITE CORP   369 Marshall Ave, St Louis, MO 63119-1897,
  Tel: (314) 961-3500
  (Mfr/prod spec chem treating programs, performance-enhancing additives & related
  equip & svces)
    Petrolite Italiana SpA, Via Sasari 86, 95127 Catania, Italy

PFIZER INC   235 E 42nd St, New York, NY 10017-5755, Tel: (212) 573-2323
  (Mfr healthcare products)
    Pfizer Italiana SpA, Italy
    Roerig Farmaceutici Italiana SRL, Italy
    SudFarma SRL, Italy

PHELPS DODGE CORP   2600 N Central Ave, Phoenix, AZ 85004-3014,
  Tel: (602) 234-8100
  (Copper, minerals, metals & spec engineered prdts for trans & elect mkts)
    Columbian Carbon Europe SRL, 10 Via P. Verri, 20121 Milan, Italy

PHILLIPS PETROLEUM CO   Phillips Bldg, Bartlesville, OK 74004,
  Tel: (918) 661-6600
  (Crude oil, natural gas, liquefied petroleum gas, gasoline & petro-chems)
    Phillips Petroleum Intl. SRL, Via Cavallotti 13, 20122 Milan, Italy

PIONEER HI-BRED INTL INC   700 Capital Sq, 400 Locust St, Des Moines,
  IA 50309, Tel: (515) 245-3500
  (Agricultural chemicals, farm supplies, biological prdts, research)
    Pioneer Hi-Bred Italia SpA, Corte Sala, 43018 Sissa, Italy

PITNEY BOWES INC   Wheeler Dr, Stamford, CT 06926-0700, Tel: (203) 356-5000
  (Mfr postage meters, mailroom equip, copiers, bus supplies; bus servs)
    Pitney Bowes Italy, Via Vincenzo Russo 28, 20127 Milan, Italy

PLAYTEX APPAREL INC   700 Fairfield Ave, Stamford, CT 06904,
  Tel: (203) 356-8000
  (Mfr intimate apparel)
    Playtex Italia SpA, Piazza L. Sturzo 31, 00144 Rome, Italy

POLAROID CORP   549 Technology Sq, Cambridge, MA 02139, Tel: (617) 386-2000
  (Photographic equip & supplies, optical prdts)
    Polaroid Corp., Casella Postale 13, 6911 Brusino Ticino Arsizio, Italy

PPG INDUSTRIES   One PPG Place, Pittsburgh, PA 15272, Tel: (412) 434-3131
  (Mfr flat glass, fiber glass, chems, coatings)
    Ampaspace SRL, Via Montello 40, 26010 Casaletto Vaprio (Cremona), Italy
    PPG Industries Glass SpA, Via Rubaldo Merello 8-8A, 16100 Genoa, Italy
    PPG Industries Italia SRLe SpA, Via Giuseppe la Masa 20, 20158 Milan, Italy

PRECISION VALVE CORP   PO Box 309, Yonkers, NY 10702, Tel: (914) 969-6500
  (Mfr aerosol valves)
    Precision Valve Italia SpA, Via Ravello 1/3, 20081 Vermezzo (Milan), Italy

PREMARK INTL INC   1717 Deerfield Rd, Deerfield, IL 60015, Tel: (708) 405-6000
  (Mfr/sale diversified consumer & coml prdts)
    Premark Italia SpA, Via Mascagni 1, 20129 Milan, Italy

PREMIX INC   PO Box 281, N Kingsville, OH 44068, Tel: (216) 224-2181
  (Mfr molded fiber glass, reinforced thermoset molding compounds & plastic parts)
    Pianfei - IPA SpA, Via Cuneo 27, 12080 Pianfei, Italy

PROCTER & GAMBLE CO   One Procter & Gamble Plaza, Cincinnati, OH 45202,
  Tel: (513) 983-1100
  (Personal care, food, laundry, cleaning & ind prdts)
    Procter & Gamble Italia SpA, Italy

PROSERV INC   1101 Wilson Blvd, #1800, Arlington, VA 22209,
  Tel: (703) 276-3030
  (Sports mktg, mgt & consult)
    ProServ Italy, Italy

PUROLATOR COURIER CORP   3240 Hillview Ave, Palo Alto, CA 94304,
  Tel: (415) 494-2900
  (Time-sensitive package delivery)
    Executive Air Courier SRL, Milan, Italy

QUAKER CHEMICAL CORP   Elm & Lee Sts, Conshohocken, PA 19428-0809,
  Tel: (610) 832-4000
  (Mfr chem specialties; total fluid mgmt services)
    Quaker Chemical SpA, Via Polonia 7, 20157 Milan, Italy

THE QUAKER OATS CO   321 N Clark St, PO Box 049001, Chicago, IL 60604-9001,
  Tel: (312) 222-7111
  (Mfr foods & beverages)
    Chiari & Forti, Via Cendon 20, 31057 Silea, Treviso, Italy
    Quaker Chiari & Forti SpA, Viale Monterosa 21, 20149 Milan, Italy

QUIGLEY CO INC   235 E 42nd St, New York, NY 10017, Tel: (212) 573-3444
  (Mfr refractory specs, application equip)
    Quigley Italiana SpA, Via Creta 8, Brescia, Italy

K J QUINN & CO INC   135 Folly Mill Rd, PO Box 158, Seabrook, NH 03874,
  Tel: (603) 474-7177
  (Mfr spec coatings, adhesives, polyurethane polymers, shoe finishes, UV/EB cure
  coatings)
    Quinn Italiana SRL, Via Gherardini 6, 20145 Milan, Italy

RALSTON PURINA CO   Checkerboard Sq, St Louis, MO 63164, Tel: (314) 982-1000
  (Poultry & live stock feed, cereals, food prdts)
    Purina Italia SpA, Italy

RAMSEY TECHNOLOGY INC   501 90th Ave NW, Minneapolis, MN 55433,
  Tel: (612) 783-2500
  (Mfr in-motion weighing, inspection, monitoring & control equip for the process inds)
    Ramsey Italia SRL, Via Perugino 44, 20093 Cologno Monzese, Milan, Italy

RANCO INC   555 Metro Pl N, PO Box 248, Dublin, OH 43017, Tel: (614) 764-3733
  (Controls for appliance, automotive, comfort, commercial & consumer mkts)
    Ranco Italian Controls, Via del Seprio 42, 22074 Lomazzo, Italy

RAND McNALLY   8255 N Central Park Ave, Skokie, IL 60076, Tel: (708) 329-8100
  (Publishing & book services, docusystems, media services)
    Instituto Geografico de Agostini, Via Giovanni de Verrazano 15, 28100 Novara, Italy

RANSBURG CORP   3939 W 56th St, Indianapolis, IN 46208, Tel: (317) 298-5000
  (Mfr electrostatic coating sys)
    Ransburg-Gema SRL, Via la Spezia 35, 20142 Milan, Italy

RAYCHEM CORP   300 Constitution Dr, Menlo Park, CA 94025, Tel: (415) 361-3333
  (Devel/mfr/mkt materials science products for electronics, telecommunications &
  industry)
    Raychem SpA, Centro Direzionale Milanofiori, Palazzo E5, 20090 Assago (Milan), Italy
    Raychem SpA, also in La Spezia & Rome, Italy

RAYTHEON CO   141 Spring St, Lexington, MA 02173, Tel: (617) 862-6600
  (Mfr divers electronics, appliances, aviation, energy & environ prdts; publishing,
  ind & constr servs)
    Badger Italiana SRL, Via Vincenzo Monti 51, 20123 Milan, Italy

READER'S DIGEST ASSOCIATION INC   PO Box 235, Pleasantville, NY 10570,
  Tel: (914) 238-1000
  (Publisher magazines & books, direct mail marketer)
    Selezione dal Reader's Digest SpA, Via Alserio 10, 20159 Milan, Italy

READING & BATES CORP   901 Threadneedle, #200, Houston, TX 77079,
  Tel: (713) 496-5000
  (Offshore contract drilling)
    Reading & Bates Drilling Co./Shore Services Inc., Corso Vittorio Emanuele 3,
      66026 Ortona, Italy

REEBOK INTL LTD   100 Technology Center Dr, Stoughton, MA 02072,
  Tel: (617) 341-5000
  (Mfr footwear & apparel)
    Reebok Italia SRL, Viale Enrico Fermi 17, 20052 Monza (MI), Italy

REED TOOL CO   6501 Navigation Blvd, Houston, TX 77001, Tel: (713) 924-5200
  (Mfr rock bits for oil & gas explor)
    Reed Tool Co., Via Raiale 187, 65128 Pescara, Italy

REEVES BROTHERS INC   PO Box 1898, Hwy 29 South, Spartanburg, SC 29304,
  Tel: (803) 576-1210
  (Woven cotton & synthetic fabrics, textile job finishing, filter cloth, ind fabric
  prdts)
    Reeves SpA, 20090 Lodivecchio, Milan, Italy

REGAL-BELOIT CORP   200 State St, Beloit, WI 53511-6254, Tel: (608) 364-8800
  (Mfr power transmission equip, perishable cutting tools)
    Costruzioni Meccaniche Legnanesi SRL (CML), Via San Bernardino 129,
      20025 Legnano (Milan), Italy

RELIANCE ELECTRIC CO   24701 Euclid Ave, Cleveland, OH 44117,
  Tel: (216) 266-7000
  (Equip & sys for ind automation, telecom equip)
    Reliance Electric SpA, Via Volturno 46, 20124 Milan, Italy

REPUBLIC NEW YORK CORP   452 Fifth Ave, New York, NY 10018,
  Tel: (212) 525-6901
  (Banking)
    Republic National Bank of New York, Milan, Italy

REVLON INC   625 Madison Ave, New York, NY 10022, Tel: (212) 527-4000
(Mfr cosmetics, fragrances, toiletries, beauty care prdts)
  Revlon SpA, Casella Postale 4128, Via Appia Nuova Km. 17.850, 00100 Rome, Italy

RHONE-POULENC RORER INC   PO Box 1200, Collegeville, PA 19426-0107,
  Tel: (215) 454-8000
  (R&D/mfr human pharmaceuticals)
    Rorer Italiana SpA, Via Valosa di Sopra 9, 20050 Monza Milan, Italy

RIDGE TOOL CO   400 Clark St, Elyria, OH 44035, Tel: (216) 323-5581
  (Hand & power tools for working pipe, drain cleaning equip, etc)
    Ridge Tool Div. Emerson Electric SRL, Milan, Italy

A H ROBINS CO INC   1407 Cummings Dr, PO Box 26609, Richmond, VA 23261-6609,
  Tel: (804) 257-2000
  (Mfr ethical pharms & consumer prdts)
    Eurand Intl. SpA, Milan, Italy

THE ROCKPORT CO   220 Donald J Lynch Blvd, Marlboro, MA 01752,
  Tel: (508) 485-2090
  (Mfr/imp dress & casual footwear)
    Rockport Intl. Trading Co., Via Don Lorenzo Peroso 14, 50018 Scandicci, Italy

ROCKWELL INTL CORP   2201 Seal Beach Blvd, PO Box 4250, Seal Beach,
  CA 90740-8250, Tel: (310) 797-3311
  (Prdts & serv for aerospace, automotive, electronics, graphics & automation inds)
    Allen-Bradley Italia SRL, Via Tortona 33, 20144 Milan, Italy
    Allen-Bradley Italia SRL, also in Rome & Turin, Italy
    Nuova OSAI SRL, Via Persicetana 12, 40012 Calderara di Reno Bo, Italy
    Nuova OSAI SRL, also in Ivrea, Corsico (Milan) & Turin, Italy
    ROR Rockwell Italiana SRL, Via Monte Fiorino 23, 37057 S. Giovanni Lupatoto,
      Verona, Italy
    Rockwell Automotive Body Systems, Via Leonardo da Vinci 32,
      10095 Grugliasco (Turin), Italy
    Rockwell Automotive Body Systems, also in Avellino, Cassino & Como, Italy
    Rockwell CVC SpA, Viale Liegi 41, 00198 Rome, Italy

ROHM AND HAAS CO   100 Independence Mall West, Philadelphia, PA 19106,
  Tel: (215) 592-3000
  (Mfr ind & agric chems, plastics)
    Rohm and Haas Italia SpA, Via della Filanda, 20060 Gessate, Milan, Italy

RUSSELL REYNOLDS ASSOCIATES INC   200 Park Ave, New York, NY 10166,
  Tel: (212) 351-2000
  (Exec recruiting services)
    Russell Reynolds Associates Inc., Via Andrea Appiani 7, 20121 Milan, Italy

SALEM CORP   PO Box 2222, Pittsburgh, PA 15230, Tel: (412) 923-2200
  (Mfr ind furnaces, coal processing equip, metal finishing equip)
    Fersalem SpA, Milan, Italy

SAMSONITE CORP   11200 E 45th Ave, Denver, CO 80239-3018, Tel: (303) 373-2000
  (Mfr luggage & leather goods)
    Samsonite Italy, Via Enrico de Nicola 18, 20090 Cesano Boscone, Italy

SARA LEE CORP   3 First National Plaza, Chicago, IL 60602-4260,
  Tel: (312) 726-2600
  (Mfr/distr food & consumer packaged goods, tobacco prdts, intimate apparel & knitwear)
    Maglificio Bellia SpA, Via C. Bellia 34, 13050 Pettinengo, Italy
    Playtex Italia SpA, Via Laurentina Km. 27,200, 00040 Pomezia (Rome), Italy

R P SCHERER CORP   2075 W Big Beaver Rd, Troy, MI 48084, Tel: (810) 649-0900
  (Mfr soft gelatin & two-piece hard shell capsules)
    R.P. Scherer SpA, Via Nettunese, 04011 Aprilia, Latina, Italy

SCHLEGEL CORP   1555 Jefferson Rd, PO Box 23197, Rochester, NY 14692-3197,
  Tel: (716) 427-7200
  (Mfr engineered perimeter sealing systems for residential & commercial constr)
    Schlegel SRL, Via Miglioli 9, 20090 Segrate, Milan, Italy

SCIENTIFIC ATLANTA INC   1 Technology Pkwy, PO Box 105600, Atlanta, GA 30348,
  Tel: (404) 441-4000
  (Telecommun instru & equip, energy mgmt & home security equip, test & measurement
  instru)
    Scientific Atlanta SA, Via Benedetto Croce 19, 00142 Rome, Italy

SCOTSMAN ICE SYSTEMS   775 Corporate Woods Pkwy, Vernon Hills, IL 60061,
  Tel: (708) 215-4500
  (Mfr ice machines & refrigerators, drink dispensers)
    Castelmac SpA, Via del Lavoro 9, 31033 Castelfranco, Veneto, Italy
    Frimont SpA, Via Puccini 22, 20010 Bettolino di Pogliano (M), Italy

SEA-LAND SERVICE INC   150 Allen Rd, Liberty Corner, NJ 07920,
  Tel: (201) 558-6000
  (Container transport)
    Sea-Land Service Inc., Via Ravasco 10, 16128 Genoa, Italy
    Sea-Land Service Inc., Calata del Magnale, Caselle Postale 736, Porto di Livorno,
      57100 Livorno, Italy
    Sea-Land Service Inc., Molobausan, Porto di Napoli, 80133 Naples, Italy
    Sea-Land Service Inc., Terminal Containers, Porto di Palermo, 90139 Palermo, Italy

SEALED AIR CORP   Park 80 Plaza E, Saddle Brook, NJ 07662-5291,
  Tel: (201) 791-7600
  (Mfr protective packaging prdts)
    Instapak Italia SpA, Via Belvedere 18, 20043 Arcore, Milan, Italy

SEALOL INC   Warwick Industrial Park, PO Box 2158, Providence, RI 02905,
  Tel: (401) 781-4700
  (Mfr seals, joints, valves)
    EG&G Sealol Inc. SpA, Via Bernardo Rucellai 23, 20126 Milan, Italy

G D SEARLE & CO   5200 Old Orchard Rd, Skokie, IL 60077, Tel: (708) 982-7000
  (Mfr pharms, health care & optical prdts, specialty chems)
    Schiapparelli Searle, Corso Belgio 86, 10153 Turni, Italy

SELAS CORP OF AMERICA   2034 S Limekiln Pike, Dresher, PA 19025,
  Tel: (215) 646-6600
  (Mfr heat treating equip for metal, glass, ceramic & chem inds)
    Selas Italiana SRL, Via delle Tuberose 14, 20146 Milan, Italy

SHEAFFER EATON INC   1 Crown Mark Dr, Lincoln, RI   02865, Tel: (401) 333-0303
  (Mfr writing instruments)
    Sheaffer (Italy), Via Gostavo Modena 16, 20193 Milan, Italy

SHIPLEY CO INC   455 Forest St, Marlborough, MA   01752, Tel: (508) 481-7950
  (Mfr chems for printed circuit boards & microelectronic mfg)
    Shipley Italia SRL, Viale Delle Industrie 10/23, 20020 Arese-Milan, Italy

SMITH INTL INC   16740 Hardy St, Houston, TX   77032, Tel: (713) 443-3370
  (Mfr/serv downhole drilling equip)
    Smith Intl. Italia SpA, Via Grandi 1, Castel Maggiore, 40013 Bologna, Italy

SOFTWARE DEVELOPERS CO INC   90 Industrial Park Rd, Hingham, MA   02043,
  Tel: (617) 740-0101
  (Prepackaged software)
    SDC South Europe, Italy

SPECTRA-PHYSICS ANALYTICAL INC   45757 Northport Loop W, Fremont, CA   94537,
  Tel: (510) 657-1100
  (Mfr liquid chromatography equip)
    Spectra-Physics SRL, Centro Direzionale Lombardo, Palazzo E, Via Roma 108,
      20060 Cassina de'Pecchi, Italy

SPECTRAL DYNAMICS CORP   4141 Ruffin Rd, San Diego, CA   92123,
  Tel: (619) 496-3400
  (Mfr Vibration monitoring, analysis & control equip)
    Scientific-Atlanta SpA, Via Benedetto Croce 19, 00142 Rome, Italy

SPRINT INTERNATIONAL   12490 Sunrise Valley Dr, Reston, VA   22096,
  Tel: (703) 689-6000
  (Telecommunications)
    Sprint Intl. Italia SpA (Central/Southern Europe), Centro Direzionale Lombardo,
      Palazzo CD, Via Roma 108, 20060 Cassina de'Pecchi, Milan, Italy

SPS TECHNOLOGIES INC   301 Highland Ave, Jenkintown, PA   19046-2630,
  Tel: (215) 572-3000
  (Mfr aerospace & ind fasteners, tightening sys, magnetic materials, superalloys)
    Unbrako SRL, Via XXV Aprile 19, 20097 San Donato (Milan), Italy

SPX CORP   700 Terrace Point Dr, PO Box 3301, Muskegon, MI   49443-3301,
  Tel: (616) 724-5000
  (Mfr spec service tools, engine & drive-train parts)
    Bear Italiana SRL, Via dei Confini 201, 50010 Capalle, Florence, Italy

SRI INTL   333 Ravenswood Ave, Menlo Park, CA   94025-3493, Tel: (415) 326-6200
  (Intl consulting & research)
    SRI Italy, Via Lanzone 6, 20123 Milan, Italy

STA-RITE INDUSTRIES INC   293 Wright St, Delavan, WI   53115,
  Tel: (414) 728-5551
  (Mfr water pumps, filters & systems)
    Nocchi Pompe SPA, Via Masaccio 13, 56010 Lugnano, Pisa, Italy

STANDEX INTL CORP   6 Manor Pkwy, Salem, NH   03079, Tel: (603) 893-9701
  (Mfr diversified graphics, institutional, ind/electr & consumer prdts)
    Standex Intl. SRL, Via Maggio 20, 20064 Gorgonzola (Milan), Italy

THE STANLEY WORKS   1000 Stanley Dr, PO Box 7000, New Britain, CT 06050,
   Tel: (203) 225-5111
   (Mfr hand tools & hardware)
      Stanley Mediterranea SpA, Via Motolense Supino, Frosinone, Italy
      Stanley Tools SpA, Via Trieste 1, 22060 Figino Serenza Como, Italy
      Stanley Works (Italia) SRL, Via Leopardi 9, 22060 Figino Serenza Como, Italy

STEINER CO   1 E Superior St, Chicago, IL 60611, Tel: (312) 642-1242
   (Soap & towel dispensers)
      L.S.I., Piazza de Angeli 9, 20146 Milan, Italy

STERLING SOFTWARE INC   8080 N Central Expy, #1100, Dallas, TX 75206-1895,
   Tel: (214) 891-8600
   (Sales/serv software prdts; tech servs)
      Sterling Software Intl., Corso Svizzera 185, 10149 Turin, Italy

STIEFEL LABORATORIES INC   255 Alhambra Circle, Coral Gables, FL 33134,
   Tel: (305) 443-3807
   (Mfr pharmaceuticals, dermatological specialties)
      Stiefel Laboratories SRL, Via Calabria 15, 20090 Redecesio Di Segrate, Milan, Italy

STORAGE TECHNOLOGY CORP   2270 S 88th St, Louisville, CO 80028-0001,
   Tel: (303) 673-5151
   (Mfr/mkt/serv info storage & retrieval sys)
      Storage Technology Italia SpA, Via Cina 413, 00144 Rome, Italy

SUDLER & HENNESSEY   1633 Broadway, New York, NY 10019, Tel: (212) 969-5800
   (Healthcare prdts advertising)
      G&R Pubblicita/Sudler & Hennessey, Via Guerrazzi 1, 20145 Milan, Italy

SYBRON INTL CORP   411 E Wisconsin Ave, Milwaukee, WI 53202,
   Tel: (414) 274-6600
   (Mfr prdts for laboratories, professional orthodontic & dental mkts)
      Kerr Italia SpA, Via Passanti 332, Casella Postale 46, 84018 Scafati (Salerno),
      Italy

SYSTEMS ENGINEERING LABS INC   6901 W Sunrise Blvd, Fort Lauderdale,
   FL 33313, Tel: (305) 587-2900
   (Digital computers)
      SEL Computer SpA, Filiale de Bologna, Via Byron 18, 20129 Bologna, Italy

TECHNICON INSTRUMENTS CORP   511 Benedict Ave, Tarrytown, NY 10591-5097,
   Tel: (914) 631-8000
   (Mfr/serv automated blook anal equip, reagents & diagnostics)
      Technicon Italiana SpA, Via Riccardo Gigante 20, 00143 Rome, Italy

TECUMSEH PRODUCTS CO   100 E Patterson St, Tecumseh, MI 49286-1899,
   Tel: (517) 423-8411
   (Mfr refrig & A/C compressors & units, small engines, pumps)
      Tecnamotor SRL, Casella Postale 1221, 10100 Torino, Italy

TEKTRONIX INC   26660 SW Parkway, Wilsonville, OR 97070, Tel: (503) 627-7111
   (Mfr test & meas, visual sys & commun prdts)
      Tektronix SpA, Milan, Turin & Rome, Italy

TELEDYNE INC   2049 Century Park East, Los Angeles, CA 90067-3101,
Tel: (310) 277-3311
(Divers mfg: aviation & electronics, specialty metals, industrial & consumer prdts)
   Teledyne Italy, Corso de Porta Romana 2, 20122 Milan, Italy

TELXON CORP   3330 W Market St, PO Box 5582, Akron, OH 44334-0582,
Tel: (216) 867-3700
(Devel/mfr portable computer sys & related equip)
   Telxon Italia SRL, Palazzo Cimabue, Via Cassanese 224, 20090 Segrate Milan, Italy

TENNECO AUTOMOTIVE   111 Pfingsten Rd, Deerfield, IL 60015,
Tel: (708) 948-0900
(Automotive parts, exhaust sys, service equip)
   Monroe Italia SRL, Via Plinio 43, 20129 Milan, Italy

TERADYNE INC   321 Harrison Ave, Boston, MA 02118, Tel: (617) 482-2700
(Mfr electronic test equip & blackplane connection sys)
   Teradyne Italia SRL, Via Modigliani 27, 20090 Segrate, Italy

TEXAS INSTRUMENTS INC   13500 N Central Expwy, Dallas, TX 75265,
Tel: (214) 995-2011
(Mfr semiconductor devices, electr/electro-mech sys, instr & controls)
   Texas Instruments Italia SpA, Via John F. Kennedy 141, Aversa, Italy

TEXON INC   1190 Huntington Rd, Russell, MA 01071, Tel: (413) 862-3652
(Mfr latex & resin impregnated fibre prdts)
   Texon Italia SRL, Via Cimitero Vecchio 8, 27023 Cassolnovo, Pavia, Italy

THERMON   100 Thermon Dr, PO Box 609, San Marcos, TX 78667-0609,
Tel: (512) 396-5801
(Mfr steam & electric heat tracing sys, components & accessories)
   Thermon Italia SpA, Viale Lomellina 12A (ang. Via Piemonte),
      20090 Buccinasco (Milan), Italy

THOMAS & BETTS CORP   1555 Lynnfield Rd, Memphis, TN 38119,
Tel: (901) 682-7766
(Mfr elect/electr connectors & accessories)
   T & B SpA, Via Archimede Angola Piazzale Labriola, 20092 Balsamo, Italy

THOR POWER TOOL CO   72 Bayside Rd, Virginia Beach, VA 23455,
Tel: (804) 323-5666
(Mfr portable air-operated & elect tools)
   Thor FIAP, Casella Postale 608, Via Piscina 43, 10060 Frossasco, Turin, Italy

TIDEWATER INC   Tidewater Place, 1440 Canal St, New Orleans, LA 70112,
Tel: (504) 568-1010
(Marine serv & equip to companies engaged in explor, development & prod of oil, gas & minerals)
   Tidewater Marine Service Inc., Via Piemonte 59, 20093 Cologno Monzese, Milan, Italy

TIFFANY & CO   727 Fifth Ave, New York, NY 10022, Tel: (212) 755-8000
(Mfr/retail fine jewelry, silverware, china, crystal, leather goods, etc)
   Faraone Milan, Via Montenapoleone 7A, 20121 Milan, Italy

THE TIMBERLAND CO   200 Domain Dr, Stratham, NH 03885, Tel: (603) 772-9500
  (Design/mfr footwear, apparel & accessories for men & women)
     Timberland Europe Inc., Centro Direczionale Colleoni, Palazzo Orione,
        Viale Colleoni, 20041 Agrate Brianza, Italy

TIME WARNER INC   75 Rockefeller Plaza, New York, NY 10019,
  Tel: (212) 484-8000
  (Communications, publishing, entertainment)
     Time-Life Intl. SARL, Via Turati 29, Milan, Italy

TOWERS PERRIN   245 Park Ave, New York, NY 10167, Tel: (212) 309-3400
  (Management consultants)
     Towers, Perrin, Forster & Crosby, Italy

TRANE CO   3600 Pammel Creek Rd, La Crosse, WI 54601, Tel: (608) 787-2000
  (Mfr/distr/svce A/C sys & equip)
     Trane Italia SRL, Via Enrico Fermi 21/23, 20090 Assago, Italy

TRANS WORLD AIRLINES INC   505 N 6th St, St Louis, MO 63101,
  Tel: (314) 589-3000
  (Air transportation)
     Trans World Airlines, Via Partemope 23, Naples, Italy
     Trans World Airlines, Via Berberini 59, Rome, Italy
     Trans World Airlines Inc., II Corsa Europa, Milan, Italy
     Trans World Airlines Inc., Via dei Vecchietti 4, Florence, Italy

TRANTER INC   1054 Claussen Rd, #314, Augusta, GA 30907, Tel: (706) 738-7900
  (Mfr heat exchangers)
     SWEP Italia SRL, Via E Toti 36/A, 2002 Monza, Italy

TRINOVA CORP   3000 Strayer, PO Box 50, Maumee, OH 43537-0050,
  Tel: (419) 867-2200
  (Mfr engr components & sys for ind)
     Trinova SpA, Via A. Nicolodi 31-33, Casella Postale 158, 57121 Livorno, Italy
     Vickers, Via Amperes 11, Settimo, 20019 Milan, Italy
     Vickers Polymotor, Via Avosso 94, 16015 Casella, Genoa, Italy
     Vickers Systems Div. Trinova SpA, Reg S. Martino, Strada Statale 460 Km. 36,
        Valperga, 10087 Turin, Italy
     Vickers Systems SA, Via Monzesen 34, Vignate, 20060 Milan, Italy

TRW INC   1900 Richmond Rd, Cleveland, OH 44124, Tel: (216) 291-7000
  (Electr & energy-related prdts, automotive & aerospace prdts, tools & fasteners)
     TRW Italia SpA, Via Valtrompia 87, 25063 Gardone Valtrompia, Brescial, Italy

TWIN DISC INC   1328 Racine St, Racine, WI 53403-1758, Tel: (414) 638-4000
  (Mfr ind clutches, reduction gears, transmissions)
     Twin Disc Italia SRL, Via Coppino 425-427, 55049 Viareggio (Lu), Italy

U S SURGICAL CORP   150 Glover Ave, Norwalk, CT 06856, Tel: (203) 845-1000
  (Mfr/devel/mkt surgical staplers, laparoscopic instru & sutures)
     Auto Suture Italia SpA, all mail to U.S. address

UNION CARBIDE CORP   39 Old Ridgebury Rd, Danbury, CT 06817,
  Tel: (203) 794-2000
  (Mfr industrial chemicals, plastics, resins)
     Union Carbide Chemicals SpA, Zona Industriale, Casella Postale 53, Termoli, Italy

UNION SPECIAL CORP   One Union Special Plaza, Huntley, IL 60142,
Tel: (708) 669-4345
(Mfr sewing machs)
  Union Special Italia SpA, Via Bergamo 4, 20020 Lainate (MI), Italy

UNIROYAL INC   World Headquarters, Middlebury, CT 06749, Tel: (203) 573-2000
(Tires, tubes & other rubber prdts, chems, plastics, textiles)
  Uniroyal Chemica SpA, Viale XVIII Dicembre, Palazzo Rocco, Latina, Italy
  Uniroyal Manull SpA, Zona Industriale Compolunga, 63100 Ascoli Piceno, Italy
  Uniroyal SpA, Via Volantari della Liberta 21, 20010 Vittuone, Italy

UNISYS CORP   PO Box 500, Blue Bell, PA 19424, Tel: (215) 986-4011
(Mfg/mktg/serv electr info sys)
  Unisys Italia SpA, Via B. Crespi 57, 20159 Milan, Italy

UNITED TECHNOLOGIES CORP   United Technologies Bldg, Hartford, CT 06101,
Tel: (203) 728-7000
(Mfr aircraft engines, elevators, A/C, auto equip, space & military electr, rocket
propulsion sys)
  Carnier Italia SpA, Via Boccaccio 35, 20090 Trezzano Sul Naviglio, Milan, Italy
  Marlo SpA, Via Vincenzo Monti 23, 20016 Pero, Milan, Italy
  S.P. Elettronica, Via Carlo Pisacane 7, 20016 Pero Milan, Italy

UNITEK CORP/3M   2724 S Peck Rd, Monrovia, CA 91016-7118, Tel: (818) 574-4000
(Mfr orthodontic prdts)
  Unital SRL, Italy

UNITRODE CORP   7 Continental Blvd, Merrimack, NH 03054, Tel: (603) 424-2410
(Mfr electronic components)
  Unitrode SRL, Via Dei Carracci 5, 20149 Milan, Italy

UNIVERSAL CORP   PO Box 25099, Richmond, VA 23260, Tel: (804) 359-9311
(Holding co: tobacco, commodities)
  Deltafina SpA, Via Donizetti 10, 00198 Rome, Italy

UNIVERSAL FOODS CORP   433 E Michigan St, Milwaukee, WI 53202,
Tel: (414) 271-6755
(Mfr food prdts & food ingredients)
  Curt Georgi Imes SpA, Milan, Italy

UNIVERSAL WEATHER & AVIATION INC   8787 Tallyho Rd, Houston, TX 77061,
Tel: (713) 944-1622
(Airport services)
  Universal Aviation Italy SRL, Aereoporto Malpensa, 21013 Gallarte, Italy

UPJOHN CO   7000 Portage Rd, Kalamazoo, MI 49001, Tel: (616) 323-4000
(Mfr pharms, agric prdts, ind chems)
  Asgrow Italia SpA, Corso Mazzahi 9, 20075 Lodi Milan, Italy

USF&G FINANCIAL SERVICES CORP   100 Light St, Baltimore, MD 21202,
Tel: (301) 547-3000
(Investment mgt, real estate, computer leasing, fin prdt mktg & admin, strategic
consult)
  F&G Computer Leasing Italia SRL, Via Ruffini 2A, 00195 Rome, Italy

VALENITE INC   PO Box 9636, Madison Heights, MI 48071-9636,
  Tel: (810) 589-1000
  (Cemented carbide, high speed steel, ceramic & diamond cutting tool prdts, etc)
    Valenite-Modco SRL, Direzione Commerciale, Via C. Battisti 3,
      20070 Vizzolo Predabissi (Milan), Italy

VARIAN ASSOCIATES INC   3100 Hansen Way, Palo Alto, CA 94304-1030,
  Tel: (415) 493-4000
  (Mfr microwave tubes & devices, analytical instru, semiconductor process & med equip,
  vacuum sys)
    Varian SpA, Via Varian 54, 10040 Lenini (Turin), Italy
    Varian SpA, Via Rivoltana 8, 20090 Segrate (Milan), Italy

VENDO CO   7209 N Ingram, Pinedale, CA 93650, Tel: (209) 439-1770
  (Mfr coin-op automatic vending machs)
    Vendo (Italia) SRL, Casella Postale 59, 15033 Casale Monferrato, Alessandria, Italy

VERNAY LABORATORIES INC   120 E South College St, Yellow Springs, OH 45387,
  Tel: (513) 767-7261
  (Mechanical prdts, spec molded shapes, rubber goods)
    Vernay Italia SRL, Localita Rilate 21, 14100 Asti Piemonte, Italy

WARNER BROS INTL TELEVISION DISTRIBUTION   4000 Warner Blvd, Burbank,
  CA 91522, Tel: (818) 954-4068
  (Distr TV programming & theatrical features)
    Warner Bros. Italia SRL, Via G. Avezzana 51, 00195 Rome, Italy

WARNER ELECTRIC BRAKE & CLUTCH CO   449 Gardner St, South Beloit, IL 61080,
  Tel: (815) 389-3771
  (Automotive & ind brakes & clutches)
    Warner Electric SpA, Via Puccini 3, 20121 Milan, Italy

WATERS CHROMATOGRAPHY DIV   34 Maple St, Milford, MA 01757,
  Tel: (617) 478-2000
  (Mfr/distr liquid chromatographic instru/accessories/tech)
    Millipore SpA, Via Cassanese 218, 20090 Segrate, Milan, Italy

WATKINS-JOHNSON CO   3333 Hillview Ave, Palo Alto, CA 94304-1204,
  Tel: (415) 493-4141
  (Mfr defense electronic prdts)
    W-J Italiana SpA, Piazza G. Marconi 25, 00144 Rome EUR, Italy

WATLOW ELECTRIC MFG CO   12001 Lackland Rd, St Louis, MO 63146-4039,
  Tel: (314) 878-4600
  (Mfr elec heating units, electr controls, thermocouple wire, metal-sheathed cable,
  infrared sensors)
    Watlow Italy SRL, Via Adige 13, 20135 Milan, Italy

WATTS INDUSTRIES INC   815 Chestnut St, North Andover, MA 01845,
  Tel: (508) 688-1811
  (Mfr ind valves & safety control prdts)
    ISI Industria Saracinesche Idrauliche SpA, Zona Industriale, Localita Ischiello,
      38015 Lavis (TN), Italy
    Intermes SpA, Zona Industriale, 39052 Caldaro (BZ), Italy
    Intermes SpA, Via Bellini 30, 20095 Cusano Milanino (Milan), Italy
    Pibiviesse SpA, Via di Vittorio 43, 20017 Mazza DiRho (MI), Italy

WEATHERFORD INTL INC   1360 Post Oak Blvd, PO Box 27608, Houston,
TX 77227-7608, Tel: (713) 439-9400
(Oilfield servs, prdts & equip; mfr marine cranes)
    Weatherford Italiana SpA, Via Pirano 19, 48100 Ravenna, Italy

THE WEST CO   101 Gordon Dr, PO Box 645, Lionville, PA 19341-0645,
Tel: (610) 594-2900
(Mfr prdts for filling, sealing, dispensing & delivering needs of health care &
consumer prdts mkts)
    Pharma-Gummi Italia SRL, Milan, Italy

WESTERN ATLAS INTL INC   10205 Westheimer, PO Box 1407, Houston,
TX 77251-1407, Tel: (713) 266-5700
(Full service to the oil industry)
    Western Atlas Logging Services, Geoscience Center, Via Angelo Moro 115,
       20097 San Donato, Milan, Italy

WEYERHAEUSER CO   Tacoma, WA 98477, Tel: (206) 924-2345
(Wood & wood fiber products)
    Weyerhauser Italia SRL, Viale Tunisia 38, 20124 Milan, Italy

WHIRLPOOL CORP   2000 N M-63, Benton Harbor, MI 49022-2692,
Tel: (616) 923-5000
(Mfr/mkt home appliances)
    Whirlpool Europe BV, Cassinetta, Naples, Siena & Trento, Italy
    Whirlpool Italia SRL, Viale G. Borghi 27, 21025 Comerio, Italy

W A WHITNEY CO   650 Race St, PO Box 1206, Rockford, IL 61105-1206,
Tel: (815) 964-6771
(Mfr hydraulic punch/plasma cutting metal fabricating equip)
    W.A. Whitney Italia SpA, Strada Del Francese 132/9, 10156 Turin, Italy

WINCHESTER ELECTRONICS   400 Park Rd, Watertown, CT 06795-0500,
Tel: (203) 945-5000
(Mfr elec & electr connectors, PCB assemblies & hardware)
    Veam SpA, Via Statuto 2, 20020 Arese, Milan, Italy

WITCO CORP   1 American Lane, Greenwich, CT 06831-4236, Tel: (203) 552-2000
(Mfr chem & petroleum prdts)
    Witco Chemical Italiana SRL, Via Vincenzo Monti 79/2, 20145 Milan, Italy
    Witco Italiana SRL, Div. SITECH, Via Roccavecchia 9, 27029 Vigevano, PV, Italy

WMX TECHNOLOGIES INC   3003 Butterfield Rd, Oak Brook, IL 60563,
Tel: (708) 572-8800
(Environmental services)
    Waste Management Italia SRL, Via XXV Aprile 59, 22070 Guanzate (CO), Italy

WORLD COURIER INC   46 Trinity Pl, New York, NY 10006, Tel: (718) 978-9400
(Intl courier serv)
    World Courier Italia SRL, Via Mecenate 30/6, Milan, Italy

XEROX CORP   800 Long Ridge Rd, PO Box 1600, Stamford, CT 06904,
Tel: (203) 968-3000
(Mfr document processing equip, sys & supplies)
    Xerox Corp., Milan & Rome, Italy

YOUNG & RUBICAM INC   285 Madison Ave, New York, NY 10017, Tel: (212) 210-3000
  (Advertising, public relations, direct marketing & sales promotion, corp & product ID management)
    Young & Rubicam Italia SpA, Piazza Eleonora Duse 2, 20122 Milan, Italy

IVORY COAST

AMERICAN INTL GROUP INC   70 Pine St, New York, NY 10270, Tel: (212) 770-7000
  (Insurance, financial services)
    American Intl. Assurance Co. Ltd., 08 Boite Postale 873, Abidjan, Ivory Coast

BANKERS TRUST CO   280 Park Ave, New York, NY 10017, Tel: (212) 250-2500
  (Banking)
    Societe Generale de Banques, Boite Postale 1355, Abidjan, Ivory Coast

CHASE MANHATTAN BANK N A   1 Chase Manhattan Plaza, New York, NY 10081,
  Tel: (212) 552-2222
  (Intl banking)
    Chase Manhattan Bank NA, 01 Boite Postale 4107, Abidjan, Ivory Coast

CITICORP   399 Park Ave, New York, NY 10043, Tel: (212) 559-1000
  (Banking & financial services)
    Citibank NA, Ivory Coast

COLGATE-PALMOLIVE CO   300 Park Ave, New York, NY 10022, Tel: (212) 310-2000
  (Mfr pharms, cosmetics, toiletries, detergents)
    Colgate-Palmolive Cote d'Ivoire, Blvd. Giscard d'Estaing, 01 Boite Postale 1283,
      Abidjan, Ivory Coast

THE DOW CHEMICAL CO   2030 Dow Center, Midland, MI 48674, Tel: (517) 636-1000
  (Mfr chems, plastics, pharms, agric prdts, consumer prdts)
    Dow Chemical Co., Boite Postale 1521, Abidjan, Ivory Coast

FIDELITY BANK   135 S Broad St, Philadelphia, PA 19109, Tel: (215) 985-6000
  (Investments & banking)
    Fidelity Bank, Boite Postale V245, Abidjan, Ivory Coast

FMC CORP   200 E Randolph Dr, Chicago, IL 60601, Tel: (312) 861-6000
  (Produces chems & precious metals, mfr machinery, equip & sys for ind, agric & govt)
    FMC Overseas Ltd., Ivory Coast

FRANK B HALL & CO INC   549 Pleasantville Rd, Briarcliff Manor, NY 10510,
  Tel: (914) 769-9200
  (Insurance)
    Sogerco, 43 Ave. de Gen. de Gaulle, 01 Boite Postale 1539, Abidjan, Ivory Coast

H J HEINZ CO   PO Box 57, Pittsburgh, PA 15230-0057, Tel: (412) 456-5700
(Processed food prdts & nutritional services)
  Star-Kist Foods Inc., Abidjan, Ivory Coast

IMCO SERVICES   5950 N Course Dr, Houston, TX 70072, Tel: (713) 561-1300
(Drilling fluids)
  Imco Services, Div. of Halliburton Ltd., Boite Postale 1115, 15 Abidjan, Ivory Coast

ITT CORP   1330 Ave of the Americas, New York, NY 10019-5490,
 Tel: (212) 258-1000
(Design/mfr communications & electronic equip, hotels, insurance)
  ITT Africa & Middle East, Boite Postale 8078, Abidjan, Ivory Coast

S C JOHNSON & SON INC   1525 Howe St, Racine, WI 53403, Tel: (414) 631-2000
(Home, auto, commercial & personal care prdts, specialty chems)
  S.C. Johnson & Son Inc., c/o CFCI Div. Technique, Boite Postale 1844, Abidjan,
    Ivory Coast

McCANN-ERICKSON WORLDWIDE   750 Third Ave, New York, NY 10017,
 Tel: (212) 697-6000
(Advertising)
  Edition Publicite, Ave. Giscard d'Estaing face a "La Galerie",
    01 Boite Postale 3420, Abidjan, Ivory Coast

PHILLIPS PETROLEUM CO   Phillips Bldg, Bartlesville, OK 74004,
 Tel: (918) 661-6600
(Crude oil, natural gas, liquefied petroleum gas, gasoline & petro-chems)
  Phillips Petroleum, Boite Postale 20947, Abidjan, Ivory Coast

TEXACO INC   2000 Westchester Ave, White Plains, NY 10650, Tel: (914) 253-4000
(Explor/mktg crude oil, mfr petro chems & prdts)
  Texaco Cote d'Ivoire, Boite Postale 1782, Abidjan, Ivory Coast

WACKENHUT CORP   1500 San Remo Ave, Coral Gables, FL 33146,
 Tel: (305) 666-5656
(Security systems & services)
  Wackenhut Seges, 2 Plateaux Rue des Jardins, Lot 2159, Abidjan, Ivory Coast

HARRY WINSTON INC   718 Fifth Ave, New York, NY 10019, Tel: (212) 245-2000
(Diamonds, lapidary work)
  Societe Wharton, Boite Postale 2816, Abidjan, Ivory Coast

XEROX CORP   800 Long Ridge Rd, PO Box 1600, Stamford, CT 06904,
 Tel: (203) 968-3000
(Mfr document processing equip, sys & supplies)
  Xerox Corp., Abidjan, Ivory Coast

JAMAICA

3M   3M Center, St Paul, MN 55144-1000, Tel: (612) 733-1110
(Mfr diversified prdts for industry, health care, imaging, commun, transport, safety, consumer, etc)
   3M Interamerica Inc. (Jamaica Div.), 218 Marcus Garvey Lane, Kingston 11, Jamaica

ACCO INTL INC   770 S Acco Plaza, Wheeling, IL 60090, Tel: (708) 541-9500
(Paper fasteners & clips, metal fasteners, binders, staplers)
   Acco Jamaica Ltd., P.O. Box 51, Kingston, Jamaica

ALUMINUM CO OF AMERICA (ALCOA)   425 6th Ave, Pittsburgh, PA 15219,
Tel: (412) 553-4545
(Aluminum mining, refining, processing, prdts)
   Alcoa Minerals of Jamaica Inc., P.O. Box 241, Kingston 6, Jamaica

AMERICAN AIRLINES INC   PO Box 619616, Dallas-Ft Worth Arpt, TX 75261-9616,
Tel: (817) 355-1234
(Air transp)
   American Airlines, P.O. Box 159, Windward Rd. Station, Kingston 2, Jamaica

AMERICAN INTL GROUP INC   70 Pine St, New York, NY 10270, Tel: (212) 770-7000
(Insurance, financial services)
   American Intl. Underwriters (Jamaica) Ltd., P.O. Box 102, Kingston, Jamaica

AVIS INC   900 Old Country Rd, Garden City, NY 11530, Tel: (516) 222-3000
(Car rental serv)
   Avis Rental Office, 3 Oxford Rd., New Kingston, Jamaica

D D BEAN & SONS CO   Peterborough Rd, PO Box 348, Jaffrey, NH 03452,
Tel: (603) 532-8311
(Mfr paper book & wooden stick matches)
   Jamaica Match Holdings Ltd., P.O. Box 370, Kingston 11, Jamaica

SAMUEL BINGHAM CO   1555 N Mittel Blvd, #T, Wood Dale, IL 60191-1046,
Tel: (708) 238-4000
(Print & industrial rollers, inks)
   Coates Bros. (Jamaica) Ltd., P.O. Box 317, Kingston 11, Jamaica

CARBOLINE CO   350 Hanley Industrial Ct, St Louis, MO 63144,
Tel: (314) 644-1000
(Mfr coatings, sealants)
   Berger Paints Jamaica Ltd., P.O. Box 8, 256 Spanish Town Rd., Kingston 11, Jamaica

CIGNA CORP   One Liberty Place, Philadelphia, PA 19192, Tel: (215) 523-4000
(Ins, invest, health care & other fin servs)
   Insurance Co. of North America, 21 Constant Spring Rd., Kingston, Jamaica

CITICORP   399 Park Ave, New York, NY 10043, Tel: (212) 559-1000
(Banking & financial services)
   Citibank NA, Jamaica

CITIZENS & SOUTHERN NATL BANK   35 Broad St, Atlanta, GA 30399,
Tel: (404) 581-2121
(Banking)
   Jamaica Citizens Bank, 4 King St., Kingston, Jamaica

COLGATE-PALMOLIVE CO   300 Park Ave, New York, NY 10022, Tel: (212) 310-2000
(Mfr pharms, cosmetics, toiletries, detergents)
   Colgate-Palmolive (Jamaica) Ltd., 26 Marcus Garvey Dr., Kingston 11, Jamaica

CRAY RESEARCH INC   655 Lone Oak Dr, Eagan, MN 55121, Tel: (612) 452-6650
(Supercomputer systems & services)
   Cray Foreign Sales Corp. Ltd., c/o Livingston Alexander & Levy, 7276 Harbour St.,
   Kingston, Jamaica

CUNA MUTUAL INSURANCE SOCIETY   5910 Mineral Point Road, PO Box 391, Madison,
WI 53701, Tel: (608) 238-5851
(Insurance)
   Cuna Mutual Insurance, 2A Manhattan Rd., P.O. Box 396, Kingston 5, Jamaica

FOOTE CONE & BELDING COMMUNICATIONS INC   101 E Erie St, Chicago,
IL 60611-2897, Tel: (312) 751-7000
(Advertising agency)
   Lindo/FCB Ltd., 14 Ruthven Rd., Kingston 10, Jamaica

THE GILLETTE CO   Prudential Tower, Boston, MA 02199, Tel: (617) 421-7000
(Devel/mfr personal care/use prdts: blades & razors, toiletries, cosmetics,
stationery)
   Gillette Cribbean Ltd., Kingston, Jamaica
   Gillette Foreign Sales Corp. Ltd., Kingston, Jamaica

THE GOODYEAR TIRE & RUBBER CO   1144 E Market St, Akron, OH 44316,
Tel: (216) 796-2121
(Mfr tires, automotive belts & hose, conveyor belts, chemicals; oil pipeline
transmission)
   Goodyear (Jamaica) Ltd., 29 Tobago Ave., Kingston 10, Jamaica

HOLIDAY INNS INC   3742 Lamar Ave, Memphis, TN 38195, Tel: (901) 362-4001
(Hotels, restaurants, casinos)
   Rose Hall, P.O. Box 480, Montego Bay, Jamaica

HORWATH INTL   415 Madison Ave, New York, NY 10017, Tel: (212) 838-5566
(Public accountants & auditors)
   Horwath & Horwath (Jamaica), P.O. Box 26, 2 Ripon Rd., Kingston 5, Jamaica

JOHNSON & JOHNSON   One Johnson & Johnson Plaza, New Brunswick, NJ 08933,
Tel: (908) 524-0400
(R&D/mfr/sale health care prdts)
   Johnson & Johnson Ltd., P.O. Box 8103, Kingston 11, Jamaica

KAISER ALUMINUM & CHEMICAL CORP   6177 Sunol Blvd, Pleasanton, CA 94566,
  Tel: (510) 462-1122
  (Mfr aluminum & aluminum prdts, chems)
    Alumina Partners of Jamaica, Spurtree, Jamaica (all mail to P.O. box 529, Arabi,
    LA 70032)
    Kaiser Jamaica Bauxite Co., Discovery Bay, Jamaica (all mail to P.O. Box 529,
    Arabi, LA 70032)

KOPPERS CO INC   Koppers Bldg, 437 Seventh Ave, Pittsburgh, PA 15219,
  Tel: (412) 227-2000
  (Constr materiald & serv; chem & bldg prdts)
    Wood Preservation Ltd., Kingston, Jamaica

LANNON MFG CO   PO Box 550, Tullahoma, TN 37388, Tel: (615) 455-0691
  (Sporting goods)
    West Indies Mfg. Co., P.O. Box 49, Lucea, Jamaica

MAIDENFORM INC   90 Park Ave, New York, NY 10016, Tel: (212) 953-1400
  (Mfr intimate apparel)
    Jamaica Needlecraft Ltd., P.O. Box 28, Kingston 15, Jamaica

McCANN-ERICKSON WORLDWIDE   750 Third Ave, New York, NY 10017,
  Tel: (212) 697-6000
  (Advertising)
    McCann-Erickson (Jamaica) Ltd., 7 Knutsford St., P.O. Box 168, Kingston 5

NATIONAL CAR RENTAL SYSTEM INC   7700 France Ave S, Minneapolis, MN 55435,
  Tel: (612) 830-2121
  (Car rental)
    National Car Rental, 16 Beechwood Ave., Kingston 5, Jamaica

THE PROTANE CORP   1400 Smith St, Houston, TX 77210, Tel: (713) 853-7047
  (Holding co: foreign invest in LPG ind & distribution)
    Industrial Gases Ltd., P.O. Box 224, Kingston 11, Jamaica

RADISSON HOTELS INTL   Carlson Pkwy, PO Box 59159, Minneapolis,
  MN 55459-8204, Tel: (612) 540-5526
  (Hotels)
    Ciboney, Ocho Rios, Main St., P.O. Box 728, Ocho Rios, St. Ann, Jamaica, W.I.
    Poinciana Beach Resort, Negril, Jamaica, W.I.

RJR NABISCO INC   1301 Ave of the Americas, New York, NY 10019,
  Tel: (212) 258-5600
  (Mfr consumer packaged food prdts & tobacco prdts)
    West Indies Yeast Co. Ltd., 38 Jobs Lane, Spanish Town, Jamaica

SEA-LAND SERVICE INC   150 Allen Rd, Liberty Corner, NJ 07920,
  Tel: (201) 558-6000
  (Container transport)
    Sea-Land Service Inc., P.O. Box 293, Kingston 11, Jamaica

SHERWIN-WILLIAMS CO INC   101 Prospect Ave NW, Cleveland, OH 44115,
  Tel: (216) 566-2000
  (Mfr paint, wallcoverings, related prdts)
    Sherwin-Williams West Indies Ltd., P.O. Box 35, Spanish Town, St. Catherine, Jamaica

TEXACO INC   2000 Westchester Ave, White Plains, NY 10650, Tel: (914) 253-4000
(Explor/mktg crude oil, mfr petro chems & prdts)
   Texaco Caribbean Inc., Mutual Life Centre, 2 Oxford St., Kingston 5, Jamaica

TRANS WORLD AIRLINES INC   505 N 6th St, St Louis, MO 63101,
  Tel: (314) 589-3000
(Air transportation)
   Trans World Airlines, Montego Bay, Jamaica

UNION CAMP CORP   1600 Valley Rd, Wayne, NJ 07470, Tel: (201) 628-2000
(Mfr paper, packaging, chems, wood prdts)
   Bush Boake Allen Ltd., P.O. Box 379, Kingston 11, Jamaica

XEROX CORP   800 Long Ridge Rd, PO Box 1600, Stamford, CT 06904,
  Tel: (203) 968-3000
(Mfr document processing equip, sys & supplies)
   Xerox Corp., Kingston, Jamaica

JAPAN

3COM CORP   5400 Bayfront Plaza, Santa Clara, CA 95052-8145,
  Tel: (408) 764-5000
(Devel/mfr computer networking prdts & sys)
   3Com, Japan

3M   3M Center, St Paul, MN 55144-1000, Tel: (612) 733-1110
(Mfr diversified prdts for industry, health care, imaging, commun, transport, safety,
consumer, etc)
   Sumitomo 3M Ltd., 33-1 Tamagawa-dai 2-chome, Setagaya-ku, Tokyo 158, Japan

AAF INTL   215 Central Ave, PO Box 35690, Louisville, KY 40232-5690,
  Tel: (502) 637-0011
(Mfr air filtration/pollution control & noise control equip)
   Japan Air Filter Co. Ltd., 1-37 Kuryozutsumi, Hiratsuka, Kanagawa 254, Japan

ABBOTT LABORATORIES   100 Abbott Park Rd, Abbott Park, IL 60064-3500,
  Tel: (708) 937-6100
(Devel/mfr/sale diversified health care prdts & services)
   Abbott Ltd., Tokyo, Japan

ACADEMIC PRESS INC   1250 Sixth Ave, San Diego, CA 92101, Tel: (619) 231-6616
(Publ scientific books)
   Academic Press Japan, Lidabashi Hokoku Bldg., 3-11-13 Lidabashi, Chiyoda-ku,
    Tokyo 102, Japan

ACCLAIM ENTERTAINMENT INC   71 Audrey Ave, Oyster Bay, NY 11771,
 Tel: (516) 624-8888
 (Mfr video games)
   Acclaim Japan Ltd., 2/F Meijiseimei-Kamata Higashi Bldg., 5-28-4, Ohta-ku,
   Tokyo 144, Japan

ACCO INTL INC   770 S Acco Plaza, Wheeling, IL 60090, Tel: (708) 541-9500
 (Paper fasteners & clips, metal fasteners, binders, staplers)
   Acco Japan, Suite 513, 2-1-15 Takanawa, Minato-ku, Tokyo 108, Japan

ACCURAY CORP   650 Ackerman Rd, PO Box 02248, Columbus, OH 43202,
 Tel: (614) 261-2000
 (Computer-based process mgmt sys for forest prdts, metals rolling, textiles, tobacco
 ind)
   Accuray Japan Ltd., Tokyo, Japan

ACCURIDE   12311 Shoemaker Ave, Santa Fe Springs, CA 90670,
 Tel: (310) 903-0200
 (Mfr drawer slides)
   Accuride, 2-5-13 Nihonbashi Muromachi, Chuo-ku, Tokyo 103, Japan

ACHESON COLLOIDS CO   PO Box 611747, Port Huron, MI 48061-1747,
 Tel: (810) 984-5581
 (Graphite, lubricants & specialty chems)
   Acheson Colloids Japan Ltd., P.O. Box 538, Kobe Port 651-01, Japan

ADAPTEC INC   691 S Milpitas Blvd, Milpitas, CA 95035, Tel: (408) 945-8600
 (Design/mfr/mkt hardware & software solutions)
   Adaptec Japan Ltd., Kioicho Hills 4/F, 3-32 Kioichi, Chiyoda-ku, Tokyo 102, Japan

ADC TELECOMMUNICATIONS INC   4900 W 78th St, Minneapolis, MN 55435,
 Tel: (612) 835-6800
 (Mfr telecom equip)
   ADC Japan, c/o Kanematsu-Gosho Ltd., 14-1 Kyobushi 2-chome, Chuo-ku, Tokyo 104,
   Japan

ADVANCED MICRO DEVICES INC   PO Box 3453, Sunnyvale, CA 94088-3000,
 Tel: (408) 732-2400
 (Mfr integrated circuits for commun & computation ind)
   Advanced Micro Devices, Atsugi, Japan

AEC INC   801 AEC Drive, Wood Dale, IL 60191, Tel: (708) 595-1090
 (Mfr/serv aux equip for plastics ind)
   The Sysko Corp., 8-9 Higeshiueno 4-chome, Taito-ku, Tokyo, Japan

AFLAC INC   1932 Wynnton Rd, Columbus, GA 31999, Tel: (706) 323-3431
 (Insurance, TV broadcasting)
   AFLAC Japan, Shinjuku Mitsui Bldg. 12/F, 2-1-1 Nishishinjuku, Shinjuku-ku,
   Tokyo 103-04, Japan

AIC PHOTO INC   117 E 57th St, New York, NY 10022, Tel: (212) 838-3220
 (Imp/distr photo equip)
   Soligor Corp. of Japan, 15-14 Roppongi 7-chome, Minato-ku, Tokyo, Japan

AIR EXPRESS INTL CORP   120 Tokeneke Rd, PO Box 1231, Darien, CT 06820,
  Tel: (203) 655-7900
  (Air frt forwarder)
    Maruzenair Express Intl. Ltd., Nakamachi Bldg., 2-13 Akasaka 6-chome, Minato-ku,
    Tokyo 107, Japan

AIR PRODUCTS & CHEMICALS INC   7201 Hamilton Blvd, Allentown, PA 18195-1501,
  Tel: (215) 481-4911
  (Mfr ind gases & related equip, spec chems, environmental/energy sys)
    Air Products Asia Inc., Shuwa 2, Kamiyacho Bldg., 3-18-19 Toranomon, Minato-ku,
    Tokyo 105, Japan

AIRBORNE EXPRESS   3101 Western Ave, PO Box 662, Seattle, WA 98111,
  Tel: (206) 285-4600
  (Air transp serv)
    Airborne, Akabanebashi Bldg., 26-6 Higashi Azabu 1-chome, Minato-ku, Tokyo 106,
    Japan
    Airborne Express, Intl. Cargo Bldg., Osaka Intl. Airport, Toyonaka-shi, Osaka 560,
    Japan

AJAX MAGNETHERMIC CORP   1745 Overland Ave NE, PO Box 991, Warren, OH 44482,
  Tel: (216) 372-8511
  (Mfr induction heating & melting equip)
    Japan Ajax Magnethermic Co. Ltd., Kyodo Bldg. 6/F, 13-4 Kodenma-cho, Nihonbashi,
    Chuo-ku, Tokyo 103, Japan

ALBANY INTL CORP   PO Box 1907, Albany, NY 12201, Tel: (518) 445-2200
  (Paper mach clothing, engineered fabrics, plastic prdts, filtration media)
    Albany Intl. of Japan Ltd., 3rd Fl., Akasaka Sanno Bldg., 5-11 Akasaka 2-chome,
    Minato-ku, Tokyo 107, Japan

ALCOA FUJIKURA LTD   105 Westpark Dr, Brentwood, TN 37027, Tel: (615) 370-2100
  (Mfr optical groundwire, tube cable, fiber optic connectors, automotive wiring
  harnesses)
    Alcoa Fujikura Ltd., Dai-Ni Yuuraku Bldg., 4th Fl., 2-30 Komachi,
    Naka-ku Hiroshima City, Japan

ALDUS CORP   411 First Ave South, Seattle, WA 98104-2871, Tel: (206) 622-5500
  (Devel/mfr computer software)
    Aldus KK, NES Bldg., 22-14 Sakuragaoka-cho, Shibuya-ku, Tokyo 150, Japan

ALLEN-BRADLEY CO   PO Box 2086, Milwaukee, WI 53201, Tel: (414) 382-2000
  (Mfr eletrical controls & info devices)
    Allen-Bradley Japan Co. Ltd., Shinkawa Sanko Bldg., 3-17 Shinkawa 1-chome,
    Tokyo 104, Japan

ALLERGAN INC   2525 Dupont Dr, PO Box 19534, Irvine, CA 92713-9534,
  Tel: (714) 752-4500
  (Mfr therapeutic eye care prdts, skin & neural care pharms)
    Allergan Inc., Tokyo, Japan

ALLIED AFTERMARKET DIV   105 Pawtucket Ave, East Providence, RI 02916,
  Tel: (401) 434-7000
  (Mfr spark plugs, filters, brakes)
    Wako-Fram Co. Ltd., Katakura Bldg., 2-1 Kyobashi 3-chome, Chuo-ku, Tokyo, Japan

ALLIEDSIGNAL INC   101 Columbia Rd, PO Box 2245, Morristown, NJ 07962-2245,
  Tel: (201) 455-2000
  (Mfr aerospace & automotive prdts, engineered materials)
    AlliedSignal Aerospace Asia, Mori Bldg. 43, 4th Fl., 13-16 Mita 3-chome, Minato-ku,
      Tokyo 108, Japan
    AlliedSignal Automotive, Mori Bldg. 43, 13-16 Mita 3-chome, Minato-ku, Tokyo 108,
      Japan
    AlliedSignal Turbo, 350-17 Minami-Kyowa, Koyei Kodama Cho, Kodama-Gun, Saitama Ken,
      367-02, Japan

ALUMINUM CO OF AMERICA (ALCOA)   425 6th Ave, Pittsburgh, PA 15219,
  Tel: (412) 553-4545
  (Aluminum mining, refining, processing, prdts)
    Aluminum Co. of America, 6-1 Marunouchi 2-chome, Lhiyoda-ku, Tokyo 100, Japan

ALVEY INC   9301 Olive Blvd, St Louis, MO 63132, Tel: (314) 993-4700
  (Mfr automatic case palletizers, package & pallet conveyor sys)
    Toyo Kanetsu KK, 19-20 Higashisuna 8-chome, Koto-ku, Tokyo 136, Japan

AM INTL INC   9399 W Higgins Rd, Rosemont, IL 60618, Tel: (708) 292-0600
  (Mfr/sale/serv printing & print prod equip, mailroom/bindery sys, svces & supplies
  for graphics ind)
    AM Japan Co. Ltd., Yamato Bldg., 3-1 Kojimachie 5-chome, Chiyoda-ku, Tokyo 102,
      Japan

AMERACE CORP   2 N Riverside Plaza, #1160, Chicago, IL 60606,
  Tel: (312) 906-8700
  (Chems, rubber prdts, plastics, electrical components & controls)
    Fujimold Ltd., 5-1 Kiba 1-chome, Koto-ku, Tokyo 135, Japan

AMEREX TRADING CORP   350 Fifth Ave, New York, NY 10016, Tel: (212) 967-3330
  (General merchandise)
    Amerex Intl. Corp., Amerex Bldg., 5-7 Azabudai 3-chome, Tokyo, Japan

AMERICAN AIRLINES INC   PO Box 619616, Dallas-Ft Worth Arpt, TX 75261-9616,
  Tel: (817) 355-1234
  (Air transp)
    American Airlines Inc., 231 Kokusai Bldg., 1-1 Marunouchi 3-chome, Chiyoda-ku,
      Tokyo 100, Japan
    American Airlines Inc., KAL Bldg. 12-1 Honmachi 3-chome, Higashi-ku, Osaka 541,
      Japan

AMERICAN AMICABLE LIFE INSURANCE CO   American-Amicable Bldg, Waco, TX 76703,
  Tel: (817) 753-7311
  (Life, accident & health ins)
    American Amicable Life Insurance Co., 607 Nikkatsu Apartment Bldg., 13-gochi,
      Shiba Koen, Minato-ku, Japan
    American Amicable Life Insurance Co., Shiba P.O. Box 118, Tokyo 105-91, Japan

AMERICAN APPRAISAL ASSOCS INC   411 E Wisconsin Ave, Milwaukee, WI 53202,
  Tel: (414) 271-7240
  (Valuation consulting serv)
    American Appraisal Japan Co. Ltd., Kabutocho Yachiyo Bldg., 20-5 Kabotocho,
      Nihonbashi, Chuo-ku, Tokyo 103, Japan

AMERICAN BROADCASTING COS INC   77 W 66th St, New York, NY 10023,
   Tel: (212) 456-7777
   (Radio/TV prod & broadcast)
      ABC News, Rokugo-ku Bldg., 6-5-9 Roppongi, Minato-ku, Tokyo 106, Japan

AMERICAN BUREAU OF SHIPPING   2 World Trade Center, 106th Fl, New York,
   NY 10048, Tel: (212) 839-5000
   (Classification/certification of ships & offshore structures, devel & tech assistance)
      ABS Pacific, Kiyoken Bldg., 12-6 Takahima 2-chome, Nishi-ku, Yokohama 220, Japan

AMERICAN COMMERCIAL INC   25 Enterprise Ave, Secaucus, NJ 07094,
   Tel: (201) 867-9210
   (Dinnerware, crystal & gifts)
      American Commercial Inc., 1-1 Shumoku-cho 3 chome, Higashi-ku, Nagoya, Japan

AMERICAN EXPRESS CO   World Financial Center, New York, NY 10285-4765,
   Tel: (212) 640-2000
   (Travel, travelers cheques, charge card & financial services)
      Amex Marketing Japan Ltd., all inquiries to U.S. address
      Amex Sumigin Service Co. Ltd., all inquiries to U.S. address

AMERICAN FAMILY LIFE ASSURANCE CO   American Family Center, Columbus,
   GA 31906, Tel: (404) 323-3431
   (Insurance)
      Aflac-Japan, Shinjuku Mitsui Bldg., 10th Fl., 1-1 Nishishinjuku 2-chome,
      Shinjuku-ku, Tokyo 163, Japan

AMERICAN INTL GROUP INC   70 Pine St, New York, NY 10270, Tel: (212) 770-7000
   (Insurance, financial services)
      American Home Assurance Co., American Intl Bldg., 20-5 Ichibancho, Chiyoda-ku,
      Tokyo 102, Japan

AMERICAN MUTUAL SERVICES CORP   100 Crossways Park Dr W, PO Box 304, Woodbury,
   NY 11797, Tel: (516) 921-2540
   (Consumer credit)
      American Mutual Services Corp., Noguchi Bldg., Akebono-cho 2-chome, Tachikawa City,
      Japan

AMERICAN PRECISION INDUSTRIES INC   2777 Walden Ave, Buffalo, NY 14225,
   Tel: (716) 684-9700
   (Mfr heat transfer equip, coils, capacitors, electro-mech clutches & brakes)
      Nitta-Apitron Co. Ltd., 4-30 Bakuro-Machi, Higashi-ku, Oaska 541, Japan

AMERICAN PRESIDENT LINES LTD   1111 Broadway, Oakland, CA 94607,
   Tel: (415) 272-8000
   (Intermodal shipping serv)
      American President Lines Ltd., Shin Aoyama Bldg., East Wing 8th Fl.,
      1-1 Minami-Aoyama 1-chome, Minato-ku, Tokyo 107, Japan

AMICON INC   72 Cherry Hill Dr, Beverly, MA 01915, Tel: (508) 777-3622
   (Mfr/sale/svce bioseparation, membrane ultrafiltration, chromatography)
      Grace Japan KK, Amicon, 2-31-1 Yushima, Bunkyo-ku, Tokyo 113, Japan

AMP INC   PO Box 3608, Harrisburg, PA 17105-3608, Tel: (717) 564-0100
   (Devel/mfr electronic & electrical connection prdts & sys)
      AMP (Japan) Ltd., 87 Hisamoto, Takatsu-ku, Kawasaki-shi, Kanagawa 213, Japan

(cont)

Businessland Japan Co. Ltd., Tokyo, Japan
Carroll Touch Intl. Ltd., Tokyo, Japan

AMPEX SYSTEMS CORP   401 Broadway, Redwood City, CA 94063-3199,
   Tel: (415) 367-2011
   (Mfr hi-perf helical scanning recording sys & associated tape media)
      Ampex Japan Ltd., Tokyo Ryutsu Center, 6-1-1 Heiwajima, Ota-ku, Tokyo 143, Japan

AMPHENOL PRODUCTS   1925A Ohio St, Lisle, IL 60532, Tel: (708) 960-1010
   (Elect interconnect/penetrate sys & assemblies)
      Daiichi Denshi Kogyo KK, Shinjuku Bldg., 7-12 Yoyogi 2-chome, Shibuya-ku,
      Tokyo 151, Japan
      Nippon Interconnect Co., 689-1 Nogami, Aze Iseochi, Ritto-cho, Shiga-ken 520-30,
      Japan
      Nippon Interconnect Co., Aya Kudan Bldg., 2-3-27 Kudan Minami, Chiyoda-ku,
      Tokyo 102, Japan

AMSCO INTL INC   One Mellon Bank Center, #5000, Pittsburgh, PA 15219,
   Tel: (412) 338-6500
   (Mfr sterilization/infection control equip, surgical tables, lighting sys for
   health/pharm/sci ind)
      AMSCO Intl. Co., Koji Kazuma, 6-11 Sakushindai 1-chome, Hanamigawa-ku,
      Chiba City 262, Japan

AMWAY CORP   7575 E Fulton Rd, Ada, MI 49355, Tel: (616) 676-6000
   (Mfr/sale home care, personal care, nutrition & houseware prdts)
      Amway (Japan) Ltd., Arco Tower, 1-8-1 Shimomeguro, Meguro-ku, Tokyo 153, Japan

ANALOG DEVICES INC   1 Technology Way, Box 9106, Norwood, MA 02062,
   Tel: (617) 329-4700
   (Mfr integrated circuits & related devices)
      Analog Devices of Japan Inc., Jibiki Bldg., 7-8 Kojimachi 4-chome, Chiyoda-ku,
      Tokyo 102, Japan

ANEMOSTAT PRODUCTS DIV   888 N Keyser Ave, Scranton, PA 18501,
   Tel: (717) 346-6586
   (Mfr air diffusers, grilles & related equip for A/C, heating & ventilation)
      Okamura Corp., 2-14-2 Nagata-cho, Chiyoda-ku, Tokyo, Japan

ANGLO-AMERICAN AVIATION CO   9740 Telfair Ave, Arleta, CA 91331,
   Tel: (818) 896-0333
   (Aviation spare parts, hardware)
      Anglo-American Aviation Co., Okura Co. Ltd., 6-12 Ginza 2-chome, Chuo-ku,
      Tokyo 104, Japan

ANHEUSER-BUSCH INTL INC   One Busch Place, St Louis, MO 63118-1852,
   Tel: (314) 577-2591
   (Beer)
      Anheuser-Busch Asia Inc., Akasalee Twin Tower, 17-22 Akasalee 2-chome, Minato-ku,
      Tokyo 107, Japan

ANVIL INDUSTRIES INC   10100 Brecksville Rd, PO Box 151, Brecksville,
   OH 44141, Tel: (216) 526-0560
   (Prefab piping sys)
      Ricwil Japan Ltd., Hasegawa Bldg. 12-9 Hamamatsu-cho 1-chome, Minato-ku, Tokyo,
      Japan

APPLE COMPUTER INC   1 Infinite Loop, Cupertino, CA 95014, Tel: (408) 996-1010
(Personal computers, peripherals & software)
   Apple Computer Japan Inc., Akasaka Twin Tower, Main Bldg. 16th Fl., 217-22 Akasaka,
   Minato-ku, Tokyo 107, Japan

APPLIED POWER INC   13000 W Silver Spring Dr, Butler, WI 53007,
   Tel: (414) 781-6600
(Mfr hi-pressure tools, vibration control prdts, electrical tools & consumables, tech
furniture)
   Applied Power Japan Ltd., 10-17 Sasame Kita-cho, Toda-City, Saitama 335, Japan

ARAMARK CORP   1101 Market St, Philadelphia, PA 19107-2988,
   Tel: (215) 238-3000
(Diversified managed services)
   AIM Services Co. Ltd., Bussam Bldg. Annex, 1-15 Nishi-Shinbashi 1-chome, Minato-ku,
   Tokyo, Japan

ARBOR ACRES FARM INC   439 Marlborough Rd, Glastonbury, CT 06033,
   Tel: (860) 633-4681
(Producers of male & female broiler breeders, commercial egg layers)
   Arbor Acres Japan Co. Ltd., Kitamatsuno Sujikawa-cho, Ihara-gun, Shizwoka Pref.,
   Japan

ARMSTRONG WORLD INDUSTRIES INC   PO Box 3001, Lancaster, PA 17604,
   Tel: (717) 397-0611
(Mfr/mkt interior furnishings & spec prdts for bldg, auto & textile inds)
   Armstrong (Japan) KK, Tokyo, Japan (all inquiries to U.S. address)
   Armstrong-ABC Co. Ltd., Tokyo, Japan (all inquiries to U.S. address)
   ISA Co. Ltd., Shizouka City, Japan (all inquiries to U.S. address)

ARVIN INDUSTRIES INC   One Noblitt Plaza, Columbus, IN 47201-6079,
   Tel: (812) 379-3000
(Mfr motor vehicle parts, springs, relays & ind controls, aircraft engines & parts)
   Arvin Intl. Inc., Kaneko Bldg., 3-25 Koraku 2-chome, Bunkyo-ku, Tokyo 112, Japan

ASARCO INC   180 Maiden Lane, New York, NY 10038, Tel: (212) 510-2000
(Nonferrous metals, specialty chems, minerals, mfr industrial prdts, environmental
services)
   Enthone-Omi Inc., Japan

ASHLAND OIL INC   1000 Ashland Dr, Russell, KY 41169, Tel: (606) 329-3333
(Petroleum exploration, refining & transportation; mfr chemicals, oils & lubricants)
   Hodogaya Ashland Co. Ltd., 4-2 Toranomon 1-chome, Minato-ku, Tokyo 105, Japan

ASSOCIATED MERCHANDISING CORP   1440 Broadway, New York, NY 10018,
   Tel: (212) 536-4000
(Retail service organization)
   Associated Merchandising Corp., Nakanoshima Center Bldg., 2-27 Nakanoshima 6-chome,
   Kita-ku, Osaka 530, Japan

ASSOCIATED METALS & MINERALS CORP   3 N Corporate Park Dr, White Plains,
   NY 10604, Tel: (914) 251-5400
(Metals & ores)
   Asoma Intl. KK, World Trade Center, P.O. Box 22, Tokyo 105, Japan

ASSOCIATED PRESS INC   50 Rockefeller Plaza, New York, NY 10020-1605,
  Tel: (212) 621-1500
  (News gathering agency)
    Associated Press, CPO Box 607, Tokyo 100-91, Japan

AST RESEARCH INC   16215 Alton Parkway, PO Box 19658, Irvine, CA 92713-9658,
  Tel: (714) 727-4141
  (Design/devel/mfr hi-perf desktop, server & notebook computers)
    AST Japan, AST Bldg., 3-59-23 Izumi, Suginami, Tokyo 168, Japan

AT&T INTERNATIONAL   412 Mt Kemble Ave, Morristown, NJ 07962-1995,
  Tel: (810) 262-6646
  (Telecommunications)
    AT&T Japan Ltd., 25 Mori Bldg., 1-4-30 Roppongi, Minato-ku, Tokyo 106, Japan

AT&T PARADYNE   8545 Ulmerton Rd, PO Box 2826, Largo, FL 34294-2826,
  Tel: (813) 530-2000
  (Mfr data commun prdts)
    AT&T Paradyne Japan, Eitai Bldg., 7 & 8/F, 1-22-11 Shinkawa, Chuo-ku, Tokyo 104,
    Japan

AUGAT INC   89 Forbes Blvd, Mansfield, MA 02048, Tel: (508) 543-4300
  (Interconnection prdts)
    Augat KK, Ace Shoto Bldg., 1-4-7 Shoto, Shibuya-ku, Tokyo 150-91, Japan

AUTODESK INC   2320 Marinship Way, Sausalito, CA 94965, Tel: (415) 332-2344
  (Devel/mkt/support computer-aided design, engineering, scientific & multimedia
  software prdts)
    Autodesk Ltd. Japan, Unosawa Tokyu Bldg. 4/F, 19-15 Ebisu, Shibuya-ku, Tokyo 150,
    Japan

AUTOMATIC SWITCH CO   Hanover Rd, Florham Park, NJ 07932, Tel: (201) 966-2000
  (Mfr solenoid valves, emergency power controls, pressure & temp switches)
    Asco (Japan) Ltd., 89-1 Takahata-cho, Nishinomiya, Hyogo 663, Japan

AUTOSPLICE INC   10121 Barnes Canyon Rd, San Diego, CA 92121,
  Tel: (619) 535-0079
  (Mfr electronic components)
    Autosplice Japan, 3-7-39 Minami-cho, Higashi, Kurume-chi, Tokyo 203, Japan

AUTOTROL CORP   5730 N Glen Park Rd, Milwaukee, WI 53209, Tel: (414) 228-9100
  (Mfr microprocessor controls & valves for water treatment sys)
    Autotrol Far East Ltd., Ozeki Bldg. 3/F, 87 Okayama-cho, 1-chome, Koshigaya,
      Saitama Pref. 343, Japan
    Nippon Autotrol KK, Shuwa-Onaromimon Bldg., 1-11 Shinbashi 6-chome, Minato-ku,
      Tokyo, Japan

AVERY DENNISON CORP   150 N Orange Grove Blvd, Pasadena, CA 91103,
  Tel: (818) 304-2000
  (Mfr pressure-sensitive adhesives & materials, office prdts, labels, tags, retail
  sys, spec chems)
    Dennison Transoceanic Corp., Kojima Bldg., 4-1 Yotsuya Shinjuku-ku, Tokyo 160, Japan
    Fasson-Sanyo Kokusaku Pulp Co., Sanyo Kokusaku Pulp Bldg., 1-4-5 Marunouchi,
      Chiyoda-ku, Tokyo, Japan

AVON PRODUCTS INC   9 W 57th St, New York, NY 10019, Tel: (212) 546-6015
(Mfr/distr beauty & related prdts, fashion jewelry, gifts & collectibles)
　　Avon Allied Co. Ltd., Totate Int. Bldg., 12-19 Shibuya 2-chome, Shibuya-ku,
　　　Tokyo 150, Japan

BAIN & CO INC   2 Copley Place, Boston, MA 02117-0897, Tel: (617) 572-2000
(Strategic management consulting services)
　　Bain & Co. Japan Inc., Hibiya Kokusai Bldg. 14/F, 2-2-3 Uchisaiwai-cho, Chiyoda-ku,
　　　Tokyo 100, Japan

BAKER & McKENZIE   2800 Prudential Plaza, Chicago, IL 60601,
　Tel: (312) 861-8000
(Lawyers)
　　Baker & McKenzie, 2-3 Kita-Aoyama 1-chome, Minato-ku, Tokyo 107, Japan

BALTIMORE AIRCOIL CO INC   7595 Montevideo Rd, Jessup, MD 20794,
　Tel: (410) 799-6200
(Mfr evaporative cooling & heat transfer equip for A/C, refrig & industrial process
cooling)
　　BAG Japan Co. Ltd., 34-6 Bodal Hadano, Kanagawa 259-13, Japan

THE BANK OF CALIFORNIA NA   400 California St, San Francisco, CA 94104,
　Tel: (415) 765-0400
(Banking)
　　The Bank of California, 1-1 Marurouchi 1-chome, Chiyoda-ku, Tokyo 100, Japan

THE BANK OF NEW YORK   48 Wall St, New York, NY 10286, Tel: (212) 495-1784
(Banking)
　　The Bank of New York, Fukoku Seimei Bldg., 2-2 Uchisaiwai-cho 2-chome, Chiyoda-ku,
　　　Tokyo 100, Japan

BANKAMERICA CORP   555 California St, San Francisco, CA 94104,
　Tel: (415) 622-3456
(Financial services)
　　Bank of America NT & SA, ARK Mori Bldg. 34/F, 1-12-32 Akasaka, Minato-ku,
　　　P.O. Box 511, Tokyo 107, Japan

BANKERS TRUST CO   280 Park Ave, New York, NY 10017, Tel: (212) 250-2500
(Banking)
　　Bankers Trust Co., CPO Box 1568, 1-6 Ohtemachi 1-chome, Chiyoda-ku, Tokyo 100-91,
　　　Japan

C R BARD INC   730 Central Ave, Murray Hill, NJ 07974, Tel: (908) 277-8000
(Mfr health care prdts)
　　Bard (Japan) Ltd., 3-4-6 Hongo, Bunkyo-ku, Tokyo 113, Japan

BAUSCH & LOMB INC   1 Chase Square, Rochester, NY 14601, Tel: (716) 338-6000
(Mfr vision care prdts & accessories)
　　B.L.J. Co. Ltd., Tokyo, Japan
　　Bausch & Lomb Far East Pte., Minato-ku, Tokyo, Japan

BAXTER HEALTHCARE CORP   1 Baxter Pky, Deerfield, IL 60015,
　Tel: (708) 948-2000
(Mfr disposable medical prdts)
　　Baxter Ltd., 4 Rokubancho, Chiyoda-ku, Tokyo 102, Japan
　　Baxter Ltd., also in Miyazaki & Gifu City, Japan

BEAR STEARNS & CO INC　　245 Park Ave, New York, NY　10167, Tel: (212) 272-2000
(Investment banking)
　　Bear Stearns Japan Ltd., Shiroyama Hills, 3-1 Toranomon 4-chome, Minato-ku,
　　Tokyo 105, Japan

BECHTEL GROUP INC　　50 Beale St, PO Box 3965, San Francisco, CA　94119,
　Tel: (415) 768-1234
　(Engineering & constr)
　　Bechtel International Corp., 410 Fuji Bldg., 2-3 Marunouchi 3-chome, Chiyoda-ku,
　　Tokyo 100, Japan

BECKMAN INSTRUMENTS INC　　2500 Harbor Blvd, Fullerton, CA　92634,
　Tel: (714) 871-4848
　(Devel/mfr/mkt automated systems & supplies for biological analysis)
　　Beckman Instruments (Japan) Ltd., 6 Sanbancho, Chiyoda, Tokyo 102, Japan

BECTON DICKINSON AND CO　　1 Becton Dr, Franklin Lakes, NJ　07417,
　Tel: (201) 847-6800
　(Mfr/sale medical supplies, devices & diagnostic sys)
　　Nippon Becton Dickinson, Shimato Bldg., 5-34 Akasaka 8-chome, Minato-ku, Tokyo 107,
　　Japan

BEE CHEMICAL CO　　2700 E 170th St, Lansing, IL　60438, Tel: (708) 758-0500
　(Coatings & finishes for plastics & metals)
　　Nippon Bee Chemical, 19-26 Ikeda Nakamachi, Neyagawa City, Osaka 575, Japan

BELL & HOWELL CO　　5215 Old Orchard Rd., Skokie, IL　60077, Tel: (708) 470-7100
　(Diversified info prdts & servs)
　　Bell & Howell Japan Ltd., Andoh Fukuyoshi Bldg., 11-28 Akasaka 1-chome, Minato-ku,
　　Tokyo 107, Japan

BENTLY NEVADA CORP　　PO Box 157, Minden, NV　89423, Tel: (702) 782-3611
　(Electronic monitoring system)
　　Rikei Corp., Shinjuku Normura Bldg., 1-26-2 Nishi-Shinjuku, Shinjuku-ku, Tokyo 160,
　　Japan
　　Rikei Corp., Nichimen Bldg., 4th Fl., 2-2-3 Nakanoshima, Kita-ku, Osaka 530, Japan

LOUIS BERGER INTL INC　　100 Halsted St, East Orange, NJ　07019,
　Tel: (201) 678-1960
　(Consulting engineers, architects, economists & planners)
　　Louis Berger Intl. Inc., Shirakawa Bldg. 4/F, 3-23-6 Nishi Shimbashi, Minato-ku,
　　Tokyo 105, Japan

BEVERLY ENTERPRISES INC　　1200 S Waldron Rd, Ft Smith, AR　72903,
　Tel: (501) 452-6712
　(Nursing homes, retirement living centers, pharmacies)
　　Beverly Japan Corp. (JV), Tohgeki Bldg., 1-1 Tsukiji 4-chome, Chuo-ku, Tokyo, Japan

BINKS MFG CO　　9201 W Belmont Ave, Franklin Park, IL　60131,
　Tel: (708) 671-3000
　(Mfr of spray painting & finishing equip)
　　Binks Japan Ltd., Akasaka Intl. Bldg., 16-10 Akaska 8-chome, Minato-ku, Tokyo, Japan

BIO-RAD LABORATORIES INC   1000 Alfred Nobel Dr, Hercules, CA 94547,
Tel: (510) 724-7000
(Mfr life science research prdts, clinical diagnostics, analytical instruments)
   Nippon Bio-Rad Laboratories KK, Fukuoka, Nagoya, Osaka, Tokyo & Tsukuba, Japan

BLACK & DECKER CORP   701 E Joppa Road, Towson, MD 21286, Tel: (410) 716-3900
(Mfr power tools & accessories, security hardware, small appliances, fasteners, info
sys & servs)
   Black & Decker Corp., all mail to U.S. address

BLACK & VEATCH INTL   8400 Ward Pkwy, PO Box 8405, Kansas City, MO 64114,
Tel: (913) 339-2000
(Engineering/architectural servs)
   M&B Engineering Co. Ltd., 1-2 Uchikanda 2-chome, Chiyoda-ku, Tokyo 101, Japan

BLACK BOX CORP   1000 Park Dr, Lawrence, PA 15055, Tel: (412) 746-5500
(Direct marketer & tech service provider of commun, networking & related computer
connectivity prdts)
   Black Box Japan, Nec Eitai Bldg., 16-10 Fuyuki, Koto-ku, Tokyo 135, Japan

BLOUNT INC   4520 Executive Park Drive, Montgomery, AL 36116-1602,
Tel: (205) 244-4000
(Mfr cutting chain & equip, timber harvest/handling equip, sporting ammo, riding
mowers; gen contract)
   Blount Japan Ltd., Toranomon Kotohira Kaikan, 2-8 Toranomon 1-chome, Minato-ku,
   Tokyo, Japan

BOOZ ALLEN & HAMILTON INC   101 Park Ave, New York, NY 10178,
Tel: (212) 697-1900
(Mgmt consultants)
   Booz Allen & Hamilton Inc., Imperial Tower Bldg., 13th Fl.,
   1-1 Uchisaiwai-cho 1-chome, Chiyoda-Ku, Tokyo 100, Japan

BORDEN INC   180 E Broad St, Columbus, OH 43215-3799, Tel: (614) 225-4000
(Mfr foods, snacks & beverages, adhesives)
   Borden Intl. (Japan) Inc., all mail to U.S. address

BORG-WARNER AUTOMOTIVE INC   200 S Michigan Ave, Chicago, IL 60604,
Tel: (312) 322-8500
(Mfr automotive components; provider of security services)
   Borg-Warner Automotive KK, 1300-50 Yabata, Nabari City, Mie Prefecture 518-04, Japan
   NSK-Warner KK, 2345 Aino, Fikuroi City, Shizuoka 437, Japan

BOSE CORP   The Mountain, Framingham, MA 01701-9168, Tel: (508) 879-7330
(Mfr audio equip)
   Bose KK, Shibuya YT Bldg., 28-3 Maruyamacho, Shibuya-ku, Tokyo, Japan

BOYDEN CONSULTING CORP   375 Park Ave, #1008, New York, NY 10152,
Tel: (212) 980-6480
(Executive search)
   Boyden Assoc. (Japan) Ltd., 1307 Aoyama Bldg., 1-2-3 Kita Aoyama, Minato-ku,
   Tokyo 107, Japan

BOZELL JACOBS KENYON & ECKHARDT INC   40 West 23rd St, New York, NY 10010,
Tel: (212) 727-5000
(Advertising agency)
   Namboskusha Advertising Agency Inc., 3-10-5 Ginza, Chou-ku, Tokyo 104, Japan

W H BRADY CO   6555 W Good Hope Rd, Milwaukee, WI 53223, Tel: (414) 358-6600
(Mfr ind ID for wire marking, circuit boards; facility ID & signage)
    Nippon Brady KK, Room 301, German Industry Center, 1-18-2 Hakusan, Midori-ku,
    Yokohama 226, Japan

BRANSON ULTRASONICS CORP   41 Eagle Rd, Danbury, CT 06813-1961,
Tel: (203) 796-0400
(Mfr plastics assembly equip, ultrasonic cleaning equip)
    Branson Ultrasonics, 4-3-14 Okada, Atsugi-shi, Kanagawa 243, Japan
    Central Scientific Commerce Ind., 2-2-7 Minowa, Taitoh-ku, Tokyo 110, Japan
    Simco Intl. Ltd., Konan Hirose Bldg., 3-5-16 Konan, Minato-ku, Tokyo 108, Japan

BROOKS INSTRUMENT DIV   407 W Vine St, Hatfield, PA 19440, Tel: (215) 362-3500
(Mfr flowmeters & parts)
    Ueshima/Brooks, 362 Waseda Tsurumaki-cho, Shinjuku-ku, Tokyo, Japan

BROWN & ROOT INC   4100 Clinton Dr, Houston, TX 77020-6299,
Tel: (713) 676-3011
(Engr, constr & maintenance)
    Brown & Root Intl. Inc., Maruyama Bldg., 5th Fl., 3-8 Azabudai 2-chome, Minato-ku,
    Tokyo 106, Japan

BROWN & WOOD   One World Trade Center, New York, NY 10048, Tel: (212) 839-5300
(Lawyers)
    Brown & Wood, Kioicho K Bldg. 6/F, 3-28 Kioicho, Chiyoda-ku, Tokyo 102, Japan

BROWN BROTHERS HARRIMAN & CO   59 Wall St, New York, NY 10005,
Tel: (212) 483-1818
(Financial services)
    Brown Brothers Harriman & Co., 8-14 Nihombashi 3-chome, Chuo-ku, Tokyo 103, Japan

BRUNSWICK CORP   1 N Field Court, Lake Forest, IL 60045-4811,
Tel: (708) 735-4700
(Mfr recreational boats, marine engines, bowling centers & equip, fishing equip,
defense/aerospace)
    Nippon Brunswick KK, Nippon Brunswick Bldg., 27-7 Sendagaya 5-chome, Skibuya-ku,
    Tokyo, Japan

BRUSH WELLMAN INC   17876 St Clair Ave, Cleveland, OH 44110,
Tel: (216) 486-4200
(Mfr beryllium, beryllium alloys & ceramics, spec metal sys, precious metal prdts)
    Brush Wellman (Japan) Ltd., Dai-Ichi Marusan Bldg, 9 Kanda Jimbocho 3-chome,
    Chiyoda-ku, Tokyo 101, Japan

BULAB HOLDINGS INC   1256 N McLean Blvd, Memphis, TN 38108,
Tel: (901) 278-0330
(Mfr microbicides, biocides, additives, corrosion inhibitors, chems)
    Buckman Laboratories KK, Ogawa Bldg. 4/F, 7-16 Nihonbashi Kodenmacho, Chuo-ku,
    Tokyo 103, Japan

BURLINGTON AIR EXPRESS   18200 Van Karman Ave, Irvine, CA 92715,
Tel: (714) 752-4000
(Air freight)
    Burlington Air Express, Hany Kodenmacho Bldg., 18-1 Nihonbashi Kodenmacho, Chuo-ku,
    Tokyo 103, Japan

LEO BURNETT CO INC   35 West Wacker Dr, Chicago, IL 60601, Tel: (312) 220-5959
  (Advertising agency)
    Leo Burnett-Kyodo Co. Ltd., 18F Akasaka Twin Tower, 17-22 Akasaka 2-chome,
    Minato-ku, Tokyo 107, Japan

BURR-BROWN RESEARCH CORP   PO Box 11400, Tucson, AZ 85734, Tel: (602) 746-1111
  (Electronic components & sys modules)
    Burr-Brown Japan Ltd., Natural House Bldg., 2nd Fl., 14-15 Akasaka 6-chome,
    Minato-Ku, Tokyo 107, Japan

BURSON-MARSTELLER   230 Park Ave, New York, NY 10003-1566, Tel: (212) 614-4000
  (Public relations/public affairs consultants)
    Dentsu Burson-Marsteller Co. Ltd., Sogo 3 Bldg., 6 Kojimachi 1-chome, Chiyoda-Ku,
    Tokyo 102, Japan

CARL BYOIR & ASSOCIATES INC   420 Lexington Ave, New York, NY 10017,
  Tel: (212) 210-6000
  (Public relations, intl commun)
    PRAP Japan Inc., Kasuya Bldg., 2-9 Sakuragaoka-cho, Shibuya-ku, Tokyo, Japan

CABOT CORP   75 State St, Boston, MA 02109-1807, Tel: (617) 890-0200
  (Mfr carbon blacks, plastics; oil & gas, info sys)
    Cabot Far East Inc., 8-15 Akasaka 4-chome, Minato-ku, Tokyo 107, Japan

CALCOMP INC   2411 W La Palma Ave, Anaheim, CA 92801, Tel: (714) 821-2000
  (Mfr computer graphics peripherals)
    NS CalComp, 2-3-1 Shintomi Chuo-ku, Tokyo 104, Japan

CALGON CORP   PO Box 1346, Pittsburgh, PA 15230, Tel: (412) 777-8000
  (Mfr. cosmetic, personal care & water treatment prdts)
    Calgon Div. MSD (Japan) Co. Ltd., Kowa Bldg., 16 Annex, 9-20 Akasaka 1-chome,
    Minato-ku, Tokyo 107, Japan

CALTEX PETROLEUM CORP   PO Box 619500, Dallas, TX 75261, Tel: (214) 830-1000
  (Petroleum prdts)
    Caltex Oil Japan KK, Hisseki Honkan, 9th Fl., 3-12 Nishi Shinbashi 1-chome,
    Minato-ku, Tokyo 105, Japan
    Caltraport (Far East) Co., 703 Uschisaiwaicho Osaka Bldg.,
    3-3 Uchisaiwai-cho 1-chome, Chiyoda-ku, Tokyo 100, Japan

CAMPBELL SOUP CO   Campbell Place, Camden, NJ 08103-1799, Tel: (609) 342-4800
  (Food prdts)
    Campbell Japan Inc., Japan

CANBERRA INDUSTRIES INC   One State St, Meriden, CT 06450, Tel: (203) 238-2351
  (Mfr instru for nuclear research)
    Packard Japan KK, Kansai Iwamotocho Bldg., 19-8 Iwamoto-cho 2-chome, Chiyoda-Ku,
    Tokyo 101, Japan

CANDELA LASER CORP   530 Boston Post Rd, Wayland, MA 01778,
  Tel: (508) 358-7400
  (Mfr/serv medical laser systems)
    Candela Japan, 3/F Tokyo Knit Bldg., 9-5 Ryogoku 2-chome, Sumida-ku, Tokyo 130,
    Japan

CARBOLINE CO   350 Hanley Industrial Ct, St Louis, MO 63144,
  Tel: (314) 644-1000
  (Mfr coatings, sealants)
    Japan Carboline Co. Ltd., Wakura Bldg., 1-5 Fukagawa 1-chome, Koto-ku, Tokyo, Japan

CARGILL   PO Box 9300, Minneapolis, MN 55440, Tel: (612) 475-7575
  (Food prdts, feeds, animal prdts)
    Cargill Japan, Fugi Bldg., 3-2-3 Marunouchi, Chiyoda-ku, Tokyo 100, Japan

CARRIER CORP   One Carrier Place, Farmington, CT 06034-4015,
  Tel: (203) 674-3000
  (Mfr/distr/svce A/C, heating & refrigeration equip)
    Carrier Higashi-Chugoku Co. Ltd., Okayama, Japan
    Carrier Nishi Chugoku Co. Ltd., Hiroshima, Japan
    Carrier Transicold Japan Ltd., Yokohama, Japan
    Ebara Carrier Co. Ltd., Tokyo, Japan
    General Aircon Tecnica Inc., Tokyo, Japan
    Keihin Sobi Co. Ltd., Tokyo, Japan
    NIT Intelligent Planning & Development Co. Ltd., Tokyo, Japan
    Nippon Building Systems Co. (NBS), Tokyo, Japan
    Toyo Carrier Engineering Co. Ltd., Mitshui Annex Bldg. #2,
      4-4-20 Nihonbashi-Hongoku-cho, Chuo-ku, Tokyo 103, Japan
    United Technologies Building Systems Co., Tokyo, Japan

J C CARTER CO   671 W 17th St, Costa Mesa, CA 92627, Tel: (714) 548-3421
  (Mfr aerospace valves & pumps, cryogenic pumps)
    Nippon Carter, Rokko Atelier House, 1-15 Yamadacho 3-chome, Nada-ku, Kobe 657, Japan

CASCADE CORP   2020 SW First Ave, Portland, OR 97201, Tel: (503) 227-0024
  (Mfr hydraulic forklift truck attachments)
    Cascade (Japan) Ltd., 5-5-41 Torikai Kami, Settsu, Osaka 566, Japan

CATERPILLAR INC   100 N E Adams St, Peoria, IL 61629, Tel: (309) 675-1000
  (Mfr earth/material-handling & constr mach & equip, engines, generators)
    Shin Caterpillar Mitsubishi Ltd., 3700 Tana, Sagamihara-shi, Kanagawaken 229, Japan

CCH INC   2700 Lake Cook Rd, Riverwoods, IL 60015, Tel: (708) 267-7000
  (Tax & busines law info, software & services)
    CCH Japan Ltd., Ginza TK Bldg. 3/F, 1-1-7 Shintomi, Chuo-ku, Tokyo 104, Japan

CEILCOTE CO   140 Sheldon Rd, Berea, OH 44017, Tel: (216) 243-0700
  (Mfr corrosion-resistant material, air pollution control equip, cons serv)
    Ceilcote Japan Ltd., Port P.O. Box 1, Yokohama 231-91, Japan

CENTOCOR INC   200 Great Valley Pkwy, Malvern, PA 19355, Tel: (610) 651-6000
  (Devel/mfr/mktg diagnostic & therapeutic pdts for human health care)
    Nippon Centocor, Landmark Shiba Park, Bldg. 7E, 1-7-6 Shibakoen, Minato-ku,
      Tokyo 105, Japan

CENTRAL NATIONAL-GOTTESMAN INC   3 Manhattanville Rd, Purchase,
  NY 10577-2110, Tel: (914) 696-9000
  (Worldwide sales pulp & paper prdts)
    Central National Pacific Ltd., Ginza Sunny Bldg., 4-16 Ginza 3-chome, Chuo-ku,
      Tokyo 104, Japan

CENTURY 21 REAL ESTATE CORP   2601 SE Main, PO Box 19564, Irvine,
  CA 92713-9564, Tel: (714) 553-2100
  (Real estate)
    Century 21 Real Estate of Japan Ltd., Akasaka Twin Tower - East Bldg. 13th Fl.,
    17-22 Akasaka 2-chome, Minato-ku, Tokyo 107, Japan

CHAMPION INTERNATIONAL CORP   One Champion Plaza, Stamford, CT 06921,
  Tel: (213) 358-7000
  (Mfr pulp & paper)
    Champion Intl. (Asia) Ltd., Izuya Bldg., 4-12 Nishi-Shimbashi 1-chome, Minato-ku,
    Tokyo 105, Japan

CHASE MANHATTAN BANK N A   1 Chase Manhattan Plaza, New York, NY 10081,
  Tel: (212) 552-2222
  (Intl banking)
    Chase Manhattan Bank NA, 1-3 Marunouchi 1-chome, Chiyoda-ku, CPO Box 383,
    Tokyo 100, Japan
    Chase Manhattan Bank NA, Osaka, Japan

CHEMICAL BANK   270 Park Ave, New York, NY 10017-2070, Tel: (212) 270-6000
  (Banking & financial services)
    Chemical Bank, Nichimen Bldg., 2-2 Nakanoshima 2-chome, Kita-ku, Osaka 530, Japan
    Chemical Bank, Asahi Tokai Bldg., 6-1 Otemachi 2-chome, Chiyoda-ku, Tokyo 100, Japan
    Chemical Securities Asia Ltd., Asahi Tokai Bldg., 6-1 Otemachi 2-chome, Chiyoda-ku,
    Tokyo 100, Japan
    Chemical Trust & Banking Co. Ltd., Mitsubishi Shoji Bldg. Annex,
    3-1 Marunouchi 2-chome, Chiyoda-ku, Tokyo 100, Japan

THE CHERRY CORP   3600 Sunset Ave, PO Box 718, Waukegan, IL 60087,
  Tel: (708) 662-9200
  (Mfr electrical switches, electronic keyboards, controls & displays, semiconductors)
    Cherry Automotive-Japan, 20-20 Hiradai, Midori-ku, Yokohama-shi, Japan
    Hirose Cherry Precision Co. Ltd., 5-30-11 Shukugawara, Tama-ku, Kawasaki,
    Kanagawa 214, Japan

CHESTERTON BINSWANGER INTL   Two Logan Sq, 4th fl, Philadelphia,
  PA 19103-2759, Tel: (215) 448-6000
  (Real estate & related svces)
    Sotsu Corp., 69 Waseda-Machi, Shinjuku-ku, Tokyo 162, Japan

CHEVRON CHEMICAL CO   PO Box 5047, San Ramon, CA 94583-0947,
  Tel: (510) 842-5500
  (Chemicals)
    Oronite Japan Ltd., Landmark Plaza 7/F, 1-6-7 Shiba-Koen, Minato-ku, Tokyo 105,
    Japan

CHEVRON CORP   225 Bush St, San Francisco, CA 94104, Tel: (415) 894-7700
  (Oil & gas exploration, production, refining, products; oilfield & financial services)
    Chevron Corp., all mail to U.S. address

CHICAGO RAWHIDE MFG CO   900 N State Street, Elgin, IL 60120,
  Tel: (708) 742-7840
  (Seals & filters)
    Koyo Chicago Rawhide Co. Ltd., 39 Baluro-machi 3-chome, Sueyoshi-bashi, Osaka, Japan

CHINET CO   101 Merritt 7, Norwalk, CT 06851, Tel: (203) 846-1499
(Mfr molded containers)
  Keyes Fibre Japan Branch, 505 Koshi-Ichi Bldg., 19-16 Jingumae 6-chome, Shibuya-ku,
    Tokyo 150, Japan
  Sekisui Plastics Co. Ltd., 2-4-4 Nishi-temma, Kita-ku, Osaka 530, Japan

CHIQUITA BRANDS INTL INC   250 E Fifth St, Cincinnati, OH 45202,
  Tel: (513) 784-8000
(Distribution food products)
  United Brands Japan Ltd., Shichijo Bldg. 7/F, 2-20-10 Higashi Nihonbashi, Chuo-ku,
    Tokyo 103, Japan

CHIRON CORP   4560 Horton St, Emeryville, CA 94608-2916, Tel: (510) 601-2412
(Research/mfg/mktg therapeutics, vaccines, diagnostics, ophthalmics)
  Ciba Corning Diagnostics KK, Unosawa Tokyu Bldg. 3F, 1-19-15 Ebisu, Shibuya-ku,
    Tokyo 150, Japan

THE CHRISTIAN SCIENCE PUBLISHING SOCIETY   1 Norway St, Boston, MA 02115,
  Tel: (617) 450-2000
(Publishing, broadcasting)
  The Christian Science Monitor, 209 Sanbancho Park Life Bldg., 20-2 Sanbancho,
    Chiyoda-ku, Tokyo 102, Japan

THE CHUBB CORP   15 Mountain View Rd, Warren, NJ 07060, Tel: (908) 580-2000
(Holding co: property/casualty ins)
  Federal Insurance Co., Japan

CIGNA CORP   One Liberty Place, Philadelphia, PA 19192, Tel: (215) 523-4000
(Ins, invest, health care & other fin servs)
  Cigna Insurance Co., Akasaka Eight-One Bldg., 7th Fl., 13-5 Mayata-cho 2-chome,
    Chiyoda-ku, Tokyo 100, Japan
  Cigna Intl. Investment Advisors KK, Tobaya Bldg., 9-22 Akasaka 4-chome, Minato-ku,
    Tokyo, Japan
  Esis Intl. Inc., Akasaka 81 Bldg., 13-5 Nagata-Cho 2-chome, Chiyoda-ku, Tokyo 100,
    Japan
  INA Life Insurance Co. Ltd., Shinjuku Center Bldg., 48th Fl.,
    1-25 Nishi-Shinjuku 1-chome, Shinjuku-ku, Tokyo 160, Japan

CINCINNATI INCORPORATED   PO Box 11111, Cincinnati, OH 45211,
  Tel: (513) 367-7100
(Mfr metal forming machines)
  Cincinnati-Japan Ltd., CPO Box 1643, Tokyo, Japan

CINCINNATI MILACRON INC   4701 Marburg Ave, Cincinnati, OH 45209,
  Tel: (513) 841-8100
(Devel/mfr technologies for metalworking & plastics processing ind)
  Cincinnati Milacron Inc., Tokyo, Japan

CINCOM SYSTEMS INC   2300 Montana Ave, Cincinnati, OH 45211,
  Tel: (513) 662-2300
(Devel/distr computer software)
  Cincom Systems Inc., Tokyo, Japan
  Cincom Systems Inc., Osaka, Japan

CITICORP   399 Park Ave, New York, NY 10043, Tel: (212) 559-1000
(Banking & financial services)
   Citibank, Japan

CLEARY GOTTLIEB STEEN & HAMILTON   1 Liberty Plaza, New York, NY 10006,
   Tel: (212) 225-2000
(Lawyers)
   Morgan Belar Terai Gaikokuho Jimubengoshi Jimusho, Shin Kasumigaseki Bldg.,
      20th Fl., 3-2 Kasumigaseki 3-chome, Chiyoda-ku, Tokyo 100, Japan

CLIMAX MOLYBDENUM CORP   1370 Washington Pike, Bridgeville, PA 15017,
   Tel: (412) 257-5181
(Molybdenum, tungsten)
   Climax Molybdenum Development Co. Ltd., P.O. Box 58, Kasumigaseki Bldg.,
      3-2-5 Kasumigaseki, Chiyoda-ku, Tokyo 100, Japan

COBE LABORATORIES INC   1185 Oak St, Lakewood, CO 80215, Tel: (303) 232-6800
(Mfr med equip & supplies)
   COBE Far East, Tokyo, Japan
   COBE Laboratories KK, Tokyo, Japan

THE COCA-COLA CO   PO Drawer 1734, Atlanta, GA 30301, Tel: (404) 676-2121
(Mfr/mkt/distr soft drinks, syrups & concentrates, juice & juice-drink prdts)
   The Coca-Cola (Japan) Co., Shibuya P.O. Box 10, Tokyo 150, Japan

COHERENT INC   PO Box 54980, Santa Clara, CA 95056, Tel: (408) 764-4000
(Mfr lasers for sci, ind & med)
   Coherent Japan Inc., 2 Asanuma Bldg. 6F, 21-10 Hongo 3-chome, Bunkyo-ku, Tokyo 113,
      Japan
   lambda Physik Japan Co. Ltd., German Industry Center, 1-18-2 Hakusan, Midori-ku,
      Yokohama 226, Japan

THE COLEMAN CO INC   1526 Cole Blvd, #300, Golden, CO 80401,
   Tel: (303) 202-2470
(Mfr/distr/sales camping & outdoor recreation prdts)
   Coleman Japan Ltd., JBP Hakozaki Bldg 2/F, Nihonbashi Hakozakicho 5-14, Chuo-ku,
      Tokyo 103, Japan

COLGATE-PALMOLIVE CO   300 Park Ave, New York, NY 10022, Tel: (212) 310-2000
(Mfr pharms, cosmetics, toiletries, detergents)
   CKR (Japan) Co. Ltd., Kakihara Asahi Eitai Bldg. 7/F, 3-7-13 Toyo, Koto-ku,
      Tokyo 135, Japan

COLUMBIA PICTURES INDUSTRIES INC   711 Fifth Ave, New York, NY 10022,
   Tel: (212) 751-4400
(Producer & distributor of motion pictures)
   Columbia Films Ltd., P.O. Box 135, Kanesaka Bldg., 5-4 Shimbashi 2-chome,
      Minato-ku, Tokyo 105, Japan

COMBINED INSURANCE CO OF AMERICA   123 N Wacker Dr, Chicago, IL 60606,
   Tel: (312) 701-3000
(Insurance)
   Combined Insurance Co. of America, Shinjuku Mitsui Bldg., 2-1-1 Nishi,
      Shinjuku-ku, Tokyo 160, Japan

COMBUSTION ENGINEERING INC   900 Long Ridge Road, Stamford, CT 06902,
Tel: (203) 329-8771
(Tech constr)
   Lummus Japan Co. Ltd., Checker Bldg., 5-29 Akasaka 8-chome, Minato-ku, Tokyo, Japan

COMDISCO INC   6111 N River Rd, Rosemont, IL 60018, Tel: (708) 698-3000
(Hi-tech asset & facility mgmt, equip leasing)
   Comdisco Japan Inc., Nagoya, Osaka & Tokyo, Japan

COMMERCIAL INTERTECH CORP   1775 Logan Ave, PO Box 239, Youngstown,
OH 44501-0239, Tel: (216) 746-8011
(Mfr hydraulic com, fluid purification sys, pre-engineered bldgs, stamped metal prdts)
   Cuno KK, Hodogaya Sta., Bldg 6F, 1-7 Iwai-cho, Hodagaya-ku, Yokohama 240, Japan
   The Oilgear Japan Co., 204 Nishikan, Daini Toyoda Bldg., 4-10-27 Meieki,
     Nakamura-ku, Nagoya 450, Japan

COMMERCIAL METALS CO   PO Box 1046, Dallas, TX 75221, Tel: (214) 689-4300
(Metal collecting/processing, steel mills, metal trading)
   Cometals Far East Inc., Daiichi Seimei Sogo-kan, 7-1 Kyobashi 3-chome, Chuo-ku,
     Tokyo 104, Japan

COMPAQ COMPUTER CORP   PO Box 692000, Houston, TX 77269-2000,
Tel: (713) 370-0670
(Devel/mfr personal computers)
   Compaq KK, Kamiya-cho Mori Bldg., 4-3-20 Toranomon, Minato-ku, Tokyo 105, Japan

COMPUTERVISION CORP   100 Crosby Dr, Bedford, MA 01730-1480,
Tel: (617) 275-1800
(Supplier of mechanical design automation & prdt data mgmt software & services)
   Computervision, Shinjuku Dai-Ichi Seimei Bldg. 7/F, 7-1 Nishi Shinjuku 2-chome,
     Shinjuku-ku, Tokyo 163-07, Japan

CONAGRA INC   1 ConAgra Dr, Omaha, NE 68102, Tel: (402) 595-4000
(Prepared & frozen foods, grains, flour, animal feeds, agric chems, poultry, meat,
dairy prdts)
   ConAgra Nissui Inc. (JV), 2-6-2 Ohtemachi, Chiyoda-ku, Tokyo 100, Japan

CONCURRENT COMPUTER CORP   2 Crescent Pl, Oceanport, NJ 07757,
Tel: (908) 870-4500
(Mfr computer systems & software)
   Concurrent Nippon Corp., 10-20 Akasaka 7-chome, Minato-ku, tokyo 107, Japan

CONOCO INC   600 N Dairy Ashford Rd, Houston, TX 77079, Tel: (713) 293-1000
(Oil, gas, coal, chems, minerals)
   Conoco Chemical Far East Inc., P.O. Box 110, Kasumigaseki Bldg., 25th Fl., Tokyo,
     Japan

CONTINENTAL BANK NA   231 S LaSalle St, Chicago, IL 60697, Tel: (312) 828-2345
(Coml banking servs)
   Continental Bank Corp., CPO Box 481, Mitsui Seimei Bldg., 2-3 Ohtemachi 1-chome,
     Chiyoda-ku, Tokyo 100, Japan
   Continental Capital Markets Ltd., CPO Box 481, Mitsui Seimei Bldg.,
     2-3 Ohtemachi 1-chome, Chiyoda-ku, Tokyo 100, Japan

CONTINENTAL INSURANCE CO   180 Maiden Lane, New York, NY 10038,
Tel: (212) 440-3000
(Insurance)
The Continetal Insurance Co., Tokio Kaijo Bldg., 6th Fl., 2-1 Marunouchi 1-chome,
Chiyoda-ku, Tokyo 100, Japan

THE CONTINUUM CO INC   9500 Arboretum Blvd, Austin, TX 78759,
Tel: (512) 345-5700
(Design & mkt software for ins & fin svces)
Continuum Japan, ABS Bldg., 2-4-16 Kudan Minami, Chiyoda-ku, Tokyo 102, Japan

COOK & CO   Omulgee St, Lumber City, GA 31549, Tel: (912) 363-4371
(Forestry; mfr steel, tire cord)
Cook & Co. Far East Agencies Inc., Chiyoda House 2-A, 17-8 Nagata-cho 2-chome,
Chiyoda-ku, Tokyo 100, Japan

CORESTATES FINANCIAL CORP   1500 Market St, Philadelphia, PA 19101,
Tel: (215) 973-3100
(Banking)
Corestates Bank, 919 Tohgin Bldg., 4-2 Marunouchi 1-chome, Chiyoda-ku, Tokyo, Japan
Philadelphia National Ltd., Yamato Intl. Bldg. 8/F,
1-3 Nihonbashi Horidome-cho 2-chome, Chuo-ku, Tokyo, Japan

CORNING HAZLETON INC   9200 Leesburg Pike, Vienna, VA 22182,
Tel: (703) 893-5400
(Contract research)
Nippon Hazleton, Suzuwa Bldg., 4-7-10 Nihonbashi Honcho, Chuo-ku, Tokyo 103, Japan

CORNING INC   One Riverfront Plaza, Corning, NY 14831, Tel: (607) 974-9000
(Mfr glass & specialty materials, consumer prdts; communications, lab services)
Corning Inc., Shizuoka, Japan
Corning Intl. KK, Tokyo, Japan
N-Cor Ltd., Tokyo, Japan

COUDERT BROTHERS   1114 Ave of the Americas, New York, NY 10036-7794,
Tel: (212) 626-4400
(Lawyers)
Coudert Brothers, 1355 West Tower, Aoyama Twin Towers, 1-1 Minami-Aoyama 1-chome,
Tokyo 107, Japan

COULTER CORP   PO Box 169015, Miami, FL 33116-9015, Tel: (305) 885-0131
(Mfr blood analysis sys, flow cytometers, chem sys, scientific sys & reagents)
Japan Scientific Instrument Co. Ltd., 6-7-5 Higashi-Kasai, Edogawa-ku, Tokyo 134,
Japan

CPC INTERNATIONAL INC   PO Box 8000, Englewood Cliffs, NJ 07632,
Tel: (201) 894-4000
(Consumer foods, corn refining)
CPC Intl. Japan Ltd., Yushima Sanyu Bldg., 2-31-1 Yushima, Bunkyo-ku, Tokyo 113,
Japan
Nihon Shokuhin Kako Co. Ltd., 8/F Shinkokusai Bldg., 4-1 Marunouchi 3-chome,
Chiyoda-ku, Tokyo 100, Japan

CR INDUSTRIES   900 N State St, Elgin, IL 60123, Tel: (708) 742-7840
(Mfr shaft & face seals)
Koyo Chicago Rawhide Co. Ltd., Aizumi, Itanogun, Tokushima 771-12, Japan

CRAY RESEARCH INC   655 Lone Oak Dr, Eagan, MN 55121, Tel: (612) 452-6650
(Supercomputer systems & services)
   Cray Research Japan Ltd., Nikko Ichibancho Bldg., 13-3 Ichibancho, Chiyoda-ku,
     Tokyo 102, Japan
   Yokogawa Cray ELS Ltd., c/o Cray Research Japan, Ichibancho Eight One Bldg.,
     6-4 Ichibancho, Chiyoda-ku, Tokyo 102, Japan

CRC PRESS INC   2000 Corporate Blvd NW, Boca Raton, FL 33431,
  Tel: (407) 994-0555
(Publishing: sci, tech & med books & journals)
   CRC Press, Misuzu Bldg. 2/F, 2-42-14 Matsubara, Setagaya-ku, Tokyo 156, Japan

CRITICARE SYSTEMS INC   20925 Crossroads Circle, Waukesha, WI 53186,
  Tel: (414) 798-8282
(Develop/mfr diagnostic & therapeutic prdts)
   Criticare Systems Inc. Japan, Maruki Bldg., 3-6-11 Hongo, Bunkyo-ku, Tokyo 113,
    Japan

CUMMINS ENGINE CO INC   PO Box 3005, Columbus, IN 47202, Tel: (812) 377-5000
(Mfr diesel engines)
   Cummins Diesel Sales Corp., 1-12-10 Shintomi, Chuo-ku, Tokyo 104, Japan

D'ARCY MASIUS BENTON & BOWLES INC (DMB&B)   1675 Broadway, New York,
  NY 10019, Tel: (212) 468-3622
(Advertising & communications)
   Tokyo Agency Intl. Inc. DMB&B, Akasaka Daiichi Bldg., 4-9-17 Akasaka, Minato-ku,
    Tokyo 107, Japan

D-M-E COMPANY   29111 Stephenson Highway, Madison Heights, MI 48071,
  Tel: (313) 398-6000
(Basic tooling for plastic molding & die casting)
   Japan DME Corp., Harumi Park Bldg., 3rd Fl., 2-22 Harumi 3-chome, Chuo-ku, Tokyo,
    Japan

LEO A DALY   8600 Indian Hills Dr, Omaha, NE 68114, Tel: (402) 391-8111
(Planning, arch, engr & interior design servs)
   ND Consultants Inc., Shinjuko Mitsui Bldg., 43rd Fl., Shinjuku-Ku, Tokyo 163, Japan

DAMES & MOORE   911 Wilshire Blvd, Los Angeles, CA 90017, Tel: (213) 683-1560
(Engineering, environmental & construction mgmt services)
   Dames & Moore Ltd., Asahi Bldg., 7th Fl., 38-3 Kamata 5-chome, Ota-Ku, Tokyo 144,
    Japan

DANA CORP   PO Box 1000, Toledo, OH 43697, Tel: (419) 535-4500
(Engineer/mfr/mkt prdts & sys for vehicular, ind & mobile off-highway mkt & related
aftermarkets)
   Daido-Sprag Ltd., Central Bldg. 6, 19-10 Toranomon 1-chome, Minato-ku, Tokyo 105,
    Japan
   Koshin-Racine, 1-12 Shin-Sayama 1-chome, Sayama-shi, Saitama-ken 350-15, Japan
   Najico Spicer Co. Ltd., Central Shintomi-cho Bldg., 5-10 Minato 3-chome, Chuo-ku,
    Tokyo, Japan

DATA I/O CORP   10525 Willows Rd NE, Redmond, WA 98053, Tel: (206) 881-6444
(Mfr computer testing devices)
   Data I/O Japan, Sumitumoseimei Higashishinbashi Bldg. 8/F, 2-1-7 Higashi-Shinbashi,
    Minato-ku, Tokyo 105, Japan

DAVIS POLK & WARDWELL   450 Lexington Ave, New York, NY 10017,
  Tel: (212) 450-4000
  (Lawyers)
    Davis Polk & Wardwell, Tokio Kaijo Bldg. Shinkan, 2-1 Marunouchi 1-chome,
    Chiyoda-Ku, Tokyo 100, Japan

DDB NEEDHAM WORLDWIDE INC   437 Madison Ave, New York, NY 10022,
  Tel: (212) 415-2000
  (Advertising)
    DDB Needham Japan Inc., Hibiya Kokusai Bldg., 2-3 Uchisaiwai-cho 2-chome,
    Chiyoda-ku, Tokyo 100, Japan
    Dai-Ichi Kikaku Co. Ltd., Hibiya Kokusai Bldg., 2-3 Uchisaiwai-cho 2-chome,
    Chiyoda-ku, Tokyo 100 Japan

DE ZURIK   250 Riverside Ave N, Sartell, MN 56377, Tel: (612) 259-2000
  (Mfr manual, process & control valves)
    DeZurik Japan, 1-11 Ueno 6-chome, Taito-ku, Tokyo 110, Japan

DELL COMPUTER CORP   2214 W Braker Ln, Austin, TX 78758-4063,
  Tel: (512) 338-4400
  (Design/mfr personal computers)
    Dell Computer Corp. Far East, 7-1-5 Minami Aoyama, Minato-ku, Tokyo, Japan

DELTA AIR LINES INC   PO Box 20706, Atlanta, GA 30320-6001,
  Tel: (404) 715-2600
  (Airline)
    Delta Air Lines Inc., Kioicho Bldg. 9/F, 3-2 Kioicho, Chiyoda-ku, Tokyo 102, Japan

DENTSPLY INTL INC   PO Box 872, York, PA 17405, Tel: (717) 845-7511
  (Mfr dental, medical & ind supplies & equip)
    Dentsply Japan, Sanada Bldg., 7-2 Sotokanda 6-chome, Chiyoda-ku, Tokyo 101, Japan

THE DEXTER CORP   1 Elm Street, Windsor Locks, CT 06096, Tel: (203) 627-9051
  (Mfr nonwovens, polymer prdts, magnetic materials, biotechnology)
    D & S Plastics Intl., 6 Kowa Bldg., 15-21 Nishi-azabu 4-chome, Minato-ku,
    Tokyo 106, Japan
    Dexter Midland Co. Ltd., 37-2 Minamisuna 2-chome, Koto-ku, Tokyo 136, Japan
    Dexter Pacific Inc., Kowa Bldg. 6, 15-21 Nishi-Azabu 4-chome, Minato-ku, Tokyo 106,
    Japan
    Hysol Ltd., 2050 Kamiyabe-cho, Totsuka-ku, Yokohama-shi 245, Japan
    Life Technologies Inc., Tejima Bldg. 3/F, 1-12-8 Toranomon, Minato-ku, Tokyo 105,
    Japan
    Life Technologies Oriental Inc., Landic Nihonbashi #3 Bldg., 9/F,
    14-4 Kodenmacha-cho, Nihonbashi, Chuo-ku, Tokyo 103, Japan

DIGITAL EQUIPMENT CORP   146 Main St, Maynard, MA 01754-2571,
  Tel: (508) 493-5111
  (Networked computer systems & services)
    Digital Equipment Corp. Japan, 1-1 Higashi Ikebukuro, Tokyo 170 Japan

DIONEX CORP   1228 Tital Way, PO Box 3603, Sunnyvale, CA 94088-3603,
  Tel: (408) 737-0700
  (Devel/mfr/mktg/svce chromatography sys & relted prdts)
    Nippon Dionex KK, Shin-Osaka Bldg. #205, 9-20 Nishi-Nakajima 6-chome, Yodogawa-ku,
    Osaka 532, Japan

WALT DISNEY CO   500 S Buena Vista St, Burbank, CA 91521, Tel: (818) 560-1000
(Film/TV prod, theme parks, resorts, publishing, recording, retail stores)
   Walt Disney Enterprises of Japan Ltd., Kanesaka Bldg., 5-4 Shimbashi 2-chome,
   Minato-ku, Tokyo 105, Japan

DONALDSON CO INC   PO Box 1299, Minneapolis, MN 55440, Tel: (612) 887-3131
(Mfr filtration prdts & sys)
   Nippon Donaldson Ltd., 13-2 Imadera 5-chome, Ome City, Tokyo 198, Japan

R R DONNELLEY & SONS CO   77 W Wacker Dr, Chicago, IL 60601-1696,
Tel: (312) 326-8000
(Coml printing, allied commun servs)
   R. R. Donnelley Far East Ltd., 1-12-6 Nihonbashi, Kayabacho, Chuo-ku, Tokyo 103,
   Japan

THE DOW CHEMICAL CO   2030 Dow Center, Midland, MI 48674, Tel: (517) 636-1000
(Mfr chems, plastics, pharms, agric prdts, consumer prdts)
   Dow Chemical Japan Ltd., Hibiya Chunichi Bldg., 6th Fl., 2-1-4 Uchisaiwai-cho,
   Chiyoda-ku, Tokyo 100, Japan
   Dow Chemical Japan Ltd., Osaka, Japan

DRAKE BEAM MORIN INC   100 Park Ave, New York, NY 10017, Tel: (212) 692-7700
(Human resource mgmt consulting & training)
   Drake Beam Morin - Japan Inc., MS Bldg. 9/F, 11-5 Shiba 4-chome, Minato-ku,
   Tokyo 108, Japan

DRESSER INDUSTRIES INC   PO Box 718, Dallas, TX 75221-0718,
Tel: (214) 740-6000
(Diversified supplier of equip & tech serv to energy & natural resource ind)
   Dresser Japan Ltd., Shin Tokyo Bldg., 3-3-1 Tokyo, Tokyo 100, Japan

DRG INTERNATIONAL INC   PO Box 1188, Mountainside, NJ 07092,
Tel: (908) 233-2075
(Mfr/sale/svce medical devices, diagnostic kits, clinical equip)
   DRG KK, IEDA Trading Corp., Hongo EK Bldg., 3-14-16 Hongo, Bunkyo-ku, Tokyo 113,
   Japan

DRIVER-HARRIS CO   308 Middlesex St, Harrison, NJ 07029, Tel: (201) 483-4802
(Mfr non-ferrous alloys)
   Driver-Harris Japan Co. Ltd., 13-27 Takakuracho 1-chome, Miyakojima, Osaka, Japan

DU BOIS CHEMICAL   255 E 5th St, Cincinnati, OH 45202-4799,
Tel: (513) 762-6000
(Mfr spec chems & maintenance prdts)
   Nippon DuBois Co. Ltd., 2 Doi Bldg., 12-8 Banchi 2-chome, Nishi-Shinbashi,
   Minato-ku, Tokyo 105, Japan
   Toso DuBois Chemicals Co. Ltd., 7-7 Akasaka 1-chome, Minato-ku, Tokyo, Japan

E I DU PONT DE NEMOURS & CO   1007 Market St, Wilmington, DE 19898,
Tel: (302) 774-1000
(Mfr/sale diversified chems, plastics, specialty prdts & fibers)
   DuPont Far East Inc., Kowa Bldg., 11-39 Akasaka 1-chome, Minato-ku, Tokyo 107, Japan

DUNHILL INTL SEARCH   59 Elm St, #520, New Haven, CT 06510,
Tel: (203) 562-0511
(Intl recruiting services: sales/mktg, accounting/finance, gen mgrs)
  Dunhill Intl. Search, Far East Div., Tokyo, Japan

DURACELL INTL INC   Berkshire Industrial Park, Bethel, CT 06801,
Tel: (203) 796-4000
(Mfr batteries)
  Duracell Battery Japan Ltd., Masudaya Bldg., 8th Fl., 2-6-4 Kuramae, Taito-ku,
  Tokyo 111, Japan

DURO-TEST CORP   9 Law Dr, Fairfield, NJ 07004, Tel: (201) 808-0905
(Mfr fluorescent, incandescent & fluomeric lamps)
  Duro-Test Japan Inc., Shiba 3-chome Bldg., 3-2-14 Shiba, Minato-ku, Tokyo, Japan

DYNATECH CORP   3 New England Executive Park, Burlington, MA 01803,
Tel: (617) 272-6100
(Devel/mfr communications equip)
  Dynatech Japan Inc., Tokyo, Japan

E-Z-EM INC   717 Main St, Westbury, NY 11590, Tel: (516) 333-8230
(Mfr prdts for med contrast media, lead protective wear & surg prdts)
  Toho Kagaku Kenkyusho Co. Inc., 3-11-11 Tatekawa, Sumida-ku, Tokyo 130, Japan

EAGLE-PICHER INDUSTRIES INC   580 Walnut St, Cincinnati, OH 45202,
Tel: (513) 721-7010
(Mfr industrial, machinery & automotive parts)
  Eagle-Picher Far East Inc., Nagoya Chogin Bldg. 4/F, 1-17-19 Marunouchi, Naka-ku,
  Nagoya 460, Japan

EASTMAN & BEAUDINE INC   13355 Noel Rd, #1370, Dallas, TX 75240,
Tel: (214) 661-5520
(Investments)
  Eastman & Beaudine Inc., 401 Akasaka Heights Bldg., 5-26 Akasaka 9-chome,
  Minato-ku, Tokyo 107, Japan

EASTMAN CHEMICAL   PO Box 511, Kingsport, TN 37662, Tel: (423) 229-2000
(Mfr plastics, chems, fibers)
  Eastman Chemical, Osaka, Japan

EASTMAN KODAK CO   343 State St, Rochester, NY 14650, Tel: (716) 724-4000
(Devel/mfr photo & chem prdts, info mgmt/video/copier sys, fibers/plastics for
various ind)
  Eastman Chemical Japan Ltd., Gotenyama Mori Bldg., 4-7-35 Kita-Shinagawa,
  Shinagawa-ku, Tokyo 140, Japan
  Eastman Kodak Asia-Pacific Ltd., Gotenyama Mori Bldg., 4-7-35 Kita-Shinagawa,
  Shinagawa-ku, Tokyo 140, Japan
  KK Kodak Information Systems, Gotenyama Mori Bldg., 4-7-35 Kita-Shinagawa,
  Shinagawa-ku, Tokyo 140, Japan
  Kodak Far East Purchasing Co. Inc., Gotenyama Mori Bldg., 4-7-35 Kita-Shinagawa,
  Shinagawa-ku, Tokyo 140, Japan
  Kodak Imagica KK, Gotenyama Mori Bldg., 4-7-35 Kita-Shinagawa, Shinagawa-ku,
  Tokyo 140, Japan
  Kodak Japan Industries Ltd., 18-2 Hakusan 1-chome, Midori-ku, Kanagawa 226, Japan
  Kodak Japan Ltd., Gotenyama Mori Bldg., 4-7-35 Kita-Shinagawa, Shinagawa-ku,
  Tokyo 140, Japan

EATON CORP   1111 Superior Ave, Cleveland, OH 44114, Tel: (216) 523-5000
(Advanced tech prdts for transp & ind mkts)
   Eaton Japan Co. Ltd., Ohno Bldg., 1-19-8 Kyobashi, Chuo-ku, Tokyo 104, Japan
   Nitta-Moore Co. Ltd., Osaka, Japan

ECONOMIST INTELLIGENCE UNIT   111 W 57th St, New York, NY 10019,
Tel: (212) 554-0600
(Business publications)
   Business Intl. Delaware, Pola Aoyama Bldg., 2-5 Minami Aoyama, Minato-ku,
      Tokyo 107, Japan

EG&G INC   45 William St, Wellesley, MA 02181-4078, Tel: (617) 237-5100
(Diversified R/D, mfg & services)
   EG&G Japan, Shuwa Kioicho TBR #1223, 7 Kojimachi 5-chome, Chiyoda-ku, Tokyo 102,
      Japan
   Eagle EG&G Aerospace Co. Ltd., 1-12-15 Shiba-Daimon, Minato-ku, Tokyo 105, Japan
   Eagle Industry Co. Ltd., 1-12-15 Shiba-Daimon, Minato-ku, Tokyo 105, Japan
   Nok EG&G Optoelectronics Corp., 4-3-1 Tsujido-Shinmachi, Fujisawa-shi,
      Kanagawa-ken 251, Japan
   Seiko EG&G Co. Ltd., 31-1 Kameido 6-chome, Koto-ku, Tokyo 136, Japan

ELECTRO-SCIENCE LABORATORIES   416 E Church Rd, King of Prussia, PA 19406,
Tel: (610) 272-8000
(Mfr thick film materials & solder pastes)
   ESL Nippon Co. Ltd., Sukegawa Bldg. 6/F, 1-3-4 Yangibashi, Taito-ku, Tokyo 111,
      Japan

ELECTROGLAS INC   2901 Coronado Dr, Santa Clara, CA 95054, Tel: (408) 727-6500
(Mfr semi-conductor test equip, automatic wafer probers)
   Electroglas KK, 8-3 Funado 1-chome, Itabashi-ku, Tokyo 174, Japan

ELECTRONIC ASSOCIATES INC   185 Monmouth Park Hwy, West Long Branch,
NJ 07764, Tel: (201) 229-1100
(Analog/hybrid computers, training simulators, energy measurement sys)
   Electronic Associates (Japan) Inc., Mori Bldg., 1-2-2 Atago, Minato-ku, Tokyo 105,
      Japan

EMCO WHEATON INC   409A Airport Blvd, Morrisville, NC 27560,
Tel: (919) 467-5878
(Mfr petroleum handling equip)
   Emco Wheaton (Japan) Ltd., 2-4 Tsunashima Higashi 4-chome, Kottoku-ku,
      Yokohama 223, Japan

EMERSON ELECTRIC CO   8000 W Florissant Ave, St Louis, MO 63136,
Tel: (314) 553-2000
(Electrical & electronic prdts, ind components & sys, consumer, government & defense
prdts)
   Emerson Electric Co., Daini-Koscen Bldg., 1-7-13 Tsuku, Chuo-ku, Tokyo 104, Japan

EMERY WORLDWIDE   One Lagoon Dr, #400, Redwood City, CA 94065,
Tel: (800) 227-1981
(Freight transport, global logistics, air cargo)
   Emery Worldwide, 2 Shuwa Nihombashi Honcho Bldg., 3-2 Nihombashi Ohdemmacho,
      Chuo-ku, Tokyo 103, Japan

ENCYCLOPAEDIA BRITANNICA INC   310 S Michigan Ave, Chicago, IL 60604,
  Tel: (312) 321-7000
  (Publishing)
    Encyclopaedia Britannica (Japan) Inc., Meiho Bldg., 1-21-1 Nishi Shinjuku,
      Shinjuku-ku, Tokyo 160, Japan
    TBS-Britannica Ltd., Shuwa Sanbancho Bldg., 28-1 Sanbancho, Chiyoda-ku, Tokyo 102,
      Japan

ENERPAC   13000 W Silver Spring Dr, Butler, WI 53007, Tel: (414) 781-6600
  (Mfr/sale high pressure hydraulic maint tools)
    Enerpac, 10-17 Sasame, Kita-cho, Toda-shi, Saitama 335, Japan

ERIEZ MAGNETICS   PO Box 10652, Erie, PA 16514, Tel: (814) 833-9881
  (Mfr magnets, vibratory feeders, metal detectors, screeners/sizers, mining equip,
  current separators)
    Eriez Magnetics Japan Co. Ltd., Shinkawa Ohara Bldg., 4th Fl.,
      27-8 Chinkawa 1-chome, Chuo-ku, Tokyo 104, Japan

ESTEE LAUDER INTL INC   767 Fifth Ave, New York, NY 10019, Tel: (212) 572-4600
  (Cosmetics)
    Estee Lauder Cosmetics (Japan) Ltd., Nihon Seimei Akasaka Bldg.,
      1-19 Akasaka 8-chome, Minato-ku, Tokyo 107, Japan

EVEREX SYSTEMS INC   901 Page Ave, Fremont, CA 94538, Tel: (510) 498-1111
  (Mfr computer systems & peripherals)
    Otokuni Denshi, 2-14-18 Hashirii, Toyonaka-shi, Osaka-fu, Osaka 516, Japan

EXPEDITORS INTL OF WASHINGTON INC   PO Box 69620, Seattle, WA 98168-9620,
  Tel: (206) 246-3711
  (Air/ocean freight forwarding, customs brokerage, intl logistics solutions)
    Expeditors Intl. Service Center, c/o Pegasus, 1-2-11 Minami-Shinagwa, Shinagawa-ku,
      Tokyo 140, Japan
    Pegasus Expeditors Intl. Inc., Nanko Aircargo Terminal 2F, 4-11-43 Nanko-Higashi,
      Suminoe-ku, Osaka, Japan

EXXON CORP   225 E John W Carpenter Freeway, Irving, TX 75062-2298,
  Tel: (214) 444-1000
  (Petroleum explor, prod, refining; mfr petrol & chem prdts; coal & minerals)
    Esso Sekiyu KK, TBS Kaikan Bldg., 3-3 Akasaka 5-chome, Minato-ku, Tokyo 107, Japan
    General Sekiyu KK, TBS Kaikan Bldg., 3-3 Akasaka 5-chome, Minato-ku, Tokyo, Japan
    Tonen KK, Palace Side Bldg., 1-1 Hitotsubashi 1-chome, Chiyoda-ku, Tokyo 100, Japan

FAIRCHILD PUBLICATIONS INC   7 W 34th St, New York, NY 10001,
  Tel: (212) 630-4000
  (Publishers)
    Fairchild Publications, Kawate Bldg., 2 Kanda Ogawa-Machi 2-chome, Chiyoda-ku,
      Tokyo, Japan

FAIRCHILD SEMICONDUCTOR DIV   PO Box 58090, Santa Clara, CA 95052-8090,
  Tel: (408) 743-3355
  (Mfr semiconductor components)
    Fairchild Semiconductor Inc., Sanyo Kokusaku Pulp Bldg., 7-8 Shibuya 1-chome,
      Shibuya-ku, Tokyo 150, Japan

FALK CORP   3001 W Canal St, Milwaukee, WI 53208, Tel: (414) 342-3131
  (Mfr gears, geared reducers & drives, couplings)
    Osaka Chain & Machinery Ltd., Osaka Shinko Bldg., 8th Fl., 5 Kitahama 3-chome,
    Higashi-ku, Osaka 541, Japan

FANSTEEL INC   1 Tantalum Pl, North Chicago, IL 60064, Tel: (708) 689-4900
  (Mfr refractory metals, cutting & mining tools, aerospace fabrications)
    V Tech-Fansteel, Mitsui Seimei Bldg., 8th Fl., 84-2 Ohtacho 6-chome, Naka-ku,
    Yokohama 231, Japan

FARAH INC   8889 Gateway Blvd W, El Paso, TX 79925, Tel: (915) 593-4000
  (Mfr wearing apparel)
    Farah Japan Ltd., 2 Mochizuki Bldg., 6-16 Shibaura 2-chome, Minato-ku, Tokyo 108,
    Japan

FEDERAL EXPRESS CORP   PO Box 727, Memphis, TN 38194, Tel: (901) 369-3600
  (Package express delivery service)
    Federal Express (Japan) KK, Akaishi Bldg., 9-3 Higashi Azabu 1-chome, Minato-ku,
    Tokyo, Japan

FEDERAL-MOGUL CORP   PO Box 1966, Detroit, MI 48235, Tel: (810) 354-7700
  (Mfr/distr precision parts for automobiles, trucks, & farm/constrution vehicles)
    Federal-Mogul Japan KK, Japan

FELTON INTERNATIONAL INC   599 Johnson Ave, Brooklyn, NY 11237,
  Tel: (212) 497-4664
  (Essential oils & extracts, perfumes & flavor material, aromatic chems)
    Felton Japan Co. Ltd., Nittoku Bldg., 3-14 Shiba 3-chome, Minato-ku, Tokyo 105,
    Japan

FENWALL INC   400 Main St, Ashland, MA 01721, Tel: (617) 881-2000
  (Temperature controls, ignition sys, fire/smoke detection & supression sys)
    Fenwal Controls of Japan Ltd., 3 Mori Bldg., 4-10 Nishi Shinbashi 1-chome,
    Minato-ku, Tokyo 105, Japan

FERRO CORPORATION   1000 Lakeside Ave, Cleveland, OH 44114,
  Tel: (216) 641-8580
  (Mfr chems, coatings, plastics, colors, refractories)
    Ferro (Enamel) Japan Ltd., 1-27 Oyodokita 2-chome, Kita-ku, Osaka, Japan
    Nissan Ferro Electronics Co. Ltd., Nissan Edobashi Bldg.,
      10-5 Nihonbashi Honcho 1-chome, Chuo-ku, Tokyo 103, Japan
    Nissan Ferro Organic Chemical Co. Ltd., Nissan Edobashi Bldg.,
      10-5 Nihonbashi Honcho 1-chome, Chuo-ku, Tokyo 103, Japan

FERROFLUIDICS CORP   40 Simon St, Nashua, NH 03061, Tel: (603) 883-9800
  (Mfr rotary feedthrough designs, emission seals, automated crystal-growing sys,
  bearings, ferrofluids)
    Ferrofluidics Japan Corp., 1001 Chisan Mansion, 24-8 Sakuragaoka-cho, Shibuya-ku,
    Tokyo 150, Japan

FILTRA SYSTEMS/HYDROMATION   30000 Beck Rd, Wixom, MI 48393,
  Tel: (313) 669-0300
  (Ind filter sys)
    Daido Hydromation Co., Ashi Seimei Nagoya Higashi Bldg., 1-3 Ayuchi-Dori 4-chome,
    Showa-ku, Nagoya 466, Japan

FINNIGAN CORP   355 River Oaks Parkway, San Jose, CA 95134-1991,
   Tel: (408) 433-4800
   (Mfr mass spectrometers)
      Finnigan MAT Instruments Inc., Nishishinjuku-Toyokuni Bldg., 2-5-8 Hatsudai,
      Shibuya-ku, Tokyo 151, Japan
      Finnigan MAT Instruments Inc., Tosabori I-N Bldg, 1-5 Tosabori 11-chome, Nishi-ku,
      Osaka 550, Japan

FIRST CHICAGO CORP   One First National Plaza, Chicago, IL 60670,
   Tel: (312) 732-4000
   (Banking)
      First Chicago Corp., Tokyo, Japan

FIRST HAWAIIAN INC   165 King St, Honolulu, HI 96813, Tel: (808) 525-7000
   (Bank holding co)
      First Hawaiian Bank Japan, Ohtemachi Bldg., 6-1 Ohtemachi 1-chome, Chiyoda-ku,
      Tokyo 100, Japan

FIRST NATIONAL BANK IN DALLAS   PO Box 6031, Dallas, TX 75283,
   Tel: (214) 744-8000
   (Commercial banking)
      First National Bank in Dallas, 330 Fuji Bldg., 2-3 Marunouchi 1-chome, Chiyoda-ku,
      Tokyo 100, Japan

FIRST NATIONAL BANK OF BOSTON   100 Federal St, Boston, MA 02110,
   Tel: (617) 434-2200
   (Commercial banking)
      First National Bank of Boston, CPO Box 643, AIU Bldg., 7th Fl.,
      1-3 Marunouchi 1-chome, Chiyoda-ku, Tokyo 100, Japan

FIRST NATIONAL BANK OF CHICAGO   One First National Plaza, Chicago, IL 60670,
   Tel: (312) 732-4000
   (Financial services)
      First Chicago Capital Markets Asia Ltd., Hibiya Central Bldg., 7th Fl.,
      2-9 Nishi-Shimbashi 1-chome, Minato-ku, Tokyo 105, Japan
      First National Bank of Chicago, Hibiya Central Bldg., 7th Fl.,
      2-9 Nishi-Shimbashi 1-chome, Minato-ku, Tokyo 105, Japan

FISHER CONTROLS INTL INC   8000 Maryland Ave, Clayton, MO 63105,
   Tel: (314) 746-9900
   (Mfr ind process control equip)
      Nippon Fisher Co. Ltd., Empire Bldg., 10th Fl., 23-1 Hatchobori 2-chome, Chuo-ku,
      Tokyo 104, Japan

FLORASYNTH INC   300 North St, Teterboro, NJ 07608, Tel: (201) 288-3200
   (Mfr fragrances & flavors)
      Florasynth-Lautier KK, Kanda Shibasaki Bldg., 16-7 Higashi Kanda 1-chome,
      Chiyoda-ku, Tokyo 101, Japan

FLUOR DANIEL INC   3333 Michelson Dr, Irvine, CA 92730, Tel: (714) 975-2000
   (Engineering, construction, maintenance & technical services)
      Fluor Daniel Japan, Sanno Grand Bldg., 2-14-2 Nagata-cho, Chiyoda-ku, Tokyo 100,
      Japan

FMC CORP   200 E Randolph Dr, Chicago, IL 60601, Tel: (312) 861-6000
   (Produces chems & precious metals, mfr machinery, equip & sys for ind, agric & govt)
      Asia Lithium Corp., Japan

(cont)

FMC Asia Pacific Inc., Sanbancho KS Bldg. 7/F, 2 Sanbancho, Chiyoda-ku, Tokyo 102, Japan
L.H. Co. Ltd., Japan
Tokai Danka Kogyo KK, Japan

FOOTE CONE & BELDING COMMUNICATIONS INC   101 E Erie St, Chicago, IL 60611-2897, Tel: (312) 751-7000
(Advertising agency)
   Accari/FCB, Dai-Ni Toshiba Bldg., 8th Fl., 6-4-4 Ginza, Chuo-ku, Tokyo 104, Japan
   Daiko/FCB Impact, Shiba Shimizu Bldg., 2-3-11 Shiba Diamon, Minato-ku, Tokyo 105, Japan

FORD MOTOR CO   The American Road, Dearborn, MI 48121, Tel: (313) 322-3000
(Mfr motor vehicles)
   Ford Motor Co. (Japan) Ltd., Mori Bldg., 5-1 Toranomon 3-chome, Minato-ku, Tokyo 105, Japan

FOUR WINDS INTL GROUP   1500 SW First Ave, #850, Portland, OR 97201, Tel: (503) 241-2732
(Transp of household goods & general cargo, third party logistics)
   Four Winds Japan, 23 Mori Bldg. 5/F, 23-7 Toranomon 1-chome, Minato-ku, Tokyo 105, Japan

FRANK RUSSELL CO   909 A St, PO Box 1616, Tacoma, WA 98401-1616, Tel: (206) 572-9500
(Investment mgmt consulting)
   Frank Russell Japan Co. Ltd., 49-13 Nishihara 3-chome, Shibuya-ku, Tokyo 151, Japan

THE FRANKLIN MINT   Franklin Center, PA 19091, Tel: (610) 459-6000
(Creation/mfr/mktg collectibles & luxury items)
   Franklin Mint Co. Ltd., Recruit Kachidoki Bldg., 2-11-9 Kachidoki, Chuo-ku, Tokyo 104, Japan

FRITZ COMPANIES INC   706 Mission St, San Francisco, CA 94103, Tel: (415) 904-8360
(Integrated transportation, sourcing, distribution & customs brokerage services)
   Suzuyo/Fritz Ltd., Suzuyo Tokyo Bldg. 3/F, 1-2-12 Shibakoen, Minato-ku, Tokyo 105, Japan

FRUEHAUF TRAILER CORP   PO Box 44913, Indianapolis, IN 46244-0913, Tel: (317) 630-3000
(Mfr truck trailers)
   Nippon Fruehauf Co. Ltd., Yokohama Nishiguchi KN Bldg. 11/F, 2-84 Kita-Saiwai Nishi-ku, Kanagawa, Yokohama, Japan

H B FULLER CO   2400 Energy Park Dr, St Paul, MN 55108, Tel: (612) 645-3401
(Mfr/distr adhesives, sealants, coatings, paints, waxes, sanitation chems)
   H.B. Fuller Japan Co. Ltd., 3-6 Kanda Nishihicho, Chiyoda-ku, Tokyo 101, Japan

GAF CORP   1361 Alps Rd, Wayne, NJ 07470, Tel: (201) 628-3000
(Chems, bldg materials, commun)
   GAF Japan Ltd., Kogen Bldg., 17-2 Shinbashi 6-chome, Minato-ku, Tokyo, Japan

THE GATES RUBBER CO   PO Box 5887, Denver, CO 80217-5887, Tel: (303) 744-1911
  (Mfr automotive & industrial belts & hose)
    Gates Export Corp., Mori Bldg. 28, 16-13 Nishi Azabu 4-chome, Minato-ku, Tokyo 106,
    Japan

GATX CAPITAL CORP   Four Embarcadero Center, #2200, San Francisco, CA 94111,
  Tel: (415) 955-3200
  (Lease & loan financing, residual guarantees)
    GATX Capital (Japan) Ltd., 4th Fl., Sogo Bldg., 8-15 Toranomon 5-chome, Minato-ku,
    Tokyo 105, Japan

GCA CORP   7 Shattuck Rd, Andover, MA 01810, Tel: (508) 837-3000
  (Mfr imaging sys for semiconductor ind)
    General Signal Corp, 17-13 Kamitoda 4-chome, Toda City, Saitama Ken 335, Japan

GELMAN SCIENCES INC   600 S Wagner Rd, Ann Arbor, MI 48106-1448,
  Tel: (313) 665-0651
  (Mfr microporous membrane filters & devices)
    Gelman Sciences Japan Ltd., Mani Bldg., 5-16-22 Roppongi, Minato-ku, Tokyo 106,
    Japan

GENERAL BINDING CORP   One GBC Plaza, Northbrook, IL 60062,
  Tel: (708) 272-3700
  (Binding & laminating equip & associated supplies)
    GBC Japan KK, Aya Kudan Bldg., 3-27 Kudan Minami 2-chome, Chiyoda-ku, Tokyo 102,
    Japan

GENERAL DYNAMICS CORP   3190 Fairview Park Dr, Falls Church, VA 22042-4523,
  Tel: (703) 876-3000
  (Mfr aerospace equip, submarines, strategic sys, armored vehicles, defense support
  sys)
    General Dynamics Intl. Corp., 30 Mori Bldg., 2-2 Toranomon 3-chome, Minato-ku,
    Tokyo 105, Japan

GENERAL ELECTRIC CO   3135 Easton Tpk, Fairfield, CT 06431,
  Tel: (203) 373-2211
  (Diversified manufacturing, technology & services)
    General Electric Co.,
    all mail to U.S. address; phone (800) 626-2004 or (518) 438-6500

GENERAL FOODS CORP   250 North St, White Plains, NY 10625, Tel: (914) 335-2500
  (Processor, distributor & mfr of foods)
    Ajinomoto General Foods Inc., Yotsuya Bldg., 8 Honshio-cho, Shinjuku-ku, Tokyo,
    Japan

GENERAL INSTRUMENT CORP   181 W Madison, Chicago, IL 60602,
  Tel: (312) 541-5000
  (Mfr broadband communications & power rectifying components)
    General Instrument Japan Ltd., 5/F, 4-1-13 Toramonom, Minato-ku, Tokyo 105, Japan

GENERAL MOTORS CORP   3044 W Grand Blvd, Detroit, MI 48202-3091,
  Tel: (313) 556-5000
  (Mfr full line vehicles, automotive electronics, coml technologies, telecom, space,
  finance)
    Isuzu Motors Ltd., Tokyo, Japan
    Suzuki Motor Co. Ltd., Hamamatsu, Japan

GENERAL REINSURANCE CORP   PO Box 10350, Stamford, CT 06904-2350,
  Tel: (203) 328-5000
  (Reinsurance)
    General Re Financial Products (Japan) Inc., Toranomon Y Koh Bldg.,
    12-1 Toranomon 5-chome, Minato-ku, Tokyo 105, Japan
    General Reinsurance Corp., Toranomon Y Koh Bldg., 12-1 Toranomon 5-chome,
    Minato-ku, Tokyo 105, Japan

GENETICS INSTITUTE INC   87 Cambridge Park Dr, Cambridge, MA 02140,
  Tel: (617) 876-1170
  (Devel/commercialize biopharmaceutical therapeutic prdts)
    Genetics Institute Inc. of Japan, 1-10-13 Higashi Azabu, Minato-ku, Tokyo 106, Japan

GENRAD INC   300 Baker Ave, Concord, MA 01742, Tel: (508) 369-4400
  (Mfr automatic test equip)
    GenRad Japan, c/o Tokyo Electron Ltd., 2-30-7 Sumiyoshi-cho, Fuchu, Tokyo 183, Japan

GETZ BROS & CO INC   150 Post St, #500, San Francisco, CA 94108,
  Tel: (415) 772-5500
  (Divers mfg, mktg/distr serv, travel serv)
    Getz Bros. & Co. Ltd., Sumitomo Seimei Aoyama Bldg., 1-30 Minami-Aoyama 3-chome,
    Minato-ku, Tokyo 107, Japan
    Muller & Phipps (Japan) Ltd., Sumitomo Seimei Aoyama Bldg.,
    1-30 Minami-Aoyama 3-chome, Minato-ku, Tokyo 107, Japan

THE GILLETTE CO   Prudential Tower, Boston, MA 02199, Tel: (617) 421-7000
  (Devel/mfr personal care/use prdts: blades & razors, toiletries, cosmetics,
  stationery)
    Braun Japan KK, Yokohama, Japan
    Gillette (Japan) Inc., Tokyo, Japan

GLITSCH INC   PO Box 660053, Dallas, TX 75266-0053, Tel: (214) 631-3841
  (Mfr/svce mass transfer/chem separation equip, process engr)
    Glitsch Japan, 3-1-4 Ikegamishincho, Kawasaki-ku, Kawasaki 210, Japan

GLOBAL INTERNATIONAL   1304 Willow St, Martinez, CA 94553, Tel: (510) 229-9330
  (International moving & forwarding)
    Global International Inc., Rohsei Bldg., 1-4-2 Higashi Azabu, Minato-ku, Tokyo 106,
    Japan

THE GOODYEAR TIRE & RUBBER CO   1144 E Market St, Akron, OH 44316,
  Tel: (216) 796-2121
  (Mfr tires, automotive belts & hose, conveyor belts, chemicals; oil pipeline
  transmission)
    Nippon Goodyear KK, Sankaido Bldg., 9-13 Akasaka 1-chome, Minato-ku, Tokyo 107,
    Japan

W R GRACE & CO   One Town Center Rd, Boca Raton, FL 33486-1010,
  Tel: (407) 362-2000
  (Mfr spec chems & materials: packaging, health care, catalysts, construction, water
  treatment/process)
    Fuji-Davison Chemical Ltd., 1846, 2-chome, Kozoji-cho, Kusagai-shi, Aichi-ken 487,
    Japan
    Grace Japan KK, Shinjuku Green Tower Bldg. 11/F, 14-1 Nushi-Shinjuku 6-chome,
    Shinjuku-ku, Tokyo 160, Japan

Nippon Belt Kogyo KK, 700 Oaza Yasutsuga, Godo-cho, Anpachi-gum, Gifu-ken 503-23, Japan

GRACE SPECIALTY POLYMERS   77 Dragon Ct, Woburn, MA 01888-4014,
  Tel: (617) 938-8630
  (Mfr spec polymers)
    Grace Specialty Polymers, Grace Atsugi Center, 100 Kaneda, Atsugi-shi, Kanagawa-ken 243, Japan

GRACO INC   4050 Olson Memorial Hwy, PO Box 1441, Minneapolis, MN 55440-1441,
  Tel: (612) 623-6000
  (Mfr/serv fluid handling equip & sys)
    Graco KK, 1-26-10 Hayabuchi, Tsuzuki-ku, Yokohama 224, Japan

GRADCO SYSTEMS INC   3753 Howard Hughes Pkwy, #200, Las Vegas, NV 89109,
  Tel: (702) 892-3714
  (Paper-handling systems for office automation mkt)
    Gradco (Japan) Ltd., Toho Seimei Bldg. 25/F, 15-1 Shibuya 2-chome, Shibuya-ku, Tokyo 150, Japan

GREY ADVERTISING INC   777 Third Ave, New York, NY 10017, Tel: (212) 546-2000
  (Advertising)
    Grey-Daiko Advertising, Grey-Daiko Bldg., 2-3-20 Motoazabu, Minato-ku, Tokyo 106, Japan

GRIFFITH LABORATORIES INC   I Griffith Center, Alsip, IL 60658,
  Tel: (708) 371-0900
  (Ind food ingredients & equip)
    Griffith Laboratories Japan KK, Nissei Bldg., 13-31 Konan 2-chome, Minato-ku, Tokyo 108, Japan

GTE CORP   One Stamford Forum, Stamford, CT 06904, Tel: (203) 965-2000
  (Electr prdts, telecom sys, publ & commun)
    NEC Sylvania Corp., Minakuchi, Japan

FRANK B HALL & CO INC   549 Pleasantville Rd, Briarcliff Manor, NY 10510,
  Tel: (914) 769-9200
  (Insurance)
    Kyoritsu Co. Ltd., Kyoritsu Bldg., Nihonbashi, Chuo-ku, Tokyo 103, Japan

HALLIBURTON NUS CORP   910 Clopper Rd, Gaithersburg, MD 20878-1399,
  Tel: (301) 258-6000
  (Tech consultants in energy & environmental fields)
    Japan NUS Co. Ltd., Shinjuku Daiichi Seimei Bldg., Nishi-Shinjuku 2-chome, Shinjuku-ku, Tokyo 160, Japan

HANDY & HARMAN   555 Theodore Fremd Ave, Rye, NY 10580, Tel: (914) 921-5200
  (Precious & specialty metals for industry, refining, scrap metal; diversified ind mfg)
    Mizuno Handy Harman Ltd., 11-12 Kitaueno 2-chome, Taitoh-ku, Tokyo, Japan

HARCOURT BRACE & CO   Orlando, FL 32887, Tel: (407) 345-2000
  (Book publ, tests & related serv, journals, facisimile reprints, mgmt consult, operates parks/shows)
    Harcourt Brace KK, Ichibancho Central Bldg., Tokyo 102, Japan

HARCOURT GENERAL   27 Boylston St, Chestnut Hill, MA 02167,
   Tel: (617) 232-8200
   (Publishing, specialty retailing, professional services)
      Harcourt Brace KK, Ichibancho Central Bldg., Tokyo, Japan

HARLEY-DAVIDSON INTL   3700 W Juneau Ave, Milwaukee, WI 53208,
   Tel: (414) 342-4680
   (Mfr motorcycles, recreational & coml vehicles, parts & accessories)
      Harley-Davidson Japan KK, P.O. Box 39, 718 Shin Nihon Kaikan Bldg.,
      7-18 Mita 3-chome, Minato-ku, Tokyo, Japan

HARMAN INTL INDUSTRIES INC   1101 Pennsylvania Ave NW, Washington, DC 20004,
   Tel: (202) 393-1101
   (Mfr audio & video equipment)
      Harman Intl. Japan Co. Ltd., Hinoki Bldg. 3/F, 1-5 Azabudai 3-chome, Minato-ku,
      Tokyo 106, Japan

HARNISCHFEGER INDUSTRIES INC   PO Box 554, Milwaukee, WI 53201,
   Tel: (414) 671-4400
   (Mfr mining & material handling equip, papermaking mach, computer sys)
      Beloit Nippon Ltd., 2-5-1 Marunouchi, Chiyoda-ku, Tokyo 100, Japan
      Kobe Steel Ltd., 3-18 Wakinohama-cho 1-chome, Chuo-ku, Kobe 651, Japan

THE HARPER GROUP   260 Townsend St, PO Box 77933, San Francisco,
   CA 94107-1719, Tel: (415) 978-0600
   (Ocean/air freight fwdg, customs brokerage, packing & whse, logistics mgt, ins)
      Circle Airfreight Japan Ltd., The Harper Plaza Tokyo, 11-7 Motonakayama 6-chome,
      Funabashi-shi, Chiba 273, Japan
      Circle Freight Intl. Japan Inc., The Harper Plaza Tokyo, 11-7 Motonakayama 6-chome,
      Funabashi-shi, Chiba 273, Japan
      Western Nagivation (Far East) Ltd., Manbu Bldg. 4/F,
      5-12 Nihonbashi-Ningyocho 1-chome, Chuo-ku, Tokyo 103, Japan

HARTMARX CORP   101 N Wacker Dr, Chicago, IL 60606, Tel: (312) 372-6300
   (Mfr/licensing men's & women's apparel)
      Hartmarx Japan, 4-2-1 Kyutaromachi, Chuo-ku, Osaka, Japan

H J HEINZ CO   PO Box 57, Pittsburgh, PA 15230-0057, Tel: (412) 456-5700
   (Processed food prdts & nutritional services)
      Heinz Japan Ltd., Tokyo, Japan
      Star-Kist Foods Inc., Tokyo, Japan

HELENE CURTIS INDUSTRIES INC   325 N Wells St, Chicago, IL 60610-4791,
   Tel: (312) 661-0222
   (Mfr personal care prdts)
      Helene Curtis Japan Inc., Daiichi Seimei Bldg., 7-1 Nishi-Shinjuku 2-chome,
      Shinjuku-ku, Tokyo 163, Japan

HERCULES INC   Hercules Plaza, Wilmington, DE 19894-0001, Tel: (302) 594-5000
   (Mfr spec chems, plastics, film & fibers, coatings, resins, food ingredients)
      Hercules Japan Ltd., Seiwa Bldg., 9th Fl., 3-4 Minami Aoyama 2-chome, Minato-ku,
      Tokyo 107, Japan

HERSHEY FOODS CORP   100 Crystal A Dr, Hershey, PA 17033, Tel: (717) 534-6799
(Mfr chocolate, food & confectionery prdts)
  Hershey Japan, Keikyu Nakahara Bldg. 6/F, 30-6 Shinbashi 4-chome, Minato-ku,
  Tokyo 105, Japan

HEWLETT-PACKARD CO   3000 Hanover St, Palo Alto, CA 94304-0890,
  Tel: (415) 857-1501
(Mfr computing, communications & measurement prdts & services)
  Hewlett-Packard Japan Ltd., 3-29-21 Takaido-Higashi, Suginami-ku, Tokyo 168, Japan

HEXCEL CORP   20701 Nordhoff St, Chatsworth, CA 91311, Tel: (213) 882-3022
(Honeycomb core materials, specialty chems, resins & epoxies)
  Hexcel, 22-1 Ichiban-cho, Chiyoda-ku, Tokyo 102, Japan

HOLIDAY INNS INC   3742 Lamar Ave, Memphis, TN 38195, Tel: (901) 362-4001
(Hotels, restaurants, casinos)
  Holiday Inns (Far East Ltd. Inc.), Niben Bldg., 5th Fl., 2-8 Muromachii,
  Nihonbashi, Chuo-ku, Tokyo 103, Japan
  Holiday Inns (Far East Ltd. Inc.), Kyoto, Japan

HONEYWELL INC   PO Box 524, Minneapolis, MN 55440-0524, Tel: (612) 951-1000
(Devel/mfr controls for home & building, industry, space & aviation)
  Yamatake-Honeywell Co. Ltd., Totate Intl. Bldg., 2-12-19 Shibuya-ku, Tokyo 150,
  Japan

HORWATH INTL   415 Madison Ave, New York, NY 10017, Tel: (212) 838-5566
(Public accountants & auditors)
  Horwath & Showa Co. Ltd. Japan/Showa Audit Corp., Daiko Bldg., 3-2 Umeda 14-chome,
  Kita-ku, Osaka 530, Japan

HOUGHTON INTL INC   PO Box 930, Valley Forge, PA 19482-0930,
  Tel: (610) 666-4000
(Mfr spec chems, hydraulic fluids, lubricants)
  Houghton Japan Co. Ltd., Shibahata Bldg. 4/F, 12-6 Shiba-Daimon 2-chome, Minato-ku,
  Tokyo 105, Japan

HOWMET CORP   475 Steamboat Rd, PO Box 1960, Greenwich, CT 06836-1960,
  Tel: (203) 661-4600
(Mfr precision investment castings, alloys, engineering & refurbishment)
  Komatsu-Howmet Ltd., 1-1 Ueno 3-chome, Hirakata-shi, Osaka-fu 573, Japan

HUCK INTL INC   6 Thomas, PO Box 19590, Irvine, CA 92713, Tel: (714) 855-9000
(Mfr advanced fastening sys)
  Huck Ltd., Yodogawa-Gobankan 11/F, 2-1 Toyosaki 3-chome, Kita-ku, Osaka 531, Japan

HUGHES AIRCRAFT CO   PO Box 80028, Los Angeles, CA 90080-0028,
  Tel: (310) 568-6904
(Mfr electronics equip & sys)
  Hughes Aircraft Intl. Service Co., Sumitomo Tamura-cho Bldg.,
  15-1 Nishi Shinbashi 1-chome, Minato-ku, Tokyo 105, Japan

HYATT INTL CORP   200 West Madison, Chicago, IL 60606, Tel: (312) 750-1234
(Intl hotel mgmt)
  Hyatt Intl. Hotels, Fukuoka, Nagoya & Tokyo, Japan

IBM CORP   Old Orchard Rd, Armonk, NY 10504, Tel: (914) 765-1900
  (Information products, technology & services)
    IBM Japan Ltd., 2-12 Roppongi 3-chome, Minato-ku, Tokyo, Japan
    ROLM Intl. Japan Co. Ltd., Japan

IBP INC   PO Box 515, Dakota City, NE 68731, Tel: (402) 494-2061
  (Produce beef & pork, hides & associated prdts, animal feeds, pharms)
    IBP Inc., Tokyo, Japan

ILLINOIS TOOL WORKS INC   3600 W Lake Ave, Glenview, IL 60025,
  Tel: (708) 724-7500
  (Mfr gears, tools, fasteners, sealants, plastic & metal components for ind, med, etc.)
    Nifco Inc., Tokyo, Yokahama & Kanagawa, Japan

IMO INDUSTRIES INC   1009 Lenox Dr, Bldg 4 West, Lawrenceville,
  NJ 08648-0550, Tel: (609) 896-7600
  (Mfr/support mech & electr controls, engineered power prdts)
    NHK Morse Co. Ltd., 3-21-10 Shin-Yokohama, Kohoku-ku, Yokohama 222, Japan

IMS INTERNATIONAL INC   100 Campus Rd, Totowa, NJ 07512, Tel: (201) 790-0700
  (Market research reports)
    IMS Japan, CPO 2147, Tokyo 100-91, Japan

INCOM INTERNATIONAL INC   3450 Princeton Pike, Lawrenceville, NJ 08648,
  Tel: (609) 896-7600
  (Roller & motorcycle chains, drive components, marine controls)
    NHK Teleflex Morse Co. Ltd., 42 Baba-cho 1-chome, Isogo-ku, Yokohama 235, Japan

INDUCTOTHERM CORP   10 Indel Ave, Rancocas, NJ 08073-0157, Tel: (609) 267-9000
  (Mfr induction melting furnaces)
    Inductotherm Japan Ltd., 3-10 Minamibefu 1-chome, Nishi-ku, Kobe 651-21, Japan

INGERSOLL-RAND CO   200 Chestnut Ridge Rd, Woodcliff Lake, NJ 07675,
  Tel: (201) 573-0123
  (Mfr compressors, rock drills, pumps, air tools, door hardware, ball bearings)
    Ingersoll-Rand (Japan) Ltd., Kowa Bldg. #17, 1-2-7 Nishi-Azabu, Minato-ku,
      Tokyo 106, Japan

INSTRON CORP   100 Royall St, Canton, MA 02021-1089, Tel: (617) 828-2500
  (Mfr material testing instruments)
    Instron Japan Co. Ltd., 1-8-9 Miyamaodaira, Miyamae-ku, Kawaskai-shi,
      Kanagawa-ken 216, Japan
    Instron Japan Co. Ltd., 1-30 Toyotsucho, Shuita-shi, Osaka 584, Japan
    Instron Japan Co. Ltd., 2-9-30 Sakaa, Naka-ku, Nagoya 460, Japan

INTER-TEL INC   7300 W Boston St, Chandler, AZ 85226, Tel: (602) 961-9000
  (Design/mfr business communications systems)
    Nihon Inter-Tel KK, 18-11 Uchikanda 1-chome, Chioyda-ku, Tokyo, Japan

INTERMEC CORP   6001 36th Ave West, PO Box 4280, Everett, WA 98203-9280,
  Tel: (206) 348-2600
  (Mfr/distr automated data collection sys)
    Matsushita Electric Industrial Co. Ltd., 1-61 Shiromi 2-chome, Chuo-ku, Osaka 540,
      Japan
    Nissho Iwai Corp., 4-5 Akasaka 2-chome, Minato-ku, Tokyo 107, Japan

INTERMETRICS INC   733 Concord Ave, Cambridge, MA 02138, Tel: (617) 576-3266
  (Software & systems engineering services)
    Nihon Intermetrics KK, Fukozawa Bldg. 2/F, 36-3 Higashi Nakono 1-chome, Nakono-ka,
    Tokyo 164, Japan

INTERNATIONAL COMPONENTS CORP   420 N May St, Chicago, IL 60622,
  Tel: (312) 829-2525
  (Mfr/sale/svce portable DC battery chargers)
    International Components Corp. (Japan) Ltd., Glory Bldg.,
    35-13 Nishikamata 6-chome, Ohta-ku, Tokyo 144, Japan

INTERNATIONAL FLAVORS & FRAGRANCES INC   521 W 57th St, New York, NY 10019,
  Tel: (212) 765-5500
  (Create/mfr flavors, fragrances & aroma chems)
    Intl. Flavors & Fragrances (Japan) Ltd., Green Fantasia Bldg.,
    11-11 Jingumae 1-chome, Shibuya-ku, Tokyo 150, Japan

INTERNATIONAL PAPER   2 Manhattanville Rd, Purchase, NY 10577,
  Tel: (914) 397-1500
  (Mfr/distr container board, paper, wood prdts)
    IPI Corp., 9-6 Nagata-cho 2-chome, Chiyoda-ku, Tokyo, Japan
    Ilford Anitec Ltd., 4-7 Minamishinagawa 2-chome, Shinagawa-ku, Tokyo 140, Japan
    International Paper (Asia) Ltd., 14-11 Ginza 4-chome, Chuo-ku, Tokyo 10, Japan
    Rengo Intl. Products Co., 900-5 Kuboki, Soja City, Oklayama, Japan
    Veratec Japan Ltd., 14-11 Ginza 4-chome, Chuo-ku, Tokyo 104, Japan

ITEL CORP   2 N Riverside Plaza, Chicago, IL 60606, Tel: (312) 902-1515
  (Transport & equip leasing & serv)
    Itel Container Intl., 30 Mori Bldg., 9th Fl., 2-2 Toranomon 3-chome, Minato-ku,
    Tokyo, Japan

ITT CORP   1330 Ave of the Americas, New York, NY 10019-5490,
  Tel: (212) 258-1000
  (Design/mfr communications & electronic equip, hotels, insurance)
    ITT Far East & Pacific Inc., Shinjuku Sumitomo Bldg., P.O. Box 21,
    6-1 Nishi-Shinjuku 2-chome, Shinjuku-ku, Tokyo 160, Japan

ITT SHERATON CORP   60 State St, Boston, MA 02108, Tel: (617) 367-3600
  (Hotel operations)
    Sheraton Intl. Sales & Reservations, Hotel New Otami, 4 Kioi-cho, Chiyoda-ku,
    Tokyo 102, Japan
    Sheraton Intl. Sales & Reservations, Sumitomo Seimei Midosuji Bldg.,
    4-4-3 Nishi Tenma, Kita-ku, Osaka 530, Japan

JAMESBURY CORP   640 Lincoln St, Worcester, MA 01605, Tel: (617) 852-0200
  (Mfr valves & accessories)
    Jamesbury Nippon Ltd., Shuwa Shibazonobashi Bldg., 1-20 Shiba 2-chome, Minato-ku,
    Tokyo 105, Japan

JBL INTERNATIONAL   8500 Balboa Blvd, Northridge, CA 91329,
  Tel: (818) 893-8411
  (Mfr loudspeakers, sound reinforcement equip)
    Harman Intl. Industries Asia, Hinoki Bldg., 3rd Fl., 1-5 Azabudai 3-chome,
    Minato-ku, Tokyo 106, Japan

JCPENNEY PURCHASING CORP   PO Box 10001, Dallas, TX 75301-0001,
  Tel: (214) 431-5380
  (Department stores)
    JCPenney Purchasing Corp., Shoho Bldg., 7th Fl., 6-2 Bingo-Machi 3-chome, Chuo-ku,
    Osaka 541, Japan

JOHNSON & HIGGINS   125 Broad St, New York, NY 10004-2424, Tel: (212) 574-7000
  (Ins brokerage, employee benefit conslt, risk mgmt, human resource conslt, ins/reins
  servs)
    Johnson & Higgins of Japan Inc., DF Bldg., 2-8 Minami-Aoyama 2-chome, Minato-ku,
    Tokyo 107, Japan

JOHNSON & JOHNSON   One Johnson & Johnson Plaza, New Brunswick, NJ 08933,
  Tel: (908) 524-0400
  (R&D/mfr/sale health care prdts)
    Cilag Pharmaceutical KK, Tokyo, Japan
    Janssen KK, Tokyo, Japan
    Janssen-Kyowa Co. Ltd., Tokyo, Japan
    Johnson & Johnson Japan Inc., Tokyo, Japan
    Johnson & Johnson KK, 3-2 Toya 6-chome, Koto-ku, Tokyo 135, Japan
    Johnson & Johnson Medical Inc., 3-2 Toyo 6-chome, Koto-ku, Tokyo 135, Japan
    Ortho Diagnostic Systems KK, Tokyo, Japan

S C JOHNSON & SON INC   1525 Howe St, Racine, WI 53403, Tel: (414) 631-2000
  (Home, auto, commercial & personal care prdts, specialty chems)
    Johnson Co. Ltd., P.O. Box 7, Kanagawa-ken 259-01, Japan

JOHNSON CONTROLS INC   5757 N Green Bay Ave, PO Box 591, Milwaukee,
  WI 53201-0591, Tel: (414) 228-1200
  (Mfr facility mgmt & control sys, auto seating, batteries & plastics)
    Yokogawa Johnson Controls Corp., Shin-Hitokuchizaka Bldg., 3-9 Kudankita 3-chome,
    Chiyoda-ku, Tokyo, Japan

THE JOURNAL OF COMMERCE   2 World Trade Center, New York, NY 10048,
  Tel: (212) 837-7000
  (Newspaper publisher)
    The Journal of Commerce, c/o The Nihon Keizai Shimbun, 1-9-5 Otemachi, Chiyoda-ku,
    Tokyo, Japan

JOY ENVIRONMENTAL TECHNOLOGIES INC   10700 North Freeway, Houston, TX 77037,
  Tel: (713) 878-1000
  (Design/eng air pollution control & material handling sys)
    Sumitomo Heavy Industries Ltd., 2 Ohtemachi 2-chome, Chiyoda-ku, Tokyo 100, Japan

A T KEARNEY INC   222 West Adams St, Chicago, IL 60606, Tel: (312) 648-0111
  (Mgmt consultants, executive search)
    A.T. Kearney Intl. Inc., Akasaka Twin Tower Annex 11-7 Akasaka 2-chome, Minato-ku,
    Tokyo 107, Japan

KEITHLEY INSTRUMENTS INC   28775 Aurora Rd, Cleveland, OH 44139,
  Tel: (216) 248-0400
  (Mfr electr test/meas instru, PC-based data acquisition hdwe/software)
    Keithley Instruments Far East KK, 201 Sumiyoshi 24 Bldg., 2-24-2 Sumiyoshi-cho,
    Naka-ku, Yokohama 231, Japan

KELLOGG CO   One Kellogg Sq, PO Box 3599, Battle Creek, MI   49016-3599,
   Tel: (616) 961-2000
   (Mfr ready-to-eat cereals, convenience foods)
      Kellogg (Japan) KK, Takasaki, Japan (all inquiries to U.S. address)

THE KENDALL CO   15 Hampshire St, Mansfield, MA   02048, Tel: (508) 261-8000
   (Mfr medical disposable prdts, home health care prdts, spec adhesive prdts)
      Nihon Kendall KK, UK Hongo 4/F, 3-44-2 Hongo, Bunkyo-ku, Tokyo 113, Japan

KENNEDY VAN SAUN CORP   PO Box 500, Danville, PA   17821, Tel: (717) 275-3050
   (Mineral processing & handling equip)
      Kubota Ltd., 2-47 Shikitsunhigashi 1-chome, Naniwa-ku, Osaka 556-91, Japan

KENT-MOORE DIV   28635 Mound Rd, Warren, MI   48092, Tel: (313) 574-2332
   (Mfr service equip for auto, constr, recreational, military & agric vehicles)
      Jatek, Dai-Ni Maruzen Bldg., 8th Fl., 9-2 Nihonbashi 3-chome, Chou-ku, Tokyo 103,
      Japan

KEPNER-TREGOE INC   PO Box 704, Princeton, NJ   08542-0740, Tel: (609) 921-2806
   (Mgmt consulting & training)
      Kepner-Tregoe (Japan) Inc., Moto-Akasaka Kikutei Bldg., 7-18 Moto-Akasaka 1-chome,
      Minato-ku, Tokyo 107, Japan

KETCHUM COMMUNICATIONS   6 PPG Pl, Pittsburgh, PA   15222, Tel: (412) 456-3500
   (Advertising, public relations, mgmt consulting)
      Ketchum Advertising (Japan) Ltd., Gotanda Trade Center Bldg.,
      25-5 Nishigotanda 7-chome, Shinagawa-ku, Tokyo 141, Japan

KEYSTONE INTL INC   PO Box 40010, Houston, TX   77040, Tel: (713) 466-1176
   (Mfr butterfly valves, actuators & control accessories)
      Nippon Keystone Corp., Japan

KIDDER PEABODY GROUP INC   10 Hanover Sq, New York, NY   10005,
   Tel: (212) 510-3000
   (Investment banking)
      Kidder, Peabody Intl. Corp., Tokio Kaijo Bldg., 13th Fl., 2-1 Marunouchi 1-chome,
      Chiyoda-ku, Tokyo 100, Japan
      Kidder, Peabody Intl. Corp., 4-21 Minami-Senba 4-chome, Minami-ku, Osaka 542, Japan

KIMBERLY-CLARK CORP   PO Box 619100, Dallas, TX   75261, Tel: (214) 281-1200
   (Mfr fiber-based prdts for personal care, lumber & paper prdts)
      Kimberly-Clark Japan Ltd., Japan

THE KNOLL GROUP   105 Wooster St, New York, NY   10021, Tel: (212) 343-4000
   (Mfr/sale office furnishings)
      Knoll Intl. Japan, Kokusai Bldg., 3-1-1 Marunouchi, Chiyoda-ku, Tokyo 100, Japan

KOEHRING CO   PO Box 312, Milwaukee, WI   53201, Tel: (414) 784-5800
   (Pulp mill & constr equip)
      Koehring Co., 930 Hibiya Park Bldg., 1 Yuraku-cho 1-chome, Chiyoda-ku, Tokyo 100,
      Japan

THE KOHLER CO   444 Highland Dr, Kohler, WI   53044, Tel: (414) 457-4441
   (Plumbing prdts, engines, generators)
      Kohler Japan KK, 3-19-23 Minami Azabu, Minato-ku, Tokyo 106, Japan

KOHN PEDERSEN FOX ASSOCIATES PC   111 W 57th St, New York, NY 10019,
   Tel: (212) 977-6500
   (Architectural design)
      Kohn Pedersen Fox Associates KK, 2-17-42 Akasaka, Minato-ku, Tokyo 107, Japan

KOMAG INC   275 S Hillview Dr, Milpitas, CA 95035, Tel: (408) 946-2300
   (Mfr magnetic-optic media, disk drive discs & heads)
      Asahi Komag Co. Ltd., 2837-9 Hachimanpara Yonezawa-shi, Yamagata 922-11, Japan

KORN/FERRY INTL   1800 Century Park East, Los Angeles, CA 90067,
   Tel: (310) 552-1834
   (Executive search)
      Korn/Ferry Intl. Japan, AIG Bldg. 7/F, 1-3 Marunouchi 1-chome, Chiyoda-ku,
      Tokyo 100, Japan

KROLL ASSOCIATES   900 Third Ave, New York, NY 10022, Tel: (212) 593-1000
   (Consulting services)
      Kroll Associates (Asia) Ltd., 1-3 Marunouchi 1-chome, Choyoda-ku, Tokyo 100, Japan

KULICKE & SOFFA INDUSTRIES INC   2101 Blair Mill Rd, Willow Grove, PA 19090,
   Tel: (215) 784-6000
   (Semiconductor assembly systems & services)
      Kulicke & Soffa (Japan) Ltd., 5 Koike Bldg. 3/F, 1-3-12 Kita-Shinagawa,
      Shinagawa-ku, Tokyo 140, Japan

KWIK LOK CORP   PO Box 9548, Yakima, WA 98909, Tel: (509) 248-4770
   (Mfr bag closing mach)
      Kwik Lok Japan, 4-12 Motogo 2-chome, Kawaguchi City, Saitama, Japan

LANDAUER INC   2 Science Rd, Glenwood, IL 60425-1586, Tel: (708) 755-7000
   (Radiation dosimetry & radon detection servs)
      Nagase-Landauer Ltd., Saimo Bldg., 9-8 Kobuna-cho, Nihonbashi, Chuo-ku, Tokyo 103,
      Japan

LANDIS TOOL CO   20 E Sixth St., Waynesboro, PA 17268-2050,
   Tel: (717) 762-2161
   (Mfr precision cylindrical grinding mach)
      Nippei Toyama Corp., World Trade Centre Bldg., 2-4-1 Hamamatsucho, Minato-ku,
      Tokyo 105, Japan

LE BLOND MAKINO INC   7680 Innovation Way, PO Box 8003, Mason, OH 45040-8003,
   Tel: (513) 573-7200
   (Mfr machine tools)
      Makino Milling Machine Co., 3-19 Nakane 2-chome, Meguro-ku, Tokyo 152, Japan

LEAF CONFECTIONERY INC   500 N Field Dr, Lake Forest, IL 60045-2595,
   Tel: (708) 735-7500
   (Chewing gum)
      Kabaya-Leaf Inc., Okayama, Japan

LEARONAL INC   272 Buffalo Ave, Freeport, NY 11520, Tel: (516) 868-8800
   (Mfr chem specialties)
      LeaRonal Japan, 14-5 Nihonbashi-Bakurocho 1-chome, Chuo-ku, Tokyo 103, Japan

LEDERLE LABS   Middletown Rd, Pearl River, NY 10965, Tel: (914) 735-5000
  (Antibiotics, pharms)
    Lederle (Japan) Ltd., 1 Kyobashi 1-chome, Chuo-ku, Tokyo 104, Japan
    Lederle (Japan) Ltd., CPO Box 957, Tokyo 100-91, Japan

LEVI STRAUSS & CO   1155 Battery, San Francisco, CA 94111, Tel: (415) 544-6000
  (Mfr casual wearing apparel)
    Levi Strauss Japan KK, Sumitomo-Seime Aoyama Bldg., 5th Fl.,
      1-30 Minami Aoyama 3-chome, Minato-ku, Tokyo 107, Japan

ELI LILLY & CO   Lilly Corporate Center, Indianapolis, IN 46285,
  Tel: (317) 276-2000
  (Mfr pharmaceuticals, animal health prdts)
    Eli Lilly Japan KK, 7-1-5 Isogami-dori, Chuo-ku, Kobe 651, Japan

THE LINCOLN ELECTRIC CO   22801 St Clair Ave, Cleveland, OH 44117-1199,
  Tel: (216) 481-8100
  (Mfr arc welding & welding related prtds, oxy-fuel & thermal cutting equip, integral
  AC motors)
    Nippon Lincoln Electric KK, 1-45 Aza-Nakamaru, Ohaza-Yamadaoka, Naraha-Machi,
      Futaba-Gun, Fukushima-Ken 979-05, Japan

LINTAS:WORLDWIDE   1 Dag Hammarskjold Plaza, New York, NY 10017,
  Tel: (212) 605-8000
  (Advertising agency)
    Hakuhodo:Lintas, Tokyo Bldg., 7-3 Marunouchi 2-chome, Chiyoda-ku, Tokyo 100, Japan

ARTHUR D LITTLE INC   25 Acorn Park, Cambridge, MA 02140-2390,
  Tel: (617) 498-5000
  (Mgmt, environ, health & safety consulting; tech & prdt development)
    Arthur D. Little (Japan) Inc., Fukide Bldg., 4-1-13 Toranomon, Minato-ku,
      Tokyo 105, Japan

LITTON INDUSTRIES INC   21240 Burbank Blvd, Woodland Hills, CA 91367,
  Tel: (818) 598-5000
  (Elec sys, ind automation, resource explor)
    Litton Industries Far East, CPO Box 760, Tokyo, Japan

LNP ENGINEERING PLASTICS   475 Creamery Way, Exton, PA 19341,
  Tel: (215) 363-4500
  (Mfr thermoplastic composites)
    ICI Japan Ltd., 47 Wadai, Tsukuba, Iboraki 300-42, Japan

LOCKHEED MARTIN CORP   6801 Rockledge Dr, Bethesda, MD 20817,
  Tel: (301) 897-6000
  (Design/mfr/mgmt sys in fields of space, defense, energy, electronics, materials,
  info & tech svces)
    Lockheed Martin Intl. Ltd., Kowa Bldg. #35, 5th fl., 1-14-14 Akasaka, 1-chome,
      Minato-ku, Tokyo 107, Japan

LOCTITE CORP   10 Columbus Blvd, Hartford, CT 06106, Tel: (203) 520-5000
  (Mfr/sale ind adhesives & sealants)
    Loctite (Japan) Corp., 15-13 Fukuura 1-chome, Kanazawa-ku, Yokohama 236, Japan

LORD CORP   2000 W Grandview Blvd, Erie, PA 16514, Tel: (814) 868-0924
  (Adhesives, coatings, chems, film prdts)
    Lord Far East Inc., 903 Kowa Bldg., 15-21 Nishi Azabu 4-chome, Minato-ku,

(cont)

Tokyo 106, Japan
Special Paint Co. Ltd., 4-15-1 Higashiogu, Arakawa-ku, Tokyo, Japan
Sunstar Chemical Inc., 7-1 Aketa-cho, Takatsuki, Osaka 569, Japan

LSI LOGIC CORP 1551 McCarthy Blvd, Milpitas, CA 95035, Tel: (408) 433-8000
(Devel/mfr semiconductors)
LSI Logic KK, 4-1-8 Konan, Minato-ku, Tokyo 108, Japan
Nihon Semiconductor Inc., 10 Kitahara, Tsukuba-shi, Ibaraki-ken 300-32, Japan

LTX CORP LTX Park, University Ave, Westwood, MA 02090, Tel: (617) 461-1000
(Design/mfr computer-controlled semiconductor test systems)
LTX Co. Ltd., Daison Kubo Bldg. 1/F, 2-5-47 Hirose, Kokubu-shi,
Kagoshima-ken 899-43, Japan

THE LUBRIZOL CORP 29400 Lakeland Blvd, Wickliffe, OH 44092-2298,
Tel: (216) 943-4200
(Mfr chem additives for lubricants & fuels)
Lubrizol Japan Ltd., Mori Bldg., 5th Fl., 23-7 Toranomon 1-chome, Minato-ku,
Tokyo 105, Japan

LYDALL INC 1 Colonial Rd, Manchester, CT 06040, Tel: (203) 646-1233
(Mfr converted paper prdts, paperboard, non-woven specialty media)
Lydall Intl. Inc., Rippongi SK Bldg., 3-15 Rippongi 3-chome, Minato-ku, Tokyo 106,
Japan

LYKES BROS STEAMSHIP CO INC Lykes Center, 300 Poydras St, New Orleans,
LA 70130, Tel: (504) 523-6611
(Ocean frt trans)
Lykes Lines Agency Inc., CPO Box 63, Tameike Tokyo Bldg., 4th Fl., Akasaka 1-chome,
Minato-ku, Tokyo 100-91, Japan

R H MACY & CO INC 151 West 34th St, New York, NY 10001, Tel: (212) 695-4400
(Department stores, importers)
R.H. Macy & Co. Inc., Daiwa Bank Semba Bldg., 6th Fl., Minami-ku, Osaka 542, Japan

MALLINCKRODT MEDICAL INC 675 McDonnell Blvd, PO Box 5840, St Louis,
MO 63134, Tel: (314) 895-2000
(Mfr specialty medical prdts)
Mallinckrodt Medical Co. Ltd., Tokyo, Japan

MANPOWER INTL INC 5301 N Ironwood Rd, PO Box 2053, Milwaukee,
WI 53201-2053, Tel: (414) 961-1000
(Temporary help service)
Manpower Japan Co. Ltd., CS Tower 3/F, 11-30 Skasaka 1-chome, Minato-ku, Tokyo 107,
Japan

MARATHON LE TOURNEAU CO PO Box 2307, Longview, TX 75606, Tel: (903) 237-7000
(Mfr heavy constr, mining mach & equip)
C. Itoh & Co. Ltd., 5-1 Kita-Aoyama 2-chome, Minato-ku, Tokyo, Japan

MARKEM CORP 150 Congress St, Keene, NH 03431, Tel: (603) 352-1130
(Marking and printing mach; hot stamping foils)
Markem-Asiatic Co. Inc., Fujikoshi Bldg., 5-23-5 Higashi Gotanda, Shinagawa-ku,
Tokyo 141, Japan

MARSH & McLENNAN COS INC   1166 Ave of the Americas, New York, NY 10036-1011,
Tel: (212) 345-5000
(Insurance)
   Marsh & McLennan Japan Ltd., 522/3 Yurakucho Bldg., 1-10-1 Yuraku-cho, Chiyoda-ku,
   Tokyo 100, Japan

MAXTOR CORP   211 River Oaks Pkwy, San Jose, CA 95134, Tel: (408) 432-1700
(Design/mfr magnetic storage prdts)
   Maxtor Japan Ltd., Tokyo, Japan

MAYFRAN INC   PO Box 43038, Cleveland, OH 44143, Tel: (216) 461-4100
(Mfr conveyors for metal working & refuse)
   Tsubakimoto Mayfran Inc., 5001 Ohno, Tsuchiyama-cho, Kouga-gun, Shiga 528-02, Japan

MCI INTERNATIONAL   2 International Dr, Rye Brook, NY 10573,
Tel: (914) 937-3444
(Telecommunications)
   MCI Intl Japan Co. Ltd., KDD Bldg., P.O. Box 17, 3-2 Nishi Shinjuku 2-chome,
   Shinjuku-ku, Tokyo 163-03, Japan

MEAD CORP   Courthouse Plaza, NE, Dayton, OH 45463, Tel: (513) 222-6323
(Mfr paper, packaging, pulp, lumber & other wood prdts, school & office prdts; electr
pub, distri)
   Mead Packaging KK, Japan
   Mead Paperboard Japan KK, Tokyo, Japan

THE MEARL CORP   320 Old Briarcliff Rd, Briarcliff Manor, NY 10510,
Tel: (914) 923-8500
(Mfr pearlescent luster pigments, mica, decorative iridescent film)
   The Mearl Corp. Japan, Room 802, Mido-Suji Urban-Life Bldg.,
   4-3 Minami Semba 4-chome, Chuo-ku, Osaka 542, Japan

MEASUREX CORP   One Results Way, Cupertino, CA 95014-5991, Tel: (408) 255-1500
(Mfr computer integrated mfg sys)
   Measurex Japan Ltd., Toyo Bldg., 12-20 Jingumae 6-chome, Shibuya-ku, Tokyo 150,
   Japan

MEDTRONIC INC   7000 Central Ave, NE, Minneapolis, MN 55432,
Tel: (612) 574-4000
(Mfr/sale/svce therapeutic medical devices)
   Medtronic Japan Co. Ltd., Shuwa Kioi-cho Park Bldg. 5/F, 3-6 Kioi-cho, Chiyoda-ku,
   Tokyo 102, Japan

MELLON BANK NA   One Mellon Bank Center, Pittsburgh, PA 15258,
Tel: (412) 234-5000
(Commercial & trade banking, foreign exchange)
   Mellon Bank NA, New Yurakucho Bldg., 12-1 Yuraku-cho 1-chome, Chiyoda-ku,
   Tokyo 100, Japan

MEMOREX CORP   San Thomas at Central Expressway, Santa Clara, CA 95052,
Tel: (408) 987-1000
(Magnetic recording tapes, etc)
   Memorex Japan Ltd., Yaesuguchi Kaikan, 3rd Fl., 1-7-20 Yaesu, Chuo-ku, Tokyo, Japan

MEMTEC AMERICA CORP   2033 Greenspring Dr, Timonium, MD 21093,
Tel: (410) 252-0800
(Mfr purification & separation sys & prdts)

(cont)

Memtec Ltd. Japan, 3-1-16 Chigasaki-Minami, Kohoku-ku, Yokohama-shi, Kanagawa 223, Japan

THE MENTHOLATUM CO INC   1360 Niagara St, Buffalo, NY 14213,
  Tel: (716) 882-7660
  (Mfr/distr proprietary medicines, drugs, OTC's)
    Mentholatum Intl. Ltd., 802 Mori Bldg., Nishikubo Sakuragawa-cho, Shiba, Minato-ku, Tokyo 105, Japan

MERCK SHARP & DOHME INTL   PO Box 2000, Rahway, NJ 07065, Tel: (201) 574-4000
  (Pharms, chems & biologicals)
    MSD (Japan) Co. Ltd., Kowa Bldg. 7th Fl., 9-20 Akasaka 1-chome, Minato-ku, Tokyo 107, Japan

METAL-CLADDING INC   PO Box 630, 470 Niagara Way, North Tonawanda, NY 14120,
  Tel: (716) 693-6205
  (FRP tanks & custom constr, scrubbers, odor control equip)
    KAO-Chemical Co., 14-10 Nihonbashi Kayaba-cho 1-chome, Chyo-ku, Tokyo 103, Japan

METALLURG INC   25 E 39th St, New York, NY 10016, Tel: (212) 686-4010
  (Mfr ferrous & nonferrous alloys & metals)
    Metallurg (Far East) Ltd., P.O. Box 5221, Tokyo Intl. 100-31, Tokyo, Japan

METCO DIV OF PERKIN-ELMER   1101 Prospect Ave, PO Box 1006, Westbury,
  NY 11590-0201, Tel: (516) 334-1300
  (Mfr/serv thermal spray coating equip & supplies)
    Daiichi Metco Co. Ltd., Kanda Union Bldg., 20 Kanda Nishiki-cho 3-chome, Chiyoda-ku, Tokyo 101, Japan

MICROSOFT CORP   One Microsoft Way, Redmond, WA 98052-6399,
  Tel: (206) 882-8080
  (Computer software, peripherals & services)
    Microsoft Japan KK, Sasazuka NA Bldg., 50-1 Sasazuka 1-chome, Shibuyo-ku, Tokyo 151, Japan

MICROTEC RESEARCH   2350 Mission College Blvd, Santa Clara, CA 95054,
  Tel: (408) 980-1300
  (Devel/mfr software tools for embedded systems market)
    Nihon Microtec Research KK, Sanbancho MS Bldg., 20 Sanbancho, Chiyoda-ku, Tokyo 102, Japan

MILLIPORE CORP   Ashley Rd, Bedford, MA 01730, Tel: (617) 275-9205
  (Mfr precision filters, hi-performance liquid chromatography instru)
    Niho Millipore Ltd., Dai 5 Koike Bldg., 3-12 Kitashinagawa 1-chome, Shinagawa-ku, Tokyo 140, Japan

MILTON ROY CO   14845 W 64th Ave, PO Box FH, Arvada, CO 80004,
  Tel: (303) 425-0800
  (Med & ind equip, process control instru)
    Milton Roy Co., Takanawa Daiichi Bldg., 9th Fl., 1-41-2 Takanawa, Minato-ku, Tokyo 108, Japan

MINE SAFETY APPLIANCES CO   PO Box 426, Pittsburgh, PA 15230,
  Tel: (421) 273 5000
  (Safety equip, ind filters)
    MSA Japan Ltd., Crest Bldg., 12-8 Roppongi 4-chome, Minatoku, Tokyo 106, Japan

MISSION DRILLING PRODUCTS DIV   PO Box 40402, Houston, TX 77240,
  Tel: (713) 460-6200
  (Oilfield equip, drilling & mining equip, ind valves)
    TRW Mission Japan Inc., 3 Bunsei Bldg., 5-8-1 Toranoman, Minato-ku, Tokyo 105, Japan

MOBIL CORP   3225 Gallows Rd, Fairfax, VA 22037-0001, Tel: (703) 846-3000
  (Petroleum explor & refining, mfr petrol prdts, chems, petrochems)
    Mobil Sekiyu KK, P.O. Box 5010, Tokyo International, Tokyo 100-31, Japan

MOEN INC   377 Woodland Ave, Elyria, OH 44036, Tel: (216) 323-3341
  (Mfr/serv plumbing prdts)
    Stanadyne Ltd., Royal Mansion Bldg., 5-1-1 Shinjuku, Shinjuku-ku, Tokyo 160, Japan

MOLEX INC   2222 Wellington Ct, Lisle, IL 60532, Tel: (708) 969-4550
  (Mfr electronic, electrical & fiber optic interconnection prdts & sys, switches,
  application tooling)
    Molex Inc., 4-21-1 Minami-Naruse, Machida, Tokyo 196, Japan

MONSANTO CO   800 N Lindbergh Blvd, St Louis, MO 63167, Tel: (314) 694-1000
  (Mfr agric & food prdts, chems, plastics, fibers, pharms, process control equip,
  performance material)
    Monsanto Japan Ltd., Kokusai Bldg. 5/F, 1-1 Marunouchi 3-chome, Chiyoda-ku,
    Tokyo 100, Japan

MOOG INC   East Aurora, NY 14052-0018, Tel: (716) 652-2000
  (Mfr precision control components & sys)
    Moog Japan Ltd., 1532 Shindo, Hiratsuka, Kanagawa-ken 254, Japan

SAMUEL MOORE GROUP   1199 S Cillicothe Rd, Aurora, OH 44202,
  Tel: (216) 562-9111
  (Mfr hose, tubing, wire, cables)
    Nitta-Moore Co. Ltd., 8-12 Hommachi 1-chome, Chuo-ku, Osaka, Japan

MOORE PRODUCTS CO   Sumneytown Pike, Spring House, PA 19477,
  Tel: (215) 646-7400
  (Mfr process control instru)
    Moore Products Co. (Japan) KK, Mikuni Bldg. 5/F, 3-6-14 Shibaura, Minato-ku,
    Tokyo 108, Japan

MORGAN GUARANTY TRUST CO   23 Wall St, New York, NY 10260, Tel: (212) 483-2323
  (Banking)
    Morgan Guaranty Trust Co. of New York, Shin Yurakucho Bldg.,
    12-1 Yurakucho 1-chome, Chiyoda-ku, Tokyo 100, Japan

MORRISON & FOERSTER   345 California St, San Francisco, CA 94104-2675,
  Tel: (415) 677-7000
  (Lawyers)
    Morrison & Foerster, AIG Bldg. 7/F, 1-1-3 Marunouchi, Chiyoda-ku, Tokyo 100, Japan

MORTON INTERNATIONAL INC   100 N Riverside Plaza, Chicago, IL 60606-1596,
  Tel: (312) 807-2000
  (Mfr adhesives, coatings, finishes, spec chems, advanced & electr materials, salt,
  airbags)
    Morton International, Premier K1 Bldg., 5th Fl., 1 Kanda Mikura-cho, Chiyoda-ku,
    Tokyo 101, Japan
    Morton Intl. Ltd., Shinjuku Koyo Bldg., 7th Fl., 19-5 Nishishinjuku 1-chome,
    Shinjuku-ku, Tokyo 160, Japan

(cont)

Nippon Bee Chemical Co. Ltd., 2-14 Shodai-Ohtani 1-chome, Hirakata, Osaka 573, Japan
Toray Thiokol Co. Ltd., 3-16 Nihonbashi-Hongokucho 3-chome, Chuo-ku, Tokyo 103, Japan
Toyo-Morton Ltd., Toin Bldg., 8th Fl., 1-12 Shinkawa 15-chome, Chuo-ku, Tokyo 104, Japan

MOTOROLA INC   1303 E Algonquin Rd, Schaumburg, IL 60196, Tel: (708) 576-5000
(Mfr commun equip, semiconductors, cellular phones)
Nippon Motorola Ltd., 5-2-32 Minami Azabu, Minato-ku, Tokyo 106, Japan
Nippon Motorola Ltd., 1 Ohyaji Kofune, Shiokawa-machi, Yama-gun, Fukushima-Ken 969-35, Japan
Nippon Motorola Ltd., 2-4-5 Roppongi, Minato-ku, Tokyo 106, Japan
Tegal Intl., Tamahan Bldg., 1-1 Kugenuma-Higashi, Fujisawa-Shi, Kanagawa, Prefecture 251, Japan

MTS SYSTEMS CORP   14000 Technology Dr, Eden Prairie, MN 55344-2290, Tel: (612) 937-4000
(Devel/mfr mechanical testing & simulation prdts & servs, ind meas & automation instrumentation)
MTS Japan Ltd., Izumikan Gobancho, 12-11 Gobancho, Chiyoda-ku, Tokyo 102, Japan

MULLER & PHIPPS INTL CORP   Box 3994, San Francisco, CA 94119, Tel: (415) 772-5650
(General merchandise)
Muller & Phipps (Japan) Ltd., CPO Box 322, Tokyo 100, Japan
Muller & Phipps Ltd., Central P.O. Box 373, Naha, Okinawa, Japan

MacDERMID INC   245 Freight St, Waterbury, CT 06702, Tel: (203) 575-5700
(Chem processing for metal ind, plastics, electronics cleaners, strippers)
Nippon MacDermid Co. Ltd., 35-5 Sakuradai, Midori-ku, Yokohama-Shi, Kanagawa-Kan, Japan

THE MacNEAL-SCHWENDLER CORP   815 Colorado Blvd, Los Angeles, CA 90041, Tel: (213) 258-9111
(Devel/mfr computer-aided engineering software)
MSC Japan Ltd., Entsuji-Gadelius Bldg., 2-39 Akasaka 5-chome, Minato-ku, Tokyo 107, Japan

McCANN-ERICKSON WORLDWIDE   750 Third Ave, New York, NY 10017, Tel: (212) 697-6000
(Advertising)
McCann-Erickson Hakuhodo Inc., P.O. Box 90, Tokyo 107-91, Japan
McCann-Erickson Hakuhodo Inc., other locations in Japan

McCORMICK & CO INC   18 Loveton Circle, Sparks, MD 21152-6000, Tel: (410) 771-7301
(Mfr/dist/sale seasonings, flavorings, specialty foods)
McCormick-Lion Ltd., 3 Honso 1-chome, Sumida-ku, Tokyo 130, Japan
Stange (Japan) KK, 5-3 Kayabacho 3-chome, Nihonbashi, Chuo-ku, Tokyo 103, Japan

THE McGRAW-HILL COS   1221 Ave of the Americas, New York, NY 10020, Tel: (212) 512-2000
(Books, magazines, info sys, financial serv, broadcast operations)
McGraw-Hill Kogakusha Ltd., 77 Bldg. 7/F, 14-11 Ginza 4-chome, Chuo-ku, Tokyo 104, Japan

McKINSEY & CO INC   55 E 52nd St, New York, NY 10022, Tel: (212) 446-7000
  (Mgmt consultants)
    McKinsey & Co., Juji Bldg., 10th Fl., 2-3 Marunouchi 3-chome, Chiyoda-ku,
      Tokyo 100, Japan
    McKinsey & Co., Osaka, Japan

NACCO INDUSTRIES INC   5875 Landerbrook Dr, Mayfield Hgts, OH 44124-4017,
  Tel: (216) 449-9600
  (Mining/mktg lignite & metals, mfr forklift trucks & small electric appliances,
  specialty retailers)
    NACCO Materials Handling Group, Obu, Japan

NALCO CHEMICAL CO   One Nalco Center, Naperville, IL 60563-1198,
  Tel: (708) 305-1000
  (Chems for water & waste water treatment, oil prod & refining, ind processes;
  water/energy mgmt serv)
    Nalco Japan Co. Ltd., Atlantic Bldg., 5th Fl., 3-3 Azabudai 2-chome, Minato-ku,
      Tokyo 106, Japan

NANOMETRICS INC   310 DeGuigne Dr, Sunnyvale, CA 94086-3906,
  Tel: (408) 746-1600
  (Mfr optical measurement & inspection sys for semiconductor ind)
    Nanometrics Japan Ltd., Shin-isumi 34, Narita-shi, Chiba Ken T286, Japan

NASHUA CORP   44 Franklin St, PO Box 2002, Nashua, NH 03061-2002,
  Tel: (603) 880-2323
  (Mail order film processing)
    Nashua Tokyo/High-C Inc., Onarimon Bldg., 3-23-11 Nishi-Shimbashi, Minato-ku,
      Tokyo 105, Japan

NATCO   PO Box 1710, Tulsa, OK 74101, Tel: (918) 663-9100
  (Mfr/sale/serv oil & gas prdts)
    NATCO Japan Co. Ltd., 20 Kanda Nishikicho 3-chome, Chiyoda-ku, Tokyo 101, Japan

NATIONAL BANK OF DETROIT   611 Woodward, PO Box 116, Detroit, MI 48232,
  Tel: (313) 225-1000
  (Banking)
    Natl. Bank of Detroit, Togin Bldg., 5th Fl., 4-2 Marunouchi 1-chome, Chiyoda-ku,
      Tokyo 100, Japan

NATIONAL BULK CARRIERS INC   1345 Ave of the Americas, New York, NY 10105,
  Tel: (212) 765-3000
  (Real estate development, mgmt serv)
    Natl. Bulk Carriers Inc., Showa-dori 2-chome, Kure City 737, Hiroshima-ken, Japan

NATIONAL DATA CORP   National Data Plaza, Atlanta, GA 30329-2010,
  Tel: (404) 728-2000
  (Info sys & servs for retail, healthcare, govt & corporate mkts)
    National Data Corp., Uchisaiwaicho-Dai Bldg., 1-3-3 Uchisaiwaicho, Chiyoda-ku,
      Tokyo 100, Japan

NATIONAL GYPSUM CO   2001 Rexford Rd., Charlotte, NC 28211,
  Tel: (704) 365-7300
  (Building prdts & servs)
    The Austin Co., Tokyo, Japan

NATIONAL PATENT DEVELOPMENT CORP   9 W 57th St, New York, NY 10019,
Tel: (212) 230-9500
(Mfr/distr medical, health care & specialty prdts)
  Hydron Japan KK, 1-14-18 Shironganedai, Minato-ku, Tokyo 108, Japan

NATIONAL STARCH & CHEMICAL CO   10 Finderne Ave, Bridgewater, NJ 08807-3300,
Tel: (908) 685-5000
(Mfr adhesives & sealants, resins & spec chems, electr materials & adhesives, food
prdts, ind starch)
  Ablestik (Japan) Co. Ltd., Yokohama, Japan
  Kanebo-NSC Ltd., Osaka, Japan
  National Starch & Chemical Co. Ltd., Chiba, Japan

NBD BANK   611 Woodward Ave, Detroit, MI 48226, Tel: (313) 225-1000
(Banking services)
  NBD Bank, Togin Bldg. 5/F, 4-2 Marunouchi 1-chome, Chiyoda-ku, Tokyo 100, Japan

NETMANAGE INC   10725 N De Anza Blvd, Cupertino, CA 95014, Tel: (408) 973-7171
(Devel/mfr computer software applications & tools)
  NetManage Inc., Tokyo, Japan

NEWPORT CORP   PO Box 19607, Irvine, CA 92714, Tel: (714) 863-3144
(Mfr/distr precision components & sys for laser/optical technology, vibration/motion
meas & control)
  KK Newport/Hakato, 1-13 Shinjuku 1-chome, Shinjuku-ku, Tokyo 160, Japan

NEWSWEEK INTL INC   444 Madison Ave, New York, NY 10022, Tel: (212) 350-4000
(Publishing)
  Newsweek Inc., Sumitomo Seimei Aoyama Bldg., 3rd Fl., 3-1-30 Minami-Aoyama,
    Minato-ku, Tokyo 107, Japan

NICOLET INSTRUMENT CORP   5225 Verona Rd, Madison, WI 53711-4495,
Tel: (608) 271-3333
(Mfr infrared spectrometers, oscilloscopes, med electro-diag equip)
  Nicolet Japan Corp., Ryokuchi-Eki Bldg., 6th Fl., 4-1 Terauchi 2-chome, Toyonaka,
    Osaka 560, Japan
  Nicolet Japan Corp., 7-1 Hirakawa-cho 2-chome, Chiyoda-ku, Tokyo 102, Japan
  Nicolet Japan Corp., 17-10 Uchiyama 3-chome, Chikusa-ku, Nagoya 464, Japan

A C NIELSEN CO   Nielsen Plaza, Northbrook, IL 60062-6288, Tel: (708) 498-6300
(Market research)
  A.C. Nielsen Co., Nielsen Bldg., 1-1-71 Nakameguro, Meguro-ku, Tokyo 153, Japan

NORDSON CORP   28601 Clemens Rd, Westlake, OH 44145, Tel: (216) 892-1580
(Mfr ind application equip & packaging mach)
  Nordson KK, 11-13 Kita-Shinagawa 3-chome, Shinagawa-ku, Tokyo 140, Japan

NOVELLUS SYSTEMS INC   81 Vista Montana, San Jose, CA 95134,
Tel: (408) 943-9700
(Mfr advanced processing systems used in fabrication of integrated circuits)
  Nippon Novellus KK, 1-12-3 Kamitsuruma, Sagamihara-shi, Kanagawa-Ken 228, Japan

OAKITE PRODUCTS INC   50 Valley Rd, Berkeley Heights, NJ 07922,
Tel: (908) 464-6900
(Mfr chem prdts for ind cleaning & metal treating)
  Diafloc Co. Ltd., Oakite Div., 5-1 Marunouchi 1-chome, Chiyoda-ku, Tokyo, Japan

OGDEN ENVIRONMENTAL & ENERGY SERVICES CO   3211 Jermantown Rd, Fairfax,
VA 22053, Tel: (703) 246-0500
(Environ & energy consulting svces for commercial clients & govt agencies)
   I.E.A. of Japan, 4 Sumitomo Higashi-Shimbashi Bldg., 9-6 Shimbashi 6-chome,
   Minato-ku, Tokyo 105, Japan

THE OILGEAR CO   2300 S 51st St, Milwaukee, WI 53219, Tel: (414) 327-1700
(Mfr hydraulic power transmission mach)
   The Oilgear Japan Co., 204 Nishikan, Daini Toyoda Bldg., 4-10-27 Meieki,
   Nakamara-ku, Nagoya 450, Japan

OLIN CORP   120 Long Ridge Rd, PO Box 1355, Stamford, CT 06904-1355,
Tel: (203) 356-2000
(Mfr chems, metals, applied physics in elect, defense, aerospace inds)
   Olin Japan Inc., Shiozaki Bldg., 7-1 Hirakawa-cho 2-chome, Chiyoda-ku, Tokyo 102,
   Japan

ONAN CORP   1400 73rd Ave NE, Minneapolis, MN 55432, Tel: (612) 574-5000
(Mfr electric generators, controls & switchgears)
   Onan Intl., 106 Sengokuyama Annex, 12-10 Shantome 1-chome, Chuo-ku, Tokyo 104, Japan

ORIENTAL EXPORTERS INC   2 Pennsylvania Plaza, New York, NY 10001,
Tel: (212) 594-7800
(General merchandise)
   Oriental Exporters (Japan) Ltd., CPO Box 375, 4 Ohtemachi 1-chome, Chiyoda-ku,
   Tokyo, Japan

OSCAR MAYER & CO   PO Box 7188, Madison, WI 53707, Tel: (608) 241-3311
(Meat & food prdts)
   Oscar Mayer & Co. Inc., P.O. Box 55, Kasumigaseki Bldg., Tokyo 100, Japan

OTIS ELEVATOR CO   10 Farm Springs, Farmington, CT 06032, Tel: (860) 676-6528
(Mfr elevators & escalators)
   Nippon Otis Elevator Co., Shinjuku NS Bldg., 17/F, 4-1 Nishishinjuku 2-chome,
   Shinjuku-ku, Tokyo 163, Japan

OWENS-ILLINOIS INC   1 Seagate, Toledo, OH 43666, Tel: (419) 247-5000
(Glass & plastic containers, house- hold & ind prdts, packaging)
   Sasaki-Owens Glass Co. Ltd., 4-9 Nihonbashi Bakuro-cho, Chuo-ku, Tokyo, Japan

PACIFIC ARCHITECTS & ENGINEERS INC   1111 W Sixth St, Los Angeles, CA 90017,
Tel: (213) 481-2311
(Tech engineering serv)
   PAE Intl., Halifax Shiba Bldg., 6th/7th Fl., 3-10 Shiba Park 1-chome, Minato-ku,
   Tokyo 105, Japan

PACIFIC TELESIS GROUP   130 Kearney St, San Francisco, CA 94108,
Tel: (415) 394-3000
(Telecommun & info sys)
   Pacific Telesis Japan KK, Toranomon Cntr. Bldg., 1-16-17 Toranomon, Minato-ku,
   Tokyo 105, Japan

PACKAGING CORP OF AMERICA   1603 Orrington Ave, Evanston, IL 60201-3853,
Tel: (708) 492-5713
(Mfr custom packaging, aluminum & plastic molded fibre, corrugated containers)
   Toyo Ekco Co. Ltd., Sumisei Shimojima Bldg., 3-8 Kitakyuhoji-machi 3-chome,
   Chuo-ku, Osala 541, Japan

PAINEWEBBER GROUP INC   1285 Ave of the Americas, New York, NY 10019,
  Tel: (212) 713-2000
  (Stock brokerage serv & invest)
    PaineWebber Intl., AIU Bldg., 1-3 Marounouchi 1-chome, Chiyoda-ku, Tokyo, Japan

PALL CORP   30 Sea Cliff Ave, Glen Cove, NY 11542, Tel: (516) 671-4000
  (Filters & related fluid clarification equip)
    Nihon Pall Ltd., Tokyo, Japan

PANDUIT CORP   17301 Ridgeland Ave, Tinley Park, IL 60477-0981,
  Tel: (708) 532-1800
  (Mfr elec/electr wiring comps)
    Panduit Corp. (Japan), 31-5 Omori Kita 6-chome, Ota-ku, Tokyo 143, Japan

PARKER HANNIFIN CORP   17325 Euclid Ave, Cleveland, OH 44112,
  Tel: (216) 531-3000
  (Mfr motion-control prdts)
    Parker Hannifin Japan Ltd., 626 Totsuka-cho, Totsuka-ku, Yokohama-shi 244, Japan

THE PARSONS CORP   100 W Walnut St, Pasadena, CA 91124, Tel: (818) 440-2000
  (Engineering & construction)
    Parsons Polytech Inc., Place Astre Bldg. 8/F, 2-3 Azabu Juban 1-chome, Minato-ku,
      Tokyo 106, Japan

PARSONS ENGINEERING SCIENCE INC   100 W Walnut St, Pasadena, CA 91124,
  Tel: (818) 440-6000
  (Environmental engineering)
    Parsons Engineering Science Inc., c/Parsons Polytech Inc.,
      Kyobashi Maruki Bldg. 3/F, 17-9 Kyobashi 2-chome, Chuo-ku, Tokyo 104, Japan

PDA ENGINEERING   2975 Redhill Ave, Costa Mesa, CA 92626, Tel: (714) 540-8900
  (Computer-aided engineering software & services, advanced materials technology &
  training)
    Nippon PDA Engineering KK, Madre Matsuda Bldg. 4/F, 4-13 Kioi-cho, Chiyoda-ku,
      Tokyo 102, Japan

PEAVEY CO/CONAGRA TRADING COS   730 Second Ave, Minneapolis, MN 55402,
  Tel: (612) 370-7500
  (Flour, feeds, seeds)
    Conagra Trading Co., Tokyo, Japan

PEPSICO INC   700 Anderson Hill Rd, Purchase, NY 10577-1444,
  Tel: (914) 253-2000
  (Beverages, snack foods, restaurants)
    Japan Frito-Lay Ltd., Japan

THE PERKIN-ELMER CORP   761 Main Ave, Norwalk, CT 06859-0001,
  Tel: (203) 762-1000
  (Mfr analytical instrumentation sys, high performance thermal spray coatings)
    Perkin-Elmer Japan Ltd., Yokohama Nishiguchi K.N. Bldg., 2-8-4 Kita-Siwai,
      Nishi-ku, Japan

PETERSON AMERICAN CORP   21200 Telegraph Rd, Southfield, MI 48034,
  Tel: (810) 799-5400
  (Mfr springs & wire prdts, metal stampings, ind machinery)
    K.P. Products Corp., 252-5 Katsu-Uri-cho, Mooka City, Tochigi Prefecture, Japan

PETROLITE CORP   369 Marshall Ave, St Louis, MO 63119-1897,
Tel: (314) 961-3500
(Mfr/prod spec chem treating programs, performance-enhancing additives & related
equip & svces)
   Toyo-Petrolite Co., Toin Bldg., 12-15 Shinkawa 2-chome, Chuo-ku, Tokyo 104, Japan

PFIZER INC   235 E 42nd St, New York, NY 10017-5755, Tel: (212) 573-2323
(Mfr healthcare products)
   Pfizer KK, Japan
   Pfizer Oral Care Inc., Japan
   Pfizer Pharmaceuticals Inc., Japan
   Pfizer Shoji Co. Ltd., Japan
   Schneider Japan KK, Japan

PHELPS DODGE CORP   2600 N Central Ave, Phoenix, AZ 85004-3014,
Tel: (602) 234-8100
(Copper, minerals, metals & spec engineered prdts for trans & elect mkts)
   Columbian Carbon Japan Ltd., 8-12 Nihonbashi Haridomecho 1-chome, Chuo-ku,
   Tokyo 103, Japan

PHILIP MORRIS COS INC   120 Park Ave, New York, NY 10017, Tel: (212) 880-5000
(Mfr cigarettes, food prdts, beer)
   Philip Morris KK, Akasaka Twin Tower, Main Tower 14/F, 2-17-22 Akasaka, Minato-ku,
   Tokyo 107, Japan

PHILIPP BROTHERS CHEMICALS INC   1 Parker Plaza, Fort Lee, NJ 07029,
Tel: (201) 944-6020
(Mfr ind & agric chems)
   Philipp Bros. Far East Inc., 933 Kokusai Bldg., 1-1 Marunouchi 3-chome, Chiyoda-ku,
   Tokyo 100, Japan

PHILLIPS PETROLEUM CO   Phillips Bldg, Bartlesville, OK 74004,
Tel: (918) 661-6600
(Crude oil, natural gas, liquefied petroleum gas, gasoline & petro-chems)
   Phillips Petroleum Intl. Ltd., 606 Shin Tokyo Bldg., 3-1 Marunouchi 3-chome,
   Chiyoda-ku, Tokyo 100, Japan

PICTURETEL CORP   222 Rosewood Dr, Danvers, MA 01923, Tel: (508) 762-5000
(Mfr video conferencing systems, network bridging & multiplexing prdts, system
peripherals)
   PictureTel Japan Inc., URD Bldg. 5/F, 3-19-6 Shirogane-dai, Minato-ku, Tokyo 108,
   Japan

PILLAR INDUSTRIES   N92 W15800 Megal Dr, Menomonee Falls, WI 53051,
Tel: (414) 255-6470
(Mfr induction heating & melting equip)
   Pillar Orient Corp., 1-11-5 Hiroo 1308, Shibuya-ku, Tokyo 150, Japan

PINKERTON SECURITY & INVESTIGATION SERVICES   6727 Odessa Ave, Van Nuys,
CA 91406-5796, Tel: (818) 373-8800
(Security & investigation services)
   Pinkerton Consulting & Investigation Services, Matsuoka Kudan Bldg.,
   8-2-2 Kudan Minami, Chiyoda-ku, Tokyo 102, Japan

PITNEY BOWES INC   Wheeler Dr, Stamford, CT 06926-0700, Tel: (203) 356-5000
(Mfr postage meters, mailroom equip, copiers, bus supplies; bus servs)
   Dodwell, Kowa Bldg. 35, 14-14 Akasaka 1-chome, Minato-ku, Tokyo 107, Japan

PITTSBURGH CORNING CORP   800 Presque Isle Dr, Pittsburgh, PA 15239-2799,
 Tel: (412) 327-6100
 (Mfr glass block, cellular glass insulation)
   Nippon Pittsburgh Corning, Sankyo Bldg. 6/F, 2-11-2 Kayabacho, Nihonbashi, Chuo-ku,
   Tokyo 103, Japan

PLIBRICO CO   1800 Kingsbury St, Chicago, IL 60614, Tel: (312) 549-7014
 (Refractories, engineering, constr)
   Plibrico Japan Ltd., 33-7 Shiba 5-chome, Minato-ku, Tokyo, Japan

PLOUGH INC   PO Box 377, Memphis, TN 38151, Tel: (901) 320-2011
 (Proprietary drug & cosmetic prdts)
   Coppertone (Japan) Ltd., P.O. Box 36, Akasaka, Tokyo, Japan

POLAROID CORP   549 Technology Sq, Cambridge, MA 02139, Tel: (617) 386-2000
 (Photographic equip & supplies, optical prdts)
   Nippon Polaroid KK, 30 Mori Bldg., 2-2 Torinomon 3-chome, Minato-ku, Tokyo 105,
   Japan

POTTERS INDUSTRIES INC   PO Box 840, Valley Forge, PA 19482-0840,
 Tel: (610) 651-4700
 (Mfr glass spheres for road marking & ind applications)
   Toshiba-Ballotini Co. Ltd., Meguro Suda Bldg. 6/F, 9-1 Meguro-ku, Tokyo 153, Japan

PPG INDUSTRIES   One PPG Place, Pittsburgh, PA 15272, Tel: (412) 434-3131
 (Mfr flat glass, fiber glass, chems, coatings)
   Asahi-Penn Chemical Co. Ltd., Chiyoda-ku, Tokyo, Japan
   PPG Industries Asia/Pacific Ltd., Takanawa Court, 13-1 Takanawa 3-chome, Minato-ku,
   Tokyo 108, Japan

PRATT & LAMBERT INC   PO Box 22, Buffalo, NY 14240-0022, Tel: (716) 873-6000
 (Mfr paints, coatings, adhesives)
   Sanko-Stevens Chemicals Inc., 1-12 Akasaka 1-chome, Minato-ku, Tokyo 107, Japan

PRECISION VALVE CORP   PO Box 309, Yonkers, NY 10702, Tel: (914) 969-6500
 (Mfr aerosol valves)
   Precision Valve Japan Ltd., 76 Niizo, Toda-shi, Saitama-Ken 335, Japan

PREMARK INTL INC   1717 Deerfield Rd, Deerfield, IL 60015, Tel: (708) 405-6000
 (Mfr/sale diversified consumer & coml prdts)
   Japan Tupperware Co. Ltd., Bungei-Shunju Bldg., 3-23 Kioicho, Chiyoda-ku, Tokyo,
   Japan

PREMIX INC   PO Box 281, N Kingsville, OH 44068, Tel: (216) 224-2181
 (Mfr molded fiber glass, reinforced thermoset molding compounds & plastic parts)
   Dia-Premix Co. Ltd., 1-2 Ushikawa-Dori 4-chome, Toyohashi City, Aichi 440, Japan
   Dia-Premix Co. Ltd., 3-19 Kyobashi 2-chome, Chuo-ku, Tokyo 104, Japan
   Takeda Chemical Industries Ltd., Chemical Prdts Div., 27 Doshomachi 2-chome,
   Higashi-ku, Osaka, Japan
   Takeda Chemical Industries Ltd., Chemical Prdts. Div., 2-17-85 Juso-Honmachi,
   Yodogawa-ku, Osaka 532, Japan

PROCTER & GAMBLE CO   One Procter & Gamble Plaza, Cincinnati, OH 45202,
 Tel: (513) 983-1100
 (Personal care, food, laundry, cleaning & ind prdts)

Procter & Gamble Sunhome Co. Ltd., Asahi Seimei-kan 50, Koraibashi 5-chome, Higashi-ku, Osaka 541, Japan

PRUDENTIAL INSURANCE CO OF AMERICA   751 Broad St, Newark, NJ 07102,
   Tel: (201) 802-6000
   (Insurance, financial services)
      Sony Prudential Life Insurance Co. Ltd., 1-1 Minami Aoyama 1-chome, Minato-ku, Tokyo 107, Japan

QMS INC   One Magnum Pass, Mobile, AL 36618, Tel: (205) 633-4300
   (Mfr monochrome & color computer printers)
      QMS Japan Inc., Shiba Dai-ichi Bldg., 5-3-2 Shiba, Minato-ku, Tokyo 108, Japan

QUAKER CHEMICAL CORP   Elm & Lee Sts, Conshohocken, PA 19428-0809,
   Tel: (610) 832-4000
   (Mfr chem specialties; total fluid mgmt services)
      Nippon Quaker Chemical Ltd., 1-3 Shibukawa-cho 2-chome, Yao City, Osaka, Japan

QUAKER STATE CORP   225 E John Carpenter Frwy, Irving, TX 75062,
   Tel: (214) 868-0400
   (Mfr motor oil, lubricants, automotive chems, waxes)
      Quaker State Japan Co. Ltd., Kairaku Bldg., 6-5-12 Soto Kanda, Chiyoda-ku, Tokyo 101, Japan

QUIGLEY CO INC   235 E 42nd St, New York, NY 10017, Tel: (212) 573-3444
   (Mfr refractory specs, application equip)
      Quigley Div. Pfizer MSP KK, Shinjuku Mitsui Bldg., P.O. Box 316, Shinjuku-ku, Tokyo 163, Japan

RADIUS INC   1710 Fortune Dr, San Jose, CA 95131, Tel: (408) 434-1010
   (Mfr graphic interface cards, displays, accelerators & multiprocessing software)
      Radius KK, Yanaba Bldg. 5/F, 6-7-10 Roppongi, Minato-ku, Tokyo, Japan

RANCO INC   555 Metro Pl N, PO Box 248, Dublin, OH 43017, Tel: (614) 764-3733
   (Controls for appliance, automotive, comfort, commercial & consumer mkts)
      Ranco Japan Ltd., Shiozaki Bldg., 7-2-2 Hirakawa-cho, Chiyoda-ku, Tokyo 102, Japan

RANSBURG CORP   3939 W 56th St, Indianapolis, IN 46208, Tel: (317) 298-5000
   (Mfr electrostatic coating sys)
      Ransburg-Gema KK, 3-5-3 Higashi-Rokugo, Ota-ku, Tokyo 144, Japan
      Simco Japan Inc., 12-12 Sumiyoshi 1-chome, Minami-Machi, Higashinada-ku, Kobe 658, Japan

RAYCHEM CORP   300 Constitution Dr, Menlo Park, CA 94025, Tel: (415) 361-3333
   (Devel/mfr/mkt materials science products for electronics, telecommunications & industry)
      KK Raychem, Nagoya Chogin Bldg. 9/F, 1-17-19 Marunouchi, Naka-ku, Nagoya 460, Japan
      KK Raychem, also in Osaka, Sapporo & Yokohama, Japan

RAYTHEON CO   141 Spring St, Lexington, MA 02173, Tel: (617) 862-6600
   (Mfr divers electronics, appliances, aviation, energy & environ prdts; publishing, ind & constr servs)
      New Japan Radio Co. Ltd., 5 Mitsuya-Toranomon Bldg., 22-14 Toranomon, Minato-ku, Tokyo 105, Japan

RECOGNITION EQUIPMENT INC   PO Box 660204, Dallas, TX 75266-0204,
  Tel: (214) 579-6000
  (Mfr hi-perf document recognition sys, image & workflow software; related customer serv)
    Recognition Equipment (Japan), 6 Kowa Bldg., 15-21 Nishi-Azabu 4-chome, Minato-ku, Tokyo 106, Japan

REDKEN LABORATORIES INC   6625 Variel Ave, Canoga Park, CA 91303,
  Tel: (818) 992-2700
  (Mfr hair & skin care prdts)
    Nihon Redken KK, Hirakawa-chuo Bldg., 2-4-16 Hirakawa-chuo, Chiyoda-ku, Tokyo, Japan

REFAC TECHNOLOGY DEVELOPMENT CORP   122 E 42nd St, #4000, New York, NY 10168,
  Tel: (212) 687-4741
  (Consult, intl tech transfer, foreign trade, power supplies)
    REFAC Intl. Japan Ltd., 19 Mori Bldg., 2-20 Toranomon 1-chome, Tokyo 109, Japan

REGAL WARE INC   1675 Reigle Dr, PO Box 395, Kewaskum, WI 53040-0395,
  Tel: (414) 626-2121
  (Mfr cookware, small electrical appliances, water purification & filtration prdts for home)
    Regal Japan Co. Ltd., Taishoseimei Nishiki Bldg., 18-24 Nishiki 1-chome, Naka-ku, Nagoya 460, Japan

RELIANCE ELECTRIC CO   24701 Euclid Ave, Cleveland, OH 44117,
  Tel: (216) 266-7000
  (Equip & sys for ind automation, telecom equip)
    Reliance Electric Ltd., 3-2 Fakuura 2-chome, Kanazana-ku, Yokohama 326, Japan

RELIANCE GROUP INC   55 E 52nd St, New York, NY 10055, Tel: (212) 909-1100
  (Financial serv, ins, mgmt serv)
    Moody-Tottrup Intl. Ltd., 5 Kowa Bldg., 15-23 Nishi Azabu 4-chome, Minato-ku, Tokyo 106, Japan

REMINGTON PRODUCTS INC   60 Main St, Bridgeport, CT 06604, Tel: (203) 367-4400
  (Mfr home appliances, electric shavers)
    Remington Japan Ltd., Central 246 Bldg., 12-13 Minami Aoyama 2-chome, Minato-ku, Tokyo 107, Japan

REPUBLIC NATIONAL BANK OF DALLAS   310 N Ervay St, Dallas, TX 75265,
  Tel: (214) 653-5000
  (Banking)
    Republic National Bank of Dallas, 601 Yurakucho Bldg., 10-1 Yurakucho 1-chome, Chiyoda-ku, Tokyo 100, Japan

REPUBLIC NEW YORK CORP   452 Fifth Ave, New York, NY 10018,
  Tel: (212) 525-6901
  (Banking)
    Republica National Bank of New York, Tokyo, Japan

REVLON INC   625 Madison Ave, New York, NY 10022, Tel: (212) 527-4000
  (Mfr cosmetics, fragrances, toiletries, beauty care prdts)
    Revlon KK, 2-3 Minami-Aoyama 2-chome, Minato-ku, Tokyo 107, Japan

RHEOMETRIC SCIENTIFIC INC   1 Possumtown Rd, Piscataway, NJ 08854,
  Tel: (908) 560-8550
  (Design/mfr rheological instruments & systems)
    Rheometric Scientific F.E. Ltd., 19-6 Yanagibashi 2-chome, Taito-ku, Tokyo 111,
    Japan

RHONE-POULENC RORER INC   PO Box 1200, Collegeville, PA 19426-0107,
  Tel: (215) 454-8000
  (R&D/mfr human pharmaceuticals)
    Kyoritzu Pharmaceutical Industries Ltd., Kaminoyama City, Japan

RICH PRODUCTS CORP   1 West Ferry, Buffalo, NY 14213, Tel: (716) 878-8000
  (Mfr non-dairy prdts)
    Rich Products Corp., Ginza-Yamamato Bldg., 16-11 Ginza 6-chome, Chuo-ku, Tokyo 104,
    Japan

RIDGE TOOL CO   400 Clark St, Elyria, OH 44035, Tel: (216) 323-5581
  (Hand & power tools for working pipe, drain cleaning equip, etc)
    Ridge Div. Emerson Japan Ltd., Kobe, Japan

RIGHT ASSOCIATES   1818 Market St, 14th Fl, Philadelphia, PA 19103-3614,
  Tel: (215) 988-1588
  (Outplacement & human resources consult servs)
    Right Associates, 1-5 Hakozaki-cho Nihonbashi, Chuo-ku, Tokyo 103, Japan

RJR NABISCO INC   1301 Ave of the Americas, New York, NY 10019,
  Tel: (212) 258-5600
  (Mfr consumer packaged food prdts & tobacco prdts)
    R.J. Reynolds/MC Tobacco Co. Ltd., 3-6 Minami-Aoyama 7-chome, Minato-ku, Tokyo 107,
    Japan

RMS GROUP INC   43-59 10th St, Long Island City, NY 11101, Tel: (212) 684-5470
  (Technology-transfer development & sales)
    Deltac, Daihatsu Bldg. 4-11 Higashi Temma 2-chome, Kita-ku, Osaka, Japan

A H ROBINS CO INC   1407 Cummings Dr, PO Box 26609, Richmond, VA 23261-6609,
  Tel: (804) 257-2000
  (Mfr ethical pharms & consumer prdts)
    A.H. Robins Intl. Co., Dai 7 Chuo Bldg., 26-1 Hamamatsu-cho 1-chome, Minato-ku,
    Tokyo 105, Japan

ROCK OF AGES CORP   PO Box 482, Barre, VT 05641-0482, Tel: (802) 476-3115
  (Quarrier; dimension granite blocks, memorials, precision industrial granite)
    Rock of Ages Asia Corp., 3-8 Uchihonmachi 2-chome, Chuo-ku, Osaka 540, Japan

ROCKWELL INTL CORP   2201 Seal Beach Blvd, PO Box 4250, Seal Beach,
  CA 90740-8250, Tel: (310) 797-3311
  (Prdts & serv for aerospace, automotive, electronics, graphics & automation inds)
    Allen-Bradley Japan Co. Ltd., 8/F Shinkawa Sanko Bldg., 1-3-17 Shinkawa, Chuo-ku,
    Tokyo 104, Japan
    Allen-Bradley Japan Co. Ltd., also in Aichi, Nagoya & Osaka, Japan
    Rockwell Graphic Systems-Japan Corp., Mitsuya Toranomon Bldg.,
    22-14 Toranomon 1-chome, Minato-ku, Tokyo 105, Japan
    Rockwell Intl. Japan Co. Ltd., Sogo Hanzomon Bldg., 1-7 Kojimachi, Chiyoda-ku,
    Tokyo 102, Japan

ROGERS CORP   One Technology Dr, Rogers, CT 06263, Tel: (203) 774-9605
(Mfr flexible, molded, die-stamped & microwave circuits; engineered polymer prdts)
   Rogers Japan Inc., Svax Hamamatsu-cho II Bldg., 2-1-16 Hamamatsu-cho, Minato-ku,
   Tokyo 105, Japan

ROHM AND HAAS CO   100 Independence Mall West, Philadelphia, PA 19106,
Tel: (215) 592-3000
(Mfr ind & agric chems, plastics)
   Rohm and Haas Japan KK, Kaisei Bldg., 4th Fl., 8-10 Azabudai 1-chome, Minato-ku,
   Tokyo 106, Japan

ROSS OPERATING VALVE CO   PO Box 7015, Troy, MI 48007, Tel: (810) 362-1250
(Mfr air valves, pneumatic controls & accessories)
   Ross Asia KK, 2-3-14 Kanumadai, Sagamihara-shi, Kanagawa 229, Japan

ROSTONE CORP   2450 Sagamore Pkwy S, PO Box 7497, Lafayette, IN 47902,
Tel: (317) 474-2421
(Custom molded glass, reinforced thermoset polyester prdts)
   Asahi Glass Co. Ltd., 1-2 Marunouchi 2-chome, Chiyoda-ku, Tokyo, Japan

RUBBERMAID OFFICE PRODUCTS GROUP   1427 William Blount Dr, Maryville,
TN 37801, Tel: (615) 977-5477
(Mfr sign boards, office furniture & accessories)
   Rubbermaid Office Products of Japan, Tenkoh Bldg., 4th Fl., 220 Sakai, Atsugi City,
   Kanagawa, Japan

RUDER FINN INC   301 E 57th St, New York, NY 10022, Tel: (212) 593-6400
(Public relations serv, broadcast commun)
   Ruder Finn Japan, Akasaka Q Bldg. 207, 9-5 Akasake 7-chome, Minato-ku, Tokyo 107,
   Japan

RUSSELL REYNOLDS ASSOCIATES INC   200 Park Ave, New York, NY 10166,
Tel: (212) 351-2000
(Exec recruiting services)
   Russell Reynolds Assoc. Inc., Time & Life Bldg., 3-6 Ohtemachi 2-chome, Chiyoda-ku,
   Tokyo 100, Japan

SALEM CORP   PO Box 2222, Pittsburgh, PA 15230, Tel: (412) 923-2200
(Mfr ind furnaces, coal processing equip, metal finishing equip)
   Nippon-Herr Co. Ltd., Tokyo, Japan

SALOMON BROTHERS INC   7 World Trade Center, New York, NY 10048,
Tel: (212) 783-7000
(Securities dealers & underwriters)
   Salomon Bros., Fukoku-Seimei Bldg., 2-2 Uchsaiwai-cho 2-chome, Chiyoda-ku, Tokyo,
   Japan

W B SAUNDERS CO   Curtis Cntr, Independence Sq W, Philadelphia, PA 19106,
Tel: (215) 238-7800
(Med & tech book publishers)
   W.B. Saunders Co., Ichibancho Central Bldg., 22-1 Ichibancho, Chiyoda-ku,
   Tokyo 102, Japan

SCHENECTADY INTERNATIONAL INC   PO Box 1046, Schenectady, NY 12301,
Tel: (518) 370-4200
(Mfr elec insulating varnishes, enamels, phenolic resins, alkylphenols)

Nisshoku Schenectady Kagaku Inc., 4-1-1 Koraibashi, Chuo-ku, Osaka 541, Japan
Yuka-Schenectady Co. Ltd., Mitsubishi Bldg., 5-2 Marunuchi 2-chome, Chiyoda-ku, Tokyo 100, Japan

R P SCHERER CORP   2075 W Big Beaver Rd, Troy, MI 48084, Tel: (810) 649-0900
(Mfr soft gelatin & two-piece hard shell capsules)
P.R. Scherer KK, Shin Tokyo Akasaka Bldg., 9-25 Akasaka 4-chome, Minato-ku, Tokyo 107, Japan

SCHERING INTL   PO Box 500, Kenilworth, NJ 07033, Tel: (201) 558-4000
(Pharms, medicines, toiletries, cosmetics, human & animal health prdts)
Essex Nippon KK (Schering Corp. USA), CPO Box 1235, Osaka 530-91, Japan

SCHLEGEL CORP   1555 Jefferson Rd, PO Box 23197, Rochester, NY 14692-3197, Tel: (716) 427-7200
(Mfr engineered perimeter sealing systems for residential & commercial constr)
Schlegel Engineering KK, 4/F Iwanami Shoten Annex, 3-1 Kanda Jinbocho 2-chome, Chiyoda-ku, Tokyo 101, Japan

SCHULLER INTL INC   PO Box 5108, Denver, CO 80217-5108, Tel: (303) 978-4900
(Mfr fiberglass insulations, roofing prdts & sys, fiberglass mat & reinforcements, filtration mats)
Schuller Intl. Japan, Neyasu #1 Bldg. 3/F, 1-21 Kanda Nishikicho, Chiyoda-ku, Tokyo 101, Japan

SEA-LAND SERVICE INC   150 Allen Rd, Liberty Corner, NJ 07920, Tel: (201) 558-6000
(Container transport)
Sea-Land Service Inc., CPO Box 1325, Tokyo 100-91, Japan
Sea-Land Service Inc., Osaka, Kobe, Nagoya & Yokohama, Japan

SEALED AIR CORP   Park 80 Plaza E, Saddle Brook, NJ 07662-5291, Tel: (201) 791-7600
(Mfr protective packaging prdts)
Instapak Ltd., 3-20-5 Shiba, Minato-ku, Tokyo 105, Japan
Instapak Ltd., 2-53 Kamioka-cho, Meito-ku, Nagoya, Japan
Instapak Ltd., Kano Bldg., 2-5-14 Nanbanaka, Naniwa-ku, Osaka, Japan

SEALOL INC   Warwick Industrial Park, PO Box 2158, Providence, RI 02905, Tel: (401) 781-4700
(Mfr seals, joints, valves)
Engle EG&G, Kokuryu Shibakoen Bldg., Minato-ku, Tokyo 105, Japan

G D SEARLE & CO   5200 Old Orchard Rd, Skokie, IL 60077, Tel: (708) 982-7000
(Mfr pharms, health care & optical prdts, specialty chems)
Searle Yakuhin KK, Miki Sangyo Bldg., 12-23 Kitahorie 3-chome, P.O. Box 550-91, Nishi-ku, Osaka 550, Japan

SELAS CORP OF AMERICA   2034 S Limekiln Pike, Dresher, PA 19025, Tel: (215) 646-6600
(Mfr heat treating equip for metal, glass, ceramic & chem inds)
Nippon Selas Co. Ltd., 4-3 Arakawa 7-chome, Arakawa-ku, Tokyo 116, Japan

SENCO PRODUCTS INC   8485 Broadwell Rd, Cincinnati, OH 45244, Tel: (513) 388-2000
(Mfr ind nailers, staplers, fasteners & accessories)

(cont)

Senco Products (Japan) Ltd., Wakasugi Grand Bldg. 11-D, 25-5 Tenjinbashi 2-chome, Kita-ku, Osaka 530, Japan

SEQUENT COMPUTER SYSTEMS INC   15450 SW Koll Pkwy, Beaverton, OR 97006-6063,
Tel: (503) 626-5700
(Mfr symmetric multiprocessing technology computers)
Sequent Computers Japan Co. Ltd., Marumasu Kojimachi Bldg., 3-3 Kojimachi, Chiyoda-ku, Tokyo 102, Japan

THE SERVICEMASTER CO   One Servicemaster Way, Downers Grove, IL 60515,
Tel: (708) 964-1300
(Mgmt serv to health care, school & ind facilities; divers residential & commercial services)
ServiceMaster Japan Inc., PJ Bldg., 22 Kaikyo-cho, Shinjuku-ku, Tokyo 160, Japan

SHAKESPEARE FISHING TACKLE GROUP   611 Shakespeare Rd, Columbia, SC 29204,
Tel: (803) 754-7000
(Mfr fishing tackle)
Shakespeare Japan Ltd., Nishiwaki Bldg., 1 Kohjimachi 4-chome, Chiyoda ku, Tokyo, Japan

SHEARMAN & STERLING   599 Lexington Ave, New York, NY 10022-6069,
Tel: (212) 848-4000
(Lawyers)
Shearman & Sterling, Fukoku Seimei Bldg. 5/F, 2-2-2 Uchisaiwaicho, Chiyoda-ku, Tokyo 100, Japan

SHIPLEY CO INC   455 Forest St, Marlborough, MA 01752, Tel: (508) 481-7950
(Mfr chems for printed circuit boards & microelectronic mfg)
Shipley Far East Ltd., Nishidai NC Bldg., 1-83-1 Takashimadaira, Itabashi-ku, Tokyo 175, Japan

SIGNETICS CORP   PO Box 3409, Sunnyvale, CA 94088-3409, Tel: (408) 991-2000
(Solid state circuits)
Signetics Japan Ltd., 25 Kowa Bldg., 8-7 Sanban-cho, Chiyoda-ku, Tokyo 102, Japan

SIGNODE PACKAGING SYSTEMS   3600 W Lake Ave, Glenview, IL 60025,
Tel: (708) 724-6100
(Mfr packaging systems)
Signode KK, Sannomiya Intl. Bldg., 1-30 Hamabe-dori 2-chome, Chuo-ku, Kobe 651, Japan

THE SIMCO CO INC   2257 N Penn Rd, Hatfield, PA 19440-1998,
Tel: (215) 248-2171
(Mfr apparatus for electrostatic charge neutralization)
The Simco Co., 12-12 Sumiyoshi Minami-machi 1-chome, Higashinada-ku, Kobe 658, Japan

SIMON & SCHUSTER INC   1230 Ave of the Americas, New York, NY 10020,
Tel: (212) 698-7000
(Publisher)
Prentice-Hall of Japan Inc., Jochi Kojimachi Bldg., 1-25 Kojimachi 6-chome, Chiyoda-ku, Tokyo 102, Japan

SIMPSON INVESTMENT CO INC   1201 3rd Ave, #4900, Seattle, WA 98101,
Tel: (206) 224-5000
(Paper, pulp & saw mills, wood prdts)

Simpson Far East KK, 2 Onishi Bldg., 1-6 Toranomon 4-chome, Minato-ku, Tokyo 105, Japan

SNAP-ON TOOLS CORP   2801 80th St, Kenosha, WI 53141-1410, Tel: (414) 656-5200
(Mfr automotive & ind maint serv tools)
   Snap-On Tools Japan KK (SOJ), 8-10 Shinkiba 1-chome, Kotoh-ku, Tokyo 136, Japan

SONOCO PRODUCTS CO   North Second St, PO Box 160, Hartsville, SC 29550,
Tel: (803) 383-7000
(Mfr packaging for consumer & ind mkt)
   Showa Products Co. Ltd., Nittochi Dojima Hama, 4-19 Dojima-Hama 1-chome, Kita-ku,
   Osaka 530, Japan
   Showa Products Co. Ltd., other locations in Japan

SOUNDESIGN CORP   Harborside Finance Ctr, 400 Plaza 2, Jersey City, NJ 07311,
Tel: (201) 434-1050
(Radios, electronic prdts)
   Soundesign Corp. Ltd., 9-14 Nihonbashi 2-chome, Chuo-ku, Tokyo, Japan

SPRAYING SYSTEMS CO   PO Box 7900, Wheaton, IL 60188, Tel: (708) 665-5000
(Fabricated metal prdts)
   Spraying Systems Co. Japan, 5-10-18 Higashi-Gotanda, Shinagawa-ku, Tokyo 141, Japan

SPRINGS INDUSTRIES INC   205 N White St, PO Box 70, Fort Mill, SC 29716,
Tel: (803) 547-1500
(Mfr & sales home furnishings, finished fabrics, ind textiles)
   Asahi-Schwebel Co. Ltd., Imperial Tower, 1-1 Uchisaiwai-cho, Chiyoda-ku, Tokyo 100,
   Japan

SPRINT INTERNATIONAL   12490 Sunrise Valley Dr, Reston, VA 22096,
Tel: (703) 689-6000
(Telecommunications)
   Sprint Japan Inc., 21-13 Himonya 4-chome, Meguro-ku, Tokyo 152, Japan

SPS TECHNOLOGIES INC   301 Highland Ave, Jenkintown, PA 19046-2630,
Tel: (215) 572-3000
(Mfr aerospace & ind fasteners, tightening sys, magnetic materials, superalloys)
   SPS/Unbrako KK, 25 Ichibancho, Chiyoda-ku, Tokyo 102, Japan

SPSS INC   444 N Michigan Ave, Chicago, IL 60611, Tel: (312) 329-2400
(Mfr statistical software)
   SPSS Japan Inc., AY Bldg., 3-2-2 Kitaaoyama, Minato-ku, Tokyo 107, Japan

SPX CORP   700 Terrace Point Dr, PO Box 3301, Muskegon, MI 49443-3301,
Tel: (616) 724-5000
(Mfr spec service tools, engine & drive-train parts)
   Kent-Moore Japan (JATEK), Dai-Ni Maruzen Bldg. 8/F, 9-2 Nihonbashi 3-chome,
   Chuo-ku, Tokyo 103, Japan
   RSV Corp., 4-38 Hokuto-cho, Kashiwazaki, Nigata 945, Japan
   Robinair Japan, c/o JATEK Ltd., Dai-Ni Maruzen Bldg., 9/2 Nihonbashi 3-chome,
   Chuo-ku, Tokyo 103, Japan

SRI INTL   333 Ravenswood Ave, Menlo Park, CA 94025-3493, Tel: (415) 326-6200
(Intl consulting & research)
   SRI East Asia, Shin-Nikko Bldg., East Wing 15/F, 10-1 Toranoman 2-chome, Minato-ku,
   Tokyo 105, Japan

STANDARD & POOR'S CORP   25 Broadway, New York, NY 10004, Tel: (212) 208-8000
(Invest, fin, economic & mktg info)
    Standard & Poor's Corp., Nihon Keisa Shambun, 5 Otemachi 1-chome, Chiyoda-ku,
      Tokyo, Japan

STATE STREET BANK & TRUST CO   225 Franklin St, Boston, MA 02101,
    Tel: (617) 786-3000
(Banking & financial services)
    State Street Trust & Banking Co. Ltd., Toranomon Mori 37 Bldg. 5/F,
      2-5-1 Toranomon, Minato-ku, Tokyo 105, Japan

STEELCASE INC   901 44th St SE, Grand Rapids, MI 49508, Tel: (616) 247-2710
(Mfr office, computer-support & systems furniture)
    Steelcase Japan Ltd., 32 Kowa Bldg., 5-2-32 Minami-Azabu, Minato-ku, Tokyo 106,
      Japan

STEINER CORP   505 E South Temple St, Salt Lake City, UT 84102,
    Tel: (801) 328-8831
(Linen supply service)
    Nippon Steiner Co. Ltd., 6-1 Ohtemachi 1-chome, Chiyoda-ku, Tokyo 100, Japan

STERLING SOFTWARE INC   8080 N Central Expy, #1100, Dallas, TX 75206-1895,
    Tel: (214) 891-8600
(Sales/serv software prdts; tech servs)
    Sterling Software Intl., Trio Akasaka Bldg. 4/F, 16-20 Akasaka 2-chome, Minato-ku,
      Tokyo 107, Japan

STIEFEL LABORATORIES INC   255 Alhambra Circle, Coral Gables, FL 33134,
    Tel: (305) 443-3807
(Mfr pharmaceuticals, dermatological specialties)
    Stiefel Laboratories Japan Inc., 704 Ichibancho Central Bldg., 22-1 Ichiban-cho,
      Chiyoda-ku, Tokyo 102, Japan

STOKES DIV   5500 Tabor Rd, Philadelphia, PA 19120, Tel: (215) 289-5671
(Vacuum pumps & components, vacuum dryers, oil-upgrading equip)
    Tamoe Engineering Co. Ltd., Daini Maruzen Bldg., 9-2 Nihonbashi 3-chome, Chuo-ku,
      Tokyo, Japan

STORAGE TECHNOLOGY CORP   2270 S 88th St, Louisville, CO 80028-0001,
    Tel: (303) 673-5151
(Mfr/mkt/serv info storage & retrieval sys)
    Storage Technology of Japan Ltd., Entsuji Gadelius Bldg., 5-2-39 Akasaka,
      Minato-ku, Tokyo 107, Japan

SUDLER & HENNESSEY   1633 Broadway, New York, NY 10019, Tel: (212) 969-5800
(Healthcare prdts advertising)
    Dentsu Sudler & Hennessey Havas KK, Tsukiji MK Bldg., 2-11-26 Tsukiji, Chuo-ku,
      Tokyo 14, Japan

SULLIVAN & CROMWELL   125 Broad St, New York, NY 10004-2498,
    Tel: (212) 558-4000
(Lawyers)
    Sullivan & Cromwell, 2-1 Marunouchi 1-chome, Chiyoda-ku, Tokyo 100, Japan

SUMMIT INDUSTRIAL CORP   600 Third Ave, New York, NY 10016,
  Tel: (212) 490-1100
  (Pharms, agric chem prdts)
    Summit Co. Ltd., 4 Highashi Ginza 8-chome, Chuo-ku, Tokyo, Japan

SUNDSTRAND CORP   PO Box 7003, Rockford, IL 61125-7003, Tel: (815) 226-6000
  (Design/mfr proprietary technology based comps & sub-sys for aerospace & ind)
    Sundstrand Service Corps., Reinazaka Annex, 3rd Fl., 11-3 Akasaka 1-chome,
      Minato-ku, Tokyo 107, Japan

SUNKIST GROWERS INC   14130 Riverside Dr, Van Nuys, CA 91423,
  Tel: (818) 423-4800
  (Fruits & vegetables)
    Sunkist Pacific Ltd., 5-19 Akasaka 4-chome, Minato-ku, Tokyo, Japan

SUNRISE MEDICAL INC   2355 Crenshaw Blvd, #150, Torrance, CA 90501,
  Tel: (213) 328-8018
  (Mfr medical appliances & supplies, furniture)
    Sunrise Medical Japan, Higashi-Nakano Green 202, 32-8 Higashi-Nikano 1-chrome,
      Nakano-ku, Tokyo, Japan

SYBRON INTL CORP   411 E Wisconsin Ave, Milwaukee, WI 53202,
  Tel: (414) 274-6600
  (Mfr prdts for laboratories, professional orthodontic & dental mkts)
    Sybron Dental Specialties Japan Inc., Onarimon #2 Bldg. 2/F,
      16-12 Shimbashi 6-chome, Minato-ku, Tokyo 107, Japan

SYSTEMS ENGINEERING LABS INC   6901 W Sunrise Blvd, Fort Lauderdale,
  FL 33313, Tel: (305) 587-2900
  (Digital computers)
    Sumitomo Corp., CPO Box 1524, Tokyo 100-91, Japan

TANDY CORP   1800 One Tandy Center, Fort Worth, TX 76102, Tel: (817) 390-3700
  (Electronic & acoustic equip)
    A&A Japan Ltd., 1-21-1 Nishi-Shinjuku, Tokyo 160, Japan
    Tandy Radio Shack Japan Ltd., 1-44-1 Tamagawa, Chofu City, Tokyo, Japan

TECHNICON INSTRUMENTS CORP   511 Benedict Ave, Tarrytown, NY 10591-5097,
  Tel: (914) 631-8000
  (Mfr/serv automated blook anal equip, reagents & diagnostics)
    Nihon Technicon KK, Hazama Bldg., 5-8 Kita-Aoyama 2-chome, Minato-ku, Tokyo 107,
      Japan

TEKELEC   26580 W Agoura Rd, Calabasas, CA 91302, Tel: (818) 880-5656
  (Mfr telecommunications testing equip)
    Tekelec Ltd., Daiichi Ogikubo Bldg., 27-8 Ogikubo 5-chome, Suginami-ku, Tokyo 167,
      Japan

TEKTRONIX INC   26660 SW Parkway, Wilsonville, OR 97070, Tel: (503) 627-7111
  (Mfr test & meas, visual sys & commun prdts)
    Sony/Tektronix Corp. (JV), Tokyo, Atsugi, Fukuoka, Gotemba, Nagoya, Osaka, Omiya,
      Sendai, Tama & Tsuchiura, Japan

TELEDYNE INC   2049 Century Park East, Los Angeles, CA 90067-3101,
  Tel: (310) 277-3311
  (Divers mfg: aviation & electronics, specialty metals, industrial & consumer prdts)

(cont)

Teledyne Japan, Nihon Seimei Akasaka Bldg. 3/F, 8-1-19 Akasaka, Minato-ku,
   Tokyo 107, Japan

TELEDYNE WATER PIK   1730 E Prospect Rd, Fort Collins, CO 80553-0001,
   Tel: (303) 484-1352
   (Mfr oral hygiene appliances, shower massage equip, water filtration prdts)
      Teledyne Water Pik Japan, Nihonseimei Akasaka Bldg. 3/F, 81-1-19Akasaka, Minato-ku,
         Tokyo 107, Japan

TELXON CORP   3330 W Market St, PO Box 5582, Akron, OH 44334-0582,
   Tel: (216) 867-3700
   (Devel/mfr portable computer sys & related equip)
      Telxon Japan, Oxson Bldg. 6/F, 102013 Shintomi, Chou-ku, Tokyo, Japan

TENNANT CO   701 N Lilac Dr, Minneapolis, MN 55440, Tel: (612) 540-1200
   (Mfr ind floor maint sweepers & scrubbers, floor coatings)
      Tennant Japan, Sanka Bldg. 5/F, 2-9 Minami Saiwai-cho, Saiwai-ku, Kawasaki 210,
         Japan

TENNECO AUTOMOTIVE   111 Pfingsten Rd, Deerfield, IL 60015,
   Tel: (708) 948-0900
   (Automotive parts, exhaust sys, service equip)
      Tenneco Automotive Japan Ltd., 20-20 Hiradai, Tsuzuke-ku, Yokohama-shi,
         Kanagawa Prefecture 224, Japan

TENNECO INC   PO Box 2511, Houston, TX 77252-2511, Tel: (713) 757-2131
   (Natural gas pipelines, shipbuilding & repair, construction & farm equip, chemicals,
   packaging)
      Albright & Wilson Ltd. Japan, 2 Okamotoya Bldg. 6/F, 1-24 Toranomon 1-chome,
         Tokyo 105, Japan
      Tenneco Automotive Japan Ltd., 2020 Hiradai, Midori-ku, Yokohama-shi,
         Kanagawa Pref. 226, Japan

TERADYNE INC   321 Harrison Ave, Boston, MA 02118, Tel: (617) 482-2700
   (Mfr electronic test equip & blackplane connection sys)
      Toyo Glove KK, 1295-6 Sanbonmatsu Ochi-cho, Okawa-gun, Kagawa 0769, Japan

TEXACO INC   2000 Westchester Ave, White Plains, NY 10650, Tel: (914) 253-4000
   (Explor/mktg crude oil, mfr petro chems & prdts)
      Texaco Japan Inc., c/o NOEC Producing Japan, 18-1 Shingashi 1-chome, Minato-ku,
         1-chome, Tokyo 105, Japan

TEXAS INSTRUMENTS INC   13500 N Central Expwy, Dallas, TX 75265,
   Tel: (214) 995-2011
   (Mfr semiconductor devices, electr/electro-mech sys, instr & controls)
      Texas Instruments Japan Ltd., 305 Tangashira, Oyama-cho, Suntoh-gun, Shizuoka-ken,
         Oyama Plant 410-13, Japan
      Texas Instruments Japan Ltd., 18-36 Minami 3-chome, Hatagoya City 334, Japan
      Texas Instruments Japan Ltd., 4260 Aza-Takao, Oaza-Kawasaki, Hayami-gun,
         Hiji-machi 879-15, Japan
      Texas Instruments Japan Ltd., 2355 Kihara Miho-mura, Inashiki-gun, Ibaragi-ken,
         Miho Plant 300-04, Japan

THERM-O-DISC INC   1320 S Main St, Mansfield, OH 44907-0538,
  Tel: (419) 525-8500
  (Mfr thermostats, controls, sensor & thermal cutoffs, switches)
    Therm-O-Disc/Japan, 102 Takasago Bldg., 100 Edo-Machi, Chuo-ku, Kobe 650, Japan

THERMADYNE INDUSTRIES INC   101 S Hanley, St Louis, MO 63105,
  Tel: (314) 721-5573
  (Mfr cutting & welding apparatus & prdts)
    Thermadyne Japan Ltd., Shiba White Bldg., 5th Fl., 2-13-9 Shiba, Minato-ku,
    Tokyo 105, Japan

THERMO ELECTRIC CO   109 Fifth St, Saddle Brook, NJ 07662, Tel: (201) 843-5800
  (Mfr temp/meas control prdts)
    Tel-Thermco Engineering Co. Inc., 32-10 Kawajiri Shiroyama 1-chome, Tsukui,
    Kanakawa Pref. 220-01, Japan

THERMO ELECTRON CORP   101 First Ave, Waltham, MA 02154, Tel: (617) 890-8700
  (Devel/mfr of process equip & instru for energy intensive inds)
    Thermo Electron Nippon Co. Ltd., 3-5-11 Minami-Nakaburi, Hiakaba, Osaka, Japan

THERMON   100 Thermon Dr, PO Box 609, San Marcos, TX 78667-0609,
  Tel: (512) 396-5801
  (Mfr steam & electric heat tracing sys, components & accessories)
    Thermon Far East, Sotetsu Tsuruya-Cho Bldg. 3/F, 2-17-1 Tsuruya-cho, Kanagawa-ku,
    yokohama 221, Japan

THOMAS & BETTS CORP   1555 Lynnfield Rd, Memphis, TN 38119,
  Tel: (901) 682-7766
  (Mfr elect/electr connectors & accessories)
    Thomas & Betts Japan Ltd., 44 Kowa Bldg., 2-7 Higashiyama 1-chome, Meguru-Ku,
    Tokyo 153, Japan

THOMAS INTL PUBLISHING CO   5 Penn Plaza, New York, NY 10001,
  Tel: (212) 290-7213
  (Publ ind magazines & directories)
    Incom Co. Ltd., Plaza Edo Gawabashi, 1-23-6 Sekiguchi, Bunkyo-ku, Tokyo 112, Japan

TIFFANY & CO   727 Fifth Ave, New York, NY 10022, Tel: (212) 755-8000
  (Mfr/retail fine jewelry, silverware, china, crystal, leather goods, etc)
    Tiffany & Co. Japan, 6-16 Ginza 4-chome, Chuo-ku, Tokyo 104, Japan

TOWERS PERRIN   245 Park Ave, New York, NY 10167, Tel: (212) 309-3400
  (Management consultants)
    Towers, Perrin, Forster & Crosby, Imperial Tower, 1-1 Uchisaiwai-cho 1-chome,
    Chiyoda-ku, Tokyo 100, Japan

TOYS R US INC   461 From Rd, Paramus, NJ 07652, Tel: (201) 262-7800
  (Retail stores: toys & games, sporting goods, computer software, books, records)
    Toys R Us Japan Ltd., 3-1 Ekimae Honcho, Kawasaki, Kanagawa 0210, Japan

TRANE CO   3600 Pammel Creek Rd, La Crosse, WI 54601, Tel: (608) 787-2000
  (Mfr/distr/svce A/C sys & equip)
    Trane Japan, Tokyodo Nishi-Cho Bldg. 5/F, 3-7-2 Kanda Nishi-cho, Chiyoda-ku, Tokyo,
    Japan

TRANS WORLD AIRLINES INC   505 N 6th St, St Louis, MO 63101,
  Tel: (314) 589-3000
  (Air transportation)
    Trans World Airlines, Kokusai Bldg. #234, 3-1-1 Manunouchi, Chiyoda-ku, Tokyo, Japan

TRAVELERS GROUP INC   388 Greenwich St, New York, NY 10013,
  Tel: (212) 816-8000
  (Insurance, financial services)
    Smith Barney Asset Management Co. Ltd., Yuraku-cho Bldg.,
    1-10-1 Yuraku-cho. Chiyoda-ku, Tokyo 0100, Japan

TRIBOL   21031 Ventura Blvd, Woodland Hills, CA 91364-2297,
  Tel: (818) 888-0808
  (Mfr industrial lubricants)
    ICI Japan Ltd., Palace Bldg., 8th Fl., 1-1 Marunouchi 1-chome, Chiyoda-ku, Tokyo,
    Japan

TRIMBLE NAVIGATION LTD   585 N Mary Ave, Sunnyvale, CA 94086,
  Tel: (408) 481-2900
  (Design/mfr electronic geographic instrumentation)
    Trimble Navigation Japan, Makuhari Techno Garden D-21, 1-3 Nakase, Chiba, Japan

TRINOVA CORP   3000 Strayer, PO Box 50, Maumee, OH 43537-0050,
  Tel: (419) 867-2200
  (Mfr engr components & sys for ind)
    Yokohama Aeroquip KK, Dowa Bldg., 10-5 Shimbashi 5-chome, Minato-ku, Tokyo 105,
    Japan

TRW INC   1900 Richmond Rd, Cleveland, OH 44124, Tel: (216) 291-7000
  (Electr & energy-related prdts, automotive & aerospace prdts, tools & fasteners)
    TRW Automotive-Electronics Asia Inc., Tameike Meisan Bldg., 8th Fl.,
    1-12 Akasaka 1-chome, Minato-ku, Tokyo 107, Japan

TWIN DISC INC   1328 Racine St, Racine, WI 53403-1758, Tel: (414) 638-4000
  (Mfr ind clutches, reduction gears, transmissions)
    Nigata Converter Co. Ltd., 27-9 Sendagaya 5-chome, Shibuya-ku, Tokyo 151, Japan

TYLAN GENERAL INC   9577 Chesapeake Dr, San Diego, CA 92123,
  Tel: (619) 571-1222
  (Mfr flow & pressure measurement & control components)
    Tylan General KK, 1-18-2 Hakusan, Midori-ku, Yokohama 226, Japan

U S WHEAT ASSOCIATES   1200 NW Front Ave, #600, Portland, OR 97209,
  Tel: (503) 223-8123
  (Market development for wheat prdts)
    U.S. Wheat Associates Inc., 1-14 Akasaka 1-chome, Minato-ku, Tokyo 107, Japan

UNION CARBIDE CORP   39 Old Ridgebury Rd, Danbury, CT 06817,
  Tel: (203) 794-2000
  (Mfr industrial chemicals, plastics, resins)
    Nippon Uninar Co., Asahi Bldg. 16-17/F, 6-1 Ohtemachi 2-chome, Minato-ku,
    Tokyo 100, Japan
    Union Carbide Japan KK, Hiroo SK Bldg., 36-13 Ebisu 2-chome, Shibuya-ku, Tokyo 150,
    Japan
    Union Carbide Middle East Ltd., 6 Ibn El Nabih St. #3, 1/F, Zamalek, Cairo, Egypt

UNION OIL INTL DIV   Union Oil Center, PO Box 7600, Los Angeles, CA 90017,
Tel: (213) 977-7600
(Petroleum prdts, petrochems)
Unoco (Japan) Ltd., Akasaka Tokyo Bldg., 14-3 Nagata-cho 2-chome, Chiyoda-ku,
Tokyo 100, Japan

UNION PACIFIC CORP   Eighth & Eaton Aves, Bethlehem, PA 18018,
Tel: (215) 861-3200
(Holding co: railroad, crude oil, natural gas, petroleum refining, metal mining serv,
real estate)
Union Pacific Railroad, Satoh Bldg., 4th Fl., 1-19-4 Hamamatsu-cho, Minato-ku,
Tokyo 105, Japan

UNION SPECIAL CORP   One Union Special Plaza, Huntley, IL 60142,
Tel: (708) 669-4345
(Mfr sewing machs)
Union Special Japan Ltd., 1-5-17 Mikuni-Honmachi, Yodogawa-ku, Osaka 532, Japan

UNISYS CORP   PO Box 500, Blue Bell, PA 19424, Tel: (215) 986-4011
(Mfg/mktg/serv electr info sys)
Nihon Unisys Ltd., 17-15 Akasaka 2-chome, Minato-ku, Tokyo 107, Japan
Nippon Univac Ltd., 17-51 Akasaka 2-chome, Minato-ku, Tokyo 107, Japan
Unisys Japan Ltd., Mori Bldg. #31, Tokyo 102, Japan

UNITED AIRLINES INC   PO Box 66100, Chicago, IL 60666, Tel: (708) 952-4000
(Air transp)
United Airlines, Honmachi Nomura Bldg., 3-4-10 Honmachi, Chuo-ku, Osaka 541, Japan

UNITED CALIFORNIA BANK   PO Box 54191, Los Angeles, CA 90054,
Tel: (213) 624-0111
(Banking)
United California Bank, CPO Box 1833, Tokyo 100, Japan

UNITED CATALYSTS INC   1227 S 12th St, PO Box 32370, Louisville, KY 40232,
Tel: (502) 634-7200
(Mfr catalysts for petroleum, chem & food inds)
Catalysts & Chemicals Inc. Far East, Sankaido Bldg., 3rd Fl., 9-13 Alasaka 1-chome,
Minato-ku, Tokyo, Japan

UNITED TECHNOLOGIES CORP   United Technologies Bldg, Hartford, CT 06101,
Tel: (203) 728-7000
(Mfr aircraft engines, elevators, A/C, auto equip, space & military electr, rocket
propulsion sys)
United Technologies Intl. Operations Inc., 408 Jibiki No. 2 Bldg.,
7-8 Kokimachi 4 chome, Chiyoda-ku, Tokyo 100, Japan

UNITEK CORP/3M   2724 S Peck Rd, Monrovia, CA 91016-7118, Tel: (818) 574-4000
(Mfr orthodontic prdts)
Unitek Japan Corp., Tokyo Reiki Bldg., 6-24-5 Honkomagome, Bunkyo-ku, Tokyo, Japan

UOP INC   Ten UOP Plaza, Des Plaines, IL 60016, Tel: (708) 391-2000
(Diversified research, development & mfr of ind prdts & sys mgmt studies & serv)
Nikki Universal Co., 2-4 Ohtemachi, Chiyoda-ku, Tokyo, Japan

UPJOHN CO   7000 Portage Rd, Kalamazoo, MI 49001, Tel: (616) 323-4000
(Mfr pharms, agric prdts, ind chems)
Japan Upjohn Ltd., Shinjuku Sumitomo Bldg., P.O. Box 49, Tokyo 160-91, Japan

URSCHEL LABORATORIES INC   2503 Calumet Ave, PO Box 2200, Valparaiso,
   IN 46384-2200, Tel: (219) 464-4811
   (Design/mfr precision food processing equip)
      Urschel Japan, 2-18-9 Ningyocho, Nihonbashi, Chuo-ku, Tokyo, Japan

VALENITE INC   PO Box 9636, Madison Heights, MI 48071-9636,
   Tel: (810) 589-1000
   (Cemented carbide, high speed steel, ceramic & diamond cutting tool prdts, etc)
      Valenite-WIDIA Japan Inc., 21-10 Kita-Kohjiya 1-chome, Ohta-ku, Tokyo 144, Japan

VARIAN ASSOCIATES INC   3100 Hansen Way, Palo Alto, CA 94304-1030,
   Tel: (415) 493-4000
   (Mfr microwave tubes & devices, analytical instru, semiconductor process & med equip,
   vacuum sys)
      TEL-Varian Ltd. Varian Ltd., 2381-1 Kitagejo Fujii-cho, Nirasaki City, Yamanashi,
      Japan
      Varian Instruments Ltd., 3 Matsuda Bldg., 2-2-6 Ohkubo-Shinjuku, Tokyo 169, Japan

VERNAY LABORATORIES INC   120 E South College St, Yellow Springs, OH 45387,
   Tel: (513) 767-7261
   (Mechanical prdts, spec molded shapes, rubber goods)
      Vernay Japan, Shanshin Bldg., 1-14-15 Okubo 6/F, Shinjuku-ku, Tokyo 0169, Japan

VIACOM INC   200 Elm St, Dedham, MA 02026, Tel: (617) 461-1600
   (Communications, publishing, entertainment)
      Prentice Hall of Japan Inc., Jochi Kojimachi Bldg. 3/F, 1-25 Kojimachi 6-chome,
      Chigoda-ku, Tokyo 102, Japan
      Viacom Japan Inc., Mitsuwa Bldg., 7-2 Ginza 6-chome, Chuo-ku, Tokyo 104, Japan

VISHAY INTERTECHNOLOGY INC   63 Lincoln Highway, Malvern, PA 19355,
   Tel: (215) 644-1300
   (Mfr resistors, strain gages, capacitors, inductors, printed circuit boards)
      Nippon Vishay Co. Ltd., 4-15=4 Haramachida, Machida-shi, Tokyo 194, Japan

VIVITAR CORP   1280 Rancho Conejo Blvd, Newbury Park, CA 91320,
   Tel: (805) 498-7008
   (Mfr photographic equip, electr supplies)
      Vivitar Japan Ltd., Marusho Bldg., 6th Fl., 12 Yotsuyu 3-chome, Shinyuku-ku,
      Tokyo 160, Japan

VLSI TECHNOLOGY INC   1109 McKay Dr, San Jose, CA 95131, Tel: (408) 434-3000
   (Mfr custom & standard integrated circuits for computing, commun & ind applications)
      COMPASS Japan KK, 1-8-1 Shinjuku, Shinjuku, Tokyo 160, Japan
      VLSI Technology KK, Nikko Motoyoyogi Bldg. 1/F, 30-13 Motoyoyogi-cho, Shibuya-ku,
      Tokyo 151, Japan

WACHOVIA BANK OF GEORGIA NA   PO Box 4148, Atlanta, GA 30302-4148,
   Tel: (404) 332-5000
   (Commercial banking)
      Wachovia Bank of Georgia N.A., Toranomon ACT Bldg., 21-1 Toranomon 5-chome,
      Minato-ku, Tokyo, Japan

WACHOVIA BANK OF NORTH CAROLINA   PO Box 3099, Winston- Salem, NC 27150,
   Tel: (919) 770-5000
   (Commercial banking)

Wachovia Bank of North Carolina, Toranomon ACT Bldg., 21-1 Toranomon 5-chome,
Minato-ku, Tokyo, Japan

WACKENHUT CORP   1500 San Remo Ave, Coral Gables, FL 33146,
Tel: (305) 666-5656
(Security systems & services)
Wackenhut Keibi Co., Ginza-Matsuyoshi Bldg., 7-17-8 Ginza, Chuo-ku, Tokyo 104, Japan

WALBRO CORP   6242 Garfield Ave, Cass City, MI 48762, Tel: (517) 872-2131
(Mfr motor vehicle accessories & parts)
Walbro Far East Inc., 2-9-25 Shinmaru-shiHigashi Nakahara-ku, Kawasaki,
Kanagawa 211, Japan

WANG LABORATORIES INC   1 Industrial Ave, Lowell, MA 01851,
Tel: (508) 459-5000
(Mfr computer info processing sys)
Wang Computer Ltd., 5 Shin Daiso Bldg., 2-10-7 Dohgenzaka, Shibuya-ku, Tokyo 150,
Japan

WARD HOWELL INTL INC   99 Park Ave, New York, NY 10016-1699,
Tel: (212) 697-3730
(Executive recruiting)
Tokyo Executive Search Co. Ltd. (TESCO), Kioicho TBR Bldg. 10/F,
7 Kohjimachi 5-chome, Chiyoda-ku, Tokyo 102, Japan

WARNER ELECTRIC BRAKE & CLUTCH CO   449 Gardner St, South Beloit, IL 61080,
Tel: (815) 389-3771
(Automotive & ind brakes & clutches)
Shinko Electric Co. Ltd., Asahi Bldg., 12-2 Nihonbashi 3-chome, Chuo-ku, Tokyo,
Japan

WATERS CHROMATOGRAPHY DIV   34 Maple St, Milford, MA 01757,
Tel: (617) 478-2000
(Mfr/distr liquid chromatographic instru/accessories/tech)
Nihon Waters Ltd., Shuwa Kioicho Park Bldg., 3 Kioi-cho, Chiyoda-ku, Tokyo 102,
Japan

WEBER MARKING SYSTEMS INC   711 W Algonquin Rd, Arlington Heights, IL 60005,
Tel: (708) 364-8500
(Mfr label printing sys, custom labels)
Weber Marking Systems Far East Co. Ltd., 3-6 Tsukiji 1-chome, Chuo-ku, Tokyo 104,
Japan

THE WEST CO   101 Gordon Dr, PO Box 645, Lionville, PA 19341-0645,
Tel: (610) 594-2900
(Mfr prdts for filling, sealing, dispensing & delivering needs of health care &
consumer prdts mkts)
Daikyo Seiko Ltd., Tokyo, Japan

WESTERN DIGITAL CORP   8105 Irvine Center Dr, Irvine, CA 92718,
Tel: (714) 932-5000
(Mfr hard disk drives, video graphics boards, VLSI)
Western Digital Japan Ltd., 44 Kowa Bldg. 8/F, 1-2-7 Higashiyama, Megoro-ku, Tokyo,
Japan

WESTVACO CORP   299 Park Ave, New York, NY 10171, Tel: (212) 688-5000
  (Mfr paper, packaging, chems)
     Westvaco Asia KK, Shoyo Kaikan Bldg., 3-3-1 Kasumigaseki, Chiyoda-ku, Tokyo 100,
     Japan

WEYERHAEUSER CO   Tacoma, WA 98477, Tel: (206) 924-2345
  (Wood & wood fiber products)
     Weyerhaeuser Japan Ltd., P.O. Box 18, Tokyo 107, Japan

WHIRLPOOL CORP   2000 N M-63, Benton Harbor, MI 49022-2692,
  Tel: (616) 923-5000
  (Mfr/mkt home appliances)
     Whirlpool Corp., Tokyo, Japan

WHITE CONSOLIDATED INDUSTRIES INC   11770 Berea Rd, Cleveland, OH 44111,
  Tel: (216) 252-3700
  (Major household appliances, ind mach & equip)
     Blaw-Knox Japan Co. Ltd., Toho Bldg., 5-1 Akasaka 2-chome, Minato-ku, Tokyo 107,
     Japan

WILBUR-ELLIS CO   320 California St, #200, San Francisco, CA 94104,
  Tel: (415) 772-4000
  (Intl merchants & distributors)
     Connell Bros. Co. (Japan) Ltd., 2-12-18 Minato-machi, Naha, Okinawa 900, Japan
     Wilbur-Ellis Co. (Japan) Ltd., 308 Sanshin Bldg., 4-1 Yuraku-cho 1-chome,
     Chiyoda-ku, Tokyo 100, Japan
     Wilbur-Ellis Co. (Japan) Ltd., 1-7 Hommachi 4-chome, Chuo-ku, Osala 541, Japan

WINCHESTER ELECTRONICS   400 Park Rd, Watertown, CT 06795-0500,
  Tel: (203) 945-5000
  (Mfr elec & electr connectors, PCB assemblies & hardware)
     Winchester Electronics Japan, c/o Litton Westrex Co., Chiyoda Bldg.,
     2-1-2 Marunochi, Chiyoda-ku, Tokyo 100, Japan

WOMETCO ENTERPRISES INC   306 N Miami Ave, Miami, FL 33128,
  Tel: (305) 374-6262
  (Television broadcasting, film distribution, bottling, vending machs)
     Intl. Leisure Corp., Tokyo Tower Wax Museum, 20-1 Shiba Park, Minato-ku, Tokyo,
     Japan

WOODWARD GOVERNOR CO   5001 North 2nd St, PO Box 7001, Rockford,
  IL 61125-7001, Tel: (815) 877-7441
  (Mfr speed control governors)
     Woodward Governor (Japan) Ltd., P.O. Box 1, Inba-gun, Chiba-ken 286-02, Japan
     Woodward Governor Co., Kobe Service Station, 86-1 Edayashi 4-chome, Nishi-ku,
     Kobe-shi, Hyogo-ken 651-21, Japan

WORLD COURIER INC   46 Trinity Pl, New York, NY 10006, Tel: (718) 978-9400
  (Intl courier serv)
     World Courier Japan, Ginza Chuo Bldg. 7/F, 3-10 Ginza 4-chome, Chuo-ku, Tokyo 104,
     Japan

WM WRIGLEY JR CO   410 N Michigan Ave, Chicago, IL 60611-4287,
  Tel: (312) 644-2121
  (Mfr chewing gum)
     Wrigley & Co. Ltd. Japan, Tokyo, Japan

XEROX CORP   800 Long Ridge Rd, PO Box 1600, Stamford, CT   06904,
   Tel: (203) 968-3000
   (Mfr document processing equip, sys & supplies)
      Fuji Xerox Co. Ltd., 3-5 Akasaka 3-chome, Minato-ku, Tokyo 107, Japan
      Xerox Corp., also in Ebina, Iwatsuki, Suzuka & Takematsu, Japan

XILINX INC   2100 Logic Dr, San Jose, CA   95124-3400, Tel: (408) 559-7779
      (Programmable logic & related development sys software)
      Xilinx KK, Daini-Nagoaka Bldg. 2/F, 2-8-5 Hatchobori, Chuo-ku, Tokyo 104, Japan

YOUNG & RUBICAM INC   285 Madison Ave, New York, NY   10017, Tel: (212) 210-3000
      (Advertising, public relations, direct marketing & sales promotion, corp & product ID
      management)
      Dentsu Young & Rubicam, Kyobashi K-1 Bldg., 2-7-12 Yaesu, Chuo-ku, Tokyo 104, Japan

YSI INC   1725 Brannum Lane, PO Box 279, Yellow Springs, OH   45387,
   Tel: (513) 767-7241
   (Mfr analyzers, meas instru & elec components)
      Nikkiso/YSI, 43-2 Ebisu 3-chome, Shibuya-ku, Tokyo, Japan

ZIEBART INTL CORP   1290 E Maple Rd, Troy, MI   48084, Tel: (810) 588-4100
   (Automotive aftermarket servs)
      Ziebart Japan Ltd., 40 Kojimachi Annex, 4-5-10 Kojimachi, Chiyoda-ku, Tokyo 102,
      Japan

ZIPPERTUBING CO   13000 S Broadway, PO Box 61129, Los Angeles, CA   90061,
   Tel: (310) 527-0488
   (Mfr zip-on plastic tubing, wire markers, pipe insulation, EMI shielding)
      Zippertubing (Japan) Ltd., 3-2-56 Takatsukadai, Nishi-ku, Kobe 651-22, Japan

ZYCAD CORP   47100 Bayside Pkwy, Fremont, CA   94538-9942, Tel: (510) 623-4400
   (Design/devel/mfr/mkt logic & fault simulation acceleration prdts; system engineering
   services)
      Zycad Japan KK, Toshin 24, Shin-Yokohama Bldg. B-8F, 2-3-8 Shin-Yokohama,
      Kohoku-ku, Yokohama 222, Japan

JORDAN

BECHTEL GROUP INC   50 Beale St, PO Box 3965, San Francisco, CA   94119,
   Tel: (415) 768-1234
   (Engineering & constr)
      Bechtel Corp., P.O. Box 5226, Amman, Jordan

CDM INTL INC   Ten Cambridge Center, Cambridge, MA   02142, Tel: (617) 252-8000
   (Consulting engineers)
      Camp Dresser & McKee Intl. Inc., c/o Sigma Consulting Engineers, P.O. Box 20076,
      Amman, Jordan

CH2M HILL INC   PO Box 428, Corvallis, OR 97339, Tel: (503) 752-4271
   (Consulting engrs, planners, economists, scientists)
      CH2M Hill Inc., c/o Arabtech, P.O. Box 7323, Amman, Jordan

CHASE MANHATTAN BANK N A   1 Chase Manhattan Plaza, New York, NY 10081,
   Tel: (212) 552 2222
   (Intl banking)
      Chase Manhattan Bank N.A., P.O. Box 20191, First Circle, Jebal, Amman, Jordan

CITICORP   399 Park Ave, New York, NY 10043, Tel: (212) 559-1000
   (Banking & financial services)
      Citibank, Jordan

HOLIDAY INNS INC   3742 Lamar Ave, Memphis, TN 38195, Tel: (901) 362-4001
   (Hotels, restaurants, casinos)
      Holiday Inn, P.O. Box 6399, Amman, Jordan

THE KULJIAN CO   3624 Science Center, Philadelphia, PA 19104,
   Tel: (215) 243-1900
   (Studies, design, engineeering, constr mgmt, site supervision)
      Kuljian Corp., P.O. Box 2749, Amman, Jordan

MERCK SHARP & DOHME INTL   PO Box 2000, Rahway, NJ 07065, Tel: (201) 574-4000
   (Pharms, chems & biologicals)
      Charles E. Frosst & Co., P.O. Box 20604, Amman, Jordan

OTIS ELEVATOR CO   10 Farm Springs, Farmington, CT 06032, Tel: (860) 676-6528
   (Mfr elevators & escalators)
      Otis/Jordan Elevator Overseas Ltd., P.O. Box 7490, Amman, Jordan

RAYTHEON CO   141 Spring St, Lexington, MA 02173, Tel: (617) 862-6600
   (Mfr divers electronics, appliances, aviation, energy & environ prdts; publishing,
   ind & constr servs)
      Raytheon Technical Assistance Co., P.O. Box 3414, Jebal, Amman, Jordan

UNION CARBIDE CORP   39 Old Ridgebury Rd, Danbury, CT 06817,
   Tel: (203) 794-2000
   (Mfr industrial chemicals, plastics, resins)
      Union Carbide Europe SA, P.O. Box 927277, Amman, Jordan

WACKENHUT CORP   1500 San Remo Ave, Coral Gables, FL 33146,
   Tel: (305) 666-5656
   (Security systems & services)
      WII/Sound & Security Eng. Co., P.O. Box 9881, Amman, Jordan

KAZAKHSTAN

CARANA CORP   4350 N Fairfax Dr, #500, Arlington, VA 22203,
  Tel: (703) 243-1700
  (Foreign trade consulting)
    CARANA Corp., ul. Ablai-Khan 93/95, Suite 528, Almaty, Kazakhstan

FRITZ COMPANIES INC   706 Mission St, San Francisco, CA 94103,
  Tel: (415) 904-8360
  (Integrated transportation, sourcing, distribution & customs brokerage services)
    Kaz-Fritz Transportation (Ltd.), 127 Furmanov St., Almaty, Kazakhstan

U S FUR EXCHANGE   515 Lake St S, Kirkland, WA 98033, Tel: (206) 828-6774
  (Fur auctioning, distr & sale)
    Palms & Co. Inc., Pr. Asddirova 46/2 Kv. 66, Karaganda 470055, Kazakhstan

WESTERN ATLAS INTL INC   10205 Westheimer, PO Box 1407, Houston,
  TX 77251-1407, Tel: (713) 266-5700
  (Full service to the oil industry)
    Western Atlas Intl. Inc., 153 Abaya St. #4, Almaty 480009, Kazakhstan

KENYA

3M   3M Center, St Paul, MN 55144-1000, Tel: (612) 733-1110
  (Mfr diversified prdts for industry, health care, imaging, commun, transport, safety,
  consumer, etc)
    3M Kenya Ltd., 3M House, Ngong Rd., Nairobi, Kenya

AIR EXPRESS INTL CORP   120 Tokeneke Rd, PO Box 1231, Darien, CT 06820,
  Tel: (203) 655-7900
  (Air frt forwarder)
    Air Express Intl. Kenya Ltd., Rahimtulla Trust Bldg., Moi Ave., P.O. Box 44469,
    Nairobi, Kenya

ASSOCIATED PRESS INC   50 Rockefeller Plaza, New York, NY 10020-1605,
   Tel: (212) 621-1500
   (News gathering agency)
      Associated Press (JV), P.O. Box 47590, Nairobi, Kenya

SAMUEL BINGHAM CO   1555 N Mittel Blvd, #T, Wood Dale, IL 60191-1046,
   Tel: (708) 238-4000
   (Print & industrial rollers, inks)
      Coates Bros. (East Africa) Ltd., P.O. Box 30607, Addis Ababa Rd., Industrial Area,
      Nairobi, Kenya

CALTEX PETROLEUM CORP   PO Box 619500, Dallas, TX 75261, Tel: (214) 830-1000
   (Petroleum prdts)
      Caltex Oil Kenya Ltd., Caltex House, Koinange St., Nairobi, Kenya

CHASE MANHATTAN BANK N A   1 Chase Manhattan Plaza, New York, NY 10081,
   Tel: (212) 552-2222
   (Intl banking)
      Chase Manhattan Overseas Corp., Kencom House, 7th Fl., P.O. Box 57051, Nairobi,
      Kenya

CHEMICAL BANK   270 Park Ave, New York, NY 10017-2070, Tel: (212) 270-6000
   (Banking & financial services)
      Chemical Bank, International House 13/F, Mama Ngina St., Nairobi, Kenya

THE CHRISTIAN SCIENCE PUBLISHING SOCIETY   1 Norway St, Boston, MA 02115,
   Tel: (617) 450-2000
   (Publishing, broadcasting)
      Robert Press, P.O. Box 59237, Nairobi, Kenya

CITICORP   399 Park Ave, New York, NY 10043, Tel: (212) 559-1000
   (Banking & financial services)
      Citibank NA, Kenya

THE COCA-COLA CO   PO Drawer 1734, Atlanta, GA 30301, Tel: (404) 676-2121
   (Mfr/mkt/distr soft drinks, syrups & concentrates, juice & juice-drink prdts)
      The Coca-Cola Co. Kenya, all mail to U.S. address

COLGATE-PALMOLIVE CO   300 Park Ave, New York, NY 10022, Tel: (212) 310-2000
   (Mfr pharms, cosmetics, toiletries, detergents)
      Colgate-Palmolive (E.A.) Ltd., P.O. Box 30264, Nairobi, Kenya

COLUMBIA PICTURES INDUSTRIES INC   711 Fifth Ave, New York, NY 10022,
   Tel: (212) 751-4400
   (Producer & distributor of motion pictures)
      Columbia Pictures, c/o Cosmopolitan Film B.V., P.O. Box 74244, Nairobi, Kenya

COULTER CORP   PO Box 169015, Miami, FL 33116-9015, Tel: (305) 885-0131
   (Mfr blood analysis sys, flow cytometers, chem sys, scientific sys & reagents)
      Coulter Electronics Kenya Ltd., Valley Arcade Shopping Centre, Gitanga Rd.,
      P.O. Box 25157, Lavington, Nairobi, Kenya

CPC INTERNATIONAL INC   PO Box 8000, Englewood Cliffs, NJ 07632,
   Tel: (201) 894-4000
   (Consumer foods, corn refining)

CPC Industrial Products (Kenya) Ltd., P.O. Box 11889, Nairobi, Kenya
CPC Kenya Ltd., P.O. Box 41045, Nairobi, Kenya

CROWN CORK & SEAL CO INC   9300 Ashton Rd, Philadelphia, PA 19136,
  Tel: (215) 698-5100
  (Mfr cans, bottle caps; filling & packaging mach)
    Crown Cork E.A. Ltd., P.O. Box 46408, Nairobi, Kenya

EASTMAN KODAK CO   343 State St, Rochester, NY 14650, Tel: (716) 724-4000
  (Devel/mfr photo & chem prdts, info mgmt/video/copier sys, fibers/plastics for
  various ind)
    Kodak Kenya Ltd., P.O. Box 18210, Funzi Rd., Nairobi, Kenya

FMC CORP   200 E Randolph Dr, Chicago, IL 60601, Tel: (312) 861-6000
  (Produces chems & precious metals, mfr machinery, equip & sys for ind, agric & govt)
    FMC Intl. AG, Kenya

GENERAL MOTORS CORP   3044 W Grand Blvd, Detroit, MI 48202-3091,
  Tel: (313) 556-5000
  (Mfr full line vehicles, automotive electronics, coml technologies, telecom, space,
  finance)
    General Motors Corp., P.O. Box 30527, Nairobi, Kenya

THE GILLETTE CO   Prudential Tower, Boston, MA 02199, Tel: (617) 421-7000
  (Devel/mfr personal care/use prdts: blades & razors, toiletries, cosmetics,
  stationery)
    Gillette Interproducts Ltd., Nairobi, Kenya

GTE CORP   One Stamford Forum, Stamford, CT 06904, Tel: (203) 965-2000
  (Electr prdts, telecom sys, publ & commun)
    Eastern Telecommunications, Nairobi, Kenya

HORWATH INTL   415 Madison Ave, New York, NY 10017, Tel: (212) 838-5566
  (Public accountants & auditors)
    Muchekehu & Co., 5th Fl. Nationwide House, Koinange St., Nairobi, Kenya

ITT CORP   1330 Ave of the Americas, New York, NY 10019-5490,
  Tel: (212) 258-1000
  (Design/mfr communications & electronic equip, hotels, insurance)
    ITT, P.O. Box 25224, Nairobi, Kenya

JOHNSON & JOHNSON   One Johnson & Johnson Plaza, New Brunswick, NJ 08933,
  Tel: (908) 524-0400
  (R&D/mfr/sale health care prdts)
    Johnson & Johnson Kenya Ltd., P.O. Box 47591, Nairobi, Kenya

S C JOHNSON & SON INC   1525 Howe St, Racine, WI 53403, Tel: (414) 631-2000
  (Home, auto, commercial & personal care prdts, specialty chems)
    Johnson's Wax E.A. Ltd., Lunga Lunga Rd., P.O. Box 18373, Nairobi, Kenya

THE KULJIAN CO   3624 Science Center, Philadelphia, PA 19104,
  Tel: (215) 243-1900
  (Studies, design, engineeering, constr mgmt, site supervision)
    Kuljian Corp., P.O. Box 53295, Nairobi, Kenya

LEDERLE LABS   Middletown Rd, Pearl River, NY 10965, Tel: (914) 735-5000
(Antibiotics, pharms)
   Lederle Labs., Div. American Cyanamid, P.O. Box 47341, Nairobi, Kenya

MERCK SHARP & DOHME INTL   PO Box 2000, Rahway, NJ 07065, Tel: (201) 574-4000
(Pharms, chems & biologicals)
   Merck, Sharp & Dohme Intl., P.O. Box 30676, Arwings-Kodhek Rd., Nairobi, Kenya

MOBIL CORP   3225 Gallows Rd, Fairfax, VA 22037-0001, Tel: (703) 846-3000
(Petroleum explor & refining, mfr petrol prdts, chems, petrochems)
   Mobil Africa Sales Inc., P.O. Box 40719, Longonot Place, Kijabe St., Nairobi, Kenya

McCANN-ERICKSON WORLDWIDE   750 Third Ave, New York, NY 10017,
   Tel: (212) 697-6000
   (Advertising)
   McCann-Erickson (Kenya) Ltd., P.O. Box 48541, Nairobi, Kenya

OTIS ELEVATOR CO   10 Farm Springs, Farmington, CT 06032, Tel: (860) 676-6528
(Mfr elevators & escalators)
   East African Elevator Co. Ltd., Finance House, 9th Fl., Bondo Rd., Industrial Area,
      P.O. Box 20014, Nairobi, Kenya

PARKER DRILLING CO   8 E Third St, Tulsa, OK 74103-3637, Tel: (918) 585-8221
(Drilling contractor)
   Parker Drilling Co., P.O. Box 45075, Nairobi, Kenya

PFIZER INC   235 E 42nd St, New York, NY 10017-5755, Tel: (212) 573-2323
(Mfr healthcare products)
   Pfizer Laboratories Ltd., Kenya

SCHERING INTL   PO Box 500, Kenilworth, NJ 07033, Tel: (201) 558-4000
(Pharms, medicines, toiletries, cosmetics, human & animal health prdts)
   Essex East Africa Ltd., P.O. Box 30409, Nairobi, Kenva,

SIGNODE PACKAGING SYSTEMS   3600 W Lake Ave, Glenview, IL 60025,
   Tel: (708) 724-6100
   (Mfr packaging systems)
   Signode Packaging Systems Ltd., Mombasa Rd., P.O. Box 78160, Nairobi, Kenya

WM WRIGLEY JR CO   410 N Michigan Ave, Chicago, IL 60611-4287,
   Tel: (312) 644-2121
   (Mfr chewing gum)
   Wrigley Co. E.A. Ltd., P.O. Box 30767, Nairobi, Kenya

XEROX CORP   800 Long Ridge Rd, PO Box 1600, Stamford, CT 06904,
   Tel: (203) 968-3000
   (Mfr document processing equip, sys & supplies)
   Xerox Corp., Nairobi, Kenya

KOREA
(South)

3COM CORP   5400 Bayfront Plaza, Santa Clara, CA 95052-8145,
Tel: (408) 764-5000
(Devel/mfr computer networking prdts & sys)
  3Com Asia Ltd., South Korea

3M   3M Center, St Paul, MN 55144-1000, Tel: (612) 733-1110
(Mfr diversified prdts for industry, health care, imaging, commun, transport, safety, consumer, etc)
  3M Korea Ltd., Daehan Investment Trust Bldg. 22/F, 27-3 Yoido-dong, Yongdungpo-Ku, Seoul 150-010, South Korea

AIR PRODUCTS & CHEMICALS INC   7201 Hamilton Blvd, Allentown, PA 18195-1501,
Tel: (215) 481-4911
(Mfr ind gases & related equip, spec chems, environmental/energy sys)
  Korea Industrial Gases Ltd., Han Il Bldg. 10/F, 64-5 Chung Mu-ro Chung-Ku, Seoul, South Korea

ALLEN-BRADLEY CO   PO Box 2086, Milwaukee, WI 53201, Tel: (414) 382-2000
(Mfr eletrical controls & info devices)
  Allen-Bradley Div., Rockwell Intl. Korea, 4/F Seocho Bldg., 1365-10 Seocho-Dong, Seocho-Ku, Seoul 137 070, South Korea
  Hyundai A-B Ltd., 178 Sejong-Ro, Chongro-ku, Seoul 110-050, South Korea
  Korea A-B Ltd., 546-4 Ami-Ri, Bubai-Eup, Ichon-Kun, Kyonggi-Do 467-860, South Korea

AMERICAN & EFIRD INC   PO Box 507, Mt Holly, NC 28120, Tel: (704) 827-4311
(Mfr ind thread, yarn & consumer sewing prdts)
  A&E (Korea) Ltd., Kikwang Bldg. #501, 949-20 Bongchon-Dong, Kwanak-gu, CPO Box 1124, Seoul, South Korea

AMERICAN AIRLINES INC   PO Box 619616, Dallas-Ft Worth Arpt, TX 75261-9616,
Tel: (817) 355-1234
(Air transp)
  American Airlines Inc., Samkoo Bldg., 70 Sokong-dong, Choong-ku, Seoul, South Korea

AMERICAN PRESIDENT LINES LTD   1111 Broadway, Oakland, CA 94607,
Tel: (415) 272-8000
(Intermodal shipping serv)
  American President Lines Ltd., Daehan Fire Insurance Bldg. 14/F, 51-1 Namchang-dong, Chung-ku, Seoul 100-060, South Korea

AMOCO CHEMICAL CO   200 E Randolph Dr, Chicago, IL 60601, Tel: (312) 856-3200
(Mfr/sale petrol based chems, plastics, chem/plastic prdts)
  Samsung Petrochemical Co. Ltd., South Korea

AMP INC   PO Box 3608, Harrisburg, PA 17105-3608, Tel: (717) 564-0100
  (Devel/mfr electronic & electrical connection prdts & sys)
    AMP Korea Ltd., Seoul, South Korea

AMWAY CORP   7575 E Fulton Rd, Ada, MI 49355, Tel: (616) 676-6000
  (Mfr/sale home care, personal care, nutrition & houseware prdts)
    Amway Korea Ltd., 12/F Dongsung Bldg., 158-24 Samsung-dong, Kangham-ku,
      Seoul 135 090, South Korea

ANALOG DEVICES INC   1 Technology Way, Box 9106, Norwood, MA 02062,
  Tel: (617) 329-4700
  (Mfr integrated circuits & related devices)
    Analog Devices Korea Ltd., Union Bldg., 961-3 Dae Chi-Dong Nam-Ku, Seoul,
      South Korea

ANGLO-AMERICAN AVIATION CO   9740 Telfair Ave, Arleta, CA 91331,
  Tel: (818) 896-0333
  (Aviation spare parts, hardware)
    Anglo-American Aviation Co., c/o Hannah Intl. Ltd., Hong Ik Bldg., Rm 902,
      198-1 Kwanhoon-dong, Chongro-ku, Seoul, South Korea

APPLIED MAGNETICS CORP   75 Robin Hill Rd, Goleta, CA 93117,
  Tel: (805) 683-5353
  (Mfr magnetic recording heads)
    Applied Magnetics Korea Ltd., KPO Box 2801, Seoul, South Korea

APPLIED POWER INC   13000 W Silver Spring Dr, Butler, WI 53007,
  Tel: (414) 781-6600
  (Mfr hi-pressure tools, vibration control prdts, electrical tools & consumables, tech
  furniture)
    Applied Power Korea Ltd., 163-12 Dodang-Dong, Wonmi-Ku, Buchun-Shi, Kyunggi-Do,
      South Korea

ARAMARK CORP   1101 Market St, Philadelphia, PA 19107-2988,
  Tel: (215) 238-3000
  (Diversified managed services)
    ARAKOR Korea, Byucksan Bldg. 19/F, 12-6 Donja-Dong, Yongsan-Ku, Seoul, South Korea

ARBOR ACRES FARM INC   439 Marlborough Rd, Glastonbury, CT 06033,
  Tel: (860) 633-4681
  (Producers of male & female broiler breeders, commercial egg layers)
    Hanil Poultry Farms, Arbor Acres Korea Farm, 97 Chunghak-ri, Osan-Eup, Hwasung-Kun,
      Kyunggi-do, South Korea

ARMSTRONG WORLD INDUSTRIES INC   PO Box 3001, Lancaster, PA 17604,
  Tel: (717) 397-0611
  (Mfr/mkt interior furnishings & spec prdts for bldg, auto & textile inds)
    Armstrong World Industries Korea Ltd., Seoul,
      South Korea (all inquiries to U.S. address)

ASHLAND OIL INC   1000 Ashland Dr, Russell, KY 41169, Tel: (606) 329-3333
  (Petroleum exploration, refining & transportation; mfr chemicals, oils & lubricants)
    Ashland Korea Foundry Products, Sambuk Bldg. 4/F, 50 AKA, Jung Ang-Dong,
      P.O. Box 968, Pusan, South Korea

ASSOCIATED MERCHANDISING CORP   1440 Broadway, New York, NY 10018,
  Tel: (212) 536-4000
  (Retail service organization)
    Associated Merchandising Corp., Trade Center P.O. Box 56, Seoul 135-091, South Korea

AST RESEARCH INC   16215 Alton Parkway, PO Box 19658, Irvine, CA 92713-9658,
  Tel: (714) 727-4141
  (Design/devel/mfr hi-perf desktop, server & notebook computers)
    AST Korea, 17/F Taewon Bldg., 143-40/41 Samsung-Dong, Kangnam-Ku, Seoul 135-090,
      South Korea

AT&T INTERNATIONAL   412 Mt Kemble Ave, Morristown, NJ 07962-1995,
  Tel: (810) 262-6646
  (Telecommunications)
    AT&T Korea Ltd., Securities Supervisory Board Bldg. 16-17/F, 27 Yoido-Dong,
      Youngdeungpo-Ku, Seoul 150-010, S. Korea

AVIS INC   900 Old Country Rd, Garden City, NY 11530, Tel: (516) 222-3000
  (Car rental serv)
    Avis Rent A Car (Korea), 89-14 4-ga Jung Ang-dong, Jung-ku, Seoul, South Korea

THE BANK OF NEW YORK   48 Wall St, New York, NY 10286, Tel: (212) 495-1784
  (Banking)
    The Bank of New York, 1410 Samsung Main Bldg., 2-250 Taepyung-ro, Chung-Ku,
      CPO Box 4906, Seoul 100-649, South Korea

BANKAMERICA CORP   555 California St, San Francisco, CA 94104,
  Tel: (415) 622-3456
  (Financial services)
    Bank of America NT & SA, CPO Box 3026, Seoul 100-630, South Korea

BANKERS TRUST CO   280 Park Ave, New York, NY 10017, Tel: (212) 250-2500
  (Banking)
    Bankers Trust Co., Center Bldg., 10th Floor, 91-1 Sokong-dong, Chung-ku, Seoul,
      South Korea

BAUSCH & LOMB INC   1 Chase Square, Rochester, NY 14601, Tel: (716) 338-6000
  (Mfr vision care prdts & accessories)
    Bausch & Lomb Korea Ltd., Seoul, South Korea

BAXTER HEALTHCARE CORP   1 Baxter Pky, Deerfield, IL 60015,
  Tel: (708) 948-2000
  (Mfr disposable medical prdts)
    Baxter Healthcare Ltd., Ma Po Chang Bldg. 922, 18-10 Do Wha Dong, Ma Po K.U.,
      Seoul, South Korea

BDM INTL INC   7915 Jones Branch Dr, McLean, VA 22102, Tel: (703) 848-5000
  (Professional & technical services)
    BDM Management Service Co., Seoul, South Korea

BECHTEL GROUP INC   50 Beale St, PO Box 3965, San Francisco, CA 94119,
  Tel: (415) 768-1234
  (Engineering & constr)
    Bechtel Overseas Corp., 87 Sokong-dong, Chung-ku, Seoul 100, South Korea

BENTLY NEVADA CORP   PO Box 157, Minden, NV 89423, Tel: (702) 782-3611
  (Electronic monitoring system)
    C&M Brothers, 53-1 Haeng-Jin Bldg., Yoido-dong, Youngdeungpo-gu, Seoul, South Korea

E W BLISS CO   1004 E State St, Hastings, MI 49058, Tel: (616) 948-3300
  (Mfr metal-forming presses)
    Gold Star Cable Co. Ltd., 537 Namdaemun-ro 5-ga, Jung-Gu, Seoul 100, South Korea

BORG-WARNER AUTOMOTIVE INC   200 S Michigan Ave, Chicago, IL 60604,
  Tel: (312) 322-8500
  (Mfr automotive components; provider of security services)
    Borg-Warner Automotive Korea Inc., 65-4 Samjung-Ri, Daeso-Myun, Eumsung-Kun,
    Choongbuk 369-820, South Korea

BOURNS INC   1200 Columbia Ave, Riverside, CA 92507, Tel: (909) 781-5500
  (Mfr resistive com & networks, precision potentiometers, panel controls, switches,
  transducers)
    Bourns Intl. Services Inc., Anjin Bldg. 5/F, 995-21 Daechi-dong, Kangnam-ku, Seoul,
    South Korea

BOYDEN CONSULTING CORP   375 Park Ave, #1008, New York, NY 10152,
  Tel: (212) 980-6480
  (Executive search)
    Boyden/Perron Associates, 1301 Lemma Bldg., 146-1 Soosong-dong, Chongro-ku, Seoul,
    South Korea

BRANSON ULTRASONICS CORP   41 Eagle Rd, Danbury, CT 06813-1961,
  Tel: (203) 796-0400
  (Mfr plastics assembly equip, ultrasonic cleaning equip)
    Branson Korea Co. Ltd., 66-9 Nonhyun-Dong, Kangnam-Ku, Seoul, South Korea

BROWN & ROOT INC   4100 Clinton Dr, Houston, TX 77020-6299,
  Tel: (713) 676-3011
  (Engr, constr & maintenance)
    Brown & Root Intl. Inc., P.O. Box 603-21, 825 Ayang-ri Janspungo-Eub,
    Geoje-Kin Kyungnam, South Korea

LEO BURNETT CO INC   35 West Wacker Dr, Chicago, IL 60601, Tel: (312) 220-5959
  (Advertising agency)
    Dong Bank Advertising Co. Ltd., Sungam Bldg. 5-6/F, 114 Nonhuyn-dong, Kangham-ku,
    Seoul, South Korea

BURSON-MARSTELLER   230 Park Ave, New York, NY 10003-1566, Tel: (212) 614-4000
  (Public relations/public affairs consultants)
    Burson Marsteller Korea Inc., DLI 63 Bldg. 42/F, 60 Yoido-dong, Youngdeungpo-ku,
    Seoul, South Korea

CALTEX PETROLEUM CORP   PO Box 619500, Dallas, TX 75261, Tel: (214) 830-1000
  (Petroleum prdts)
    Honam Oil Refinery Co. Ltd., Lucky Goldstar Twin Towers, 20 Yoido-dong,
    Yongdungpo-ku, Seoul 150-721, South Korea

CARBOLINE CO   350 Hanley Industrial Ct, St Louis, MO 63144,
  Tel: (314) 644-1000
  (Mfr coatings, sealants)

Carboline Korea Ltd., 43-1 Jin Young-Ri, Jin Young-EUB, Kim Hae-Gun, Kyoung-Nam, South Korea

CARRIER CORP   One Carrier Place, Farmington, CT 06034-4015,
  Tel: (203) 674-3000
  (Mfr/distr/svce A/C, heating & refrigeration equip)
    Daewoo Crarier Corp., Yong San Bldg., 92 Kalwol-Dong, Yongsan-Ku, Swang-ju,
    South Korea

CBI INDUSTRIES INC   800 Jorie Blvd, Oak Brook, IL 60521, Tel: (708) 654-7000
  (Holding co: metal plate fabricating, constr, oil & gas drilling)
    Korea Shipbuilding & Construction Business Inc., CPO Box 8624, Chosan Hotel, Seoul,
    South Korea

CHASE MANHATTAN BANK N A   1 Chase Manhattan Plaza, New York, NY 10081,
  Tel: (212) 552-2222
  (Intl banking)
    Chase Manhattan Bank N.A., 50 1-ka Ulchiro, Choong-ku, CPO Box 2249, Seoul 100,
    South Korea

CHEMICAL BANK   270 Park Ave, New York, NY 10017-2070, Tel: (212) 270-6000
  (Banking & financial services)
    Chemical Bank, Daewoo Center Bldg. 11/F, 541 5-ka Namdaemun-ro, Chung-ku, Seoul,
    South Korea
    Chemical Securities, Daewoo Center Bldg. 11/F, 541 5-ka Namdaemun-ro, Chung-ku,
    Seoul, South Korea

CHEVRON CORP   225 Bush St, San Francisco, CA 94104, Tel: (415) 894-7700
  (Oil & gas exploration, production, refining, products; oilfield & financial services)
    Chevron Corp., all mail to U.S. address

CHIRON CORP   4560 Horton St, Emeryville, CA 94608-2916, Tel: (510) 601-2412
  (Research/mfg/mktg therapeutics, vaccines, diagnostics, ophthalmics)
    Ciba Corning Korea Ltd., Kye Myung Bldg. 4F, Myundil Dong 48-7, Kangdong-Gu,
    Seoul 134 070, Korea

CIGNA CORP   One Liberty Place, Philadelphia, PA 19192, Tel: (215) 523-4000
  (Ins, invest, health care & other fin servs)
    Cigna Insurance Co., Suhwoo Bldg. 8/F, 17-10 Yoido-dong, Yungdungpo-ku, 159 Seoul,
    South Korea
    Life Insurance Co. of North America, Kukje Center Bldg. 18/F, 191 2-ka, Hankang-ro,
    Yong San-ku, Seoul 140-012, South Korea

CITICORP   399 Park Ave, New York, NY 10043, Tel: (212) 559-1000
  (Banking & financial services)
    Citibank NA, South Korea

THE CLOROX CO   1221 Broadway, PO Box 24305, Oakland, CA 94623-1305,
  Tel: (510) 271-7000
  (Mfr domestic consumer packaged prdts)
    Clorox Korea Ltd., Seoul, South Korea
    Yuhan-Clorox Co. Ltd., South Korea

COBE LABORATORIES INC   1185 Oak St, Lakewood, CO 80215, Tel: (303) 232-6800
  (Mfr med equip & supplies)
    COBE Far East, Seoul, South Korea

COMBUSTION ENGINEERING INC   900 Long Ridge Road, Stamford, CT 06902,
Tel: (203) 329-8771
(Tech constr)
  Combustion Engineering Inc., Hotel Shilla, Rm. 509, 202-2-ga Jangchung-dong,
  Chung-ku, Seoul, South Korea

COMPUTER ASSOCIATES INTL INC   One Computer Associates Plaza, Islandia,
NY 11788, Tel: (516) 342-5224
(Devel/mkt/mgt info mgt & bus applications software)
  Computer Associates Korea Ltd., Textile Center Bldg., 944-31 Daechi-Dong,
  Kang Nam-Ku, Seoul, South Korea

CONTINENTAL CAN CO   PO Box 5410, Stamford, CT 06856, Tel: (203) 357-8110
(Packaging prdts & mach, metal, plastic & paper containers)
  Doosan Continental Can Mfg. Co. Ltd., Han Hyo Bldg., Yoido-dong, Youngdeunpo-ku,
  Seoul, South Korea

CORESTATES FINANCIAL CORP   1500 Market St, Philadelphia, PA 19101,
Tel: (215) 973-3100
(Banking)
  Corestates Bank, Samwhan Bldg. 10/F, Unni-Dong, Chongro-ku, Seoul, South Korea

CORNING INC   One Riverfront Plaza, Corning, NY 14831, Tel: (607) 974-9000
(Mfr glass & specialty materials, consumer prdts; communications, lab services)
  Samsung-Corning Co. Ltd., Seoul, South Korea

CPC INTERNATIONAL INC   PO Box 8000, Englewood Cliffs, NJ 07632,
Tel: (201) 894-4000
(Consumer foods, corn refining)
  Best Foods-Miwon Ltd., Baby-Ra Bldg. 5/F, 1433 Song-In-Dong, Chong-Ro-Ku,
    Seoul 110-550, South Korea
  Doosan Grain Co. Ltd., 15-1 2-Ga, Dangsan-Dong, Youngdeungpo-Ku, Seoul, South Korea

CRAY RESEARCH INC   655 Lone Oak Dr, Eagan, MN 55121, Tel: (612) 452-6650
(Supercomputer systems & services)
  CRS Korea Ltd., Plaza 654 Bldg. 4/F, 654-3 Yeoksam-Dong, Kangnam-Ku, Seoul,
    South Korea
  Cray Research Korea Ltd., Plaza 654 Bldg. 4/F, 654-3 Yeoksam-Dong, Kangnam-Ku,
    Seoul, South Korea

D'ARCY MASIUS BENTON & BOWLES INC (DMB&B)   1675 Broadway, New York,
NY 10019, Tel: (212) 468-3622
(Advertising & communications)
  Seoul/DMB&B Inc., Dong-hwa Bldg. 15/F, 58-7 Seasomoon-dong, Jung-gu, Seoul,
    South Korea

DANA CORP   PO Box 1000, Toledo, OH 43697, Tel: (419) 535-4500
(Engineer/mfr/mkt prdts & sys for vehicular, ind & mobile off-highway mkt & related
aftermarkets)
  Korea Spicer Corp., P.O. Box 26, Bupyong 211-3, Samsan-Dong, Buk-ku, Inchon,
    South Korea

DIGITAL EQUIPMENT CORP   146 Main St, Maynard, MA 01754-2571,
Tel: (508) 493-5111
(Networked computer systems & services)
  Digital Equipment Korea Inc.,

THE DOW CHEMICAL CO   2030 Dow Center, Midland, MI 48674, Tel: (517) 636-1000
    (Mfr chems, plastics, pharms, agric prdts, consumer prdts)
        Dow Chemical Korea Ltd., CPO Box 1583, 118 2-ka, Namdaemun-ro, Chung-ku, Seoul 100,
        South Korea
        Korea Pacific Chemical Corp., CPO Box 2626, 118 2-ka Namdaemun-ro, Chung-Ku,
        Seoul 100, South Korea

DOW CORNING CORP   2220 W Salzburg Rd, PO Box 1767, Midland, MI 48640,
    Tel: (517) 496-4000
    (Silicones, silicon chems, solid lubricants)
        Dow Corning Korea Ltd., 102 Namsong Mansion, 260-199 Itaweon-dong, Yonsan-Ku,
        CPO Box 7217, Seoul, South Korea

E I DU PONT DE NEMOURS & CO   1007 Market St, Wilmington, DE 19898,
    Tel: (302) 774-1000
    (Mfr/sale diversified chems, plastics, specialty prdts & fibers)
        Du Pont Korea Ltd., South Korea

DURAMETALLIC CORP   2104 Factory St, Kalamazoo, MI 49001, Tel: (616) 382-8720
    (Mfr mech seals, compression packings, auxiliaries)
        Korea Seal Master Co. Ltd., 600 Kamjungri, Kimpoup, Kimpogun, Kyunggido, South Korea

DYN CORP   2000 Edmund Halley Dr, Reston, VA 22091, Tel: (703) 264-0330
    (Diversified tech services)
        Dyn Corp, all mail to 45th Transportation, APO San Francisco, CA 96271

EASTMAN KODAK CO   343 State St, Rochester, NY 14650, Tel: (716) 724-4000
    (Devel/mfr photo & chem prdts, info mgmt/video/copier sys, fibers/plastics for
    various ind)
        Eastman Chemical Korea Ltd., 7/F Marine Ctr. Bldg., 118 2-Ka Namdaenum-Ro, Jung-Ku,
        Seoul 100-770, South Korea
        Kodak Korea Ltd., KPO Box 1089, Seoul 110-610, South Korea

EBASCO SERVICES INC   2 World Trade Center, New York, NY 10048-0752,
    Tel: (212) 839-1000
    (Engineering, constr)
        Ebasco Qualtech Korea Inc., 8/F Dong Sung Bldg., 158-9 Samsung-Dong Kangnam-ju,
        Seoul 135-090, South Korea

ELECTROGLAS INC   2901 Coronado Dr, Santa Clara, CA 95054, Tel: (408) 727-6500
    (Mfr semi-conductor test equip, automatic wafer probers)
        Electroglas Intl. Inc., Hamshin Bldg. 16/F, 98-4 Karak-Dong, Songpa-Ku, Seoul,
        South Korea

EMERSON RADIO CORP   1 Emerson Lane, N Bergen, NJ 07047, Tel: (201) 854-6600
    (Consumer electronics, radios, TV & VCR, tape recorders & players, computer prdts)
        Emerson Radio/Korea, 701 Daehan Bldg., 75 Seosomun-dung, Jung-gu, Seoul, South Korea

ENCYCLOPAEDIA BRITANNICA INC   310 S Michigan Ave, Chicago, IL 60604,
    Tel: (312) 321-7000
    (Publishing)
        Korea Britannica Corp., Ssanglim Bldg. 5/F, Ssanglim-Dong, Chung-Ku, Seoul 100-400,
        South Korea

EXPEDITORS INTL OF WASHINGTON INC   PO Box 69620, Seattle, WA 98168-9620,
    Tel: (206) 246-3711
    (Air/ocean freight forwarding, customs brokerage, intl logistics solutions)

(cont)

EI (Korea) Co. Ltd., Kyungnam Bldg. #6, 4KA 56-4 Jungang-Dong, Jung-Ku, Busan,·
  South Korea

FAIRCHILD CAMERA & INSTRUMENT CORP   PO Box 58090, Santa Clara,
  CA 95052-8090, Tel: (408) 743-3355
  (Mfr electr instru & controls)
    Fairchild Semiconductor (Korea) Ltd., CPO Box 2806, 4759 Shinkil-dong,
    Yungdungpo-ku, Seoul 150, South Korea

FELTON INTERNATIONAL INC   599 Johnson Ave, Brooklyn, NY 11237,
  Tel: (212) 497-4664
  (Essential oils & extracts, perfumes & flavor material, aromatic chems)
    Teejei Intl. Co., Bokchang Bldg., 80 Sokong-dong, Chung-ku, Seoul, South Korea

FIRST CHICAGO CORP   One First National Plaza, Chicago, IL 60670,
  Tel: (312) 732-4000
  (Banking)
    First Chicago Corp., Seoul, South Korea

FIRST NATIONAL BANK OF BOSTON   100 Federal St, Boston, MA 02110,
  Tel: (617) 434-2200
  (Commercial banking)
    First Natl. Bank of Boston, CPO Box 313, Dong Sung Bldg. 4/F,
    17-7 7-ka Namdaemun-ro, Chung-ku, Seoul, South Korea

FIRST NATIONAL BANK OF CHICAGO   One First National Plaza, Chicago, IL 60670,
  Tel: (312) 732-4000
  (Financial services)
    First Natl. Bank of Chicago, CPO Box 7239, Oriental Chemical Industry Bldg. 15/F,
    50 Sogong-dong, Chung-ku, Seoul, South Korea

FLUOR DANIEL INC   3333 Michelson Dr, Irvine, CA 92730, Tel: (714) 975-2000
  (Engineering, construction, maintenance & technical services)
    Fluor Daniel Eastern Inc., Samboo Bldg. 17/F, 676 Yoksam-Dong, Kangnam-ku,
    Seoul 135-080, South Korea

FMC CORP   200 E Randolph Dr, Chicago, IL 60601, Tel: (312) 861-6000
  (Produces chems & precious metals, mfr machinery, equip & sys for ind, agric & govt)
    FMC Intl. AG, South Korea

FOUR WINDS INTL GROUP   1500 SW First Ave, #850, Portland, OR 97201,
  Tel: (503) 241-2732
  (Transp of household goods & general cargo, third party logistics)
    Four Winds A-1 Trans Korea, Myung San Bldg. #203, 646 Itaewon-Dong, Yong San Ku,
    Seoul 140-202, South Korea

FRITZ COMPANIES INC   706 Mission St, San Francisco, CA 94103,
  Tel: (415) 904-8360
  (Integrated transportation, sourcing, distribution & customs brokerage services)
    Fritz Air Freight (Korea) Co. Ltd., Soo Sung Bldg. 1/F, 198-31 Dong Kyo-Dong,
    Mapo-Ku, Seoul, South Korea
    Fritz Transportation Intl. (Korea) Co., Jeoksun Hyundae Bldg. 7/F, Jeoksun-Dong,
    Chongro-Ku, Seoul, South Korea

GENERAL DYNAMICS CORP   3190 Fairview Park Dr, Falls Church, VA 22042-4523,
Tel: (703) 876-3000
(Mfr aerospace equip, submarines, strategic sys, armored vehicles, defense support sys)
  General Dynamics Intl Corp., 3-block, Sungjoo Danji, Changwon City, Kyung Nam, South Korea

GENERAL ELECTRIC CO   3135 Easton Tpk, Fairfield, CT 06431,
Tel: (203) 373-2211
(Diversified manufacturing, technology & services)
  General Electric Co.,
    all mail to U.S. address; phone (800) 626-2004 or (518) 438-6500

GENERAL FOODS CORP   250 North St, White Plains, NY 10625, Tel: (914) 335-2500
(Processor, distributor & mfr of foods)
  Dong Suh Foods Corp., 994-4 Daerimdong, Youngdungpo-ku, Seoul, South Korea

GENERAL MOTORS CORP   3044 W Grand Blvd, Detroit, MI 48202-3091,
Tel: (313) 556-5000
(Mfr full line vehicles, automotive electronics, coml technologies, telecom, space, finance)
  Daewoo Motor Co. Ltd., Seoul, South Korea

GEORGIA BONDED FIBERS INC   1040 W 29th St, PO Box 751, Buena Vista,
VA 24416, Tel: (703) 261-2181
(Mfr insole & luggage material)
  Bontex Korea, Song Nam Bldg., P.O. Box Pusan 581, Chung-gu, Pusan, South Korea

GETZ BROS & CO INC   150 Post St, #500, San Francisco, CA 94108,
Tel: (415) 772-5500
(Divers mfg, mktg/distr serv, travel serv)
  GETEC, 50-10 2-Ka, Chungmu-Ro, Chung-ku, GPO Box 3704, Seoul, South Korea

GIBBS & HILL INC   11 Penn Plaza, New York, NY 10001, Tel: (212) 216-6000
(Consulting engineers)
  Gibbs & Hill Inc., Lodge Hotel, Suite 631, CPO Box 3500, Seoul 77110, South Korea

THE GILLETTE CO   Prudential Tower, Boston, MA 02199, Tel: (617) 421-7000
(Devel/mfr personal care/use prdts: blades & razors, toiletries, cosmetics, stationery)
  Gillette Korea Ltd., Seoul, South Korea

W R GRACE & CO   One Town Center Rd, Boca Raton, FL 33486-1010,
Tel: (407) 362-2000
(Mfr spec chems & materials: packaging, health care, catalysts, construction, water treatment/process)
  Grace Korea Inc., DLI 63 Bldg, 43/F, 60 Yoeido-dong, Youngdeungpo-ku, Seoul, South Korea

GRACO INC   4050 Olson Memorial Hwy, PO Box 1441, Minneapolis, MN 55440-1441,
Tel: (612) 623-6000
(Mfr/serv fluid handling equip & sys)
  Graco Korea Inc., Dae-A Bldg. 3/F, 707-7/8 Yoksam-Dong, Gangnam-Ku, Seoul 135-080, South Korea

GRUMMAN INTL INC   1111 Stewart Ave, Bethpage, NY 11714, Tel: (516) 575-4806
  (Mfr/sale aerospace prdts, aircraft, software, automated test equip, C3 projects)
    Grumman Korea Ltd., Leema Bldg. 1405, 146-1 Soosong-Dong, Chongro-ku,
      Seoul 110-140, South Korea

FRANK B HALL & CO INC   549 Pleasantville Rd, Briarcliff Manor, NY 10510,
  Tel: (914) 769-9200
  (Insurance)
    Frank B. Hall & Co. Korea Inc., 58-4 1-ga Bongrae-dong, Choong-ku, CPO Box 9733,
      Seoul, South Korea

THE HARPER GROUP   260 Townsend St, PO Box 77933, San Francisco,
  CA 94107-1719, Tel: (415) 978-0600
  (Ocean/air freight fwdg, customs brokerage, packing & whse, logistics mgt, ins)
    Circle Airfreight Intl. Korea, 903 Kumjung Bldg., 192-11 Chung-ku, CPO Box 592,
      Seoul, South Korea

THE HARTFORD STEAM BOILER INSPECTION & INSURANCE CO   1 State St, Hartford,
  CT 06102, Tel: (203) 722-1866
  (Inspection & quality assurance, asbestos monitoring)
    Hartford Steam Boiler, 97-7, 603, Chungho Bldg., Nonhycon-Dong, Kangnam-Ku,
      Seoul 135-010, South Korea

H J HEINZ CO   PO Box 57, Pittsburgh, PA 15230-0057, Tel: (412) 456-5700
  (Processed food prdts & nutritional services)
    Seoul-Heinz Ltd., Seoul, South Korea

HEWLETT-PACKARD CO   3000 Hanover St, Palo Alto, CA 94304-0890,
  Tel: (415) 857-1501
  (Mfr computing, communications & measurement prdts & services)
    Hewlett-Packard Korea Ltd., SHP House, 25-12 Yoido-Dong, Youngdeungpo-Gu,
      Seoul 150-010, South Korea

HONEYWELL INC   PO Box 524, Minneapolis, MN 55440-0524, Tel: (612) 951-1000
  (Devel/mfr controls for home & building, industry, space & aviation)
    Lucky Goldstar-Honeywell Co. Ltd., Kukje Center Bldg. 18/F, 191 Hangangro-Ga,
      Yongsan-Gu, Seoul 140-702, South Korea

HORWATH INTL   415 Madison Ave, New York, NY 10017, Tel: (212) 838-5566
  (Public accountants & auditors)
    Chong-Un Accounting Co. Inc., Room 704, Sampoong Bldg., 310-4-ka Eulji-ro,
      Choong-ku, Seoul, South Korea

HUGHES AIRCRAFT CO   PO Box 80028, Los Angeles, CA 90080-0028,
  Tel: (310) 568-6904
  (Mfr electronics equip & sys)
    Hughes Aircraft Intl. Service Co., Kyobo Bldg., Room 1606, 1-1 Jongro 1-ka,
      Jongro-ku, Seoul 110, South Korea

HYATT INTL CORP   200 West Madison, Chicago, IL 60606, Tel: (312) 750-1234
  (Intl hotel mgmt)
    Hyatt Intl. Hotels, Cheju, Pusan & Seoul, South Korea

IBM CORP   Old Orchard Rd, Armonk, NY 10504, Tel: (914) 765-1900
  (Information products, technology & services)
    IBM Korea Inc., Seoul, South Korea

INDUCTOTHERM CORP   10 Indel Ave, Rancocas, NJ 08073-0157, Tel: (609) 267-9000
  (Mfr induction melting furnaces)
    Inductotherm Korea Ltd., 18-40 Banwol Industrial Complex, Ansan, Kyunggi-Do 425110,
    South Korea

INSTRON CORP   100 Royall St, Canton, MA 02021-1089, Tel: (617) 828-2500
  (Mfr material testing instruments)
    Instron Corp. (Korea), Seo Woo Bldg. 837-12, 7/F, Yeoksang-Dong, Kangnam-Ku, Seoul,
    South Korea

INTERGRAPH CORP   Huntsville, AL 35894-0001, Tel: (205) 730-2000
  (Devel/mfr interactive computer graphic systems)
    Intergraph Korea Ltd., Young Dong P.O. Box 6, Kangnam-Ku, Seoul 135-600, South Korea

INTERMEC CORP   6001 36th Ave West, PO Box 4280, Everett, WA 98203-9280,
  Tel: (206) 348-2600
  (Mfr/distr automated data collection sys)
    Sammi Computer Service Co. Ltd., 907-4 Bangbae-dong, Socho-ku, Seoul, South Korea

INTERNATIONAL CLOSEOUT EXCHANGE SYS INC   220 W 19th St, #1200, New York,
  NY 10011, Tel: (212) 647-8901
  (Online service listing off-price merchandise)
    SEMI ICES Korea, Han-Duk Bldg. 3/F, 45-6 Jamwong-Dong, Secho-Ku, Seoul, South Korea

INTERNATIONAL PAPER   2 Manhattanville Rd, Purchase, NY 10577,
  Tel: (914) 397-1500
  (Mfr/distr container board, paper, wood prdts)
    International Paper Korea Ltd., 552-19 Shinsa-Dong, Kangnam-Ku, Seoul, South Korea

INTERTRANS CORP   125 E John Carpenter Frwy, Irving, TX 75062,
  Tel: (214) 830-8888
  (Intl freight forwarding)
    Intertrans Corp., Sukchun Bldg. 3/F, 169-14 Dongyo-Dong, Mapo-gu, Seoul, South Korea

ITT CORP   1330 Ave of the Americas, New York, NY 10019-5490,
  Tel: (212) 258-1000
  (Design/mfr communications & electronic equip, hotels, insurance)
    ITT Far East & Pacific Inc., CPO Box 1201, Seoul 100, South Korea

ITT SHERATON CORP   60 State St, Boston, MA 02108, Tel: (617) 367-3600
  (Hotel operations)
    Sheraton Walker Hill Hotel, San 21, Kwangiang-dong, Sungdong-ku, South Korea

JCPENNEY PURCHASING CORP   PO Box 10001, Dallas, TX 75301-0001,
  Tel: (214) 431-5380
  (Department stores)
    JCPenney Purchasing Corp., OCI Bldg. 11/F, 50 Sokong-dong, Chung-ku, Seoul 100-070,
    South Korea

JOHNSON & HIGGINS   125 Broad St, New York, NY 10004-2424, Tel: (212) 574-7000
  (Ins brokerage, employee benefit conslt, risk mgmt, human resource conslt, ins/reins
  servs)
    Johnson & Higgins Agency of Korea Ltd., Seoul, South Korea

JOHNSON & JOHNSON   One Johnson & Johnson Plaza, New Brunswick, NJ 08933,
  Tel: (908) 524-0400
  (R&D/mfr/sale health care prdts)

(cont)

Cilag Korea Ltd., Do Bong P.O. Box 24, Seoul, South Korea
Janssen Korea Ltd., Kangnam, P.O. Box 1111, Seoul 135-611, South Korea
Johnson & Johnson Korea Ltd., Yongsan P.O. Box 175, Seoul, South Korea
Johnson & Johnson Medical Korea Ltd., Yongsan P.O. Box 175, Seoul, South Korea

S C JOHNSON & SON INC   1525 Howe St, Racine, WI 53403, Tel: (414) 631-2000
(Home, auto, commercial & personal care prdts, specialty chems)
S.C. Johnson (Korea) Co. Ltd., Sungdong P.O. Box 39, Seoul, South Korea

JOY ENVIRONMENTAL TECHNOLOGIES INC   10700 North Freeway, Houston, TX 77037,
Tel: (713) 878-1000
(Design/eng air pollution control & material handling sys)
Hansung Power & Industrial Corp., CPO Box 993, Seoul, South Korea

A T KEARNEY INC   222 West Adams St, Chicago, IL 60606, Tel: (312) 648-0111
(Mgmt consultants, executive search)
A.T. Kearney Inc., Intercontinental Hotel #525, 159-8 Samsung-Dong Kangnam-Ku,
Seoul 135-732, South Korea

KELLOGG CO   One Kellogg Sq, PO Box 3599, Battle Creek, MI 49016-3599,
Tel: (616) 961-2000
(Mfr ready-to-eat cereals, convenience foods)
Nhong Shim Kellogg Co. Ltd., Kyeongki-do, Korea (all inquiries to U.S. address)

KEYSTONE INTL INC   PO Box 40010, Houston, TX 77040, Tel: (713) 466-1176
(Mfr butterfly valves, actuators & control accessories)
Keystone Valve, South Korea

KIMBERLY-CLARK CORP   PO Box 619100, Dallas, TX 75261, Tel: (214) 281-1200
(Mfr fiber-based prdts for personal care, lumber & paper prdts)
Ssangyong Paper Co. Ltd., Korea
Yuhan-Kimberly Ltd. (JV), CPO Box 2537, 302-75 Dongbu Echon-dong, Yongsan-ku,
Seoul 140, South Korea

LESTER B KNIGHT & ASSOC INC   549 W Randolph St, Chicago, IL 60661,
Tel: (312) 346-2300
(Architecture, engineering, planning, operations & mgmt consulting)
Knight Korea, Boram Savings and Finance Bldg. 12/F, 705-19 Yok Sam Dong,
Kang Nam-Ku, Seoul, South Korea

KYSOR INDUSTRIAL CORP   One Madison Ave, Cadillac, MI 49601-9785,
Tel: (616) 779-2200
(Mfr commercial refrigeration, commercial vehicle components)
Kysor/Asia Ltd., Room 505, Chungdong Bldg., 1659-2 Bongchun-Dong, Kwanak-Ku,
Seoul 151-061, South Korea

LEARONAL INC   272 Buffalo Ave, Freeport, NY 11520, Tel: (516) 868-8800
(Mfr chem specialties)
LeaRonal Korea, Dong-Ah Bldg. 6/F, 14-6 Youido-Dong, Youngdungpo-Gu, Seoul,
South Korea

ELI LILLY & CO   Lilly Corporate Center, Indianapolis, IN 46285,
Tel: (317) 276-2000
(Mfr pharmaceuticals, animal health prdts)
Eli Lilly Asia Inc., 802 Changhak-Hall Bldg., 945-15 Daechi-Dong, Kangnam-Ku,
Seoul 135-283, South Korea

LIQUID CARBONIC INDUSTRIES CORP   810 Jorie Blvd, Oak Brook, IL 60521,
Tel: (708) 572-7500
(Mfr compressed gasses)
　　Korea Liquid Carbonic Co. Ltd., CPO Box 4123, Doksan-dong, Guro-Ku, Seoul 150,
　　South Korea

ARTHUR D LITTLE INC   25 Acorn Park, Cambridge, MA 02140-2390,
Tel: (617) 498-5000
(Mgmt, environ, health & safety consulting; tech & prdt development)
　　Arthur D. Little Korea Inc., Kyobo Bldg. 13/F, 1-1 Chongro, Chongro-Ku,
　　Seoul 110-714, South Korea

LOCKHEED MARTIN CORP   6801 Rockledge Dr, Bethesda, MD 20817,
Tel: (301) 897-6000
(Design/mfr/mgmt sys in fields of space, defense, energy, electronics, materials,
info & tech svces)
　　Lockheed Martin Intl. Ltd., DLI 63 Bldg. 46/F, 60 Yoido-Dong, Youngdeungpo-Ku,
　　Seoul 150-763, South Korea

LOCTITE CORP   10 Columbus Blvd, Hartford, CT 06106, Tel: (203) 520-5000
(Mfr/sale ind adhesives & sealants)
　　Loctite Korea Inc., Chungsan Bldg. 4/F, 262-1 Hannam-dong, Yongsan-Ku, Seoul,
　　South Korea

LORAL INTL INC   999 Central Park Ave, Yonkers, NY 10704-1013,
Tel: (914) 964-6520
(Mktg coordination: defense electronics, communications sys)
　　Loral Intl. Systems Ltd., 27th Floor, Korean World Trade Center, 159 Samsung-Dong,
　　Kangnam-ku, Seoul 135-729, South Korea

THE LUBRIZOL CORP   29400 Lakeland Blvd, Wickliffe, OH 44092-2298,
Tel: (216) 943-4200
(Mfr chem additives for lubricants & fuels)
　　Lubrizol Korea, South Korea

R H MACY & CO INC   151 West 34th St, New York, NY 10001, Tel: (212) 695-4400
(Department stores, importers)
　　R.H. Macy & Co. Inc., 903 Samkoo Bldg., 70 Sockong-dong, Joong-ku, Seoul 100,
　　South Korea

MARSH & McLENNAN COS INC   1166 Ave of the Americas, New York, NY 10036-1011,
Tel: (212) 345-5000
(Insurance)
　　March & McLennan (Korea) Ltd., 2404 Kukong Bldg., 60-1 3-ka Chungmi-ro, Chung-ku,
　　Seoul, South Korea

MAXTOR CORP   211 River Oaks Pkwy, San Jose, CA 95134, Tel: (408) 432-1700
(Design/mfr magnetic storage prdts)
　　Maxtor Asia Pacific Ltd., Seoul, South Korea

MERCK SHARP & DOHME INTL   PO Box 2000, Rahway, NJ 07065, Tel: (201) 574-4000
(Pharms, chems & biologicals)
　　Merck Sharp & Dohme, 501-B Dae Kyung Bldg., 199 Wonnam-dong, Chongro-ku, Seoul,
　　South Korea

METROPOLITAN LIFE INSURANCE CO   1 Madison Ave, New York, NY   10010-3690,
  Tel: (212) 578-2211
  (Insurance & retirement savings prdts & services)
     Kolon-Met Life Insurance Co., 141 Samsung-Dong, Kangnam-Ku, Sungwon B/D 6-8/F,
     Seoul 135-090, South Korea

MICROSOFT CORP   One Microsoft Way, Redmond, WA   98052-6399,
  Tel: (206) 882-8080
  (Computer software, peripherals & services)
     Microsoft Korea CH, Dong Seong Bldg., 158-9 Samseong-Dong, Gangnam-Gu,
     Seoul 135-090, South Korea

MICROTEC RESEARCH   2350 Mission College Blvd, Santa Clara, CA   95054,
  Tel: (408) 980-1300
  (Devel/mfr software tools for embedded systems market)
     Hankuk Microtec Research, 302 Kyunghee Bldg., 109-18 Samsung-Dong, Kangnam-Ku,
     Seoul 135-090, South Korea

MILLIPORE CORP   Ashley Rd, Bedford, MA   01730, Tel: (617) 275-9205
  (Mfr precision filters, hi-performance liquid chromatography instru)
     Millipore Korea Ltd., Room 202, Junwha Bldg., 157-10 Samsung-Dong, Kangnam-ku,
     Seoul, South Korea

MOLEX INC   2222 Wellington Ct, Lisle, IL   60532, Tel: (708) 969-4550
  (Mfr electronic, electrical & fiber optic interconnection prdts & sys, switches,
  application tooling)
     Molex Inc., Ansan City, South Korea

MOOG INC   East Aurora, NY   14052-0018, Tel: (716) 652-2000
  (Mfr precision control components & sys)
     Moog Korea Ltd., 505-4 Yeolmi-Ri, Shilchou-myon, Kwangju-kun, Kyunggi-do,
     South Korea

MOTOROLA INC   1303 E Algonquin Rd, Schaumburg, IL   60196, Tel: (708) 576-5000
  (Mfr commun equip, semiconductors, cellular phones)
     Motorola Korea Ltd., 445 Kwangjank-dong, Sungdong-ku, Seoul 133, South Korea
     Motorola Korea Ltd., Kangnam Jeil Bldg., 822-4 Yuksam-dong, Kangnam-ku,
     Seoul 134-03, South Korea

MTS SYSTEMS CORP   14000 Technology Dr, Eden Prairie, MN   55344-2290,
  Tel: (612) 937-4000
  (Devel/mfr mechanical testing & simulation prdts & servs, ind meas & automation
  instrumentation)
     MTS Korea Inc., Sungdam Bldg. 3/F, 142-35 Samsung-Dong, Gangnam-Ku, Seoul 135-090,
     South Korea

NASH INTL CO   3 Trefoil Dr, Trumbull, CT   06611, Tel: (203) 459-3900
  (Mfr air & gas compressors, vacuum pumps)
     Nash-Korea Ltd., 17 Block 8 Lot, Namdong Industrial Complex, Namdong-ku,
     Inchon 405-300, South Korea

NATIONAL STARCH & CHEMICAL CO   10 Finderne Ave, Bridgewater, NJ   08807-3300,
  Tel: (908) 685-5000
  (Mfr adhesives & sealants, resins & spec chems, electr materials & adhesives, food
  prdts, ind starch)
     IPCO-National Ltd., Seoul, South Korea

A C NIELSEN CO   Nielsen Plaza, Northbrook, IL 60062-6288, Tel: (708) 498-6300
  (Market research)
    Nielsen Korea Ltd., Namkyung Bldg., 8-2 Samsung-dong, Kangnam-ku, Seoul, South Korea

NORDSON CORP   28601 Clemens Rd, Westlake, OH 44145, Tel: (216) 892-1580
  (Mfr ind application equip & packaging mach)
    Nordson Sang San Ltd., 324-2 Gosan-Ri, Ohpo-Myun, Kwangju-Gun, Kyunggi-Do,
    Seoul 464-890, South Korea

NOVELLUS SYSTEMS INC   81 Vista Montana, San Jose, CA 95134,
  Tel: (408) 943-9700
  (Mfr advanced processing systems used in fabrication of integrated circuits)
    Novellus Korea, 3/F WMU Bldg., 239-16 Poi Dong, Kang Nam-Ku, Seoul, South Korea

ONAN CORP   1400 73rd Ave NE, Minneapolis, MN 55432, Tel: (612) 574-5000
  (Mfr electric generators, controls & switchgears)
    Onan Korea, Joyang Bldg., 113 Sam-Sung-dong, Kang-Nam Gu, Seoul 135-090, South Korea

OTIS ELEVATOR CO   10 Farm Springs, Farmington, CT 06032, Tel: (860) 676-6528
  (Mfr elevators & escalators)
    Hankook Otis Elevator Co. Ltd., KFSB Bldg., 16-2 Yoido-Dong, Yeong Deungpo-gu,
    Seoul, South Korea

PACIFIC TELESIS GROUP   130 Kearney St, San Francisco, CA 94108,
  Tel: (415) 394-3000
  (Telecommun & info sys)
    Pacific Telesis Korea Ltd., 1141 Chamber of Commerce & Industry Bldg.,
    4-45 Namdenmun-ro, Chung-Gu, Seoul, South Korea

PANDUIT CORP   17301 Ridgeland Ave, Tinley Park, IL 60477-0981,
  Tel: (708) 532-1800
  (Mfr elec/electr wiring comps)
    Panduit Korea Ltd., Insung Bldg. 3/F, 102-9 Samjun-Dong, Songpa-Ku, Seoul,
    South Korea

PARKER HANNIFIN CORP   17325 Euclid Ave, Cleveland, OH 44112,
  Tel: (216) 531-3000
  (Mfr motion-control prdts)
    Parker Hannifin Asia Pacific Co. Ltd., 902 Dae Heung Bldg., 648-23 Yeoksam-dong,
    Kangnam-ku, Seoul 135-080, South Korea

PFIZER INC   235 E 42nd St, New York, NY 10017-5755, Tel: (212) 573-2323
  (Mfr healthcare products)
    Pfizer Korea Ltd., South Korea
    Pfizer Ltd., South Korea

PPG INDUSTRIES   One PPG Place, Pittsburgh, PA 15272, Tel: (412) 434-3131
  (Mfr flat glass, fiber glass, chems, coatings)
    Dongju Industrial Co. Ltd., 128-7 Yongdang-dong, Nam-ku, Pusan 608-080, South Korea

PREMARK INTL INC   1717 Deerfield Rd, Deerfield, IL 60015, Tel: (708) 405-6000
  (Mfr/sale diversified consumer & coml prdts)
    Premiere Korea Ltd., Samwhan Bldg. 2/F, 98-5 Wooni-dong, Chongro-ku, Seoul,
    South Korea

RALSTON PURINA CO   Checkerboard Sq, St Louis, MO 63164, Tel: (314) 982-1000
(Poultry & live stock feed, cereals, food prdts)
Purina Korea Inc., Intl. Insurance Bldg., Namdaemun Rd., Choong-ku, Seoul,
South Korea

RAY BURNER CO   401 Parr Blvd, Richmond, CA 94801, Tel: (510) 236-4972
(Mfr gas & oil burners, controls, oil pump sets, boilers)
Ray of New Korea Ind. Co. Ltd., No. 304, 18-2 Dohwa-Dong, Mapo-ku, Seoul 121 040,
South Korea

RAYCHEM CORP   300 Constitution Dr, Menlo Park, CA 94025, Tel: (415) 361-3333
(Devel/mfr/mkt materials science products for electronics, telecommunications &
industry)
Raychem Korea Ltd., 73-62 Youngho-Dong, Changwon City 641-041, South Korea
Raychem Korea Ltd., also in Seoul & Suwon, South Korea

READING & BATES CORP   901 Threadneedle, #200, Houston, TX 77079,
Tel: (713) 496-5000
(Offshore contract drilling)
Reading & Bates Drilling Co., temporary address: Hyatt Regency-Pusan,
1405-16 Jung-Dong, Haeundae-Ku, Pusan, South Korea

REGAL WARE INC   1675 Reigle Dr, PO Box 395, Kewaskum, WI 53040-0395,
Tel: (414) 626-2121
(Mfr cookware, small electrical appliances, water purification & filtration prdts for
home)
Regal Ware Korea Co. Ltd., Wooduk Bldg. 3/F, 770-20 Yeoksam-Dong, Kang Nam Ku,
Seoul, South Korea

ROCKWELL INTL CORP   2201 Seal Beach Blvd, PO Box 4250, Seal Beach,
CA 90740-8250, Tel: (310) 797-3311
(Prdts & serv for aerospace, automotive, electronics, graphics & automation inds)
Allen-Bradley/Rockwell Intl. Korea Ltd., 42/F DLI 63 Bldg., 60 Yoido,
Yongdungpo-ku, Seoul, South Korea
Rockwell-Collins Intl. Inc., 608 Lee Ma Bldg., 146-1 Soosong-Dong, Chongro-ku,
KPO Box 527, Seoul, South Korea

ROHM AND HAAS CO   100 Independence Mall West, Philadelphia, PA 19106,
Tel: (215) 592-3000
(Mfr ind & agric chems, plastics)
Rohm and Haas Korea Co. Ltd., 802 Poong Lim Bldg., 823 Yeoksam-dong, Kangnam-ku,
Seoul, South Korea

SBC COMMUNICATIONS INC   175 E Houston, San Antonio, TX 78205,
Tel: (210) 821-4105
(Telecommunications)
SBC Communications Inc., South Korea

R P SCHERER CORP   2075 W Big Beaver Rd, Troy, MI 48084, Tel: (810) 649-0900
(Mfr soft gelatin & two-piece hard shell capsules)
R.P. Scherer Korea Ltd., Youngdong Bldg., 832 Yeogsam-dong, Kangnam-gu, Seoul,
South Korea

SEA-LAND SERVICE INC   150 Allen Rd, Liberty Corner, NJ 07920,
Tel: (201) 558-6000
(Container transport)

Sea-Land Service Inc., CPO Box 5390, 51 Sokong-dong, Chung-ku, Seoul 100, South Korea
Sea-Land Service Inc., CPO Box 85, 703 New Kal Bldg., Inchon 160, Seoul, South Korea
Sea-Land Service Inc., CPO Box 54, 18 Jaesong-dong, Dongrae-ku, Pusan, South Korea

G D SEARLE & CO   5200 Old Orchard Rd, Skokie, IL 60077, Tel: (708) 982-7000
(Mfr pharms, health care & optical prdts, specialty chems)
Searle Ciba-Geigy Korea Ltd., CPO Box 9047, Life Bldg. 15/F, 61 Youido-Dong, Youngeungpo-ku, Seoul, South Korea

SENCO PRODUCTS INC   8485 Broadwell Rd, Cincinnati, OH 45244,
Tel: (513) 388-2000
(Mfr ind nailers, staplers, fasteners & accessories)
Senco Korea, 22-1 Palryong-Dong, Changwon City, South Korea

SIGNETICS CORP   PO Box 3409, Sunnyvale, CA 94088-3409, Tel: (408) 991-2000
(Solid state circuits)
Signetics-Korea Co., 272 Yomchong-dong, Kangsu-ku, Seoul, South Korea

SPRINT INTERNATIONAL   12490 Sunrise Valley Dr, Reston, VA 22096,
Tel: (703) 689-6000
(Telecommunications)
Sprint Korea Inc., City Air Terminal Bldg. #509, 159-6 Samsung-Dong, Kangnam-Ku, Seoul, South Korea

SRI INTL   333 Ravenswood Ave, Menlo Park, CA 94025-3493, Tel: (415) 326-6200
(Intl consulting & research)
SRI-Seoul, Seok Tan Hoi Kwan Bldg. 3/F, 80-6 Soosong-Dong, Chongro-Ku, Seoul 110-140, South Korea

STANDARD COMMERCIAL CORP   PO Box 450, Wilson, NC 27893, Tel: (919) 291-5507
(Leaf tobacco dealers/processors, wool processors)
Kortec Ltd., Choongju, South Korea

STIEFEL LABORATORIES INC   255 Alhambra Circle, Coral Gables, FL 33134,
Tel: (305) 443-3807
(Mfr pharmaceuticals, dermatological specialties)
Stiefel Laboratories (Korea) Ltd., Wonjin Bldg. 6/F, 1626-2 Seocho-Dong, Seocho-ku, Seoul, South Korea

STOKES DIV   5500 Tabor Rd, Philadelphia, PA 19120, Tel: (215) 289-5671
(Vacuum pumps & components, vacuum dryers, oil-upgrading equip)
Connell Bros Co. (Korea) Ltd., CPO Box 1190, Seoul, South Korea

STONE & WEBSTER ENGINEERING CORP   245 Summer St, Boston, MA 02210-2288,
Tel: (617) 589-5111
(Engineering, constr & environmental & mgmt services)
Stone & Webster Korea Corp., Stone & Webster Suite, 42/F DLI 63 Bldg., 60 Yoido-Dong, Youngdeungpo-Ku, Seoul 150-763, South Korea

SUMMIT INDUSTRIAL CORP   600 Third Ave, New York, NY 10016,
Tel: (212) 490-1100
(Pharms, agric chem prdts)
Summit Industrial Corp., CPO Box 1078, 70-5 2-ka, Taepyung-ro, Chung-ku, Seoul 100, South Korea
Summit Service Corp. (Korea), CPO Box 4318, 73-1 Dungchon-dong, Yungdungpo-ku, Seoul 150, South Korea

TACO INC   1160 Cranston St, Cranston, RI   02920, Tel: (401) 942-8000
  (Mfr HVAC pumps & equip)
    Taco Korea Ltd., Daeha Bldg. #812, 14-11 Yoido-Dong, Youngdeungpo-Ku, Seoul,
    South Korea

TANDY CORP   1800 One Tandy Center, Fort Worth, TX   76102, Tel: (817) 390-3700
  (Electronic & acoustic equip)
    A&A Intl., Han Hyo Bldg., Yong Dong Pu-Ku, Seoul, South Korea
    TC Electronics (Korea) Corp., Masan P.O. Box 320, Masan Free Export Zone,
    South Korea

TELEDYNE INC   2049 Century Park East, Los Angeles, CA   90067-3101,
  Tel: (310) 277-3311
  (Divers mfg: aviation & electronics, specialty metals, industrial & consumer prdts)
    Teledyne Korea, Nam Song Mansion #403, 260-139 Itaewon-Dong, Yongsan-Ku,
    CPO Box 3599, Seoul, South Korea

TELLABS INC   4951 Indiana Ave, Lisle, IL   60532, Tel: (708) 969-8800
  (Design/mfr/svce voice/data transport & network access sys)
    Tellabs Korea, B1209 SamHo Bldg., 275-6 Yangjae-Dong, Seocho-ku, Seoul, South Korea

TEXACO INC   2000 Westchester Ave, White Plains, NY   10650, Tel: (914) 253-4000
  (Explor/mktg crude oil, mfr petro chems & prdts)
    Texaco Korea Inc., CPO Box 3257, Seoul, South Korea

THERMON   100 Thermon Dr, PO Box 609, San Marcos, TX   78667-0609,
  Tel: (512) 396-5801
  (Mfr steam & electric heat tracing sys, components & accessories)
    Thermon Korea Ltd., KWTC Bldg. #2602, 159-1 Samsung-Dong, Kangnam-Ku,
    Seoul 135-729, Korea

TIME WARNER INC   75 Rockefeller Plaza, New York, NY   10019,
  Tel: (212) 484-8000
  (Communications, publishing, entertainment)
    Hankook Ilbo Time Life Ltd., 14 Chunghak-dong, Chongro-gu, Seoul, South Korea

TRANE CO   3600 Pammel Creek Rd, La Crosse, WI   54601, Tel: (608) 787-2000
  (Mfr/distr/svce A/C sys & equip)
    Trane Korea, Han Duk Bldg. 901, 1337-33 Seocho-Dong, Seocho-Ku, Seoul, South Korea

TYLAN GENERAL INC   9577 Chesapeake Dr, San Diego, CA   92123,
  Tel: (619) 571-1222
  (Mfr flow & pressure measurement & control components)
    Tylan General Korea Ltd., 31-6 Mango-Dong, Paldal-Ku, Suwon City, Kyunggi-Do, Korea

U S WHEAT ASSOCIATES   1200 NW Front Ave, #600, Portland, OR   97209,
  Tel: (503) 223-8123
  (Market development for wheat prdts)
    U.S. Wheat Associates Inc., c/o Agricultural Trade Office, U.S. Embassy,
    63 Euljiro 1-ka, Chung-ku, Seoul, South Korea
    U.S. Wheat Associates Inc., P.O. Box 1004, Seoul, South Korea

UNION CARBIDE CORP   39 Old Ridgebury Rd, Danbury, CT   06817,
  Tel: (203) 794-2000
  (Mfr industrial chemicals, plastics, resins)

Union Carbide Chemicals Korea Ltd., 945-1 Hongwoo Bldg. 3/F, Daechi-Dong, Kangnam-Ku, Seoul 135-280, South Korea

UNION OIL INTL DIV   Union Oil Center, PO Box 7600, Los Angeles, CA 90017, Tel: (213) 977-7600
(Petroleum prdts, petrochems)
Kyung Energy Co. Ltd. (JV), Chemical Bldg., 35 Seosomoon-dong, Choong-ku, Seoul 100, South Korea

UNISYS CORP   PO Box 500, Blue Bell, PA 19424, Tel: (215) 986-4011
(Mfg/mktg/serv electr info sys)
Unisys Ltd., 60 Yoido Dong Bldg., Yongdungpo-gu, Seoul, South Korea

UNITED AIRLINES INC   PO Box 66100, Chicago, IL 60666, Tel: (708) 952-4000
(Air transp)
United Airlines, Ankuk Ins. Bldg. 15/F, 87 1-ka Eulchi-ro, Chung-ku, Seoul 100-191, South Korea

UNIVERSAL CORP   PO Box 25099, Richmond, VA 23260, Tel: (804) 359-9311
(Holding co: tobacco, commodities)
Oriental Processors & Exporters of Korea Ltd., P.O. Box CPO 2137, Seoul, South Korea

UPJOHN CO   7000 Portage Rd, Kalamazoo, MI 49001, Tel: (616) 323-4000
(Mfr pharms, agric prdts, ind chems)
Korea Upjohn Ltd., CPO Box 5816, 8 Yang-dong, Chung-ku, Seoul 100, South Korea

VARIAN ASSOCIATES INC   3100 Hansen Way, Palo Alto, CA 94304-1030, Tel: (415) 493-4000
(Mfr microwave tubes & devices, analytical instru, semiconductor process & med equip, vacuum sys)
Varian Korea Ltd., 433-1 Mogok-Dong, Songtan, Kyunaggi-Do 459-040, South Korea

WARD HOWELL INTL INC   99 Park Ave, New York, NY 10016-1699, Tel: (212) 697-3730
(Executive recruiting)
Top Business Consultants Services Inc., Korea World Trade Center #3505, 159-1 Samsung-Dong, Kangnam-Ku, Seoul 135-729, South Korea

WATLOW ELECTRIC MFG CO   12001 Lackland Rd, St Louis, MO 63146-4039, Tel: (314) 878-4600
(Mfr elec heating units, electr controls, thermocouple wire, metal-sheathed cable, infrared sensors)
Watlow Korea, 302 Samsung Bldg., 945-3 Daechi-Dong, Kangnam-Ku, Seoul 135-283, South Korea

THE WEST CO   101 Gordon Dr, PO Box 645, Lionville, PA 19341-0645, Tel: (610) 594-2900
(Mfr prdts for filling, sealing, dispensing & delivering needs of health care & consumer prdts mkts)
The West Co., Seoul, South Korea

WESTERN DIGITAL CORP   8105 Irvine Center Dr, Irvine, CA 92718, Tel: (714) 932-5000
(Mfr hard disk drives, video graphics boards, VLSI)
Western Digital Korea, Hanjin Bldg. 6/F, 169-11 Samsung-Dong, Kangnam-Ku, Seoul, South Korea

WESTINGHOUSE ELECTRIC CORP   11 Stanwix St, Pittsburgh, PA 15222-1384,
  Tel: (412) 244-2000
  (TV/radio broadcasting, mfr electr sys for ind/defense, fin & environmental servs)
    Westinghouse Electric SA, CPO Box 8069, Seoul, South Korea

WILBUR-ELLIS CO   320 California St, #200, San Francisco, CA 94104,
  Tel: (415) 772-4000
  (Intl merchants & distributors)
    Connell Bros. Co. (Korea) Ltd., 1708 Intl. Insurance Bldg., 120 5-ka Namdaemoon-ro,
    Chunk-gu, Seoul, South Korea

XEROX CORP   800 Long Ridge Rd, PO Box 1600, Stamford, CT 06904,
  Tel: (203) 968-3000
  (Mfr document processing equip, sys & supplies)
    Xerox Corp., Inchon & Seoul, South Korea

KUWAIT

THE ARCHITECTS COLLABORATIVE INC   46 Brattle St, Cambridge, MA 02138,
  Tel: (617) 868-4200
  (Arch/interior/landscape, master planning, graphic design)
    The Architects Collaborative Inc., P.O. Box 23548, 13096 Safat, Kuwait

BECHTEL GROUP INC   50 Beale St, PO Box 3965, San Francisco, CA 94119,
  Tel: (415) 768-1234
  (Engineering & constr)
    Eastern Bechtel Corp., P.O. Box 23930, Safat, Kuwait

BENTLY NEVADA CORP   PO Box 157, Minden, NV 89423, Tel: (702) 782-3611
  (Electronic monitoring system)
    A.Z. Trading Co. WWL, P.O. Box 25752, Safat, Kuwait

LEO BURNETT CO INC   35 West Wacker Dr, Chicago, IL 60601, Tel: (312) 220-5959
  (Advertising agency)
    Radius Advertising, Al Khalcejia Bldg., P.O. Box 26100, Safat 13121, Kuwait

CARRIER CORP   One Carrier Place, Farmington, CT 06034-4015,
  Tel: (203) 674-3000
  (Mfr/distr/svce A/C, heating & refrigeration equip)
    Kuwait American Airconditioning Co., P.O. Box 146, 13002 Safat, Kuwait

COMBUSTION ENGINEERING INC   900 Long Ridge Road, Stamford, CT 06902,
  Tel: (203) 329-8771
  (Tech constr)
    Al Julaiah General Irading & Contracting Co., P.O. Box 173, Kuwait, Kuwait
    P.S.C. Supply Co., P.O. Box 9465, Ahmadi, Kuwait

CONTINENTAL CAN CO   PO Box 5410, Stamford, CT 06856, Tel: (203) 357-8110
  (Packaging prdts & mach, metal, plastic & paper containers)
    Kuwait Metal Container Co. Ltd., P.O. Box 9295, Ahmadi, Kuwait

DANIEL MANN JOHNSON & MENDENHALL   3250 Wilshire Blvd, Los Angeles, CA 90010,
  Tel: (213) 381-3663
  (Architects & engineers)
    DMJM Intl., P.O. Box 23406, 13095 Safat, Kuwait

EXPEDITORS INTL OF WASHINGTON INC   PO Box 69620, Seattle, WA 98168-9620,
  Tel: (206) 246-3711
  (Air/ocean freight forwarding, customs brokerage, intl logistics solutions)
    Expeditors Intl., P.O. Box 27063, Safat 13131, Kuwait

GLOBAL INTERNATIONAL   1304 Willow St, Martinez, CA 94553, Tel: (510) 229-9330
  (International moving & forwarding)
    Global International, P.O. Box 42065, 70651 Shuwaikh, Kuwait

GREY ADVERTISING INC   777 Third Ave, New York, NY 10017, Tel: (212) 546-2000
  (Advertising)
    CSS & Grey, Fisheries Bldg. 4/F, Al Hilali St., Safat 13103, Kuwait

HONEYWELL INC   PO Box 524, Minneapolis, MN 55440-0524, Tel: (612) 951-1000
  (Devel/mfr controls for home & building, industry, space & aviation)
    Honeywell Kuwait Ksc., P.O. Box 20825, Safat 13069, Kuwait

ITT SHERATON CORP   60 State St, Boston, MA 02108, Tel: (617) 367-3600
  (Hotel operations)
    Kuwait Sheraton Hotel, P.O. Box 5902, Fahd al Salem St., Kuwait, Kuwait

KEYSTONE INTL INC   PO Box 40010, Houston, TX 77040, Tel: (713) 466-1176
  (Mfr butterfly valves, actuators & control accessories)
    Keystone Kuwait, Kuwait

KIRBY BUILDING SYSTEMS INC   555 Marriott Dr, PO Box 140700, Nashville,
  TN 37214, Tel: (615) 889-0020
  (Steel building sys)
    Kirby Building Systems SFK, P.O. Box 23933, Safat, Kuwait

MARRIOTT CORP   Marriott Dr, Washington, DC 20058, Tel: (301) 380-9000
  (Lodging, contract food & beverage serv, restaurants)
    Marriott Corp., P.O. Box 24285, Safat, Kuwait

NATIONAL CAR RENTAL SYSTEM INC   7700 France Ave S, Minneapolis, MN 55435,
  Tel: (612) 830-2121
  (Car rental)
    National Car Rental, P.O. Box 81, Safat, Kuwait

OTIS ELEVATOR CO   10 Farm Springs, Farmington, CT 06032, Tel: (860) 676-6528
  (Mfr elevators & escalators)
    Otis Elevator Co. (Kuwait), P.O. Box 11169, Dasma 35152, Kuwait

PARKER DRILLING CO   8 E Third St, Tulsa, OK 74103-3637, Tel: (918) 585-8221
  (Drilling contractor)
    Parker Drilling Co., P.O. Box 9277, Ahmadi, Kuwait

THE PARSONS CORP   100 W Walnut St, Pasadena, CA 91124, Tel: (818) 440-2000
  (Engineering & construction)
    Parsons Engineering Ltd., P.O. Box 9912, Ahmadi 61008, Kuwait

PARSONS DE LEUW INC   1133 15th St NW, Washington, DC 20005,
  Tel: (202) 775-3300
  (Consulting engineers)
    De Leuw Cather Intl. Ltd., P.O. Box 25582, Safat, Kuwait

PARSONS ENGINEERING SCIENCE INC   100 W Walnut St, Pasadena, CA 91124,
  Tel: (818) 440-6000
  (Environmental engineering)
    Parsons Engineering Science Inc., c/o Gulf Consult, P.O. Box 22412, Safat 13085,
    Kuwait

RAYTHEON CO   141 Spring St, Lexington, MA 02173, Tel: (617) 862-6600
  (Mfr divers electronics, appliances, aviation, energy & environ prdts; publishing,
  ind & constr servs)
    Raytheon Gulf Systems Co., P.O. Box 33147, Rawda, Kuwait

THE RENDON GROUP INC   2000 S St. NW, Washington, DC 20009,
  Tel: (202) 745-4900
  (Public relations, print & video production, strategic communicaitons)
    The Rendon Group Inc., Flat 802, Tower 8, Floor 3, Bneid Al Ghar, Kuwait City,
    Kuwait

STANLEY CONSULTANTS INC   225 Iowa Ave, Muscatine, IA 52761,
  Tel: (319) 264-6600
  (Engineering, architectural, planning & management services)
    Stanley/AKO, P.O. Box 3834 Safat, Kuwait City 13039, Kuwait

UOP INC   Ten UOP Plaza, Des Plaines, IL 60016, Tel: (708) 391-2000
  (Diversified research, development & mfr of ind prdts & sys mgmt studies & serv)
    Procon Middle East Inc., Safat, Kuwait

WEATHERFORD INTL INC   1360 Post Oak Blvd, PO Box 27608, Houston,
  TX 77227-7608, Tel: (713) 439-9400
  (Oilfield servs, prdts & equip; mfr marine cranes)
    Weatherford Intl. Inc., c/o Ajal Contracting & General Trading Co., P.O. Box 26256,
    Safat, Kuwait

WESTERN ATLAS INTL INC   10205 Westheimer, PO Box 1407, Houston,
  TX 77251-1407, Tel: (713) 266-5700
  (Full service to the oil industry)
    Western Atlas Intl. Inc., c/o Exim Trading Co., P.O. Box 25371, Safat 13113, Kuwait

LATVIA

KELLOGG CO   One Kellogg Sq, PO Box 3599, Battle Creek, MI 49016-3599,
  Tel: (616) 961-2000
  (Mfr ready-to-eat cereals, convenience foods)
    Kellogg Latvia Inc., Riga District, Latvia (all inquiries to U.S. address)

XEROX CORP   800 Long Ridge Rd, PO Box 1600, Stamford, CT 06904,
  Tel: (203) 968-3000
  (Mfr document processing equip, sys & supplies)
    Xerox Corp., Riga, Latvia

LEBANON

AMERICAN BROADCASTING COS INC   77 W 66th St, New York, NY 10023,
  Tel: (212) 456-7777
  (Radio/TV prod & broadcast)
    American Broadcasting Co., Gefinar Center, Block B, Rm. 1602, Beirut, Lebanon

ASSOCIATED PRESS INC   50 Rockefeller Plaza, New York, NY 10020-1605,
  Tel: (212) 621-1500
  (News gathering agency)
    Associated Press, 121 Rue Clemenceau, P.O. Box 3780, Beirut, Lebanon

LEO BURNETT CO INC   35 West Wacker Dr, Chicago, IL 60601, Tel: (312) 220-5959
  (Advertising agency)
    H&C Leo Burnett, Sofil Center, P.O. Box 55369, Beirut, Lebanon

CHASE MANHATTAN BANK N A   1 Chase Manhattan Plaza, New York, NY 10081,
  Tel: (212) 552-2222
  (Intl banking)
    The Chase Manhattan Bank N.A., Riad Solh St., P.O. Box 3684, Beirut, Lebanon

CHEMICAL BANK   270 Park Ave, New York, NY 10017-2070, Tel: (212) 270-6000
  (Banking & financial services)
    Chemical Bank, Gefinor Center, Block C, 2nd Fl., 201 Clemenceau St., Beirut, Lebanon

CIGNA CORP   One Liberty Place, Philadelphia, PA 19192, Tel: (215) 523-4000
(Ins, invest, health care & other fin servs)
    Insurance Co. of North America, c/o Joseph E. Zakhour & Co. SARL, Ashrafieh,
    Rmeil/Liberty Bldg., Beirut, Lebanon

COBB INC   Great Road, Littleton, MA 01460, Tel: (617) 486-3535
(Poultry)
    Cobb Middle East SAL, Zahle, Lebanon

COLUMBIA PICTURES INDUSTRIES INC   711 Fifth Ave, New York, NY 10022,
Tel: (212) 751-4400
(Producer & distributor of motion pictures)
    Les Fils De Georges Haddad & Co., Empire Cinema Bldg., P.O. Box 4680, Beirout,
    Lebanon

DAMES & MOORE   911 Wilshire Blvd, Los Angeles, CA 90017, Tel: (213) 683-1560
(Engineering, environmental & construction mgmt services)
    Dames & Moore, P.O. Box 116-5249 Museum, Achrafieh-Beirut, Lebanon

EASTMAN KODAK CO   343 State St, Rochester, NY 14650, Tel: (716) 724-4000
(Devel/mfr photo & chem prdts, info mgmt/video/copier sys, fibers/plastics for
various ind)
    Kodak (Near East) Inc., Beirut, Lebanon, c/o Kodak (Near East) Inc.,
    P.O. Box 11460, Dubai, United Arab Emirates

EMCO ENGINEERING INC   25 North St, Canton, MA 02021, Tel: (617) 828-7340
(Water purification & sewage treatment)
    Emco Group, P.O. Box 113-5993, Beirut, Lebanon

EXPEDITORS INTL OF WASHINGTON INC   PO Box 69620, Seattle, WA 98168-9620,
Tel: (206) 246-3711
(Air/ocean freight forwarding, customs brokerage, intl logistics solutions)
    Expeditors Intl. Service Center, P.O. Box 50252, Furn El Chebback, Lebanon

JOHN FABICK TRACTOR CO   1 Fabick Dr, Fenton, MO 63026, Tel: (314) 343-5900
(Wheel tractors, excavating & road building equip)
    A.K. Zarby & Associates, Ardeti Bldg., Bliss St., Manara, Beirut, Lebanon

FEL-PRO INC   7450 N McCormick Blvd, Skokie, IL 60076, Tel: (708) 674-7700
(Oil gaskets)
    Intraco Corp., Barazi Bldg., P.O. Box 7771, Beirut, Lebanon

FRANCHI CONSTRUCTION CO INC   183 W Central St, Natick, MA 01750-3715,
Tel: (617) 655-8330
(General contractors)
    Franchi Construction Co. Inc., c/o Special Construction Projects,
    American University of Beirut, Beirut, Lebanon

GRANT THORNTON INTL   Prudential Plaza, Chicago, IL 60601, Tel: (312) 856-0001
(Intl accountants)
    Grant Thornton Intl., Minkara Bldg., Clemenceau St., P.O. Box 11-5075, Beirut,
    Lebanon

GREY ADVERTISING INC   777 Third Ave, New York, NY 10017, Tel: (212) 546-2000
(Advertising)
    CSS & Grey, Beitmery Roundabout, Beitmery, Beirut, Lebanon

GTE CORP   One Stamford Forum, Stamford, CT 06904, Tel: (203) 965-2000
(Electr prdts, telecom sys, publ & commun)
GTE Sylvania SA, Dessouki Bldg., 6th Floor, Patriarch Hoyek St., P.O. Box 3455,
Beirut, Lebanon

FRANK B HALL & CO INC   549 Pleasantville Rd, Briarcliff Manor, NY 10510,
Tel: (914) 769-9200
(Insurance)
Astra Insurance Co. SAL, Centre Ivoire, Commodore St., Hamra, P.O. Box 113-6025,
Beirut, Lebanon

HORWATH INTL   415 Madison Ave, New York, NY 10017, Tel: (212) 838-5566
(Public accountants & auditors)
Horwath Abou Chakra Co., Minkara Bldg., Clemenceau St., Beirut, Lebanon

INTRACO CORP   530 Stephenson Hwy, Troy, MI 48083, Tel: (810) 585-6900
(Export mgmt & mktg consultants)
Intraco Corp., P.O. Box 135714 Shouran, Beirut, Lebanon

MERCK SHARP & DOHME INTL   PO Box 2000, Rahway, NJ 07065, Tel: (201) 574-4000
(Pharms, chems & biologicals)
Merck, Sharp & Dohme Intl. Middle East, Naji Itani Bldg., Jeanne d'Arc St.,
Ras Beirut, Lebanon

MOBIL CORP   3225 Gallows Rd, Fairfax, VA 22037-0001, Tel: (703) 846-3000
(Petroleum explor & refining, mfr petrol prdts, chems, petrochems)
Mobil Oil Lebanon Inc., Wardieh Holdings Inc., Room 2925, Beirut, Lebanon

MORGAN GUARANTY TRUST CO   23 Wall St, New York, NY 10260, Tel: (212) 483-2323
(Banking)
Morgan Guaranty Trust Co. of NY, Beirut Riyad Bldg., 5th Floor, Rue Riyad Solh,
P.O. Box 5752, Beirut, Lebanon

NATIONAL CAR RENTAL SYSTEM INC   7700 France Ave S, Minneapolis, MN 55435,
Tel: (612) 830-2121
(Car rental)
National Car Rental, P.O. Box 5965, Ain-Al-Mraisse St., Nsouli Bldg., Beirut,
Lebanon

OTIS ELEVATOR CO   10 Farm Springs, Farmington, CT 06032, Tel: (860) 676-6528
(Mfr elevators & escalators)
Otis Elevator Co. SAL, Drab Bldg.- Mekalles, P.O. Box 11-7968, Beirut, Lebanon

PHILLIPS PETROLEUM CO   Phillips Bldg, Bartlesville, OK 74004,
Tel: (918) 661-6600
(Crude oil, natural gas, liquefied petroleum gas, gasoline & petro-chems)
Phillips Petroleum Intl. Corp., Shell Bldg., 14th Floor, 8 Raouche, P.O. Box 6106,
Beirut, Lebanon

PROCTER & GAMBLE CO   One Procter & Gamble Plaza, Cincinnati, OH 45202,
Tel: (513) 983-1100
(Personal care, food, laundry, cleaning & ind prdts)
Procter & Gamble Mfg. Co. of Lebanon SAL, P.O. Box 4992, Beirut, Lebanon

U S INDUSTRIES INC   PO Box 629, Evansville, IN 47704, Tel: (812) 425-2428
(Diversified prdts & sys for industry, agribusiness & retail markets)
Big Dutchman Intl SA, P.O. Box 5012, Beirut, Lebanon

UNITED CENTRIFUGAL PUMPS INC   1132 N 7th St, San Jose, CA 95112,
   Tel: (408) 298-0123
   (Pumps)
      United Centrifugal Pumps Netherlands NV, Sabbagh Center, Hamra St., P.O. Box 4641,
      Beirut, Lebanon

UPJOHN CO   7000 Portage Rd, Kalamazoo, MI 49001, Tel: (616) 323-4000
   (Mfr pharms, agric prdts, ind chems)
      The Upjohn Scientific Office, Wahab Bldg., 6th Floor, 213 Fouad Chelab St.,
      P.O. Box 6305, Beirut, Lebanon

LIBERIA

AIR EXPRESS INTL CORP   120 Tokeneke Rd, PO Box 1231, Darien, CT 06820,
   Tel: (203) 655-7900
   (Air frt forwarder)
      Air Express Intl., Scanship Inc., P.O. Box 209, Monrovia, Liberia

CHASE MANHATTAN BANK N A   1 Chase Manhattan Plaza, New York, NY 10081,
   Tel: (212) 552-2222
   (Intl banking)
      Chase Manhattan Bank, P.O. Box 181, Ashmun & Randall Sts., Monrovia, Liberia
      Chase Manhattan Bank, P.O. Box 46, Harbel, Monrovia, Liberia

CIGNA CORP   One Liberty Place, Philadelphia, PA 19192, Tel: (215) 523-4000
   (Ins, invest, health care & other fin servs)
      Cigna Worldwide Insurance Co., c/o Lone Star Insurances Inc., 51 Broad St.,
      PO Box 1142, Monrovia, Liberia

THE DOW CHEMICAL CO   2030 Dow Center, Midland, MI 48674, Tel: (517) 636-1000
   (Mfr chems, plastics, pharms, agric prdts, consumer prdts)
      Chief Shipping Co., Liberia

E I DU PONT DE NEMOURS & CO   1007 Market St, Wilmington, DE 19898,
   Tel: (302) 774-1000
   (Mfr/sale diversified chems, plastics, specialty prdts & fibers)
      World Wide Transport Inc., Liberia

C T MAIN INTL INC   Southeast Tower, Prudential Center, Boston, MA 02199,
   Tel: (617) 262-3200
   (Engineering consultants)
      Charles T. Main Intl. Inc., P.O. Box 165, Monrovia, Liberia

MOBIL CORP   3225 Gallows Rd, Fairfax, VA 22037-0001, Tel: (703) 846-3000
   (Petroleum explor & refining, mfr petrol prdts, chems, petrochems)
      Mobil Oil Liberia Inc., P.O. Box 342, Monrovia, Liberia

REPUBLIC STEEL CORP   PO Box 6778, Cleveland, OH 44101, Tel: (216) 622-5000
  (Alloy, carbon & stainless steel, chems, electrical conduit, etc)
    Liberia Mining Co., P.O. Box 252, Monrovia, Liberia

LIECHTENSTEIN

BLACK & DECKER CORP   701 E Joppa Road, Towson, MD 21286, Tel: (410) 716-3900
  (Mfr power tools & accessories, security hardware, small appliances, fasteners, info
  sys & servs)
    Black & Decker Corp., all mail to U.S. address

CARRIER CORP   One Carrier Place, Farmington, CT 06034-4015,
  Tel: (203) 674-3000
  (Mfr/distr/svce A/C, heating & refrigeration equip)
    Clymalynx AG, Vaduz, Liechtenstein

SUPRADUR COMPANIES INC   411 Theodore Fremd Ave, Rye, NY 10580,
  Tel: (914) 967-8230
  (Mfr siding & roofing materials, precision sheet metal components)
    Ambit AG, Postfach 127, 9494 Vaduz, Liechtenstein
    Brixite AG, Postfach 127, 9494 Vaduz, Liechtenstein

LUXEMBOURG

ADVANCE MACHINE CO   14600 21st Ave N, Plymouth, MN 55447, Tel: (612) 473-2235
  (Ind floor cleaning equip)
    Advanced Intl. SA, 4 rue Jean Engling, Parc de l'Europe, Dommeldange, Luxembourg

AMDAHL CORP   1250 E Arques Ave, PO Box 3470, Sunnyvale, CA 94088-3470,
  Tel: (408) 746-6000
  (Devel/mfr large scale computers, software, data storage prdts, info-technology
  solutions & support)
    Amdahl Luxembourg, Regus Luxembourg Route de Treves 6, Bldg. B,
      L-2633 Senningerberg, Luxembourg

AMERACE CORP   2 N Riverside Plaza, #1160, Chicago, IL   60606,
  Tel: (312) 906-8700
  (Chems, rubber prdts, plastics, electrical components & controls)
    Amersil SA, Kehlen, Luxembourg City, Luxembourg

BROWN BROTHERS HARRIMAN & CO   59 Wall St, New York, NY   10005,
  Tel: (212) 483-1818
  (Financial services)
    Brown Brothers Harriman (Luxembourg) SA, 23 rue Beaumont, BP 403, L-2014 Luxembourg

CAFCO INTERNATIONAL LTD   Furnace St, Stanhope, NJ   07874, Tel: (201) 347-1200
  (Insulation, fire-proofing materials)
    Cafco Europe SARL, 1 rue l'Industrie, L-3895 Fuetz, Luxembourg

CHASE MANHATTAN BANK N A   1 Chase Manhattan Plaza, New York, NY   10081,
  Tel: (212) 552-2222
  (Intl banking)
    Chase Manhattan Bank SA, 47 boulevard Royal, BP 240, Luxembourg City, Luxembourg
    Kredietbank SA Luxembourgeoise, 37 rue Notre Dame, Luxembourg City, Luxembourg

CITICORP   399 Park Ave, New York, NY   10043, Tel: (212) 559-1000
  (Banking & financial services)
    Citibank NA, Luxembourg

COMMERCIAL INTERTECH CORP   1775 Logan Ave, PO Box 239, Youngstown,
  OH   44501-0239, Tel: (216) 746-8011
  (Mfr hydraulic com, fluid purification sys, pre-engineered bldgs, stamped metal prdts)
    Commercial Intertech SA, P.O. Box 152, Route d'Ettelbruck, L-9202 Diekirch,
    Luxembourg

THE DOW CHEMICAL CO   2030 Dow Center, Midland, MI   48674, Tel: (517) 636-1000
  (Mfr chems, plastics, pharms, agric prdts, consumer prdts)
    Administration de Participations Etrangeres SA, 13 boulevard Royal,
    L-2449 Luxembourg City, Luxembourg

DUKANE CORP   2900 Dukane Drive, St Charles, IL   60174, Tel: (708) 584-2300
  (Mfr facility intercommun, optoelectronic device assembly, plastics welding, local
  area network equip)
    Dukane Corp., Regus Centre/Bldg. A, Route de Treves 6, L-2633 Senningerberg,
    Luxembourg

ESKIMO PIE CORP   530 E Main St, Richmond, VA   23219, Tel: (804) 782-1800
  (Frozen food prdts)
    Eskimo Europe SARL, 16 boulevard d'Avranches, Luxembourg City, Luxembourg

FIRST NATIONAL BANK OF BOSTON   100 Federal St, Boston, MA   02110,
  Tel: (617) 434-2200
  (Commercial banking)
    First National Bank of Boston, 41 boulevard Royal, BP 209, L-2012 Luxembourg City,
    Luxembourg

GENERAL MOTORS CORP   3044 W Grand Blvd, Detroit, MI   48202-3091,
  Tel: (313) 556-5000
  (Mfr full line vehicles, automotive electronics, coml technologies, telecom, space,
  finance)

General Motors Luxembourg Operations SA, Route de Luxembourg, BP 29, 4901 Bascharage, Luxembourg

THE GOODYEAR TIRE & RUBBER CO   1144 E Market St, Akron, OH 44316, Tel: (216) 796-2121
(Mfr tires, automotive belts & hose, conveyor belts, chemicals; oil pipeline transmission)
Goodyear SA, Avenue Gordon Smith, L-7750 Colmar-Berg, Luxembourg

HOLIDAY INNS INC   3742 Lamar Ave, Memphis, TN 38195, Tel: (901) 362-4001
(Hotels, restaurants, casinos)
Holiday Inn, BP 512, Luxembourg City, Luxembourg

HORWATH INTL   415 Madison Ave, New York, NY 10017, Tel: (212) 838-5566
(Public accountants & auditors)
Hoogewerf & Co., 19 Rue Aldringen, L-1118 Luxembourg City, Luxembourg

ITT SHERATON CORP   60 State St, Boston, MA 02108, Tel: (617) 367-3600
(Hotel operations)
Aerogulf Sheraton Hotel, BP 1793, Luxembourg City, Luxembourg

KORN/FERRY INTL   1800 Century Park East, Los Angeles, CA 90067, Tel: (310) 552-1834
(Executive search)
Korn/Ferry Intl., 19 Cote d'Eich, L-1450 Luxembourg

MANPOWER INTL INC   5301 N Ironwood Rd, PO Box 2053, Milwaukee, WI 53201-2053, Tel: (414) 961-1000
(Temporary help service)
Manpower SARL, 19 rue Glesener, Luxembourg City, Luxembourg

MARWAIS STEEL CO   655 Montgomery St, #600, San Francisco, CA 94111, Tel:
(Steel shelters, metal coil coating)
Marwais Intl. SA, 3 rue Aldringer, Luxembourg City, Luxembourg

MILLICOM INC   153 E 53rd St, #5500, New York, NY 10022, Tel: (212) 355-3440
(Cellular communications, satellite TV transmission, public phone & paging services)
Millicom Intl. Cellular SARL, 65 ave. de la Gare, L-1611 Luxembourg

MINERAIS U S INC   122 Route 22 East, Bridgewater, NJ 08807, Tel: (908) 722-8111
(Mktg/distr ferro alloys, ores, minerals)
S.A. des Minerais, 13 rue Robert Stumper, BP 5, L-2010 Luxembourg City, Luxembourg

MNC INTERNATIONAL BANK   2 N Charles St, Baltimore, MD 21201, Tel: (301) 244-6804
(Intl banking)
Maryland Bank Intl. SA, 33 boulevard Prince Henri, BP 11, L-2010 Luxembourg City, Luxembourg

NATIONAL CAR RENTAL SYSTEM INC   7700 France Ave S, Minneapolis, MN 55435, Tel: (612) 830-2121
(Car rental)
National Car Rental, 33 boulevard Prince Henri, Luxembourg City, Luxembourg

NORTON CO   1 New Bond St, Worcester, MA 01606, Tel: (508) 795-5000
  (Abrasives, drill bits, constr & safety prdts, plastics)
    Norton SA, Chemin Rouge Belvaux, Luxembourg City, Luxembourg

OTIS ELEVATOR CO   10 Farm Springs, Farmington, CT 06032, Tel: (860) 676-6528
  (Mfr elevators & escalators)
    General Technic-Otis SARL, 44 rue des Bruyeres, BP 1056, L-1274 Howald, Luxembourg

RPM INC   2628 Pearl Rd, Medina, OH 44256, Tel: (216) 225-3192
  (Protective coatings, paint)
    Akron SARL, 3 rue de la Sapiniere, Bridel, Luxembourg

STANDARD OIL CO OF CALIFORNIA   225 Bush St, San Francisco, CA 94104,
  Tel: (415) 894-7700
  (Oil explor & prod, petroleum prdts)
    Chevron Petroleu SA, 10 boulevard Roosevelt, Luxembourg City, Luxembourg

STATE STREET BANK & TRUST CO   225 Franklin St, Boston, MA 02101,
  Tel: (617) 786-3000
  (Banking & financial services)
    State Street Bank Luxembourg SA, 47 Boulevard Royal, L-2449 Luxembourg

TEXAS REFINERY CORP   840 North Main, Fort Worth, TX 76101,
  Tel: (817) 332-1161
  (Mfr bldg maintenance prdts & spec lubricants)
    Texas Refinery Corp. Inter-Continental SA, BP 4, Zone Industrielle Echternach,
    L-6401 Echternach, Luxembourg

THOMAS & BETTS CORP   1555 Lynnfield Rd, Memphis, TN 38119,
  Tel: (901) 682-7766
  (Mfr elect/electr connectors & accessories)
    Thomas & Betts (Luxembourg) SA, Zone Industrielle, rue de l'Industrie,
    L-2895 Fuetz, Luxembourg

UNIROYAL INC   World Headquarters, Middlebury, CT 06749, Tel: (203) 573-2000
  (Tires, tubes & other rubber prdts, chems, plastics, textiles)
    Uniroyal Luxembourg SA, Steinfort, Luxembourg

THE VIKING CORP   210 N Ind Rd, Hastings, MI 49058, Tel: (616) 945-9501
  (Mfr fire extinguishing equip)
    Sprinkler Viking SA, Zone Industrial Haneboesch, BP 88, L-4501 Differdange,
    Luxembourg

MACAU

AMWAY CORP   7575 E Fulton Rd, Ada, MI 49355, Tel: (616) 676-6000
  (Mfr/sale home care, personal care, nutrition & houseware prdts)
    Amway Macau Lda., Rua de Pedro Coutinbo, Np. 52 Edificio Hio Fai, Bloco D R/C, Macau

BEL FUSE INC   198 Van Vorst St, Jersey City, NJ 07302, Tel: (201) 432-0463
  (Mfr electronic components for networking, fuses, delay lines, hybrids & magnetic
  prdts)
    Bel Fuse Macau Lda., 218 Largo do Pac On, Taipa Macau

MADEIRA

MOBIL CORP   3225 Gallows Rd, Fairfax, VA 22037-0001, Tel: (703) 846-3000
  (Petroleum explor & refining, mfr petrol prdts, chems, petrochems)
    Mobil Oil SARL, Rua da Se 34, Funchal, Madeira

MALAWI

AIR EXPRESS INTL CORP   120 Tokeneke Rd, PO Box 1231, Darien, CT 06820,
  Tel: (203) 655-7900
  (Air frt forwarder)
    Air Express Intl., P.O. Box 30471, Chichiri Blantyre 3, Malawi

BURLINGTON AIR EXPRESS   18200 Van Karman Ave, Irvine, CA 92715,
  Tel: (714) 752-4000
  (Air freight)
    Burlington Air Express Malawi, P.O. Box 40132, Kaneneo, Lilongwe, Malawi

CALTEX PETROLEUM CORP   PO Box 619500, Dallas, TX 75261, Tel: (214) 830-1000
  (Petroleum prdts)
    Caltex Oil (Malawi) Ltd., Old Sites, Mission Rd., Blantyre, Malawi

LINTAS:WORLDWIDE   1 Dag Hammarskjold Plaza, New York, NY 10017,
  Tel: (212) 605-8000
  (Advertising agency)
    Graphic Lintas, P.O. Box 835, Blantyre, Malawi

PARSONS DE LEUW INC   1133 15th St NW, Washington, DC 20005,
  Tel: (202) 775-3300
  (Consulting engineers)
    De Leuw Cather Intl. Ltd., P.O. Box 30394, Area 9164, Ulongwe, Malawi

STANDARD COMMERCIAL CORP   PO Box 450, Wilson, NC 27893, Tel: (919) 291-5507
  (Leaf tobacco dealers/processors, wool processors)
    Stancom Tobacco Co. (Malawi) Ltd., Limbe, Malawi
    Stancom Tobacco Packers (Malawi) Ltd., Lilongwe, Malawi
    Tobacco Processors (Malawi) Ltd., Limbe, Malawi

NELLO L TEER CO   PO Box 1131, Durham, NC 27702, Tel: (919) 682-6191
  (Heavy highway constr, building constr)
    Nello L. Teer Co., P.O. Box 30060, Lilongwe 3, Malawi

MALAYSIA

3COM CORP   5400 Bayfront Plaza, Santa Clara, CA 95052-8145,
  Tel: (408) 764-5000
  (Devel/mfr computer networking prdts & sys)
    3Com Asia Ltd., Malaysia

3M   3M Center, St Paul, MN 55144-1000, Tel: (612) 733-1110
  (Mfr diversified prdts for industry, health care, imaging, commun, transport, safety,
  consumer, etc)
    3M Malaysia Sdn. Bhd., Lot 16, Jalan 225, Section 51A, 46100 Petaling Jaya,
      Selangor, Malaysia

ADVANCED MICRO DEVICES INC   PO Box 3453, Sunnyvale, CA 94088-3000,
  Tel: (408) 732-2400
  (Mfr integrated circuits for commun & computation ind)

Advanced Micro Devices Sdn. Ghd., Bayan Lepas Free Trade Zone, Phase II,
Pulau Pinang, Malaysia

AIR PRODUCTS & CHEMICALS INC   7201 Hamilton Blvd, Allentown, PA 18195-1501,
Tel: (215) 481-4911
(Mfr ind gases & related equip, spec chems, environmental/energy sys)
Sitt Tatt Industrial Gases Sdn. Bhd., Lot 54, Jalan Jitra 26/7,
Sec. 26 (Hicom Sector B), 4000 Shah Alam, Selangor, Malaysia

AMERICAN EXPRESS CO   World Financial Center, New York, NY 10285-4765,
Tel: (212) 640-2000
(Travel, travelers cheques, charge card & financial services)
American Express (Malaysia) Sdn. Bhd., all inquiried to U.S. address

AMP INC   PO Box 3608, Harrisburg, PA 17105-3608, Tel: (717) 564-0100
(Devel/mfr electronic & electrical connection prdts & sys)
AMP Products (Malaysia) Sdn. Bhd., Lot 11/3, 11/F, Menara Tun Razak,
Jalan Raja Laut, 50350 Kuala Lumpur, Malaysia

AMWAY CORP   7575 E Fulton Rd, Ada, MI 49355, Tel: (616) 676-6000
(Mfr/sale home care, personal care, nutrition & houseware prdts)
Amway Malaysia Sdn. Bhd., No. 34, Jalan 223, 46100 Petaling Jaya, Selangor, Malaysia

APPLIED MAGNETICS CORP   75 Robin Hill Rd, Goleta, CA 93117,
Tel: (805) 683-5353
(Mfr magnetic recording heads)
Applied Magnetics (Malaysia) Sdn. Bhd., Penang, Malaysia

ASARCO INC   180 Maiden Lane, New York, NY 10038, Tel: (212) 510-2000
(Nonferrous metals, specialty chems, minerals, mfr industrial prdts, environmental
services)
Enthone-Omi Inc., Malaysia

ASSOCIATED PRESS INC   50 Rockefeller Plaza, New York, NY 10020-1605,
Tel: (212) 621-1500
(News gathering agency)
Associated Press, China Insurance Bldg., 174 Jalan Tuanku Abdul Rahman,
Kuala Lumpur, Malaysia

AST RESEARCH INC   16215 Alton Parkway, PO Box 19658, Irvine, CA 92713-9658,
Tel: (714) 727-4141
(Design/devel/mfr hi-perf desktop, server & notebook computers)
AST Malaysia, 8A/F Wisma Genting Annexe, Jalan Sultan Ismail, 50250 Kuala Lumpur,
Malaysia

AVIS INC   900 Old Country Rd, Garden City, NY 11530, Tel: (516) 222-3000
(Car rental serv)
Avis Rent A Car, 40 Jalan Suttan, Ismail 50250, Kuala Lumpur, Malaysia

AVON PRODUCTS INC   9 W 57th St, New York, NY 10019, Tel: (212) 546-6015
(Mfr/distr beauty & related prdts, fashion jewelry, gifts & collectibles)
Avon Cosmetics (Malaysia) Sdn. Bhd., Lot 13-A, Jalan 219, Section 51A,
46100 Petaling Jaya, Malaysia

BAKER OIL TOOLS   PO Box 40129, Houston, TX 77240-0129, Tel: (713) 466-1322
(Mfr/serv oil/gas well completions equip)
   Baker Oil Tools, Lot 2065, Piasau Ind. Estate, Jalan Bulatan, 98000 Miri, Sarawak,
   E. Malaysia

BANDAG INC   2905 NW 61, Muscatine, IA 52761, Tel: (319) 262-1400
(Mfr/sale retread tires)
   Bandag (Malaysia) Sdn. Bhd., Kuala Lumpur, Malaysia

BANKAMERICA CORP   555 California St, San Francisco, CA 94104,
Tel: (415) 622-3456
(Financial services)
   Bank of America Malaysia Bhd., P.O. Box 10950, 50730 Kuala Lumpur, Malaysia

BAXTER HEALTHCARE CORP   1 Baxter Pky, Deerfield, IL 60015,
Tel: (708) 948-2000
(Mfr disposable medical prdts)
   Baxter Healthcare SA, P.O. Box 515, 10760 Penang, Malaysia
   Euromedical Industries Sdn. Bhd., P.O. Box 18, Sungei Patani, Kedah, Malaysia

BENTLY NEVADA CORP   PO Box 157, Minden, NV 89423, Tel: (702) 782-3611
(Electronic monitoring system)
   Satupadu Sdn. Bhd., 210-1 Jin Ipoh, Kuala Lumpur, Malaysia

LOUIS BERGER INTL INC   100 Halsted St, East Orange, NJ 07019,
Tel: (201) 678-1960
(Consulting engineers, architects, economists & planners)
   Louis Berger Intl. Inc., P.O. Box 10, Kuala Lumpur 50450, Malaysia

BORDEN INC   180 E Broad St, Columbus, OH 43215-3799, Tel: (614) 225-4000
(Mfr foods, snacks & beverages, adhesives)
   Borden Sdn. Bhd., all mail to U.S. address

BOYDEN CONSULTING CORP   375 Park Ave, #1008, New York, NY 10152,
Tel: (212) 980-6480
(Executive search)
   Boyden Associates Sdn. Bhd., Menara Kewangen, Jalan Sultan Ismail,
      50258 Kuala Lumpur, Malaysia

BRANSON ULTRASONICS CORP   41 Eagle Rd, Danbury, CT 06813-1961,
Tel: (203) 796-0400
(Mfr plastics assembly equip, ultrasonic cleaning equip)
   Branson Ultrasonics (Malaysia) Sdn. Bhd., Lot 46, Jalan PJS 11/20, Bandar Sunway,
      46150 Petaling Jaya, Selangor, Malaysia

BROWN & ROOT INC   4100 Clinton Dr, Houston, TX 77020-6299,
Tel: (713) 676-3011
(Engr, constr & maintenance)
   Brown & Root (Malaysia) Sdn. Bhd., P.O. Box 502, 55100 Kuala Lumpur, Malaysia

BRY-AIR INC   PO Box 269, Rte 37 W, Sunbury, OH 43074, Tel: (614) 965-2974
(Mfr industrial dehumidifiers/auxiliary equip for plastics ind)
   Bry-Air Malaysia, 92-A Jalan SS21/35, Damansara Utama, 47400 Petaling Jaya,
      Selangor, Malaysia

BURLINGTON AIR EXPRESS   18200 Van Karman Ave, Irvine, CA 92715,
  Tel: (714) 752-4000
  (Air freight)
    Burlington Air Express, 1 Jalan SS 15/8B, Subang Jaya, 47500 Petaling Jaya,
    Selangor, Malaysia

LEO BURNETT CO INC   35 West Wacker Dr, Chicago, IL 60601, Tel: (312) 220-5959
  (Advertising agency)
    Leo Burnett Sdn. Bhd., 8th Fl., Wisma Damansara, Damansara Heights, Jalan Semantan,
    50490 Kuala Lumpur, Malaysia

BURSON-MARSTELLER   230 Park Ave, New York, NY 10003-1566, Tel: (212) 614-4000
  (Public relations/public affairs consultants)
    Burson-Marsteller (Malaysia) Sdn. Bhd., 11th Fl., Wisma Getah Asli,
    148 Jalan Ampang, 50450 Kuala Lumpur, Malaysia

CABOT CORP   75 State St, Boston, MA 02109-1807, Tel: (617) 890-0200
  (Mfr carbon blacks, plastics; oil & gas, info sys)
    Malaysia Carbon Sdn. Bhd., Affiliates Div., P.O. Box 30, Port Dickson,
    Negeri Sembilan, Malaysia

CALTEX PETROLEUM CORP   PO Box 619500, Dallas, TX 75261, Tel: (214) 830-1000
  (Petroleum prdts)
    Caltex Oil Malaysia Ltd., Wisma Mirama, Jalan Wisma Putra, 50460 Kuala Lumpur,
    Malaysia

CARRIER CORP   One Carrier Place, Farmington, CT 06034-4015,
  Tel: (203) 674-3000
  (Mfr/distr/svce A/C, heating & refrigeration equip)
    Carrier (Malaysia) Sdn. Bhd., Kajang Selangor, Malaysia
    Carrier Experts Service (Central Malaysia) Sdn. Bhd., Kuala Lumpur, Malaysia
    Carrier Intl. Sdn. Bhd., Lot 4, Jln P/6, Bandhar Baru Bangi, 43650 Bangi, Selangor,
    Malaysia

CENTRAL NATIONAL-GOTTESMAN INC   3 Manhattanville Rd, Purchase,
  NY 10577-2110, Tel: (914) 696-9000
  (Worldwide sales pulp & paper prdts)
    Central National-Gottesman (M) Sdn. Bhd., 15-2B Jalan Perdana 4/1, Pandan Perdana,
    55300 Kuala Lumpur, Malaysia

CHASE MANHATTAN BANK N A   1 Chase Manhattan Plaza, New York, NY 10081,
  Tel: (212) 552-2222
  (Intl banking)
    Chase Manhattan Bank N.A., P.O. Box 1090, Wisma Stephens, 88 Jalan Raja Chulan,
    Kuala Lumpur, Malaysia

CHEMICAL BANK   270 Park Ave, New York, NY 10017-2070, Tel: (212) 270-6000
  (Banking & financial services)
    Chemical Bank, 148 Jalan Ampang, 50450 Kuala Lumpur, Malaysia

CHESTERTON BINSWANGER INTL   Two Logan Sq, 4th fl, Philadelphia,
  PA 19103-2759, Tel: (215) 448-6000
  (Real estate & related svces)
    Chesterton Intl. (Malaysia) Sdn. Bhd., Suite 18.04, 18th fl., Plaza See Hoy Chan,
    Jalan Raja Chulan, 50200 Kuala Lumpur, Malaysia

CIGNA CORP   One Liberty Place, Philadelphia, PA 19192, Tel: (215) 523-4000
(Ins, invest, health care & other fin servs)
   Insurance Co. of North America, Apera-ULG Centre 8/F, Jalan Raja Chulan,
     Kuala Lumpur, Malaysia

CITICORP   399 Park Ave, New York, NY 10043, Tel: (212) 559-1000
(Banking & financial services)
   Citibank NA, Malaysia

THE CLOROX CO   1221 Broadway, PO Box 24305, Oakland, CA 94623-1305,
 Tel: (510) 271-7000
(Mfr domestic consumer packaged prdts)
   Clorox (Malaysia) Industries Sdn. Bhd, Kuala Lumpur, Malaysia
   Clorox (Malaysia) Sdn. Bhd., Kuala Lumpur, Malaysia

COLGATE-PALMOLIVE CO   300 Park Ave, New York, NY 10022, Tel: (212) 310-2000
(Mfr pharms, cosmetics, toiletries, detergents)
   Colgate-Palmolive (Malaysia) Sdn. Bhd., Jalan Semangat/Bersatu, Sec. 13,
     Petaling Jaya, Selangor, Malaysia

COLUMBIA PICTURES INDUSTRIES INC   711 Fifth Ave, New York, NY 10022,
 Tel: (212) 751-4400
(Producer & distributor of motion pictures)
   Cathay Organlzation (Malaysia) Sdn. Bhd., 4 Jalan Bukit Bintang, Kuala Lumpur,
     Malaysia

COMBUSTION ENGINEERING INC   900 Long Ridge Road, Stamford, CT 06902,
 Tel: (203) 329-8771
(Tech constr)
   Combustion Engineering Inc. (Div. Gray Tool Co.), Kuala Lumpur, Malaysia
   Combustion Engineering Inc., C-E Crest Div., Crest Engrg., Suite 12-06, 12th Fl.,
     Wisma Stephens, 88 Jalan Raja Chulan, Kuala Lumpur, Malaysia

COMPUTER ASSOCIATES INTL INC   One Computer Associates Plaza, Islandia,
 NY 11788, Tel: (516) 342-5224
(Devel/mkt/mgt info mgt & bus applications software)
   Computer Associates (Malaysia) Sdn. Bhd., Menara Maybank 34-1, 34th Fl.,
     100 Jalan Tun Perak, 50050 Kuala Lumpur, Malaysia

CORE LABORATORIES   10205 Westheimer, Houston, TX 77042, Tel: (713) 972-6311
(Petroleum testing/analysis, analytical chem, lab & octane analysis instrumentation)
   Core Laboratories (Malaysia) Sdn. Bhd., Lot 10B, Jalan 51A/223,
     46100 Petaling Jaya, Selangor, Malaysia

CORESTATES FINANCIAL CORP   1500 Market St, Philadelphia, PA 19101,
 Tel: (215) 973-3100
(Banking)
   Corestates Bank, UOA Centre, 19 Jln Pinang, #19-15-3A, 50450 Kuala Lumpur, Malaysia

CORNING INC   One Riverfront Plaza, Corning, NY 14831, Tel: (607) 974-9000
(Mfr glass & specialty materials, consumer prdts; communications, lab services)
   Iwaki-Corning Malaysia Ltd., Jahore Baru, Malaysia

CPC INTERNATIONAL INC   PO Box 8000, Englewood Cliffs, NJ 07632,
 Tel: (201) 894-4000
(Consumer foods, corn refining)

CPC/AJI (Malaysia) Sdn. Bhd., P.O. Box 56, 46700 Petaling Jaya, Selangor, Malaysia
Stamford Food Industries Sdn. Bhd., P.O. Box 531, 46760 Petaling Jaya, Selangor, Malaysia

CRAY RESEARCH INC   655 Lone Oak Dr, Eagan, MN 55121, Tel: (612) 452-6650
(Supercomputer systems & services)
   Cray Research (Malaysia) Sdn. Bhd., Suite 7.06, MCB Plaza, 6 Cangkat Raja Chulan, 50200 Kuala Lumpur, Malaysia

CROWN CORK & SEAL CO INC   9300 Ashton Rd, Philadelphia, PA 19136,
   Tel: (215) 698-5100
(Mfr cans, bottle caps; filling & packaging mach)
   Crown Corks of Malaysia Sdn. Bhd., Jalan Tampoi, P.O. Box 252, Johor Bahru, Johor, Malaysia

D'ARCY MASIUS BENTON & BOWLES INC (DMB&B)   1675 Broadway, New York,
   NY 10019, Tel: (212) 468-3622
(Advertising & communications)
   KHK DMB&B Standard, 6 Jalan Wan Kadir, Taman Tun Dr. Ismail, Kuala Lumpur, Malaysia

D-M-E COMPANY   29111 Stephenson Highway, Madison Heights, MI 48071,
   Tel: (313) 398-6000
(Basic tooling for plastic molding & die casting)
   Leong Bee & Soo Bee Sdn. Bhd., 1-3 Mac Callum St., P.O. Box 23, Pulau Pinang, Malaysia

DAMES & MOORE   911 Wilshire Blvd, Los Angeles, CA 90017, Tel: (213) 683-1560
(Engineering, environmental & construction mgmt services)
   Dames & Moore Malaysia Sdn. Bhd., 7th Floor, Wisma Budiman, Jalan Raja Chulan, 50200 Kuala Lumpur, Malaysia

DANA CORP   PO Box 1000, Toledo, OH 43697, Tel: (419) 535-4500
(Engineer/mfr/mkt prdts & sys for vehicular, ind & mobile off-highway mkt & related aftermarkets)
   APD Enterprise (M) Sdn. Bhd., Lot 1035-1043, 1/F, Block D, Resource Comples 33, Jalan Segambut Atas, 51299 Kuala Lumpur, Malaysia

DDB NEEDHAM WORLDWIDE INC   437 Madison Ave, New York, NY 10022,
   Tel: (212) 415-2000
(Advertising)
   Naga DDB Needham DIK Sdn. Bhd., Jalan SS 6/8-#8, Kelana Jaya, 47301 Petaling Jaya, Selangor, Malaysia

THE DEXTER CORP   1 Elm Street, Windsor Locks, CT 06096, Tel: (203) 627-9051
(Mfr nonwovens, polymer prdts, magnetic materials, biotechnology)
   Dexter Electronic Materials, BHD, A506, 5/F, West Wing, Wisma Tractors, 7 Jalan SS 16/1, 47500 Petaling Jaya, Selangor, Malaysia

DIGITAL EQUIPMENT CORP   146 Main St, Maynard, MA 01754-2571,
   Tel: (508) 493-5111
(Networked computer systems & services)
   Digital Equipment Malaysia Sdn. Bhd., Menara Maybank 100, Jl. Tun Perak, Ipoh, Perak, Malaysia

THE DOW CHEMICAL CO   2030 Dow Center, Midland, MI   48674, Tel: (517) 636-1000
  (Mfr chems, plastics, pharms, agric prdts, consumer prdts)
    Dow Chemical Pacific Ltd., P.O. Box 714, Kuala Lumpur, Malaysia
    Pacific Chemicals Bhd., Malaysia

DOW CORNING CORP   2220 W Salzburg Rd, PO Box 1767, Midland, MI   48640,
  Tel: (517) 496-4000
  (Silicones, silicon chems, solid lubricants)
    Sch Malaysia Snd. Bhd., Lot 2 Loring Eng Gang 35, Ulu Kland Free Trading Zone,
      Selangor, Malaysia

DRAKE BEAM MORIN INC   100 Park Ave, New York, NY   10017, Tel: (212) 692-7700
  (Human resource mgmt consulting & training)
    DBM (Malaysia) Sdn. Bhd., 11.02 Level 11, Amoda Bldg., 22 Jalan Imbi,
      55100 Kuala Lumpur, Malaysia

EASTMAN CHEMICAL   PO Box 511, Kingsport, TN   37662, Tel: (423) 229-2000
  (Mfr plastics, chems, fibers)
    Esterol Sdn. Bhd., Kuala Lumpur, Malaysia

EASTMAN KODAK CO   343 State St, Rochester, NY   14650, Tel: (716) 724-4000
  (Devel/mfr photo & chem prdts, info mgmt/video/copier sys, fibers/plastics for
  various ind)
    Kodak Malaysia Sdn. Bhd., Jalan Semangat, 46860 Petaling Jaya,
      Selangor Darul Ehsan, Malaysia

EATON CORP   1111 Superior Ave, Cleveland, OH   44114, Tel: (216) 523-5000
  (Advanced tech prdts for transp & ind mkts)
    Tamco Cutler-Hammer Snd. Bhd., Lot 9D Jalan, Kemajuan 12/18, P.O. Box 156,
      Petaling Jaya, Selangor, Malaysia

EATON CORP/CUTLER HAMMER   4201 North 27th St, Milwaukee, WI   53216,
  Tel: (414) 449-6000
  (Electric control apparatus, mfr of advanced technologic prdts)
    Tamco Cutler-Hammer Sdn. Bhd., P.O. Box 156, 46710 Petaling Jaya, Selangor, Malaysia

EXPEDITORS INTL OF WASHINGTON INC   PO Box 69620, Seattle, WA   98168-9620,
  Tel: (206) 246-3711
  (Air/ocean freight forwarding, customs brokerage, intl logistics solutions)
    EI Freight Sdn. Bhd., Unit 4, Block B, MAS Cargo Comples, Jalan Garuda,
      Bayan Lepas, 11900 Penang, Malaysia

EXXON CORP   225 E John W Carpenter Freeway, Irving, TX   75062-2298,
  Tel: (214) 444-1000
  (Petroleum explor, prod, refining; mfr petrol & chem prdts; coal & minerals)
    Esso Malaysia Bhd., Kompleks Antarabangs, Jalan Sultan Ismail, 50250 Kuala Lumpur,
      Malaysia
    Esso Production Malaysia Inc., Kompleks Antarabangsa, Jalan Sultan Ismail,
      50250 Kuala Lumpur, Malaysia

FEDERAL-MOGUL CORP   PO Box 1966, Detroit, MI   48235, Tel: (810) 354-7700
  (Mfr/distr precision parts for automobiles, trucks, & farm/constrution vehicles)
    Federal-Mogul World Trade Sdn. Bhd., Malaysia

FLUOR DANIEL INC   3333 Michelson Dr, Irvine, CA 92730, Tel: (714) 975-2000
(Engineering, construction, maintenance & technical services)
   Fluor Daniel Malaysia Sdn. Bhd., Box 80, Menara Maybank 44/F, 100 Jalan Tun Perak,
   50050 Kuala Lumpur, Malaysia

FMC CORP   200 E Randolph Dr, Chicago, IL 60601, Tel: (312) 861-6000
(Produces chems & precious metals, mfr machinery, equip & sys for ind, agric & govt)
   Antah FMC Supplies & Services Sdn. Bhd., Malaysia
   FMC Petroleum Equipment (Malaysia) Sdn. Bhd., Malaysia

FOOTE CONE & BELDING COMMUNICATIONS INC   101 E Erie St, Chicago,
   IL 60611-2897, Tel: (312) 751-7000
(Advertising agency)
   AP:Foote, Cone & Belding Sdn. Bhd., Menara HPPJ 21-22, Jalan Tengah, P.O. Box 102,
   46710 Petaling Jaya, Selangor, Malaysia

FORD MOTOR CO   The American Road, Dearborn, MI 48121, Tel: (313) 322-3000
(Mfr motor vehicles)
   AMIM Holdings Sdn. Bhd., GPO Box 12612, 50784 Kuala Lumpur, Malaysia

FOUR WINDS INTL GROUP   1500 SW First Ave, #850, Portland, OR 97201,
   Tel: (503) 241-2732
(Transp of household goods & general cargo, third party logistics)
   Four Winds Malaysia, 656, 2/F, 4th Mile, Jalan Ipoh Rd., 51200 Kuala Lumpur,
   Malaysia

THE FRANKLIN MINT   Franklin Center, PA 19091, Tel: (610) 459-6000
(Creation/mfr/mktg collectibles & luxury items)
   Franklin Porcelain Sdn. Bhd., Kulim Industrial Estate, 09000 Kulim, Kedah, Malaysia

FRITZ COMPANIES INC   706 Mission St, San Francisco, CA 94103,
   Tel: (415) 904-8360
(Integrated transportation, sourcing, distribution & customs brokerage services)
   FTI-Fritz Transportation (Malaysia) Sdn. Bhd., Level 50 Unit 12, Komtar Tower,
   10000 Panang, Malaysia
   Fritz Air Freight (Malaysia) Sdn. Bhd., Lot 1 & 2, Cargo Agent Bonded Complex,
   Subang Intl. Airport, 47200 Kuala Lumpur, Malaysia

GENERAL ELECTRIC CO   3135 Easton Tpk, Fairfield, CT 06431,
   Tel: (203) 373-2211
(Diversified manufacturing, technology & services)
   General Electric Co.,
   all mail to U.S. address; phone (800) 626-2004 or (518) 438-6500

THE GILLETTE CO   Prudential Tower, Boston, MA 02199, Tel: (617) 421-7000
(Devel/mfr personal care/use prdts: blades & razors, toiletries, cosmetics,
stationery)
   Gilco (Malaysia) Sdn. Bhd., Selangor, Malaysia
   Gillette (Malaysia) Sdn. Bhd., Selangor, Malaysia
   Interpena Sdn. Bhd., Selangor, Malaysia
   Jafra Cosmeticos (Malaysia) Sdn. Bhd., Selangor, Malaysia
   Moorgate Industries Sdn. Bhd., Selangor, Malaysia

THE GOODYEAR TIRE & RUBBER CO   1144 E Market St, Akron, OH 44316,
   Tel: (216) 796-2121
(Mfr tires, automotive belts & hose, conveyor belts, chemicals; oil pipeline
transmission)

(cont)

Goodyear Malaysia Bhd., P.O. Box 7049, 40914 Shah Alam, Selangor Darul Ehsan, Malaysia

GREY ADVERTISING INC   777 Third Ave, New York, NY 10017, Tel: (212) 546-2000
(Advertising)
Grey Malaysia, Empire Tower 37/F, 182 Jalan Tun Razak, 50400 Kuala Lumpur, Malaysia

GTE CORP   One Stamford Forum, Stamford, CT 06904, Tel: (203) 965-2000
(Electr prdts, telecom sys, publ & commun)
GTE Intl Inc., 112 Jalan Pudu, Kuala Lumpur, Malaysia

FRANK B HALL & CO INC   549 Pleasantville Rd, Briarcliff Manor, NY 10510,
Tel: (914) 769-9200
(Insurance)
Frank B. Hall Insurance Brokers Sdn. Bhd., Lot 1909, Wisma MPI, Jalan Raja Chulan, 50200 Kuala Lumpur, Malaysia

THE HARPER GROUP   260 Townsend St, PO Box 77933, San Francisco,
CA 94107-1719, Tel: (415) 978-0600
(Ocean/air freight fwdg, customs brokerage, packing & whse, logistics mgt, ins)
Circle Freight (Malaysia) Sdn. Bhd., B7 MAS Cargo Complex, 11900 Bayan Lepas, Penang, Malaysia
Circle Freight (Malaysia) Sdn. Bhd., also in Ipoh, Johor Bahru, Kuala Lumpur & Port Klang, Malaysia

HARRIS SEMICONDUCTOR SECTOR   PO Box 883, Melbourne, FL 32902,
Tel: (407) 724-7000
(Mfr communications & info handling equip)
Harris Semiconductor Malaysia, P.O. Box 4, JLC Gurney, 54007 Kuala Lumpur, Malaysia

HARSCO CORP   PO Box 8888, Camp Hill, PA 17001-8888, Tel: (717) 763-7064
(Metal reclamation & mill svces, infrastructure & construction, process industry prdts)
Taylor-Wharton Asis (M) Sdn. Bhd., Hicom Ind. Park, PO Box 7193, Pejabat Pos Besar, 40706 Shah Alam, Selangor Darul Ehsan, Malaysia

HEWLETT-PACKARD CO   3000 Hanover St, Palo Alto, CA 94304-0890,
Tel: (415) 857-1501
(Mfr computing, communications & measurement prdts & services)
Hewlett-Packard Sales (Malaysia) Sdn. Bhd., Ground Floor, Wisma Cyclecarri, 288 Jalan Raja Laut, 50350 Kuala Lumpur, Malaysia

HOLIDAY INNS INC   3742 Lamar Ave, Memphis, TN 38195, Tel: (901) 362-4001
(Hotels, restaurants, casinos)
Holiday Inn, 23111 Jalan Tunku Abdul Rahman, Kuching, Sarawak, Malaysia

HONEYWELL INC   PO Box 524, Minneapolis, MN 55440-0524, Tel: (612) 951-1000
(Devel/mfr controls for home & building, industry, space & aviation)
Berkat-Honeywell Sdn. Bhd., No. 4, 2nd fl., Wisma CSA, Jalan Bersatu 13/4, 46200 Petaling Jaya, Selangor, Malaysia

HORWATH INTL   415 Madison Ave, New York, NY 10017, Tel: (212) 838-5566
(Public accountants & auditors)
Horwath & Hals & Oh, 17th Fl., UMBC Annexe Bldg., Jalan Sulaiman, 50000 Kuala Lumpur, Malaysia

HUGHES AIRCRAFT CO   PO Box 80028, Los Angeles, CA 90080-0028,
  Tel: (310) 568-6904
  (Mfr electronics equip & sys)
    Hughes Aircraft Intl. Service Co., Suite 1701, Pernas Intl. Bldg.,
      Jalan Sultan Ismail, 50250 Kuala Lumpur, Malaysia

HUGHES TOOL CO   PO Box 2539, Houston, TX 77001, Tel: (713) 924-2222
  (Equip & serv to oil & gas explor & prod ind)
    BJ Service (Malaysia) Sdn. Bhd., Rm. 32, Mezzanine Fl., Kuala Lumpur Hilton,
      Jalan Sultan Ismail, Kuala Lumpur, Malaysia

HYATT INTL CORP   200 West Madison, Chicago, IL 60606, Tel: (312) 750-1234
  (Intl hotel mgmt)
    Hyatt Intl. Hotels, Kota Kinabalu, Kuala Lumpur & Kuantan, Malaysia

INTERGRAPH CORP   Huntsville, AL 35894-0001, Tel: (205) 730-2000
  (Devel/mfr interactive computer graphic systems)
    Intergraph Systems (Malaysia) Sdn. Bhd., 46-1 Jalan Twlawi, Bangsar Baru,
      Kuala Lumpur 59100, Malaysia

ITT CORP   1330 Ave of the Americas, New York, NY 10019-5490,
  Tel: (212) 258-1000
  (Design/mfr communications & electronic equip, hotels, insurance)
    ITT Far East & Pacific Inc., P.O. Box 2182, Kuala Lumpur, Malaysia
    ITT Transelectronics (Malaysia) Sdn. Bhd., P.O. Box 1119, Pulau Pinang, Malaysia

FRED S JAMES & CO OF NY   230 W Monroe St, Chicago, IL 60606,
  Tel: (312) 726-4080
  (Group pension consultants, actuarial serv, ins brokerage)
    Malaysia Minet Sdn. Bhd., P.O. Box 2355, Kuala Lumpur, Malaysia

JOHNSON & HIGGINS   125 Broad St, New York, NY 10004-2424, Tel: (212) 574-7000
  (Ins brokerage, employee benefit conslt, risk mgmt, human resource conslt, ins/reins
  servs)
    Johnson & Higgins Insurance Brokers Sdn. Bhd., Kuala Lumpur & Penang, Malaysia

JOHNSON & JOHNSON   One Johnson & Johnson Plaza, New Brunswick, NJ 08933,
  Tel: (908) 524-0400
  (R&D/mfr/sale health care prdts)
    Johnson & Johnson Medical Malaysia, P.O. Box 7188, 40706 Selangor, Malaysia
    Johnson & Johnson Sdn. Bhd., P.O. Box 8017, Petaling Jaya, Selangor, Malaysia

S C JOHNSON & SON INC   1525 Howe St, Racine, WI 53403, Tel: (414) 631-2000
  (Home, auto, commercial & personal care prdts, specialty chems)
    S.C. Johnson & Pte. Ltd., P.O. Box 1079, Jalan Semangat, Petaling Jaya, Selangor,
      Malaysia

THE M W KELLOGG CO   601 Jefferson Ave, Houston, TX 77002, Tel: (713) 753-2000
  (Design, engr, procurement & constr for process & energy ind)
    W. M. Kellogg Co., Wisma Genting 6th Fl., Bldg. Letter Box 20, Jalan Sultan Ismail,
      50250 Kuala Lumpur, Malaysia

THE KENDALL CO   15 Hampshire St, Mansfield, MA 02048, Tel: (508) 261-8000
  (Mfr medical disposable prdts, home health care prdts, spec adhesive prdts)
    Lovytex Sdn. Bhd., Lot 8, Jalan Suasa, 42500 Telok Panglima Garang,
      Selangor Darul Ehsan, Malaysia

(cont)

Mediquip Sdn. Bhd., Padang Lati, Mukim Paya, P.O. Box 25, 01700 Kangar, Perlis, West Malaysia

KEPNER-TREGOE INC   PO Box 704, Princeton, NJ 08542-0740, Tel: (609) 921-2806
   (Mgmt consulting & training)
      Kepner-Tregoe (m) Sdn. Bhd., Suite 1707, 17th fl., Bangunan AMDB, 1 Jalan Lumut,
      50400 Kuala Lumpur, Malaysia

KEYSTONE INTL INC   PO Box 40010, Houston, TX 77040, Tel: (713) 466-1176
   (Mfr butterfly valves, actuators & control accessories)
      Keystone Valve, Malaysia

KIMBERLY-CLARK CORP   PO Box 619100, Dallas, TX 75261, Tel: (214) 281-1200
   (Mfr fiber-based prdts for personal care, lumber & paper prdts)
      Kimberly-Clark (Malaysia) Sdn. Bhd., Malaysia
      Kimberly-Clark Malaysia Sdn. Bhd., Petaling Jaya, Selangor, Malaysia

KORN/FERRY INTL   1800 Century Park East, Los Angeles, CA 90067,
   Tel: (310) 552-1834
   (Executive search)
      Korn/Ferry Intl. Sdn. Bhd., UBN Tower 6/F, Letter Box 33, 10 Jalan P. Ramlee,
      50250 Kuala Lumpur, Malaysia

LEARONAL INC   272 Buffalo Ave, Freeport, NY 11520, Tel: (516) 868-8800
   (Mfr chem specialties)
      LeaRonal (SE Asia)Ltd., 56, 1/F, Jalan Mahsuri, 11900 Bayan Baru, Penang, Malaysia

LEVI STRAUSS & CO   1155 Battery, San Francisco, CA 94111, Tel: (415) 544-6000
   (Mfr casual wearing apparel)
      Levi's (Malaysia) Sdn. Bhd., 78 Lorong Selamat, 10400 Pulau Pinang, Malaysia

ELI LILLY & CO   Lilly Corporate Center, Indianapolis, IN 46285,
   Tel: (317) 276-2000
   (Mfr pharmaceuticals, animal health prdts)
      Eli Lilly Malaysia Sdn. Bhd., Menara Cold Storage #7-4, Ltr Box 21, Sec. 14,
      Jl. Semanaat, 46100 Petaling Jaya, Selangor, Malaysia

LILLY INDUSTRIES INC   733 S West St, Indianapolis, IN 46225,
   Tel: (317) 687-6700
   (Mfr industrial finishes, coatings & fillers)
      Lilly Industries Inc., 11 7 12 Chempaka Emas Industrial Park, Japan Pandamaran,
      Port Klang, 4200 Salango, Malaysia

LINTAS:WORLDWIDE   1 Dag Hammarskjold Plaza, New York, NY 10017,
   Tel: (212) 605-8000
   (Advertising agency)
      Lintas:Kuala Lumpur, Wisma Perdana, Jalan Dungun, Damansara Heights,
      50490 Kuala Lumpur, Malaysia

ARTHUR D LITTLE INC   25 Acorn Park, Cambridge, MA 02140-2390,
   Tel: (617) 498-5000
   (Mgmt, environ, health & safety consulting; tech & prdt development)
      Arthur D. Little (Malaysia) Sdn. Bhd., Office Suite 19-16-3A, UOA Centre,
      19 Jalan Pinang, 50450 Kuala Lumpur, Malaysia

LOCKHEED MARTIN CORP   6801 Rockledge Dr, Bethesda, MD 20817,
   Tel: (301) 897-6000
   (Design/mfr/mgmt sys in fields of space, defense, energy, electronics, materials,
   info & tech svces)
      Lockheed Martin Intl. Ltd., UBN Tower, 10th fl., Letter Box 123,
      10 Jalan P. Ramlee, 50250 Kuala Lumpur, Malaysia

LOCTITE CORP   10 Columbus Blvd, Hartford, CT 06106, Tel: (203) 520-5000
   (Mfr/sale ind adhesives & sealants)
      Loctite (Malaysia) Sdn. Bhd., 5 Jalan 2/118B, Desa Tun Razak Ind. Park,
      56000 Cheras, Kuala Lumpur, Malaysia

MARSTELLER INTL   1 E Wacker Dr, Chicago, IL 60601, Tel: (312) 329-1100
   (Advertising, marketing research, sales promotion)
      Burson-Marsteller (Malaysia) Sdn. Bhd., 105-A Jalan Ampang, Kuala Lumpur, Malaysia

MECHANICAL SYSTEMS INC   4110 Romaine, Greensboro, NC 27407,
   Tel: (910) 292-4956
   (Mechanical & electrical contractors)
      Mechanical Systems (Malaysia) Sdn. Bhd., Paramount Gardens, Petaling Jaya,
      Kuala Lumpur, Malaysia

MICROSOFT CORP   One Microsoft Way, Redmond, WA 98052-6399,
   Tel: (206) 882-8080
   (Computer software, peripherals & services)
      Microsoft Malaysia, MCB Bldg. 9/F, 6 Cangkat Raja, Chulan, 50200 Kuala Lupur,
      Malaysia

MOLEX INC   2222 Wellington Ct, Lisle, IL 60532, Tel: (708) 969-4550
   (Mfr electronic, electrical & fiber optic interconnection prdts & sys, switches,
   application tooling)
      Molex Inc., Prai, Penang, Malaysia

MORGAN GUARANTY TRUST CO   23 Wall St, New York, NY 10260, Tel: (212) 483-2323
   (Banking)
      Morgan Guaranty Trust Co., 1201 Wisma Stephens, 88 Jalan Raja, Kuala Lumpur,
      Malaysia

MOTOROLA INC   1303 E Algonquin Rd, Schaumburg, IL 60196, Tel: (708) 576-5000
   (Mfr commun equip, semiconductors, cellular phones)
      Motorola Malaysia Sdn. Bhd., 116 Jalan Semangat, Petaling Jaya, Selangor, Malaysia
      Motorola Malaysia Sdn. Bhd., P.O. Box 420, Pulau Pinang, Malaysia
      Motorola Military & Aerospace Electronics Inc., Sungei Way Free Trade Zone,
      Singei Way/Subang, Selangor, Malaysia
      Motorola Semiconductor Sdn. Bhd., Lot 122, Senawang Ind. Estate, Seremban,
      Negeri Sembilan, Malaysia

MTEL INTERNATIONAL   1350 I St NW, #1100, Washington, DC 20005,
   Tel: (202) 336-5211
   (Radio paging services & sys implementation)
      Skytel Systems Malaysia, Kuala Lumpur, Malaysia

McCANN-ERICKSON WORLDWIDE   750 Third Ave, New York, NY 10017,
   Tel: (212) 697-6000
   (Advertising)
      McCann-Erickson (Malaysia) Sdn. Bhd., Menara Aik Hua, Jalan Hicks,
      50200 Kuala Lumpur, Malaysia

(cont)

Mutiara-McCann (Malaysia) Sdn. Bhd., Menara Aik Hua, Jalan Hicks,
50200 Kuala Lumpur, Malaysia

NATIONAL CAR RENTAL SYSTEM INC   7700 France Ave S, Minneapolis, MN 55435,
Tel: (612) 830-2121
(Car rental)
Natlional Car Rental, G10 Ground Floor, Wisma Stephens, 88 Jalan Raja Chula,
Kuala Lumpur, Malaysia

NATIONAL SEMICONDUCTOR CORP   PO Box 58090, Santa Clara, CA 95052-8090,
Tel: (408) 721-5000
(Mfr semiconductors, design/devel sys)
National Semiconductor, Malacca & Penang, Malaysia

NATIONAL STARCH & CHEMICAL CO   10 Finderne Ave, Bridgewater, NJ 08807-3300,
Tel: (908) 685-5000
(Mfr adhesives & sealants, resins & spec chems, electr materials & adhesives, food
prdts, ind starch)
National Starch & Chemical (M) Sdn. Bhd., Selangor Darul Ehsan, Malaysia

NORDSON CORP   28601 Clemens Rd, Westlake, OH 44145, Tel: (216) 892-1580
(Mfr ind application equip & packaging mach)
Nordson (Mayalsia) Sdn. Bhd., 3 Jalan SS-13/6C, Subang Jaya Industrial Estate,
Subang Jaya, 47500 Selangor Darul Ehsan, Malaysia

OCEANEERING INTL INC   PO Box 218130, Houston, TX 77218-8130,
Tel: (713) 578-8868
(Underwater serv to offshore oil & gas ind)
Oceaneering Intl. Inc., Operational bases in Kuala Lumpur,
Miri (Sarawak) & Tanjong Berhala

OTIS ELEVATOR CO   10 Farm Springs, Farmington, CT 06032, Tel: (860) 676-6528
(Mfr elevators & escalators)
Pernas Otis Elevator Co. Sdn. Bhd., P.O. Box 11242, Kuala Lumpur 50740, Malaysia

PACIFIC TELESIS GROUP   130 Kearney St, San Francisco, CA 94108,
Tel: (415) 394-3000
(Telecommun & info sys)
Pacific Telesis (Malaysia) Sdn. Bhd., Lot 420, Kompleks Antarabangsa,
Jalan Sultan Ismail, 50250 Kuala Lumpur, Malaysia

PARKER HANNIFIN CORP   17325 Euclid Ave, Cleveland, OH 44112,
Tel: (216) 531-3000
(Mfr motion-control prdts)
Parker Hannifin Malaysia, 16B Jalan SS21/35 Damansara Utama, 47400 Petaling Jaya,
Selangor, Malaysia

PETROLITE CORP   369 Marshall Ave, St Louis, MO 63119-1897,
Tel: (314) 961-3500
(Mfr/prod spec chem treating programs, performance-enhancing additives & related
equip & svces)
Petrolite (Malaysia) Sdn. Bhd., 2.12, 2nd Floor, Angkasa Raya Bldg., Jalan Ampang,
50450 Kuala Lumpur, Malaysia

PFIZER INC   235 E 42nd St, New York, NY 10017-5755, Tel: (212) 573-2323
(Mfr healthcare products)
   Pfizer (Malaysia) Sdn. Bhd., Malaysia

PINKERTON SECURITY & INVESTIGATION SERVICES   6727 Odessa Ave, Van Nuys,
   CA 91406-5796, Tel: (818) 373-8800
(Security & investigation services)
   Pinkerton Consulting & Investigation Services, 1/F Kangunan KUB, Jalan 2/87G,
      Off Jalan Syed Putra, 58000 Kuala Lumpur, Malaysia

POWER TECHNOLOGIES INC   1482 Erie Blvd, PO Box 1058, Schenectady, NY 12301,
   Tel: (518) 395-5000
(Power sys engineering, consulting, services & related control software; power
quality hdwe)
   PTI Asia, 17-B, PJS 10/32, Bandar SRI Subang, 46000 Petaling Jaya, Selangor,
      Malaysia

THE QUAKER OATS CO   321 N Clark St, PO Box 049001, Chicago, IL 60604-9001,
   Tel: (312) 222-7111
(Mfr foods & beverages)
   Quaker Products (Malaysia) Sdn. Bhd., 7 Jalan SS 16/1, 12/F, Wisma Tractors,
      Subang Jaya, 47500 Petaling Jaya, Selangor, Malaysia

RAYCHEM CORP   300 Constitution Dr, Menlo Park, CA 94025, Tel: (415) 361-3333
(Devel/mfr/mkt materials science products for electronics, telecommunications &
industry)
   Raychem Sdn. Bhd., 3/F Wisma Ali Bawal, Lot 11 Jalan Tandang, 46050 Petaling Jaya,
      Selangor, Malaysia

READING & BATES CORP   901 Threadneedle, #200, Houston, TX 77079,
   Tel: (713) 496-5000
(Offshore contract drilling)
   Reading & Bates (M) Sdn. Bhd., P.O. Box 2156, Lot 2066, Block 4, MCLD, Jl. Bulatan,
      Piasau Ind. Area, Miri, Sarawak 98000, Malaysia

RJR NABISCO INC   1301 Ave of the Americas, New York, NY 10019,
   Tel: (212) 258-5600
(Mfr consumer packaged food prdts & tobacco prdts)
   R.J. Reynolds Tobacco Sdr. Bhd., Jalan Perbadanan 3/5, Kelangor, Malaysia

ROCKWELL INTL CORP   2201 Seal Beach Blvd, PO Box 4250, Seal Beach,
   CA 90740-8250, Tel: (310) 797-3311
(Prdts & serv for aerospace, automotive, electronics, graphics & automation inds)
   Rockwell Electronics (Australasia) Pty. Ltd., Suite 14.01, Wisma Stephens,
      88 Jalan Raja Chulan, 50200 Kuala Lumpur, Malaysia

SEALED AIR CORP   Park 80 Plaza E, Saddle Brook, NJ 07662-5291,
   Tel: (201) 791-7600
(Mfr protective packaging prdts)
   Sealed Air Malaysia Sdn Bhd., 10 Lorong 13/6B, Subang Jaya 47500, Petaling Jaya,
      Selangor, Malaysia

SERVCO CORP OF AMERICA   111 New South Rd, Hicksville, NY 11802,
   Tel: (516) 938-9700
(Electronic equip)
   Servco Co., Suite A, 14th Fl., Angkasaraya Jalan Ampang, Kuala Lumpur, Malaysia

WILBUR SMITH ASSOCS   NationsBank Tower, PO Box 92, Columbia, SC 29202,
  Tel: (803) 708-4500
  (Consulting engineers)
     Wilbur Smith Associates, Suite 8-04, Wisma Stephens, 88 Jalan Raja Chulan,
        50200 Kuala Lumpur, Malaysia

SONAT OFFSHORE DRILLING INC   PO Box 2765, Houston, TX 77252-2765,
  Tel: (713) 871-7500
  (Offshore oil well drilling)
     Asie Sonat Offshore Sdn. Bhd., 10/F Menara Apera, 84 Jalan Raja Chulan,
        50200 Kuala Lumpur, Malaysia

STEPAN CO   22 W Frontage Rd, Northfield, IL 60093, Tel: (708) 446-7500
  (Mfr basic & intermediate chems)
     Stepan Asia, 35A Jalan SS 18/6, Subang Jaya, 47500 Petaling Jaya, Selangor, Malaysia

STOKES DIV   5500 Tabor Rd, Philadelphia, PA 19120, Tel: (215) 289-5671
  (Vacuum pumps & components, vacuum dryers, oil-upgrading equip)
     Connell Bros. Co. Ltd., 11A Jalan S.S., 15/4B, Subang Jaya, Selangor, Malaysia

STONE & WEBSTER ENGINEERING CORP   245 Summer St, Boston, MA 02210-2288,
  Tel: (617) 589-5111
  (Engineering, constr & environmental & mgmt services)
     Stone & Webster Services Sdn. Bhd., Suite 25A-B, Empire Tower 25/F,
        City Sq. Center, 182 Jalan Tun Razak, 50400 Kuala Lumpur, Malaysia

SULLAIR CORP   3700 E Michigan Blvd, Michigan City, IN 46360,
  Tel: (219) 879-5451
  (Refrigeration sys, vacuum pumps, generators, etc)
     Sullair Malaysia Ltd., 17 Jalan 4906 off Jalan SS 13/3 Subang,
        Jaya Industrial Estate, Subang Jaya, Selangor, Malaysia

SUMMIT INDUSTRIAL CORP   600 Third Ave, New York, NY 10016,
  Tel: (212) 490-1100
  (Pharms, agric chem prdts)
     Summit Co. (Malaysia) Sdn. Bhd., P.O. Box 1088, Jalan Semangat, Petaling Jaya,
        Selangor, Malaysia

TELEDYNE INC   2049 Century Park East, Los Angeles, CA 90067-3101,
  Tel: (310) 277-3311
  (Divers mfg: aviation & electronics, specialty metals, industrial & consumer prdts)
     Teledyne Malaysia, Wisma Consplant 4/F, 2 Jalan SS16/4, Sugang Jaya,
        47500 Petaling Jaya, Selangor, Malaysia

TEXAS INSTRUMENTS INC   13500 N Central Expwy, Dallas, TX 75265,
  Tel: (214) 995-2011
  (Mfr semiconductor devices, electr/electro-mech sys, instr & controls)
     Texas Instruments Malaysia Sdn. Bhd., 1 Lorong Enggang 33, Ampang/Ulu, Keland,
        Kuala Lumpur, Malaysia

TRANE CO   3600 Pammel Creek Rd, La Crosse, WI 54601, Tel: (608) 787-2000
  (Mfr/distr/svce A/C sys & equip)
     TM Sales & Services Sdn. Bhd., Lot 3 & 5, Jalan PJS 11/1, Bandar Sunway,
        46150 Petaling Jaya, Selangor, Darul Ehsan, W. Malaysia

U S SUMMIT CORP   600 Third Ave, New York, NY 10016, Tel: (212) 490-1100
(Mktg/distrib pharms, chems)
   Summit Co. (Malaysia) Sdn. Bhd., P.O. Box 1088, Jalan Semangat, Petaling Jaya,
     Selangor, Malaysia

UNION CAMP CORP   1600 Valley Rd, Wayne, NJ 07470, Tel: (201) 628-2000
(Mfr paper, packaging, chems, wood prdts)
   Bush Boake Allen (Malaysia) Sdn. Bhd., 90B Jalan SS 15/4, Subang Jaya, Selangor,
     Malaysia

UNION CARBIDE CORP   39 Old Ridgebury Rd, Danbury, CT 06817,
  Tel: (203) 794-2000
(Mfr industrial chemicals, plastics, resins)
   UC Chemicals (Malaysia) Sdn. Bhd., Suite 3, Level 28, Fujitsu Plaza,
     1A Jalan Tangdang 204, 46050 Petaling Selangor, Malaysia

UNISYS CORP   PO Box 500, Blue Bell, PA 19424, Tel: (215) 986-4011
(Mfg/mktg/serv electr info sys)
   Unisys (Malaysia) Sdn. Bhd., 10 Jalan P. Ramlee, UBN Tower, 50250 Kuala Lumpur,
     Malaysia

UPRIGHT INC   1775 Park St, Selma, CA 93662, Tel: (209) 891-5200
(Mfr aluminum scaffolds & aerial lifts)
   UpRight (Far East) Inc., 22 King St., 10200 Penang, Malaysia

WD-40 COMPANY   1061 Cudahy Pl, San Diego, CA 92110-3998, Tel: (619) 275-1400
(Mfr lubricant/cleaner)
   WD-40 Company (Malaysia), Suite 1302, West Tower, Wisma Consplant #2,
     Jalan SS 16/4, Subang Jaya, 47500 Selangor, Malaysia

WEATHERFORD INTL INC   1360 Post Oak Blvd, PO Box 27608, Houston,
  TX 77227-7608, Tel: (713) 439-9400
(Oilfield servs, prdts & equip; mfr marine cranes)
   Weatherford Intl., 10F Wisma On Tai, 161-8 Jalan Ampang, 50450 Kuala Lumpur,
     Malaysia
   Weatherford/Lamb (Malaysia) Sdn. Bhd., Sangara & Co., P.O. Box WDT 33,
     214 Jalan Kolam, Labuan, Sabah, Malaysia

WESTERN ATLAS INTL INC   10205 Westheimer, PO Box 1407, Houston,
  TX 77251-1407, Tel: (713) 266-5700
(Full service to the oil industry)
   Western Atlas Logging Services, Lot 35, Block 4, SEDC Piasau Industrial Estate,
     98000 Miri, Sarawak, Malaysia
   Western Atlas Software, Letter Box 41, 14th fl., Menara Haw Par,
     Jalan Sultan Ismail, 50250 Kuala Lumpur, Malaysia

WILBUR-ELLIS CO   320 California St, #200, San Francisco, CA 94104,
  Tel: (415) 772-4000
(Intl merchants & distributors)
   Connell Bros. Co. Ltd., A606, 6/F West, Wisma Tractors, 7 Jalan SS16/1,
     Subang Jaya, 47500 Petaling Jaya, Selangor, Malaysia

WM WRIGLEY JR CO   410 N Michigan Ave, Chicago, IL 60611-4287,
  Tel: (312) 644-2121
(Mfr chewing gum)
   The Wrigley Co. (Malaysia) Sdn. Bhd., Kuala Lumpur, Malaysia

XEROX CORP   800 Long Ridge Rd, PO Box 1600, Stamford, CT 06904,
   Tel: (203) 968-3000
   (Mfr document processing equip, sys & supplies)
     Xerox Corp., Selangor, Malaysia

YORK INTERNATIONAL CORP   PO Box 1592, York, PA 17405-1592,
   Tel: (717) 771-7890
   (Mfr A/C, heating & refrig sys & equip)
     York (Malaysia) Service Sdn. Bhd., 51B SS21/A1 Damansara Utama,
       47400 Petaling Jaya, Selangor, Malaysia

ZEMEX CORP   1 West Pack Sq, Asheville, NC 28801, Tel: (704) 255-4900
   (Tin mining, industrial minerals & metal powders)
     Perangsang Pasifik Sdn. Bhd., 161-B Jalan Ampang, 50450 Kuala Lumpur, Malaysia
     Zemex Corp., P.O. Box 10292, Kuala Lumpur, Malaysia

MALTA

BAXTER HEALTHCARE CORP   1 Baxter Pky, Deerfield, IL 60015,
   Tel: (708) 948-2000
   (Mfr disposable medical prdts)
     Baxter Ltd., A47 Industrial Estate, Marsa, Malta

HORWATH INTL   415 Madison Ave, New York, NY 10017, Tel: (212) 838-5566
   (Public accountants & auditors)
     Diamantino, Mizzi & Co., Valletta Bldgs, South St., Valletta, Malta

SEA-LAND SERVICE INC   150 Allen Rd, Liberty Corner, NJ 07920,
   Tel: (201) 558-6000
   (Container transport)
     Sea Malta Co. Ltd., P.O. Box 555, Europa Centre, Floriana, Malta

MEXICO

3COM CORP   5400 Bayfront Plaza, Santa Clara, CA 95052-8145,
  Tel: (408) 764-5000
  (Devel/mfr computer networking prdts & sys)
    3Com Latim America, Mexico

3M   3M Center, St Paul, MN 55144-1000, Tel: (612) 733-1110
  (Mfr diversified prdts for industry, health care, imaging, commun, transport, safety,
  consumer, etc)
    3M Mexico SA de CV, Calz. San Juan de Aragon 516, Col. Carrera Lardizabal,
      Del. Gustavo Madero, 07070 Mexico DF, Mexico

AAF INTL   215 Central Ave, PO Box 35690, Louisville, KY 40232-5690,
  Tel: (502) 637-0011
  (Mfr air filtration/pollution control & noise control equip)
    AAF SA de CV, Aptdo. Postal 292, Av. Progreso 85, Tlalnepantla, 54000 Mexico DF,
      Mexico

AAF-McQUAY INC   111 S Calvert St, #2800, Baltimore, MD 21202,
  Tel: (410) 528-2755
  (Mfr air quality control prdts: heating, ventilating, air-conditioning & filtration
  prdts & services)
    SnyderGeneral SA de CV, Avda. 1 de Mayo 85, Tlalnepantla, Mexico

ABBOTT LABORATORIES   100 Abbott Park Rd, Abbott Park, IL 60064-3500,
  Tel: (708) 937-6100
  (Devel/mfr/sale diversified health care prdts & services)
    Abbott Laboratories de Mexico SA, Mexico DF, Mexico

ABF FREIGHT SYSTEM INC   PO Box 10048, Fort Smith, AR 72917-0048,
  Tel: (501) 785-8928
  (Motor carrier)
    ABF Freight Canada Ltd., Calle de Parque 44, Col. Napoles, 03810 Mexico DF, Mexico

ACCO INTL INC   770 S Acco Plaza, Wheeling, IL 60090, Tel: (708) 541-9500
  (Paper fasteners & clips, metal fasteners, binders, staplers)
    Acco Mexicana SA de CV, Av. Sara 4441, Mexico DF, Mexico

ACCURAY CORP   650 Ackerman Rd, PO Box 02248, Columbus, OH 43202,
  Tel: (614) 261-2000
  (Computer-based process mgmt sys for forest prdts, metals rolling, textiles, tobacco
  ind)
    Accuray Mexico SA de CV, Mexico DF, Mexico

AIR PRODUCTS & CHEMICALS INC   7201 Hamilton Blvd, Allentown, PA 18195-1501,
   Tel: (215) 481-4911
   (Mfr ind gases & related equip, spec chems, environmental/energy sys)
      Cryoinfra SA de CV, Felix Guzman 16, Col. el Parque, 53390 Naucalpan, Mexico DF,
      Mexico

AJAY LEISURE PRODUCTS INC   1501 E Wisconsin St, Delavan, WI 53115,
   Tel: (414) 728-5521
   (Mfr golf bags)
      Richard Milton SA, all mail to P.O. Box 3507, Calexico, CA 92232

ALBANY INTL CORP   PO Box 1907, Albany, NY 12201, Tel: (518) 445-2200
   (Paper mach clothing, engineered fabrics, plastic prdts, filtration media)
      Albany Equipos y Sistemas SA de CV, Aptdo. Postal 5-989, Guadalajara, Jalisco,
      Mexico
      Albany Nordiska de Mexico SA de CV, Aptdo. Postal 94-60, Mexico DF, Mexico

ALBERTO-CULVER CO   2525 Armitage Ave, Melrose Park, IL 60160,
   Tel: (708) 450-3000
   (Mfr/mktg personal care & beauty prdts, household & grocery prdts, institutional food
   prdts)
      Alberto-Culver de Mexico SA de CV, Alce Blanco 11, Naucalpan de Juarez, Mexico

ALLEN-BRADLEY CO   PO Box 2086, Milwaukee, WI 53201, Tel: (414) 382-2000
   (Mfr eletrical controls & info devices)
      Controlmatic Allen-Bradley SA de CV, Patriotismo 579, Col. Nochebuena,
      03720 Mexico DF, Mexico
      Electrica Allen-Bradley SA de CV, Constituyentes 1154, Piso 10, Col. Lomas Altas,
      11950 Mexico DF, Mexico

ALLENBERG COTTON CO INC   PO Box 3254, Cordova, TN 38018-3254,
   Tel: (901) 383-5000
   (Raw cotton)
      Algodonera Comercial Mexicana SA, Av. las Granjas y Calz. Acalotenco, Mexico DF,
      Mexico
      Algodonera Comercial Mexicana SA, Av. Madero 42, Mexico DF, Mexico

ALLIED AFTERMARKET DIV   105 Pawtucket Ave, East Providence, RI 02916,
   Tel: (401) 434-7000
   (Mfr spark plugs, filters, brakes)
      Filtram SA, Gral. P.A. Gonzalez 500 PTE, Aptdo. Postal 1869, Monterrey, NL, Mexico

ALLIEDSIGNAL INC   101 Columbia Rd, PO Box 2245, Morristown, NJ 07962-2245,
   Tel: (201) 455-2000
   (Mfr aerospace & automotive prdts, engineered materials)
      Bendix Mexicana SA de CV, Av. de las Granjas 47A, Aptdo. Postal 63-255,
      02530 Mexico DF, Mexico
      Bendix Safety Restraints Div., Parque Industrial Gema, Aptdo. Postal 1701-D,
      Juarez, Chihuahua, Mexico

ALUMINUM CO OF AMERICA (ALCOA)   425 6th Ave, Pittsburgh, PA 15219,
   Tel: (412) 553-4545
   (Aluminum mining, refining, processing, prdts)
      Alcomex SA, Paseo de la Reforma 403, Mexico DF, Mexico
      Alcomex SA, Veracruz, Mexico

Tapas y Evases SA de CV, Poniente 150 #660, Col. Industrial Vallejo, Mexico DF, Mexico

AMATEX CORP   1030 Standbridge St, Norristown, PA 19404, Tel: (215) 277-6100
(Mfr textile, fiberglass prdts)
Maquilladoras Fronterizas SA, Calle 6 #361, Agua Prieta, Sonora, Mexico

AMERICAN & EFIRD INC   PO Box 507, Mt Holly, NC 28120, Tel: (704) 827-4311
(Mfr ind thread, yarn & consumer sewing prdts)
A&E de Mexico SA de CV, Calle 8 #17A, Fracc. Industrial Alce Blanco, 53370 Naucalpan de Juarez, Mexico

AMERICAN AIRLINES INC   PO Box 619616, Dallas-Ft Worth Arpt, TX 75261-9616, Tel: (817) 355-1234
(Air transp)
American Airlines Inc., Paseo de la Reforma 300, Mexico DF, Mexico

AMERICAN APPRAISAL ASSOCS INC   411 E Wisconsin Ave, Milwaukee, WI 53202, Tel: (414) 271-7240
(Valuation consulting serv)
Panamericano de Avaluos SA, Bufete Bldg., Moras 850, Colonia del Valle, 03100 Mexico DF, Mexico

AMERICAN EXPRESS CO   World Financial Center, New York, NY 10285-4765, Tel: (212) 640-2000
(Travel, travelers cheques, charge card & financial services)
American Express Co. (Mexico) SA de CV
Banamsa, all inquiries to U.S. address

AMERICAN GREETINGS CORP   10500 American Rd, Cleveland, OH 44144, Tel: (216) 252-7300
(Mfr/distr greeting cards, gift wrappings, tags, seals, ribbons & party goods)
Felicitaciones Nacionales, Calzada Tulyehualco 4513, San Nicolas Tolentino, Mexico 13 DF, Mexico

AMERICAN OPTICAL CORP   14 Mechanic St, Southbridge, MA 01550, Tel: (508) 765-9711
(Mfr opthalmic lenses & frames, custom molded prdts, specialty lenses)
American Optical de Mexico SA de CV, Av. San Andres Atoto 165-B, Naucalpan de Juarez, 53550 Edo de Mexico, Mexico
Industrias Opticas SA de CV, Tijuana, Mexico (all mail to P.O. Box 439026, San Diego, CA 92143-9026)

AMERICAN STANDARD INC   1 Centennial Ave, Piscataway, NJ 08855, Tel: (908) 980-3000
(Mfr heating & sanitary equip)
Ideal Standard SA de CV, Aptdo. Postal 291, Mexico DF, Mexico

AMERICAN TELESOURCE INTL INC   12500 Network Blvd, #407, San Antonio, TX 78249, Tel: (210) 558-6090
(Long distance commun, payphones, private satellite commun networks)
American Telesource Intl. de Mexico SA de CV, Division del Norte 421, Despacho 403, 03100 Mexico DF, Mexico

THE AMERICAN TOBACCO CO   PO Box 10380, Stamford, CT 06904,
  Tel: (203) 325-4900
  (Tobacco prdts)
    AT&T Intl., Paseo de la Reforma 300, 06600 Mexico DF, Mexico

AMERON INC   PO Box 7007, Pasadena, CA 91109-7007, Tel: (818) 683-4000
  (Mfr steel pipe sys, concrete prdts, traffic & lighting poles, protective coatings)
    Amercoat Mexicana SA, Aptdo. Postal 7-1525, Mexico DF, Mexico

AMP INC   PO Box 3608, Harrisburg, PA 17105-3608, Tel: (717) 564-0100
  (Devel/mfr electronic & electrical connection prdts & sys)
    AMP de Mexico SA, Mexico DF, Mexico

AMWAY CORP   7575 E Fulton Rd, Ada, MI 49355, Tel: (616) 676-6000
  (Mfr/sale home care, personal care, nutrition & houseware prdts)
    Amway de Mexico SA de CV, Washington 539 Ote., 64000 Monterrey, NL, Mexico

ANACONDA CO   555 17th St, Denver, CO 80202, Tel: (303) 575-4000
  (Copper mining)
    Cia. Minera de Cananea SA de CV, Av. Insurgentes Sur 1377, Mexico DF, Mexico

ANAMET INC   698 S Main St, Waterbury, CT 06706, Tel: (203) 574-8500
  (Mfr ind machinery, wiring devices, measure & control devices)
    Anamet SA de CV, Calle 16 26, Ecatepec de Morelos, Mexico DF, Mexico

ANCHOR LABORATORIES INC   2621 N Belt Hwy, St Joseph, MO 64501,
  Tel: (816) 233-1385
  (Vaccines & serums)
    Anchor SA de CV, Calle 30 #2812, Zona Industrial, Guadalajara, Jalisco, Mexico

ANDREW CORP   10500 W 153rd St, Orlando Park, IL 60462, Tel: (708) 349-3300
  (Mfr antenna sys, coaxial cable, electronic commun & network connectivity sys)
    Andrew Corp. Mexico, Homero 1804, Of. 903, Col. Polanco Reforma, 11510 Mexico DF,
    Mexico

APPLE COMPUTER INC   1 Infinite Loop, Cupertino, CA 95014, Tel: (408) 996-1010
  (Personal computers, peripherals & software)
    Apple de Mexico, Blvd. M. Avila Comacho 1, Plaza Comermex, Piso 2, 11000 Mexico DF,
    Mexico

APPLIED POWER INC   13000 W Silver Spring Dr, Butler, WI 53007,
  Tel: (414) 781-6600
  (Mfr hi-pressure tools, vibration control prdts, electrical tools & consumables, tech
  furniture)
    Applied Power Mexico SA de CV, Av. Ind. La Paz Lotes 36 y 37, Fracc. Ind. La Paz,
    Pachuca, Hidalgo, Mexico

ARBOR ACRES FARM INC   439 Marlborough Rd, Glastonbury, CT 06033,
  Tel: (860) 633-4681
  (Producers of male & female broiler breeders, commercial egg layers)
    Arbor Acres de Mexico SA de CV, Aptdo. Postal 732-733, Queretaro, Mexico

ARMSTRONG WORLD INDUSTRIES INC   PO Box 3001, Lancaster, PA 17604,
  Tel: (717) 397-0611
  (Mfr/mkt interior furnishings & spec prdts for bldg, auto & textile inds)
    Armstrong World Industries de Mexic SA de CV, Mexico City,

Mexico (all inquiries to U.S. address)
Recubrimientos Interceramic SA de CV, Chihuahua,
Mexico (all inquiries to U.S. address)

ARROW CO   530 Fifth Ave, New York, NY 10036, Tel: (212) 930-2900
(Men's apparel)
Arrow de Mexico SA, Aptdo. Postal 1395, Mexico DF, Mexico

ARVIN INDUSTRIES INC   One Noblitt Plaza, Columbus, IN 47201-6079,
Tel: (812) 379-3000
(Mfr motor vehicle parts, springs, relays & ind controls, aircraft engines & parts)
AP de Mexico SA de CV, Aptdo. Postal 229, Km. 9.5 Carretera Constitucion,
76000 Queretaro, Mexico

ARVINAIR   500 S 15th St, Phoenix, AZ 85034, Tel: (602) 257-0060
(Mfr evaporative air coolers & portable elec heaters)
Impco SA de CV, Aptdo. Postal 260, 67100 Guadalupe, NL, Mexico

ASARCO INC   180 Maiden Lane, New York, NY 10038, Tel: (212) 510-2000
(Nonferrous metals, specialty chems, minerals, mfr industrial prdts, environmental
services)
Enthone-Omi Inc., Mexico City, Mexico
Mexico Desarrollo Industrial Minero SA de CV, Cananea & La Caridad, Mexico

ASGROW SEED CO   2605 E Kilgore Rd, Kalamazoo, MI 49002, Tel: (616) 384-5675
(Research/mfr agronomic & vegetable seeds; seed technologies)
Asgrow Mexicana SA de CV, Av. Mariano Otero 2347, Col. Verde Valle,
44550 Guaalajara, Jal., Mexico

ASHLAND OIL INC   1000 Ashland Dr, Russell, KY 41169, Tel: (606) 329-3333
(Petroleum exploration, refining & transportation; mfr chemicals, oils & lubricants)
Ashland de Mexico SA de CV, Apartado Postal 5-294, Col. Cuauhtemoc,
06500 Mexico DF, Mexico

ASKO INC   501 W 7th Ave, PO Box 355, Homestead, PA 15120, Tel: (412) 461-4110
(Mfr ind knives & saws for metal ind)
SOTEC, Apartado Postal 6-bis, 06000 Mexico D.F., Mexico

ASSOCIATED PRESS INC   50 Rockefeller Plaza, New York, NY 10020-1605,
Tel: (212) 621-1500
(News gathering agency)
The Associated Press, Aptdo. Postal 1181, Mexico DF, Mexico

ASSOCIATED SPRING   18 Main St, Bristol, CT 06010, Tel: (203) 583-1331
(Mfr precision springs & stampings)
Resortes Mecanicos, Aptdo. Postal 756, 06000 Mexico DF, Mexico

AT&T INTERNATIONAL   412 Mt Kemble Ave, Morristown, NJ 07962-1995,
Tel: (810) 262-6646
(Telecommunications)
AT&T de Mexico, Edificio Omega, Campos Eliseos 345 - PH2, 11560 Mexico DF, Mexico

AUTOMATIC SWITCH CO   Hanover Rd, Florham Park, NJ 07932, Tel: (201) 966-2000
(Mfr solenoid valves, emergency power controls, pressure & temp switches)
Ascomatica SA de CV, Bosques de Duraznos 65-1003A, Fracc. Bosques de las Lomas,
Deleg. Miguel Hidalgo, Mexico

AVERY DENNISON CORP   150 N Orange Grove Blvd, Pasadena, CA   91103,
Tel: (818) 304-2000
(Mfr pressure-sensitive adhesives & materials, office prdts, labels, tags, retail
sys, spec chems)
   Dennison de Mexico SA de CV, Sto. Estaban 88, Z.P. 16, Mexico DF, Mexico
   Tasson de Mexico SA, Avda. Circunvalacion Pte. 53-F, Naucalpan de Juarez, Mexico

AVON PRODUCTS INC   9 W 57th St, New York, NY   10019, Tel: (212) 546-6015
(Mfr/distr beauty & related prdts, fashion jewelry, gifts & collectibles)
   Avon Cosmetics SA de CV, Aptdo. Postal 591, Mexico DF, Mexico

AVX CORP   750 Lexington Ave, New York, NY   10022-1208, Tel: (212) 935-6363
(Mfr multilayer ceramic capacitors)
   Avio Excellente SA de CV, Ing. Rafael Parez Serna y Henry Dunant, Area Riberena,
   Aptdo. Postal 1709-D, 32310 Juarez, Mexico

BAILEY-FISCHER & PORTER CO   125 E County Line Rd, Warminster, PA   18974,
Tel: (215) 674-6000
(Design/mfr meas, recording & control instru & sys; mfr ind glass prdts)
   FISPO SA, Aptdo. Postal M-9307, Mexico DF, Mexico

J T BAKER INC   222 Red School Lane, Phillipsburg, NJ   08865,
Tel: (201) 859-2151
(Mfr/sale/serv lab & process chems)
   J.T. Baker SA de CV, Aptdo. Postal 75595, Col. Lindavista,
   Deleg. Gustavo A. Madero, 07300 Mexico DF, Mexico

BAKER OIL TOOLS   PO Box 40129, Houston, TX   77240-0129, Tel: (713) 466-1322
(Mfr/serv oil/gas well completions equip)
   Baker Mexico, Avda. Ejercito Nacional 579, 3 Piso, Col. Granada, 11520 Mexico DF,
   Mexico

BALDWIN PIANO & ORGAN CO   422 Wards Corder Rd, Loveland, OH   45140-8390,
Tel: (513) 576-4500
(Mfr pianos, organs, clocks)
   Pratt-Win, Aptdo. Postal 1537, Sucursal de Correos "B", Ciudad Juarez, Chihuahua,
   Mexico

BANDAG INC   2905 NW 61, Muscatine, IA   52761, Tel: (319) 262-1400
(Mfr/sale retread tires)
   Vitafrio SA de CV, Aptdo. Postal 29, Leon, Gto., Mexico

BANKAMERICA CORP   555 California St, San Francisco, CA   94104,
Tel: (415) 622-3456
(Financial services)
   Arrendadora BankAmerica SA, Paseo de la Reforma 116, 06600 Mexico DF, Mexico
   Bank of America Mexico SA, Paseo de la Reforma 116, Piso 12, 06600 Mexico DF, Mexico
   Bank of America NT & SA, Paseo de la Reforma 116, Piso 12, 06600 Mexico DF, Mexico

BANKERS TRUST CO   280 Park Ave, New York, NY   10017, Tel: (212) 250-2500
(Banking)
   Bankers Trust Co., Paseo de la Reforma 199, Mexico DF, Mexico

BARNES GROUP INC   123 Main St, PO Box 409, Bristol, CT 06011-0489,
  Tel: (860) 583-7070
  (Mfr maint parts & supplies)
    Associated Spring, Mexico City, Mexico

R G BARRY CORP   13405 Yarmouth Dr, Pickerington, OH 43147,
  Tel: (614) 864-6400
  (Mfr slippers & footwear)
    Barry de Mexico SA de CV, Cesar Lopez de Lara 3130, 88000 Monterrey, NL, Mexico

BAUSCH & LOMB INC   1 Chase Square, Rochester, NY 14601, Tel: (716) 338-6000
  (Mfr vision care prdts & accessories)
    Optima Industrial, Mexico DF, Mexico

BAXTER HEALTHCARE CORP   1 Baxter Pky, Deerfield, IL 60015,
  Tel: (708) 948-2000
  (Mfr disposable medical prdts)
    Antonio J. Bermudez, Apartado Postal 1706-D, Cd. Juarez, Chihuahua, mexico
    Baxter SA de CV, Apartado Postal 13-279, Mexico 13 DF, Mexico
    Cirmax de Chihuahua SA de CV, Parque Industrial las Americas,
      Proj. Av. de las Americas, Chihuahua, Mexico
    Cirpro de Delicias SA de CV, Apartado Postal 715, Delicias, Chihuahua, Mexico
    Convertos de Mexico SA de CV, Apartado Postal 1519, Cd. Juarez, Chihuahua, Mexico
    Productos Urologos de Mexico SA de CV, Saturno 90, Mexicali, Baja California 21210,
      Mexico
    Quiro Productos de Cuauhtemoc SA de CV, Parque Cuauhtemoc, Carr. Anahuac K-3,
      Cd. Cuauhtemoc, Chihuahua, Mexico

BECHTEL GROUP INC   50 Beale St, PO Box 3965, San Francisco, CA 94119,
  Tel: (415) 768-1234
  (Engineering & constr)
    Bechtel de Mexico SA de CV, Paseo de la Reforma 381, Mexico DF, Mexico
    Bicomp SA de CV, Mexicali, Mexico

BECKMAN INSTRUMENTS INC   2500 Harbor Blvd, Fullerton, CA 92634,
  Tel: (714) 871-4848
  (Devel/mfr/mkt automated systems & supplies for biological analysis)
    Beckman Instruments de Mexico SA de CV, Angel Urraza 1119, Colonia del Valle,
      A.P. 44-100, 03100 Mexico DF, Mexico

BECTON DICKINSON AND CO   1 Becton Dr, Franklin Lakes, NJ 07417,
  Tel: (201) 847-6800
  (Mfr/sale medical supplies, devices & diagnostic sys)
    Becton Dickinson Mexico, Monte Pelvous 111, 11000 Mexico DF, Mexico

BELVEDERE CO   One Belvedere Blvd, Belvidere, IL 61008-8596,
  Tel: (815) 544-3131
  (Mfr beauty salon equip)
    Ensanibles de Silleria Mexicana SA, Local 22 Parque Industrial, El Virgia 12.5 Km.,
      Baja California, Mexico

BENTLY NEVADA CORP   PO Box 157, Minden, NV 89423, Tel: (702) 782-3611
  (Electronic monitoring system)
    Maquinaria Rotative SA, Tramonte 33, Fracc. los Pastores, 53340 Naucalpan, Mexico

BEROL CORP   105 Westpark Dr, Brentwood, TN 37027, Tel: (615) 370-9700
  (Mfr writing instru, sharpeners, drafting prdts, templates, coloring prdts)
    Berol SA de CV, Aptdo. Postal 289, Mexico DF, Mexico

BICKLEY INC   PO Box 369, Bensalem, PA 19020, Tel: (215) 638-4500
  (Mfr high temp furnaces)
    Bickley Mexico SA de CV, Mariano Escobedo 353A, Chapultepec, 11570 Morales, Mexico

SAMUEL BINGHAM CO   1555 N Mittel Blvd, #T, Wood Dale, IL 60191-1046,
  Tel: (708) 238-4000
  (Print & industrial rollers, inks)
    Bingham de Mexico, Galeana 3033, Apartado Postal 1070, Col. del Norte, Monterrey,
    NL, Mexico

BINKS MFG CO   9201 W Belmont Ave, Franklin Park, IL 60131,
  Tel: (708) 671-3000
  (Mfr of spray painting & finishing equip)
    Binks de Mexico SA, San Andres Atoto 155-C, Naucalpan de Juarez, Edo. de Mexico,
    Mexico

BINNEY & SMITH INC   1100 Church Lane, PO Box 431, Easton, PA 18044-0431,
  Tel: (610) 253-6271
  (Mfr art supplies, craft kits)
    Binney & Smith (Mexico) SA de CV, Escape #10, Fracc. Ind. Alce Blanco,
    53370 Naucalpan, Edo de Mexico, Mexico

BLACK & DECKER CORP   701 E Joppa Road, Towson, MD 21286, Tel: (410) 716-3900
  (Mfr power tools & accessories, security hardware, small appliances, fasteners, info
  sys & servs)
    Black & Decker Corp., all mail to U.S. address

BLACK BOX CORP   1000 Park Dr, Lawrence, PA 15055, Tel: (412) 746-5500
  (Direct marketer & tech service provider of commun, networking & related computer
  connectivity prdts)
    Black Box de Mexico SA de CV, Prolongacion Ixcatcopan 310, Col. Sta. Cruz Aloyac,
    CP 03310 Mexico DF, Mexico

BLACKSTONE CORP   1111 Allen St, Jamestown, NY 14701, Tel: (716) 665-2620
  (Heat transfer prdts, heaters, coolers)
    Blackstone de Mexico SA de CV, 130 Esq. Ave. CFE, Zona Industrial del Potosi,
    78090 San Luis Potosi , Mexico

BLACKSTONE MFG CO INC   4630 W Harrison Ave, Chicago, IL 60644,
  Tel: (312) 378-7800
  (Automotive prdts)
    Dinamica Automotriz, Fuente de Barco 17, Tecamachalco, Edo. de Mexico, Mexico

BLUE BIRD CORP   3920 Arkwright Rd, PO Box 7839, Macon, GA 31210,
  Tel: (912) 757-7100
  (Mfr/sale/svce buses, parts & access)
    Blue Bird de Mexico SA de CV, Apartado Postal 658, 66250 Col. del Valle, NL, Mexico

BOOZ ALLEN & HAMILTON INC   101 Park Ave, New York, NY 10178,
  Tel: (212) 697-1900
  (Mgmt consultants)

Booz Allen & Hamilton de Mexico SA de CV, Monte Pelvoux 130, Lomas de Chapultepec, 11000 Mexico DF, Mexico

BORG-WARNER AUTOMOTIVE INC   200 S Michigan Ave, Chicago, IL 60604,
  Tel: (312) 322-8500
  (Mfr automotive components; provider of security services)
    B.W. Componentes Mexicanos de Transmisiones SA de CV, Rio Altar 2250,
    Fracc. El Rosario, 44890 Guadalajara, Jalisco, Mexico
    Borg-Warner de Mexico SA de CV, Av. las Granjas 473-C, Col. Jardin Azpeitia,
    Deleg. Atzcapotzalco, 02530 Mexico DF, Mexico

BOSS MANUFACTURING CO   221 W First St, Kewanee, IL 61443, Tel: (309) 852-2131
  (Safety prdts, protective clothing, sport/work gloves)
    Boss de Mexico SA, Calle Abraham Gonzalez 127, Esqu. Av. Francisco, Villa Juarez,
    26246 Chihuahua, Mexico

BOSTITCH DIV   815 Briggs St, East Greenwich, RI 02818, Tel: (401) 884-2500
  (Stapling machs & supplies, wire)
    Bostitch de Mexico SA, 122 Poniente 419, Col. Industrial Vallego,
    Aptdo. Postal 15-066, Mexico DF, Mexico

BOURNS INC   1200 Columbia Ave, Riverside, CA 92507, Tel: (909) 781-5500
  (Mfr resistive com & networks, precision potentiometers, panel controls, switches,
  transducers)
    Bourns de Mexico SA, all mail to P.O. Box 439040, San Diego, CA 92143-9040

BOWNE INTL INC   345 Hudson St, New York, NY 10014, Tel: (212) 924-5500
  (Financial printing & foreign language translation)
    Bowne of Mexico City, Buffon 12, Col. Nueva Anzures, 11590 Mexico DF, Mexico

BOYDEN CONSULTING CORP   375 Park Ave, #1008, New York, NY 10152,
  Tel: (212) 980-6480
  (Executive search)
    Boyden Latin America SA, Paseo de la Reforma 509, Mexico DF, Mexico

BRANSON ULTRASONICS CORP   41 Eagle Rd, Danbury, CT 06813-1961,
  Tel: (203) 796-0400
  (Mfr plastics assembly equip, ultrasonic cleaning equip)
    Grupo Stevi SA de CV, Antiguo Camino a Culhuacan 100, Col. Sta. Isabel Industrial,
    09820 Mexico DF, Mexico
    Ultrasonido Industrial, Ricardo Adalid 3, Col. Elias Perez Avalos, 52210 Morelia,
    Mexico

W BRAUN CO   300 N Canal St, Chicago, IL 60606, Tel: (312) 346-6500
  (Design/mfr/supply packaging)
    W. Braun Co., all mail to 13165 NW 45th Ave., Opa Locka, FL 33054

BRISTOL BABCOCK INC   1100 Buckingham St, Watertown, CT 06795,
  Tel: (203) 575-3000
  (Mfr process control instru & SCADA sys)
    Instrumentos Bristol SA, Parque Rio Frio 14, 53390 Naucalpan, Edo de Mexico,
    11220 Mexico DF, Mexico

BRK BRANDS INC   3901 Liberty Street Rd, Aurora, IL 60504-8122,
  Tel: (708) 851-7330
  (Mfr CO detectors, smoke detectors, fire extinguishers, lights, timers & sensor sys)

(cont)

Electronica BRK de Mexico SA de CV, Av. Fernando Borrequero, Parque Indus. Juarez,
Cd. Juarez, Chihuahua, Mexico

BROWN & ROOT INC   4100 Clinton Dr, Houston, TX 77020-6299,
Tel: (713) 676-3011
(Engr, constr & maintenance)
Brown & Root de Mexico SA de CV, Campos Eliseos 385, Piso 2, Torre A, Col. Polanco,
Mexico DF, Mexico
Taylor Diving, Aptdo. Postal 110, Ciudad del Carmen, Campeche, Mexico

BRUNSWICK CORP   1 N Field Court, Lake Forest, IL 60045-4811,
Tel: (708) 735-4700
(Mfr recreational boats, marine engines, bowling centers & equip, fishing equip,
defense/aerospace)
Productos Marine de Mexico SA de CV, Parque Industrial Bermudez, Ciudad Juarez,
Chihuahua, Mexico

BUCK CONSULTANTS INC   Two Pennsylvania Plaza, New York, NY 10121,
Tel: (212) 330-1000
(Employee benefit, actuarial & compensation conslt serv)
Buck Actuarios Consultores SA de CV, Alfonso Esparaza Oteo 63, Guadalupe Inn,
01020 Mexico DF, Mexico

BUDGET RENT-A-CAR CORP OF AMERICA   4225 Napierville Rd, Lisle, IL 60532,
Tel: (708) 955-1900
(Self-drive car hire)
Budget Rent-A-Car de Mexico SA, Av. Rio Mixcoac 36-6, Mexico DF, Mexico
Budget Rent-A-Car de Mexico SA, Ribera de San Cosme 137, Mexico DF, Mexico

BUFFALO FORGE CO   PO Box 985, Buffalo, NY 14240, Tel: (716) 847-5121
(Fans, air-handling units)
Buffalo Forge SA de CV, Aptdo. Postal 34-032, 11619 Mexico, Mexico

BULAB HOLDINGS INC   1256 N McLean Blvd, Memphis, TN 38108,
Tel: (901) 278-0330
(Mfr microbicides, biocides, additives, corrosion inhibitors, chems)
Buckman Laboratories SA de CV, Paseo Cuauhnahuac Km. 13.5, Jiutepec, Morelos,
62550 Cuernavaca, Mexico

BURLINGTON INDUSTRIES INC   3330 W Friendly Ave, PO Box 21207, Greensboro,
NC 27420, Tel: (919) 379-2000
(Textiles)
Nobiles Lees SA de CV, Blvd. A. Lopez Mateos 2601, San Angel, 01080 Mexico, DF,
Mexico
Textiles Morelos SA de CV, Blvd. A. Lopez Mateos 2601, San Angel, 01080 Mexico, DF,
Mexico

LEO BURNETT CO INC   35 West Wacker Dr, Chicago, IL 60601, Tel: (312) 220-5959
(Advertising agency)
Leo Burnett SA de CV, Bosque de Duraznos 65-8 P, Bosques de las Lomas,
11700 Mexico DF, Mexico

BURSON-MARSTELLER   230 Park Ave, New York, NY 10003-1566, Tel: (212) 614-4000
(Public relations/public affairs consultants)
Omo-Delta Burson-Marsteller, Luz y Fuerza 9, Colonia Las Aguilas, 01710 Mexico DF,
Mexico

BUSSMANN   PO Box 14460, St Louis, MO 63178-4460, Tel: (314) 394-2877
   (Mfr electr fuses & acces, terminal strips, interconnect devices & circuit breakers)
     Bussmann, Juarez, Mexico

CARL BYOIR & ASSOCIATES INC   420 Lexington Ave, New York, NY 10017,
   Tel: (212) 210-6000
   (Public relations, intl commun)
     Robert S. Benjamin & Associates, Insurgentes 76-502, 06600 Mexico DF, Mexico

CALCOMP INC   2411 W La Palma Ave, Anaheim, CA 92801, Tel: (714) 821-2000
   (Mfr computer graphics peripherals)
     CalComp Mexico, Plateros 7, Piso 1, Col. San Jose Insurgentes, 03900 Mexico DF,
     Mexico

CALGON CORP   PO Box 1346, Pittsburgh, PA 15230, Tel: (412) 777-8000
   (Mfr. cosmetic, personal care & water treatment prdts)
     Proveedores Techicos SA de CV, Aptdo. Postal 40-149, 06140 Mexico DF, Mexico
     Proveedores Tecnicos SA de CV, 16 de Septiembre 203-302, Coatzacoalcos, Ver., Mexico

CALIFORNIA BUFF CO INC   1612 N Indiana St, Los Angeles, CA 90063,
   Tel: (213) 268-7884
   (Mfr. buffs, satin finishing wheels, abrasive wheels, cotton polishing)
     American Buff de Mexico SA, Emilion Cardenas 211, Centro Ind., Tlalnepantla,
     Edo. de Mexico, Mexico
     Ruenas Poleas y Abrasivos, Lopez Portillo 222, Pte. Col. Nueva, Tijuana, Mexico

CAMBRIDGE WIRE CLOTH CO   105 Goodwill Road, PO Box 399, Cambridge, MD 21613,
   Tel: (301) 228-3000
   (Mfr ind wire cloth, women wire conveyor belting, ind mesh)
     Cambridge Intl. SA de CV, Prol. Av. Uniones 2500, Parque Ind. del Norte,
     H. Matamoros, Tamps., Mexico

CAMP INTL INC   PO Box 89, Jackson, MI 49204, Tel: (517) 787-1600
   (Mfr orthotics & prosthetics)
     Ortiz Intl. SA, Galeana 237-239, Guadalajara, Jal., Mexico

CAMPBELL SOUP CO   Campbell Place, Camden, NJ 08103-1799, Tel: (609) 342-4800
   (Food prdts)
     Campbell's de Mexico SA de CV, Mexico

CARBOLINE CO   350 Hanley Industrial Ct, St Louis, MO 63144,
   Tel: (314) 644-1000
   (Mfr coatings, sealants)
     Carboline SA de CV, Ganaderos 234, Colonia Granjas Esmeralda, Deleg. Iztapalapa,
     Mexico

CARGILL   PO Box 9300, Minneapolis, MN 55440, Tel: (612) 475-7575
   (Food prdts, feeds, animal prdts)
     Cargill de Mexico SA de CV, Aptdo. Postal M-7137, Mexico DF, Mexico

CAROTRANS INTL INC   PO Box 1060, Cherryville, NC 28021, Tel: (704) 435-8356
   (Non-vessel operating common carrier)
     CaroTrans Intl. de Mexico, Av. 16 de Septiembre 182, Col. San Martin Xochinahuac,
     Azcapotzalco 02210 Mexico DF, Mexico

CARPENTER TECHNOLOGY CORP   101 W Bern St, PO Box 14662, Reading,
  PA 19612-4662, Tel: (610) 208-2000
  (Mfr specialty steels & structural ceramics for casting ind)
    Aceros Fortuna SA de CV, Av. Lic. Juan Gernandez Albarran 31,
      Frac. Industrial San Pablo Salpa, Tlalnepantla, Mexico

CARRIER CORP   One Carrier Place, Farmington, CT 06034-4015,
  Tel: (203) 674-3000
  (Mfr/distr/svce A/C, heating & refrigeration equip)
    Carrier Mexico SA de CV, Galeana 469 Ote., 66350 Santa Catarina, NL, Mexico
    Carrier Transicold de Mexico SA de CV, Col. La Joya, Mexico
    Entalpia SA de CV, Tlalpan, Mexico
    Industrias Consolidadas de Monterrey SA de CV, Nuevo Leon, Mexico
    Manufacturas Especializadas SA (MESA), Monterrey, NL, Mexico

CARTER'S INK CO   300 Howard St, Farmingham, MA 01701, Tel: (617) 890-2950
  (Inks, adhesives, ribbons)
    Dennison de Mexico SA, San Esteban 88, Arztazopalco, Mexico DF, Mexico

CARTER-WALLACE INC   1345 Ave of the Americas, New York, NY 10105,
  Tel: (212) 339-5000
  (Mfr personal care prdts, pet prdts)
    Carter-Wallace SA, Aptdo. Postal 2612, Blvd. Miguel de Cervantes 193, Mexico DF,
      Mexico

CASAS INTL BROKERAGE INC   10030 Marconi Dr, San Diego, CA 92173-3255,
  Tel: (619) 661-6162
  (Customhouse brokerage, freight fwdr, warehousing, imp/exp)
    Agencia Aduanal Obregon, Blvd. Tercera Oeste, 17522 Fracc. Garita de Otay,
      22509 Tijuana, Mexico
    Casas International, Blvd. Tercera Oeate, 17522 Fracc. Garita de Otay,
      22509 Tijuana, Mexico

CATERPILLAR INC   100 N E Adams St, Peoria, IL 61629, Tel: (309) 675-1000
  (Mfr earth/material-handling & constr mach & equip, engines, generators)
    Conek SA de CV, Aptdo. Postal 278, 69000 Monterrey, NL, Mexico

CEILCOTE CO   140 Sheldon Rd, Berea, OH 44017, Tel: (216) 243-0700
  (Mfr corrosion-resistant material, air pollution control equip, cons serv)
    Ceilcote Ingenieros en Corrosion SA de CV, Jaime Bames 11, Edif. Plaza, Polanco,
      Mexico 11510 DF, Mexico

CELITE CORP   PO Box 519, Lompoc, CA 93438, Tel: (805) 735-7791
  (Mining/process diatomaceous earth (diatomite))
    Celite Mexico SA de CV, Alejandro Dumas 103, Col. Polanco, 11560 Mexico DF, Mexico

CENTRAL NATIONAL-GOTTESMAN INC   3 Manhattanville Rd, Purchase,
  NY 10577-2110, Tel: (914) 696-9000
  (Worldwide sales pulp & paper prdts)
    Central National de Mexico SA, Av. Juarez 56, 7 piso,
      Zona Centro Delegacion Cuauhtemoc, 06050 Mexico DF, Mexico

CENTURY 21 REAL ESTATE CORP   2601 SE Main, PO Box 19564, Irvine,
  CA 92713-9564, Tel: (714) 553-2100
  (Real estate)

Century 21 Mexico SA de CV, Monte Libano 245, Lomas de Chapultepec, Mexico DF,
   Mexico

CERTRON CORP   1545 Sawtelle Blvd, Los Angeles, CA 90025, Tel: (213) 954-0477
   (Mfr/distr audio/video tapes & disks)
   Certron Audio SA, Mexicali, B.C., Mexico

CHAMPION INTERNATIONAL CORP   One Champion Plaza, Stamford, CT 06921,
   Tel: (213) 358-7000
   (Mfr pulp & paper)
   Champion International de Mexico SA de CV, Bosque de Duraznos 75, Oficina 202,
      Col. Bosques de las Lomas, 11700 Mexico DF, Mexico

CHAMPION SPARK PLUG CO   PO Box 910, Toledo, OH 43661-0001,
   Tel: (419) 535-2567
   (Mfr spark plugs, wiper blades & related prdts)
   Bujias Champion de Mexico SA de CV, Aptdo. Postal 16-282, Deleg. Azcapotzalco,
      02000 Mexico DF, Mexico

CHASE MANHATTAN BANK N A   1 Chase Manhattan Plaza, New York, NY 10081,
   Tel: (212) 552-2222
   (Intl banking)
   The Chase Manhattan Bank SA, Paseo de la Reforma 300, Mexico DF, Mexico

CHEMICAL BANK   270 Park Ave, New York, NY 10017-2070, Tel: (212) 270-6000
   (Banking & financial services)
   Chemical Bank, Campos Eliseos 400, Col. Polancio Chapultepec, 11000 Mexico DF,
      Mexico

CHESTERTON BINSWANGER INTL   Two Logan Sq, 4th fl, Philadelphia,
   PA 19103-2759, Tel: (215) 448-6000
   (Real estate & related svces)
   Grupo Bermudez Network, Blvd. Thomas Fernandez 7930, Cd. Juarez, Chih. 32470, Mexico

A W CHESTERTON CO   Middlesex Industrial Park, Stoneham, MA 02180,
   Tel: (617) 438-7000
   (Packing gaskets, sealing prdts sys, etc)
   Chesterton Mexicana, Naucalpan de Juarez, Mexico

CHEVRON CHEMICAL CO   PO Box 5047, San Ramon, CA 94583-0947,
   Tel: (510) 842-5500
   (Chemicals)
   Aditivos Mexicanos SA, Carretera Mexico Cuautitlan Km. 19.5, Aptdo. Postal 259,
      Tlalnepantla, Edo de Mexico, Mexico

CHEVRON CORP   225 Bush St, San Francisco, CA 94104, Tel: (415) 894-7700
   (Oil & gas exploration, production, refining, products; oilfield & financial services)
   Chevron Corp., all mail to U.S. address

CHICAGO PNEUMATIC TOOL CO   2200 Bleecker St, Utica, NY 13501,
   Tel: (315) 792-2600
   (Mfr air tools & equip)
   Chicago Pneumatic de Mexico SA, Blvd. Puerto Aereo 169, Col. Federal,
      Deleg. V. Carranza, 15700 Mexico DF, Mexico

CHICAGO RAWHIDE MFG CO   900 N State Street, Elgin, IL 60120,
  Tel: (708) 742-7840
  (Seals & filters)
    C/R Mexicana SA, Governador Curiel 2690, Zona Industrial, Guadalajara, Jalisco,
    Mexico

CHINET CO   101 Merritt 7, Norwalk, CT 06851, Tel: (203) 846-1499
  (Mfr molded containers)
    Productora de Articulos de Celulosa Keyes SA, Blvd. Adolfo Lopes Mateos 165,
    01010 Mexico DF, Mexico

CHIRON CORP   4560 Horton St, Emeryville, CA 94608-2916, Tel: (510) 601-2412
  (Research/mfg/mktg therapeutics, vaccines, diagnostics, ophthalmics)
    Ciba Corning Diagnostics de Mexico SA de CV, Av. Periferico Sur 6677,
      Col. Ejidos de Tepepan, Xochimilco 16018, Mexico

THE CHRISTIAN SCIENCE PUBLISHING SOCIETY   1 Norway St, Boston, MA 02115,
  Tel: (617) 450-2000
  (Publishing, broadcasting)
    The Christian Science Monitor, all mail to P.O. Box 60326, Houston, TX 77205

CHRYSLER CORP   12000 Chrysler Dr, Highland Park, MI 48288-1919,
  Tel: (313) 956-5741
  (Mfr/mktg cars & light trucks, electr & aerospace prdts & sys)
    Chrysler de Mexico SA, Aptdo. Postal 53-951, Mexico DF, Mexico

CHRYSLER FINANCIAL CORP   27777 Franklin Rd, Southfield, MI 48034,
  Tel: (313) 948-2890
  (Financial serv)
    Chrysler Comercial SA de CV, Paseo de las Palmas 735, 11010 Mexico DF, Mexico

CIGNA CORP   One Liberty Place, Philadelphia, PA 19192, Tel: (215) 523-4000
  (Ins, invest, health care & other fin servs)
    Inamex SA, Viena #71, Col. del Carmen, Coyoacan, 04100 Mexico DF, Mexico

CINCINNATI MILACRON INC   4701 Marburg Ave, Cincinnati, OH 45209,
  Tel: (513) 841-8100
  (Devel/mfr technologies for metalworking & plastics processing ind)
    Cincinnati Milacron SA de CV, Nogales, Mexico

CINCOM SYSTEMS INC   2300 Montana Ave, Cincinnati, OH 45211,
  Tel: (513) 662-2300
  (Devel/distr computer software)
    Cincom Systems Inc., Mexico City, Mexico

CITICORP   399 Park Ave, New York, NY 10043, Tel: (212) 559-1000
  (Banking & financial services)
    Citibank Mexico SA, Grupo Financiero Citibank, Mexico
    Citibank NA, Mexico

CLAYTON INDUSTRIES   4213 N Temple City Blvd, El Monte, CA 91731,
  Tel: (213) 443-9381
  (Mfr steam generators, dynamometers, water treatment chems)
    Clayton de Mexico SA, Manuel L. Stampa 54, Nueva Industrial Vallejo,
      07000 Mexico DF, Mexico

CLEVELAND TWIST DRILL CO   470 Old Evans Rd, Evans, GA 30809,
  Tel: (706) 650-4253
  (Mfr metal cutting/threading tools, related prdts)
    Herramientas Cleveland SA, Aptdo. Postal 314, Prol. Ave. Juarez 1602, Pachuca,
    Hgo., Mexico

THE CLOROX CO   1221 Broadway, PO Box 24305, Oakland, CA 94623-1305,
  Tel: (510) 271-7000
  (Mfr domestic consumer packaged prdts)
    Clorox de Mexico SA de CV, Mexico City, Mexico

COBE LABORATORIES INC   1185 Oak St, Lakewood, CO 80215, Tel: (303) 232-6800
  (Mfr med equip & supplies)
    COBE Laboratories Inc., Tijuana, Mexico

THE COCA-COLA CO   PO Drawer 1734, Atlanta, GA 30301, Tel: (404) 676-2121
  (Mfr/mkt/distr soft drinks, syrups & concentrates, juice & juice-drink prdts)
    Coca-Cola FEMSA SA de CV, all mail to U.S. address
    Coca-Cola North Latin America, Aptdo. Postal 57-211, 06500 Mexico DF, Mexico
    Grupo Continental, all mail to U.S. address

COILCRAFT INC   1102 Silver Lake Rd, Cary, IL 60013, Tel: (708) 639-2361
  (Leaded & surface-mount coils & transformers)
    Coilcraft de Mexico SA, Melquiades Alanes y Fray Marcos de Risga,
    Aptdo. Postal 2518 E, CD Juarez Chieh, Mexico

COLGATE-PALMOLIVE CO   300 Park Ave, New York, NY 10022, Tel: (212) 310-2000
  (Mfr pharms, cosmetics, toiletries, detergents)
    Colgate-Palmolive SA, Presa La Angosture 225, 11500 Mexico DF, Mexico

COLUMBIA PICTURES INDUSTRIES INC   711 Fifth Ave, New York, NY 10022,
  Tel: (212) 751-4400
  (Producer & distributor of motion pictures)
    Columbia Pictures SA, Sinaloa 20, Aptdo. Postal 911, Mexico DF, Mexico

COMBUSTION ENGINEERING INC   900 Long Ridge Road, Stamford, CT 06902,
  Tel: (203) 329-8771
  (Tech constr)
    EPN SA, Hegel 153, Col. Polanco, Mexico DF, Mexico
    EPN-Gray SA, Av. Central 235, Unidad Industrial Vallejo, Mexico DF, Mexico

CONTINENTAL BANK NA   231 S LaSalle St, Chicago, IL 60697, Tel: (312) 828-2345
  (Coml banking servs)
    Continental Bank Corp., Blvd. Manuel Avila Camacho #191,
    Colonia Los Morales Polanco, 11510 Mexico DF, Mexico

CONTINENTAL CAN CO   PO Box 5410, Stamford, CT 06856, Tel: (203) 357-8110
  (Packaging prdts & mach, metal, plastic & paper containers)
    Envases Generales Continental de Mexico SA, Calle Oriente 107 #114, Col. Bondojito,
    Mexico

COOK & CO   Omulgee St, Lumber City, GA 31549, Tel: (912) 363-4371
  (Forestry; mfr steel, tire cord)
    Servicios Agricolas Cook SA, Av. de las Palmas 765, Mexico DF, Mexico

COOPER INDUSTRIES INC   1001 Fannin St, PO Box 4446, Houston, TX 77210-4446,
  Tel: (713) 739-5400
  (Mfr/distr electrical prdts, tools & hardware, automotive prdts)
    Bussmann Division, Juarez, Chihuahua, Mexico
    Cooper Automotive, Azcapotzalco, Edo. de Mexico, Mexico
    Cooper Automotive, Matamoros, Tamaulipas, Mexico
    Cooper Automotive, Tlalnepantla, Edo. de Mexico, Mexico
    Cooper Hand Tools Div., Guadalajara, Jalisco, Mexico
    Cooper Hand Tools Div., Tlalnepantla, Edo. de Mexico, Mexico
    Cooper Lighting Div., Juarez, Chihuahua, Mexico
    Cooper Lighting Div., Mexicali, Baja California, Mexico
    Crouse-Hinds Div., Ixtapalapa, Edo. de Mexico, Mexico
    Crouse-Hinds Div., Mexico City, Mexico
    Moog Automotive, Tijuana, Baja California, Mexico

COPELAND CORP   Campbell Road, Sidney, OH 45365, Tel: (513) 498-3011
  (Ind refrigeration equip)
    Gilbert-Copeland SA de CV, Av. Sor Juana 555, Tlalnepantla, Edo. de Mexico, Mexico

CORE LABORATORIES   10205 Westheimer, Houston, TX 77042, Tel: (713) 972-6311
  (Petroleum testing/analysis, analytical chem, lab & octane analysis instrumentation)
    Rotenco SA de CV, Paseo de la Reforma 295, Col. Cuauhtemoc, 06500 Mexico DF, Mexico

CORESTATES FINANCIAL CORP   1500 Market St, Philadelphia, PA 19101,
  Tel: (215) 973-3100
  (Banking)
    Corestates Bank, Moliere 39, piso 5, Colonia Polcano, 11560 Mexico DF, Mexico

COULTER CORP   PO Box 169015, Miami, FL 33116-9015, Tel: (305) 885-0131
  (Mfr blood analysis sys, flow cytometers, chem sys, scientific sys & reagents)
    Coulter de Mexico SA de CV, Av. Popocatepetl 396, Esq. Palomar,
      Deleg. Benito Juarez, 03340 Mexico DF, Mexico

CPC INTERNATIONAL INC   PO Box 8000, Englewood Cliffs, NJ 07632,
  Tel: (201) 894-4000
  (Consumer foods, corn refining)
    Arancia CPC Industrial SA de CV, Lopez Cotilla 2030, Col. Arcos Sur,
      44100 Guadalajara, Jalisco, Mexico
    Productos Modificados SA de CV, San Francisco 657-A, Piso 11, Col. del Valle,
      03100 Mexico DF, Mexico
    Productos de Maiz SA, Av. Rio Consulado 721, Aptdo. Postal 2936, 06430 Mexico DF,
      Mexico

CRAY RESEARCH INC   655 Lone Oak Dr, Eagan, MN 55121, Tel: (612) 452-6650
  (Supercomputer systems & services)
    Cray Research de Mexico SA de CV, Tuxpan 10-401, 06760 Mexico DF, Mexico

CROWN CORK & SEAL CO INC   9300 Ashton Rd, Philadelphia, PA 19136,
  Tel: (215) 698-5100
  (Mfr cans, bottle caps; filling & packaging mach)
    Crown Cork de Mexico SA, Poniente 134 #583, Aptdo. Postal 16-184, Mexico DF, Mexico

CTS CORP   905 N West Blvd, Elkhart, IN 46514, Tel: (215) 293-7511
  (Mfr electr components)
    CTS de Mexico SA, c/o CTS Electronics Corp., 1100 Roosevelt St., Brownsville,
      TX 78521

CUMMINS ENGINE CO INC   PO Box 3005, Columbus, IN 47202, Tel: (812) 377-5000
  (Mfr diesel engines)
    Cummins SA de CV, Arquimedes 209, Col. Polanco, 11560 Mexico DF, Mexico

D'ARCY MASIUS BENTON & BOWLES INC (DMB&B)   1675 Broadway, New York,
  NY 10019, Tel: (212) 468-3622
  (Advertising & communications)
    Noble/DMB&B, Constituyentes 908, 11950 Mexico DF, Mexico

D-M-E COMPANY   29111 Stephenson Highway, Madison Heights, MI 48071,
  Tel: (313) 398-6000
  (Basic tooling for plastic molding & die casting)
    Partes para Moldes D-M-E SA, Avda. 1, Lote 20-A Parque Indistrial,
      Cartagena Tultitlan, Mexico

DANA CORP   PO Box 1000, Toledo, OH 43697, Tel: (419) 535-4500
  (Engineer/mfr/mkt prdts & sys for vehicular, ind & mobile off-highway mkt & related
  aftermarkets)
    Direcspicer SA, Apartado 41-949, Mexico 10 DF, Mexico

DATA GENERAL CORP   4400 Computer Dr, Westboro, MA 01580, Tel: (617) 366-8911
  (Design, mfr gen purpose computer sys & peripheral prdts & servs)
    Data General de Mexico SA de CV, Vasconcelos 449 PTE, Col. del Valle,
      Aptdo. Postal 24A, Garza, NL, Monterrey, Mexico

DATAEASE INTL INC   7 Cambridge Dr, Trumbull, CT 06611, Tel: (203) 374-8000
  (Mfr applications devel software)
    Sistemas Expertos en Red. SA, Mirlo 11, Las Arboledas, Tialnepantla,
      Edo. de Mexico, Mexico

DATAPRODUCTS CORP   6200 Canada Ave, PO Box 746, Woodland Hills, CA 91365,
  Tel: (818) 887-8000
  (Mfr computer printers & supplies)
    Dataproducts de Mexico SA de CV, Shakespeare 19-60, Col. Nueva Anzures,
      11590 Mexico DF, Mexico

DAY INTL   333 W First St, Dayton, OH 45412, Tel: (513) 226-7000
  (Diversified auto, ind & household prdts)
    Dayco de Mexico SA de CV, Bosque de Duraznos 304-305, Col. Bosque de, la Lomas,
      11700 Mexico DF, Mexico

DAYTON-WALTHER CORP   PO Box 1022, Dayton, OH 45401, Tel: (513) 296-3113
  (Mfr heavy duty components for truck/trailer chassis)
    Industrias Fontana SA, Tilos 56, Mexico DF, Mexico

DDB NEEDHAM WORLDWIDE INC   437 Madison Ave, New York, NY 10022,
  Tel: (212) 415-2000
  (Advertising)
    DDB Needham Worldwide SA de CV, Bosque de Duraznos #55/4,
      Fracc. Bosques de las Lomas, Deleg. M. Hidalgo, 11700 Mexico DF, Mexico

DE ZURIK   250 Riverside Ave N, Sartell, MN 56377, Tel: (612) 259-2000
  (Mfr manual, process & control valves)
    Dezurik Mexico SA de CV, Nueva Jersey 4331, Fracc. Industrial Lincoln, Monterrey,
      NL, Mexico

DEERE & CO   John Deere Rd, Moline, IL 61265, Tel: (309) 765-8000
  (Mfr/sale agri/constr/utility/forestry & lawn/grounds care equip)
    Industrias John Deere SA de CV, Aptdo. Postal 1153, Carretera A. Sattillo Km. 333,
      Monterrey, NL, Mexico

DEKALB PLANT GENETICS   3100 Sycamore Rd, DeKalb, IL 60115,
  Tel: (815) 753-7333
  (Devel/produce hybrid corn, sorghum, sunflowers, sudax, varietal soybeans, alfalfa)
    Semillas Hibridas SA de CV, Aptdo. Postal 1618, Av. Hidalgo 2375,
      44100 Guadalajara, Mexico

DEL MONTE FOODS   PO Box 93575, San Francisco, CA 94119-3575,
  Tel: (415) 442-4000
  (Food processor)
    Productos del Monte SA de CV, Av. Colonia de Valle 615, 03100 Mexico DF, Mexico

DENTSPLY INTL INC   PO Box 872, York, PA 17405, Tel: (717) 845-7511
  (Mfr dental, medical & ind supplies & equip)
    Dentsply-Caulk de Mexico SA de CV, Calzada Vallejo 846, Col. Industrial,
      02300 Mexico DF, Mexico

DENVER EQUIPMENT DIV   PO Box 340, Colorado Springs, CO 80901,
  Tel: (303) 471-3443
  (Ind process equip)
    Maquinas de Proceso SA de CV, Aptdo. Postal 438, Queretaro, Quo., Mexico

THE DEXTER CORP   1 Elm Street, Windsor Locks, CT 06096, Tel: (203) 627-9051
  (Mfr nonwovens, polymer prdts, magnetic materials, biotechnology)
    Danomex SA de CV, Benito Juarez 102, San Lucas, Tlalnepantla, Mexico
    Dexter Indael de Mexico SA, Azcapotzalco la Villa 774, Col. Industrial Vallejo,
      Aptdo. Postal 16-276, CP 02300 Mexico DF, Mexico
    Dexter Midland Mexicana SA de CV, Cipres 403, Mexico 4 DF, Mexico

DIETZGEN CORP   250 Wille Rd, Des Plaines, IL 60018-1866, Tel: (708) 635-5200
  (Mfr reprographic & drafting equip, acces & supplies)
    Dietzgen de Mexico SA de CV, Belisario Dominguez 155, Col. del Carmen Coyoacan,
      04100 Mexico DF, Mexico

DIGITAL EQUIPMENT CORP   146 Main St, Maynard, MA 01754-2571,
  Tel: (508) 493-5111
  (Networked computer systems & services)
    Digital Equipment de Mexico SA de CV, Lane 80, 03810 Mexico DF, Mexico

DIODES INC   3050 E Hillcrest Dr, #200, Westlake Village, CA 91362,
  Tel: (805) 446-4800
  (Mfr semiconductor devices)
    Diomex SA, Reforma 90 Altos, Mexicali, Baja California, Mexico

DIXON TICONDEROGA CO   2600 Maitland Center Pkwy, #200, Maitland, FL 32751,
  Tel: (407) 875-9000
  (Mfr/serv writing implements & art supplies)
    Dixon Ticonderoga de Mexico, Aptdo. Postal M-9531, Mexico DF, Mexico

R R DONNELLEY & SONS CO   77 W Wacker Dr, Chicago, IL 60601-1696,
Tel: (312) 326-8000
(Coml printing, allied commun servs)
   Impresora Donneco Intl. SA de CV, Reynosa, Mexico

DONNELLY CORP   414 E Fortieth St, Holland, MI 49423, Tel: (616) 786-7000
(Mfr mirrors, interior lighting & modular window sys for transp & elec info display
mkt)
   Donnelly de Mexico SA de CV, Calle Dia del Empresario 2000, 67110 Guadalupe, NL,
   Mexico

DORR-OLIVER INC   612 Wheeler's Farm Rd, PO Box 3819, Milford, CT 06460,
Tel: (203) 876-5400
(Mfr process equip for food, pulp & paper, mineral & chem ind; & municipal/ind waste
treatment)
   Dorr-Oliver de Mexico SA, Cuauhtemoc 1338, Col. Sta. Cruz Atoyac,
      Del. Benito Juarez, 03310 Mexico DF, Mexico

DOUGLAS & LOMASON CO   24600 Hallwood Ct, Farmington Hills, MI 48335-1671,
Tel: (313) 478-7800
(Mfr automotive seating, hardware & ornamentation)
   Douglas & Lomason de Coahuila SA de CV, Blvd. Nazario Ortiz Garza 4021,
      Pte. Saltillo, Coahuila, Mexico
   Douglas & Lomason de Mexico SA de CV, Km. 5 Carretera Presa la Amistad, Acuna,
   Mexico

THE DOW CHEMICAL CO   2030 Dow Center, Midland, MI 48674, Tel: (517) 636-1000
(Mfr chems, plastics, pharms, agric prdts, consumer prdts)
   Dow Quimica Mexicana SA de CV, Paseo de las Palmas 555-1, Mexico DF, Mexico
   Dow Quimica Mexicana SA de CV, Planta Filiberto Gomez 46, Tlalnepantla, Mexico DF,
   Mexico
   Laboratorios Lepetit de Mexico SA de CV, Carr. Cuernavaca a Cuautla, Civac,
      Morelos, Mexico
   Terminales Maritimas SA de CV, Aptdo. Postal 168, Tuxpan, Vera Cruz, Mexico

DOW CORNING CORP   2220 W Salzburg Rd, PO Box 1767, Midland, MI 48640,
Tel: (517) 496-4000
(Silicones, silicon chems, solid lubricants)
   Dow Corning de Mexico SA de CV, Paseo de las Palmas 751, Mexico DF, Mexico

DRESSER INDUSTRIES INC   PO Box 718, Dallas, TX 75221-0718,
Tel: (214) 740-6000
(Diversified supplier of equip & tech serv to energy & natural resource ind)
   Masoneilan Internacional SA de CV, Henry Ford 114, 54030 Tlalnepantla, Mexico
   Turbo Productos Dresser SA, Acceso 3, Parque Industrial 15, Queretaro, Mexico

DU BOIS CHEMICAL   255 E 5th St, Cincinnati, OH 45202-4799,
Tel: (513) 762-6000
(Mfr spec chems & maintenance prdts)
   DuBois Quimica SA de CV, Calz. Atacapotzalco, La Villa 260, Codigo Postal 02250,
   Mexico DF, Mexico

E I DU PONT DE NEMOURS & CO   1007 Market St, Wilmington, DE 19898,
Tel: (302) 774-1000
(Mfr/sale diversified chems, plastics, specialty prdts & fibers)
   Du Pont SA de CV, Mexico DF, Mexico

DURACELL INTL INC   Berkshire Industrial Park, Bethel, CT 06801,
Tel: (203) 796-4000
(Mfr batteries)
    Duracell de Mexico SA de CV, Aptdo. Postal 421, Montana 166,
        53340 Naucalpan de Juarez, Edo. de Mexico, Mexico

DURAMETALLIC CORP   2104 Factory St, Kalamazoo, MI 49001, Tel: (616) 382-8720
(Mfr mech seals, compression packings, auxiliaries)
    Durametallic Mexicana SA de CV, Calzado St. Thomas 115-B, Mexico DF, Mexico

DURO-TEST CORP   9 Law Dr, Fairfield, NJ 07004, Tel: (201) 808-0905
(Mfr fluorescent, incandescent & fluomeric lamps)
    Duro de Mexico SA, Paseo de la Reforma 195, 10 Piso, Mexico DF 06500, Mexico

EAGLE-PICHER INDUSTRIES INC   580 Walnut St, Cincinnati, OH 45202,
Tel: (513) 721-7010
(Mfr industrial, machinery & automotive parts)
    Eagle-Picher (Construction Equip. Div.), Equipos de Acuna SA de CV,
        Parque Ind. Modelo, Km. 8.5 Presa de Amistad, CD Acuna, Coahuila, Mexico

EASTMAN CHEMICAL   PO Box 511, Kingsport, TN 37662, Tel: (423) 229-2000
(Mfr plastics, chems, fibers)
    Eastman Chemical, Cosoleacaque, Mexico

EASTMAN KODAK CO   343 State St, Rochester, NY 14650, Tel: (716) 724-4000
(Devel/mfr photo & chem prdts, info mgmt/video/copier sys, fibers/plastics for
various ind)
    Industria Fotografica Interamericana SA de CV, Apartado Postal 31-44,
        Guadalajara 5, Jalisco, Mexico
    Industria Mexicana de Fotocopiadoras SA de CV, Tijuana,
        Mexico (all mail to P.O. Box 98, Imperial Beach, CA 91933)
    Kodak Mexicana SA de CV, Calzada de Tlalpan 2980, Admon de Correos 68M,
        04851 Mexico DF, Mexico

EATON CORP   1111 Superior Ave, Cleveland, OH 44114, Tel: (216) 523-5000
(Advanced tech prdts for transp & ind mkts)
    Cutler-Hammer Mexicana SA, Mexico DF, Mexico
    Eaton Manufacturera SA, San Francisco 400, Mexico DF, Mexico
    Fawick de Mexico SA, Francisco Novoa 105, Col. Aragon, Mexico DF, Mexico

EATON CORP/CUTLER HAMMER   4201 North 27th St, Milwaukee, WI 53216,
Tel: (414) 449-6000
(Electric control apparatus, mfr of advanced technologic prdts)
    Cutler-Hammer Mexicana SA, Calz. Javier Rojo Gomez 1300, 09360 Ixtapalapa, Mexico

ECOLOGY AND ENVIRONMENT INC   368 Pleasant View Dr, East Amherst,
NY 14086-1397, Tel: (716) 684-8060
(Environmental, scientific & engineering consulting)
    Ecology and Environment Inc., Rio Ebro 53-Bis, 06500 Mexico DF, Mexico

EFCO   1800 NE Broadway Ave, Des Moines, IA 50316-0386, Tel: (515) 266-1141
(Mfr systems for concrete construction)
    EFCO, Circunvalacion 127 esq. Divison Del Norte, Col. Atlantida, 04370 Mexico DF,
        Mexico

ELANCO PRODUCTS CO   PO Box 1750, Indianapolis, IN 46206, Tel: (317) 261-2000
(Antibiotics, fine chems)
  Elanco Mexicana SA de CV, Calz. de Tlalpan 2034, Mexico DF, Mexico

EMERY WORLDWIDE   One Lagoon Dr, #400, Redwood City, CA 94065,
  Tel: (800) 227-1981
  (Freight transport, global logistics, air cargo)
    Consolidora de Fletes, Irapuato 188, Piso 1, Penon de los Banos, 15520 Mexico DF,
    Mexico

ENDO LABORATORIES INC   1000 Stewart Ave, Garden City, NY 11530,
  Tel: (516) 832-2002
  (Ethical pharms)
    Laboratorios Endo de Mexico SA, Amores 1734, Mexico DF, Mexico

ENGINE PRODUCTS DIV   PO Box 1166, Richmond, IN 47374, Tel: (317) 966-8111
  (Gaskets, seals, packings, etc)
    Direcspicer SA, Aptdo. Postal 41-949, Mexico DF, Mexico

EQUIFAX INC   PO Box 4081, Atlanta, GA 30302, Tel: (404) 885-8000
  (Information services)
    Equifax de Mexico SA, Monte Pelvoux 111, Piso 1, Lomas de Chapultepec,
    Miguel Hidalgo, 11000 Mexico DF, Mexico

ERICO PRODUCTS INC   34600 Solon Road, Cleveland, OH 44139,
  Tel: (216) 248-0100
  (Mfr electric welding apparatus & hardware, metal stampings, specialty fasteners)
    Mexerico SA, Recursos Hydraulicos 3, Tlalnepantla, Edo. de Mexico, Mexico

ERIEZ MAGNETICS   PO Box 10652, Erie, PA 16514, Tel: (814) 833-9881
  (Mfr magnets, vibratory feeders, metal detectors, screeners/sizers, mining equip,
  current separators)
    Eriez Equipos Magneticos SA, Autopista Mexico Queretaro 2500 Km 23.5,
    54020 Tlalnepantla, Mexico

FAIRCHILD SEMICONDUCTOR DIV   PO Box 58090, Santa Clara, CA 95052-8090,
  Tel: (408) 743-3355
  (Mfr semiconductor components)
    Fairchild Mexicana SA, Blvd. Adolfo Lopez Mateas 163, Col. Mixoac, Mexico DF, Mexico

FALK CORP   3001 W Canal St, Milwaukee, WI 53208, Tel: (414) 342-3131
  (Mfr gears, geared reducers & drives, couplings)
    Mecanica Falk SA de CV, Poniente 150 #842, Col. Ind. Vallejo,
    Delag. 02300 Azcapotzalco DF, Mexico

FARMLAND INDUSTRIES INC   PO Box 7305, Kansas City, MO 64116,
  Tel: (816) 459-6000
  (Food production & marketing)
    Farmland Industries SA de CV, Mexico City, Mexico

FEDERAL-MOGUL CORP   PO Box 1966, Detroit, MI 48235, Tel: (810) 354-7700
  (Mfr/distr precision parts for automobiles, trucks, & farm/constrution vehicles)
    Conaba SA de CV (CONABA), Mexico
    Federal-Mogul SA de CV (PUEBLA), Mexico
    Femosa Mexico SA, Mexico
    Manufacturas Metalicas Linan SA (LINAN), Mexico
    Raimsa SA de CV (RAIMSA), Mexico

(cont)

Servicios Administrativos Industriales SA (SAISA), Mexico
Servicios de Components Automotrices SA (SEDECA), Mexico
Subensambles Internacionales SA de CV, Mexico

FELTON INTERNATIONAL INC   599 Johnson Ave, Brooklyn, NY 11237,
  Tel: (212) 497-4664
  (Essential oils & extracts, perfumes & flavor material, aromatic chems)
    Felton Chemical Compania de Mexico SA, Poniente 128 #561, Industrial Vallejo,
      Mexico DF, Mexico

FERRO CORPORATION   1000 Lakeside Ave, Cleveland, OH 44114,
  Tel: (216) 641-8580
  (Mfr chems, coatings, plastics, colors, refractories)
    Metquim SA de CV, Km. 12.5 Carr. Celaya-Salamanca, Municipio de Villagran,
      Edo. de Guanjuato, Mexico
    Quimica Colfer SA de CV, Oriente 171 #450, Col. Prol. Aragon-Inguaran,
      Deleg. G.A. Madero, 07490 Mexico DF, Mexico

FIBRE METAL PRODUCTS INC   PO Box 248, Concordville, PA 19331,
  Tel: (215) 459-5300
  (Welding accessories, ind safety equip)
    Fibre Metal Mexicana SA de CV, Industria 130, Mexico DF, Mexico

FIRST NATIONAL BANK OF BOSTON   100 Federal St, Boston, MA 02110,
  Tel: (617) 434-2200
  (Commercial banking)
    Bank of Boston, Campos Eliseos 345, Edif. Omega, Col. Polanco, Aptdo. Postal 6699,
      11560 Mexico DF, Mexico

FIRST NATIONAL BANK OF CHICAGO   One First National Plaza, Chicago, IL 60670,
  Tel: (312) 732-4000
  (Financial services)
    Inversionista Latina SA, Edif. Omega, Campos Eliseos 345, 4 piso, 11560 Mexico DF,
      Mexico

FISHER CONTROLS INTL INC   8000 Maryland Ave, Clayton, MO 63105,
  Tel: (314) 746-9900
  (Mfr ind process control equip)
    Fisher Governor de Mexico SA, Homero 229, Quinto Piso, Col. Chapultepec Morales,
      11560 Mexico DF, Mexico
    Fisher Governor de Mexico SA, Calle 1a con 12a Avenida, Zona Industrial,
      Aptdo. Postal 29, Toluca, Mexico

FLORASYNTH INC   300 North St, Teterboro, NJ 07608, Tel: (201) 288-3200
  (Mfr fragrances & flavors)
    Florasynth SA de CV, Apartado Postal 158, Cuautitlan de Romero Rubio,
      54800 Estado de Mexico, Mexico

FMC CORP   200 E Randolph Dr, Chicago, IL 60601, Tel: (312) 861-6000
  (Produces chems & precious metals, mfr machinery, equip & sys for ind, agric & govt)
    E.M.D. SA de CV, Mexico
    Electro Quimica Mexicana SA de CV, Mexico
    FMC Agroquimica de Mexico, Mexico
    FMC Ingrediantes Alimenticos, Mexico
    FMC de Mexico SA de CV, Arquimeded 130, Piso 7, Colonia Polanco, 11560 Mexico DF,
      Mexico

Fabricacion Maquinaria y Ceras SA de CV, Mexico
Minera FMC SA de CV, Mexico

FMC PACKAGING & MATERIAL HANDLING DIV   57 Cooper Ave, Homer City,
 PA 15748-1306, Tel: (412) 479-4500
 (Mfr bulk material handling & automation equip)
   FMC de Mexico, Av. Lopez Mateos Sur 1480, Piso 5, 45040 Guadalajara, Jalisco, Mexico

FOAMEX INTL   1000 Columbia Ave, Linwood, PA 19061, Tel: (800) 776-3626
 (Mfr polyurethane foam)
   Foamex de Mexico (TEFSA), Calz. Azcapotzalco La Villa 846, Col. Industrial Vallejo,
    02300 Mexico DF, Mexico

FOOTE CONE & BELDING COMMUNICATIONS INC   101 E Erie St, Chicago,
 IL 60611-2897, Tel: (312) 751-7000
 (Advertising agency)
   FCB/Maqueda, Presidente Mazaryk 61, Col. Polanco, 11560 Mexico DF, Mexico

FORD MOTOR CO   The American Road, Dearborn, MI 48121, Tel: (313) 322-3000
 (Mfr motor vehicles)
   Ford Motor Co. SA, Aptdo. Postal 39 bis, Mexico DF, Mexico

FRANKLIN ELECTRIC CO INC   400 E Spring St, Bluffton, IN 46714,
 Tel: (219) 824-2900
 (Mfr fractional hp motors, submersible motors & controls)
   Franklin Electrica SA de CV, all mail to P.O. Box 332, El Centro Station, Laredo,
    TX 78040

FRIES & FRIES INC   110 East 70th St, Cincinnati, OH 45216,
 Tel: (513) 948-8000
 (Flavoring compounds for food & pharm industries)
   Fries Intl. de Mexico SA, Chicago 162, Mexico DF, Mexico

FRITZ COMPANIES INC   706 Mission St, San Francisco, CA 94103,
 Tel: (415) 904-8360
 (Integrated transportation, sourcing, distribution & customs brokerage services)
   Fritz Companies Mexico SA de CV, Av. del Penon 106, Col. Revolucion,
    15460 Mexico City, Mexico

FRUEHAUF TRAILER CORP   PO Box 44913, Indianapolis, IN 46244-0913,
 Tel: (317) 630-3000
 (Mfr truck trailers)
   Fruehauf de Mexico SA de CV, Via Jose Portillo Km. 28.5,
    55700 Coacalco de Berriozabal, Mexico

H B FULLER CO   2400 Energy Park Dr, St Paul, MN 55108, Tel: (612) 645-3401
 (Mfr/distr adhesives, sealants, coatings, paints, waxes, sanitation chems)
   H.B. Fuller Mexico SA de CV, Calzada Vallejo 1023, Mexico DF, Mexico
   H.B. Fuller Mexico SA de CV, Aptdo. Postal 450, Ensenada, Baja California, Mexico

GAF CORP   1361 Alps Rd, Wayne, NJ 07470, Tel: (201) 628-3000
 (Chems, bldg materials, commun)
   GAF Corp. de Mexico SA de CV, Aptdo. Postal M-9474, Calle Lopez 15-403/4,
    06050 Mexico DF, Mexico

GARLOCK INC 1666 Division St, Palmyra, NY 14522, Tel: (315) 597-4811
(Mfr mechanical packings)
Garlock de Mexico SA, Aptdo. Postal 15-103, Poniente 116 #571, Mexico DF, Mexico

THE GATES RUBBER CO PO Box 5887, Denver, CO 80217-5887, Tel: (303) 744-1911
(Mfr automotive & industrial belts & hose)
Gates Rubber de Mexico, Cerrada de Galeana 5, Fracc. Industrial La Loma,
54060 Tlalnepantla, Edo de Mexico, Mexico

GATX LOGISTICS INC 1301 Gulf Life Dr, #1800, Jacksonville, FL 32207-0000,
Tel: (904) 396-2517
(Warehouse-based third party logistics)
Unit de Mexico (GATX Logistics), Parque Industrial La Luz,
Autopesta Mexico-Queretaro Km. 43, 68340 Cuautitlan Izcalle, Mexico

GENERAL BINDING CORP One GBC Plaza, Northbrook, IL 60062,
Tel: (708) 272-3700
(Binding & laminating equip & associated supplies)
GBC Mexicana SA de CV, Neptuno 43, Unid. Industrial Vallejo,
Deleg. Gustavo A. Madero, 07700 Mexico DF, Mexico

GENERAL CABLE CORP 4 Tesseneer Dr, Highland Heights, KY 41076,
Tel: (606) 572-8000
(Mfr wire & cable)
General Cable de Mexico del Norte SA de CV, all mail to 2328 El Indino Hwy.,
Eagle Pass, TX 78852

GENERAL DATACOMM INC 1579 Straits Tpk, PO Box 1299, Middlebury,
CT 06762-1299, Tel: (203) 574-1118
(Mfr/sale/svce trans equip for commun networks)
General Telecomm SA de CV, Periferico Sur 4225, Desp. 306,
14210 Jardines de la Montana, Mexico

GENERAL ELECTRIC CO 3135 Easton Tpk, Fairfield, CT 06431,
Tel: (203) 373-2211
(Diversified manufacturing, technology & services)
General Electric de Mexico,
all mail to U.S. address; phone (800) 626-2004 or (518) 438-6500

GENERAL FOODS CORP 250 North St, White Plains, NY 10625, Tel: (914) 335-2500
(Processor, distributor & mfr of foods)
General Foods de Mexico SA, Constituyentes 908B, Col. Lomas Altas, 11950 Mexico DF,
Mexico

GENERAL INSTRUMENT CORP 181 W Madison, Chicago, IL 60602,
Tel: (312) 541-5000
(Mfr broadband communications & power rectifying components)
Jerrold Communications, Jesus Garcia 6, Nogales, Sonora, Mexico
Jerrold Communications/Ensambladora de Matamoros SA, Avda. Lauro Villar 565,
H. Matamoros, Tamps., Mexico

GENERAL MOTORS ACCEPTANCE CORP 3044 West Grand Blvd, Detroit, MI 48202,
Tel: (313) 556-5000
(Automobile financing)
GMAC de Mexico SA, Lago Victoria 74, Planta Baja, Col. Granada,
Aptdo. Postal 5-561, Mexico DF, Mexico

GENERAL MOTORS CORP   3044 W Grand Blvd, Detroit, MI   48202-3091,
  Tel: (313) 556-5000
  (Mfr full line vehicles, automotive electronics, coml technologies, telecom, space, finance)
    General Motors de Mexico SA de CV, Aptdo. Postal 107-bis, Mexico DF, Mexico

GENICOM CORP   14800 Conference Center Dr, #400, Chantilly, VA   22021-3806,
  Tel: (703) 802-9200
  (Supplier of network sys, service & printer solutions)
    Datacom de Mexico SA de CV, Carretera a Matamoros con Brecha E-99,
      Aptdo Postal 775, Parque Ind. Reynosa, Reynosa 88780, Mexico

GENISCO TECHNOLOGY CORP   1230 S Lewis St, Anaheim, CA   92626,
  Tel: (714) 563-4300
  (Mfr rugged computers, DMI filters, power supplies)
    Genisco Electronics de Mexico, Calle Uno Poniente 13, Ciudad Industrial,
      22520 Tijuana, Mexico

GERALD METALS INC   PO Box 10134, Stamford, CT   06904, Tel: (203) 329-4700
  (Minerals & metals)
    Gerald de Mexico SA, Paseo de la Reforma 444, Mexico DF, Mexico

GERBER PRODUCTS CO   445 State St, Fremont, MI   49412, Tel: (616) 928-2000
  (Mfr/distr baby food & related prdts)
    Productos Gerber SA de CV, Ejercito Nacional 404, Col. Polanco,
      Delegacion Miguel Hidalgo, 11570 Mexico DF, Mexico

GIBSON GREETINGS INC   2100 Section Rd, Cincinnati, OH   45237,
  Tel: (513) 841-6600
  (Design/mfr greetings cards, gift wrap & trim, paper partywares, related spec prdts)
    Gibson de Mexico SA de CV, Mexico City, Mexico

THE GILLETTE CO   Prudential Tower, Boston, MA   02199, Tel: (617) 421-7000
  (Devel/mfr personal care/use prdts: blades & razors, toiletries, cosmetics, stationery)
    Braun de Mexico y Compania de Capital Variable, Mexico City, Mexico
    Cofiad SA de CV, Mexico City, Mexico
    Dirsamex SA de CV, Mexico DF, Mexico
    Distribuidora Venus SA de CV, Mexico DF, Mexico
    Gillette de Mexico SA de CV, Mexico DF, Mexico
    Grupo Jafra SA de CV, Mexico City, Mexico
    Jafra Cosmetics SA de CV, Mexico City, Mexico
    Oral-B Laboratories SA de CV, Mexico City, Mexico
    Plumibol SA de CV, Mexico City, Mexico
    Prodenob SA de CV, Mexico City, Mexico
    Qualifax SA de CV, Mexico DF, Mexico
    Reday SA de CV, Mexico DF, Mexico

THE GOODYEAR TIRE & RUBBER CO   1144 E Market St, Akron, OH   44316,
  Tel: (216) 796-2121
  (Mfr tires, automotive belts & hose, conveyor belts, chemicals; oil pipeline transmission)
    Compania Hulera Goodyear-Oxo SA de CV, Varsavia 44, Piso 9, Mexico 6, DF, Mexico

GOULDS PUMPS INC   240 Fall St, Seneca Falls, NY   13148, Tel: (315) 568-2811
  (Mfr ind & water sys pumps)
    Bombas Goulds de Mexico SA de CV, Cincinnati 40, 03720 Mexico DF, Mexico

W R GRACE & CO   One Town Center Rd, Boca Raton, FL 33486-1010,
  Tel: (407) 362-2000
  (Mfr spec chems & materials: packaging, health care, catalysts, construction, water
  treatment/process)
    Grace de Mexico SA de CV, Av. de la Fuentes 41-A, Techamachalco,
      53950 Edo. de Mexico, Mexico

GRANT THORNTON INTL   Prudential Plaza, Chicago, IL 60601, Tel: (312) 856-0001
  (Intl accountants)
    Grant Thornton Intl., Paseo de la Reforma 610, Lomas de Chapultepec, Mexico 10 DF,
      Mexico

GREAT WESTERN CHEMICAL CO   808 SW Fifteenth Ave, Portland, OR 97205,
  Tel: (503) 228-2600
  (Industrial chemical distribution & logistics)
    Great Western de Mexico SA de CV, Periferico Sur 8565-A, Colonia El Mante,
      45090 Tlaquepaque, Jal., Mexico

GREFCO INC   3435 W Lomita Blvd, Torrance, CA 90505, Tel: (213) 517-0700
  (Filter powders)
    Dicalite de Mexico SA, Rio Delta Plata 56-401, Mexico DF, Mexico

GREY ADVERTISING INC   777 Third Ave, New York, NY 10017, Tel: (212) 546-2000
  (Advertising)
    Grey Mexico, Horacio 1844, pisos 2 y 6, Esq. Periferico., Col. Polanco Reforma,
      11550 Mexico DF, Mexico

GRIFFITH LABORATORIES INC   I Griffith Center, Alsip, IL 60658,
  Tel: (708) 371-0900
  (Ind food ingredients & equip)
    Laboratorios Griffith de Mexico SA, Aptdo. Postal 1832, Monterrey, NL, Mexico

GTE CORP   One Stamford Forum, Stamford, CT 06904, Tel: (203) 965-2000
  (Electr prdts, telecom sys, publ & commun)
    Focos SA, Monterrey, Mexico
    General de Telecomunicaciones SA, Sabinas, Mexico
    Materiales de Precision SA de CV, Monterrey, Mexico
    Unisistemas Estructurales SA de CV, Mexico DF, Mexico

FRANK B HALL & CO INC   549 Pleasantville Rd, Briarcliff Manor, NY 10510,
  Tel: (914) 769-9200
  (Insurance)
    Ramos, Rosado y Asociados Agente de Seguros SA de CV, Boxque de Duraznos 65,
      Col. Bosques de las Lomas, 11700 Mexico DF, Mexico
    Ramos, Rosado y Asociados Agente de Seguros SA de CV, Calle 24 #2311, Col. Mirador,
      31270 Chihuahua, Mexico
    Ramos, Rosado y Asociados Agente de Seguros SA de CV,
      Jose Guadalupe Hernandez 2122A, Sector Juarez, Guadalajara, Jal., Mexico
    Ramos, Rosado y Asociados Agente de Seguros SA de CV, Mariano Avila 297,
      78230 San Luis Potosi, Mexico

HALLMARK CARDS INC   PO Box 419580, Kansas City, MO 64141, Tel: (816) 274-5100
  (Mfr greeting cards & related prdts)
    Hallmark De Mexico SA de CV, Aptdo. Postal #129, 53370 Naucalpan de Juarez, Mexico

THE HARPER GROUP   260 Townsend St, PO Box 77933, San Francisco,
  CA 94107-1719, Tel: (415) 978-0600
  (Ocean/air freight fwdg, customs brokerage, packing & whse, logistics mgt, ins)
    Circle Air Freight de Mexico SA de CV, Av. Texcoco #18, Col. Penon de los Banos,
      15520 Mexico DF, Mexico
    Circle Freight Intl. de Mexico SA de CV, Calle Colonias 188, Despacho 401,
      44100 Guadalajara, Jalisco, Mexico

HARSCO CORP   PO Box 8888, Camp Hill, PA 17001-8888, Tel: (717) 763-7064
  (Metal reclamation & mill svces, infrastructure & construction, process industry
  prdts)
    Andamios Patentados SA de CV, Calle Guillermo Gonzalez, Camarena #25,
      Parque Ind. Cuamatla, Cuautitlan Izcalli, CP 54730, Mexico
    Electroforjados Nacionales SA de CV, Corregidora Norte 487, 76160 Queretaro, Qro.,
      Mexico

HECKETT   PO Box 1071, Butler, PA 16001-1071, Tel: (412) 283-5741
  (Metal reclamation, steel mill services)
    Heckett Mexicana SA de CV, Aptdo. Postal 98, Sucursal A, C.P. 66480,
      Nicolas de los Garza, NL, Mexico

HECLA MINING CO   PO C-8000, Coeur d'Alene, ID 83814, Tel: (208) 769-4100
  (Non-ferrous & industrial metals mining, mfg)
    Minerva Hecla SA de CV, Concepcion L. de Sona 70, Hermosillo, Sonora, Mexico

HENNINGSON DURHAM & RICHARDSON INC   8404 Indian Hiills Dr, Omaha, NE 68114,
  Tel: (402) 399-1000
  (Consulting architects & engineers)
    HDR Mexicana SA de CV, Tenayuca 55-A, Mezzanine, 03800 Mexico City, Mexico

HERCULES INC   Hercules Plaza, Wilmington, DE 19894-0001, Tel: (302) 594-5000
  (Mfr spec chems, plastics, film & fibers, coatings, resins, food ingredients)
    Quimica Hercules SA de CV, Saltillo 19, 1er Piso, Col. Condesa/D. Miguel Hidalgo,
      06140 Mexico DF, Mexico

HEWLETT-PACKARD CO   3000 Hanover St, Palo Alto, CA 94304-0890,
  Tel: (415) 857-1501
  (Mfr computing, communications & measurement prdts & services)
    Hewlett-Packard de Mexico SA de CV, Prolong. Paseo de la Reforma 700,
      Col. Lomas de Santa Fe, Del. A. Obregon, 01210 Mexico DF, Mexico
    Microcomputadoras Hewlett-Packard SA de CV, Montemorelos 299, Fracc. Loma Bonita,
      Guadalajara, Jalisco 45060, Mexico

HOLIDAY INNS INC   3742 Lamar Ave, Memphis, TN 38195, Tel: (901) 362-4001
  (Hotels, restaurants, casinos)
    Holiday Inn, Liverpool 155, Mexico DF, Mexico

HOLLINGSWORTH & VOSE CO   112 Washington St, East Walpole, MA 02032,
  Tel: (508) 668-0295
  (Mfr tech & ind papers & non-wovens)
    Hovomex SA de CV, Km. 1.2 Camino Morelos, 90308 Apizaco, Tlaxcala, Mexico

HOLOPHANE CORP   250 E Broad St, #1400, Columbus, OH 43215,
  Tel: (614) 345-9631
  (Mfr ind, coml, outdoor, roadway & emergency lighting fixtures; inverters,
  programmable controllers)
    Holophane SA de CV, Km. 31 Carretera Mexico-Cuautitlan, Mexico DF, Mexico

O HOMMEL CO　　Hope & Maple Sts, Carnegie, PA　15106, Tel: (412) 923-2233
(Ceramic colors for glass)
　　Colores Ceramicos Mexicanos SA, Aptdo. Postal 2586, Monterrey, NL, Mexico

HONEGGERS CO　　PO Box 109, Forrest, IL　61741, Tel: (815) 692-2511
(livestock & poultry feeds, storage)
　　Honeggers Intl. Latinoamericana SA, Insurgentes Sur 1023, Mexico DF, Mexico

HONEYWELL INC　　PO Box 524, Minneapolis, MN　55440-0524, Tel: (612) 951-1000
(Devel/mfr controls for home & building, industry, space & aviation)
　　Honeywell SA de CV, Av. Constituyentes 900, Col. Lomas Altas, 11950 Mexico City,
　　　DF, Mexico

HORWATH INTL　　415 Madison Ave, New York, NY　10017, Tel: (212) 838-5566
(Public accountants & auditors)
　　Castillo Miranda, Moliere 450 AB-1 Fl., 11520 Mexico D.F, Mexico

HOUGHTON INTL INC　　PO Box 930, Valley Forge, PA　19482-0930,
Tel: (610) 666-4000
(Mfr spec chems, hydraulic fluids, lubricants)
　　Especialidades Quimicas Monterrey SA, Aptdo. Postal 1230, 64000 Monterrey, NL,
　　　Mexico

HUCK INTL INC　　6 Thomas, PO Box 19590, Irvine, CA　92713, Tel: (714) 855-9000
(Mfr advanced fastening sys)
　　Huck Intl. Ltd., Av. Parque Lira 79-402, Tacubaya, 11850 Mexico DF, Mexico

HUGHES TOOL CO　　PO Box 2539, Houston, TX　77001, Tel: (713) 924-2222
(Equip & serv to oil & gas explor & prod ind)
　　Hughes Tool Co. de Mexico SA de CV, Aptdo. Postal 14-102, Km. 12.5 Carretera Libre,
　　　Mexico DF, Mexico

HYATT INTL CORP　　200 West Madison, Chicago, IL　60606, Tel: (312) 750-1234
(Intl hotel mgmt)
　　Hyatt Intl. Hotels, Acapulco, Cancun, Guadalajara, Puerto Vallarta & Villahermosa,
　　　Mexico

IBM CORP　　Old Orchard Rd, Armonk, NY　10504, Tel: (914) 765-1900
(Information products, technology & services)
　　IBM de Mexico SA, Mariano Escobedo 595, Col. Chapultepec, Morales, 41560 Mexico DF,
　　　Mexico

ICF KAISER INTL INC　　9300 Lee Hwy, Fairfax, VA　22031, Tel: (703) 934-3600
(Engineering, construction & consulting services)
　　ICF Kaiser Servicios Ambientales SA de CV, Perif. Sur 3343, Desp. 301,
　　　entre L. Cabarera y Renencion, 10200 Deleg. Magdelena Contreras, Mexico

IKG INDUSTRIES　　270 Terminal Ave, Clark, NJ　07066, Tel: (908) 815-9500
(Mfr metal gratings)
　　Irving SA de CV, Aptdo. Postal 18-897, Mexico DF, Mexico

ILLINOIS TOOL WORKS INC　　3600 W Lake Ave, Glenview, IL　60025,
Tel: (708) 724-7500
(Mfr gears, tools, fasteners, sealants, plastic & metal components for ind, med, etc.)
　　Devcon de Mexico SA de CV, R.A. de la Pena 89, Mexico DF, Mexico

INDUCTOTHERM CORP   10 Indel Ave, Rancocas, NJ 08073-0157, Tel: (609) 267-9000
(Mfr induction melting furnaces)
   Inductotherm SA de CV, Aptdo. Postal 123, Calle Industria Siderugica 2036,
     Parque Ind. Saltillo-Ramos, 25900 Arizpe, Mexico

INGERSOLL-RAND CO   200 Chestnut Ridge Rd, Woodcliff Lake, NJ 07675,
Tel: (201) 573-0123
(Mfr compressors, rock drills, pumps, air tools, door hardware, ball bearings)
   Ingersoll-Rand SA de CV, Blvd. Centro Industrial 11,
     Fracc. Industrial Puente de Vigas, 54090 Tlalnepantla, Mexico

INSTEEL INDUSTRIES INC   1373 Boggs Dr, Mt Airy, NC 27030, Tel: (910) 786-2141
(Mfr wire products)
   Insteel Panel-Mex SA de CV, Mexicali, Baja California, Mexico

INTERGRAPH CORP   Huntsville, AL 35894-0001, Tel: (205) 730-2000
(Devel/mfr interactive computer graphic systems)
   Intergraph de Mexico SA de CV, Durango 263, Col. Roma, Piso 7, 06700 Mexico DF,
     Mexico

INTERMEC CORP   6001 36th Ave West, PO Box 4280, Everett, WA 98203-9280,
Tel: (206) 348-2600
(Mfr/distr automated data collection sys)
   Intermec de Mexico, Pedro Rosales de Leon 7020 #207, Ciudad Juarez, Chihuahua,
     Mexico

INTERNATIONAL FLAVORS & FRAGRANCES INC   521 W 57th St, New York, NY 10019,
Tel: (212) 765-5500
(Create/mfr flavors, fragrances & aroma chems)
   Intl. Flavors & Fragrances de Mexico SA de CV, Aptdo. Postal M-7663, Mexico DF,
     Mexico

INTERNATIONAL RECTIFIER CORP   233 Kansas St, El Segundo, CA 90245,
Tel: (310) 322-3331
(Mfr semiconductor components)
   Rectificadores Internacionales SA, Durazno 30, Centro Industrial Los Olivos,
     La Mesa de Tijuana, Baja California, Mexico

IRECO INC   Crossroads Tower, 11th Fl, Salt Lake City, UT 84144,
Tel: (801) 364-4800
(Mfr explosive supplies, accessories for ind & military applications; aluminum
granules)
   Ireco/ASA-Mexico, Av. Lazaro Cardenas 2885, Jardines del Bosque, Guadalajara 44520,
     Mexico

ITT CORP   1330 Ave of the Americas, New York, NY 10019-5490,
Tel: (212) 258-1000
(Design/mfr communications & electronic equip, hotels, insurance)
   ITT de Mexico SA, Bosque de Duraznos 127, Mexico DF, Mexico

ITT SHERATON CORP   60 State St, Boston, MA 02108, Tel: (617) 367-3600
(Hotel operations)
   Maria Isabel Sheraton Hotel & Towers, Paseo de la Reforma 325, Mexico DF, Mexico

ITW RANSBURG ELECTROSTATIC SYSTEMS   PO Box 913, Toledo, OH 43697-0913,
Tel: (419) 470-2000
(Mfr rotary atomizers, electrostatic guns, paint finishing sys)

(cont)

DeVilbiss Ransburg de Mexico SA de CV, Via Dr. Gustavo Baz 3990, Aptdo. Postal 349, 54110 Tlalnepantla, Edo. de Mexico, Mexico

JAMESBURY CORP   640 Lincoln St, Worcester, MA 01605, Tel: (617) 852-0200
  (Mfr valves & accessories)
    Jamesbury Oym SA, Alfredo Nobel 39, Aptdo. Postal 574, Tlalnepantla, Mexico

JEUNIQUE INTL INC   19501 E Walnut Dr, City of Industry, CA 91748,
  Tel: (909) 598-8598
  (Mfr/sale vitamins, food supplements, cosmetics, diet prdts)
    Jeunique Intl. Mexico SA de CV, Av. La Patria 290, Jardines de la Patria, 45110 Zapopan, Jalisco, Mexico

JOHNSON & JOHNSON   One Johnson & Johnson Plaza, New Brunswick, NJ 08933,
  Tel: (908) 524-0400
  (R&D/mfr/sale health care prdts)
    Cilag de Mexico SA de CV, Mexico DF, Mexico
    Jansen Farmaceutica SA de CV, Aptdo. Postal 20-759, Col. San Angel, Deleg. Alvaro Obregon, 01000 Mexico DF, Mexico
    Johnson & Johnson de Mexico SA, Aptdo. Postal 74062, 09081 Mexico DF, Mexico

S C JOHNSON & SON INC   1525 Howe St, Racine, WI 53403, Tel: (414) 631-2000
  (Home, auto, commercial & personal care prdts, specialty chems)
    S.C. Johnson & Son. SA de CV, Calle Poniente 140 #717, Col. Industrial Vallejo, Mexico DF, Mexico

JONES APPAREL GROUP INC   250 Rittenhouse Circle, Bristol, PA 19007,
  Tel: (215) 785-4000
  (Mfr women's apparel, knitting mills)
    Camisas de Juarez SA de CV, Faraday S/N, Parque Industrial Antonio J Bermudez, Ciudad Juarez, Mexico
    Vestamex SA de CV, Faraday S/N, Parque Industrial Antonio J Bermudez, Ciudad Juarez, Mexico

KAPPLER SAFETY GROUP   PO Box 490, Guntersville, AL 35976, Tel: (205) 505-4005
  (Mfr of protective apparel & fabrics)
    Kappler de Mexico SA de CV, Circ. Aguascalientes Norte 136, Parque Industrial, CP 20140 Aguascalientes, AGS, Mexico

KAYDON CORP   19329 U S 19 North, #101, Clearwater, FL 34624,
  Tel: (813) 531-1101
  (Design/mfr custom engineered prdts: bearings, rings, seals, etc)
    Kaydon SA de CV, Parque Industrial La Silb, Av. Sierra con Pablo Livas 1303, 67190 Guadalupe, Mexico

A T KEARNEY INC   222 West Adams St, Chicago, IL 60606, Tel: (312) 648-0111
  (Mgmt consultants, executive search)
    A.T. Kearney Inc., Ruben Dario 281, Piso 17, Col. Bosques de Chapultepec, CP 11580 Mexico DF, Mexico

KELLOGG CO   One Kellogg Sq, PO Box 3599, Battle Creek, MI 49016-3599,
  Tel: (616) 961-2000
  (Mfr ready-to-eat cereals, convenience foods)
    Kellogg de Mexico SA de CV, Queretaro, Qro., Mexico (all inquiries to U.S. address)

KELLY SERVICES   999 W Big Beaver Rd, Troy, MI   48084, Tel: (810) 244-4313
(Temporary help placement)
   Kelly de Mexico SA de CV, Paseo Triunfo de la Republica 215, Local 13 y 14 CD,
      32320 Juarez, Chihuahua, Mexico

KELSEY-HAYES CO   38481 Huron River Dr, Romulus, MI   48174, Tel: (313) 941-2000
(Automotive & aircraft parts)
   Kelsey-Hayes de Mexico SA, Aptdo. Postal 41-668, Admon de Correos 41, Mexico DF,
      Mexico

THE KENDALL CO   15 Hampshire St, Mansfield, MA   02048, Tel: (508) 261-8000
(Mfr medical disposable prdts, home health care prdts, spec adhesive prdts)
   Kendall de Mexico SA de CV, Aptdo. Postal 2113, 06000 Mexico DF, Mexico

KENNAMETAL INC   PO Box 231, Latrobe, PA   15650, Tel: (412) 539-5000
(Tools, hard carbide & tungsten alloys)
   Kennamex SA de CV, Aptdo. Postal 269A, Centro Civico, 53100 CD Satelite,
      Edo. de Mexico, Mexico

KEYSTONE INTL INC   PO Box 40010, Houston, TX   77040, Tel: (713) 466-1176
(Mfr butterfly valves, actuators & control accessories)
   Valvulos Keystone de Mexico SA, Mexico

KIMBALL INTERNATIONAL INC   1600 Royal St, Jasper, IN   47546,
Tel: (812) 482-1600
(Mfr office furn & seating, pianos, wood veneers, plywood prdts)
   Kimco SA, Carretera Matamoros Km. 9, Aptdo. Postal 386, Reynosa, Tamaulipas, Mexico

KIMBERLY-CLARK CORP   PO Box 619100, Dallas, TX   75261, Tel: (214) 281-1200
(Mfr fiber-based prdts for personal care, lumber & paper prdts)
   Compania Industrial de San Cristobal SA, Mexico
   Kimberly-Clark de Mexico SA de CV, Av. 1 #9., Naucalpan de Juarez, Mexico DF, Mexico

KIRKWOOD INDUSTRIES INC   4855 W 130th St, Cleveland, OH   44135-5182,
Tel: (216) 267-6200
(Mfr elect components, commutators, mica insulation, slip rings, carbon brushes)
   Industrias Kirkwood SA, Poniente 150 #978, Col. Industrial Vallejo, Mexico DF,
      Mexico

THE KNOLL GROUP   105 Wooster St, New York, NY   10021, Tel: (212) 343-4000
(Mfr/sale office furnishings)
   Mobel Internacional SA de CV, Insurgentes Sur 1188, Mexico DF, Mexico

KOEHRING CO   PO Box 312, Milwaukee, WI   53201, Tel: (414) 784-5800
(Pulp mill & constr equip)
   Codeca SA, La Morena 1213, Col. Narvarte, Mexico DF, Mexico
   Equipos Belther, Av. Ferrocarril de Cuernavaca 520, Mexico DF, Mexico
   Maquinas del Norte SA, Ruiz Cortines 983 PTE, Monterrey, NL, Mexico

THE KOHLER CO   444 Highland Dr, Kohler, WI   53044, Tel: (414) 457-4441
(Plumbing prdts, engines, generators)
   Kohler de Mexico SA, Calle Norte 45 #766, Fracc. Inc. Vallejo, Codigo Postal 2300,
      Mexico DF, Mexico

KORN/FERRY INTL   1800 Century Park East, Los Angeles, CA   90067,
Tel: (310) 552-1834
(Executive search)

(cont)

Korn/Ferry Hazzard Intl. SA de CV, Montes Urales 641, Lomas de Chapultepec,
  Deleg. Miguel Hidalgo, 11000 Mexico DF, Mexico
Korn/Ferry Hazzard del Norte SA de CV, Daniel Zambrano 525, Col. Chepe Vera,
  Monterrey, NL, Mexico

KORODY-COLYER CORP   700 W Artesia Blvd, Compton, CA 90220,
  Tel: (310) 639-9511
  (Fuel injection equip, etc)
    Industrias K-C de Mexico SA, San Andres Atoto 12, Naucalpan de Juarez, Mexico DF,
    Mexico

KRAFT INC   Kraft Court, Glenview, IL 60025, Tel: (708) 998-2000
  (Dairy prdts, processed food, chems)
    Kraft Foods de Mexico SA de CV, Pino 459, Mexico DF, Mexico

LEEDS+NORTHRUP   795 Horsham Rd, PO Box 1010, Horsham, PA 19044-8010,
  Tel: (215) 442-8000
  (Mfr process control instrumentation, liquid & particle analysis)
    Leeds+Northrup Mexicana SA, Aptdo. Postal 339, 53560 Mexico DF, Mexico

LEVI STRAUSS & CO   1155 Battery, San Francisco, CA 94111, Tel: (415) 544-6000
  (Mfr casual wearing apparel)
    Levi Strauss de Mexico SA, Horacio 1844 4/F, Col. Polanco Reforma, 11550 Mexico DF,
    Mexico

LIGHTNIN   135 Mt Read Blvd, PO Box 1370, Rochester, NY 14611,
  Tel: (716) 436-5550
  (Mfr/sale/svce ind mixing mach, aerators)
    Lightnin de Mexico SA de CV, Aptdo. Postal 42023, Alfonso Herrera 106,
    06470 Mexico DF, Mexico

LIGHTOLIER   100 Lighting Way, Secaucus, NJ 07096, Tel: (201) 864-3000
  (Mfr lighting fixtures, portable lamps)
    ILTEC SA de CV, Insurgentes Sur 585, 03810 Mexico DF, Mexico

ELI LILLY & CO   Lilly Corporate Center, Indianapolis, IN 46285,
  Tel: (317) 276-2000
  (Mfr pharmaceuticals, animal health prdts)
    Eli Lilly y Cia. de Mexico SA de CV, Galzade de Tlalpan 2024, Campestre Churubusco,
    Coyoacan, Aptdo. Postal 864, 04200 Mexico DF, Mexico
    Eli Lilly y Cia. de Mexico SA de CV, Aptdo. Postal 864, Mexico DF, Mexico

THE LINCOLN ELECTRIC CO   22801 St Clair Ave, Cleveland, OH 44117-1199,
  Tel: (216) 481-8100
  (Mfr arc welding & welding related prtds, oxy-fuel & thermal cutting equip, integral
  AC motors)
    Lincoln Electric Mexicana SA de CV, Poniente 122 #550, Col. Industrial Vallejo,
    Deleg. Azcapotzalco, 02300 Mexico DF, Mexico

LINTAS:WORLDWIDE   1 Dag Hammarskjold Plaza, New York, NY 10017,
  Tel: (212) 605-8000
  (Advertising agency)
    Lintas:Mexico, Jose Vasconcelos 208, Col. Condesa, 06140 Mexico DF, Mexico

LIQUID CARBONIC INDUSTRIES CORP   810 Jorie Blvd, Oak Brook, IL 60521,
  Tel: (708) 572-7500
  (Mfr compressed gasses)
    Liquid Carbonic de Mexico SA, Apartado 9590, Admon. 1, Mexico City, Mexico

ARTHUR D LITTLE INC   25 Acorn Park, Cambridge, MA 02140-2390,
  Tel: (617) 498-5000
  (Mgmt, environ, health & safety consulting; tech & prdt development)
    Arthur D. Little Mexicana SA de CV, Editicio San Pedro, Av. San Pedro 300,
      Desp. 303, 66220 Monterrey, Mexico
    Arthur D. Little Mexicana SA de CV, Av. Sinaloa 149, 10 piso, Col. Roma,
      06700 Mexico DF, Mexico

LOCTITE CORP   10 Columbus Blvd, Hartford, CT 06106, Tel: (203) 520-5000
  (Mfr/sale ind adhesives & sealants)
    Loctite Company de Mexico SA de CV, Bosques de Radiatas 18, pisos 3 y 4,
      Bosques de Las Lomas, 11700 Mexico DF, Mexico

LONGYEAR CO   PO Box 27314, Salt Lake City, UT 84127, Tel: (801) 972-1395
  (Mfr diamond drills, concrete cutting equip; drill serv)
    Longyear de Mexico SA de CV, Aptdo. Postal 325, Tlalnepantla, Edo. de Mexico, Mexico

LORD CORP   2000 W Grandview Blvd, Erie, PA 16514, Tel: (814) 868-0924
  (Adhesives, coatings, chems, film prdts)
    Hughson Quimicade Mexico, Aptdo. Postal M-9123, 06000 Mexico DF, Mexico

LOUISIANA-PACIFIC CORP   111 SW Fifth Ave, Portland, OR 97204-3601,
  Tel: (503) 221-0800
  (Mfr lumber & building products)
    Louisiana-Pacific de Mexico SA de CV, Km. 100.5 Cart. Escan. Ens., Tijuana,
      Mexico (mail to: 555 Saturn Blvd., B-515, San Diego, CA 92154

THE LUBRIZOL CORP   29400 Lakeland Blvd, Wickliffe, OH 44092-2298,
  Tel: (216) 943-4200
  (Mfr chem additives for lubricants & fuels)
    Industrias Lubrizol SA de CV, Mexico
    Lubrizol Servicios Technicos S de RL, Av. Paseo de la Reforma 381-601,
      06500 Mexico DF, Mexico
    Lubrizol de Mexico S de RL, Mexico

MAGNETIC METALS CORP   Box 351, Camden, NJ 08105, Tel: (609) 964-7842
  (Magnetic alloys, shields; lamina- tions & special stampings)
    Metales Magneticos SA de CV, Cedro 429, Mexico DF, Mexico

MAIDENFORM INC   90 Park Ave, New York, NY 10016, Tel: (212) 953-1400
  (Mfr intimate apparel)
    Creaciones Textiles de Merida SA de CV, Yucatan Industrial Park,
      Apdo. Postal 38 CordeMex, 97000 Merida, Yucatan, Mexico

MALLINCKRODT MEDICAL INC   675 McDonnell Blvd, PO Box 5840, St Louis,
  MO 63134, Tel: (314) 895-2000
  (Mfr specialty medical prdts)
    Mallinckrodt Medical SA de CV, Ixtapalapa, Mexico

MANPOWER INTL INC   5301 N Ironwood Rd, PO Box 2053, Milwaukee,
WI 53201-2053, Tel: (414) 961-1000
(Temporary help service)
  Manpower SA, Miguel Laurent 15, Col. del Valle, 03100 Mexico DF, Mexico

MARATHON LE TOURNEAU CO   PO Box 2307, Longview, TX 75606, Tel: (903) 237-7000
(Mfr heavy constr, mining mach & equip)
  Macroequipos y Aceros SA, Bl. Puerto del Sol 502, Edif. Plaza Puerta del Sol,
    Col. Colinas de San Jeronimo, Monterrey, Mexico

MARKEM CORP   150 Congress St, Keene, NH 03431, Tel: (603) 352-1130
(Marking and printing mach; hot stamping foils)
  Markem SA de CV, Aptdo. Postal 5-077, Rio Guadalquivir 66, Mexico DF, Mexico

MARLEY CO   1900 Johnson Dr, Mission Woods, KS 66205, Tel: (913) 362-5440
(Cooling & heating towers, waste treatment sys)
  Marley de Mexico SA de CV, Carr. Circunvalacion 258, Tlalnepantla, Mexico DF, Mexico

J B MARTIN CO   10 E 53rd St, #3100, New York, NY 10022, Tel: (212) 421-2020
(Mfr/sale velvets)
  Martin Mexicana SA, Montes Urales 520, Mexico DF, Mexico

MASCO CORP   21001 Van Born Rd, Taylor, MI 48180, Tel: (313) 274-7400
(Mfr home improvement, building & home furnishings prdts)
  MascoMex SA de CV, Mexico

MATTEL INC   333 Continental Blvd, El Segundo, CA 90245, Tel: (310) 252-2000
(Mfr toys, dolls, games, crafts & hobbies)
  Fisher-Price de Mexico SA de CV, Apartado 1019, Matamoros, Mexico

MEAD CORP   Courthouse Plaza, NE, Dayton, OH 45463, Tel: (513) 222-6323
(Mfr paper, packaging, pulp, lumber & other wood prdts, school & office prdts; electr
pub, distri)
  Productos para Escuela y Oficina de Mexico SA de CV, Mexico City, Mexico

THE MEARL CORP   320 Old Briarcliff Rd, Briarcliff Manor, NY 10510,
Tel: (914) 923-8500
(Mfr pearlescent luster pigments, mica, decorative iridescent film)
  Mearl de Mexico SA de CV, Mexico City, Mexico

MEASUREX CORP   One Results Way, Cupertino, CA 95014-5991, Tel: (408) 255-1500
(Mfr computer integrated mfg sys)
  Measurex SA de CV, Mazatlan 43, Col. Condesa, 06140 Mexico DF, Mexico

MEMOREX CORP   San Thomas at Central Expressway, Santa Clara, CA 95052,
Tel: (408) 987-1000
(Magnetic recording tapes, etc)
  Memorex SA de CV, Campos Eliseos 67, Col. Polanco, Mexico DF, Mexico

THE MENTHOLATUM CO INC   1360 Niagara St, Buffalo, NY 14213,
Tel: (716) 882-7660
(Mfr/distr proprietary medicines, drugs, OTC's)
  Mentholatum de Mexico SA de CV, Pico de Verpaz 435, 14210 Mexico DF, Mexico

MERCK SHARP & DOHME INTL   PO Box 2000, Rahway, NJ 07065, Tel: (201) 574-4000
  (Pharms, chems & biologicals)
    Merck, Sharp & Dohme de Mexico SA de CV, Av. Division del Norte 3377, Mexico DF,
    Mexico

MERGENTHALER LINOTYPE CO   201 Old Country Rd, Melville, NY 11747,
  Tel: (516) 673-4197
  (Photocomposition machs, sys & equip)
    Distribuidora MerLino SA de CV, Guanajuato 215, Mexico DF, Mexico

METAL-CLADDING INC   PO Box 630, 470 Niagara Way, North Tonawanda, NY 14120,
  Tel: (716) 693-6205
  (FRP tanks & custom constr, scrubbers, odor control equip)
    FRP de Mexico SA, Trigo 30, Col. Granjas Esmeralda, Mexico DF, Mexico

METCO DIV OF PERKIN-ELMER   1101 Prospect Ave, PO Box 1006, Westbury,
  NY 11590-0201, Tel: (516) 334-1300
  (Mfr/serv thermal spray coating equip & supplies)
    Metco de Mexico, Obrero Mundial 678, Col. Atenor Salas, 03010 Mexico DF, Mexico

METROPOLITAN LIFE INSURANCE CO   1 Madison Ave, New York, NY 10010-3690,
  Tel: (212) 578-2211
  (Insurance & retirement savings prdts & services)
    Seguros Genesis SA, Blvd. Manuel Avila Camacho 36, Col. Lomas de Chapultepec,
    11000 Mexico DF, Mexico

MICROSOFT CORP   One Microsoft Way, Redmond, WA 98052-6399,
  Tel: (206) 882-8080
  (Computer software, peripherals & services)
    Microsoft Mexico, Blvd. M.A. Comacho 21, Piso 2, Lomas de Chaputepec,
    11000 Mexico DF, Mexico

MILCHEM INC   3900 Essex Lane, PO Box 22111, Houston, TX 77027,
  Tel: (214) 439-8000
  (Gas & oil well drilling fluids & chem additives)
    Quimotecnica SA, Av. Insurgentes Sur 933-201, Mexico DF, Mexico

MILLIPORE CORP   Ashley Rd, Bedford, MA 01730, Tel: (617) 275-9205
  (Mfr precision filters, hi-performance liquid chromatography instru)
    Millipore SA de CV, Av. Ingenieros Militares 85-PB, 11230 Mexico DF, Mexico

MINE SAFETY APPLIANCES CO   PO Box 426, Pittsburgh, PA 15230,
  Tel: (421) 273 5000
  (Safety equip, ind filters)
    MSA de Mexico SA de CV, Francisco 1 Madero 84, Naucalpan de Juarez,
    53500 Mexico DF, Mexico

MISSION DRILLING PRODUCTS DIV   PO Box 40402, Houston, TX 77240,
  Tel: (713) 460-6200
  (Oilfield equip, drilling & mining equip, ind valves)
    Manufacturas y Servicios Industriales, Aptdo. Postal 16-157, Mexico DF, Mexico

MISSION ENERGY CO   18101 Von Karman Ave, #1700, Irvine, CA 92715-1007,
  Tel: (714) 752-5588
  (Independent power producer)
    Mission Energy Mexico, 190 Bosque de Ciruelos A-303, Bosques de las Lomas,
    11700 Mexico DF, Mexico

MOBIL CORP   3225 Gallows Rd, Fairfax, VA 22037-0001, Tel: (703) 846-3000
  (Petroleum explor & refining, mfr petrol prdts, chems, petrochems)
    Mobil Atlas SA, 146 Poniente 700, Col. Industrial Vallejo, Mexico DF, Mexico
    Mobil Oil de Mexico SA, Aptdo. Postal 22, Centro de la Ciudad, Cuauhtemoc ZPI,
      0600 Mexico DF, Mexico

MODINE MANUFACTURING CO   1500 DeKoven Ave, Racine, WI 53403,
  Tel: (414) 636-1200
  (Mfr heat-transfer prdts)
    Modine Transferencia de Calor SA de CV, Av. Los Dos Laredos,
      Parque Ind. Los Dos Laredos, Nuevo Laredo, 88000 Tamaulipas, Mexico

MOLEX INC   2222 Wellington Ct, Lisle, IL 60532, Tel: (708) 969-4550
  (Mfr electronic, electrical & fiber optic interconnection prdts & sys, switches,
  application tooling)
    Molex Inc., Guadalajara, Magdalena & Nogales, Mexico

MONARCH MARKING SYSTEM INC   PO Box 608, Dayton, OH 45401, Tel: (513) 865-2123
  (Marking devices, tickets, tags)
    Monarch Marking System de Mexico SA de CV, Aptdo. Postal 15-054, Mexico DF, Mexico

MONSANTO CO   800 N Lindbergh Blvd, St Louis, MO 63167, Tel: (314) 694-1000
  (Mfr agric & food prdts, chems, plastics, fibers, pharms, process control equip,
  performance material)
    G.D. Searle & Co., Coapa, Mexico

MONTICELLO DRUG CO   1604 Stockton St, Jacksonville, FL 32204,
  Tel: (904) 384-3666
  (Cold preparations)
    Monticello Drug Co SA, Joyas 16 Esq. Amatista 54, Col. Estrella, Mexico DF, Mexico

MOORE PRODUCTS CO   Sumneytown Pike, Spring House, PA 19477,
  Tel: (215) 646-7400
  (Mfr process control instru)
    Moore Products de Mexico SA de CV, Tintoreto 32, Desp. 302, Col. Nonoalco, Mixcoac,
      Mexico DF, Mexico

MORTON INTERNATIONAL INC   100 N Riverside Plaza, Chicago, IL 60606-1596,
  Tel: (312) 807-2000
  (Mfr adhesives, coatings, finishes, spec chems, advanced & electr materials, salt,
  airbags)
    Morton Intl. SA de CV, Av. 16 de Septiembre 445, Naucalpan de Juarez,
      Edo. de Mexico, Mexico

MOSLER INC   1561 Grand Blvd, Hamilton, OH 45012, Tel: (513) 867-4000
  (Mfr security prdts, sys, & servs to fin, coml, & govt mkt)
    Mosler SA de CV, Rio Lerma 69, Mexico DF, Mexico

MOTOROLA INC   1303 E Algonquin Rd, Schaumburg, IL 60196, Tel: (708) 576-5000
  (Mfr commun equip, semiconductors, cellular phones)
    Motorola de Mexico SA, Av. Curtidor 218, 37510 Leon, Guanajuato, Mexico
    Motorola de Mexico SA, Guanajuato 114, Col. Roma, Mexico DF, Mexico
    Motorola de Mexico SA, Tonala 59 (Antes 63), Mexico DF, Mexico
    Motorola de Mexico SA, Amado Nervo 1437, Japopan, Jalisco, Mexico
    Motorola de Mexico SA, Montes Urales 760-3P, Lomas de Chapultepec, Mexico City DF,

Mexico
Motorola de Mexico SA, Av. Lopez Mateos Sur 2220, 44530 Guadalajara, Jalisco, Mexico

MTEL INTERNATIONAL   1350 I St NW, #1100, Washington, DC 20005,
 Tel: (202) 336-5211
 (Radio paging services & sys implementation)
   Comunicaciones Mtel, Mexico City, Mexico

MULTIGRAPHICS DIV   1800 W Central Rd, Mt Prospect, IL 60056,
 Tel: (708) 398-1900
 (Offset duplicating & graphic commun sys)
   AM Intl. SA de CV, Aptdo. Postal 30-633, Mexico DF, Mexico

MYERS INTL INC   1293 South Main St, Akron, OH 44301, Tel: (216) 253-5592
 (Mfr tire retreading & maintenance equip & supplies)
   Cia. Myers Zulueta De Mexico SA, Dr. Navarro 58, Colonia Doctores, 06720 Mexico DF,
   Mexico

McCANN-ERICKSON WORLDWIDE   750 Third Ave, New York, NY 10017,
 Tel: (212) 697-6000
 (Advertising)
   McCann-Erickson (Div. Corp. Interpublic Mexicana), Londres 259, Esq. Seville,
   Col. Juarez, 06600 Mexico DF, Mexico

McCORMICK & CO INC   18 Loveton Circle, Sparks, MD 21152-6000,
 Tel: (410) 771-7301
 (Mfr/dist/sale seasonings, flavorings, specialty foods)
   McCormick de Mexico SA de CV, Apartado Postal 17540, 11230 Mexico DF, Mexico

THE McGRAW-HILL COS   1221 Ave of the Americas, New York, NY 10020,
 Tel: (212) 512-2000
 (Books, magazines, info sys, financial serv, broadcast operations)
   Libros McGraw-Hill de Mexico SA de CV, Altacomulco 499-501,
   Fracc. Indl. San Andres, 53500 Naucalpan, Mesico

McKINSEY & CO INC   55 E 52nd St, New York, NY 10022, Tel: (212) 446-7000
 (Mgmt consultants)
   Plaza Comermex, Blvd. Manuel Avila Camacho 1, Mexico DF, Mexico

NACCO INDUSTRIES INC   5875 Landerbrook Dr, Mayfield Hgts, OH 44124-4017,
 Tel: (216) 449-9600
 (Mining/mktg lignite & metals, mfr forklift trucks & small electric appliances,
 specialty retailers)
   Hamilton Beach/Proctor-Silex Inc., Juarez, Mexico

NALCO CHEMICAL CO   One Nalco Center, Naperville, IL 60563-1198,
 Tel: (708) 305-1000
 (Chems for water & waste water treatment, oil prod & refining, ind processes;
 water/energy mgmt serv)
   Nalcomex SA de CV, Tlaxcala 177-5 piso, Col. Hipodromo, 06100 Mexico DF, Mexico

NATIONAL CAR RENTAL SYSTEM INC   7700 France Ave S, Minneapolis, MN 55435,
 Tel: (612) 830-2121
 (Car rental)
   National Car Rental, Marsella 48, Col. Juarez, Mexico DF, Mexico

NATIONAL CHEMSEARCH CORP   2727 Chemsearch Blvd, Irving, TX 75061,
Tel: (214) 438-0211
(Commercial chem prdts)
  Laboratorios Certificados SA, Henry Ford 163, Col. Guadalupe Tepeyace, Mexico DF,
  Mexico

NATIONAL STARCH & CHEMICAL CO   10 Finderne Ave, Bridgewater, NJ 08807-3300,
Tel: (908) 685-5000
(Mfr adhesives & sealants, resins & spec chems, electr materials & adhesives, food
prdts, ind starch)
  Aranal Comercial SA de CV, Mexico City, Mexico
  National Starch & Chemical de Mexico SA de CV, Mexico City, Mexico

NATIONAL TECHNICAL SCHOOLS   4000 S Figueroa St, Los Angeles, CA 90037,
Tel: (213) 234-9061
(Correspondence schools)
  National Schools, Instituto Practico Rosenkranz, Av. Morelos 85, Mexico DF, Mexico

NELLCOR INC   4280 Hacienda Dr, Pleasanton, CA 94588-2719, Tel: (510) 463-4000
(Mfr medical patient safety & management monitoring instruments)
  Nellcor de Mexico SA de CV, La Mesa Parque Industrial, Paseo Reforma S/N,
    Fracc. Rubio, Las Mesa, Tijuana, BC, Mexico

NELSON INDUSTRIES INC   Highway 51, W Stoughton, WI 53589, Tel: (608) 873-4373
(Mfr automotive parts & accessories, ind machinery)
  Nelson Industries Mexico SA de CV, Calle Cinco 187, Col. Pantitlan,
    08100 Mexico DF, Mexico

NEUTROGENA CORP   5760 W 96th St, Los Angeles, CA 90045, Tel: (310) 642-1150
(Mfr facial cleansing, moisturizing prdts; body care, sun & hair care specialty prdts)
  Neutrogena Mexico, Sur 128 No. 143, Interior 11, Colonia Cove, Alvaro Obregon,
    01120 Mexico DF, Mexico

A C NIELSEN CO   Nielsen Plaza, Northbrook, IL 60062-6288, Tel: (708) 498-6300
(Market research)
  A.C. Nielsen Co. de Mexico SA, Av. Lerdo 251 Norte, Ciudad Juarez, Chihuahua, Mexico

NORDSON CORP   28601 Clemens Rd, Westlake, OH 44145, Tel: (216) 892-1580
(Mfr ind application equip & packaging mach)
  Nordson de Mexico SA de CV, Prolongacion 5 de Mayo 27, Parque Industrial Naucalpan,
    53489 Naucalpan, Mexico

NORTON CO   1 New Bond St, Worcester, MA 01606, Tel: (508) 795-5000
(Abrasives, drill bits, constr & safety prdts, plastics)
  Boyles Bros. Drilling de Mexico SA de CV, Aptdo. Postal 251, Naucalpan, Mexico
  Christensen Diamond Products de Mexico SA de CV, Aptdo. Postal 57, Naucalpan, Mexico
  Norton SA, Homero 526-501, Mexico DF, Mexico
  Norton SA, Aptdo. Postal 325, Puebla, Pue., Mexico

OCEANEERING INTL INC   PO Box 218130, Houston, TX 77218-8130,
Tel: (713) 578-8868
(Underwater serv to offshore oil & gas ind)
  Oceaneering Intl. Inc., Operational base in Ciudad del Carmen

ODI   25 Mall Rd, Burlington, MA 01803, Tel: (617) 272-8040
  (Mgt & consul serv)
    ODI Mexico/Fundameca, Loma Bonita 24, Col. Lomas Altas, 11950 Mexico DF, Mexico

OHAUS CORP   29 Hanover Rd, PO Box 900, Florham Park, NJ 07932-0900,
  Tel: (201) 377-9000
  (Mfr balances & scales for labs, ind & education)
    Ohaus de Mexico SA de CV, Managua 697, Desp. 404, Col. Lindavista, 07300 Mexico DF,
    Mexico

THE OILGEAR CO   2300 S 51st St, Milwaukee, WI 53219, Tel: (414) 327-1700
  (Mfr hydraulic power transmission mach)
    Oilgear Mexicana SA de CV, Rafael Vega 100-203, Esq. Revolucion, Pachuca,
    42000 Hidalgo, Mexico

OLIN CORP   120 Long Ridge Rd, PO Box 1355, Stamford, CT 06904-1355,
  Tel: (203) 356-2000
  (Mfr chems, metals, applied physics in elect, defense, aerospace inds)
    Olin Quimica SA de CV, Campos Eliseos 385, Torre A, Piso 9, Col. Polanco,
    Delg. Miguel Hidalgo, 11560 Mexico DF, Mexico

OLSTEN CORP   175 Broad Hollow Rd, Melville, NY 11747-8905,
  Tel: (516) 844-7800
  (Staffing, home health care & info technology svces (642,000 assignment employees
  worldwide))
    Olsten Staff, Tijuana 19, Col. de Valle, 03100 Mexico DF, Mexico

ONEIDA LTD   Kenwood Ave, Oneida, NY 13421, Tel: (315) 361-3000
  (Mfr cutlery, holloware, china, crystal)
    Oneida Mexicana SA, Balderas 27, Mexico DF, Mexico

OPTEK TECHNOLOGY INC   1215 W Crosby Rd, Carrollton, TX 75006,
  Tel: (214) 323-2200
  (Mfr electronic components)
    Optron de Mexico SA de CV, Parque Industrial Rio Bravo S/N, Ciudad Juarez, Mexico
    Semiconductores Opticos SA de CV, Juarez Porvenir 8419, Ciudad Juarez, Mexico

ORACLE CORP   500 Oracle Parkway, Redwood Shores, CA 94065,
  Tel: (415) 506-7000
  (Develop/mfr software)
    Oracle Mexico SA de CV, Ejercito Nacional 579, Piso 1, Col. Granada,
    11550 Mexico DF, Mexico

OSMOSE INTL INC   980 Ellicott St, Buffalo, NY 14209, Tel: (716) 882-5905
  (Mfr wood preservatives; maint & inspec utility poles, railroad track & marine piling)
    Osmose Mexicana SA de CV, Fracc. de Cuernavaca 344, Mexico DF, Mexico

OTIS ELEVATOR CO   10 Farm Springs, Farmington, CT 06032, Tel: (860) 676-6528
  (Mfr elevators & escalators)
    Elevadores Otis SA de CV, Aptdo. Postal 44, 06000 Mexico DF, Mexico

OUTBOARD MARINE CORP   100 Sea Horse Dr, Waukegan, IL 60085,
  Tel: (708) 689-6200
  (Mfr/mkt marine engines, boats & accessories)
    Outboard Marine Power Products Group, Mexico

OXFORD INDUSTRIES INC   222 Piedmont Ave NE, Atlanta, GA 30308,
  Tel: (404) 659-2424
  (Design/mfr/mktng consumer apparel prdts)
    Camisas Bahio Kino SA de CV, Aqua Prieta, Sonora, Mexico
    Industrias Oxford de Merida SA de CV, Parque Industrial Yucatan,
      Km. 12.5 Carr. Merida-Progreso, Merida, Yucatan, Mexico

PADCO INC   2220 Elm St SE, Minneapolis, MN 55414, Tel: (612) 378-7270
  (Mfr paint sundries)
    Padco Mexico SA de CV, Presas 3, Fraccionamiento de los Frenos,
      53250 Naucalpan de Juarez, Mexico

PANDUIT CORP   17301 Ridgeland Ave, Tinley Park, IL 60477-0981,
  Tel: (708) 532-1800
  (Mfr elec/electr wiring comps)
    Panduit Mexico S. en N.C., Lazard Cardenas 2785, Col. Alamo Industrial,
      CP 44490 Guadalajara, Jalisco, Mexico

PARKER HANNIFIN CORP   17325 Euclid Ave, Cleveland, OH 44112,
  Tel: (216) 531-3000
  (Mfr motion-control prdts)
    Arosellos SA de CV, Rio Lerma 221, Tlalnepantla, Mexico
    Brownville Rubber Co. SA de CV, Sexta y Vix caya 95, Matamoros, Tam., Mexico
    Conductores de Fluidos Parker SA de CV, Primero de Mayo 1496 Ote., Zona Industrial,
      Aptdo. Postal 504, 50070 Toluca, Mexico
    Parker Seal de Baja SA de CV, Calle Siete Norte 111, Esq. con Calle Uno Poniente,
      Ciudad Ind. Nueva Tijuana, Tijuana, Mexico
    Parker Seal de Mexico SA, Rio Lerma 221, Fracc. Industrial San Nicolas,
      Tlalnepantla, Edo. de Mexico, Mexico
    Parker Zenith, Av. Morones Prieto, Pte. 1300, Monterrey, NL, Mexico
    Schrader Bellows Parker SA de CV, Calle 9 #6 Alce Blanco, 053370 Naucalpan, Mexico

THE PARSONS CORP   100 W Walnut St, Pasadena, CA 91124, Tel: (818) 440-2000
  (Engineering & construction)
    Latinoamericana de Ingenieria SA de CV, Culiacan 108, 06170 Mexico DF, Mexico

PEAVEY CO/CONAGRA TRADING COS   730 Second Ave, Minneapolis, MN 55402,
  Tel: (612) 370-7500
  (Flour, feeds, seeds)
    Conagra Trading Co., Mexico City, Mexico

PEPSICO INC   700 Anderson Hill Rd, Purchase, NY 10577-1444,
  Tel: (914) 253-2000
  (Beverages, snack foods, restaurants)
    Empresas Gamesa SA de CV, Mexico
    Groupo Gamesa SA de CV, Mexico
    Pepsi-Cola Mexicana SA de CV, Mexico
    Sabritas SA de CV, Mexico

PERIPHONICS CORP   4000 Veterans Hwy, Bohemia, NY 11716, Tel: (516) 467-0500
  (Mfr voice processing systems)
    Periphonics SA de CV, San Francisco 1626-301, Colonia del Valle, 03100 Mexico DF,
      Mexico

PETERSON AMERICAN CORP   21200 Telegraph Rd, Southfield, MI   48034,
  Tel: (810) 799-5400
  (Mfr springs & wire prdts, metal stampings, ind machinery)
    Resortes y Productos Metalicos SA, Privada de Rio Pilcomayo 183-A,
    Aptdo. Postal 17549, 11230 Mexico DF, Mexico

PETROLITE CORP   369 Marshall Ave, St Louis, MO   63119-1897,
  Tel: (314) 961-3500
  (Mfr/prod spec chem treating programs, performance-enhancing additives & related
  equip & svces)
    Petrolite de Mexico SA de CV, Mercurio 126, Fracc. Galaxia, Villahermosa, Tabasco,
    Mexico

PETTIBONE CORP   4225 Naperville Rd, Lisle, IL   60532-3657, Tel: (708) 955-0220
  (Mfr material-handling, forestry, foundry & crushing equip, castings, plastic knobs,
  tow tractors)
    Pettibone de Mexico SA de CV, Fundidores 5, Distrito I 71-B, Aptdo. 61/62,
    Cuautitlan Izcallala, Mexico

PFAUDLER CO   PO Box 1600, Rochester, NY   14692, Tel: (716) 235-1000
  (Mfr glass lined reactor vessels)
    Pfaudler SA de CV, Av. Encarnacion Ortiz 1860, Apartado 15-184, Col. Cosmopolita,
    02670 Mexico DF, Mexico

PFIZER INC   235 E 42nd St, New York, NY   10017-5755, Tel: (212) 573-2323
  (Mfr healthcare products)
    Compania Distribuidora del Centro SA de CV, Mexico
    Pfizer SA de CV, Mexico
    Tenedora Pfizer SA de CV, Mexico

PHELPS DODGE CORP   2600 N Central Ave, Phoenix, AZ   85004-3014,
  Tel: (602) 234-8100
  (Copper, minerals, metals & spec engineered prdts for trans & elect mkts)
    Phelps Dodge Exploration Corp., Mexico

PHILLIPS PETROLEUM CO   Phillips Bldg, Bartlesville, OK   74004,
  Tel: (918) 661-6600
  (Crude oil, natural gas, liquefied petroleum gas, gasoline & petro-chems)
    Negromex SA, Bosques de los Ciruelos 180, Mexico DF, Mexico
    Phillips Quimica SA de CV, Bosques de Duraznos 69, Mexico DF, Mexico

PILGRIM'S PRIDE CORP   PO Box 93, Pittsburgh, TX   75686, Tel: (903) 855-1000
  (Broiler & egg production, poultry & livestock feed)
    Alimentos Balanceados Pilgrim's Pride, Avda. 5 de Febrero 1048, 76130 Queretaro,
    Mexico
    Avicola Pilgrim's Pride de Mexico SA de CV, Oklahoma 112, Piso 3, Col. Napoles,
    03810 Mexico DF, Mexico

PIONEER HI-BRED INTL INC   700 Capital Sq, 400 Locust St, Des Moines,
  IA   50309, Tel: (515) 245-3500
  (Agricultural chemicals, farm supplies, biological prdts, research)
    Hibridos Mexicanos SA de CV, Avda. Americas 1297, Sector Hidalgo, Guadalajara,
    Jalisco, Mexico
    Investigaciones Pioneer SA de CV, Avda. Americas 1297, Sector Hidalgo, Guadalajara,
    Mexico

PLANTRONICS   337 Encinal St, Santa Cruz, CA 95060, Tel: (408) 426-6060
   (Mfr commun equip, elect & electr appliances & apparatus)
      Plamex SA, Centro Industrial Barranquita 19, 22000 Tijuana, Mexico

PLAYTEX APPAREL INC   700 Fairfield Ave, Stamford, CT 06904,
   Tel: (203) 356-8000
   (Mfr intimate apparel)
      Playtex de Mexico SA, Ave. Constituyantes 908-C, Col. Lomas Altas, Mexico 10 DF,
      Mexico

PLIBRICO CO   1800 Kingsbury St, Chicago, IL 60614, Tel: (312) 549-7014
   (Refractories, engineering, constr)
      Plibrico de Mexico SA de CV, Martin Mendalde 1451, Col. del Valle,
      Deleg. Benito Juarez, 03100 Mexico DF, Mexico

PNEUMO ABEX CORP   485 Frontage Rd, Burr Ridge, IL 60521, Tel: (708) 323-4446
   (Mfr aerospace & automotive friction materials & equip)
      Abex Industrial SA de CV, Poniente 128, 02300 Mexico DF, Mexico

POLYCHROME CORP   222 Bridge Plaza S, Fort Lee, NJ 07024, Tel: (201) 346-8800
   (Metal offset plates, coating specialties, graphic arts films)
      Polychrome de Mexico SA, Poniente 128 #745B, Mexico DF, Mexico

POTTERS INDUSTRIES INC   PO Box 840, Valley Forge, PA 19482-0840,
   Tel: (610) 651-4700
   (Mfr glass spheres for road marking & ind applications)
      Ballotini Panamericana SA, Cordoba 131-101, Col. Roma, 06700 Mexico DF, Mexico

POWERS REGULATOR CO   3400 Oakton St, Skokie, IL 60076, Tel: (708) 673-6700
   (Control devices)
      Reguladores Powers de Mexico SA de CV, Oriente 259 y Ave. Sur 12, Mexico DF, Mexico

PPG INDUSTRIES   One PPG Place, Pittsburgh, PA 15272, Tel: (412) 434-3131
   (Mfr flat glass, fiber glass, chems, coatings)
      PPG Industrias de Mexico SA, Av. Presidente Juarez 1978, 54090 Tlalnepantla,
      Edo. de Mexico, Mexico

PRECISION VALVE CORP   PO Box 309, Yonkers, NY 10702, Tel: (914) 969-6500
   (Mfr aerosol valves)
      Valvulas de Precision SA, Goma 160 Esq. Azafran, Col. Granjas de Mexico, Mexico DF,
      Mexico

PREFORMED LINE PRODUCTS CO   PO Box 91129, Cleveland, OH 44101,
   Tel: (216) 461-5200
   (Mfr pole line hardware for elec transmission lines; splice closures & related prdts
   for telecom)
      Preformados de Mexico SA de CV, Poniente 140 #526, Mexico DF, Mexico

PREMARK INTL INC   1717 Deerfield Rd, Deerfield, IL 60015, Tel: (708) 405-6000
   (Mfr/sale diversified consumer & coml prdts)
      Dart SA de CV, Ejercito Nacional 579, Colonia Granada, 11520 Mexico DF, Mexico

PREMIX INC   PO Box 281, N Kingsville, OH 44068, Tel: (216) 224-2181
   (Mfr molded fiber glass, reinforced thermoset molding compounds & plastic parts)
      Vitro Fibras SA, Av. Ingenieros Militares 85-4 piso, 11230 Mexico DF, Mexico

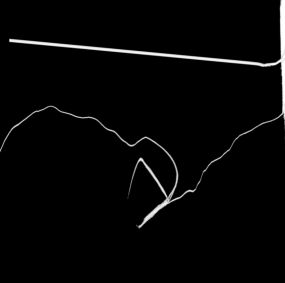

PROCTER & GAMBLE CO   One Procter & Gamble Plaza, Cincinnati, OH 45202,
  Tel: (513) 983-1100
  (Personal care, food, laundry, cleaning & ind prdts)
    Proctor & Gamble de Mexico SA de CV, Loma Florida 32, Col. Vistahermosa,
      05100 Mexico DF, Mexico

QUAKER CHEMICAL CORP   Elm & Lee Sts, Conshohocken, PA 19428-0809,
  Tel: (610) 832-4000
  (Mfr chem specialties; total fluid mgmt services)
    TecniQuimia Mexicana SA de CV, Aptdo. Postal 4425, Suc. de Correos "H", Monterrey,
      NL, Mexico

QUAKER FABRIC CORP   941 Grinnell St, Fall River, MA 02721,
  Tel: (508) 678-1951
  (Mfr upholstery fabrics, yarns)
    Quaker Fabric Mexico SA de CV, Av. Urbina 41, Parque Industrial Naucalpan,
      53489 Naucalpan de Juarez, Mexico

QUIGLEY CO INC   235 E 42nd St, New York, NY 10017, Tel: (212) 573-3444
  (Mfr refractory specs, application equip)
    Quigley Div., Bolivar 782, 03400 Mexico DF, Mexico

RADISSON HOTELS INTL   Carlson Pkwy, PO Box 59159, Minneapolis,
  MN 55459-8204, Tel: (612) 540-5526
  (Hotels)
    Hotel El Presidente Acapulco, Acapulco, Mexico
    Las Misiones de San Jose, San Jose del Cabo, B.C.S., Mexico
    Radisson Hotels Intl., Acapulco, Cancun, Manzanillo, Mexico City, Monterrey,
      Tijuana, Zacatecas (inquiries to U.S. address)

RALSTON PURINA CO   Checkerboard Sq, St Louis, MO 63164, Tel: (314) 982-1000
  (Poultry & live stock feed, cereals, food prdts)
    Eveready de Mexico SA de CV, Paseo de la Reforma 295, 06500 Mexico DF, Mexico
    Industrias Purina SA de CV, Av. Constituyentes 956, 11950 Mexico DF, Mexico

RAMSEY TECHNOLOGY INC   501 90th Ave NW, Minneapolis, MN 55433,
  Tel: (612) 783-2500
  (Mfr in-motion weighing, inspection, monitoring & control equip for the process inds)
    Ingenieria Ramsey Mexicana SA de CV, Carpio 127, Col. Santa Maria la Ribera,
      06400 Mexico DF, Mexico

RANCO INC   555 Metro Pl N, PO Box 248, Dublin, OH 43017, Tel: (614) 764-3733
  (Controls for appliance, automotive, comfort, commercial & consumer mkts)
    Electronic Control Corp. de Mexico SA, Primera 230 Norte/Col. Jardin, H. Matamoros,
      Tam., Mexico
    Fricon SA de CV, Av. Lauro Villar 726 OTE, H. Matamoros, Tam., Mexico

RAND McNALLY   8255 N Central Park Ave, Skokie, IL 60076, Tel: (708) 329-8100
  (Publishing & book services, docusystems, media services)
    Rand McNally-Book Services, Av. Mexico 51, Colonia Hipodromo, 06100 Mexico DF,
      Mexico

RAYCHEM CORP   300 Constitution Dr, Menlo Park, CA 94025, Tel: (415) 361-3333
  (Devel/mfr/mkt materials science products for electronics, telecommunications &
  industry)
    Raychem Technologies SA, Melchor Ocampo 193-A-13, Col. Veronica Anzures,
      11300 Mexico DF, Mexico

(cont)

Raychem Technologies SA, Calle 11 Norte y 1 Poniente 110,
Cd. Industrial Nueva Tijuana, Tijuana, Mexico

READER'S DIGEST ASSOCIATION INC   PO Box 235, Pleasantville, NY   10570,
Tel: (914) 238-1000
(Publisher magazines & books, direct mail marketer)
Reader's Digest Mexico SA de CV, Lomas de Sotele 1102, Col. Loma Hermosa,
11200 Mexico DF, Mexico

RELIANCE ELECTRIC CO   24701 Euclid Ave, Cleveland, OH   44117,
Tel: (216) 266-7000
(Equip & sys for ind automation, telecom equip)
Administrativa Industry Reliance SA de CV, Aptdo. Postal 77-311, Mexico DF, Mexico
Dodge de Mexico SA de CV, Aptdo. Postal 239, 53370 Mexico DF, Mexico

REVLON INC   625 Madison Ave, New York, NY   10022, Tel: (212) 527-4000
(Mfr cosmetics, fragrances, toiletries, beauty care prdts)
Barnes-Hind Pharmaceuticals de Mexico SA de CV, Mexico DF, Mexico
Laboratorios Grossman SA, Mexico DF, Mexico

RHONE-POULENC RORER INC   PO Box 1200, Collegeville, PA   19426-0107,
Tel: (215) 454-8000
(R&D/mfr human pharmaceuticals)
Rorer de Mexico SA de CV, Av. Insurgentes Sur 1991, Mexico DF, Mexico

RIEKE CORP   500 W 7th St, Auburn, IN   46706, Tel: (219) 925-3700
(Mfr steel drum closures, plugs, seals, faucets, rings, combination pail spout &
closure, etc)
Rieke de Mexico SA, Aptdo. 75-3, Col. Linda Vista, 07300 Mexico DF, Mexico

RJR NABISCO INC   1301 Ave of the Americas, New York, NY   10019,
Tel: (212) 258-5600
(Mfr consumer packaged food prdts & tobacco prdts)
Nabisco Famosa SA, Poniente 116 #536, Col. Industrial Vallejo, 02300 Mexico DF,
Mexico

ROADWAY EXPRESS INC   1077 George Blvd, Akron, OH   44309, Tel: (216) 384-1717
(Motor carrier, long haul trucking)
Roadway Bodegas y Consolidacion, all mail to U.S. address

A H ROBINS CO INC   1407 Cummings Dr, PO Box 26609, Richmond, VA   23261-6609,
Tel: (804) 257-2000
(Mfr ethical pharms & consumer prdts)
A.H. Robins de Mexico SA de CV, Cuautitlan, Mexico

ROCHESTER GAUGES INC   PO Box 29242, Dallas, TX   75229-0242,
Tel: (214) 241-2161
(Liquid-level gauges, level switches, pressured gauges, electric panel gauges, etc)
Medidores Internacionales Rochester SA, Aptdo. Postal 51-604, 07600 Mexico DF,
Mexico

ROCKWELL INTL CORP   2201 Seal Beach Blvd, PO Box 4250, Seal Beach,
CA 90740-8250, Tel: (310) 797-3311
(Prdts & serv for aerospace, automotive, electronics, graphics & automation inds)
Controlmatic Allen-Bradley SA de CV, Avda. Patriotismo 579, Colonia Nochebuena,
03720 Mexico DF, Mexico

R A RODRIGUEZ INC   320 Endo Blvd, Garden City, NY 11530, Tel: (516) 832-2600
  (Distribution ball & roller bearings, mechanical sys)
    R. A. Rodriguez de Mexico SA de CV, Calle Sabino 154, Col. Santa Maria La Rivera,
    U6400 Mexico DF, Mexico

ROHM AND HAAS CO   100 Independence Mall West, Philadelphia, PA 19106,
  Tel: (215) 592-3000
  (Mfr ind & agric chems, plastics)
    Rohm and Haas Mexico SA de CV, Insurgentes Sur 1106, 10 Piso, 03720 Mexico DF,
    Mexico

SYDNEY ROSS CO   90 Park Ave, New York, NY 10016, Tel: (212) 907-2000
  (Pharms, toiletries & cosmetics)
    Sydney Ross Co. SA, Agencia de Correos 291, Mexico DF, Mexico

SALEM OIL & GREASE CO   60 Grove St, Salem, MA 01970, Tel: (617) 745-0505
  (Tanning oils & greases)
    Salem Oil & Grease Mexico, Calle el Catorce 19-A, Mexico DF, Mexico

SAMSONITE CORP   11200 E 45th Ave, Denver, CO 80239-3018, Tel: (303) 373-2000
  (Mfr luggage & leather goods)
    Samsonite Mexico, Calzado a la Venta 25, Complejo Industrial Cuamatla,
    54730 Cuautitlan, Mexico

SARA LEE CORP   3 First National Plaza, Chicago, IL 60602-4260,
  Tel: (312) 726-2600
  (Mfr/distr food & consumer packaged goods, tobacco prdts, intimate apparel & knitwear)
    House of Fuller SA de CV, Francisco Villa 5, Tepepan Xochimilco, 16020 Mexico DF,
    Mexico
    Playtex Mexicana SA de DV, Av. Constituyentes 908-C, Col. Lomas Altas,
    Mexico 10 DF, Mexico

SBC COMMUNICATIONS INC   175 E Houston, San Antonio, TX 78205,
  Tel: (210) 821-4105
  (Telecommunications)
    SBC Communications Inc., Mexico

SCHENECTADY INTERNATIONAL INC   PO Box 1046, Schenectady, NY 12301,
  Tel: (518) 370-4200
  (Mfr elec insulating varnishes, enamels, phenolic resins, alkylphenols)
    Schenectady Mexico SA de CV, Col. Aragon, Deleg. Gustavo A. Madero,
    Patdo. Postal 118-014, 07000 Mexico DF, Mexico

SCHLAGE LOCK CO   2401 Bayshore Blvd, San Francisco, CA 94134,
  Tel: (415) 467-1100
  (Locks, builders hardware)
    Schlage de Mexico SA, Viaducto Miguel Aleman 525, Mexico DF, Mexico

SCHOLASTIC INC   555 Broadway, New York, NY 10012, Tel: (212) 343-6100
  (Pub/distr educational & children's magazines, books, software)
    Scholastic Mexico, Bretana 99, Col. Zacahuitzco, 03550 Mexico DF, Mexico

A SCHULMAN INC   3550 W Market St, Akron, OH 44333, Tel: (216) 666-3751
  (Mfr/sale plastic resins & compounds)
    A. Schulman, Bosques de Duraznas 65 #401B, 11700 Bosques de las Lomas, Mexico DF,
    Mexico

(cont)

A. Schulman, Camino del Lago 4517, Sector 4, Colonia Cortijo del Rio, 64890 Monterrey, NL, Mexico

SCI SYSTEMS INC   PO Box 1000, Huntsville, AL 35807, Tel: (205) 882-4800
(R/D & mfr electronics systems for commerce, industry, aerospace, etc)
Adelantos de Tecnologia SA de CV, Apartado Postal 1-1874, Guadalajara, Mexico

SEA-LAND SERVICE INC   150 Allen Rd, Liberty Corner, NJ 07920,
Tel: (201) 558-6000
(Container transport)
AEM Representates, Calle Vallejo 1830, Edif. Administration, Mexico DF, Mexico
Sea-Land Service Inc., Tuxpan 2-504, Col. Roma, Mexico DF, Mexico

G D SEARLE & CO   5200 Old Orchard Rd, Skokie, IL 60077, Tel: (708) 982-7000
(Mfr pharms, health care & optical prdts, specialty chems)
Searle de Mexico SA de CV, Aptdo. Postal 1848, 06000 Mexico DF, Mexico

SEARS ROEBUCK & CO   Sears Tower, Chicago, IL 60684, Tel: (312) 875-2500
(Diversified general merchandise)
Sears Roebuck de Mexico SA, San Luis Potosi 214, Mexico DF, Mexico

SEVEN OAKS INTL INC   700 Colonial Rd, #100, Memphis, TN 38117,
Tel: (901) 683-7055
(Marketing coupon processing)
Siete Robles Intl., Prolongacion Hermanos Escobar 6965, Apartado Postal 3113-J, 32320 Juarez, Mexico

SHURE BROS INC   222 Hartrey Ave, Evanston, IL 60202-3696, Tel: (708) 866-2200
(Mfr microphones, teleconferencing sys, circuitry prdts)
Sonidos Selectos de Sonora SA de CV, Calle 12, Av. 10 y 11, Agua Prieta, Sonora, Mexico
Sonidos Selectos de Sonora SA de CV, Melquiades Alanis 5885, Cd. Juarez, Chih., Mexico

SIMON & SCHUSTER INC   1230 Ave of the Americas, New York, NY 10020,
Tel: (212) 698-7000
(Publisher)
Prentice-Hall Hispanoamericana SA, Aptdo. Postal 126, Naucalpan, Edo. de Mexico, Mexico

J R SIMPLOT CO INC   999 Main St, #1300, Boise, ID 83702, Tel: (208) 336-2110
(Fresh/frozen fruits & vegetables, animal feeds, fertilizers)
Congeladora y Empacadora Peninsular SA, Carretera Campeche Lerma, Campeche 24000, Mexico

SKIL CORP   4801 W Peterson Ave, Chicago, IL 60646, Tel: (312) 286-7330
(Portable electric power tools)
Skiltools de Mexico SA de CV, Calz. Proton 14, Parque Industrial Naucalpan, Mexico DF, Mexico

A O SMITH CORP   11270 W Park Pl, Milwaukee, WI 53224, Tel: (414) 359-4000
(Auto & truck frames, motors, water heaters, storage/handling sys, plastics, railroad prdts)
Metalsa SA de CV, Av. Churubusco Nte. 3890, Monterrey, NL, Mexico

SMITH INTL INC   16740 Hardy St, Houston, TX 77032, Tel: (713) 443-3370
   (Mfr/serv downhole drilling equip)
      Industrias Smith Intl. SA de CV, San Nicolas #56, Fracc. Ind. San Nicolas,
         54030 Tlalnepantla, Edo. de Mexico, Mexico

SNAP-ON TOOLS CORP   2801 80th St, Kenosha, WI 53141-1410, Tel: (414) 656-5200
   (Mfr automotive & ind maint serv tools)
      Herramientas Snap-On de Mexico SA, Aptdo. Postal 78-035,
         Av. M. Othon de Mendizabel Ote. 497-A, Col. Nueva Ind. Vallejo, 07700 Mexico

SONOCO PRODUCTS CO   North Second St, PO Box 160, Hartsville, SC 29550,
   Tel: (803) 383-7000
   (Mfr packaging for consumer & ind mkt)
      Especialidades Cilindricas de Carton SA de CV, Av. San Lorenzo 279 Local 8,
         Iztapalapa, 09860 Mexico DF, Mexico
      Fibro Tambor SA de CV, 16 de Septiembre 200, Aptdo. Postal 615,
         53370 Naucalpan de Juarez, Edo. de Mexico, Mexico
      Manufacturos Gargo SA de CV, Ignacio Zaragoza 15, Apdto. Postal 7, Edo. de Mexico,
         Mexico
      Sonoco de Mexico SA, Aptdo. Postal 92 bis, Centro de la Ciudad, Deleg. Cuauhtemoc,
         Mexico DF, Mexico

SPALDING & EVENFLO COS INC   5750A N Hoover Blvd, Tampa, FL 33614,
   Tel: (813) 887-5200
   (Mfr sports equip, infant & juvenile furniture & accessories)
      Evenflo Mexico SA, Aptdo. Postal 18939, Mexico DF, Mexico

SPI PHARMACEUTICALS INC   ICN Plaza, 3300 Hyland Ave, Costa Mesa, CA 92626,
   Tel: (714) 545-0100
   (Mfr pharms, biochems, radioactive materials)
      ICN Farmaceutica/ICN Grossman SA, Cal. de Tlanpan 2021, 04040 Mexico DF, Mexico

SPRAGUE DEVICES INC   107 Eastwood Rd, Michigan City, IN 46360,
   Tel: (219) 872-7295
   (Mfr heavy duty windshield wiper/washer sys & components)
      Sprague SA de CV, Calle 9 #6, Fracc. Alce Blanco, Naucalpan, Edo. de Mexico, Mexico

SPRINGFIELD WIRE INC   243 Cottage St, Box 638, Springfield, MA 01102-0638,
   Tel: (413) 781-6950
   (Mfr heating elements for ind)
      Springfield Wire de Mexico, all mail to Box 638, Springfield, MA 01101

SPRINGS INDUSTRIES INC   205 N White St, PO Box 70, Fort Mill, SC 29716,
   Tel: (803) 547-1500
   (Mfr & sales home furnishings, finished fabrics, ind textiles)
      Springs de Mexico, Benjamin Franklin 161, Piso 4, Col. Condesa, 06140 Mexico DF,
         Mexico

SPRINT INTERNATIONAL   12490 Sunrise Valley Dr, Reston, VA 22096,
   Tel: (703) 689-6000
   (Telecommunications)
      Sprint International Mexico SA de CV, Paseo de la Reforma 51, Oficina 1703,
         Col. Revolucion, 06030 Mexico DF, Mexico

SPS TECHNOLOGIES INC   301 Highland Ave, Jenkintown, PA 19046-2630,
   Tel: (215) 572-3000
   (Mfr aerospace & ind fasteners, tightening sys, magnetic materials, superalloys)

(cont)

Unbrako Mexicana SA de CV, Aptdo. Postal 55424, Paseo de Antioquia 14,
  Col. Lomas Estrella, 09890 Mexico DF, Mexico

SPX CORP   700 Terrace Point Dr, PO Box 3301, Muskegon, MI   49443-3301,
  Tel: (616) 724-5000
  (Mfr spec service tools, engine & drive-train parts)
    Camisa SA de CV, Privado los Trevina 500, Aptdo. Postal 1126, CP 64000 Monterrey,
      NL, Mexico
    Promec, M. de Cervantes Saavedra 255, Col. Ampliacion Granada, Del. Miguel Hidalgo,
      11520 Mexico DF, Mexico
    Sealed Power Mexicana SA de CV, Calle 8 #6, Aptdo. Postal 104,
      CP 53370 Naucalpan de Juarez, Mexico
    Sealed Power Mexicana SA de CV, Km. 0.3 Carretera Maravillas Jesus Maria,
      Aptdo. Postal 1766, CP 20900 Aguascalientes, Mexico

STA-RITE INDUSTRIES INC   293 Wright St, Delavan, WI   53115,
  Tel: (414) 728-5551
  (Mfr water pumps, filters & systems)
    Sta-Rite Foreign Sales Corp., Rio Tiber 99-601B, Col. Cuauhtemoc, 06500 Mexico DF,
      Mexico

STANDEX INTL CORP   6 Manor Pkwy, Salem, NH   03079, Tel: (603) 893-9701
  (Mfr diversified graphics, institutional, ind/electr & consumer prdts)
    S.I. de Mexico SA de CV, Calle Primera 2550, Agua Prieta, Sonora, Mexico

THE STANLEY WORKS   1000 Stanley Dr, PO Box 7000, New Britain, CT   06050,
  Tel: (203) 225-5111
  (Mfr hand tools & hardware)
    Bostitch-Mexico, Aptdo. Postal 15-066, 02300 Mexico DF, Mexico
    Bostitch-Mexico, Defensores de la Republica 999, Fracc. los Pinos, Col. Obrera,
      Puebla, Pue., Mexico
    Herramientas Stanley SA de CV, Aptdo. Postal 675, Puebla, Pue., Mexico

STEINER CORP   505 E South Temple St, Salt Lake City, UT   84102,
  Tel: (801) 328-8831
  (Linen supply service)
    Blacomex, Postes 227, Tadubaya, Mexico DF, Mexico

STEPAN CO   22 W Frontage Rd, Northfield, IL   60093, Tel: (708) 446-7500
  (Mfr basic & intermediate chems)
    Stepan Mexico, Avda. Uniones, Zona Industrial, Matamoros, Mexico

STIEFEL LABORATORIES INC   255 Alhambra Circle, Coral Gables, FL   33134,
  Tel: (305) 443-3807
  (Mfr pharmaceuticals, dermatological specialties)
    Stiefel Mexicana SA de CV, Eje Nte., Sur No. 11, Neuvo Parque Industrial,
      76808 San Juan del Rio, Qro., Mexico

STOKES DIV   5500 Tabor Rd, Philadelphia, PA   19120, Tel: (215) 289-5671
  (Vacuum pumps & components, vacuum dryers, oil-upgrading equip)
    Pennwalt Inter-Americana SA, Aptdo. Postal 24, Suc. "A" Ciudad Satelite,
      Estado de Mexico, Mexico

STONE CONTAINER CORP   150 N Michigan Ave, Chicago, IL   60601-7568,
  Tel: (312) 346-6600
  (Mfr paper & paper packaging)

Empaques de Carton Titan, Aptdo. Postal 339, Col. Del Valle, 66220 Garza Gardia,
   NL, Mexico

STUART ENTERTAINMENT INC   400 E Mineral Ave, Littleton, CO   80122,
   Tel: (303) 795-2625
   (Mfr bingo equip & supplies)
      Stuart Entertainment SA de CV, Avda. Industrial Falcon,
      Parque Industrial del Norte, Reynosa, Mexico

SULLAIR CORP   3700 E Michigan Blvd, Michigan City, IN   46360,
   Tel: (219) 879-5451
   (Refrigeration sys, vacuum pumps, generators, etc)
      Sullair Mexicana SA de CV, Av. Coyoacan 806, Esq. San Borja, Mexico DF, Mexico

SUN ELECTRIC CORP   One Sun Pkwy, Crystal Lake, IL   60014-2299,
   Tel: (815) 459-7700
   (Mfr auto tune-up, diagnostic & emission testing equip)
      Sun Electric de Mexico SA de CV, Aptdo. Postal 525, Mexico DF, Mexico

SUNBEAM CORP   200 E Las Olas Blvd, #2100, Ft Lauderdale, FL   33301,
   Tel: (305) 767-2100
   (Mfr household & personal grooming appliances)
      Sunbeam Mexicana SA de CV, Via Dr. Gustavo Baz P. 180, Tlalnepantla,
      Edo. de Mexico, Mexico

SUPERIOR GRAPHITE CO   120 S Riverside Plaza, Chicago, IL   60606,
   Tel: (312) 559-2999
   (Mfr natural & synthetic graphites, electrodes, lubricants, suspensions, carbide &
   carbon)
      Grafito Superior SA, Blvd. Rodriguez y Veracruz, Edificio Isabel, Hermosillo,
      Sonora, Mexico

SUPERIOR INDUSTRIES INTL INC   7800 Woodley Ave, Van Nuys, CA   91406,
   Tel: (818) 781-4973
   (Mfr cast aluminum auto wheels & auto accessories)
      Industrias Universales Unidas de Mexico, Tijuana, Mexico

SWECO INC   7120 New Buffington Rd, PO Box 1509, Florence, KY   41042-1509,
   Tel: (606) 727-5100
   (Mfr vibratory process & solids control equip)
      Swequipos SA, Av. Ejercito Nacional 752, Mexico DF, Mexico

SYBRON INTL CORP   411 E Wisconsin Ave, Milwaukee, WI   53202,
   Tel: (414) 274-6600
   (Mfr prdts for laboratories, professional orthodontic & dental mkts)
      ETM Corp. de Mexico SA de CV, Blvd. Benito Juarez Km. 5.5,
      Centro Industrial Nelson, Mexicali, BC, Mexico
      Ormco de Mexico SA de CV, Insurgentes Sur 263, Piso 5, Esquina con Alvaro Obregon,
      Col. Roma, CP 06700, Mexico
      Ormex SA de CV, Apartdo Postal 25F, Aeropuerto Merida, Mexico

SYSTEMS ENGINEERING LABS INC   6901 W Sunrise Blvd, Fort Lauderdale,
   FL 33313, Tel: (305) 587-2900
   (Digital computers)
      Sistemas Interactivos Cientificos SA de CV, Colorado 24, Col. Napoles, Mexico DF,
      Mexico

TEKTRONIX INC   26660 SW Parkway, Wilsonville, OR 97070, Tel: (503) 627-7111
  (Mfr test & meas, visual sys & commun prdts)
    Tektronix SA de CV, Coyoacan (Mexico City), Mexico

TELEDYNE INC   2049 Century Park East, Los Angeles, CA 90067-3101,
  Tel: (310) 277-3311
  (Divers mfg: aviation & electronics, specialty metals, industrial & consumer prdts)
    Teledyne Mexico, Av. Sonora 166, 3 piso, 06100 Mexico DF, Mexico

TELLABS INC   4951 Indiana Ave, Lisle, IL 60532, Tel: (708) 969-8800
  (Design/mfr/svce voice/data transport & network access sys)
    Tellabs SA de CV, Presidente Masarik 274, Colonia Chapultepec Morales,
      11560 Mexico, Mexico

TEMPLE-INLAND INC   Drawer N, Diboll, TX 75941, Tel: (409) 829-1313
  (Mfr paper, packaging, bldg prdts; financial services)
    Temple-Inland Inc., San Jose Iturbide & Monterrey, Mexico

TENNECO AUTOMOTIVE   111 Pfingsten Rd, Deerfield, IL 60015,
  Tel: (708) 948-0900
  (Automotive parts, exhaust sys, service equip)
    Monroe Mexico SA de CV, Av. Poniente 4, #118, CD Industrial, 38010 Celaya, Gto.,
      Mexico

TENNESSEE ASSOCIATES INTL   223 Associates Blvd, PO Box 710, Alcoa,
  TN 37701-0710, Tel: (423) 982-9514
  (Mgt consulting servs)
    TAI de Mexico SA de CV, Paseo Pinos 5516, Col. Lomas del Paseo, 64920 Monterrey,
      NL, Mexico

TEXAS INSTRUMENTS INC   13500 N Central Expwy, Dallas, TX 75265,
  Tel: (214) 995-2011
  (Mfr semiconductor devices, electr/electro-mech sys, instr & controls)
    Texas Instruments de Mexico SA, Calle 18E 507, Ciudad Industrial, Aguascalientes,
      Ags., Mexico

TEXAS REFINERY CORP   840 North Main, Fort Worth, TX 76101,
  Tel: (817) 332-1161
  (Mfr bldg maintenance prdts & spec lubricants)
    Texas Refinery Corp. de Mexico SA, Mier y Peasdo 26, Esq. Netzahualcoyotl 82,
      Mexico DF, Mexico

TEXTRON INC   40 Westminster St, Providence, RI 02903, Tel: (401) 421-2800
  (Mfr aerospace, ind & consumer prdts; fin servs)
    Textron SA de CV, 159 Sinaloa St. Colonia Roma, Industrial Vallejo,
      06700 Mexico DF, Mexico

THERMO ELECTRON CORP   101 First Ave, Waltham, MA 02154, Tel: (617) 890-8700
  (Devel/mfr of process equip & instru for energy intensive inds)
    Thermo Electron SA de CV, Div. AER, Campos Eliseos 115, Polanco, Mexico DF, Mexico

THOMAS & BETTS CORP   1555 Lynnfield Rd, Memphis, TN 38119,
  Tel: (901) 682-7766
  (Mfr elect/electr connectors & accessories)
    Thomas & Betts de Mexico SA de CV, Carlos Areliano 6, Centro Comercial Satelite,
      53100 Naucalpan, Mexico

THOMAS BUILT BUSES INC   1408 Courtesy Rd, PO Box 2450, High Point, NC 27261,
  Tel: (910) 889-4871
  (Mfr buses & bus chassis)
    Thomas Build Buses de Mexico SA de CV, Apdo. Postal 105, CP 66600 Apodaca, NL,
    Mexico

THOR POWER TOOL CO   72 Bayside Rd, Virginia Beach, VA 23455,
  Tel: (804) 323-5666
  (Mfr portable air-operated & elect tools)
    Herramientas Thor de Mexico SA, Aptdo. Postal 12-642, Mexico DF, Mexico

TIDEWATER INC   Tidewater Place, 1440 Canal St, New Orleans, LA 70112,
  Tel: (504) 568-1010
  (Marine serv & equip to companies engaged in explor, development & prod of oil, gas &
  minerals)
    Servicios Maritimos des SA de RL, Calle 26A x37 x23B, Centro,
      24100 Ciudad del Carmen, Campeche, Mexico
    Transportadora y Abastecedora del Gulfo SA, Calle 26A x37 x23B, Centro,
      24100 Ciudad del Carmen, Campeche, Mexico

TIME WARNER INC   75 Rockefeller Plaza, New York, NY 10019,
  Tel: (212) 484-8000
  (Communications, publishing, entertainment)
    Time-Life de Mexico SA de CV, Leibnitz 13-8, Aptdo. Postal 5-592, Mexico DF, Mexico

TOOTSIE ROLL INDUSTRIES INC   7401 S Cicero Ave, Chicago, IL 60629,
  Tel: (312) 838-3400
  (Mfr candies, chocolate prd*s)
    Tutsi SA de CV, Caneis 277, Col. Granjas Mexico, 08400 Mexico DF, Mexico

TORK INC   1 Grove St, Mount Vernon, NY 10550, Tel: (914) 664-3542
  (Mfr time & photoelectric controls)
    Tork Electro Sistemas SA de CV, Calle Hortensia 97, Col. los Angeles,
      Delg. Iztapalapa DF, Mexico

TOWERS PERRIN   245 Park Ave, New York, NY 10167, Tel: (212) 309-3400
  (Management consultants)
    Towers, Perrin, Forster & Crosby de Mexico, Bosque de Duraznos 65, 101B-C,
      Bosques de Las Lomas, 11700 Mexico DF, Mexico
    Towers, Perrin, Forster & Crosby de Mexico, also in Chihuahua,
      Guadalajara & Juarez, Mexico

TRACOR INC   6500 Tracor Lane, Austin, TX 78725-2000, Tel: (512) 926-2800
  (Time & frequency prdts, gas & liquid chromatographs, eng serv, ship repair)
    Tracor Littlefuse SA de CV, Xicotencatl 306 Sur, Piedras Negras, Coahuila, Mexico

TRANE CO   3600 Pammel Creek Rd, La Crosse, WI 54601, Tel: (608) 787-2000
  (Mfr/distr/svce A/C sys & equip)
    Trane Mexico, Felix Guzman 21, Col. El Parque, 53390 Naucalpan, Edo. de Mexico,
      Mexico
    Trane Monterrey, Av. San Jeronimo 401-B Pte., Col. San Jeronimo, 64640 Monterrey,
      NL, Mexico

TRANS WORLD AIRLINES INC   505 N 6th St, St Louis, MO 63101,
  Tel: (314) 589-3000
  (Air transportation)
    Trans World Airlines, Cancun, Mexico

(cont)

Trans World Airlines, Ixtapa-Zihuatanejo, Mexico
Trans World Airlines, Mexico DF, Mexico
Trans World Airlines Inc., Puerto Vallarta, Mexico
Trans World Airlines Inc., Intl. Playa de Oro, Manzanilla, Mexico

TRICO TECHNOLOGIES CORP   1995 Billy Mitchell, Brownsville, TX 78521,
 Tel: (512) 544-2722
 (Mfr windshield wiper sys & components)
  Trico Componentes SA de CV, Av. Michigan 200, Parque Finsa H. Matamaoros,
   Tamaulipas, Mexico

TRINITY INDUSTRIES INC   PO Box 568887, Dallas, TX 75356-8887,
 Tel: (214) 631-4420
 (Mfr heavy metal prdts)
  Grupo TATSA SA de CV, Mexico City, Mexico

TRINOVA CORP   3000 Strayer, PO Box 50, Maumee, OH 43537-0050,
 Tel: (419) 867-2200
 (Mfr engr components & sys for ind)
  Aeroquip Mexicana SA de CV, Ingenieros Militares 105, Mexico DF, Mexico

TRW INC   1900 Richmond Rd, Cleveland, OH 44124, Tel: (216) 291-7000
 (Electr & energy-related prdts, automotive & aerospace prdts, tools & fasteners)
  Industrias Medina SA de CV, Aptdo. Postal E-29, Leon, Gto., Mexico
  Manufacturas y Servicios Industriales SA, Aptdo. Postal 16-157, Mexico DF, Mexico
  Mo-Re-Sa, Calle Norte 35 #895, Col. Industrial Vallejo, Mexico DF, Mexico
  TRW Electronics SA de CV, Administration de Correos 5, Guadalajara, Jalisco, Mexico

TYSON FOODS INC   P.O. Box 2020, Springdale, AR 72765, Tel: (501) 290-4000
 (Production/mfr/distr poultry, beef, port & seafood prdts)
  Trasgo, Valle del Guadiana y Cuatrocienegas, Gomez Palacio, 35070 Durango, Mexico

UNION CARBIDE CORP   39 Old Ridgebury Rd, Danbury, CT 06817,
 Tel: (203) 794-2000
 (Mfr industrial chemicals, plastics, resins)
  Union Carbide Mexicana, Chemicals & Plastics, Caragoca South 1300, Apt. 204,
   Monterrey, NL, Mexico

UNION PACIFIC CORP   Eighth & Eaton Aves, Bethlehem, PA 18018,
 Tel: (215) 861-3200
 (Holding co: railroad, crude oil, natural gas, petroleum refining, metal mining serv,
 real estate)
  Union Pacific Railroad Co., Homero 1804-802, Col. Los Morales,
   Deleg. Miguel Hidalgo, 11510 Mexico DF, Mexico

UNIROYAL INC   World Headquarters, Middlebury, CT 06749, Tel: (203) 573-2000
 (Tires, tubes & other rubber prdts, chems, plastics, textiles)
  Uniroyal SA, Lago Aullagas 60, Mexico DF, Mexico
  Uniroyal SA, Queretaro, Que., Mexico

UNISYS CORP   PO Box 500, Blue Bell, PA 19424, Tel: (215) 986-4011
 (Mfg/mktg/serv electr info sys)
  Compubur SA de CV, 1338 Calle 3, 44940 Guadalajara, Mexico
  Sperry SA de CV, Presidente Masaryk 291, Col. Palanco, 11560 Mexico DF, Mexico
  Unisys de Mexico SA de CV, Londres 102, 06600 Mexico DF, Mexico

UNITED CATALYSTS INC   1227 S 12th St, PO Box 32370, Louisville, KY 40232,
Tel: (502) 634-7200
(Mfr catalysts for petroleum, chem & food inds)
  Quimica Somex SA de CV, Aptdo. Postal 19-201, 03910 Mexico DF, Mexico

UNITED PRESS INTL   1400 I St, Washington, DC 20005, Tel: (202) 898-8000
(Collection & distributor of news, newspictures, fin data)
  United Press Intl., Aptdo. Postal 91, Mexico DF, Mexico

UNITEK CORP/3M   2724 S Peck Rd, Monrovia, CA 91016-7118, Tel: (818) 574-4000
(Mfr orthodontic prdts)
  Unitek/3M Mexico SA de CV, Calz. San Juan de Aragon 516, Col. C. Lardizabael,
  Del. G. A. Madero, 07070 Mexico DF, Mexico

UNIVERSAL CORP   PO Box 25099, Richmond, VA 23260, Tel: (804) 359-9311
(Holding co: tobacco, commodities)
  Casa Export Ltd., Aptdo. Postal 490, Tepic, Nayarit, Mexico

UNIVERSAL FOODS CORP   433 E Michigan St, Milwaukee, WI 53202,
Tel: (414) 271-6755
(Mfr food prdts & food ingredients)
  Warner-Jenkinson SA de CV, Hacienda de la Gabia 35, 53310 Exhegaray, Mexico

UNIVERSAL WEATHER & AVIATION INC   8787 Tallyho Rd, Houston, TX 77061,
Tel: (713) 944-1622
(Airport services)
  UASCO SA de CV, Fuerza Aerea Mexicana 380-C, Mexico DF, Mexico

UPJOHN CO   7000 Portage Rd, Kalamazoo, MI 49001, Tel: (616) 323-4000
(Mfr pharms, agric prdts, ind chems)
  Asgrow Mexicana SA de CV, Bravoy Septima, Matamoros, Tamps., Mexico
  Upjohn SA de CV, Calz. de Tlalpan 2962, Mexico DF, Mexico

USG CORP   125 S Franklin, Chicago, IL 60606, Tel: (312) 606-4122
(Holding co: bldg prdts ind)
  Yeso Panamericano, Providencia 334-7, Aptdo. Postal 27-418, 03100 Mexico DF, Mexico

VALENITE INC   PO Box 9636, Madison Heights, MI 48071-9636,
Tel: (810) 589-1000
(Cemented carbide, high speed steel, ceramic & diamond cutting tool prdts, etc)
  Valenite de Mexico SA de CV, Blvd. Plan de Guadalupa 100, Esquina con Matamoros,
  25900 Ramos Arizpe, Coahuila, Mexico

VAN HEUSEN CO   1290 Ave of the Americas, New York, NY 10019,
Tel: (212) 541-5200
(Wearing apparel)
  Van Heusen de Mexico SA, Paseo de la Reforma 509, Mexico DF, Mexico

VAREL MFG CO   9230 Denton Rd, PO Box 540157, Dallas, TX 75354-0157,
Tel: (214) 351-6486
(Mfr oil, mining, geophysical, water-well & constr equip)
  VMC de Matamoros, Calle 3a Sur y Michoacan 312, Apdo. Postal 217, H. Matamoros,
  Tamps. Mexico
  Varel de Mexico, Calle 3a Sur y Michoacan 312, H. Matamoros, Tamps., Mexico

VARIAN ASSOCIATES INC   3100 Hansen Way, Palo Alto, CA 94304-1030,
   Tel: (415) 493-4000
   (Mfr microwave tubes & devices, analytical instru, semiconductor process & med equip,
   vacuum sys)
      Varian SA, Liverpool 96, Col. Juarez, 06600 Mexico DF, Mexico

VARITY CORP   672 Delaware Ave, Buffalo, NY 14209, Tel: (716) 888-8000
   (Mfr farm & ind machinery, diesel engines, automotive components, electromechanical
   prdts)
      Min-Cer SA, Madrid 21, Colonia Tabaciera, 03060 Mexico DF, Mexico

VIACOM INC   200 Elm St, Dedham, MA 02026, Tel: (617) 461-1600
   (Communications, publishing, entertainment)
      Prentice Hall Hispanoamerica SA, San Andres Atato 157, 53500 Naucalpan de Juarez,
      Mexico

VIRCO MANUFACTURING CORP   2027 Harpers Way, Torrance, CA 90501,
   Tel: (310) 533-0474
   (Mfr non-wood office furniture, public bldg furniture)
      Virsan SA de CV, Calz Constitucion y Rio Mayo S/N, San Luis Rio Colorado, Sonora,
      Mexico

VULCAN MATERIALS CO   1 Metroplex Dr, Birmingham, AL 35209,
   Tel: (205) 877-3000
   (Mfr constr materials & ind chems)
      Vulcan Materials Co., all mail to PO Box 531207, Birmingham, AL 35253

WACKENHUT CORP   1500 San Remo Ave, Coral Gables, FL 33146,
   Tel: (305) 666-5656
   (Security systems & services)
      Grupo Wackenhut SA de CV, Mar Mediterraneo 133, Col. Popotla, 11400 Mexico DF,
      Mexico
      Grupo Wackenhut SA de CV, other locations in Mexico

WAL-MART STORES INC   702 SW 8th St, Bentonville, AR 72716-8611,
   Tel: (501) 273-4000
   (Retailer)
      Wal-Mart Stores Inc., Mexico

WARD HOWELL INTL INC   99 Park Ave, New York, NY 10016-1699,
   Tel: (212) 697-3730
   (Executive recruiting)
      Rexer Seleccion de Ejecutivos SC, Blvd. Adolfo Lopez Mateos 20, Col. San Angel Inn,
      01060 Mexico DF, Mexico

WARNACO INC   90 Park Ave, New York, NY 10016, Tel: (212) 661-1300
   (Intimate apparel, men's & women's shirts, ski & sportswear)
      Warner's de Mexico SA de CV, Londres 75, Mexico DF, Mexico

WARNER BROS INTL TELEVISION DISTRIBUTION   4000 Warner Blvd, Burbank,
   CA 91522, Tel: (818) 954-4068
   (Distr TV programming & theatrical features)
      Warner Bros. (Mexico) SA, Acapulco 37, 06140 Mexico DF, Mexico

WARNER-JENKINSON CO INC   2526 Baldwin St, St Louis, MO 63106,
  Tel: (314) 889-7600
  (Mfr synthetic & natural colors for food, drugs & cosmetics)
    Warner-Jenkinson Mexico, Av. Lomas Verdes 791, piso 1, Col. Jardines de Satelite,
      CP 53000 Naucalpan, Mexico

WARNER-LAMBERT CO   201 Tabor Road, Morris Plains, NJ 07950,
  Tel: (201) 540-2000
  (Mfr ethical & proprietary pharms, confectionary & consumer prdts)
    Cia. Mecidinal la Campana SA, Av. Division del Norte 3443, 04620 Mexico DF, Mexico

WATLOW ELECTRIC MFG CO   12001 Lackland Rd, St Louis, MO 63146-4039,
  Tel: (314) 878-4600
  (Mfr elec heating units, electr controls, thermocouple wire, metal-sheathed cable,
  infrared sensors)
    Watlow de Mexico, Colon 6, Despacho 103, Col. Centro, CP 76000 Queretaro, Mexico

THE WEST BEND CO   400 Washington St, West Bend, WI 53095, Tel: (414) 334-2311
  (Mfr small elec appliances, cookware, water distillers, timers)
    West Bend de Mexico, all mail to P.O. Box 5479, McAllen, TX 78502

WEST CHEMICAL PRODUCTS INC   1000 Herrontown Rd, Princeton, NJ 08540,
  Tel: (609) 921-0501
  (Sanitary equip & supplies)
    West de Mexico SA, Pultarco-Elias Calles 27, Mexico DF, Mexico

THE WEST CO   101 Gordon Dr, PO Box 645, Lionville, PA 19341-0645,
  Tel: (610) 594-2900
  (Mfr prdts for filling, sealing, dispensing & delivering needs of health care &
  consumer prdts mkts)
    Aluplast SA de CV, Mexico
    Pharma-Tap SA de CV, Mexico
    West Rubber de Mexico SA, Mexico DF, Mexico

WESTERN ATLAS INTL INC   10205 Westheimer, PO Box 1407, Houston,
  TX 77251-1407, Tel: (713) 266-5700
  (Full service to the oil industry)
    Western Geophysical, Gral. Garcia Conde Palomas 64, Col. Reforma Social,
      11650 Mexico DF, Mexico

WESTINGHOUSE ELECTRIC CORP   11 Stanwix St, Pittsburgh, PA 15222-1384,
  Tel: (412) 244-2000
  (TV/radio broadcasting, mfr electr sys for ind/defense, fin & environmental servs)
    Westinghouse Electric Co. SA, Homero 1804, Col. Chapultepec Morales,
      Aptdo. Postal 10-1023, Mexico DF, Mexico

WHEATON INDUSTRIES   1101 Wheaton Ave, Milville, NJ 08332, Tel: (609) 825-1400
  (Mfr glass & plastic containers, plastic prdts)
    Plasticos Wheaton de Mexico SA, Naucalpan, Edo. de Mexico, Mexico

WHIRLPOOL CORP   2000 N M-63, Benton Harbor, MI 49022-2692,
  Tel: (616) 923-5000
  (Mfr/mkt home appliances)
    Vitromatic SA de CV, Avda. San Nicolas 2121 N, Monterrey, N.L., Mexico

WHITE CONSOLIDATED INDUSTRIES INC   11770 Berea Rd, Cleveland, OH 44111,
    Tel: (216) 252-3700
    (Major household appliances, ind mach & equip)
      Wirz & Machuca SA, Xocotitia 119, Mexico DF, Mexico

W A WHITNEY CO   650 Race St, PO Box 1206, Rockford, IL 61105-1206,
    Tel: (815) 964-6771
    (Mfr hydraulic punch/plasma cutting metal fabricating equip)
      W.A. Whitney de Mexico SA, Viveros de la Colina 24, 54080 Tlalnepantla, Mexico

WITCO CORP   1 American Lane, Greenwich, CT 06831-4236, Tel: (203) 552-2000
    (Mfr chem & petroleum prdts)
      Argus Quimica Mexicana SA, Paseo de Guadalupe 410, 8 Cuautitlan, Edo. de Mexico,
      Mexico

WOODHEAD INDUSTRIES INC   2150 E Lake Cook Rd, #400, Buffalo Grove, IL 60089,
    Tel: (708) 465-8300
    (Devel/mfr/sale/distr elect/electr, fiber optic & ergonomic special-function,
    non-commodity prdts)
      Woodhead de Mexico SA de CV, Carretera Waterfill y Calle Manuel Quinones Ponce 2,
      32550 Nuevo Zaragosa, Chihuahua, Mexico

WOOLWORTH CORP   Woolworth Bldg, 233 Broadway, New York, NY 10279,
    Tel: (212) 553-2000
    (Retail stores, footwear, men's clothing)
      F.W. Woolworth Co., 250 Colonia Polanca, Mexico DF, Mexico

WORLD COURIER INC   46 Trinity Pl, New York, NY 10006, Tel: (718) 978-9400
    (Intl courier serv)
      World Courier de Mexico, Paseo de la Reforma 390, Mexico DF, Mexico
      World Couriers Inc., Mexico DF, Mexico

WYATT INDUSTRIES INC   6200 Kansas St, PO Box 3052, Houston, TX 77001,
    Tel: (713) 861-6141
    (Steel plate fabrications, prdts for energy ind)
      Corporacion de Suministros Petroleros, Cruz Galoca 169, Col. Nueva Santa Maria,
      Mexico DF, Mexico

WYNN OIL CO   1050 W Fifth St, Azusa, CA 91702-9510, Tel: (818) 334-0231
    (Mfr chem additives for oil, grease & fuels; hardware)
      Wynn's Friction Proofing Mexico SA de CV, Municipio Libre 114-A, Colonial Portales,
      03300 Mexico DF, Mexico

XEROX CORP   800 Long Ridge Rd, PO Box 1600, Stamford, CT 06904,
    Tel: (203) 968-3000
    (Mfr document processing equip, sys & supplies)
      Xerox Corp., Aguascalientes, Mexico
      Xerox Mexicana SA de CV, Bosque de Duraznos 61, Bosque de las Lomas,
      11700 Mexico DF, Mexico

YELLOW FREIGHT SYSTEM INC   10990 Roe Ave, Overland Park, KS 66211,
    Tel: (913) 345-3000
    (Commodity transportation)
      Yellow Freight Mexicana, Calzada Santa Cecilia, Tlanepantla, 54130 Mexico City,
      Mexico
      Yellow Freight Mexicana, also in Guadalajara, Monterrey & Nuevo Laredo, Mexico

YORK INTERNATIONAL CORP   PO Box 1592, York, PA   17405-1592,
   Tel: (717) 771-7890
   (Mfr A/C, heating & refrig sys & equip)
      York Aire SA, Carr. Miguel Aleman Km. 11.2, 66600 Apodaca, Aptdo. Postal 1900,
      Monterrey, N.L., Mexico

YOUNG & RUBICAM INC   285 Madison Ave, New York, NY   10017, Tel: (212) 210-3000
   (Advertising, public relations, direct marketing & sales promotion, corp & product ID
   management)
      Young & Rubicam SA de CV, Leibnitz 13, Col. Polanco, Mexico 5, DF, Mexico

ZEIGLER CATTLE CORP   Plaza Motor Hotel, Suite 1, El Paso, TX   79943,
   Tel: (915) 532-2401
   (Cattle)
      Zeigler Cattle Corp., Hotel Victoria, Juarez & Colon, Chihuahua, Mexico

ZENITH ELECTRONICS CORP   1000 Milwaukee Ave, Glenview, IL   60025,
   Tel: (708) 391-7000
   (Mfr/sales/svce consumer electronics, cable prdts, electr components)
      Cableproductos de Chihuahua SA de CV, Parque Industrial Las Americas,
      Prolong. Av. de Las Americas, Chihuahua, Mexico
      Electro Partes de Matamoros SA de CV, Carretera General Lauro Villar Km 4,
      #700 H. Matamoros, Tamaulipas, Mexico
      Partes de Television de Reynosa SA de CV, Matamoros y Brecha E-99, Carretera A,
      Aptdo. Postal 178, Reynosa, Tamaulipas, Mexico
      Zenco de Chihuahua SA de CV, Carretera Pan Americana, Parque Industrial Aeropuerto,
      32690 Ciudad Juarez, Chihuahua, Mexico

MONACO

BULAB HOLDINGS INC   1256 N McLean Blvd, Memphis, TN   38108,
   Tel: (901) 278-0330
   (Mfr microbicides, biocides, additives, corrosion inhibitors, chems)
      Buckman Laboratories SAM, 23 Boulevard Albert I, 98000 Monaco

CINCOM SYSTEMS INC   2300 Montana Ave, Cincinnati, OH   45211,
   Tel: (513) 662-2300
   (Devel/distr computer software)
      Cincom Systems Inc., Monaco

CITICORP   399 Park Ave, New York, NY   10043, Tel: (212) 559-1000
   (Banking & financial services)
      Citibank NA, Monaco

EATON CORP   1111 Superior Ave, Cleveland, OH   44114, Tel: (216) 523-5000
   (Advanced tech prdts for transp & ind mkts)
      Eaton SAM, 14 Boulevard du Bord de Mer, Monaco

FERREX INTL INC   26 Broadway, New York, NY 10004, Tel: (212) 509-7030
(Mfg/distr of road maint mach, welding & ind equip & supplies)
   Ferrex-Near East, Monte Carlo, Monaco

HORWATH INTL   415 Madison Ave, New York, NY 10017, Tel: (212) 838-5566
(Public accountants & auditors)
   Hoogewerf & Co. Secoma, 57 rue Grimaldi, 98000 Monaco

PAINEWEBBER GROUP INC   1285 Ave of the Americas, New York, NY 10019,
Tel: (212) 713-2000
(Stock brokerage serv & invest)
   PaineWebber Intl., Le George V, 14 Ave. de Grande-Bretagne, 98000 Monte Carlo,
   Monaco

MOROCCO

AIR EXPRESS INTL CORP   120 Tokeneke Rd, PO Box 1231, Darien, CT 06820,
Tel: (203) 655-7900
(Air frt forwarder)
   Air Express Intl., c/o T.S.T. Aeromaritime, 26 Blvd. de la Resistance, Casablanca,
   Morocco

AMERICAN APPRAISAL ASSOCS INC   411 E Wisconsin Ave, Milwaukee, WI 53202,
Tel: (414) 271-7240
(Valuation consulting serv)
   American Appraisal Maroc SA, Avenue des Far 28, 2100 Casablanca, Morocco

CITICORP   399 Park Ave, New York, NY 10043, Tel: (212) 559-1000
(Banking & financial services)
   Citibank, Morocco

COLGATE-PALMOLIVE CO   300 Park Ave, New York, NY 10022, Tel: (212) 310-2000
(Mfr pharms, cosmetics, toiletries, detergents)
   Colgate-Palmolive, Rue Fatima Bent M'Barek Azlif, Quarter Industriel Ain Sebaa,
   Boite Bostale 7565, Casablanca, Morocco

CPC INTERNATIONAL INC   PO Box 8000, Englewood Cliffs, NJ 07632,
Tel: (201) 894-4000
(Consumer foods, corn refining)
   CPC Maghreb SA, Bd Abdelmoumen/Angle Ave. des Pleides, 20100 Casablanca, Morocco

CROWN CORK & SEAL CO INC   9300 Ashton Rd, Philadelphia, PA 19136,
Tel: (215) 698-5100
(Mfr cans, bottle caps; filling & packaging mach)
   Crown Cork Co., Boite Postale 998, Chemin des Dahlias, Casablanca, Morocco

THE DOW CHEMICAL CO   2030 Dow Center, Midland, MI 48674, Tel: (517) 636-1000
(Mfr chems, plastics, pharms, agric prdts, consumer prdts)
   Lepetit-Pharmaghreb SA, 280 Blvd. Yacoub El Manscur, Casablanca, Morocco

THE GILLETTE CO   Prudential Tower, Boston, MA 02199, Tel: (617) 421-7000
(Devel/mfr personal care/use prdts: blades & razors, toiletries, cosmetics,
stationery)
   Gillette Interlame SA, Casablanca, Morocco
   Intermaghreb SA, Casablanca, Morocco

THE GOODYEAR TIRE & RUBBER CO   1144 E Market St, Akron, OH 44316,
Tel: (216) 796-2121
(Mfr tires, automotive belts & hose, conveyor belts, chemicals; oil pipeline
transmission)
   Goodyear Maroc SA, Autoroute de Rabat, Boite Postale 2550, Ain-es-Sebaa,
      Casablanca, Morocco

HORWATH INTL   415 Madison Ave, New York, NY 10017, Tel: (212) 838-5566
(Public accountants & auditors)
   Fiduciaire des Societies Marocaines, 7 rue Bendahan, DH-R.C. 18719 Casablanca,
      Morocco

HYATT INTL CORP   200 West Madison, Chicago, IL 60606, Tel: (312) 750-1234
(Intl hotel mgmt)
   Hyatt Intl. Hotels, Casablanca & Rabat, Morocco

ITT CORP   1330 Ave of the Americas, New York, NY 10019-5490,
Tel: (212) 258-1000
(Design/mfr communications & electronic equip, hotels, insurance)
   ITT Maroc, 1 Rue Louis Guillotte, Casablanca, Morocco

ITT SHERATON CORP   60 State St, Boston, MA 02108, Tel: (617) 367-3600
(Hotel operations)
   Sheraton Casablanca Hotel, 100 Ave. des F.A.R. Angle Rue Colbert,
      Boite Postale 15870, Casablanca 21804, Morocco

JOHNSON & JOHNSON   One Johnson & Johnson Plaza, New Brunswick, NJ 08933,
Tel: (908) 524-0400
(R&D/mfr/sale health care prdts)
   Johnson & Johnson Morocco SA, Boite Postale 15979, Casablanca, Morocco

MERCK SHARP & DOHME INTL   PO Box 2000, Rahway, NJ 07065, Tel: (201) 574-4000
(Pharms, chems & biologicals)
   Merck, Sharp & Dohme Intl., Immeuble Oceania, 1 Place Mirabeau, Casablanca, Morocco

MICROSOFT CORP   One Microsoft Way, Redmond, WA 98052-6399,
Tel: (206) 882-8080
(Computer software, peripherals & services)
   Microsoft Morocco, Casablanca, Morocco

MOBIL CORP   3225 Gallows Rd, Fairfax, VA 22037-0001, Tel: (703) 846-3000
(Petroleum explor & refining, mfr petrol prdts, chems, petrochems)
   Mobil Oil Maroc, 23 Rue Ali Ben Abdellah, Boite Postale 485, Casablanca, Morocco

McCANN-ERICKSON WORLDWIDE   750 Third Ave, New York, NY 10017,
   Tel: (212) 697-6000
   (Advertising)
     Shem's Publicite, 162 Blvd. d'Anfa, Casablanca, Morocco

OTIS ELEVATOR CO   10 Farm Springs, Farmington, CT 06032, Tel: (860) 676-6528
   (Mfr elevators & escalators)
     Otis Maroc SA, 39 Rue Vouziers, Angle Bd. Emile Zola, Casablanca, Morocco

PFIZER INC   235 E 42nd St, New York, NY 10017-5755, Tel: (212) 573-2323
   (Mfr healthcare products)
     Laboratoires Pfizer SA, Morocco
     Pfizer SA, Morocco

PROCTER & GAMBLE CO   One Procter & Gamble Plaza, Cincinnati, OH 45202,
   Tel: (513) 983-1100
   (Personal care, food, laundry, cleaning & ind prdts)
     Industries Marocaines Modernes SA, Km. 10, 400 Ancianne Route de Rabat,
       Ain-es-Sebaa, Casablanca, Morocco

STIEFEL LABORATORIES INC   255 Alhambra Circle, Coral Gables, FL 33134,
   Tel: (305) 443-3807
   (Mfr pharmaceuticals, dermatological specialties)
     Stiefel Maroc SA, Angel Bd., Abdelmoumen et Rue Soumaya, Imm. Renault, etage 6 #27,
       Casablanca, Morocco

U S WHEAT ASSOCIATES   1200 NW Front Ave, #600, Portland, OR 97209,
   Tel: (503) 223-8123
   (Market development for wheat prdts)
     U.S. Wheat Associates, 201 Rue Mustapha El Maani, Casablanca, Morocco

WACKENHUT CORP   1500 San Remo Ave, Coral Gables, FL 33146,
   Tel: (305) 666-5656
   (Security systems & services)
     Wackenhut Morocco Inc., 37 Rue 22 Hay el Have, Hay Hassani, Casablanca 02, Morocco

XEROX CORP   800 Long Ridge Rd, PO Box 1600, Stamford, CT 06904,
   Tel: (203) 968-3000
   (Mfr document processing equip, sys & supplies)
     Xerox Corp., Casablanca, Morocco

MOZAMBIQUE

LOUIS BERGER INTL INC   100 Halsted St, East Orange, NJ 07019,
      Tel: (201) 678-1960
      (Consulting engineers, architects, economicst & planners)
        Louis Berger Intl. Inc., P.O. Box 1947, Maputo, Mozambique

JOHNSON & JOHNSON   One Johnson & Johnson Plaza, New Brunswick, NJ 08933,
  Tel: (908) 524-0400
  (R&D/mfr/sale health care prdts)
    Johnson & Johnson (Mozambique) Ltda., Caixa Postal 2687, Maputo, Mozambique

PFIZER INC   235 E 42nd St, New York, NY 10017-5755, Tel: (212) 573-2323
  (Mfr healthcare products)
    Pfizer Ltda., Mozambique

WACKENHUT CORP   1500 San Remo Ave, Coral Gables, FL 33146,
  Tel: (305) 666-5656
  (Security systems & services)
    Wackenhut Intl., Av. Paulo Samuel, Kankhomba 280, Maputo, Mozambique

XEROX CORP   800 Long Ridge Rd, PO Box 1600, Stamford, CT 06904,
  Tel: (203) 968-3000
  (Mfr document processing equip, sys & supplies)
    Xerox Corp., Maputo, Mozambique

NETHERLANDS

3COM CORP   5400 Bayfront Plaza, Santa Clara, CA 95052-8145,
  Tel: (408) 764-5000
  (Devel/mfr computer networking prdts & sys)
    3Com Benelux BV, Netherlands

3M   3M Center, St Paul, MN 55144-1000, Tel: (612) 733-1110
  (Mfr diversified prdts for industry, health care, imaging, commun, transport, safety,
  consumer, etc)
    3M Nederland BV, The Industrieweg 24, 2382 NW Zoeterwoude, Netherlands

AAF INTL   215 Central Ave, PO Box 35690, Louisville, KY 40232-5690,
  Tel: (502) 637-0011
  (Mfr air filtration/pollution control & noise control equip)
    AAF-Intl. BV, P.O. Box 60, 7800 Abemmen, Netherlands
    AAF-Intl. BV, Egelenburg 2, P.O. Box 7928, 1008 AC Amsterdam, Netherlands

AAF-McQUAY INC   111 S Calvert St, #2800, Baltimore, MD 21202,
  Tel: (410) 528-2755
  (Mfr air quality control prdts: heating, ventilating, air-conditioning & filtration
  prdts & services)

(cont)

AAF International BV, Egelenburg 2, 1081 GK Amsterdam, Netherlands
SnyderGeneral Netherlands BV, Egelenburg 2, 1081 GK Amsterdam, Netherlands

AAR CORP   1111 Nicholas Blvd, Elk Grove Village, IL 60007,
  Tel: (708) 439-3939
  (Aviation repair & supply provisioning)
    AAR Allen Group Intl., Kruisweg 705, 2132 ND Hoofddorp, Netherlands

ABBOTT LABORATORIES   100 Abbott Park Rd, Abbott Park, IL 60064-3500,
  Tel: (708) 937-6100
  (Devel/mfr/sale diversified health care prdts & services)
    Abbott NV, Amsterdam, Netherlands

ACCO INTL INC   770 S Acco Plaza, Wheeling, IL 60090, Tel: (708) 541-9500
  (Paper fasteners & clips, metal fasteners, binders, staplers)
    Acco Nederland BV, Willem Alexanderweg 71, P.O. Box 150, Cothen/Utrecht, Netherlands

ACHESON COLLOIDS CO   PO Box 611747, Port Huron, MI 48061-1747,
  Tel: (810) 984-5581
  (Graphite, lubricants & specialty chems)
    Acheson Colloiden BV, Netherlands

ADAMAS CARBIDE CORP   Market & Passaic St, Kenilworth, NJ 07033,
  Tel: (201) 241-1000
  (Metal prdts)
    Duracarb BV, Parallelweg 25, P.O Box 52, Weert, Netherlands

AIR EXPRESS INTL CORP   120 Tokeneke Rd, PO Box 1231, Darien, CT 06820,
  Tel: (203) 655-7900
  (Air frt forwarder)
    Air Express Intl. Corp., Bldg. No. 105, Schiphol East, Netherlands

AIR PRODUCTS & CHEMICALS INC   7201 Hamilton Blvd, Allentown, PA 18195-1501,
  Tel: (215) 481-4911
  (Mfr ind gases & related equip, spec chems, environmental/energy sys)
    Air Products Nederland BV, P.O. Box 56, 100 Noordkade, 2740 AB Waddinxveen,
      Netherlands

ALBANY INTL CORP   PO Box 1907, Albany, NY 12201, Tel: (518) 445-2200
  (Paper mach clothing, engineered fabrics, plastic prdts, filtration media)
    Albany Nordiska (Nederland) BV, Industrieterrein, P.O. Box 32, 6950 AA Direen,
      Netherlands
    Hollandse Plastic Industrie BV, Netherlands

ALBERTO-CULVER CO   2525 Armitage Ave, Melrose Park, IL 60160,
  Tel: (708) 450-3000
  (Mfr/mktg personal care & beauty prdts, household & grocery prdts, institutional food
  prdts)
    Cederroth BV, P.O. Box 565, 5000 NK an Tilburg, Netherlands
    Indola Cosmetics Nederland BV, Verrijin Stuartlaan 42, 2288 EM Rijswijk, Netherlands

ALDUS CORP   411 First Ave South, Seattle, WA 98104-2871, Tel: (206) 622-5500
  (Devel/mfr computer software)
    Aldus Software Benelux BV, Printerweg 3-5, 3800 BN Amersfoort, Netherlands

THE ALLEN GROUP INC 25101 Chagrin Blvd, Beachwood, OH 44122,
Tel: (216) 765-5800
(Mfr communications equip, automotive bodies & parts, electronic components)
Allen Rohe BV, Netherlands

ALLEN-BRADLEY CO PO Box 2086, Milwaukee, WI 53201, Tel: (414) 382-2000
(Mfr eletrical controls & info devices)
Allen-Bradley Nederland BV, J.N. Wagenaarweg 6, 1422 AK Uithoorn, Netherlands

ALLIS-CHALMERS CORP 1126 S 70th St, West Allis, WI 53214,
Tel: (414) 475-3552
(Mfr molded fabric prdts for apparel ind; service industrial equip)
AAF International BV, P.O. Box 7928, 1008 AC Amsterdam, Netherlands

AM INTL INC 9399 W Higgins Rd, Rosemont, IL 60618, Tel: (708) 292-0600
(Mfr/sale/serv printing & print prod equip, mailroom/bindery sys, svces & supplies
for graphics ind)
AM Finance BV, P.O. Box 130, 2280 AC Rijswijk, Netherlands
AM Netherlands BV, P.O. Box 130, 2280 AC Rijswijk, Netherlands

AMDAHL CORP 1250 E Arques Ave, PO Box 3470, Sunnyvale, CA 94088-3470,
Tel: (408) 746-6000
(Devel/mfr large scale computers, software, data storage prdts, info-technology
solutions & support)
Amdahl Nederland BV, Weg der Verenigde Naties 1, 3527 KT Utrecht, Netherlands

AMERICAN AIRLINES INC PO Box 619616, Dallas-Ft Worth Arpt, TX 75261-9616,
Tel: (817) 355-1234
(Air transp)
American Airlines Inc., Carlton House, Vijezelstraat 2-18, Amsterdam, Netherlands

AMERICAN MANAGEMENT SYSTEMS INC 4050 Legato Rd, Fairfax, VA 22033,
Tel: (703) 267-8000
(Systems integration & consulting)
AMS Management Systems Netherlands BV, Koninginnegracht 14J, 2514 AA The Hague,
Netherlands

AMERICAN METER CO 300 Welsh Rd, Bldg #1, Horsham, PA 19044-2234,
Tel: (215) 830-1800
(Meas & control serv for natural gas inds)
Intl. Gas Apparaten BV, P.O. Box 410, 5140 AK Waaiwijk, Netherlands

AMERICAN NICKEL ALLOY MFG CORP 30 Vesey St, New York, NY 10007,
Tel: (212) 267-6420
(Nickel, nickel alloys & spec metals for melting & alloying)
Nederlandsche Nikkel Mil. BV, Netherlands

AMERICAN STANDARD INC 1 Centennial Ave, Piscataway, NJ 08855,
Tel: (908) 980-3000
(Mfr heating & sanitary equip)
Ideal Standard (Holland) BV, Lange Herenstraat 45-47, Haarlem, Netherlands

AMERON INC PO Box 7007, Pasadena, CA 91109-7007, Tel: (818) 683-4000
(Mfr steel pipe sys, concrete prdts, traffic & lighting poles, protective coatings)
Amercoat Europa BV, J.F. Kennedylam 7, P.O. Box 6, 4190 CA Geldermalsen, Netherlands

AMES TEXTILE CORP   710 Chelmsford St, Lowell, MA 01851, Tel: (508) 458-3321
   (Textile prdts)
      Eurames NV, P.O. Box 2242, 7500 CE Enschede, Netherlands

AMICON INC   72 Cherry Hill Dr, Beverly, MA 01915, Tel: (508) 777-3622
   (Mfr/sale/svce bioseparation, membrane ultrafiltration, chromatography)
      Grace BV, Amicon Div., Esseboon 19A-B, 2908 LJ Capelle a/d Ijssel, Netherlands

AMP INC   PO Box 3608, Harrisburg, PA 17105-3608, Tel: (717) 564-0100
   (Devel/mfr electronic & electrical connection prdts & sys)
      AMP-Holland BV, P.O. Box 288, 5201 AG 'S-Hertogenbosch, Netherlands

AMPCO METAL INC   1745 S 38th St, PO Box 2004, Milwaukee, WI 53201,
   Tel: (414) 645-3750
   (Mfr/distr/sale cast & wrought copper-based alloys)
      Ampco Metal Woerden (Nederland) BV, Kerkplein 2, P.O. Box 56, Ampereivet,
         3440 AB Woerden, Netherlands

AMPEX SYSTEMS CORP   401 Broadway, Redwood City, CA 94063-3199,
   Tel: (415) 367-2011
   (Mfr hi-perf helical scanning recording sys & associated tape media)
      Ampex BV, Netherlands

AMPHENOL PRODUCTS   1925A Ohio St, Lisle, IL 60532, Tel: (708) 960-1010
   (Elect interconnect/penetrate sys & assemblies)
      Amphenol Benelux c/o Instru. Lab. BV, Netherlands

AMWAY CORP   7575 E Fulton Rd, Ada, MI 49355, Tel: (616) 676-6000
   (Mfr/sale home care, personal care, nutrition & houseware prdts)
      Amway Netherlands Ltd., Edisonstraat 18, P.O. Box 278, 4000 AG Tiel, Netherlands

ANACOMP INC   PO Box 509005, San Diego, CA 92150-8729, Tel: (619) 679-9797
   (Mfr electronic computing equip)
      Anacomp SA, Coehoornstraat 71, Hilversum, Netherlands

ANALOG DEVICES INC   1 Technology Way, Box 9106, Norwood, MA 02062,
   Tel: (617) 329-4700
   (Mfr integrated circuits & related devices)
      Analog Devices Inc., Beneluxweg 27, 4904 SJ Oosterhout, Netherlands

ANAMET INC   698 S Main St, Waterbury, CT 06706, Tel: (203) 574-8500
   (Mfr ind machinery, wiring devices, measure & control devices)
      Anamet Europe BV, Transformatorweg 30, 1014 AK Amsterdam, Netherlands
      Anamet Holland BV, Transformatorweg 30, 1014 AK Amsterdam, Netherlands

ANGLO-AMERICAN AVIATION CO   9740 Telfair Ave, Arleta, CA 91331,
   Tel: (818) 896-0333
   (Aviation spare parts, hardware)
      Anglo American Aviation Co., Building 112, Rooms 185-187, P.O. Box 7650,
         Schiphol-East, Netherlands

AP PARTS CO   1800 Indianwood Circle, Maumee, OH 43537-4073,
   Tel: (419) 891-8400
   (Mfr auto parts & accessories)
      United Parts Holding NV, World Trade Center, Strawinskylaan 745, 1077 XX Amsterdam,
         Netherlands

APPLE COMPUTER INC   1 Infinite Loop, Cupertino, CA 95014, Tel: (408) 996-1010
(Personal computers, peripherals & software)
   Apple Computer BV, P.O. Box 600, 7300 AP Apeldoorn, Netherlands

APPLIED POWER INC   13000 W Silver Spring Dr, Butler, WI 53007,
   Tel: (414) 781-6600
(Mfr hi-pressure tools, vibration control prdts, electrical tools & consumables, tech furniture)
   Power-Packer Europa BV, Edisonstraat 2, P.O. Box 327, 7570 AH Oldenzaal, Netherlands

ARBOR ACRES FARM INC   439 Marlborough Rd, Glastonbury, CT 06033,
   Tel: (860) 633-4681
(Producers of male & female broiler breeders, commercial egg layers)
   Arbor Acres Farm BV, Elburgerweg 13, P.O. Box 24, 8180 AA Heerde, Netherlands

ARCHER-DANIELS-MIDLAND CO   PO Box 1470, Decatur, IL 62525,
   Tel: (217) 424-5200
(Flours, grains, oils, flax fibre)
   Archer Daniels Midland Nederland BV Groothandelsgebouw AL, Netherlands

ARMSTRONG WORLD INDUSTRIES INC   PO Box 3001, Lancaster, PA 17604,
   Tel: (717) 397-0611
(Mfr/mkt interior furnishings & spec prdts for bldg, auto & textile inds)
   Armstrong World Industries Netherlands BV, Hoogezand,
      Netherlands (all inquiries to U.S. address)

ARTOS ENGINEERING CO INC   W228 N2792 Duplainville Rd, Waukesha, WI 53186,
   Tel: (414) 524-6600
(Mfr metalworking machinery)
   Artos Engineering Benelux BV, Pettelaar 33. 5216 PJ 's Hertogenbosch, Netherlands

ARVIN INDUSTRIES INC   One Noblitt Plaza, Columbus, IN 47201-6079,
   Tel: (812) 379-3000
(Mfr motor vehicle parts, springs, relays & ind controls, aircraft engines & parts)
   Arvin Cheswick Intl. (Netherlands) BV, Keulsbaan 507, Roermond, 6045 GG Limburg,
      Netherlands
   Masterparts BV, Strijkviertel 39, 3454 PJ Utrecht, Netherlands

ASARCO INC   180 Maiden Lane, New York, NY 10038, Tel: (212) 510-2000
(Nonferrous metals, specialty chems, minerals, mfr industrial prdts, environmental services)
   Enthone-Omi Inc., Netherlands

ASGROW SEED CO   2605 E Kilgore Rd, Kalamazoo, MI 49002, Tel: (616) 384-5675
(Research/mfr agronomic & vegetable seeds; seed technologies)
   Bruinsma Seed Co., P.O. Box 24, 2670 AA Naaldwyk, Netherlands

ASHLAND OIL INC   1000 Ashland Dr, Russell, KY 41169, Tel: (606) 329-3333
(Petroleum exploration, refining & transportation; mfr chemicals, oils & lubricants)
   BV Ashland-Suedchemie V.H. Necof, P.O. Box 6, 4930 AA Geertruidenberg, Netherlands
   Valvoline Oil Co., 3300 AA Dordrecht, Netherlands
   Valvoline Oil Nederland BV, Wieldrechtseweg 39, Dordrecht, Netherlands

ASKO INC   501 W 7th Ave, PO Box 355, Homestead, PA 15120, Tel: (412) 461-4110
(Mfr ind knives & saws for metal ind)
   Asko BV, Willem Fenengastraat 10, 1096 BN Amsterdam, Netherlands

AST RESEARCH INC   16215 Alton Parkway, PO Box 19658, Irvine, CA 92713-9658,
  Tel: (714) 727-4141
  (Design/devel/mfr hi-perf desktop, server & notebook computers)
    AST Netherlands, Computerweg 12E, 3821 AB Amersfoot, Netherlands

ATLANTIC RICHFIELD CO (ARCO)   515 S Flower St, Los Angeles, CA 90071-2256,
  Tel: (213) 486-3511
  (Petroleum & natural gas, chemicals, service stations)
    Arco Chemie Technologie Nederland BV, Theemsweg 14, 3197 KM Rotterdam, Netherlands

THE AUSTIN CO   3650 Mayfield Rd, Cleveland, OH 44121, Tel: (216) 382-6600
  (Consulting, design, engineering & construction)
    Austin-Nederland BV, Airport Office Center, Schipholweg 297, 1171 PK Badhoevedorp,
    Netherlands

AUTODESK INC   2320 Marinship Way, Sausalito, CA 94965, Tel: (415) 332-2344
  (Devel/mkt/support computer-aided design, engineering, scientific & multimedia
  software prdts)
    Autodesk BV, Druivenstraat 1, 4816 KB Breda, Netherlands

AUTOMATIC DATA PROCESSING INC   1 ADP Blvd, Roseland, NJ 07068,
  Tel: (201) 994-5000
  (Data processing services)
    ADP Nederland BV, Lylantsebaan 1, 2908 LG Capelle aan den IJssel

AUTOMATIC SPRINKLER CORP OF AMERICA   1000 E Edgerton Rd, Cleveland,
  OH 44147, Tel: (216) 526-9900
  (Fire protection & detection sys)
    Automatic Sprinkler-Holland BV, P.O. Box 211, 3800 AE Amersfoort, Netherlands

AUTOMATIC SWITCH CO   Hanover Rd, Florham Park, NJ 07932, Tel: (201) 966-2000
  (Mfr solenoid valves, emergency power controls, pressure & temp switches)
    Asco Controls BV, Industrielaan 21, P.O. Box 3, 3925 ZG Scherpenzeel, Netherlands

AVERY DENNISON CORP   150 N Orange Grove Blvd, Pasadena, CA 91103,
  Tel: (818) 304-2000
  (Mfr pressure-sensitive adhesives & materials, office prdts, labels, tags, retail
  sys, spec chems)
    Fasson Nederland BV, Lammenschansweg 140, 2321 JX, Leiden, Netherlands
    Fasson Producten Verkoopmaatshappij BV, Rijndijk 86, 2934 AJ Hazerwovde, Netherlands

AVON PRODUCTS INC   9 W 57th St, New York, NY 10019, Tel: (212) 546-6015
  (Mfr/distr beauty & related prdts, fashion jewelry, gifts & collectibles)
    Avon Cosmetics GmbH, Vestigney in Nederland, Leidsevaantweg 99, 2106 AS Heemstede,
    Netherlands

THE BADGER CO INC   One Broadway, Cambridge, MA 02142, Tel: (617) 494-7312
  (Engr & const serv to process ind)
    Badger BV, Binckhorstlaan 117, 2516 BA The Hague, Netherlands

BAILEY-FISCHER & PORTER CO   125 E County Line Rd, Warminster, PA 18974,
  Tel: (215) 674-6000
  (Design/mfr meas, recording & control instru & sys; mfr ind glass prdts)
    Bailey-Fischer & Porter BV, Avelingen West 3, 4202 MS Gorinchem, Netherlands

BAIRD CORP   125 Middlesex Turnpike, Bedford, MA   01730, Tel: (617) 276-6000
  (Scientific instru)
    Baird (Europe) BV, Produktieweg 20, 2382 PC Zoeterwoude, Netherlands

J T BAKER INC   222 Red School Lane, Phillipsburg, NJ   08865,
  Tel: (201) 859-2151
  (Mfr/sale/serv lab & process chems)
    J.T. Baker BV, Rijstenborgherweg 20, 7400 AA Deventer, Netherlands

BAKER OIL TOOLS   PO Box 40129, Houston, TX   77240-0129, Tel: (713) 466-1322
  (Mfr/serv oil/gas well completions equip)
    Baker Oil Tools UK Ltd., Zuiderkade 25A, 1948 NG Beverwijk, Netherlands

BALDWIN TECHNOLOGY CO INC   65 Rowayton Ave, Rowayton, CT   06853,
  Tel: (203) 838-7470
  (Mfr/serv mat handling, acces, control & prepress equip for print ind)
    Baldwin Europe Consolidated, Nijverheidsweg 21, P.O. Box 371, 5680 AJ Best,
    Netherlands

BANDAG INC   2905 NW 61, Muscatine, IA   52761, Tel: (319) 262-1400
  (Mfr/sale retread tires)
    Bandag BV, Born, Netherlands

BANKAMERICA CORP   555 California St, San Francisco, CA   94104,
  Tel: (415) 622-3456
  (Financial services)
    Bank of America NT & SA, P.O. Box 1638, 1000 BP Amsterdam, Netherlands

BANKERS TRUST CO   280 Park Ave, New York, NY   10017, Tel: (212) 250-2500
  (Banking)
    Bankers Trust Co., Herengracht 418, 1017 BZ Amsterdam, Netherlands

BARBER-COLMAN CO   555 Colman Center Dr, Rockford, IL   61125,
  Tel: (815) 397-7400
  (Mfr controls, motors)
    Barcol-Air BV, Maaldery 30, 1185 ZC Amstelveen, Netherlands

BARBER-GREENE CO   3000 Baraber-Greene Rd, DeKalb, IL   60115,
  Tel: (815) 756-5600
  (Mfr heavy road constr equip)
    Barber-Greene Europa BV, P.O. Box 149, 8000 AC Zwolle, Netherlands

C R BARD INC   730 Central Ave, Murray Hill, NJ   07974, Tel: (908) 277-8000
  (Mfr health care prdts)
    Bard Nederland BV, Ravenswade 94, 3439 LD Nieuwegein, Netherlands

BATTEN BARTON DURSTINE & OSBORN INC   1285 Ave of the Americas, New York,
  NY   10019, Tel: (212) 459-5000
  (Advertising agency)
    Franzen, Hey & Veltman, Cronenburg 2, Amsterdam, Netherlands

BAUSCH & LOMB INC   1 Chase Square, Rochester, NY   14601, Tel: (716) 338-6000
  (Mfr vision care prdts & accessories)
    Bausch & Lomb BV, Heemstede, Netherlands

BAXTER HEALTHCARE CORP   1 Baxter Pky, Deerfield, IL 60015,
  Tel: (708) 948-2000
  (Mfr disposable medical prdts)
    Baxter BV, P.O. Box 1536, 3600 BM Maarssen (Utrecht), Netherlands
    Baxter Healthcare Corp., P.O. Box 169, 5400 AD Uden, Netherlands
    Bentley Laboratories Europe BV, P.O. Box 169, 5400 AD Uden, Netherlands
    Edwards CVS Europe, P.O. Box 169, 5400 AD Uden, Netherlands

BEAR STEARNS & CO INC   245 Park Ave, New York, NY 10167, Tel: (212) 272-2000
  (Investment banking)
    Bear Stearns Netherlands Holding BV, Rivierstaete, Amsteldjik 166,
      1079 LH Amsterdam, Netherlands

BECHTEL GROUP INC   50 Beale St, PO Box 3965, San Francisco, CA 94119,
  Tel: (415) 768-1234
  (Engineering & constr)
    Bechtel Inc., Netherlands

BECKMAN INSTRUMENTS INC   2500 Harbor Blvd, Fullerton, CA 92634,
  Tel: (714) 871-4848
  (Devel/mfr/mkt automated systems & supplies for biological analysis)
    Beckman Instruments BV, Nijverheidsweg 21, 3641 RP Mijdrecht, Netherlands

BELL HELICOPTER CO   PO Box 482, Ft Worth, TX 76101, Tel: (817) 280-2011
  (Helicopters, air cushion vehicles, rocket engines)
    Bell Helicopter Supply Center, Div. of Textron Atlantic, Bldg. 112, P.O. Box 7534,
      Schiphol-East, Netherlands

BENTLY NEVADA CORP   PO Box 157, Minden, NV 89423, Tel: (702) 782-3611
  (Electronic monitoring system)
    Bently Nevada Europa BV, Weteringweg 14, 2641 KM Pijnacker, Netherlands

BERG ELECTRONICS DIV   Route 83, New Cumberland, PA 17070, Tel: (717) 938-6711
  (Mfr & sales of strip terminals)
    Berg Electronics, Div. of Du Pont De Nemours (Nederland) BV, Helftheuvelweg 1,
      P.O. Box 2060, 4004 'S-Hertogenbosch 4004, Netherlands

BIO-RAD LABORATORIES INC   1000 Alfred Nobel Dr, Hercules, CA 94547,
  Tel: (510) 724-7000
  (Mfr life science research prdts, clinical diagnostics, analytical instruments)
    Bio-Rad Laboratories BV, Veenendaal, Netherlands

BLACK & DECKER CORP   701 E Joppa Road, Towson, MD 21286, Tel: (410) 716-3900
  (Mfr power tools & accessories, security hardware, small appliances, fasteners, info
  sys & servs)
    Black & Decker Corp., all mail to U.S. address

BLACK BOX CORP   1000 Park Dr, Lawrence, PA 15055, Tel: (412) 746-5500
  (Direct marketer & tech service provider of commun, networking & related computer
  connectivity prdts)
    Black Box Datacom BV, Saannehweg 60, 3542 AW Utrecht, Netherlands

BLACKSTONE CORP   1111 Allen St, Jamestown, NY 14701, Tel: (716) 665-2620
  (Heat transfer prdts, heaters, coolers)
    Bloksma BV, Industrieterrein De Vaart 1, Draaibrugweg 15, P.O. Box 50045,
      1305 AA Almere, Netherlands

BONDED SERVICES 520 Main St, Fort Lee, NJ 07024, Tel: (201) 592-9044
(Storage, distribution & service of film & tape libraries)
Bonded Services Intl., Bldg. 72, 1117 ZJ Schiphol East, Amsterdam, Netherlands

BOOLE & BABBAGE INC 510 Oakmead Pkwy, Sunnyvale, CA 94086,
Tel: (408) 735-9550
(Devel/support enterprise automation & systems mgmt software)
Boole & Babbage Europe, Laan 20, 2512 GH The Hague, Netherlands

BOOZ ALLEN & HAMILTON INC 101 Park Ave, New York, NY 10178,
Tel: (212) 697-1900
(Mgmt consultants)
Booz Allen & Hamilton Inc., Rust En Vreugdiann 2, 2243 AS Wassenaar, Netherlands

BORDEN INC 180 E Broad St, Columbus, OH 43215-3799, Tel: (614) 225-4000
(Mfr foods, snacks & beverages, adhesives)
Borden Packaging & Industrial Products, P.O. Box 66, 7300 AB Apeldoorn, Netherlands

BOSE CORP The Mountain, Framingham, MA 01701-9168, Tel: (508) 879-7330
(Mfr audio equip)
Bose BV, Nijverheidstraat 8, 1135 GE Edam, Netherlands

BOURNS INC 1200 Columbia Ave, Riverside, CA 92507, Tel: (909) 781-5500
(Mfr resistive com & networks, precision potentiometers, panel controls, switches,
transducers)
Bourns BV, Van Tuyl/Van Serooskerkenstraat 81-85, P.O. Box 37, 2273 CD Voorburg,
Netherlands

BOWEN TOOLS INC PO Box 3186, Houston, TX 77253-3186, Tel: (713) 868-8888
(Mfr drilling & specialty tools for oil/gas ind)
Bowen Tools Inc., Netherlands

BOZELL JACOBS KENYON & ECKHARDT INC 40 West 23rd St, New York, NY 10010,
Tel: (212) 727-5000
(Advertising agency)
C.P.V. Nederland NV, Stadhouderskade 31, Amsterdam, Netherlands

BRANSON ULTRASONICS CORP 41 Eagle Rd, Danbury, CT 06813-1961,
Tel: (203) 796-0400
(Mfr plastics assembly equip, ultrasonic cleaning equip)
Branson Ultraonics BV, Energieweg 2, P.O. Box 9, 3760 AA Soest, Netherlands

BROWN & ROOT INC 4100 Clinton Dr, Houston, TX 77020-6299,
Tel: (713) 676-3011
(Engr, constr & maintenance)
Brown & Root Nederland BV, P.O. Box 125, Nieuwe Waterwegstraat 1, 3115 HE Schiedam,
Rotterdam, Netherlands

BRY-AIR INC PO Box 269, Rte 37 W, Sunbury, OH 43074, Tel: (614) 965-2974
(Mfr industrial dehumidifiers/auxiliary equip for plastics ind)
Delair, P.O. Box 570, 4870 AN Etten-Leur, Netherlands

BURLINGTON AIR EXPRESS 18200 Van Karman Ave, Irvine, CA 92715,
Tel: (714) 752-4000
(Air freight)
Burlington Air Express, Freight Station 1, #503/513, 1118 AA Schiphol Airport,
Netherlands

LEO BURNETT CO INC   35 West Wacker Dr, Chicago, IL 60601, Tel: (312) 220-5959
(Advertising agency)
    Noordervliet & Winninnghoff/Leo Burnett BV, Drentestraat 5, 1083 HK Amsterdam,
    Netherlands

BURR-BROWN RESEARCH CORP   PO Box 11400, Tucson, AZ 85734, Tel: (602) 746-1111
(Electronic components & sys modules)
    Burr-Brown Intl. BV, Netherlands

BURSON-MARSTELLER   230 Park Ave, New York, NY 10003-1566, Tel: (212) 614-4000
(Public relations/public affairs consultants)
    Burson-Marsteller BV, Sophialaan 1a, 2514 JP The Hague, Netherlands

CARL BYOIR & ASSOCIATES INC   420 Lexington Ave, New York, NY 10017,
Tel: (212) 210-6000
(Public relations, intl commun)
    Boetes Publiciteit BV, Netherlands
    Boetes Publiciteit BV, Hofpleinbuilding, Hofplein 19, 3032 AC Rotterdam, Netherlands

C-COR ELECTRONICS INC   60 Decible Rd, State College, PA 16801,
Tel: (814) 238-2461
(Design/mfr amplifiers, electronic equip for data & cable TV systems)
    C-Cor Europe BV, 1301 AG Almere, Netherlands

CABOT CORP   75 State St, Boston, MA 02109-1807, Tel: (617) 890-0200
(Mfr carbon blacks, plastics; oil & gas, info sys)
    Ketjen-Carbon BV (JV), Botlekweg, Rozenburg ZH, P.O. Box 1009, 3180 AA, Rotterdam,
    Netherlands
    NV Kawecki-Billiton Metaalindustrie (KBI Div.), P.O. Box 38, 6800 LH Arnbem,
    Netherlands

CALCOMP INC   2411 W La Palma Ave, Anaheim, CA 92801, Tel: (714) 821-2000
(Mfr computer graphics peripherals)
    CalComp BV, Dr. Willem Dreesweg 6-8, P.O. Box 444, 1185 VB Amstelveen, Netherlands

CALIFORNIA PELLET MILL CO   221 Main St, #420, San Francisco, CA 94105,
Tel: (415) 431-3800
(Mfr mach for pelleting)
    CPM/Europe BV, Distelweg 89, Amsterdam, Netherlands

CAMP INTL INC   PO Box 89, Jackson, MI 49204, Tel: (517) 787-1600
(Mfr orthotics & prosthetics)
    Basko Camp, P.O. Box 8359, Haspelsstraat 6, Amsterdam, Netherlands

CANBERRA INDUSTRIES INC   One State St, Meriden, CT 06450, Tel: (203) 238-2351
(Mfr instru for nuclear research)
    Canberra-Packard Benelux NV, Ringbaan Noord 89, 5046 AA Tilburg, Netherlands
    Packard Instrument BV, P.O. Box 9403, 9703 LP Groningen, Netherlands

CANDELA LASER CORP   530 Boston Post Rd, Wayland, MA 01778,
Tel: (508) 358-7400
(Mfr/serv medical laser systems)
    Candela Europe, Vestdijk 9, 5611 CA Eindhoven, Netherlands

CARBOLINE CO   350 Hanley Industrial Ct, St Louis, MO 63144,
  Tel: (314) 644-1000
  (Mfr coatings, sealants)
    Carboline Benelux BV, P.O. Box 62, 2964 ZH Groot Ammers, Netherlands

CARGILL   PO Box 9300, Minneapolis, MN 55440, Tel: (612) 475-7575
  (Food prdts, feeds, animal prdts)
    Cargil BV, P.O. Box 8074, 1005 AB Amsterdam, Netherlands

CARON SPINNING CO   Avenue E, Rochelle, IL 61068, Tel: (815) 562-4121
  (Carpet & texture yarns)
    Carolan (Holland) BV, Industrielaam 38, P.O. Box 44, Veenendaal, Netherlands

CAROTRANS INTL INC   PO Box 1060, Cherryville, NC 28021, Tel: (704) 435-8356
  (Non-vessel operating common carrier)
    CaroTrans Intl., Vlaardingweg 65, 3044 CJ Rotterdam, Netherlands

CARRIER CORP   One Carrier Place, Farmington, CT 06034-4015,
  Tel: (203) 674-3000
  (Mfr/distr/svce A/C, heating & refrigeration equip)
    Carrier BV, Rijnkijk 141, P.O. Box 151, 2394 ZH Hazerswoude, Netherlands
    United Technologies Corp., The Hague, Netherlands

CASCADE CORP   2020 SW First Ave, Portland, OR 97201, Tel: (503) 227-0024
  (Mfr hydraulic forklift truck attachments)
    Cascade NV, Achterwerf 240, 1357 CB Almere-Haven, Netherlands

A M CASTLE & CO   3400 N Wolf Rd, Franklin Park, IL 60131, Tel: (708) 455-7111
  (Metals distribution)
    Castle Metals Europe, Netherlands

CBI INDUSTRIES INC   800 Jorie Blvd, Oak Brook, IL 60521, Tel: (708) 654-7000
  (Holding co: metal plate fabricating, constr, oil & gas drilling)
    CBI Nederland BV, Van Rie Madijkweg 20, Rotterdam, Netherlands

CENTOCOR INC   200 Great Valley Pkwy, Malvern, PA 19355, Tel: (610) 651-6000
  (Devel/mfr/mktg diagnostic & therapeutic pdts for human health care)
    Centocor BV, P.O. Box 251, 2300 AG Leiden, Netherlands

CENTRAL GULF LINES INC   650 Poydras St, New Orleans, LA 70130,
  Tel: (504) 529-5461
  (Steamship service)
    Netherlands Maritime Agencies, Strevelsweg 700, P.O. Box 5019, 3008 AA Rotterdam,
      Netherlands

CENTRAL NATIONAL-GOTTESMAN INC   3 Manhattanville Rd, Purchase,
  NY 10577-2110, Tel: (914) 696-9000
  (Worldwide sales pulp & paper prdts)
    Central National Co. BV, World Trade Center, Tower C, 8th fl., Strawinskylaan 847,
      1077 XX Amsterdam, Netherlands

CHARBERT INC   Church St, Alton, RI 02803, Tel: (401) 364-7751
  (Mfg & sales of elastic fabric)
    Charbert-Blydenstein NV (JV), Netherlands

CHASE MANHATTAN BANK N A   1 Chase Manhattan Plaza, New York, NY 10081,
Tel: (212) 552-2222
(Intl banking)
   Chase Manhattan Bank, Soetensteeg 65, P.O. Box 974, Rotterdam, Netherlands
   Chase Manhattan Bank, Keizersgracht 515-521, Amsterdam, Netherlands
   Chase Manhattan Overseas Corp., Netherlands
   Nederlandse Credietbank NV, Herengracht 458, P.O. Box 941, Amsterdam, Netherlands

CHESTERTON BINSWANGER INTL   Two Logan Sq, 4th fl, Philadelphia,
PA 19103-2759, Tel: (215) 448-6000
(Real estate & related svces)
   Chesterton (Netherlands) NV, Parkweg 2, 2585 JJ The Hague, Netherlands

CHIQUITA BRANDS INTL INC   250 E Fifth St, Cincinnati, OH 45202,
Tel: (513) 784-8000
(Distribution food products)
   Chiquita Europe BV, Netherlands

CHIRON CORP   4560 Horton St, Emeryville, CA 94608-2916, Tel: (510) 601-2412
(Research/mfg/mktg therapeutics, vaccines, diagnostics, ophthalmics)
   Chiron Therapeutics, Paasheuvelweg 30, 1105 BJ Amsterdam-Zuidoost, Netherlands
   Ciba Corning Diagnostics NV, Peppelkade 64 D/E, P.O. Box 111, 3990 DC Houten,
   Netherlands

CIGNA CORP   One Liberty Place, Philadelphia, PA 19192, Tel: (215) 523-4000
(Ins, invest, health care & other fin servs)
   Cigna Insurance Co. of Europe SA/NV, Netherlands
   Esis Intl. Inc., Gebouw Blakeburg, Blaak 22, 3011 TA Rotterdam, Netherlands

CINCINNATI MILACRON INC   4701 Marburg Ave, Cincinnati, OH 45209,
Tel: (513) 841-8100
(Devel/mfr technologies for metalworking & plastics processing ind)
   Cincinnati Milacron BV, Vlaardingen, Netherlands

CINCOM SYSTEMS INC   2300 Montana Ave, Cincinnati, OH 45211,
Tel: (513) 662-2300
(Devel/distr computer software)
   Cincom Systems Inc., Nieuwegein, Netherlands

CITICORP   399 Park Ave, New York, NY 10043, Tel: (212) 559-1000
(Banking & financial services)
   Citibank NA, Netherlands

COBE LABORATORIES INC   1185 Oak St, Lakewood, CO 80215, Tel: (303) 232-6800
(Mfr med equip & supplies)
   COBE Laboratories Inc., Venendaal, Netherlands

THE COCA-COLA CO   PO Drawer 1734, Atlanta, GA 30301, Tel: (404) 676-2121
(Mfr/mkt/distr soft drinks, syrups & concentrates, juice & juice-drink prdts)
   NCCB, all mail to U.S. address

COEN CO INC   1510 Rollins Road, Burlingame, CA 94010, Tel: (415) 697-0440
(Ind burners)
   De Jong-Coen BV, Postbus 5, 3100 AA Schiedam, Netherlands

COHERENT INC   PO Box 54980, Santa Clara, CA 95056, Tel: (408) 764-4000
  (Mfr lasers for sci, ind & med)
    Coherent Benelux, Argonstraat 136, 2718 SP Zoetermeer, Netherlands

THE COLEMAN CO INC   1526 Cole Blvd, #300, Golden, CO 80401,
  Tel: (303) 202-2470
  (Mfr/distr/sales camping & outdoor recreation prdts)
    Coleman Holland BV, Galileistraat 28, 1704 SE Heerugowaard, Netherlands

COLGATE-PALMOLIVE CO   300 Park Ave, New York, NY 10022, Tel: (212) 310-2000
  (Mfr pharms, cosmetics, toiletries, detergents)
    Colgate-Palmolive Handelmaatschappij BV, Amstellandlaan 84, 1382 CM Weesp,
    Netherlands

COMBUSTION ENGINEERING INC   900 Long Ridge Road, Stamford, CT 06902,
  Tel: (203) 329-8771
  (Tech constr)
    C-E Natco Netherlands BV, Netherlands
    C-E Vetco Services, c/o Peterson Ijmuiden BV, P.O. Box 513, Westerdiunweg 7,
    Netherlands
    Gray Tool Co. (Europe) Ltd., Westerduinweg 4, Ijmuiden, Netherlands

COMDISCO INC   6111 N River Rd, Rosemont, IL 60018, Tel: (708) 698-3000
  (Hi-tech asset & facility mgmt, equip leasing)
    Comdisco Nederland BV, Maarssen, Netherlands

COMPAQ COMPUTER CORP   PO Box 692000, Houston, TX 77269-2000,
  Tel: (713) 370-0670
  (Devel/mfr personal computers)
    Compaq Computer Intl. Corp., Gorinchem, Netherlands

COMPUTER ASSOCIATES INTL INC   One Computer Associates Plaza, Islandia,
  NY 11788, Tel: (516) 342-5224
  (Devel/mkt/mgt info mgt & bus applications software)
    Computer Associates Products Nederland BV, Wattbaan 27, 3439 ML Nieuwegein,
    Netherlands

COMPUTER SCIENCES CORP   2100 E Grand Ave, El Segundo, CA 90245,
  Tel: (310) 615-0311
  (Info technology servs, management consulting, systems integration, outsourcing)
    CSC Computer Sciences BV, Van Heuven Goedhartlaan 121, P.O. Box 2086,
    1180 EM Amstelveen, Netherlands

COMSHARE INC   3001 S State St, Ann Arbor, MI 48108, Tel: (313) 994-4800
  (Managerial application software)
    Comshare BV, Netherlands

CONOCO INC   600 N Dairy Ashford Rd, Houston, TX 77079, Tel: (713) 293-1000
  (Oil, gas, coal, chems, minerals)
    Continental Oil Co. (Nederland) BV, The Hague, Netherlands

CONTINENTAL CAN CO   PO Box 5410, Stamford, CT 06856, Tel: (203) 357-8110
  (Packaging prdts & mach, metal, plastic & paper containers)
    Thomassen & Drijver Verblifa NV, Zutphenseweg 51, P.O. Box 103, 7400 GB Deventer,
    Netherlands

THE CONTINUUM CO INC   9500 Arboretum Blvd, Austin, TX 78759,
  Tel: (512) 345-5700
  (Design & mkt software for ins & fin svces)
    Continuum, Hoogstraat 64, P.O. Box 57, 3417 ZH Montfoort, Netherlands

COOPER INDUSTRIES INC   1001 Fannin St, PO Box 4446, Houston, TX 77210-4446,
  Tel: (713) 739-5400
  (Mfr/distr electrical prdts, tools & hardware, automotive prdts)
    Cooper Hand Tools Div., Emmen, Drenthe, Netherlands

CORDIS CORP   PO Box 025700, Miami, FL 33102-5700, Tel: (305) 824-2000
  (Mfr med devices & sys)
    Cordis Europa NV, Postbus 38, 9300 AA Roden, Netherlands

CORE LABORATORIES   10205 Westheimer, Houston, TX 77042, Tel: (713) 972-6311
  (Petroleum testing/analysis, analytical chem, lab & octane analysis instrumentation)
    Core Laboratories, Heulweg 28-30, 2288 GN Rijswijk, Netherlands

COSTAR CORP   One Alewife Center, Cambridge, MA 02140, Tel: (617) 868-6200
  (Mfr disposable products for life science research labs)
    Costar Europe Ltd., Sloterweg 305A, 1171 VC Badhoevedorp, Netherlands

COULTER CORP   PO Box 169015, Miami, FL 33116-9015, Tel: (305) 885-0131
  (Mfr blood analysis sys, flow cytometers, chem sys, scientific sys & reagents)
    Coulter Electronics Nederland, Industrieweg 42, 3641 RM Mijdrecht, Netherlands

CPC INTERNATIONAL INC   PO Box 8000, Englewood Cliffs, NJ 07632,
  Tel: (201) 894-4000
  (Consumer foods, corn refining)
    CPC Benelux BV, Rading 1, P.O. Box 62, 1200 AB Hilversum, Netherlands

CRAY RESEARCH INC   655 Lone Oak Dr, Eagan, MN 55121, Tel: (612) 452-6650
  (Supercomputer systems & services)
    Cray Research BV, P.O. Box 3105, 2280 GC Rijswijk, Netherlands

CROMPTON & KNOWLES CORP   1 Station Pl Metro Center, Stamford, CT 06902,
  Tel: (203) 353-5400
  (Mfr dyes, colors, flavors, fragrances, spec chems, ind prdts)
    Althouse Tertre SA, Netherlands
    Gruno BV, Essencefabriek, Nijverheidslaan 10, Weesp, Netherlands

CROWN ANDERSON INC   306 Dividend Dr, Peachtree City, GA 30269,
  Tel: (770) 486-2000
  (Holding co: design/mfr/install ind pollution control, heat recovery, air handling &
  waste systems)
    Montair Anderson BV, Heuvelsestraat 14, 5976 NG Sevenum, Netherlands

CYBEREX INC   7171 Industrial Park Blvd, Mentor, OH 44060, Tel: (216) 946-1783
  (Mfr uninterruptible power sys, line voltage regulators, static switches, power line
  filters)
    Cyberex Intl. Services, Torenstraat 54, 9643 CV Wildervank, Netherlands

D'ARCY MASIUS BENTON & BOWLES INC (DMB&B)   1675 Broadway, New York,
  NY 10019, Tel: (212) 468-3622
  (Advertising & communications)
    DMB&B BV, P.O. Box 71219, 1008 BE Amsterdam, Netherlands

DAMES & MOORE 911 Wilshire Blvd, Los Angeles, CA 90017, Tel: (213) 683-1560
(Engineering, environmental & construction mgmt services)
   Bureau voor Milieumanagement BV, P.O. Box 45, 4780 AA Moerdijk, Netherlands
   Bureau voor Milieumanagement BV, Treubstraat 33, 2288 EH Rijswijk, Netherlands
   Dames & Moore, Treubstratt 33, 2288 EH Rijswijk, Netherlands

DANA CORP PO Box 1000, Toledo, OH 43697, Tel: (419) 535-4500
(Engineer/mfr/mkt prdts & sys for vehicular, ind & mobile off-highway mkt & related
aftermarkets)
   Aftermarket Distribution Div., P.O. Box 868, 3160 AB Rhoon, Netherlands
   Spicer Nederland BV, Neevwal 286, 3871 KG Hoevelaken, Netherlands

DATA GENERAL CORP 4400 Computer Dr, Westboro, MA 01580, Tel: (617) 366-8911
(Design, mfr gen purpose computer sys & peripheral prdts & servs)
   Data General Holland BV, Laan Van de Helende Meesters 13, 1186 AC Amstelveen,
   Netherlands

DATA I/O CORP 10525 Willows Rd NE, Redmond, WA 98053, Tel: (206) 881-6444
(Mfr computer testing devices)
   Data I/O Amsterdam, Amsterdam, Netherlands

DATAEASE INTL INC 7 Cambridge Dr, Trumbull, CT 06611, Tel: (203) 374-8000
(Mfr applications devel software)
   DataEase Europe, Elisabethhof 21, 2353 EW Leiderdorp, Netherlands
   Software Solutions Benelux, Elisabethhof 21, 2353 EW Leiderdorp, Netherlands

DATASCOPE CORP 14 Philips Pkwy, Montvale, NJ 07645, Tel: (201) 391-8100
(Mfr medical devices)
   Bioplex Medical BV, Vaals, Netherlands
   Datascope BV, Cyftenbeltlaan 6, P.O. Box 26, Hoevelaken, Netherlands

DAUBERT INDUSTRIES INC One Westbrook Corporate Center, Westchester,
IL 60154, Tel: (708) 409-5000
(Mfr chem spec, adhesive sealers, rust films, release papers)
   Daubert Intl., Netherlands

DAY-GLO COLOR CORP 4732 St Clair Ave, Cleveland, OH 44103,
Tel: (216) 391-7070
(Flourescent dyes & pigments)
   Day-Glo Color Corp., Netherlands

DDB NEEDHAM WORLDWIDE INC 437 Madison Ave, New York, NY 10022,
Tel: (212) 415-2000
(Advertising)
   DDB Needham Worldwide BV, Josef Israelskade 46, 1072 SB Amsterdam, Netherlands

THE DEXTER CORP 1 Elm Street, Windsor Locks, CT 06096, Tel: (203) 627-9051
(Mfr nonwovens, polymer prdts, magnetic materials, biotechnology)
   AD Aerospace Finishes BV, P.O. Box 3, Rijksstraatweg 31, 2170 BA Sassenheim,
   Netherlands

DIBRELL BROS INC 512 Bridge St, Danville, VA 24543, Tel: (804) 792-7511
(Sale leaf tobacco, cut flowers)
   Dibrell Bros. Intl. BV, Zwarteweg 149, 1430 BH Aalsmeer, Netherlands

DIGITAL EQUIPMENT CORP   146 Main St, Maynard, MA 01754-2571,
  Tel: (508) 493-5111
  (Networked computer systems & services)
    Digital Equipment Foreign Sales BV, Netherlands
    Digital Equipment Holdings BV, St. Theunismolenweg 15, 6534 AG Nymegen, Netherlands

DIONEX CORP   1228 Tital Way, PO Box 3603, Sunnyvale, CA 94088-3603,
  Tel: (408) 737-0700
  (Devel/mfr/mktg/svce chromatography sys & relted prdts)
    Dionex BV, Takkebijsters 65, 4817 BL Breda, Netherlands

DO ALL COMPANY   254 N Laurel Ave, Des Plaines, IL 60016, Tel: (708) 824-1122
  (Distributors of mach tools, metal cutting tools, instru & ind supplies)
    DoAll Nederland BV, Debijestraat 14, 3316 GE Dordrecht, Netherlands

DONALDSON CO INC   PO Box 1299, Minneapolis, MN 55440, Tel: (612) 887-3131
  (Mfr filtration prdts & sys)
    Donaldson Europe NV, P.O. Box 770, 2003 Route Haarlem, Netherlands

DORR-OLIVER INC   612 Wheeler's Farm Rd, PO Box 3819, Milford, CT 06460,
  Tel: (203) 876-5400
  (Mfr process equip for food, pulp & paper, mineral & chem ind; & municipal/ind waste
  treatment)
    Dorr-Oliver BV, Wegalaan 38-44, 2132 JC Hoofdoorp, Netherlands

THE DOW CHEMICAL CO   2030 Dow Center, Midland, MI 48674, Tel: (517) 636-1000
  (Mfr chems, plastics, pharms, agric prdts, consumer prdts)
    Dow Chemical (Nederland) BV, Herbert H. Dowweg, P.O. Box 48, Terneuzen, Netherlands
    Lurex BV, Netherlands

DRAKE BEAM MORIN INC   100 Park Ave, New York, NY 10017, Tel: (212) 692-7700
  (Human resource mgmt consulting & training)
    DBM Nederland, P.O. Box 85557, 2508 CD The Hague, Netherlands

DRESSER INDUSTRIES INC   PO Box 718, Dallas, TX 75221-0718,
  Tel: (214) 740-6000
  (Diversified supplier of equip & tech serv to energy & natural resource ind)
    Dresser Netherlands BV, Leidseplein 29, 1017 PS Amsterdam, Netherlands
    Kellogg Continental BV, Netherlands
    Kellogg Continental Construction BV, Leidseplein 29, 2240 BA Amsterdam, Netherlands
    Worthington Pump Nederland BV, Bijlmermeerstraat 12, 2130 AM Hoofddorp, Netherlands

E I DU PONT DE NEMOURS & CO   1007 Market St, Wilmington, DE 19898,
  Tel: (302) 774-1000
  (Mfr/sale diversified chems, plastics, specialty prdts & fibers)
    Continental Netherlands Oil Co., The Hague, Netherlands
    DuPont de Nemours (Nederland) BV, Netherlands

DURAMETALLIC CORP   2104 Factory St, Kalamazoo, MI 49001, Tel: (616) 382-8720
  (Mfr mech seals, compression packings, auxiliaries)
    Durametallic Benelux, Netherlands

THE DURIRON CO INC   PO Box 8820, Dayton, OH 45401-8820, Tel: (513) 476-6100
  (Mfr chem equip, pumps, valves, filters, fans, heat exchangers)
    Durco BV, Elleboog 52, 4822 NA Breda, Netherlands

E-Z-EM INC   717 Main St, Westbury, NY 11590, Tel: (516) 333-8230
(Mfr prdts for med contrast media, lead protective wear & surg prdts)
   E-Z-EM Nederland BV, Planckstraat 69, 3316 GS Dordrecht, Netherlands

EASTMAN & BEAUDINE INC   13355 Noel Rd, #1370, Dallas, TX 75240,
   Tel: (214) 661-5520
(Investments)
   Eastman & Beaudine Inc., Netherlands

EASTMAN CHEMICAL   PO Box 511, Kingsport, TN 37662, Tel: (423) 229-2000
(Mfr plastics, chems, fibers)
   Eastman Chemical, Rotterdam, Netherlands

EASTMAN KODAK CO   343 State St, Rochester, NY 14650, Tel: (716) 724-4000
(Devel/mfr photo & chem prdts, info mgmt/video/copier sys, fibers/plastics for
various ind)
   Kodak Nederland BV, P.O. Box 1000, Driebergen, Netherlands

EBASCO SERVICES INC   2 World Trade Center, New York, NY 10048-0752,
   Tel: (212) 839-1000
(Engineering, constr)
   Ebasco BV Netherlands, Verrign Stuartlaan 7, 2288 EK Rijswijk, The Hague,
      Netherlands
   Ebasco Overseas Corp., Verrijn Stuartlaan 7, 2288 EK Rijswijk, The Hague,
      Netherlands

ECLIPSE INC   1665 Elmwood Rd, Rockford, IL 61103, Tel: (815) 877-3031
(Mfr ind process heating equip & sys)
   Eclipse Combustion Ltd., Postbus 37, 2800 AA Gouda, Netherlands

EG&G INC   45 William St, Wellesley, MA 02181-4078, Tel: (617) 237-5100
(Diversified R/D, mfg & services)
   EG&G Benelux BV, P.O. Box 3198, 4800 DD Breda, Netherlands
   EG&G Sealol, Marconiweg 69, 3225 LV Hellevoetsluis, Netherlands

EMERY WORLDWIDE   One Lagoon Dr, #400, Redwood City, CA 94065,
   Tel: (800) 227-1981
(Freight transport, global logistics, air cargo)
   Con-Way Intermodal BV Holland Ltd., Netherlands

ENCYCLOPAEDIA BRITANNICA INC   310 S Michigan Ave, Chicago, IL 60604,
   Tel: (312) 321-7000
(Publishing)
   Encyclopaedia Britannica (The Netherlands), Burgemeester Hazenberglaan 405,
      3078 HG Rotterdam, Netherlands

ENERPAC   13000 W Silver Spring Dr, Butler, WI 53007, Tel: (414) 781-6600
(Mfr/sale high pressure hydraulic maint tools)
   Enerpac BV, P.O. Box 269, 3900 AB Veenendaal, Netherlands

ENGELHARD CORP   101 Wood Ave S, CN 770, Iselin, NJ 08830, Tel: (908) 205-5000
(Mfr pigments, additives, catalysts, chemicals, engineered materials)
   Engelhard DeMeern BV, Strijkviertel 67, 3454 ZG De Meern, Netherlands
   Engelhard Terneuzen BV, P.O. Box 404, Finlandweg 21, 4530 AK Terneuzen, Netherlands

ENTERPRISES INTL INC   P.O. Box 293, Hoquiam, WA 98550, Tel: (360) 533-6222
  (Mfr/sale/svce capital equip for pulp, paper & newsprint ind)
    Machinefabriek Roosendaal BV, Schotsbossenstraat 16, 4705 AG Roosendaal, Netherlands

EQUIFAX INC   PO Box 4081, Atlanta, GA 30302, Tel: (404) 885-8000
  (Information services)
    Equifax Decision Systems BV, Museumplein 11, 1071 DJ Amsterdam, Netherlands

ERICO PRODUCTS INC   34600 Solon Road, Cleveland, OH 44139,
  Tel: (216) 248-0100
  (Mfr electric welding apparatus & hardware, metal stampings, specialty fasteners)
    Erico Europa BV, Netherlands

EXCELLON AUTOMATION   23915 Garnier, Torrance, CA 90509, Tel: (213) 534-6300
  (PCB drilling & routing machs; optical inspection equip)
    Excellon Europa BV, Vijhutzerkijk 158, P.O. Box 6, Vijfhutzen, Netherlands

EXPEDITORS INTL OF WASHINGTON INC   PO Box 69620, Seattle, WA 98168-9620,
  Tel: (206) 246-3711
  (Air/ocean freight forwarding, customs brokerage, intl logistics solutions)
    Expeditors Intl. BV, Freightway Bldg. #142, Flamingoweg 54, 1118 EG Schiphol South,
      Amsterdam, Netherlands

EXXON CORP   225 E John W Carpenter Freeway, Irving, TX 75062-2298,
  Tel: (214) 444-1000
  (Petroleum explor, prod, refining; mfr petrol & chem prdts; coal & minerals)
    Esso Capital BV, 129-131 Jan van Nassaustraat, 4837 DS Breda, Netherlands
    Esso Holding Co. Holland Inc., Graaf Engelbertlaan 75, 4837 DS Breda, Netherlands
    Esso Nederland BV, Jan van Nassaustraat 129-131, The Hague, Netherlands
    NV Nederlandse Gasunie, Laan Corpus den Hoorn 102, 9728 JR Groningen, Netherlands
    Nederlandse Aardolie Maatschappij BV, Schepersmaat 2, 9405 TA Assen, Netherlands

FALLEK CHEMICAL CORP   770 Lexington Ave, New York, NY 10017,
  Tel: (212) 223-3353
  (Petrochems, spec chems)
    Fallek Chemical (Europe) Ltd., Apollolaan 153, P.O. Box 7494, Amsterdam, Netherlands

FATMAN INTL PRIVATE DETECTIVE AGENCY   6638 Cascade Rd SE, Grand Rapids,
  MI 49546-6896, Tel: (616) 949-1790
  (Private investigation)
    The Fatman Intl. Private Detective Service, P.O. Box 39, 2240 AA Wassenaar,
      Netherlands

FEDERAL EXPRESS CORP   PO Box 727, Memphis, TN 38194, Tel: (901) 369-3600
  (Package express delivery service)
    Federal Express, Netherlands

FEDERAL-MOGUL CORP   PO Box 1966, Detroit, MI 48235, Tel: (810) 354-7700
  (Mfr/distr precision parts for automobiles, trucks, & farm/constrution vehicles)
    Glyco BV, Netherlands

FERRO CORPORATION   1000 Lakeside Ave, Cleveland, OH 44114,
  Tel: (216) 641-8580
  (Mfr chems, coatings, plastics, colors, refractories)
    Ferro (Holland) BV, Van Helmontstraat 20, P,O. Box 6088, 3002 Rotterdam, Netherlands

FINNIGAN CORP   355 River Oaks Parkway, San Jose, CA 95134-1991,
  Tel: (408) 433-4800
  (Mfr mass spectrometers)
    Finnigan MAT Benelux, Landjuweel 7, 3905 PE Veenendaal, Netherlands

FIRST NATIONAL BANK OF BOSTON   100 Federal St, Boston, MA 02110,
  Tel: (617) 434-2200
  (Commercial banking)
    Intl Factors Nederland NV, Netherlands

FISHER CONTROLS INTL INC   8000 Maryland Ave, Clayton, MO 63105,
  Tel: (314) 746-9900
  (Mfr ind process control equip)
    Fisher Controls BV, P.O. Box 212, 2280 AE Rijiswijk, 21-23 Treubstraat,
    2288 EH Rijswijk, Netherlands

FLUKE CORP   PO Box 9090, Everett, WA 98206-9090, Tel: (206) 347-6100
  (Mfr electronic test tools)
    Fluke Europe BV, P.O. Box 1186, Eindhoven, Netherlands

FLUOR DANIEL INC   3333 Michelson Dr, Irvine, CA 92730, Tel: (714) 975-2000
  (Engineering, construction, maintenance & technical services)
    Fluor Daniel BV, Surinameweg 17, 2035 VA Haarlem, Netherlands
    Fluor Daniel Consultants BV, Netherlands

FMC CORP   200 E Randolph Dr, Chicago, IL 60601, Tel: (312) 861-6000
  (Produces chems & precious metals, mfr machinery, equip & sys for ind, agric & govt)
    FMC Fluid Control (Nederland) BV, Netherlands
    FMC Food Machinery & Chemical Holding Co. BV, Netherlands
    FMC Industrial Chemicals (Netherlands) BV, Netherlands
    FMC Nederland BV, Netherlands

FOOTE CONE & BELDING COMMUNICATIONS INC   101 E Erie St, Chicago,
  IL 60611-2897, Tel: (312) 751-7000
  (Advertising agency)
    EMC Rotterdam, Netherlands
    Publicis-FCB, Metropool Bldg., Weesperstraat 63, 1018 VN Amsterdam, Netherlands

FORD MOTOR CO   The American Road, Dearborn, MI 48121, Tel: (313) 322-3000
  (Mfr motor vehicles)
    Ford Nederland BV, P.O. Box 795, 1000 AT Amsterdam, Netherlands

FORMICA CORP   1680 Route 23 North, Wayne, NJ 07474-0980, Tel: (201) 305-9400
  (Mfr decorative laminate, adhesives & solvents)
    Formica Nederland BV, Dobbeweg 15, P.O. Box 44, Voorschoten, Netherlands

FOSTER REFRIGERATOR CORP   247 N Second, Hudson, NY 12534, Tel: (518) 828-3311
  (Refrigerators, freezers)
    Foster Refrigerator Continental BV, Netherlands

FOUR WINDS INTL GROUP   1500 SW First Ave, #850, Portland, OR 97201,
  Tel: (503) 241-2732
  (Transp of household goods & general cargo, third party logistics)
    Four Winds KHZ Group, P.O. Box 354, 2400 AJ Alphen Aan Den Rijn, Netherlands

THE FRANKLIN MINT   Franklin Center, PA 19091, Tel: (610) 459-6000
  (Creation/mfr/mktg collectibles & luxury items)
     Franklin Mint BV, Willem Barentszstraat 11-19, 3165 AA Rotterdam, Albrandswaard,
       Netherlands

FURON CO   29982 Ivy Glenn Dr, Laguna Niguel, CA 92677, Tel: (714) 831-5350
  (Mfr of ind components)
     Furon CHR Europe BV, Netherlands

GAF CORP   1361 Alps Rd, Wayne, NJ 07470, Tel: (201) 628-3000
  (Chems, bldg materials, commun)
     GAF Corp., P.O. Box 4005, 3102 GA Schiedam, Netherlands

GENERAL BINDING CORP   One GBC Plaza, Northbrook, IL 60062,
  Tel: (708) 272-3700
  (Binding & laminating equip & associated supplies)
     General Binding (Nederland) BV, Graftermeerstraat 36-38, 2131 AC Hoofddorp,
       Netherlands

GENERAL ELECTRIC CO   3135 Easton Tpk, Fairfield, CT 06431,
  Tel: (203) 373-2211
  (Diversified manufacturing, technology & services)
     General Electric Co.,
       all mail to U.S. address; phone (800) 626-2004 or (518) 438-6500

GENERAL MILLS INC   1 General Mills Blvd, PO Box 1113, Minneapolis, MN 55440,
  Tel: (612) 540-2311
  (Mfr consumer foods)
     Snack Ventures Europe, Zonnebaan 35, 3606 CH Maarssen, Netherlands

GENERAL MOTORS ACCEPTANCE CORP   3044 West Grand Blvd, Detroit, MI 48202,
  Tel: (313) 556-5000
  (Automobile financing)
     GMAC, Hoofdweg 486, 3067 GK Rotterdam, Netherlands
     GMAC Nederland NV, Blaak 22, P.O. Box 715, 3000 AS Rotterdam, Netherlands

GENERAL MOTORS CORP   3044 W Grand Blvd, Detroit, MI 48202-3091,
  Tel: (313) 556-5000
  (Mfr full line vehicles, automotive electronics, coml technologies, telecom, space,
  finance)
     General Motors Nederland BV, Netherlands

GENERAL RAILWAY SIGNAL CO   PO Box 20600, Rochester, NY 14602-0600,
  Tel: (716) 783-2000
  (Mfr railway, rapid transit & vehicle control sys)
     Algemene Sein Industrie BV, Moeder Teresalaan 100, Utrecht, Netherlands

GENRAD INC   300 Baker Ave, Concord, MA 01742, Tel: (508) 369-4400
  (Mfr automatic test equip)
     GenRad Benelux BV, Netherlands

THE GILLETTE CO   Prudential Tower, Boston, MA 02199, Tel: (617) 421-7000
  (Devel/mfr personal care/use prdts: blades & razors, toiletries, cosmetics,
  stationery)
     Braun Nederland BV, Rijswijk (ZH), Netherlands
     Gilfin BV, Netherlands

Gillette Finance BV, Amsterdam, Netherlands
Gillette Intl. BV, Netherlands
Gillette Nederland BV, Rijswijk (ZH), Netherlands
Jafra Cosmetics Intl. BV, Leiderdorp, Netherlands

GLOBAL INTERNATIONAL 1304 Willow St, Martinez, CA 94553, Tel: (510) 229-9330
(International moving & forwarding)
  GVL International BV, Rozenhof 33, 3311 JT Dordrecht, Netherlands

GOLODETZ GROUP CORP 142 W 57th St, New York, NY 10019, Tel: (212) 887-1600
(Commodity dealer)
  Lonconex BV, Londensche & Continentale Export-Mij., Netherlands
  Prohama BV, Producten Handelmij., Rokin 54, P.O. Box 3251, Amsterdam, Netherlands

W R GRACE & CO One Town Center Rd, Boca Raton, FL 33486-1010,
  Tel: (407) 362-2000
(Mfr spec chems & materials: packaging, health care, catalysts, construction, water
treatment/process)
  Cacao de Zaan BV, Stationsstraat 76, Koog aan de Zaan, Netherlands

GRANT THORNTON INTL Prudential Plaza, Chicago, IL 60601, Tel: (312) 856-0001
(Intl accountants)
  Grant Thornton Intl, Noordsingel 250, 3032 BN Rotterdam, Netherlands

GREY ADVERTISING INC 777 Third Ave, New York, NY 10017, Tel: (212) 546-2000
(Advertising)
  Grey, Parnassusweg 103, 1077 DE Amsterdam, Netherlands

GROUNDWATER TECHNOLOGY INC 100 River Ridge Dr, Norwood, MA 02062,
  Tel: (617) 769-7600
(Industrial site cleanup, mgmt & consulting)
  Groundwater Technology BV, Canaalstaete-Kanaalweg 33, 2903 LR Capelle a/d IJssel,
    Netherlands

GTE CORP One Stamford Forum, Stamford, CT 06904, Tel: (203) 965-2000
(Electr prdts, telecom sys, publ & commun)
  GTE Atea NV, Netherlands
  GTE Sylvanla NV, Riethil 7, Breda, Netherlands

FRANK B HALL & CO INC 549 Pleasantville Rd, Briarcliff Manor, NY 10510,
  Tel: (914) 769-9200
(Insurance)
  Blom and Van Der Aa Holdings BV, Netherlands

HANNON ELECTRIC CO 1605 Waynesburg Rd, SE, Canton, OH 44707,
  Tel: (216) 456-4728
(Specialized heating equip)
  Hanco Intl Europa BV, Netherlands

THE HARPER GROUP 260 Townsend St, PO Box 77933, San Francisco,
  CA 94107-1719, Tel: (415) 978-0600
(Ocean/air freight fwdg, customs brokerage, packing & whse, logistics mgt, ins)
  Circle Freight Intl. (Holland) BV, P.O. Box 7503, 1118 ZG Schiphol C, Amsterdam,
    Netherlands
  Con-Carriers, P.O. Box 12023, 3047 GA Rotterdam, Netherlands
  Max Gruenhut BV, P.O. Box 12023, 3047 GA Rotterdam, Netherlands

HECKETT   PO Box 1071, Butler, PA 16001-1071, Tel: (412) 283-5741
  (Metal reclamation, steel mill services)
    Heckett (Holland) BV, P.O. Box 83, 1970 AB Ijmuiden, Netherlands

H J HEINZ CO   PO Box 57, Pittsburgh, PA 15230-0057, Tel: (412) 456-5700
  (Processed food prdts & nutritional services)
    H.J. Heinz BV, Elst, Gelderland, Netherlands

HENNINGSEN FOODS INC   2 Corporate Park Dr, White PLains, NY 10604,
  Tel: (914) 694-1000
  (Dehyd egg, poultry & meat prdts)
    Hennigsen Nederland BV, P.O. Box 344, Schouwslootweg 3, Waalwyjk, Netherlands
    Henningsen/Van Den Burg BV, 20 Sluisweg, P.O. Box 220, Waalwyjk, Netherlands

HERCULES INC   Hercules Plaza, Wilmington, DE 19894-0001, Tel: (302) 594-5000
  (Mfr spec chems, plastics, film & fibers, coatings, resins, food ingredients)
    Hercules BV, Veraartlaan 8, P.O. Box 5832, 2280 HV Rijswijk, Netherlands

HETEROCHEMICAL CORP   111 E Hawthorne Ave, Valley Stream, NY 11580,
  Tel: (516) 561-8225
  (Chloride prdts, germicides, etc)
    Randstad BV Chemische Industrie, Eikenlaan 65, P.O. Box 26, Soest, Netherlands

HEWLETT-PACKARD CO   3000 Hanover St, Palo Alto, CA 94304-0890,
  Tel: (415) 857-1501
  (Mfr computing, communications & measurement prdts & services)
    Hewlett-Packard Nederland BV, Startbaan 16, 1187 XR Amstelveen, Netherlands

HIGH VOLTAGE ENGINEERING CO   401 Edgewater Pl, Wakefield, MA 01880,
  Tel: (617) 224-1001
  (Holding co: industrial & scientific instruments)
    High Voltage Engineering BV, Amsterdamseweg 61, Amersfoort, Netherlands

HOLIDAY INNS INC   3742 Lamar Ave, Memphis, TN 38195, Tel: (901) 362-4001
  (Hotels, restaurants, casinos)
    Holiday Inn, 1 Veldmaarschalk, Montgomery-laan, Eindhoven, Netherlands

A J HOLLANDER & CO INC   257 Park Ave So, New York, NY 10010,
  Tel: (212) 353-8000
  (Hides, skins & leather)
    Julius Hollander BV, P.O. Box 8373, Amsterdam, Netherlands

HOMELITE TEXTRON   14401 Carowinds Blvd, Charlotte, NC 28217,
  Tel: (704) 588-3200
  (Mfr pumps, generators, lawn/garden equip, outdoor power equip)
    Homelite Textron, Haverstraat 24, 2153 GB Nieuw Vennep, Netherlands

HONEYWELL INC   PO Box 524, Minneapolis, MN 55440-0524, Tel: (612) 951-1000
  (Devel/mfr controls for home & building, industry, space & aviation)
    Honeywell BV, Laarderhoogtweg 18, 1101 EA Amsterdam ZO, Netherlands

HORWATH INTL   415 Madison Ave, New York, NY 10017, Tel: (212) 838-5566
  (Public accountants & auditors)
    Horwath Tax Holland, Weerdestein 117, 1083 GH Amsterdam, Netherlands
    Walgemoed, Weerdestein 117, 1083 GH Amsterdam, Netherlands

HOUGHTON INTL INC   PO Box 930, Valley Forge, PA 19482-0930,
  Tel: (610) 666-4000
  (Mfr spec chems, hydraulic fluids, lubricants)
    Houghton Benelux BV, Energieweg 26, 4096 CG Oosterhout, Netherlands

HUBBARD FARMS INC   PO Box 415, Walpole, NH 03608, Tel: (603) 756-3311
  (Poultry breeding R&D, poultry foundation breeding stock)
    Hubbard Nederland BV, P.O. Box 31, 8090 AA Wezep, Netherlands

HUGHES TOOL CO   PO Box 2539, Houston, TX 77001, Tel: (713) 924-2222
  (Equip & serv to oil & gas explor & prod ind)
    BJ-Hughes BV, Nijverheidsweg 45, 4879 AC Etten-Leur, Netherlands

HUTCHINSON TECHNOLOGY INC   40 W Highland Pk, Hutchinson, MN 55350-9784,
  Tel: (612) 587-1900
  (Mfr suspension assembly components for rigid disk drives)
    Hutchinson Technology Inc., Schuttersveld 4A, 2316 ZA Leiden, Netherlands

HYSTER CO   PO Box 2902, Portland, OR 97208, Tel: (503) 280-7000
  (Fork lifts, trucks, trailers, towing winches, personnel lifts, compaction equip)
    Hyster BV, Nijverheidsweg 26-29, P.O. Box 136, Nijmegen, Netherlands

IBM CORP   Old Orchard Rd, Armonk, NY 10504, Tel: (914) 765-1900
  (Information products, technology & services)
    IBM Nederland NV, Johan Huizingalaan 265, 1066 AP Amsterdam, Netherlands

IDEX CORP   630 Dundee Rd, #400, Northbrook, IL 60062, Tel: (708) 498-7070
  (Mfr ind pumps, lubrication sys, metal fabrication equip, bending & clamping devices)
    Viking Pump Intl. Inc., Prins Bernhardlaan 10, 2405 VT Alphen A/d Rijn, Netherlands

IMCO SERVICES   5950 N Course Dr, Houston, TX 70072, Tel: (713) 561-1300
  (Drilling fluids)
    Imco Services BV, Emmapark 3, 2595 ES The Hague, Netherlands

IMS INTERNATIONAL INC   100 Campus Rd, Totowa, NJ 07512, Tel: (201) 790-0700
  (Market research reports)
    IMS Nederland BV, Netherlands

INFORMATION BUILDERS INC   1250 Broadway, New York, NY 10001,
  Tel: (212) 736-4433
  (Devel/mfr/serv computer software)
    Information Builders Nederland BV, Stroombahn 4, 1181 Amstelveen, Netherlands

INGERSOLL-RAND CO   200 Chestnut Ridge Rd, Woodcliff Lake, NJ 07675,
  Tel: (201) 573-0123
  (Mfr compressors, rock drills, pumps, air tools, door hardware, ball bearings)
    CPM/Europe BV, Distelweg 89, 1031 HD Amsterdam, Netherlands
    Ingersoll-Rand Benelux, Std. Machin Prof. Tool Group ISO, Produktieweg 10,
    2382 PB Zoeterwoude-Rinjdijk, Netherlands

INSTRUMENTATION LABORATORY   113 Hartwell Ave, Lexington, MA 02173-3190,
  Tel: (617) 861-0710
  (Med & sci analyzers & meas instru)
    Instrumentation Laboratory BV, P.O. Box 253, Ambachstweg 304, 3400 AB Ijsselstein,
    Netherlands

INTERGRAPH CORP   Huntsville, AL 35894-0001, Tel: (205) 730-2000
(Devel/mfr interactive computer graphic systems)
    Intergraph Benelux BV, Siriusdreef 2, 2130 AH Hoofddorp, Netherlands
    Intergraph Europe Inc., Siriusdreef 2, 2130 AH Netherlands

INTERMEC CORP   6001 36th Ave West, PO Box 4280, Everett, WA 98203-9280,
Tel: (206) 348-2600
(Mfr/distr automated data collection sys)
    Intermec Netherlands, P.O. Box 115, 3440 AC Woerden, Netherlands

INTERMODAL TECHNICAL SERVICES INC   9 Campus Dr #7, PO Box 316, Parsippany,
NJ 07054, Tel: (201) 993-3634
(Damage survey & inspection services)
    Intermodal Technical Services Inc., Teilingerstraat 53G, 3032 AS Rotterdam,
    Netherlands

INTERNATIONAL BANK WASHINGTON DC   1701 Pennsylvania Ave NW, Washington,
DC 20006, Tel: (202) 452-6500
(Banking)
    Europabank NV, Westblaak 147, P.O. Box 2585, Rotterdam, Netherlands

INTERNATIONAL CHEMICAL CORP   720 Fifth Ave, New York, NY 10019,
Tel: (212) 397-3300
(Chemicals, pharmaceuticals)
    Barberot BV, Etablissementen JV, Netherlands

INTERNATIONAL FLAVORS & FRAGRANCES INC   521 W 57th St, New York, NY 10019,
Tel: (212) 765-5500
(Create/mfr flavors, fragrances & aroma chems)
    Intl. Flavors & Fragrances (Nederland) BV, P.O. Box 309, 1200 AH Hilversum,
    Netherlands

INTERNATIONAL GAME TECHNOLOGY INC   5270 Neil Rd, Reno, NV 89502,
Tel: (702) 688-0100
(Mfr games, hobby goods; equip leasing, amusements, computers)
    IGT Europe BV, Daalmeerstraat 16, 2131 HC Hoofdorp, Netherlands

INTERNATIONAL PAPER   2 Manhattanville Rd, Purchase, NY 10577,
Tel: (914) 397-1500
(Mfr/distr container board, paper, wood prdts)
    Akrosil Europe BV, P.O. Box 6080, Imstenraderweg 15, 6401 SC Heerlen, Netherlands
    Anitec Image Nederland BV, P.O. Box 1125, 2302 BC Leiden, Netherlands
    Aussedat Rey Netherland BV, De Boelelaan 575A, 1082 RM Amsterdam, Netherlands
    Bergvik Chemie BV, Hellingstraat 22h, P.O. Box 1172, 1270 BC Huizen, Netherlands
    Forest Lines Agencies BV, Woudrichemstraat, Steiger 2216, P.O. Box 54128,
       3008 JC Rotterdam, Netherlands
    Horsell Graphic Industries BV, Netherlands
    Ilford Photo BV, P.O. Box 1125, 2302 BC Leiden, Netherlands

INTRALOX INC   PO Box 50699, New Orleans, LA 70150, Tel: (504) 733-0463
(Mfr plastic, modular conveyor belts & access)
    Intralox Benelux BV, P.O. Box 23280, 1100 DT Amsterdam, Netherlands

ITEL CORP   2 N Riverside Plaza, Chicago, IL 60606, Tel: (312) 902-1515
(Transport & equip leasing & serv)
    Itel Container Intl. BV, Netherlands

ITT CORP 1330 Ave of the Americas, New York, NY 10019-5490,
Tel: (212) 258-1000
(Design/mfr communications & electronic equip, hotels, insurance)
Conoflow Europa BV, Vierlinghstraat 10, P.O. Box 40, Dordrecht, Netherlands
Ergon Electric BV, Zwaansprengweg 20, P.O. Box 111, Apeldoorn, Netherlands
Flygt Pompen BV, Netherlands
ITT Grinnell Piping Products BV, Lorentzstraat 8, P.O. Box 43, Ede, Netherlands
ITT Nova, Netherlands
ITT Standard Nederland, Netherlands
Koni BV, Langeweg 1, P.O. Box 1014, Duo Beiuerland, Netherlands
Lowew Pompen Nederland BV, Netherlands
Markant BV, Netherlands
Metalight BV, Handelskade W. 17, Enschede, Netherlands
Muelink & Grol BV, Loodind En Metaalwarenfabriek, Paradijsvdgelstraat 11,
  P.O. Box 509, Groningen, Netherlands
Nederlandsche Standard Electric Mij. BV, Netherlands
Payot-Holland BV, Dr. N.G. Keizersgracht 12, Amsterdam, Netherlands
Publimedia BV, Laan Van Kronenburg 14, Amstelveen, Netherlands
Zwolsche Algemeene Verzekering Mij. NV, Netherlands

ITT HARTFORD INSURANCE GROUP Hartford Plaza, Hartford, CT 06115,
Tel: (203) 547-5000
(Insurance)
Zwolsche Group, Buizerdlaan 12, 3435 SB Nieuwegein, Netherlands

JEUNIQUE INTL INC 19501 E Walnut Dr, City of Industry, CA 91748,
Tel: (909) 598-8598
(Mfr/sale vitamins, food supplements, cosmetics, diet prdts)
Jeunique Intl. (Nederland) BV, Pampuslaan 161, 1382 JP Weesp, Netherlands

JOHNSON & JOHNSON One Johnson & Johnson Plaza, New Brunswick, NJ 08933,
Tel: (908) 524-0400
(R&D/mfr/sale health care prdts)
Chicopee BV, Lange Oyen 16, P.O. Box 15, Cuijk, Netherlands
Janssen Pharmaceutica BV, P.O. Box 90240, 5000 LT Tilburg, Netherlands
Johnson & Johnson Medical BV, P.O. Box 188, 3800 AD Amersfoort, Netherlands
Taxandria Pharmaceutica BV, Tilburg, Netherlands

S C JOHNSON & SON INC 1525 Howe St, Racine, WI 53403, Tel: (414) 631-2000
(Home, auto, commercial & personal care prdts, specialty chems)
Johnson Wax Nederland BV, Groot Mijdrechtstraat 81, P.O. Box 22, Mikdrecht,
  Netherlands

JOHNSON CONTROLS INC 5757 N Green Bay Ave, PO Box 591, Milwaukee,
WI 53201-0591, Tel: (414) 228-1200
(Mfr facility mgmt & control sys, auto seating, batteries & plastics)
Johnson Control Nederland BV, James Wattstraat, P.O. Box 230, 8901 BA Leeuwarden,
  Netherlands

THE JOHNSON CORP 805 Wood St, Three Rivers, MI 49093, Tel: (616) 278-1715
(Mfr rotary joints & syphon sys)
Johnson-Hamstra BV, P.O. Box 68, 1380 AB Weesp, Netherlands

THE JOURNAL OF COMMERCE 2 World Trade Center, New York, NY 10048,
Tel: (212) 837-7000
(Newspaper publisher)
A. Arnold Teesing BV, Tulipstraat 17, 1018 GZ Amsterdam, Netherlands

K-SWISS INC   20664 Bahama St, Chatsworth, CA   91311, Tel: (818) 998-3388
(Mfr casual & athletic shoes, socks, leisure apparel)
    K-Swiss BV, Spring Bldg., Overschiestraat 186F, 1062 XK Amsterdam, Netherlands

KARTRIDG PAK CO   807 W Kimberly Road, Davenport, IA   52808,
   Tel: (319) 391-1100
(Meat packaging & aerosol filling equip)
    Seffelaar & Looyen BV, Eektestraat 1, P.O. Box 24, Oldenzaal, Netherlands

KAWNEER CO INC   555 Guthridge Ct, Norcross, GA   30092, Tel: (404) 449-5555
(Mfr arch aluminum prdts for commercial constr)
    Alumax Extrusions BV, P.O. Box 248, 6040 AE Roermond, Netherlands
    Kawneer Europe BV, P.O. Box 1105, 6201 BC Maastricht, Netherlands

A T KEARNEY INC   222 West Adams St, Chicago, IL   60606, Tel: (312) 648-0111
(Mgmt consultants, executive search)
    A.T. Kearney Inc., P.O. Box 22926, 1100 DK Amsterdam, Netherlands

KEITHLEY INSTRUMENTS INC   28775 Aurora Rd, Cleveland, OH   44139,
   Tel: (216) 248-0400
(Mfr electr test/meas instru, PC-based data acquisition hdwe/software)
    Keithley Instruments BV, Avelingen West 49, 4202 MS Gorinchem, Netherlands

KELLOGG CO   One Kellogg Sq, PO Box 3599, Battle Creek, MI   49016-3599,
   Tel: (616) 961-2000
(Mfr ready-to-eat cereals, convenience foods)
    Kellogg's Nederland, Amersfoort, Netherlands (all inquiries to U.S. address)

KELLY SERVICES   999 W Big Beaver Rd, Troy, MI   48084, Tel: (810) 244-4313
(Temporary help placement)
    Kelly Services (Nederland) BV, 14 branches throughout Netherlands
    Kelly Services (Nederland) BV (HQ), De Horst 2, 2592 HA The Hague, Netherlands

KENNAMETAL INC   PO Box 231, Latrobe, PA   15650, Tel: (412) 539-5000
(Tools, hard carbide & tungsten alloys)
    Kennametal Nederland BV, Netherlands

KETCHUM COMMUNICATIONS   6 PPG Pl, Pittsburgh, PA   15222, Tel: (412) 456-3500
(Advertising, public relations, mgmt consulting)
    Ketchum Brunning Intl. BV, Weena 127, 3013 CK Rotterdam, Netherlands

KEYSTONE INTL INC   PO Box 40010, Houston, TX   77040, Tel: (713) 466-1176
(Mfr butterfly valves, actuators & control accessories)
    Keystone Nederland, Netherlands
    Keystone Valve Breda, Netherlands

KIMBERLY-CLARK CORP   PO Box 619100, Dallas, TX   75261, Tel: (214) 281-1200
(Mfr fiber-based prdts for personal care, lumber & paper prdts)
    Kimberly-Clark Benelux Operations BV, Groeneveldselaan 10, P.O. Box 72, Veenendaal,
       Netherlands
    Kimberly-Clark Page BV, Netherlands
    Kimberly-Clark Sales Corp., Veenendaal, Netherlands

LESTER B KNIGHT & ASSOC INC   549 W Randolph St, Chicago, IL   60661,
   Tel: (312) 346-2300
(Architecture, engineering, planning, operations & mgmt consulting)

Knight Wendling Consulting BV, Prins Hendriklaan 56, P.O. Box 75235, 1070 AE Amsterdam, Netherlands

KNOGO CORP   350 Wireless Blvd, Hauppauge, NY 11788-3907, Tel: (516) 232-2100
(Mfr electr article surveillance sys)
Knogo Nederland BV, Netherlands

THE KNOLL GROUP   105 Wooster St, New York, NY 10021, Tel: (212) 343-4000
(Mfr/sale office furnishings)
Knoll Intl., Netherlands

KOEHRING CO   PO Box 312, Milwaukee, WI 53201, Tel: (414) 784-5800
(Pulp mill & constr equip)
Koehring Europe BV, Netherlands

KORN/FERRY INTL   1800 Century Park East, Los Angeles, CA 90067,
Tel: (310) 552-1834
(Executive search)
Korn/Ferry Intl., Stawinskylaan 545, 1077 XX Amsterdam, Netherlands

KOSTER KEUNEN WAXES LTD   90 Bourne Blvd, Sayville, NY 11782,
Tel: (516) 589-0400
(Mfr waxes)
Koster Keunen (Holland) BV, Losweg 14, P.O. Box 25, Geldrop, Netherlands

KRATOS ANALYTICAL   535 E Crescent Ave, Ramsey, NJ 07466, Tel: (201) 825-7500
(Mfr liq chromatography, mass spectrometry & surface analysis instru)
Kratos Analytical BV, Buizenwerf 93, 3063 AB Rotterdam, Netherlands

LEVI STRAUSS & CO   1155 Battery, San Francisco, CA 94111, Tel: (415) 544-6000
(Mfr casual wearing apparel)
Levi Strauss Nederland BV, Schurenbergweg 6, 1105 AR Amsterdam, Netherlands

ELI LILLY & CO   Lilly Corporate Center, Indianapolis, IN 46285,
Tel: (317) 276-2000
(Mfr pharmaceuticals, animal health prdts)
Eli Lilly Nederland, City Kantoren, Roadstede 15, 3431 HA Nievwegein, Netherlands

LINTAS:WORLDWIDE   1 Dag Hammarskjold Plaza, New York, NY 10017,
Tel: (212) 605-8000
(Advertising agency)
Lintas:Amsterdam, World Trade Center Amsterdam, Tower C, Strawinskylaan 1641, 1077 XX Amsterdam, Netherlands

ARTHUR D LITTLE INC   25 Acorn Park, Cambridge, MA 02140-2390,
Tel: (617) 498-5000
(Mgmt, environ, health & safety consulting; tech & prdt development)
Arthur D. Little Intl. Inc., Willemswerf, Boompjes 40, 3011 XB Rotterdam, Netherlands

LITTON INDUSTRIES INC   21240 Burbank Blvd, Woodland Hills, CA 91367,
Tel: (818) 598-5000
(Elec sys, ind automation, resource explor)
Litton Business Systems Holland BV, Vrijzicht 79, P.O. Box 9267, 1006 AG Amsterdam, Netherlands

LNP ENGINEERING PLASTICS   475 Creamery Way, Exton, PA 19341,
  Tel: (215) 363-4500
  (Mfr thermoplastic composites)
    LNP Engineering Plastics, Ottergeerde 24, 4941 VM, Raamsdonksveer, Netherlands

LONGYEAR CO   PO Box 27314, Salt Lake City, UT 84127, Tel: (801) 972-1395
  (Mfr diamond drills, concrete cutting equip; drill serv)
    Longyear (Nederland) BV, Nijverheidsweg 47, P.O. Box 56, 4870 AB Etten-Leur (N.B.),
    Netherlands

LTX CORP   LTX Park, University Ave, Westwood, MA 02090, Tel: (617) 461-1000
  (Design/mfr computer-controlled semiconductor test systems)
    LTX Benelux BV, Stratumsedyk 29B, Eindhoven, Netherlands

LUFKIN RULE CO   PO Box 728, Apex, NC 27502, Tel: (919) 362-7510
  (Mfr measuring tapes & rules, hand tools)
    Lufkin Ruropa BV, Phinias Foggstraat 16, P.O. Box 53, Emmen, Netherlands

MALLINCKRODT MEDICAL INC   675 McDonnell Blvd, PO Box 5840, St Louis,
  MO 63134, Tel: (314) 895-2000
  (Mfr specialty medical prdts)
    Mallinckrodt Medical BV, Petten, Netherlands

MANPOWER INTL INC   5301 N Ironwood Rd, PO Box 2053, Milwaukee,
  WI 53201-2053, Tel: (414) 961-1000
  (Temporary help service)
    Manpower BV NV, P.O. Box 12150, 1100 AD Amsterdam, Netherlands

MARATHON LE TOURNEAU CO   PO Box 2307, Longview, TX 75606, Tel: (903) 237-7000
  (Mfr heavy constr, mining mach & equip)
    H.S.B. Boumachines, Europaweg 212, 7300 AJ Apeldoorn, Netherlands

MARCAM CORP   95 Wells Ave, Newton, MA 02159, Tel: (617) 965-0220
  (Applications software & services)
    Mar Computeraided Mfg. BV, DeWaal 20, 5684 PH Best, Netherlands

MARK IV INDUSTRIES INC   PO Box 810, Amherst, NY 14226-0810,
  Tel: (716) 689-4972
  (Mfr diversified prdts: timers & controls, power equip, loudspeaker sys, etc)
    Vapor Intl. Holland BV, Atoomweg 496, 3542 AB Utrecht, Netherlands

MARKEM CORP   150 Congress St, Keene, NH 03431, Tel: (603) 352-1130
  (Marking and printing mach; hot stamping foils)
    Markem (Europa) BV, Netherlands

MARS INC   6885 Elm St, McLean, VA 22101, Tel: (703) 821-4900
  (Mfr candy, snack foods, cat food)
    Effem BV, Nijenburg 152, P.O. Box 7893, Amsterdam, Netherlands
    Mars Chocoladefabriek BV, Taylorweg 5, Veghel, Netherlands

MARSH & McLENNAN COS INC   1166 Ave of the Americas, New York, NY 10036-1011,
  Tel: (212) 345-5000
  (Insurance)
    Hudig-Langeveldt Insurance Brokers, P.O. Box 518, 3000 AM Rotterdam, Netherlands

MARSTELLER INTL   1 E Wacker Dr, Chicago, IL 60601, Tel: (312) 329-1100
  (Advertising, marketing research, sales promotion)
    Burson-Marsteller BV, Netherlands

MARYLAND CUP CORP   10100 Reistertown Rd, Owings Mills, MD 21117,
  Tel: (301) 363-1111
  (Paper cups, drinking straws, ice cream cones, packaging equip, etc)
    Sweetheart-Monocon BV JV, Houtwal 3, P.O. Box 8, Groenlo, Netherlands

MATHEWS & CLARK COMMUNICATIONS   710 Lakeway, #170, Sunnyvale, CA 94086-4013,
  Tel: (408) 736-1120
  (Public relations: hi-tech industry)
    Franssen Communications, Dennenweg 14, 3735 MS Bosch en Duin, Netherlands

MATTEL INC   333 Continental Blvd, El Segundo, CA 90245, Tel: (310) 252-2000
  (Mfr toys, dolls, games, crafts & hobbies)
    Mattel BV, Schurenbergweg 5, 1105 AP Amsterdam, Netherlands

MAYFRAN INC   PO Box 43038, Cleveland, OH 44143, Tel: (216) 461-4100
  (Mfr conveyors for metal working & refuse)
    Mayfran Limburg BV, Netherlands

MEAD CORP   Courthouse Plaza, NE, Dayton, OH 45463, Tel: (513) 222-6323
  (Mfr paper, packaging, pulp, lumber & other wood prdts, school & office prdts; electr
  pub, distri)
    Mead Coated Board Europe BV, Netherlands
    Mead Holdings BV, Netherlands
    Mead Verpakking BV, Ettenseweg 46, P.O. Box 1134, Roosendaal (N.B.), Netherlands

THE MEARL CORP   320 Old Briarcliff Rd, Briarcliff Manor, NY 10510,
  Tel: (914) 923-8500
  (Mfr pearlescent luster pigments, mica, decorative iridescent film)
    Mearl Intl. BV, Emrikweg 18, 2031 BT Haarlem, Netherlands

MEASUREX CORP   One Results Way, Cupertino, CA 95014-5991, Tel: (408) 255-1500
  (Mfr computer integrated mfg sys)
    Measurex BV, Stephensonstraat 4, 4004 JA Tiel, Netherlands

MEDTRONIC INC   7000 Central Ave, NE, Minneapolis, MN 55432,
  Tel: (612) 574-4000
  (Mfr/sale/svce therapeutic medical devices)
    Vitatron Medical BV, Kanaalweg 24, P.O. Box 76, 6950 Dierem, Netherlands

MEMOREX CORP   San Thomas at Central Expressway, Santa Clara, CA 95052,
  Tel: (408) 987-1000
  (Magnetic recording tapes, etc)
    Memorex BV, Netherlands

MERCK SHARP & DOHME INTL   PO Box 2000, Rahway, NJ 07065, Tel: (201) 574-4000
  (Pharms, chems & biologicals)
    Merck, Sharp & Dohme BV, Waarderweg 39, P.O. Box 581, 2031 BN Haarlem, Netherlands

MERIDIAN DATA INC   5615 Scotts Valley Dr, Scotts Valley, CA 95062,
  Tel: (408) 438-3100
  (Mfr computer sys & equip)
    Meridian Data Europe, Mierloseweg 53, PO Box 384, 5660 AJ Geldrop, Netherlands

METCO DIV OF PERKIN-ELMER   1101 Prospect Ave, PO Box 1006, Westbury,
  NY 11590-0201, Tel: (516) 334-1300
  (Mfr/serv thermal spray coating equip & supplies)
    Metco Nederland BV, P.O. Box 3464, 4800 DL Breda, Netherlands

MICROSOFT CORP   One Microsoft Way, Redmond, WA 98052-6399,
  Tel: (206) 882-8080
  (Computer software, peripherals & services)
    Microsoft Netherlands BV, P.O. Box 364, Jupiterstraat 190, 2132 HH Hoofddorp,
      Netherlands

MILCHEM INC   3900 Essex Lane, PO Box 22111, Houston, TX 77027,
  Tel: (214) 439-8000
  (Gas & oil well drilling fluids & chem additives)
    Milchem Nederland BV Intl. Ltd., Regentesselaan 18, The Hague, Netherlands

MILLIPORE CORP   Ashley Rd, Bedford, MA 01730, Tel: (617) 275-9205
  (Mfr precision filters, hi-performance liquid chromatography instru)
    Millipore BV, Penningweg 33, P.O. Box 166, 4870 AD Etten, Netherlands

MINE SAFETY APPLIANCES CO   PO Box 426, Pittsburgh, PA 15230,
  Tel: (421) 273 5000
  (Safety equip, ind filters)
    MSA Nederland NV, Kernweg 20, P.O. Box 39, 1620 AA Hoorn, Netherlands

MOBIL CORP   3225 Gallows Rd, Fairfax, VA 22037-0001, Tel: (703) 846-3000
  (Petroleum explor & refining, mfr petrol prdts, chems, petrochems)
    Mobil Chemie BV, P.O. Box 130, Delft, Netherlands
    Mobil Chemie Mfg. BV, P.O. Box 130, Delft, Netherlands
    Mobil Oil BV, Westblaak 163, 3012 KJ Rotterdam, Netherlands
    Mobil Oil BV, P.O. Box 8125, Amsterdam, Netherlands

MODINE MANUFACTURING CO   1500 DeKoven Ave, Racine, WI 53403,
  Tel: (414) 636-1200
  (Mfr heat-transfer prdts)
    Modine Europe BV, P.O. Box 83, 5450 AB Mill, Netherlands
    NRF Holding BV, Langenboomseweg 64, P.O. Box 1, 5450 AA Mill, Netherlands
    NRF Thermal Engineering BV, Netherlands

MOGUL CORP   PO Box 200, Chagrin Falls, OH 44022, Tel: (216) 247-5000
  (Water treatment chems, equip)
    Mogul BV, P.O. Box 72, 3640 AB Mijdrecht, Netherlands
    Mogul BV, Groot Mijdrechtstraat 31-35, 3641 RV Mijdrecht, Netherlands

MONMOUTH PLASTICS INC   PO Box 921, Asbury Park, NJ 07712, Tel: (201) 775-5100
  (Flame retardant concentrates, thermoplastic sys, spec formulations)
    Integrated Chemicals, Netherlands

MOORE PRODUCTS CO   Sumneytown Pike, Spring House, PA 19477,
  Tel: (215) 646-7400
  (Mfr process control instru)
    Moore Products Co. BV, Wagenmakerstraat 3, Industrieterrein "Donkersloot-Noord",
      2984 BD Ridderkerk, Netherlands

MORGAN GUARANTY TRUST CO   23 Wall St, New York, NY 10260, Tel: (212) 483-2323
   (Banking)
      Bank Morgan Labouchere NV, Netherlands

MORTON INTERNATIONAL INC   100 N Riverside Plaza, Chicago, IL 60606-1596,
   Tel: (312) 807-2000
   (Mfr adhesives, coatings, finishes, spec chems, advanced & electr materials, salt,
   airbags)
      Morton Intl. BV, Valgenweg 7, P.O. Box 273, 9930 AG Delfzijl, Netherlands
      Morton Intl. BV, Special Chemicals Group, Kleine Koppel 31, P.O. Box 32,
        3800 AA Amersfoort, Netherlands

MOTOROLA INC   1303 E Algonquin Rd, Schaumburg, IL 60196, Tel: (708) 576-5000
   (Mfr commun equip, semiconductors, cellular phones)
      Motorola BV, Emmalaan 41, 3581 HP Utrecht, Netherlands

MULTIGRAPHICS DIV   1800 W Central Rd, Mt Prospect, IL 60056,
   Tel: (708) 398-1900
   (Offset duplicating & graphic commun sys)
      AM Intl. BV, P.O. Box 130, 2280 AC Rijswijk, Netherlands

MacDERMID INC   245 Freight St, Waterbury, CT 06702, Tel: (203) 575-5700
   (Chem processing for metal ind, plastics, electronics cleaners, strippers)
      MacDermid Benelux BV, Mon Plaisir 89C, 4879 AN Etten-Leur, Netherlands

THE MacNEAL-SCHWENDLER CORP   815 Colorado Blvd, Los Angeles, CA 90041,
   Tel: (213) 258-9111
   (Devel/mfr computer-aided engineering software)
      MacNeal-Schwendler Benelux BV, Groningenweg 6, 2803 PV Gouda, Netherlands
      MacNeal-Schwendler EDC BV, Groningenweg 6, 2803 PV Gouda, Netherlands

McCANN-ERICKSON WORLDWIDE   750 Third Ave, New York, NY 10017,
   Tel: (212) 697-6000
   (Advertising)
      McCann Industrieel, Netherlands
      McCann Retail, Netherlands
      McCann-Direct, Netherlands
      McCann-Erickson (Nederland) BV, Amsterdam, Netherlands
      Universal-Media, Netherlands

McKINSEY & CO INC   55 E 52nd St, New York, NY 10022, Tel: (212) 446-7000
   (Mgmt consultants)
      McKinsey & Co. Benelux, Amstel 344, 1017 AS Amsterdam, Netherlands

NALCO CHEMICAL CO   One Nalco Center, Naperville, IL 60563-1198,
   Tel: (708) 305-1000
   (Chems for water & waste water treatment, oil prod & refining, ind processes;
   water/energy mgmt serv)
      Nalco Chemicals BV, P.O. Box 5131, Swaardvenstraat 5, 5004 EC Tilburg, Netherlands
      Nalco Europe SARL, P.O. Box 627, 2300 AP Leiden, Netherlands

NATIONAL CAR RENTAL SYSTEM INC   7700 France Ave S, Minneapolis, MN 55435,
   Tel: (612) 830-2121
   (Car rental)
      Holland Rent-A-Car BV, Overtoom 51-53, Amsterdam W & Schiphol Airport, Netherlands

NATIONAL GYPSUM CO   2001 Rexford Rd., Charlotte, NC 28211,
Tel: (704) 365-7300
(Building prdts & servs)
  Austin Nederland BV, Netherlands

NATIONAL SERVICE INDUSTRIES INC   1420 Peachtree St NE, Atlanta, GA 30309,
Tel: (404) 853-1000
(Mfr lighting equip, spec chems; textile rental)
  Zep Europe, Bergen op Zoom, Netherlands

NATIONAL STARCH & CHEMICAL CO   10 Finderne Ave, Bridgewater, NJ 08807-3300,
Tel: (908) 685-5000
(Mfr adhesives & sealants, resins & spec chems, electr materials & adhesives, food
prdts, ind starch)
  National Starch & Chemical BV, Zutphen, Netherlands
  Vinamul BV, Geleen, Netherlands

NELLCOR INC   4280 Hacienda Dr, Pleasanton, CA 94588-2719, Tel: (510) 463-4000
(Mfr medical patient safety & management monitoring instruments)
  Nellcor BV, Hambakenwetering 1, 5231 DD 's-Hertogenbosch, Netherlands

NEVILLE CHEMICAL CO   2800 Neville Rd, Pittsburgh, PA 15225-1496,
Tel: (412) 331-4200
(Mfr hydrocarbon resins)
  Nevcin Polymers BV, Amstedlijk 66, 1420 AD Vithoorn, Netherlands

NEW BRUNSWICK SCIENTIFIC CO INC   44 Talmadge Rd, Edison, NJ 08818-4005,
Tel: (201) 287-1200
(Mfr research & production equip for life sciences)
  New Brunswick Scientific Benelux BV, P.O. Box 6826, 6503 GH Nijmegen, Netherlands

NEW VALLEY CORP   One Lake St, Upper Saddle River, NJ 07458,
Tel: (201) 818-5000
(Financial & messaging services)
  Western Union Financial Services Intl., La Vie/Lange Viestraat 333,
    3511 BK Utrecht, Netherlands

NIBCO CORP   500 Simpson Ave, PO Box 1167, Elkhart, IN 46515,
Tel: (219) 295-3000
(Mfr fluid handling prdts for residential, commercial, industrial & fire protection
markets)
  Nibco Inc., World Trade Center, Beursplein 37, P.O. Box 30222, 3001 DE Rotterdam,
    Netherlands

A C NIELSEN CO   Nielsen Plaza, Northbrook, IL 60062-6288, Tel: (708) 498-6300
(Market research)
  A.C. Nielsen (Nederland) BV, Diemerhop 2, 1112 XL Diemen, Netherlands

NORDSON CORP   28601 Clemens Rd, Westlake, OH 44145, Tel: (216) 892-1580
(Mfr ind application equip & packaging mach)
  Nordson Nederland BV, Peppelkade 40, Industrieterrein Doornkade, 3992 AK Houten,
    Netherlands
  Nordson Walcom BV, Nijverheidsweg 23, 5071 NL Udenhout, Netherlands

NORTHERN TELECOM SYSTEMS CORP   PO Box 1222, Minneapolis, MN 55440,
  Tel: (612) 932-8000
  (Remote information processing sys)
    Data 100 BV, Bldg. Bavinckstate, Prof. J.H., Bavinckloon 5, P.O. Box 852,
      1183 AT Amstelucen, Netherlands

NORTON CO   1 New Bond St, Worcester, MA 01606, Tel: (508) 795-5000
  (Abrasives, drill bits, constr & safety prdts, plastics)
    Norton BV, Wijingaardsweg 73, Hoensbroek, Netherlands
    Norton Chemical Process Products Div., Jan Van Nassaustraat 12, The Hague,
      Netherlands

NOVELLUS SYSTEMS INC   81 Vista Montana, San Jose, CA 95134,
  Tel: (408) 943-9700
  (Mfr advanced processing systems used in fabrication of integrated circuits)
    Novellus Systems BV, Dillenburgstraat 5B, 5662 Am Eindhoven, Netherlands

ODI   25 Mall Rd, Burlington, MA 01803, Tel: (617) 272-8040
  (Mgt & consul serv)
    ODI Nederland, Australielaan 9a, 3526 AB Utrecht, Netherlands

OMI INTERNATIONAL CORP   21441 Hoover Rd, Warren, MI 48089,
  Tel: (313) 497-9100
  (Mfr spec chems & equip for metal finishing & surface treatment)
    OMI Intl. (Benelux) BV, Koenendelseweg 29, 5222 BG S'Hertogenhosh, Netherlands

OPW FUELING COMPONENTS   PO Box 405003, Cincinnati, OH 45240-5003,
  Tel: (513) 870-3100
  (Mfr fueling & vapor recovery nozzles, service station equip, aboveground storage
  tank equip)
    OPW Fueling Components Europe, P.O. Box 113, 1160 AC Zwanenburg, Netherlands

OTIS ELEVATOR CO   10 Farm Springs, Farmington, CT 06032, Tel: (860) 676-6528
  (Mfr elevators & escalators)
    Otis BV, Willem Fenengastraat 21-27, 1096 BL Amsterdam, Netherlands

OWENS-CORNING FIBERGLAS CORP   Fiberglas Tower, Toledo, OH 43659,
  Tel: (419) 248-8000
  (Mfr insulation, building materials, glass fiber prdts)
    Owens-Corning Fiberglas Netherlands BV, Apeldoorn, Netherlands

PANDUIT CORP   17301 Ridgeland Ave, Tinley Park, IL 60477-0981,
  Tel: (708) 532-1800
  (Mfr elec/electr wiring comps)
    Panduit Netherland, Eikenburglan 11e, 5248 BJ Rosmalen, Netherlands

PARKER HANNIFIN CORP   17325 Euclid Ave, Cleveland, OH 44112,
  Tel: (216) 531-3000
  (Mfr motion-control prdts)
    Atlas Automation, Merwedeweg 7, 3336 LG Zwijndrecht, Netherlands
    Parker Hannifin Hoogezand BV, Foxham 57, P.O. Box 338, 9611 AA Hoogezand,
      Netherlands
    Parker-Hannifin BV, Netherlands

PDA ENGINEERING   2975 Redhill Ave, Costa Mesa, CA   92626, Tel: (714) 540-8900
  (Computer-aided engineering software & services, advanced materials technology &
  training)
    PDA Engineering Intl. BV, Netherlands

PEAVEY CO/CONAGRA TRADING COS   730 Second Ave, Minneapolis, MN   55402,
  Tel: (612) 370-7500
  (Flour, feeds, seeds)
    Conagra Trading Co. Netherlands BV, Rotterdam, Netherlands

PENNZOIL CO   PO Box 2967, Houston, TX   77252-2967, Tel: (713) 546-4000
  (Producer, refiner, marketer of oil, natural gas, sulphur)
    Pennzoil Overseas BV, Sluispolderweg 11, P.O. Box 20, 1500 EA Zaandam, Netherlands

PEPSICO INC   700 Anderson Hill Rd, Purchase, NY   10577-1444,
  Tel: (914) 253-2000
  (Beverages, snack foods, restaurants)
    Seven-Up Nederland BV, Netherlands

PET INC   400 S 4th St, St Louis, MO   63102, Tel: (314) 622-7700
  (Mfr packaged foods)
    Old El Paso Foods BV (Netherlands), Flevolaan 4, 1382 JZ Weesp, Netherlands

PFIZER INC   235 E 42nd St, New York, NY   10017-5755, Tel: (212) 573-2323
  (Mfr healthcare products)
    Cadsand Medica NV, Netherlands
    Pfizer BV, Netherlands
    Pfizer Hospital Products (Netherlands) BV, Netherlands
    Roerig BV, Netherlands
    Van Cadsand Beheer BV, Netherlands

PLACID OIL CO   1601 Elm St, #3800, Dallas, TX   75201-7243, Tel: (214) 880-1000
  (Petroleum explor)
    Placid Intl. Oil Ltd., Eleanor Rooseveltlaan 3, 2719 AB Zoetermeer, Netherlands

PLAYBOY ENTERPRISES INC   680 N Lake Shore Dr, Chicago, IL   60611,
  Tel: (312) 751-8000
  (Publishing & entertainment)
    Playboy Products & Services Intl. BV, all mail to U.S. address

PLIBRICO CO   1800 Kingsbury St, Chicago, IL   60614, Tel: (312) 549-7014
  (Refractories, engineering, constr)
    Plibrico BV, Postbus 278, 4900 AG Oosterhout (NB), Netherlands

POLAROID CORP   549 Technology Sq, Cambridge, MA   02139, Tel: (617) 386-2000
  (Photographic equip & supplies, optical prdts)
    Polaroid (Europa) BV, Markt 24, P.O. Box 316, Enschede, Netherlands

POWER-PACKER   12801 W Silver Spring Rd, Butler, WI   53007, Tel: (414) 781-5000
  (Mfr OEM hydraulic sys)
    Power-Packer Europe BV, P.O. Box 327, Edisonstraat 2, 7570 AH Oldenzaal, Netherlands

POWERS CHEMCO INC   PO Box 151, Glen Cove, NY   11542, Tel: (516) 676-4000
  (Photographic supplies)
    Dalco Inc., De Beaufortlaan 28, P.O. Box 2, Soest, Netherlands

PPG INDUSTRIES   One PPG Place, Pittsburgh, PA 15272, Tel: (412) 434-3131
  (Mfr flat glass, fiber glass, chems, coatings)
    PPG Industries Fiber Glass BV, P.O. Box 50, 9600 AB Hoogezand, Netherlands

PRECISION SCIENTIFIC GROUP   3737 Cortland St, Chicago, IL 60647,
  Tel: (312) 227-2660
  (Laboratory apparatus)
    Precision Scientific Development Co., Netherlands

PREMARK INTL INC   1717 Deerfield Rd, Deerfield, IL 60015, Tel: (708) 405-6000
  (Mfr/sale diversified consumer & coml prdts)
    Dart Industries Nederland BV, Rijkstraatweg 113-117, 3632 AB Loenen Aan De Vecht,
      Netherlands

PRINTRONIX INC   17500 Cartwright Rd, Irvine, CA 92715, Tel: (714) 863-1900
  (Mfr computer printers)
    Printronix Nederland BV, Nieuweweg 283, P.O. Box 163, 6600 AD Wijchen, Netherlands

PROCTER & GAMBLE CO   One Procter & Gamble Plaza, Cincinnati, OH 45202,
  Tel: (513) 983-1100
  (Personal care, food, laundry, cleaning & ind prdts)
    Procter & Gamble Benelux NV, Heer Bokelweg 25, P.O. Box 1345, Rotterdam, Netherlands

PROCTER & GAMBLE PHARMACEUTICALS   17 Eaton Ave, Norwich, NY 13815-1799,
  Tel: (607) 335-2111
  (Devel/mfr pharms, chems, health prdts)
    Norwich Benelux SA, Netherlands

PRUDENTIAL INSURANCE CO OF AMERICA   751 Broad St, Newark, NJ 07102,
  Tel: (201) 802-6000
  (Insurance, financial services)
    Bache Halsey Stuart Shields Inc., Gebouw Rivierstaete, Amstedijk 166,
      1074 LH Amsterdam, Netherlands

QMS INC   One Magnum Pass, Mobile, AL 36618, Tel: (205) 633-4300
  (Mfr monochrome & color computer printers)
    QMS Europe/Middle East/Africa, Apollolaan 171, 1077 AX Amsterdam, Netherlands

QUAKER CHEMICAL CORP   Elm & Lee Sts, Conshohocken, PA 19428-0809,
  Tel: (610) 832-4000
  (Mfr chem specialties; total fluid mgmt services)
    Quaker Chemical (Holland) BV, P.O. Box 39, 1420 AA Uithoorn, Netherlands
    Quaker Chemical Europe BV, P.O. Box 579, 1420 CB Uithoorn, Netherlands

THE QUAKER OATS CO   321 N Clark St, PO Box 049001, Chicago, IL 60604-9001,
  Tel: (312) 222-7111
  (Mfr foods & beverages)
    Quaker Oats BV, Brielselaan 7, 3081 AA Rotterdam, Netherlands

RADISSON HOTELS INTL   Carlson Pkwy, PO Box 59159, Minneapolis,
  MN 55459-8204, Tel: (612) 540-5526
  (Hotels)
    Cadettt Hotel Movenpick, Pettelaar Park 90, 5216 DC 's-Hertogenbosch, Netherlands

RAMSEY TECHNOLOGY INC   501 90th Ave NW, Minneapolis, MN 55433,
  Tel: (612) 783-2500
  (Mfr in-motion weighing, inspection, monitoring & control equip for the process inds)
    Ramsey Engineering BV, Hardwareweg 3, 3821 BL Amersfoort, Netherlands

RANSBURG CORP   3939 W 56th St, Indianapolis, IN 46208, Tel: (317) 298-5000
  (Mfr electrostatic coating sys)
    Simco (Nederland) BV, Kwinkweerd 2, P.O. Box 11, 7240 AA Lochem, Netherlands

RAYCHEM CORP   300 Constitution Dr, Menlo Park, CA 94025, Tel: (415) 361-3333
  (Devel/mfr/mkt materials science products for electronics, telecommunications &
  industry)
    Raychem Nederland BV, Benelux Bldg., Van Heuven Goedhartiaan 121,
      1181 KK Amstelveen, Netherlands

RAYTHEON CO   141 Spring St, Lexington, MA 02173, Tel: (617) 862-6600
  (Mfr divers electronics, appliances, aviation, energy & environ prdts; publishing,
  ind & constr servs)
    Badger BV, Binckhorstlaan 117, 2516 BA The Hague, Netherlands

READER'S DIGEST ASSOCIATION INC   PO Box 235, Pleasantville, NY 10570,
  Tel: (914) 238-1000
  (Publisher magazines & books, direct mail marketer)
    Vitgeversmaatschappij The Reader's Digest NV, Hogehilwig 17, 1101 CB Amsterdam,
      Zuidoost, Netherlands

RECOGNITION EQUIPMENT INC   PO Box 660204, Dallas, TX 75266-0204,
  Tel: (214) 579-6000
  (Mfr hi-perf document recognition sys, image & workflow software; related customer
  serv)
    Recognition Equipment Nederland BV, Buikslotermeerplein 418, 1025 NL Amsterdam,
      Netherlands

REED TOOL CO   6501 Navigation Blvd, Houston, TX 77001, Tel: (713) 924-5200
  (Mfr rock bits for oil & gas explor)
    Reed Tool Co., Netherlands

RENA-WARE DISTRIBUTORS INC   8383 158th Ave NE, Redmond, WA 98052,
  Tel: (206) 881-6171
  (Cookware & china)
    Rena-Ware (Holland) BV, Netherlands

RHONE-POULENC RORER INC   PO Box 1200, Collegeville, PA 19426-0107,
  Tel: (215) 454-8000
  (R&D/mfr human pharmaceuticals)
    Pharbil-Rorer BV, Rotterdam, Netherlands

RJR NABISCO INC   1301 Ave of the Americas, New York, NY 10019,
  Tel: (212) 258-5600
  (Mfr consumer packaged food prdts & tobacco prdts)
    R.J. Reynolds BV, Vreelandsweg 46, 1200 AW Hilversum, Netherlands

ROCKWELL INTL CORP   2201 Seal Beach Blvd, PO Box 4250, Seal Beach,
  CA 90740-8250, Tel: (310) 797-3311
  (Prdts & serv for aerospace, automotive, electronics, graphics & automation inds)

Allen-Bradley Nederland BV, J.N. Wagenaarweg 6, 1422 AK Uithoorn, Netherlands
ROR Rockwell BV, Middendijk 40, 5705 CC Helmond, Netherlands

ROLSCREEN CO   102 Main St, Pella, IA 50129, Tel: (515) 628-1000
(Mfr wood windows, glass sliding & folding doors)
    Pella BV, P.O. Box NR 7044, 5980 AA Panningen, Netherlands

ROTRON INC   7 Hasbrouck Lane, Woodstock, NY 12498, Tel: (914) 679-2401
(Mfr fans & blowers for cooling electr equip & ind application)
    Rotron BV, Terheijdenseweg 441, P.O. Box 405, Breda, Netherlands

ROWAN COMPANIES INC   2800 Post Oak Blvd, Houston, TX 77056-6196,
  Tel: (713) 621-7800
(Contract drilling & air charter service)
    NZD Noordzee Drill BV, Akerdijk 150A, 1171 PV Badhoevedorp, Netherlands

RUBBERMAID INC   1147 Akron Rd, Wooster, OH 44691, Tel: (216) 264-6464
(Mfr rubber & plastic home, commercial & ind prdts)
    Dupol-Rubbermaid Nederland BV, Zandweg 6, De Meern, Netherlands
    Fuston Rubbermaid BV, Zweedsestraat 61010, P.O. Box 41, Deventer, Netherlands

RUST-OLEUM CORP   11 Hawthorne Parkway, Vernon Hill, IL 60061,
  Tel: (708) 367-7700
(Rust preventive coatings)
    Rust-Oleum Nederland BV, Braak 1, P.O. Box 138, Roosendaal, Netherlands

SARA LEE CORP   3 First National Plaza, Chicago, IL 60602-4260,
  Tel: (312) 726-2600
(Mfr/distr food & consumer packaged goods, tobacco prdts, intimate apparel & knitwear)
    Sara Lee/DE, Vieutensevaart 100, 3532 AD Utrecht, Netherlands

SCIENTIFIC AMERICAN INC   415 Madison Ave, New York, NY 10017,
  Tel: (212) 754-0550
(Magazine & textbook publ)
    Scientific American Inc., Apollolaan 127, Amsterdam, Netherlands

SCIENTIFIC ATLANTA INC   1 Technology Pkwy, PO Box 105600, Atlanta, GA 30348,
  Tel: (404) 441-4000
(Telecommun instru & equip, energy mgmt & home security equip, test & measurement
instru)
    Dymac-Europe, P.O. Box 329, Oss, Netherlands

SEA-LAND SERVICE INC   150 Allen Rd, Liberty Corner, NJ 07920,
  Tel: (201) 558-6000
(Container transport)
    RJR Industries Inc., Johan de Witlaan 15, The Hague, Netherlands
    Sea-Land Service Inc., Striendwaalseweg 30, P.O. Box 3000, Rotterdam (Pernis),
    Netherlands

SEALED AIR CORP   Park 80 Plaza E, Saddle Brook, NJ 07662-5291,
  Tel: (201) 791-7600
(Mfr protective packaging prdts)
    Sealed Air BV, Lindenhoutseweg 45, 6545 AH Nijmegen, Netherlands

G D SEARLE & CO   5200 Old Orchard Rd, Skokie, IL 60077, Tel: (708) 982-7000
(Mfr pharms, health care & optical prdts, specialty chems)
    Searle Netherlands BV, P.O. Box 1402, 3600 BK Maarssen, Netherlands

SEARS WORLD TRADE   633 Pennsylvania Ave, NW, Washington, DC 20004,
  Tel: (202) 626-1600
  (Consumer & light ind goods, processed foods)
    Hageneyer NV, Rijksweg 69, 1411 GE Naarden, Netherlands

SENCO PRODUCTS INC   8485 Broadwell Rd, Cincinnati, OH 45244,
  Tel: (513) 388-2000
  (Mfr ind nailers, staplers, fasteners & accessories)
    Verpa-Senco BV, P.O. Box 5135, 6802 EC Arnhem, Netherlands

SEQUENT COMPUTER SYSTEMS INC   15450 SW Koll Pkwy, Beaverton, OR 97006-6063,
  Tel: (503) 626-5700
  (Mfr symmetric multiprocessing technology computers)
    Sequent Computer Systems Inc., Rijnzathe 7A2, 3454 PV DeMeern, Netherlands

SHAKESPEARE FISHING TACKLE GROUP   611 Shakespeare Rd, Columbia, SC 29204,
  Tel: (803) 754-7000
  (Mfr fishing tackle)
    Shakespear Hengelsport BV, Reeweg 16, P.O. Box 23, 1394 ZG Nederhorst den Berg,
    Netherlands

SHARED MEDICAL SYSTEMS CORP   51 Valley Stream Pkwy, Malvern, PA 19355,
  Tel: (215) 219-6300
  (Computer-based info processing for healthcare ind)
    SMS/Medisys BV, Netherlands

SHEAFFER EATON INC   1 Crown Mark Dr, Lincoln, RI 02865, Tel: (401) 333-0303
  (Mfr writing instruments)
    Sheaffer Pen Co., P.O. Box 1930, 2280 DX Rijswijk, Netherlands

SHIPLEY CO INC   455 Forest St, Marlborough, MA 01752, Tel: (508) 481-7950
  (Mfr chems for printed circuit boards & microelectronic mfg)
    Shipley BV, Siriusstraat 45, 5015 BT Tilburg, Netherlands

SIGNETICS CORP   PO Box 3409, Sunnyvale, CA 94088-3409, Tel: (408) 991-2000
  (Solid state circuits)
    Philips Nederland BV, Eindhoven, Netherlands

SIGNODE PACKAGING SYSTEMS   3600 W Lake Ave, Glenview, IL 60025,
  Tel: (708) 724-6100
  (Mfr packaging systems)
    Signode BV, Graftermeerstraat 18, P.O. Box 26, 2130 AA Hoofddorp, Netherlands

THE SIMCO CO INC   2257 N Penn Rd, Hatfield, PA 19440-1998,
  Tel: (215) 248-2171
  (Mfr apparatus for electrostatic charge neutralization)
    Simco (Nederland) BV, Aalsvoort 5, P.O. Box 11, 7240 AA Lochem, Netherlands

SKIL CORP   4801 W Peterson Ave, Chicago, IL 60646, Tel: (312) 286-7330
  (Portable electric power tools)
    Skil (Nederland) BV, Konijnenberg 60, 3267 DG Breda, Netherlands

SKINNER VALVE   95 Edgewood Ave, New Britain, CT 06051, Tel: (203) 827-2300
  (Mfr solenoid valves)
    Skinner Europa BV, Scherpdeel 30, Roosendaal (N.B.), Netherlands

A O SMITH CORP   11270 W Park Pl, Milwaukee, WI 53224, Tel: (414) 359-4000
   (Auto & truck frames, motors, water heaters, storage/handling sys, plastics, railroad
   prdts)
      A.O. Smith Water Products Co., Industrieweg 27, 5500 AB Veldhoven, Netherlands

SMITH INTL INC   16740 Hardy St, Houston, TX 77032, Tel: (713) 443-3370
   (Mfr/serv downhole drilling equip)
      S.I. Nederland BV, Netherlands

SNAP-ON TOOLS CORP   2801 80th St, Kenosha, WI 53141-1410, Tel: (414) 656-5200
   (Mfr automotive & ind maint serv tools)
      Snap-On Tools BV, Schipholweg 1003, 2143 CH Boesingheliede, Netherlands

SOLIDYNE INC   60 Spence St, Bay Shore, NY 11706, Tel: (516) 231-7800
   (Heat sealing generators, dielectric equip)
      Colpitt BV, Kamerlingh Onnesstraat 40, Zandvoort, Aan Zee, Netherlands

SONOCO PRODUCTS CO   North Second St, PO Box 160, Hartsville, SC 29550,
   Tel: (803) 383-7000
   (Mfr packaging for consumer & ind mkt)
      Sonoco Nederland BV, P.O. Box 19, 7120 AA Aalten, Netherlands

SPARKLER FILTERS INC   PO Box 19, Conroe, TX 77305-0019, Tel: (713) 756-4471
   (Mfr liquid filtration sys)
      Sparkler Intl. Ltd., P.O. Box 94142, 1090 GC Amsterdam, Netherlands

SPECTRA-PHYSICS ANALYTICAL INC   45757 Northport Loop W, Fremont, CA 94537,
   Tel: (510) 657-1100
   (Mfr liquid chromatography equip)
      Spectra-Physics BV, Prof. Dr. Dorgelolaan 20, P.O. Box 2264, 5613 AM Eindhoven,
      Netherlands

SPECTRAL DYNAMICS CORP   4141 Ruffin Rd, San Diego, CA 92123,
   Tel: (619) 496-3400
   (Mfr Vibration monitoring, analysis & control equip)
      Scientific-Atlanta, Netherlands

SPI PHARMACEUTICALS INC   ICN Plaza, 3300 Hyland Ave, Costa Mesa, CA 92626,
   Tel: (714) 545-0100
   (Mfr pharms, biochems, radioactive materials)
      ICN Pharmaceuticals Inc., Stephensonstraat 45, 2723 RM Zoetermeer, Netherlands

SPSS INC   444 N Michigan Ave, Chicago, IL 60611, Tel: (312) 329-2400
   (Mfr statistical software)
      SPSS Benelux BV, P.O. Box 115, 4200 AC Gorinchem, Netherlands

SPX CORP   700 Terrace Point Dr, PO Box 3301, Muskegon, MI 49443-3301,
   Tel: (616) 724-5000
   (Mfr spec service tools, engine & drive-train parts)
      Power Team Europe, Junostraat 2, 6468 EW Kerkrade, Netherlands

ST JOHNSBURY TRUCKING CO   119 Jeffrey Ave, Holliston, MA 01746,
   Tel: (508) 429-5920
   (Transportation service)
      St. Johnsbury Worldlink Logistics BV, Columbusstraat 22-26, Distripark Eemhaven,
      Havennummer 2501, 3165 AD Rotterdam, Netherlands

THE STANLEY WORKS   1000 Stanley Dr, PO Box 7000, New Britain, CT 06050,
Tel: (203) 225-5111
(Mfr hand tools & hardware)
Stanley Works (Nederland) BV, Sand-Ambachtstraat 95, 'S Gravenzande, Netherlands

STAPLING MACHINES CO   41 Pine St, Rockaway, NJ 07866, Tel: (201) 627-4400
(Mfr wirebound box making mach for fruit/veg ind & industrial applications)
Package Research Laboratory, Dorpstraat 42B, 1688 CG Nibbixwoud, Netherlands

STEWART & STEVENSON SERVICES INC   2707 N Loop W, Houston, TX 77008,
Tel: (713) 868-7700
(Design/mfr customized diesel & turbine power sys)
Thomassen/Stewart & Stevenson (TSSI), P.O. Box 95, 6990 AB Rheden, Netherlands

STORAGE TECHNOLOGY CORP   2270 S 88th St, Louisville, CO 80028-0001,
Tel: (303) 673-5151
(Mfr/mkt/serv info storage & retrieval sys)
Storage Tek (The Netherlands) BV, IR.D.S. Tuynmanweg 6, 4131 PN Vianen, Netherlands

SULLAIR CORP   3700 E Michigan Blvd, Michigan City, IN 46360,
Tel: (219) 879-5451
(Refrigeration sys, vacuum pumps, generators, etc)
Sullair Schroefcompressoren, P.O. Box 178, 2700 AD Zoetermeer, Netherlands

SUN ELECTRIC CORP   One Sun Pkwy, Crystal Lake, IL 60014-2299,
Tel: (815) 459-7700
(Mfr auto tune-up, diagnostic & emission testing equip)
Sun Electric Europa BV, Sparlerweg 69, 1099 BB Amsterdam, Netherlands

THE SUPERIOR ELECTRIC CO   383 Middle St, Bristol, CT 06010,
Tel: (203) 582-9561
(Mfr voltage regulators/conditioners, transformers, motion control prdts)
Superior Electric Nederland BV, Netherlands

SYSTEMS ENGINEERING LABS INC   6901 W Sunrise Blvd, Fort Lauderdale,
FL 33313, Tel: (305) 587-2900
(Digital computers)
Systems Engineering Labs BV, P.O. Box 56, 4000 AB Tiel, Netherlands

TAB PRODUCTS CO   1400 Page Mill Rd, PO Box 10269, Palo Alto, CA 94303,
Tel: (415) 852-2400
(Mfr filing sys, electronic office prdts)
TAB Products Europa BV, Netherlands

TANDEM COMPUTERS INC   19333 Valco Pkwy, Cupertino, CA 95014,
Tel: (408) 725-6000
(Mfr multiple processor computer sys)
Tandem Computers BV, The Hague, Netherlands

TECHNICON INSTRUMENTS CORP   511 Benedict Ave, Tarrytown, NY 10591-5097,
Tel: (914) 631-8000
(Mfr/serv automated blook anal equip, reagents & diagnostics)
Technicon Instruments BV, Netherlands

TEEPAK INC   3 Westbrook Corp Center, Westchester, IL 60154,
  Tel: (708) 409-3000
  (Mfr cellulose, fibrous, collegen sausage casings & plastic packaging)
    Tee-Pak BV, P.O. Box 126, Rondebroslaan 18, Delfzijl, Netherlands
    Tee-Pak Intl., Huidekoperstraat 26, Amsterdam, Netherlands

TEKTRONIX INC   26660 SW Parkway, Wilsonville, OR 97070, Tel: (503) 627-7111
  (Mfr test & meas, visual sys & commun prdts)
    Tektronix Holland NV, Hoofddorp (Amsterdam) & Heerenven, Netherlands

TENNANT CO   701 N Lilac Dr, Minneapolis, MN 55440, Tel: (612) 540-1200
  (Mfr ind floor maint sweepers & scrubbers, floor coatings)
    Tennant NV, Industrielaan 6, P.O. Box 6, 5400 AA Uden, Netherlands

TENNECO INC   PO Box 2511, Houston, TX 77252-2511, Tel: (713) 757-2131
  (Natural gas pipelines, shipbuilding & repair, construction & farm equip, chemicals,
  packaging)
    Tenneco Automotive Europe Inc., P.O. Box 547, 1180 AM Amstelveen, Netherlands
    Tenneco Holdings BV, de Lairessestrat 133, 1075 HJ Amsterdam, Netherlands

TEXAS INSTRUMENTS INC   13500 N Central Expwy, Dallas, TX 75265,
  Tel: (214) 995-2011
  (Mfr semiconductor devices, electr/electro-mech sys, instr & controls)
    Texas Instruments Holland BV, 1100 AZ Amsterdam Zuid-oost, Netherlands

TEXTRON INC   40 Westminster St, Providence, RI 02903, Tel: (401) 421-2800
  (Mfr aerospace, ind & consumer prdts; fin servs)
    Textron Atlantic Netherlands NV, Haverstraat 24, 2153 GB Nieuw Vennep, Netherlands

THERM-O-DISC INC   1320 S Main St, Mansfield, OH 44907-0538,
  Tel: (419) 525-8500
  (Mfr thermostats, controls, sensor & thermal cutoffs, switches)
    Capax BV, Rooyakkersstraat, P.O. Box 7017, 5605 JA Eindhoven, Netherlands
    Therm-O-Disc/Europe, Rooyakkersstraat4A, P.O. Box 7125, 5625 BB Eindhoven,
    Netherlands

THERMO ELECTRIC CO   109 Fifth St, Saddle Brook, NJ 07662, Tel: (201) 843-5800
  (Mfr temp/meas control prdts)
    Thermo Electric Intl. BV, P.O. Box 65, 2360 AB Warmond, Netherlands

THERMO ELECTRON CORP   101 First Ave, Waltham, MA 02154, Tel: (617) 890-8700
  (Devel/mfr of process equip & instru for energy intensive inds)
    Van Hengel Instruments BV, Heerbaan 220, Breda, Netherlands

THERMON   100 Thermon Dr, PO Box 609, San Marcos, TX 78667-0609,
  Tel: (512) 396-5801
  (Mfr steam & electric heat tracing sys, components & accessories)
    Thermon Benelux BV, P.O. Box 205, 2640 AE Pijnacker, Netherlands
    Thermon Europe BV, P.O. Box 205, 2640 AE Pijnacker, Netherlands

THETFORD CORP   7101 Jackson Rd, PO Box 1285, Ann Arbor, MI 48106,
  Tel: (313) 769-6000
  (Mfr sanitation prdts & chems)
    Thetford Producten BV, Nijverheidsweg 29, P.O. Box 169, 4870 AD Etten-Leur,
    Netherlands

TIDEWATER INC   Tidewater Place, 1440 Canal St, New Orleans, LA 70112,
Tel: (504) 568-1010
(Marine serv & equip to companies engaged in explor, development & prod of oil, gas & minerals)
   Tidewater Marine Service (UK) Ltd., Parallalweg 6A, 3131 DG Vlaardingen, Netherlands

TIME WARNER INC   75 Rockefeller Plaza, New York, NY 10019,
Tel: (212) 484-8000
(Communications, publishing, entertainment)
   Time-Life Books BV, Ottho Heldring Straat 5, 1066 AZ Amsterdam, Netherlands
   Time-Life International BV, Ottho Heldring Straat 5, 1066 AZ Amsterdam, Netherlands

TOKHEIM CORP   PO Box 360, Fort Wayne, IN 46801, Tel: (219) 470-4600
(Mfr gasoline service station dispensers, access, hand & in-tank fuel pumps)
   Tokheim BV, Splinterlaan 152, P.O. Box 143, Leiderdorp, Netherlands

TOPFLIGHT CORP   160 E 9th Ave, York, PA 17404, Tel: (717) 843-9901
(Commercial printing, service paper)
   Adhesives Research Europe BV, Bisonspoor 354, 3605 JW Maarssen, Utrecht, Netherlands

TORIT PRODUCTS   1400 W 94th St, Minneapolis, MN 55431, Tel: (612) 887-3900
(Mfr dust collectors, fume extractors)
   Torit Netherlands, Waardeweg 45, P.O. Box 770, Haarlem, Netherlands

TOWERS PERRIN   245 Park Ave, New York, NY 10167, Tel: (212) 309-3400
(Management consultants)
   Tillinghast, Leuven Actuarissen, Netherlands
   Towers, Perrin, Forster & Crosby, Smit & Bunschoten, Emmastraat 36,
      1075 HW Amsterdam, Netherlands
   Towers, Perrin/Nijhoff, Verbeekstraat 5, 2332 CA Leiden, Netherlands

TOWNSEND ENGINEERING CO INC   2425 Hubbell Ave, Des Moines, IA 50317,
Tel: (515) 265-8181
(Mfr machinery for food ind)
   Townsend Engineering Verkoopmaatschappij BV, Philipstraat 1, 2722 NA Zoetermeer,
      Netherlands

TOYS R US INC   461 From Rd, Paramus, NJ 07652, Tel: (201) 262-7800
(Retail stores: toys & games, sporting goods, computer software, books, records)
   Toys R Us Intl. BV, Atoomweg 400, 3542 AB Utrecht, Netherlands

TRACOR INC   6500 Tracor Lane, Austin, TX 78725-2000, Tel: (512) 926-2800
(Time & frequency prdts, gas & liquid chromatographs, eng serv, ship repair)
   Olvis Smeltzekeringenfabriek BV, Kanosistraat 36-38, 3531 BM Utrecht, Netherlands
   Tracor Europa BV, Netherlands

TRANE CO   3600 Pammel Creek Rd, La Crosse, WI 54601, Tel: (608) 787-2000
(Mfr/distr/svce A/C sys & equip)
   Trane Air Conditioning BV, Koningsweg 4, P.O. Box 58, 3760 AB Soest, Netherlands
   Wabco Standard Trane BV, Jupiterstraat 254, 2132 HK Hoofddorp, Netherlands

TRANS WORLD AIRLINES INC   505 N 6th St, St Louis, MO 63101,
Tel: (314) 589-3000
(Air transportation)
   Trans World Airlines, Singel 540, Amsterdam, Netherlands

TRANTER INC 1054 Claussen Rd, #314, Augusta, GA 30907, Tel: (706) 738-7900
(Mfr heat exchangers)
SWEP Marketing BV Benelux, Rijksstraatweg 36, 7231 AG Warnsveld, Netherlands

TREDEGAR INDUSTRIES INC 1100 Boulders Pkwy, Richmond, VA 23225,
Tel: (804) 330-1000
(Mfr plastics & aluminum prdts; energy (oil & gas))
Tredegar Film Products BV, P.O. Box 1059, 6460 BB Kerkrape, Netherlands

U S SURGICAL CORP 150 Glover Ave, Norwalk, CT 06856, Tel: (203) 845-1000
(Mfr/devel/mkt surgical staplers, laparoscopic instru & sutures)
Auto Suture Co. Netherlands, all mail to U.S. address

U S WHEAT ASSOCIATES 1200 NW Front Ave, #600, Portland, OR 97209,
Tel: (503) 223-8123
(Market development for wheat prdts)
U.S. Wheat Associates Inc., Netherlands

UNION CAMP CORP 1600 Valley Rd, Wayne, NJ 07470, Tel: (201) 628-2000
(Mfr paper, packaging, chems, wood prdts)
Bush Boake Allen Nederland BV, Netherlands

UNION OIL INTL DIV Union Oil Center, PO Box 7600, Los Angeles, CA 90017,
Tel: (213) 977-7600
(Petroleum prdts, petrochems)
Union Oil Co. of the Netherlands, Corsicaweg 2, Amsterdam, Netherlands

UNISYS CORP PO Box 500, Blue Bell, PA 19424, Tel: (215) 986-4011
(Mfg/mktg/serv electr info sys)
Omnicon BV, Wattbaan 12, 3439 ML Utrecht, Netherlands
Unisys Intl. Services BV, Hoogoorddreef 11, 1100 DD Amsterdam, Netherlands
Unisys Nederland NV, Hoogoorddreef 11, 1100 DD Amsterdam, Netherlands

UNITED CENTRIFUGAL PUMPS INC 1132 N 7th St, San Jose, CA 95112,
Tel: (408) 298-0123
(Pumps)
United Centrifugal Pumps (Netherlands) NV, Van Stolkweg 32, The Hague, Netherlands

UNITED TECHNOLOGIES CORP United Technologies Bldg, Hartford, CT 06101,
Tel: (203) 728-7000
(Mfr aircraft engines, elevators, A/C, auto equip, space & military electr, rocket
propulsion sys)
Otis Liften BV, P.O. Box 4059, 1009 AB Amsterdam, Netherlands
Otis Liften BV, Willem Fenengastraat 21-27, 1096 BL Amsterdam, Netherlands

UNIVAR CORP 6100 Carillon Point, Kirkland, WA 98004, Tel: (206) 889-3400
(Industrial chemicals)
Univar Europe, Blaak 28-34, 3011 TA Rotterdam, Netherlands

UNIVERSAL CORP PO Box 25099, Richmond, VA 23260, Tel: (804) 359-9311
(Holding co: tobacco, commodities)
Europee Tabak Maatschappij BV, Kanaaldvk Noord 123, 7565 JA Eindhoven, Netherlands
NV Deli-Universal, P.O. Box 689, 3000 AR Rotterdam, Netherlands

UPJOHN CO   7000 Portage Rd, Kalamazoo, MI 49001, Tel: (616) 323-4000
  (Mfr pharms, agric prdts, ind chems)
    Upjohn (Nederland), Morsestraat 15, P.O. Box 252, Ede, Netherlands
    Upjohn Polymer BV, Heemskesweg 53, P.O. Box 80, Delfzijl, Netherlands

UROPLASTY INC   2718 Summer St NE, Minneapolis, MN 55413-2820,
  Tel: (612) 378-1180
  (Mfr urology prdts)
    Uroplasty BV, Hertogsingel 54, 6214 AE Maastricht, Netherlands

URSCHEL LABORATORIES INC   2503 Calumet Ave, PO Box 2200, Valparaiso,
  IN 46384-2200, Tel: (219) 464-4811
  (Design/mfr precision food processing equip)
    Urschel Intl. Ltd., Hogemaat 1, 3961 MG Wijk bij Duurstede, Netherlands

USF&G FINANCIAL SERVICES CORP   100 Light St, Baltimore, MD 21202,
  Tel: (301) 547-3000
  (Investment mgt, real estate, computer leasing, fin prdt mktg & admin, strategic
  consult)
    Megaleasing Intl. BV, World Trade Center, Strawlinskylaan 1341, 1077 XX Amsterdam,
    Netherlands

USX CORP   600 Grant St, Pittsburgh, PA 15219-4776, Tel: (412) 433-1121
  (Steel & related resources, oil & gas, engineering, real estate)
    Marathon Petroleum Netherlands Ltd., Wolwevershave 24, Dordrecht, Netherlands

VALMONT INDUSTRIES INC   One Valmont Pkwy, PO Box 358, Valley, NE 68064-0358,
  Tel: (402) 359-2201
  (Mfr irrigation sys, steel lighting, utility & communication poles)
    Valmont Nederlands BV, Den Engelsman 3, 6026 RB Maarheeze, Netherlands

VAPOR   6420 W Howard St, Niles, IL 60714-3302, Tel: (847) 967-8300
  (Mfr bus & rail transit automatic door sys, railcar/locomotive relays & contactors,
  vehicle ID sys)
    Vapor Intl. Holland, Atoomweg 498, 3452 AM Utrecht, Netherlands

VARIAN ASSOCIATES INC   3100 Hansen Way, Palo Alto, CA 94304-1030,
  Tel: (415) 493-4000
  (Mfr microwave tubes & devices, analytical instru, semiconductor process & med equip,
  vacuum sys)
    Varlan Benelux BV, De Molen 2, P.O. Box 266, 3994 DB Houten, Netherlands

VERMEER MFG CO   PO Box 200, Pella, IA 50219-0200, Tel: (515) 628-3141
  (Mfr agri & ind equip)
    Vermeer Intl. BV, P.O. Box 323, 4460 AS Goes, Netherlands

VERNAY LABORATORIES INC   120 E South College St, Yellow Springs, OH 45387,
  Tel: (513) 767-7261
  (Mechanical prdts, spec molded shapes, rubber goods)
    Vernay Europa BV, Kelvinstraat 6, 7575 AS Oldenzaal, Netherlands

VERSA PRODUCTS CO INC   22 Spring Valley Rd, Paramus, NJ 07652,
  Tel: (201) 843-2400
  (Mfr pneumatic & hydraulic directional control valves)
    Versa BV, Halstraat 3, 7321 AG Apeldoorn, Netherlands

VIACOM INC   200 Elm St, Dedham, MA 02026, Tel: (617) 461-1600
(Communications, publishing, entertainment)
  Paramount Pictures Intl., Rikswijkstraat 175, 1062 EZ Amsterdam, Netherlands

VIVITAR CORP   1280 Rancho Conejo Blvd, Newbury Park, CA 91320,
  Tel: (805) 498-7008
(Mfr photographic equip, electr supplies)
  Vivitar BV, Netherlands
  Vivitar Europe, Netherlands

WANG LABORATORIES INC   1 Industrial Ave, Lowell, MA 01851,
  Tel: (508) 459-5000
(Mfr computer info processing sys)
  Wang Nederlands BV, Produktieweg L-1, 3401 MG Ijsselspein, Netherlands

WARD HOWELL INTL INC   99 Park Ave, New York, NY 10016-1699,
  Tel: (212) 697-3730
(Executive recruiting)
  Maes & Lunau, Keizersgracht 560-562, 1017 EM Amsterdam, Netherlands

WARNER-JENKINSON CO INC   2526 Baldwin St, St Louis, MO 63106,
  Tel: (314) 889-7600
(Mfr synthetic & natural colors for food, drugs & cosmetics)
  Warner-Jenkinson Netherlands, Kleine Koppel 39-40, P.O. Box 1493,
    3800 BL Amersfoort, Netherlands

WATERS CHROMATOGRAPHY DIV   34 Maple St, Milford, MA 01757,
  Tel: (617) 478-2000
(Mfr/distr liquid chromatographic instru/accessories/tech)
  Millipore BV, Waters Chromatography Div., Penningweg 33, P.O. Box 166,
    4870 AD Etten-Leur, Netherlands

WATTS INDUSTRIES INC   815 Chestnut St, North Andover, MA 01845,
  Tel: (508) 688-1811
(Mfr ind valves & safety control prdts)
  Watts Industries Europe BV, P.O. Box 152, 6960 AD Eerbeek, Netherlands
  Watts Ocean BV, P.O. Box 98, 6960 AB Eerbeek, Netherlands

WEATHERFORD INTL INC   1360 Post Oak Blvd, PO Box 27608, Houston,
  TX 77227-7608, Tel: (713) 439-9400
(Oilfield servs, prdts & equip; mfr marine cranes)
  Weatherford Oil Tool Nederland BV, Steenkade 3A, 1948 NH Beverwijk, Netherlands

WEATHERHEAD DIV   6615 Brotherhood Way, Fort Wayne, IN 46825,
  Tel: (219) 481-3500
(Mfr fluid power prdts, hose assys, tube & pipe fittings & valves)
  Dana Distribution BV, P.O. Box 868, 3160 AB Rhoon, Netherlands

WEDCO TECHNOLOGY INC   PO Box 397, Bloomsbury, NJ 08804, Tel: (908) 479-4181
(Plastics grinding & related services, machinery & equip for plastics ind)
  Wedco Holland BV, Mijlweg 7, 3295 ZH 's Gravendeel, Netherlands

WELLMAN INC   1040 Broad St, #302, Shrewsbury, NJ 07702, Tel: (908) 542-7300
(Plastic recycler; mfr polyester fibres & resins)
  Wellman Recycling, P.O. Box 51, 6916 ZH Tolkamer, Gelderland, Netherlands

WEST POINT-PEPPERELL INC   400 W 10th St, PO Box 71, West Point, GA 31833,
Tel: (205) 756-7111
(Ind, household & apparel fabrics, bed & bath products)
  First BV, Verlaat 22, P.O. Box 45, Veenendaal, Netherlands

WESTERN ATLAS INTL INC   10205 Westheimer, PO Box 1407, Houston,
TX 77251-1407, Tel: (713) 266-5700
(Full service to the oil industry)
  Western Atlas Logging Services, Bedrijifsweg 12, 1785 AK Den Helder, Netherlands

WHIRLPOOL CORP   2000 N M-63, Benton Harbor, MI 49022-2692,
Tel: (616) 923-5000
(Mfr/mkt home appliances)
  Whirlpool Europe BV, Eindhoven, Netherlands

WINCHESTER ELECTRONICS   400 Park Rd, Watertown, CT 06795-0500,
Tel: (203) 945-5000
(Mfr elec & electr connectors, PCB assemblies & hardware)
  Litton Precision Products Intl. Inc., Griendstraat 10, 2921 LA Krimpen a/d Ljssel,
    Netherlands

WITCO CORP   1 American Lane, Greenwich, CT 06831-4236, Tel: (203) 552-2000
(Mfr chem & petroleum prdts)
  Witco BV, Wezelstraat, P.O. Box 5, 1540 AD Zaan, Netherlands
  Witco Chemical BV, Spaarndamseweg 466, P.O. Box 577, Haarlem, Netherlands
  Witco Polymers & Resins BV, P.O. Box 37, 6669 ZG Dodewaard, Netherlands
  Witco Polymers & Resins BV, P.O. Box 116, 1380 AC Weesp, Netherlands

WMX TECHNOLOGIES INC   3003 Butterfield Rd, Oak Brook, IL 60563,
Tel: (708) 572-8800
(Environmental services)
  Waste Management Nederland, Kruisplein 25, 3014 DB Rotterdam, Netherlands

WOODHEAD INDUSTRIES INC   2150 E Lake Cook Rd, #400, Buffalo Grove, IL 60089,
Tel: (708) 465-8300
(Devel/mfr/sale/distr elect/electr, fiber optic & ergonomic special-function,
non-commodity prdts)
  AKAPP Electro Industrie BV, Nijverheidsweg 14, 3771 ME Barneveld, Netherlands

WOODWARD GOVERNOR CO   5001 North 2nd St, PO Box 7001, Rockford,
IL 61125-7001, Tel: (815) 877-7441
(Mfr speed control governors)
  Woodward Governor Nederland BV, Hoofdweg 601, P.O. Box 34, 2130 AA Hoofddorp,
    Netherlands

WORCESTER CONTROLS CORP   33 Lott Dr, Marlboro, MA 01752, Tel: (508) 481-4800
(Mfr ball valves, control devices)
  Worcester Nederland BV, Netherlands

WORLD COURIER INC   46 Trinity Pl, New York, NY 10006, Tel: (718) 978-9400
(Intl courier serv)
  World Courier Holland, Freeport Bldg., Rm. 214, P.O. Box 75528, Schiphol/Centre,
    Amsterdam, Netherlands

WM WRIGLEY JR CO   410 N Michigan Ave, Chicago, IL 60611-4287,
  Tel: (312) 644-2121
  (Mfr chewing gum)
    Wrigley NV, Amsterdam, Netherlands

XEROX CORP   800 Long Ridge Rd, PO Box 1600, Stamford, CT 06904,
  Tel: (203) 968-3000
  (Mfr document processing equip, sys & supplies)
    Xerox Corp., Amsterdam & Venray, Netherlands

YORK INTERNATIONAL CORP   PO Box 1592, York, PA 17405-1592,
  Tel: (717) 771-7890
  (Mfr A/C, heating & refrig sys & equip)
    York Intl. BV, P.O. Box 3453, Tinstraaat 15, 4800 DL Breda, Netherlands

YOUNG & RUBICAM INC   285 Madison Ave, New York, NY 10017, Tel: (212) 210-3000
  (Advertising, public relations, direct marketing & sales promotion, corp & product ID
  management)
    Prins Meijer, Stamenkovits en Van Walbeek/Young & Rubicam BV,
      Frans van Mierisstraat 92, 1071 RZ Amsterdam, Netherlands

NETHERLANDS ANTILLES

THE BANK OF NEW YORK   48 Wall St, New York, NY 10286, Tel: (212) 495-1784
  (Banking)
    The Bank of New York Overseas Finance NV, 15 Pietermaai, Curacao,
      Netherlands Antilles

BAXTER HEALTHCARE CORP   1 Baxter Pky, Deerfield, IL 60015,
  Tel: (708) 948-2000
  (Mfr disposable medical prdts)
    American Hospital Supply, 15 Pietermaai, Curacao, Netherlands Antilles

CIGNA CORP   One Liberty Place, Philadelphia, PA 19192, Tel: (215) 523-4000
  (Ins, invest, health care & other fin servs)
    Cigna Overseas Finance NV, Handelskade 8, PO Box 3115, Curacao, Netherlands Antilles

MANPOWER INTL INC   5301 N Ironwood Rd, PO Box 2053, Milwaukee,
  WI 53201-2053, Tel: (414) 961-1000
  (Temporary help service)
    Manpower Curacao, P.O. Box 132, Curacao, Netherlands Antilles

NYCAL CORP   3050 K St NW, #310, Washington, DC 20007, Tel: (202) 944-4424
  (Resource & financial services)
    I-Cal Finance NV, Netherlands Antilles

PEPSICO INC   700 Anderson Hill Rd, Purchase, NY 10577-1444,
  Tel: (914) 253-2000
  (Beverages, snack foods, restaurants)
    PARCO NV, Netherlands Antilles
    PEI NV, Netherlands Antilles
    Paige NV, Netherlands Antilles
    Paine Corp. NV, Netherlands Antilles
    PepsiCo Finance (Antilles A/B) NV, Netherlands Antilles
    PepsiCo Overseas Finance NV, Netherlands Antilles

RALSTON PURINA CO   Checkerboard Sq, St Louis, MO 63164, Tel: (314) 982-1000
  (Poultry & live stock feed, cereals, food prdts)
    Ralston Purina Overseas Finance NV, De Ruyterkade 62, Willemstad, Curacao,
      Netherlands Antilles

VARITY CORP   672 Delaware Ave, Buffalo, NY 14209, Tel: (716) 888-8000
  (Mfr farm & ind machinery, diesel engines, automotive components, electromechanical
  prdts)
    Massey-Ferguson NV, Abraham DeVeerstraat 7A, Curacao, Netherlands Antilles

XEROX CORP   800 Long Ridge Rd, PO Box 1600, Stamford, CT 06904,
  Tel: (203) 968-3000
  (Mfr document processing equip, sys & supplies)
    Xerox Corp., Willemstad (Curacao) & Aruba, Netherlands Antilles

NEW ZEALAND

3M   3M Center, St Paul, MN 55144-1000, Tel: (612) 733-1110
  (Mfr diversified prdts for industry, health care, imaging, commun, transport, safety,
  consumer, etc)
    3M New Zealand Ltd., 250 Archers Rd., Glenfield, Auckland, New Zealand

ACCO INTL INC   770 S Acco Plaza, Wheeling, IL 60090, Tel: (708) 541-9500
  (Paper fasteners & clips, metal fasteners, binders, staplers)
    Acco Intl. (NZ) Ltd., 2 Nelson St., P.O. Box 6382, Wellington, New Zealand

ACCURAY CORP   650 Ackerman Rd, PO Box 02248, Columbus, OH 43202,
  Tel: (614) 261-2000
  (Computer-based process mgmt sys for forest prdts, metals rolling, textiles, tobacco
  ind)
    Accuray Australia Pty. Ltd., Rotorua, New Zealand

AIR EXPRESS INTL CORP   120 Tokeneke Rd, PO Box 1231, Darien, CT 06820,
  Tel: (203) 655-7900
  (Air frt forwarder)
    Air Express Intl., Air Cargo Agents Bldg., Christchurch Intl. Airport,

Christchurch, New Zealand
Air Express Intl., other locations in New Zealand

AIRBORNE EXPRESS   3101 Western Ave, PO Box 662, Seattle, WA 98111,
  Tel: (206) 285-4600
  (Air transp serv)
    Airborne Express, P.O. Box 73-034, 17 Aintree Ave., Airport Oaks, Mangere,
    Auckland, New Zealand

ALLEN-BRADLEY CO   PO Box 2086, Milwaukee, WI 53201, Tel: (414) 382-2000
  (Mfr eletrical controls & info devices)
    Allen-Bradley (NZ) Ltd., 343 Church St., P.O. Box 13-262, Onehunga, Auckland 6,
    New Zealand

ALLIED AFTERMARKET DIV   105 Pawtucket Ave, East Providence, RI 02916,
  Tel: (401) 434-7000
  (Mfr spark plugs, filters, brakes)
    Sphinx Mfg. Co. Ltd., P.O. Box 12315, 31 Olive Rd., Penrose, Auckland, New Zealand

ALLIEDSIGNAL INC   101 Columbia Rd, PO Box 2245, Morristown, NJ 07962-2245,
  Tel: (201) 455-2000
  (Mfr aerospace & automotive prdts, engineered materials)
    Allied Chemical (NZ) Ltd., P.O. Box 39-189, MLC Bldg., Symonds St., Auckland,
    New Zealand

ALVEY INC   9301 Olive Blvd, St Louis, MO 63132, Tel: (314) 993-4700
  (Mfr automatic case palletizers, package & pallet conveyor sys)
    CBS Engineering Ltd., 48 Wharf Rd., P.O. Box 45032, Te Atatu North, New Zealand

AMDAHL CORP   1250 E Arques Ave, PO Box 3470, Sunnyvale, CA 94088-3470,
  Tel: (408) 746-6000
  (Devel/mfr large scale computers, software, data storage prdts, info-technology
  solutions & support)
    Amdahl Intl. Corp., ASB Bank Tower, Level 8, 2 Hunter St., P.O. Box 5004,
    Wellington, New Zealand

AMERICAN AIRLINES INC   PO Box 619616, Dallas-Ft Worth Arpt, TX 75261-9616,
  Tel: (817) 355-1234
  (Air transp)
    American Airlines Inc., CPO Box 4258, Auckland, New Zealand

AMERICAN EXPRESS CO   World Financial Center, New York, NY 10285-4765,
  Tel: (212) 640-2000
  (Travel, travelers cheques, charge card & financial services)
    Centurion Finance Ltd., all inquiries to U.S. address

AMERICAN INTL GROUP INC   70 Pine St, New York, NY 10270, Tel: (212) 770-7000
  (Insurance, financial services)
    American Intl. Underwriters (New Zealand) Ltd., P.O. Box 1745, Auckland, New Zealand

AMP INC   PO Box 3608, Harrisburg, PA 17105-3608, Tel: (717) 564-0100
  (Devel/mfr electronic & electrical connection prdts & sys)
    New Zealand AMP Ltd., 51 Mahunga Dr., Mangere, P.O. Box 59-121, Auckland,
    New Zealand

AMWAY CORP   7575 E Fulton Rd, Ada, MI 49355, Tel: (616) 676-6000
  (Mfr/sale home care, personal care, nutrition & houseware prdts)
    Amway of New Zealand Ltd., 25 Springs Rd., East Tamaki, Auckland, New Zealand

AST RESEARCH INC   16215 Alton Parkway, PO Box 19658, Irvine, CA 92713-9658,
  Tel: (714) 727-4141
  (Design/devel/mfr hi-perf desktop, server & notebook computers)
    AST New Zealand, Level 5, 197-201 Willis St., Wellington, New Zealand

ATLANTIC RICHFIELD CO (ARCO)   515 S Flower St, Los Angeles, CA 90071-2256,
  Tel: (213) 486-3511
  (Petroleum & natural gas, chemicals, service stations)
    Arco Petroleum Taranaki Ltd., 337 Devon St., New Plymouth, New Zealand

AVCO FINANCIAL SERVICES INC   600 Anto Blvd, PO Box 5011, Costa Mesa,
  CA 92628-5011, Tel: (714) 435-1200
  (Financial services, loans)
    Avco Financial Services Ltd., Unit 3, 7 Rata St., New Lynn (Auckland), New Zealand

AVIS INC   900 Old Country Rd, Garden City, NY 11530, Tel: (516) 222-3000
  (Car rental serv)
    Avis Rent A Car (NZ), 22 Wakefield St., Auckland, New Zealand

AVNET INC   80 Cutter Mill Rd, Great Neck, NY 11021, Tel: (516) 466-7000
  (Distr electr components, computers & peripherals)
    Avnet VSI Electronics (NZ) Ltd., 274 Church St., Penrose, Auckland, New Zealand

AVON PRODUCTS INC   9 W 57th St, New York, NY 10019, Tel: (212) 546-6015
  (Mfr/distr beauty & related prdts, fashion jewelry, gifts & collectibles)
    Avon Cosmetics Ltd., Auckland, New Zealand

BANDAG INC   2905 NW 61, Muscatine, IA 52761, Tel: (319) 262-1400
  (Mfr/sale retread tires)
    Bandag Group Ltd., Auckland, New Zealand

BAUSCH & LOMB INC   1 Chase Square, Rochester, NY 14601, Tel: (716) 338-6000
  (Mfr vision care prdts & accessories)
    Bausch & Lomb (New Zealand) Ltd., Auckland, New Zealand

BAXTER HEALTHCARE CORP   1 Baxter Pky, Deerfield, IL 60015,
  Tel: (708) 948-2000
  (Mfr disposable medical prdts)
    Baxter Healthcare Ltd., P.O. Box 14-062, Panmure, Auckland 6, New Zealand

BECHTEL GROUP INC   50 Beale St, PO Box 3965, San Francisco, CA 94119,
  Tel: (415) 768-1234
  (Engineering & constr)
    Bechtel Pacific Corp., 32 The Terrace, Wellington, New Zealand

BENTLY NEVADA CORP   PO Box 157, Minden, NV 89423, Tel: (702) 782-3611
  (Electronic monitoring system)
    W. Arthur Fisher Ltd., Box 12-747, Penrose, Auckland, New Zealand

SAMUEL BINGHAM CO   1555 N Mittel Blvd, #T, Wood Dale, IL 60191-1046,
  Tel: (708) 238-4000
  (Print & industrial rollers, inks)
    Coates Brothers (New Zealand) Ltd., P.O. Box 12748, Penrose, Auckland 6, New Zealand

BIO-RAD LABORATORIES INC   1000 Alfred Nobel Dr, Hercules, CA 94547,
  Tel: (510) 724-7000
  (Mfr life science research prdts, clinical diagnostics, analytical instruments)
    Bio-Rad Laboratories Inc., Auckland, New Zealand

BLACK & DECKER CORP   701 E Joppa Road, Towson, MD 21286, Tel: (410) 716-3900
  (Mfr power tools & accessories, security hardware, small appliances, fasteners, info
  sys & servs)
    Black & Decker Corp., all mail to U.S. address

H & R BLOCK INC   4410 Main St, Kansas City, MO 64111, Tel: (816) 753-6900
  (Income tax preparation)
    H&R Block, the Income Tax People Ltd., P.O. Box 333-79, Takapuna North, Auckland 9,
    New Zealand

BORDEN INC   180 E Broad St, Columbus, OH 43215-3799, Tel: (614) 225-4000
  (Mfr foods, snacks & beverages, adhesives)
    Borden Inc., all mail to U.S. address

BOYDEN CONSULTING CORP   375 Park Ave, #1008, New York, NY 10152,
  Tel: (212) 980-6480
  (Executive search)
    Boyden Associates Ltd., P.O. Box 3270, Auckland 1, New Zealand

BRANSON ULTRASONICS CORP   41 Eagle Rd, Danbury, CT 06813-1961,
  Tel: (203) 796-0400
  (Mfr plastics assembly equip, ultrasonic cleaning equip)
    Techspan New Zealand Ltd., P.O. Box 80055, Green Bay, Auckland 7, New Zealand

BRIGGS & STRATTON CORP   PO Box 702, Milwaukee, WI 53201, Tel: (414) 259-5333
  (Mfr engines, auto locking devices)
    Briggs & Stratton New Zealand Ltd., all mail to U.S. address

BURLINGTON AIR EXPRESS   18200 Van Karman Ave, Irvine, CA 92715,
  Tel: (714) 752-4000
  (Air freight)
    Burlington Air Express (NZ) Ltd., 95-101 Tirangi Rd., Rongotai, Wellington,
    New Zealand

LEO BURNETT CO INC   35 West Wacker Dr, Chicago, IL 60601, Tel: (312) 220-5959
  (Advertising agency)
    Leo Burnett Ltd., 85-87 Ghuznee St., P.O. Box 10-430, Wellington, New Zealand
    Leo Burnett Ltd., 150 Hobson St., Auckland 1, New Zealand

BURSON-MARSTELLER   230 Park Ave, New York, NY 10003-1566, Tel: (212) 614-4000
  (Public relations/public affairs consultants)
    Burson-Marsteller, P.O. Box 37196, Parnell, Auckland, New Zealand

BUTTERICK CO INC   161 Ave of the Americas, New York, NY 10013,
  Tel: (212) 620-2500
  (Sewing patterns)
    Butterick Fashion Marketing Co., 38 Kalmia St., Ellerslie, Auckland 5, New Zealand

CALTEX PETROLEUM CORP   PO Box 619500, Dallas, TX 75261, Tel: (214) 830-1000
   (Petroleum prdts)
      Caltex Oil (NZ) Ltd., Caltex Tower, 141 The Terrace, Wellington 1, New Zealand

CARBOLINE CO   350 Hanley Industrial Ct, St Louis, MO 63144,
   Tel: (314) 644-1000
   (Mfr coatings, sealants)
      Polymer Developments Group Ltd., P.O. Box 58256, Greenmount, Auckland, New Zealand

CARRIER CORP   One Carrier Place, Farmington, CT 06034-4015,
   Tel: (203) 674-3000
   (Mfr/distr/svce A/C, heating & refrigeration equip)
      Carrier A/C Ltd., 25 Springs Rd E., Tamaki, New Zealand

CCH INC   2700 Lake Cook Rd, Riverwoods, IL 60015, Tel: (708) 267-7000
   (Tax & busines law info, software & services)
      CCH New Zealand Ltd., 17 Kahika Rd., Beach Haven, Auckland 10, New Zealand

CEILCOTE CO   140 Sheldon Rd, Berea, OH 44017, Tel: (216) 243-0700
   (Mfr corrosion-resistant material, air pollution control equip, cons serv)
      Ceilcote (NZ) Ltd., P.O. Box 3046, New Plymouth, New Zealand

CHAMPION SPARK PLUG CO   PO Box 910, Toledo, OH 43661-0001,
   Tel: (419) 535-2567
   (Mfr spark plugs, wiper blades & related prdts)
      Champion Spark Plug (NZ) Ltd., 51-53 Carbine Rd., P.O. Box 14-219, Panmure,
      Auckland, New Zealand

CHASE MANHATTAN BANK N A   1 Chase Manhattan Plaza, New York, NY 10081,
   Tel: (212) 552-2222
   (Intl banking)
      Chase-NBA New Zealand Ltd., P.O. Box 3975, CML Centre, Queens & Wyndham Sts.,
      Auckland, New Zealand
      Chase-NBA New Zealand Ltd., 155-161 The Terrace, P.O. Box 2266, Wellington,
      New Zealand

CHEVRON CORP   225 Bush St, San Francisco, CA 94104, Tel: (415) 894-7700
   (Oil & gas exploration, production, refining, products; oilfield & financial services)
      Chevron Corp., all mail to U.S. address

CHINET CO   101 Merritt 7, Norwalk, CT 06851, Tel: (203) 846-1499
   (Mfr molded containers)
      Fibre Products (New Zealand) Ltd., P.O. Box 22-550, Otahuhu, Auckland 6, New Zealand

CIGNA CORP   One Liberty Place, Philadelphia, PA 19192, Tel: (215) 523-4000
   (Ins, invest, health care & other fin servs)
      Cigna Insurance New Zealand Ltd., Cigna House, 345 Queen St., Auckland 1,
      New Zealand
      Cigna Life Insurance New Zealand Ltd., 104 The Terrace, Wellington, New Zealand
      Cigna Reinsurance New Zealand Ltd., Quay Tower-29, Customs St., Auckland 1,
      New Zealand
      Esis Intl. Inc., Level 1G, Cigna House, 345 Queen St., Auckland 1, New Zealand

CINCOM SYSTEMS INC   2300 Montana Ave, Cincinnati, OH 45211,
Tel: (513) 662-2300
(Devel/distr computer software)
  Cincom Systems Inc., Wellington, New Zealand

CITICORP   399 Park Ave, New York, NY 10043, Tel: (212) 559-1000
(Banking & financial services)
  Citibank NA, New Zealand

COLGATE-PALMOLIVE CO   300 Park Ave, New York, NY 10022, Tel: (212) 310-2000
(Mfr pharms, cosmetics, toiletries, detergents)
  Colgate Palmolive Inc., Navis St. & Hutt Rd., P.O. Box 38-077, Petone, New Zealand

COLUMBIA PICTURES INDUSTRIES INC   711 Fifth Ave, New York, NY 10022,
Tel: (212) 751-4400
(Producer & distributor of motion pictures)
  Columbia Warner Distributors, 24/26 Nikau St., Auckland 3, New Zealand
  Columbia Warner Distributors, P.O. Box 8687, Upper Symonds St., Auckland 3,
  New Zealand

COMPUTER ASSOCIATES INTL INC   One Computer Associates Plaza, Islandia,
NY 11788, Tel: (516) 342-5224
(Devel/mkt/mgt info mgt & bus applications software)
  Computer Associates NZ Ltd., Rural Bank Bldg., 9th Fl., 32-34 Manners St.,
  Wellington, New Zealand

CORE LABORATORIES   10205 Westheimer, Houston, TX 77042, Tel: (713) 972-6311
(Petroleum testing/analysis, analytical chem, lab & octane analysis instrumentation)
  Core Laboratories Inc., P.O. Box 3206, New Plymouth, New Zealand

COULTER CORP   PO Box 169015, Miami, FL 33116-9015, Tel: (305) 885-0131
(Mfr blood analysis sys, flow cytometers, chem sys, scientific sys & reagents)
  Coulter Electronics New Zealand Ltd., 2/63 Lansford Crescent, Avondale, Auckland,
  New Zealand

CPC INTERNATIONAL INC   PO Box 8000, Englewood Cliffs, NJ 07632,
Tel: (201) 894-4000
(Consumer foods, corn refining)
  New Zealand Starch Products, P.O. Box 13-024, Onehunga, Auckland 6, New Zealand

CROWN EQUIPMENT CORP   40 S Washington St, New Bremen, OH 45869,
Tel: (419) 629-2311
(Mfr/sales/svce forklift trucks, stackers)
  Crown Equipment Pty. Ltd., Pakuranga, Auckland, New Zealand

D'ARCY MASIUS BENTON & BOWLES INC (DMB&B)   1675 Broadway, New York,
NY 10019, Tel: (212) 468-3622
(Advertising & communications)
  DMB&B, CPO Box 4085, Auckland, New Zealand

DATA GENERAL CORP   4400 Computer Dr, Westboro, MA 01580, Tel: (617) 366-8911
(Design, mfr gen purpose computer sys & peripheral prdts & servs)
  Data General New Zealand Ltd., B level, Grand Arcade Bldg., Willis St.,
    P.O. Box 9735, Wellington, New Zealand

DDB NEEDHAM WORLDWIDE INC   437 Madison Ave, New York, NY 10022,
  Tel: (212) 415-2000
  (Advertising)
    DDB Needham New Zealand Ltd., DDB Needham House, 16 Liverpool St., Auckland,
      New Zealand
    DDB Needham New Zealand Ltd., DDB Needham House, 120 Victoria St., Wellington,
      New Zealand
    DDB Needham New Zealand Ltd., Clarendon Tower-17 Level,
      Cor. Worcester St. & Oxford Terrace, Christchurch, New Zealand
    DDB Needham Worldwide Ltd., DDB Needham House, 16 Liverpool St., Auckland,
      New Zealand

THE DEXTER CORP   1 Elm Street, Windsor Locks, CT 06096, Tel: (203) 627-9051
  (Mfr nonwovens, polymer prdts, magnetic materials, biotechnology)
    Life Technologies (NZ) Ltd., 18-24 Botha Rd., P.O. Box 12-502, Penrose, Auckland 6,
      New Zealand

DIGITAL EQUIPMENT CORP   146 Main St, Maynard, MA 01754-2571,
  Tel: (508) 493-5111
  (Networked computer systems & services)
    Digital Equipment Corp. (New Zealand) Ltd., Auckland Club Tower, 34 Shortland St.,
      Auckland, New Zealand

DONN PRODUCTS INC   1000 Crocker Rd, Westlake, OH 44145, Tel: (216) 871-1000
  (Suspended ceiling sys)
    Donn Pacific Ltd., Monier Place, P.O. Box 11-155, Ellerslie, Mt. Wellington,
      Auckland 6, New Zealand

DOW CORNING CORP   2220 W Salzburg Rd, PO Box 1767, Midland, MI 48640,
  Tel: (517) 496-4000
  (Silicones, silicon chems, solid lubricants)
    Dow Corning (NZ), 3001 Great North Rd., P.O. Box 15-404, New Lynn, Auckland 7,
      New Zealand

E I DU PONT DE NEMOURS & CO   1007 Market St, Wilmington, DE 19898,
  Tel: (302) 774-1000
  (Mfr/sale diversified chems, plastics, specialty prdts & fibers)
    DuPont (NZ) Ltd., New Zealand

DURAMETALLIC CORP   2104 Factory St, Kalamazoo, MI 49001, Tel: (616) 382-8720
  (Mfr mech seals, compression packings, auxiliaries)
    Petch/Duramteallic (NA) Ltd., P.O. Box 12245, 6 Fairfax Ave., Penrose, Auckland,
      New Zealand

EASTMAN KODAK CO   343 State St, Rochester, NY 14650, Tel: (716) 724-4000
  (Devel/mfr photo & chem prdts, info mgmt/video/copier sys, fibers/plastics for
  various ind)
    Kodak New Zealand Ltd., P.O. Box 2198, 70 Stanley St., Auckland, New Zealand
    Kodak New Zealand Ltd., also in Christchurch & Wellington, New Zealand

EATON CORP   1111 Superior Ave, Cleveland, OH 44114, Tel: (216) 523-5000
  (Advanced tech prdts for transp & ind mkts)
    Cutler Hammes (NZ) Ltd., Hansford Cies, Avondale, Auckland 7, New Zealand

EATON CORP/CUTLER HAMMER   4201 North 27th St, Milwaukee, WI 53216,
  Tel: (414) 449-6000
  (Electric control apparatus, mfr of advanced technologic prdts)
    Cutler-Hammer New Zealand Ltd., P.O. Box 11-129, Ellerslie, Auckland, New Zealand

EG&G INC   45 William St, Wellesley, MA 02181-4078, Tel: (617) 237-5100
  (Diversified R/D, mfg & services)
    EG&G Canada Ltd., 22001 Dumberry Rd., Vaudreuil, PQ, Canada J7V 8P7

EMERY WORLDWIDE   One Lagoon Dr, #400, Redwood City, CA 94065,
  Tel: (800) 227-1981
  (Freight transport, global logistics, air cargo)
    Emery Worldwide, P.O. Box 73002, Auckland Intl. Airport, AFCA Bldg.,
    George Bolt Dr., Auckland, New Zealand

EXPEDITORS INTL OF WASHINGTON INC   PO Box 69620, Seattle, WA 98168-9620,
  Tel: (206) 246-3711
  (Air/ocean freight forwarding, customs brokerage, intl logistics solutions)
    Expeditors Intl. (NZ) Ltd., P.O. Box 43202, Mangere, Auckland, New Zealand

FEDERAL-MOGUL CORP   PO Box 1966, Detroit, MI 48235, Tel: (810) 354-7700
  (Mfr/distr precision parts for automobiles, trucks, & farm/constrution vehicles)
    Federal-Mogul New Zealand Ltd., New Zealand

FELTON INTERNATIONAL INC   599 Johnson Ave, Brooklyn, NY 11237,
  Tel: (212) 497-4664
  (Essential oils & extracts, perfumes & flavor material, aromatic chems)
    Chemby Marketing Ltd., 17-21 Maidstone St., Auckland 2, New Zealand

FERRO CORPORATION   1000 Lakeside Ave, Cleveland, OH 44114,
  Tel: (216) 641-8580
  (Mfr chems, coatings, plastics, colors, refractories)
    Ferro Plastics (NZ) Ltd., 26 Poland Rd., Takapuna, Auckland, New Zealand
    Ferro Stratos Ltd., 6 Woodruffe Ave., Henderson, Auckland, New Zealand

FOOTE CONE & BELDING COMMUNICATIONS INC   101 E Erie St, Chicago,
  IL 60611-2897, Tel: (312) 751-7000
  (Advertising agency)
    Mainstream/FCB, 89-91 Grafton Rd., Auckland, New Zealand

FORD MOTOR CO   The American Road, Dearborn, MI 48121, Tel: (313) 322-3000
  (Mfr motor vehicles)
    Ford Motor Co. of (NZ) Ltd., Private Bag, Auckland, New Zealand

FRANK RUSSELL CO   909 A St, PO Box 1616, Tacoma, WA 98401-1616,
  Tel: (206) 572-9500
  (Investment mgmt consulting)
    Frank Russell Co. (NZ) Ltd., P.O. Box 105-191, Auckland, New Zealand

THE FRANKLIN MINT   Franklin Center, PA 19091, Tel: (610) 459-6000
  (Creation/mfr/mktg collectibles & luxury items)
    Franklin Mint Ltd., 6 Clayton St., New Market, Auckland, New Zealand

H B FULLER CO   2400 Energy Park Dr, St Paul, MN 55108, Tel: (612) 645-3401
  (Mfr/distr adhesives, sealants, coatings, paints, waxes, sanitation chems)
    H.B. Fuller Co. (NZ) Ltd., Box 43-164, Mangere, Auckland, New Zealand

GAF CORP   1361 Alps Rd, Wayne, NJ 07470, Tel: (201) 628-3000
  (Chems, bldg materials, commun)
    GAF (Australasia) Pty Ltd., Box 78073, 2 Monmouth St., Grey Lynn, Auckland 2,
    New Zealand

GENERAL BINDING CORP   One GBC Plaza, Northbrook, IL 60062,
  Tel: (708) 272-3700
  (Binding & laminating equip & associated supplies)
    GBC New Zealand Ltd., 169 Pilkington Rd., Panmure, Auckland, New Zealand

GENERAL MOTORS ACCEPTANCE CORP   3044 West Grand Blvd, Detroit, MI 48202,
  Tel: (313) 556-5000
  (Automobile financing)
    GMAC N.Z., Level 6, 40-44 Queens Dr., Lower Hutt, New Zealand

GENERAL MOTORS CORP   3044 W Grand Blvd, Detroit, MI 48202-3091,
  Tel: (313) 556-5000
  (Mfr full line vehicles, automotive electronics, coml technologies, telecom, space,
  finance)
    General Motors Ltd., Trentham Plant #1, Private Bag, Upper Hutt, New Zealand

GEORGIA GULF CORP   400 Perimeter Center Terrace, Atlanta, GA 30346,
  Tel: (404) 395-4500
  (Mfr/mkt commodity chems & polymers)
    Georgia Gulf Corp., Tauranga, New Zealand

THE GILLETTE CO   Prudential Tower, Boston, MA 02199, Tel: (617) 421-7000
  (Devel/mfr personal care/use prdts: blades & razors, toiletries, cosmetics,
  stationery)
    Gillette (New Zealand) Ltd., Auckland, New Zealand
    Oral-B Laboratories Ltd., Auckland, New Zealand
    Wilkinson Sword (New Zealand) Ltd., Auckland, New Zealand

W R GRACE & CO   One Town Center Rd, Boca Raton, FL 33486-1010,
  Tel: (407) 362-2000
  (Mfr spec chems & materials: packaging, health care, catalysts, construction, water
  treatment/process)
    W.R. Grace (NZ) Ltd., Prosser St., Elsdon, Porirua, New Zealand

GREY ADVERTISING INC   777 Third Ave, New York, NY 10017, Tel: (212) 546-2000
  (Advertising)
    Grey New Zealand, Level 7, 73 Symonds St., Auckland, New Zealand

GRIFFITH LABORATORIES INC   I Griffith Center, Alsip, IL 60658,
  Tel: (708) 371-0900
  (Ind food ingredients & equip)
    Griffith Labs (NZ) Ltd., P.O. Box 22-434, 11-13 Bell Ave., Otahuhu, Auckland 6,
    New Zealand

GROUNDWATER TECHNOLOGY INC   100 River Ridge Dr, Norwood, MA 02062,
  Tel: (617) 769-7600
  (Industrial site cleanup, mgmt & consulting)
    Groundwater Technology (NZ), Level 4, 195 Khyber Pass Rd., Grafton, Aukland,
    New Zealand

GUEST SUPPLY INC   720 U S Hwy 1, PO Box 6018, N Brunswick, NJ 08902,
Tel: (908) 246-3011
(Mfr personal care & housekeeping prdts)
  Guest Intl. (New Zealand) Ltd., 31 Princess St., Auckland, New Zealand

HALLMARK CARDS INC   PO Box 419580, Kansas City, MO 64141, Tel: (816) 274-5100
(Mfr greeting cards & related prdts)
  Hallmark Cards New Zealand Ltd., 59 Mahunga Dr., Private Bag, Onehunga Mangere,
  Auckland, New Zealand

THE HARPER GROUP   260 Townsend St, PO Box 77933, San Francisco,
CA 94107-1719, Tel: (415) 978-0600
(Ocean/air freight fwdg, customs brokerage, packing & whse, logistics mgt, ins)
  CFS New Zealand Ltd., P.O. Box 53095, Auckland Airport, New Zealand
  CFS New Zealand Ltd., also in Christchurch & Wellington, New Zealand
  Circle Freight Intl. (NZ), P.O. Box 53095, Auckland Airport, New Zealand
  Circle Freight Intl. (NZ), also in Christchurch & Wellington, New Zealand
  Marshall Customs & Forwarding Services, P.O. Box 43-233, Mangere, Auckland,
  New Zealand

HARRAH'S ENTERTAINMENT INC   1023 Cherry Rd, Memphis, TN 38139,
Tel: (901) 762-8600
(Casino entertainment)
  Harrah's Sky City, Nelson House Bldg., 93 Wellesley St., Auckland, New Zealand

H J HEINZ CO   PO Box 57, Pittsburgh, PA 15230-0057, Tel: (412) 456-5700
(Processed food prdts & nutritional services)
  Heinz-Wattie's Australasia, Auckland, New Zealand
  Wattie's Ltd., Auckland, New Zealand

HELENE CURTIS INDUSTRIES INC   325 N Wells St, Chicago, IL 60610-4791,
Tel: (312) 661-0222
(Mfr personal care prdts)
  Helene Curtis (New Zealand) Ltd., 171 Main North Rd., Christchurch, New Zealand

HERCULES INC   Hercules Plaza, Wilmington, DE 19894-0001, Tel: (302) 594-5000
(Mfr spec chems, plastics, film & fibers, coatings, resins, food ingredients)
  A.C. Hatrick (NZ) Ltd., 22 York St., P.O. Box 2359, Auckland 1, New Zealand

HEWLETT-PACKARD CO   3000 Hanover St, Palo Alto, CA 94304-0890,
Tel: (415) 857-1501
(Mfr computing, communications & measurement prdts & services)
  Hewlett-Packard (NZ) Ltd., 186-190 Willis St., Wellington 1, New Zealand

HONEYWELL INC   PO Box 524, Minneapolis, MN 55440-0524, Tel: (612) 951-1000
(Devel/mfr controls for home & building, industry, space & aviation)
  Honeywell Ltd., 264 Mount Eden Rd., Mount Eden, Auckland, New Zealand

HORWATH INTL   415 Madison Ave, New York, NY 10017, Tel: (212) 838-5566
(Public accountants & auditors)
  Horwath International (NZ) Ltd., 10th Fl. Barclays Bldg., 70 Shortland St.,
  Auckland, New Zealand
  Hunter & Brockelbank & Dey, 56 York Place, Dunedin, New Zealand

HOUGHTON INTL INC   PO Box 930, Valley Forge, PA 19482-0930,
  Tel: (610) 666-4000
  (Mfr spec chems, hydraulic fluids, lubricants)
    Paykel Engineering Ltd., P.O. Box 5046, Wellesley St., Auckland 6, New Zealand

HYATT INTL CORP   200 West Madison, Chicago, IL 60606, Tel: (312) 750-1234
  (Intl hotel mgmt)
    Hyatt Intl. Hotels, Auckland, New Zealand

IBM CORP   Old Orchard Rd, Armonk, NY 10504, Tel: (914) 765-1900
  (Information products, technology & services)
    IBM New Zealand, New Zealand

ICS INTERNATIONAL INC   125 Oak St, Scranton, PA 18515, Tel: (717) 342-7701
  (Correspondence courses)
    ICS (NZ) Ltd., 1F Athenic Bldg., 45 Courtenay Pl., Wellington, New Zealand

ILLINOIS TOOL WORKS INC   3600 W Lake Ave, Glenview, IL 60025,
  Tel: (708) 724-7500
  (Mfr gears, tools, fasteners, sealants, plastic & metal components for ind, med, etc.)
    W.A. Deutsher Pty. (NZ) Ltd., Auckland, New Zealand

INGERSOLL-RAND CO   200 Chestnut Ridge Rd, Woodcliff Lake, NJ 07675,
  Tel: (201) 573-0123
  (Mfr compressors, rock drills, pumps, air tools, door hardware, ball bearings)
    Ingersoll-Rand Schlage (NA) Ltd., 437 Rosebank Rd., P.O. Box 19347, Avondale,
      Auckland, New Zealand

INTERGRAPH CORP   Huntsville, AL 35894-0001, Tel: (205) 730-2000
  (Devel/mfr interactive computer graphic systems)
    Intergraph Corp. (NZ) Ltd., Level 3, Sequent House, 8-10 Whitaker Place, Auckland,
      New Zealand

INTERMEC CORP   6001 36th Ave West, PO Box 4280, Everett, WA 98203-9280,
  Tel: (206) 348-2600
  (Mfr/distr automated data collection sys)
    Walker Datavision, P.O. Box 12343, Penrose, 666 Gt. South Rd., Auckland 5,
      New Zealand

ITT CORP   1330 Ave of the Americas, New York, NY 10019-5490,
  Tel: (212) 258-1000
  (Design/mfr communications & electronic equip, hotels, insurance)
    Standard Telephone & Cables (NZ) Ltd., Lane St., P.O. Box 40-140, Upper Hutt,
      New Zealand

ITT SHERATON CORP   60 State St, Boston, MA 02108, Tel: (617) 367-3600
  (Hotel operations)
    Sheraton Auckland Hotel, P.O. Box 2771, Auckland 1, New Zealand

JOHNSON & JOHNSON   One Johnson & Johnson Plaza, New Brunswick, NJ 08933,
  Tel: (908) 524-0400
  (R&D/mfr/sale health care prdts)
    Johnson & Johnson (NZ) Ltd., P.O. Box 97-027, South Auckland Mail Centre, Wiri,
      New Zealand
    Johnson & Johnson Medical New Zealand, P.O. Box 97561, Wiri, South Auckland,
      New Zealand

S C JOHNSON & SON INC   1525 Howe St, Racine, WI 53403, Tel: (414) 631-2000
(Home, auto, commercial & personal care prdts, specialty chems)
   Johnson's Wax of (NZ) Ltd., Mahunga Dr., P.O. Box Private Bag, Onehunga,
   Auckland 6, New Zealand

KELLY SERVICES   999 W Big Beaver Rd, Troy, MI 48084, Tel: (810) 244-4313
(Temporary help placement)
   Kelly Services (New Zealand) Ltd., 4 branches throughout New Zealand
   Kelly Services (New Zealand) Ltd. (HQ), Price Waterhouse Centre, Floor 10,
      119 Armaugh St., Christchurch, New Zealand

KEYSTONE INTL INC   PO Box 40010, Houston, TX 77040, Tel: (713) 466-1176
(Mfr butterfly valves, actuators & control accessories)
   Keystone Pacific, locations throughout New Zealand

KWIK-SEW PATTERN CO INC   3000 Washington Ave N, Minneapolis, MN 55411,
   Tel: (612) 521-7651
(Mfr patterns & instruction books for home sewing)
   Kwik-Sew Patterns (NZ) Inc., P.O. Box 58541, Greenmount, Auckland, New Zealand

LEEDS+NORTHRUP   795 Horsham Rd, PO Box 1010, Horsham, PA 19044-8010,
   Tel: (215) 442-8000
(Mfr process control instrumentation, liquid & particle analysis)
   Leeds+Northrup New Zealand Ltd., 81 Hugo Johnson Dr., Penrose, Auckland, New Zealand

LEVI STRAUSS & CO   1155 Battery, San Francisco, CA 94111, Tel: (415) 544-6000
(Mfr casual wearing apparel)
   Levi Strauss (NZ) Ltd., 30 Heather St., Parnell, Auckland, New Zealand

ELI LILLY & CO   Lilly Corporate Center, Indianapolis, IN 46285,
   Tel: (317) 276-2000
(Mfr pharmaceuticals, animal health prdts)
   Eli Lilly & Co. (NZ) Ltd., 9 Gladding Pl., Manukau City, Auckland, New Zealand

LINTAS:WORLDWIDE   1 Dag Hammarskjold Plaza, New York, NY 10017,
   Tel: (212) 605-8000
(Advertising agency)
   Lintas:Auckland, 100 Greys Ave., Auckland 1, New Zealand

LONGYEAR CO   PO Box 27314, Salt Lake City, UT 84127, Tel: (801) 972-1395
(Mfr diamond drills, concrete cutting equip; drill serv)
   Longyear Co., P.O. Box 43030, Mangere, Auckland, New Zealand

MARATHON LE TOURNEAU CO   PO Box 2307, Longview, TX 75606, Tel: (903) 237-7000
(Mfr heavy constr, mining mach & equip)
   Cable Price Corp. Ltd., P.O. Box 10042, Wellington, New Zealand

MARSH & McLENNAN COS INC   1166 Ave of the Americas, New York, NY 10036-1011,
   Tel: (212) 345-5000
(Insurance)
   Marsh & McLennan Ltd., 5/F NZFP House, 110 Symonds St., P.O. Box 2221, Auckland,
   New Zealand

MATTEL INC   333 Continental Blvd, El Segundo, CA 90245, Tel: (310) 252-2000
(Mfr toys, dolls, games, crafts & hobbies)
   Mattel Toys New Zealand Ltd., 13-15 Bath St., Auckland, New Zealand

MEASUREX CORP   One Results Way, Cupertino, CA 95014-5991, Tel: (408) 255-1500
  (Mfr computer integrated mfg sys)
    Measurex Systems (NZ) Ltd., P.O. Box 1547, Ngongotaha, Rotorua, New Zealand

MERCK SHARP & DOHME INTL   PO Box 2000, Rahway, NJ 07065, Tel: (201) 574-4000
  (Pharms, chems & biologicals)
    Merck, Sharp & Dohme (NZ) Ltd., Plunket Ave., P.O. Box 23-244, Papatoetoe,
    Auckland, New Zealand

MICROSOFT CORP   One Microsoft Way, Redmond, WA 98052-6399,
  Tel: (206) 882-8080
  (Computer software, peripherals & services)
    Microsoft New Zealand (Pty.), 12th Fl., Amex House, 67-69 Symonds St.,
    P.O. Box 8070, Auckland 1, New Zealand

MOBIL CORP   3225 Gallows Rd, Fairfax, VA 22037-0001, Tel: (703) 846-3000
  (Petroleum explor & refining, mfr petrol prdts, chems, petrochems)
    Mobil Oil New Zealand Ltd., Aurora House, 5464 The Terrace, Wellington 1,
    New Zealand

MULTIGRAPHICS DIV   1800 W Central Rd, Mt Prospect, IL 60056,
  Tel: (708) 398-1900
  (Offset duplicating & graphic commun sys)
    AM Intl. Ltd., P.O. Box 163, Wellington, New Zealand

MYERS INTL INC   1293 South Main St, Akron, OH 44301, Tel: (216) 253-5592
  (Mfr tire retreading & maintenance equip & supplies)
    Myers Tyre Supply (NZ) Ltd., 14 Seaview Rd., P.O. Box 1072, Wellington, New Zealand

McCANN-ERICKSON WORLDWIDE   750 Third Ave, New York, NY 10017,
  Tel: (212) 697-6000
  (Advertising)
    McCann-Erickson Ltd., Greenpark, 382 Manukau Rd., Epsom, P.O. Box 830, Auckland,
    New Zealand
    McCann-Erickson Ltd., 8 Lipman St., Wellington, New Zealand

THE McGRAW-HILL COS   1221 Ave of the Americas, New York, NY 10020,
  Tel: (212) 512-2000
  (Books, magazines, info sys, financial serv, broadcast operations)
    McGraw-Hill Book Co. (NZ) Ltd., 5 Joval Pl., P.O. Box 97-082, Manukau, Wiri,
    New Zealand

NATIONAL CAR RENTAL SYSTEM INC   7700 France Ave S, Minneapolis, MN 55435,
  Tel: (612) 830-2121
  (Car rental)
    Natl. Car Rental System Inc., 87 St. Asaph St., Christchurch, New Zealand
    Natl. Car Rental System Inc., 220 Hardy St., Nelson, New Zealand
    Natl. Car Rental System Inc., High St., Picton, New Zealand

NATIONAL STARCH & CHEMICAL CO   10 Finderne Ave, Bridgewater, NJ 08807-3300,
  Tel: (908) 685-5000
  (Mfr adhesives & sealants, resins & spec chems, electr materials & adhesives, food
  prdts, ind starch)
    National Starch & Chemical NZ Ltd., Auckland, New Zealand

A C NIELSEN CO   Nielsen Plaza, Northbrook, IL 60062-6288, Tel: (708) 498-6300
(Market research)
    A.C. Nielsen (NZ) Ltd., 107 Great South Rd., One Tree Hill, Auckland, New Zealand

NORTON CO   1 New Bond St, Worcester, MA 01606, Tel: (508) 795-5000
(Abrasives, drill bits, constr & safety prdts, plastics)
    Norton Australia Pty. Ltd., Wharf Rd., Te Atatu North, P.O. Box 45005, Auckland 8,
    New Zealand

OCCIDENTAL PETROLEUM CORP   10889 Wilshire Blvd, Los Angeles, CA 90024,
  Tel: (213) 879-1700
(Petroleum & petroleum prdts, chems, plastics)
    Occidental Chemical Co. Ltd., P.O. Box 2786, Auckland, New Zealand

ODI   25 Mall Rd, Burlington, MA 01803, Tel: (617) 272-8040
(Mgt & consul serv)
    ODI New Zealand, 54 Porritt Ave., P.O. Box 6262, Te Aro, Wellington, New Zealand

OLIN CORP   120 Long Ridge Rd, PO Box 1355, Stamford, CT 06904-1355,
  Tel: (203) 356-2000
(Mfr chems, metals, applied physics in elect, defense, aerospace inds)
    Olin Corp (NZ) Ltd., 9 Joval Pl., Manukau City, Auckland, New Zealand

OTIS ELEVATOR CO   10 Farm Springs, Farmington, CT 06032, Tel: (860) 676-6528
(Mfr elevators & escalators)
    Otis Elevator Co. Ltd., 60 Stanley St., Parnell, Auckland, New Zealand

PARKER DRILLING CO   8 E Third St, Tulsa, OK 74103-3637, Tel: (918) 585-8221
(Drilling contractor)
    Parker Drilling Co. of New Zealand Ltd., P.O. Box 144, New Plymouth, New Zealand

PARKER HANNIFIN CORP   17325 Euclid Ave, Cleveland, OH 44112,
  Tel: (216) 531-3000
(Mfr motion-control prdts)
    Parker Hannifin (NZ) Ltd./Parker Enzed (NZ) Ltd., 3 Bowden Rd., Mt. Wellington,
    Auckland, New Zealand

PFIZER INC   235 E 42nd St, New York, NY 10017-5755, Tel: (212) 573-2323
(Mfr healthcare products)
    Pfizer (NZ) Ltd., New Zealand
    Pfizer Laboratories Ltd., New Zealand

PLOUGH INC   PO Box 377, Memphis, TN 38151, Tel: (901) 320-2011
(Proprietary drug & cosmetic prdts)
    Scholl (NZ) Ltd., P.O. Box 2370, Wellington 35, New Zealand

POLAROID CORP   549 Technology Sq, Cambridge, MA 02139, Tel: (617) 386-2000
(Photographic equip & supplies, optical prdts)
    Polaroid (NZ), Augustus House, 15 Augustus Terrace, P.O. Box 37046, Parnell,
    Auckland, New Zealand

PRECISION VALVE CORP   PO Box 309, Yonkers, NY 10702, Tel: (914) 969-6500
(Mfr aerosol valves)
    Precision Valve New Zealand, 12 Donner Pl., P.O. Box 62-111, Sylvia Park,
    Auckland 6, New Zealand

PREMARK INTL INC   1717 Deerfield Rd, Deerfield, IL 60015, Tel: (708) 405-6000
(Mfr/sale diversified consumer & coml prdts)
    Dart Industries (New Zealand) Ltd., 47-49 The Concourse, Hendrson, Auckland,
    New Zealand

RAYCHEM CORP   300 Constitution Dr, Menlo Park, CA 94025, Tel: (415) 361-3333
(Devel/mfr/mkt materials science products for electronics, telecommunications &
industry)
    Raychem New Zealand Ltd., P.O. Box 52-211, Mt. Wellington, 4 Arthur Brown Pl.,
    Auckland, New Zealand

READER'S DIGEST ASSOCIATION INC   PO Box 235, Pleasantville, NY 10570,
Tel: (914) 238-1000
(Publisher magazines & books, direct mail marketer)
    Readers Digest (NZ) Ltd., 11 York St., Parnell, Auckland, New Zealand

REDKEN LABORATORIES INC   6625 Variel Ave, Canoga Park, CA 91303,
Tel: (818) 992-2700
(Mfr hair & skin care prdts)
    Redken New Zealand, P.O. Box 22022, Otahuhu, Auckland, New Zealand

RELIANCE ELECTRIC CO   24701 Euclid Ave, Cleveland, OH 44117,
Tel: (216) 266-7000
(Equip & sys for ind automation, telecom equip)
    Reliance Electric (NZ) Ltd., 44-46 Walls Rd., P.O. Box 12016, Penrose, Auckland 6,
    New Zealand

REVLON INC   625 Madison Ave, New York, NY 10022, Tel: (212) 527-4000
(Mfr cosmetics, fragrances, toiletries, beauty care prdts)
    Middows Taylor Ltd., New Zealand

ROCKWELL INTL CORP   2201 Seal Beach Blvd, PO Box 4250, Seal Beach,
CA 90740-8250, Tel: (310) 797-3311
(Prdts & serv for aerospace, automotive, electronics, graphics & automation inds)
    Allen-Bradley (NZ) Ltd., 343 Church St., P.O. Box 13-262, Onehunga, Auckland 6,
    New Zealand
    Allen-Bradley (NZ) Ltd., also in Christchurch & Wellington, New Zealand

ROHM AND HAAS CO   100 Independence Mall West, Philadelphia, PA 19106,
Tel: (215) 592-3000
(Mfr ind & agric chems, plastics)
    Rohm and Haas (NZ) Ltd., 16 Beach Rd., Otahuhu, Auckland 6, New Zealand

SCHOLASTIC INC   555 Broadway, New York, NY 10012, Tel: (212) 343-6100
(Pub/distr educational & children's magazines, books, software)
    Ashton Scholastic Ltd., 21 Lady Ruby Dr., East Tanaki, Private Bag 94407,
    Greenmont, Auckland, New Zealand

SEQUENT COMPUTER SYSTEMS INC   15450 SW Koll Pkwy, Beaverton, OR 97006-6063,
Tel: (503) 626-5700
(Mfr symmetric multiprocessing technology computers)
    Sequent Computer Systems Inc., Sequent House, Level 6, 8-10 Whitaker Pl.,
    P.O. Box 4518, Auckland, New Zealand

SIMPLICITY PATTERN CO INC   2 Park Ave, New York, NY 10016,
Tel: (212) 372-0500
(Dress patterns)
   Simplicity Patterns (NZ) Ltd., P.O. Box 41011, Auckland 3, New Zealand

SONOCO PRODUCTS CO   North Second St, PO Box 160, Hartsville, SC 29550,
Tel: (803) 383-7000
(Mfr packaging for consumer & ind mkt)
   Sonoco Australia Pty. Ltd., Hickory Ave., P.O. Box 21-163, Henderson, New Zealand

STA-RITE INDUSTRIES INC   293 Wright St, Delavan, WI 53115,
Tel: (414) 728-5551
(Mfr water pumps, filters & systems)
   Onga (New Zealand) Ltd., P.O. Box 12637, Penrose, Auckland, New Zealand

THE STANLEY WORKS   1000 Stanley Dr, PO Box 7000, New Britain, CT 06050,
Tel: (203) 225-5111
(Mfr hand tools & hardware)
   Stanley Tools (NZ) Ltd., P.O. Box 12-582, Penrose, Auckland, New, Zealand

STATE STREET BANK & TRUST CO   225 Franklin St, Boston, MA 02101,
Tel: (617) 786-3000
(Banking & financial services)
   State Street New Zealand Ltd., 50-64 Customhouse Quay, Wellington 6001, New Zealand

STOKES DIV   5500 Tabor Rd, Philadelphia, PA 19120, Tel: (215) 289-5671
(Vacuum pumps & components, vacuum dryers, oil-upgrading equip)
   Barry-Huber & Associates Ltd., P.O. Box 153, Hamilton, New Zealand

SUB SEA INTL INC   701 Engineers Rd, Belle Chasse, LA 70037,
Tel: (504) 393-7744
(Service oil/gas industry: diving, ROV's, offshore construction, engineering,
pipeline services)
   Sub Sea Intl. New Zealand Inc., 146 Devon St. E., P.O. Box 599, New Plymouth,
   New Zealand

SULLAIR CORP   3700 E Michigan Blvd, Michigan City, IN 46360,
Tel: (219) 879-5451
(Refrigeration sys, vacuum pumps, generators, etc)
   Sullair (NZ) Inc., 196 Station Rd., Penrose, P.O. Box 12-627, Auckland, New Zealand

TRITON ENERGY CORP   6688 N Central Expressway, #1400, Dallas, TX 75206,
Tel: (214) 691-5200
(Energy explor & prod)
   New Zealand Petroleum Co. Ltd., 100 Willis St., Wellington, New Zealand

UNION CAMP CORP   1600 Valley Rd, Wayne, NJ 07470, Tel: (201) 628-2000
(Mfr paper, packaging, chems, wood prdts)
   Bush Boake Allen Ltd., P.O. Box 27-162, 128-130 Stoddard Rd., Auckland 4,
   New Zealand

UNION CARBIDE CORP   39 Old Ridgebury Rd, Danbury, CT 06817,
Tel: (203) 794-2000
(Mfr industrial chemicals, plastics, resins)
   Union Carbide (New Zealand) Ltd., Private Bag 102960, North Shore Mail Center,
   Auckland 10, New Zealand

WANG LABORATORIES INC   1 Industrial Ave, Lowell, MA 01851,
   Tel: (508) 459-5000
   (Mfr computer info processing sys)
      Wang Computer Ltd., Eden House, 44 Khyber, Pass Rd., Auckland, New Zealand

WARD HOWELL INTL INC   99 Park Ave, New York, NY 10016-1699,
   Tel: (212) 697-3730
   (Executive recruiting)
      Executive Search Intl. Ltd., Level 11, Forsyth Barr House, 764 Colombo St.,
         Christchurch, New Zealand
      Executive Search Intl. Ltd., Level 17, Phillips Fox Tower, National Bank Centre,
         209 Queen St., Auckland, New Zealand
      Executive Search Intl. Ltd., 4th Floor, 32 The Terrace, Wellington, New Zealand

WARNER-LAMBERT CO   201 Tabor Road, Morris Plains, NJ 07950,
   Tel: (201) 540-2000
   (Mfr ethical & proprietary pharms, confectionary & consumer prdts)
      Warner-Lambert (New Zealand) Ltd., P.O. Box 430, Auckland, New Zealand

WEATHERFORD INTL INC   1360 Post Oak Blvd, PO Box 27608, Houston,
   TX 77227-7608, Tel: (713) 439-9400
   (Oilfield servs, prdts & equip; mfr marine cranes)
      Weatherford Intl. Inc., Box 4033, New Plymouth East, New Zealand

WMX TECHNOLOGIES INC   3003 Butterfield Rd, Oak Brook, IL 60563,
   Tel: (708) 572-8800
   (Environmental services)
      Waste Management N.Z. Ltd., 86 Lunn Ave., Mount Wellington, Auckland 6, New Zealand

WM WRIGLEY JR CO   410 N Michigan Ave, Chicago, IL 60611-4287,
   Tel: (312) 644-2121
   (Mfr chewing gum)
      Wrigley Co. (NZ) Ltd., 393 Ellerslie-Panmure Hwy., P.O. Box 14-140, Panmure,
         Mt. Wellington, Auckland 6, New Zealand

XEROX CORP   800 Long Ridge Rd, PO Box 1600, Stamford, CT 06904,
   Tel: (203) 968-3000
   (Mfr document processing equip, sys & supplies)
      Xerox Corp., Auckland, New Zealand

NICARAGUA

LOUIS BERGER INTL INC   100 Halsted St, East Orange, NJ 07019,
   Tel: (201) 678-1960
   (Consulting engineers, architects, economists & planners)

Louis Berger Intl. Inc., Aptdo. 6016, Palacio de Telecommunicaciones y Correos, Managua, Nicaragua

COLGATE-PALMOLIVE CO   300 Park Ave, New York, NY 10022, Tel: (212) 310-2000
  (Mfr pharms, cosmetics, toiletries, detergents)
    Colgate-Palmolive Inc., Km 11.5 Carretera Nueva a Leon, Managua, Nicaragua

COTTON STATES CHEMICAL CO   PO Box 157, West Monroe, LA 71291,
  Tel: (318) 388-4271
  (Agric chems)
    Cotton States Chemical SA, Managua, Nicaragua

DEVELOPMENT ASSOCIATES INC   1730 N Lynn St, Arlington, VA 22209-2023,
  Tel: (703) 276-0677
  (Mgt consulting servs)
    Development Associates Inc., Del Intercontinental, 1 c. Abajo, Casa 1014, Managua,
      Nicaragua

H B FULLER CO   2400 Energy Park Dr, St Paul, MN 55108, Tel: (612) 645-3401
  (Mfr/distr adhesives, sealants, coatings, paints, waxes, sanitation chems)
    Kativo de Nicaragua SA, Aptdo. Postal 2135, Managua, Nicaragua

RJR NABISCO INC   1301 Ave of the Americas, New York, NY 10019,
  Tel: (212) 258-5600
  (Mfr consumer packaged food prdts & tobacco prdts)
    Pan American Standard Brands Inc., Carretera Norte Kilometro 5,
      Detras de la Ferreteria Bunge, Aptdo. 656, Managua, Nicaragua

SEA-LAND SERVICE INC   150 Allen Rd, Liberty Corner, NJ 07920,
  Tel: (201) 558-6000
  (Container transport)
    India Transport, Aptdo. Postal 956, Managua, Nicaragua

TEXACO INC   2000 Westchester Ave, White Plains, NY 10650, Tel: (914) 253-4000
  (Explor/mktg crude oil, mfr petro chems & prdts)
    Texaco Caribbean Inc., Km. 3 Carretera Sur, Aptdo. Postal 647, Managua, Nicaragua

WACKENHUT CORP   1500 San Remo Ave, Coral Gables, FL 33146,
  Tel: (305) 666-5656
  (Security systems & services)
    Wackenhut de Nicaragua SA, Aptdo. Postal P-163, Managua, Nicaragua

XEROX CORP   800 Long Ridge Rd, PO Box 1600, Stamford, CT 06904,
  Tel: (203) 968-3000
  (Mfr document processing equip, sys & supplies)
    Xerox Corp., Managua, Nicaragua

NIGERIA

AEROFLEX SYSTEMS CORP/T-CAS CORP   1749 Old Meadow Rd, McLean, VA 22102,
   Tel: (703) 556-0330
   (Engineer/install commun sys)
      T-CAS (Nigeria) Ltd., 24 Modjidi St. (off Toyin St.), Ikeja, Lagos 12705, Nigeria

AIR EXPRESS INTL CORP   120 Tokeneke Rd, PO Box 1231, Darien, CT 06820,
   Tel: (203) 655-7900
   (Air frt forwarder)
      Air Express Intl., c/o Bems, 16 Francis St., P.M.B. 1335, Ikeja, Lagos, Nigeria

ARBOR ACRES FARM INC   439 Marlborough Rd, Glastonbury, CT 06033,
   Tel: (860) 633-4681
   (Producers of male & female broiler breeders, commercial egg layers)
      Food & Commodities Production Group, Ltd., P.O. Box 117, Agege, Lagos, Nigeria

BAKER OIL TOOLS   PO Box 40129, Houston, TX 77240-0129, Tel: (713) 466-1322
   (Mfr/serv oil/gas well completions equip)
      Baker Nigeria Ltd., Plot 1435, Victoria Island, Sanusi Fafunwa, Lagos, Nigeria

BANKERS TRUST CO   280 Park Ave, New York, NY 10017, Tel: (212) 250-2500
   (Banking)
      BT Intl. Nigeria Ltd., 122/124 Broad St., P.O. Box 3444, Lagos, Nigeria

BECHTEL GROUP INC   50 Beale St, PO Box 3965, San Francisco, CA 94119,
   Tel: (415) 768-1234
   (Engineering & constr)
      Bechtel Intl. Corp., 8-B Ademola St., P.O. Box 3992, Lagos, Nigeria

BENTLY NEVADA CORP   PO Box 157, Minden, NV 89423, Tel: (702) 782-3611
   (Electronic monitoring system)
      Petrochem Services (Nigeria) Ltd., P.O. Box 8080, Lagos, Nigeria

LOUIS BERGER INTL INC   100 Halsted St, East Orange, NJ 07019,
   Tel: (201) 678-1960
   (Consulting engineers, architects, economists & planners)
      Louis Berger Inc. Nigeria, P.O. Box 53559, Falomo Ikoyi, Lagos, Nigeria

SAMUEL BINGHAM CO   1555 N Mittel Blvd, #T, Wood Dale, IL 60191-1046,
   Tel: (708) 238-4000
   (Print & industrial rollers, inks)
      Coates Brothers (West Africa) Ltd., Nes Isheri Rd., Agidingbi, P.O. Box 395, Ikeja,
      Lagos, Nigeria

CAMCO INC   7010 Ardmore St, Houston, TX 77021, Tel: (713) 747-4000
   (Oil field equip)
      Camco Ltd., 9 Nnamdi Azikiwe St., Lagos Island, P.O. Box 5009, Lagos, Nigeria

CHASE MANHATTAN BANK N A   1 Chase Manhattan Plaza, New York, NY 10081,
   Tel: (212) 552-2222
   (Intl banking)
      Chase Merchant Bank (Nigeria) Ltd., 23 Awolowo Rd., Ikoyi, P.M.B. 12035, Lagos,
      Nigeria

CHEVRON CORP   225 Bush St, San Francisco, CA 94104, Tel: (415) 894-7700
   (Oil & gas exploration, production, refining, products; oilfield & financial services)
      Chevron Nigeria Ltd., all mail to U.S. address

CITICORP   399 Park Ave, New York, NY 10043, Tel: (212) 559-1000
   (Banking & financial services)
      Citibank NA, Nigeria

THE COCA-COLA CO   PO Drawer 1734, Atlanta, GA 30301, Tel: (404) 676-2121
   (Mfr/mkt/distr soft drinks, syrups & concentrates, juice & juice-drink prdts)
      Coca-Cola Nigeria, all mail to U.S. address

COMBUSTION ENGINEERING INC   900 Long Ridge Road, Stamford, CT 06902,
   Tel: (203) 329-8771
   (Tech constr)
      Service & Supply Co. of West Africa, Plot 52, Transamadi, P.O. Box 387,
      Port Harcourt, Nigeria

CONOCO INC   600 N Dairy Ashford Rd, Houston, TX 77079, Tel: (713) 293-1000
   (Oil, gas, coal, chems, minerals)
      Continental Oil Co., Lagos, Nigeria

CONTINENTAL CAN CO   PO Box 5410, Stamford, CT 06856, Tel: (203) 357-8110
   (Packaging prdts & mach, metal, plastic & paper containers)
      Continental Can Nigeria Ltd., P.O. Box 965, 94 Broad St., Lagos, Nigeria

CORE LABORATORIES   10205 Westheimer, Houston, TX 77042, Tel: (713) 972-6311
   (Petroleum testing/analysis, analytical chem, lab & octane analysis instrumentation)
      Core Laboratories, c/o Western Geophysical Niberia, 11 Industry Rd.,
      Trans Amadi Ind. Park, Port Harcourt, Nigeria

CROWN CORK & SEAL CO INC   9300 Ashton Rd, Philadelphia, PA 19136,
   Tel: (215) 698-5100
   (Mfr cans, bottle caps; filling & packaging mach)
      Crown Cork & Seal Co. (Nigeria) Ltd., Ikeja Industrial Estate, P.O. Box 142, Ikeja,
      Lagos, Nigeria

DRESSER INDUSTRIES INC   PO Box 718, Dallas, TX 75221-0718,
   Tel: (214) 740-6000
   (Diversified supplier of equip & tech serv to energy & natural resource ind)
      Dresser Nigeria Ltd., 38 Adeola Hopewell St., Victoria Island, Lagos, Nigeria

EATON CORP   1111 Superior Ave, Cleveland, OH 44114, Tel: (216) 523-5000
   (Advanced tech prdts for transp & ind mkts)
      Cutler-Hammer Nigeria Ltd., P.O. Box 490, Cutler-Hammer House, Ikeja, Nigeria

EATON CORP/CUTLER HAMMER   4201 North 27th St, Milwaukee, WI 53216,
Tel: (414) 449-6000
(Electric control apparatus, mfr of advanced technologic prdts)
  Cutler-Hammer Nigeria Ltd., P.O. Box 1107 Mushin, Ilasamaja Scheme, Isolo, Lagos,
  Nigeria

FIRST NATIONAL BANK OF BOSTON   100 Federal St, Boston, MA 02110,
Tel: (617) 434-2200
(Commercial banking)
  Nigeria-American Merchant Bank Ltd., P.M.B. Box 12759, Lagos, Nigeria
  Nigeria-American Merchant Bank Ltd., P.M.B. 3150, Kano, Nigeria

GENERAL ELECTRIC CO   3135 Easton Tpk, Fairfield, CT 06431,
Tel: (203) 373-2211
(Diversified manufacturing, technology & services)
  General Electric Co.,
    all mail to U.S. address; phone (800) 626-2004 or (518) 438-6500

GLOBAL MARINE INC   777 N Eldridge, Houston, TX 77079, Tel: (713) 596-5100
(Offshore contract drilling, turnkey drilling, oil & gas explor & prod)
  Global Marine Inc., Port Harcourt, Nigeria

GTE CORP   One Stamford Forum, Stamford, CT 06904, Tel: (203) 965-2000
(Electr prdts, telecom sys, publ & commun)
  GTE Nigeria Ltd., 2 Tinubu Square, 1st Floor, P.O. Box 5154, Lagos, Nigeria

HOLIDAY INNS INC   3742 Lamar Ave, Memphis, TN 38195, Tel: (901) 362-4001
(Hotels, restaurants, casinos)
  Iko Holiday Inn Inc., c/o Iko Hotel, Victoria Island, P.M.B. 12724, Lagos, Nigeria

HORWATH INTL   415 Madison Ave, New York, NY 10017, Tel: (212) 838-5566
(Public accountants & auditors)
  Alabl, Bakoh, Ekundare & Co., P.O. Box 4542, 2A Montgomery Rd., Yaba, Lagos, Nigeria
  Alabl, Eakoh, Ekundare & Co., also in Minna & Kaduna, Nigeria

HUGHES TOOL CO   PO Box 2539, Houston, TX 77001, Tel: (713) 924-2222
(Equip & serv to oil & gas explor & prod ind)
  Alea Co. Ltd., P.O. Box 51377, Ikoyi Falonx, Lagos, Nigeria

ITT CORP   1330 Ave of the Americas, New York, NY 10019-5490,
Tel: (212) 258-1000
(Design/mfr communications & electronic equip, hotels, insurance)
  ITT Nigeria Ltd., Ikorodu Rd., Yaba 19, P.O. Box 3197, Lagos, Nigeria

ITT SHERATON CORP   60 State St, Boston, MA 02108, Tel: (617) 367-3600
(Hotel operations)
  Lagos Sheraton Hotel, 30 Airport Rd., P.M.B. 21109, Ikeja, Nigeria

JOHNSON & JOHNSON   One Johnson & Johnson Plaza, New Brunswick, NJ 08933,
Tel: (908) 524-0400
(R&D/mfr/sale health care prdts)
  Health Care Products (Nigeria) Ltd., P.O. Box 3136, Lagos, Nigeria

S C JOHNSON & SON INC   1525 Howe St, Racine, WI   53403, Tel: (414) 631-2000
(Home, auto, commercial & personal care prdts, specialty chems)
   Johnson Wax Nigeria Ltd., Plot 5, Block H, Isolo Industrial Estate, P.M.B. 1279,
   Ikeja, Nigeria

THE M W KELLOGG CO   601 Jefferson Ave, Houston, TX   77002, Tel: (713) 753-2000
(Design, engr, procurement & constr for process & energy ind)
   Kellogg Nigeria Inc., 36 Kofo Abayomi St., Victoria Island, Lagos, Nigeria

LINTAS:WORLDWIDE   1 Dag Hammarskjold Plaza, New York, NY   10017,
Tel: (212) 605-8000
(Advertising agency)
   Lintas:Lagos, 202 Awolowo Rd., Falomo SW, Ikoyi, Lagos, Nigeria

MERCK SHARP & DOHME INTL   PO Box 2000, Rahway, NJ   07065, Tel: (201) 574-4000
(Pharms, chems & biologicals)
   Associated Pharmaceutical Products Ltd., Lagos, Nigeria
   Merck, Sharp & Dohme (Nigeria) Ltd., 23 Warehouse Rd., Apapa, P.O. Box 5571, Lagos,
   Nigeria

MOBIL CORP   3225 Gallows Rd, Fairfax, VA   22037-0001, Tel: (703) 846-3000
(Petroleum explor & refining, mfr petrol prdts, chems, petrochems)
   Mobil Producing Nigeria & Mobil Oil Nigeria Ltd., Mobil House, Lekki Expressway,
   Victoria Island, PMB 12054, Lagos, Nigeria

MORGAN GUARANTY TRUST CO   23 Wall St, New York, NY   10260, Tel: (212) 483-2323
(Banking)
   ICON Ltd., NIDB House, 63 Broad St., Lagos, Nigeria

McCANN-ERICKSON WORLDWIDE   750 Third Ave, New York, NY   10017,
Tel: (212) 697-6000
(Advertising)
   Grant Advertising Nigeria Ltd., 48 Bode Thomas St., Surulere, P.O. Box 3930, Lagos,
   Nigeria

NATIONAL CAR RENTAL SYSTEM INC   7700 France Ave S, Minneapolis, MN   55435,
Tel: (612) 830-2121
(Car rental)
   Natl. Car Rental, P.O. Box 6569, Lagos, Nigeria
   Natl. Car Rental, INV House, 21-25 Broad St., Lagos, Nigeria

OCEANEERING INTL INC   PO Box 218130, Houston, TX   77218-8130,
Tel: (713) 578-8868
(Underwater serv to offshore oil & gas ind)
   Oceaneering Intl. Inc., Operational bases in Escravos, Lagos, Port Harcourt & Warri

PARSONS DE LEUW INC   1133 15th St NW, Washington, DC   20005,
Tel: (202) 775-3300
(Consulting engineers)
   De Leuw, Cather Intl. Ltd., P.O. Box 6138, Aladinma Owerri, Imo State, Nigeria

PFIZER INC   235 E 42nd St, New York, NY   10017-5755, Tel: (212) 573-2323
(Mfr healthcare products)
   Livestock Feeds PLC, Nigeria
   Pfizer Products PLC, Nigeria

PHILLIPS PETROLEUM CO   Phillips Bldg, Bartlesville, OK 74004,
   Tel: (918) 661-6600
   (Crude oil, natural gas, liquefied petroleum gas, gasoline & petro-chems)
      Phillips Oil Co. (Nigeria) Ltd., Western House, 3rd Fl., 8/10 Yakubu Gowon St.,
         Lagos Island, P.M.B. 12612, Lagos, Nigeria

TEXACO INC   2000 Westchester Ave, White Plains, NY 10650, Tel: (914) 253-4000
   (Explor/mktg crude oil, mfr petro chems & prdts)
      Texaco Nigeria, Ltd., 241 Igbosere Rd., Lagos Island, P.O. Box 166, Lagos, Nigeria
      Texaco Overseas Nigeria Petroleum Co., Western House, 6th Fl.,
         8/10 Yakubu Gowon St., Lagos Island, P.O. Box 1986, Lagos, Nigeria

TIDEWATER INC   Tidewater Place, 1440 Canal St, New Orleans, LA 70112,
   Tel: (504) 568-1010
   (Marine serv & equip to companies engaged in explor, development & prod of oil, gas &
   minerals)
      Tidex Nigeria Ltd., 10 Elsie Femi Pearse St., Victoria Island, Lagos, Nigeria

UNION CAMP CORP   1600 Valley Rd, Wayne, NJ 07470, Tel: (201) 628-2000
   (Mfr paper, packaging, chems, wood prdts)
      W. J. Bush & Co. Ltd., P.O. Box 350, 168-170 Mission Rd., Kano, Nigeria

WEATHERFORD INTL INC   1360 Post Oak Blvd, PO Box 27608, Houston,
   TX 77227-7608, Tel: (713) 439-9400
   (Oilfield servs, prdts & equip; mfr marine cranes)
      Weatherford Oil Tool GmbH, c/o Remm Oil Service Ltd., P.O. Box 1164,
         Plot 52 Trans Amadi Ind. Park, Port Harcourt, Nigeria

WESTERN ATLAS INTL INC   10205 Westheimer, PO Box 1407, Houston,
   TX 77251-1407, Tel: (713) 266-5700
   (Full service to the oil industry)
      Western Atlas Logging Services, 17 Menkunwen Rd. #2, Ikoyi, Lagos, Nigeria
      Western Geophysical, 17 Mekunwen Rd., Flat 2, Ikoyi, Lagos, Nigeria
      Western Geophysical, Plot 468, Trans Amadi Layout, P.O. Box 7056, Port Harcourt,
         Nigeria

WORLD COURIER INC   46 Trinity Pl, New York, NY 10006, Tel: (718) 978-9400
   (Intl courier serv)
      World Courier Nigeria, 302 B Murtala Muhammed Way, Yaba Lagos, Nigeria

XEROX CORP   800 Long Ridge Rd, PO Box 1600, Stamford, CT 06904,
   Tel: (203) 968-3000
   (Mfr document processing equip, sys & supplies)
      Xerox Corp., Lagos, Nigeria

NORTHERN IRELAND

AVX CORP   750 Lexington Ave, New York, NY 10022-1208, Tel: (212) 935-6363
  (Mfr multilayer ceramic capacitors)
    AVX Ltd., 5 Hillmans Way, Ballycastle Rd., Coleraine BT52 2Da, Northern Ireland

CHASE MANHATTAN BANK N A   1 Chase Manhattan Plaza, New York, NY 10081,
  Tel: (212) 552-2222
  (Intl banking)
    Chase Bank Ireland Ltd., 11 Donegal Square So., P.O. Box 86, Belfast BT1 5DL,
      Northern Ireland

CHINET CO   101 Merritt 7, Norwalk, CT 06851, Tel: (203) 846-1499
  (Mfr molded containers)
    Lurgan Fibre Ltd., Inn Rd., Dollingstown, Lurgan, Co. Armagh BT66 7JW,
      Northern Ireland

CONOCO INC   600 N Dairy Ashford Rd, Houston, TX 77079, Tel: (713) 293-1000
  (Oil, gas, coal, chems, minerals)
    Conoco Ltd., 176-184 Woodstock Rd., Belfast BT6 8AG, Northern Ireland

DATA-DESIGN LABORATORIES INC   1270 NW 167th Pl, Beaverton, OR 97006,
  Tel: (503) 645-3807
  (Mfr printed circuit boards)
    DDL Electronics Ltd., 72 Silverwood Rd., Armagh BT6 6NB, N. Ireland
    DDL Europe Ltd., 72 Silverwood Rd., Armagh, Co. Lurgan BT6 6NB, N. Ireland
    Irlandus Circuits Ltd., Annesborough 3, Craigavon BT67 9JJ, N. Ireland

HATHAWAY CORP   8228 Park Meadows Dr, Littleton, CO 80124, Tel: (303) 799-8200
  (Mfr monitoring & test instrumentation & motors, optical encoders)
    CSD Hathaway Ltd., 21-23 Market Square, Lisburn, N. Ireland

HUGHES TOOL CO   PO Box 2539, Houston, TX 77001, Tel: (713) 924-2222
  (Equip & serv to oil & gas explor & prod ind)
    Hughes Tool Co. Ltd., Montgomery Rd., Castlereagh, Belfast BT6 9HQ, Northern Ireland

MISSION DRILLING PRODUCTS DIV   PO Box 40402, Houston, TX 77240,
  Tel: (713) 460-6200
  (Oilfield equip, drilling & mining equip, ind valves)
    TRW Mission Ltd., Alexander Rd., Cregagh, Belfast BT6 9HJ, Northern Ireland

McCANN-ERICKSON WORLDWIDE   750 Third Ave, New York, NY 10017,
  Tel: (212) 697-6000
  (Advertising)
    McCann-Erickson Belfast, 31 Bruce St., Great Victoria St., Belfast BT2 7JD,
      Northern Ireland

NACCO INDUSTRIES INC   5875 Landerbrook Dr, Mayfield Hgts, OH 44124-4017,
Tel: (216) 449-9600
(Mining/mktg lignite & metals, mfr forklift trucks & small electric appliances,
specialty retailers)
NACCO Materials Handling Group, Craigavon, Northern Ireland

NORTON CO   1 New Bond St, Worcester, MA 01606, Tel: (508) 795-5000
(Abrasives, drill bits, constr & safety prdts, plastics)
Norton Abrasives Ltd., 405 Castlereagh Rd., Belfast BT7 56RB, Northern Ireland

PAPER MANUFACTURERS CO   9800 Bustleton Ave, Philadelphia, PA 19115,
Tel: (215) 673-4500
(Mfr packaging materials & converted prdts for med & pharm prdts)
Perfecseal Nuprint Ltd., Springtown Industrial Estate, Londonderry BT48 OLY,
Northern Ireland

SONOCO PRODUCTS CO   North Second St, PO Box 160, Hartsville, SC 29550,
Tel: (803) 383-7000
(Mfr packaging for consumer & ind mkt)
Sonoco Products Co., Portadown Rd., Craigavon, Lurgan, Armagh BT66 8RA,
Northern Ireland

TRW INC   1900 Richmond Rd, Cleveland, OH 44124, Tel: (216) 291-7000
(Electr & energy-related prdts, automotive & aerospace prdts, tools & fasteners)
TRW Mission Ltd., Alexander Rd., Cregagh, Belfast BT6 9HJ, Northern Ireland

NORWAY

3COM CORP   5400 Bayfront Plaza, Santa Clara, CA 95052-8145,
Tel: (408) 764-5000
(Devel/mfr computer networking prdts & sys)
3Com Nordic AB, Norway

3M   3M Center, St Paul, MN 55144-1000, Tel: (612) 733-1110
(Mfr diversified prdts for industry, health care, imaging, commun, transport, safety,
consumer, etc)
3M Norge A/S, Hvamvelen 6, P.O. Box 100, 2013 Skjetten, Norway

A-Z INTL TOOL CO   PO Box 7108, Houston, TX 77248-7108, Tel: (713) 880-8888
(Mfr oil field, milling & casing cutting tools)
A-Z International Norge A/S, P.O. Box 1035, 4001 Stavanger, Norway

AIR EXPRESS INTL CORP   120 Tokeneke Rd, PO Box 1231, Darien, CT 06820,
Tel: (203) 655-7900
(Air frt forwarder)
Air Express Intl., Drammensvei 130-C, Skoeyen, Oslo, Norway

AIR PRODUCTS & CHEMICALS INC   7201 Hamilton Blvd, Allentown, PA 18195-1501,
  Tel: (215) 481-4911
  (Mfr ind gases & related equip, spec chems, environmental/energy sys)
    Gardner Cryogenic A/S, Luramyrveien 27, 4300 Sandnes, Norway

ALBANY INTL CORP   PO Box 1907, Albany, NY 12201, Tel: (518) 445-2200
  (Paper mach clothing, engineered fabrics, plastic prdts, filtration media)
    Nordiska Filtog Virer A/S, P.O. Box 117, 2020 Skedsmokorset, Norway

ALUMINUM CO OF AMERICA (ALCOA)   425 6th Ave, Pittsburgh, PA 15219,
  Tel: (412) 553-4545
  (Aluminum mining, refining, processing, prdts)
    Norsk Alcoa A/S, Oslo, Norway

AMDAHL CORP   1250 E Arques Ave, PO Box 3470, Sunnyvale, CA 94088-3470,
  Tel: (408) 746-6000
  (Devel/mfr large scale computers, software, data storage prdts, info-technology
  solutions & support)
    Amdahl Norge A/S, Brynsveien 13, P.O. Box 6221, Etterstad, 0603 Oslo, Norway

AMERADA HESS CORP   1185 Ave of the Americas, New York, NY 10036,
  Tel: (212) 997-8500
  (Crude oil, natural gas)
    Amerada Hess Norge A/S, Langkaien 1, 0150 Oslo, Norway

AMERICAN EXPRESS CO   World Financial Center, New York, NY 10285-4765,
  Tel: (212) 640-2000
  (Travel, travelers cheques, charge card & financial services)
    American Express Co. A/S
    American Express Reisebyria A/S

AMP INC   PO Box 3608, Harrisburg, PA 17105-3608, Tel: (717) 564-0100
  (Devel/mfr electronic & electrical connection prdts & sys)
    AMP Norge A/S, Oslo, Norway

ANIXTER BROS INC   4711 Golf Rd, Skokie, IL 60076, Tel: (708) 677-2600
  (Dist wiring sys/prdts for voice, video, data & power applications)
    Anixter Norway, P.O. Box 8, Loxaveien 11, 1350 Rud, Norway

ANTHONY INDUSTRIES INC   4900 S Eastern Ave, Los Angeles, CA 90040,
  Tel: (213) 724-2800
  (Mfr sporting goods, recreational & ind prdts)
    Maelshus AG, Biri, Norway

ASSOCIATED PRESS INC   50 Rockefeller Plaza, New York, NY 10020-1605,
  Tel: (212) 621-1500
  (News gathering agency)
    Associated Press A/S, Fridtlof Nansens Plass 5, Oslo, Norway

AST RESEARCH INC   16215 Alton Parkway, PO Box 19658, Irvine, CA 92713-9658,
  Tel: (714) 727-4141
  (Design/devel/mfr hi-perf desktop, server & notebook computers)
    AST Norway, P.O. Box 26, 1371 Asker, Norway

AVERY DENNISON CORP   150 N Orange Grove Blvd, Pasadena, CA 91103,
  Tel: (818) 304-2000
  (Mfr pressure-sensitive adhesives & materials, office prdts, labels, tags, retail

(cont)

sys, spec chems)
   Fasson Norge A/S, Elveveijen 26/28, 1472 Fjellhamar, Norway

BAKER OIL TOOLS   PO Box 40129, Houston, TX   77240-0129, Tel: (713) 466-1322
   (Mfr/serv oil/gas well completions equip)
   Baker Oil Tools Norway A/S, 4056 Tananger, Norway

BAUSCH & LOMB INC   1 Chase Square, Rochester, NY   14601, Tel: (716) 338-6000
   (Mfr vision care prdts & accessories)
   Bausch & Lomb Norway A/S, Oslo, Norway

BAXTER HEALTHCARE CORP   1 Baxter Pky, Deerfield, IL   60015,
   Tel: (708) 948-2000
   (Mfr disposable medical prdts)
   Baxter A/S, Gjerdrumsvej 10B, 0486 Oslo 4, Norway

BENTLY NEVADA CORP   PO Box 157, Minden, NV   89423, Tel: (702) 782-3611
   (Electronic monitoring system)
   Bently Nevada Norge, P.O. Box 99, Kokstaddalen 4, 5061 Kokstad, Norway
   Petrovest A/S, P.O. Box 93, Kokstaddalen 4, 5061 Kokstad, Norway

BLACK & DECKER CORP   701 E Joppa Road, Towson, MD   21286, Tel: (410) 716-3900
   (Mfr power tools & accessories, security hardware, small appliances, fasteners, info
   sys & servs)
   Black & Decker Corp., all mail to U.S. address

BORDEN INC   180 E Broad St, Columbus, OH   43215-3799, Tel: (614) 225-4000
   (Mfr foods, snacks & beverages, adhesives)
   Borden Norge A/S, all mail to U.S. address

BOSE CORP   The Mountain, Framingham, MA   01701-9168, Tel: (508) 879-7330
   (Mfr audio equip)
   Bose A/S, Solheimsgt. 11, 2001 Lillestrom, Norway

LEO BURNETT CO INC   35 West Wacker Dr, Chicago, IL   60601, Tel: (312) 220-5959
   (Advertising agency)
   Nordskar & Thorkildsen A/S, Fritzners Gate 12, 0264 Oslo 2, Norway

BURSON-MARSTELLER   230 Park Ave, New York, NY   10003-1566, Tel: (212) 614-4000
   (Public relations/public affairs consultants)
   Burson-Marsteller A/S, Drammensveien 302-304, P.O. Box 233, 1324 Lysaker, Norway

CALCOMP INC   2411 W La Palma Ave, Anaheim, CA   92801, Tel: (714) 821-2000
   (Mfr computer graphics peripherals)
   CalComp A/S, Billingstadsletta 83, 1362 Billingstad, Norway

CARBOLINE CO   350 Hanley Industrial Ct, St Louis, MO   63144,
   Tel: (314) 644-1000
   (Mfr coatings, sealants)
   Carboline Norge A/S, P.O. Box 540, 3412 Lierstranda, Norway

CARRIER CORP   One Carrier Place, Farmington, CT   06034-4015,
   Tel: (203) 674-3000
   (Mfr/distr/svce A/C, heating & refrigeration equip)
   CA-NOR Kjoleindustri AS, Oslo, Norway

CHASE MANHATTAN BANK N A   1 Chase Manhattan Plaza, New York, NY   10081,
Tel: (212) 552-2222
(Intl banking)
  Chase Manhattan Overseas Corp., Akersgt 1, 6th Fl., Oslo, Norway

CHEMICAL BANK   270 Park Ave, New York, NY   10017-2070, Tel: (212) 270-6000
(Banking & financial services)
  Chemical Bank Norge AS, Karl Johans Gate 41B, 0162 Oslo, Norway

CHINET CO   101 Merritt 7, Norwalk, CT   06851, Tel: (203) 846-1499
(Mfr molded containers)
  Keyes Norway A/S, Viul, 3500 Honefoss, Norway

CIGNA CORP   One Liberty Place, Philadelphia, PA   19192, Tel: (215) 523-4000
(Ins, invest, health care & other fin servs)
  Cigna Insurance Co. of Europe SA/NV, Teatergaten 5, 0180 Oslo 1, Norway

CINCOM SYSTEMS INC   2300 Montana Ave, Cincinnati, OH   45211,
Tel: (513) 662-2300
(Devel/distr computer software)
  Cincom Systems Inc., Oslo, Norway

CITICORP   399 Park Ave, New York, NY   10043, Tel: (212) 559-1000
(Banking & financial services)
  Citibank NA, Norway

THE COCA-COLA CO   PO Drawer 1734, Atlanta, GA   30301, Tel: (404) 676-2121
(Mfr/mkt/distr soft drinks, syrups & concentrates, juice & juice-drink prdts)
  Coca-Cola Norge A/S, P.O. Box 37, Lilleaker, Oslo, Norway

COLUMBIA PICTURES INDUSTRIES INC   711 Fifth Ave, New York, NY   10022,
Tel: (212) 751-4400
(Producer & distributor of motion pictures)
  Columbia Kamerafilm A/S, Stortingsgaten 30, Oslo, Norway

COMBUSTION ENGINEERING INC   900 Long Ridge Road, Stamford, CT   06902,
Tel: (203) 329-8771
(Tech constr)
  Gray Tool Co. (Norway) A/S, P.O. Box 4, 4033 Forus, Norway
  Gray Tool Co. (Norway) A/S, P.O. Box 1569, Sandivika, 5001 Bergen, Norway
  Vetco Offshore Inc., c/o Norsea Base, P.O. Box 5036, 4001 Stauanger, Norway

COMPUTER ASSOCIATES INTL INC   One Computer Associates Plaza, Islandia,
NY   11788, Tel: (516) 342-5224
(Devel/mkt/mgt info mgt & bus applications software)
  Computer Associates Norway A/S, Brynsveien 13, 0667 Oslo, Norway

CONOCO INC   600 N Dairy Ashford Rd, Houston, TX   77079, Tel: (713) 293-1000
(Oil, gas, coal, chems, minerals)
  Conoco Norway Inc., Ovre Stokkavei 42, P.O. Box 488, 4001 Stavanger, Norway
  Conoco Norway Inc., P.O. Box 1752 Vika, Thilbagaarden, Haakon 7, Oslo, Norway

CPC INTERNATIONAL INC   PO Box 8000, Englewood Cliffs, NJ   07632,
Tel: (201) 894-4000
(Consumer foods, corn refining)
  CPC Foods A/S, Billingstadsletta 25, Postboks 134, 1361 Billingstad, Norway

CRAY RESEARCH INC   655 Lone Oak Dr, Eagan, MN 55121, Tel: (612) 452-6650
  (Supercomputer systems & services)
    Cray Research Scandinavia A/S, Radhusgt 7B, 0141 Oslo, Norway

D'ARCY MASIUS BENTON & BOWLES INC (DMB&B)   1675 Broadway, New York,
  NY 10019, Tel: (212) 468-3622
  (Advertising & communications)
    DMB&B/Lund & Lommer A/S, P.O. Box 7645, Skillebekk, 0205 Oslo 2, Norway

DATA GENERAL CORP   4400 Computer Dr, Westboro, MA 01580, Tel: (617) 366-8911
  (Design, mfr gen purpose computer sys & peripheral prdts & servs)
    Data General, Oslo, Norway

DATAEASE INTL INC   7 Cambridge Dr, Trumbull, CT 06611, Tel: (203) 374-8000
  (Mfr applications devel software)
    West Soft A/S, Box 98, 6018 MDA Aalesund, Norway

DDB NEEDHAM WORLDWIDE INC   437 Madison Ave, New York, NY 10022,
  Tel: (212) 415-2000
  (Advertising)
    Uvanti DDB Needham, Inkognitogaten 18, Oslo 2, Norway

DIGITAL EQUIPMENT CORP   146 Main St, Maynard, MA 01754-2571,
  Tel: (508) 493-5111
  (Networked computer systems & services)
    Digital Equipment Corp AS, Ammerudy 22, Oslo, Norway

THE DOW CHEMICAL CO   2030 Dow Center, Midland, MI 48674, Tel: (517) 636-1000
  (Mfr chems, plastics, pharms, agric prdts, consumer prdts)
    Dow Chemical International Inc. A/S, Fridtjof Nansens Vei 2, Oslo 3, Norway

DRAKE BEAM MORIN INC   100 Park Ave, New York, NY 10017, Tel: (212) 692-7700
  (Human resource mgmt consulting & training)
    DBM Outplacement Scandinavia, Drammensveien 214, 0277 Oslo 2, Norway

DRESSER INDUSTRIES INC   PO Box 718, Dallas, TX 75221-0718,
  Tel: (214) 740-6000
  (Diversified supplier of equip & tech serv to energy & natural resource ind)
    Dresser Norway A/S, P.O. Box 55, Kvernevik Rings, 4042 Hafrsfjord, Norway

E I DU PONT DE NEMOURS & CO   1007 Market St, Wilmington, DE 19898,
  Tel: (302) 774-1000
  (Mfr/sale diversified chems, plastics, specialty prdts & fibers)
    Conoco Norway Inc., Norway

EASTMAN KODAK CO   343 State St, Rochester, NY 14650, Tel: (716) 724-4000
  (Devel/mfr photo & chem prdts, info mgmt/video/copier sys, fibers/plastics for
  various ind)
    Kodak Norge A/S, Trollasveien 6, 1410 Kolbot, Norway

EG&G INC   45 William St, Wellesley, MA 02181-4078, Tel: (617) 237-5100
  (Diversified R/D, mfg & services)
    Wallac Norge, Gjerdrumsvei 12, 0486 Oslo, Norway

EXOLON-ESK CO   1000 E Niagara St, PO Box 590, Tonawanda, NY 14151-0590,
  Tel: (716) 693-4550
  (Mfr fused aluminum oxide & silicon carbide abrasive grains)
    Orkla/Exolon A/S & Co. K/S, P.O. Box 25, 7301 Orkanger, Norway

EXXON CORP   225 E John W Carpenter Freeway, Irving, TX 75062-2298,
  Tel: (214) 444-1000
  (Petroleum explor, prod, refining; mfr petrol & chem prdts; coal & minerals)
    Esso Exploration & Production Norway Inc., Grenseveien 6, 4033 Forus, Norway
    Esso Norge A/S, Drammensveien 149, Oslo, Norway

FISHER CONTROLS INTL INC   8000 Maryland Ave, Clayton, MO 63105,
  Tel: (314) 746-9900
  (Mfr ind process control equip)
    Fisher Controls, Haukedalen 1, 5095 Ulset, Bergen, Norway

FMC CORP   200 E Randolph Dr, Chicago, IL 60601, Tel: (312) 861-6000
  (Produces chems & precious metals, mfr machinery, equip & sys for ind, agric & govt)
    Kongsberg Offshore Services A/S, Box 1012, 3601 Kongsberg, Norway

FOOTE CONE & BELDING COMMUNICATIONS INC   101 E Erie St, Chicago,
  IL 60611-2897, Tel: (312) 751-7000
  (Advertising agency)
    Art & Copy/FCB, Bygdoy Alle 4, 0257 Oslo 2, Norway

FORD MOTOR CO   The American Road, Dearborn, MI 48121, Tel: (313) 322-3000
  (Mfr motor vehicles)
    Ford Motor Norge A/S, Kolbotn 1410, Oslo, Norway

GENERAL MOTORS ACCEPTANCE CORP   3044 West Grand Blvd, Detroit, MI 48202,
  Tel: (313) 556-5000
  (Automobile financing)
    General Motors Norge A/S, P.O. Box 163, 2001 Lillestrom, Norway

GENERAL MOTORS CORP   3044 W Grand Blvd, Detroit, MI 48202-3091,
  Tel: (313) 556-5000
  (Mfr full line vehicles, automotive electronics, coml technologies, telecom, space,
  finance)
    General Motors Norge A/S, P.O. Box 205, 2001 Lillestrom, Norway

THE GILLETTE CO   Prudential Tower, Boston, MA 02199, Tel: (617) 421-7000
  (Devel/mfr personal care/use prdts: blades & razors, toiletries, cosmetics,
  stationery)
    Braun Norge A/S, Oslo, Norway
    Gillette Norge A/S, Oslo, Norway

GRACO INC   4050 Olson Memorial Hwy, PO Box 1441, Minneapolis, MN 55440-1441,
  Tel: (612) 623-6000
  (Mfr/serv fluid handling equip & sys)
    Graco A/S, Lommedalsveien 281, 1350 Lommedalen, Norway

GREY ADVERTISING INC   777 Third Ave, New York, NY 10017, Tel: (212) 546-2000
  (Advertising)
    GCG Norge, Kirkegt 1-3, P.O. Box 722 Sentrum, 0105 Oslo, Norway

HEWLETT-PACKARD CO   3000 Hanover St, Palo Alto, CA 94304-0890,
  Tel: (415) 857-1501
  (Mfr computing, communications & measurement prdts & services)
    Hewlett-Packard Norge A/S, Drammensveien 169, 0212 Oslo, Norway

HONEYWELL INC   PO Box 524, Minneapolis, MN 55440-0524, Tel: (612) 951-1000
  (Devel/mfr controls for home & building, industry, space & aviation)
    Honeywell AS, Askerveien 61, 1371 Asker, Norway

HORWATH INTL   415 Madison Ave, New York, NY 10017, Tel: (212) 838-5566
  (Public accountants & auditors)
    Revisor-Kontoret A/S, Sandakervn 35 B, Oslo, Norway

HOUGHTON INTL INC   PO Box 930, Valley Forge, PA 19482-0930,
  Tel: (610) 666-4000
  (Mfr spec chems, hydraulic fluids, lubricants)
    Andersen & Odegaard, Fyrstikkalleen 17, Oslo 6, Norway

HUGHES TOOL CO   PO Box 2539, Houston, TX 77001, Tel: (713) 924-2222
  (Equip & serv to oil & gas explor & prod ind)
    BJ-Hughes BV, Aker-Norsco Base, 4056 Tananger, Norway

INGERSOLL-RAND CO   200 Chestnut Ridge Rd, Woodcliff Lake, NJ 07675,
  Tel: (201) 573-0123
  (Mfr compressors, rock drills, pumps, air tools, door hardware, ball bearings)
    Ingersoll-Rand Scandinavian Operations, Dronningen, Bygdoy, 0211 Oslo 2, Norway

INTERGRAPH CORP   Huntsville, AL 35894-0001, Tel: (205) 730-2000
  (Devel/mfr interactive computer graphic systems)
    Intergraph Norge AS, Nesoyveien 4, P.O. Box 8, 1361 Billingstadsletta, Norway

INTERMEC CORP   6001 36th Ave West, PO Box 4280, Everett, WA 98203-9280,
  Tel: (206) 348-2600
  (Mfr/distr automated data collection sys)
    Intermec Norge A/S, Vakaasveien 16, P.O. Box 134, 1364 Hvalstad, Norway

INTERNATIONAL PAPER   2 Manhattanville Rd, Purchase, NY 10577,
  Tel: (914) 397-1500
  (Mfr/distr container board, paper, wood prdts)
    Horsell Norge A/S, P.O. Box 28, Oslo Rudssletta 97, 1351 Rud, Norway

ITT CORP   1330 Ave of the Americas, New York, NY 10019-5490,
  Tel: (212) 258-1000
  (Design/mfr communications & electronic equip, hotels, insurance)
    Standard Telefon Og Kabelfabrik A/S, P.O. Box 60, Okern, Oslo, Norway

S C JOHNSON & SON INC   1525 Howe St, Racine, WI 53403, Tel: (414) 631-2000
  (Home, auto, commercial & personal care prdts, specialty chems)
    Norsk Johnson's Wax A/S, P.O. Box 53, 2013 Skjetten, Norway

JOHNSON CONTROLS INC   5757 N Green Bay Ave, PO Box 591, Milwaukee,
  WI 53201-0591, Tel: (414) 228-1200
  (Mfr facility mgmt & control sys, auto seating, batteries & plastics)
    Johnson Controls Norge A/S, Frysjaveien 35, 0883 Oslo, Norway

A T KEARNEY INC   222 West Adams St, Chicago, IL 60606, Tel: (312) 648-0111
(Mgmt consultants, executive search)
A.T. Kearney A/S, P.O. Box 7, O.H. Bangs vei 70, 1322 Hovik (Oslo), Norway

KELLOGG CO   One Kellogg Sq, PO Box 3599, Battle Creek, MI 49016-3599,
Tel: (616) 961-2000
(Mfr ready-to-eat cereals, convenience foods)
Kellogg Norge, Drammen, Norway (all inquiries to U.S. address)

KELLY SERVICES   999 W Big Beaver Rd, Troy, MI 48084, Tel: (810) 244-4313
(Temporary help placement)
Kelly Services Norge AS (HQ), Karl Johansgate 35, 0162 Oslo, Norway
Kelly Services Norge SA, 4 branches throughout Norway

KEYSTONE INTL INC   PO Box 40010, Houston, TX 77040, Tel: (713) 466-1176
(Mfr butterfly valves, actuators & control accessories)
Keystone Oslo, Norway

LESTER B KNIGHT & ASSOC INC   549 W Randolph St, Chicago, IL 60661,
Tel: (312) 346-2300
(Architecture, engineering, planning, operations & mgmt consulting)
Knight Wendling Consulting AS, c/o Advakatfirmaet Schjodt AS, P.O. Box 2444 Soli,
0201 Oslo, Norway

KORN/FERRY INTL   1800 Century Park East, Los Angeles, CA 90067,
Tel: (310) 552-1834
(Executive search)
Korn/Ferry Intl., Haakon VII's gate 2, 0161 Oslo, Norway

LEVI STRAUSS & CO   1155 Battery, San Francisco, CA 94111, Tel: (415) 544-6000
(Mfr casual wearing apparel)
Levi-Strauss Norway A/S, Marcus Thranesgt 2, Oslo 4, Norway

THE LINCOLN ELECTRIC CO   22801 St Clair Ave, Cleveland, OH 44117-1199,
Tel: (216) 481-8100
(Mfr arc welding & welding related prtds, oxy-fuel & thermal cutting equip, integral
AC motors)
Lincoln Norweld Management A/S, Stasjonsveien 18, 1361 Billingstadadsletta, Norway

LINTAS:WORLDWIDE   1 Dag Hammarskjold Plaza, New York, NY 10017,
Tel: (212) 605-8000
(Advertising agency)
Myres:Lintas, Hausmannsgate 17, Oslo 1, Norway

LOCTITE CORP   10 Columbus Blvd, Hartford, CT 06106, Tel: (203) 520-5000
(Mfr/sale ind adhesives & sealants)
Loctite Norway, Sandakerveien 102, 0483 Oslo, Norway

MANPOWER INTL INC   5301 N Ironwood Rd, PO Box 2053, Milwaukee,
WI 53201-2053, Tel: (414) 961-1000
(Temporary help service)
Manpower A/S, Dronning Maudsgate 10, P.O. Box 2506, Solli, 0202 Oslo, Norway

MARATHON LE TOURNEAU CO   PO Box 2307, Longview, TX 75606, Tel: (903) 237-7000
(Mfr heavy constr, mining mach & equip)
A/S G. Hartmann Velog Anlegg, P.O. Box 1, Sentrum, 0580 Oslo 5, Norway

MICROSOFT CORP   One Microsoft Way, Redmond, WA 98052-6399,
  Tel: (206) 882-8080
  (Computer software, peripherals & services)
    Microsoft Norway, Gjerdrumsvei 21, 0881 Oslo, Norway

MILCHEM INC   3900 Essex Lane, PO Box 22111, Houston, TX 77027,
  Tel: (214) 439-8000
  (Gas & oil well drilling fluids & chem additives)
    Promud A/S, 4056 Tanager, Tanager, Norway

MILLIPORE CORP   Ashley Rd, Bedford, MA 01730, Tel: (617) 275-9205
  (Mfr precision filters, hi-performance liquid chromatography instru)
    Millipore A/S, Enebakkveien 119, 0680 Oslo 6, Norway

MOTOROLA INC   1303 E Algonquin Rd, Schaumburg, IL 60196, Tel: (708) 576-5000
  (Mfr commun equip, semiconductors, cellular phones)
    Motorola Norway A/S, P.O. Box 188, Leirdal, Oslo 10, Norway

NATIONAL CAR RENTAL SYSTEM INC   7700 France Ave S, Minneapolis, MN 55435,
  Tel: (612) 830-2121
  (Car rental)
    National Car Rental, Fredensborgveien 33, Oslo 1, Norway

NATIONAL STARCH & CHEMICAL CO   10 Finderne Ave, Bridgewater, NJ 08807-3300,
  Tel: (908) 685-5000
  (Mfr adhesives & sealants, resins & spec chems, electr materials & adhesives, food
  prdts, ind starch)
    National Starch & Chemical A/S, Oslo, Norway

NETWORK EQUIPMENT TECHNOLOGIES INC   800 Saginaw Dr, Redwood City, CA 94063,
  Tel: (415) 366-440
  (Mfr/serv networking prdts to info-intensive organizations)
    NET Ltd., P.O. Box 239, Eyvind Lyches vei 13B, 1301 Sandvika, Norway

A C NIELSEN CO   Nielsen Plaza, Northbrook, IL 60062-6288, Tel: (708) 498-6300
  (Market research)
    Nielsen Norge A/S, P.O. Box 100-Kjelsas, 0411 Oslo 4, Norway

NORDSON CORP   28601 Clemens Rd, Westlake, OH 44145, Tel: (216) 892-1580
  (Mfr ind application equip & packaging mach)
    Nordson Norge A/S, Stromsveien 125, P.O. Box 6213, Etterstad, 0603 Oslo 6, Norway

OCEANEERING INTL INC   PO Box 218130, Houston, TX 77218-8130,
  Tel: (713) 578-8868
  (Underwater serv to offshore oil & gas ind)
    Oceaneering Intl. Inc., Operational base in Stavanger

OLSTEN CORP   175 Broad Hollow Rd, Melville, NY 11747-8905,
  Tel: (516) 844-7800
  (Staffing, home health care & info technology svces (642,000 assignment employees
  worldwide))
    Norsk Personal AS, Bryggen 3, P.O. Box 671, 5001 Bergen, Norway

OWENS-CORNING FIBERGLAS CORP   Fiberglas Tower, Toledo, OH 43659,
  Tel: (419) 248-8000
  (Mfr insulation, building materials, glass fiber prdts)

Norsk Glassfiber A/S, Birkeland, Norway
Veroc Technology A/S, Birkeland, Norway

PARKER HANNIFIN CORP   17325 Euclid Ave, Cleveland, OH 44112,
  Tel: (216) 531-3000
  (Mfr motion-control prdts)
    Parker Hannifin A/S, Postveien 12, Breivika, P.O. Box 7619, Moa, 6018 Aalesund,
      Norway
    Parker Hannifin A/S, Lervigsvein 32, P.O. Box 491, 4001 Stavanger, Norway
    Parker Hannifin A/S, Kokstadflaten 19B, P.O. Box 79, 5061 Kokstad, Bergen, Norway
    Parker-Hannifin A/S, Handverksveien, Berghagan, P.O. Box 8, 1405 Langhus, Norway

PETROLITE CORP   369 Marshall Ave, St Louis, MO 63119-1897,
  Tel: (314) 961-3500
  (Mfr/prod spec chem treating programs, performance-enhancing additives & related
  equip & svces)
    Petrolite A/S, Harestadvike, 4070 Randaberg, Norway

PFIZER INC   235 E 42nd St, New York, NY 10017-5755, Tel: (212) 573-2323
  (Mfr healthcare products)
    Pfizer A/S, Norway

PHILLIPS PETROLEUM CO   Phillips Bldg, Bartlesville, OK 74004,
  Tel: (918) 661-6600
  (Crude oil, natural gas, liquefied petroleum gas, gasoline & petro-chems)
    Phillips Petroleum Co., Akersgaten 45, Oslo 1, Norway

POLICY MANAGEMENT SYS CORP   PO Box 10, Columbia, SC 29202,
  Tel: (803) 735-4000
  (Computer software, insurance industry support services)
    PMS Norden AS, Vollsveien 13, Bldg. C, 4th floor, 1324 Lysake, Oslo, Norway
    PMS Norden AS, Folke Bernadottes vei 38, 5033 Fyllingsdalen, Bergen, Norway

RAYCHEM CORP   300 Constitution Dr, Menlo Park, CA 94025, Tel: (415) 361-3333
  (Devel/mfr/mkt materials science products for electronics, telecommunications &
  industry)
    Raychem A/S, Trollaasveien 36, P.O. Box 31, 1414 Trollaasen, Norway

READING & BATES CORP   901 Threadneedle, #200, Houston, TX 77079,
  Tel: (713) 496-5000
  (Offshore contract drilling)
    Reading & Bates, c/o Srcade Drilling AS, P.O. Box 1715 Vika, Stortingsgt. 8,
      0121 Oslo, Norway

RIGHT ASSOCIATES   1818 Market St, 14th Fl, Philadelphia, PA 19103-3614,
  Tel: (215) 988-1588
  (Outplacement & human resources consult servs)
    Right Associates, P.O. Box 8, 1414 Oslo-Trollasen, Norway

SEA-LAND SERVICE INC   150 Allen Rd, Liberty Corner, NJ 07920,
  Tel: (201) 558-6000
  (Container transport)
    Skandinavisk Billspedition A/S, Verkseier Furulundsvei 5, P.O. Box 66, Alnabru,
      Oslo 6, Norway

SONAT OFFSHORE DRILLING INC   PO Box 2765, Houston, TX 77252-2765,
   Tel: (713) 871-7500
   (Offshore oil well drilling)
      Polar Frontier Drilling A/S, Kikstaddalen 26, P.O. Box 74, 5061 Kokstad, Norway

SONOCO PRODUCTS CO   North Second St, PO Box 160, Hartsville, SC 29550,
   Tel: (803) 383-7000
   (Mfr packaging for consumer & ind mkt)
      Sonoco Norge, P.O. Box 32, 3191 Horten, Norway

STANDEX INTL CORP   6 Manor Pkwy, Salem, NH 03079, Tel: (603) 893-9701
   (Mfr diversified graphics, institutional, ind/electr & consumer prdts)
      Standex Intl. AS, P.O. Box 607, Lisleby, 1616 Fredrikstad, Norway

THE STANLEY WORKS   1000 Stanley Dr, PO Box 7000, New Britain, CT 06050,
   Tel: (203) 225-5111
   (Mfr hand tools & hardware)
      Stanley Norge A/S, Okernveien 145, P.O. Box 220, Okern, Oslo 5, Norway

STERLING SOFTWARE INC   8080 N Central Expy, #1100, Dallas, TX 75206-1895,
   Tel: (214) 891-8600
   (Sales/serv software prdts; tech servs)
      Sterling Software Scandinavia A/S, Rektor Natvig Pedersenvei 29, P.O. Box 459,
      4001 Stavanger, Norway

STORAGE TECHNOLOGY CORP   2270 S 88th St, Louisville, CO 80028-0001,
   Tel: (303) 673-5151
   (Mfr/mkt/serv info storage & retrieval sys)
      Storage Tek AS, Lars Hillesg. 20B, P.O. Box 4264, 5028 Nygaardstangen, Bergen,
      Norway

SUB SEA INTL INC   701 Engineers Rd, Belle Chasse, LA 70037,
   Tel: (504) 393-7744
   (Service oil/gas industry: diving, ROV's, offshore construction, engineering,
   pipeline services)
      Sub Sea Dolphin A/S, P.O. Box 138, 4956 Tananger, Norway

SULLAIR CORP   3700 E Michigan Blvd, Michigan City, IN 46360,
   Tel: (219) 879-5451
   (Refrigeration sys, vacuum pumps, generators, etc)
      Sullair Skruekompressorer A/S, Industrieveien 11, 1400 Ski, Norway

TEKTRONIX INC   26660 SW Parkway, Wilsonville, OR 97070, Tel: (503) 627-7111
   (Mfr test & meas, visual sys & commun prdts)
      Tektronix Norge A/S, Oslo, Norway

TEXAS EASTERN TRANSMISSION CORP   PO Box 2521, Houston, TX 77252,
   Tel: (713) 759-3131
   (Energy pipeliner, oil/gas explor & prod)
      Texas Eastern Norwegian Inc, P.O. Box 399, 4001 Stavanger, Norway

THERMO ELECTRIC CO   109 Fifth St, Saddle Brook, NJ 07662, Tel: (201) 843-5800
   (Mfr temp/meas control prdts)
      Thermo-Electric Co. Inc. A/S, P.O. Box 1, Oslo 1, Norway

TRINOVA CORP   3000 Strayer, PO Box 50, Maumee, OH 43537-0050,
  Tel: (419) 867-2200
  (Mfr engr components & sys for ind)
    Vickers Systems A/S, P.O. Box 5881, Hegderhaugen, 0308 Oslo 3, Norway

UNION OIL INTL DIV   Union Oil Center, PO Box 7600, Los Angeles, CA 90017,
  Tel: (213) 977-7600
  (Petroleum prdts, petrochems)
    Unionoil Norge A/S, P.O. Box 377, 4301 Sandnes, Norway

UNISYS CORP   PO Box 500, Blue Bell, PA 19424, Tel: (215) 986-4011
  (Mfg/mktg/serv electr info sys)
    Sperry A/S, Sandakerveien 74, 0401 Oslo, Norway
    Unisys Norge AS, Sandakerveien 74, 0401 Oslo, Norway

UNITED TECHNOLOGIES CORP   United Technologies Bldg, Hartford, CT 06101,
  Tel: (203) 728-7000
  (Mfr aircraft engines, elevators, A/C, auto equip, space & military electr, rocket
  propulsion sys)
    Carrier Intl Corp., Kjelsasveien 174, P.O. Box 18, Korsvoll, Oslo 8, Norway
    Otis Heis A/S, P.O. Box 3676 Gamlebyen, Oslo 1, Norway

USX CORP   600 Grant St, Pittsburgh, PA 15219-4776, Tel: (412) 433-1121
  (Steel & related resources, oil & gas, engineering, real estate)
    Marathon Petroleum Co., Tollbodgaten 27, Oslo, Norway

VALHI INC   5430 LBJ Freeway, Dallas, TX 75240, Tel: (214) 233-1700
  (Chemicals, hardware, sugar, mining)
    Kronos Norge A/S, 1601 Fredrikstad, Norway
    Kronos Titan A/S, 1601 Fredrikstad, Norway
    Titania A/S, 4380 Hauge, Norway

WARD HOWELL INTL INC   99 Park Ave, New York, NY 10016-1699,
  Tel: (212) 697-3730
  (Executive recruiting)
    Ward Howell Intl., Drammensvien 4, P.O. Box 2679 Solli, 0203 Oslo, Norway

WEATHERFORD INTL INC   1360 Post Oak Blvd, PO Box 27608, Houston,
  TX 77227-7608, Tel: (713) 439-9400
  (Oilfield servs, prdts & equip; mfr marine cranes)
    Weatherford Norge A/S, P.O. Box 5053, Norsea Base, Dusevik, 4001 Stavanger, Norway

WESTERN ATLAS INTL INC   10205 Westheimer, PO Box 1407, Houston,
  TX 77251-1407, Tel: (713) 266-5700
  (Full service to the oil industry)
    Western Atlas Logging Services, P.O. Box 55, Sundebrotet, 4040 Hafrsfjord,
      Stavanger, Norway
    Western Geophysical, Kvemevik Ring 177, P.O. Box 55, Sundebrotet, 4040 Hafrsfjord,
      Stavanger, Norway

WESTERN TEMPORARY SERVICES INC   301 Lennon Lane, Walnut Creek, CA 94598,
  Tel: (510) 930-5300
  (Secretarial & clerical temporary service)
    Kontorservice Inc., P.O. Box 599, Eyvind Lyches Vei 13B, 1301 Sandvika, Norway

WORLD COURIER INC   46 Trinity Pl, New York, NY 10006, Tel: (718) 978-9400
  (Intl courier serv)
    World Courier Norway, c/o Ships Sped Ais, Bekkelagskaia, Oslo, Norway

WM WRIGLEY JR CO   410 N Michigan Ave, Chicago, IL 60611-4287,
  Tel: (312) 644-2121
  (Mfr chewing gum)
    Wrigley Scandinavia A/S, Dag Hammarskjoldsvei 48, Oslo 5, Norway

XEROX CORP   800 Long Ridge Rd, PO Box 1600, Stamford, CT 06904,
  Tel: (203) 968-3000
  (Mfr document processing equip, sys & supplies)
    Xerox Corp., Oslo, Norway

YOUNG & RUBICAM INC   285 Madison Ave, New York, NY 10017, Tel: (212) 210-3000
  (Advertising, public relations, direct marketing & sales promotion, corp & product ID
  management)
    Young & Rubicam Norway, Stranden 3, 0250 Oslo, Norway

OMAN

A-Z INTL TOOL CO   PO Box 7108, Houston, TX 77248-7108, Tel: (713) 880-8888
  (Mfr oil field, milling & casing cutting tools)
    Sharikat Hani LLC, Div. A-Z Intl., P.O. Box 4618, Ruwi, Muscat, Oman

CARBOLINE CO   350 Hanley Industrial Ct, St Louis, MO 63144,
  Tel: (314) 644-1000
  (Mfr coatings, sealants)
    Sadolin Paints (Oman) Ltd., P.O. Box 531, Muscat 112, Oman

CDM INTL INC   Ten Cambridge Center, Cambridge, MA 02142, Tel: (617) 252-8000
  (Consulting engineers)
    Camp Dresser & McKee Intl. Inc., P.O. Box 18201, Salalah, Oman

CITICORP   399 Park Ave, New York, NY 10043, Tel: (212) 559-1000
  (Banking & financial services)
    Citibank NA, Oman

THE HARPER GROUP   260 Townsend St, PO Box 77933, San Francisco,
  CA 94107-1719, Tel: (415) 978-0600
  (Ocean/air freight fwdg, customs brokerage, packing & whse, logistics mgt, ins)
    Circle Freight Intl. LLC, P.O. Box 1077, Central Post Office, Muscat, Oman

HOLIDAY INNS INC   3742 Lamar Ave, Memphis, TN 38195, Tel: (901) 362-4001
  (Hotels, restaurants, casinos)
    Holiday Inn, Holisal MB, P.O. Box 8870, Salalah, Oman

HONEYWELL INC   PO Box 524, Minneapolis, MN 55440-0524, Tel: (612) 951-1000
  (Devel/mfr controls for home & building, industry, space & aviation)
    Honeywell & Co. Oman LLC, P.O. Box 482, Mina-Al-Fahal 116, Oman

IMCO SERVICES   5950 N Course Dr, Houston, TX 70072, Tel: (713) 561-1300
  (Drilling fluids)
    Imco Services BV, c/o OOSC, P.O. Box 5796/4, 160 Ruwi, Oman

ITT SHERATON CORP   60 State St, Boston, MA 02108, Tel: (617) 367-3600
  (Hotel operations)
    Oman Sheraton Hotel, P.O. Box 6260, Muscat, Oman

OCEANEERING INTL INC   PO Box 218130, Houston, TX 77218-8130,
  Tel: (713) 578-8868
  (Underwater serv to offshore oil & gas ind)
    Oceaneering Intl. Inc., Operational base in Muscat

PARSONS ENGINEERING SCIENCE INC   100 W Walnut St, Pasadena, CA 91124,
  Tel: (818) 440-6000
  (Environmental engineering)
    Parsons Engineering Science Inc., P.O. Box 43162, Wadi Al Kabir, Muscat, Oman

WEATHERFORD INTL INC   1360 Post Oak Blvd, PO Box 27608, Houston,
  TX 77227-7608, Tel: (713) 439-9400
  (Oilfield servs, prdts & equip; mfr marine cranes)
    Weatherford Intl. Inc., P.O. Box 3510, Muscat, Oman

WESTERN ATLAS INTL INC   10205 Westheimer, PO Box 1407, Houston,
  TX 77251-1407, Tel: (713) 266-5700
  (Full service to the oil industry)
    Western Geophysical, P.O. Box 14, Min Al Fahal, Muscat, Oman

PAKISTAN

3M   3M Center, St Paul, MN 55144-1000, Tel: (612) 733-1110
  (Mfr diversified prdts for industry, health care, imaging, commun, transport, safety,
  consumer, etc)
    3M Pakistan (Pvt.) Ltd., Lakson Square Bldg 1, 3D 3/F, Sarwar Shaheed Rd.,
      Karachi 74200, Pakistan

AMERICAN PRESIDENT LINES LTD   1111 Broadway, Oakland, CA 94607,
  Tel: (415) 272-8000
  (Intermodal shipping serv)
    American President Lines Ltd., P.O. Box 4037, 2 West Wharf Rd., Karachi 2, Pakistan

AST RESEARCH INC   16215 Alton Parkway, PO Box 19658, Irvine, CA 92713-9658,
   Tel: (714) 727-4141
   (Design/devel/mfr hi-perf desktop, server & notebook computers)
     AST Pakistan, 509 5th fl. Clifton Centre, Block 5, KDA Scheme 5, Kahkashan,
     Clifton, Karachi, Pakistan

AVIS INC   900 Old Country Rd, Garden City, NY 11530, Tel: (516) 222-3000
   (Car rental serv)
     Avis Rent Office, Waljis Bldg., 10 Khayaban Suhrawardy, P.O. Box 1088, Islamabad,
     Pakistan

BAKER OIL TOOLS   PO Box 40129, Houston, TX 77240-0129, Tel: (713) 466-1322
   (Mfr/serv oil/gas well completions equip)
     Baker Eastern SA, c/o Nuricon Union Ltd., House 303-A, Street 18, Sector E-7,
     Islambad, Pakistan

BANKAMERICA CORP   555 California St, San Francisco, CA 94104,
   Tel: (415) 622-3456
   (Financial services)
     Bank of America NT & SA, Jubilee Insurance House, Ismail Ibrahim Chundrigar Rd.,
     P.O. Box 3715, Karachi, Pakistan

BEAR STEARNS & CO INC   245 Park Ave, New York, NY 10167, Tel: (212) 272-2000
   (Investment banking)
     Bear Stearns Jahangir Siddiqui Ltd., Chapel Plaza, Hasrat Mohani Rd.,
     Karachi 74000, Pakistan

LOUIS BERGER INTL INC   100 Halsted St, East Orange, NJ 07019,
   Tel: (201) 678-1960
   (Consulting engineers, architects, economists & planners)
     Louis Berger Intl. Inc., Coverdale Organization, 2 Railroad Rd., University Town,
     Peshawar, Pakistan

BRANSON ULTRASONICS CORP   41 Eagle Rd, Danbury, CT 06813-1961,
   Tel: (203) 796-0400
   (Mfr plastics assembly equip, ultrasonic cleaning equip)
     Farooq Ahmad Partnership, Nasir Rd., Chah Piswan, Sialkot 1, Pakistan

CALTEX PETROLEUM CORP   PO Box 619500, Dallas, TX 75261, Tel: (214) 830-1000
   (Petroleum prdts)
     Caltex Oil (Pakistan) Ltd., Press Trust House, 11 Chundrigar Rd., Karachi 74200,
     Pakistan

CHASE MANHATTAN BANK N A   1 Chase Manhattan Plaza, New York, NY 10081,
   Tel: (212) 552-2222
   (Intl banking)
     Chase Manhattan Bank N.A., Shaheen Commercial Complex, M.R. Kayanl Rd., Karachi,
     Pakistan
     Chase Manhattan Bank N.A., P.O. Box 1161, Karachi, Pakistan

CIGNA CORP   One Liberty Place, Philadelphia, PA 19192, Tel: (215) 523-4000
   (Ins, invest, health care & other fin servs)
     Insurance Co. of North America, National Insurance Corp. Bldg.,
     Abbasi Shaheed Rd. off Sharea Faisal, Karachi, Pakistan

CITICORP   399 Park Ave, New York, NY 10043, Tel: (212) 559-1000
   (Banking & financial services)
     Citibank NA, Pakistan

COMBUSTION ENGINEERING INC   900 Long Ridge Road, Stamford, CT 06902,
   Tel: (203) 329-8771
   (Tech constr)
     Intl. Products Co., 1 Mayfair Court, Canal Bank, Lahore, Pakistan

CORE LABORATORIES   10205 Westheimer, Houston, TX 77042, Tel: (713) 972-6311
   (Petroleum testing/analysis, analytical chem, lab & octane analysis instrumentation)
     Core Laboratories Inc., P.O. Box 5912, Karachi, Pakistan

CPC INTERNATIONAL INC   PO Box 8000, Englewood Cliffs, NJ 07632,
   Tel: (201) 894-4000
   (Consumer foods, corn refining)
     Rafhan Maize Products Co. Ltd., Rakh Canal E. Rd., P.O. Box 62, Faisalabad, Punjab,
     Pakistan

D'ARCY MASIUS BENTON & BOWLES INC (DMB&B)   1675 Broadway, New York,
   NY 10019, Tel: (212) 468-3622
   (Advertising & communications)
     The Advertising Agency, A-9 A-1 Sunset Blvd., Deference Housing Authority, Karachi,
     Pakistan

DILLINGHAM CONSTRUCTION CORP   5944 Inglewood Dr, Pleasanton, CA 94566,
   Tel: (415) 847-7700
   (General contracting)
     Dillingham Pakistan Ltd., P.O. Box 3, Tarbela Dam Colony, Dist. Abbottabad, NWFP,
     Pakistan
     Dillingham Pakistan Ltd., 14-B Agha Khan Rd., Sector F-6/4, P.O. Box 1559,
     Islamabad, Pakistan

EASTMAN KODAK CO   343 State St, Rochester, NY 14650, Tel: (716) 724-4000
   (Devel/mfr photo & chem prdts, info mgmt/video/copier sys, fibers/plastics for
   various ind)
     Kodak Ltd., P.O. Box 4956, 4th Floor Bahria Complex, Mavlvi Tamizuddin Khan Rd.,
     Karachi, Pakistan

FMC CORP   200 E Randolph Dr, Chicago, IL 60601, Tel: (312) 861-6000
   (Produces chems & precious metals, mfr machinery, equip & sys for ind, agric & govt)
     FMC Intl. SA, Pakistan
     FMC United (Pvt.) Ltd., Pakistan

GENERAL ELECTRIC CO   3135 Easton Tpk, Fairfield, CT 06431,
   Tel: (203) 373-2211
   (Diversified manufacturing, technology & services)
     General Electric Co.,
       all mail to U.S. address; phone (800) 626-2004 or (518) 438-6500

GEONEX CORP   150 Second Ave North, St Petersburg, FL 33701,
   Tel: (813) 823-3300
   (Geo-information services: mapping, resource interpretation, analysis & testing, data
   base mgmt)
     Geonex Corp., 63-D Model Town, Lahore, Pakistan

GETZ BROS & CO INC   150 Post St, #500, San Francisco, CA 94108,
  Tel: (415) 772-5500
  (Divers mfg, mktg/distr serv, travel serv)
    Muller & Phipps Pakistan (Pvt.) Ltd., Uzma Court, 1/F, Main Clifton Rd.,
    P.O. Box 3880, Karachi, Pakistan

THE GILLETTE CO   Prudential Tower, Boston, MA 02199, Tel: (617) 421-7000
  (Devel/mfr personal care/use prdts: blades & razors, toiletries, cosmetics,
  stationery)
    Interpak Shaving Products Ltd., Karachi, Pakistan

HOLIDAY INNS INC   3742 Lamar Ave, Memphis, TN 38195, Tel: (901) 362-4001
  (Hotels, restaurants, casinos)
    Holiday Inn, Agha Kahn Rd., Islamabad Intl. Airport, Islamabad, Pakistan

HORWATH INTL   415 Madison Ave, New York, NY 10017, Tel: (212) 838-5566
  (Public accountants & auditors)
    United Consultants (Pvt.) Ltd., Hassan Rehman & Co., 44 Warris Rd., Lahore, Pakistan

INTERNATIONAL TANK TERMINALS LTD   321 St Charles Ave, New Orleans, LA 70130,
  Tel: (504) 586-8300
  (Storage tank facilities)
    Intl. Tank Terminals Ltd., W. Wharf, Dockyard Rd., Karachi, Pakistan

ITT SHERATON CORP   60 State St, Boston, MA 02108, Tel: (617) 367-3600
  (Hotel operations)
    Karachi Sheraton Hotel, Club Rd., P.O. Box 3918, Karachi, Pakistan

JOHNSON & JOHNSON   One Johnson & Johnson Plaza, New Brunswick, NJ 08933,
  Tel: (908) 524-0400
  (R&D/mfr/sale health care prdts)
    Johnson & Johnson Pakistan Ltd., P.O. Box 8033, Kirachi 75180, Pakistan

LINTAS:WORLDWIDE   1 Dag Hammarskjold Plaza, New York, NY 10017,
  Tel: (212) 605-8000
  (Advertising agency)
    Lintas:Karachi, Hashoo Chambers, Abdullah Haroon Rd., Karachi, Pakistan

MERCK SHARP & DOHME INTL   PO Box 2000, Rahway, NJ 07065, Tel: (201) 574-4000
  (Pharms, chems & biologicals)
    Merck, Sharp & Dohme of Pakistan Ltd., 2 American Life Square, I.I. Chundrigar Rd.,
    Karachi, Pakistan

MULLER & PHIPPS INTL CORP   Box 3994, San Francisco, CA 94119,
  Tel: (415) 772-5650
  (General merchandise)
    M & P Pakistan Ltd., P.O. Box 6713, Karachi 2, Pakistan

McCANN-ERICKSON WORLDWIDE   750 Third Ave, New York, NY 10017,
  Tel: (212) 697-6000
  (Advertising)
    Paragon Advertising (Pte.) Ltd., Panorama Centre, Raja Ghazanfar Ali Rd.,
    Karachi 4, Pakistan

OCCIDENTAL PETROLEUM CORP   10889 Wilshire Blvd, Los Angeles, CA 90024,
  Tel: (213) 879-1700
  (Petroleum & petroleum prdts, chems, plastics)
    Occidental of Pakistan Inc., 230 Nazimuddin Rd., Sector F-7/4, Islamabad, Pakistan

PARKER DRILLING CO   8 E Third St, Tulsa, OK 74103-3637, Tel: (918) 585-8221
  (Drilling contractor)
    Parker Drilling Co. Intl. Ltd., House 5, Street 66, Sector F7/3, Islamabad, Pakistan

PARSONS DE LEUW INC   1133 15th St NW, Washington, DC 20005,
  Tel: (202) 775-3300
  (Consulting engineers)
    De Leuw, Cather Intl. Ltd., P.O. Box 1725, Islamabad, Pakistan

PARSONS ENGINEERING SCIENCE INC   100 W Walnut St, Pasadena, CA 91124,
  Tel: (818) 440-6000
  (Environmental engineering)
    Parsons Engineering Science Inc., c/o Indus Associated Consultants,
      18A FCC Maratab Ali Rd., Bulberg 4, Lahaore, Pakistan
    Parsons Engineering Science Inc., F61/II-Block, 4 Kehkeshan-Clifton, Karachi 75500,
      Pakistan

PEPSICO INC   700 Anderson Hill Rd, Purchase, NY 10577-1444,
  Tel: (914) 253-2000
  (Beverages, snack foods, restaurants)
    Pepsi-Cola Intl. (Pvt.) Ltd., Pakistan

PFIZER INC   235 E 42nd St, New York, NY 10017-5755, Tel: (212) 573-2323
  (Mfr healthcare products)
    Pfizer Laboratories Ltd., Pakistan

RAYCHEM CORP   300 Constitution Dr, Menlo Park, CA 94025, Tel: (415) 361-3333
  (Devel/mfr/mkt materials science products for electronics, telecommunications &
  industry)
    Raychem Pakistan, Shaheen Chambers, A-4 Central Commercial Area, Block 7/8 KHCS,
      Karachi, Pakistan

ROHM AND HAAS CO   100 Independence Mall West, Philadelphia, PA 19106,
  Tel: (215) 592-3000
  (Mfr ind & agric chems, plastics)
    Rohm and Haas Asia Inc., Ispahani Tea Factory Bldg., 31 West Wharf Rd., Karachi 01,
      Pakistan

G D SEARLE & CO   5200 Old Orchard Rd, Skokie, IL 60077, Tel: (708) 982-7000
  (Mfr pharms, health care & optical prdts, specialty chems)
    Searle (Pakistan) Ltd., 58 West Wharf Rd., KDLB Bldg. 5/F, Karachi 1, Pakistan

STIEFEL LABORATORIES INC   255 Alhambra Circle, Coral Gables, FL 33134,
  Tel: (305) 443-3807
  (Mfr pharmaceuticals, dermatological specialties)
    Stiefel Laboratories Scientific Services, 2 Gulberg Rd., Gulberg-V, Lahore 54660,
      Pakistan

WACKENHUT CORP   1500 San Remo Ave, Coral Gables, FL 33146,
  Tel: (305) 666-5656
  (Security systems & services)

(cont)

Wackenhut Pakistan (Pvt.) Ltd., 19-1A Bloc 6 PECHS, Shahrah-El-Faisal,
Karachi 75400, Pakistan

WARNER-LAMBERT CO   201 Tabor Road, Morris Plains, NJ 07950,
Tel: (201) 540-2000
(Mfr ethical & proprietary pharms, confectionary & consumer prdts)
Parke-Davis & Co. Ltd., P.O. Box 3621, B/2 S.I.T.E., Karachi 75700, Pakistan

PANAMA

3M   3M Center, St Paul, MN 55144-1000, Tel: (612) 733-1110
(Mfr diversified prdts for industry, health care, imaging, commun, transport, safety,
consumer, etc)
3M Panama SA, Calle D y Alberto Navarro, El Cangrejo, Aptdo. Postal 4454, Panama 5,
Panama

AMERICAN EXPRESS CO   World Financial Center, New York, NY 10285-4765,
Tel: (212) 640-2000
(Travel, travelers cheques, charge card & financial services)
Sociedad Internacional de Servicios de Panama SA, all inquiries to U.S. address

AMWAY CORP   7575 E Fulton Rd, Ada, MI 49355, Tel: (616) 676-6000
(Mfr/sale home care, personal care, nutrition & houseware prdts)
Amway de Panama SA, Apartado 6-4200, El Dorado, Panama

AVIS INC   900 Old Country Rd, Garden City, NY 11530, Tel: (516) 222-3000
(Car rental serv)
Avis Rent A Car System Inc., Edif. Castilla de Oro Calle, El Cangrejo, Panama,
Panama

BANKERS TRUST CO   280 Park Ave, New York, NY 10017, Tel: (212) 250-2500
(Banking)
Bankers Trust Co., Apartado 6360, Panama 5, Panama

BATA SHOE CO INC   U S Rt 40, Pulaski Hwy, Belcamp, MD 21017,
Tel: (301) 272-2000
(Rubber, canvas & plastic footwear)
Bata Shoe Co., Inc., Apartado 1347, Panama, Panama

LOUIS BERGER INTL INC   100 Halsted St, East Orange, NJ 07019,
Tel: (201) 678-1960
(Consulting engineers, architects, economists & planners)
Louis Berger Intl. Inc., c/o COPISA, Calle G y F, Parque Lefevre,
Entrada por la Paz, Panama, Panama

BORDEN INC   180 E Broad St, Columbus, OH 43215-3799, Tel: (614) 225-4000
  (Mfr foods, snacks & beverages, adhesives)
    Borden SA, all mail to U.S. address

CALMAQUIP ENGINEERING CORP   7240 NW 12th St, Miami, FL 33121,
  Tel: (305) 592-4510
  (Engineering)
    Calmaquip Panama, Apartado 6-3001, El Dorado, Panama

CARBOLINE CO   350 Hanley Industrial Ct, St Louis, MO 63144,
  Tel: (314) 644-1000
  (Mfr coatings, sealants)
    Sun Chemical de Panama SA, Apartado 6-896, El Dorado, Panama

CHASE MANHATTAN BANK N A   1 Chase Manhattan Plaza, New York, NY 10081,
  Tel: (212) 552-2222
  (Intl banking)
    Chase Manhattan Bank N.A., 120 Via Espana, Panama 9A, Panama
    Chase Manhattan Bank N.A., other locations in Panama

CHIQUITA BRANDS INTL INC   250 E Fifth St, Cincinnati, OH 45202,
  Tel: (513) 784-8000
  (Distribution food products)
    Chiriqui Land Co., Aptdo. Aereo 6-2637/6-2638, Estafeta El Dorado, Panama City,
      Panama

CIGNA CORP   One Liberty Place, Philadelphia, PA 19192, Tel: (215) 523-4000
  (Ins, invest, health care & other fin servs)
    Cigna Compania de Seguros de Panama SA, Torre Banco Exterior, Apartado 6-8909,
      El Dorado, Panama
    Cigna Reaseguros SA, Av. Samuel Lewis, Torre Banco Union, Panama, Panama
    DelPanama SA, c/o Arias, Fabrega & Fabrega, Bank America Bldg., Calle 50, Panama,
      Panama

CITICORP   399 Park Ave, New York, NY 10043, Tel: (212) 559-1000
  (Banking & financial services)
    Citibank NA, Panama

THE CLOROX CO   1221 Broadway, PO Box 24305, Oakland, CA 94623-1305,
  Tel: (510) 271-7000
  (Mfr domestic consumer packaged prdts)
    Clorox de Panama SA, Panama City, Panama

COLGATE-PALMOLIVE CO   300 Park Ave, New York, NY 10022, Tel: (212) 310-2000
  (Mfr pharms, cosmetics, toiletries, detergents)
    Colgate-Palmolive (West Indies) Inc., Apartado 64998, El Dorado, Panama 6, Panama

COLUMBIA PICTURES INDUSTRIES INC   711 Fifth Ave, New York, NY 10022,
  Tel: (212) 751-4400
  (Producer & distributor of motion pictures)
    Columbia Pictures de Panama Inc., Apartado 4492, Panama 5, Panama
    Columbia Pictures de Panama Inc., Edif. Elga, Via Espana 46-50, Panama

CORESTATES FINANCIAL CORP   1500 Market St, Philadelphia, PA 19101,
  Tel: (215) 973-3100
  (Banking)
    Corestates Bank, P.O. Box 55-2203, Panama City, Panama

DEVELOPMENT ASSOCIATES INC　　1730 N Lynn St, Arlington, VA　22209-2023,
　Tel: (703) 276-0677
　(Mgt consulting servs)
　　Development Associates Inc., Edif. Tribunal Maritimo, Calle Herrick 310, Ancon,
　　　Panama City, Panama

THE DOW CHEMICAL CO　　2030 Dow Center, Midland, MI　48674, Tel: (517) 636-1000
　(Mfr chems, plastics, pharms, agric prdts, consumer prdts)
　　Coral Navigation Co. Inc., Panama, Panama

EASTMAN KODAK CO　　343 State St, Rochester, NY　14650, Tel: (716) 724-4000
　(Devel/mfr photo & chem prdts, info mgmt/video/copier sys, fibers/plastics for
　various ind)
　　Kodak Panama Ltd., P.O. Box 7333, Via Israel 96, Panama 5, Panama

FEDERAL-MOGUL CORP　　PO Box 1966, Detroit, MI　48235, Tel: (810) 354-7700
　(Mfr/distr precision parts for automobiles, trucks, & farm/construction vehicles)
　　Federal-Mogul Panama SA, Panama

FIRST NATIONAL BANK OF BOSTON　　100 Federal St, Boston, MA　02110,
　Tel: (617) 434-2200
　(Commercial banking)
　　Bank of Boston, Edif. Banco de Boston, Via Espana 22, Apartado 5368, Panama 5,
　　　Panama
　　Bank of Boston, Apartado 3024, Av. Roosevelt, Zona Libre de Colon, Panama

GENERAL FOODS CORP　　250 North St, White Plains, NY　10625, Tel: (914) 335-2500
　(Processor, distributor & mfr of foods)
　　General Foods Panama SA, Apartadoo 2016, Balboa-Ancon, Panama City, Panama

THE GILLETTE CO　　Prudential Tower, Boston, MA　02199, Tel: (617) 421-7000
　(Devel/mfr personal care/use prdts: blades & razors, toiletries, cosmetics,
　stationery)
　　Compania Interamericana Gillette SA, Panama City, Panama
　　Compania Interamericana de Prestamos SA, Panama City, Panama

GLOBAL ASSOCIATES　　2420 Camino Ramon, #236, San Ramon, CA　94583,
　Tel: (415) 275-9010
　(Logistic support services)
　　Global Associates, all mail to APO Miami, FL 34704

GRIFFITH LABORATORIES INC　　I Griffith Center, Alsip, IL　60658,
　Tel: (708) 371-0900
　(Ind food ingredients & equip)
　　Laboratorios Panama SA, Apartado 1391, Panama 9A, Panama

GTE DIRECTORIES CORP　　West Airport Dr, DFW Airport, TX　75261-9810,
　Tel: (214) 453-7000
　(Pub telephone directories)
　　GTD SA, Apartado 5394, Panama 5, Panama

FRANK B HALL & CO INC　　549 Pleasantville Rd, Briarcliff Manor, NY　10510,
　Tel: (914) 769-9200
　(Insurance)
　　Kam y Associados SA, Apartado 3049, Zona Libre de Colon, Panama

THE HARPER GROUP   260 Townsend St, PO Box 77933, San Francisco,
  CA 94107-1719, Tel: (415) 978-0600
  (Ocean/air freight fwdg, customs brokerage, packing & whse, logistics mgt, ins)
    Circle Freight Intl. de Panama SA, Apartado 6-4181, El Dorado, Panama

HCA INTL CO   1 Park Plaza, PO Box 550, Nashville, TN 37202,
  Tel: (615) 327-9551
  (Hospital & health care mgmt)
    Clinicas y Hospitales Centro Medico Paitilla, Av. Balboa y Calle 53, Apartado 7503,
      Panama 5, Panama

HOLIDAY INNS INC   3742 Lamar Ave, Memphis, TN 38195, Tel: (901) 362-4001
  (Hotels, restaurants, casinos)
    Posadas de America Central SA, Apartado 1807, Panama 1, Panama

HORWATH INTL   415 Madison Ave, New York, NY 10017, Tel: (212) 838-5566
  (Public accountants & auditors)
    Horwath & Co., Edificio Vallarino, Area Bancaria, Calle 52 y Elvira Mendez 4 Piso,
      Zona 5, Panama

IBM CORP   Old Orchard Rd, Armonk, NY 10504, Tel: (914) 765-1900
  (Information products, technology & services)
    IBM de Panama SA, Panama, Panama

INTRUSION-PREPAKT INC   5353 W 161st St, Cleveland, OH 44142,
  Tel: (216) 267-7300
  (Contractor: preplaced aggregate concrete, concrete repirs, erosion control,
  underwater concrete, etc)
    Intrusion-Prepakt Interamerica SA, Apartado 6, 194 El Dorado, Panama, Panama

JOHNSON & JOHNSON   One Johnson & Johnson Plaza, New Brunswick, NJ 08933,
  Tel: (908) 524-0400
  (R&D/mfr/sale health care prdts)
    Ethnor del Istmo SA, P.O. Box 64576, El Dorado, Panama, Panama
    Johnson & Johnson Central America Area, P.O. Box 10569, Panama 4, Panama

THE KENDALL CO   15 Hampshire St, Mansfield, MA 02048, Tel: (508) 261-8000
  (Mfr medical disposable prdts, home health care prdts, spec adhesive prdts)
    Kendall SA, P.O. Box 55-0739 Paitilla, Calle Primera (Harry Eno),
      Urbanizacion Industrial Los Angeles, Panama

KIMBERLY-CLARK CORP   PO Box 619100, Dallas, TX 75261, Tel: (214) 281-1200
  (Mfr fiber-based prdts for personal care, lumber & paper prdts)
    Kimberly-Clark Intl. SA, Panama, Panama

KRAFT INC   Kraft Court, Glenview, IL 60025, Tel: (708) 998-2000
  (Dairy prdts, processed food, chems)
    Kraft Foods SA, Urbanizacion Industrial San Cristobal, Calle Harry Eno,
      Los Angeles, Panama City, Panama
    Kraft Foods SA, Apartado 6-2596, El Dorado, Panama

MANPOWER INTL INC   5301 N Ironwood Rd, PO Box 2053, Milwaukee,
  WI 53201-2053, Tel: (414) 961-1000
  (Temporary help service)
    Manpower-Servex SA, Apartado 134-9A, Panama, Panama

MARCO   2300 W Commodore Way, Seattle, WA 98199, Tel: (206) 285-3200
  (Shipbldg & repair, coml fishing equip & sys, hydraulic pumps)
    Marco Panama, Apartado 10356, Panama 4, Panama

MERRILL LYNCH   World Financial Center, New York, NY 10281-1323,
  Tel: (212) 449-1000
  (Security brokers & dealers, investment & business services)
    Merrill Lynch Intl. Bank Inc., Calle Aquilino de la Guardia 18, Panama 5, Panama

McCANN-ERICKSON WORLDWIDE   750 Third Ave, New York, NY 10017,
  Tel: (212) 697-6000
  (Advertising)
    McCann-Erickson de Panama SA, Campo Alegre, Calle Gerardo Ortega 10, Apartado 4248,
      Panama 5, Panama

McKESSON CORP   One Post St, San Francisco, CA 94104-5296, Tel: (415) 983-8300
  (Mfr drugs, car-care prdts, toiletries)
    Calox Panamena, Apartado 6-3369, El Dorado, Panama, Panama

NATIONAL BULK CARRIERS INC   1345 Ave of the Americas, New York, NY 10105,
  Tel: (212) 765-3000
  (Real estate development, mgmt serv)
    Citricos de Chiriqui SA, Apartado 7121, Panama, Panama
    Refineria Panama SA, Apartado 5270, Panama 5, Panama

NATIONAL CAR RENTAL SYSTEM INC   7700 France Ave S, Minneapolis, MN 55435,
  Tel: (612) 830-2121
  (Car rental)
    Natl. Car Rental, Apartado 6-2899, Calle 55, El Cangrejo, Panama, Panama

NEW YORK AIR BRAKE CO   Starbuck Ave, Watertown, NY 13601, Tel: (315) 782-7000
  (Hydraulic pumps)
    New York Air Brake Intl. SA, Av. Central 8-16, Panama, Panama

PAN-AMERICAN LIFE INSURANCE CO   Pan American Life Center, PO Box 60219,
  New Orleans, LA 70130-0219, Tel: (504) 566-1300
  (Insurance)
    Pan-American de Panama SA, Calle Aquilino de la Guardia, entre Calles 47 y 48,
      Panama, Panama

PFIZER INC   235 E 42nd St, New York, NY 10017-5755, Tel: (212) 573-2323
  (Mfr healthcare products)
    Harmag Inc., Panama
    Howmedica Intl. Inc., Panama
    Pfizer Corp., Panama
    Pfizer Holding Corp., Panama
    Pfizer International Corp. SA, Panama
    Pfizer Pharmaceuticals Production Corp., Panama

PHELPS DODGE CORP   2600 N Central Ave, Phoenix, AZ 85004-3014,
  Tel: (602) 234-8100
  (Copper, minerals, metals & spec engineered prdts for trans & elect mkts)
    Alambres y Cables de Panama SA (ALCAP), Apartado Postal 11186, Panama 6, Panama

SEA-LAND SERVICE INC   150 Allen Rd, Liberty Corner, NJ 07920,
Tel: (201) 558-6000
(Container transport)
  Ocean Trucking Co., Apartado 2078, Balboa, Zona Canal, Panama

SEARS ROEBUCK & CO   Sears Tower, Chicago, IL 60684, Tel: (312) 875-2500
(Diversified general merchandise)
  Sears Roebuck SA, Apartado 4374, Panama 5, Panama

SHERWIN-WILLIAMS CO INC   101 Prospect Ave NW, Cleveland, OH 44115,
Tel: (216) 566-2000
(Mfr paint, wallcoverings, related prdts)
  Sherwin-Williams de Panama SA, Juan Diaz Rd., Panama 5, Panama

TEXACO INC   2000 Westchester Ave, White Plains, NY 10650, Tel: (914) 253-4000
(Explor/mktg crude oil, mfr petro chems & prdts)
  Texaco Antilles Ltd., Transisthmian Hwy., Panama, Panama

UNITED MERCHANTS & MANUFACTURERS INC   1650 Palisade Ave, Teaneck, NJ 07666,
Tel: (201) 837-1700
(Rayon, cotton, print cloth, nylon, sheeting & drills, glass & plastic fabrics)
  Panameritex de Panama, Panama, Panama

UPJOHN CO   7000 Portage Rd, Kalamazoo, MI 49001, Tel: (616) 323-4000
(Mfr pharms, agric prdts, ind chems)
  Upjohn Co. SA, Apartado 536, Colon, Panama

WACKENHUT CORP   1500 San Remo Ave, Coral Gables, FL 33146,
Tel: (305) 666-5656
(Security systems & services)
  Seguridad Tecnica SA (SETECSA), Apto. 4284, Panama 5, Panama
  Wackenhut Intl. (Panama) SA, Apartado Postal 850, Panama 1, Panama

WORLD COURIER INC   46 Trinity Pl, New York, NY 10006, Tel: (718) 978-9400
(Intl courier serv)
  World Courier Panama SA, IBM Tower 5/F, Av. Balboa y Calle 39, Panama, Panama

XEROX CORP   800 Long Ridge Rd, PO Box 1600, Stamford, CT 06904,
Tel: (203) 968-3000
(Mfr document processing equip, sys & supplies)
  Xerox Corp., Panama City, Panama

PAPUA NEW GUINEA

ASARCO INC   180 Maiden Lane, New York, NY 10038, Tel: (212) 510-2000
   (Nonferrous metals, specialty chems, minerals, mfr industrial prdts, environmental
   services)
     MIM Holdings Ltd., Porgera, Papua New Guinea

CARRIER CORP   One Carrier Place, Farmington, CT 06034-4015,
   Tel: (203) 674-3000
   (Mfr/distr/svce A/C, heating & refrigeration equip)
     Carrier Air Conditioning (PNG) Pty. Ltd., Boroko, New Guinea

CHEVRON CORP   225 Bush St, San Francisco, CA 94104, Tel: (415) 894-7700
   (Oil & gas exploration, production, refining, products; oilfield & financial services)
     Chevron Corp., all mail to U.S. address

THE GILLETTE CO   Prudential Tower, Boston, MA 02199, Tel: (617) 421-7000
   (Devel/mfr personal care/use prdts: blades & razors, toiletries, cosmetics,
   stationery)
     Gillette (PNG) Pty. Ltd., Port Moresby, Papua New Guinea

THE HARPER GROUP   260 Townsend St, PO Box 77933, San Francisco,
   CA 94107-1719, Tel: (415) 978-0600
   (Ocean/air freight fwdg, customs brokerage, packing & whse, logistics mgt, ins)
     Chards Forwarding Services Pty. Ltd., P.O. Box 1150, Port Moresby, Papua New Guinea

HELMERICH & PAYNE INC   1579 E 21st St, Tulsa, OK 74114, Tel: (918) 742-5531
   (Oil/gas exploration & drilling, real estate, mfr gas odorants)
     Helmerich & Payne Investments Ltd., Investmen Haus 6/F, Douglas St.,
       P.O. Box 1045 POM, Port Moresby, Papua New Guinea

OCEANEERING INTL INC   PO Box 218130, Houston, TX 77218-8130,
   Tel: (713) 578-8868
   (Underwater serv to offshore oil & gas ind)
     Oceaneering Intl. Inc., Operational base in Port Moresby

PARKER DRILLING CO   8 E Third St, Tulsa, OK 74103-3637, Tel: (918) 585-8221
   (Drilling contractor)
     Parker Drilling Co. Eastern Hemisphere ltd., ANG House 8/F, Hunter St.,
       P.O. Box 478, Port Moresby, Papua New Guinea

WM WRIGLEY JR CO   410 N Michigan Ave, Chicago, IL 60611-4287,
   Tel: (312) 644-2121
   (Mfr chewing gum)
     The Wrigley Co. (PNG) Pty. Ltd., Port Moresby, Papua New Guinea

PARAGUAY

AVON PRODUCTS INC   9 W 57th St, New York, NY 10019, Tel: (212) 546-6015
  (Mfr/distr beauty & related prdts, fashion jewelry, gifts & collectibles)
    Productos Avon Ltd., Asuncion, Paraguay

CHASE MANHATTAN BANK N A   1 Chase Manhattan Plaza, New York, NY 10081,
  Tel: (212) 552-2222
  (Intl banking)
    Chase Manhattan Bank N.A., Vitor Haedo 103, Esquina Ind. Nacional,
      Casilla de Correo 317, Asuncion, Paraguay

CIGNA CORP   One Liberty Place, Philadelphia, PA 19192, Tel: (215) 523-4000
  (Ins, invest, health care & other fin servs)
    Cigna Worldwide Insurance Co., 15 de Agosto 112, Asuncion, Paraguay

CITICORP   399 Park Ave, New York, NY 10043, Tel: (212) 559-1000
  (Banking & financial services)
    Citibank NA, Paraguay

CPC INTERNATIONAL INC   PO Box 8000, Englewood Cliffs, NJ 07632,
  Tel: (201) 894-4000
  (Consumer foods, corn refining)
    Maizena SA, Teniente Cusmanich 947, Las Mercedes, Asuncion, Paraguay

FIRST NATIONAL BANK OF BOSTON   100 Federal St, Boston, MA 02110,
  Tel: (617) 434-2200
  (Commercial banking)
    First National Bank of Boston, Pte. Franco 706, Casilla de Correo 325, Asuncion,
      Paraguay

HORWATH INTL   415 Madison Ave, New York, NY 10017, Tel: (212) 838-5566
  (Public accountants & auditors)
    Horwath & Co., Victor Haedo 179, piso 17, Asuncion, Paraguay

LOS PINOS II CORP   1111 Park Centre Blvd #245, Miami, FL 33169,
  Tel: (305) 625-1151
  (On-line service internet provider)
    Los Pinos II Paraguay, Mariscal Lopez 3791, P.1 "A", Asuncion, Paraguay

MARATHON LE TOURNEAU CO   PO Box 2307, Longview, TX 75606, Tel: (903) 237-7000
  (Mfr heavy constr, mining mach & equip)
    Ramon Martinez Blanco, Casilla 2131, Chile 645, Asuncion, Paraguay

MORRISON-KNUDSEN ENGINEERS INC   180 Howard St, San Francisco, CA 94105,
  Tel: (415) 442-7300
  (Engineering & cons mgmt)

(cont)

Cia. Internacional de Ingenieria SA, Casilla de Correo 1691, B. Constant 977,
Asuncion, Paraguay

McCANN-ERICKSON WORLDWIDE   750 Third Ave, New York, NY 10017,
Tel: (212) 697-6000
(Advertising)
Publicitaria Nasta SRL, Paraguari 852, Asuncion, Paraguay

NATIONAL CAR RENTAL SYSTEM INC   7700 France Ave S, Minneapolis, MN 55435,
Tel: (612) 830-2121
(Car rental)
National Car Rental, Yegros 501, Asuncion, Paraguay

WACKENHUT CORP   1500 San Remo Ave, Coral Gables, FL 33146,
Tel: (305) 666-5656
(Security systems & services)
Wackenhut Paraguay SA, Nery Quevedo 315, Es. H. Harron, Barrio San Miguel,
Asuncion, Paraguay

WORLD COURIER INC   46 Trinity Pl, New York, NY 10006, Tel: (718) 978-9400
(Intl courier serv)
World Courier, Presidente Franco 663, Asuncion, Paraguay

XEROX CORP   800 Long Ridge Rd, PO Box 1600, Stamford, CT 06904,
Tel: (203) 968-3000
(Mfr document processing equip, sys & supplies)
Xerox Corp., Asuncion, Paraguay

PERU

3M   3M Center, St Paul, MN 55144-1000, Tel: (612) 733-1110
(Mfr diversified prdts for industry, health care, imaging, commun, transport, safety,
consumer, etc)
3M Peru SA, Av. Canaval y Moreyra 641 (Ex-Corpac), San Isidro, Lima 27, Peru

AIR EXPRESS INTL CORP   120 Tokeneke Rd, PO Box 1231, Darien, CT 06820,
Tel: (203) 655-7900
(Air frt forwarder)
Air Express Intl. Corp. del Peru SA, Aeropuerto Intl. Jorge Chavez, Oficina 11,
Edif. de Carga, Zona Comercial, Callao 1, Peru

AMERICAN CHICLE CO   201 Tabor Rd, Morris Plains, NJ 07950,
Tel: (201) 540-2000
(Chewing gum)
Chicle Adams SA, Av. Bolivar 550-556, Pueblo Libre, Apartado 4264, Lima, Peru

ARBOR ACRES FARM INC   439 Marlborough Rd, Glastonbury, CT 06033,
  Tel: (860) 633-4681
  (Producers of male & female broiler breeders, commercial egg layers)
    Avicola del Norte SA, Apartado 6028, Lima, Peru

ASARCO INC   180 Maiden Lane, New York, NY 10038, Tel: (212) 510-2000
  (Nonferrous metals, specialty chems, minerals, mfr industrial prdts, environmental
  services)
    Corporacion Minera Nor Peru SA, Peru
    Southern Peru Copper Corp., Peru

ASSOCIATED PRESS INC   50 Rockefeller Plaza, New York, NY 10020-1605,
  Tel: (212) 621-1500
  (News gathering agency)
    Associated Press, Kiron Cailloma 377, Oficina 200, Apartado 119, Lima, Peru

AVIS INC   900 Old Country Rd, Garden City, NY 11530, Tel: (516) 222-3000
  (Car rental serv)
    Avis Rent A Car System Inc., Sherator Hotel Shopping Arcade,
      Paseo de la Republica 170, Lima, Peru

BECHTEL GROUP INC   50 Beale St, PO Box 3965, San Francisco, CA 94119,
  Tel: (415) 768-1234
  (Engineering & constr)
    Bechtel Corp. SA, Lima, Peru

BELCO OIL & GAS CORP   767 Fifth Ave, 46th fl, New York, NY 10153,
  Tel: (212) 644-2200
  (Expl & prod crude oil & natural gas)
    Belco Petroleum Corp. of Peru, Av. Los Incas 460, Apartado 3153, Lima 1, Peru

SAMUEL BINGHAM CO   1555 N Mittel Blvd, #T, Wood Dale, IL 60191-1046,
  Tel: (708) 238-4000
  (Print & industrial rollers, inks)
    Stimgraf SA, Apartado Postal 4757, Lima 100, Peru

BRANSON ULTRASONICS CORP   41 Eagle Rd, Danbury, CT 06813-1961,
  Tel: (203) 796-0400
  (Mfr plastics assembly equip, ultrasonic cleaning equip)
    Plasticos y Maquinarias SRL, Av. Grau 260, Casilla 18-0084, Lima 18, Peru

LEO BURNETT CO INC   35 West Wacker Dr, Chicago, IL 60601, Tel: (312) 220-5959
  (Advertising agency)
    Causa Publicidad, Tarata 269, Oficina 210, Miraflores, Lima 18, Peru

CARBOLINE CO   350 Hanley Industrial Ct, St Louis, MO 63144,
  Tel: (314) 644-1000
  (Mfr coatings, sealants)
    Quimica Industrial SA, Aptdo. Postal 2831, Lima 100, Peru

CARGILL   PO Box 9300, Minneapolis, MN 55440, Tel: (612) 475-7575
  (Food prdts, feeds, animal prdts)
    Cargill Peru SA, Apartado 2924, Lima 1, Peru

CHASE MANHATTAN BANK N A   1 Chase Manhattan Plaza, New York, NY 10081,
  Tel: (212) 552-2222
  (Intl banking)

(cont)

Chase Manhattan Overseas Corp., Calle Juan De Arona 893, Piso 13, San Isidro, Lima, Peru

CITICORP   399 Park Ave, New York, NY 10043, Tel: (212) 559-1000
(Banking & financial services)
Citibank NA, Peru

THE CLOROX CO   1221 Broadway, PO Box 24305, Oakland, CA 94623-1305,
Tel: (510) 271-7000
(Mfr domestic consumer packaged prdts)
Clorox del Peru SA, Lima, Peru

COLGATE-PALMOLIVE CO   300 Park Ave, New York, NY 10022, Tel: (212) 310-2000
(Mfr pharms, cosmetics, toiletries, detergents)
C.P. Peru SA, Jr. Chinchon 944, Piso 4, San Isidro, Lima 27, Peru

COLUMBIA PICTURES INDUSTRIES INC   711 Fifth Ave, New York, NY 10022,
Tel: (212) 751-4400
(Producer & distributor of motion pictures)
Columbia Pictures of Peru Inc., Apartado 2532, Jr. Lampa 1115, Oficina 1002, Lima, Peru

COMBUSTION ENGINEERING INC   900 Long Ridge Road, Stamford, CT 06902,
Tel: (203) 329-8771
(Tech constr)
Gray Tool Intl. Inc., c/o General Well Service S.A., Apartado 657, Lima, Peru

CONTINENTAL CAN CO   PO Box 5410, Stamford, CT 06856, Tel: (203) 357-8110
(Packaging prdts & mach, metal, plastic & paper containers)
Industrias Reunidas SA, Apartado 2645, Av. Argentina 5260, Lima, Peru

CPC INTERNATIONAL INC   PO Box 8000, Englewood Cliffs, NJ 07632,
Tel: (201) 894-4000
(Consumer foods, corn refining)
Alimentos y Productos de Maiz SA, Av. Elmer J. Faucett 3825, Apartado 288, Callao 1, Peru

CROWN CORK & SEAL CO INC   9300 Ashton Rd, Philadelphia, PA 19136,
Tel: (215) 698-5100
(Mfr cans, bottle caps; filling & packaging mach)
Crown Cork del Peru SA, Av. Minerales 487, Apartado 1692, Lima, Peru

DATA GENERAL CORP   4400 Computer Dr, Westboro, MA 01580, Tel: (617) 366-8911
(Design, mfr gen purpose computer sys & peripheral prdts & servs)
Data General de Peru SA, Av. Paseo de la Republica 3615, San Isidro, Lima 27, Peru

DENVER EQUIPMENT DIV   PO Box 340, Colorado Springs, CO 80901,
Tel: (303) 471-3443
(Ind process equip)
Denver Equipment Co. (Peru) SA, Maquinarias 270, Lima, Peru

THE DOW CHEMICAL CO   2030 Dow Center, Midland, MI 48674, Tel: (517) 636-1000
(Mfr chems, plastics, pharms, agric prdts, consumer prdts)
Productos Quimicos Peruanos SA, Paseo de la Republica 3587, Oficina 1001, San Isidro, Lima, Peru

DRAKE BEAM MORIN INC   100 Park Ave, New York, NY 10017, Tel: (212) 692-7700
(Human resource mgmt consulting & training)
   DBM Peru, 460 Nicolas de Rivera, Lima 27, Peru

EASTMAN KODAK CO   343 State St, Rochester, NY 14650, Tel: (716) 724-4000
(Devel/mfr photo & chem prdts, info mgmt/video/copier sys, fibers/plastics for various ind)
   Foto Interamericana de Peru Ltd., Casilla 2557, Lima 100, Peru

EATON CORP   1111 Superior Ave, Cleveland, OH 44114, Tel: (216) 523-5000
(Advanced tech prdts for transp & ind mkts)
   Eaton Corp., Apartado 129, Lima 100, Peru

EFCO   1800 NE Broadway Ave, Des Moines, IA 50316-0386, Tel: (515) 266-1141
(Mfr systems for concrete construction)
   EFCO, Avda. Del Pinar 415, Chac. Del Estanque, Lima, Peru

H B FULLER CO   2400 Energy Park Dr, St Paul, MN 55108, Tel: (612) 645-3401
(Mfr/distr adhesives, sealants, coatings, paints, waxes, sanitation chems)
   H.B. Fuller Peru SA, Apartado 3079, Lima, Peru

THE GILLETTE CO   Prudential Tower, Boston, MA 02199, Tel: (617) 421-7000
(Devel/mfr personal care/use prdts: blades & razors, toiletries, cosmetics, stationery)
   Gillette del Peru SC, Lima, Peru
   Jafra Cosmeticos (Peru) SC, San Isidro, Lima, Peru
   Oral-B Laboratories SA, Peru

THE GOODYEAR TIRE & RUBBER CO   1144 E Market St, Akron, OH 44316,
Tel: (216) 796-2121
(Mfr tires, automotive belts & hose, conveyor belts, chemicals; oil pipeline transmission)
   Compania Goodyear del Peru SA, Av. Republica de Panama 3055, piso 12, San Isidro, Lima 27, Peru

GORTON GROUP   327 Main Street, Gloucester, MA 01930, Tel: (617) 283-3000
(Frozen fish)
   Gloucester Peruvian SA, Av. Nicolas de Pierola 611, Lima, Peru

GREY ADVERTISING INC   777 Third Ave, New York, NY 10017, Tel: (212) 546-2000
(Advertising)
   Grey Peru, Las Camelias 891, San Isidro, Lima 27, Peru

FRANK B HALL & CO INC   549 Pleasantville Rd, Briarcliff Manor, NY 10510,
Tel: (914) 769-9200
(Insurance)
   B.I. David & Cia. Asesores y Corredores de Seguros SA, Jr. Camana 780, Lima 1, Peru

HOLIDAY INNS INC   3742 Lamar Ave, Memphis, TN 38195, Tel: (901) 362-4001
(Hotels, restaurants, casinos)
   Holiday Inn, Av. El Sol 954, Apartado 543, Cusco, Lima, Peru
   Holiday Inn, Apartado 2466, Lima, Peru

HOMESTAKE MINING CO   650 California St, San Francisco, CA 94108,
Tel: (415) 981-8150
(Precious metal & mineral mining)
   Compania Minera del Madrigal, Jiron de la Union 264, Apartado 5979, Lima, Peru

HORWATH INTL   415 Madison Ave, New York, NY 10017, Tel: (212) 838-5566
(Public accountants & auditors)
   Del Bosque Roncal D'Angelo y Asociados, Av. Republica de Chile 376, Lima 11, Peru

J M HUBER CORP   PO Box 277, Rumson, NJ 07760, Tel: (201) 291-1880
(Inks, crude oil, gas, carbon black, kaolin clay, rubber & paper pigments, timber &
minerals)
   Huber del Peru SA, Av. Mariscal Benavides 1225, Apartado 3744, Lima, Peru

HUGHES TOOL CO   PO Box 2539, Houston, TX 77001, Tel: (713) 924-2222
(Equip & serv to oil & gas explor & prod ind)
   Hughes Tool Co., Sucursal del Peru, Paseo de la Republica 2582, Apartado 11288,
   Santa Beatriz, Lima 14, Peru

IBM CORP   Old Orchard Rd, Armonk, NY 10504, Tel: (914) 765-1900
(Information products, technology & services)
   IBM del Peru SA, Camino Real 456, Nibel B. Inda, Lima, Peru

IRECO INC   Crossroads Tower, 11th Fl, Salt Lake City, UT 84144,
Tel: (801) 364-4800
(Mfr explosive supplies, accessories for ind & military applications; aluminum
granules)
   Seminco SA, Av. Separdora Industrial Mz., I Lote 11, Urb. Los Alamos, Lima 3, Peru

ITT CORP   1330 Ave of the Americas, New York, NY 10019-5490,
Tel: (212) 258-1000
(Design/mfr communications & electronic equip, hotels, insurance)
   Fabrica de Equipo de Telefonia SA, Jiron Iquique 191, Brena, Apartado 10309, Lima,
   Peru

ITT SHERATON CORP   60 State St, Boston, MA 02108, Tel: (617) 367-3600
(Hotel operations)
   Lima Sheraton Hotel & Towers, Apartado 588, Lima 1, Peru

JOHNSON & HIGGINS   125 Broad St, New York, NY 10004-2424, Tel: (212) 574-7000
(Ins brokerage, employee benefit conslt, risk mgmt, human resource conslt, ins/reins
servs)
   Consultores de Seguros SA, Nicolas de Rivera 502, San Isidro, Lima 27, Peru

LANMAN & KEMP-BARCLAY & CO   25 Woodland Ave, Westwood, NJ 07675,
Tel: (201) 666-4990
(Mfr pharms, toiletries)
   Lanman & Kemp-Barclay & Co. of Peru, Tacna 751, Apartado 3076, Magdalena del Mar,
   Lima, Peru

ELI LILLY & CO   Lilly Corporate Center, Indianapolis, IN 46285,
Tel: (317) 276-2000
(Mfr pharmaceuticals, animal health prdts)
   Eli Lilly Interamerica Inc., Las Begonias 441, piso 11, San Isidro, Lima 27, Peru

LIQUID CARBONIC INDUSTRIES CORP   810 Jorie Blvd, Oak Brook, IL 60521,
Tel: (708) 572-7500
(Mfr compressed gasses)
   Liquid Carbonic del Peru SA, Av. Venezuela 2597, Bellavista, Callao, Apartado 4057,
   Lima, Peru

LYKES BROS STEAMSHIP CO INC   Lykes Center, 300 Poydras St, New Orleans,
  LA 70130, Tel: (504) 523-6611
  (Ocean frt trans)
    Lykes Lines Agency Inc., Chamber of Commerce Bldg., Miller 450, Apartado 160,
    Callao, Peru

MARCO   2300 W Commodore Way, Seattle, WA 98199, Tel: (206) 285-3200
  (Shipbldg & repair, coml fishing equip & sys, hydraulic pumps)
    Marco Peruana SA, Apartado 01-0415, Callao 1, Peru

MARRIOTT CORP   Marriott Dr, Washington, DC 20058, Tel: (301) 380-9000
  (Lodging, contract food & beverage serv, restaurants)
    Marriott Peru SA, Aeropuerto Intl. Jorge Chavez, Callao, Apartado 60971, Lima, Peru

MERCK SHARP & DOHME INTL   PO Box 2000, Rahway, NJ 07065, Tel: (201) 574-4000
  (Pharms, chems & biologicals)
    Laboratorios Prosalud SA, Urbanizacion Limatambo, Lima, Peru
    Merck, Sharp & Dohme SA, Av. Republica de Panama 3852, Surquillo, Apartado 1231,
    Lima, Peru

MICROSOFT CORP   One Microsoft Way, Redmond, WA 98052-6399,
  Tel: (206) 882-8080
  (Computer software, peripherals & services)
    Microsoft Peru, all mail to Multicento Oficina #403, Av. 6 Dicienbre 4, La Nina,
    Quito, Ecuador

MINE SAFETY APPLIANCES CO   PO Box 426, Pittsburgh, PA 15230,
  Tel: (421) 273 5000
  (Safety equip, ind filters)
    MSA del Peru SA, Apartado 5809, Lima 100, Peru

MOBIL CORP   3225 Gallows Rd, Fairfax, VA 22037-0001, Tel: (703) 846-3000
  (Petroleum explor & refining, mfr petrol prdts, chems, petrochems)
    Mobil Oil del Peru (Compania Commercial) SA, Apartado 1272, Lima 100, Peru

McCANN-ERICKSON WORLDWIDE   750 Third Ave, New York, NY 10017,
  Tel: (212) 697-6000
  (Advertising)
    McCann-Erickson Corp. Publicidad SA, Calle Tripoli 102, Miraflores,
    Apartado 180368, Lima 18, Peru

NATIONAL CAR RENTAL SYSTEM INC   7700 France Ave S, Minneapolis, MN 55435,
  Tel: (612) 830-2121
  (Car rental)
    Natl. Car Rental System Inc., Av. Garcilaso de la Vega 1287, Apartado 10351,
    Lima 1, Peru

NEWMONT GOLD CORP   1700 Lincoln St, Denver, CO 80203, Tel: (303) 863-7414
  (Gold mining)
    Minera Yanacocha SA, Av. Camino Real 348, Torre El Pilar, Of. 1004, Lima 27, Peru

NORTON CO   1 New Bond St, Worcester, MA 01606, Tel: (508) 795-5000
  (Abrasives, drill bits, constr & safety prdts, plastics)
    Boyles Bros. Diamantina SA, Apartado 5166, Lima, Peru
    Christensen Diamond Products del Peru SA, Apartado 5788, Lima, Peru
    Geotec SA, Calle Uno 416, Urbaniz. Corpac, Lima, Peru

OCCIDENTAL PETROLEUM CORP   10889 Wilshire Blvd, Los Angeles, CA 90024,
  Tel: (213) 879-1700
  (Petroleum & petroleum prdts, chems, plastics)
    Occidental Petroleum Corp. of Peru, Los Nardos 1018, San Isidro, Lima 27, Peru

PARKER DRILLING CO   8 E Third St, Tulsa, OK 74103-3637, Tel: (918) 585-8221
  (Drilling contractor)
    Parker Drilling Co. of Oklahoma Inc., Sucursal del Peru,
      Paseo de la Republica 3557, Piso 3, San Isidro, Lima, Peru
    Parker Drilling Co. of Oklahoma Inc., Sucursal del Peru, Casilla 355, Iquitos, Peru

PFIZER INC   235 E 42nd St, New York, NY 10017-5755, Tel: (212) 573-2323
  (Mfr healthcare products)
    Corporacion Farmaceutica SA (COFASA), Peru

PHELPS DODGE CORP   2600 N Central Ave, Phoenix, AZ 85004-3014,
  Tel: (602) 234-8100
  (Copper, minerals, metals & spec engineered prdts for trans & elect mkts)
    Southern Peru Copper Corp., Toquepala, Peru

PHILLIPS PETROLEUM CO   Phillips Bldg, Bartlesville, OK 74004,
  Tel: (918) 661-6600
  (Crude oil, natural gas, liquefied petroleum gas, gasoline & petro-chems)
    Phillips Petrochemical Sales Inc., Las Magnolias 791, San Isidro, Apartado 2876,
      Lima, Peru

PROCTER & GAMBLE CO   One Procter & Gamble Plaza, Cincinnati, OH 45202,
  Tel: (513) 983-1100
  (Personal care, food, laundry, cleaning & ind prdts)
    Deterperu SA, Lino Alarco 270, 4 piso, Miraflores, Apartado 3848, Lima, Peru

RJR NABISCO INC   1301 Ave of the Americas, New York, NY 10019,
  Tel: (212) 258-5600
  (Mfr consumer packaged food prdts & tobacco prdts)
    F & R Peru SA, Calle Daniel Olaechea 273, Lima, Peru

ROHM AND HAAS CO   100 Independence Mall West, Philadelphia, PA 19106,
  Tel: (215) 592-3000
  (Mfr ind & agric chems, plastics)
    Rohm and Haas Peru, Richard O. Custer SA, Av. Bolivar 2100, Pueblo Libre,
      Casilla 681, Lima, Peru

SYDNEY ROSS CO   90 Park Ave, New York, NY 10016, Tel: (212) 907-2000
  (Pharms, toiletries & cosmetics)
    Sydney Ross SA, Av. Republica de Panama 4825, Surquillo, Apartado 1454, Lima, Peru

SCHERING INTL   PO Box 500, Kenilworth, NJ 07033, Tel: (201) 558-4000
  (Pharms, medicines, toiletries, cosmetics, human & animal health prdts)
    Schering Corp. del Peru SA, Augusto Tamayo 154, San Isidro, Apartado 2130, Lima,
      Peru

SEARS ROEBUCK & CO   Sears Tower, Chicago, IL 60684, Tel: (312) 875-2500
  (Diversified general merchandise)
    Sears, Roebuck del Peru SA, Paseo de la Republica 3220, San Isidro, Apartado 567,
      Lima, Peru

STOKES DIV 5500 Tabor Rd, Philadelphia, PA 19120, Tel: (215) 289-5671
(Vacuum pumps & components, vacuum dryers, oil-upgrading equip)
Centrifugas Peruanas SA, Apartado 1729, Lima, Peru

SULLAIR CORP 3700 E Michigan Blvd, Michigan City, IN 46360,
Tel: (219) 879-5451
(Refrigeration sys, vacuum pumps, generators, etc)
Sullair del Pacifico, Av. Pershing 908, Magdalena, Lima, Peru

TEXACO INC 2000 Westchester Ave, White Plains, NY 10650, Tel: (914) 253-4000
(Explor/mktg crude oil, mfr petro chems & prdts)
Texas Petroleum Co., Apartado 2906, San Isidro, Lima, Peru

UNION CARBIDE CORP 39 Old Ridgebury Rd, Danbury, CT 06817,
Tel: (203) 794-2000
(Mfr industrial chemicals, plastics, resins)
Union Carbide Inter-America Inc., Av. La Paz 1417, Miraflores 18, Peru

UPJOHN CO 7000 Portage Rd, Kalamazoo, MI 49001, Tel: (616) 323-4000
(Mfr pharms, agric prdts, ind chems)
Upjohn Inter-American Corp., Natalio Sanchez 220-1202, Apartado 4825, Lima, Peru

WACKENHUT CORP 1500 San Remo Ave, Coral Gables, FL 33146,
Tel: (305) 666-5656
(Security systems & services)
Peruana de Seguridad y Vigilancia SA (PESEVISA), Av. Arequipa 4856, Lima 18, Peru

WARNER-LAMBERT CO 201 Tabor Road, Morris Plains, NJ 07950,
Tel: (201) 540-2000
(Mfr ethical & proprietary pharms, confectionary & consumer prdts)
Laboratorios Promaceo SA, Apartado 3527, Lima, Peru
Labs Indufarma SA, Apartado 800, Lima, Peru

WESTERN ATLAS INTL INC 10205 Westheimer, PO Box 1407, Houston,
TX 77251-1407, Tel: (713) 266-5700
(Full service to the oil industry)
Western Atlas Intl. Inc., Sucursal del Peru, Av. Carlos Villaran 508, Ofic. 302,
Urbanizacion Santa Catalina-La Victoria, Lima 13, Peru

WORLD COURIER INC 46 Trinity Pl, New York, NY 10006, Tel: (718) 978-9400
(Intl courier serv)
World Courier del Peru SA, Av. Jose Pardo 231, Oficina 601, Miraflores, Lima, Peru

XEROX CORP 800 Long Ridge Rd, PO Box 1600, Stamford, CT 06904,
Tel: (203) 968-3000
(Mfr document processing equip, sys & supplies)
Xerox Corp., Lima, Peru

PHILIPPINES

3M   3M Center, St Paul, MN 55144-1000, Tel: (612) 733-1110
(Mfr diversified prdts for industry, health care, imaging, commun, transport, safety, consumer, etc)
  3M Philippines Inc., PCI Bank Tower 2, 18th fl., Makati Ave., Makati 1200, Metro Manila, Philippines

AIR EXPRESS INTL CORP   120 Tokeneke Rd, PO Box 1231, Darien, CT 06820,
Tel: (203) 655-7900
(Air frt forwarder)
  Air Express Intl. Philippines Inc., Corner Domestic Rd., MIA Mobil Compound, Pasay City, Metro Manila, Philippines

AMERICAN AIRLINES INC   PO Box 619616, Dallas-Ft Worth Arpt, TX 75261-9616,
Tel: (817) 355-1234
(Air transp)
  American Airlines Inc., P.O. Box 4297, Manila, Philippines

AMERICAN INTL GROUP INC   70 Pine St, New York, NY 10270, Tel: (212) 770-7000
(Insurance, financial services)
  Philippine American Accident Insurance Co. Inc., United Nations Ave., Manila, Philippines
  Philippine American Life Insurance Co., United Nations Ave., Manila, Philippines

AMERICAN PRESIDENT LINES LTD   1111 Broadway, Oakland, CA 94607,
Tel: (415) 272-8000
(Intermodal shipping serv)
  American President Lines Ltd., P.O. Box 7592 ACD NAIA, Pasay City 1300, Philippines

AMERICAN STANDARD INC   1 Centennial Ave, Piscataway, NJ 08855,
Tel: (908) 980-3000
(Mfr heating & sanitary equip)
  Sanitary Wares Mfg. Corp., P.O. Box 499, Makati, Metro Manila, Philippines

AMP INC   PO Box 3608, Harrisburg, PA 17105-3608, Tel: (717) 564-0100
(Devel/mfr electronic & electrical connection prdts & sys)
  AMP Philippines Inc., Manila, Philippines

ASSOCIATED MERCHANDISING CORP   1440 Broadway, New York, NY 10018,
Tel: (212) 536-4000
(Retail service organization)
  Associated Merchandising Corp., P.O. Box 7323, Airmail Distribution Center, Naia, Pasay City, 1300 Philippines

AVIS INC   900 Old Country Rd, Garden City, NY 11530, Tel: (516) 222-3000
(Car rental serv)
  Avis Rental Office, 311 P. Casal St., Manila, Philippines

AVON PRODUCTS INC   9 W 57th St, New York, NY 10019, Tel: (212) 546-6015
(Mfr/distr beauty & related prdts, fashion jewelry, gifts & collectibles)
  Avon Pacific Inc., Fortune Bldg., 160 Legaspi St., Legaspi Village, Makati,
    Metro Manila, Philippines

THE BANK OF CALIFORNIA NA   400 California St, San Francisco, CA 94104,
  Tel: (415) 765-0400
(Banking)
  Manila Offshore Banking Unit, Corinthian Plaza Condominium, 121 Paseo de Roxas,
    Makati, Metro Manila, Philippines

BANKAMERICA CORP   555 California St, San Francisco, CA 94104,
  Tel: (415) 622-3456
(Financial services)
  Bank of America NT & SA, BA Lepanto Bldg. 2/F, 8747 Paseo de Roxas, P.O. Box 1767,
    Makati, Metro Manila, Philippines

BANKERS TRUST CO   280 Park Ave, New York, NY 10017, Tel: (212) 250-2500
(Banking)
  Bankers Trust Co., P.O. Box 341, Makati Commercial Center, Makati, Metro Manila,
    Philippines

BAUSCH & LOMB INC   1 Chase Square, Rochester, NY 14601, Tel: (716) 338-6000
(Mfr vision care prdts & accessories)
  Bausch & Lomb Intl. Inc., Manila, Philippines

BEAR STEARNS & CO INC   245 Park Ave, New York, NY 10167, Tel: (212) 272-2000
(Investment banking)
  Bear Stearns Philippines Ltd., Greenbelt Mansion, 106 Perea St., Legaspi Village,
    Makati, Metro Manila, Philippines
  Bear Stearns State Asia Inc., Greenbelt Mansion, 106 Perea St., Legaspi Village,
    Makati, Metro Manila, Philippines

BECHTEL GROUP INC   50 Beale St, PO Box 3965, San Francisco, CA 94119,
  Tel: (415) 768-1234
(Engineering & constr)
  Bechtel Overseas Corp., FNCB Bldg., Paseo de Roxas, Makati, Rizal, Manila,
    Philippines

LOUIS BERGER INTL INC   100 Halsted St, East Orange, NJ 07019,
  Tel: (201) 678-1960
(Consulting engineers, architects, economists & planners)
  Louis Berger Intl. Inc., P.O. Box 1262, MCPO, 1252 Makati, Metro Manila, Philippines

BORDEN INC   180 E Broad St, Columbus, OH 43215-3799, Tel: (614) 225-4000
(Mfr foods, snacks & beverages, adhesives)
  Borden Inc., all mail to U.S. address

BRANSON ULTRASONICS CORP   41 Eagle Rd, Danbury, CT 06813-1961,
  Tel: (203) 796-0400
(Mfr plastics assembly equip, ultrasonic cleaning equip)
  Mesco, Reliance corner Brixton St., P.O. Box 468, Pasig, Metro Manila, Philippines

LEO BURNETT CO INC　　35 West Wacker Dr, Chicago, IL　60601, Tel: (312) 220-5959
(Advertising agency)
　　Hemisphere-Leo Burnett Inc., Planters Products Inc. Bldg., Esteban St.,
　　Legaspi Village, Makati, Metro Manila, Philippines

CALTEX PETROLEUM CORP　　PO Box 619500, Dallas, TX　75261, Tel: (214) 830-1000
(Petroleum prdts)
　　Caltex (Philippines) Inc., 540 P. Faura St., Ermita, Manila, Philippines
　　Caltex Batangas Refinery, San Pascual, Batangas 4204, Philippines

CARBOLINE CO　　350 Hanley Industrial Ct, St Louis, MO　63144,
　Tel: (314) 644-1000
(Mfr coatings, sealants)
　　Technoline Corp., Room 512, SMS Bldg., 213 Sen. Gil J. Puyat Ave., Makati,
　　Metro Manila, Philippines

CBI INDUSTRIES INC　　800 Jorie Blvd, Oak Brook, IL　60521, Tel: (708) 654-7000
(Holding co: metal plate fabricating, constr, oil & gas drilling)
　　CBI Philippines Inc., G&A Bldg., 3rd Fl., Metro Manila, Philippines

CDM INTL INC　　Ten Cambridge Center, Cambridge, MA　02142, Tel: (617) 252-8000
(Consulting engineers)
　　Camp Dresser & McKee Intl. Inc., PWA Bldg.,
　　Katipunan & Shuster Rds. Balara Diliman, Quezon City, Philippines

CENTRAL NATIONAL-GOTTESMAN INC　　3 Manhattanville Rd, Purchase,
　NY　10577-2110, Tel: (914) 696-9000
(Worldwide sales pulp & paper prdts)
　　Central National (Philippines) Inc., Exec. Suite 221, Nikko Manila Garden Hotel,
　　Makati Com'l Center, Makati, Metro Manila, Philippines

CHASE MANHATTAN BANK N A　　1 Chase Manhattan Plaza, New York, NY　10081,
　Tel: (212) 552-2222
(Intl banking)
　　Chase Manhattan Bank N.A., P.O. Box 1399, Filinvest Financial Center,
　　Paseo de Roxas, Makati, Metro Manila, Philippines
　　Philippine American Investments Corp. (PAIC), PAIC Bldg., 105 Paseo de Roxas,
　　Manila, Philippines

CHEMICAL BANK　　270 Park Ave, New York, NY　10017-2070, Tel: (212) 270-6000
(Banking & financial services)
　　Chemical Bank, Corinthian Plaza, 121 Paseo de Roxas, Makati, Metro Manila,
　　Philippines

CHEVRON CORP　　225 Bush St, San Francisco, CA　94104, Tel: (415) 894-7700
(Oil & gas exploration, production, refining, products; oilfield & financial services)
　　Chevron Corp., all mail to U.S. address

CHIQUITA BRANDS INTL INC　　250 E Fifth St, Cincinnati, OH　45202,
　Tel: (513) 784-8000
(Distribution food products)
　　Mindanao Fruit Co., P.O. Box 301, Davao City, Philippines

CIGNA CORP   One Liberty Place, Philadelphia, PA 19192, Tel: (215) 523-4000
(Ins, invest, health care & other fin servs)
   Insurance Co. of North America, Afia Monarch Bldg., Legaspi Village, Makati,
     Metro-Manila, Philippines

CITICORP   399 Park Ave, New York, NY 10043, Tel: (212) 559-1000
(Banking & financial services)
   Citibank, Philippines

THE COCA-COLA CO   PO Drawer 1734, Atlanta, GA 30301, Tel: (404) 676-2121
(Mfr/mkt/distr soft drinks, syrups & concentrates, juice & juice-drink prdts)
   Coca-Cola Philippines, all mail to U.S. address

COLGATE-PALMOLIVE CO   300 Park Ave, New York, NY 10022, Tel: (212) 310-2000
(Mfr pharms, cosmetics, toiletries, detergents)
   Colgate Palmolive Philippines Inc., 1049 J.P. Rizal Ave., Makati, Metro Manila,
     Philippines

COLUMBIA PICTURES INDUSTRIES INC   711 Fifth Ave, New York, NY 10022,
Tel: (212) 751-4400
(Producer & distributor of motion pictures)
   Columbia Pictures Industries Inc., Rm. 307-308 Philippines President Lines Bldg.,
     1000 United Nations Ave., Manila, Philippines

COLUMBIAN ROPE CO   PO Box 270, Guntown, MS 38849-0270, Tel: (601) 348-2241
(Mfr rope, twine & ind fiber prdts)
   Columbian Philippines Inc., P.O. Box 7501, Airmail Exchange Office,
     Manila Intl. Airport 3120, Philippines
   TCG Fibers Philippines Inc., P.O. Box 162, Sasa, Davao City 9501, Philippines

COMBUSTION ENGINEERING INC   900 Long Ridge Road, Stamford, CT 06902,
Tel: (203) 329-8771
(Tech constr)
   Gray Tool Intl. Inc., c/o Wammco Philippines Co. Ltd., 235 Salcedost,
     Legaspi Village, Makati, Metro Manila, Philippines

COMPUTER ASSOCIATES INTL INC   One Computer Associates Plaza, Islandia,
NY 11788, Tel: (516) 342-5224
(Devel/mkt/mgt info mgt & bus applications software)
   Philippine Computer Associates Intl. Inc., Pacific Star Bldg.,
     Sen. Gil J Puyat Ave., Cor. Makati Ave., Metro Manila, Philippines

CORESTATES FINANCIAL CORP   1500 Market St, Philadelphia, PA 19101,
Tel: (215) 973-3100
(Banking)
   Corestates Bank, 2 PCI Bank Tower 12/F, Makati Ave., Makati, Metro Manila,
     Philippines

CPC INTERNATIONAL INC   PO Box 8000, Englewood Cliffs, NJ 07632,
Tel: (201) 894-4000
(Consumer foods, corn refining)
   California Mfg. Co. Inc., P.O. Box 7149, Airmail Exchange Office,
     Ninoy Aquino Intl. Airport 1399, Philippines

D-M-E COMPANY   29111 Stephenson Highway, Madison Heights, MI 48071,
  Tel: (313) 398-6000
  (Basic tooling for plastic molding & die casting)
    Mesco, P.O. Box 468 MCC, Makati, Metro Manila 3117, Philippines

DAMES & MOORE   911 Wilshire Blvd, Los Angeles, CA 90017, Tel: (213) 683-1560
  (Engineering, environmental & construction mgmt services)
    Dames & Moore, Adamson Center Bldg., Suite A, 5/F, 121 Alfaro St., Salcedo Vlg.,
      Makati, Metro Manila, Philippines

DANIEL MANN JOHNSON & MENDENHALL   3250 Wilshire Blvd, Los Angeles, CA 90010,
  Tel: (213) 381-3663
  (Architects & engineers)
    DMJM Far East Inc., 4/5 Raha Sulayman Bldg., 108 Benavidez St., Makati,
      Metro Manila, Philippines
    DMJM Far East Inc., Katipunan Bldg. 3/F, 95 E. Rodriguez Sr. Ave., Quezon City,
      Metro Manila, Philippines

DEL MONTE FOODS   PO Box 93575, San Francisco, CA 94119-3575,
  Tel: (415) 442-4000
  (Food processor)
    Del Monte Philippines Inc., Citibank Center, 8741 Paseo de Roxas, Makati,
      Metro Manila, Philippines

DEVELOPMENT ASSOCIATES INC   1730 N Lynn St, Arlington, VA 22209-2023,
  Tel: (703) 276-0677
  (Mgt consulting servs)
    Development Associates Inc., 3/F Filipino Merchant Bldg., 135 Del Rosa St.,
      Legaspi Village, Makat, Metro Manila, Philippines

DIGITAL EQUIPMENT CORP   146 Main St, Maynard, MA 01754-2571,
  Tel: (508) 493-5111
  (Networked computer systems & services)
    Digital Equipment Filipinas Inc., 41 Constellation St., Bel Air, Manila, Philippines

DOW CORNING CORP   2220 W Salzburg Rd, PO Box 1767, Midland, MI 48640,
  Tel: (517) 496-4000
  (Silicones, silicon chems, solid lubricants)
    Dow Corning Asia Ltd., Filinvest Financial Center, 8753 Paseo de Roxas, Makati,
      Metro Manila, Philippines

DRAVO CORP   1 Oliver Plaza, Pittsburgh, PA 15222, Tel: (412) 777-5000
  (Material handling equip, process plants)
    Dravo Corp., Air Mail Distribution Center, International Airport, P.O. Box 7570,
      Manila 3120, Philippines

EAGLE ELECTRIC MFG CO INC   45-31 Court Sq, Long Island City, NY 11101,
  Tel: (718) 937-8000
  (Mfr electrical wiring devices & switchgear)
    Eagle Electric of the Philippines, P.O. Box 1519, Manila, Philippines

EASTMAN KODAK CO   343 State St, Rochester, NY 14650, Tel: (716) 724-4000
  (Devel/mfr photo & chem prdts, info mgmt/video/copier sys, fibers/plastics for
  various ind)
    Kodak Philippines Ltd., P.O. Box 620, Commercial Center, Makati Rizal 3117,
      Philippines

EATON CORP 1111 Superior Ave, Cleveland, OH 44114, Tel: (216) 523-5000
(Advanced tech prdts for transp & ind mkts)
Asiaphll Cutler-Hammer Inc., 1150 Pres Quirino Ave., Paco, Manila, Philippines

EBASCO SERVICES INC 2 World Trade Center, New York, NY 10048-0752,
Tel: (212) 839-1000
(Engineering, constr)
Ebasco Services Intl. Inc., Belson House 2/F, 271-E De Los Santos Ave. (EDSA),
Mandalvyong, Metro Manila, Philippines

EG&G INC 45 William St, Wellesley, MA 02181-4078, Tel: (617) 237-5100
(Diversified R/D, mfg & services)
EG&G Vactec Philippines, Light Industry & Science Park, 3 Ampere St., Cabuyao,
Laguna 4205, Philippines

ENCYCLOPAEDIA BRITANNICA INC 310 S Michigan Ave, Chicago, IL 60604,
Tel: (312) 321-7000
(Publishing)
Encyclopaedia Britannica Philippines, 7/f Kings Court I Bldg.,
2129 Chino Roces Ave., Makati City, Philippines

ENDO LABORATORIES INC 1000 Stewart Ave, Garden City, NY 11530,
Tel: (516) 832-2002
(Ethical pharms)
Endo Labs Philippines, P.O. Box 2150, Makati, Rizal, Philippines

EXPEDITORS INTL OF WASHINGTON INC PO Box 69620, Seattle, WA 98168-9620,
Tel: (206) 246-3711
(Air/ocean freight forwarding, customs brokerage, intl logistics solutions)
Expeditors Intl. Philippines Inc., Pascor Dr., Pascor Bldg. 3,
Sto. Nino Paranaque 1700, Metro Manila, Philippines

FIRST BRANDS CORP 83 Wooster Heights Rd, Danbury, CT 06813-1911,
Tel: (203) 731-2300
(Mfr automotive products, plastic wrap & bags, pet prdts)
First Brands Philippines, 622 Shaw Blvd. cor. Samat St., Mandaluyong, Metro Manila,
Philippines

FIRST NATIONAL BANK OF BOSTON 100 Federal St, Boston, MA 02110,
Tel: (617) 434-2200
(Commercial banking)
First Natl. Bank of Boston, Solidbank Bldg., 777 Paseo de Roxas, P.O. Box 1180,
Makati, Metro Manila, Philippines

FIRST NATIONAL BANK OF CHICAGO One First National Plaza, Chicago, IL 60670,
Tel: (312) 732-4000
(Financial services)
The First Natl. Bank of Chicago, Solidbank Bldg., P.O. Box 2146,
777 Paseo de Roxas, Makat, Manila, Philippines

FLUOR DANIEL INC 3333 Michelson Dr, Irvine, CA 92730, Tel: (714) 975-2000
(Engineering, construction, maintenance & technical services)
Fluor Daniel/AG&P Inc., 9th Fl., Pacific Star Bldg., Makati Ave., Makati Metro,
Manila, Philippines

FMC CORP   200 E Randolph Dr, Chicago, IL 60601, Tel: (312) 861-6000
  (Produces chems & precious metals, mfr machinery, equip & sys for ind, agric & govt)
    FMC Intl. SA, P.O. Box 7080 ACD, Metro Manila, Philippines
    Marine Colloids (Philippines) Inc., Philippines

FOOTE CONE & BELDING COMMUNICATIONS INC   101 E Erie St, Chicago,
  IL 60611-2897, Tel: (312) 751-7000
  (Advertising agency)
    Basic/Foote, Cone & Belding, Zaragoza Bldg., 102 Gamboa, Legaspi Village Makati,
      Metro Manila, Philippines
    Park/Adformatix Inc., Arco Bldg., 196 Salcedo, Legaspi Village Makati,
      Metro Manila, Philippines

FOUR WINDS INTL GROUP   1500 SW First Ave, #850, Portland, OR 97201,
  Tel: (503) 241-2732
  (Transp of household goods & general cargo, third party logistics)
    Four Winds Philippines, 2241 Pasong Tamo, Makati, Metro Manila, Philippines

FOWNES BROTHERS & CO INC   411 Fifth Ave, New York, NY 10016,
  Tel: (212) 683-0150
  (Dress & sport gloves)
    Phil Gloves Inc., P.O. Box 2348, Makati, Metro Manila, Philippines

FRITZ COMPANIES INC   706 Mission St, San Francisco, CA 94103,
  Tel: (415) 904-8360
  (Integrated transportation, sourcing, distribution & customs brokerage services)
    FTI (Philippines) Inc., Oyster Industrial Complex, Ninoy Aquino Ave., Paranque,
      Metro Manila, Philippines
    Fritz Airfreight (Philippines) Inc., Oyster Industrial Complex, Ninoy Aquino Ave.,
      Paranaque, Metro Manila, Philippines

GENERAL ELECTRIC CO   3135 Easton Tpk, Fairfield, CT 06431,
  Tel: (203) 373-2211
  (Diversified manufacturing, technology & services)
    General Electric Co.,
      all mail to U.S. address; phone (800) 626-2004 or (518) 438-6500

GENERAL FOODS CORP   250 North St, White Plains, NY 10625, Tel: (914) 335-2500
  (Processor, distributor & mfr of foods)
    General Foods Philippines Inc., Km. 16 Severina Ind. Compound, South Super Hwy.,
      Paranagua, Metro Manila, Philippines

GENERAL MOTORS CORP   3044 W Grand Blvd, Detroit, MI 48202-3091,
  Tel: (313) 556-5000
  (Mfr full line vehicles, automotive electronics, coml technologies, telecom, space,
  finance)
    General Motors Philippines Inc., P.O. Box 7061, Airmail Exchange Office,
      Manila Intl. Airport 3120, Philippines

GETZ BROS & CO INC   150 Post St, #500, San Francisco, CA 94108,
  Tel: (415) 772-5500
  (Divers mfg, mktg/distr serv, travel serv)
    Getz Bros. Philippines Inc., P.O. Box 421, MCPO Makati, Metro Manila, Philippines

THE GILLETTE CO   Prudential Tower, Boston, MA 02199, Tel: (617) 421-7000
(Devel/mfr personal care/use prdts: blades & razors, toiletries, cosmetics, stationery)
 Gillette (Philippines) Inc., Metro Manila, Philippines
 Oral-B Laboratories (Philippines) Inc., Metro Manila, Philippines

GLOBAL INTERNATIONAL   1304 Willow St, Martinez, CA 94553, Tel: (510) 229-9330
(International moving & forwarding)
 Global International, 147 Yakal St., P.O. Box 7143, Makati, Metro Manila, Philippines

THE GOODYEAR TIRE & RUBBER CO   1144 E Market St, Akron, OH 44316,
Tel: (216) 796-2121
(Mfr tires, automotive belts & hose, conveyor belts, chemicals; oil pipeline transmission)
 Goodyear Philippines Inc., 790 Pasay Rd., Makati, Metro Manila, Philippines

GOULDS PUMPS INC   240 Fall St, Seneca Falls, NY 13148, Tel: (315) 568-2811
(Mfr ind & water sys pumps)
 Goulds Pumps Philippines Inc., Natividad 1 Bldg., 2308 Pasong Tamo Ext., Makati, Metro Manila, Philippines

W R GRACE & CO   One Town Center Rd, Boca Raton, FL 33486-1010,
Tel: (407) 362-2000
(Mfr spec chems & materials: packaging, health care, catalysts, construction, water treatment/process)
 W.R. Grace (Philippines) Inc., P.O. Box 7249, Domestic Airport PO Lock Box, Pasay City 1300, Philippines

GREFCO INC   3435 W Lomita Blvd, Torrance, CA 90505, Tel: (213) 517-0700
(Filter powders)
 Induplex Inc., DCG Bldg., 167 Le Gaspi St., Makati, Metro Manila, Philippines

GREY ADVERTISING INC   777 Third Ave, New York, NY 10017, Tel: (212) 546-2000
(Advertising)
 Campaigns & Grey, 12/F Valero, Valero St., Salcedo Village, Makati, Metro Manila, Philippines

GRIFFITH LABORATORIES INC   I Griffith Center, Alsip, IL 60658,
Tel: (708) 371-0900
(Ind food ingredients & equip)
 Griffith Labs (Philippines) Inc., P.O. Box 1908 MCC, Makati, Metro Manila, Philippines

GTE CORP   One Stamford Forum, Stamford, CT 06904, Tel: (203) 965-2000
(Electr prdts, telecom sys, publ & commun)
 Asia-Pacific Telecommunications, MCCPO Box 1747, Makati, Manila, Philippines
 Sylvania Div., 45 Libertad St., Mandaluyong, Rizal, Manila, Philippines

GTE DIRECTORIES CORP   West Airport Dr, DFW Airport, TX 75261-9810,
Tel: (214) 453-7000
(Pub telephone directories)
 GTE Directories Corp., Majalco Bldg., Trasierra cor. Benavides St., P.O. Box 513, Makati, Metro Manila, Philippines
 GTE Directories Corp., Metro Bank Bldg., G. Payat Ave., Makati, Metro Manila, Philippines

FRANK B HALL & CO INC   549 Pleasantville Rd, Briarcliff Manor, NY 10510,
  Tel: (914) 769-9200
  (Insurance)
    Anscor Insurance Brokers Inc., A. Soriano Bldg., Paseo de Roxas, P.O. Box 319,
    Makati, Metro Manila, Philippines

HAMBRECHT & QUIST   One Bush St, San Francisco, CA 94104, Tel: (415) 576-3300
  (Invest banking & venture capital serv)
    H&Q Philippines Inc., Corinthian Plaza, Paseo de Roxas, Legaspi Village, Makati,
    Metro Manila, Philippines

THE HARPER GROUP   260 Townsend St, PO Box 77933, San Francisco,
  CA 94107-1719, Tel: (415) 978-0600
  (Ocean/air freight fwdg, customs brokerage, packing & whse, logistics mgt, ins)
    Circle Freight Intl. (Philippines) Ltd., CFIP Bldg.,
      Corner Pascor Dr. & Johann St., Ninoy Aquino Ave., Paranque, Metro Manila,
      Philippines
    Circle Freight Intl. (Philippines) Ltd., also in Bataan, Cagayan de Oro, Cavite,
      Cebu & Legaspi, Philippines
    Gus Banks Training Center, CFIP Bldg., Corner Pascor Dr. & Johann St.,
      Ninoy Aquino Ave., Paranque, Metro Manila, Philippines

HEWLETT-PACKARD CO   3000 Hanover St, Palo Alto, CA 94304-0890,
  Tel: (415) 857-1501
  (Mfr computing, communications & measurement prdts & services)
    HP Philippines, Rufina Pacific Tower 9/F, 6784 Ayala Ave., Makati, Metro Manila,
    Philippines

HOLIDAY INNS INC   3742 Lamar Ave, Memphis, TN 38195, Tel: (901) 362-4001
  (Hotels, restaurants, casinos)
    Holiday Inn, Roxas Blvd., Manila, Philippines

HORWATH INTL   415 Madison Ave, New York, NY 10017, Tel: (212) 838-5566
  (Public accountants & auditors)
    Alas & Co., 2nd Fl. Priscilla Bldg., 2278 Pasong Tamo Extension Makati,
    Meto Manila, Philippines

HYATT INTL CORP   200 West Madison, Chicago, IL 60606, Tel: (312) 750-1234
  (Intl hotel mgmt)
    Hyatt Intl. Hotels, Manila, Philippines

IBM CORP   Old Orchard Rd, Armonk, NY 10504, Tel: (914) 765-1900
  (Information products, technology & services)
    IBM Philippines Inc., Manila, Philippines

ICS INTERNATIONAL INC   125 Oak St, Scranton, PA 18515, Tel: (717) 342-7701
  (Correspondence courses)
    I.C.S. Philippines, 203 Alcco Bldg., Greenhills, San Juan 1502, Metro Manila,
    Philippines

INGERSOLL-RAND CO   200 Chestnut Ridge Rd, Woodcliff Lake, NJ 07675,
  Tel: (201) 573-0123
  (Mfr compressors, rock drills, pumps, air tools, door hardware, ball bearings)
    Ingersoll-Rand Philippines Inc., 2300 Pasong Tamo Ext. 1231, Makati, Metro Manila,
    Phillipines

INTERNATIONAL PAPER   2 Manhattanville Rd, Purchase, NY 10577,
   Tel: (914) 397-1500
   (Mfr/distr container board, paper, wood prdts)
      Paper Industries Corp., P.O. Box 502, Makati Central P.O., Makati, Metro Manila,
      Philippines

ITT SHERATON CORP   60 State St, Boston, MA 02108, Tel: (617) 367-3600
   (Hotel operations)
      Century Park Sheraton Manila, P.O. Box 117, Manila, Philippines

JOHNSON & HIGGINS   125 Broad St, New York, NY 10004-2424, Tel: (212) 574-7000
   (Ins brokerage, employee benefit conslt, risk mgmt, human resource conslt, ins/reins
   servs)
      H.I. Group-Johnson & Higgins Philippines Inc., Manila, Philippines

JOHNSON & JOHNSON   One Johnson & Johnson Plaza, New Brunswick, NJ 08933,
   Tel: (908) 524-0400
   (R&D/mfr/sale health care prdts)
      Janssen Pharmaceutica, P.O. Box 12981, Pasig, Metro Manila, Philippines
      Johnson & Johnson Philippines, Inc., MCCPO Box 2007, Makati, Metro Manila,
      Philippines

S C JOHNSON & SON INC   1525 Howe St, Racine, WI 53403, Tel: (414) 631-2000
   (Home, auto, commercial & personal care prdts, specialty chems)
      S.C. Johnson & Sons Inc., MCCPO Box 505, Makati, Metro Manila, Philippines

KEYSTONE INTL INC   PO Box 40010, Houston, TX 77040, Tel: (713) 466-1176
   (Mfr butterfly valves, actuators & control accessories)
      Keystone Philippines, Philippines

KIMBERLY-CLARK CORP   PO Box 619100, Dallas, TX 75261, Tel: (214) 281-1200
   (Mfr fiber-based prdts for personal care, lumber & paper prdts)
      Kimberly-Clark Philippines Inc., P.O. Box 451, Makati, Metro Manila, Philippines

KRAFT INC   Kraft Court, Glenview, IL 60025, Tel: (708) 998-2000
   (Dairy prdts, processed food, chems)
      Kraft Foods Inc., P.O. Box 7411, Airmail Exchange Office,
         Manila Intl. Airport 3120, Philippines
      Kraft Foods Inc., Dr. A. Santos Ave., Paranaque, Metro Manila 3128, Philippines

L&F PRODUCTS   225 Summit Ave, Montvale, NJ 07645-1575, Tel: (201) 573-5700
   (Mfr household, personal care, woodworking & ind prdts)
      L&F Products Philippines, 74 Epifanio de los Santos Ave., Mandaluyong,
      Metro Manila 3119, Philippines

LEVI STRAUSS & CO   1155 Battery, San Francisco, CA 94111, Tel: (415) 544-6000
   (Mfr casual wearing apparel)
      Levi Strauss Philippines Inc., 2264 Pasong Tamo Ext., Makati, Metro Manila,
      Philippines

ELI LILLY & CO   Lilly Corporate Center, Indianapolis, IN 46285,
   Tel: (317) 276-2000
   (Mfr pharmaceuticals, animal health prdts)
      Eli Lilly (Philippines) Inc., Galleria Corporate Center 18/F, Robinsons Galleria,
      EDSA cor. Ortigas Ave., Quezon City, Philippines

LINCOLN NATIONAL LIFE REINSURANCE   PO Box 7808, Ft Wayne, IN 46801,
  Tel: (219) 455-2000
  (Reinsurance)
    Lincoln Natl. Life Reinsurance, MCCPO Box 1340, Makati, Metro Manila 3117,
    Philippines

LINTAS:WORLDWIDE   1 Dag Hammarskjold Plaza, New York, NY 10017,
  Tel: (212) 605-8000
  (Advertising agency)
    Lintas: Manila, Producers Bank Centre 12/14F, 8737 Paseo de Roxas, Makati,
    Metro Manila, Philippines

LONGYEAR CO   PO Box 27314, Salt Lake City, UT 84127, Tel: (801) 972-1395
  (Mfr diamond drills, concrete cutting equip; drill serv)
    Long Year Co., P.O. Box 308, 7232 Malugay St., Makati, Rizal, Manila 3117,
    Philippines

R H MACY & CO INC   151 West 34th St, New York, NY 10001, Tel: (212) 695-4400
  (Department stores, importers)
    R.H. Macy & Co. Inc., Bancom 111 Bldg., Legaspi & Radai Sts., Legaspi Village,
    Makati, Metro Manila, Philippines

MARATHON LE TOURNEAU CO   PO Box 2307, Longview, TX 75606, Tel: (903) 237-7000
  (Mfr heavy constr, mining mach & equip)
    Abominco Equipment Corp., 3rd Fl., 110 Legaspi St., Legaspi Village, Makati,
    Metro Manila, Philippines

MOBIL CORP   3225 Gallows Rd, Fairfax, VA 22037-0001, Tel: (703) 846-3000
  (Petroleum explor & refining, mfr petrol prdts, chems, petrochems)
    Mobil Oil Philippines Inc., Makati Commercial Center, P.O. Box 246, Makati,
    Metro Manila 3117, Philippines

MOOG INC   East Aurora, NY 14052-0018, Tel: (716) 652-2000
  (Mfr precision control components & sys)
    Moog Controls Corp., Philippines

MORGAN GUARANTY TRUST CO   23 Wall St, New York, NY 10260, Tel: (212) 483-2323
  (Banking)
    Morgan Guaranty Trust Co., BPI Bldg., Ayala Ave. & Paseo de Roxas, Makati, Rizal,
    Philippines

MOSLER INC   1561 Grand Blvd, Hamilton, OH 45012, Tel: (513) 867-4000
  (Mfr security prdts, sys, & servs to fin, coml, & govt mkt)
    Mosler Inc., Unit 405, Centerpoint Bldg. 4/F, Ortigas Complex, PASIG, Metro Manila,
    Philippines

MOTION PICTURE EXPORT ASSN OF AMERICA   1133 Ave of the Americas, New York,
  NY 10036, Tel: (212) 840-6161
  (Motion picture trade association)
    MPEAA, P.O. Box LA-424, Ermita, Manila, 2801, Philippines

MOTOROLA INC   1303 E Algonquin Rd, Schaumburg, IL 60196, Tel: (708) 576-5000
  (Mfr commun equip, semiconductors, cellular phones)
    Motorola Philippines Inc., Bormaheco Bldg., Km. 17 West Service Rd.,
    South Superhwy., Paranaque, Metro Manila, Philippines

MULLER & PHIPPS INTL CORP   Box 3994, San Francisco, CA 94119,
Tel: (415) 772-5650
(General merchandise)
    Muller & Phipps Group of Companies, P.O. Box 7078, Airport Rep., Manila, Philippines

McCANN-ERICKSON WORLDWIDE   750 Third Ave, New York, NY 10017,
Tel: (212) 697-6000
(Advertising)
    McCann-Erickson Philippines Inc., 118 Herrera St., Legaspi Village, P.O. Box 2006,
    MCC, Makati, Metro Manila, Philippines

NALCO CHEMICAL CO   One Nalco Center, Naperville, IL 60563-1198,
Tel: (708) 305-1000
(Chems for water & waste water treatment, oil prod & refining, ind processes;
water/energy mgmt serv)
    Nalco Chemical Co. Philippines Inc., P.O. Box 1064, MCC, Makati, Metro Manila,
    Philippines

NATIONAL CAR RENTAL SYSTEM INC   7700 France Ave S, Minneapolis, MN 55435,
Tel: (612) 830-2121
(Car rental)
    Natl Car Rental System Inc., Manila Gardens Hotel,
    Cor. E. de los Santos Ave. & Pasay Rd., Makati, Metro Manila, Philippines

NATIONAL SEMICONDUCTOR CORP   PO Box 58090, Santa Clara, CA 95052-8090,
Tel: (408) 721-5000
(Mfr semiconductors, design/devel sys)
    National Semiconductor, Cebu, Philippines

NATIONAL STARCH & CHEMICAL CO   10 Finderne Ave, Bridgewater, NJ 08807-3300,
Tel: (908) 685-5000
(Mfr adhesives & sealants, resins & spec chems, electr materials & adhesives, food
prdts, ind starch)
    Inter-National Starch & Chemical Co. Inc., Manila, Philippines

OCEANEERING INTL INC   PO Box 218130, Houston, TX 77218-8130,
Tel: (713) 578-8868
(Underwater serv to offshore oil & gas ind)
    Oceaneering Intl. Inc., Operational base in Manila

OSMOSE INTL INC   980 Ellicott St, Buffalo, NY 14209, Tel: (716) 882-5905
(Mfr wood preservatives; maint & inspec utility poles, railroad track & marine piling)
    Osmose Philippines Inc., 218 Socorro Fernandez St., Mandaluyong, Metro Manila,
    Philippines

OTIS ELEVATOR CO   10 Farm Springs, Farmington, CT 06032, Tel: (860) 676-6528
(Mfr elevators & escalators)
    Otis Elevator Co. (Philippines) Inc., 808 Romvaldez St., Ermita, Metro Manila 1000,
    Philippines

THE PARSONS CORP   100 W Walnut St, Pasadena, CA 91124, Tel: (818) 440-2000
(Engineering & construction)
    Parsons Intl. Ltd., Rufino Pacific Tower 10/F, 6784 Ayala Ave., 1226 Makati,
    Metro Manila, Philipines

PARSONS DE LEUW INC   1133 15th St NW, Washington, DC 20005,
  Tel: (202) 775-3300
  (Consulting engineers)
    De Leuw Cather Intl. Ltd., 107 Herrera St., Legaspi Village, Makati, Metro Manila,
      Philippines

PARSONS ENGINEERING SCIENCE INC   100 W Walnut St, Pasadena, CA 91124,
  Tel: (818) 440-6000
  (Environmental engineering)
    Parsons Engineering Science Inc., Suite 401, Gedisco Bldg., 1564A Mabini St.,
      Ermita, Manila, Philippines
    Parsons Engineering Science Inc., Rufino Pacific Tower 10/F, 6784 Ayala Ave.,
      Makati, Metro Manila, Philippines

PEPSICO INC   700 Anderson Hill Rd, Purchase, NY 10577-1444,
  Tel: (914) 253-2000
  (Beverages, snack foods, restaurants)
    Pepsi-Cola Far East Trade Development Co., Philippines

PETROLEUM HELICOPTERS INC   5728 Jefferson Hwy, Box 23502, Harahan, LA 70183,
  Tel: (504) 733-6790
  (Aerial transp, helicopter charter)
    Asia Aircraft Overseas Philippines, Domestic Rd. corner Mia Rd., Pasay City,
      Metro Manila, Philippines

PFIZER INC   235 E 42nd St, New York, NY 10017-5755, Tel: (212) 573-2323
  (Mfr healthcare products)
    Pfizer Inc., Philippines

PHELPS DODGE CORP   2600 N Central Ave, Phoenix, AZ 85004-3014,
  Tel: (602) 234-8100
  (Copper, minerals, metals & spec engineered prdts for trans & elect mkts)
    Columbian Carbon Philippines Inc., TMBC Bldg. 5/F, 6772 Ayala Ave., Makati,
      Metro Manila 1200, Philippines
    Phelps Dodge Philippines Inc., A. Soriana Bldg., 8776 Paseo de Raxas, Makati,
      Rizal Philippines

PINKERTON SECURITY & INVESTIGATION SERVICES   6727 Odessa Ave, Van Nuys,
  CA 91406-5796, Tel: (818) 373-8800
  (Security & investigation services)
    Pinkerton Consulting & Investigation Services, Thomas Jefferson Cultural Center,
      395 Senator Gil Puyat Ave., Makati, Metro Manila, Philippines

PLOUGH INC   PO Box 377, Memphis, TN 38151, Tel: (901) 320-2011
  (Proprietary drug & cosmetic prdts)
    Schering Corp. Philippines Inc., P.O. Box 297, Manila, Philippines

PREMARK INTL INC   1717 Deerfield Rd, Deerfield, IL 60015, Tel: (708) 405-6000
  (Mfr/sale diversified consumer & coml prdts)
    Dart (Philippines) Inc., P.O. Box 83, Makati Commercial Center, Makati,
      Metro Manila, Philippines   ·

PROCTER & GAMBLE CO   One Procter & Gamble Plaza, Cincinnati, OH 45202,
  Tel: (513) 983-1100
  (Personal care, food, laundry, cleaning & ind prdts)
    Procter & Gamble Philippine Mfg. Corp., P.O. Box 302, Manila, Philippines

RESERVE INDUSTRIES CORP   20 First Plaza, #308, Albuquerque, NM 87102,
Tel: (505) 247-2384
(Mineral exploration, recycling, mfr abrasives & chem prdts)
   Industrial Mineral Products, P.O. Box 1008, Cebu 6400, Philippines

RHONE-POULENC RORER INC   PO Box 1200, Collegeville, PA 19426-0107,
Tel: (215) 454-8000
(R&D/mfr human pharmaceuticals)
   Rorer-Philippines Inc., Manila, Philippines

A H ROBINS CO INC   1407 Cummings Dr, PO Box 26609, Richmond, VA 23261-6609,
Tel: (804) 257-2000
(Mfr ethical pharms & consumer prdts)
   A.H. Robins (Philippines) Co., Pasig, Metro Manila, Philippines

ROHM AND HAAS CO   100 Independence Mall West, Philadelphia, PA 19106,
Tel: (215) 592-3000
(Mfr ind & agric chems, plastics)
   Rohm and Haas Philipines Inc., PCI Bank Tower II 12/F,
      Makati Ave. cor H.V. de la Costa St., Salcedo Village, Philippines

SEA-LAND SERVICE INC   150 Allen Rd, Liberty Corner, NJ 07920,
Tel: (201) 558-6000
(Container transport)
   Sea-Land Service Inc., MCCPO Box 1575, Makati, Manila, Philippines

G D SEARLE & CO   5200 Old Orchard Rd, Skokie, IL 60077, Tel: (708) 982-7000
(Mfr pharms, health care & optical prdts, specialty chems)
   Searle (Philippines) Inc., P.O. Box 7287, Airmail Exchange Center,
      Manila Intl. Airport, Pasay City, Philippines

SPALDING & EVENFLO COS INC   5750A N Hoover Blvd, Tampa, FL 33614,
Tel: (813) 887-5200
(Mfr sports equip, infant & juvenile furniture & accessories)
   Evenflo (Philippines) Inc., P.O. Box 421, Makati, Metro Manila, Philippines

STANDARD & POOR'S CORP   25 Broadway, New York, NY 10004, Tel: (212) 208-8000
(Invest, fin, economic & mktg info)
   Standard Brands of the Philippines Inc., P.O. Box 586, Manila, Philippines

THE STANLEY WORKS   1000 Stanley Dr, PO Box 7000, New Britain, CT 06050,
Tel: (203) 225-5111
(Mfr hand tools & hardware)
   Stanley Consultants Inc., P.O. Box 7065, Air Mail Exchange Office,
      Manila Intl. Airport 3120, Philippines
   Stanley Works Sales Philippines Inc., PAIC Bldg., 105 Paseo de Roxas, Makati,
      Metro Manila 3117, Philippines

STIEFEL LABORATORIES INC   255 Alhambra Circle, Coral Gables, FL 33134,
Tel: (305) 443-3807
(Mfr pharmaceuticals, dermatological specialties)
   Stiefel Philippines Inc., Kalaw-Ledesma Condo. #403, 117 Gamboa St.,
      Legaspi Village, Makati, Metro Manila 1200, Philippines

STOKES DIV   5500 Tabor Rd, Philadelphia, PA 19120, Tel: (215) 289-5671
(Vacuum pumps & components, vacuum dryers, oil-upgrading equip)
   Morris Corp., P.O. Box 1451, Manila, Philippines

STV GROUP   11 Robinson St, PO Box 459, Pottstown, PA 19464-0459,
  Tel: (215) 326-4600
  (Engineering, architectural, planning, environmental & construction mgmt services)
    STV Inc., 1680 Roxas Blvd. 5/F, Manila 1000, Philippines

SUNDT INTL   PO Box 26685, Tucson, AZ 85726, Tel: (602) 790-0295
  (Holding company)
    Sundt Intl. Philippines Inc., c/o Tierra Intl. Construction Co.,
      cor. Osmena & Augono Sts., Makati, Metro Manila, Philippines

SUNWARD TECHNOLOGIES INC   5828 Pacific Center Blvd, San Diego, CA 92121,
  Tel: (619) 587-9140
  (Mfr computer components & peripherals)
    Sunward Technologies Philippines Inc., Km. 19 West Service Rd., South Expressway,
      Metro Manila, Philippines

TENNESSEE ASSOCIATES INTL   223 Associates Blvd, PO Box 710, Alcoa,
  TN 37701-0710, Tel: (423) 982-9514
  (Mgt consulting servs)
    Tennessee Associates Asia Pacific, RCI Bldg., 105 Rada St., Legaspi Village,
      Makati, Metro Manila, Philippines

TEXAS INSTRUMENTS INC   13500 N Central Expwy, Dallas, TX 75265,
  Tel: (214) 995-2011
  (Mfr semiconductor devices, electr/electro-mech sys, instr & controls)
    Texas Instruments (Philippines) Inc., Baguio City Export Processing Zone,
      Loakan Rd., Baguio City 0201, Philippines

TRANE CO   3600 Pammel Creek Rd, La Crosse, WI 54601, Tel: (608) 787-2000
  (Mfr/distr/svce A/C sys & equip)
    Trane Philippines, 1423 Vito Cruz Extension, Makati, Metro Manila, Philippines

U S ELECTRICAL MOTOR CO   58-C Robinson Blvd, Orange, CT 06477,
  Tel: (203) 891-1080
  (Mfr elect motors, components)
    Emerson Electric Intl. Inc., P.O. Box 781 MCCPO, Makati, Metro Manila, Philippines

U S WHEAT ASSOCIATES   1200 NW Front Ave, #600, Portland, OR 97209,
  Tel: (503) 223-8123
  (Market development for wheat prdts)
    U.S. Wheat Associates Inc., P.O. Box 146, Makati, Metro Manila 3117, Philippines

UNION CAMP CORP   1600 Valley Rd, Wayne, NJ 07470, Tel: (201) 628-2000
  (Mfr paper, packaging, chems, wood prdts)
    Bush Boake Allen Philippines Inc., WC1 Bldg., Fairlane St., Pasig, Metro Manila,
      Philippines

UNION CARBIDE CORP   39 Old Ridgebury Rd, Danbury, CT 06817,
  Tel: (203) 794-2000
  (Mfr industrial chemicals, plastics, resins)
    Union Carbide Philippines (Far East) Inc., CPO Box 2572, Makati, Metro Manila 1299,
      Philippines

UNION OIL INTL DIV   Union Oil Center, PO Box 7600, Los Angeles, CA 90017,
  Tel: (213) 977-7600
  (Petroleum prdts, petrochems)

Philippine Geothermal Inc., Metro Bank Plaza, Buendia Ave. Ext., P.O. Box 7336, Airport, Philippines

UNISYS CORP   PO Box 500, Blue Bell, PA 19424, Tel: (215) 986-4011
  (Mfg/mktg/serv electr info sys)
     Unisys Philippines Ltd., De la Rose & Estaban Sts., Legaspi Village, Makati, Rizal, Philippines

UNITED CALIFORNIA BANK   PO Box 54191, Los Angeles, CA 90054,
  Tel: (213) 624-0111
  (Banking)
     United California Bank (Manila Branch), P.O. Box 2093, Metrobank Plaza, Buendia Ave. Ext., Makati, Metro Manila, Philippines

UNIVERSAL CORP   PO Box 25099, Richmond, VA 23260, Tel: (804) 359-9311
  (Holding co: tobacco, commodities)
     Orient Leaf Tobacco Co. Ltd., Manila Intl. Airport, P.O. Box 7406, Manila, Philippines

UPJOHN CO   7000 Portage Rd, Kalamazoo, MI 49001, Tel: (616) 323-4000
  (Mfr pharms, agric prdts, ind chems)
     Upjohn Inc., MCCPO Box 57, Makati, Metro Manila, Philippines

VELSICOL CHEMICAL CORP   10400 W Higgins Rd, #600, Rosemont, IL 60018-3728,
  Tel: (708) 298-9000
  (Mfr pesticides & ind chems)
     Velsicol Chemical Corp., 44th Fl., Marsman Bldg., Buendia Ave. corner Washington St., Makati, Metro Manila, Philippines

WARNER-LAMBERT CO   201 Tabor Road, Morris Plains, NJ 07950,
  Tel: (201) 540-2000
  (Mfr ethical & proprietary pharms, confectionary & consumer prdts)
     Warner-Lambert Philippines Inc., P.O. Box 65, Makati Commercial Center, Makati, Metro Manila, Philippines

WEST CHEMICAL PRODUCTS INC   1000 Herrontown Rd, Princeton, NJ 08540,
  Tel: (609) 921-0501
  (Sanitary equip & supplies)
     West Chemicals Philippines Inc., 5486 South Super Hwy., Makati, Philippines

WILBUR-ELLIS CO   320 California St, #200, San Francisco, CA 94104,
  Tel: (415) 772-4000
  (Intl merchants & distributors)
     Connell Bros. Co. Pilipinas Inc., Agustin I Bldg. 4/F, Emerald Ave, Ortigas Center, Pasig, Metro Manila 1600, Philippines
     Connell Bros. Co. Pilipinas Inc. (CEBU), Ros-Mel Arcade, A.C. Cortes Ave., Mandaue City, Philippines

WORLD COURIER INC   46 Trinity Pl, New York, NY 10006, Tel: (718) 978-9400
  (Intl courier serv)
     World Courier Philippines Inc., 1-D Torre de Salced, Salcedo St., Legaspi Village, Makati, Metro Manila, Philippines

WM WRIGLEY JR CO   410 N Michigan Ave, Chicago, IL 60611-4287,
  Tel: (312) 644-2121
  (Mfr chewing gum)
     Wrigley Philippines Inc., MCCPO Box 661, Makati, Manila 1299, Philippines

XEROX CORP   800 Long Ridge Rd, PO Box 1600, Stamford, CT 06904,
  Tel: (203) 968-3000
  (Mfr document processing equip, sys & supplies)
    Xerox Corp., Manila, Philippines

POLAND

3COM CORP   5400 Bayfront Plaza, Santa Clara, CA 95052-8145,
  Tel: (408) 764-5000
  (Devel/mfr computer networking prdts & sys)
    3Com GmbH, Poland

3M   3M Center, St Paul, MN 55144-1000, Tel: (612) 733-1110
  (Mfr diversified prdts for industry, health care, imaging, commun, transport, safety,
  consumer, etc)
    3M Poland sp. z o.o, Bema Str 57A, 01-244 Warsaw, Poland

ADAMS & ASSOCIATES INTL   978 Hampton Park, Barrington, IL 60010,
  Tel: (708) 304-5300
  (Mgt conslt exec search)
    Adams & Associates Intl., Rutkowskiego 8 #310, 00-950 Warsaw, Poland

ADEMCO INTL   165 Eileen Way, Syosset, NY 11791, Tel: (516) 921-6704
  (Mfr security, fire & burglary sys & prdts)
    Ademco Italia SpA, Stepinska 49a/9, 00-739 Warsaw, Poland

ALTHEIMER & GRAY   10 S Wacker Dr, #4000, Chicago, IL 60606-7482,
  Tel: (312) 715-4000
  (Lawyers)
    Altheimer & Gray, ul. Nowogrodzka 50, Room 204, 00-950 Warsaw, Poland

AMERICAN APPRAISAL ASSOCS INC   411 E Wisconsin Ave, Milwaukee, WI 53202,
  Tel: (414) 271-7240
  (Valuation consulting serv)
    American Appraisal Poland Ltd., 43 Filtrowa St., 02-057 Warsaw, Poland

AMERICAN EXPRESS CO   World Financial Center, New York, NY 10285-4765,
  Tel: (212) 640-2000
  (Travel, travelers cheques, charge card & financial services)
    American Express Travel Poland Sp. z o.o.

AMP INC   PO Box 3608, Harrisburg, PA 17105-3608, Tel: (717) 564-0100
  (Devel/mfr electronic & electrical connection prdts & sys)
    AMP Polska Sp. z o.o, Poznan, Poland

AMWAY CORP   7575 E Fulton Rd, Ada, MI 49355, Tel: (616) 676-6000
  (Mfr/sale home care, personal care, nutrition & houseware prdts)
    Amway Polska Sp. z o.o, ul. Mangalia 4, 02-758 Warsaw, Poland

BAXTER HEALTHCARE CORP   1 Baxter Pky, Deerfield, IL 60015,
  Tel: (708) 948-2000
  (Mfr disposable medical prdts)
    Baxter Polska Sp. z o.o, Lowicka 33/1, 02-502 Warsaw, Poland

CARANA CORP   4350 N Fairfax Dr, #500, Arlington, VA 22203,
  Tel: (703) 243-1700
  (Foreign trade consulting)
    CARANA Corp., Batoszka 4/18, 00-710 Warsaw, Poland

CARBOLINE CO   350 Hanley Industrial Ct, St Louis, MO 63144,
  Tel: (314) 644-1000
  (Mfr coatings, sealants)
    Polifarb Cieszyn Carboline, ul. Przeclawska 5, 03-879 Warsaw, Poland

CARGILL   PO Box 9300, Minneapolis, MN 55440, Tel: (612) 475-7575
  (Food prdts, feeds, animal prdts)
    Cargill Enterprises Inc., ul. Szpacza 2, 04-238 Warsaw, Poland

CHESTERTON BINSWANGER INTL   Two Logan Sq, 4th fl, Philadelphia,
  PA 19103-2759, Tel: (215) 448-6000
  (Real estate & related svces)
    Blumenauer Immobilien, ul. Czeczota 10/1, 02-607 Warsaw, Poland

CHIRON CORP   4560 Horton St, Emeryville, CA 94608-2916, Tel: (510) 601-2412
  (Research/mfg/mktg therapeutics, vaccines, diagnostics, ophthalmics)
    Ciba Corning Diagnostics, ul. Wiktorii Wiedenskiej 17m2, 02-954 Warsaw, Poland

CITICORP   399 Park Ave, New York, NY 10043, Tel: (212) 559-1000
  (Banking & financial services)
    Citibank NA, Poland

THE CLOROX CO   1221 Broadway, PO Box 24305, Oakland, CA 94623-1305,
  Tel: (510) 271-7000
  (Mfr domestic consumer packaged prdts)
    The Clorox Co., Poland

THE COCA-COLA CO   PO Drawer 1734, Atlanta, GA 30301, Tel: (404) 676-2121
  (Mfr/mkt/distr soft drinks, syrups & concentrates, juice & juice-drink prdts)
    Coca-Cola Amatil Ltd., all mail to U.S. address

CPC INTERNATIONAL INC   PO Box 8000, Englewood Cliffs, NJ 07632,
  Tel: (201) 894-4000
  (Consumer foods, corn refining)
    CPC Polska Sp. z o.o, Ul. Baltycka 32, 60-960 Poznan 10, Poland

CRAY RESEARCH INC   655 Lone Oak Dr, Eagan, MN 55121, Tel: (612) 452-6650
  (Supercomputer systems & services)
    Cray Research (Eastern Europe) Ltd., Warsaw, Poland - all mail to U.S. address

DELL COMPUTER CORP   2214 W Braker Ln, Austin, TX 78758-4063,
  Tel: (512) 338-4400
  (Design/mfr personal computers)
    Dell Poland, Warsaw, Poland

DRG INTERNATIONAL INC   PO Box 1188, Mountainside, NJ 07092,
  Tel: (908) 233-2075
  (Mfr/sale/svce medical devices, diagnostic kits, clinical equip)
    DRG MedTek Sp. z o.o, ul. F-Joliot-Curie 17/13, 02-646 Warsaw, Poland

E I DU PONT DE NEMOURS & CO   1007 Market St, Wilmington, DE 19898,
  Tel: (302) 774-1000
  (Mfr/sale diversified chems, plastics, specialty prdts & fibers)
    E.I. du Pont de Namours & Co. Inc., Intraco Bldg., ul. Stawki 2, 00-193 Warsaw,
      Poland

EPSTEIN ENGINEERING EXPORT LTD   600 W Fulton St, Chicago, IL 60606-1199,
  Tel: (312) 454-9100
  (Engr & constr)
    Epstein Engineering Export Ltd., Al. Armii Wojska Polskiego, 16 m 3, 00-582 Warsaw,
      Poland

FMC CORP   200 E Randolph Dr, Chicago, IL 60601, Tel: (312) 861-6000
  (Produces chems & precious metals, mfr machinery, equip & sys for ind, agric & govt)
    FMC Poland LLC, Poland

GENERAL ELECTRIC CO   3135 Easton Tpk, Fairfield, CT 06431,
  Tel: (203) 373-2211
  (Diversified manufacturing, technology & services)
    General Electric Poland,
      all mail to U.S. address; phone (800) 626-2004 or (518) 438-6500

GETZ BROS & CO INC   150 Post St, #500, San Francisco, CA 94108,
  Tel: (415) 772-5500
  (Divers mfg, mktg/distr serv, travel serv)
    Getz Intl. Travel, ul. Wareckra 9, P.O. Box 17, Warsaw, Poland

THE GILLETTE CO   Prudential Tower, Boston, MA 02199, Tel: (617) 421-7000
  (Devel/mfr personal care/use prdts: blades & razors, toiletries, cosmetics,
  stationery)
    Wizamet SA, Lodz, Poland

GLOBAL COMMUNICATION NETWORK INC   12750 Ventura Blvd, #202, Studio City,
  CA 91604, Tel: (818) 755-9589
  (Commun, pub, electr typesetting)
    Global Communication Network, ul. Koralowa 51, Szczecin, Poland

THE GOODYEAR TIRE & RUBBER CO   1144 E Market St, Akron, OH 44316,
  Tel: (216) 796-2121
  (Mfr tires, automotive belts & hose, conveyor belts, chemicals; oil pipeline
  transmission)
    Debica SA, Poland

GREY ADVERTISING INC   777 Third Ave, New York, NY 10017, Tel: (212) 546-2000
  (Advertising)
    Grey Warsaw, ul. Krolewska 27, 00-060 Warsaw, Poland

HARNISCHFEGER INDUSTRIES INC   PO Box 554, Milwaukee, WI 53201,
  Tel: (414) 671-4400
  (Mfr mining & material handling equip, papermaking mach, computer sys)
    Beloit Poland SA, ul. Fabryczna 1, Jelenia Gora-Cieplice, Poland

H J HEINZ CO   PO Box 57, Pittsburgh, PA 15230-0057, Tel: (412) 456-5700
  (Processed food prdts & nutritional services)
    Heinz Polska Sp., Warsaw, Poland

HEWLETT-PACKARD CO   3000 Hanover St, Palo Alto, CA 94304-0890,
  Tel: (415) 857-1501
  (Mfr computing, communications & measurement prdts & services)
    Hewlett Packard Polska Sp. z o.o, ul. Newelska 6, 01-447 Warsaw, Poland

HOLIDAY INNS INC   3742 Lamar Ave, Memphis, TN 38195, Tel: (901) 362-4001
  (Hotels, restaurants, casinos)
    Holiday Inn, Hotel Orbis-Holiday Inn, ul. Konlewa 7, 03-150 Krakow, Poland

HONEYWELL INC   PO Box 524, Minneapolis, MN 55440-0524, Tel: (612) 951-1000
  (Devel/mfr controls for home & building, industry, space & aviation)
    Honeywell Ltd., Augustowka 3, 02-981 Warsaw, Poland

HUNTON & WILLIAMS   951 E Byrd St, East Tower, Richmond, VA 23219-4074,
  Tel: (804) 788-8200
  (Lawyers)
    Hunton & Williams, Ul. Bagatela 14, V p., 00-585 Warsaw, Poland

IBM CORP   Old Orchard Rd, Armonk, NY 10504, Tel: (914) 765-1900
  (Information products, technology & services)
    IBM Poland, ul. Marszalkowska 6/6, 00-590 Warsaw, Poland

INTERMODAL TECHNICAL SERVICES INC   9 Campus Dr #7, PO Box 316, Parsippany,
  NJ 07054, Tel: (201) 993-3634
  (Damage survey & inspection services)
    ITS Polska Sp. z o.o, Zmudzka Str. 4, 60-604 Poznan, Poland

INTERNATIONAL PAPER   2 Manhattanville Rd, Purchase, NY 10577,
  Tel: (914) 397-1500
  (Mfr/distr container board, paper, wood prdts)
    Zaklady Celulozowo-Papierneicze SA, Poland

JOHNSON & JOHNSON   One Johnson & Johnson Plaza, New Brunswick, NJ 08933,
  Tel: (908) 524-0400
  (R&D/mfr/sale health care prdts)
    Johnson & Johnson Sp. z o.o, ul. Korkowa 89, 02-954 Warsaw, Poland

KEYSTONE INTL INC   PO Box 40010, Houston, TX 77040, Tel: (713) 466-1176
  (Mfr butterfly valves, actuators & control accessories)
    Keystone Poland, Poland

KORN/FERRY INTL   1800 Century Park East, Los Angeles, CA 90067,
  Tel: (310) 552-1834
  (Executive search)
    Korn/Ferry Intl., Frascati 3/6, 00-492 Warsaw, Poland

LOCTITE CORP   10 Columbus Blvd, Hartford, CT 06106, Tel: (203) 520-5000
(Mfr/sale ind adhesives & sealants)
  Loctite Polska Sp. z o.o, ul. Felinskiego 37, 01-569 Warsaw, Poland

MACRO INTL INC   11785 Beltsville Dr, Calverton, MD 20705-3119,
Tel: (301) 572-0200
(Research, evaluation, mkt research, surveys, mgmt consult/training, info sys)
  Macro-PJG Ltd., ul. Jerozolimskie 560, 00-803 Warsaw, Poland

NATIONAL CAR RENTAL SYSTEM INC   7700 France Ave S, Minneapolis, MN 55435,
Tel: (612) 830-2121
(Car rental)
  National Car Rental, P.O. Box 67, Warsaw, Poland

NORDSON CORP   28601 Clemens Rd, Westlake, OH 44145, Tel: (216) 892-1580
(Mfr ind application equip & packaging mach)
  Nordson Polska Sp. z o.o, ul. Lektykarska 29/8, 01-687 Warsaw, Poland

NYNEX CORP   1095 Ave of the Americas, New York, NY 10036, Tel: (212) 370-7400
(Telecom & info servs)
  NYNEX, ul. Nowogrodzka 50, 00-695 Warsaw, Poland

OTIS ELEVATOR CO   10 Farm Springs, Farmington, CT 06032, Tel: (860) 676-6528
(Mfr elevators & escalators)
  Otis Sp. z o.o, ul. Szpitalna 1, 00-020 Warsaw, Poland

PEPSICO INC   700 Anderson Hill Rd, Purchase, NY 10577-1444,
Tel: (914) 253-2000
(Beverages, snack foods, restaurants)
  E Wedel SA, Poland

PROCTER & GAMBLE CO   One Procter & Gamble Plaza, Cincinnati, OH 45202,
Tel: (513) 983-1100
(Personal care, food, laundry, cleaning & ind prdts)
  Procter & Gamble, c/o OMC Poll, ul. Hibnera 6, 00-018 Warsaw, Poland

THE STANLEY WORKS   1000 Stanley Dr, PO Box 7000, New Britain, CT 06050,
Tel: (203) 225-5111
(Mfr hand tools & hardware)
  Stanley Tools Poland Ltd., ul. 1 Maja 70, 32-440 Sulkowice, Poland

STIEFEL LABORATORIES INC   255 Alhambra Circle, Coral Gables, FL 33134,
Tel: (305) 443-3807
(Mfr pharmaceuticals, dermatological specialties)
  Stiefel Polska Sp. z o.o, ul Litewska 3/5, 00-589 Warsaw, Poland

TENNECO AUTOMOTIVE   111 Pfingsten Rd, Deerfield, IL 60015,
Tel: (708) 948-0900
(Automotive parts, exhaust sys, service equip)
  Monroe Poland, ul. Wisnlowa 57/3, 02-520 Warsaw, Poland

TENNECO INC   PO Box 2511, Houston, TX 77252-2511, Tel: (713) 757-2131
(Natural gas pipelines, shipbuilding & repair, construction & farm equip, chemicals,
packaging)
  Tenneco Europe (Warsaw) Ltd., ul. Pesztenska 10, 03-912 Warsaw, Poland

UPJOHN CO   7000 Portage Rd, Kalamazoo, MI 49001, Tel: (616) 323-4000
(Mfr pharms, agric prdts, ind chems)
   Upjohn, ul. Kubickjego 27/29 m 12, 00-676 Warsaw, Poland

VALMONT INDUSTRIES INC   One Valmont Pkwy, PO Box 358, Valley, NE 68064-0358,
   Tel: (402) 359-2201
   (Mfr irrigation sys, steel lighting, utility & communication poles)
   Valmont Polska, Ul Terespolska 12, 08-110 Siedlec, Poland

WARD HOWELL INTL INC   99 Park Ave, New York, NY 10016-1699,
   Tel: (212) 697-3730
   (Executive recruiting)
   Dr. Prasuhn & Partner Sp. z o.o, Pl. 1 Maja 1/2, 50-136 Wroclaw, Poland
   Ward Howell Intl., ul. Polna 50, 00-644 Warsaw, Poland

WOODWARD GOVERNOR CO   5001 North 2nd St, PO Box 7001, Rockford,
   IL 61125-7001, Tel: (815) 877-7441
   (Mfr speed control governors)
   Woodward Governor Poland Sp. z o.o, ul. Chmielna 8, 00-950 Warsaw, Poland

WM WRIGLEY JR CO   410 N Michigan Ave, Chicago, IL 60611-4287,
   Tel: (312) 644-2121
   (Mfr chewing gum)
   Wrigley Poland Ltd., Poznan, Poland

XEROX CORP   800 Long Ridge Rd, PO Box 1600, Stamford, CT 06904,
   Tel: (203) 968-3000
   (Mfr document processing equip, sys & supplies)
   Xerox Corp., Warsaw, Poland

PORTUGAL

3M   3M Center, St Paul, MN 55144-1000, Tel: (612) 733-1110
   (Mfr diversified prdts for industry, health care, imaging, commun, transport, safety,
   consumer, etc)
   Minnesota (3M) de Portugal Lda., Rua Conde de Redondo 98, P-1169 Lisbon Codex,
   Portugal

AERONAUTICAL INSTRUMENTS & RADIO CO   234 Garibaldi Ave, Lodi, NJ 07644,
   Tel: (201) 473-0034
   (Mfr aeronautical instru)
   Cinave, Rua do Quelhas 27, P-2000 Lisbon, Portugal

AIR EXPRESS INTL CORP   120 Tokeneke Rd, PO Box 1231, Darien, CT 06820,
   Tel: (203) 655-7900
   (Air frt forwarder)

(cont)

Air Express Intl., c/o Germano Serrao Arnaud, Ltd., Avenida 24 Julio 22-D,
P-2000 Lisbon, Portugal

ALLIEDSIGNAL INC   101 Columbia Rd, PO Box 2245, Morristown, NJ 07962-2245,
Tel: (201) 455-2000
(Mfr aerospace & automotive prdts, engineered materials)
AlliedSignal Auomotive Portugal, Olho de Boi, Alferrarede, P-2200 Abrantes, Portugal

AMDAHL CORP   1250 E Arques Ave, PO Box 3470, Sunnyvale, CA 94088-3470,
Tel: (408) 746-6000
(Devel/mfr large scale computers, software, data storage prdts, info-technology
solutions & support)
Amdahl Intl. Corp., Av. Marques de Tomar 35-4 Esq., P-1000 Lisbon, Portugal

AMERICAN APPRAISAL ASSOCS INC   411 E Wisconsin Ave, Milwaukee, WI 53202,
Tel: (414) 271-7240
(Valuation consulting serv)
American Appraisal Consultores de Avaliacao Lda., Av. Miguel Bombarda 36,
P-1000 Lisbon, Portugal

AMP INC   PO Box 3608, Harrisburg, PA 17105-3608, Tel: (717) 564-0100
(Devel/mfr electronic & electrical connection prdts & sys)
AMP Portugal Lda., Rua Joaquin Antonio de Aquiar 66-1, P-1000 Lisbon, Portugal

AMPCO METAL INC   1745 S 38th St, PO Box 2004, Milwaukee, WI 53201,
Tel: (414) 645-3750
(Mfr/distr/sale cast & wrought copper-based alloys)
Ampco Metal Portugal Lda., Rua de Recarei 312, Leca do Balio,
P-4465 S Mamede de Infesta, Portugal

AMWAY CORP   7575 E Fulton Rd, Ada, MI 49355, Tel: (616) 676-6000
(Mfr/sale home care, personal care, nutrition & houseware prdts)
Amway Portugal, Av. do Forte 10, Carnaxide, P-2795 Linda-a-Velha, Portugal

ASHLAND OIL INC   1000 Ashland Dr, Russell, KY 41169, Tel: (606) 329-3333
(Petroleum exploration, refining & transportation; mfr chemicals, oils & lubricants)
Ashland Quimica Portuguesa Lda., Rua Cova da Moura 2-6, P-1300 Liston, Portugal

ASSOCIATED MERCHANDISING CORP   1440 Broadway, New York, NY 10018,
Tel: (212) 536-4000
(Retail service organization)
Associated Merchandising Corp., Rua do Bom Sucesso 372-4, P-4100 Porto, Portugal

ASSOCIATED PRESS INC   50 Rockefeller Plaza, New York, NY 10020-1605,
Tel: (212) 621-1500
(News gathering agency)
Associated Press, Praca de Alegria 58-3 A, Lisbon, Portugal

BANKERS TRUST CO   280 Park Ave, New York, NY 10017, Tel: (212) 250-2500
(Banking)
Bankers Trust Co., Edif. Aviz, Bloco 3A, Rua Latino Coelho 1-12DT, P-1000 Lisbon,
Portugal

C R BARD INC 730 Central Ave, Murray Hill, NJ 07974, Tel: (908) 277-8000
(Mfr health care prdts)
   C.R. Bard Portugal Lda., Praceta Acacio Lino 5B/7B, Funchalinho,
    P-2825 Monte de Caparica, Portugal

BRANSON ULTRASONICS CORP 41 Eagle Rd, Danbury, CT 06813-1961,
Tel: (203) 796-0400
(Mfr plastics assembly equip, ultrasonic cleaning equip)
   Zima Comercio International Lda., R. Ros Arneiros 96, P-1500 Lisbon, Portugal

BULAB HOLDINGS INC 1256 N McLean Blvd, Memphis, TN 38108,
Tel: (901) 278-0330
(Mfr microbicides, biocides, additives, corrosion inhibitors, chems)
   Buckman Laboratories Quimica (Portugal) Lda., Av. da Republica 1261, 3 Esq. Sala 5,
    P-2775 Parede, Portugal

CHASE MANHATTAN BANK N A 1 Chase Manhattan Plaza, New York, NY 10081,
Tel: (212) 552-2222
(Intl banking)
   Chase Manhattan Bank, NA, Avenida da Republica 9, P-1000 Lisbon, Portugal

CHEMICAL BANK 270 Park Ave, New York, NY 10017-2070, Tel: (212) 270-6000
(Banking & financial services)
   Banco Chemical (Portugal) SA, Rua Barata Salgueiro 33, P-1200 Lisbon, Portugal
   Banco Chemical (Portugal) SA, also in Aveiro, Guimaraes, Porto, Setubal & Viseu,
    Portugal

CIGNA CORP One Liberty Place, Philadelphia, PA 19192, Tel: (215) 523-4000
(Ins, invest, health care & other fin servs)
   Cigna Insurance Co. of Europe SA/NV, Avenida Fontes Pereira de Melo 31,
    P-2000 Lisbon, Portugal

CITICORP 399 Park Ave, New York, NY 10043, Tel: (212) 559-1000
(Banking & financial services)
   Citibank NA, Portugal

COLGATE-PALMOLIVE CO 300 Park Ave, New York, NY 10022, Tel: (212) 310-2000
(Mfr pharms, cosmetics, toiletries, detergents)
   Colgate-Palmolive Portuguesa Lda., Rua Mario Castelhano 1, Queluz, Portugal

COLUMBIA PICTURES INDUSTRIES INC 711 Fifth Ave, New York, NY 10022,
Tel: (212) 751-4400
(Producer & distributor of motion pictures)
   Columbia a Warner-Filmes de Portugal Lda., Avenida Duque de Loule 90-3o, Lisbon,
    Portugal

COMPUTER ASSOCIATES INTL INC One Computer Associates Plaza, Islandia,
NY 11788, Tel: (516) 342-5224
(Devel/mkt/mgt info mgt & bus applications software)
   Computer Associates Intl. Inc., Sucursal en Portugal,
    Av. Columbano Bordalo Pinheiro 108, P-1000 Lisbon, Portugal

CONAGRA INC 1 ConAgra Dr, Omaha, NE 68102, Tel: (402) 595-4000
(Prepared & frozen foods, grains, flour, animal feeds, agric chems, poultry, meat,
dairy prdts)
   Sapropur, Rua Dr. Antonio Candido 10-40, P-1000 Lisbon, Portugal

COULTER CORP   PO Box 169015, Miami, FL 33116-9015, Tel: (305) 885-0131
   (Mfr blood analysis sys, flow cytometers, chem sys, scientific sys & reagents)
      Coulter Cientifica SA, Rua Manual dos Santos 23 A/B, Encosta das Olaias,
        P-1900 Lisbon, Portugal

CPC INTERNATIONAL INC   PO Box 8000, Englewood Cliffs, NJ 07632,
   Tel: (201) 894-4000
   (Consumer foods, corn refining)
      Knorr Portuguesa-Produtos Alimentares SARL,
        Avenida Antonio Augusto de Aguiar 108-2, P-1088 Lisbon, Portugal

CROWN CORK & SEAL CO INC   9300 Ashton Rd, Philadelphia, PA 19136,
   Tel: (215) 698-5100
   (Mfr cans, bottle caps; filling & packaging mach)
      Produtos Corticeiros Portugueses SARL, Apartado 2307, P-1108 Lisbon, Portugal

D'ARCY MASIUS BENTON & BOWLES INC (DMB&B)   1675 Broadway, New York,
   NY 10019, Tel: (212) 468-3622
   (Advertising & communications)
      DMB&B Inc., Rua Tierno Galvan, Torre 3, 5-512, Amoreiras, P-1200 Lisbon, Portugal

D-M-E COMPANY   29111 Stephenson Highway, Madison Heights, MI 48071,
   Tel: (313) 398-6000
   (Basic tooling for plastic molding & die casting)
      Soteime Lda., Rua Sociedade Farmaceutica N-20 4B, Lisbon, Portugal

DATA GENERAL CORP   4400 Computer Dr, Westboro, MA 01580, Tel: (617) 366-8911
   (Design, mfr gen purpose computer sys & peripheral prdts & servs)
      Data General Sociedade de Computadores, Lisbon-Sintra Rd., Casal de Garoto,
        Amadora, P-1002 Lisbon, Portugal

DATAEASE INTL INC   7 Cambridge Dr, Trumbull, CT 06611, Tel: (203) 374-8000
   (Mfr applications devel software)
      Tempo Real, Avenida Duque d'Avila 66-4, P-1000 Lisbon, Portugal

DDB NEEDHAM WORLDWIDE INC   437 Madison Ave, New York, NY 10022,
   Tel: (212) 415-2000
   (Advertising)
      DDB Needham & Guerreiro Publicidade SARL, Rua D. Carlos de Mascarenhas 75,
        P-1000 Lisbon, Portugal

DIGITAL EQUIPMENT CORP   146 Main St, Maynard, MA 01754-2571,
   Tel: (508) 493-5111
   (Networked computer systems & services)
      Digital Equipment Portugal Lda., Avda. Engenheiro Duarte Pacheco Torre,
        P-1000 Lisbon, Portugal

WALT DISNEY CO   500 S Buena Vista St, Burbank, CA 91521, Tel: (818) 560-1000
   (Film/TV prod, theme parks, resorts, publishing, recording, retail stores)
      Walt Disney Portuguesa Criacoes Artisticas Lda., Portugal

THE DOW CHEMICAL CO   2030 Dow Center, Midland, MI 48674, Tel: (517) 636-1000
   (Mfr chems, plastics, pharms, agric prdts, consumer prdts)
      Sociedade Quimica Lepetit SARL, Lisbon, Portugal

DRAKE BEAM MORIN INC   100 Park Ave, New York, NY 10017, Tel: (212) 692-7700
(Human resource mgmt consulting & training)
  DBM Portugal, Rua Soldados da India 50, Restelo, P-1400 Lisbon, Portugal

EASTMAN KODAK CO   343 State St, Rochester, NY 14650, Tel: (716) 724-4000
(Devel/mfr photo & chem prdts, info mgmt/video/copier sys, fibers/plastics for
various ind)
  Kodak Portuguesa Lda., Apartado 12, P-2796 Linda-a-Velha, Portugal

EXPEDITORS INTL OF WASHINGTON INC   PO Box 69620, Seattle, WA 98168-9620,
  Tel: (206) 246-3711
(Air/ocean freight forwarding, customs brokerage, intl logistics solutions)
   Expeditors (Portugal) Transitarios Internacionais Lda., Rua C, Edif. 124 Piso 2,
     Gabinete 11, Aeroporto de Lisboa, P-1700 Lisbon, Portugal

FERRO CORPORATION   1000 Lakeside Ave, Cleveland, OH 44114,
  Tel: (216) 641-8580
(Mfr chems, coatings, plastics, colors, refractories)
  Metal Portuguesa SA, Apartado 10, Castanheira do Ribatejo,
    P-2600 Vila Franca de Zira, Portugal

FIRST NATIONAL BANK OF BOSTON   100 Federal St, Boston, MA 02110,
  Tel: (617) 434-2200
(Commercial banking)
   International-Factors Portugal SARL, Apartado 21161, Rua Castilho 71-5, Lisbon,
     Portugal

FOOTE CONE & BELDING COMMUNICATIONS INC   101 E Erie St, Chicago,
  IL 60611-2897, Tel: (312) 751-7000
(Advertising agency)
   CIESA/NCK Publicidade, Rua Goncalves Zarco 14, P-1499 Lisbon, Portugal
   Comunicar, Travessa Cova da Moura 2, P-1300 Lisbon, Portugal
   FCB Publicidade, Avenida de Liberdata 13-3, P-1200 Lisbon, Portugal
   Park Publicidade, Rua Braamcamp 14-4o, P-1200 Lisbon, Portugal
   Publicis, Avenida Almirante Gago Coutinho 113, P-1700 Lisbon, Portugal

GENERAL ELECTRIC CO   3135 Easton Tpk, Fairfield, CT 06431,
  Tel: (203) 373-2211
(Diversified manufacturing, technology & services)
   General Electric Co.,
     all mail to U.S. address; phone (800) 626-2004 or (518) 438-6500

GENERAL MOTORS ACCEPTANCE CORP   3044 West Grand Blvd, Detroit, MI 48202,
  Tel: (313) 556-5000
(Automobile financing)
  GMAC de Portugal, Avenida Eng. Durate Pacheco 827, Amoreiras, Torre 1-6,
    P-1000 Lisbon, Portugal

GENERAL MOTORS CORP   3044 W Grand Blvd, Detroit, MI 48202-3091,
  Tel: (313) 556-5000
(Mfr full line vehicles, automotive electronics, coml technologies, telecom, space,
finance)
   Cablesa-Industria de Componentes Electricos Lda., Apartado 82, Linho,
     P-2710 Sintra, Portugal
   General Motors de Portugal Lda., Apartado 8115, P-1802 Lisbon, Portugal
   Inlan-Industria de Componentes Mecanicos Lda., Apartado 40, P-7400 Ponte de Sor,
     Portugal

THE GILLETTE CO   Prudential Tower, Boston, MA 02199, Tel: (617) 421-7000
(Devel/mfr personal care/use prdts: blades & razors, toiletries, cosmetics,
stationery)
   Gillette Portuguesa Lda., Lisbon, Portugal

FRANK B HALL & CO INC   549 Pleasantville Rd, Briarcliff Manor, NY 10510,
Tel: (914) 769-9200
(Insurance)
   Joao Mata Lda., Rua Chmico Castelo Branco 21, P-1100 Lisbon, Portugal

THE HARPER GROUP   260 Townsend St, PO Box 77933, San Francisco,
CA 94107-1719, Tel: (415) 978-0600
(Ocean/air freight fwdg, customs brokerage, packing & whse, logistics mgt, ins)
   Circle Freight Intl. (Portugal) Lda., Rua C Edificio 124, Gabinete 8,
      Aeroporto de Lisboa, P-1700 Lisbon, Portugal
   Circle Freight Intl. (Portugal) Lda., also in Marinha & Oporto, Portugal

H J HEINZ CO   PO Box 57, Pittsburgh, PA 15230-0057, Tel: (412) 456-5700
(Processed food prdts & nutritional services)
   IDAL (Industrias de Alimentacao Lda.), Lisbon, Portugal
   Marie Elisabeth Produtos Alimentares SA, Peniche, Portugal

HEWLETT-PACKARD CO   3000 Hanover St, Palo Alto, CA 94304-0890,
Tel: (415) 857-1501
(Mfr computing, communications & measurement prdts & services)
   Hewlett-Packard Portugal SA, Rua Gregoria Lopes, Lote 1732A, P-1400 Lisbon, Portugal

HONEYWELL INC   PO Box 524, Minneapolis, MN 55440-0524, Tel: (612) 951-1000
(Devel/mfr controls for home & building, industry, space & aviation)
   Honeywell Lda., Edificio Suecia II, Av. do Forte 3, Piso 3, Carnaxide,
      2795 Linda a Velha, Portugal

HORWATH INTL   415 Madison Ave, New York, NY 10017, Tel: (212) 838-5566
(Public accountants & auditors)
   Horwath & Horwath (Portugal), Rua Joao da Silva, Lote 33, P-1900 Lisbon, Portugal

IBM CORP   Old Orchard Rd, Armonk, NY 10504, Tel: (914) 765-1900
(Information products, technology & services)
   Companhia IBM Portuguesa SARL, Lisbon, Portugal

ICF KAISER INTL INC   9300 Lee Hwy, Fairfax, VA 22031, Tel: (703) 934-3600
(Engineering, construction & consulting services)
   Kaiser Engineers, Edificio Monumental, Av. Fontes Pereira de Melo 51-20-D,
      P-1050 Lisbon, Portugal

ITT SHERATON CORP   60 State St, Boston, MA 02108, Tel: (617) 367-3600
(Hotel operations)
   Lisboa Sheraton Hotel, Rua Latino Coelho 1, P-1097 Lisbon, Portugal
   Madeira Sheraton Hotel, Apartado 598, P-9007 Funchal, Madeira, Portugal
   Porto Sheraton Hotel, Avenida da Boavista 1269, P-4100 Porto, Portugal

JOHNSON & JOHNSON   One Johnson & Johnson Plaza, New Brunswick, NJ 08933,
Tel: (908) 524-0400
(R&D/mfr/sale health care prdts)
   Janssen Farmaceutica Portugal Lda., Campo Grande 281D, P-1700 Lisbon, Portugal
   Johnson & Johnson Lda., Apartado 17, P-2746 Quelerz, Portugal

S C JOHNSON & SON INC   1525 Howe St, Racine, WI 53403, Tel: (414) 631-2000
  (Home, auto, commercial & personal care prdts, specialty chems)
    Ceras Johnson de Portugal Lda., Rua Maestro Raul Portela 1, Lagoal, Caxias, Portugal

KELLOGG CO   One Kellogg Sq, PO Box 3599, Battle Creek, MI 49016-3599,
  Tel: (616) 961-2000
  (Mfr ready-to-eat cereals, convenience foods)
    Kellogg Portugal, Lisbon, Portugal (all inquiries to U.S. address)

KIMBERLY-CLARK CORP   PO Box 619100, Dallas, TX 75261, Tel: (214) 281-1200
  (Mfr fiber-based prdts for personal care, lumber & paper prdts)
    Kimberly-Clark Portugal Ltda., Portugal

KNOGO CORP   350 Wireless Blvd, Hauppauge, NY 11788-3907, Tel: (516) 232-2100
  (Mfr electr article surveillance sys)
    Knogo Equipamentos de Seguranca Lda., Rua Ivone Silva 2B, Reboleira,
      P-2700 Amadora, Portugal

LINTAS:WORLDWIDE   1 Dag Hammarskjold Plaza, New York, NY 10017,
  Tel: (212) 605-8000
  (Advertising agency)
    Lintas:Lisbon, Avenida Conselheiro Fernando de Sousa 19-7o, P-1092 Lisbon, Portugal

ARTHUR D LITTLE INC   25 Acorn Park, Cambridge, MA 02140-2390,
  Tel: (617) 498-5000
  (Mgmt, environ, health & safety consulting; tech & prdt development)
    Arthur D. Little Inc., Edificio Monumental 2-C, Av. Praia de Vitoroa 71-A,
      P-1050 Lisbon, Portugal

MANPOWER INTL INC   5301 N Ironwood Rd, PO Box 2053, Milwaukee,
  WI 53201-2053, Tel: (414) 961-1000
  (Temporary help service)
    Manpower Portuguesa, Praca Jose Fontana 9-C, P-1000 Lisbon, Portugal

MEASUREX CORP   One Results Way, Cupertino, CA 95014-5991, Tel: (408) 255-1500
  (Mfr computer integrated mfg sys)
    Measurex Sistemas de Controle Lda., Avenida 22 de Dezembro 21-7C, P-2900 Setubal,
      Portugal

MERCK SHARP & DOHME INTL   PO Box 2000, Rahway, NJ 07065, Tel: (201) 574-4000
  (Pharms, chems & biologicals)
    Merck, Sharp & Dohme Lda., Rua Barata S. Igueiro 37-1o, Lisbon, Portugal

METROPOLITAN LIFE INSURANCE CO   1 Madison Ave, New York, NY 10010-3690,
  Tel: (212) 578-2211
  (Insurance & retirement savings prdts & services)
    Seguros Genesis SA, Av. Fontes Pereira de Melo 51-6E, P-1050 Lisbon, Portugal

MICROSOFT CORP   One Microsoft Way, Redmond, WA 98052-6399,
  Tel: (206) 882-8080
  (Computer software, peripherals & services)
    Microsoft Portugal, Galerias Alto da Barra, Piso 3, Av. Das Descobertas,
      P-2780 Oeiras, Portugal

MOBIL CORP   3225 Gallows Rd, Fairfax, VA 22037-0001, Tel: (703) 846-3000
  (Petroleum explor & refining, mfr petrol prdts, chems, petrochems)
    Mobil Oil Portuguesa Lda., Edif. Mobil, Rua Castillo 165, P-1903 Lisbon Codex,
    Portugal

MORGAN GUARANTY TRUST CO   23 Wall St, New York, NY 10260, Tel: (212) 483-2323
  (Banking)
    MDM-Estudos Tecnicos e Financeiros Lda., Rua Rodrigues Sampaio 50-2, P-1100 Lisbon,
    Portugal

McCANN-ERICKSON WORLDWIDE   750 Third Ave, New York, NY 10017,
  Tel: (212) 697-6000
  (Advertising)
    McCann-Erickson/Hora Publicidade Lda., Avenida Antonio Jose de Almeida 7,
    P-1093 Lisbon, Portugal

THE McGRAW-HILL COS   1221 Ave of the Americas, New York, NY 10020,
  Tel: (212) 512-2000
  (Books, magazines, info sys, financial serv, broadcast operations)
    Editora McGraw-Hill de Portugal Lda., Avenida Almicante Reis 59-6, P-1100 Lisbon,
    Portugal

A C NIELSEN CO   Nielsen Plaza, Northbrook, IL 60062-6288, Tel: (708) 498-6300
  (Market research)
    A.C. Nielsen Co., Rua D. Filipa de Vilhena 38, P-1000 Lisbon, Portugal

NORDSON CORP   28601 Clemens Rd, Westlake, OH 44145, Tel: (216) 892-1580
  (Mfr ind application equip & packaging mach)
    Nordson Portugal Equipamento Industrial Lda., Rua Sidonio Pais 30-34,
    Nogueira da Maia, P-4470 Maia, Portugal

OTIS ELEVATOR CO   10 Farm Springs, Farmington, CT 06032, Tel: (860) 676-6528
  (Mfr elevators & escalators)
    Otis Elevadores SA, SAO Carlos, Apartado 4, P-2725 Mem Martins, Sintra, Portugal

PFIZER INC   235 E 42nd St, New York, NY 10017-5755, Tel: (212) 573-2323
  (Mfr healthcare products)
    Laboratorios Pfizer SA, Portugal
    Pfizer S.G.P.S. Lda., Portugal

PINKERTON SECURITY & INVESTIGATION SERVICES   6727 Odessa Ave, Van Nuys,
  CA 91406-5796, Tel: (818) 373-8800
  (Security & investigation services)
    Pinkerton Security Services, Praga de Alvalade 4, 11-D, P-1700 Lisbon, Portugal

PREMARK INTL INC   1717 Deerfield Rd, Deerfield, IL 60015, Tel: (708) 405-6000
  (Mfr/sale diversified consumer & coml prdts)
    Dartluso-Industria Lusitana de Artigos Domesticos Lda., Avenida da Republica 83-3,
    Lisbon, Portugal
    Tupperware (Portugal) Artigos Domesticos Lda., Avenida da Republica 83-3, Lisbon,
    Portugal

RAYCHEM CORP   300 Constitution Dr, Menlo Park, CA 94025, Tel: (415) 361-3333
  (Devel/mfr/mkt materials science products for electronics, telecommunications &
  industry)
    Raychem Produtos Quimicos Lda., Avda. Miguel Bombarda 36-82, P-1000 Lisbon, Portugal

READER'S DIGEST ASSOCIATION INC   PO Box 235, Pleasantville, NY 10570,
  Tel: (914) 238-1000
  (Publisher magazines & books, direct mail marketer)
     Seleccnoes do Reader's Digest (Portugal) SARL, Rua Francisco Manuel de Melo 21,
       P-1000 Lisbon, Portugal

REEVES BROTHERS INC   PO Box 1898, Hwy 29 South, Spartanburg, SC 29304,
  Tel: (803) 576-1210
  (Woven cotton & synthetic fabrics, textile job finishing, filter cloth, ind fabric
  prdts)
     Intebis-Industrias Texteis de Beiriz SARL, Rua da Constituicao, 797-1o, Porto,
       Portugal
     Reeves Portuguesa - Revestimentos SARL, Rua da Constituicao 797, Porto, Portugal

RJR NABISCO INC   1301 Ave of the Americas, New York, NY 10019,
  Tel: (212) 258-5600
  (Mfr consumer packaged food prdts & tobacco prdts)
     R.J. Reynolds (Portugal) Lda., Rua do Proletariado 14, Lisbon, Portugal

THE ROCKPORT CO   220 Donald J Lynch Blvd, Marlboro, MA 01752,
  Tel: (508) 485-2090
  (Mfr/imp dress & casual footwear)
     Reebok Worldwide Trading Co., Av. D. Afonso Henriques 1196, Sala 502-5,
       P-4450 Matosinhos, Portugal

SEA-LAND SERVICE INC   150 Allen Rd, Liberty Corner, NJ 07920,
  Tel: (201) 558-6000
  (Container transport)
     A.J. Concalves de Moraes Lda., 22 Rua do Alecrim, Apartado 2772, Lisbon, Portugal
     A.J. Concalves de Moraes Lda., Rua da Nova Alfandega 18, Apartado 185, Porto,
       Portugal

G D SEARLE & CO   5200 Old Orchard Rd, Skokie, IL 60077, Tel: (708) 982-7000
  (Mfr pharms, health care & optical prdts, specialty chems)
     Searle Farmaceutical Lda., Rua Sanches Coelho 1 - 8 Esq., P-1600 Lisbon, Portugal

STANDEX INTL CORP   6 Manor Pkwy, Salem, NH 03079, Tel: (603) 893-9701
  (Mfr diversified graphics, institutional, ind/electr & consumer prdts)
     Mold-Tech Portugal Lda., Rua da Estrada 266, Crestins, P-4470 Maia, Portugal

THE STANLEY WORKS   1000 Stanley Dr, PO Box 7000, New Britain, CT 06050,
  Tel: (203) 225-5111
  (Mfr hand tools & hardware)
     Stanley Portugal Lda., Edif. Mobil, Rua Castilho 165, P-1000 Lisbon, Portugal

STIEFEL LABORATORIES INC   255 Alhambra Circle, Coral Gables, FL 33134,
  Tel: (305) 443-3807
  (Mfr pharmaceuticals, dermatological specialties)
     Laboratorios Farmaceuticos Stiefel (Portugal) Lda., Rua Oliveria Martins,
       Lote 243 - LJ, Esq. Casal de S. Bras, P-2700 Amadora, Portugal

TEXAS INSTRUMENTS INC   13500 N Central Expwy, Dallas, TX 75265,
  Tel: (214) 995-2011
  (Mfr semiconductor devices, electr/electro-mech sys, instr & controls)
     Texas Instruments Equipamento Electronico (Portugal) Lda.,
       Rua Eng. Frederico Ulrich 2650, Moreira da Maia, P-4470 Maia, Portugal

TRANE CO   3600 Pammel Creek Rd, La Crosse, WI 54601, Tel: (608) 787-2000
  (Mfr/distr/svce A/C sys & equip)
    Ava Norte Lda., Porto, Portugal
    Trane Espanola, Sucural Em Portugal, Av. Miguel Bombarda 120-A, P-1000 Lisbon,
      Portugal

TRANS WORLD AIRLINES INC   505 N 6th St, St Louis, MO 63101,
  Tel: (314) 589-3000
  (Air transportation)
    Trans World Airlines Inc., Avenida da Liberdade 258A, Lisbon, Portugal

UNISYS CORP   PO Box 500, Blue Bell, PA 19424, Tel: (215) 986-4011
  (Mfg/mktg/serv electr info sys)
    Burroughs Electronica Portugal Lda., Rua Actor Antonio Silva 7, P-1600 Lisbon,
      Portugal
    Unisys (Portugal) Sistemas de Informac, Rua Actor Antonio Silva 7, P-1600 Lisbon,
      Portugal

URSCHEL LABORATORIES INC   2503 Calumet Ave, PO Box 2200, Valparaiso,
  IN 46384-2200, Tel: (219) 464-4811
  (Design/mfr precision food processing equip)
    Urschel Intl. Ltd., World Trade Center, Av. do Brasil 1, P-1700 Lisbon, Portugal

XEROX CORP   800 Long Ridge Rd, PO Box 1600, Stamford, CT 06904,
  Tel: (203) 968-3000
  (Mfr document processing equip, sys & supplies)
    Xerox Corp., Lisbon, Portugal

QATAR

ANEMOSTAT PRODUCTS DIV   888 N Keyser Ave, Scranton, PA 18501,
  Tel: (717) 346-6586
  (Mfr air diffusers, grilles & related equip for A/C, heating & ventilation)
    KMC, P.O. Box 1038, Doha, Qatar

CHASE MANHATTAN BANK N A   1 Chase Manhattan Plaza, New York, NY 10081,
  Tel: (212) 552-2222
  (Intl banking)
    The Commercial Bank of Qatar Ltd., P.O. Box 3232, Doha, Qatar

DRILCO DIV   16740 Hardy Rd, PO Box 60068, Houston, TX 77205,
  Tel: (713) 443-3370
  (Oil well down-hole drilling tools)
    Drilco Inc., P.O. Box 150, Doha, Qatar

ITT SHERATON CORP   60 State St, Boston, MA   02108, Tel: (617) 367-3600
  (Hotel operations)
    Doha Sheraton Hotel, P.O. Box 6000, Doha, Qatar

OCEANEERING INTL INC   PO Box 218130, Houston, TX   77218-8130,
  Tel: (713) 578-8868
  (Underwater serv to offshore oil & gas ind)
    Oceaneering Intl. Inc., Operational base in Doha

WEATHERFORD INTL INC   1360 Post Oak Blvd, PO Box 27608, Houston,
  TX   77227-7608, Tel: (713) 439-9400
  (Oilfield servs, prdts & equip; mfr marine cranes)
    Weatherford Oil Tool Middle East Ltd., P.O. Box 150, Doha, Qatar

REUNION

CALTEX PETROLEUM CORP   PO Box 619500, Dallas, TX   75261, Tel: (214) 830-1000
  (Petroleum prdts)
    Caltex Oil (Reunion) Ltd., 46 Rue Labourdonnais, 97462 St. Denis, Reunion

THE STANLEY WORKS   1000 Stanley Dr, PO Box 7000, New Britain, CT   06050,
  Tel: (203) 225-5111
  (Mfr hand tools & hardware)
    Stanley Works, 1A Ravate, BP 450, 97471 St. Denis, Reunion

ROMANIA

LOUIS BERGER INTL INC   100 Halsted St, East Orange, NJ   07019,
  Tel: (201) 678-1960
  (Consulting engineers, architects, economists & planners)
    Louis Berger SA, CP 374, 2900 Arad 8, Romania

CHEMICAL BANK   270 Park Ave, New York, NY   10017-2070, Tel: (212) 270-6000
  (Banking & financial services)
    Chemical Bank, 16 Bulevardul Republicii, P.O. Box 1-750, Bucharest, Romania

THE COCA-COLA CO   PO Drawer 1734, Atlanta, GA 30301, Tel: (404) 676-2121
  (Mfr/mkt/distr soft drinks, syrups & concentrates, juice & juice-drink prdts)
   Coca-Cola Bucharest, all mail to U.S. address

COMTEK INTL   43 Danbury Rd, Wilton, CT 06897, Tel: (203) 834-1122
  (Produce intl trade fairs)
   Contek Romania SRL, Str Cezikovschi 13, Sector 2, Bucharest, Romania

CPC INTERNATIONAL INC   PO Box 8000, Englewood Cliffs, NJ 07632,
  Tel: (201) 894-4000
  (Consumer foods, corn refining)
   CPC International Inc., C.P. 41-118, Bucharest, Romania

GENERAL ELECTRIC CO   3135 Easton Tpk, Fairfield, CT 06431,
  Tel: (203) 373-2211
  (Diversified manufacturing, technology & services)
   GE Technical Services Co.,
    all mail to U.S. address; phone (800) 626-2004 or (518) 438-6500

GREY ADVERTISING INC   777 Third Ave, New York, NY 10017, Tel: (212) 546-2000
  (Advertising)
   Grey Bucharest, Bucuresti, Sector 1, Str. Buzesti 61, Bloc A6, Apt. 55, Bucharest,
   Romania

HONEYWELL INC   PO Box 524, Minneapolis, MN 55440-0524, Tel: (612) 951-1000
  (Devel/mfr controls for home & building, industry, space & aviation)
   Honeywell Bucharest, St. Aurel Vlaicu 147/20/2/4/62, 72921 Bucharest, Romania

KORN/FERRY INTL   1800 Century Park East, Los Angeles, CA 90067,
  Tel: (310) 552-1834
  (Executive search)
   Korn/Ferry Intl., World Trade Centre, Bd Expozitiei 2, Principal Bldg. 3.01 bis,
   78334 Bucharest, Romania

WARD HOWELL INTL INC   99 Park Ave, New York, NY 10016-1699,
  Tel: (212) 697-3730
  (Executive recruiting)
   Ward Howell Intl., 78 Popa Savu St., 71262 Bucharest, Romania

WESTERN ATLAS INTL INC   10205 Westheimer, PO Box 1407, Houston,
  TX 77251-1407, Tel: (713) 266-5700
  (Full service to the oil industry)
   Western Geophysical, Str. Scoala Herestrau, Interarea Catedrei 5, Sector 1,
   Bucharest, Romania

XEROX CORP   800 Long Ridge Rd, PO Box 1600, Stamford, CT 06904,
  Tel: (203) 968-3000
  (Mfr document processing equip, sys & supplies)
   Xerox Corp., Bucharest, Romania

RUSSIA

3M   3M Center, St Paul, MN 55144-1000, Tel: (612) 733-1110
(Mfr diversified prdts for industry, health care, imaging, commun, transport, safety, consumer, etc)
  3M Russia, Samarsky Per 3. Moscow 129110, Russia

AMERICAN APPRAISAL ASSOCS INC   411 E Wisconsin Ave, Milwaukee, WI 53202,
  Tel: (414) 271-7240
(Valuation consulting serv)
  American Appraisal St. Petersburg, 24 Shpalernaya St., St. Petersburg, Russia

AMERICAN EXPRESS CO   World Financial Center, New York, NY 10285-4765,
  Tel: (212) 640-2000
(Travel, travelers cheques, charge card & financial services)
  American Express Russia Ltd.

AMERICOM BUSINESS CENTERS   2010 Main St, #410, Irvine, CA 92714,
  Tel: (714) 752-6577
(Office leasing, office servs, consult, desktop pub, trade seminars)
  RadAmer Hotel & Business Center, Berezhkovskaya Naberezhnaya 2, Moscow 121059,
    Russia

ANALOGIC CORP   8 Centennial Dr, Peabody, MA 01960, Tel: (508) 977-3000
(Conceive/design/mfr precision meas, signal processing & imaging equip for med, sci, ind & commun)
  Analogic Scientific, Russia

APPLIED POWER INC   13000 W Silver Spring Dr, Butler, WI 53007,
  Tel: (414) 781-6600
(Mfr hi-pressure tools, vibration control prdts, electrical tools & consumables, tech furniture)
  Applied Power Moscow, Leninski Prospekt 95a, Moscow 117313, Russia

ARMSTRONG WORLD INDUSTRIES INC   PO Box 3001, Lancaster, PA 17604,
  Tel: (717) 397-0611
(Mfr/mkt interior furnishings & spec prdts for bldg, auto & textile inds)
  Armstrong Insulation, Moscow, Russia (all inquiries to U.S. address)

ASTRONAUTICS CORP OF AMERICA   PO Box 523, Milwaukee, WI 53201-0523,
  Tel: (414) 447-8200
(Design/devel/mfr aircraft instru, avionic & electronics sys)
  AKE, 40 Marshall Govorova, St. Petersburg 198096, Russia

AUTODESK INC   2320 Marinship Way, Sausalito, CA 94965, Tel: (415) 332-2344
(Devel/mkt/support computer-aided design, engineering, scientific & multimedia
software prdts)
    Parallel Joint Venture, 2 Baumanskaya, dom 9/23, Korpus 18, Moscow 107005, Russia

BAIN & CO INC   2 Copley Place, Boston, MA 02117-0897, Tel: (617) 572-2000
(Strategic management consulting services)
    Bain Link, Scherbakovskaya Str. 40-42, Moscow 105187, Russia

BANKAMERICA CORP   555 California St, San Francisco, CA 94104,
Tel: (415) 622-3456
(Financial services)
    Bank of America NT & SA, Krasnopresnenskaya Na 12, Suite 1605, Moscow, Russia

CARANA CORP   4350 N Fairfax Dr, #500, Arlington, VA 22203,
Tel: (703) 243-1700
(Foreign trade consulting)
    CARANA Corp., Ulitsa Dostoevskogo 21/23, Moscow 103030, Russia

CARLISLE SYNTEC SYSTEMS   PO Box 7000, Carlisle, PA 17013, Tel: (717) 245-7000
(Mfr elastomeric roofing & waterproofing sys)
    Kroytex, 1st Kolobovsky Pereulok 11, Moscow 103051, Russia

CHADBOURNE & PARKE   30 Rockefeller Plaza, New York, NY 10112-0127,
Tel: (212) 408-5100
(Lawyers)
    Chadbourne, Parke, Hedman & Union of Advocates, 38 Maxim Gorky Naberezhnaya,
    Moscow 113035, Russia

CHASE MANHATTAN BANK N A   1 Chase Manhattan Plaza, New York, NY 10081,
Tel: (212) 552-2222
(Intl banking)
    Chase Manhattan Bank NA, WTC/Krasnopresnenskaya Embankment 12, 1709, Moscow 123610,
    Russia

CHESTERTON BINSWANGER INTL   Two Logan Sq, 4th fl, Philadelphia,
PA 19103-2759, Tel: (215) 448-6000
(Real estate & related svces)
    Blumenauer Immobilien, 15 Parkovaja 8, 105203 Moscow, Russia

THE CHRISTIAN SCIENCE PUBLISHING SOCIETY   1 Norway St, Boston, MA 02115,
Tel: (617) 450-2000
(Publishing, broadcasting)
    The Christian Science Monitor, 12/24 Sadovo-Samotechnaya, Apt. 54, Moscow 103051,
    Russia

CITICORP   399 Park Ave, New York, NY 10043, Tel: (212) 559-1000
(Banking & financial services)
    Citibank NA, Russia

COMPUTER ASSOCIATES INTL INC   One Computer Associates Plaza, Islandia,
NY 11788, Tel: (516) 342-5224
(Devel/mkt/mgt info mgt & bus applications software)
    Computer Associates CIS Ltd., Business Complex Bldg. 1, Prospect Mira, VDNH,
    Moscow 129223, Russia

COMTEK INTL   43 Danbury Rd, Wilton, CT 06897, Tel: (203) 834-1122
(Produce intl trade fairs)
   Comtek Intl., 4 Kulneva St. #426, Moscow 121170, Russia

COUDERT BROTHERS   1114 Ave of the Americas, New York, NY 10036-7794,
Tel: (212) 626-4400
(Lawyers)
   Coudert Brothers, Ulitsa Staraya Basmannaya 14, Moscow, Russia

CPC INTERNATIONAL INC   PO Box 8000, Englewood Cliffs, NJ 07632,
Tel: (201) 894-4000
(Consumer foods, corn refining)
   CPC Foods Co. Inc., 53 Leningradsky Prospekt, Moscow 125468, Russia

CRAY RESEARCH INC   655 Lone Oak Dr, Eagan, MN 55121, Tel: (612) 452-6650
(Supercomputer systems & services)
   Cray Research (Eastern Europe) Ltd., Moscow, Russia - all mail to U.S. address

D'ARCY MASIUS BENTON & BOWLES INC (DMB&B)   1675 Broadway, New York,
NY 10019, Tel: (212) 468-3622
(Advertising & communications)
   Promstroybank/DMB&B, 13 Tverskoy Blvd., Moscow 013867, Russia

THE DEXTER CORP   1 Elm Street, Windsor Locks, CT 06096, Tel: (203) 627-9051
(Mfr nonwovens, polymer prdts, magnetic materials, biotechnology)
   The Dexter Corp., Park Place Moscow, Apt. E0513, 113/1 Leninsky Prospect,
     Moscow 117198, Russia

DRESSER INDUSTRIES INC   PO Box 718, Dallas, TX 75221-0718,
Tel: (214) 740-6000
(Diversified supplier of equip & tech serv to energy & natural resource ind)
   Dresser Industries, Ulitsa Lunacharskoyo 7, Moscow, Russia

DRG INTERNATIONAL INC   PO Box 1188, Mountainside, NJ 07092,
Tel: (908) 233-2075
(Mfr/sale/svce medical devices, diagnostic kits, clinical equip)
   DRG Biomedical A/O, ul. Serdobolskaja 1 #183, St. Petersburg 194156, Russia
   DRG TechSystems, Krasnopresnenskaya nab. 12, Mezhdunarodnaya II, Office 721,
     Moscow 123610, Russia

E I DU PONT DE NEMOURS & CO   1007 Market St, Wilmington, DE 19898,
Tel: (302) 774-1000
(Mfr/sale diversified chems, plastics, specialty prdts & fibers)
   Du Pont Russia, Moscow, Russia

FMC CORP   200 E Randolph Dr, Chicago, IL 60601, Tel: (312) 861-6000
(Produces chems & precious metals, mfr machinery, equip & sys for ind, agric & govt)
   A/O FMC Overseas, Russia
   FMC Corp., 3rd Samotechny Per 11, 6th fl., Moscow 103473, Russia
   FMC Tyumen Petroleum Equipment, Russia

FRITZ COMPANIES INC   706 Mission St, San Francisco, CA 94103,
Tel: (415) 904-8360
(Integrated transportation, sourcing, distribution & customs brokerage services)
   Fritz Companies (CIS), J. Hohermuth AG Business Center II,
     Bol. Tcherjomushinskaia Ulica 25, Korpus 40, Moscow, Russia

GENERAL ELECTRIC CO   3135 Easton Tpk, Fairfield, CT 06431,
  Tel: (203) 373-2211
  (Diversified manufacturing, technology & services)
    General Electric Co.,
      all mail to U.S. address; phone (800) 626-2004 or (518) 438-6500

GENERAL MOTORS CORP   3044 W Grand Blvd, Detroit, MI 48202-3091,
  Tel: (313) 556-5000
  (Mfr full line vehicles, automotive electronics, coml technologies, telecom, space,
  finance)
    General Motors, Moscow & St. Petersburg, Russia

THE GILLETTE CO   Prudential Tower, Boston, MA 02199, Tel: (617) 421-7000
  (Devel/mfr personal care/use prdts: blades & razors, toiletries, cosmetics,
  stationery)
    Petersburg Products Intl., Russia

GLOBAL MANAGEMENT & TECHNOLOGY   229 Broadway, Lynbrook, NY 11563,
  Tel: (516) 887-0763
  (Executive education, travel, event organization, consulting)
    Global Management & Technology, Dmitrovsky Hwy. 9, Unit B, Suite 409,
      Moscow 127434, Russia

GREY ADVERTISING INC   777 Third Ave, New York, NY 10017, Tel: (212) 546-2000
  (Advertising)
    Grey Moscow, Kursovoy pereulok 17, Moscow 119034, Russia

H J HEINZ CO   PO Box 57, Pittsburgh, PA 15230-0057, Tel: (412) 456-5700
  (Processed food prdts & nutritional services)
    H.J. Heinz Co. CIS, Moscow, Russia

HEWLETT-PACKARD CO   3000 Hanover St, Palo Alto, CA 94304-0890,
  Tel: (415) 857-1501
  (Mfr computing, communications & measurement prdts & services)
    Hewlett-Packard AO, Pokrovski Blvd. 4/17 KV12, Moscow 101000, Russia

HONEYWELL INC   PO Box 524, Minneapolis, MN 55440-0524, Tel: (612) 951-1000
  (Devel/mfr controls for home & building, industry, space & aviation)
    Honeywell Home & Building Control, Ulitsa Zakharevskaya 31, St. Petersburg 191194,
      Russia
    Honeywell Inc., Tryokprudny per 11/13, Moscow 103001, Russia
    Honeywell Sterch Industrial Automation, Partizanskaya ul 27, Moscow 121351, Russia

ICF KAISER INTL INC   9300 Lee Hwy, Fairfax, VA 22031, Tel: (703) 934-3600
  (Engineering, construction & consulting services)
    ICF/EKO, Novoalekseevska 20A, Moscow 129626, Russia

INGERSOLL-RAND CO   200 Chestnut Ridge Rd, Woodcliff Lake, NJ 07675,
  Tel: (201) 573-0123
  (Mfr compressors, rock drills, pumps, air tools, door hardware, ball bearings)
    Ingersoll-Rand Co./Instrum Rand Co., Kuznetsky Most 21/5, Moscow 103895, Russia

INTERGRAPH CORP   Huntsville, AL 35894-0001, Tel: (205) 730-2000
  (Devel/mfr interactive computer graphic systems)
    Intergraph Graphic Systems Ltd. (Russia), Bakrushina 20, Room 401, Moscow 130054,
      Russia

INTERMODAL TECHNICAL SERVICES INC   9 Campus Dr #7, PO Box 316, Parsippany,
NJ 07054, Tel: (201) 993-3634
(Damage survey & inspection services)
  Marinex/ITS Ltd., Prospekt Vernadskogo 41, 5th Fl., Rooms 517-719, Moscow 117981,
  Russia

INTEROCCIDENTAL INC   PO Box 20548, Riverside, CA 92516-0548,
Tel: (909) 274-9119
(Real estate & business consulting)
  InterOccidental, 33 Ryleeva St., Suite 25, St. Petersburg, Russia

JOHNSON & JOHNSON   One Johnson & Johnson Plaza, New Brunswick, NJ 08933,
Tel: (908) 524-0400
(R&D/mfr/sale health care prdts)
  Johnson & Johnson Ltd., P.O. Box 42, Moscow 11728, Russia

A T KEARNEY INC   222 West Adams St, Chicago, IL 60606, Tel: (312) 648-0111
(Mgmt consultants, executive search)
  A.T. Kearney, 24/27 Sadovaya-Samotyochnaya, Mosenka Plaza, Moscow 103051, Russia

KEYSTONE INTL INC   PO Box 40010, Houston, TX 77040, Tel: (713) 466-1176
(Mfr butterfly valves, actuators & control accessories)
  Keystone Russia, Russia

KORN/FERRY INTL   1800 Century Park East, Los Angeles, CA 90067,
Tel: (310) 552-1834
(Executive search)
  Korn/Ferry Intl., 20 Voznesensky per, Korpus 3, Moscow 103009, Russia
  Korn/Ferry Intl., Ul Gorohovaya 12, St. Petersburg 191186, Russia

ARTHUR D LITTLE INC   25 Acorn Park, Cambridge, MA 02140-2390,
Tel: (617) 498-5000
(Mgmt, environ, health & safety consulting; tech & prdt development)
  Arthur D. Little Intl. Inc., 3rd Khoroshevsky Proyezd 3V, Bldg. 2, Moscow 123007,
  Russia

LORAL INTL INC   999 Central Park Ave, Yonkers, NY 10704-1013,
Tel: (914) 964-6520
(Mktg coordination: defense electronics, communications sys)
  Spacesystems/Loral, Russia

THE LUBRIZOL CORP   29400 Lakeland Blvd, Wickliffe, OH 44092-2298,
Tel: (216) 943-4200
(Mfr chem additives for lubricants & fuels)
  Solub Product Application Laboratory, Russia

MICROSOFT CORP   One Microsoft Way, Redmond, WA 98052-6399,
Tel: (206) 882-8080
(Computer software, peripherals & services)
  Microsoft Russia, Ulitsa Staraya Basmannaya 14, Moscow 103064, Russia

MOTOROLA INC   1303 E Algonquin Rd, Schaumburg, IL 60196, Tel: (708) 576-5000
(Mfr commun equip, semiconductors, cellular phones)
  Motorola Moscow, Moscow, Russia

THE MacNEAL-SCHWENDLER CORP   815 Colorado Blvd, Los Angeles, CA 90041,
  Tel: (213) 258-9111
  (Devel/mfr computer-aided engineering software)
    MacNeal-Schwendler GmbH, ul. 26 Bakinsky Komissarov, 11 Whg. 96, Moscow 117571,
    Russia

NATIONAL PATENT DEVELOPMENT CORP   9 W 57th St, New York, NY 10019,
  Tel: (212) 230-9500
  (Mfr/distr medical, health care & specialty prdts)
    St. Petersburg Technologies (JV), St. Petersburg, Russia

NORDSON CORP   28601 Clemens Rd, Westlake, OH 44145, Tel: (216) 892-1580
  (Mfr ind application equip & packaging mach)
    Nordson Deutschland GmbH, 37 Energetikov Ave. 6/F, St. Petersburg 195248, Russia

OCCIDENTAL PETROLEUM CORP   10889 Wilshire Blvd, Los Angeles, CA 90024,
  Tel: (213) 879-1700
  (Petroleum & petroleum prdts, chems, plastics)
    Occidental Petroleum Corp., Krasnopresnenskaya Naberejnaya, 12 World Trade Center,
    14th Floor, Moscow 123610, Russia
    Permaneft, Russia

ORION MARINE CORP   79 W Monroe #1105, Chicago, IL 60603, Tel: (312) 263-5153
  (Ocean transportation)
    CBT Vostochny, Wrangel - 1 Primoskiy Krai, Vostochny 692903, Russia
    Wal-Rus Ltd., Nekrasova 40-1, St. Petersburg 191014, Russia

OTIS ELEVATOR CO   10 Farm Springs, Farmington, CT 06032, Tel: (860) 676-6528
  (Mfr elevators & escalators)
    Otis St. Petersburg, Khimichasky Pereulok 14, St. Petersburg 198095, Russia

PARKER DRILLING CO   8 E Third St, Tulsa, OK 74103-3637, Tel: (918) 585-8221
  (Drilling contractor)
    Parker Drilling Co., c/o White Knights Joint Enterpirse, 25 Agan, White Nights Sq.,
    Raduzhnyy, Russia

RADISSON HOTELS INTL   Carlson Pkwy, PO Box 59159, Minneapolis,
  MN 55459-8204, Tel: (612) 540-5526
  (Hotels)
    Slavjanskaya Hotel, Berezhkovskaya Nabereznaya 2, Moscow 121059, Russia

RJR NABISCO INC   1301 Ave of the Americas, New York, NY 10019,
  Tel: (212) 258-5600
  (Mfr consumer packaged food prdts & tobacco prdts)
    RJR-Petro, St. Petersburg, Russia

ROCKWELL INTL CORP   2201 Seal Beach Blvd, PO Box 4250, Seal Beach,
  CA 90740-8250, Tel: (310) 797-3311
  (Prdts & serv for aerospace, automotive, electronics, graphics & automation inds)
    Rockwell Intl. Ltd., Suite 403, Bolshoi Strochenovsky Pereulok 22/25,
    Moscow 113054, Russia

RUSSIN & VECCHI   1140 Connecticut Ave, #250, Washington, DC 20036,
  Tel: (202) 223-4793
  (Lawyers)

Russin & Vecchi, Danilovsky Hotel Complex, Bolshoy Starodanilovsky Perulok 5, Moscow 113191, Russia

SPRINT INTERNATIONAL   12490 Sunrise Valley Dr, Reston, VA 22096,
  Tel: (703) 689-6000
  (Telecommunications)
    Sprint Networks, 7 Tverskaya Ulitsa, 103375 Moscow, Russia

TELEDYNE INC   2049 Century Park East, Los Angeles, CA 90067-3101,
  Tel: (310) 277-3311
  (Divers mfg: aviation & electronics, specialty metals, industrial & consumer prdts)
    Teledyne Russia, Leningradsky Prospekt 55, Moscow 125468, Russia

TRANSCISCO INDUSTRIES INC   601 California St, #1301, San Francisco,
  CA 94108-2818, Tel: (415) 477-9700
  (Railcar leasing, maintenance & transportation svces)
    Sovfinamtrans (SFAT), Krasnoprudnaja 26/1, Moscow 107170, Russia

U S FUR EXCHANGE   515 Lake St S, Kirkland, WA 98033, Tel: (206) 828-6774
  (Fur auctioning, distr & sale)
    Palms & Co. Inc., 22 Myasnitskaya St., Moscow 101000, Russia
    Palms & Co. Inc., Vasilovsky St. 21, #18, Konokova 171280, Tver Region, Russia
    Palms & Co. Inc., Zelenograd K-460, Korpus 1126 rv. 659, Moscow 103460, Russia
    Palms & Co. Inc., P. Lumumba St. 50-57, Vladivostok 690037, Russia
    Palms & Co. Inc., Gagarin St. 21a #45, Magadan 685027, Russia
    Russian Venture Capital Fund of America, Ultisa Sverdlova 3, Box 263,
      Novosibirsk 630093, Russia
    U.S. Interbank Currency Exchange, Argakain Per 1, St. Petersburg 191023, Russia

U S SURGICAL CORP   150 Glover Ave, Norwalk, CT 06856, Tel: (203) 845-1000
  (Mfr/devel/mkt surgical staplers, laparoscopic instru & sutures)
    Auto Suture Instruments (ASI), all mail to U.S. address
    Auto Suture Russia Inc., all mail to U.S. address

UNION CARBIDE CORP   39 Old Ridgebury Rd, Danbury, CT 06817,
  Tel: (203) 794-2000
  (Mfr industrial chemicals, plastics, resins)
    Union Carbide Moscow, ul Mytnaja 3, Pom 1, Moscow 117049, Russia

WACKENHUT CORP   1500 San Remo Ave, Coral Gables, FL 33146,
  Tel: (305) 666-5656
  (Security systems & services)
    Wackenhut A/O, Verhnyaya Syromain, Coscow 103001, Russia

WARD HOWELL INTL INC   99 Park Ave, New York, NY 10016-1699,
  Tel: (212) 697-3730
  (Executive recruiting)
    Deloitte & Touche/Ward Howell Intl., 15 Bolshoi Troykhgorny Pereulok,
      Moscow 123022, Russia
    Deloitte & Touche/Ward Howell Intl., 5A First Beriozovaya Alleya,
      St. Petersburg 197042, Russia

WESTERN ATLAS INTL INC   10205 Westheimer, PO Box 1407, Houston,
  TX 77251-1407, Tel: (713) 266-5700
  (Full service to the oil industry)
    Western Atlas Intl. Inc., Grokholsky Per 19-27, Moscow 129010, Russia
    Western Atlas Software, Grokholsky Per 19-27, Moscow 129010, Russia

XEROX CORP   800 Long Ridge Rd, PO Box 1600, Stamford, CT 06904,
   Tel: (203) 968-3000
   (Mfr document processing equip, sys & supplies)
      Xerox Corp., Chimkent, Moscow, & St. Petersburg, Russia

SAUDI ARABIA

3D/INTERNATIONAL INC   1900 W Loop South, Houston, TX 77027,
   Tel: (713) 871-7000
   (Design, management, environmental services)
      3D/I-Saudi Arabia, P.O. Box 4030, Riyadh 11491, Saudi Arabia

ALLIEDSIGNAL TECHNICAL SERVICES CORP   One Bendix Rd, Ellicott City,
   MD 21045, Tel: (410) 964-7000
   (Technical services)
      Allied-Signal Technical Services Corp., P.O. Box 8822, Jeddah, Saudi Arabia

AMERICAN AIRLINES INC   PO Box 619616, Dallas-Ft Worth Arpt, TX 75261-9616,
   Tel: (817) 355-1234
   (Air transp)
      American Airlines Inc., P.O. Box 7747, Jeddah, Saudi Arabia

AMERON INC   PO Box 7007, Pasadena, CA 91109-7007, Tel: (818) 683-4000
   (Mfr steel pipe sys, concrete prdts, traffic & lighting poles, protective coatings)
      Ameron Saudi Arabia Ltd., P.O. Box 589, Damman, Saudi Arabia

ASHLAND OIL INC   1000 Ashland Dr, Russell, KY 41169, Tel: (606) 329-3333
   (Petroleum exploration, refining & transportation; mfr chemicals, oils & lubricants)
      Saudi Industrial Resins Ltd., P.O. Box 7764, Jeddah 21472, Saudi Arabia

BAKER OIL TOOLS   PO Box 40129, Houston, TX 77240-0129, Tel: (713) 466-1322
   (Mfr/serv oil/gas well completions equip)
      Baker Mira Saudi Arabia Ltd., c/o Al Rushaid Trading Co., P.O. Box 540,
         Dhahran Airport 31932, Saudi Arabia

BDM INTL INC   7915 Jones Branch Dr, McLean, VA 22102, Tel: (703) 848-5000
   (Professional & technical services)
      The BDM Corp., P.O. Box 6872, Riyadh, Saudi Arabia

BECHTEL GROUP INC   50 Beale St, PO Box 3965, San Francisco, CA 94119,
   Tel: (415) 768-1234
   (Engineering & constr)
      Arabian Bechtel Co., P.O. Box 88, Dhahran Airport, Dhahran, Saudi Arabia
      Arabian Bechtel Co., P.O. Box 5963, Jeddah, Saudi Arabia
      Intl. Bechtel Inc., P.O. Box 4103, Riyadh, Saudi Arabia

BENTLY NEVADA CORP   PO Box 157, Minden, NV 89423, Tel: (702) 782-3611
  (Electronic monitoring system)
     Bently Nevada Corp., c/o A.A. Turki Corp., P.O. Box 136, Dhahran Airport, Dhahran,
     Saudi Arabia

C F BRAUN & CO   1000 S Fremont Ave, Alhambra, CA 91802, Tel: (213) 570-1000
  (Engineering/constr/mgmt for energy & power ind)
     Arabian Industrial & Petroleum Facilities Construction Co., Dhahran Airport,
       P.O. Box 4, Al-Khobar, Saudi Arabia
     Saudi Braun Ltd., Abraj Bldg., Al Bin Abu Talib St., Sharafia, Jeddah, Saudi Arabia

BROWN & ROOT INC   4100 Clinton Dr, Houston, TX 77020-6299,
  Tel: (713) 676-3011
  (Engr, constr & maintenance)
     Brown & Root Arabia Ltd., P.O. Box 10255, Madinat Al-Jubail, Al-Sinaiyah 31961,
       Saudi Arabia
     Brown & Root Saudi Ltd., P.O. Box 52926,, Riyadh, Saudi Arabia
     Rezayat Brown & Root Saudi Ltd., P.O. Box 90, Al-Khobar 31952, Saudi Arabia

LEO BURNETT CO INC   35 West Wacker Dr, Chicago, IL 60601, Tel: (312) 220-5959
  (Advertising agency)
     Targets Advertising, P.O. Box 6093, Jeddah 21442, Saudi Arabia

BUTLER MFG CO   PO Box 917, Kansas City, MO 64141, Tel: (816) 968-3000
  (Pre-engineered steel struc sys, curtain wall & elec dist sys, grain storage &
  handling sys)
     Saudi Building Systems, P.O. Box 3643, Jeddah, Saudi Arabia

CARL BYOIR & ASSOCIATES INC   420 Lexington Ave, New York, NY 10017,
  Tel: (212) 210-6000
  (Public relations, intl commun)
     Tihama for Advertising, Public Relations & Marketing, Al Andalus St.,
       P.O. Box 5455, Jeddah 21422, Saudi Arabia

CALGON CORP   PO Box 1346, Pittsburgh, PA 15230, Tel: (412) 777-8000
  (Mfr. cosmetic, personal care & water treatment prdts)
     Abdel Hadi Abdallah Al-Quahtani & Sons, P.O. Box 20, Damman 31411, Saudi Arabia

CALMAQUIP ENGINEERING CORP   7240 NW 12th St, Miami, FL 33121,
  Tel: (305) 592-4510
  (Engineering)
     Calmaquip Engineering Corp., P.O. Box 1312, Queens Bldg., Jeddah, Saudi Arabia

CALTEX PETROLEUM CORP   PO Box 619500, Dallas, TX 75261, Tel: (214) 830-1000
  (Petroleum prdts)
     Caltex (Overseas) Ltd. SA, Ace Bldg., 2nd fl., Al Hamra - Yousuf Nassif St.,
       Jeddah 21492, Saudi Arabia

CARRIER CORP   One Carrier Place, Farmington, CT 06034-4015,
  Tel: (203) 674-3000
  (Mfr/distr/svce A/C, heating & refrigeration equip)
     Arabian Air Conditioning Co., P.O. Box 349, Jeddah, Saudi Arabia
     Carrier Saudi Service Co., P.O. Box 9784, Off Khurais Rd., Riyadh 11423,
       Saudi Arabia
     Saudi Air Conditioning Mfg. Co. (SAMCO), Jeddah, Saudi Arabia

CBI INDUSTRIES INC   800 Jorie Blvd, Oak Brook, IL 60521, Tel: (708) 654-7000
  (Holding co: metal plate fabricating, constr, oil & gas drilling)
    Arabian CBI Ltd., R.T. Box 610, Dhahran, Saudi Arabia

CH2M HILL INC   PO Box 428, Corvallis, OR 97339, Tel: (503) 752-4271
  (Consulting engrs, planners, economists, scientists)
    CH2M Hill Inc., P.O. Box 26739, Riyadh 11496, Saudi Arabia

CHASE MANHATTAN BANK N A   1 Chase Manhattan Plaza, New York, NY 10081,
  Tel: (212) 552-2222
  (Intl banking)
    Saudi Industrial Development Fund, P.O. Box 4143, Samatowers Airport Rd., Riyadh,
      Saudi Arabia
    Saudi Investment Banking Corp., P.O. Box 3553, Riyadh, Saudi Arabia
    Saudi Investment Banking Corp., P.O. Box 6330 & 5577, Jeddah, Saudi Arabia

CHESTERTON BINSWANGER INTL   Two Logan Sq, 4th fl, Philadelphia,
  PA 19103-2759, Tel: (215) 448-6000
  (Real estate & related svces)
    Dabbagh Group Holding Co. Ltd., P.O. Box 1039, Jeddah 21431, Saudi Arabia

CIGNA CORP   One Liberty Place, Philadelphia, PA 19192, Tel: (215) 523-4000
  (Ins, invest, health care & other fin servs)
    Cigna Worldwide Insurance Co., Al Melaihi Bldg., corner of St. 1 & King Saud St.,
      Dammam 31411, Saudi Arabia

CITICORP   399 Park Ave, New York, NY 10043, Tel: (212) 559-1000
  (Banking & financial services)
    Citibank NA, Saudi Arabia

THE CLOROX CO   1221 Broadway, PO Box 24305, Oakland, CA 94623-1305,
  Tel: (510) 271-7000
  (Mfr domestic consumer packaged prdts)
    Mohammed Ali Abudawood & Co. for Industry, Jeddah, Saudi Arabia
    National Cleaning Products Ltd., Damman, Saudi Arabia

COMBUSTION ENGINEERING INC   900 Long Ridge Road, Stamford, CT 06902,
  Tel: (203) 329-8771
  (Tech constr)
    Combustion Engineering Inc., 19 Bandar St., P.O. Box 245, Dhahran Airport, Dhahran,
      Saudi.Arabia
    Gray Tool Intl. Inc., c/o Drilling Equipment & Chemicals Co., P.O. Box 132, Dammam,
      Saudi Arabia
    Lummus Alireza Ltd., P.O. Box 8321, Riyadh, Saudi Arabia

CONTINENTAL CAN CO   PO Box 5410, Stamford, CT 06856, Tel: (203) 357-8110
  (Packaging prdts & mach, metal, plastic & paper containers)
    Continental Can of Saudi Arabia Ltd., Al-Khobar, Saudi Arabia
    Jeddah Beverage Can Making Co. Ltd., P.O. Box 16626, Jeddah 21474, Saudi Arabia

CONTINENTAL INSURANCE CO   180 Maiden Lane, New York, NY 10038,
  Tel: (212) 440-3000
  (Insurance)
    Continental Insurance Cos., P.O. Box 5511, Jeddah, Saudi Arabia
    Continental Insurance Cos., P.O. Box 4024, Riyadh, Saudi Arabia
    Continental Insurance Cos., P.O. Box 1021, Dammam, Saudi Arabia

CPC INTERNATIONAL INC   PO Box 8000, Englewood Cliffs, NJ 07632,
   Tel: (201) 894-4000
   (Consumer foods, corn refining)
      Best Foods Saudi Arabia Ltd., P.O. Box 16319, Ali-Reza Tower, Medina Rd.,
      Jeddah 21464, Saudi Arabia

D'ARCY MASIUS BENTON & BOWLES INC (DMB&B)   1675 Broadway, New York,
   NY 10019, Tel: (212) 468-3622
   (Advertising & communications)
      ZeeAd DMB&B, P.O. Box 20702, Alireza Tower, Medinah Rd., Jeddah 21465, Saudi Arabia

LEO A DALY   8600 Indian Hills Dr, Omaha, NE 68114, Tel: (402) 391-8111
   (Planning, arch, engr & interior design servs)
      Saudi Consulting House-Leo A. Daly (SCH/LAD), Al Amal Sq., P.O. Box 1267,
         Riyadh 11431, Saudi Arabia

DAMES & MOORE   911 Wilshire Blvd, Los Angeles, CA 90017, Tel: (213) 683-1560
   (Engineering, environmental & construction mgmt services)
      Saudi Arabian Dames & Moore, P.O. Box 2384, Riyadh, Saudi Arabia
      Walk Haydel & Associates, Prince Tarner/12th St., Al-Khobar 31952, Saudi Arabia

DANIEL INDUSTRIES INC   9753 Pine Lake Dr, PO Box 19097, Houston, TX 77224,
   Tel: (713) 467-6000
   (Oil/gas equip & sys, geophysical servs)
      Al-Qahtani-Daniel Ltd., P.O. Box 20, Dammam, Saudi Arabia

DANIEL INTERNATIONAL CORP   100 Fluor Daniel Dr, Greenville, SC 29607-2762,
   Tel: (803) 281-4400
   (Gen contractor, engr & constr)
      Daniel Intl. (Saudi Arabia) Ltd., P.O. Box 8120, Jeddah, Saudi Arabia

DANIEL MANN JOHNSON & MENDENHALL   3250 Wilshire Blvd, Los Angeles, CA 90010,
   Tel: (213) 381-3663
   (Architects & engineers)
      DMJM, P.O. Box 58729, Riyadh 11515, Saudi Arabia

DMJM/TECHNICAL MGMT SERVICES   3250 Wilshire Blvd, Los Angeles,
   CA 90010-1599, Tel: (213) 381-3663
   (Tech consultants)
      DMJM/Technical Services Inc., P.O. Box 1779, Dhahran, Saudi Arabia

THE DOW CHEMICAL CO   2030 Dow Center, Midland, MI 48674, Tel: (517) 636-1000
   (Mfr chems, plastics, pharms, agric prdts, consumer prdts)
      Arabian Chemical Co. Inc., P.O. Box 24, Dammam, Saudi Arabia
      Arabian Chemical Co. Inc., P.O. Box 86, Riyadh, Saudi Arabia

DRAVO CORP   1 Oliver Plaza, Pittsburgh, PA 15222, Tel: (412) 777-5000
   (Material handling equip, process plants)
      Dravo Arabia, P.O. Box 10365, Riyadh, Saudi Arabia

EBASCO SERVICES INC   2 World Trade Center, New York, NY 10048-0752,
   Tel: (212) 839-1000
   (Engineering, constr)
      Ebasco Arabia Ltd., 28th St., Hilal Bldg., Al Khobar, Saudi Arabia

ECOLOGY AND ENVIRONMENT INC   368 Pleasant View Dr, East Amherst,
 NY 14086-1397, Tel: (716) 684-8060
 (Environmental, scientific & engineering consulting)
    Ecology & Environment of Saudi Arabia Ltd., c/o Petrostar/Star Navigation,
      P.O. Box 3793, Jeddah, Saudi Arabia

EMCO ENGINEERING INC   25 North St, Canton, MA 02021, Tel: (617) 828-7340
 (Water purification & sewage treatment)
    National Co. for Water & Waste Treatment Ltd., P.O Box 852-80, Riyadh, Saudi Arabia

EMERSON ELECTRIC CO   8000 W Florissant Ave, St Louis, MO 63136,
 Tel: (314) 553-2000
 (Electrical & electronic prdts, ind components & sys, consumer, government & defense
 prdts)
    Emerson Electric Co., P.O. Box 9, Al-Khobar, Saudi Arabia

EXPEDITORS INTL OF WASHINGTON INC   PO Box 69620, Seattle, WA 98168-9620,
 Tel: (206) 246-3711
 (Air/ocean freight forwarding, customs brokerage, intl logistics solutions)
    Expeditors Intl., P.O. Box 41924, Jeddah 21531, Saudi Arabia
    Expeditors Intl., P.O. Box 92788, Riyadh 11663, Saudi Arabia

EXXON CORP   225 E John W Carpenter Freeway, Irving, TX 75062-2298,
 Tel: (214) 444-1000
 (Petroleum explor, prod, refining; mfr petrol & chem prdts; coal & minerals)
    Al-Jubail Petrochemical Co., Tareet 183/272, Industrial Area, Saudi Arabia

FIRST EMPLOYMENT CONSULTANTS   6175 NW 153rd St, #230, Miami Lakes,
 FL 33014-2435, Tel: (305) 825-8900
 (Employment consultants)
    First Employment Riyadh, P.O. Box 391, Riyadh, Saudi Arabia

FLUOR DANIEL INC   3333 Michelson Dr, Irvine, CA 92730, Tel: (714) 975-2000
 (Engineering, construction, maintenance & technical services)
    Fluor Daniel Arabia, P.O. Box 360, Dhahran Airport 31932, Dhahran, Saudi Arabia
    Fluor Daniel Arabia, P.O. Box 8120, Jeddah 21482, Saudi Arabia

FMC CORP   200 E Randolph Dr, Chicago, IL 60601, Tel: (312) 861-6000
 (Produces chems & precious metals, mfr machinery, equip & sys for ind, agric & govt)
    FMC Arabia, Saudi Arabia

FOSTER WHEELER CORP   Perryville Corporate Park, Clinton, NJ 08809-4000,
 Tel: (908) 730-4000
 (Engr, constr, mfg)
    Foster Wheeler Saudi Arabia Ltd., P.O. Box 5250, Al-Hamrz Bldg., Jeddah,
      Saudi Arabia

FOUR WINDS INTL GROUP   1500 SW First Ave, #850, Portland, OR 97201,
 Tel: (503) 241-2732
 (Transp of household goods & general cargo, third party logistics)
    Four Winds Saudi Arabia, P.O. Box 4223, Jeddah, Saudi Arabia

GENERAL ELECTRIC CO   3135 Easton Tpk, Fairfield, CT 06431,
 Tel: (203) 373-2211
 (Diversified manufacturing, technology & services)

General Electric Co.,
    all mail to U.S. address; phone (800) 626-2004 or (518) 438-6500

GREY ADVERTISING INC   777 Third Ave, New York, NY 10017, Tel: (212) 546-2000
(Advertising)
    CSS & Grey, Sultan Centre #105, Medina Rd. (North), Jeddah 21511, Saudi Arabia

HAINES LUNDBERG WAEHLER   115 Fifth Ave, New York, NY 10003,
    Tel: (212) 353-4600
(Architecture, engineering, planning, interior design)
    Radicon/HLW Intl., P.O. Box 1097, Al-Khobar, Saudi Arabia

FRANK B HALL & CO INC   549 Pleasantville Rd, Briarcliff Manor, NY 10510,
    Tel: (914) 769-9200
(Insurance)
    Commercial Svcs. Co. Ltd., P.O. Box 11210, Jeddah 21453, Saudi Arabia
    Commercial Svcs. Co. Ltd., P.O. Box 800, Al-Khobar 31952, Saudi Arabia
    Commercial Svcs. Co. Ltd., P.O. Box 21944, Riyadh, Saudi Arabia

HARCO TECHNOLOGIES CORP   1055 W Smith Rd, Medina, OH 44256,
    Tel: (216) 725-6681
(Full-serv corrosion engr, cathodic protection)
    Harco Arabia C.P. Ltd. Co., P.O. Box 444, Dhahran Airport, Dhahran, Saudi Arabia

THE HARPER GROUP   260 Townsend St, PO Box 77933, San Francisco,
    CA 94107-1719, Tel: (415) 978-0600
(Ocean/air freight fwdg, customs brokerage, packing & whse, logistics mgt, ins)
    Circle Freight Intl. Ltd., P.O. Box 12725, Jeddah 21483, Saudi Arabia
    Circle Freight Intl. Ltd., also in Dhahran & Riyadh, Saudi Arabia

HCA INTL CO   1 Park Plaza, PO Box 550, Nashville, TN 37202,
    Tel: (615) 327-9551
(Hospital & health care mgmt)
    HCA Mideast Ltd., P.O. Box 22490, Riyadh, Saudi Arabia

HENNINGSON DURHAM & RICHARDSON INC   8404 Indian Hiills Dr, Omaha, NE 68114,
    Tel: (402) 399-1000
(Consulting architects & engineers)
    Henningson, Durham & Richardson Intl., P.O. Box 6261, Jeddah, Saudi Arabia

HOLIDAY INNS INC   3742 Lamar Ave, Memphis, TN 38195, Tel: (901) 362-4001
(Hotels, restaurants, casinos)
    Holiday Inn, Yanbu, Saudi Arabia

HOLMES & NARVER INC   999 Town & Country Road, Orange, CA 92668,
    Tel: (714) 567-2400
(Arch/engr, constr/constr mgmt, O&M serv)
    Holmes & Narver Inc., P.O. Box 1272, Al-Khobar, Saudi Arabia

HONEYWELL INC   PO Box 524, Minneapolis, MN 55440-0524, Tel: (612) 951-1000
(Devel/mfr controls for home & building, industry, space & aviation)
    Honeywell Turki Arabia Ltd., P.O. Box 718, King Khalid St., Damman 31421,
        Saudi Arabia

HORWATH INTL   415 Madison Ave, New York, NY 10017, Tel: (212) 838-5566
  (Public accountants & auditors)
    Al-Saleh Certified Accountants & Auditors, Al-Mousa Commercial Complex, Tower B,
    3rd Fl., Suite 240, Olaya St, Riyadh, Saudi Arabia

HOSPITAL CORP OF AMERICA   Park Plaza, PO Box 550, Nashville, TN 37203,
  Tel: (615) 327-9551
  (Med equip)
    Hospital Corp. Intl. Ltd., P.O. Box 3354, Riyadh, Saudi Arabia

HUGHES AIRCRAFT CO   PO Box 80028, Los Angeles, CA 90080-0028,
  Tel: (310) 568-6904
  (Mfr electronics equip & sys)
    Hughes Saudi Arabia Ltd., P.O. Box 69357, Riyadh, Saudi Arabia

HYATT INTL CORP   200 West Madison, Chicago, IL 60606, Tel: (312) 750-1234
  (Intl hotel mgmt)
    Hyatt Intl. Hotels, Jeddah & Riyadh, Saudi Arabia

IONICS INC   65 Grove St, Watertown, MA 02172, Tel: (617) 926-2500
  (Mfr desalination equip)
    Ionics Inc., P.O. Box 10983, Riyadh 11445, Saudi Arabia
    Saif/Ionics Co., P.O. Box 1749, Dammam 31441, Saudi Arabia

ITT CORP   1330 Ave of the Americas, New York, NY 10019-5490,
  Tel: (212) 258-1000
  (Design/mfr communications & electronic equip, hotels, insurance)
    ITT-Africa-Middle East SA, P.O. Box 361, Riyadh, Saudi Arabia
    ITT-Africa-Middle East SA, P.O. Box 8, Jeddah, Saudi Arabia
    ITT/AME Saudi Arabia, P.O. Box 8, Jeddah, Saudi Arabia

ITT SHERATON CORP   60 State St, Boston, MA 02108, Tel: (617) 367-3600
  (Hotel operations)
    Al Hada Sheraton, P.O. Box 999, Al Haida (TAIF), Saudi Arabia
    Medina Sheraton Hotel, P.O. Box 1735, Sultanah Rd., Sultanah, Medina, Saudi Arabia
    Riyadh Sheraton, Makkah Rd., Riyadh 11441, Saudi Arabia

JOHNSON & HIGGINS   125 Broad St, New York, NY 10004-2424, Tel: (212) 574-7000
  (Ins brokerage, employee benefit conslt, risk mgmt, human resource conslt, ins/reins
  servs)
    Johnson & Higgins Management Services Ltd., P.O. Box 106, Al-Khobar, Saudi Arabia

KEYSTONE INTL INC   PO Box 40010, Houston, TX 77040, Tel: (713) 466-1176
  (Mfr butterfly valves, actuators & control accessories)
    Keystone Saudi, Saudi Arabia

THE KULJIAN CO   3624 Science Center, Philadelphia, PA 19104,
  Tel: (215) 243-1900
  (Studies, design, engineeering, constr mgmt, site supervision)
    The Kuljian Corp., P.O. Box 4191, Riyadh, Saudi Arabia

L&F PRODUCTS   225 Summit Ave, Montvale, NJ 07645-1575, Tel: (201) 573-5700
  (Mfr household, personal care, woodworking & ind prdts)
    L&F Products, c/o Saudi Import Co., P.O. Box 42, Jeddah 21411, Saudi Arabia

LAW INTERNATIONAL INC 1000 Abernathy Rd NE, Atlanta, GA 30328,
Tel: (404) 396-8000
(Consulting engrs & archs)
Al Rajehi Law Engineering Ltd., P.O. Box 51179, Riyadh 11543, Saudi Arabia

ARTHUR D LITTLE INC 25 Acorn Park, Cambridge, MA 02140-2390,
Tel: (617) 498-5000
(Mgmt, environ, health & safety consulting; tech & prdt development)
Arthur D. Little Intl. Inc., P.O. Box 3266, Riyadh 11471, Saudi Arabia
Arthur D. Little Intl. Inc., P.O. Box 9251, Jeddah 21413, Saudi Arabia

LOCKHEED MARTIN CORP 6801 Rockledge Dr, Bethesda, MD 20817,
Tel: (301) 897-6000
(Design/mfr/mgmt sys in fields of space, defense, energy, electronics, materials,
info & tech svces)
Lockheed Martin Intl. SA, Box 2811, Riyadh 11461, Saudi Arabia

THE LUBRIZOL CORP 29400 Lakeland Blvd, Wickliffe, OH 44092-2298,
Tel: (216) 943-4200
(Mfr chem additives for lubricants & fuels)
Lubrizol Transarabian Co. Ltd., Saudi Arabia

MARRIOTT CORP Marriott Dr, Washington, DC 20058, Tel: (301) 380-9000
(Lodging, contract food & beverage serv, restaurants)
Khurais Marriott Hotel, P.O. Box 2086, Riyadh, Saudi Arabia

MECHANICAL SYSTEMS INC 4110 Romaine, Greensboro, NC 27407,
Tel: (910) 292-4956
(Mechanical & electrical contractors)
Mechanical Systems, P.O. Box 2774, Riyadh, Saudi Arabia

METCALF & EDDY INTL INC 30 Harvard Mill Sq, Wakefield, MA 01880,
Tel: (617) 246-5200
(Consulting engineers)
Metcalf & Eddy/Saudi Consolidated Engineering Co., P.O. Box 1713, Al-Khobar,
Saudi Arabia

MOBIL CORP 3225 Gallows Rd, Fairfax, VA 22037-0001, Tel: (703) 846-3000
(Petroleum explor & refining, mfr petrol prdts, chems, petrochems)
Mobil Saudi Arabia Inc., P.O. Box 5335, Jeddah, Saudi Arabia
Mobil Saudi Arabia Inc., P.O. Box 40228, Riyadh 11499, Saudi Arabia

MORGAN EQUIPMENT CO 131 Stuart St., #300, San Francisco, CA 94105,
Tel: (415) 227-4070
(Engineers, builders)
Saudi Heavy Equipment, P.O. Box 3412, Riyadh, Saudi Arabia
Saudi Morgan Equipment Co. Inc., P.O. Box 394, Dhahran Airport, Dhahran,
Saudi Arabia

NALCO CHEMICAL CO One Nalco Center, Naperville, IL 60563-1198,
Tel: (708) 305-1000
(Chems for water & waste water treatment, oil prod & refining, ind processes;
water/energy mgmt serv)
Nalco Saudi Co. Ltd., P.O. Box 7372, Dammam 31462, Saudi Arabia

NATIONAL CAR RENTAL SYSTEM INC   7700 France Ave S, Minneapolis, MN 55435,
  Tel: (612) 830-2121
  (Car rental)
    National Car Rental, P.O. Box 5241, Jeddah, Saudi Arabia

NATIONAL STARCH & CHEMICAL CO   10 Finderne Ave, Bridgewater, NJ 08807-3300,
  Tel: (908) 685-5000
  (Mfr adhesives & sealants, resins & spec chems, electr materials & adhesives, food
  prdts, ind starch)
    National Adhesives Ltd., Damman, Saudi Arabia

OCCIDENTAL PETROLEUM CORP   10889 Wilshire Blvd, Los Angeles, CA 90024,
  Tel: (213) 879-1700
  (Petroleum & petroleum prdts, chems, plastics)
    Occidental Corp. Saudi Arabia, P.O. Box 572, Dammam, Saudi Arabia

OCEANEERING INTL INC   PO Box 218130, Houston, TX 77218-8130,
  Tel: (713) 578-8868
  (Underwater serv to offshore oil & gas ind)
    Oceaneering Intl. Inc., Operational bases in Al-Khobar & Dhahran

OTIS ELEVATOR CO   10 Farm Springs, Farmington, CT 06032, Tel: (860) 676-6528
  (Mfr elevators & escalators)
    Otis Elevator Co., P.O. Box 4256, Jeddah 21491, Saudi Arabia

OWENS-CORNING FIBERGLAS CORP   Fiberglas Tower, Toledo, OH 43659,
  Tel: (419) 248-8000
  (Mfr insulation, building materials, glass fiber prdts)
    Arabian Fiberglass Insulation Co. (Saudi Arabia), Saudi Arabia

OWL COMPANIES   2465 Campus Dr, Irvine, CA 92715, Tel: (714) 660-4966
  (General contractor)
    Owl Constructors, P.O. Box 209, Al-Khobar, Saudi Arabia

THE PARSONS CORP   100 W Walnut St, Pasadena, CA 91124, Tel: (818) 440-2000
  (Engineering & construction)
    Saudi Arabian Parsons Ltd., Corporate Office, P.O. Box 727, Dhahran, Saudi Arabia

PETROLITE CORP   369 Marshall Ave, St Louis, MO 63119-1897,
  Tel: (314) 961-3500
  (Mfr/prod spec chem treating programs, performance-enhancing additives & related
  equip & svces)
    Petrolite Saudi Arabia Ltd., P.O. Box 1940, Dammam 31441, Saudi Arabia

PITT-DES MOINES INC   3400 Grand Ave, Neville Island, Pittsburgh, PA 15225,
  Tel: (412) 331-3000
  (Mfr water & petrol storage sys, low temp & cryogenic tanks & sys, waste water
  treatment facilities)
    PDM Saudi Arabia Ltd., P.O. Box 30075, Madinat Yanbu al Sinaiyah, Saudi Arabia

PROCTER & GAMBLE CO   One Procter & Gamble Plaza, Cincinnati, OH 45202,
  Tel: (513) 983-1100
  (Personal care, food, laundry, cleaning & ind prdts)
    Modern Industries Co., Saudi Arabia

RADISSON HOTELS INTL   Carlson Pkwy, PO Box 59159, Minneapolis,
  MN 55459-8204, Tel: (612) 540-5526
  (Hotels)
    Al Khozama Hotel Movenpick, Oleya Rd., P.O. Box 4148, Riyadh 11491, Saudi Arabia
    Albilad Hotel Movenpick, Al Corniche Hwy., P.O. Box 6788, Jeddah 21452, Saudi Arabia

RAYCHEM CORP   300 Constitution Dr, Menlo Park, CA 94025, Tel: (415) 361-3333
  (Devel/mfr/mkt materials science products for electronics, telecommunications &
  industry)
    Raychem Saudi Arabia Ltd., P.O. Box 24, Damman 31411, Saudi Arabia
    Raychem Saudi Arabia Ltd., also in Jeddah & Riyadh, Saudi Arabia

RAYTHEON CO   141 Spring St, Lexington, MA 02173, Tel: (617) 862-6600
  (Mfr divers electronics, appliances, aviation, energy & environ prdts; publishing,
  ind & constr servs)
    Raytheon Middle East Systems Co., P.O. Box 2714, Riyadh, Saudi Arabia

RAYTHEON MISSILE SYSTEMS DIV   350 Lowell St, Andover, MA 01810,
  Tel: (617) 475-5000
  (Electronic commun equip)
    Raytheon Middle East Systems, P.O. Box 1348, Jeddah, Saudi Arabia

REAL ESTATE RESEARCH CORP   2 N LaSalle St, #400, Chicago, IL 60602,
  Tel: (312) 346-5885
  (Real estate research & appraisal)
    Real Estate Research Corp., P.O. Box 5847, Riyadh, Saudi Arabia

ROCKWELL INTL CORP   2201 Seal Beach Blvd, PO Box 4250, Seal Beach,
  CA 90740-8250, Tel: (310) 797-3311
  (Prdts & serv for aerospace, automotive, electronics, graphics & automation inds)
    Collins Systems Intl. Inc., P.O. Box 2375, Riyadh 11451, Saudi Arabia

SEA-LAND SERVICE INC   150 Allen Rd, Liberty Corner, NJ 07920,
  Tel: (201) 558-6000
  (Container transport)
    Sea-Land Service Inc., c/o Resayat Trading Co., P.O. Box 6670, Jeddah, Saudi Arabia
    Sea-Land Service Inc., P.O. Box 445, Dhahran Airport, Dhahran, Saudi Arabia

SPERRY-SUN INC   104 Industrial Blvd, Sugar Land, TX 77478,
  Tel: (713) 491-2280
  (Oilfield serv)
    Sperry Sun Intl., P.O. Box 2224, Dhahran, Saudi Arabia

STANDARD OIL CO OF CALIFORNIA   225 Bush St, San Francisco, CA 94104,
  Tel: (415) 894-7700
  (Oil explor & prod, petroleum prdts)
    Arabian American Oil Co., Saudi Arabia
    Arabian Chevron Inc., Saudi Arabia

STONE & WEBSTER ENGINEERING CORP   245 Summer St, Boston, MA 02210-2288,
  Tel: (617) 589-5111
  (Engineering, constr & environmental & mgmt services)
    Bugshan S&W Co. Ltd., Damman Tower #29, First St., Damman 67KNLI, Saudi Arabia
    Stone & Webster Saudi Arabia Inc., P.O. Box 4639, Dammam 31412, Saudi Arabia

SUNDT INTL   PO Box 26685, Tucson, AZ 85726, Tel: (602) 790-0295
(Holding company)
  Arabian-Sundt Ltd., P.O. Box 392, Dhahran Airport, Dhahran, Saudi Arabia

TEXACO INC   2000 Westchester Ave, White Plains, NY 10650, Tel: (914) 253-4000
(Explor/mktg crude oil, mfr petro chems & prdts)
  Texaco Saudi Inc., P.O. Box 5572, Riyadh, Saudi Arabia

TEXAS EASTERN TRANSMISSION CORP   PO Box 2521, Houston, TX 77252,
Tel: (713) 759-3131
(Energy pipeliner, oil/gas explor & prod)
  National Methanol Co., P.O. Box 10003, Al-Sinaiyah 31433, Saudi Arabia

TRANE CO   3600 Pammel Creek Rd, La Crosse, WI 54601, Tel: (608) 787-2000
(Mfr/distr/svce A/C sys & equip)
  Societe Trane, P.O. Box 13558, 21414 Jeddah, Saudi Arabia

UOP INC   Ten UOP Plaza, Des Plaines, IL 60016, Tel: (708) 391-2000
(Diversified research, development & mfr of ind prdts & sys mgmt studies & serv)
  Al Hazza Procon Ltd., Al-Khobar, Saudi Arabia
  Fluid Systems (Saudi Arabia) Ltd., Riyadh, Saudi Arabia
  UOP Management Services (Saudi Arabia) Ltd., Jeddah, Saudi Arabia

UOP MANAGEMENT SERVICES INC   25 East Algonquin Rd, Des Plaines,
IL 60017-5017, Tel: (708) 391-2654
(Ind devel planning, project implementation, operations mgmt serv)
  UOP Management Services (Saudi Arabia) Ltd., P.O. Box 7989, Jeddah 21472,
    Saudi Arabia

WACKENHUT CORP   1500 San Remo Ave, Coral Gables, FL 33146,
Tel: (305) 666-5656
(Security systems & services)
  Al-Mona Wackenhut Saudi Arabia, Al Olaya Business District, P.O. Box 3901,
    Riyadh 11481, Saudi Arabia

WEATHERFORD INTL INC   1360 Post Oak Blvd, PO Box 27608, Houston,
TX 77227-7608, Tel: (713) 439-9400
(Oilfield servs, prdts & equip; mfr marine cranes)
  Weatherford (Saudi Arabia) Intl., P.O. Box 623, Dhahran Airport 31932, Saudi Arabia

WESTERN ATLAS INTL INC   10205 Westheimer, PO Box 1407, Houston,
TX 77251-1407, Tel: (713) 266-5700
(Full service to the oil industry)
  Western Atlas Arabia Ltd., P.O. Box 721, Dhahran Airport 31932, Saudi Arabia
  Western Geophysical, P.O. Box 1927, Al-Khobar 31952, Saudi Arabia

WORLD COURIER INC   46 Trinity Pl, New York, NY 10006, Tel: (718) 978-9400
(Intl courier serv)
  Bandar Agencies/World Courier Div., P.O. Box 2682, Jeddah, Saudi Arabia

YORK INTERNATIONAL CORP   PO Box 1592, York, PA 17405-1592,
Tel: (717) 771-7890
(Mfr A/C, heating & refrig sys & equip)
  MARCO, P.O. Box 6290, Jeddah 21442, Saudi Arabia

H B ZACHRY CO   PO Box 21130, San Antonio, TX 78221-0130, Tel: (210) 922-1213
   (Construction)
   Zachry Saudi Arabian Contracting Co. Ltd., P.O. Box 9184, Riyadh, Saudi Arabia

SCOTLAND

AIR EXPRESS INTL CORP   120 Tokeneke Rd, PO Box 1231, Darien, CT 06820,
   Tel: (203) 655-7900
   (Air frt forwarder)
   Air Express Intl., Bldg. 388, Cargo House, Prestwick Airport, Ayrshire, Scotland

ALBANY INTL CORP   PO Box 1907, Albany, NY 12201, Tel: (518) 445-2200
   (Paper mach clothing, engineered fabrics, plastic prdts, filtration media)
   Albany Intl., J.K. Industrial Fabric Esk Mills, Musselburg, Edinburgh EH21 7PA,
      Scotland

ALBERTO-CULVER CO   2525 Armitage Ave, Melrose Park, IL 60160,
   Tel: (708) 450-3000
   (Mfr/mktg personal care & beauty prdts, household & grocery prdts, institutional food
   prdts)
   Wallace, Cameron & Co. Ltd., 303 Drakemire Dr., Glasgow G45 9SU, Scotland

ALDUS CORP   411 First Ave South, Seattle, WA 98104-2871, Tel: (206) 622-5500
   (Devel/mfr computer software)
   Aldus Europe Ltd., Aldus House, West One Business Park, 5 Mid New Cultins,
      Edinburgh EH11 4DU, Scotland
   Aldus UK Ltd., 39 Palmerton Place, Edinburgh EH12 5AU, Scotland

ANDREW CORP   10500 W 153rd St, Orlando Park, IL 60462, Tel: (708) 349-3300
   (Mfr antenna sys, coaxial cable, electronic commun & network connectivity sys)
   Andrew Antenna, Lochgelly, Fife KY5 9HG, Scotland

ARMSTRONG ENGINEERING ASSOCIATES INC   PO Box 566, West Chester, PA 19380,
   Tel: (215) 436-6080
   (Heat exchangers & process equip for chem plants & oil refineries)
   Chemtec BV, P.O. Box 3 Willowyard Rd., Beith, Ayrshire KA15 1JQ, Scotland

AST RESEARCH INC   16215 Alton Parkway, PO Box 19658, Irvine, CA 92713-9658,
   Tel: (714) 727-4141
   (Design/devel/mfr hi-perf desktop, server & notebook computers)
   AST Scotland Mfg., 18 W. Mains Rd., College Milton North, East Kilbride G74 1PQ,
      Scotland

BAKER OIL TOOLS   PO Box 40129, Houston, TX 77240-0129, Tel: (713) 466-1322
   (Mfr/serv oil/gas well completions equip)
   Baker Oil Tools (UK) Ltd., Woodside Rd., Bridge of Don Ind. Estate,
      Aberdeen AB2 8BW, Scotland

BOURNS INC   1200 Columbia Ave, Riverside, CA 92507, Tel: (909) 781-5500
  (Mfr resistive com & networks, precision potentiometers, panel controls, switches,
  transducers)
     Bourns Electronics Ltd., Hillend Ind. Estate, Dunfermline, Fife KY11 5JO, Scotland

BOWEN TOOLS INC   PO Box 3186, Houston, TX 77253-3186, Tel: (713) 868-8888
  (Mfr drilling & specialty tools for oil/gas ind)
     Bowen Tools Inc., Kirkton Ave., Pitmedden Road Ind. Estate, Dyce, Aberdeen AB2 0BF,
     Scotland

BROWN & ROOT INC   4100 Clinton Dr, Houston, TX 77020-6299,
  Tel: (713) 676-3011
  (Engr, constr & maintenance)
     Brown & Root (UK) Ltd., Wellheads Pl., Wellheads Ind. Estate, Dyce,
       Aberdeen AB2 0GG, Scotland
     Brown & Root-Wimpey Highlands Fabricators Ltd., P.O. Box 4, Nigg, Tain,
       Ross-Shire 1V19 1GY, Scotland
     Wharton Williams Taylor BV, Farburn Ind. Estate, Dyce, Aberdeen AB2 0HG, Scotland

BURR-BROWN RESEARCH CORP   PO Box 11400, Tucson, AZ 85734, Tel: (602) 746-1111
  (Electronic components & sys modules)
     Burr-Brown Ltd., Simpson Pkwy, Kirkton Campus, Livingston, West Lothian EH54 7BG,
     Scotland

BUTLER MFG CO   PO Box 917, Kansas City, MO 64141, Tel: (816) 968-3000
  (Pre-engineered steel struc sys, curtain wall & elec dist sys, grain storage &
  handling sys)
     Butler Bldg. Products Ltd., Mitchelston Ind. Estate, Kirkcaldy, Fife, Scotland

CHIRON CORP   4560 Horton St, Emeryville, CA 94608-2916, Tel: (510) 601-2412
  (Research/mfg/mktg therapeutics, vaccines, diagnostics, ophthalmics)
     Chiron Vision Corp., 3 Fleming Rd., Kirkton Campus, West Lothian EH54 7BN, Scotland

CIGNA CORP   One Liberty Place, Philadelphia, PA 19192, Tel: (215) 523-4000
  (Ins, invest, health care & other fin servs)
     Crusader Insurance PLC, Reigate, Surrey RH2 8BL, Scotland

CINCOM SYSTEMS INC   2300 Montana Ave, Cincinnati, OH 45211,
  Tel: (513) 662-2300
  (Devel/distr computer software)
     Cincom Systems Inc., Edinburgh, Scotland

CITICORP   399 Park Ave, New York, NY 10043, Tel: (212) 559-1000
  (Banking & financial services)
     Citibank NA, Scotland

COMBUSTION ENGINEERING INC   900 Long Ridge Road, Stamford, CT 06902,
  Tel: (203) 329-8771
  (Tech constr)
     C-E Vetco Service, Bridge of Don Ind. Estate, Broadfold Rd., Aberdeen AB2 3EY,
       Scotland
     Douglas Lanark Gray Tool Co. Ltd., Douglas Ind. Estate, Scotland
     Gray Tool Co. Ltd., A-2 A-3, Wellhead Ind. Centre, Dyce, Aberdeen, Scotland
     Gray Tool Co. Ltd., East Kolbride, P.O. Box 6, 8 Singer Rd., Glasgow G75 0YW,
       Scotland

COMPAQ COMPUTER CORP   PO Box 692000, Houston, TX 77269-2000,
  Tel: (713) 370-0670
  (Devel/mfr personal computers)
    Compaq Computer Mfg. Ltd., Erskine, Scotland

CONOCO INC   600 N Dairy Ashford Rd, Houston, TX 77079, Tel: (713) 293-1000
  (Oil, gas, coal, chems, minerals)
    Conoco Ltd., Rubislaw House, North Anderson Dr., Aberdeen AB2 4AZ, Scotland

CORE LABORATORIES   10205 Westheimer, Houston, TX 77042, Tel: (713) 972-6311
  (Petroleum testing/analysis, analytical chem, lab & octane analysis instrumentation)
    Core Lab. Ltd., Howe Moss Rd., Kirkhill Ind. Estate, Dyce, Aberdeen AB2 OES,
      Scotland

CTS CORP   905 N West Blvd, Elkhart, IN 46514, Tel: (215) 293-7511
  (Mfr electr components)
    CTS Corp. UK Ltd., Blantyre Ind. Estate, High Blantyre, Glasgow G72 OXA, Scotland

DAMES & MOORE   911 Wilshire Blvd, Los Angeles, CA 90017, Tel: (213) 683-1560
  (Engineering, environmental & construction mgmt services)
    Dames & Moore, 1 St. Colme St. #29, Edinburgh EH3 6AA, Scotland

DAY INTL   333 W First St, Dayton, OH 45412, Tel: (513) 226-7000
  (Diversified auto, ind & household prdts)
    Dayco Rubber Ltd., Balgray St., Dundee Angus DD3 8HN, Scotland

THE DEXTER CORP   1 Elm Street, Windsor Locks, CT 06096, Tel: (203) 627-9051
  (Mfr nonwovens, polymer prdts, magnetic materials, biotechnology)
    Dexter Nonwovens, Chirnside, Duns TD11 3JU, Scotland
    Life Technologies Ltd., P.O. Box 35, Trident House, Renfrew Rd., Paisley,
      Renfrewshire PA3 4EF, Scotland

DIAMOND POWER SPECIALTY CORP   PO Box 415, Lancaster, OH 43130,
  Tel: (614) 687-6500
  (Mfr sootblowers & controls, rodding robots, drum level indicators & gauges)
    Diamond Power Specialty Ltd., Glasgow Rd., Dumbarton G82 1ES, Scotland

DIGITAL EQUIPMENT CORP   146 Main St, Maynard, MA 01754-2571,
  Tel: (508) 493-5111
  (Networked computer systems & services)
    Digital Equipment Scotland Ltd., Mosshill Ind. Estate, Ayr, Strathclyde KA6 68E,
      Scotland

DRAKE BEAM MORIN INC   100 Park Ave, New York, NY 10017, Tel: (212) 692-7700
  (Human resource mgmt consulting & training)
    Drake Beam Morin PLC, 4 Wemyss Place, Edinburgh EH3 6DH, Scotland

DRESSER INDUSTRIES INC   PO Box 718, Dallas, TX 75221-0718,
  Tel: (214) 740-6000
  (Diversified supplier of equip & tech serv to energy & natural resource ind)
    Dresser Oilfield Products, Pocra Quay, Aberdeen AB2 1DQ, Scotland

EASTMAN KODAK CO   343 State St, Rochester, NY 14650, Tel: (716) 724-4000
  (Devel/mfr photo & chem prdts, info mgmt/video/copier sys, fibers/plastics for
  various ind)
    Kodak Ltd., Scottish Business Centre, Pegasus House, 375 W. George St.,
      Glasgow G2 4NT, Scotland

EFCO   1800 NE Broadway Ave, Des Moines, IA 50316-0386, Tel: (515) 266-1141
(Mfr systems for concrete construction)
   EFCO, Office 6, Axwel House, East Mains Ind. Estate, Broxburn,
      West Lothian EH52 5AU, Scotland

ELECTROGLAS INC   2901 Coronado Dr, Santa Clara, CA 95054, Tel: (408) 727-6500
(Mfr semi-conductor test equip, automatic wafer probers)
   Electroglas Intl. Inc., Unit 44, West Calder Workspace, Society Place, West Calder,
      West Lothian EH55 8EA, Scotland

EXPEDITORS INTL OF WASHINGTON INC   PO Box 69620, Seattle, WA 98168-9620,
   Tel: (206) 246-3711
(Air/ocean freight forwarding, customs brokerage, intl logistics solutions)
   Expeditors Intl. (UK) Ltd., Unit 3D, Lyon Rd., Linwood Ind. Estate, Linwood,
      Renfrewshire PA3 3BQ, Scotland

FISHER CONTROLS INTL INC   8000 Maryland Ave, Clayton, MO 63105,
   Tel: (314) 746-9900
(Mfr ind process control equip)
   Fisher Controls Ltd., Hareness Circle, Altens Ind. Estate, Aberdeen, AB1 4LY,
      Scotland
   Fisher Controls Ltd., Carlyle House, Carlyle Rd., Kirkcaldy, Fife, KY1 1DB, Scotland

THE GATES RUBBER CO   PO Box 5887, Denver, CO 80217-5887, Tel: (303) 744-1911
(Mfr automotive & industrial belts & hose)
   The Gates Rubber Co. Ltd., Heathhall Factory, Edinburgh Rd., Heathhall,
      Dumfries DC1 1QA, Scotland

GENERAL MOTORS ACCEPTANCE CORP   3044 West Grand Blvd, Detroit, MI 48202,
   Tel: (313) 556-5000
(Automobile financing)
   GMAC (UK) PLC, 389 Argyle St., Glasgow G2 8LR, Scotland

GENERAL MOTORS CORP   3044 W Grand Blvd, Detroit, MI 48202-3091,
   Tel: (313) 556-5000
(Mfr full line vehicles, automotive electronics, coml technologies, telecom, space,
finance)
   Terex Equip. Ltd., Newhouse Ind. Estate, Motherwell, Lanarks. ML1 5RY, Scotland

GIRARD INDUSTRIES   6531 N Eldridge Pkwy, Houston, TX 77041-3507,
   Tel: (713) 466-3100
(Mfr polyurethane foam pipeline cleaners)
   Girard Industries Europe Ltd., 21/23 Kelvin Ave., Nethermains Industrial Estate,
      Ayrshire KA13 6PS, Scotland

GLOBAL MARINE INC   777 N Eldridge, Houston, TX 77079, Tel: (713) 596-5100
(Offshore contract drilling, turnkey drilling, oil & gas explor & prod)
   Global Marine Integrated Services, North Norfolk House, Pitmedden d., Dyce AB2 0DP,
      Scotland

W L GORE & ASSOCIATES INC   555 Paper Mill Road, Newark, DE 19711,
   Tel: (302) 738-4880
(Mfr electr, ind filtration, med & fabric prdts)
   Gore & Associates Ltd., Queens Fairy Rd., Dunfermline, Fife, Scotland

HALLMARK CARDS INC   PO Box 419580, Kansas City, MO 64141, Tel: (816) 274-5100
  (Mfr greeting cards & related prdts)
    Valentines of Dundee Ltd., Kinnoull Rd., P.O. Box 74, Dundee, Scotland

HARNISCHFEGER INDUSTRIES INC   PO Box 554, Milwaukee, WI 53201,
  Tel: (414) 671-4400
  (Mfr mining & material handling equip, papermaking mach, computer sys)
    Joy Manufacturing Co. (UK) Ltd., Peel Park Place, East Kilbride G74 5LN, Scotland

THE HARPER GROUP   260 Townsend St, PO Box 77933, San Francisco,
  CA 94107-1719, Tel: (415) 978-0600
  (Ocean/air freight fwdg, customs brokerage, packing & whse, logistics mgt, ins)
    Harper Freight Intl. UK Ltd., Airlink Ind. Estate, Inchinnan Rd., Paisley PA3 2RS,
      Scotland
    Harper Freight Intl. UK Ltd., also in Aberdeen, Edinburgh & Prestwick, Scotland

HENRY VALVE CO   3215 North Ave, Melrose Park, IL 60160, Tel: (708) 344-1100
  (Mfr components for coml A/C & refrig sys)
    Henry Valve (UK) Ltd., Block 76, Mossland Rd., Hillington, Glasgow G52 4JZ, Scotland

HOLIDAY INNS INC   3742 Lamar Ave, Memphis, TN 38195, Tel: (901) 362-4001
  (Hotels, restaurants, casinos)
    Holiday Inn, Riverview Dr., Farbum Dyce, Aberdeen, Scotland

HUGHES TOOL CO   PO Box 2539, Houston, TX 77001, Tel: (713) 924-2222
  (Equip & serv to oil & gas explor & prod ind)
    BJ Hughes BV, Wellheads Crescent, Dyce Ind. Estate Park, Aberdeen AB2 0EZ, Scotland

ICS INTERNATIONAL INC   125 Oak St, Scranton, PA 18515, Tel: (717) 342-7701
  (Correspondence courses)
    ICS Ltd., Intertext House, 8 Elliot Pl., Clydeway Centre, Glasgow G3 8EF, Scotland

IMCO SERVICES   5950 N Course Dr, Houston, TX 70072, Tel: (713) 561-1300
  (Drilling fluids)
    Imco Services Div. Halliburton Mfg. Ltd., Unit 5, Palmerston Rd., Aberdeen AB1 2QW,
      Scotland

ITT SHERATON CORP   60 State St, Boston, MA 02108, Tel: (617) 367-3600
  (Hotel operations)
    Edinburgh Sheraton, 1 Festival Sq., Lothian Rd., Edinburgh EH3 9SR, Scotland

JACOBS ENGINEERING GROUP INC   251 S Lake Ave, Pasadena, CA 91101,
  Tel: (818) 449-2171
  (Engineering, design & consulting; construction & construction mgmt; process plant
  maintenance)
    Jacobs Engineering Ltd., Park House, Park Circus Place, Glasgow G3 6AN, Scotland

JET-LUBE INC   4849 Homestead Fr, Houston, TX 77028, Tel: (713) 674-7617
  (Mfr anti-seize compounds, thread sealants, lubricants, greases)
    Jet-Lube (UK) Inc., Aberdeen Freight Centre, 12 Baltic Place, Aberdeen AB2 1AE,
      Scotland

JOHNSON & HIGGINS   125 Broad St, New York, NY 10004-2424, Tel: (212) 574-7000
  (Ins brokerage, employee benefit conslt, risk mgmt, human resource conslt, ins/reins
  servs)
    Johnson & Higgins UK Ltd., Glasgow, Scotland

JOHNSON & JOHNSON   One Johnson & Johnson Plaza, New Brunswick, NJ 08933,
   Tel: (908) 524-0400
   (R&D/mfr/sale health care prdts)
      Ethicon Ltd., P.O. Box 408, Bankhead Ave., Edinburgh EH11 4HE, Scotland

JOHNSON CONTROLS INC   5757 N Green Bay Ave, PO Box 591, Milwaukee,
   WI 53201-0591, Tel: (414) 228-1200
   (Mfr facility mgmt & control sys, auto seating, batteries & plastics)
      Johnson Controls Maclaren Products, 333 West St., Glasgow GS 8JE, Scotland

JOY TECHNOLOGIES INC   301 Grant St, Pittsburgh, PA 15219-1490,
   Tel: (412) 562-4500
   (Mfr coal mining, air pollution control, materials mgmt & incineration equip, fans)
      Joy Manufacturing Co. (UK) Ltd., Peel Park Place, East Kilbride, Glasgow G74 5LN,
      Scotland

KELLY SERVICES   999 W Big Beaver Rd, Troy, MI 48084, Tel: (810) 244-4313
   (Temporary help placement)
      Kelly Services (UK) Ltd., 5 branches throughout Scotland

KERR-McGEE CORP   PO Box 25861, Oklahoma City, OK 73125, Tel: (405) 270-1313
   (Oil & gas exploration & production, ind chems, coal)
      Kerr-McGee Oil (UK) Ltd., The Regent Centre, Regent Rd., Aberdeen AB9 8UQ, Scotland

KEYSTONE INTL INC   PO Box 40010, Houston, TX 77040, Tel: (713) 466-1176
   (Mfr butterfly valves, actuators & control accessories)
      Keystone Scotland, Scotland

MARTIN-DECKER TOTCO INC   1200 Cypress Creek Rd, Cedar Park, TX 78613-3614,
   Tel: (512) 331-0411
   (Mfr oilfield & ind weight & meas sys)
      M/D Totco Inc., Silverburn Pl., Bridge of Don Ind. Estate, Aberdeen AB2 8EG,
      Scotland

THE MENTHOLATUM CO INC   1360 Niagara St, Buffalo, NY 14213,
   Tel: (716) 882-7660
   (Mfr/distr proprietary medicines, drugs, OTC's)
      Mentholatum Co. Ltd., 1 Redwood Ave., Peel Park Campus, East Kilbride G74 5PE,
      Scotland

MILCHEM INC   3900 Essex Lane, PO Box 22111, Houston, TX 77027,
   Tel: (214) 439-8000
   (Gas & oil well drilling fluids & chem additives)
      Milchem Drilling Fluids, Souter Heap Rd., Aberdeen AB1 4LF, Scotland

MINE SAFETY APPLIANCES CO   PO Box 426, Pittsburgh, PA 15230,
   Tel: (421) 273 5000
   (Safety equip, ind filters)
      Mine Safey Appliances Co. Ltd., East Shawhead, Coatbridge ML5 4TD, Scotland

MOUNT HOPE MACHINERY CO   15 Fifth St, Taunton, MA 02780, Tel: (508) 824-6994
   (Web control equip for paper, plastics, textiles)
      Mount Hope Scotland, Boston Rd., Viewfield Ind. Estate, Glenrothe, Fife, Scotland

McCANN-ERICKSON WORLDWIDE   750 Third Ave, New York, NY 10017,
Tel: (212) 697-6000
(Advertising)
  McCann-Erickson Scotland Ltd., Woolward House, Marine Dr., Edinburgh EH4 5EW,
    Scotland

NABORS INDUSTRIES INC   515 W Greens Rd, #1200, Houston, TX 77067,
Tel: (713) 874-0035
(Oil & gas drilling, petrol prdts)
  Nabors Europe Ltd., Kirkton Ave., Pitmedden Rd. Ind. Estate, Dyce,
    Aberdeen AB2 ODP, Scotland

NACCO INDUSTRIES INC   5875 Landerbrook Dr, Mayfield Hgts, OH 44124-4017,
Tel: (216) 449-9600
(Mining/mktg lignite & metals, mfr forklift trucks & small electric appliances,
specialty retailers)
  NACCO Materials Handling Group, Irvine, Scotland

NATIONAL SEMICONDUCTOR CORP   PO Box 58090, Santa Clara, CA 95052-8090,
Tel: (408) 721-5000
(Mfr semiconductors, design/devel sys)
  National Semiconductor, Greenock, Scotland

NATIONAL-OILWELL   PO Box 4638, Houston, TX 77210-4638, Tel: (713) 960-5100
(Mfr/distr oilfield drills & tubulars)
  National-Oilwell U.K. Ltd., W. Tullos Industrial Estate, Aberdeen AB1 4AB, Scotland

NATIONAL-STANDARD CO   1618 Terminal Rd, Niles, MI 49120, Tel: (616) 683-8100
(Mfr wire, wire related prdts, mach & med prdts)
  National-Standard Co. Ltd., Arran Rd., North Muirton, Perth PH1 3DX, Scotland

NOBLE DRILLING CORP   10370 Richmond Ave, #400, Houston, TX 77042,
Tel: (713) 974-3131
(Drilling contractor, engineering services)
  Noble Drilling (UK) Ltd./Noble Engineering Services, Ltd.,
    Farburn Industrial Estate, Dyce, Aberdeen AB2 OHG, Scotland

NORTON CO   1 New Bond St, Worcester, MA 01606, Tel: (508) 795-5000
(Abrasives, drill bits, constr & safety prdts, plastics)
  Christensen Diamond Products (UK) Ltd., Kirkhill Rd., Kirkhill Ind. Estate, Dyce,
    Aberdeen, Scotland

OCEANEERING INTL INC   PO Box 218130, Houston, TX 77218-8130,
Tel: (713) 578-8868
(Underwater serv to offshore oil & gas ind)
  Oceaneering Intl. Inc., Operational base in Edinburgh
  Oceaneering Intl. Services Ltd., Pitmedden Rd., Dyce, Aberdeen AB2 ODP, Scotland

OPTICAL COATING LAB INC (OCLI)   2789 Northpoint Pkwy, Santa Rosa,
CA 95407-7397, Tel: (707) 545-6440
(Mfr thin film precision coated optical devices)
  OCLI Optical Coatings Ltd., Ridge Way, Hillend Ind. Estate,
    Dalgety Bay near Dunfermline, Fife KY11 5FR, Scotland

ORION RESEARCH INC   529 Main St, Boston, MA 02129, Tel: (617) 242-3900
(Mfr laboratory & industrial prdts, measure & display instruments)
  Russell pH Ltd., Station Rd., Auchtermuchty, Fife KY14 7DP, Scotland

PFAUDLER CO   PO Box 1600, Rochester, NY 14692, Tel: (716) 235-1000
(Mfr glass lined reactor vessels)
    Pfaudler Balfour & Co. Ltd., Leven, Fife KY8 4RW, Scotland

PHILLIPS DRILL CO INC   PO Box 364, Michigan City, IN 46360,
Tel: (219) 874-4217
(Concrete anchor sys for constr ind)
    Phillips Drill Co. Inc., Queenslie Ind. Estate, Glasgow E3, Scotland

PINKERTON SECURITY & INVESTIGATION SERVICES   6727 Odessa Ave, Van Nuys,
CA 91406-5796, Tel: (818) 373-8800
(Security & investigation services)
    Pinkerton Security Services Ltd., Fleming House, 134 Renfrew St., Glasgow G3 6ST,
    Scotland

PLAYTEX APPAREL INC   700 Fairfield Ave, Stamford, CT 06904,
Tel: (203) 356-8000
(Mfr intimate apparel)
    Playtex Ltd., Playtex Park, Port Glasgow, Renfrewshire KA14, Scotland

PROCTOR & SCHWARTZ INC   251 Gibraltar Rd, Horsham, PA 19044,
Tel: (215) 443-5200
(Mfr ind drying mach for food, tobacco, chem & textile ind)
    Proctor & Schwartz, Thornlie Bank Ind. Estate, Glasgow G46 8JA, Scotland

RAYCHEM CORP   300 Constitution Dr, Menlo Park, CA 94025, Tel: (415) 361-3333
(Devel/mfr/mkt materials science products for electronics, telecommunications &
industry)
    Raychem Ltd., 7 Melville Terrace, Stirling FK8 2ND, Scotland

REED TOOL CO   6501 Navigation Blvd, Houston, TX 77001, Tel: (713) 924-5200
(Mfr rock bits for oil & gas explor)
    Reed Tool Co., Burnside Rd., Farburn Ind. Estate, Dyce, Scotland

RUSSELL CORP   PO Box 272, Alexander City, AL 35010, Tel: (205) 329-4000
(Mfr athletic & leisure apparel)
    Russell Corp. UK Ltd., Unit 28, First Rd., Houstoun Ind. Estate, Livingston,
    West Lothian EH54 5DJ, Scotland

RUSSELL REYNOLDS ASSOCIATES INC   200 Park Ave, New York, NY 10166,
Tel: (212) 351-2000
(Exec recruiting services)
    Russell Reynolds Associates Inc., 25A Stafford St., Edinburgh EH3 78J, Scotland

SANDUSKY INTL   615 W Market St, PO Box 5012, Sandusky, OH 44871-8012,
Tel: (419) 626-8012
(Mfr roll shells for paper machines, centrifugal tubular prdts)
    Sandusky Ltd., Glenrothes, Fife KY6 2RQ, Scotland

SARA LEE CORP   3 First National Plaza, Chicago, IL 60602-4260,
Tel: (312) 726-2600
(Mfr/distr food & consumer packaged goods, tobacco prdts, intimate apparel & knitwear)
    Playtex Ltd., Playtex Park, Port Glasgow, Renfrewshire, Scotland

SCI SYSTEMS INC   PO Box 1000, Huntsville, AL 35807, Tel: (205) 882-4800
(R/D & mfr electronics systems for commerce, industry, aerospace, etc)
  SCI UK Ltd., 1 Crompton Way, N. Newmoor Ind. Estate, Irvine KA11 4HU, Scotland

SCIENTIFIC ATLANTA INC   1 Technology Pkwy, PO Box 105600, Atlanta, GA 30348,
Tel: (404) 441-4000
(Telecommun instru & equip, energy mgmt & home security equip, test & measurement
instru)
  Optima Enclosures Ltd., Great North Rd., Macmerry, East Lothian EH33 1EX, Scotland

SEA-LAND SERVICE INC   150 Allen Rd, Liberty Corner, NJ 07920,
Tel: (201) 558-6000
(Container transport)
  Freight Sales Intl. Ltd., 4 Ingram St., Glasgow, Scotland
  Sea-Land Containership Ltd., P.O. Box 24, Grangedock, Grangemouth, Stirlingshire,
  Scotland

SEMTECH CORP   652 Mitchell Rd, PO Box 367, Newbury Park, CA 91320,
Tel: (805) 498-2111
(Mfr silicon rectifiers, rectifier assemblies, capacitors, switching regulators,
AC/DC converters)
  Semtech Ltd., Newark Road S, Eastfield Ind. Estate, Glenrothes, Fide KY7 4NF,
  Scotland

SEQUENT COMPUTER SYSTEMS INC   15450 SW Koll Pkwy, Beaverton, OR 97006-6063,
Tel: (503) 626-5700
(Mfr symmetric multiprocessing technology computers)
  Sequent Computer Systems Inc., 1 St. Colme St., Edinburgh EH3 6AA, Scotland

SNAP-ON TOOLS CORP   2801 80th St, Kenosha, WI 53141-1410, Tel: (414) 656-5200
(Mfr automotive & ind maint serv tools)
  Snap-On Tools Ltd., 69 Colvilles Place, Kelvin Industrial Estate,
  East Kilbride G75 0XJ, Scotland

SONAT OFFSHORE DRILLING INC   PO Box 2765, Houston, TX 77252-2765,
Tel: (713) 871-7500
(Offshore oil well drilling)
  Sonat Offshore (UK) Ltd., Barclayhill Pl., Aberdeen AB1 4PF, Scotland

SONOCO PRODUCTS CO   North Second St, PO Box 160, Hartsville, SC 29550,
Tel: (803) 383-7000
(Mfr packaging for consumer & ind mkt)
  Sonoco Products Co., Montrose Rd., Brechin, Tayside, Scotland

SUB SEA INTL INC   701 Engineers Rd, Belle Chasse, LA 70037,
Tel: (504) 393-7744
(Service oil/gas industry: diving, ROV's, offshore construction, engineering,
pipeline services)
  Sub Sea Offshore Ltd., Greenwell Base, Greenwell Rd., Aberdeen AB1 4AX, Scotland

SUN COMPANY INC   1801 Market St, Philadelphia, PA 19103-1699,
Tel: (215) 977-3000
(Petroleum refining & marketing, petroleum prdts, oil/gas exploration & production,
oil sands mining)
  Sun Oil Britain Ltd., 26 Union Terrace, Aberdeen AB1 1NN, Scotland

TEKTRONIX INC   26660 SW Parkway, Wilsonville, OR 97070, Tel: (503) 627-7111
  (Mfr test & meas, visual sys & commun prdts)
    Tektronix Inc., Livingston, Scotland

TIDEWATER INC   Tidewater Place, 1440 Canal St, New Orleans, LA 70112,
  Tel: (504) 568-1010
  (Marine serv & equip to companies engaged in explor, development & prod of oil, gas &
  minerals)
    Tidewater Marine Service (UK) Ltd., 63 Regent Quay, Aberdeen AB1 2AR, Scotland

TOKHEIM CORP   PO Box 360, Fort Wayne, IN 46801, Tel: (219) 470-4600
  (Mfr gasoline service station dispensers, access, hand & in-tank fuel pumps)
    Tokheim Ltd., Newark Rd. S., Glenrothes, Fife KY7 4NJ, Scotland

TRANE CO   3600 Pammel Creek Rd, La Crosse, WI 54601, Tel: (608) 787-2000
  (Mfr/distr/svce A/C sys & equip)
    Trane (UK) Ltd., 10 Nappier Ct, Wardpark North Industrial Estate,
      Cumbernauld G68 OLG, Scotland

TURBOCOMPRESSOR   3101 Broadway, PO Box 209, Buffalo, NY 14225-0209,
  Tel: (716) 896-6600
  (Mfr air & gas compressors)
    Turbocompressor, East Kilbride, Glasgow, Scotland

TYLAN GENERAL INC   9577 Chesapeake Dr, San Diego, CA 92123,
  Tel: (619) 571-1222
  (Mfr flow & pressure measurement & control components)
    Tylan General Scotland, 12 Crofthead Centre, Livingston EH54 6DG, Scotland

UNION OIL INTL DIV   Union Oil Center, PO Box 7600, Los Angeles, CA 90017,
  Tel: (213) 977-7600
  (Petroleum prdts, petrochems)
    Union Oil Co., Salvesen Tower, Blaikies Quay, Aberdeen AB1 2PU, Scotland

UNIROYAL INC   World Headquarters, Middlebury, CT 06749, Tel: (203) 573-2000
  (Tires, tubes & other rubber prdts, chems, plastics, textiles)
    Uniroyal Ltd., Newbridge, Midlothian EH28 8LG, Scotland
    Uniroyal Ltd., Heathall Factory, Dumfries, Scotland

UNITED TECHNOLOGIES CORP   United Technologies Bldg, Hartford, CT 06101,
  Tel: (203) 728-7000
  (Mfr aircraft engines, elevators, A/C, auto equip, space & military electr, rocket
  propulsion sys)
    United Technologies Corp., Essex Group Ind. Estate, Kilwinning, Ayrshire KA1 36EX,
      Scotland

VALENITE INC   PO Box 9636, Madison Heights, MI 48071-9636,
  Tel: (810) 589-1000
  (Cemented carbide, high speed steel, ceramic & diamond cutting tool prdts, etc)
    Valenite-Modco (UK) Ltd., Clydeway Industrial Centre, Unit 5C, 45 Finnieston St.,
      Glasgow G3 8JU, Scotland

VALHI INC   5430 LBJ Freeway, Dallas, TX 75240, Tel: (214) 233-1700
  (Chemicals, hardware, sugar, mining)
    Abbey Chemicals Ltd., Nettlehill Rd., Livingston, West Lothian EH54 5DL, Scotland

NL Specialty Chemicals Ltd., Nettlehill Rd., Livingston, West Lothian EH54 5DL, Scotland

VEEDER-ROOT CO   125 Powder Forest Dr, PO Box 2003, Simsbury, CT 06070-2003,
Tel: (203) 651-2700
(Mfr counting, controlling & sensing devices)
  Veeder-Root Ltd., Kilspindie Rd., Dundee DD2 3QJ, Scotland

WEATHERFORD INTL INC   1360 Post Oak Blvd, PO Box 27608, Houston,
TX 77227-7608, Tel: (713) 439-9400
(Oilfield servs, prdts & equip; mfr marine cranes)
  Weatherford Ltd., Kirkhill Ind. Estate, Walton Rd., Dyce, Aberdeen AB2 0ES, Scotland

WEBER MARKING SYSTEMS INC   711 W Algonquin Rd, Arlington Heights, IL 60005,
Tel: (708) 364-8500
(Mfr label printing sys, custom labels)
  Weber Marking Systems Ltd., Macmerry Ind. Estate, Tranent, East Lothian, EH33 1HD, Scotland

WESTERN ATLAS INTL INC   10205 Westheimer, PO Box 1407, Houston,
TX 77251-1407, Tel: (713) 266-5700
(Full service to the oil industry)
  Western Atlas Logging Services, Stoneywood Park, Dyce, Aberdeen AB2 0DF, Scotland

WESTERN OCEANIC INC   515 Post Oak Blvd, Houston, TX 77027,
Tel: (713) 629-2700
(Oil explor, drilling)
  Western Oceanic (UK) Ltd., North Esplanade West, Aberdeen AB1 2OS, Scotland

WINCHESTER ELECTRONICS   400 Park Rd, Watertown, CT 06795-0500,
Tel: (203) 945-5000
(Mfr elec & electr connectors, PCB assemblies & hardware)
  Interconnection Products, 72 Whitecraigs Rd., Whitehill Ind. Estate, Glenrothes,
  Fife KY6 2RX, Scotland

WYMAN-GORDON CO   244 Worcester St, N Grafton, MA 01536-8001,
Tel: (508) 839-4441
(Mfr forging & investment casting components, composite airframe structures)
  Wyman-Gordon Co., Livingston, Scotland

XILINX INC   2100 Logic Dr, San Jose, CA 95124-3400, Tel: (408) 559-7779
(Programmable logic & related development sys software)
  Xilinx Development Corp., 52 Mortonhall Gate, Frogston Rd. E., Edinburgh EH16 6TJ,
  Scotland

ZURN INDUSTRIES INC   1 Zurn Place, Erie, PA 16505, Tel: (814) 452-2111
(Heavy construction; mfr instru & ind machinery, sporting goods)
  Lynx Golf (Scotland) Ltd., 9/11 Langlands Place, Kelvin South Business Park,
  E. Kilbride, Glasgow G75 0YF, Scotland

SENEGAL

AVON PRODUCTS INC   9 W 57th St, New York, NY 10019, Tel: (212) 546-6015
  (Mfr/distr beauty & related prdts, fashion jewelry, gifts & collectibles)
    Avon Cosmetics SARL, Dakar Yves Repesse, Senegal

LOUIS BERGER INTL INC   100 Halsted St, East Orange, NJ 07019,
  Tel: (201) 678-1960
  (Consulting engineers, architects, economists & planners)
    Louis Berger Intl. Inc., P.O. Box 21 104, Dakar Ponty, Senegal

CHASE MANHATTAN BANK N A   1 Chase Manhattan Plaza, New York, NY 10081,
  Tel: (212) 552-2222
  (Intl banking)
    Chase Manhattan Bank Overseas Corp., 4 Ave. Roume Angel, Boite Postale 89, Dakar,
      Senegal

CITICORP   399 Park Ave, New York, NY 10043, Tel: (212) 559-1000
  (Banking & financial services)
    Citibank, Senegal

COLGATE-PALMOLIVE CO   300 Park Ave, New York, NY 10022, Tel: (212) 310-2000
  (Mfr pharms, cosmetics, toiletries, detergents)
    Societe Africaine de Detergents (SAD), Km 2,
      Blvd. du Centenaire de la Commune de Dakar, Dakar, Senegal

FRANK B HALL & CO INC   549 Pleasantville Rd, Briarcliff Manor, NY 10510,
  Tel: (914) 769-9200
  (Insurance)
    Societe Africaine d'Assurances (SAFRA), Ave. Roume, Boite Postale 508, Dakar,
      Senegal

SIERRA LEONE

MOBIL CORP   3225 Gallows Rd, Fairfax, VA 22037-0001, Tel: (703) 846-3000
  (Petroleum explor & refining, mfr petrol prdts, chems, petrochems)
    Mobil Oil Ltd., P.O. Box 548, Freetown, Sierra Leone

WACKENHUT CORP   1500 San Remo Ave, Coral Gables, FL 33146,
  Tel: (305) 666-5656
  (Security systems & services)
    Wackenhut Sierra Leone, 58 Campbell St., P.O. Box 1464, Freetown, Sierra Leone

SINGAPORE

3COM CORP   5400 Bayfront Plaza, Santa Clara, CA 95052-8145,
  Tel: (408) 764-5000
  (Devel/mfr computer networking prdts & sys)
    3Com Asia Ltd., Singapore

3M   3M Center, St Paul, MN 55144-1000, Tel: (612) 733-1110
  (Mfr diversified prdts for industry, health care, imaging, commun, transport, safety,
  consumer, etc)
    3M Singapore Pte. Ltd., 9 Tagore Lane, Singapore 2678

A-Z INTL TOOL CO   PO Box 7108, Houston, TX 77248-7108, Tel: (713) 880-8888
  (Mfr oil field, milling & casing cutting tools)
    Grant Oil Tool Co., Loyang Offshore Supply Base, Loyang Crescent, Singapore 1750

AAF INTL   215 Central Ave, PO Box 35690, Louisville, KY 40232-5690,
  Tel: (502) 637-0011
  (Mfr air filtration/pollution control & noise control equip)
    AAF Asia Pte. Ltd., P.O. Box 375, Jurong Town Post Office, Singapore 9161

AAF-McQUAY INC   111 S Calvert St, #2800, Baltimore, MD 21202,
  Tel: (410) 528-2755
  (Mfr air quality control prdts: heating, ventilating, air-conditioning & filtration
  prdts & services)
    SnyderGeneral Pte. Ltd., 450 Alexandra Rd., #04-07 Inchcape House, Singapore 0511

AAR CORP   1111 Nicholas Blvd, Elk Grove Village, IL   60007,
  Tel: (708) 439-3939
  (Aviation repair & supply provisioning)
    AAR Allen Group Intl., 1 Loyang St., Singapore 1750

ADAPTEC INC   691 S Milpitas Blvd, Milpitas, CA   95035, Tel: (408) 945-8600
  (Design/mfr/mkt hardware & software solutions)
    Adaptec Mfg. (S) Pte. Ltd., Block 1003, Bukit Merah Central #07-09, Singapore 0315

ADC TELECOMMUNICATIONS INC   4900 W 78th St, Minneapolis, MN   55435,
  Tel: (612) 835-6800
  (Mfr telecom equip)
    ADC Singapore, 10 Anson Rd., Aex 24-06 International Plaza, Singapore 0207

ADVANCED LOGIC RESEARCH INC   9401 Jeronimo Rd, Irvine, CA   92718,
  Tel: (714) 581-6770
  (Computers)
    ALR Intl. (Pte.) Ltd., 140 Pays Lebar Rd., #04-11 A-Z Bldg., Singapore 1440

ADVANCED MICRO DEVICES INC   PO Box 3453, Sunnyvale, CA   94088-3000,
  Tel: (408) 732-2400
  (Mfr integrated circuits for commun & computation ind)
    Advanced Micro Devices Intl. Ltd., P.O. Box 512, Chai Chee Lane 07 to 0706,
      Bedok Ind. Estate, Singapore

AERO SYSTEMS AVIATION CORP   PO Box 52-2221, Miami, FL   33152,
  Tel: (305) 871-1300
  (Aviation equip sales & serv sys)
    Aero Systems Pte. Ltd., 290 Oxford St., Seletar Airport, Singapore 2879

AIR EXPRESS INTL CORP   120 Tokeneke Rd, PO Box 1231, Darien, CT   06820,
  Tel: (203) 655-7900
  (Air frt forwarder)
    Air Express Intl. (S) Pte. Ltd., Third Cargo Complex, Singapore Airport, Singapore

AIRBORNE EXPRESS   3101 Western Ave, PO Box 662, Seattle, WA   98111,
  Tel: (206) 285-4600
  (Air transp serv)
    Airborne Express, P.O. Box 551, Airmail Transit Centre, Singapore 9181

ALLIEDSIGNAL INC   101 Columbia Rd, PO Box 2245, Morristown, NJ   07962-2245,
  Tel: (201) 455-2000
  (Mfr aerospace & automotive prdts, engineered materials)
    AlliedSignal Aerospace Co., Shaw Ctr., Suite 15-07, 1 Scotts Rd., Singapore 0922
    AlliedSignal Air Transport Avionics, 512 Chai Chee Ln. 05-01/06,
      Bedok Industrial Estate, Singapore 1646
    Garrett Singapore (Pte.) Ltd., 161 Gul Ctr., Jurong Industrial Estate,
      Singapore 2262

AMDAHL CORP   1250 E Arques Ave, PO Box 3470, Sunnyvale, CA   94088-3470,
  Tel: (408) 746-6000
  (Devel/mfr large scale computers, software, data storage prdts, info-technology
  solutions & support)
    Amdahl Intl. Corp., 152 Beach Rd., #22-06/08 Gateway East, Signapore 0718

AMERICAN & EFIRD INC   PO Box 507, Mt Holly, NC 28120, Tel: (704) 827-4311
(Mfr ind thread, yarn & consumer sewing prdts)
   American & Efird (S) Pte. Ltd., 10 Tuas Drive 2, Jurong Town, Singapore 2263

AMERICAN AIRLINES INC   PO Box 619616, Dallas-Ft Worth Arpt, TX 75261-9616,
   Tel: (817) 355-1234
   (Air transp)
   American Airlines Inc., UOL Bldg. 2/F, 96 Somerset Rd., Singapore 0923

AMERICAN BUREAU OF SHIPPING   2 World Trade Center, 106th Fl, New York,
   NY 10048, Tel: (212) 839-5000
   (Classification/certification of ships & offshore structures, devel & tech assistance)
   ABS Pacific, SLF Bldg., 510 Thomson Rd. #06-00, Singapore 1129

AMERICAN OPTICAL CORP   14 Mechanic St, Southbridge, MA 01550,
   Tel: (508) 765-9711
   (Mfr opthalmic lenses & frames, custom molded prdts, specialty lenses)
   American Optical Co. (S) Pte. Ltd., 1002 Jalan Bukit Merah, #02-13/20,
      Singapore 0315

AMERICAN PRESIDENT LINES LTD   1111 Broadway, Oakland, CA 94607,
   Tel: (415) 272-8000
   (Intermodal shipping serv)
   American President Line Ltd., Maxwell P.O. Box 193, Singapore 9003

AMERICAN RE-INSURANCE CO   555 College Rd East, Princeton, NJ 08543,
   Tel: (609) 243-4200
   (Reinsurance)
   American Re-Insurance Co., 17/05-07 The Gateway East, 152 Beach Rd., Singapore 0718

AMETEK INC   Station Sq, Paoli, PA 19301, Tel: (610) 647-2121
   (Mfr instru, elect motors, engineered materials)
   Ametek Singapore Pte. Ltd., 10 Ang Mo Kio St. 65, #05-12 TechPoint, Singapore 2056

AMP INC   PO Box 3608, Harrisburg, PA 17105-3608, Tel: (717) 564-0100
   (Devel/mfr electronic & electrical connection prdts & sys)
   AMP Singapore (Pte) Ltd., 26 Ang Mo Kio Industrial Park 2, Singapore 2056

ANGLO-AMERICAN AVIATION CO   9740 Telfair Ave, Arleta, CA 91331,
   Tel: (818) 896-0333
   (Aviation spare parts, hardware)
   Anglo-American Aviation Co. (S) Pte., World Trade Center 8/F, 1 Maritime Square,
      Singapore 0409

APPLIED MAGNETICS CORP   75 Robin Hill Rd, Goleta, CA 93117,
   Tel: (805) 683-5353
   (Mfr magnetic recording heads)
   Applied Magnetics (Singapore) Pte. Ltd., Singapore

APPLIED POWER INC   13000 W Silver Spring Dr, Butler, WI 53007,
   Tel: (414) 781-6600
   (Mfr hi-pressure tools, vibration control prdts, electrical tools & consumables, tech
   furniture)
   Applied Power Asia Pte. Ltd., 47 Jalan Pemimpin, Sin Cheong Bldg. #01-02/03,
      Singapore 577200

ARGO INTL CORP   140 Franklin St, New York, NY 10013, Tel: (212) 431-1700
  (Distr electrical spare parts)
    Argo Intl. Europe Ltd., 150 Orchard Rd., Singapore 0923

ARMSTRONG ENGINEERING ASSOCIATES INC   PO Box 566, West Chester, PA 19380,
  Tel: (215) 436-6080
  (Heat exchangers & process equip for chem plants & oil refineries)
    Chemtec Pte. Ltd., 9 Gul Ave., Jurong, Singapore 2266

ARMSTRONG WORLD INDUSTRIES INC   PO Box 3001, Lancaster, PA 17604,
  Tel: (717) 397-0611
  (Mfr/mkt interior furnishings & spec prdts for bldg, auto & textile inds)
    Armstrong (Singapore) Pte. Ltd., Singapore (all inquiries to U.S. address)

ASARCO INC   180 Maiden Lane, New York, NY 10038, Tel: (212) 510-2000
  (Nonferrous metals, specialty chems, minerals, mfr industrial prdts, environmental
  services)
    Enthone-Omi Inc., Singapore

ASSOCIATED MERCHANDISING CORP   1440 Broadway, New York, NY 10018,
  Tel: (212) 536-4000
  (Retail service organization)
    Associated Merchandising Corp., 250 North Bridge Rd., Raffles City Tower 20-03/04,
      Singapore 0617

ASSOCIATED SPRING   18 Main St, Bristol, CT 06010, Tel: (203) 583-1331
  (Mfr precision springs & stampings)
    Associated Spring Asia, 28 Tuas Ave. 2, Jurong, Singapore 2263

AST RESEARCH INC   16215 Alton Parkway, PO Box 19658, Irvine, CA 92713-9658,
  Tel: (714) 727-4141
  (Design/devel/mfr hi-perf desktop, server & notebook computers)
    AST Singapore, 401 Commonwealth Dr., #06-02 Haw Par Technocentre, Singapore 0314

AT&T INTERNATIONAL   412 Mt Kemble Ave, Morristown, NJ 07962-1995,
  Tel: (810) 262-6646
  (Telecommunications)
    AT&T Singapore Pte. Ltd., 150 Beach Rd., #36-00 Gateway West, Singapore 0718

ATLANTIC RICHFIELD CO (ARCO)   515 S Flower St, Los Angeles, CA 90071-2256,
  Tel: (213) 486-3511
  (Petroleum & natural gas, chemicals, service stations)
    Arco Chemical (Singapore) Pte. Ltd., 152 Beach Rd, The Gateway East #37-00,
      Singapore 0718

ATWOOD OCEANICS INTL   PO Box 218350, Houston, TX 77218, Tel: (713) 492-2929
  (Offshore drilling for gas/oil)
    Atwood Oceanics (S) Pte. Ltd., 1205 Orchard Towers, 400 Orchard Rd., Singapore

AUTODESK INC   2320 Marinship Way, Sausalito, CA 94965, Tel: (415) 332-2344
  (Devel/mkt/support computer-aided design, engineering, scientific & multimedia
  software prdts)
    Autodesk Inc., A-Z Bldg. #04-07, 140 Paya Lebar Rd., Singapore 1440

AUTOMATIC SPRINKLER CORP OF AMERICA   1000 E Edgerton Rd, Cleveland,
   OH 44147, Tel: (216) 526-9900
   (Fire protection & detection sys)
      Automatic Sprinkler Corp. of America, 59B Duxton Rd., Singapore 0208

AUTOMATIC SWITCH CO   Hanover Rd, Florham Park, NJ 07932, Tel: (201) 966-2000
   (Mfr solenoid valves, emergency power controls, pressure & temp switches)
      ASCO Asia, 63 Hillview Ave 07-04, Lam Soon Industrial Bldg., Singapore 2366

AUTOSPLICE INC   10121 Barnes Canyon Rd, San Diego, CA 92121,
   Tel: (619) 535-0079
   (Mfr electronic components)
      Autosplice Asia Pte. Ltd., 1002 Jalan Bukit Merah, Unit #05-11,
         Redhill Ind. Estate, Singapore 0315

AVIS INC   900 Old Country Rd, Garden City, NY 11530, Tel: (516) 222-3000
   (Car rental serv)
      Avis Rental Services Office, Boon Liew Bldg. 204B, Bukit Timah Rd., Singapore 0922

J T BAKER INC   222 Red School Lane, Phillipsburg, NJ 08865,
   Tel: (201) 859-2151
   (Mfr/sale/serv lab & process chems)
      J.T. Baker Inc., 51 Newton Rd. 17-04/05, Tower Block, Goldhill Plaza, Singapore 1130

BAKER OIL TOOLS   PO Box 40129, Houston, TX 77240-0129, Tel: (713) 466-1322
   (Mfr/serv oil/gas well completions equip)
      Baker Oil Tools-Asia Pacific, 273 Jalan Ahmad Ibrahim, Singapore 2262

BAND-IT IDEX CORP   4799 Dahlia St, Denver, CO 80216, Tel: (303) 320-4555
   (Mfr pressure clamps)
      Band-It Clamps (Asia) Pte. Ltd., Block 19, No. 73, Pandan Loop,
         Pandan Light Industry Park, Singapore 0512

THE BANK OF NEW YORK   48 Wall St, New York, NY 10286, Tel: (212) 495-1784
   (Banking)
      The Bank of New York, 10 Collyer Quay, Ocean Bldg. #14-02/03, Singapore 0104

BANKAMERICA CORP   555 California St, San Francisco, CA 94104,
   Tel: (415) 622-3456
   (Financial services)
      Bank of America NT & SA, 78 Shenton Way, #20-00, Singapore 0207
      BankAmerica Singapore Ltd., 78 Shenton Way, #20-00, Singapore 0207

BANKERS TRUST CO   280 Park Ave, New York, NY 10017, Tel: (212) 250-2500
   (Banking)
      Bankers Trust Co. Singapore Branch, Ocean Bldg. 5/F, Collyer Quay, Singapore

C R BARD INC   730 Central Ave, Murray Hill, NJ 07974, Tel: (908) 277-8000
   (Mfr health care prdts)
      Bard International, Level 36, Hong Leong Bldg., 16 Raffles Quay, Singapore 0104

BARNES GROUP INC   123 Main St, PO Box 409, Bristol, CT 06011-0489,
   Tel: (860) 583-7070
   (Mfr maint parts & supplies)
      Associated Spring-Asia Pte. Ltd., Singapore
      Windsor Airmotive Asia Pte. Ltd., Singapore

BAUSCH & LOMB INC   1 Chase Square, Rochester, NY 14601, Tel: (716) 338-6000
   (Mfr vision care prdts & accessories)
      Bausch & Lomb (Singapore) Pte. Ltd., Singapore

BAXTER HEALTHCARE CORP   1 Baxter Pky, Deerfield, IL 60015,
   Tel: (708) 948-2000
   (Mfr disposable medical prdts)
      Baxter Healthcare Pte. Ltd., 1 Scotts Rd., Shaw Centre, Unit 2605-06, Singapore 0922

BEAR STEARNS & CO INC   245 Park Ave, New York, NY 10167, Tel: (212) 272-2000
   (Investment banking)
      Bear Stearns Singapore Pte. Ltd., 24 Raffles Place, #26-05 Clifford Centre,
         Singapore 0104

BECHTEL GROUP INC   50 Beale St, PO Box 3965, San Francisco, CA 94119,
   Tel: (415) 768-1234
   (Engineering & constr)
      Bechtel Inc., 66/68B Cecil St., Singapore

BECKMAN INSTRUMENTS INC   2500 Harbor Blvd, Fullerton, CA 92634,
   Tel: (714) 871-4848
   (Devel/mfr/mkt automated systems & supplies for biological analysis)
      Beckman Instruments (Singapore) Pte. Ltd., 331 N. Bridge Rd.,
         Odeon Towers #07-01/02, Singapore 0718

BECTON DICKINSON AND CO   1 Becton Dr, Franklin Lakes, NJ 07417,
   Tel: (201) 847-6800
   (Mfr/sale medical supplies, devices & diagnostic sys)
      Becton Dickinson, 30 Tuas Ave. 2, Singapore 2263

BENTLY NEVADA CORP   PO Box 157, Minden, NV 89423, Tel: (702) 782-3611
   (Electronic monitoring system)
      Bently Nevada Singapore Pte. Ltd., 19 Tanglin Rd., 09-06 Tanglin Shopping Centre,
         Singapore 1024

SAMUEL BINGHAM CO   1555 N Mittel Blvd, #T, Wood Dale, IL 60191-1046,
   Tel: (708) 238-4000
   (Print & industrial rollers, inks)
      Coates Brothers (Singapore) Ptd. Ltd., 19 International Rd., Jurong, Singapore 2261

BLACK & DECKER CORP   701 E Joppa Road, Towson, MD 21286, Tel: (410) 716-3900
   (Mfr power tools & accessories, security hardware, small appliances, fasteners, info
   sys & servs)
      Black & Decker Corp., all mail to U.S. address

BOOZ ALLEN & HAMILTON INC   101 Park Ave, New York, NY 10178,
   Tel: (212) 697-1900
   (Mgmt consultants)
      Booz Allen & Hamilton Management Consultants Pte. Ltd., 10 College Quay,
         #05-01 Ocean Bldg., Singapore 0104

BOURNS INC   1200 Columbia Ave, Riverside, CA 92507, Tel: (909) 781-5500
   (Mfr resistive com & networks, precision potentiometers, panel controls, switches,
   transducers)
      Bourns Asia Pacific Pte. Ltd., 400 Orchard Rd #06-20, Orchard Towers, Singapore 0923

BOWEN TOOLS INC   PO Box 3186, Houston, TX 77253-3186, Tel: (713) 868-8888
   (Mfr drilling & specialty tools for oil/gas ind)
      Bowen Tools Inc., Unit 1, Block 2, Terrace Warehouse, Loyang Offshore Supply Base,
      Loyang Crescent, Singapore 1750

BOWNE INTL INC   345 Hudson St, New York, NY 10014, Tel: (212) 924-5500
   (Financial printing & foreign language translation)
      Bowne of Singapore, Standard Chartered Bldg. #09-06, 6 Battery Rd., Singapore 0104

BOYDEN CONSULTING CORP   375 Park Ave, #1008, New York, NY 10152,
   Tel: (212) 980-6480
   (Executive search)
      Boyden Associates Pte. Ltd., 50 Raffles Pl., 19-02 Shell Tower, Singapore 0104

BOZELL JACOBS KENYON & ECKHARDT INC   40 West 23rd St, New York, NY 10010,
   Tel: (212) 727-5000
   (Advertising agency)
      Grant K &.E (S) Pte. Ltd., MacDonald House 6/F, Orchard Rd., P.O. Box 2196,
      Singapore

W H BRADY CO   6555 W Good Hope Rd, Milwaukee, WI 53223, Tel: (414) 358-6600
   (Mfr ind ID for wire marking, circuit boards; facility ID & signage)
      W.H. Brady Pte. Ltd., 55 Ayer Rajah Crescent 03-01, Ayer Rajah Industrial Estate,
      Singapore 0513

BRANSON ULTRASONICS CORP   41 Eagle Rd, Danbury, CT 06813-1961,
   Tel: (203) 796-0400
   (Mfr plastics assembly equip, ultrasonic cleaning equip)
      Branson Ultrasonics, 63 Hillview Ave. #07-04, Lam Soon Industrial Bldg.,
      Singapore 2366

BROWN & ROOT INC   4100 Clinton Dr, Houston, TX 77020-6299,
   Tel: (713) 676-3011
   (Engr, constr & maintenance)
      Brown & Root (Singapore) Pte. Ltd., P.O. Box 104, Killiney Rd. Post Office,
      Singapore 9123
      Taylor Diving (SE Asia) Pte. Ltd., 19 Tuas Crescent, Jurong 2263, Singapore 2262

BULAB HOLDINGS INC   1256 N McLean Blvd, Memphis, TN 38108,
   Tel: (901) 278-0330
   (Mfr microbicides, biocides, additives, corrosion inhibitors, chems)
      Buckman Laboratories (Asia) Pte. Ltd., 33 Gul Dr., Singapore 629481

BURLINGTON AIR EXPRESS   18200 Van Karman Ave, Irvine, CA 92715,
   Tel: (714) 752-4000
   (Air freight)
      Burlington Air Express, Unit 01-28/29 Cargo Agents Bldg. C., 115 Airport Cargo Rd.,
      Singapore 1781

LEO BURNETT CO INC   35 West Wacker Dr, Chicago, IL 60601, Tel: (312) 220-5959
   (Advertising agency)
      Leo Burnett Pte. Ltd., 11 Beach Rd., Singapore

BURSON-MARSTELLER   230 Park Ave, New York, NY 10003-1566, Tel: (212) 614-4000
   (Public relations/public affairs consultants)
      Burson Marsteller, 100 Beach Rd., 14-08 Shaw Towers, Singapore 0718

CARL BYOIR & ASSOCIATES INC   420 Lexington Ave, New York, NY 10017,
Tel: (212) 210-6000
(Public relations, intl commun)
  Gibson Public Relations (Pte.) Ltd., 100 Beach St., 33-01 Shaw Towers,
    Singapore 0718

CABLETRON SYSTEM   35 Industrial Way, PO Box 5005, Rochester, NY 03866-5005,
Tel: (603) 332-9400
(Devel/mfr/mkt/install/support local & wide area network connectivity hardware &
software)
  Cabletron System, 85 Science Park Dr., #03-03/04 The Cavendish, Singapore 0511

CALIFORNIA PELLET MILL CO   221 Main St, #420, San Francisco, CA 94105,
Tel: (415) 431-3800
(Mfr mach for pelleting)
  CPM/Pacific (Pte.) Ltd., 17 Liu Fang Rd., Singapore 2263

CALTEX PETROLEUM CORP   PO Box 619500, Dallas, TX 75261, Tel: (214) 830-1000
(Petroleum prdts)
  Caltex (Asia) Ltd., Robinson Rd., P.O. Box 646, Singapore 9012
  Caltex Operations Ltd., Robinson Rd., Box 646, Singapore 9012
  Caltex Services Pte. Ltd., Robinson Rd., Box 646, Singapore 9012
  Caltex Trading Pte. Ltd., 17-01 Tong Bldg., 302 Orchard Rd., Singapore 0923

CAMCO INC   7010 Ardmore St, Houston, TX 77021, Tel: (713) 747-4000
(Oil field equip)
  Camco Asia (Pte.) Ltd., Loyang Offshore Base, Kuala Loyang Rd., P.O. Box 23,
    Singapore

CARBOLINE CO   350 Hanley Industrial Ct, St Louis, MO 63144,
Tel: (314) 644-1000
(Mfr coatings, sealants)
  Carboline South East Asia Pte. Ltd., 400 Orchard Rd. #06-15, Orchard Towers,
    Singapore 0923

CARGILL   PO Box 9300, Minneapolis, MN 55440, Tel: (612) 475-7575
(Food prdts, feeds, animal prdts)
  Cargill Southeast Asia, 300 Beach Rd., #23-01, The Concourse, Singapore 0719

CARRIER CORP   One Carrier Place, Farmington, CT 06034-4015,
Tel: (203) 674-3000
(Mfr/distr/svce A/C, heating & refrigeration equip)
  Carrier Intl. Corp., 76 Shenton Way, #17-00 Ong Bldg., Singapore 0207
  Comfortair (Singapore) Pte. Ltd., 28 Teban Gardens Crescent, Singapore 2260

J I CASE CO   700 State St, Racine, WI 53404, Tel: (414) 636-6011
(Mfr/sale agric & constr equip)
  J.I. Case Co., Yen San Bldg. 12/F, 268 Orchard Rd., Singapore 0923

CATERPILLAR INC   100 N E Adams St, Peoria, IL 61629, Tel: (309) 675-1000
(Mfr earth/material-handling & constr mach & equip, engines, generators)
  Caterpillar Far East Ltd., 14 Tractor Rd., Jurong Town, P.O. Box 105, Singapore

CBI INDUSTRIES INC   800 Jorie Blvd, Oak Brook, IL 60521, Tel: (708) 654-7000
   (Holding co: metal plate fabricating, constr, oil & gas drilling)
      CBI Overseas Inc., Tan Chwee Boon Bldg., 921 Bukit Timah Rd., Singapore
      CBI Overseas Inc., Loyang Offshore Base, Kualya Loyang Rd., Singapore 1750

CCH INC   2700 Lake Cook Rd, Riverwoods, IL 60015, Tel: (708) 267-7000
   (Tax & busines law info, software & services)
      CCH Asia Limited, 139 Cecil St., #02-00, Singapore 0106

CDM INTL INC   Ten Cambridge Center, Cambridge, MA 02142, Tel: (617) 252-8000
   (Consulting engineers)
      Camp, Dresser & McKee Inc., World Trade Center, 1 Maritime Sq., Singapore 0409

CEILCOTE CO   140 Sheldon Rd, Berea, OH 44017, Tel: (216) 243-0700
   (Mfr corrosion-resistant material, air pollution control equip, cons serv)
      Ceilcote Pte. Ltd., P.O. Box 183, Jurong, Singapore 9161

CENTRAL GULF LINES INC   650 Poydras St, New Orleans, LA 70130,
   Tel: (504) 529-5461
   (Steamship service)
      Marco Shipping Co. (Pte.) Ltd., 200 Cantonment Rd. 16/03, Southpoint, Singapore 0208

CENTRAL NATIONAL-GOTTESMAN INC   3 Manhattanville Rd, Purchase,
   NY 10577-2110, Tel: (914) 696-9000
   (Worldwide sales pulp & paper prdts)
      Central Asia Sales Pte. Ltd., 171 Chin Swee Rd., #10-08 San Centre, Singapore 0316

CHASE MANHATTAN BANK N A   1 Chase Manhattan Plaza, New York, NY 10081,
   Tel: (212) 552-2222
   (Intl banking)
      The Chase Manhattan Bank N.A., Shing Kwan House, 4 Shenton Way, GPO Box 3012,
         Singapore
      United Chase Merchant Bankers Ltd., Straits Trading Bldg. 12/F, 9 Battery Rd.,
         Singapore

CHEMICAL BANK   270 Park Ave, New York, NY 10017-2070, Tel: (212) 270-6000
   (Banking & financial services)
      Chemical Bank, 150 Beach St., #23-00 Gateway West, Singapore 0718

CHESTERTON BINSWANGER INTL   Two Logan Sq, 4th fl, Philadelphia,
   PA 19103-2759, Tel: (215) 448-6000
   (Real estate & related svces)
      Chesterton Intl. Property Consultants Pte. Ltd., 20 Cecil St., #17-02 The Exchange,
         Singapore 0104

CHEVRON CHEMICAL CO   PO Box 5047, San Ramon, CA 94583-0947,
   Tel: (510) 842-5500
   (Chemicals)
      Chevron Chemical (Far East) Ltd., One Scotts Rd., #20-13 Shaw Centre, Singapore 0922

CHEVRON CORP   225 Bush St, San Francisco, CA 94104, Tel: (415) 894-7700
   (Oil & gas exploration, production, refining, products; oilfield & financial services)
      Chevron Corp., all mail to U.S. address

CHIRON CORP   4560 Horton St, Emeryville, CA 94608-2916, Tel: (510) 601-2412
  (Research/mfg/mktg therapeutics, vaccines, diagnostics, ophthalmics)
     Chiron Vision Singapore Pte. Ltd., 10 Anson Rd., #19-16 International Plaza,
       Singapore 0923

THE CHUBB CORP   15 Mountain View Rd, Warren, NJ 07060, Tel: (908) 580-2000
  (Holding co: property/casualty ins)
     Federal Insurance Co., Singapore

CIGNA CORP   One Liberty Place, Philadelphia, PA 19192, Tel: (215) 523-4000
  (Ins, invest, health care & other fin servs)
     Esis Intl. Inc., 5 Shenton Way- #12.01, UIC Bldg., Singapore 0106
     Insurance Co. of North America, 5 Shenton Way- #12.01/UIC Bldg., Maxwell Rd.,
       PO Box 46, Singapore
     Safire Private Ltd., 24 Raffles Place, 21-01 Clifford Centre, Singapore 0104

CINCOM SYSTEMS INC   2300 Montana Ave, Cincinnati, OH 45211,
  Tel: (513) 662-2300
  (Devel/distr computer software)
     Cincom Systems Inc., Singapore

CITICORP   399 Park Ave, New York, NY 10043, Tel: (212) 559-1000
  (Banking & financial services)
     Citibank NA, Singapore

CITIZENS & SOUTHERN NATL BANK   35 Broad St, Atlanta, GA 30399,
  Tel: (404) 581-2121
  (Banking)
     Citizens & Southern Natl. Bank, Bank of East Asia Bldg. 10/F, 131-137 Market St.,
       Singapore

CLEMCO INDUSTRIES CORP   One Cable Car Dr, Washington, MO 63090,
  Tel: (314) 239-0300
  (Blast cleaning equip & sys, dust collection sys, coating & finishing sys, dry
  stripping facilities)
     Clemco Intl. GmbH, 32A Hillview Terrace, Singapore 2366

COBE LABORATORIES INC   1185 Oak St, Lakewood, CO 80215, Tel: (303) 232-6800
  (Mfr med equip & supplies)
     COBE Far East, Singapore

COLGATE-PALMOLIVE CO   300 Park Ave, New York, NY 10022, Tel: (212) 310-2000
  (Mfr pharms, cosmetics, toiletries, detergents)
     Colgate-Palmolive (Eastern) Pte. Ltd., 29 First Lokyand Rd., Jurong, P.O. Box 35,
       Singapore

COLUMBIA PICTURES INDUSTRIES INC   711 Fifth Ave, New York, NY 10022,
  Tel: (212) 751-4400
  (Producer & distributor of motion pictures)
     Cathay Film Distributors Pte. Ltd., Killiney Rd., P.O. Box 17, Singapore

COMBUSTION ENGINEERING INC   900 Long Ridge Road, Stamford, CT 06902,
  Tel: (203) 329-8771
  (Tech constr)
     Gray Service Co. AG, Loyang Offshore Base, Loyang Crescent, Singapore 1750
     Gray Service Co. AG, other locations in Singapore

COMDISCO INC   6111 N River Rd, Rosemont, IL 60018, Tel: (708) 698-3000
  (Hi-tech asset & facility mgmt, equip leasing)
    Comdisco Asia Pte. Ltd., Singapore 0106

COMMERCIAL INTERTECH CORP   1775 Logan Ave, PO Box 239, Youngstown,
  OH 44501-0239, Tel: (216) 746-8011
  (Mfr hydraulic com, fluid purification sys, pre-engineered bldgs, stamped metal prdts)
    Cuno Filtration Asia Pte. Ltd., 51 Gul Circle, Jurong, Singapore 2262
    Cuno Pacific Pty. Ltd., 19 Keppel Rd., #05-02 Jit Poh Bldg., Singapore 0208

COMMERCIAL METALS CO   PO Box 1046, Dallas, TX 75221, Tel: (214) 689-4300
  (Metal collecting/processing, steel mills, metal trading)
    CMC Intl. (SE Asia) Pte. Ltd., HEX 15-02 Tong Bldg., 302 Orchard Rd., Singapore 0923

COMPAQ COMPUTER CORP   PO Box 692000, Houston, TX 77269-2000,
  Tel: (713) 370-0670
  (Devel/mfr personal computers)
    Compaq Asia Pte. Ltd., Singapore
    Compaq Computer Asia/Pacific Pte. Ltd., 53 Yishun Industrial Park A, Singapore 2776

COMPUTER ASSOCIATES INTL INC   One Computer Associates Plaza, Islandia,
  NY 11788, Tel: (516) 342-5224
  (Devel/mkt/mgt info mgt & bus applications software)
    Computer Associates Pte. Ltd., 391B Orchard Rd., #21-01/05 Ngee Ann City,
      Singapore 0923

COMPUTERVISION CORP   100 Crosby Dr, Bedford, MA 01730-1480,
  Tel: (617) 275-1800
  (Supplier of mechanical design automation & prdt data mgmt software & services)
    Computervision Singapore Pte. Ltd., 152 Beach Rd., #07-00 Gateway East,
      Singapore 0718

CONAGRA INC   1 ConAgra Dr, Omaha, NE 68102, Tel: (402) 595-4000
  (Prepared & frozen foods, grains, flour, animal feeds, agric chems, poultry, meat,
  dairy prdts)
    ConAgra Asia Pacific, Raffles City Tower #27-04, Singapore
    ConAgra Intl. Pte. Ltd., Raffles City Tower #27-04, Singapore

CONE MILLS CORP   3101 N Elm St, Greensboro, NC 27408, Tel: (910) 545-3541
  (Mfr denims, flannels, chamois & other fabrics)
    Cone Mills Intl., 60 Martin Rd., #03-31 Trademart Singapore, Singapore 239067

CONOCO INC   600 N Dairy Ashford Rd, Houston, TX 77079, Tel: (713) 293-1000
  (Oil, gas, coal, chems, minerals)
    Conoco Western Pacific Ltd., Shaw House 9/F, Orchard Rd., Singapore
    Continental Oil Co. of Indonesia, Shaw House 9/F, Orchard Rd., Singapore

CONTINENTAL BANK NA   231 S LaSalle St, Chicago, IL 60697, Tel: (312) 828-2345
  (Coml banking servs)
    Continental Bank Corp., 10 Collyer Quay- #20-06/08, Ocean Building, Singapore 0104
    Continental First Options Inc., 10 Collyer Quay, #20-06/08 Ocean Bldg.,
      Singapore 0104

CONVEX COMPUTER CORP   3000 Waterview Pkwy, Richardson, TX 75080,
  Tel: (214) 497-4000
  (Mfr high-performance computing systems)
    Convex Computer Pte. Ltd., 1 Scotts Rd., #25-06 Shaw Center, Singapore 0922

CORE LABORATORIES   10205 Westheimer, Houston, TX 77042, Tel: (713) 972-6311
  (Petroleum testing/analysis, analytical chem, lab & octane analysis instrumentation)
    Core Laboratories Inc., 24-A Lim Teck Boo Rd., Singapore 1953

CORESTATES FINANCIAL CORP   1500 Market St, Philadelphia, PA 19101,
  Tel: (215) 973-3100
  (Banking)
    Corestates Bank, 6 Battery Rd., #13-03, Singapore 0104

CORNING INC   One Riverfront Plaza, Corning, NY 14831, Tel: (607) 974-9000
  (Mfr glass & specialty materials, consumer prdts; communications, lab services)
    Corning (Singapore) Pte. Ltd., Singapore

COUDERT BROTHERS   1114 Ave of the Americas, New York, NY 10036-7794,
  Tel: (212) 626-4400
  (Lawyers)
    Coudert Brothers, Tung Centre #21-00, 20 Collyer Quay, Singapore 0104

CPC INTERNATIONAL INC   PO Box 8000, Englewood Cliffs, NJ 07632,
  Tel: (201) 894-4000
  (Consumer foods, corn refining)
    CPC/AJI (Singapore) Pte. Ltd., Yishun Central P.O. Box 106, Singapore 9176

CROWLEY MARITIME CORP   155 Grand Ave, Oakland, CA 94612, Tel: (510) 251-7500
  (Marine transp)
    PT Patra Drilling Contractor, 53 Shipyard Rd., Jurong Town, Singapore

CROWN CORK & SEAL CO INC   9300 Ashton Rd, Philadelphia, PA 19136,
  Tel: (215) 698-5100
  (Mfr cans, bottle caps; filling & packaging mach)
    The Crown Cork Co. (Malaya) Ltd., Jalan Boon Lay, Jurong Town, Singapore 2261

CROWN EQUIPMENT CORP   40 S Washington St, New Bremen, OH 45869,
  Tel: (419) 629-2311
  (Mfr/sales/svce forklift trucks, stackers)
    Crown Equipment Pte. Ltd., 15 Tuas Ave. 8, Singapore 2263

CTS CORP   905 N West Blvd, Elkhart, IN 46514, Tel: (215) 293-7511
  (Mfr electr components)
    CTS Singapore Pte. Ltd., 14 Ang Mo Kio Industrial Park, Singapore 2056

CUMMINS ENGINE CO INC   PO Box 3005, Columbus, IN 47202, Tel: (812) 377-5000
  (Mfr diesel engines)
    Cummins Diesel Sales Corp., 8 Tanjong Perjuru, Jurong Ind. Estate, Singapore 2260

CYBORG SYSTEMS INC   2 N Riverside Plaza, Chicago, IL 60606-0899,
  Tel: (312) 454-1865
  (Devel/mfr human resources, payroll & time/attendance software)
    Cyborg Systems Asia Ltd., 73 Science Park Dr., #B1-17 CINTECH,
      Singapore Science Park, Singapore 0511

D'ARCY MASIUS BENTON & BOWLES INC (DMB&B)   1675 Broadway, New York,
  NY 10019, Tel: (212) 468-3622
  (Advertising & communications)
    DMB&B Pte. Ltd., 19 Keppel Rd., 09-08 Jit Poh Bldg., Singapore 0208

DAMES & MOORE   911 Wilshire Blvd, Los Angeles, CA 90017, Tel: (213) 683-1560
(Engineering, environmental & construction mgmt services)
   Dames & Moore, 171 Chin Swee Rd., #02-09 Sam Centre, Singapore 0316

DANA CORP   PO Box 1000, Toledo, OH 43697, Tel: (419) 535-4500
(Engineer/mfr/mkt prdts & sys for vehicular, ind & mobile off-highway mkt & related
aftermarkets)
   Dana Asia (Singapore) Pte. Ltd., 130 Hillview Ave., Singapore 2366
   Warner Electric, 58 Hillview Terrace, Singapore 2366

DANA WORLD TRADE CORP   PO Box 405, Toledo, OH 43692, Tel: (419) 535-5300
(Automotive, heavy truck, off-hwy, fluid & mech power components)
   Dana World Trade Singapore Pte. Ltd., 28 Hill View Ter., Singapore 2366

DATA GENERAL CORP   4400 Computer Dr, Westboro, MA 01580, Tel: (617) 366-8911
(Design, mfr gen purpose computer sys & peripheral prdts & servs)
   Data General Singapore Pte. Ltd., 141 Market St., Harapan Bldg., Unit 04-00,
   Singapore 0104

DATAEASE INTL INC   7 Cambridge Dr, Trumbull, CT 06611, Tel: (203) 374-8000
(Mfr applications devel software)
   Genetic Software Consultancy, 1 Selegie Rd., #03-04 Paradiz Centre, Singapore 0718

DATAWARE TECHNOLOGIES INC   222 Third St, #3300, Cambridge, MA 02142,
   Tel: (617) 621-0820
(Multi-platform, multi-lingual software solutions & services for electronic info
providers)
   Dataware Technologies Pte. Ltd., 143 Cecil St., #21-02 GB Bldg., Singapore 069542

DDB NEEDHAM WORLDWIDE INC   437 Madison Ave, New York, NY 10022,
   Tel: (212) 415-2000
(Advertising)
   DDB Needham Worldwide DIK Pte. Ltd., 545 Orchard Rd.,
   #1107 Far East Shopping Centre, Singapore 0923

DEVCON CORP   30 Endicott St, Danvers, MA 01923, Tel: (617) 777-1100
(Mfr filled epoxies, urethanes, adhesives & metal treatment prdts)
   ITW Asia (Pte.) Ltd., 8 Kaki Bukit Rd. 2, 02-34 Ruby Warehouse Complex,
   Singapore 1440

DEWITT INTERNATIONAL CORP   5 N Watson Rd, Taylors, SC 29687,
   Tel: (803) 244-8521
(Mfr over-counter pharms)
   DeWitt Intl. (S) Pte. Ltd., P.O. Box 2292, Singapore

THE DEXTER CORP   1 Elm Street, Windsor Locks, CT 06096, Tel: (203) 627-9051
(Mfr nonwovens, polymer prdts, magnetic materials, biotechnology)
   Dexter Asia Pacific Ltd., 6 Tuas Ave. 8, Singapore 2263
   Dexter Asia Pacific Ltd., 6 Tuas Ave. 8, Singapore 2263
   Dexter Asia Pacific Ltd., 6 Tuas Ave. 8, Singapore 2263
   Dexter Nonwovens, 6 Tuas Ave. 8, Singapore 2263

DIGICON INC   3701 Kirby Drive, Houston, TX 77096, Tel: (713) 526-5611
(Geophysical services)
   Earth Search Processing, Union Bldg., Unit 06-01, 37 Jalan Pemimpin, Singapore

DIGITAL EQUIPMENT CORP   146 Main St, Maynard, MA 01754-2571,
  Tel: (508) 493-5111
  (Networked computer systems & services)
    Digital Equipment Singapore Pte. Ltd., 152 Beach Rd., #36-00, Singapore 0718

DOBOY PACKAGING MACHINERY INC   869 S Knowles Ave, New Richmond,
  WI 54017-1797, Tel: (715) 246-6511
  (Mfr packaging machinery)
    SIG Asia Pte. Ltd., 1 Tannery Rd. #01-00, Singapore 1334

THE DOW CHEMICAL CO   2030 Dow Center, Midland, MI 48674, Tel: (517) 636-1000
  (Mfr chems, plastics, pharms, agric prdts, consumer prdts)
    Dow Chemical (Singapore) Pte. Ltd., Singapore
    Dow Chemical Pacific Ltd., 806 Cathay Bldg., P.O. Box 2985, Singapore
    Pacific Terminals Pte. Ltd., Singapore

DOW CORNING CORP   2220 W Salzburg Rd, PO Box 1767, Midland, MI 48640,
  Tel: (517) 496-4000
  (Silicones, silicon chems, solid lubricants)
    Dow Corning Asia Ltd., 806 Cathay Bldg., P.O. Box 2985, Singapore

DRAKE BEAM MORIN INC   100 Park Ave, New York, NY 10017, Tel: (212) 692-7700
  (Human resource mgmt consulting & training)
    Drake Beam Morin - Singapore, 5 Shenton Way, #30-01 UIC Bldg., Singapore 0106

DRESSER INDUSTRIES INC   PO Box 718, Dallas, TX 75221-0718,
  Tel: (214) 740-6000
  (Diversified supplier of equip & tech serv to energy & natural resource ind)
    Dresser (Singapore) Pte. Ltd., 1 Scott's Rd., #21-01, Singapore 0922
    Masoneilan (SEA) Pvt. Ltd., 16 Tuas Ave, Singapore 2262

DRILCO DIV   16740 Hardy Rd, PO Box 60068, Houston, TX 77205,
  Tel: (713) 443-3370
  (Oil well down-hole drilling tools)
    Drilco, Div. of Smith Intl. Inc., Loyang Offshore Base, Kuala Loyang Rd., Singapore
    Smith Intl. Inc., Loyang Offshore Base, Kuala Loyang Rd., Singapore

E I DU PONT DE NEMOURS & CO   1007 Market St, Wilmington, DE 19898,
  Tel: (302) 774-1000
  (Mfr/sale diversified chems, plastics, specialty prdts & fibers)
    DuPont (Singapore) Electronics Pte. Ltd., Singapore
    DuPont Far East Inc., 604 Cathay Bldg., Mt. Sophia Rd., Newton P.O. Box 73,
      Singapore

DURAMETALLIC CORP   2104 Factory St, Kalamazoo, MI 49001, Tel: (616) 382-8720
  (Mfr mech seals, compression packings, auxiliaries)
    Durametallic Asia Pte. Ltd., 12 Loring Baker Batu, 01-07/8 Kolam Ayer Ind. Park,
      Singapore 1334

THE DURIRON CO INC   PO Box 8820, Dayton, OH 45401-8820, Tel: (513) 476-6100
  (Mfr chem equip, pumps, valves, filters, fans, heat exchangers)
    Durco-Valtek (Asia Pacific) Pte. Ltd., 12 Tuas Ave 20, Singapore 2263

EASTMAN CHEMICAL .   PO Box 511, Kingsport, TN 37662, Tel: (423) 229-2000
  (Mfr plastics, chems, fibers)
    Eastman Chemical, Singapore

EASTMAN KODAK CO   343 State St, Rochester, NY 14650, Tel: (716) 724-4000
(Devel/mfr photo & chem prdts, info mgmt/video/copier sys, fibers/plastics for various ind)
    Atex Asia, 305 Alexandra Rd., Singapore 0315
    Eastman Chemical Intl. Ltd., World Trade Center #09-01, One Maritime Sq.,
      Singapore 0409
    Eastman Kodak Co., Godown P8, Pasir Panjang Wharves, PSA Gate 5, Pasir Panjang Rd.,
      Singapore 0511
    Kodak (Singapore) Pte. Ltd., 305 Alexandra Rd., Singapore 0315
    Sterling Pacific Pte. Ltd., 11 Dhoby Ghaut, Unit 10-01 Cathay Bldg., Singapore 0922

EATON CORP   1111 Superior Ave, Cleveland, OH 44114, Tel: (216) 523-5000
(Advanced tech prdts for transp & ind mkts)
    Eaton Intl. Inc., SIA Bldg. 16/F, 77 Robinson Rd., P.O. Box 21, Singapore
    Tamco Cutler-Hammer Pte. Ltd., Hokyand Rd., P.O. Box 48, Tomon Jarong, Singapore

EATON CORP/CUTLER HAMMER   4201 North 27th St, Milwaukee, WI 53216,
Tel: (414) 449-6000
(Electric control apparatus, mfr of advanced technologic prdts)
    Tamco Cutler-Hammer, 1 Jalan Remaja #05-501/502, Hillview House, Singapore 2366

EBASCO SERVICES INC   2 World Trade Center, New York, NY 10048-0752,
Tel: (212) 839-1000
(Engineering, constr)
    Ebasco Services Singapore Pty. Ltd., Wallich Bldg. #02-59, Wallich St.,
      Singapore 0207

EG&G INC   45 William St, Wellesley, MA 02181-4078, Tel: (617) 237-5100
(Diversified R/D, mfg & services)
    EG&G Heimann Optoelectronics, Block 47, Ayer Rajah Crescent #06-12, Singapore 0513
    Eagle EG&G Aerospace Pte. Ltd., 18 Tractor Rd., Jurong Town, Singapore 2262

ELECTROGLAS INC   2901 Coronado Dr, Santa Clara, CA 95054, Tel: (408) 727-6500
(Mfr semi-conductor test equip, automatic wafer probers)
    Electroglas Intl. Inc., 5004 Ang Mo Kio Ave. 5, #02-09/10 TECHplace II,
      Singapore 2056

EMERY WORLDWIDE   One Lagoon Dr, #400, Redwood City, CA 94065,
Tel: (800) 227-1981
(Freight transport, global logistics, air cargo)
    Emery Worldwide, P.O. Box 507, Singapore Changi Airport, Singapore 9181

ENTERRA CORP   13100 Northwest Freeway, Houston, TX 77040, Tel: (713) 462-7300
(Provides specialized services, products & equip for oil/gas wells & pipelines)
    Enterra Oilfield Rentals Pte. Ltd., Singapore

ESCO CORP   2141 NW 25th Ave, Portland, OR 97210, Tel: (503) 228-2141
(Mfr equip for mining, constr, forestry ind)
    ESCO Pacific, 1 Scotts Rd., #16-08 Shaw Centre, Singapore 0922

ETHYL CORP   330 South 4th St, PO Box 2189, Richmond, VA 23219,
Tel: (804) 788-5000
(Mfr fuel & lubricant additives)
    Ethyl Asia Pacific Co., 13-06 PUB Bldg., Devonshire Road Wing, 111 Somerset Rd.,
      Singapore 0923

EXPEDITORS INTL OF WASHINGTON INC   PO Box 69620, Seattle, WA 98168-9620,
  Tel: (206) 246-3711
  (Air/ocean freight forwarding, customs brokerage, intl logistics solutions)
    Expeditors (S) Pte. Ltd., Cargo Agents Bldg C, #06-14/15,
      Box 577 Changi Airfreight Centre, Singapore 1781

EXXON CORP   225 E John W Carpenter Freeway, Irving, TX 75062-2298,
  Tel: (214) 444-1000
  (Petroleum explor, prod, refining; mfr petrol & chem prdts; coal & minerals)
    Esso Singapore Pte. Ltd., 1 Raffles Pl., 28-38/F, Singapore 0104

FAIRCHILD AIRCRAFT CORP   PO Box 790490, San Antonio, TX 78279-0490,
  Tel: (512) 824-9421
  (Mfr turboprop aircraft)
    Fairchild Aircraft Corp., 20 Leonie Hill, 06-24 Leonie Towers, Block B,
      Singapore 0923

FAIRCHILD CAMERA & INSTRUMENT CORP   PO Box 58090, Santa Clara,
  CA 95052-8090, Tel: (408) 743-3355
  (Mfr electr instru & controls)
    Fairchild Singapore Pte. Ltd., 11 Lorong 3, Toa Payoh,
      Toa Payoh Central P.O. Box 311, Singapore

FEDERAL EXPRESS CORP   PO Box 727, Memphis, TN 38194, Tel: (901) 369-3600
  (Package express delivery service)
    Federal Express Courier Svcs. Pte. Ltd., 3 Kaki Bukit Rd. 2, Blk. A, Unit 3E,
      Eunos Warehouse Complex, Singapore 1441

FEDERAL-MOGUL CORP   PO Box 1966, Detroit, MI 48235, Tel: (810) 354-7700
  (Mfr/distr precision parts for automobiles, trucks, & farm/constrution vehicles)
    Federal-Mogul World Trade Pte. Ltd., Singapore

FIRST CHICAGO CORP   One First National Plaza, Chicago, IL 60670,
  Tel: (312) 732-4000
  (Banking)
    First Chicago Corp., Singapore

FIRST NATIONAL BANK IN DALLAS   PO Box 6031, Dallas, TX 75283,
  Tel: (214) 744-8000
  (Commercial banking)
    First Natl. Bank in Dallas, UIC Bldg. 10/F, 5 Shenton Way, P.O. Box 1574, Singapore

FIRST NATIONAL BANK OF BOSTON   100 Federal St, Boston, MA 02110,
  Tel: (617) 434-2200
  (Commercial banking)
    The First Natl. Bank of Boston, 21 Collyer Quay, 13-01 Hong Kong Bank Bldg.,
      P.O. Box 2900, Singapore 9048

FIRST NATIONAL BANK OF CHICAGO   One First National Plaza, Chicago, IL 60670,
  Tel: (312) 732-4000
  (Financial services)
    Ong First Chicago Futures Pte. Ltd., Ong Group Bldg., 76 Shenton Way 10-00,
      Singapore 0207

FIRST PENNSYLVANIA BANK   16th & Market St, Philadelphia, PA 19101,
  Tel: (215) 786-5000
  (Bank holding company)
    First Pennsylvania Bank N.A., 331 ICB Bldg., 2 Shenton Way, Singapore

FISERV INC   255 Fiserv Dr, PO Box 979, Brookfield, WI 53008-0979,
  Tel: (414) 879-5000
  (Data processing, computer services)
    Fiserv (Asia/Pacific) Pte. Ltd., 80 Raffles Place #56-02, Singapore 0104

FISHER CONTROLS INTL INC   8000 Maryland Ave, Clayton, MO 63105,
  Tel: (314) 746-9900
  (Mfr ind process control equip)
    Fisher Controls Pte. Ltd., Locked Bag Service #5, Singapore 9158,
      985 Bukit Timah Rd., Singapore 2158

FISHER SCIENTIFIC INC   Liberty Lane, Hampton, NH 03842, Tel: (603) 929-2650
  (Mfr sci instru & apparatus, chems, reagents)
    Fisher Scientific, 101 Thomson Rd., 16-05 United Sq., Singapore 1130

C B FLEET CO INC   4615 Murray Place, PO Box 11349, Lynchburg, VA 24506,
  Tel: (804) 528-4000
  (Mfr pharmaceutical, health & beauty aids)
    DeWitt International (S) Pte. Ltd., 62 Tannery Lane, Singapore 1334

FLEXTRONICS INC INTL   2241 Lundy Ave, San Jose, CA 95131-1822,
  Tel: (408) 428-1300
  (Contract mfr for electronics ind)
    Flextronics Singapore Pte. Ltd., 1 Bedok Ind. Estate, 514 Chai Chee Lane 05-12,
      Singapore 1646

FLORASYNTH INC   300 North St, Teterboro, NJ 07608, Tel: (201) 288-3200
  (Mfr fragrances & flavors)
    Florasynth (Singapore) Ptd. Ltd., 83 Science Park Dr. #04-01, The Curie,
      Singapore Science Park, Singapore 0511

FLUOR DANIEL INC   3333 Michelson Dr, Irvine, CA 92730, Tel: (714) 975-2000
  (Engineering, construction, maintenance & technical services)
    Fluor Daniel Engineers & Constructors Ltd., Inchcape House #05-01,
      450/452 Alexandra Rd., Singapore 0511

FMC CORP   200 E Randolph Dr, Chicago, IL 60601, Tel: (312) 861-6000
  (Produces chems & precious metals, mfr machinery, equip & sys for ind, agric & govt)
    FMC Southeast Asia Pte. Ltd., Singapore

FOUR WINDS INTL GROUP   1500 SW First Ave, #850, Portland, OR 97201,
  Tel: (503) 241-2732
  (Transp of household goods & general cargo, third party logistics)
    Four Winds Logistics Services, 275 Beach Rd. 03-00, Singapore 0719

FRITZ COMPANIES INC   706 Mission St, San Francisco, CA 94103,
  Tel: (415) 904-8360
  (Integrated transportation, sourcing, distribution & customs brokerage services)
    FAF-Fritz Pte. Ltd., Unit 06-12 Cargo Agents Bldg. C, 115 Airport Cargo Rd.,
      Singapore 1781
    FTI-Fritz Pte. Ltd., Unit 07-23/24, 1 Colombo Ct., Singapore 0617

GAF CORP   1361 Alps Rd, Wayne, NJ 07470, Tel: (201) 628-3000
  (Chems, bldg materials, commun)
    GAF Corp. (Singapore) Pty., 200 Cantonment Road 06-07, Southpoint, Singapore 0208

GAFFNEY CLINE & ASSOCIATES INC   PO Box 796309, Dallas, TX 75379,
  Tel: (214) 733-1183
  (Consultants to energy & mineral ind)
    Gaffney, Cline & Assoc., 04-05A SIF Bldg., 96 Robinson Rd., Singapore 0106

THE GATES RUBBER CO   PO Box 5887, Denver, CO 80217-5887, Tel: (303) 744-1911
  (Mfr automotive & industrial belts & hose)
    Gates Export Corp., 14 Tuas Ave. 8, Jurong Industrial Estate, Singapore 2263

GATX CAPITAL CORP   Four Embarcadero Center, #2200, San Francisco, CA 94111,
  Tel: (415) 955-3200
  (Lease & loan financing, residual guarantees)
    GATX Leasing (Pacific) Ltd., 11 Collyer Quay, #15-01A The Arcade, Singapore 0104

GENERAL ELECTRIC CO   3135 Easton Tpk, Fairfield, CT 06431,
  Tel: (203) 373-2211
  (Diversified manufacturing, technology & services)
    General Electric Co.,
      all mail to U.S. address; phone (800) 626-2004 or (518) 438-6500

GENERAL FOODS CORP   250 North St, White Plains, NY 10625, Tel: (914) 335-2500
  (Processor, distributor & mfr of foods)
    General Foods (Southwest Asia), 101 Thomson Rd., 10-05 Goldhill Sq., Singapore 1130

GENERAL INSTRUMENT CORP   181 W Madison, Chicago, IL 60602,
  Tel: (312) 541-5000
  (Mfr broadband communications & power rectifying components)
    General Instrument, 1 Marine Parade Central, #03-09 Parkway Builder's Centre,
      Singapore 1544
    Jerrold Communications, 16 Lady Hill Rd., Singapore 1025

GENERAL MOTORS CORP   3044 W Grand Blvd, Detroit, MI 48202-3091,
  Tel: (313) 556-5000
  (Mfr full line vehicles, automotive electronics, coml technologies, telecom, space,
  finance)
    GM Singapore Pte. Ltd., 501 Ang Mo Kio Industrial Park, Singapore 2056
    General Motors Overseas Distribution Corp., 15 Benoi Sector, Jurong Town,
      Singapore 2262

GENRAD INC   300 Baker Ave, Concord, MA 01742, Tel: (508) 369-4400
  (Mfr automatic test equip)
    GenRad Inc., 456 Alexandra Rd 15-00, NOL Bldg., Singapore 0511

GETZ BROS & CO INC   150 Post St, #500, San Francisco, CA 94108,
  Tel: (415) 772-5500
  (Divers mfg, mktg/distr serv, travel serv)
    Consmat Singapore (Pte.), 5 Gul Crescent, Jurong Town, Singapore 2262
    The Getz Corp. (Singapore) Sdn. Bhd., GPO Box 234, Singapore 9004

THE GILLETTE CO   Prudential Tower, Boston, MA 02199, Tel: (617) 421-7000
  (Devel/mfr personal care/use prdts: blades & razors, toiletries, cosmetics,
  stationery)

Gillette Asia Pacific Pte. Ltd., Singapore
Gillette Singapore Pte. Ltd., Singapore

GLOBAL INTERNATIONAL 1304 Willow St, Martinez, CA 94553, Tel: (510) 229-9330
(International moving & forwarding)
Global Forwarding (Singapore) Pte. Ltd., 54 Pandan Rd., Jurong, Singapore 2260

THE GOODYEAR TIRE & RUBBER CO 1144 E Market St, Akron, OH 44316,
Tel: (216) 796-2121
(Mfr tires, automotive belts & hose, conveyor belts, chemicals; oil pipeline
transmission)
Goodyear Singapore Pte. Ltd., 16A Bendeneer Rd (or 24A), Singapore 1233

W R GRACE & CO One Town Center Rd, Boca Raton, FL 33486-1010,
Tel: (407) 362-2000
(Mfr spec chems & materials: packaging, health care, catalysts, construction, water
treatment/process)
W.R. Grace (Singapore) Pte. Ltd., 23 Tanjong Penjuru, Jurong Ind. Town,
Singapore 2260

GREY ADVERTISING INC 777 Third Ave, New York, NY 10017, Tel: (212) 546-2000
(Advertising)
CR & Grey, 20 Maxwell Rd., #02-01 Maxwell House, Singapore 0106

GRUMMAN INTL INC 1111 Stewart Ave, Bethpage, NY 11714, Tel: (516) 575-4806
(Mfr/sale aerospace prdts, aircraft, software, automated test equip, C3 projects)
Grumman (Singapore) Pte. Ltd., 250 North Bridge Rd., Hex 15-04, Raffles City Tower,
Singapore 0617

GTE DIRECTORIES CORP West Airport Dr, DFW Airport, TX 75261-9810,
Tel: (214) 453-7000
(Pub telephone directories)
GTE Directories (S) Pte. Ltd., Tower Block, Goldhill Plaza 12-07,
12-09 Newton Place, Singapore 1130

FRANK B HALL & CO INC 549 Pleasantville Rd, Briarcliff Manor, NY 10510,
Tel: (914) 769-9200
(Insurance)
Frank B. Hall Ins. Brokers (S) Pte. Ltd., 20 McCallum St., Hex 16-05,
Asia Chambers, Singapore 0106

HALLIBURTON CO 500 N Akard St, #3600, Dallas, TX 75201-3391,
Tel: (214) 978-2600
(Energy, construction, insurance)
Halliburton, Bldg. 25, Loyang Offshore Supply Base, Loyang Crescent, Singapore 1750

HAMBRECHT & QUIST One Bush St, San Francisco, CA 94104, Tel: (415) 576-3300
(Invest banking & venture capital serv)
H&Q Asia Pacific Venture Mgmt. Pte. Ltd., 78 Shenton Way #12-02, Singapore 0207

HANDY & HARMAN 555 Theodore Fremd Ave, Rye, NY 10580, Tel: (914) 921-5200
(Precious & specialty metals for industry, refining, scrap metal; diversified ind mfg)
Handy & Harman Mfg. (Singapore) Pte. Ltd., 20 Tuas Avenue 5, Jurong, Singapore 2263

HARCO TECHNOLOGIES CORP   1055 W Smith Rd, Medina, OH 44256,
Tel: (216) 725-6681
(Full-serv corrosion engr, cathodic protection)
   Harco Pacific Technologies Ltd., 9 Pandan Rd., Singapore 2260

HARNISCHFEGER INDUSTRIES INC   PO Box 554, Milwaukee, WI 53201,
Tel: (414) 671-4400
(Mfr mining & material handling equip, papermaking mach, computer sys)
   Beloit Corp., 230 Orchard Rd. #06-230, Faber House, Singapore 0923

THE HARPER GROUP   260 Townsend St, PO Box 77933, San Francisco,
CA 94107-1719, Tel: (415) 978-0600
(Ocean/air freight fwdg, customs brokerage, packing & whse, logistics mgt, ins)
   Circle Freight Intl. (S) Pte. Ltd., 97A-100A Duxton Rd., Singapore 0208
   Gruenhut Intl. (S) Pte. Ltd., 97A-100A Duxton Rd., Singapore 0208
   Western Navigation (FE) Pte. Ltd., 97A-100A Duxton Rd., Singapore 0208

THE HARTFORD STEAM BOILER INSPECTION & INSURANCE CO   1 State St, Hartford,
CT 06102, Tel: (203) 722-1866
(Inspection & quality assurance, asbestos monitoring)
   Hartford Steam Boiler (Singapore) Pte. Ltd., 50 Florissa Park, Singapore 2678

HERCULES INC   Hercules Plaza, Wilmington, DE 19894-0001, Tel: (302) 594-5000
(Mfr spec chems, plastics, film & fibers, coatings, resins, food ingredients)
   Hersean Pte. Ltd., 101 Thomson Rd., 05-01 United Square, Singapore 1130

HEWLETT-PACKARD CO   3000 Hanover St, Palo Alto, CA 94304-0890,
Tel: (415) 857-1501
(Mfr computing, communications & measurement prdts & services)
   HP Singapore (Pte.) Ltd., 1150 Depot Rd., Singapore 0410

HOBART BROTHERS CO   Hobart Sq, 600 W Main St, Troy, OH 45373-2928,
Tel: (513) 332-4000
(Mfr arc/automatic welding sys, power sys, filler metals)
   Hobart Brothers Co., 80 Marine Parade Rd., #13-06 Parkway Parade, Singapore 1544

HOCKMAN-LEWIS LTD   200 Executive Dr, West Orange, NJ 07052,
Tel: (201) 325-3838
(Export management)
   Hockman-Lewis Ltd., Orchard P.O. Box 0457, Singapore 9123

HOLIDAY INNS INC   3742 Lamar Ave, Memphis, TN 38195, Tel: (901) 362-4001
(Hotels, restaurants, casinos)
   Holiday Inn, Singapore

HONEYWELL INC   PO Box 524, Minneapolis, MN 55440-0524, Tel: (612) 951-1000
(Devel/mfr controls for home & building, industry, space & aviation)
   Honeywell Pte. Ltd., Southeast Asia Block 750E,
      Chai Chee Rd. #06-01 Chai Chee Industrial Park, Singapore 1646

HORWATH INTL   415 Madison Ave, New York, NY 10017, Tel: (212) 838-5566
(Public accountants & auditors)
   Chio Lim & Associates, Blk 162 #06-3655, Bukit Merah Central, Singapore 0315
   Lo Hock Ling & Co., 101-A Upper Cross St., #11-22, People's Park Centre,
      Singapore 0105

HOUGHTON INTL INC   PO Box 930, Valley Forge, PA 19482-0930,
Tel: (610) 666-4000
(Mfr spec chems, hydraulic fluids, lubricants)
  Houghton Singapore, 20 Bideford Rd. #14-01/02, Wellington Bldg., Singapore 0923

HOWE RICHARDSON CO   680 Van Houten Ave, Clifton, NJ 07015,
Tel: (201) 471-3400
(Ind weighing & packaging equip)
  Howe Richardson Pte. Ltd., 131 Central Bldg., 1-2 Magazine Rd., Singapore 0105

HUCK INTL INC   6 Thomas, PO Box 19590, Irvine, CA 92713, Tel: (714) 855-9000
(Mfr advanced fastening sys)
  Huck Intl. Singapore Pte. Ltd., 130 Joo Seng Rd., #05-03 Olivine Bldg.,
  Singapore 1336

HUGHES AIRCRAFT CO   PO Box 80028, Los Angeles, CA 90080-0028,
Tel: (310) 568-6904
(Mfr electronics equip & sys)
  Hughes Aircraft Intl. Service Co., United Square Bldg. #27-01, 101 Thomson Rd.,
  Singapore 1130

HUGHES TOOL CO   PO Box 2539, Houston, TX 77001, Tel: (713) 924-2222
(Equip & serv to oil & gas explor & prod ind)
  Hughes Services, 20 Gulway Jurong, P.O. Box 333, Singapore 9161

HUTCHINSON TECHNOLOGY INC   40 W Highland Pk, Hutchinson, MN 55350-9784,
Tel: (612) 587-1900
(Mfr suspension assembly components for rigid disk drives)
  Hutchinson Technology Asia, 20 Jalan Afifi, #05-07 Cisco Centre, Singapore 409179

HYATT INTL CORP   200 West Madison, Chicago, IL 60606, Tel: (312) 750-1234
(Intl hotel mgmt)
  Hyatt Intl. Hotels, Singapore

IBM CORP   Old Orchard Rd, Armonk, NY 10504, Tel: (914) 765-1900
(Information products, technology & services)
  IBM Singapore Pte. Ltd., Shing Kwan House, 4 Shenton Way, Singapore 0106

ICS INTERNATIONAL INC   125 Oak St, Scranton, PA 18515, Tel: (717) 342-7701
(Correspondence courses)
  ICS (Overseas) Ltd., Union Bldg. #10-179, 171 Tras St., Singapore 0207

IDEX CORP   630 Dundee Rd, #400, Northbrook, IL 60062, Tel: (708) 498-7070
(Mfr ind pumps, lubrication sys, metal fabrication equip, bending & clamping devices)
  Band-It Clamps (Asia) Pte. Ltd., Block 19, #73 Pandam Loop, Singapore 0512

IMO INDUSTRIES INC   1009 Lenox Dr, Bldg 4 West, Lawrenceville,
NJ 08648-0550, Tel: (609) 896-7600
(Mfr/support mech & electr controls, engineered power prdts)
  Imo Industries Pte. Ltd., 30 Pioneer Rd., Jurong P.O. Box 119, Singapore 2262

IMODCO INC   27001 Agoura Rd, #350, Calabasas Hills, CA 91301-5359,
Tel: (818) 880-0300
(Turnkey supplier/contractor for offshore mooring sys)
  Imodco Inc., 100 Beach Rd., U-2209 Shaw Towers, Singapore 0718

INCOM INTERNATIONAL INC   3450 Princeton Pike, Lawrenceville, NJ 08648,
   Tel: (609) 896-7600
   (Roller & motorcycle chains, drive components, marine controls)
      Incom Singapore Pte. Ltd., 30 Pioneer Rd., P.O. Box 119, Jurong Town, Singapore 22

INDEL-DAVIS INC   4401 S Jackson St, Tulsa, OK 74157, Tel: (918) 587-2151
   (Mfr exploraton supplies to seismic ind)
      Indel-Davis Singapore (Pte.) Ltd., 875 Bukit Timah Rd., Singapore

INGERSOLL-RAND CO   200 Chestnut Ridge Rd, Woodcliff Lake, NJ 07675,
   Tel: (201) 573-0123
   (Mfr compressors, rock drills, pumps, air tools, door hardware, ball bearings)
      Ingersoll-Rand South East Asia (Pte.) Ltd., 42 Benoi Rd., Jurong Town,
      Singapore 2262

INTEL CORP   2200 Mission College Blvd, Santa Clara, CA 95052-8119,
   Tel: (408) 765-8080
   (Mfr semiconductor, microprocessor & microcommunications components & systems)
      Intel Singapore Ltd., Block 26, Ayer Rajah Crescent #03-01, Singapore 0513

INTERCONEX INC   50 Main St, White Plains, NY 10606-1920, Tel: (914) 328-7600
   (Freight forwarding)
      Interconex Intl. Movers Pte. Ltd., 5 Pioneer Lane, Singapore 2262

INTERGRAPH CORP   Huntsville, AL 35894-0001, Tel: (205) 730-2000
   (Devel/mfr interactive computer graphic systems)
      Intergraph Systems South-East Asia (Pte.) Ltd., 85 Science Park Dr.,
      #02-01/04 The Cavendish, Singapore 0511

INTERMEC CORP   6001 36th Ave West, PO Box 4280, Everett, WA 98203-9280,
   Tel: (206) 348-2600
   (Mfr/distr automated data collection sys)
      Peripheral Solutions (S) Pte. Ltd., 705 Sims Dr. #05-18,
      Shun Li Industrial Complex, Singapore 1438

INTERNATIONAL COMPONENTS CORP   420 N May St, Chicago, IL 60622,
   Tel: (312) 829-2525
   (Mfr/sale/svce portable DC battery chargers)
      International Components Corp. Singapore Pte. Ltd., 52 Genting Lane, #05-01/02/03,
      Hiang Kee Complex 1, Singapore 349560

INTERTRANS CORP   125 E John Carpenter Frwy, Irving, TX 75062,
   Tel: (214) 830-8888
   (Intl freight forwarding)
      Freight Intertrans Pte. Ltd., 43 Kakit Bukit Rd., Singapore 1441

INTERVEST INC   PO Box 2990, Honolulu, HI 96802, Tel: (808) 548-6611
   (Mgmt consultants)
      Intervest, Inc., 193-A Goldhill Plaza, P.O. Box 3381, Singapore 11

INTERVOICE INC   17811 Waterview Pkwy, Dallas, TX 75206, Tel: (214) 497-8862
   (Mfr voice automation systems)
      InterVoice Inc., 20 Cecil St, #25-07 The Exchange, Singapore 0104

ITT CORP   1330 Ave of the Americas, New York, NY   10019-5490,
  Tel: (212) 258-1000
  (Design/mfr communications & electronic equip, hotels, insurance)
    ITT Far East & Pacific Inc., Suite 2112, Shaw Center, Scotts Rd., Singapore 9

JAMESBURY CORP   640 Lincoln St, Worcester, MA   01605, Tel: (617) 852-0200
  (Mfr valves & accessories)
    Jamesbury Far East Pte. Ltd., 01-12 Pioneer Lane, P.O. Box 443, Jurong Town,
      Singapore 2262

JCPENNEY PURCHASING CORP   PO Box 10001, Dallas, TX   75301-0001,
  Tel: (214) 431-5380
  (Department stores)
    JCPenney Purchasing Corp., 435 Orchard Rd., #15-04 Wisma Atria, Singapore 0923

JOHNSON & HIGGINS   125 Broad St, New York, NY   10004-2424, Tel: (212) 574-7000
  (Ins brokerage, employee benefit conslt, risk mgmt, human resource conslt, ins/reins
  servs)
    Johnson & Higgins Pte. Ltd., Unity House #06-01, 1 Science Centre Rd.,
      Singapore 2260
    Johnson & Higgins Risk Management Services Pte. Ltd., Singapore

JOHNSON & JOHNSON   One Johnson & Johnson Plaza, New Brunswick, NJ   08933,
  Tel: (908) 524-0400
  (R&D/mfr/sale health care prdts)
    Johnson & Johnson Pte. Ltd., P.O. Box 189, Jurong Town Post Office, Singapore 9161

S C JOHNSON & SON INC   1525 Howe St, Racine, WI   53403, Tel: (414) 631-2000
  (Home, auto, commercial & personal care prdts, specialty chems)
    S.C. Johnson & Son Pte. Ltd., P.O. Box 2636, Singapore

JOHNSTON PUMP CO   800 Koomey Rd, Brookshire, TX   77423, Tel: (713) 391-6000
  (Mfr vertical turbine pumps)
    Johnston Pump Co. Pte. Ltd., 218 Tagore Lane, Sindo Industrial Estate,
      Upper Thompson Rd., Singapore 2678

A T KEARNEY INC   222 West Adams St, Chicago, IL   60606, Tel: (312) 648-0111
  (Mgmt consultants, executive search)
    A.T. Kearney Inc., 152 Beach Rd., #06-06 The Gateway East Tower, Singapore 0718

KELLOGG CO   One Kellogg Sq, PO Box 3599, Battle Creek, MI   49016-3599,
  Tel: (616) 961-2000
  (Mfr ready-to-eat cereals, convenience foods)
    Kellogg 20th Century Pte. Ltd., Jurong, Singapore (all inquiries to U.S. address)

THE M W KELLOGG CO   601 Jefferson Ave, Houston, TX   77002, Tel: (713) 753-2000
  (Design, engr, procurement & constr for process & energy ind)
    Kellogg Far East Inc., 541 Orchard Rd., 09-04 Liat Towers, Singapore 0923

THE KENDALL CO   15 Hampshire St, Mansfield, MA   02048, Tel: (508) 261-8000
  (Mfr medical disposable prdts, home health care prdts, spec adhesive prdts)
    The Kendall Co., 1 Selegie Rd., #06-17 Paradiz Centre, Singapore 0718

KENNAMETAL INC   PO Box 231, Latrobe, PA   15650, Tel: (412) 539-5000
  (Tools, hard carbide & tungsten alloys)
    Kennametal Tool Systems Singapore Pte. Ltd., 73 Ayer Rajah Cres., 01-20,
      Ayer Rajah Ind. Estate, Singapore 0513

KEPNER-TREGOE INC   PO Box 704, Princeton, NJ 08542-0740, Tel: (609) 921-2806
  (Mgmt consulting & training)
     Kepner-Tregoe Southeast Asia Ltd., #18-06 United Square, 101 Thompson Rd.,
       Singapore 1130

KETCHUM COMMUNICATIONS   6 PPG Pl, Pittsburgh, PA 15222, Tel: (412) 456-3500
  (Advertising, public relations, mgmt consulting)
     Ketchum Advertising (Singapore) Pte. Ltd., 5/7 Halifax Rd., Singapore 0922

KEYSTONE INTL INC   PO Box 40010, Houston, TX 77040, Tel: (713) 466-1176
  (Mfr butterfly valves, actuators & control accessories)
     Keystone Southeast Asia, Singapore

KIMBERLY-CLARK CORP   PO Box 619100, Dallas, TX 75261, Tel: (214) 281-1200
  (Mfr fiber-based prdts for personal care, lumber & paper prdts)
     Kimberly-Clark (Singapore) Pte. Ltd., Singapore
     Kimberly-Clark Far East Pte. Ltd., 34 Boon Leat Terrace, P.O. Box 191, Singapore

KORN/FERRY INTL   1800 Century Park East, Los Angeles, CA 90067,
  Tel: (310) 552-1834
  (Executive search)
     Korn/Ferry Intl. Pte. Ltd., 28-06 Shell Tower, 50 Raffles Pl., Singapore 0104

LE BLOND MAKINO INC   7680 Innovation Way, PO Box 8003, Mason, OH 45040-8003,
  Tel: (513) 573-7200
  (Mfr machine tools)
     LeBlond Asia Pte. Ltd., 2 Gul Ave., Jurong Town, Singapore 22

LEARONAL INC   272 Buffalo Ave, Freeport, NY 11520, Tel: (516) 868-8800
  (Mfr chem specialties)
     LeaRonal Singapore Pte. Ltd., 23 Joo Koon Rd., Singapore 2262

LEEDS+NORTHRUP   795 Horsham Rd, PO Box 1010, Horsham, PA 19044-8010,
  Tel: (215) 442-8000
  (Mfr process control instrumentation, liquid & particle analysis)
     Leeds+Northrup Singapore Pte. Ltd., Alexandria Distripark, Blk. 1, #08-30,
       Pasir Panjang Rd., Singpore 0511

LIGHTNIN   135 Mt Read Blvd, PO Box 1370, Rochester, NY 14611,
  Tel: (716) 436-5550
  (Mfr/sale/svce ind mixing mach, aerators)
     Lightnin Pte. Ltd., 5 Kian Tech Dr., Singapore 2262

ELI LILLY & CO   Lilly Corporate Center, Indianapolis, IN 46285,
  Tel: (317) 276-2000
  (Mfr pharmaceuticals, animal health prdts)
     Eli Lilly SA, 583 Orchard Rd., #12-01/04 Forum, Singapore 238884

LIMITORQUE   PO Box 11318, Lynchburg, VA 24506, Tel: (804) 528-4400
  (Mfr/mktg/svce electric valve actuators)
     Limitorque Asia Pte. Ltd., 22 Mandai Estate, Singapore 2572

LINTAS:WORLDWIDE   1 Dag Hammarskjold Plaza, New York, NY 10017,
  Tel: (212) 605-8000
  (Advertising agency)
     Lintas:Singapore, 133 Cecil St., Hex 1401, Keck Seng Tower, Singapore 0106

ARTHUR D LITTLE INC   25 Acorn Park, Cambridge, MA 02140-2390,
   Tel: (617) 498-5000
   (Mgmt, environ, health & safety consulting; tech & prdt development)
      Arthur D. Little Far East Inc., The Gateway, East Tower #13-06, 125 Beach Rd.,
      Singapore 0718

LITTON INDUSTRIES INC   21240 Burbank Blvd, Woodland Hills, CA 91367,
   Tel: (818) 598-5000
   (Elec sys, ind automation, resource explor)
      Western Geophysical (Singapore), 37 B Union Industrial Bldg., Thomson Rd.,
      Singapore 20

LOCKHEED MARTIN CORP   6801 Rockledge Dr, Bethesda, MD 20817,
   Tel: (301) 897-6000
   (Design/mfr/mgmt sys in fields of space, defense, energy, electronics, materials,
   info & tech svces)
      Lockheed Martin Intl. Ltd., 501 Orchard Rd., #21-00 Lane Crawford Pl.,
      Singapore 238880

LOCTITE CORP   10 Columbus Blvd, Hartford, CT 06106, Tel: (203) 520-5000
   (Mfr/sale ind adhesives & sealants)
      Loctite (Singapore) Pte. Ltd., 401 Commonwealth Dr.,
      #04-01/02 Haw Par Technocentre, Singapore 0314

THE LUBRIZOL CORP   29400 Lakeland Blvd, Wickliffe, OH 44092-2298,
   Tel: (216) 943-4200
   (Mfr chem additives for lubricants & fuels)
      Lubrizol Southeast Asia (Pte.) Ltd., Singapore

LUCAS AEROSPACE   PO Box 120039, Stamford, CT 06912, Tel: (203) 351-8400
   (Repair/overhaul/distr service parts aircraft sys & controls)
      Lucas Aerospace, 35/37 Loyang Way, Singapore 1750

MARCAM CORP   95 Wells Ave, Newton, MA 02159, Tel: (617) 965-0220
   (Applications software & services)
      Marcam Asia-Pacific Pte. Ltd., 80 Anson Rd., #30-04 IBM Towers, Singapore 0207
      Marcam Singapore, Level 36, Hong Leong Bldg., 16 Raffles Quay, Singapore 0104

MARSH & McLENNAN COS INC   1166 Ave of the Americas, New York, NY 10036-1011,
   Tel: (212) 345-5000
   (Insurance)
      Marsh & McLennan Bowring Pte. Ltd., 100 Beach Rd. #18-00, Shaw Towers,
      Singapore 0718

MARSTELLER INTL   1 E Wacker Dr, Chicago, IL 60601, Tel: (312) 329-1100
   (Advertising, marketing research, sales promotion)
      Burson-Marsteller (SEA) Pte. Ltd., Faber House, 236-J Orchard Rd., Singapore 0923

MARTIN-DECKER TOTCO INC   1200 Cypress Creek Rd, Cedar Park, TX 78613-3614,
   Tel: (512) 331-0411
   (Mfr oilfield & ind weight & meas sys)
      M/D Totco Inc., 8, 6th Lokyarg Rd., Jurong Town, Singapore 22

MATTEL INC   333 Continental Blvd, El Segundo, CA 90245, Tel: (310) 252-2000
   (Mfr toys, dolls, games, crafts & hobbies)
      Mattel Toys (Singapore) Pte. Ltd., 1 Scotts Rd., #23-06 Shaw Centre, Singapore 0922

MAXTOR CORP   211 River Oaks Pkwy, San Jose, CA 95134, Tel: (408) 432-1700
  (Design/mfr magnetic storage prdts)
    Maxtor Asia Pacific Ltd., Singapore
    Maxtor Peripherals (S) Pte. Ltd., Singapore

MECHANICAL SYSTEMS INC   4110 Romaine, Greensboro, NC 27407,
  Tel: (910) 292-4956
  (Mechanical & electrical contractors)
    Mechanical Systems (S) Pte. Ltd., 3rd Fl., Uniteers Bldg., River Valley Rd.,
      Singapore

MELROE CO   112 N University Dr, PO Box 6019, Fargo, ND 58108-6019,
  Tel: (701) 241-8700
  (Mfr heavy equip)
    Melroe Intl., 268 Orchard Rd.- #1507, Yen San Bldg., Singapore 0923

MEMTEC AMERICA CORP   2033 Greenspring Dr, Timonium, MD 21093,
  Tel: (410) 252-0800
  (Mfr purification & separation sys & prdts)
    Memtec Ltd., Block 208, #04-221, Hougang St. 21, Singapore 1953

METHODE ELECTRONICS INC   7444 W Wilson Ave, Harwood Heights, IL 60656,
  Tel: (708) 867-9600
  (Mfr electr components)
    Methode Electronics Far East Pte. Ltd., 37 Tuas Ave. 2, Jurong Town, Singapore 2263

MICROPOLIS CORP   21211 Nordhoff St, Chatsworth, CA 91311, Tel: (818) 709-3300
  (Mfr computer disk drives)
    Micropolis Corp., Block 5004, Ang Mo Kio Ave, #01-11, Singapore 2056

MICROSOFT CORP   One Microsoft Way, Redmond, WA 98052-6399,
  Tel: (206) 882-8080
  (Computer software, peripherals & services)
    Microsoft Singapore, 10 Anson Rd., #21-15 International Plaza, Singapore 0207

MIDLAND INC   PO Box 1193, Fort Wayne, IN 46801, Tel: (219) 432-3533
  (Export mgt)
    Midland Inc. (Singapore), Block A, #03-03, 60 Martin Rd., Singapore 0923

MILCHEM INC   3900 Essex Lane, PO Box 22111, Houston, TX 77027,
  Tel: (214) 439-8000
  (Gas & oil well drilling fluids & chem additives)
    Milchem Intl. Ltd., 03-16 Manhahen House, Isi Chin Swee Rd., Singapore 0316

MILLIPORE CORP   Ashley Rd, Bedford, MA 01730, Tel: (617) 275-9205
  (Mfr precision filters, hi-performance liquid chromatography instru)
    Millipore Asia Ltd., Jumbo Industrial Bldg. #07-01, 19 Kim Keat Rd, Singapore 1232

MINE SAFETY APPLIANCES CO   PO Box 426, Pittsburgh, PA 15230,
  Tel: (421) 273 5000
  (Safety equip, ind filters)
    MSA S.E. Asia Pte. Ltd., 51 Ayer Rajah Industrial Estate, 02-03, Block 7,
      Singapore 0513

MISSION DRILLING PRODUCTS DIV   PO Box 40402, Houston, TX 77240,
  Tel: (713) 460-6200
  (Oilfield equip, drilling & mining equip, ind valves)
    Mission Drilling Products Div., 4 Tuas Ave. 9, Singapore 2263

MOBIL CORP   3225 Gallows Rd, Fairfax, VA 22037-0001, Tel: (703) 846-3000
  (Petroleum explor & refining, mfr petrol prdts, chems, petrochems)
    Mobil Oil Singapore Pte. Ltd., P.O. Box 3025, Singapore 9050

MOLEX INC   2222 Wellington Ct, Lisle, IL 60532, Tel: (708) 969-4550
  (Mfr electronic, electrical & fiber optic interconnection prdts & sys, switches,
  application tooling)
    Molex Far East Management Ltd., 110 International Rd., Jurong Town, Singapore 2262

MONSANTO CO   800 N Lindbergh Blvd, St Louis, MO 63167, Tel: (314) 694-1000
  (Mfr agric & food prdts, chems, plastics, fibers, pharms, process control equip,
  performance material)
    Monsanto Singapore Co. (Pte.) Ltd., 101 Thomson Rd., #19-00 United Sq.,
      Singapore 1130

MOORE PRODUCTS CO   Sumneytown Pike, Spring House, PA 19477,
  Tel: (215) 646-7400
  (Mfr process control instru)
    Moore Products Co. (S) Pte. Ltd., Beaverton Industrial Bldg. #03-01,
      10 Tannery Lane, Singapore 1334

MORGAN GUARANTY TRUST CO   23 Wall St, New York, NY 10260, Tel: (212) 483-2323
  (Banking)
    Morgan Guaranty & Partners Ltd., DBS Bldg., 30th Fl., 6 Shenton Way, Singapore 1
    Morgan Guaranty Pacific Ltd., 3001 DBS Tower, 6 Shenton Way, Singapore 0106
    Morgan Guaranty Trust Co. of New York, 2901 DBS Tower, 6 Shenton Way, Singapore 1

MOTOROLA INC   1303 E Algonquin Rd, Schaumburg, IL 60196, Tel: (708) 576-5000
  (Mfr commun equip, semiconductors, cellular phones)
    Motorola Electronics Pte. Ltd., Blk 4012 Ang Mo Kio, Industrial Park 1,
      Singapore 2056
    Motorola Singapore Pte. Ltd., Shaw Towers 3500, 100 Beach Rd., Singapore 0718

MTS SYSTEMS CORP   14000 Technology Dr, Eden Prairie, MN 55344-2290,
  Tel: (612) 937-4000
  (Devel/mfr mechanical testing & simulation prdts & servs, ind meas & automation
  instrumentation)
    MTS Systems Corp., 14 Faber Park, Singapore 0512

MacDERMID INC   245 Freight St, Waterbury, CT 06702, Tel: (203) 575-5700
  (Chem processing for metal ind, plastics, electronics cleaners, strippers)
    MacDermid Inc., 80 Marien Parade Rd., #16-01 Parkway Parade, Singapoare 1543

McCANN-ERICKSON WORLDWIDE   750 Third Ave, New York, NY 10017,
  Tel: (212) 697-6000
  (Advertising)
    McCann-Erickson (Singapore) Pte. Ltd., 360 Orchard St., Hex 03-00 Intl. Bldg.,
      Singapore 0923

McCORMICK & CO INC   18 Loveton Circle, Sparks, MD 21152-6000,
  Tel: (410) 771-7301
  (Mfr/dist/sale seasonings, flavorings, specialty foods)

(cont)

McCormick Ingredients Southeast Asia Pte. Ltd., 4 Enterprise Rd., Jurong, Singapore 2262

McDERMOTT INTL INC   1450 Poydras St, PO Box 60035, New Orleans, LA 70160-0035, Tel: (504) 587-5400
(Engineering & construction)
  McDermott South East Asia Pty. Ltd., 1 Science Center Rd., Unity House #08-00, Singapore

NALCO CHEMICAL CO   One Nalco Center, Naperville, IL 60563-1198, Tel: (708) 305-1000
(Chems for water & waste water treatment, oil prod & refining, ind processes; water/energy mgmt serv)
  Nalco South East Asia, 21 Gul Lane, Jurong Town, Singapore 2262;,
    Boon Lay P.O. Box 861, Singapore 9164

NATCO   PO Box 1710, Tulsa, OK 74101, Tel: (918) 663-9100
(Mfr/sale/serv oil & gas prdts)
  NATCO Intl. Ltd., 200 Cantonment Rd., #14-03 Southpoint, Singapore 0208

NATIONAL CHEMSEARCH CORP   2727 Chemsearch Blvd, Irving, TX 75061, Tel: (214) 438-0211
(Commercial chem prdts)
  Natl. Chemsearch Corp. (SEA) Pte. Ltd., M & G Centre, 2nd Fl., Rm 202, 154/170 Clemenceau Ave., Singapore 9

NATIONAL SEMICONDUCTOR CORP   PO Box 58090, Santa Clara, CA 95052-8090, Tel: (408) 721-5000
(Mfr semiconductors, design/devel sys)
  National Semiconductor Pte. Ltd., 202 Cantoment Rd. #13-01, Southpoint, Singapore 0208

NATIONAL STARCH & CHEMICAL CO   10 Finderne Ave, Bridgewater, NJ 08807-3300, Tel: (908) 685-5000
(Mfr adhesives & sealants, resins & spec chems, electr materials & adhesives, food prdts, ind starch)
  Ablestik Electronic Materials & Adhesives, Singapore
  National Adhesives (Singapore) Pte. Ltd., Singapore
  National Starch & Chemical (Asia) Pte. Ltd., Singapore

NATIONAL-OILWELL   PO Box 4638, Houston, TX 77210-4638, Tel: (713) 960-5100
(Mfr/distr oilfield drills & tubulars)
  National-Oilwell Pte. Ltd., 12 Gul, Jurong Town, Singapore 2262

NATIONSBANK CORP   1 NCNB Plaza, Charlotte, NC 28255, Tel: (704) 386-5000
(Banking & financial services)
  NationsBank Corp., Maxwell Rd., 5 Shenton Way, UIC Bldg. #11-01, Singapore

NORDSON CORP   28601 Clemens Rd, Westlake, OH 44145, Tel: (216) 892-1580
(Mfr ind application equip & packaging mach)
  Nordson S.E. Asia (Pte.) Ltd., 16A Science Park Dr., #01-01 Singapore Science Park, Singapore 0511

NORTON CO   1 New Bond St, Worcester, MA 01606, Tel: (508) 795-5000
(Abrasives, drill bits, constr & safety prdts, plastics)
  Christensen Diamond Products Pte. Ltd., 1407A Far East Shopping Centre,

Orchard Rd., Jurong, Singapore
Christensen Maikai Co. Ltd., Rm 14-11 14th Fl., Far East Shopping Centre,
  Orchard Rd., Singapore
Norton Pte. Ltd., P.O. Box 510, Singapore

NORWEST BANK MINNESOTA NA   Norwest Center, 6th & Marquette, Minneapolis,
  MN 55479-0095, Tel: (612) 667-8110
  (Banking)
    Norwest Bank Minnesota NA, 100 Cecil St. #14-02, The Globe, Singapore 0106

OCEANEERING INTL INC   PO Box 218130, Houston, TX 77218-8130,
  Tel: (713) 578-8868
  (Underwater serv to offshore oil & gas ind)
    Oceaneering Intl. Pte. Ltd., 1 Kwong Min Rd., Singapore 2262

ODETICS INC   1515 S Manchester Ave, Anaheim, CA 92802-2907,
  Tel: (714) 774-5000
  (Design/mfr digital data mgmt prdts for mass data storage, commun & video security
mkts)
    Odetics Asia Pacific Pte. Ltd., 14 Upper Cross St., Singapore 0105

OLIN CORP   120 Long Ridge Rd, PO Box 1355, Stamford, CT 06904-1355,
  Tel: (203) 356-2000
  (Mfr chems, metals, applied physics in elect, defense, aerospace inds)
    Olin Pte. Ltd., 9 Tuas Avenue 10, Singapore 2263

ONAN CORP   1400 73rd Ave NE, Minneapolis, MN 55432, Tel: (612) 574-5000
  (Mfr electric generators, controls & switchgears)
    Onan Far East Pte. Ltd., 8 Tanjong Penjuru, Singapore 2260

OSMONICS INC   5951 Clearwater Dr, Minnetonka, MN 55343-8995,
  Tel: (612) 933-2277
  (Mfr fluid filtration & separation equip & components)
    Autotrol Singapore, Kent Ridge, P.O. Box 1065, Singapore 9111

OTIS ELEVATOR CO   10 Farm Springs, Farmington, CT 06032, Tel: (860) 676-6528
  (Mfr elevators & escalators)
    Otis Elevator Co., 250 North Bridge Rd., 18-00 Raffles City Tower, Singapore 0617
    Otis Elevator Co. (S) Pte. Ltd., P.O. Box 291, Robinson Rd. Post Office,
      Singapore 9005

OTIS ENGINEERING CORP   PO Box 819052, Dallas, TX 75381-9052,
  Tel: (214) 418-3932
  (Mfr oil/gas field equip; service well completion & maint)
    Otis Engineering Corp., 100 Gul Circle, Upper Jurong, Singapore 2262

OWENS-ILLINOIS INC   1 Seagate, Toledo, OH 43666, Tel: (419) 247-5000
  (Glass & plastic containers, house- hold & ind prdts, packaging)
    Owens-Illinois Inc., 3 Greenleaf Place, Singapore 10

PACCAR INTL   10604 NE 38th Place, Kirkland, WA 98033, Tel: (206) 828-8872
  (Heavy duty dump trucks, military vehicles)
    Paccar Intl., 101 Thomson Rd., #09-05 Goldhill Sq., Singapore 1130

PACIFIC ARCHITECTS & ENGINEERS INC   1111 W Sixth St, Los Angeles, CA   90017,
Tel: (213) 481-2311
(Tech engineering serv)
   PAE Singapore Pte. Ltd., 1 Scotts Rd, #19-01, Singapore 0922

PANDUIT CORP   17301 Ridgeland Ave, Tinley Park, IL   60477-0981,
Tel: (708) 532-1800
(Mfr elec/electr wiring comps)
   Panduit Singapore Pte. Ltd., 5 Gul Lane, Singapore 629404

PARK ELECTROCHEMICAL CORP   5 Dakota Dr, Lake Success, NY   11042,
Tel: (516) 354-4100
(Multi-layer laminate printed circuit materials, ind comps, plumbing hdwe prdts)
   Nelco Products Pte. Ltd., 4 Gul Crescent, Jurong, Singapore

PARKER DRILLING CO   8 E Third St, Tulsa, OK   74103-3637, Tel: (918) 585-8221
(Drilling contractor)
   Parker Drilling Co., Loyang Offshore Supply Base, Loyang Crescent Block B,
      Singapore 1750
   Parker Drilling Co. of Indonesia Inc., Shaw Centre, 17th Fl., Suite 1704,
      Singapore 9

PARKER HANNIFIN CORP   17325 Euclid Ave, Cleveland, OH   44112,
Tel: (216) 531-3000
(Mfr motion-control prdts)
   Parker Hannifin Singapore Pte. Ltd., 11-4th Chin Bee Rd., Jurong Town,
      Singapore 2261

PERIPHONICS CORP   4000 Veterans Hwy, Bohemia, NY   11716, Tel: (516) 467-0500
(Mfr voice processing systems)
   Periphonics Corp., 13-10 Chinatown Point, 133 New Bridge Rd., Singapore 0105

PETROLITE CORP   369 Marshall Ave, St Louis, MO   63119-1897,
Tel: (314) 961-3500
(Mfr/prod spec chem treating programs, performance-enhancing additives & related
equip & svces)
   Petrolite Pacific Pte. Ltd., 2 Tanjong Penjuru Crescent, Jurong, Singapore 2260

PFIZER INC   235 E 42nd St, New York, NY   10017-5755, Tel: (212) 573-2323
(Mfr healthcare products)
   Pfizer Private Ltd., Singapore

PHILLIPS PETROLEUM CO   Phillips Bldg, Bartlesville, OK   74004,
Tel: (918) 661-6600
(Crude oil, natural gas, liquefied petroleum gas, gasoline & petro-chems)
   Phillips Petroleum Co. Far East, 18th Fl., Goldhill Plaza, Newton Rd., Singapore 11

PITTSBURGH NATIONAL BANK   Fifth Ave at Wood, Pittsburgh, PA   15222,
Tel: (412) 355-2000
(Banking)
   Pittsburgh Natl. Bank, Suite 1108, Ocean Bldg., Collyer Quay, Singapore 1

PRECISION VALVE CORP   PO Box 309, Yonkers, NY   10702, Tel: (914) 969-6500
(Mfr aerosol valves)
   Precision Valve Singapore Pte. Ltd., 10 Pioneer Lane, Jurong, Singapore 2262

PRINTED CIRCUITS INTL LTD   10 Micro Dr, Woburn, MA 01801, Tel: (617) 935-9570
(Printed circuit boards)
    Printed Circuits Intl. Pte. Ltd., 23 Lok Yang Way, Jurong, Singapore 22

PRINTRONIX INC   17500 Cartwright Rd, Irvine, CA 92715, Tel: (714) 863-1900
(Mfr computer printers)
    Printronix AG, 512 Chai Chee Lane, Hex 02-15, Bedok Industrial Estate,
    Singapore 1646

RALSTON PURINA CO   Checkerboard Sq, St Louis, MO 63164, Tel: (314) 982-1000
(Poultry & live stock feed, cereals, food prdts)
    Eveready Singapore Pte. Ltd., 25 Gul Way, Singapore

RAYCHEM CORP   300 Constitution Dr, Menlo Park, CA 94025, Tel: (415) 361-3333
(Devel/mfr/mkt materials science products for electronics, telecommunications &
industry)
    Raychem Singapore Pte. Ltd., 3 Kaki Bukit Rd 2, Singapore 1441
    Sigmaform Corp.-Singapore, 434 Tagore Ave., Singapore 2678

RAYTHEON CO   141 Spring St, Lexington, MA 02173, Tel: (617) 862-6600
(Mfr divers electronics, appliances, aviation, energy & environ prdts; publishing,
ind & constr servs)
    Raytheon Overseas Ltd., 360 Orchard Rd., #07-03, Intl. Bldg., Singapore 0923

READER'S DIGEST ASSOCIATION INC   PO Box 235, Pleasantville, NY 10570,
Tel: (914) 238-1000
(Publisher magazines & books, direct mail marketer)
    Reader's Digest Asia Ltd., 03-04 Union Bldg., 37 Jalan Pemimin, Singapore 2057

REED TOOL CO   6501 Navigation Blvd, Houston, TX 77001, Tel: (713) 924-5200
(Mfr rock bits for oil & gas explor)
    Reed Tool Co., 4 Gul Way, Jurong, Singapore

RELIABILITY INC   PO Box 218370, Houston, TX 77218-8370, Tel: (713) 492-0550
(Mfr burn-in/memory test sys, DC/DC converters)
    Reliability Singapore Pte. Ltd., 5004 Ang Mo Kio Ave. 5, #04-01 Techplace II,
    Singapore 569872

REPUBLIC NATIONAL BANK OF DALLAS   310 N Ervay St, Dallas, TX 75265,
Tel: (214) 653-5000
(Banking)
    Rep. Natl. Bank of Dallas, 1408 Shenton House, 1 Shenton Way, Singapore

REPUBLIC NEW YORK CORP   452 Fifth Ave, New York, NY 10018,
Tel: (212) 525-6901
(Banking)
    Republic National Bank of New York (Singapore) Ltd., Singapore

REVLON INC   625 Madison Ave, New York, NY 10022, Tel: (212) 527-4000
(Mfr cosmetics, fragrances, toiletries, beauty care prdts)
    Revlon Health Care (SEA) Pte. Ltd., Singapore 1

RICH PRODUCTS CORP   1 West Ferry, Buffalo, NY 14213, Tel: (716) 878-8000
(Mfr non-dairy prdts)
    Rich Products Corp, 28/28A Jalan Selaseh, Singapore 2880

ROCKWELL INTL CORP   2201 Seal Beach Blvd, PO Box 4250, Seal Beach,
   CA 90740-8250, Tel: (310) 797-3311
   (Prdts & serv for aerospace, automotive, electronics, graphics & automation inds)
      Rockwell Intl. Manufacturing Pty. Ltd., 1 Gul Way, Jurong, Singapore 2262
      Rockwell-Collins Intl. Inc., 10-230/232 Faber House, 230 Orchard Rd., Singapore 0923

ROHM AND HAAS CO   100 Independence Mall West, Philadelphia, PA 19106,
   Tel: (215) 592-3000
   (Mfr ind & agric chems, plastics)
      Rohm and Haas Asia Inc., 391-B Orchard Rd., 16-05109 Ngee Ann City, Singapore 0923

ROSEMOUNT INC   12001 Technology Dr, Eden Prairie, MN 55344,
   Tel: (612) 941-5560
   (Mfr instruments & distributed control sys)
      Rosemount Singapore Pte. Ltd., 2 Ang Mo Kio St. 64, Industrial Park 3,
         Singapore 2056

ROWAN COMPANIES INC   2800 Post Oak Blvd, Houston, TX 77056-6196,
   Tel: (713) 621-7800
   (Contract drilling & air charter service)
      Rowan Intl. Inc., Rm. 203, Thong Tech Bldg., 15 Scott's Rd., Singapore 9

RUSSELL REYNOLDS ASSOCIATES INC   200 Park Ave, New York, NY 10166,
   Tel: (212) 351-2000
   (Exec recruiting services)
      Russell Reynolds Associates Inc., 6 Battery Rd. #16-08, Singapore 0104

SARA LEE CORP   3 First National Plaza, Chicago, IL 60602-4260,
   Tel: (312) 726-2600
   (Mfr/distr food & consumer packaged goods, tobacco prdts, intimate apparel & knitwear)
      Sara Lee/SE Asia Inc., 1 Shenton Way, #08-02/09, Robina House, Singapore 0106

SCI SYSTEMS INC   PO Box 1000, Huntsville, AL 35807, Tel: (205) 882-4800
   (R/D & mfr electronics systems for commerce, industry, aerospace, etc)
      SCI Singapore Pte. Ltd., Plant 7, 3 Depot Close, Singapore 0410

SEA-LAND SERVICE INC   150 Allen Rd, Liberty Corner, NJ 07920,
   Tel: (201) 558-6000
   (Container transport)
      Sea-Land Service Inc., GPO Box 316, Singapore 0104

SEALED AIR CORP   Park 80 Plaza E, Saddle Brook, NJ 07662-5291,
   Tel: (201) 791-7600
   (Mfr protective packaging prdts)
      Sealed Air (Singapore) Pte. Ltd., 2 Tuas Avenue 6, Singapore 2263

SEQUENT COMPUTER SYSTEMS INC   15450 SW Koll Pkwy, Beaverton, OR 97006-6063,
   Tel: (503) 626-5700
   (Mfr symmetric multiprocessing technology computers)
      Sequent Computer Systems Inc., 5 Shelton Way, #21-11 UIC Bldg., Singapore 0106

SIGNETICS CORP   PO Box 3409, Sunnyvale, CA 94088-3409, Tel: (408) 991-2000
   (Solid state circuits)
      Philips Singapore Pte. Ltd., Singapore

SIMON & SCHUSTER INC   1230 Ave of the Americas, New York, NY 10020,
  Tel: (212) 698-7000
  (Publisher)
    Prentice-Hall of Southeast Asia Pte. Ltd., 24 Pasir PanJang Rd. 04-31,
      PSA Multi-Storey Complex, Singapore 0511

WILBUR SMITH ASSOCS   NationsBank Tower, PO Box 92, Columbia, SC 29202,
  Tel: (803) 708-4500
  (Consulting engineers)
    Wilbur Smith Associates, 400 Orchard Rd., 09-01 Orchard Towers, Singapore 0923

SNAP-ON TOOLS CORP   2801 80th St, Kenosha, WI 53141-1410, Tel: (414) 656-5200
  (Mfr automotive & ind maint serv tools)
    Snap-On Tools Intl. Ltd., 128 Tagore Lane, Singapore 2678

SONAT OFFSHORE DRILLING INC   PO Box 2765, Houston, TX 77252-2765,
  Tel: (713) 871-7500
  (Offshore oil well drilling)
    Sonat Offshore Drilling, c/o Kim Hong Marine Pte. Ltd., 45 Shipyard Rd., TW9,
      Jurong Marine Base, Singapore 2262

SONOCO PRODUCTS CO   North Second St, PO Box 160, Hartsville, SC 29550,
  Tel: (803) 383-7000
  (Mfr packaging for consumer & ind mkt)
    Sonoco Singapore Pte. Ltd., 10 Pandan Rd., Singapore 2260

SPSS INC   444 N Michigan Ave, Chicago, IL 60611, Tel: (312) 329-2400
  (Mfr statistical software)
    SPSS Asia Pacific Pte. Ltd., 10 Anson Rd., #34-07, International Plaza,
      Singapore 0207

SPX CORP   700 Terrace Point Dr, PO Box 3301, Muskegon, MI 49443-3301,
  Tel: (616) 724-5000
  (Mfr spec service tools, engine & drive-train parts)
    Power Team Far East, 23 First Lok Yang Rd., Singapore 2262

STA-RITE INDUSTRIES INC   293 Wright St, Delavan, WI 53115,
  Tel: (414) 728-5551
  (Mfr water pumps, filters & systems)
    Sta-Rite Foreign Sales Corp., all mail to: STAFCO, 175 Wright St., Delavan,
      WI 53115

STANDEX INTL CORP   6 Manor Pkwy, Salem, NH 03079, Tel: (603) 893-9701
  (Mfr diversified graphics, institutional, ind/electr & consumer prdts)
    Mold-Tech Singapore Pte. Ltd., Block 1022, Tai Seng Ave.,
      #01-3250 Tai Seng Industrial Estate, Singapore 538890

THE STANLEY WORKS   1000 Stanley Dr, PO Box 7000, New Britain, CT 06050,
  Tel: (203) 225-5111
  (Mfr hand tools & hardware)
    Stanley Magic-Door Far East, Jurong Town P.O. Box 425, Singapore 9161
    Stanley Works Asia Pacific Pte. Ltd., Jurong Town P.O. Box 425, Singapore 9161

STIEFEL LABORATORIES INC   255 Alhambra Circle, Coral Gables, FL 33134,
  Tel: (305) 443-3807
  (Mfr pharmaceuticals, dermatological specialties)
    Stiefel Laboratories Pte. Ltd., 103 Gul Circle, Jurong, Singapore 629589

STOKES DIV   5500 Tabor Rd, Philadelphia, PA 19120, Tel: (215) 289-5671
  (Vacuum pumps & components, vacuum dryers, oil-upgrading equip)
    Connell Bros. Co. Ltd., P.O. Box 392, Tanglin Post Office, Singapore 9124

STRATEGIC PLANNING ASSOCIATES INC   2300 N St NW, Washington, DC 20037,
  Tel: (202) 778-7000
  (Mgmt consulting)
    Strategic Planning Associates Pte. Ltd., 143 Cecil St., 22-03/04 GB Bldg.,
      Singapore 0106

SUB SEA INTL INC   701 Engineers Rd, Belle Chasse, LA 70037,
  Tel: (504) 393-7744
  (Service oil/gas industry: diving, ROV's, offshore construction, engineering,
  pipeline services)
    Sub Sea Offshore Pte. Ltd., 9b Layang Offshore Supply Base, Singapore 1750

SULLAIR CORP   3700 E Michigan Blvd, Michigan City, IN 46360,
  Tel: (219) 879-5451
  (Refrigeration sys, vacuum pumps, generators, etc)
    Sullair Asia Ltd., 2602 OCBC Centre, Singapore 1

SUNDSTRAND CORP   PO Box 7003, Rockford, IL 61125-7003, Tel: (815) 226-6000
  (Design/mfr proprietary technology based comps & sub-sys for aerospace & ind)
    Sundstrand Pacific Pte. Ltd., 18 Bedok South Rd., Singapore 1646

SWECO INC   7120 New Buffington Rd, PO Box 1509, Florence, KY 41042-1509,
  Tel: (606) 727-5100
  (Mfr vibratory process & solids control equip)
    Sweco Industrial Div. (Singapore), 63 Hillview Ave.,
      03-02 Lam Soon Industrial Bldg., Singapore 2366

SYMBOL TECHNOLOGIES INC   116 Wilbur Place, Bohemia, NY 11716,
  Tel: (516) 563-2400
  (Mfr bar code-driven data mgmt sys)
    Symbol Technologies Asia Inc., Bugis Junction Office Tower, 230 Victoria St,
      #04-50, Singapore 0718

TANDEM COMPUTERS INC   19333 Valco Pkwy, Cupertino, CA 95014,
  Tel: (408) 725-6000
  (Mfr multiple processor computer sys)
    Tandem Computers Intl. Inc., Singapore

TECH-SYM CORP   10500 Westoffice Dr, #200, Houston, TX 77042,
  Tel: (713) 785-7790
  (Electronics, real estate, aeromechanics)
    Syntron Asia Pte. Ltd., 68 Loyang Way, Singapore 1750

TECHNICON INSTRUMENTS CORP   511 Benedict Ave, Tarrytown, NY 10591-5097,
  Tel: (914) 631-8000
  (Mfr/serv automated blook anal equip, reagents & diagnostics)
    Technicon AutoAnalyzer Singapore Pte. Ltd., 456 Alexandra Rd., 16-01 NOL Bldg.,
      Singapore 0511

TELEDYNE INC 2049 Century Park East, Los Angeles, CA 90067-3101,
Tel: (310) 277-3311
(Divers mfg: aviation & electronics, specialty metals, industrial & consumer prdts)
Teledyne Singapore, 11 Dhoby Ghaut, #09-06 Cathay Bldg., Singapore 0922

TELEX COMMUNICATIONS INC 9600 Aldrich Ave S, Minneapolis, MN 55420,
Tel: (612) 884-4051
(Mfr communications, audio-visual & professional audio prdts)
Telex Communications (SEA) Pte. Ltd., 3015A Ubi Road 1 #05-10, Singapore 1440

TELLABS INC 4951 Indiana Ave, Lisle, IL 60532, Tel: (708) 969-8800
(Design/mfr/svce voice/data transport & network access sys)
Tellabs Inc., Singapore

TELXON CORP 3330 W Market St, PO Box 5582, Akron, OH 44334-0582,
Tel: (216) 867-3700
(Devel/mfr portable computer sys & related equip)
Telxon Singapore, Hougang Ave., Blk 1020, Tai Seng Industrial Estate #02-3506,
Singapore 1953

TENNECO AUTOMOTIVE 111 Pfingsten Rd, Deerfield, IL 60015,
Tel: (708) 948-0900
(Automotive parts, exhaust sys, service equip)
Tenneco Automotive Trading Co., 10 Anson Rd., #17-20 International Plaza,
Singapore 0207

TEXAS EASTERN TRANSMISSION CORP PO Box 2521, Houston, TX 77252,
Tel: (713) 759-3131
(Energy pipeliner, oil/gas explor & prod)
Texas Eastern Far East Inc, 51 Goldhill Plaza, 15-07, Newton Rd., Singapore 1130

TEXAS INSTRUMENTS INC 13500 N Central Expwy, Dallas, TX 75265,
Tel: (214) 995-2011
(Mfr semiconductor devices, electr/electro-mech sys, instr & controls)
Texas Instruments Singapore Pte. Ltd., P.O. Box 2093, Singapore 1233

TEXTRON INC 40 Westminster St, Providence, RI 02903, Tel: (401) 421-2800
(Mfr aerospace, ind & consumer prdts; fin servs)
Textron Far East Pte. Ltd., 36 Robinson Rd., #18-01, Singapore 0106

THERMO ELECTRIC CO 109 Fifth St, Saddle Brook, NJ 07662, Tel: (201) 843-5800
(Mfr temp/meas control prdts)
Industrial Automation Ltd., 469 Block 62 Tamon Jurong, P.O. Box 67, Singapore 22

THOMAS & BETTS CORP 1555 Lynnfield Rd, Memphis, TN 38119,
Tel: (901) 682-7766
(Mfr elect/electr connectors & accessories)
T & B SE Asia Pte. Ltd., 50 Genting Lane, 02-05 Cideco Industrial Complex,
Singapore 1334

TIDELAND SIGNAL CORP 4310 Directors Row, PO Box 52430, Houston,
TX 77052-2430, Tel: (713) 681-6101
(Mfr/sale aids to navigation)
Tideland Signal Pte. Ltd., 124 Owens Rd., Singapore 218928

TIDEWATER INC   Tidewater Place, 1440 Canal St, New Orleans, LA 70112,
  Tel: (504) 568-1010
  (Marine serv & equip to companies engaged in explor, development & prod of oil, gas &
  minerals)
    Tidex Pte. Ltd., 21 Loyang Offshore Supply Base, Loyang Crescent, Singapore 1750

TIW CORP   12300 S Main St, PO Box 35729, Houston, TX 77235,
  Tel: (713) 729-2110
  (Mfr liner hanger equip, production packers, safety & kelly valves)
    TIW Intl. Inc., 33 Kim Chuan Dr., Singapore 1953

TOWERS PERRIN   245 Park Ave, New York, NY 10167, Tel: (212) 309-3400
  (Management consultants)
    Towers, Perrin, Forster & Crosby, 5 Shenton Way, UIC Bldg. #15-01, Singapore 0106

TRADE & INDUSTRIES CORP INC   31 Brookside Dr, Greenwich, CT 06830,
  Tel: (203) 661-5813
  (Financial services)
    Trade & Industry Acceptance Corp. Far East Pty. Ltd., Suite 707-710,
      Tong Eng Bldg., 101 Cecil St., Singapore 0106

TRANE CO   3600 Pammel Creek Rd, La Crosse, WI 54601, Tel: (608) 787-2000
  (Mfr/distr/svce A/C sys & equip)
    Trane Singapore, Bukit Timah, P.O. Box 0275, Singapore 9158

TRAVELERS GROUP INC   388 Greenwich St, New York, NY 10013,
  Tel: (212) 816-8000
  (Insurance, financial services)
    Smith Barney Harris Upham (Singapore) Pte. Ltd., 20 Collyer Quay,
      #18-00 Tung Centre, Singapore 0104

TRINOVA CORP   3000 Strayer, PO Box 50, Maumee, OH 43537-0050,
  Tel: (419) 867-2200
  (Mfr engr components & sys for ind)
    Vickers Systems Pte. Ltd., 01-420 Indus. Rd., Block 79A, Singapore 0316

TRW INC   1900 Richmond Rd, Cleveland, OH 44124, Tel: (216) 291-7000
  (Electr & energy-related prdts, automotive & aerospace prdts, tools & fasteners)
    Reda Pump Co. (S) Pte. Ltd., No. 10 Wan Shih Rd., Jurong, Singapore 22
    TRW Mission Mfg. Co., 8th Fl., Cathay Bldg., G.P.O. Box 190, Dhoby Ghanti,
      Singapore 9
    TRW Reda Intl. (Div. of TRW Energy Services Intl.), 3A Gold Hill Plaza, Newton Rd.,
      Singapore 11

TURNER INTL INDUSTRIES INC   375 Hudson St, New York, NY 10014,
  Tel: (212) 229-6000
  (General construction, construction mgmt)
    Turner East Asia Pte. Ltd., 1102 Wing on Life Bldg., 150 Cecil St., Singapore 0106

TWIN DISC INC   1328 Racine St, Racine, WI 53403-1758, Tel: (414) 638-4000
  (Mfr ind clutches, reduction gears, transmissions)
    Twin Disc (Far East) Ltd., P.O. Box 155, Jurong Town Post Office, Singapore 9161

U S INDUSTRIES INC   PO Box 629, Evansville, IN 47704, Tel: (812) 425-2428
  (Diversified prdts & sys for industry, agribusiness & retail markets)
    Axelson Inc., Sisir Bldg., 3rd Fl., 179 River Valley Rd., Singapore 0617

U S SUMMIT CORP   600 Third Ave, New York, NY 10016, Tel: (212) 490-1100
(Mktg/distrib pharms, chems)
    Summit Co. (Singapore) Pte. Ltd., P.O. Box 1896, Singapore 9037

UNION CAMP CORP   1600 Valley Rd, Wayne, NJ 07470, Tel: (201) 628-2000
(Mfr paper, packaging, chems, wood prdts)
    Bush Boake Allen Singapore Pte. Ltd., 1 Enterprise Rd., Jurong, Singapore 2262

UNION CARBIDE CORP   39 Old Ridgebury Rd, Danbury, CT 06817,
    Tel: (203) 794-2000
(Mfr industrial chemicals, plastics, resins)
    Union Carbide Asia Pacific Inc., 8 Shenton Way, #22-01 Treasury Bldg.,
        Singapore 0106
    Union Carbide Singapore Pte. Ltd., 12 Soon Lee Rd., P.O. Box 115,
        Jurong Town Post Office, Singapore 9161

UNION OIL INTL DIV   Union Oil Center, PO Box 7600, Los Angeles, CA 90017,
    Tel: (213) 977-7600
(Petroleum prdts, petrochems)
    Unocal Corp., Locked Bag Service No. 3, Killiney Rd. P.O., Singapore 9123

UNISYS CORP   PO Box 500, Blue Bell, PA 19424, Tel: (215) 986-4011
(Mfg/mktg/serv electr info sys)
    Unisys Intl. Singapore Pte. Ltd., 20 Gul Way, Singapore 2262
    Unisys Pte. Ltd., 10 Shenton Way, Singapore 0207

UNITED AIRLINES INC   PO Box 66100, Chicago, IL 60666, Tel: (708) 952-4000
(Air transp)
    United Airlines, 18-03 Hong Leong Bldg., 16 Raffles Quay, Singapore 0104

UNITED CALIFORNIA BANK   PO Box 54191, Los Angeles, CA 90054,
    Tel: (213) 624-0111
(Banking)
    United California Bank, UIC Bldg. 22/F, 5 Shenton Way, Singapore

UNITED TECHNOLOGIES CORP   United Technologies Bldg, Hartford, CT 06101,
    Tel: (203) 728-7000
(Mfr aircraft engines, elevators, A/C, auto equip, space & military electr, rocket
propulsion sys)
    United Technologies Intl., Suite 1406, Robina House, 1 Shenton Way, Singapore

UNITRODE CORP   7 Continental Blvd, Merrimack, NH 03054, Tel: (603) 424-2410
(Mfr electronic components)
    Unitrode Electronics Singapore (UES), 55 Ayer Rajah Crescent, Singapore 0413

UNIVERSAL WEATHER & AVIATION INC   8787 Tallyho Rd, Houston, TX 77061,
    Tel: (713) 944-1622
(Airport services)
    Intl. Business Aviation (Singapore) Pte. Ltd., Seletar Airport Bldg. 555, Singapore

UNOCAL CORP   PO Box 7600, Los Angeles, CA 90051, Tel: (213) 977-7600
(Fully integrated high-tech energy resources devel)
    Unocal Indonesia Ltd., Locked Bag Serv. #3, Tampines South Post Office,
        Singapore 9152

VARIAN ASSOCIATES INC   3100 Hansen Way, Palo Alto, CA 94304-1030,
   Tel: (415) 493-4000
   (Mfr microwave tubes & devices, analytical instru, semiconductor process & med equip,
   vacuum sys)
      Varian Microwave Equipment Ltd., 140 Cecil St., Unit 06-01/A Pil Pldg.,
         Singapore 0106

VELCON FILTERS INC   4525 Centennial Blvd, Colorado Springs, CO 80919-3350,
   Tel: (719) 531-5855
   (Mfr/sale filters & filtration systems)
      Hanevel Filters Pte. Ltd., Block 5071 #04-1555, Ang Mo Kio Industrial Park II,
         Singapore 2056

VIACOM INC   200 Elm St, Dedham, MA 02026, Tel: (617) 461-1600
   (Communications, publishing, entertainment)
      Simon & Schuster (Asia) Pte. Ltd., 24 Pasir Panjang Rd.,
         #04-31 PSA Multi Storey Complex, Singapore 0511

VISHAY INTERTECHNOLOGY INC   63 Lincoln Highway, Malvern, PA 19355,
   Tel: (215) 644-1300
   (Mfr resistors, strain gages, capacitors, inductors, printed circuit boards)
      Vishay Electronic Components Asia Pte. Ltd., 450-452 Alexandra Rd.,
         #08-06 Inchcape House, Singapore 0511

WALBRO CORP   6242 Garfield Ave, Cass City, MI 48762, Tel: (517) 872-2131
   (Mfr motor vehicle accessories & parts)
      Walbro Singapore Pte. Ltd., 623 Larong, 4 Toa Payoh, Singapore 1231

WANG LABORATORIES INC   1 Industrial Ave, Lowell, MA 01851,
   Tel: (508) 459-5000
   (Mfr computer info processing sys)
      Wang Computers Pte. Ltd., Tong Bldg., 302 Orchard Rd., Singapore 0923

WARD HOWELL INTL INC   99 Park Ave, New York, NY 10016-1699,
   Tel: (212) 697-3730
   (Executive recruiting)
      Strategic Executive Search Pte. Ltd., 28C Stanley St., Singapore 0106

WATERS CHROMATOGRAPHY DIV   34 Maple St, Milford, MA 01757,
   Tel: (617) 478-2000
   (Mfr/distr liquid chromatographic instru/accessories/tech)
      Waters Associates Pty. Ltd., 181 Goldhill Shopping Centre, Thompson Rd.,
         Singapore 1130

WATLOW ELECTRIC MFG CO   12001 Lackland Rd, St Louis, MO 63146-4039,
   Tel: (314) 878-4600
   (Mfr elec heating units, electr controls, thermocouple wire, metal-sheathed cable,
   infrared sensors)
      Watlow Singapore Pte. Ltd. (JV), 44 Ayer Rajah Crescent, #03-19 to #03-23,
         Ayer Rajah Ind. Estate, Singapore 0513

WEATHERFORD INTL INC   1360 Post Oak Blvd, PO Box 27608, Houston,
   TX 77227-7608, Tel: (713) 439-9400
   (Oilfield servs, prdts & equip; mfr marine cranes)
      Weatherford Oil Tool Pte. Ltd., Loyang Offshore Supply Base, Loyang Crescent,
         Singapore 1750

WEATHERHEAD DIV   6615 Brotherhood Way, Fort Wayne, IN 46825,
  Tel: (219) 481-3500
  (Mfr fluid power prdts, hose assys, tube & pipe fittings & valves)
    Dana Singapore Pte. Ltd., 130 Hillview Ave., Singapore 2366

THE WEST CO   101 Gordon Dr, PO Box 645, Lionville, PA 19341-0645,
  Tel: (610) 594-2900
  (Mfr prdts for filling, sealing, dispensing & delivering needs of health care &
  consumer prdts mkts)
    West Pharmapack Pte. Ltd., Singapore

WESTERN ATLAS INTL INC   10205 Westheimer, PO Box 1407, Houston,
  TX 77251-1407, Tel: (713) 266-5700
  (Full service to the oil industry)
    Western Atlas Logging Services, Terrace Warehouse Block 3, Unit 4,
      Loyang Offshore Supply Base, Singapore 1750
    Western Geophysical, Blk. 2, Unit 2, Terrace Warehouse, c/Offshore Supply Base,
      Box 5129, Loyang Crescent, Singapore 1750

WESTERN BANCORPORATION   707 Wilshire Blvd, Los Angeles, CA 90017,
  Tel: (213) 614-3001
  (Bank holding company)
    Pacific Natl. Bank of Washington, 22nd Fl., UIC Bldg., 5 Shenton Way, Singapore 1

WESTERN DIGITAL CORP   8105 Irvine Center Dr, Irvine, CA 92718,
  Tel: (714) 932-5000
  (Mfr hard disk drives, video graphics boards, VLSI)
    Western Digital (SEA) Ptd. Ltd., 750 Chai Chee Rd., #04-00, Lobby 1, Singapore

WESTINGHOUSE ELECTRIC CORP   11 Stanwix St, Pittsburgh, PA 15222-1384,
  Tel: (412) 244-2000
  (TV/radio broadcasting, mfr electr sys for ind/defense, fin & environmental servs)
    Westinghouse Electric SA, 111 N. Bridge Rd. 21-04, Peninsula Plaza, Singapore 0619

WHIRLPOOL CORP   2000 N M-63, Benton Harbor, MI 49022-2692,
  Tel: (616) 923-5000
  (Mfr/mkt home appliances)
    Whirlpool Corp. Regional HQ, Singapore

WILBUR-ELLIS CO   320 California St, #200, San Francisco, CA 94104,
  Tel: (415) 772-4000
  (Intl merchants & distributors)
    Connell Bros., 19-07 Orchard Towers, 400 Orchard Rd., Singapore 0923
    Harricros Chemicals Pte. Ltd., 10 & 12 Third Lok Yang Rd., Jurong, Singapore 2262

JOHN WILEY & SONS INC   605 Third Ave, New York, NY 10158-0012,
  Tel: (212) 850-6000
  (Publisher: print & electronic prdts for academic, professional, scientific,
  technical & consumer mkt)
    John Wiley & Sons (Asia) Pte. Ltd., 2 Clementi Loop, #02-01 Jin Xing Distripark,
      Singapore 0512

T D WILLIAMSON INC   PO Box 2299, Tulsa, OK 74101, Tel: (918) 254-9400
  (Mfr equip/provide service for pipeline maintenance)
    Williamson Intl. Corp., 446 Tagore Ave., Singapore 787818

WINCHESTER ELECTRONICS   400 Park Rd, Watertown, CT 06795-0500,
  Tel: (203) 945-5000
  (Mfr elec & electr connectors, PCB assemblies & hardware)
    Litton Components Pte. Ltd., 500 Chai Chee Lane, Singapore 1646

WOODHEAD INDUSTRIES INC   2150 E Lake Cook Rd, #400, Buffalo Grove, IL 60089,
  Tel: (708) 465-8300
  (Devel/mfr/sale/distr elect/electr, fiber optic & ergonomic special-function,
  non-commodity prdts)
    Woodhead Asia Pte. Ltd., 401 Commonwealth Dr. #04-04, Haw Par Technocentre,
      Singapore 0314

WOODWARD GOVERNOR CO   5001 North 2nd St, PO Box 7001, Rockford,
  IL 61125-7001, Tel: (815) 877-7441
  (Mfr speed control governors)
    Woodward Governor Asia/Pacific Pte. Ltd., 2 Alexandra Rd., #03-02A Delta House,
      Singapore 0315

WORLD COURIER INC   46 Trinity Pl, New York, NY 10006, Tel: (718) 978-9400
  (Intl courier serv)
    World Courier Singapore, 1102 Textile Centre, 200 Jalan Sultan, Singapore 0719

WM WRIGLEY JR CO   410 N Michigan Ave, Chicago, IL 60611-4287,
  Tel: (312) 644-2121
  (Mfr chewing gum)
    Malayan Guttas Pte. Ltd., Singapore

XEROX CORP   800 Long Ridge Rd, PO Box 1600, Stamford, CT 06904,
  Tel: (203) 968-3000
  (Mfr document processing equip, sys & supplies)
    Fuji Xerox Asia Pacific (Pte.) Ltd., Shing Kwan House #13-00, 4 Shenton Way,
      Singapore 0106
    Xerox Corp., Fortune Centre, Singapore

YORK INTERNATIONAL CORP   PO Box 1592, York, PA 17405-1592,
  Tel: (717) 771-7890
  (Mfr A/C, heating & refrig sys & equip)
    York Air-Conditioning & Refrigeration Inc., 29 New Industrial Rd., Singapore 1953

YOUNG & RUBICAM INC   285 Madison Ave, New York, NY 10017, Tel: (212) 210-3000
  (Advertising, public relations, direct marketing & sales promotion, corp & product ID
  management)
    Dentsu Young & Rubicam Pte. Ltd., 6th Floor, 20 Kallang Ave., Singapore 1233

SLOVAKIA

ALTHEIMER & GRAY 10 S Wacker Dr, #4000, Chicago, IL 60606-7482,
  Tel: (312) 715-4000
  (Lawyers)
    Altheimer & Gray, Namestie SNP 15, 81106 Bratislava, Slovakia

AMERICAN EXPRESS CO World Financial Center, New York, NY 10285-4765,
  Tel: (212) 640-2000
  (Travel, travelers cheques, charge card & financial services)
    American Express s.p.o.l.

GENERAL ELECTRIC CO 3135 Easton Tpk, Fairfield, CT 06431,
  Tel: (203) 373-2211
  (Diversified manufacturing, technology & services)
    General Electric Co.,
      all mail to U.S. address; phone (800) 626-2004 or (518) 438-6500

GREY ADVERTISING INC 777 Third Ave, New York, NY 10017, Tel: (212) 546-2000
  (Advertising)
    Grey & Soria, Kominarska 2, 83203 Bratislava, Slovakia

HONEYWELL INC PO Box 524, Minneapolis, MN 55440-0524, Tel: (612) 951-1000
  (Devel/mfr controls for home & building, industry, space & aviation)
    Honeywell GmbH, Trnavska 3, 83104 Bratislava, Slovakia

HORWATH INTL 415 Madison Ave, New York, NY 10017, Tel: (212) 838-5566
  (Public accountants & auditors)
    IB Interbilanz Bratislava Himmer, Egger & Partnev s.p.o.l., Panska 15,
      81101 Bratislava, Slovakia

KORN/FERRY INTL 1800 Century Park East, Los Angeles, CA 90067,
  Tel: (310) 552-1834
  (Executive search)
    Korn/Ferry Intl., Dubravska cesta 2, SR-817 03 Bratislava, Slovakia

LOCTITE CORP 10 Columbus Blvd, Hartford, CT 06106, Tel: (203) 520-5000
  (Mfr/sale ind adhesives & sealants)
    Loctite SK s.r.o, Prokopova 31, 85101 Bratislava, Slovakia

WHIRLPOOL CORP 2000 N M-63, Benton Harbor, MI 49022-2692,
  Tel: (616) 923-5000
  (Mfr/mkt home appliances)
    Whirlpool Europe BV, Poprad, Slovakia

SLOVENIA

GREY ADVERTISING INC   777 Third Ave, New York, NY 10017, Tel: (212) 546-2000
  (Advertising)
    Pristop D.O.O. Prospekt Communication Group, Dunajska 107, 61113 Ljubljana,
      p.p. 49, Slovenia

HOLIDAY INNS INC   3742 Lamar Ave, Memphis, TN 38195, Tel: (901) 362-4001
  (Hotels, restaurants, casinos)
    Holiday Inn, Miklosiceva 3, P.O. Box 64, 61000 Ljubljana, Slovenia

LOCTITE CORP   10 Columbus Blvd, Hartford, CT 06106, Tel: (203) 520-5000
  (Mfr/sale ind adhesives & sealants)
    Loctite d.o.o., Kajuhova 17, 61000 Ljubljana, Slovenia

THE ROCKPORT CO   220 Donald J Lynch Blvd, Marlboro, MA 01752,
  Tel: (508) 485-2090
  (Mfr/imp dress & casual footwear)
    Rockport Slovenija, Ste. Marie aux Mines 34, 64290 Trzic, Slovenia

SEA-LAND SERVICE INC   150 Allen Rd, Liberty Corner, NJ 07920,
  Tel: (201) 558-6000
  (Container transport)
    Sea-Land Service, P.O. Box 63, 61001 Ljubljana, Slovenia

STANLEY CONSULTANTS INC   225 Iowa Ave, Muscatine, IA 52761,
  Tel: (319) 264-6600
  (Engineering, architectural, planning & management services)
    Stanley Consultants Inc., Breg 12, 61000 Ljubljana, Slovenia

WM WRIGLEY JR CO   410 N Michigan Ave, Chicago, IL 60611-4287,
  Tel: (312) 644-2121
  (Mfr chewing gum)
    Wrigley Ljubljana Ltd., Ljubljana, Slovenia

SOUTH AFRICA

3COM CORP   5400 Bayfront Plaza, Santa Clara, CA 95052-8145,
  Tel: (408) 764-5000
  (Devel/mfr computer networking prdts & sys)
    3Com, South Africa

3M   3M Center, St Paul, MN 55144-1000, Tel: (612) 733-1110
  (Mfr diversified prdts for industry, health care, imaging, commun, transport, safety,
  consumer, etc)
    3M South Africa (Pty.) Ltd., 181 Barbara Rd., Elandsfontein 1406, South Africa

AAF INTL   215 Central Ave, PO Box 35690, Louisville, KY 40232-5690,
  Tel: (502) 637-0011
  (Mfr air filtration/pollution control & noise control equip)
    Gosair Filter Systems (Pty.) Ltd., P.O. Box 12648, Chloorkop 1624, South Africa

ACCURAY CORP   650 Ackerman Rd, PO Box 02248, Columbus, OH 43202,
  Tel: (614) 261-2000
  (Computer-based process mgmt sys for forest prdts, metals rolling, textiles, tobacco
  ind)
    Accuray S.A. (Pty.) Ltd., Pinetown, South Africa

ACUFF-ROSE PUBLICATION INC   65 Music Square W, Nashville, TN 37203,
  Tel: (615) 321-5000
  (Music publisher)
    Acuff-Rose S.A. (Pty.) Ltd., c/o Gallo Ltd., corner Kerk & Goud Sts., Gallo Center,
    Johannesburg, South Africa

AIR EXPRESS INTL CORP   120 Tokeneke Rd, PO Box 1231, Darien, CT 06820,
  Tel: (203) 655-7900
  (Air frt forwarder)
    Air Express Intl., Plot 2, Agents Site, D.F. Malan Airport, Cape Town, South Africa
    Air Express Intl., South Africa (Pty.) Ltd., 14 Pascoe Rd., Mobenl, Natal,
    South Africa

ALBANY INTL CORP   PO Box 1907, Albany, NY 12201, Tel: (518) 445-2200
  (Paper mach clothing, engineered fabrics, plastic prdts, filtration media)
    Beier Albany Co., P.O. Box 121, Pinetown, Natal 3600, South Africa

ALLERGAN INC   2525 Dupont Dr, PO Box 19534, Irvine, CA 92713-9534,
  Tel: (714) 752-4500
  (Mfr therapeutic eye care prdts, skin & neural care pharms)
    Allergan Inc., Johannesburg, South Africa

ALLIED AFTERMARKET DIV   105 Pawtucket Ave, East Providence, RI 02916,
   Tel: (401) 434-7000
   (Mfr spark plugs, filters, brakes)
      Filpro (Pty.) Ltd., P.O. Box 367, Pretermaritzburg, South Africa

AVERY DENNISON CORP   150 N Orange Grove Blvd, Pasadena, CA 91103,
   Tel: (818) 304-2000
   (Mfr pressure-sensitive adhesives & materials, office prdts, labels, tags, retail
   sys, spec chems)
      Fasson Products (Pty.) Ltd., 7 Sherwell St., Poornfontein, Johannesbury 2094,
      South Africa

BECKMAN INSTRUMENTS INC   2500 Harbor Blvd, Fullerton, CA 92634,
   Tel: (714) 871-4848
   (Devel/mfr/mkt automated systems & supplies for biological analysis)
      Beckman Instruments (Pty.) Ltd., Stand 1A Fedlife Park, Tonetti St.,
      Halfway House 1685, Johannesburg, South Africa

BENTLY NEVADA CORP   PO Box 157, Minden, NV 89423, Tel: (702) 782-3611
   (Electronic monitoring system)
      Control Logic Pty. Ltd., Conlog House, P.O. Box 729, Bergulei 2012, South Africa

SAMUEL BINGHAM CO   1555 N Mittel Blvd, #T, Wood Dale, IL 60191-1046,
   Tel: (708) 238-4000
   (Print & industrial rollers, inks)
      Rubber Rollers (Pty.) Ltd., 55 Henwood Rd., New Germany, Natal 3600, South Africa

BINKS MFG CO   9201 W Belmont Ave, Franklin Park, IL 60131,
   Tel: (708) 671-3000
   (Mfr of spray painting & finishing equip)
      Walter McNaughtan (Pty.) Ltd., P.O. Box 8666, Johannesburg 2000, South Africa

BLACK CLAWSON CO   405 Lexington Ave, New York, NY 10174, Tel: (212) 916-8000
   (Paper & pulp mill mach)
      Black-Clawson S.A. (Pty.) Ltd., 1011 Winchester House, Loveday St., P.O. Box 4236,
      Johannesburg, South Africa

BOYDEN CONSULTING CORP   375 Park Ave, #1008, New York, NY 10152,
   Tel: (212) 980-6480
   (Executive search)
      Boyden Executive Services, Hampstead House, 46 Biccard St., Braamfontein 2001,
      South Africa

BRANSON ULTRASONICS CORP   41 Eagle Rd, Danbury, CT 06813-1961,
   Tel: (203) 796-0400
   (Mfr plastics assembly equip, ultrasonic cleaning equip)
      W. Lee Ultraplast (Pty.) Ltd., P.O. Box 82097, Southdale 2135, South Africa

BUCYRUS-ERIE CO   1100 Milwaukee Ave, South Milwaukee, WI 53172,
   Tel: (414) 768-4000
   (Mfr draglines, electric shovels, blast hole drills for suface mining)
      Bucyrus-Africa Pty. Ltd., 64 Innes Rd., Jet Park Ext. 31, Boksburg 1459,
      South Africa

BULAB HOLDINGS INC   1256 N McLean Blvd, Memphis, TN 38108,
  Tel: (901) 278-0330
  (Mfr microbicides, biocides, additives, corrosion inhibitors, chems)
    Buckman Laboratories (Pty.) Ltd., P.O. Box 591, Hammarsdale, Natal 3700,
      South Africa

BURLINGTON AIR EXPRESS   18200 Van Karman Ave, Irvine, CA 92715,
  Tel: (714) 752-4000
  (Air freight)
    Burlington Air Express, Cor. Manhattan & Mobile Sts., DF Malan Airport, Industria,
      Cape Town, South Africa

BUTTERICK CO INC   161 Ave of the Americas, New York, NY 10013,
  Tel: (212) 620-2500
  (Sewing patterns)
    Butterick Fashion Marketing Co., 205 Kelhoff, 112 Pritehard St., Johannesburg 2001,
      South Africa

CALGON CORP   PO Box 1346, Pittsburgh, PA 15230, Tel: (412) 777-8000
  (Mfr. cosmetic, personal care & water treatment prdts)
    Floccotan (Pty) Ltd., P.O. Box 1818, Pietermaritzburg 3200, Natal, South Africa

CALTEX PETROLEUM CORP   PO Box 619500, Dallas, TX 75261, Tel: (214) 830-1000
  (Petroleum prdts)
    Caltex Oil (SA) (Pty) Ltd., Caltex House, 19 D F Malan St., Foreshore,
      Cape Town 8001, South Africa
    Capetown Refinery, Box 13, Milnerton 74356, Cape Town, South Africa

CARBOLINE CO   350 Hanley Industrial Ct, St Louis, MO 63144,
  Tel: (314) 644-1000
  (Mfr coatings, sealants)
    Chemrite Coatings (Pty.) Ltd., P.O. Box 2205, Halfway House 1685, South Africa

CARBONE LORRAINE INDUSTRIES INC   400 Myrtle Ave, Boonton, NJ 07005,
  Tel: (201) 334-0700
  (Carbon brushes, batteries)
    Le Carbone, P.O. Box 11269, Johannesburg, South Africa

CBI INDUSTRIES INC   800 Jorie Blvd, Oak Brook, IL 60521, Tel: (708) 654-7000
  (Holding co: metal plate fabricating, constr, oil & gas drilling)
    CBI Constructor S.A. (Pty.) Ltd., P.O. Box 260, Springs 1560, South Africa

CHICAGO PNEUMATIC TOOL CO   2200 Bleecker St, Utica, NY 13501,
  Tel: (315) 792-2600
  (Mfr air tools & equip)
    Consolidated Pneumatic Tool Co. S.A. (Pty.) Ltd., 20 Anvil Rd., P.O. Box 105,
      1600 Isando, South Africa

CHINET CO   101 Merritt 7, Norwalk, CT 06851, Tel: (203) 846-1499
  (Mfr molded containers)
    Moulded Fibre Business Unit, P.O. Box 559, Springs 1560, Transvaal, South Africa
    Sun Packaging (Pty.), P.O. Box 1452, Dassenberg 7350, South Africa
    Van Leer South Africa (Pty.) Ltd., Van Leer House, 15 Wellington Rd., Parktown,
      P.O. Box 7164, Johannesburg 2000, South Africa
    Van Leer South Africa (Pty.) Ltd., Industry Rd., New Era, Springs 1560, South Africa

THE CHRISTIAN SCIENCE PUBLISHING SOCIETY   1 Norway St, Boston, MA 02115,
   Tel: (617) 450-2000
   (Publishing, broadcasting)
     The Christian Science Monitor, P.O. Box 1212, Callo Manor, Johannesburg 2052,
       South Africa

THE COCA-COLA CO   PO Drawer 1734, Atlanta, GA 30301, Tel: (404) 676-2121
   (Mfr/mkt/distr soft drinks, syrups & concentrates, juice & juice-drink prdts)
     Coca Cola, Johannesburg/National Beverage Services, all mail to U.S. address

COLGATE-PALMOLIVE CO   300 Park Ave, New York, NY 10022, Tel: (212) 310-2000
   (Mfr pharms, cosmetics, toiletries, detergents)
     Colgate-Palmolive Ltd., 528 Commissioner St., Industrial Sites, P.O. Box 213,
       Boksburg, South Africa

COLLOIDS INC   394-400 Frelinghuysen Ave, Newark, NJ 07114,
   Tel: (201) 926-6100
   (Chem prdts)
     The Hodgson Extract Co., Merebank, Natal, South Africa

COULTER CORP   PO Box 169015, Miami, FL 33116-9015, Tel: (305) 885-0131
   (Mfr blood analysis sys, flow cytometers, chem sys, scientific sys & reagents)
     Coulter Electronics SA Pty. Ltd., P.O. Box 84, Halfway House 1685, Transvaal,
       South Africa

CPC INTERNATIONAL INC   PO Box 8000, Englewood Cliffs, NJ 07632,
   Tel: (201) 894-4000
   (Consumer foods, corn refining)
     African Products (Pty.) Ltd., P.O. Box 78954, Sandton 2146, South Africa
     CPC Tongaat Foods (Pty.) Ltd., P.O. Box 5353, Johannesburg 2000, South Africa

CRAY RESEARCH INC   655 Lone Oak Dr, Eagan, MN 55121, Tel: (612) 452-6650
   (Supercomputer systems & services)
     Cray Research (Pty.) Ltd., c/o KPMG Aiken & Peat, P.O. Box 11265, Brooklyn 0011,
       South Africa

CROWN CORK & SEAL CO INC   9300 Ashton Rd, Philadelphia, PA 19136,
   Tel: (215) 698-5100
   (Mfr cans, bottle caps; filling & packaging mach)
     Crown Cork Co. S.A. (Pty.) Ltd., P.O. Box 4, Isando 1600, South Africa

DEERE & CO   John Deere Rd, Moline, IL 61265, Tel: (309) 765-8000
   (Mfr/sale agri/constr/utility/forestry & lawn/grounds care equip)
     John Deere (Pty.) Ltd., P.O. Box 198, 40 Standard St., Nigel 1490, South Africa

DENVER EQUIPMENT DIV   PO Box 340, Colorado Springs, CO 80901,
   Tel: (303) 471-3443
   (Ind process equip)
     Joy Process Equip. Co. Pty. Ltd., Butler Rd., Nuffield Springs, P.O. Box 361,
       Spring 1560, South Africa

DONALDSON CO INC   PO Box 1299, Minneapolis, MN 55440, Tel: (612) 887-3131
   (Mfr filtration prdts & sys)
     Donaldson Filtration Systems (Pty.) Ltd., P.O. Box 149, Eppindust, Cape Town 7475,
       South Africa

DRAKE BEAM MORIN INC   100 Park Ave, New York, NY 10017, Tel: (212) 692-7700
(Human resource mgmt consulting & training)
    DBM South Africa, P.O. Box 47198, Parklands 2121, South Africa

ERIEZ MAGNETICS   PO Box 10652, Erie, PA 16514, Tel: (814) 833-9881
(Mfr magnets, vibratory feeders, metal detectors, screeners/sizers, mining equip,
current separators)
    Eriez Magnetics Pty., P.O. Box 391281, Bramley 2018, South Africa

EXPEDITORS INTL OF WASHINGTON INC   PO Box 69620, Seattle, WA 98168-9620,
    Tel: (206) 246-3711
(Air/ocean freight forwarding, customs brokerage, intl logistics solutions)
    Expeditors Intl. (Pty.) Ltd., P.O. Box 4869, Durban 4000, Natal, South Africa
    Expeditors Intl. SA (Pty.) Ltd., P.O. Box 1595, Kempton Park 1620, South Africa

FISHER CONTROLS INTL INC   8000 Maryland Ave, Clayton, MO 63105,
    Tel: (314) 746-9900
(Mfr ind process control equip)
    Control Specialists (Pty.) Ltd., 1197 Butel Rd., Robertville, Roodepoort,
      South Africa
    Control Specialists (Pty.) Ltd., P.O. Box 38216, Point 4069, 57 Smith St., Durban,
      Natal, South Africa

FOOTE CONE & BELDING COMMUNICATIONS INC   101 E Erie St, Chicago,
    IL 60611-2897, Tel: (312) 751-7000
(Advertising agency)
    Jonsson Advertising, P.O. Box 9421, Johannesburg 2000, South Africa
    Lindsay/Smithers/FCB (Pty.) Ltd., P.O. Box 1604, Johannesburg, South Africa
    Partnership in Advertising & Marketing, PH Suite, Sanlam Arena, 10 Cradock Ave.,
      Rosebank 2196, Johannesburg, South Africa

FRANKLIN ELECTRIC CO INC   400 E Spring St, Bluffton, IN 46714,
    Tel: (219) 824-2900
(Mfr fractional hp motors, submersible motors & controls)
    Franklin Electric South Africa (Pty.) Ltd., P.O. Box 3337, Randburg 2125,
      South Africa

FRUEHAUF TRAILER CORP   PO Box 44913, Indianapolis, IN 46244-0913,
    Tel: (317) 630-3000
(Mfr truck trailers)
    Henred Fruehauf Trailers (Pty.) Ltd., Private Bag X5, Kelvin 2054, South Africa

GAF CORP   1361 Alps Rd, Wayne, NJ 07470, Tel: (201) 628-3000
(Chems, bldg materials, commun)
    GAF (South Africa) Pty. Ltd., P.O. Box 78838, Sandton 2146, South Africa

THE GILLETTE CO   Prudential Tower, Boston, MA 02199, Tel: (617) 421-7000
(Devel/mfr personal care/use prdts: blades & razors, toiletries, cosmetics,
stationery)
    Gillette South Africa Ltd., Bedfordview, South Africa
    Oral-B Laboratories (South Africa) (Pty.) Ltd., Eastgate, Sandton, South Africa

GRANT THORNTON INTL   Prudential Plaza, Chicago, IL 60601, Tel: (312) 856-0001
(Intl accountants)
    Grant Thornton Intl., Annity House 1/F, 18 Rissik St., Johannesburg 2001,
      South Africa

GREY ADVERTISING INC   777 Third Ave, New York, NY 10017, Tel: (212) 546-2000
  (Advertising)
    Grey Advertising, 171 Katherine St., Bldg. 2, Sandton, South Africa

HARNISCHFEGER INDUSTRIES INC   PO Box 554, Milwaukee, WI 53201,
  Tel: (414) 671-4400
  (Mfr mining & material handling equip, papermaking mach, computer sys)
    Harnischfeger South Africa (Pty.) Ltd., P.O. Box 4087, Alrode 1450, South Africa
    Joy Manufacturing Co. (Africa) (Pty.) Ltd., P.O. Box 4070, Johannesburg 2000,
    South Africa

HECKETT   PO Box 1071, Butler, PA 16001-1071, Tel: (412) 283-5741
  (Metal reclamation, steel mill services)
    Heckett (South Africa)(Pty.) Ltd., P.O. Box 2125, Pretoria 0001, South Africa

HOLIDAY INNS INC   3742 Lamar Ave, Memphis, TN 38195, Tel: (901) 362-4001
  (Hotels, restaurants, casinos)
    Holiday Inn, Cross St., P.O. Box 233, Bellville 7530, Cape Town, South Africa
    Holiday Inn, Melbourne Rd., P.O. Box 2979, Cape Town, South Africa

HONEYWELL INC   PO Box 524, Minneapolis, MN 55440-0524, Tel: (612) 951-1000
  (Devel/mfr controls for home & building, industry, space & aviation)
    Honeywell Southern Africa Ltd., 34 Harry St., Robertsham, Johannesburg 2001,
    South Africa

HORWATH INTL   415 Madison Ave, New York, NY 10017, Tel: (212) 838-5566
  (Public accountants & auditors)
    Leveton Boner, 3/F Cedar Grove, Grove City, 198 Louis Botha Ave.,
      Houghton Estate 2198, Johannesburg, South Africa
    Michael Rogers and Mainguard, 10th Fl., Maritime House, Salmon Grove, Durbin 4001,
      South Africa
    Penkin, Zeller & Karro, 2nd Fl., Monex House, Cape Town 8001, South Africa

HOUGHTON INTL INC   PO Box 930, Valley Forge, PA 19482-0930,
  Tel: (610) 666-4000
  (Mfr spec chems, hydraulic fluids, lubricants)
    Chemserve Metal Sciences (Pty.) Ltd., P.O. Box 12055, Chloorkop 1624, South Africa

INGERSOLL-RAND CO   200 Chestnut Ridge Rd, Woodcliff Lake, NJ 07675,
  Tel: (201) 573-0123
  (Mfr compressors, rock drills, pumps, air tools, door hardware, ball bearings)
    Ingersoll-Rand Co. South Africa (Pty.) Ltd., Jurie St., Alrode 1451, South Africa

INTERMEC CORP   6001 36th Ave West, PO Box 4280, Everett, WA 98203-9280,
  Tel: (206) 348-2600
  (Mfr/distr automated data collection sys)
    ScanTech CC, Suite 13, Dayan Office Park, Dayan Rd., Dayan Glen, P.O. Box 10260,
      Fonteinriet 1464, South Africa

INTERNATIONAL FLAVORS & FRAGRANCES INC   521 W 57th St, New York, NY 10019,
  Tel: (212) 765-5500
  (Create/mfr flavors, fragrances & aroma chems)
    Intl. Flavors & Fragrances (Pty.) Ltd. (IFFSA), P.O. Box 231, Roodepport,
      South Africa

INTERNATIONAL PAPER   2 Manhattanville Rd, Purchase, NY 10577,
  Tel: (914) 397-1500
  (Mfr/distr container board, paper, wood prdts)
    Ezebilt Products Ltd., 322 Mark St., Waltloo, Silverton 0127, South Africa
    Masonite (Africa) Ltd., 14th Fl., Nedbank Center, Durban Club Place, Durban 4000,
      South Africa

JEUNIQUE INTL INC   19501 E Walnut Dr, City of Industry, CA 91748,
  Tel: (909) 598-8598
  (Mfr/sale vitamins, food supplements, cosmetics, diet prdts)
    Jeunique Intl. (South Africa)(Pty.) Ltd., 22 Commerce Crescent E.,
      Eastgate Ext. 12, Sandton 2199, South Africa

JOHNSON & JOHNSON   One Johnson & Johnson Plaza, New Brunswick, NJ 08933,
  Tel: (908) 524-0400
  (R&D/mfr/sale health care prdts)
    Janssen Pharmaceutica (Pty.) Ltd., P.O. Box 785939, Sandton 2146, South Africa
    Johnson & Johnson (Pty.) Ltd., P.O. Box 727, East London 5200, South Africa
    Johnson & Johnson Professional Products (Pty.) Ltd., P.O. Box 273, Halfway House,
      Transvaal, South Africa

JOY TECHNOLOGIES INC   301 Grant St, Pittsburgh, PA 15219-1490,
  Tel: (412) 562-4500
  (Mfr coal mining, air pollution control, materials mgmt & incineration equip, fans)
    Joy Manufacturing Co. (Africa)(Pty.) Ltd., 1 Steele St., Steeledale,
      Johannesburg 2000, South Africa

KELLOGG CO   One Kellogg Sq, PO Box 3599, Battle Creek, MI 49016-3599,
  Tel: (616) 961-2000
  (Mfr ready-to-eat cereals, convenience foods)
    Kellogg Co. of South Africa (Pty) Ltd., Springs,
      South Africa (all inquiries to U.S. address)

KENNEDY VAN SAUN CORP   PO Box 500, Danville, PA 17821, Tel: (717) 275-3050
  (Mineral processing & handling equip)
    Kennedy Van Saun (S.A.) Pty. Ltd., P.O. Box 75074, Garden View 2047, South Africa

KIMBERLY-CLARK CORP   PO Box 619100, Dallas, TX 75261, Tel: (214) 281-1200
  (Mfr fiber-based prdts for personal care, lumber & paper prdts)
    Carlton Paper Corp. Ltd., Johannesburg, South Africa
    K.C.S.A. Holdings (Pty.) Ltd., Johannesburg, South Africa

ELI LILLY & CO   Lilly Corporate Center, Indianapolis, IN 46285,
  Tel: (317) 276-2000
  (Mfr pharmaceuticals, animal health prdts)
    Eli Lilly (South Africa) (Pty.) Ltd., P.O. Box 98, Isando 1600, Transvaal,
      South Africa

LINTAS:WORLDWIDE   1 Dag Hammarskjold Plaza, New York, NY 10017,
  Tel: (212) 605-8000
  (Advertising agency)
    Lintas:South Africa, Sandton City Office Tower, Fifth St., Sandton 2146,
      South Africa

LOCTITE CORP   10 Columbus Blvd, Hartford, CT 06106, Tel: (203) 520-5000
  (Mfr/sale ind adhesives & sealants)
    Loctite SA (Pty.) Ltd., P.O. Box 543, Florida 1710, Transvaal, South Africa

THE LUBRIZOL CORP   29400 Lakeland Blvd, Wickliffe, OH 44092-2298,
  Tel: (216) 943-4200
  (Mfr chem additives for lubricants & fuels)
    Lubrizol South Africa (Pty.) Ltd., 10/22 Joyner Rd., Prospection, Isipingo 4110,
      South Africa

LYKES BROS STEAMSHIP CO INC   Lykes Center, 300 Poydras St, New Orleans,
  LA 70130, Tel: (504) 523-6611
  (Ocean frt trans)
    Lykes Lines Agency Inc., P.O. Box 1337, Trust Bank Center 14/F, 475 Smith St.,
      Durban, South Africa

MARATHON LE TOURNEAU CO   PO Box 2307, Longview, TX 75606, Tel: (903) 237-7000
  (Mfr heavy constr, mining mach & equip)
    Blackwood-Hodge S.A. (Pty.) Ltd., P.O. Box 2, Isando 1600, South Africa

MASONITE CORP   1 S Wacker Dr, Chicago, IL 60606, Tel: (312) 750-0900
  (Mfr hardboard, softboard & molded prdts)
    Masonite (Africa) Ltd., P.O. Box 671, Durban 4000, South Africa

THE MENTHOLATUM CO INC   1360 Niagara St, Buffalo, NY 14213,
  Tel: (716) 882-7660
  (Mfr/distr proprietary medicines, drugs, OTC's)
    Mentholatum South Africa (Pty) Ltd., 80 Bonza Bay Rd., Beacon Bay,
      East London 5241, South Africa

MERCK SHARP & DOHME INTL   PO Box 2000, Rahway, NJ 07065, Tel: (201) 574-4000
  (Pharms, chems & biologicals)
    MSD (Pty.) Ltd., 142 Pritchard St., P.O. Box 7748, Johannesburg, South Africa

MICROSOFT CORP   One Microsoft Way, Redmond, WA 98052-6399,
  Tel: (206) 882-8080
  (Computer software, peripherals & services)
    Microsoft South Africa, P.O. Box 5817, Rivonia 2128, South Africa

MINE SAFETY APPLIANCES CO   PO Box 426, Pittsburgh, PA 15230,
  Tel: (421) 273 5000
  (Safety equip, ind filters)
    MSA Africa (Pty.) Ltd., Stand 16, Aeroton Twp. Baragwanath, P.O. Box 1680,
      Johannesburg 2000, South Africa

MOLEX INC   2222 Wellington Ct, Lisle, IL 60532, Tel: (708) 969-4550
  (Mfr electronic, electrical & fiber optic interconnection prdts & sys, switches,
  application tooling)
    Molex Inc., Bergvlei (Johannesburg), South Africa

MYERS INTL INC   1293 South Main St, Akron, OH 44301, Tel: (216) 253-5592
  (Mfr tire retreading & maintenance equip & supplies)
    Myers Tyre Supply S.A. Pty. Ltd., 1-3 Lower Ross St., P.O. Box 15601, Doornfontein,
      Johannesburg 2028, South Africa

McCANN-ERICKSON WORLDWIDE   750 Third Ave, New York, NY 10017,
  Tel: (212) 697-6000
  (Advertising)
    McCann Group, 367 Rivonia Rd., P.O. Box 10663, Johannesburg 2000, South Africa
    McCann Group, other locations in South Africa

NALCO CHEMICAL CO   One Nalco Center, Naperville, IL 60563-1198,
  Tel: (708) 305-1000
  (Chems for water & waste water treatment, oil prod & refining, ind processes;
  water/energy mgmt serv)
    Anikem Pty. Ltd., P.O. Box 2954, Spartan, Kempton Park 1620, South Africa

NATIONAL STARCH & CHEMICAL CO   10 Finderne Ave, Bridgewater, NJ 08807-3300,
  Tel: (908) 685-5000
  (Mfr adhesives & sealants, resins & spec chems, electr materials & adhesives, food
  prdts, ind starch)
    National Starch & Chemical (Pty.) Ltd., Wadeville, South Africa

NATIONAL UTILITY SERVICE INC   One Maynard Dr, PO Box 712, Park Ridge,
  NJ 07656, Tel: (201) 391-4300
  (Utility rate consulting)
    NUS South Africa (Pty.) Ltd., P.O. Box 62346, Marshalltown 2107, Johannesburg 2001,
    South Africa

NATIONAL-STANDARD CO   1618 Terminal Rd, Niles, MI 49120, Tel: (616) 683-8100
  (Mfr wire, wire related prdts, mach & med prdts)
    National-Standard Co. (Pty.) Ltd., P.O. Box 582, 48 Mel Brookes Ave.,
    Currie Township, Uitenhage, South Africa

OTIS ELEVATOR CO   10 Farm Springs, Farmington, CT 06032, Tel: (860) 676-6528
  (Mfr elevators & escalators)
    Otis Elevator Co. Ltd., 222 Marshall St., P.O. Box 2729, Johannesburg 2000,
    South Africa

PARKER HANNIFIN CORP   17325 Euclid Ave, Cleveland, OH 44112,
  Tel: (216) 531-3000
  (Mfr motion-control prdts)
    Parker Hannifin Africa Pty. Ltd., P.O. Box 1153, Kempton Park 1620, South Africa

PFIZER INC   235 E 42nd St, New York, NY 10017-5755, Tel: (212) 573-2323
  (Mfr healthcare products)
    Pfizer (Pty.) Ltd., South Africa
    Pfizer Laboratories (Pty.) Ltd., South Africa

PHELPS DODGE CORP   2600 N Central Ave, Phoenix, AZ 85004-3014,
  Tel: (602) 234-8100
  (Copper, minerals, metals & spec engineered prdts for trans & elect mkts)
    Black Mountain Mineral Development Co. (Pty.) Ltd., Cape Province, South Africa
    Phelps Dodge Exploration Corp., Johannesburg, South Africa
    Phelps Dodge Mining (Pty.) Ltd., Johannesburg, South Africa

PRECISION VALVE CORP   PO Box 309, Yonkers, NY 10702, Tel: (914) 969-6500
  (Mfr aerosol valves)
    Precision Valve South Africa (Pty.) Ltd., P.O. Box 92, Rosslyn, South Africa

PREFORMED LINE PRODUCTS CO   PO Box 91129, Cleveland, OH 44101,
  Tel: (216) 461-5200
  (Mfr pole line hardware for elec transmission lines; splice closures & related prdts
  for telecom)
    Preformed Line Prdts. (South Africa) Pty. Ltd., Pietermaritzburg, Natal,
    South Africa

PREMARK INTL INC   1717 Deerfield Rd, Deerfield, IL 60015, Tel: (708) 405-6000
  (Mfr/sale diversified consumer & coml prdts)
    Dart Industries (Pty) Ltd., Box 78947, Sandton 2146, South Africa

QUAKER CHEMICAL CORP   Elm & Lee Sts, Conshohocken, PA 19428-0809,
  Tel: (610) 832-4000
  (Mfr chem specialties; total fluid mgmt services)
    Quaker Chemical South Africa (Pty.) Ltd., 188 Lansdowne Rd., Jacobs 4052, Natal,
    South Africa

QUIGLEY CO INC   235 E 42nd St, New York, NY 10017, Tel: (212) 573-3444
  (Mfr refractory specs, application equip)
    Quigley Div., P.O. Box 783720, Sandton 2146, South Africa

RAMSEY TECHNOLOGY INC   501 90th Ave NW, Minneapolis, MN 55433,
  Tel: (612) 783-2500
  (Mfr in-motion weighing, inspection, monitoring & control equip for the process inds)
    Ramsey Engineering Africa (Pty) Ltd., P.O. Box 70, Isando 1600, Transvaal,
    South Africa

READER'S DIGEST ASSOCIATION INC   PO Box 235, Pleasantville, NY 10570,
  Tel: (914) 238-1000
  (Publisher magazines & books, direct mail marketer)
    Reader's Digest Assn., Reader's Digest House, 130 Strand St., Cape Town 8001,
    South Africa

SCHENECTADY INTERNATIONAL INC   PO Box 1046, Schenectady, NY 12301,
  Tel: (518) 370-4200
  (Mfr elec insulating varnishes, enamels, phenolic resins, alkylphenols)
    Schenectady South Africa (Pty.) Ltd., P.O. Box 32130, Mobeni 4060, Natal,
    South Africa

G D SEARLE & CO   5200 Old Orchard Rd, Skokie, IL 60077, Tel: (708) 982-7000
  (Mfr pharms, health care & optical prdts, specialty chems)
    Searle (Pty) Ltd., P.O. Box 11128, Johannesburg, South Africa

SIMPLICITY PATTERN CO INC   2 Park Ave, New York, NY 10016,
  Tel: (212) 372-0500
  (Dress patterns)
    Simplicity Patterns S.A. (Pty.) Ltd., P.O. Box 9172, 15 Hulbert St., Genop House,
    Johannesburg, South Africa

STEINER CORP   505 E South Temple St, Salt Lake City, UT 84102,
  Tel: (801) 328-8831
  (Linen supply service)
    Steiner, P.O. Box 4091, Alrode 1450, South Africa

STIEFEL LABORATORIES INC   255 Alhambra Circle, Coral Gables, FL 33134,
  Tel: (305) 443-3807
  (Mfr pharmaceuticals, dermatological specialties)
    Stiefel Laboratories (SA) Pty. Ltd., P.O. Box 890371, Lyndhurst 2106, South Africa

TECHNICON INSTRUMENTS CORP   511 Benedict Ave, Tarrytown, NY 10591-5097,
  Tel: (914) 631-8000
  (Mfr/serv automated blook anal equip, reagents & diagnostics)
    Technicon AutoAnalyzer (Pty.) Ltd., P.O. Box 39390, Bramley 2018, South Africa

THOMAS & BETTS CORP   1555 Lynnfield Rd, Memphis, TN 38119,
  Tel: (901) 682-7766
  (Mfr elect/electr connectors & accessories)
    T & B Spa, P.O. Box 27169, 31 Raebor Rd., Benrose 2011, South Africa

THE TIMKEN CO   1835 Dueber Ave SW, PO Box 6927, Canton, OH 44706-6927,
  Tel: (216) 438-3000
  (Mfr tapered roller bearings & quality alloy steels)
    Timken South Africa Pty. Ltd., P.O. Box 5050, Edinburgh Road Ind. Sites,
      Benoni South 1502, South Africa

TOKHEIM CORP   PO Box 360, Fort Wayne, IN 46801, Tel: (219) 470-4600
  (Mfr gasoline service station dispensers, access, hand & in-tank fuel pumps)
    Tokheim South Africa (Pty.) Ltd., Private Bag 2, Wendywood, Sandton 2144,
      South Africa

TRADE & INDUSTRIES CORP INC   31 Brookside Dr, Greenwich, CT 06830,
  Tel: (203) 661-5813
  (Financial services)
    Intl. Shipping Co. (Pty.) Ltd., Wesbank House 18/F, 222 Smit St.,
      Braamfontein 2001, South Africa

TWIN DISC INC   1328 Racine St, Racine, WI 53403-1758, Tel: (414) 638-4000
  (Mfr ind clutches, reduction gears, transmissions)
    Twin Disc (South Africa)(Pty.) Ltd., P.O. Box 40542, Cleveland 2022, South Africa

UNION CAMP CORP   1600 Valley Rd, Wayne, NJ 07470, Tel: (201) 628-2000
  (Mfr paper, packaging, chems, wood prdts)
    Bush Boake Allen (Pty.) Ltd., P.O. Box 40, Isando, South Africa

UNION CARBIDE CORP   39 Old Ridgebury Rd, Danbury, CT 06817,
  Tel: (203) 794-2000
  (Mfr industrial chemicals, plastics, resins)
    Union Carbide South Africa (Pty. Ltd.), Nedbank Circle, 4th Fl. #403,
      577 Point Rd., Durban, South Africa

UNISYS CORP   PO Box 500, Blue Bell, PA 19424, Tel: (215) 986-4011
  (Mfg/mktg/serv electr info sys)
    Unidata, P.O. Box 47178, Parklands, Johannesburg 2121, South Africa

UPJOHN CO   7000 Portage Rd, Kalamazoo, MI 49001, Tel: (616) 323-4000
  (Mfr pharms, agric prdts, ind chems)
    Tuco (Pty.) Ltd., 44 Monteer Rd., P.O. Box 7779, Isando, Johannesburg, South Africa

WARD HOWELL INTL INC   99 Park Ave, New York, NY 10016-1699,
  Tel: (212) 697-3730
  (Executive recruiting)
    Woodburn Mann (Pty.) Ltd., 102 A Albertyn Ave., Wierda Valley, Sandton, Gauteng,
      South Africa

WARNER-LAMBERT CO   201 Tabor Road, Morris Plains, NJ 07950,
  Tel: (201) 540-2000
  (Mfr ethical & proprietary pharms, confectionary & consumer prdts)
    Warner-Lambert (Pty.) Ltd., Tokai 7966, Cape Town, South Africa

WILBUR-ELLIS CO   320 California St, #200, San Francisco, CA 94104,
  Tel: (415) 772-4000
  (Intl merchants & distributors)
    Wilbur-Ellis Co. (Pty) Ltd., 1 Salmon Grove, Durban 4001, South Africa
    Wilbur-Ellis Co. (Pty.) Ltd., P.O. Box 4258, Cape Town 8000, South Africa

WORLD COURIER INC   46 Trinity Pl, New York, NY 10006, Tel: (718) 978-9400
  (Intl courier serv)
    World Courier South Africa (Pty.) Ltd., P.O. Box 116, Kempton Park 1620,
      South Africa

WYNN OIL CO   1050 W Fifth St, Azusa, CA 91702-9510, Tel: (818) 334-0231
  (Mfr chem additives for oil, grease & fuels; hardware)
    Wynn's South Africa, 702 Main Pretoria Rd., Wynberg, Sandton 2090, South Africa

SPAIN

3COM CORP   5400 Bayfront Plaza, Santa Clara, CA 95052-8145,
  Tel: (408) 764-5000
  (Devel/mfr computer networking prdts & sys)
    3Com Mediterraneo, Spain

3M   3M Center, St Paul, MN 55144-1000, Tel: (612) 733-1110
  (Mfr diversified prdts for industry, health care, imaging, commun, transport, safety,
  consumer, etc)
    3M Espana SA, Juan Ignacio Luca de Tena 19-25, 28027 Madrid, Spain

AAF INTL   215 Central Ave, PO Box 35690, Louisville, KY 40232-5690,
  Tel: (502) 637-0011
  (Mfr air filtration/pollution control & noise control equip)
    American Air Filter SA, Calle Urartea 11, Victoria, Spain

AAF-McQUAY INC   111 S Calvert St, #2800, Baltimore, MD 21202,
  Tel: (410) 528-2755
  (Mfr air quality control prdts: heating, ventilating, air-conditioning & filtration
  prdts & services)
    AAF SA, Calle Uratea 11, Poligona Ali-Gobeo, 01010 Vitoria, Spain

ABRASIVE TECHNOLOGY INC   8400 Green Meadows Dr, Westerville, OH 43081,
  Tel: (614) 548-4100
  (Mfr diamond & CBN tooling: bits, blades, drills, wheels, belts, discs)
    Abrasive Technology Europe SA, c/Natacion, S/N Pol. Ind. "Can Roses" Nave 16,
      08191 Rubi, Barcelona, Spain

ACCURAY CORP   650 Ackerman Rd, PO Box 02248, Columbus, OH 43202,
  Tel: (614) 261-2000
  (Computer-based process mgmt sys for forest prdts, metals rolling, textiles, tobacco
  ind)
    Accuray Espana, Milanesado 21-23, 08017 Barcelona, Spain

ACHESON COLLOIDS CO   PO Box 611747, Port Huron, MI 48061-1747,
  Tel: (810) 984-5581
  (Graphite, lubricants & specialty chems)
    Acheson Colloiden BV, Gran Via Carlos III 58-60B, 08028 Barcelona, Spain

ADEMCO INTL   165 Eileen Way, Syosset, NY 11791, Tel: (516) 921-6704
  (Mfr security, fire & burglary sys & prdts)
    Ademco-Sontrix Espana SA, Martinez Izquierdo 6, 28028 Madrid, Spain

AIR EXPRESS INTL CORP   120 Tokeneke Rd, PO Box 1231, Darien, CT 06820,
  Tel: (203) 655-7900
  (Air frt forwarder)
    Air Express Intl., Terminal de Carga, Local No. 29, Aeropuerto de Barcelona,
    Barcelona, Spain
    Air Express Intl. (Espana), Avda. de la Hispanidad 13, 28042 Madrid, Spain

AIR PRODUCTS & CHEMICALS INC   7201 Hamilton Blvd, Allentown, PA 18195-1501,
  Tel: (215) 481-4911
  (Mfr ind gases & related equip, spec chems, environmental/energy sys)
    S. E. Carburos Metalicos, Consejo de Ciento 365, 08009 Barcelona, Spain

ALLEN-BRADLEY CO   PO Box 2086, Milwaukee, WI 53201, Tel: (414) 382-2000
  (Mfr eletrical controls & info devices)
    Allen-Bradley (Espana) SA, Avda. Gran Via 8-10, 08902 l'Hospitalet de Llobregat,
    Barcelona, Spain

ALLERGAN INC   2525 Dupont Dr, PO Box 19534, Irvine, CA 92713-9534,
  Tel: (714) 752-4500
  (Mfr therapeutic eye care prdts, skin & neural care pharms)
    Allergan Inc., Madrid, Spain

ALLIED AFTERMARKET DIV   105 Pawtucket Ave, East Providence, RI 02916,
  Tel: (401) 434-7000
  (Mfr spark plugs, filters, brakes)
    Fram Espana SA, Aptdo. 6, Llisso de Vall, Barcelona, Spain

ALLIEDSIGNAL INC   101 Columbia Rd, PO Box 2245, Morristown, NJ 07962-2245,
  Tel: (201) 455-2000
  (Mfr aerospace & automotive prdts, engineered materials)
    Allied-Signal Automocion Espana SA, Balmes 243, 08006 Barcelona, Spain
    AlliedSignal Aerospace Co., Princesa 47-3A, 28008 Madrid, Spain
    Garrett Intl. SA, Princesa 47-3A, 28008 Madrid, Spain
    Jurid Iberica SA, Poligono IZ Franca, Sector B, Calle B, 08004 Barcelona, Spain

ALTEK EQUIPMENT CORP   PO Box 353, New York, NY 10023, Tel: (212) 877-6800
  (Engineering, mktg/sales machinery & equip for aluminum ind)
    Remetal SA, Apartado 837, Bilbao, Spain

ALUMINUM CO OF AMERICA (ALCOA)   425 6th Ave, Pittsburgh, PA 15219,
Tel: (412) 553-4545
(Aluminum mining, refining, processing, prdts)
   Aluminum Co. of America, Barcelona, Spain

AMDAHL CORP   1250 E Arques Ave, PO Box 3470, Sunnyvale, CA 94088-3470,
Tel: (408) 746-6000
(Devel/mfr large scale computers, software, data storage prdts, info-technology
solutions & support)
   Amdahl Computer Systems, Edif. Iberia Mart 1, Pedro Teizeira 8, 28020 Madrid, Spain

AMERICAN AIRLINES INC   PO Box 619616, Dallas-Ft Worth Arpt, TX 75261-9616,
Tel: (817) 355-1234
(Air transp)
   American Airlines Inc., Plaza de Espana 18, Torre de Madrid 9-2, Madrid, Spain

AMERICAN APPRAISAL ASSOCS INC   411 E Wisconsin Ave, Milwaukee, WI 53202,
Tel: (414) 271-7240
(Valuation consulting serv)
   American Appraisal Espana SA, Principe de Vergara 9, 3 Dcha., 28001 Madrid, Spain

AMERICAN EXPRESS CO   World Financial Center, New York, NY 10285-4765,
Tel: (212) 640-2000
(Travel, travelers cheques, charge card & financial services)
   American Express Future Plans SA/Coreduria de Seguros, all inquiries to U.S. address
   American Express Viajes SA, all inquiries to U.S. address
   American Express de Espana SA, all inquiries to U.S. address

AMERON INC   PO Box 7007, Pasadena, CA 91109-7007, Tel: (818) 683-4000
(Mfr steel pipe sys, concrete prdts, traffic & lighting poles, protective coatings)
   Ameron Espana SA, Felix Boix 18, 28016 Madrid, Spain

AMP INC   PO Box 3608, Harrisburg, PA 17105-3608, Tel: (717) 564-0100
(Devel/mfr electronic & electrical connection prdts & sys)
   AMP Espanola SA, Aptdo. 5294, 08080 Barcelona, Spain

AMPEX SYSTEMS CORP   401 Broadway, Redwood City, CA 94063-3199,
Tel: (415) 367-2011
(Mfr hi-perf helical scanning recording sys & associated tape media)
   Ampex Iberica SA, Calle Princesa 47, 5/F C&D, 28008 Madrid, Spain

AMSTED INDUSTRIES INC   205 N Michigan, Chicago, IL 60601, Tel: (312) 645-1700
(Steel castings for railroad & ind use, wire prdts, refrig & heading equip)
   BAC Iberica SA, Calle Nuestra Senora de Lujan 5, 23016 Madrid, Spain

AMWAY CORP   7575 E Fulton Rd, Ada, MI 49355, Tel: (616) 676-6000
(Mfr/sale home care, personal care, nutrition & houseware prdts)
   Amway de Espana SA, c/o Industria 101-115, Poligono Gran Via, Zona 22A,
      08908 Hospitalet de Llobregat, Barcelona, Spain

ANIXTER BROS INC   4711 Golf Rd, Skokie, IL 60076, Tel: (708) 677-2600
(Dist wiring sys/prdts for voice, video, data & power applications)
   Anixter Spain, Avda. de la Fama 94, Poligono Industrial de Almeda, 08940 Cornella,
      Barcelona, Spain

APPLE COMPUTER INC 1 Infinite Loop, Cupertino, CA 95014, Tel: (408) 996-1010
(Personal computers, peripherals & software)
  Apple Computer Espana SA, Valencia 87-89, Aptdo. 35148, 08029 Barcelona, Spain

APPLIED POWER INC 13000 W Silver Spring Dr, Butler, WI 53007,
  Tel: (414) 781-6600
(Mfr hi-pressure tools, vibration control prdts, electrical tools & consumables, tech furniture)
  Applied Power Intl. SA, Calle de la Imprenta 7, Poligono Industrial,
    28100 Acobendas Madrid, Spain
  Power-Packer Espana SA, Apartado de Correos 27, Calle Romero 12, 45500 Torrijos,
    Toledo, Spain

ARAMARK CORP 1101 Market St, Philadelphia, PA 19107-2988,
  Tel: (215) 238-3000
(Diversified managed services)
  ARAMARK/Spain, Masia Torre Rodona, Sabino de Arana 27, 08028 Barcelona, Spain

ARBOR ACRES FARM INC 439 Marlborough Rd, Glastonbury, CT 06033,
  Tel: (860) 633-4681
(Producers of male & female broiler breeders, commercial egg layers)
  Granja Avicola Gallina Blanca SA, Fernando Gonzalez 57, 28009 Madrid, Spain

ARMSTRONG WORLD INDUSTRIES INC PO Box 3001, Lancaster, PA 17604,
  Tel: (717) 397-0611
(Mfr/mkt interior furnishings & spec prdts for bldg, auto & textile inds)
  Armstrong World Industries SA, Begur, Spain (all inquiries to U.S. address)

ARVIN INDUSTRIES INC One Noblitt Plaza, Columbus, IN 47201-6079,
  Tel: (812) 379-3000
(Mfr motor vehicle parts, springs, relays & ind controls, aircraft engines & parts)
  AP Amortiguadores SA, Carretera Iruzun S/N, Orobia, 31171 Navarra, Spain

ASARCO INC 180 Maiden Lane, New York, NY 10038, Tel: (212) 510-2000
(Nonferrous metals, specialty chems, minerals, mfr industrial prdts, environmental services)
  Enthone-Omi Inc., Spain

ASGROW SEED CO 2605 E Kilgore Rd, Kalamazoo, MI 49002, Tel: (616) 384-5675
(Research/mfr agronomic & vegetable seeds; seed technologies)
  Complejo Asgrow Semillas SA, Zurbano 67-2B, 28010 Madrid, Spain

ASHLAND OIL INC 1000 Ashland Dr, Russell, KY 41169, Tel: (606) 329-3333
(Petroleum exploration, refining & transportation; mfr chemicals, oils & lubricants)
  Iberia Ashland Chemical SA, Muelle Tomas de Olabarri 4, 48930 Las Arenas (Vizcaya),
    Spain

ASSOCIATED MERCHANDISING CORP 1440 Broadway, New York, NY 10018,
  Tel: (212) 536-4000
(Retail service organization)
  Associated Merchandising Corp., Rambla Mendez Nunez 58, Edificio Manero,
    03002 Alicante, Spain
  Associated Merchandising Corp., Barbara de Braganza 10, 28004 Madrid, Spain

AT&T INTERNATIONAL   412 Mt Kemble Ave, Morristown, NJ 07962-1995,
  Tel: (810) 262-6646
  (Telecommunications)
    AT&T Espana SA, Salvador de Madariaga 1, Planta 13, 28027 Madrid, Spain

AUTODESK INC   2320 Marinship Way, Sausalito, CA 94965, Tel: (415) 332-2344
  (Devel/mkt/support computer-aided design, engineering, scientific & multimedia
  software prdts)
    Autodesk SA, Constitucion 3, Planta Baja, 08960 San Just Desvern, Barcelona, Spain

AVCO FINANCIAL SERVICES INC   600 Anto Blvd, PO Box 5011, Costa Mesa,
  CA 92628-5011, Tel: (714) 435-1200
  (Financial services, loans)
    Avco Financial Services, Juan Esplandiu 15, 1 piso, 28007 Madrid, Spain

AVERY DENNISON CORP   150 N Orange Grove Blvd, Pasadena, CA 91103,
  Tel: (818) 304-2000
  (Mfr pressure-sensitive adhesives & materials, office prdts, labels, tags, retail
  sys, spec chems)
    Avery Dennison Spain, Spain

AVON PRODUCTS INC   9 W 57th St, New York, NY 10019, Tel: (212) 546-6015
  (Mfr/distr beauty & related prdts, fashion jewelry, gifts & collectibles)
    Avon Cosmetics SA, Carrera Barcelona Km 34.200, Alcala de Henares, Madrid, Spain

BAILEY-FISCHER & PORTER CO   125 E County Line Rd, Warminster, PA 18974,
  Tel: (215) 674-6000
  (Design/mfr meas, recording & control instru & sys; mfr ind glass prdts)
    Bailey-Fischer & Porter Iberica SA, Sanchez Pacheco 79, 28002 Madrid, Spain

BAKER OIL TOOLS   PO Box 40129, Houston, TX 77240-0129, Tel: (713) 466-1322
  (Mfr/serv oil/gas well completions equip)
    Baker Oil Tools (Espana) SA, c/o Tarragona Offshore SA, Calle Caliao 9, Tarragona,
    Spain

BANKAMERICA CORP   555 California St, San Francisco, CA 94104,
  Tel: (415) 622-3456
  (Financial services)
    Bank of America SA, Calle del Capitan Haya 1, Aptdo. 1168, 28020 Madrid, Spain

C R BARD INC   730 Central Ave, Murray Hill, NJ 07974, Tel: (908) 277-8000
  (Mfr health care prdts)
    Bard de Espana SA, Poligono Industrial Rosanes, c/Luxemburgo s/n,
      08769 Castellvi de Rosanes, Barcelona, Spain

BAUSCH & LOMB INC   1 Chase Square, Rochester, NY 14601, Tel: (716) 338-6000
  (Mfr vision care prdts & accessories)
    Bausch & Lomb Espana SA, Madrid, Spain

BAXTER HEALTHCARE CORP   1 Baxter Pky, Deerfield, IL 60015,
  Tel: (708) 948-2000
  (Mfr disposable medical prdts)
    Baxter SA, Poligono Industrial Vara de Cuart, Calle del Gremis 7,
      Aptdo. de Correos 765, 46080 Valencia, Spain
    Baxter SA, also in Barcelona & Madrid, Spain

BEAR STEARNS & CO INC   245 Park Ave, New York, NY   10167, Tel: (212) 272-2000
  (Investment banking)
    Bear Stearns Spanish Securitization Corp., c/o Titulizacion de Activos,
      Via Llanueva 19, 28001 Madrid, Spain

BECKMAN INSTRUMENTS INC   2500 Harbor Blvd, Fullerton, CA 92634,
  Tel: (714) 871-4848
  (Devel/mfr/mkt automated systems & supplies for biological analysis)
    Beckman Instruments Espana SA, Avda. del Llano Castellano 15, 28034 Madrid, Spain

BIO-RAD LABORATORIES INC   1000 Alfred Nobel Dr, Hercules, CA 94547,
  Tel: (510) 724-7000
  (Mfr life science research prdts, clinical diagnostics, analytical instruments)
    Bio-Rad Laboratories Inc., Madrid, Spain

BLACK & DECKER CORP   701 E Joppa Road, Towson, MD 21286, Tel: (410) 716-3900
  (Mfr power tools & accessories, security hardware, small appliances, fasteners, info
  sys & servs)
    Black & Decker Corp., all mail to U.S. address

BLACK BOX CORP   1000 Park Dr, Lawrence, PA 15055, Tel: (412) 746-5500
  (Direct marketer & tech service provider of commun, networking & related computer
  connectivity prdts)
    Black Box Comunicaciones SA, Avda. de la Industria 32,
      Poligono Industrial de Alcobendas, 28036 Madrid, Spain

BOOLE & BABBAGE INC   510 Oakmead Pkwy, Sunnyvale, CA 94086,
  Tel: (408) 735-9550
  (Devel/support enterprise automation & systems mgmt software)
    Boole & Babbage Espana SA, Centro Empresarial El Plantio, c/Ochandiano N 6-2 DCHA,
      28023 Madrid, Spain
    Boole & Babbage Espana SA, Edif. Autopistas, Plaza Gala Placidia, 1-2-Pita, Esc. B,
      80885 Barcelona, Spain

BOOZ ALLEN & HAMILTON INC   101 Park Ave, New York, NY 10178,
  Tel: (212) 697-1900
  (Mgmt consultants)
    Booz Allen & Hamilton Inc., Marques de la Ensenada 16, 28004 Madrid, Spain

BORDEN INC   180 E Broad St, Columbus, OH 43215-3799, Tel: (614) 225-4000
  (Mfr foods, snacks & beverages, adhesives)
    Borden SA, all mail to U.S. address

BOSTITCH DIV   815 Briggs St, East Greenwich, RI 02818, Tel: (401) 884-2500
  (Stapling machs & supplies, wire)
    Bostitch Espanola SA, Modesto Lafuente 15, 28003 Madrid, Spain
    Bostitch Espanola SA, Via Augusta 103, Barcelona, Spain
    Bostitch Espanolas SA, c/o Elro, 12 Torregon de Ardoz, Madrid, Spain

BOSTON OVERSEAS FINANCIAL CORP   100 Federal St, Boston, MA 02110,
  Tel: (617) 434-3276
  (Ind financial serv)
    Intl. Factors Espanola SA, Aptdo. 14739, 28013 Madrid, Spain

BOYDEN CONSULTING CORP   375 Park Ave, #1008, New York, NY 10152,
  Tel: (212) 980-6480
  (Executive search)

(cont)

Boyden/Ibersearch, Travesera de Garcia 73-79, 08006 Barcelona, Spain
Boyden/Ibersearch, Jorge Juan 10, 46004 Valencia, Spain
Boyden/Ibersearch, Torres de Jerez, Plaza de Colon 2, 28046 Madrid, Spain

W H BRADY CO   6555 W Good Hope Rd, Milwaukee, WI 53223, Tel: (414) 358-6600
(Mfr ind ID for wire marking, circuit boards; facility ID & signage)
W.H. Brady SARL, Rambla de San Juan 83 6/1, 08914 Badalona, Spain

BRANSON ULTRASONICS CORP   41 Eagle Rd, Danbury, CT 06813-1961,
Tel: (203) 796-0400
(Mfr plastics assembly equip, ultrasonic cleaning equip)
Branson Ultrasonidos SAE, Poligono Industrial "Can Roses",
Calle/Interior B naves 12 y 13, 08191 Rubi, Barcelona, Spain

BRINK'S INC   Thorndal Circle, Darien, CT 06820, Tel: (203) 655-8781
(Security transportation)
Brink's Emece SA, Madrid, Spain

BULAB HOLDINGS INC   1256 N McLean Blvd, Memphis, TN 38108,
Tel: (901) 278-0330
(Mfr microbicides, biocides, additives, corrosion inhibitors, chems)
Buckman Laboratories Iberica SA, Avda. de Roma 157, 08011 Barcelona, Spain

LEO BURNETT CO INC   35 West Wacker Dr, Chicago, IL 60601, Tel: (312) 220-5959
(Advertising agency)
Leo Burnett SA, Edif. Britannia, Parque de las Naciones, Guzman El Bueno 133,
28013 Madrid, Spain

BURSON-MARSTELLER   230 Park Ave, New York, NY 10003-1566, Tel: (212) 614-4000
(Public relations/public affairs consultants)
Burson-Marsteller SA, Basilica 19, 28020 Madrid, Spain

CARL BYOIR & ASSOCIATES INC   420 Lexington Ave, New York, NY 10017,
Tel: (212) 210-6000
(Public relations, intl commun)
Relaciones Publicas Internacionales SA, Nunez de Balboa 30-5B, 28001 Madrid, Spain

CABOT CORP   75 State St, Boston, MA 02109-1807, Tel: (617) 890-0200
(Mfr carbon blacks, plastics; oil & gas, info sys)
Cabot SA, Aptdo. 8, Santurce, Vizcaya, Spain
Deloro Stellite Iberica SA, Weatec Div., Aptdo. 1633, Bilbao, Spain

CALCOMP INC   2411 W La Palma Ave, Anaheim, CA 92801, Tel: (714) 821-2000
(Mfr computer graphics peripherals)
CalComp Espana SA, Basauri 17, 28023 Madrid, Spain

CAMP INTL INC   PO Box 89, Jackson, MI 49204, Tel: (517) 787-1600
(Mfr orthotics & prosthetics)
Prim SA, Poligono Ind. 1, Calle C 20, Mostoles, Madrid, Spain

CAMPBELL SOUP CO   Campbell Place, Camden, NJ 08103-1799, Tel: (609) 342-4800
(Food prdts)
Compania Envasadora Loreto SA, Spain

CARBOLINE CO   350 Hanley Industrial Ct, St Louis, MO 63144,
Tel: (314) 644-1000
(Mfr coatings, sealants)
  Carboline Iberica SA, Avda. Pio XII 6, 28016 Madrid, Spain

CARGILL   PO Box 9300, Minneapolis, MN 55440, Tel: (612) 475-7575
(Food prdts, feeds, animal prdts)
  Cargill Espana SA, Aptdo. de Correos 314, 08194 Sant Cugat del Valles, Barcelona,
  Spain

CARLISLE SYNTEC SYSTEMS   PO Box 7000, Carlisle, PA 17013, Tel: (717) 245-7000
(Mfr elastomeric roofing & waterproofing sys)
  Carlisle SynTec Systems Espana SL, Poligono Famades II, c/Crom 76,
    08940 Cornella da Llobragat, Barcelona, Spain

CARRIER CORP   One Carrier Place, Farmington, CT 06034-4015,
Tel: (203) 674-3000
(Mfr/distr/svce A/C, heating & refrigeration equip)
  Carrier Espana SA, Calle Albarracin 26, 28037 Madrid, Spain
  Global Transporte Refrigeracion Espana SA, Madrid, Spain

CENTRAL NATIONAL-GOTTESMAN INC   3 Manhattanville Rd, Purchase,
NY 10577-2110, Tel: (914) 696-9000
(Worldwide sales pulp & paper prdts)
  Central National Espanola SA, Calle Joaquin Costa 36, 28002 Madrid, Spain

CHASAN INTL INC   1251 Ave of the Americas, New York, NY 10020,
Tel: (212) 719-1320
(Real estate devel & investment mgmt)
  Chasan Intl. Desarrollo SL, 365-B Calle 17-B, Nueva Andalucia, Marbella, Spain

CHASE MANHATTAN BANK N A   1 Chase Manhattan Plaza, New York, NY 10081,
Tel: (212) 552-2222
(Intl banking)
  Chase Manhattan Bank, Avda. Diagonal 427-429, 08036 Barcelona, Spain
  Chase Manhattan Bank N.A., Paseo de la Castellana 31, Madrid, Spain

CHECK TECHNOLOGY CORP   12500 Whitewater Dr, Minnetonka, MN 55343-9420,
Tel: (612) 939-9000
(Mfr computer-controlled check/coupon print sys)
  Check Technology Espana SA, Calle General Yague 10 2/F, 02806 Madrid, Spain

CHEMICAL BANK   270 Park Ave, New York, NY 10017-2070, Tel: (212) 270-6000
(Banking & financial services)
  Chemical Bank Sucursal en Espana, Paseo de la Castellana 51, 28046 Madrid, Spain
  Chemical Bank Sucursal en Espana, also in Barcelona, Bilbao, Seville & Valencia,
  Spain

CHESTERTON BINSWANGER INTL   Two Logan Sq, 4th fl, Philadelphia,
PA 19103-2759, Tel: (215) 448-6000
(Real estate & related svces)
  Chesterton y Asociados SA, c/Serrano 77, 1 Primero Izda, 28006 Madrid, Spain

CHIRON CORP   4560 Horton St, Emeryville, CA 94608-2916, Tel: (510) 601-2412
(Research/mfg/mktg therapeutics, vaccines, diagnostics, ophthalmics)
  Ciba Corning Diagnostics SA, Edificio Dublin, Parque Empresarial San Fernando,

(cont)

28831 Madrid, Spain
Domilens Iberica SA, Bori I Fontesta 39-41, 08017 Barcelona, Spain

THE CHUBB CORP   15 Mountain View Rd, Warren, NJ 07060, Tel: (908) 580-2000
   (Holding co: property/casualty ins)
      Chubb Insurance Co. of Europe, Spain

CIGNA CORP   One Liberty Place, Philadelphia, PA 19192, Tel: (215) 523-4000
   (Ins, invest, health care & other fin servs)
      Cigna Insurance Co. of Europe SA/NV, Francisco Gervas 13, 28020 Madrid, Spain
      Esis Intl. Inc., Francisco Gervas 13, 1 Planta, 28020 Madrid, Spain

CITICORP   399 Park Ave, New York, NY 10043, Tel: (212) 559-1000
   (Banking & financial services)
      Citibank NA, Spain

THE CLOROX CO   1221 Broadway, PO Box 24305, Oakland, CA 94623-1305,
   Tel: (510) 271-7000
   (Mfr domestic consumer packaged prdts)
      Henkel Iberica SA, Barcelona, Spain

THE COCA-COLA CO   PO Drawer 1734, Atlanta, GA 30301, Tel: (404) 676-2121
   (Mfr/mkt/distr soft drinks, syrups & concentrates, juice & juice-drink prdts)
      Compania Coca-Cola de Espana SA, Autopista de Barajas Km. 6, 28027 Madrid, Spain

COLGATE-PALMOLIVE CO   300 Park Ave, New York, NY 10022, Tel: (212) 310-2000
   (Mfr pharms, cosmetics, toiletries, detergents)
      Colgate-Palmolive, General Aranaz 88, 28027 Madrid, Spain

COLUMBIA PICTURES INDUSTRIES INC   711 Fifth Ave, New York, NY 10022,
   Tel: (212) 751-4400
   (Producer & distributor of motion pictures)
      Columbia Films SA, Calle Veneras 9-6 Piso, 28013 Madrid, Spain

COMBUSTION ENGINEERING INC   900 Long Ridge Road, Stamford, CT 06902,
   Tel: (203) 329-8771
   (Tech constr)
      Combustion Engineerlng Inc., Calle del Sol, Salau Tarragona, Spain
      Services y Products SA, Plaza de Chambiri 10, 28010 Madrid, Spain

COMPUTER ASSOCIATES INTL INC   One Computer Associates Plaza, Islandia,
   NY 11788, Tel: (516) 342-5224
   (Devel/mkt/mgt info mgt & bus applications software)
      C.A. Computer Associates SA, Carabaela La Nina 12, 08017 Barcelona, Spain

CONAGRA INC   1 ConAgra Dr, Omaha, NE 68102, Tel: (402) 595-4000
   (Prepared & frozen foods, grains, flour, animal feeds, agric chems, poultry, meat,
   dairy prdts)
      Bioter-Biona SA, Bioter-Biona Bldg., Emilio Vargas 7, 28027 Madrid, Spain
      ConAgra Spain SA, Avda. del Ejercito 2-2, 15006 La Coruna, Spain

CONOCO INC   600 N Dairy Ashford Rd, Houston, TX 77079, Tel: (713) 293-1000
   (Oil, gas, coal, chems, minerals)
      Continental Oil Co. of Spain/Conoco Espanola, General Oraa, 68 5 Izqda,
         28006 Madrid, Spain
      Petroquimica Espanola SA, Orense 68-6a Planta, 28020 Madrid, Spain

COOPER INDUSTRIES INC 1001 Fannin St, PO Box 4446, Houston, TX 77210-4446,
Tel: (713) 739-5400
(Mfr/distr electrical prdts, tools & hardware, automotive prdts)
Kirsch Div., Vitoria, Spain

CORESTATES FINANCIAL CORP 1500 Market St, Philadelphia, PA 19101,
Tel: (215) 973-3100
(Banking)
Coresates Bank, Villaverde 26, Oficina 322, 28003 Madrid, Spain

COULTER CORP PO Box 169015, Miami, FL 33116-9015, Tel: (305) 885-0131
(Mfr blood analysis sys, flow cytometers, chem sys, scientific sys & reagents)
Coulter Cientifica SA, Aragon 90, 08015 Barcelona, Spain

CPC INTERNATIONAL INC PO Box 8000, Englewood Cliffs, NJ 07632,
Tel: (201) 894-4000
(Consumer foods, corn refining)
CPC Espana SA, Via Augusta 59, Aptdo. 9443, 08006 Barcelona, Spain

CRANE CO 100 First Stamford Pl, Stamford, CT 06907, Tel: (203) 363-7300
(Diversified mfr/distr engineered prdts for ind)
NRI Iberica SA, Calle Badajoz 145-147, 08018 Barcelona, Spain

CRAY RESEARCH INC 655 Lone Oak Dr, Eagan, MN 55121, Tel: (612) 452-6650
(Supercomputer systems & services)
Cray Research SAE, Paseo Castellana 141, Planta 20, 28046 Madrid, Spain

CROWN CORK & SEAL CO INC 9300 Ashton Rd, Philadelphia, PA 19136,
Tel: (215) 698-5100
(Mfr cans, bottle caps; filling & packaging mach)
Metalinas SA, Aptdo. 23, Carabanchel, Getafe, Madrid, Spain
Ruigomes y Momene SA, Aptdo. 720, Bilbao, Spain

CRSS INTL INC 1177 W Loop So, PO Box 22427, Houston, TX 77227-2427,
Tel: (713) 552-2000
(Consulting, architecture, engineering, construction mgmt)
CRSS Iberia SA, Marques de Urquijo 5, 28008 Madrid, Spain

CULLIGAN INTL CO One Culligan Parkway, Northbrook, IL 60062,
Tel: (708) 205-6000
(Water treatment prdts & serv)
Culligan Espana SA, Parc A.E. "Can Sant Joan", 08191 Rubi (Barcelona), Spain

D'ARCY MASIUS BENTON & BOWLES INC (DMB&B) 1675 Broadway, New York,
NY 10019, Tel: (212) 468-3622
(Advertising & communications)
DMB&B Madrid SA, Avda. de Brasil 6, 28020 Madrid, Spain
DMB&B SA, other locations in Spain

D-M-E COMPANY 29111 Stephenson Highway, Madison Heights, MI 48071,
Tel: (313) 398-6000
(Basic tooling for plastic molding & die casting)
DME Iberica SA, Industrialdea 3, 20180 Dyarzun (Guipuzcoa), Spain

LEO A DALY 8600 Indian Hills Dr, Omaha, NE 68114, Tel: (402) 391-8111
(Planning, arch, engr & interior design servs)
Leo A. Daly SA, Paseo de la Castellana 115, 28046 Madrid, Spain

DAMES & MOORE   911 Wilshire Blvd, Los Angeles, CA 90017, Tel: (213) 683-1560
  (Engineering, environmental & construction mgmt services)
    Dames & Moore, Caracas 6-10, 28010 Madrid, Spain

DANA CORP   PO Box 1000, Toledo, OH 43697, Tel: (419) 535-4500
  (Engineer/mfr/mkt prdts & sys for vehicular, ind & mobile off-highway mkt & related
  aftermarkets)
    Spicer Espana SA, Calle Santander 42-48, 08020 Barcelona, Spain

DATA GENERAL CORP   4400 Computer Dr, Westboro, MA 01580, Tel: (617) 366-8911
  (Design, mfr gen purpose computer sys & peripheral prdts & servs)
    Data General SA, Calle Condesa de Venadito, Madrid, Spain

DATAEASE INTL INC   7 Cambridge Dr, Trumbull, CT 06611, Tel: (203) 374-8000
  (Mfr applications devel software)
    HSC Industrial SA, Fundadores 25, 28028 Madrid, Spain

DDB NEEDHAM WORLDWIDE INC   437 Madison Ave, New York, NY 10022,
  Tel: (212) 415-2000
  (Advertising)
    Tandem DDB Needham Campmany-Guasch SA, Paseo de la Bonanova 93-95, 08017 Barcelona,
      Spain
    Tandem DDB Needham SA, Orense 6, 28020 Madrid, Spain

DEERE & CO   John Deere Rd, Moline, IL 61265, Tel: (309) 765-8000
  (Mfr/sale agri/constr/utility/forestry & lawn/grounds care equip)
    John Deere Iberica SA, Carr. de Toledo, Km 12.200, Getafe, Madrid, Spain

DEKALB PLANT GENETICS   3100 Sycamore Rd, DeKalb, IL 60115,
  Tel: (815) 753-7333
  (Devel/produce hybrid corn, sorghum, sunflowers, sudax, varietal soybeans, alfalfa)
    DeKalb Iberica, Calle Santa Engracia 4, 28010 Madrid, Spain

DIGITAL EQUIPMENT CORP   146 Main St, Maynard, MA 01754-2571,
  Tel: (508) 493-5111
  (Networked computer systems & services)
    Digital Equipment Corp. Espana Sa, Cerro del Castanar 72, 28034 Madrid, Spain

WALT DISNEY CO   500 S Buena Vista St, Burbank, CA 91521, Tel: (818) 560-1000
  (Film/TV prod, theme parks, resorts, publishing, recording, retail stores)
    Walt Disney Iberica SA, P. de La Castellana 53, 28001 Madrid, Spain

THE DOW CHEMICAL CO   2030 Dow Center, Midland, MI 48674, Tel: (517) 636-1000
  (Mfr chems, plastics, pharms, agric prdts, consumer prdts)
    Dow Chemical Iberica SA, Spain
    Labs Lepetit SA, Spain

DOW CORNING CORP   2220 W Salzburg Rd, PO Box 1767, Midland, MI 48640,
  Tel: (517) 496-4000
  (Silicones, silicon chems, solid lubricants)
    Dow Corning AG, Sucursal Enespana, Avda. General Franco 612-613, 08015 Barcelona,
      Spain

DRAKE BEAM MORIN INC   100 Park Ave, New York, NY 10017, Tel: (212) 692-7700
(Human resource mgmt consulting & training)
  DBM Spain, Hermosilla 21, 28001 Madrid Spain
  DBM Spain, Ausias March 7, 08010 Barcelona, Spain

DRESSER INDUSTRIES INC   PO Box 718, Dallas, TX 75221-0718,
  Tel: (214) 740-6000
  (Diversified supplier of equip & tech serv to energy & natural resource ind)
    Masoneilan S, Sector M, Calle 4, 08004 Barcelona, Spain
    Pleuger SA, Centra de Valencia, Km. 24.300, 28500 Madrid, Spain

DRIVER-HARRIS CO   308 Middlesex St, Harrison, NJ 07029, Tel: (201) 483-4802
  (Mfr non-ferrous alloys)
    Driver-Harris Iberica, Aptdo. 49006, 28012 Madrid, Spain

E I DU PONT DE NEMOURS & CO   1007 Market St, Wilmington, DE 19898,
  Tel: (302) 774-1000
  (Mfr/sale diversified chems, plastics, specialty prdts & fibers)
    DuPont Iberica SA, Spain

EAGLE-PICHER INDUSTRIES INC   580 Walnut St, Cincinnati, OH 45202,
  Tel: (513) 721-7010
  (Mfr industrial, machinery & automotive parts)
    Eagle-Picher Espana SA, Poligono Industrial del INUR, Aptdo. de Correos 32,
    42080 Soria, Spain

EASTMAN CHEMICAL   PO Box 511, Kingsport, TN 37662, Tel: (423) 229-2000
  (Mfr plastics, chems, fibers)
    Eastman Chemical, San Roque, Spain

EASTMAN KODAK CO   343 State St, Rochester, NY 14650, Tel: (716) 724-4000
  (Devel/mfr photo & chem prdts, info mgmt/video/copier sys, fibers/plastics for
  various ind)
    Kodak SA, Ctra. Nal. VI Km. 33, 28230 Las Rozas (Madrid), Spain
    Kodak SA, also in Bilbao, Canary Islands, Palma de Mallorca, Seville & Valencia,
    Spain

EATON CORP   1111 Superior Ave, Cleveland, OH 44114, Tel: (216) 523-5000
  (Advanced tech prdts for transp & ind mkts)
    Cutler-Hammer Espanola SA, Madrid, Spain
    Eaton Livia SA, Barcelona, Spain
    Eaton SA, Pamplona, Spain

EBASCO SERVICES INC   2 World Trade Center, New York, NY 10048-0752,
  Tel: (212) 839-1000
  (Engineering, constr)
    Ebasco Espana SA, c/o Medosa Servicios SA, Costa Brava 33-4A Centro, Madrid, Spain

ECLIPSE INC   1665 Elmwood Rd, Rockford, IL 61103, Tel: (815) 877-3031
  (Mfr ind process heating equip & sys)
    APLI Combustion SA, Santander 71, 08020 Barcelona, Spain

ENERPAC   13000 W Silver Spring Dr, Butler, WI 53007, Tel: (414) 781-6600
  (Mfr/sale high pressure hydraulic maint tools)
    Applied Power Iberica SA, Calle La Granja, s/u Poligono Industrial,
    28100 Alcobendas (Madrid), Spain

EQUIFAX INC   PO Box 4081, Atlanta, GA 30302, Tel: (404) 885-8000
  (Information services)
    ASNEF-Equifax Servicios de Informacion de Credito, SL, Paseo de la Castellana 128,
    Madrid, Spain

ERICO PRODUCTS INC   34600 Solon Road, Cleveland, OH 44139,
  Tel: (216) 248-0100
  (Mfr electric welding apparatus & hardware, metal stampings, specialty fasteners)
    Productos Erico SA, Poligono Indust.,
      Central Amarilla c/o Jose Maria Ibarra y Gomez Rull, Parcella 139, Seville, Spain

ESSEF CORPORATION   220 Park Dr, Chardon, OH 44024-1333, Tel: (216) 286-2200
  (Mfr non-metallic pressure vessels & related prdts)
    Structural Iberica SA, Sr. Pere Aulestia, Carr. de Colon 288,
      08226 Terrassa (Barcelona), Spain

ESTERLINE TECHNOLOGIES   10800 NE 8th St, Bellevue, WA 98004,
  Tel: (206) 453-9400
  (Mfr equip & instru for ind automation, precision meas, data acquisition)
    Ausitrol Iberico SA, c/o Caucho 18, Poligono Industrial, Aptdo. 30,
      28850 Torrejon de Ardoz, Madrid, Spain

EXPEDITORS INTL OF WASHINGTON INC   PO Box 69620, Seattle, WA 98168-9620,
  Tel: (206) 246-3711
  (Air/ocean freight forwarding, customs brokerage, intl logistics solutions)
    Expeditors Intl. Espana SA, Travesia Trespaderne 2, Edificio Artemisa,
      28042 Madrid, Spain

FEDERAL-MOGUL CORP   PO Box 1966, Detroit, MI 48235, Tel: (810) 354-7700
  (Mfr/distr precision parts for automobiles, trucks, & farm/constrution vehicles)
    Federal-Mogul World Trade de Espana SA, Spain

FELTON INTERNATIONAL INC   599 Johnson Ave, Brooklyn, NY 11237,
  Tel: (212) 497-4664
  (Essential oils & extracts, perfumes & flavor material, aromatic chems)
    Felton Espana, Avda. Diagonal 523 (10A), 08029 Barcelona, Spain

FERRO CORPORATION   1000 Lakeside Ave, Cleveland, OH 44114,
  Tel: (216) 641-8580
  (Mfr chems, coatings, plastics, colors, refractories)
    Ferro Enamel Espanola SA, Aptdo. 232, Castellon de La Plana, Spain

FIRST NATIONAL BANK OF CHICAGO   One First National Plaza, Chicago, IL 60670,
  Tel: (312) 732-4000
  (Financial services)
    First Natl. Bank of Chicago, Paseo de Gracia 54, 08007 Barcelona, Spain
    First Natl. Bank of Chicago (Madrid), Paseo de La Castellana 18, 28046 Madrid, Spain

FISHER CONTROLS INTL INC   8000 Maryland Ave, Clayton, MO 63105,
  Tel: (314) 746-9900
  (Mfr ind process control equip)
    Fisher Controls SA, San Nazario 1, Esc. Izq 1, 28002 Madrid, Spain

FLORASYNTH INC   300 North St, Teterboro, NJ 07608, Tel: (201) 288-3200
  (Mfr fragrances & flavors)
    Compania General de Esencias - Grupo Florasynth SA, Poligono Industrial Congost,
      Avda. Sant Julia 260-266, 08400 Granollers, Spain

FLUOR DANIEL INC   3333 Michelson Dr, Irvine, CA 92730, Tel: (714) 975-2000
  (Engineering, construction, maintenance & technical services)
    Fluor Daniel Espana SA, Capitan Haya 38, piso 1, 28020 Madrid, Spain

FMC CORP   200 E Randolph Dr, Chicago, IL 60601, Tel: (312) 861-6000
  (Produces chems & precious metals, mfr machinery, equip & sys for ind, agric & govt)
    FMC Airline Eqipment Europe Sa, Spain
    FMC Foret SA, Corcega 293, 08008 Barcelona, Spain
    FMC Spain SA, Spain
    Forsean SL, Spain
    Peroxidos Organicos SA, Spain
    Sibelco Espanola SA, Spain
    Turegano SA, Spain
    Valentin Herraiz SA, Spain

FOOTE CONE & BELDING COMMUNICATIONS INC   101 E Erie St, Chicago,
  IL 60611-2897, Tel: (312) 751-7000
  (Advertising agency)
    Arge, Paseo de la Castellana 83, 28046 Madrid, Spain
    Moline & Publicis, Sabina de Arang 54, 08028 Barcelona, Spain
    Publicis-FCB, Paseo de la Castellana 147, 28046 Madrid, Spain

FORD MOTOR CO   The American Road, Dearborn, MI 48121, Tel: (313) 322-3000
  (Mfr motor vehicles)
    Ford Espana SA, Paseo de la Castellana 135, 28046 Madrid, Spain

FOSTER WHEELER CORP   Perryville Corporate Park, Clinton, NJ 08809-4000,
  Tel: (908) 730-4000
  (Engr, constr, mfg)
    Foster Wheeler Iberia SA, Parque Empresarial Madrid-Las Razas,
      N-VI Carretera de la Coruna Km. 22, 300, 28230 Las Rozas, Spain
    Generadores de Vapor Foster Wheeler SA, Parque Empresarial Madrid-Las Rozas,
      N-VI Carretera de la Coruna Km. 22, 300, 28230 Las Rozas, Spain

THE FRANKLIN MINT   Franklin Center, PA 19091, Tel: (610) 459-6000
  (Creation/mfr/mktg collectibles & luxury items)
    Franklin Mint Commercial Office, c/o Ferran Agullo 5, 08021 Barcelona, Spain

FREEPORT-McMORAN INC   1615 Poydras St, New Orleans, LA 70112,
  Tel: (504) 582-4000
  (Natural resources exploration & processing)
    Rio Tinto Minera SA, Zurbano 76, 28010 Madrid, Spain

GAF CORP   1361 Alps Rd, Wayne, NJ 07470, Tel: (201) 628-3000
  (Chems, bldg materials, commun)
    GAF Corp. Sucursal en Espana, Loreto 42, 08029 Barcelona, Spain

GARCY CORP   1400 N 25th Ave, Melrose Park, IL 60160, Tel: (312) 261-1800
  (Commercial furniture & supplies)
    Garcy Espanola SA, Virgen de Africa 36, 28017 Madrid, Spain
    Garcy Espanola SA, Ganduzer 5, Barcelona, Spain

THE GATES RUBBER CO   PO Box 5887, Denver, CO 80217-5887, Tel: (303) 744-1911
  (Mfr automotive & industrial belts & hose)
     Gates Vulca SA, Avinguda de la Riera 3-5, Aptdo. de Correos 7,
       08960 Sant Just Desvern, Barcelona, Spain

GENERAL BINDING CORP   One GBC Plaza, Northbrook, IL 60062,
  Tel: (708) 272-3700
  (Binding & laminating equip & associated supplies)
     General Binding Corp., Sucursal Espana, Torre Catalunya, Despacho 1410,
       Avda. de Roma 2 y 4, 08014 Barcelona, Spain

GENERAL ELECTRIC CO   3135 Easton Tpk, Fairfield, CT 06431,
  Tel: (203) 373-2211
  (Diversified manufacturing, technology & services)
     General Electric Co.,
       all mail to U.S. address; phone (800) 626-2004 or (518) 438-6500

GENERAL FOODS CORP   250 North St, White Plains, NY 10625, Tel: (914) 335-2500
  (Processor, distributor & mfr of foods)
     Saimaza SA, Josefa Valcarcel 42, 28027 Madrid, Spain

GENERAL MOTORS ACCEPTANCE CORP   3044 West Grand Blvd, Detroit, MI 48202,
  Tel: (313) 556-5000
  (Automobile financing)
     GMAC Espana SA de Financiacion, Edif. Master's 1, Avda. Gen. Peron 38,
       28020 Madrid, Spain
     GMAC Expana SA de Financiacion, also in Barcelona, Las Palmas & Seville, Spain

GENERAL MOTORS CORP   3044 W Grand Blvd, Detroit, MI 48202-3091,
  Tel: (313) 556-5000
  (Mfr full line vehicles, automotive electronics, coml technologies, telecom, space,
  finance)
     Delco Products Overseas Corp & Saginaw Div. Overseas Corp, Poligono el, Trocadero,
       Puerto Real, Spain
     GM Espana-Fisher Guide, Aptdo. 281, Logrono, Rioja, Spain
     General Motors Espana SA, Poligono de Enterrios, Figueruclas, Spain
     Senalizacion y Accesorios del Automovil Yorka SA, Venezuela 76, Barcelona, Spain

GENERAL REINSURANCE CORP   PO Box 10350, Stamford, CT 06904-2350,
  Tel: (203) 328-5000
  (Reinsurance)
     General Re Correduria de Reaseguros SA, Serrano Jover 5, 6A, 28015 Madrid, Spain

GIBBS & HILL INC   11 Penn Plaza, New York, NY 10001, Tel: (212) 216-6000
  (Consulting engineers)
     Gibbs & Hill Espanola SA, Magallanes 3, Planta 9, 28015 Madrid, Spain

THE GILLETTE CO   Prudential Tower, Boston, MA 02199, Tel: (617) 421-7000
  (Devel/mfr personal care/use prdts: blades & razors, toiletries, cosmetics,
  stationery)
     Braun Espanola SA, Barcelona, Spain
     Gillette Espanola SA, Madrid, Spain
     Jafra Cosmeticos Espanola Inc., Madrid, Spain
     Oral-B Laboratories SA, Madrid, Spain

W R GRACE & CO   One Town Center Rd, Boca Raton, FL 33486-1010,
  Tel: (407) 362-2000
  (Mfr spec chems & materials: packaging, health care, catalysts, construction, water
  treatment/process)
    Grace SA, Apartado Postal 523, 08080 Barcelona, Spain

GRANT THORNTON INTL   Prudential Plaza, Chicago, IL 60601, Tel: (312) 856-0001
  (Intl accountants)
    Grant Thornton Intl. (Spain), Edificio Barcino, Tuset 20-24, 08006 Barcelona, Spain

GRAPHIC CONTROLS CORP   PO Box 1271, Buffalo, NY 14240, Tel: (716) 853-7500
  (Mfr info, medical & physiological monitoring prdts)
    Controles Graficos Ibericos SA, Samamigo 9, Poligono Las Mercedes, 28022 Madrid,
    Spain

GREY ADVERTISING INC   777 Third Ave, New York, NY 10017, Tel: (212) 546-2000
  (Advertising)
    Grey Barcelona, Ctra. de Esplugas 79, 08034 Barcelona, Spain
    Grey Madrid, Paseo de la Castellana 91, Planta 11, 28046 Madrid, Spain

GRIFFITH LABORATORIES INC   I Griffith Center, Alsip, IL 60658,
  Tel: (708) 371-0900
  (Ind food ingredients & equip)
    Griffith Laboratories Iberia SA, Aptdo. 78, 43800 Valls (Tarragon), Spain

GUARDIAN PACKAGING CORP   6590 Central Ave, Newark, CA 94560,
  Tel: (415) 797-3710
  (Mfr flexible packaging materials)
    Guardian Espanola SA, Larragana 16, Zona Industrial, Eetono, Aptdo. 305, Victoria,
    Spain

FRANK B HALL & CO INC   549 Pleasantville Rd, Briarcliff Manor, NY 10510,
  Tel: (914) 769-9200
  (Insurance)
    Frank B. Hall Iberica SA, Pedro Maguruza 5, 28036 Madrid, Spain

THE HARPER GROUP   260 Townsend St, PO Box 77933, San Francisco,
  CA 94107-1719, Tel: (415) 978-0600
  (Ocean/air freight fwdg, customs brokerage, packing & whse, logistics mgt, ins)
    Circle Espana SA, C/Ferrocarril 25 Nave 18, 28820 Coslada, Madrid, Spain
    Circle Espana SA, also in Barcelona, Deba & Valencia, Spain

THE HARTFORD STEAM BOILER INSPECTION & INSURANCE CO   1 State St, Hartford,
  CT 06102, Tel: (203) 722-1866
  (Inspection & quality assurance, asbestos monitoring)
    HSB Engineering Insurance Ltd., C/. Claudio Coello 124, 8th fl., 28006 Madrid, Spain

HECKETT   PO Box 1071, Butler, PA 16001-1071, Tel: (412) 283-5741
  (Metal reclamation, steel mill services)
    Auxihec, Apdo. de Correos 15, 33460 Llaranes, Asturias, Spain

H J HEINZ CO   PO Box 57, Pittsburgh, PA 15230-0057, Tel: (412) 456-5700
  (Processed food prdts & nutritional services)
    Heinz Iberica SA, Madrid, Spain

HERCULES INC   Hercules Plaza, Wilmington, DE 19894-0001, Tel: (302) 594-5000
  (Mfr spec chems, plastics, film & fibers, coatings, resins, food ingredients)
    Ceratonia SA, Carretera de Valencia, 43006 Tarragona, Spain

HEWLETT-PACKARD CO   3000 Hanover St, Palo Alto, CA 94304-0890,
  Tel: (415) 857-1501
  (Mfr computing, communications & measurement prdts & services)
    Hewlett-Packard Espanola SA, Crta. de la Coruna Km. 16.400, 28230 Las Rozas,
      Madrid, Spain

HOLIDAY INNS INC   3742 Lamar Ave, Memphis, TN 38195, Tel: (901) 362-4001
  (Hotels, restaurants, casinos)
    Holiday Inn, Urbanization Guadalmar, Carr. de Cadiz Km. 238, Malaga, Torremolinos,
      Spain

HONEYWELL INC   PO Box 524, Minneapolis, MN 55440-0524, Tel: (612) 951-1000
  (Devel/mfr controls for home & building, industry, space & aviation)
    Honeywell SA, Josefa Valcarcel 24, 28027 Madrid, Spain

HUGHES AIRCRAFT CO   PO Box 80028, Los Angeles, CA 90080-0028,
  Tel: (310) 568-6904
  (Mfr electronics equip & sys)
    Hughes Aircraft Intl. Service Co., Darro 13, El Viso, 28002 Madrid, Spain

HYATT INTL CORP   200 West Madison, Chicago, IL 60606, Tel: (312) 750-1234
  (Intl hotel mgmt)
    Hyatt Intl. Hotels, Madrid & Murcia, Spain

IBM CORP   Old Orchard Rd, Armonk, NY 10504, Tel: (914) 765-1900
  (Information products, technology & services)
    International Business Machines SAE, Paseo de la Castellana 4, 28001 Madrid, Spain

ILLINOIS TOOL WORKS INC   3600 W Lake Ave, Glenview, IL 60025,
  Tel: (708) 724-7500
  (Mfr gears, tools, fasteners, sealants, plastic & metal components for ind, med, etc.)
    ITW Espana SA, Centra Ribas Km. 31.7, Las Franquesas del Valles, Barcelona, Spain

IMCO CONTAINER CO   451 Florida Blvd, Baton Rouge, LA 70801,
  Tel: (504) 388-8011
  (Plastic containers)
    Imco-Bepsa, 16 Llull, Barcelona, Spain
    Imco-Litoplas, Agueda Diez 7, 28019 Madrid, Spain

IMO INDUSTRIES INC   1009 Lenox Dr, Bldg 4 West, Lawrenceville,
  NJ 08648-0550, Tel: (609) 896-7600
  (Mfr/support mech & electr controls, engineered power prdts)
    Morse Controls SL, Lo Gaiter del Llobregat 2, 1st 1a, 08820 Prat de Llobregat,
      Barcelona, Spain

IMS INTERNATIONAL INC   100 Campus Rd, Totowa, NJ 07512, Tel: (201) 790-0700
  (Market research reports)
    IMS Iberica SA, Claudio Coello 20, Madrid, Spain

INFORMATION BUILDERS INC   1250 Broadway, New York, NY 10001,
  Tel: (212) 736-4433
  (Devel/mfr/serv computer software)

Information Builders Iberica, Centro Empresarial El Plantio, c/Ochandiano S/N,
Edif. 10-2 planta, 28023 Madrid, Spain

INGERSOLL-RAND CO   200 Chestnut Ridge Rd, Woodcliff Lake, NJ 07675,
Tel: (201) 573-0123
(Mfr compressors, rock drills, pumps, air tools, door hardware, ball bearings)
Cia Ingersoll-Rand SA, Poligno Industrial de Doslada, Avda. de Fuentemer 26828,
28820 Coslada, Madrid, Spain
Industrias del Rodamiento SA, Dr. Diaz Emparanza 3, Aptdo. Postal 6138,
48080 Bilboa, Spain
Ingersoll-Rand Espanola SA, Avda. Fuentemar 26-28, Poligno Industrial de Coslada,
28820 Coslada, Spain
Pleuger SA, Ctrs. II-III Km. 24.3, 28600 Arganda del Ray, Madrid, Spain

INSTRON CORP   100 Royall St, Canton, MA 02021-1089, Tel: (617) 828-2500
(Mfr material testing instruments)
Instron Intl. Ltd., Sabina de Arana 26, 08028 Barcelona, Spain

INTERGRAPH CORP   Huntsville, AL 35894-0001, Tel: (205) 730-2000
(Devel/mfr interactive computer graphic systems)
Intergraph (Espana) SA, Calle Gobelas 47-49, La Florida, 28023 Madrid, Spain

INTERMEC CORP   6001 36th Ave West, PO Box 4280, Everett, WA 98203-9280,
Tel: (206) 348-2600
(Mfr/distr automated data collection sys)
Intermec Iberia, Apolonio Morales 13-B, 28036 Madrid, Spain

INTERNATIONAL FLAVORS & FRAGRANCES INC   521 W 57th St, New York, NY 10019,
Tel: (212) 765-5500
(Create/mfr flavors, fragrances & aroma chems)
Intl. Flavora Fragancos (Spanish) SA, Apartado de Correo 36211, Madrid, Spain

INTERNATIONAL PAPER   2 Manhattanville Rd, Purchase, NY 10577,
Tel: (914) 397-1500
(Mfr/distr container board, paper, wood prdts)
Aussedat Rey Espana SA, 95 Avenida de Madrid, Atico 2, 08028 Barcelona, Spain
Cartonajes Intl. SA, Apartado de Correos 632, Bilbao, Spain
Cartonajes Intl. SA, also in Barcelona, Las Palmas, Madrid & Valladolid, Spain
Duriron SA, Calle Ronda 38-68, 08100 Sant Fost de Campsentelles, Barcelona, Spain
Horsell Industrias Graficas SA, Avenida Torrellos 6a, 08620 San Vicente del Horts,
Barcelona, Spain
Ilford Anitec SA, Industria 473, Recinto Cros-Pje Nave 1,
08912 Badalona (Barcelona), Spain
Intamasa, Sicilia 93-97, 08013 Barcelona, Spain
International Paper (Espana) SA, Muntaner 200, Atico 7, 08036 Barcelona, Spain

INTRUSION-PREPAKT INC   5353 W 161st St, Cleveland, OH 44142,
Tel: (216) 267-7300
(Contractor: preplaced aggregate concrete, concrete repirs, erosion control,
underwater concrete, etc)
Intrusion Prepakt SA, Pio XII 57, 28016 Madrid, Spain

IONICS INC   65 Grove St, Watertown, MA 02172, Tel: (617) 926-2500
(Mfr desalination equip)
Ionics Iberia, Edif. Mercurio, 35100 Playa del Ingles, Gran Canaria, Spain

ITT CORP   1330 Ave of the Americas, New York, NY 10019-5490,
  Tel: (212) 258-1000
  (Design/mfr communications & electronic equip, hotels, insurance)
    Marconi Espanola SA, Carr. Andalucia Km. 10.300, 28001 Madrid, Spain

ITT SHERATON CORP   60 State St, Boston, MA 02108, Tel: (617) 367-3600
  (Hotel operations)
    Sheraton Sales Centre-Spain, Plaza de Manolete 5-5A, 28020 Madrid, Spain

JOHNSON & JOHNSON   One Johnson & Johnson Plaza, New Brunswick, NJ 08933,
  Tel: (908) 524-0400
  (R&D/mfr/sale health care prdts)
    Janssen-Cilag, Avda. Europa 19-3, Parque Empresarial La Moraleja, 28100 Alcobendas,
      Madrid, Spain
    Johnson & Johnson SA, Apartado 79, 28080 Madrid, Spain

S C JOHNSON & SON INC   1525 Howe St, Racine, WI 53403, Tel: (414) 631-2000
  (Home, auto, commercial & personal care prdts, specialty chems)
    Johnson's Wax Espanola SA, c/o Orense 4-6.a, 28020 Madrid, Spain
    Johnson's Wax Espanola SA, Milane Sado 21, Barcelona, Spain

JOY ENVIRONMENTAL TECHNOLOGIES INC   10700 North Freeway, Houston, TX 77037,
  Tel: (713) 878-1000
  (Design/eng air pollution control & material handling sys)
    Ecolaire Espana, Rios Rosa 44-A, 6TA Planta, Madrid, Spain

K-TEL INTL INC   2605 Fernbrook Lane N, Plymouth, MN 55447,
  Tel: (612) 559-6800
  (Sale/distr packaged consumer entertainment & convenience prdts)
    K-Tel Intl. (Spain), Paseo de la Castellana 226-5A, 28046 Madrid, Spain

A T KEARNEY INC   222 West Adams St, Chicago, IL 60606, Tel: (312) 648-0111
  (Mgmt consultants, executive search)
    A.T. Kearney, Paseo de Gracia 111, planta 17, 08008 Barcelona, Spain
    A.T. Kearney, Paseo de la Castellana 31, 28046 Madrid, Spain

KELLOGG CO   One Kellogg Sq, PO Box 3599, Battle Creek, MI 49016-3599,
  Tel: (616) 961-2000
  (Mfr ready-to-eat cereals, convenience foods)
    Kellogg Espana SA, Valls, Spain (all inquiries to U.S. address)

KENT-MOORE DIV   28635 Mound Rd, Warren, MI 48092, Tel: (313) 574-2332
  (Mfr service equip for auto, constr, recreational, military & agric vehicles)
    Kent-Moore Espanola SA, Poligono Industrial del Henares (Ampliacion), Parcela 58,
      19080 Guadalajara, Spain

KEYSTONE INTL INC   PO Box 40010, Houston, TX 77040, Tel: (713) 466-1176
  (Mfr butterfly valves, actuators & control accessories)
    Keystone, Barcelona & Madrid, Spain

KIMBERLY-CLARK CORP   PO Box 619100, Dallas, TX 75261, Tel: (214) 281-1200
  (Mfr fiber-based prdts for personal care, lumber & paper prdts)
    Kimberly-Clark Iberica SA, Spain

KIRSCH   309 N Prospect St, Sturgis, MI 49091-0370, Tel: (616) 659-5228
  (Mfr drapery hardware & accessories, wood shelving, woven wood shades, etc)
    HOFESA, Apartado 311, 01080 Vitoria, Spain

KIRSCHNER MEDICAL CORP   9690 Deereco Rd, Timonium, MD 21093,
  Tel: (410) 560-3333
  (Mfr orthopedic products)
    Industrias Quirurgicas de Levante SA, Calle Islas Baleras 50, Fuente del Jarro,
      46988 Valencia, Spain

KNOGO CORP   350 Wireless Blvd, Hauppauge, NY 11788-3907, Tel: (516) 232-2100
  (Mfr electr article surveillance sys)
    Knogo Iberica SA, General Oraa 70, 28006 Madrid, Spain

THE KNOLL GROUP   105 Wooster St, New York, NY 10021, Tel: (212) 343-4000
  (Mfr/sale office furnishings)
    Idea Madrid, Paseo de la Habana 24, 28036 Madrid, Spain

KORN/FERRY INTL   1800 Century Park East, Los Angeles, CA 90067,
  Tel: (310) 552-1834
  (Executive search)
    Korn/Ferry Espana, Calle Felipe IV #9, 28014 Madrid, Spain
    Korn/Ferry Intl., Diagonal 482-5, 08006 Barcelona, Spain

KRAFT INC   Kraft Court, Glenview, IL 60025, Tel: (708) 998-2000
  (Dairy prdts, processed food, chems)
    Kraft-Leonesas SA, Arapiles 13, Madrid, Spain

KURT SALMON ASSOCIATES INC   1355 Peachtree St NE, Atlanta, GA 30309,
  Tel: (404) 892-0321
  (Management consulting: consumer products, retailing)
    Kurt Salmon Associates/F.T. Grup SL, Avenida de Roma 2 y 4, Torre Catalunya,
      08014 Barcelona, Spain

LAW INTERNATIONAL INC   1000 Abernathy Rd NE, Atlanta, GA 30328,
  Tel: (404) 396-8000
  (Consulting engrs & archs)
    Daly-Law Iberica SA, Edificio Torres Blancas, Corazon de Maria 2 6-20,
      28002 Madrid, Spain

LEEDS+NORTHRUP   795 Horsham Rd, PO Box 1010, Horsham, PA 19044-8010,
  Tel: (215) 442-8000
  (Mfr process control instrumentation, liquid & particle analysis)
    Leeds+Northrup SA, Calle Miguel Fleta #4 - Tercero, 28037 Madrid, Spain

LEVEL EXPORT CORP   1460 Broadway, New York, NY 10018, Tel: (212) 354-2600
  (Chewing gum)
    Chicles Americanos SA, Gaztambide 11, 28015 Madrid, Spain
    Marrero y Level Ltd., Juan Padron 12, Santa Cruz de Tenerife, Canarias, Spain
    Sdad. de Importaciones Hispania, Gaztambide 11, 28015 Madrid, Spain

LEVI STRAUSS & CO   1155 Battery, San Francisco, CA 94111, Tel: (415) 544-6000
  (Mfr casual wearing apparel)
    Levi Strauss de Espana SA, Edificio Heron Barcelona, Diagonal 605, Planta 3,
      08028 Barcelona, Spain

LINTAS:WORLDWIDE   1 Dag Hammarskjold Plaza, New York, NY 10017,
  Tel: (212) 605-8000
  (Advertising agency)
    Lintas:Madrid, Edif. Sollube, Plaza Carlos Tria S Beltran S/N, 28020 Madrid, Spain

LIQUID CARBONIC INDUSTRIES CORP   810 Jorie Blvd, Oak Brook, IL 60521,
  Tel: (708) 572-7500
  (Mfr compressed gasses)
    Liquid Carbonic de Espana SA, Paseo de la Castellana 147,
      Apartado de Correos 36089, 28046 Madrid, Spain

ARTHUR D LITTLE INC   25 Acorn Park, Cambridge, MA 02140-2390,
  Tel: (617) 498-5000
  (Mgmt, environ, health & safety consulting; tech & prdt development)
    Arthur D. Little SRC, General Peron 40A, 28020 Madrid, Spain

LOCTITE CORP   10 Columbus Blvd, Hartford, CT 06106, Tel: (203) 520-5000
  (Mfr/sale ind adhesives & sealants)
    Loctite Espana SABV, Poligono Industrial Alparrache, Parcela 56,
      28600 Navalcarnero (Madrid) Spain

LONGYEAR CO   PO Box 27314, Salt Lake City, UT 84127, Tel: (801) 972-1395
  (Mfr diamond drills, concrete cutting equip; drill serv)
    Longyear Co. Spain, Avda. de Los Metales S/N, Leganes, Madrid, Spain

THE LUBRIZOL CORP   29400 Lakeland Blvd, Wickliffe, OH 44092-2298,
  Tel: (216) 943-4200
  (Mfr chem additives for lubricants & fuels)
    Lubrizol Espanola SA, General Yague 4, 28020 Madrid, Spain

R H MACY & CO INC   151 West 34th St, New York, NY 10001, Tel: (212) 695-4400
  (Department stores, importers)
    Macy May, Torre de Madrid 8-11, 28013 Madrid, Spain

MALLINCKRODT MEDICAL INC   675 McDonnell Blvd, PO Box 5840, St Louis,
  MO 63134, Tel: (314) 895-2000
  (Mfr specialty medical prdts)
    Mallinckrodt Medical SA, Madrid, Spain
    Mallinckrodt-Iberica SA, Madrid, Spain

MANPOWER INTL INC   5301 N Ironwood Rd, PO Box 2053, Milwaukee,
  WI 53201-2053, Tel: (414) 961-1000
  (Temporary help service)
    Manpower ETT, Corsega 372, 08037 Barcelona, Spain

MARATHON LE TOURNEAU CO   PO Box 2307, Longview, TX 75606, Tel: (903) 237-7000
  (Mfr heavy constr, mining mach & equip)
    Blackwood-Hodge (Espana) Ltd., Camino Monte Valdeoliva Finca El Raso,
      28750 San Agustin del Guadalix, Km. 36 Ctra., Madrid, Spain

MARCO   2300 W Commodore Way, Seattle, WA 98199, Tel: (206) 285-3200
  (Shipbldg & repair, coml fishing equip & sys, hydraulic pumps)
    Marco Espana, Las Mercedes 5, Las Arenas, Bilbao, Spain

MARSH & McLENNAN COS INC 1166 Ave of the Americas, New York, NY 10036-1011,
Tel: (212) 345-5000
(Insurance)
  Marsh & McLennan Espana SA, Avda. Diagonal, Bloque B 652-656, 08034 Barcelona, Spain
  Marsh & McLennan Espana SA, Edif. GM 15, Paseo de la Castellana 83-85,
    28046 Madrid, Spain

MARSTELLER INTL 1 E Wacker Dr, Chicago, IL 60601, Tel: (312) 329-1100
(Advertising, marketing research, sales promotion)
  Burson-Marsteller SA, Zurbano 67 1-A, 28003 Madrid, Spain

MATTEL INC 333 Continental Blvd, El Segundo, CA 90245, Tel: (310) 252-2000
(Mfr toys, dolls, games, crafts & hobbies)
  Fisher-Price SA, Craywinkel 17, 80822 Barcelona, Spain
  Mattel Espana SA, Aribau 200, 08036 Barcelona, Spain

MEASUREX CORP One Results Way, Cupertino, CA 95014-5991, Tel: (408) 255-1500
(Mfr computer integrated mfg sys)
  Measurex (Spain), Avda. de Zarauz 82-10, Edif. Oficinas Lorea, 20009 San Sebastian,
    Spain

MEDTRONIC INC 7000 Central Ave, NE, Minneapolis, MN 55432,
Tel: (612) 574-4000
(Mfr/sale/svce therapeutic medical devices)
  Medtronic Iberica SA, Travesia de Costa Brava 6, planta 6, Edifiolo a Madrid, Spain

MEMOREX CORP San Thomas at Central Expressway, Santa Clara, CA 95052,
Tel: (408) 987-1000
(Magnetic recording tapes, etc)
  Memorex AG, C/Estudio 9, Aravaca, 28023 Madrid, Spain

MERCK SHARP & DOHME INTL PO Box 2000, Rahway, NJ 07065, Tel: (201) 574-4000
(Pharms, chems & biologicals)
  Merck Sharp & Dohme de Espana SAE, Pedro Texeira 8-8a Planta, Aptdo. 36318,
    28020 Madrid, Spain
  Merck Sharp Dohme de Espana SA, Avda. Generalisimo Franco 349, Barcelona, Spain

METCO DIV OF PERKIN-ELMER 1101 Prospect Ave, PO Box 1006, Westbury,
NY 11590-0201, Tel: (516) 334-1300
(Mfr/serv thermal spray coating equip & supplies)
  Metco Iberica SA, Calle Ramon y Cajal 4, Torrejon de Ardoz, Madrid, Spain

METROPOLITAN LIFE INSURANCE CO 1 Madison Ave, New York, NY 10010-3690,
Tel: (212) 578-2211
(Insurance & retirement savings prdts & services)
  Seguros Genesis SA, Paseo de las Doce Estrellas 4, Piso 4, Campo de las Naciones,
    28042 Madrid, Spain

MICROSOFT CORP One Microsoft Way, Redmond, WA 98052-6399,
Tel: (206) 882-8080
(Computer software, peripherals & services)
  Microsoft Spain SRL, Avda. Comenar Viejo, Sector Foresta 2-3-4, 28760 Tres Cantos,
    Madrid, Spain

MILLICOM INC   153 E 53rd St, #5500, New York, NY 10022, Tel: (212) 355-3440
  (Cellular communications, satellite TV transmission, public phone & paging services)
    Millisat SA, Poligono La Ermita Fase II, Bl. 112 Ctra. de Cadiz Km. 182.75,
      29600 Marbella, Spain

MILLIPORE CORP   Ashley Rd, Bedford, MA 01730, Tel: (617) 275-9205
  (Mfr precision filters, hi-performance liquid chromatography instru)
    Millipore Iberica SA, Avda. del Llano Castellano 13-3a, 28034 Madrid, Spain

MINE SAFETY APPLIANCES CO   PO Box 426, Pittsburgh, PA 15230,
  Tel: (421) 273 5000
  (Safety equip, ind filters)
    MSA Espanola SA, Avda. Diagonal 618, 08021 Barcelona, Spain

MOBIL CORP   3225 Gallows Rd, Fairfax, VA 22037-0001, Tel: (703) 846-3000
  (Petroleum explor & refining, mfr petrol prdts, chems, petrochems)
    Mobil Oil SA, Maria de Molina 40, 28006 Madrid, Spain
    Mobil Oil de Canarias SA, Leon y Castillo 309, Las Palmas de Gran Canaria, Spain
    Mobil Oil de Espana SA, Avda. Cap. L. Varela 128, Barcelona, Spain

MORGAN GUARANTY TRUST CO   23 Wall St, New York, NY 10260, Tel: (212) 483-2323
  (Banking)
    Banco del Desarrollo Economico Espanola SA, Jose Ortega y Gasset 29, 28006 Madrid,
      Spain

MOTOROLA INC   1303 E Algonquin Rd, Schaumburg, IL 60196, Tel: (708) 576-5000
  (Mfr commun equip, semiconductors, cellular phones)
    Motorola Espana SA, Alberto Alcocer 46, 28616 Madrid, Spain

MULLER & PHIPPS INTL CORP   Box 3994, San Francisco, CA 94119,
  Tel: (415) 772-5650
  (General merchandise)
    M & P EXM Spain, Calle Moratin 14, 6-B, 46002 Valencia, Spain

MULTIGRAPHICS DIV   1800 W Central Rd, Mt Prospect, IL 60056,
  Tel: (708) 398-1900
  (Offset duplicating & graphic commun sys)
    AM Intl. SA, Garcia de Paredes 74, 28003 Madrid, Spain

MacDERMID INC   245 Freight St, Waterbury, CT 06702, Tel: (203) 575-5700
  (Chem processing for metal ind, plastics, electronics cleaners, strippers)
    MacDermid Espanola SA, Avda. Barcelona 6 y 8, Santa Coloma de Carvello, Barcelona,
      Spain

THE MacNEAL-SCHWENDLER CORP   815 Colorado Blvd, Los Angeles, CA 90041,
  Tel: (213) 258-9111
  (Devel/mfr computer-aided engineering software)
    MacNeal-Schwendler Iberica SA, P. de la Castellana 93, 28046 Madrid, Spain

McCANN-ERICKSON WORLDWIDE   750 Third Ave, New York, NY 10017,
  Tel: (212) 697-6000
  (Advertising)
    Clarin Publicidad SA, Compositor Beethoven 15, 08021 Barcelona, Spain
    EPIC Ltd., Valazquez 76-3, 28001 Madrid, Spain
    McCann Direct, Paseo de la Castellana 149, 28046 Madrid, Spain
    McCann Erickson SA, Rosario Pino 5, 28020 Madrid, Spain

McKINSEY & CO INC   55 E 52nd St, New York, NY 10022, Tel: (212) 446-7000
  (Mgmt consultants)
    McKinsey & Co. SL, Miguel Angel 11, 28010 Madrid, Spain

NALCO CHEMICAL CO   One Nalco Center, Naperville, IL 60563-1198,
  Tel: (708) 305-1000
  (Chems for water & waste water treatment, oil prod & refining, ind processes;
  water/energy mgmt serv)
    Nalco Espanola, Aptdo. 23.100, 08028 Barcelona, Spain

NATIONAL CHEMSEARCH CORP   2727 Chemsearch Blvd, Irving, TX 75061,
  Tel: (214) 438-0211
  (Commercial chem prdts)
    Chemsearch Espanola SA, Java 12, Madrid, Spain
    Chemsearch Espanola SA, Pedro J.V. 78, Barcelona, Spain

NATIONAL DATA CORP   National Data Plaza, Atlanta, GA 30329-2010,
  Tel: (404) 728-2000
  (Info sys & servs for retail, healthcare, govt & corporate mkts)
    NDC Intl. Ltd., Francisco Giralte 2, 28002 Madrid, Spain

NATIONAL GYPSUM CO   2001 Rexford Rd., Charlotte, NC 28211,
  Tel: (704) 365-7300
  (Building prdts & servs)
    The Austin Co. SA, Madrid, Spain
    The Austin Co. SA, Barcelona, Spain

NATIONAL STARCH & CHEMICAL CO   10 Finderne Ave, Bridgewater, NJ 08807-3300,
  Tel: (908) 685-5000
  (Mfr adhesives & sealants, resins & spec chems, electr materials & adhesives, food
  prdts, ind starch)
    National Starch & Chemical SA, Barcelona, Spain

NEW VALLEY CORP   One Lake St, Upper Saddle River, NJ 07458,
  Tel: (201) 818-5000
  (Financial & messaging services)
    Western Union Financial Services Intl., Montesa 35, 28006 Madrid, Spain

A C NIELSEN CO   Nielsen Plaza, Northbrook, IL 60062-6288, Tel: (708) 498-6300
  (Market research)
    A.C. Nielsen Co. SA, Plaza del Descubridor, Diego de Cordas 3, 28003 Madrid, Spain

NORDSON CORP   28601 Clemens Rd, Westlake, OH 44145, Tel: (216) 892-1580
  (Mfr ind application equip & packaging mach)
    Nordson Iberica SA, Carretera de Torrente 225, 46950 Xirivella, Valencia, Spain

NORTHERN TELECOM SYSTEMS CORP   PO Box 1222, Minneapolis, MN 55440,
  Tel: (612) 932-8000
  (Remote information processing sys)
    Data 100 SA, Edificio UAP, Avda. del Generalisimo 11, 28016 Madrid, Spain

NORTHROP CORP   1840 Century Park E, Los Angeles, CA 90067-2199,
  Tel: (213) 553-6262
  (Advanced technology for aircraft, electronics, & tech/support serv)
    Construcciones Aeronauticas SA, Calle del Rey Francisco 4, Aptdo. 193,
      28009 Madrid, Spain
    Electronica Basica SA, Carretera Nacional 2 Km. 583, Esparreguera, Barcelona, Spain

NORTON CO   1 New Bond St, Worcester, MA 01606, Tel: (508) 795-5000
  (Abrasives, drill bits, constr & safety prdts, plastics)
    Norton SA, Carretera de Guipuzcoa Km. 7, Aptdo. 162, Berriplano, Navarra, Spain
    Norton SA, Aptdo. 162, Pamplona, Navarra, Spain
    Refractarios Norton SA, Cam. Barca, S/N, Madrid, Spain
    Refractarios Norton SA, Camino de Las Piedras, Vicalvaro, 28032 Madrid, Spain

OCCIDENTAL PETROLEUM CORP   10889 Wilshire Blvd, Los Angeles, CA 90024,
  Tel: (213) 879-1700
  (Petroleum & petroleum prdts, chems, plastics)
    Occidental of Spain Inc., Paseo de la Castellana 141, 28016 Madrid, Spain
    Oxy Metal Industrias Espana SA, Carretera de Madrid 118, San Justo Desvern,
      Barcelona, Spain

OCEANEERING INTL INC   PO Box 218130, Houston, TX 77218-8130,
  Tel: (713) 578-8868
  (Underwater serv to offshore oil & gas ind)
    Oceaneering Intl. Inc., Operational base in Madrid

ODI   25 Mall Rd, Burlington, MA 01803, Tel: (617) 272-8040
  (Mgt & consul serv)
    ODI Espana, Paseo de la Castellana, 143-7 Area Cuzco, 29046 Madrid, Spain

OGDEN ENVIRONMENTAL & ENERGY SERVICES CO   3211 Jermantown Rd, Fairfax,
  VA 22053, Tel: (703) 246-0500
  (Environ & energy consulting svces for commercial clients & govt agencies)
    Compania General de Sondeos (CGS), Corazon de Maria 15, 28002 Madrid, Spain

THE OILGEAR CO   2300 S 51st St, Milwaukee, WI 53219, Tel: (414) 327-1700
  (Mfr hydraulic power transmission mach)
    Oilgear Towler SA, Entidad Zicunaga 62, Apartado 104, Hernani (Guipuzcoa), Spain

OMI INTERNATIONAL CORP   21441 Hoover Rd, Warren, MI 48089,
  Tel: (313) 497-9100
  (Mfr spec chems & equip for metal finishing & surface treatment)
    OMI Intl. (Espana) SA, Carr de Madrid 118, Sant Just Desvern, Barcelona, Spain

OPTICAL COATING LAB INC (OCLI)   2789 Northpoint Pkwy, Santa Rosa,
  CA 95407-7397, Tel: (707) 545-6440
  (Mfr thin film precision coated optical devices)
    OCLI Optical Coatings Espana SA, Antonio Vincent 23, plano 2, 28019 Madrid, Spain

ORACLE CORP   500 Oracle Parkway, Redwood Shores, CA 94065,
  Tel: (415) 506-7000
  (Develop/mfr software)
    Oracle Iberica, Gobelos 33, La Florida, 28023 Madrid, Spain

OSCAR MAYER & CO   PO Box 7188, Madison, WI 53707, Tel: (608) 241-3311
  (Meat & food prdts)
    Oscar Mayer SA, Aptdo. 21, Torrente, Valencia, Spain

OTIS ELEVATOR CO   10 Farm Springs, Farmington, CT 06032, Tel: (860) 676-6528
  (Mfr elevators & escalators)
    Zardoya Otis SA, Plaza del Liceo 3, Parque Conde de Orgaz, 28043 Madrid, Spain

OWENS-CORNING FIBERGLAS CORP   Fiberglas Tower, Toledo, OH 43659,
  Tel: (419) 248-8000
  (Mfr insulation, building materials, glass fiber prdts)
    Owens-Corning Fiberglas Espana SA, Barcelona, Spain

PACIFIC TELESIS GROUP   130 Kearney St, San Francisco, CA 94108,
  Tel: (415) 394-3000
  (Telecommun & info sys)
    Pacific Telesis Iberica SA, Torres de Jerez 1, Plaza de Colon 2, 28046 Madrid, Spain

PACKAGING CORP OF AMERICA   1603 Orrington Ave, Evanston, IL 60201-3853,
  Tel: (708) 492-5713
  (Mfr custom packaging, aluminum & plastic molded fibre, corrugated containers)
    Omni-Pac Embalajes SA, Carretera de Irun, Km. 6, Arre (Navarra), Spain

PANDUIT CORP   17301 Ridgeland Ave, Tinley Park, IL 60477-0981,
  Tel: (708) 532-1800
  (Mfr elec/electr wiring comps)
    Panduit Corp., Del Ferrers Pje., Particular Nave 3, Aptdo. 195,
      08184 Palau de Plegamans, Barcelona, Spain

PANELFOLD INC   10700 NW 36th Ave, Miami, FL 33167, Tel: (305) 688-3501
  (Mfr folding doors & partitions, operable & relocatable partition sys)
    Panelfold Doors SA, Alemania 36-38, 08201 Sabadell (Barcelona), Spain

PARKER HANNIFIN CORP   17325 Euclid Ave, Cleveland, OH 44112,
  Tel: (216) 531-3000
  (Mfr motion-control prdts)
    Parker Hannifin Espana SA, Parque Industrial Las Monjas, Calle de las Estacions 8,
      28850 Torrejon de Ardoz, Madrid, Spain

PEER INTERNATIONAL CORP   810 Seventh Ave, New York, NY 10019,
  Tel: (212) 265-3910
  (Music publishers)
    Southern Music Espanola SA, Hortaleza 18, Atico, 28004 Madrid, Spain

PEPSICO INC   700 Anderson Hill Rd, Purchase, NY 10577-1444,
  Tel: (914) 253-2000
  (Beverages, snack foods, restaurants)
    Compania de Bebides PepsiCo SA, Spain
    Kas SA, Spain
    Pepsi-Cola de Espana SA, Spain
    Pizza Hut de Espana SA, Spain
    Pizza Management de Espana SA, Spain
    Restaurant Associates SA, Spain

PETROLITE CORP   369 Marshall Ave, St Louis, MO 63119-1897,
  Tel: (314) 961-3500
  (Mfr/prod spec chem treating programs, performance-enhancing additives & related
  equip & svces)
    Petrolite Iberica SA, Marques de Urquijo 10, 28008 Madrid, Spain

PFIZER INC   235 E 42nd St, New York, NY 10017-5755, Tel: (212) 573-2323
  (Mfr healthcare products)
    Bioquimica Industrial Espanola SA (BINESA), Spain
    Howmedica Faimon Sa, Spain

(cont)

Howmedica Iberica SA, Spain
Pfizer SA, Spain

PHELPS DODGE CORP   2600 N Central Ave, Phoenix, AZ 85004-3014,
  Tel: (602) 234-8100
  (Copper, minerals, metals & spec engineered prdts for trans & elect mkts)
    Columbian Chemicals Co., Spain

PHILLIPS PETROLEUM CO   Phillips Bldg, Bartlesville, OK 74004,
  Tel: (918) 661-6600
  (Crude oil, natural gas, liquefied petroleum gas, gasoline & petro-chems)
    Calatrava, Empresa para la Industria Petroquimica, Ctan Haya 1, Madrid, Spain
    Phillips Calatrava Ventas SA, Aptdo. 50687, Madrid, Spain
    Phillips Calatrava Ventas SA, Balmes 193, Barcelona, Spain
    Plasticos Vanguardia SA, Carretera Villaverde Vallecas S/N, Madrid, Spain

PIONEER HI-BRED INTL INC   700 Capital Sq, 400 Locust St, Des Moines,
  IA 50309, Tel: (515) 245-3500
  (Agricultural chemicals, farm supplies, biological prdts, research)
    Semillas Pioneer SA, Ctra Sevilla A Cazalla, Km. 9.4, 41309 La Rinconada, Spain

PLAYTEX APPAREL INC   700 Fairfield Ave, Stamford, CT 06904,
  Tel: (203) 356-8000
  (Mfr intimate apparel)
    Playtex Espana SA, Paseo de la Castellana 93, 28046 Madrid, Spain
    Playtex Espana SA, Carretera de Sabadel S/N, 08211 Castellar del Valles, Spain

PLIBRICO CO   1800 Kingsbury St, Chicago, IL 60614, Tel: (312) 549-7014
  (Refractories, engineering, constr)
    Plibrico Espana SA, Aptdo. 4050, Gijon, Spain

POLICY MANAGEMENT SYS CORP   PO Box 10, Columbia, SC 29202,
  Tel: (803) 735-4000
  (Computer software, insurance industry support services)
    PMSE Spain, Paseo de la Castellana 93, piso 4, 20846 Madrid, Spain

POWER TECHNOLOGIES INC   1482 Erie Blvd, PO Box 1058, Schenectady, NY 12301,
  Tel: (518) 395-5000
  (Power sys engineering, consulting, services & related control software; power
  quality hdwe)
    CIDESPA, Bravo Murilla 203, 2802 Madrid, Spain

POWER-PACKER   12801 W Silver Spring Rd, Butler, WI 53007, Tel: (414) 781-5000
  (Mfr OEM hydraulic sys)
    Power-Packer Espana SA, Aptdo. 27, Carretera Toledo, Avila Km. 27.040,
      45500 Torrijos, Spain

PPG INDUSTRIES   One PPG Place, Pittsburgh, PA 15272, Tel: (412) 434-3131
  (Mfr flat glass, fiber glass, chems, coatings)
    PPG Iberica SA, Aptdo 22, Carretera Garcia Manresa Km. 19.2,
      08191 Rubi (Barcelona), Spain

PRECISION VALVE CORP   PO Box 309, Yonkers, NY 10702, Tel: (914) 969-6500
  (Mfr aerosol valves)
    Valvulas de Precision Espanola SA, Montesa 35, 28006 Madrid, Spain

PREMARK INTL INC   1717 Deerfield Rd, Deerfield, IL 60015, Tel: (708) 405-6000
(Mfr/sale diversified consumer & coml prdts)
   Dart Iberica SA, Aptdo. 203, 28100 Alcobendas, Madrid, Spain
   Tupperware Iberica SA, Aptdo. 203, 28100 Alcobendas, Madrid, Spain

PRINCIPAL INTL INC   711 High St, Des Moines, IA 50392-9950,
   Tel: (515) 247-5013
(Insurance)
   Grupo Financiero Principal SA de Seguros de Vida, c/o Alcaia Galiono 4,
      28010 Madrid, Spain

PROCTER & GAMBLE CO   One Procter & Gamble Plaza, Cincinnati, OH 45202,
   Tel: (513) 983-1100
(Personal care, food, laundry, cleaning & ind prdts)
   Procter & Gamble Espana SA, Avda. Meridiana 354, Barcelona, Spain
   Procter & Gamble Espanola SA, Jose Lazaro Galdiano 6, Madrid, Spain

PUROLATOR COURIER CORP   3240 Hillview Ave, Palo Alto, CA 94304,
   Tel: (415) 494-2900
(Time-sensitive package delivery)
   Executive Air Express, 28007 Madrid, Spain

QUAKER CHEMICAL CORP   Elm & Lee Sts, Conshohocken, PA 19428-0809,
   Tel: (610) 832-4000
(Mfr chem specialties; total fluid mgmt services)
   Quaker Quimica Espanola SA, Aptdo. 22, Santa Perpetua de Mogoda, Barcelona, Spain

QUIGLEY CO INC   235 E 42nd St, New York, NY 10017, Tel: (212) 573-3444
(Mfr refractory specs, application equip)
   Quigley Div., Aptdo. 600, 28080 Madrid, Spain

RALSTON PURINA CO   Checkerboard Sq, St Louis, MO 63164, Tel: (314) 982-1000
(Poultry & live stock feed, cereals, food prdts)
   Gallina Blanca Purina SA, Paseo San Juan 189-6, 08037 Barcelona, Spain

RAMSEY TECHNOLOGY INC   501 90th Ave NW, Minneapolis, MN 55433,
   Tel: (612) 783-2500
(Mfr in-motion weighing, inspection, monitoring & control equip for the process inds)
   Ramsey Ingenieros SA, Guzman El Bueno 12, 28100 Alcobendas (Madrid), Spain

RANSBURG CORP   3939 W 56th St, Indianapolis, IN 46208, Tel: (317) 298-5000
(Mfr electrostatic coating sys)
   Ransburg-Gema SA, Paseo de la Castellana 179, 28046 Madrid, Spain
   Ransburg-Gema SA, Edificio Torre de Cataluna, Desp. 1503, Avda. Roma 2 y 4,
      08014 Barcelona, Spain

RAYCHEM CORP   300 Constitution Dr, Menlo Park, CA 94025, Tel: (415) 361-3333
(Devel/mfr/mkt materials science products for electronics, telecommunications &
industry)
   Raychem SA, Ctra. Antigua Francia, Km. 15.100, Place Alcobendas, Alcobendas,
      Madrid, Spain
   Raynet-Spain, Ctra. Antigua Francia, Km. 15.100, Place Alcobendas, Alcobendas,
      Madrid, Spain

RECOGNITION EQUIPMENT INC   PO Box 660204, Dallas, TX 75266-0204,
   Tel: (214) 579-6000
(Mfr hi-perf document recognition sys, image & workflow software; related customer

(cont)

serv)
    Recognition Equipment Iberica SA, Paseo Castellana 45, 28046 Madrid, Spain

REEBOK INTL LTD   100 Technology Center Dr, Stoughton, MA 02072,
    Tel: (617) 341-5000
    (Mfr footwear & apparel)
    Reebok Leisure SA, c/Antonio Machado 86, 03201 Elche, Alicante, Spain

REVLON INC   625 Madison Ave, New York, NY 10022, Tel: (212) 527-4000
    (Mfr cosmetics, fragrances, toiletries, beauty care prdts)
    Haugron Cientifical SA, Spain
    Henry Cokmer SA, Spain
    Productos Cosmeticos Revlon, Camino Burgos S/N, Madrid, Spain

RHONE-POULENC RORER INC   PO Box 1200, Collegeville, PA 19426-0107,
    Tel: (215) 454-8000
    (R&D/mfr human pharmaceuticals)
    Rorer Iberica SA, Madrid, Spain

RJR NABISCO INC   1301 Ave of the Americas, New York, NY 10019,
    Tel: (212) 258-5600
    (Mfr consumer packaged food prdts & tobacco prdts)
    R.J. Reynolds Tobacco Espana SA, Marques de Villamagna 6-8, 28001 Madrid, Spain

ROCKWELL INTL CORP   2201 Seal Beach Blvd, PO Box 4250, Seal Beach,
    CA 90740-8250, Tel: (310) 797-3311
    (Prdts & serv for aerospace, automotive, electronics, graphics & automation inds)
    Allen-Bradley (Espana) SA, Sector Foresta 40, 28760 Tres Cantos (Madrid), Spain
    Allen-Bradley (Espana) SA, also in l'Hospitalet de Llobregat (Barcelona),
       Las Arenas-Getxo (Vizcaya) & Valencia, Spain
    ROR Rockwell Espana SA, Ctra. de Granollers a Sabadell Km. 13.3,
       Poligono Argelagues, 08185 Llissa de Vall, Spain
    Rockwell Automotive Body Systems Espana SA, Dr. Robert 13,
       08460 Santa Maria de Palautordera, Barcelona, Spain

ROHM AND HAAS CO   100 Independence Mall West, Philadelphia, PA 19106,
    Tel: (215) 592-3000
    (Mfr ind & agric chems, plastics)
    Rohm and Haas Espana SA, Provenza 216, 08036 Barcelona, Spain

RUSSELL REYNOLDS ASSOCIATES INC   200 Park Ave, New York, NY 10166,
    Tel: (212) 351-2000
    (Exec recruiting services)
    Russell Reynolds Associates Inc., Castellana 51, 28046 Madrid, Spain
    Russell Reynolds Associates Inc., Diputacion 246, Atico, 08007 Barcelona, Spain

RUSSIN & VECCHI   1140 Connecticut Ave, #250, Washington, DC 20036,
    Tel: (202) 223-4793
    (Lawyers)
    Russin Vecchi & Francisco Iglesias, Paseo de la Castellana 156, Piso 6,
       28046 Madrid, Spain

SAFETY-KLEEN CORP   777 Big Timber Rd, Elgin, IL 60123, Tel: (708) 697-8460
    (Solvent based parts cleaning serv, sludge/solvent recycling serv)
    CODI SA/Safety-Kleen Spain, Agustin de Foxa 25, 28036 Madrid, Spain

SARA LEE CORP   3 First National Plaza, Chicago, IL 60602-4260,
  Tel: (312) 726-2600
  (Mfr/distr food & consumer packaged goods, tobacco prdts, intimate apparel & knitwear)
    Grupo SA Sans, Carretera Cirera sn, Apartado 80, 08300 Mataro, Spain
    Playtex Espana SA, Paseo de la Castellana 93, 28046 Madrid, Spain

SCHLEGEL CORP   1555 Jefferson Rd, PO Box 23197, Rochester, NY 14692-3197,
  Tel: (716) 427-7200
  (Mfr engineered perimeter sealing systems for residential & commercial constr)
    Perfiles del Automovil SA, San Fernando s/n, Apartado 7, 08940 Cornella, Barcelona,
      Spain
    Permolca SA, Poligono Industrial La Portalada, Barrio de Varea, 26006 Logrono, Spain
    Schlegel SA/Taliana Div., Pol. Industrial Santa Margarida, Vial 3, c/Anoia 9,
      08223 Terrassa, Barcelona, Spain

SEA-LAND SERVICE INC   150 Allen Rd, Liberty Corner, NJ 07920,
  Tel: (201) 558-6000
  (Container transport)
    Naviera del Odiel SA, Alcala Galiano 3 Primero, 28004 Madrid, Spain
    Naviera del Odiel SA, other locations in Spain

SEALED AIR CORP   Park 80 Plaza E, Saddle Brook, NJ 07662-5291,
  Tel: (201) 791-7600
  (Mfr protective packaging prdts)
    Plastec Iberica SA, Calle Hostal del Pi, S/N, Poligono Industrial Barcelones,
      Abrerea (Barcelona), Spain

G D SEARLE & CO   5200 Old Orchard Rd, Skokie, IL 60077, Tel: (708) 982-7000
  (Mfr pharms, health care & optical prdts, specialty chems)
    Searle Iberica SA, La Granja 23, Poligono Industrial Alcobendas, 14478 Madrid, Spain

SEARS ROEBUCK & CO   Sears Tower, Chicago, IL 60684, Tel: (312) 875-2500
  (Diversified general merchandise)
    Sears Roebuck & Co., Paseo de la Castellana 86, 28006 Madrid, Spain
    Sears, Roebuck de Espana SA, Avda. Glmo. Franco 471-473, Barcelona, Spain

SENSORMATIC ELECTRONICS CORP   500 NW 12th Ave, Deerfield Beach, FL 33341,
  Tel: (305) 427-9700
  (Electronic article surveillance equip)
    Sensormatic Electronics Corp., Calle Velazquez 138, 28006 Madrid, Spain

SHARED MEDICAL SYSTEMS CORP   51 Valley Stream Pkwy, Malvern, PA 19355,
  Tel: (215) 219-6300
  (Computer-based info processing for healthcare ind)
    SMS Spain, Capital Haya 60, 28043 Madrid, Spain

SIGNODE PACKAGING SYSTEMS   3600 W Lake Ave, Glenview, IL 60025,
  Tel: (708) 724-6100
  (Mfr packaging systems)
    Signode Spain, Poligono Industrial El Bellots, Av. del Valles 320,
      08227 Terrassa (Barcelona), Spain

SONOCO PRODUCTS CO   North Second St, PO Box 160, Hartsville, SC 29550,
  Tel: (803) 383-7000
  (Mfr packaging for consumer & ind mkt)
    Sonoco Espana, Extremadure 2, Aptdo. 170, Poligono Ind. Fonoillar,
      Sant Boi de Llogregat, Barcelona, Spain

SPI PHARMACEUTICALS INC   ICN Plaza, 3300 Hyland Ave, Costa Mesa, CA 92626,
  Tel: (714) 545-0100
  (Mfr pharms, biochems, radioactive materials)
    ICN Hubber SA, Casanoja 27-31, 08757 Barcelona, Spain

SPS TECHNOLOGIES INC   301 Highland Ave, Jenkintown, PA 19046-2630,
  Tel: (215) 572-3000
  (Mfr aerospace & ind fasteners, tightening sys, magnetic materials, superalloys)
    Ferre Plana SA, Mosen Jacint Verdaguer 67-69, Poligano Ind. Fontsanta,
      08970 Sant Joan Despi, Barcelona, Spain

SPX CORP   700 Terrace Point Dr, PO Box 3301, Muskegon, MI 49443-3301,
  Tel: (616) 724-5000
  (Mfr spec service tools, engine & drive-train parts)
    Kent-Moore & Euroline, Poligono Industrial del Henares, (Ampliacion) Parcele 58,
      19080 Guadalajara, Spain
    Robinair Spain, c/o SPX Iberica SA, Aptdo. de Correos 295, 19880 Guadalajara, Spain
    SPX Iberica, Poligono Industrial del Henares, (Ampliacion) Parecle 58,
      19080 Guadalajara, Spain

STANDARD OIL CO OF CALIFORNIA   225 Bush St, San Francisco, CA 94104,
  Tel: (415) 894-7700
  (Oil explor & prod, petroleum prdts)
    California Oil Co. of Spain, Frapiles 13, 28015 Madrid, Spain

STANDEX INTL CORP   6 Manor Pkwy, Salem, NH 03079, Tel: (603) 893-9701
  (Mfr diversified graphics, institutional, ind/electr & consumer prdts)
    Standex Intl. SA, Calle Chromo 114, Hospitalet (Barcelona), Spain
    Standex Intl. SA, Carretera del Medio 25, Hospitalet (Barcelona), Spain

STEINER CORP   505 E South Temple St, Salt Lake City, UT 84102,
  Tel: (801) 328-8831
  (Linen supply service)
    Steiner/Thoban Spain, San Mariano 109, 28022 Madrid, Spain

STIEFEL LABORATORIES INC   255 Alhambra Circle, Coral Gables, FL 33134,
  Tel: (305) 443-3807
  (Mfr pharmaceuticals, dermatological specialties)
    Laboratorios Stiefel (Espana) SA, Soledad 47, 28330 San Martin de la Vega, Madrid,
      Spain

TECHNICON INSTRUMENTS CORP   511 Benedict Ave, Tarrytown, NY 10591-5097,
  Tel: (914) 631-8000
  (Mfr/serv automated blook anal equip, reagents & diagnostics)
    Technicon Espana SA, Llanos de Jerez 2, Poligano Industrial, Coslada (Madrid), Spain

TEKTRONIX INC   26660 SW Parkway, Wilsonville, OR 97070, Tel: (503) 627-7111
  (Mfr test & meas, visual sys & commun prdts)
    Tektronix Espanola SA, Madrid, Barcelona & Bilbao, Spain

TELEDYNE INC   2049 Century Park East, Los Angeles, CA 90067-3101,
  Tel: (310) 277-3311
  (Divers mfg: aviation & electronics, specialty metals, industrial & consumer prdts)
    Teledyne Spain, Pedro de Valdivia 10, Bajo DCHA, 28006 Madrid, Spain

TELLABS INC   4951 Indiana Ave, Lisle, IL 60532, Tel: (708) 969-8800
  (Design/mfr/svce voice/data transport & network access sys)
    Tellabs Inc., Barcelona, Spain

TELXON CORP   3330 W Market St, PO Box 5582, Akron, OH 44334-0582,
  Tel: (216) 867-3700
  (Devel/mfr portable computer sys & related equip)
    Telxon Corp. Systems Espana SA, Golfo de Salonica 27 1A, 28033 Madrid, Spain

TENNECO AUTOMOTIVE   111 Pfingsten Rd, Deerfield, IL 60015,
  Tel: (708) 948-0900
  (Automotive parts, exhaust sys, service equip)
    Monroe Espana Planta de Gijon, Alto de Pumarin S/N, 33211 Gijon, Spain
    Monroe Espana SA, Avda. Vizcaya S/N, Aptdo. 27, Ermua, Spain
    Monroe Espana SA, Av. Valdelaparra 17, Aptdo. 352, Poligono Industrial,
      18200 Alcobendas, Madrid, Spain

TENNECO INC   PO Box 2511, Houston, TX 77252-2511, Tel: (713) 757-2131
  (Natural gas pipelines, shipbuilding & repair, construction & farm equip, chemicals,
  packaging)
    Monroe Espana (Gijon), Alto de Pumarin F/N, Aptdo. de Correos 87, 33211 Gijon, Spain
    Monroe Espana SA, Avda. Vizcaya S/N, Aptdo. 27, Ermua, Vizcaya, Spain
    Poclain Hispana SA, Avda. Jose Garate 11, Coslada, 28017 Madrid, Spain
    Poclain Hispana SA, other locations in Spain

TEXTRON INC   40 Westminster St, Providence, RI 02903, Tel: (401) 421-2800
  (Mfr aerospace, ind & consumer prdts; fin servs)
    Bostitch Espanola SA, Velazquez 75, 28006 Madrid, Spain

THOMAS & BETTS CORP   1555 Lynnfield Rd, Memphis, TN 38119,
  Tel: (901) 682-7766
  (Mfr elect/electr connectors & accessories)
    T & B Spain, Pallars 65-71, 08018 Barcelona, Spain

THE TIMBERLAND CO   200 Domain Dr, Stratham, NH 03885, Tel: (603) 772-9500
  (Design/mfr footwear, apparel & accessories for men & women)
    Timberland Espana SA, Tuset 30, Piso 7 #3A, 08006 Barcelona, Spain

TOWERS PERRIN   245 Park Ave, New York, NY 10167, Tel: (212) 309-3400
  (Management consultants)
    Towers, Perrin, Forster & Crosby, Suero de Quinones 40-42, Quinta Planta,
      28002 Madrid, Spain

TOYS R US INC   461 From Rd, Paramus, NJ 07652, Tel: (201) 262-7800
  (Retail stores: toys & games, sporting goods, computer software, books, records)
    Toys R Us Iberia SA, Poligono Ind. Alcala Oeste, Alcala de Henares, 28812 Madrid,
      Spain

TRANE CO   3600 Pammel Creek Rd, La Crosse, WI 54601, Tel: (608) 787-2000
  (Mfr/distr/svce A/C sys & equip)
    Trane Espanola SA, C/Turo Blau 19-21, 08016 Barcelona, Spain
    Trane Espanola SA, PAE Neisa-Sur, Avda. de Andalucia Km. 10,500, 28021 Madrid, Spain
    Trane Espanola SA, PISA C/Horizonte 7, Nave 16, 41927 Mairena del Aljarafe, Spain
    Trane Espanola SA, C/Selva de Mar 140, 08020 Barcelona, Spain

TRANS WORLD AIRLINES INC   505 N 6th St, St Louis, MO 63101,
Tel: (314) 589-3000
(Air transportation)
   Trans World Airlines Inc., Paseo de Gracia 55-57, Barcelona, Spain
   Trans World Airlines, Inc., Plaza de Colon 2, Torres de Colon, Madrid, Spain

TRANTER INC   1054 Claussen Rd, #314, Augusta, GA 30907, Tel: (706) 738-7900
(Mfr heat exchangers)
   SWEP Iberica, Travessera de Gr coa 62 ent. 6, 08006 Barcelona, Spain

TRINOVA CORP   3000 Strayer, PO Box 50, Maumee, OH 43537-0050,
Tel: (419) 867-2200
(Mfr engr components & sys for ind)
   Aeroquip Iberica SA, Carreterra Alcala de Henares, Km 31.700, Madrid, Spain

TRW INC   1900 Richmond Rd, Cleveland, OH 44124, Tel: (216) 291-7000
(Electr & energy-related prdts, automotive & aerospace prdts, tools & fasteners)
   TRW Systems Overseas, Pedro Teixeira 8, 28020 Madrid, Spain
   TRW Systems Overseas, other locations in Spain

TWIN DISC INC   1328 Racine St, Racine, WI 53403-1758, Tel: (414) 638-4000
(Mfr ind clutches, reduction gears, transmissions)
   Twin Disc Spain SA, Poligono Industrial La Mina, Nave 61, 28770 Colmenar Viejo,
      Madrid, Spain

U S INDUSTRIES INC   PO Box 629, Evansville, IN 47704, Tel: (812) 425-2428
(Diversified prdts & sys for industry, agribusiness & retail markets)
   Big Dutchman Iberica SA, Aptdo. 374, Carretera de Salou Km 4, Reus, Tarragona, Spain

U S PLAYING CARD CO   Beech St at Park Ave, Cincinnati, OH 45212,
Tel: (513) 396-5700
(Mfr playing cards & accessories, board games)
   Fournier SA, Spain

U S SURGICAL CORP   150 Glover Ave, Norwalk, CT 06856, Tel: (203) 845-1000
(Mfr/devel/mkt surgical staplers, laparoscopic instru & sutures)
   Auto Suture Espana SA, all mail to U.S. address

UNION CAMP CORP   1600 Valley Rd, Wayne, NJ 07470, Tel: (201) 628-2000
(Mfr paper, packaging, chems, wood prdts)
   Bush Boake Allen Espana SA, c/o Baimes, 114, 3 Local A, 08008 Barcelona, Spain
   Cartonajes Union SA, Avda. del Brasil 7-6, Edificio Iberia Mart, 28020 Madrid, Spain
   Cartonera Canaria, Sucursal de Cartonjes Union SA, Aptdo. 445,
      Las Palmas de Gran Canaria, Spain

UNION CARBIDE CORP   39 Old Ridgebury Rd, Danbury, CT 06817,
Tel: (203) 794-2000
(Mfr industrial chemicals, plastics, resins)
   Union Carbide Chemicals Iberica SA, Josep Irla I Bosch 1-3, 08034 Barcelona, Spain

UNIROYAL INC   World Headquarters, Middlebury, CT 06749, Tel: (203) 573-2000
(Tires, tubes & other rubber prdts, chems, plastics, textiles)
   Uniroyal Espana SA, Jose Sanchez Saez 9, Alicante, Spain

UNISYS CORP   PO Box 500, Blue Bell, PA 19424, Tel: (215) 986-4011
  (Mfg/mktg/serv electr info sys)
    Sperry SA, Polig. Z.I. Franca CD/SV, 08004 Barcelona, Spain
    Unisys Espana SA, Martinez Villergas 52, 28027 Madrid, Spain

UNITED TECHNOLOGIES CORP   United Technologies Bldg, Hartford, CT 06101,
  Tel: (203) 728-7000
  (Mfr aircraft engines, elevators, A/C, auto equip, space & military electr, rocket
  propulsion sys)
    Zardoya Otis SA, Plaza del Liceo, Parque Conde de Orgaz, 28033 Madrid, Spain
    Zardoya Otis SA, other locations in Spain

UPJOHN CO   7000 Portage Rd, Kalamazoo, MI 49001, Tel: (616) 323-4000
  (Mfr pharms, agric prdts, ind chems)
    Laboratories Upjohn SA, Avda. Generalisimo 110, Madrid, Spain

VALENITE INC   PO Box 9636, Madison Heights, MI 48071-9636,
  Tel: (810) 589-1000
  (Cemented carbide, high speed steel, ceramic & diamond cutting tool prdts, etc)
    Valenite Inc., C/Alcarria 7, Poligono Industrial, 28820 Coslada (Madrid), Spain

VALMONT INDUSTRIES INC   One Valmont Pkwy, PO Box 358, Valley, NE 68064-0358,
  Tel: (402) 359-2201
  (Mfr irrigation sys, steel lighting, utility & communication poles)
    Valmont SA, Ctra. de Mejorada del Campo, Velilla de San Antonio Km. 0.64,
      28840 Mejorada del Campo (M), Spain

VENDO CO   7209 N Ingram, Pinedale, CA 93650, Tel: (209) 439-1770
  (Mfr coin-op automatic vending machs)
    Vendo, Calle de la Reina Victoria 22, 08021 Barcelona, Spain

VOLT INFORMATION SCIENCES INC   1221 Sixth Ave, 47th fl, New York,
  NY 10020-1001, Tel: (212) 704-2400
  (Computerized publishing, telecommunications & computer systems & services)
    Autologic Intl. Ltd., Gran Via de las Corts Catalanes 774, Barcelona, Spain

WARD HOWELL INTL INC   99 Park Ave, New York, NY 10016-1699,
  Tel: (212) 697-3730
  (Executive recruiting)
    Ward Howell Executive Search, Ferran Agullo 18, 08021 Barcelona, Spain
    Ward Howell Executive Search, Fernandez de la Hoz 53, 28003 Madrid, Spain

WARNER BROS INTL TELEVISION DISTRIBUTION   4000 Warner Blvd, Burbank,
  CA 91522, Tel: (818) 954-4068
  (Distr TV programming & theatrical features)
    Warner Bros. Intl. Television, Juan de Mena 10, 28014 Madrid, Spain

WARNER-LAMBERT CO   201 Tabor Road, Morris Plains, NJ 07950,
  Tel: (201) 540-2000
  (Mfr ethical & proprietary pharms, confectionary & consumer prdts)
    Laboratorio Substancia SA, Aptdo. 4, Prat de Llobergat, Barcelona, Spain

WATERS CHROMATOGRAPHY DIV   34 Maple St, Milford, MA 01757,
  Tel: (617) 478-2000
  (Mfr/distr liquid chromatographic instru/accessories/tech)
    Millipore Iberica SA, Etenza 28-30 Entlo., 08015 Barcelona, Spain

WATTS INDUSTRIES INC   815 Chestnut St, North Andover, MA 01845,
  Tel: (508) 688-1811
  (Mfr ind valves & safety control prdts)
    GRC Controls SA, Poligono Industrial Cros. Nare N.3, c/Julio Galvez Brusson S/N,
      089 Badalona (Barcelona), Spain

THE WEST CO   101 Gordon Dr, PO Box 645, Lionville, PA 19341-0645,
  Tel: (610) 594-2900
  (Mfr prdts for filling, sealing, dispensing & delivering needs of health care &
  consumer prdts mkts)
    West Rubber de Espana SA, San Fernando de Henares, Spain

WHEELABRATOR CLEAN WATER INC, HPD DIV   55 Shuman Blvd, Naperville, IL 60563,
  Tel: (708) 357-7330
  (Technical design & service process systems)
    Wheelabrator HPD PSS SA, Avda. Neguri 9, 48990 Guecho-Vizcaya, Spain

WINCHESTER ELECTRONICS   400 Park Rd, Watertown, CT 06795-0500,
  Tel: (203) 945-5000
  (Mfr elec & electr connectors, PCB assemblies & hardware)
    Litton Precision Products Intl. Inc., Condes de Val 8, 28036 Madrid, Spain

WITCO CORP   1 American Lane, Greenwich, CT 06831-4236, Tel: (203) 552-2000
  (Mfr chem & petroleum prdts)
    Witco Espana SL, Mendez Alvaro 55, 28045 Madrid, Spain
    Witco Espana SL, Poligono Industrial de Congost, Avda. Sant Julia s/n,
      08400 Granollers, Barcelona, Spain

WMX TECHNOLOGIES INC   3003 Butterfield Rd, Oak Brook, IL 60563,
  Tel: (708) 572-8800
  (Environmental services)
    Waste Management Espana, Saneamientos Sellberg SA, Gran Via 61, piso s6,
      28013 Madrid, Spain

WORLD COURIER INC   46 Trinity Pl, New York, NY 10006, Tel: (718) 978-9400
  (Intl courier serv)
    World Courier de Espana SA, Calle Pedro Teixera, Madrid, Spain

WM WRIGLEY JR CO   410 N Michigan Ave, Chicago, IL 60611-4287,
  Tel: (312) 644-2121
  (Mfr chewing gum)
    Wrigley Co. SA, Apdo. Correos 1014, Santa Cruz de Tenerife, Canarias, Spain

XEROX CORP   800 Long Ridge Rd, PO Box 1600, Stamford, CT 06904,
  Tel: (203) 968-3000
  (Mfr document processing equip, sys & supplies)
    Xerox Corp., Barcelona, Coslada, Madrid & Seville, Spain

YOUNG & RUBICAM INC   285 Madison Ave, New York, NY 10017, Tel: (212) 210-3000
  (Advertising, public relations, direct marketing & sales promotion, corp & product ID
  management)
    Young & Rubicam Espana SA, Edificio Windsor, 28003 Madrid, Spain

SRI LANKA

3M   3M Center, St Paul, MN 55144-1000, Tel: (612) 733-1110
(Mfr diversified prdts for industry, health care, imaging, commun, transport, safety, consumer, etc)
   3M Lanka Pvt. Ltd., Valiant Towers 8/F, 46/8 Nawam Mawatha, P.O. Box 1713, Colombo 2, Sri Lanka

ASSOCIATED MERCHANDISING CORP   1440 Broadway, New York, NY 10018,
Tel: (212) 536-4000
(Retail service organization)
   Associated Merchandising Corp., 45 Rosmead Pl., Colombo 7, Sri Lanka

SAMUEL BINGHAM CO   1555 N Mittel Blvd, #T, Wood Dale, IL 60191-1046,
Tel: (708) 238-4000
(Print & industrial rollers, inks)
   Coates Brothers (Sri Lanka) Ltd., 142 Kaluwana Industrial Estate, Homagama, Sri Lanka

CH2M HILL INC   PO Box 428, Corvallis, OR 97339, Tel: (503) 752-4271
(Consulting engrs, planners, economists, scientists)
   CH2M Hill Inc., 44 Galle Rd., Colombo 3, Sri Lanka

CITICORP   399 Park Ave, New York, NY 10043, Tel: (212) 559-1000
(Banking & financial services)
   Citibank NA, Sri Lanka

CPC INTERNATIONAL INC   PO Box 8000, Englewood Cliffs, NJ 07632,
Tel: (201) 894-4000
(Consumer foods, corn refining)
   CPC (Lanka) Ltd., 17 R.A. de Mel Mawatha, Colombo, Sri Lanka

EXPEDITORS INTL OF WASHINGTON INC   PO Box 69620, Seattle, WA 98168-9620,
Tel: (206) 246-3711
(Air/ocean freight forwarding, customs brokerage, intl logistics solutions)
   EI Freight Lanka (Pte.) Ltd., 56/3 Justice Akbar Mawatha, Colombo 2, Sri Lanka

FISHER CONTROLS INTL INC   8000 Maryland Ave, Clayton, MO 63105,
Tel: (314) 746-9900
(Mfr ind process control equip)
   Environmental Laboratories Ltd., 135/1 Old Kottawa Rd., Nawinna, P.O. Box 14, Maharaganma, Sri Lanka

FRITZ COMPANIES INC   706 Mission St, San Francisco, CA 94103,
Tel: (415) 904-8360
(Integrated transportation, sourcing, distribution & customs brokerage services)
   Fritz Air Freight (Sri Lanka) Ltd., 18/1 Lillie St., Colombo 2, Sri Lanka

GETZ BROS & CO INC   150 Post St, #500, San Francisco, CA 94108,
   Tel: (415) 772-5500
   (Divers mfg, mktg/distr serv, travel serv)
      Muller & Phipps (Ceylon) Ltd., 27-2/1 York Arcade Rd., P.O. Box 117, Colombo,
         Sri Lanka

GTE DIRECTORIES CORP   West Airport Dr, DFW Airport, TX 75261-9810,
   Tel: (214) 453-7000
   (Pub telephone directories)
      GTE Directories Lanka (Pvt) Ltd., The Regent, 345 R.A. de Mel Mn., Colombo 3,
         Sri Lanka

HOLIDAY INNS INC   3742 Lamar Ave, Memphis, TN 38195, Tel: (901) 362-4001
   (Hotels, restaurants, casinos)
      Holiday Inn, Mohamed Macan Markar Mawatha, Colombo 3, Sri Lanka

HORWATH INTL   415 Madison Ave, New York, NY 10017, Tel: (212) 838-5566
   (Public accountants & auditors)
      Manoharan & Sangakkara, 74 1/1 Park St., Colombo 2, Sri Lanka

MULLER & PHIPPS INTL CORP   Box 3994, San Francisco, CA 94119,
   Tel: (415) 772-5650
   (General merchandise)
      Muller & Phipps Ltd., Chartered Bank Bldg., P.O. Box 117, Queen St., Colombo,
         Sri Lanka

OTIS ELEVATOR CO   10 Farm Springs, Farmington, CT 06032, Tel: (860) 676-6528
   (Mfr elevators & escalators)
      Elevators Pte. Ltd., 2/F, 228 Galle Rd., Colombo 4, Sri Lanka

PARSONS ENGINEERING SCIENCE INC   100 W Walnut St, Pasadena, CA 91124,
   Tel: (818) 440-6000
   (Environmental engineering)
      Parsons Engineering Science Inc., Town East of Colombo Water Supply Project,
         1093 Pannipittiva Rd., Battaramulla, Sri Lanka
      Parsons Engineering Science Inc., 655/12 Elvitigala Mawatha, Colombo 5, Sri Lanka
      Parsons Engineering Science Inc., Sewerage Project, NWSDB Office,
         New Parliament Rd., Battaramulla, Sri Lanka

PFIZER INC   235 E 42nd St, New York, NY 10017-5755, Tel: (212) 573-2323
   (Mfr healthcare products)
      Pfizer Ltd., Sri Lanka

UNION CARBIDE CORP   39 Old Ridgebury Rd, Danbury, CT 06817,
   Tel: (203) 794-2000
   (Mfr industrial chemicals, plastics, resins)
      Union Carbide Lanka Ltd., Red Cross Society Bldg. 1/F, 106 Dharmapala Mawatha,
         Colombo 7, Sri Lanka

SUDAN

AIR EXPRESS INTL CORP   120 Tokeneke Rd, PO Box 1231, Darien, CT 06820,
  Tel: (203) 655-7900
  (Air frt forwarder)
    Air Express Intl., c/o Polytra, P.O. Box 2634, Khartoum, Sudan

AMATEX CORP   1030 Standbridge St, Norristown, PA 19404, Tel: (215) 277-6100
  (Mfr textile, fiberglass prdts)
    Amatex, Port Sudan, Sudan

CHASE MANHATTAN BANK N A   1 Chase Manhattan Plaza, New York, NY 10081,
  Tel: (212) 552-2222
  (Intl banking)
    Chase Manhattan Bank, P.O. Box 2679, Khartoum, Sudan

CITICORP   399 Park Ave, New York, NY 10043, Tel: (212) 559-1000
  (Banking & financial services)
    Citibank NA, Sudan

MOBIL CORP   3225 Gallows Rd, Fairfax, VA 22037-0001, Tel: (703) 846-3000
  (Petroleum explor & refining, mfr petrol prdts, chems, petrochems)
    Mobil Oil Ltd., P.O. Box 283, Khartoum, Sudan

PARKER DRILLING CO   8 E Third St, Tulsa, OK 74103-3637, Tel: (918) 585-8221
  (Drilling contractor)
    Parker Drilling Co. Eastern Hemisphere Ltd., Street 51, House 24, P.O. Box 2421,
      Kartoum, Sudan

SURINAM

ALCOA STEAMSHIP CO INC   1501 Alcoa Bldg, Pittsburgh, PA 15219,
  Tel: (412) 553-4545
  (Ship owners/operators)
    Alcoa Steamship Co. Inc., 55 V.H. Hogerhuysstraat, P.O. Box 1842, Paramaribo,
      Surinam

ALUMINUM CO OF AMERICA (ALCOA)   425 6th Ave, Pittsburgh, PA 15219,
  Tel: (412) 553-4545
  (Aluminum mining, refining, processing, prdts)
    Aluminum Co., Waterkant 28, Paramaribo, Surinam

ITT CORP   1330 Ave of the Americas, New York, NY 10019-5490,
  Tel: (212) 258-1000
  (Design/mfr communications & electronic equip, hotels, insurance)
    Intl. Telephone & Telegraph Co., Industriehal 2, Paramaribo, Surinam

SWEDEN

3COM CORP   5400 Bayfront Plaza, Santa Clara, CA 95052-8145,
  Tel: (408) 764-5000
  (Devel/mfr computer networking prdts & sys)
    3Com Nordic AB, Sweden

3M   3M Center, St Paul, MN 55144-1000, Tel: (612) 733-1110
  (Mfr diversified prdts for industry, health care, imaging, commun, transport, safety,
  consumer, etc)
    3M Svenska AB, Bollstanaesvaegen 3, S-191 89 Sollentuna, Sweden

AAF INTL   215 Central Ave, PO Box 35690, Louisville, KY 40232-5690,
  Tel: (502) 637-0011
  (Mfr air filtration/pollution control & noise control equip)
    IF Luftfilter AB, Industrigatan 6, S-502 60 Boras, Sweden

ACCURAY CORP   650 Ackerman Rd, PO Box 02248, Columbus, OH 43202,
  Tel: (614) 261-2000
  (Computer-based process mgmt sys for forest prdts, metals rolling, textiles, tobacco
  ind)
    Accuray Scandinavia AB, Bergshojden 32, P.O. Box 7102, S-172 07 Sundbyberg, Sweden

ACUFF-ROSE PUBLICATION INC   65 Music Square W, Nashville, TN 37203,
  Tel: (615) 321-5000
  (Music publisher)
    Acuff-Rose Scandia, P.O. Box 3094, S-171 03 Solna, Sweden

AEC INC   801 AEC Drive, Wood Dale, IL 60191, Tel: (708) 595-1090
  (Mfr/serv aux equip for plastics ind)
    AB Ewebe, Odengatan 7, S-593 00 Vastervik, Sweden

AIR EXPRESS INTL CORP   120 Tokeneke Rd, PO Box 1231, Darien, CT 06820,
  Tel: (203) 655-7900
  (Air frt forwarder)

Air Express Intl., c/o AB Olson & Wright, P.O. Box 73, S-190 45 Stockholm, Arlanda, Sweden

ALBANY INTL CORP   PO Box 1907, Albany, NY 12201, Tel: (518) 445-2200
(Paper mach clothing, engineered fabrics, plastic prdts, filtration media)
Nordiskafiltab, P.O. Box 161, S-301 03 Halmstad, Sweden

ALBERTO-CULVER CO   2525 Armitage Ave, Melrose Park, IL 60160,
Tel: (708) 450-3000
(Mfr/mktg personal care & beauty prdts, household & grocery prdts, institutional food prdts)
Cederroth Intl. AB, P.O. Box 715, S-194 27 Upplands-Vasby, Sweden

ALDUS CORP   411 First Ave South, Seattle, WA 98104-2871, Tel: (206) 622-5500
(Devel/mfr computer software)
Aldus Sverige AB, P.O. Box 47, S-164 93 Kista, Sweden

ALLEN-BRADLEY CO   PO Box 2086, Milwaukee, WI 53201, Tel: (414) 382-2000
(Mfr eletrical controls & info devices)
Allen-Bradley AB, Bryggare Bergs Vag 2, P.O. Box 4054, S-182 04 Enebyberg, Sweden

ALLIED AFTERMARKET DIV   105 Pawtucket Ave, East Providence, RI 02916,
Tel: (401) 434-7000
(Mfr spark plugs, filters, brakes)
Fram Europe (Marketing) AB, P.O. Box 84, S-124 21 Bandhagen, Sweden

AMDAHL CORP   1250 E Arques Ave, PO Box 3470, Sunnyvale, CA 94088-3470,
Tel: (408) 746-6000
(Devel/mfr large scale computers, software, data storage prdts, info-technology solutions & support)
Amdahl Svenska AB, Svardvagen 11, P.O. Box 150, S-182 12 Danderyd, Sweden

AMERICAN AIRLINES INC   PO Box 619616, Dallas-Ft Worth Arpt, TX 75261-9616,
Tel: (817) 355-1234
(Air transp)
Scandinavia Finland STC Agencies, P.O. Box 7451, S-103 92 Stockholm, Sweden

AMERICAN EXPRESS CO   World Financial Center, New York, NY 10285-4765,
Tel: (212) 640-2000
(Travel, travelers cheques, charge card & financial services)
American Express Co. AB
American Express Resebyra AB
Amex Services Sweden AB

AMERICAN MANAGEMENT SYSTEMS INC   4050 Legato Rd, Fairfax, VA 22033,
Tel: (703) 267-8000
(Systems integration & consulting)
Nordic Business Management Systems AB, Varmdovagen 84, S-131 34 Nacka, Sweden

AMICON INC   72 Cherry Hill Dr, Beverly, MA 01915, Tel: (508) 777-3622
(Mfr/sale/svce bioseparation, membrane ultrafiltration, chromatography)
W. R. Grace AB, Amicon, P.O. Box 622, S-251 06 Helsinborg, Sweden

AMP INC   PO Box 3608, Harrisburg, PA 17105-3608, Tel: (717) 564-0100
(Devel/mfr electronic & electrical connection prdts & sys)
AMP Svenska AB, Stockholm, Sweden

AMPEX SYSTEMS CORP   401 Broadway, Redwood City, CA 94063-3199,
  Tel: (415) 367-2011
  (Mfr hi-perf helical scanning recording sys & associated tape media)
    Ampex Scandinavia AB, P.O. Box 7056, Rissneleden 8, S-172 07 Sundbyberg, Sweden

AMPHENOL PRODUCTS   1925A Ohio St, Lisle, IL 60532, Tel: (708) 960-1010
  (Elect interconnect/penetrate sys & assemblies)
    Amphenol Scandinavia AB, Kanalvaegen 1, S-194 61 Upplands Vaesby, Sweden

ANALOG DEVICES INC   1 Technology Way, Box 9106, Norwood, MA 02062,
  Tel: (617) 329-4700
  (Mfr integrated circuits & related devices)
    Analog Devices AB, Mariehallsvagen 42, S-161 02 Bromma, Stockholm, Sweden

APPLE COMPUTER INC   1 Infinite Loop, Cupertino, CA 95014, Tel: (408) 996-1010
  (Personal computers, peripherals & software)
    Apple Computer AB, Industrivagen 7, S-171 48 Solna, Sweden

ASARCO INC   180 Maiden Lane, New York, NY 10038, Tel: (212) 510-2000
  (Nonferrous metals, specialty chems, minerals, mfr industrial prdts, environmental
  services)
    Enthone-Omi Inc., Sweden

ASHLAND OIL INC   1000 Ashland Dr, Russell, KY 41169, Tel: (606) 329-3333
  (Petroleum exploration, refining & transportation; mfr chemicals, oils & lubricants)
    Valvoline Sweden AB, Arstaangavagen 11B, Stockholm, Sweden

ASSOCIATED PRESS INC   50 Rockefeller Plaza, New York, NY 10020-1605,
  Tel: (212) 621-1500
  (News gathering agency)
    Associated Press AB, P.O. Box 1726, S-111 87 Stockholm Sweden

AST RESEARCH INC   16215 Alton Parkway, PO Box 19658, Irvine, CA 92713-9658,
  Tel: (714) 727-4141
  (Design/devel/mfr hi-perf desktop, server & notebook computers)
    AST Sweden, P.O. Box 997, S-191 56 Sollentuna, Sweden

AT&T INTERNATIONAL   412 Mt Kemble Ave, Morristown, NJ 07962-1995,
  Tel: (810) 262-6646
  (Telecommunications)
    AT&T Nordics AB, P.O. Box 70363, S-107 24 Stockholm, Sweden

AUGAT INC   89 Forbes Blvd, Mansfield, MA 02048, Tel: (508) 543-4300
  (Interconnection prdts)
    Augat AB, Svatgangen 1-3, S-191 41 Sollentuna, Sweden

AUTO-TROL TECHNOLOGY CORP   12500 N Washington St, Denver, CO 80241-2400,
  Tel: (303) 452-4919
  (Mfr/sale/serv systems integration, CAD/CAM/CAE software)
    Auto-trol Technology AB, Allfarvagen 1-3, S-191 47 Sollentuna, Sweden
    Auto-trol Technology AB, also in Gothenburg & Lund, Sweden

AUTODESK INC   2320 Marinship Way, Sausalito, CA 94965, Tel: (415) 332-2344
  (Devel/mkt/support computer-aided design, engineering, scientific & multimedia
  software prdts)
    Autodesk AB, Molndalsvagen 24, S-400 20 Gothenburg, Sweden

AVERY DENNISON CORP   150 N Orange Grove Blvd, Pasadena, CA 91103,
   Tel: (818) 304-2000
   (Mfr pressure-sensitive adhesives & materials, office prdts, labels, tags, retail
sys, spec chems)
      Fasson AB, Kostergatan 5, S-211 24 Malmo, Sweden

AVNET INC   80 Cutter Mill Rd, Great Neck, NY 11021, Tel: (516) 466-7000
   (Distr electr components, computers & peripherals)
      AB Avnet EMG, Huvudstagatan 1, S-171 27 Solna, Sweden

BAILEY-FISCHER & PORTER CO   125 E County Line Rd, Warminster, PA 18974,
   Tel: (215) 674-6000
   (Design/mfr meas, recording & control instru & sys; mfr ind glass prdts)
      Bailey-Fisher & Porter AB, Malmgardsvagen 16-18, P.O. Box 11124,
        S-100 61 Stockholm, Sweden

BANDAG INC   2905 NW 61, Muscatine, IA 52761, Tel: (319) 262-1400
   (Mfr/sale retread tires)
      Vakuum Vulk AB, Backakersvagen 3A, S-217 63 Malmo, Sweden

BAUSCH & LOMB INC   1 Chase Square, Rochester, NY 14601, Tel: (716) 338-6000
   (Mfr vision care prdts & accessories)
      Bausch & Lomb Svenska AB, Stockholm, Sweden

BAXTER HEALTHCARE CORP   1 Baxter Pky, Deerfield, IL 60015,
   Tel: (708) 948-2000
   (Mfr disposable medical prdts)
      Baxter Medical AB, Adolfsbergsvagen 11, P.O. Box 20115, S-161 02 Bromma, Sweden

BECKMAN INSTRUMENTS INC   2500 Harbor Blvd, Fullerton, CA 92634,
   Tel: (714) 871-4848
   (Devel/mfr/mkt automated systems & supplies for biological analysis)
      Beckman Instruments AB, Archimedesvaegen 2, P.O. Box 65, S-161 26 Bromma, Sweden

LOUIS BERGER INTL INC   100 Halsted St, East Orange, NJ 07019,
   Tel: (201) 678-1960
   (Consulting engineers, architects, economists & planners)
      Brokonsult AB, Per Sundbergs Vag 1-3, S-183 63, Sweden

L M BERRY & CO   3179 Kettering Blvd, Dayton, OH 45439, Tel: (513) 296-2121
   (Advertising)
      Teleannons AB, Fack, P.O. Box 521, S-162 Vallingby, Sweden

BINKS MFG CO   9201 W Belmont Ave, Franklin Park, IL 60131,
   Tel: (708) 671-3000
   (Mfr of spray painting & finishing equip)
      Binks-Bullows Sweden AB, P.O. Box 90, Jarnringen 17, S-433 22 Partille, Sweden

BIO-RAD LABORATORIES INC   1000 Alfred Nobel Dr, Hercules, CA 94547,
   Tel: (510) 724-7000
   (Mfr life science research prdts, clinical diagnostics, analytical instruments)
      Bio-Rad Laboratories Inc., Stockholm, Sweden

BIOMATRIX INC   65 Railroad Ave, Ridgefield, NJ 07657, Tel: (201) 945-9550
   (Mfr hylan biological polymers for therapeutic med & skin care prdts)
      Biomatrix Svenska AB, 6 Havelvagen, S-756 47 Uppsala, Sweden

BLACK & DECKER CORP   701 E Joppa Road, Towson, MD 21286, Tel: (410) 716-3900
   (Mfr power tools & accessories, security hardware, small appliances, fasteners, info
   sys & servs)
      Black & Decker AB (Sweden), all mail to U.S. address

BLACKSTONE CORP   1111 Allen St, Jamestown, NY 14701, Tel: (716) 665-2620
   (Heat transfer prdts, heaters, coolers)
      Blackstone Sweden AB, P.O. Box 2064, S-294 02 Solvesborg, Sweden
      Nordiska Kylare Blackstone AB, Odenskogsvagen 38, S-831 48 Ostersund, Sweden
      Torell AB, P.O. Box 1174, Tornbyvagen, S-581 11 Linkoping, Sweden

BLOUNT INC   4520 Executive Park Drive, Montgomery, AL 36116-1602,
   Tel: (205) 244-4000
   (Mfr cutting chain & equip, timber harvest/handling equip, sporting ammo, riding
   mowers; gen contract)
      Svenska Blount AB, P.O. Box 1104, S-432 15 Varberg, Sweden
      Svenska Oregon AB, P.O. Box 1104, S-432 15 Varberg, Sweden

BOOLE & BABBAGE INC   510 Oakmead Pkwy, Sunnyvale, CA 94086,
   Tel: (408) 735-9550
   (Devel/support enterprise automation & systems mgmt software)
      Boole & Babbage Europe SA, Skytteholmsvagen 2, P.O. Box 1065, S-171 22 Solna, Sweden

BORDEN INC   180 E Broad St, Columbus, OH 43215-3799, Tel: (614) 225-4000
   (Mfr foods, snacks & beverages, adhesives)
      Borden AB, all mail to U.S. address

BOYDEN CONSULTING CORP   375 Park Ave, #1008, New York, NY 10152,
   Tel: (212) 980-6480
   (Executive search)
      Boyden Intl. AB, Wahrendorffsgatan 8, P.O. Box 7023, S-103 86 Stockholm, Sweden

W H BRADY CO   6555 W Good Hope Rd, Milwaukee, WI 53223, Tel: (414) 358-6600
   (Mfr ind ID for wire marking, circuit boards; facility ID & signage)
      Brady AB, Box 454, Finvids Vag 8-10, S-194 04 Upplands-Vasby, Sweden

BURR-BROWN RESEARCH CORP   PO Box 11400, Tucson, AZ 85734, Tel: (602) 746-1111
   (Electronic components & sys modules)
      Burr-Brown Intl. AB, Kanalvagen 5, S-194 61 Upplands, Vasby, Sweden

BURSON-MARSTELLER   230 Park Ave, New York, NY 10003-1566, Tel: (212) 614-4000
   (Public relations/public affairs consultants)
      Burson-Marsteller AB, Klarabergsviadukten 70, S-107 24 Stockholm, Sweden

CARL BYOIR & ASSOCIATES INC   420 Lexington Ave, New York, NY 10017,
   Tel: (212) 210-6000
   (Public relations, intl commun)
      Svenska PR-Byran AB, Gyllenstiernsgatan 14, S-115 26 Stockholm, Sweden

CABOT CORP   75 State St, Boston, MA 02109-1807, Tel: (617) 890-0200
   (Mfr carbon blacks, plastics; oil & gas, info sys)
      Deloro Stellite AB (Weartec Div.), Grunnebo 5530, S-462 00 Vanersborg, Sweden

CALCOMP INC   2411 W La Palma Ave, Anaheim, CA 92801, Tel: (714) 821-2000
   (Mfr computer graphics peripherals)
      CalComp AB, Turebergsvagen 11A, S-191 47 Sollentuna, Sweden

CAMP INTL INC   PO Box 89, Jackson, MI 49204, Tel: (517) 787-1600
  (Mfr orthotics & prosthetics)
    Camp Scandinavia AB, Karbingatan 38, S-252 55 Helsingborg, Sweden

CANBERRA INDUSTRIES INC   One State St, Meriden, CT 06450, Tel: (203) 238-2351
  (Mfr instru for nuclear research)
    Canberra-Packard AB, P.O. Box 10103, S-750 10 Uppsala, Sweden

CARRIER CORP   One Carrier Place, Farmington, CT 06034-4015,
  Tel: (203) 674-3000
  (Mfr/distr/svce A/C, heating & refrigeration equip)
    Carrier AB, Gothenburg, Sweden
    Carrier Forsaljnings AB, P.O. Box 8946, Arods Industriveg 32, S-402 73 Gothenburg,
      Sweden
    Duffab AB, Stockholm, Sweden
    Frigal AB, Alingsas, Sweden
    Klimatstyrning AB, Gothenburg, Sweden
    Nordqvist & Pavst AB, Molndal, Sweden

CHASE MANHATTAN BANK N A   1 Chase Manhattan Plaza, New York, NY 10081,
  Tel: (212) 552-2222
  (Intl banking)
    Chase Manhattan Bank (Sweden), Vastra Tradgardsgatan 7, S-111 53 Stockholm, Sweden

CHIRON CORP   4560 Horton St, Emeryville, CA 94608-2916, Tel: (510) 601-2412
  (Research/mfg/mktg therapeutics, vaccines, diagnostics, ophthalmics)
    Domilens AB, Virvelvagen 1, Box 249, S-232 23 Arlov, Sweden

CIGNA CORP   One Liberty Place, Philadelphia, PA 19192, Tel: (215) 523-4000
  (Ins, invest, health care & other fin servs)
    Cigna Insurance Co. of Europe SA/NV, Fleminggatan 18, S-106 26 Stockholm, Sweden

CINCOM SYSTEMS INC   2300 Montana Ave, Cincinnati, OH 45211,
  Tel: (513) 662-2300
  (Devel/distr computer software)
    Cincom Systems Inc., Gothenburg, Sweden

CITICORP   399 Park Ave, New York, NY 10043, Tel: (212) 559-1000
  (Banking & financial services)
    Citibank NA, Sweden

COLGATE-PALMOLIVE CO   300 Park Ave, New York, NY 10022, Tel: (212) 310-2000
  (Mfr pharms, cosmetics, toiletries, detergents)
    Colgate-Palmolive AB, Kemistragen 8, P.O. Box 525, S-183 25 Taby, Sweden

COLUMBIA PICTURES INDUSTRIES INC   711 Fifth Ave, New York, NY 10022,
  Tel: (212) 751-4400
  (Producer & distributor of motion pictures)
    Warner Columbia Film AB, P.O. Box 1428, S-111 84 Stockholm, Sweden

COMBUSTION ENGINEERING INC   900 Long Ridge Road, Stamford, CT 06902,
  Tel: (203) 329-8771
  (Tech constr)
    AB Refracto, P.O. Box 41, S-123 21 Farstal, Stockholm, Sweden

COMMERCIAL INTERTECH CORP   1775 Logan Ave, PO Box 239, Youngstown,
   OH   44501-0239, Tel: (216) 746-8011
   (Mfr hydraulic com, fluid purification sys, pre-engineered bldgs, stamped metal prdts)
      Commercial Hydraulics, Veddestavagen 24, S-175 62 Jaerfaella, Sweden

COMPUTER ASSOCIATES INTL INC   One Computer Associates Plaza, Islandia,
   NY   11788, Tel: (516) 342-5224
   (Devel/mkt/mgt info mgt & bus applications software)
      Computer Associates Sweden AB, Berga Backe 4, S-182 15 Danderyd, Sweden

CONOCO INC   600 N Dairy Ashford Rd, Houston, TX   77079, Tel: (713) 293-1000
   (Oil, gas, coal, chems, minerals)
      ARA-Bolagen AB, Jakobsgatan 6, P.O. Box 16144, S-103 23 Stockholm, Sweden

COOPER INDUSTRIES INC   1001 Fannin St, PO Box 4446, Houston, TX   77210-4446,
   Tel: (713) 739-5400
   (Mfr/distr electrical prdts, tools & hardware, automotive prdts)
      Kirsch Div., Malmo, Sweden

CPC INTERNATIONAL INC   PO Box 8000, Englewood Cliffs, NJ   07632,
   Tel: (201) 894-4000
   (Consumer foods, corn refining)
      CPC Foods AB, Tegelbruksvagen 18, P.O. Box 2126, S-291 02 Kristianstad, Sweden

CRAY RESEARCH INC   655 Lone Oak Dr, Eagan, MN   55121, Tel: (612) 452-6650
   (Supercomputer systems & services)
      Cray Research AB, Teknikringen 1, S-583 30 Linkoping, Sweden

D'ARCY MASIUS BENTON & BOWLES INC (DMB&B)   1675 Broadway, New York,
   NY   10019, Tel: (212) 468-3622
   (Advertising & communications)
      DMB&B AB, Olandsgatan 42, S-116 62 Stockholm, Sweden

DANA CORP   PO Box 1000, Toledo, OH   43697, Tel: (419) 535-4500
   (Engineer/mfr/mkt prdts & sys for vehicular, ind & mobile off-highway mkt & related
   aftermarkets)
      Warner Tollo AB, P.O. Box 9053, S-291 09 Kristianstad, Sweden

DATA GENERAL CORP   4400 Computer Dr, Westboro, MA   01580, Tel: (617) 366-8911
   (Design, mfr gen purpose computer sys & peripheral prdts & servs)
      Data General AB, Armegatan 38, P.O. Box 1290, S-171 25 Solna, Stockholm, Sweden

DATAEASE INTL INC   7 Cambridge Dr, Trumbull, CT   06611, Tel: (203) 374-8000
   (Mfr applications devel software)
      West Soft AB, Osterby Gard, S-150 16 Holo, Sweden

DATAWARE TECHNOLOGIES INC   222 Third St, #3300, Cambridge, MA   02142,
   Tel: (617) 621-0820
   (Multi-platform, multi-lingual software solutions & services for electronic info
   providers)
      Dataware Technologies, P.O. Box 1273, Solnawagen 39, S-171 24 Solna, Sweden
      Dataware Technologies AB, CD Rom Plaza, Skaraborgslaan, S-541 36 Skovde, Sweden

DAYCO PRODUCTS INC   1 Prestige Place, PO Box 1004, Dayton, OH 45401-1004,
  Tel: (513) 226-7000
  (Mfr ind & automotive belts, hose & related components & systems)
    Dayco Europe AB, S-294 01 Solvesborg, Sweden

DDB NEEDHAM WORLDWIDE INC   437 Madison Ave, New York, NY 10022,
  Tel: (212) 415-2000
  (Advertising)
    Carlsson & Broman/DDB Needham AB, Biblioteksgatan 11, P.O. Box 1757,
    S-111 87 Stockholm, Sweden

DEERE & CO   John Deere Rd, Moline, IL 61265, Tel: (309) 765-8000
  (Mfr/sale agri/constr/utility/forestry & lawn/grounds care equip)
    John Deere Svenska AB, Foretagsvagen 30, S-232 00 Arlov, Sweden

DELL COMPUTER CORP   2214 W Braker Ln, Austin, TX 78758-4063,
  Tel: (512) 338-4400
  (Design/mfr personal computers)
    Dell Computer AB, Business Campus, Harvard St., S-194 61 Upplands, Vasby, Sweden

DENISON HYDRAULICS   14299 Industrial Pkwy, Marysville, OH 43040,
  Tel: (513) 644-3915
  (Mach, hydraulic presses, pumps, valves, fluid motors, hydrostatic transmissions)
    Abex Industries AB, Sporregatan 13, S-213 77 Malmo, Sweden

THE DEXTER CORP   1 Elm Street, Windsor Locks, CT 06096, Tel: (203) 627-9051
  (Mfr nonwovens, polymer prdts, magnetic materials, biotechnology)
    Dexter Nonwovens AB, S-714 03 Stalldalen, Kpparberg, Sweden

DO ALL COMPANY   254 N Laurel Ave, Des Plaines, IL 60016, Tel: (708) 824-1122
  (Distributors of mach tools, metal cutting tools, instru & ind supplies)
    Do-All Co. AB, Akerivagen 21A, S-151 42 Sodertalje, Sweden

THE DOW CHEMICAL CO   2030 Dow Center, Midland, MI 48674, Tel: (517) 636-1000
  (Mfr chems, plastics, pharms, agric prdts, consumer prdts)
    Dow Chemical AB, Sweden

DRAKE BEAM MORIN INC   100 Park Ave, New York, NY 10017, Tel: (212) 692-7700
  (Human resource mgmt consulting & training)
    DBM Outplacement Scandinavia, Arstaangsvagen 1A, S-117 43 Stockholm, Sweden
    DBM Outplacement Scandinavia, also in Gothenburg & Jonkoping, Sweden

E I DU PONT DE NEMOURS & CO   1007 Market St, Wilmington, DE 19898,
  Tel: (302) 774-1000
  (Mfr/sale diversified chems, plastics, specialty prdts & fibers)
    ARA Bolagen AB, Sweden
    Du Pont Scandinavia AB, Fack, Marsta, Stockholm, S-195 01, Sweden

EASTMAN KODAK CO   343 State St, Rochester, NY 14650, Tel: (716) 724-4000
  (Devel/mfr photo & chem prdts, info mgmt/video/copier sys, fibers/plastics for
  various ind)
    Kodak AB, S-175 85 Jarfalla, Sweden
    Kodak AB, also in Gothenburg & Veddesta, Sweden

EATON CORP   1111 Superior Ave, Cleveland, OH 44114, Tel: (216) 523-5000
  (Advanced tech prdts for transp & ind mkts)
    Cutler Hammer Soensha AB, Florehgatan 37, S-252 55 Helsingborg, Sweden

EG&G INC   45 William St, Wellesley, MA 02181-4078, Tel: (617) 237-5100
(Diversified R/D, mfg & services)
    Wallac Sverige AB, Djupdalsvagen 20-22, P.O. Box 776, S-191 27 Sollentuna, Sweden

ELECTRONIC ASSOCIATES INC   185 Monmouth Park Hwy, West Long Branch,
NJ 07764, Tel: (201) 229-1100
(Analog/hybrid computers, training simulators, energy measurement sys)
    AEI, Hagalundsgatan 40, S-171 50 Solna, Sweden

ERICO PRODUCTS INC   34600 Solon Road, Cleveland, OH 44139,
Tel: (216) 248-0100
(Mfr electric welding apparatus & hardware, metal stampings, specialty fasteners)
    AB Svenska Cadweld, Kungsgatan 42, P.O. Box 253, S-244 02 Furulund, Sweden

ESTEE LAUDER INTL INC   767 Fifth Ave, New York, NY 10019, Tel: (212) 572-4600
(Cosmetics)
    AB Lestelle, Tulegatan 47, S-113 53 Stockholm, Sweden

EXPEDITORS INTL OF WASHINGTON INC   PO Box 69620, Seattle, WA 98168-9620,
Tel: (206) 246-3711
(Air/ocean freight forwarding, customs brokerage, intl logistics solutions)
    Expeditors Intl. Sverige AB, P.O. Box 2171 S-438 14 Landvetter, Sweden

FINNIGAN CORP   355 River Oaks Parkway, San Jose, CA 95134-1991,
Tel: (408) 433-4800
(Mfr mass spectrometers)
    Finnigan MAT AB, Pyramidbacken 3, S-141 75 Huddinge, Sweden

FOOTE CONE & BELDING COMMUNICATIONS INC   101 E Erie St, Chicago,
IL 60611-2897, Tel: (312) 751-7000
(Advertising agency)
    FCB Stockholm, Kungsgatan 5, S-105 62 Stockholm, Sweden
    Intermarco, Hamngatan 2, S-103 09 Stockholm, Sweden
    Intermarco Business-to-Business, Birger Jarlsgatan 5, S-103 99 Stockholm, Sweden

FORD MOTOR CO   The American Road, Dearborn, MI 48121, Tel: (313) 322-3000
(Mfr motor vehicles)
    Ford Motor Co. AB, P.O. Box 27-303, Tullvaktsvagen 11, S-102 54 Stockholm, Sweden

FOUR WINDS INTL GROUP   1500 SW First Ave, #850, Portland, OR 97201,
Tel: (503) 241-2732
(Transp of household goods & general cargo, third party logistics)
    Four Winds Scandinavia, P.O. Box 2074, S-182 02 Danderyd, Stockholm, Sweden

THE FRANKLIN MINT   Franklin Center, PA 19091, Tel: (610) 459-6000
(Creation/mfr/mktg collectibles & luxury items)
    Franklin Mint AB, Strandgatan 50 NB, S-216 12 Malmo, Sweden

H B FULLER CO   2400 Energy Park Dr, St Paul, MN 55108, Tel: (612) 645-3401
(Mfr/distr adhesives, sealants, coatings, paints, waxes, sanitation chems)
    L.W. Fuller Sverige AB, Lona Knapes Gata 5, S-421 32 Vastra Frolunda, Sweden

GAF CORP   1361 Alps Rd, Wayne, NJ 07470, Tel: (201) 628-3000
(Chems, bldg materials, commun)
    GAF (Norden) AB, P.O. Box 824, S-121 08 Johanneshov, Sweden

GENERAL BINDING CORP   One GBC Plaza, Northbrook, IL 60062,
  Tel: (708) 272-3700
  (Binding & laminating equip & associated supplies)
    GBC Scandinavia AB, Hastholmsvagen 28, S-131 30 Nacka, Sweden

GENERAL ELECTRIC CO   3135 Easton Tpk, Fairfield, CT 06431,
  Tel: (203) 373-2211
  (Diversified manufacturing, technology & services)
    General Electric Co.,
      all mail to U.S. address; phone (800) 626-2004 or (518) 438-6500

GENERAL FOODS CORP   250 North St, White Plains, NY 10625, Tel: (914) 335-2500
  (Processor, distributor & mfr of foods)
    General Foods AB, Holmparken 1, Gavle, Sweden

GENERAL MOTORS ACCEPTANCE CORP   3044 West Grand Blvd, Detroit, MI 48202,
  Tel: (313) 556-5000
  (Automobile financing)
    GMAC Continental, Kistagaangen 2, P.O. Box 1115, S-164 22 Kista, Sweden

GENERAL MOTORS CORP   3044 W Grand Blvd, Detroit, MI 48202-3091,
  Tel: (313) 556-5000
  (Mfr full line vehicles, automotive electronics, coml technologies, telecom, space, finance)
    General Motors Nordiska AB, Armaturvaegen 4, S-126 82 Handen, Sweden

THE GILLETTE CO   Prudential Tower, Boston, MA 02199, Tel: (617) 421-7000
  (Devel/mfr personal care/use prdts: blades & razors, toiletries, cosmetics, stationery)
    Braun Svenska AB, Frolunda, Sweden
    Gillette SA, Stockholm, Sweden

THE GOODYEAR TIRE & RUBBER CO   1144 E Market St, Akron, OH 44316,
  Tel: (216) 796-2121
  (Mfr tires, automotive belts & hose, conveyor belts, chemicals; oil pipeline transmission)
    Goodyear Gummi Fabriks AB, Archimedes Vagen 2-4, Bromma, S-161 20 Stockholm, Sweden

W R GRACE & CO   One Town Center Rd, Boca Raton, FL 33486-1010,
  Tel: (407) 362-2000
  (Mfr spec chems & materials: packaging, health care, catalysts, construction, water treatment/process)
    Rexolin Chemicals AB, P.O. Box 622, S-251 06 Helsingborg, Sweden
    W.R. Grace AB, P.O. Box 622, S-251 06 Helsingborg, Sweden

GREY ADVERTISING INC   777 Third Ave, New York, NY 10017, Tel: (212) 546-2000
  (Advertising)
    Grey Communications Group, Eriksbergsgatan 27, S-103 99 Stockholm, Sweden

FRANK B HALL & CO INC   549 Pleasantville Rd, Briarcliff Manor, NY 10510,
  Tel: (914) 769-9200
  (Insurance)
    Frank B. Hall (Scandinavia) A/S, Djurholmsvagen 50A, S-183 51 Taby, Stockholm, Sweden

HARNISCHFEGER INDUSTRIES INC   PO Box 554, Milwaukee, WI 53201,
  Tel: (414) 671-4400
  (Mfr mining & material handling equip, papermaking mach, computer sys)
    Rader Intl. AB, Krossgaten 34, S-162-26 Vallingby, Stockholm, Sweden

THE HARPER GROUP   260 Townsend St, PO Box 77933, San Francisco,
  CA 94107-1719, Tel: (415) 978-0600
  (Ocean/air freight fwdg, customs brokerage, packing & whse, logistics mgt, ins)
    Harper Freight Intl. (Sweden) AB, P.O. Box 507, Arlanda, S-190 45 Stockholm, Sweden
    Harper Freight Intl. (Sweden) AB, also in Gothenburg, Malmo & Norrkoping, Sweden

H J HEINZ CO   PO Box 57, Pittsburgh, PA 15230-0057, Tel: (412) 456-5700
  (Processed food prdts & nutritional services)
    Weight Watchers Intl. Inc., Helsingborg, Sweden

HERCULES INC   Hercules Plaza, Wilmington, DE 19894-0001, Tel: (302) 594-5000
  (Mfr spec chems, plastics, film & fibers, coatings, resins, food ingredients)
    Hercules Kemiska AB, P.O. Box 300, S-401 24 Gothenburg, Sweden

HEWLETT-PACKARD CO   3000 Hanover St, Palo Alto, CA 94304-0890,
  Tel: (415) 857-1501
  (Mfr computing, communications & measurement prdts & services)
    Hewlett-Packard Sverige AB, Skalholtsgatan 9, S-164 93 Kista, Sweden

A J HOLLANDER & CO INC   257 Park Ave So, New York, NY 10010,
  Tel: (212) 353-8000
  (Hides, skins & leather)
    AB Baltiska Skinnkompaniet, P.O. Box 7674, S-103 95 Stockholm, Sweden

HONEYWELL INC   PO Box 524, Minneapolis, MN 55440-0524, Tel: (612) 951-1000
  (Devel/mfr controls for home & building, industry, space & aviation)
    Honeywell AB, Storsatragrand 5, S-127 86 Skarholmen, Stockholm

HORWATH INTL   415 Madison Ave, New York, NY 10017, Tel: (212) 838-5566
  (Public accountants & auditors)
    Horwath Consulting AB, Riddarhuskajen 5, S-111 28 Stockholm, Sweden

HOUGHTON INTL INC   PO Box 930, Valley Forge, PA 19482-0930,
  Tel: (610) 666-4000
  (Mfr spec chems, hydraulic fluids, lubricants)
    Houghton Sverige AB, Landshovdingegatan 32, S-431 38 Molndal, Sweden

IBM CORP   Old Orchard Rd, Armonk, NY 10504, Tel: (914) 765-1900
  (Information products, technology & services)
    IBM Svenska AB, Oddegatan 5, S-163 92 Stockholm, Sweden

IDAB INTERNATIONAL INC   One Enterprise Pkwy, Hampton, VA 23666-5841,
  Tel: (804) 825-2260
  (Mfr material handling sys & equip for newspaper industry)
    IDAB WAMAC AB, P.O. Box 189, S-575 22 Eksjo, Sweden

IMO INDUSTRIES INC   1009 Lenox Dr, Bldg 4 West, Lawrenceville,
  NJ 08648-0550, Tel: (609) 896-7600
  (Mfr/support mech & electr controls, engineered power prdts)
    IMO AB, Vastberga Alle 50, P.O. Box 42090, S-126 14 Stockholm, Sweden
    Morse Controls AB, P.O. Box 153, S-195 24 Marsta, Sweden

INCOM INTERNATIONAL INC   3450 Princeton Pike, Lawrenceville, NJ 08648,
  Tel: (609) 896-7600
  (Roller & motorcycle chains, drive components, marine controls)
    Telflex Morse AB, P.O. Box 153, S-195 01 Marsta, Sweden

INGERSOLL-RAND CO   200 Chestnut Ridge Rd, Woodcliff Lake, NJ 07675,
  Tel: (201) 573-0123
  (Mfr compressors, rock drills, pumps, air tools, door hardware, ball bearings)
    Ingersol-Rand Scandinavian Operations, Isafjordsgatan 19, S-164 Spanga, Sweden

INSTRON CORP   100 Royall St, Canton, MA 02021-1089, Tel: (617) 828-2500
  (Mfr material testing instruments)
    Instron Ltd. (Sweden), Hobergsgatan 59B, S-118 26 Stockholm, Sweden

INTERMEC CORP   6001 36th Ave West, PO Box 4280, Everett, WA 98203-9280,
  Tel: (206) 348-2600
  (Mfr/distr automated data collection sys)
    Optiscan Intermec AB, P.O. Box 2077, S-172 06 Sundbyberg, Sweden

INTERNATIONAL COMPONENTS CORP   420 N May St, Chicago, IL 60622,
  Tel: (312) 829-2525
  (Mfr/sale/svce portable DC battery chargers)
    International Components Corp. Nordic AB, Uddevallavagen 3, SF-452 31 Stromstad,
    Sweden

INTERNATIONAL PAPER   2 Manhattanville Rd, Purchase, NY 10577,
  Tel: (914) 397-1500
  (Mfr/distr container board, paper, wood prdts)
    Anitec Image (Svenska) AB, Stensatravagen 9, Satra Indus., P.O. Box 3060,
    S-127 03 Skarholmen, Sweden
    Bergvik Kemi AB, P.O. Box 66, S-820 22 Sandarne, Sweden
    Horsell Grafiska AB, Staffan Vag 6, S-191 78 Solentuna, Sweden
    Ilford Photo AB, P.O. Box 3052, S-400 10 Gottenburg, Sweden

ITT CORP   1330 Ave of the Americas, New York, NY 10019-5490,
  Tel: (212) 258-1000
  (Design/mfr communications & electronic equip, hotels, insurance)
    Standard Radio & Telefon AB, Johannesfredsvagen 9-11, Bromma, Sweden

ITT SHERATON CORP   60 State St, Boston, MA 02108, Tel: (617) 367-3600
  (Hotel operations)
    Sheraton Stockholm Hotel, Tegelbacken 6, S-111 52 Stockholm, Sweden

JOHNSON & JOHNSON   One Johnson & Johnson Plaza, New Brunswick, NJ 08933,
  Tel: (908) 524-0400
  (R&D/mfr/sale health care prdts)
    Janssen-Cilag AB, P.O. Box 7073, S-191 07 Sollentuna, Sweden
    Johnson & Johnson AB, S-191 84 Sollentuna, Sweden

S C JOHNSON & SON INC   1525 Howe St, Racine, WI 53403, Tel: (414) 631-2000
  (Home, auto, commercial & personal care prdts, specialty chems)
    Svenska Johnson's Vax AB, P.O. Box 2, S-183 21 Taby, Sweden

A T KEARNEY INC   222 West Adams St, Chicago, IL 60606, Tel: (312) 648-0111
  (Mgmt consultants, executive search)
    A.T. Kearney AB, Biblioleksgatan 11, Box 1751, S-111 87 Stockholm, Sweden

KELLOGG CO   One Kellogg Sq, PO Box 3599, Battle Creek, MI 49016-3599,
  Tel: (616) 961-2000
  (Mfr ready-to-eat cereals, convenience foods)
    Kellogg Sverige, Solna (Stockholm), Sweden (all inquiries to U.S. address)

KORN/FERRY INTL   1800 Century Park East, Los Angeles, CA 90067,
  Tel: (310) 552-1834
  (Executive search)
    Korn/Ferry Intl., Ostra Hamangatan 5, S-411 10 Gothenburg, Sweden
    Korn/Ferry Intl., Norrmalmstorg 14, S-111 46 Stockholm, Sweden

KRAFT INC   Kraft Court, Glenview, IL 60025, Tel: (708) 998-2000
  (Dairy prdts, processed food, chems)
    Kraft Foods Svenska AB, Sallerupesvagen 1, S-212 18 Malmo, Sweden

LEVI STRAUSS & CO   1155 Battery, San Francisco, CA 94111, Tel: (415) 544-6000
  (Mfr casual wearing apparel)
    Levi Strauss Sweden, Birger Jarlsgatan 25, S-111 45 Stockholm, Sweden

LINTAS:WORLDWIDE   1 Dag Hammarskjold Plaza, New York, NY 10017,
  Tel: (212) 605-8000
  (Advertising agency)
    Lintas:Stockholm, Grev Turegatan 11, s-114-46 Stockholm, Sweden

ARTHUR D LITTLE INC   25 Acorn Park, Cambridge, MA 02140-2390,
  Tel: (617) 498-5000
  (Mgmt, environ, health & safety consulting; tech & prdt development)
    Arthur D. Little AB, P.O. Box 70434, S-107 25 Stockholm, Sweden
    Arthur D. Little AB, Lilla Bommen 1, S-441 04 Gothenburg, Sweden

LOCTITE CORP   10 Columbus Blvd, Hartford, CT 06106, Tel: (203) 520-5000
  (Mfr/sale ind adhesives & sealants)
    Plastic Padding AB, P.O. Box 8823, S-402 71 Gothenburg, Sweden

LOUIS ALLIS CO   PO Box 2020, Milwaukee, WI 53201, Tel: (414) 481-6000
  (Elec motors, adjustable speed drives, generators, compressors)
    Litton Precision Products Intl., Warfvinges Vag 32, P.O. Box 30095,
      S-104 25 Stockholm, Sweden

THE LUBRIZOL CORP   29400 Lakeland Blvd, Wickliffe, OH 44092-2298,
  Tel: (216) 943-4200
  (Mfr chem additives for lubricants & fuels)
    Lubrizol Scandinavia AB, Sweden

MARATHON LE TOURNEAU CO   PO Box 2307, Longview, TX 75606, Tel: (903) 237-7000
  (Mfr heavy constr, mining mach & equip)
    AB Truckimport, P.O. Box 17, S-194 21 Upplands Vasby, Stockholm, Sweden

MARK IV INDUSTRIES INC   PO Box 810, Amherst, NY 14226-0810,
  Tel: (716) 689-4972
  (Mfr diversified prdts: timers & controls, power equip, loudspeaker sys, etc)
    Blackstone Europe AB, Mjallby, S-294 02 Solvesborg, Sweden

MARKEM CORP   150 Congress St, Keene, NH 03431, Tel: (603) 352-1130
  (Marking and printing mach; hot stamping foils)
    Markem AB, Karl Johansgatan 47-49, P.O. Box 12029, S-402 41 Gothenburg, Sweden

MARSTELLER INTL 1 E Wacker Dr, Chicago, IL 60601, Tel: (312) 329-1100
(Advertising, marketing research, sales promotion)
Burson-Marsteller AB, Skeppargatan 37, S-114 52 Stockholm, Sweden
Burson-Marsteller AB, Bjarshog 355, S-212 90 Malmo, Sweden

MCI INTERNATIONAL 2 International Dr, Rye Brook, NY 10573,
Tel: (914) 937-3444
(Telecommunications)
MCI Intl. Sweden AB, World Trade Center, P.O. Box 70396, S-107 24 Stockholm, Sweden

MEASUREX CORP One Results Way, Cupertino, CA 95014-5991, Tel: (408) 255-1500
(Mfr computer integrated mfg sys)
Measurex Sweden AB, P.O. Box 5091, S-781 05 Borlange, Sweden

MEMOREX CORP San Thomas at Central Expressway, Santa Clara, CA 95052,
Tel: (408) 987-1000
(Magnetic recording tapes, etc)
Memorex AB, P.O. Box 20026, S-161 20 Bromma, Sweden

MERCK SHARP & DOHME INTL PO Box 2000, Rahway, NJ 07065, Tel: (201) 574-4000
(Pharms, chems & biologicals)
Merck, Sharp & Dohme (Sweden) AB, Mariehallsvagen 42, Bromma, Sweden

METALLURG INC 25 E 39th St, New York, NY 10016, Tel: (212) 686-4010
(Mfr ferrous & nonferrous alloys & metals)
AB Ferrolgeringar, P.O. Box 7163, S-103 88 Stockholm, Sweden

METCO DIV OF PERKIN-ELMER 1101 Prospect Ave, PO Box 1006, Westbury,
NY 11590-0201, Tel: (516) 334-1300
(Mfr/serv thermal spray coating equip & supplies)
Metco Scandinavia AB, Fack 57, S-143 01 Varby, Sweden

MICROSOFT CORP One Microsoft Way, Redmond, WA 98052-6399,
Tel: (206) 882-8080
(Computer software, peripherals & services)
Microsoft Sweden AB, Finlandsgatan 30, P.O. Box 27, S-164 93 Kista, Sweden

MICROTEC RESEARCH 2350 Mission College Blvd, Santa Clara, CA 95054,
Tel: (408) 980-1300
(Devel/mfr software tools for embedded systems market)
Microtec Research AB, Arstaangvagen 17, S-117 43 Stockholm, Sweden

MILLIPORE CORP Ashley Rd, Bedford, MA 01730, Tel: (617) 275-9205
(Mfr precision filters, hi-performance liquid chromatography instru)
Millipore AB, P.O. Box 233, S-421-23 Vastra Frolunda, Sweden

MOBIL CORP 3225 Gallows Rd, Fairfax, VA 22037-0001, Tel: (703) 846-3000
(Petroleum explor & refining, mfr petrol prdts, chems, petrochems)
Mobil Oil AB Sweden, P.O. Box 502, S-182 15 Danderyd, Sweden

MOOG INC East Aurora, NY 14052-0018, Tel: (716) 652-2000
(Mfr precision control components & sys)
Moog Norden AB, Datavagen 18, S-436 32 Askim, Sweden

MOTOROLA INC   1303 E Algonquin Rd, Schaumburg, IL 60196, Tel: (708) 576-5000
  (Mfr commun equip, semiconductors, cellular phones)
    Motorola AB, Kistagaangen 2, S-163 42 Spaagna, Sweden
    Svenska Codex Data AB, Dalvaegen 2, S-171 36 Solna, Sweden

MTS SYSTEMS CORP   14000 Technology Dr, Eden Prairie, MN 55344-2290,
  Tel: (612) 937-4000
  (Devel/mfr mechanical testing & simulation prdts & servs, ind meas & automation
  instrumentation)
    MTS Systems Norden AB, Datavagen 32, S-436 32 Askim, Sweden

McCANN-ERICKSON WORLDWIDE   750 Third Ave, New York, NY 10017,
  Tel: (212) 697-6000
  (Advertising)
    McCann-Erickson AB, Sibyllegatan 17, P.O. Box 5511, S-114 85 Stockholm, Sweden
    Werne & Co. AB, Kungsgatan 2, S-111 43 Stockholm, Sweden
    Werne/McCann AB, Engelbrektsgatan 7, S-211 23 Malmo, Sweden

McKINSEY & CO INC   55 E 52nd St, New York, NY 10022, Tel: (212) 446-7000
  (Mgmt consultants)
    McKinsey & Co. Inc., Hamngatan 13, S-111 47 Stockholm, Sweden

NALCO CHEMICAL CO   One Nalco Center, Naperville, IL 60563-1198,
  Tel: (708) 305-1000
  (Chems for water & waste water treatment, oil prod & refining, ind processes;
  water/energy mgmt serv)
    Nalco Chemical AB, Lagervagen 4, S-136 50 Haninge, Sweden

NASH INTL CO   3 Trefoil Dr, Trumbull, CT 06611, Tel: (203) 459-3900
  (Mfr air & gas compressors, vacuum pumps)
    Nash Nytor AB, P.O. Box 49006, Stockholm, Sweden

NATIONAL STARCH & CHEMICAL CO   10 Finderne Ave, Bridgewater, NJ 08807-3300,
  Tel: (908) 685-5000
  (Mfr adhesives & sealants, resins & spec chems, electr materials & adhesives, food
  prdts, ind starch)
    National Starch & Chemical AB, Norrkoping, Sweden

NATIONAL UTILITY SERVICE INC   One Maynard Dr, PO Box 712, Park Ridge,
  NJ 07656, Tel: (201) 391-4300
  (Utility rate consulting)
    NUS Scandinavia AB, P.O. Box 17172, S-104 62 Stockholm, Sweden

THE NEW YORK TIMES CO   229 W 43rd St, New York, NY 10036, Tel: (212) 556-1234
  (Communications, newspaper & magazine publishing, broadcasting, forest prdts)
    Golf Digest Medstroms AB (JV), Karlbergsvagen 77-81, S-113 35 Stockholm, Sweden

A C NIELSEN CO   Nielsen Plaza, Northbrook, IL 60062-6288, Tel: (708) 498-6300
  (Market research)
    A.C. Nielsen Co. AB, Borgarfjordsgatan 13, Kista, Sweden

NORDSON CORP   28601 Clemens Rd, Westlake, OH 44145, Tel: (216) 892-1580
  (Mfr ind application equip & packaging mach)
    Nordson Sverige AB, Kabingatan 13, S-212 39 Malmo, Sweden
    Nordson Sverige AB, ICAB Div., P.O. Box 258, S-444 24 Stenungsund, Sweden

NORTON CO 1 New Bond St, Worcester, MA 01606, Tel: (508) 795-5000
(Abrasives, drill bits, constr & safety prdts, plastics)
Norton Scandinavia AB, P.O. Box 12203, S-102 25 Stockholm, Sweden

OTIS ELEVATOR CO 10 Farm Springs, Farmington, CT 06032, Tel: (860) 676-6528
(Mfr elevators & escalators)
Otis AB, P.O. Box 1187, S-172 24 Sundbyberg, Sweden

OUTBOARD MARINE CORP 100 Sea Horse Dr, Waukegan, IL 60085,
Tel: (708) 689-6200
(Mfr/mkt marine engines, boats & accessories)
Outboard Marine Power Products Group, Sweden

OUTDOOR TECHNOLOGIES GROUP One Berkley Dr, Spirit Lake, IA 51360,
Tel: (712) 336-1520
(Mfr fishing rods, reels, lines & tackle, outdoor & marine prdts, soft & hard baits)
Abu Garcia, S-376 81 Svangsta Blekinge, Sweden

OWENS-CORNING FIBERGLAS CORP Fiberglas Tower, Toledo, OH 43659,
Tel: (419) 248-8000
(Mfr insulation, building materials, glass fiber prdts)
Glasfiber AB (Sweden), Sweden
Scandinavian Glasfiber AB, Falkenberg, Sweden

PACKAGING CORP OF AMERICA 1603 Orrington Ave, Evanston, IL 60201-3853,
Tel: (708) 492-5713
(Mfr custom packaging, aluminum & plastic molded fibre, corrugated containers)
Omni-Pac AB, Wallingatan 8-10, S-111 60 Stockholm, Sweden

PARKER HANNIFIN CORP 17325 Euclid Ave, Cleveland, OH 44112,
Tel: (216) 531-3000
(Mfr motion-control prdts)
Atlas Automation, P.O. Box 110, Karlin AS Vagen 19, S-523 23 Ulricehamn, Sweden
Parker Hannifin Sweden AB, Fagerstagatan 51, P.O. Box 6314, S-163 08 Spanga, Sweden
Parker Hannifin/Finn-Filter Svenska AB, Reprovagen 3, P.O. Box 1133, S-183 11 Taby,
Sweden

PET INC 400 S 4th St, St Louis, MO 63102, Tel: (314) 622-7700
(Mfr packaged foods)
AB Estrella (Sweden), P.O. Box 2101, S-424 02 Angered, Sweden

PFIZER INC 235 E 42nd St, New York, NY 10017-5755, Tel: (212) 573-2323
(Mfr healthcare products)
Pfizer AB, Sweden
Roerig AB, Sweden
Shiley Scandinavia AB, Sweden

PHILLIPS PETROLEUM CO Phillips Bldg, Bartlesville, OK 74004,
Tel: (918) 661-6600
(Crude oil, natural gas, liquefied petroleum gas, gasoline & petro-chems)
Nordisk Philblack AB, P.O. Box 21035, Malmo, Sweden

PITNEY BOWES INC Wheeler Dr, Stamford, CT 06926-0700, Tel: (203) 356-5000
(Mfr postage meters, mailroom equip, copiers, bus supplies; bus servs)
Pitney Bowes Svenska AB, Storgatan 22, P.O. Box 9125, S-171 09 Solna, Sweden

PLIBRICO CO   1800 Kingsbury St, Chicago, IL 60614, Tel: (312) 549-7014
  (Refractories, engineering, constr)
    Plibrico Eldfast Material AB, Karrlyckegatan 7, S-417 91 Gothenburg, Sweden

POLICY MANAGEMENT SYS CORP   PO Box 10, Columbia, SC 29202,
  Tel: (803) 735-4000
  (Computer software, insurance industry support services)
    PMS Norden AB, Karlvagen 18, P.O. Box 5671, S-114 86 Stockholm, Sweden

PROCTER & GAMBLE CO   One Procter & Gamble Plaza, Cincinnati, OH 45202,
  Tel: (513) 983-1100
  (Personal care, food, laundry, cleaning & ind prdts)
    Procter & Gamble AB, Sweden

PUROLATOR COURIER CORP   3240 Hillview Ave, Palo Alto, CA 94304,
  Tel: (415) 494-2900
  (Time-sensitive package delivery)
    Sweden Courier of Sweden, Stockholm, Sweden

QMS INC   One Magnum Pass, Mobile, AL 36618, Tel: (205) 633-4300
  (Mfr monochrome & color computer printers)
    QMS Inc., Stockholm, Sweden

QUAKER CHEMICAL CORP   Elm & Lee Sts, Conshohocken, PA 19428-0809,
  Tel: (610) 832-4000
  (Mfr chem specialties; total fluid mgmt services)
    Quaker Chemical BV, S-384 80 Perstorp, Sweden

RAYCHEM CORP   300 Constitution Dr, Menlo Park, CA 94025, Tel: (415) 361-3333
  (Devel/mfr/mkt materials science products for electronics, telecommunications &
  industry)
    Raychem AB, P.O. Box 2054, Vita Lijans Vaeg 20, S-127 02 Skaerholmen, Sweden

READER'S DIGEST ASSOCIATION INC   PO Box 235, Pleasantville, NY 10570,
  Tel: (914) 238-1000
  (Publisher magazines & books, direct mail marketer)
    Reader's Digest Assn. AB, Skalholtsgatan 2, S-164 40 Kista, Sweden

RECOGNITION EQUIPMENT INC   PO Box 660204, Dallas, TX 75266-0204,
  Tel: (214) 579-6000
  (Mfr hi-perf document recognition sys, image & workflow software; related customer
  serv)
    Recognition Equipment AB, Arstaangsvagen 1C, P.O. Box 47155, S-100 74 Stockholm,
    Sweden

RELIANCE ELECTRIC CO   24701 Euclid Ave, Cleveland, OH 44117,
  Tel: (216) 266-7000
  (Equip & sys for ind automation, telecom equip)
    Toledo-Reliance Skandinavia AB, Asogatan 142, S-116 24 Stockholm Sweden

RIDGE TOOL CO   400 Clark St, Elyria, OH 44035, Tel: (216) 323-5581
  (Hand & power tools for working pipe, drain cleaning equip, etc)
    Svenska Ridge AB Huddinge, Stockholm, Sweden

RJR NABISCO INC 1301 Ave of the Americas, New York, NY 10019,
Tel: (212) 258-5600
(Mfr consumer packaged food prdts & tobacco prdts)
R.J. Reynolds Tobacco SA, Vatten Tornsvagen 18, S-180 21 Osterskar, Sweden

ROCKWELL INTL CORP 2201 Seal Beach Blvd, PO Box 4250, Seal Beach,
CA 90740-8250, Tel: (310) 797-3311
(Prdts & serv for aerospace, automotive, electronics, graphics & automation inds)
Allen-Bradley AB, Bryggate Bergs vag 2, P.O. Box 4054, S-182 04 Enebyberg, Sweden

ROHM AND HAAS CO 100 Independence Mall West, Philadelphia, PA 19106,
Tel: (215) 592-3000
(Mfr ind & agric chems, plastics)
Rohm and Haas Nordiska AB, P.O. Box 45, Osterleden 165, S-261 22 Landskrona, Sweden

RUDER FINN INC 301 E 57th St, New York, NY 10022, Tel: (212) 593-6400
(Public relations serv, broadcast commun)
Ruder Finn & Johard, Hadeholms Gard, S-810 40 Hedusunda, Sweden

THE SCOTT & FETZER CO 28800 Clemens Rd, Westlake, OH 44145,
Tel: (216) 892-3000
(Electrical & lighting fixtures, leisure prdts)
Sheraton Reservation Corp., Tegelbacken 6, P.O. Box 289, S-101 Stockholm, Sweden

SEA-LAND SERVICE INC 150 Allen Rd, Liberty Corner, NJ 07920,
Tel: (201) 558-6000
(Container transport)
Sea-Land Containerships AB, Birgerjarsgatan 33B, S-110 45 Stockholm, Sweden
Sea-Land Containerships AB, Sturepatsen 1, S-411 39 Gothenburg, Sweden
Sea-Land Containerships AB, P.O. Box 48031, Gothenburg, Sweden

SEALED AIR CORP Park 80 Plaza E, Saddle Brook, NJ 07662-5291,
Tel: (201) 791-7600
(Mfr protective packaging prdts)
Sealed Air Svenska AB, P.O. Box 146, Patorpsvagen 2, S-578 00 Aneby, Sweden

G D SEARLE & CO 5200 Old Orchard Rd, Skokie, IL 60077, Tel: (708) 982-7000
(Mfr pharms, health care & optical prdts, specialty chems)
Searle Scandinavia, Hastvagen 4A, S-212 35 Malmo, Sweden

SHIPLEY CO INC 455 Forest St, Marlborough, MA 01752, Tel: (508) 481-7950
(Mfr chems for printed circuit boards & microelectronic mfg)
Shipley Svenska AB, Vaexthusgaten, S-602 28 Norrkoeping, Sweden

SKIL CORP 4801 W Peterson Ave, Chicago, IL 60646, Tel: (312) 286-7330
(Portable electric power tools)
Skil-Europe, all mail to Konijnenberg 60, P.O. Box 32, 6748 DG Breda, Netherlands

SPSS INC 444 N Michigan Ave, Chicago, IL 60611, Tel: (312) 329-2400
(Mfr statistical software)
SPSS Scandinavia AB, Gamla Brogatan 36-38, S-111 20 Stockholm, Sweden

STANDEX INTL CORP 6 Manor Pkwy, Salem, NH 03079, Tel: (603) 893-9701
(Mfr diversified graphics, institutional, ind/electr & consumer prdts)
James Burn Intl. AB, P.O. Box 4093, Engelbrektsgatan 15, S-203 12 Malmo, Sweden

STORAGE TECHNOLOGY CORP   2270 S 88th St, Louisville, CO 80028-0001,
  Tel: (303) 673-5151
  (Mfr/mkt/serv info storage & retrieval sys)
    Storage Tek AB, P.O. Box 336, S-191 30 Sollentuna, Stockholm, Sweden

SYSTEMS ENGINEERING LABS INC   6901 W Sunrise Blvd, Fort Lauderdale,
  FL 33313, Tel: (305) 587-2900
  (Digital computers)
    Systems Associates AB, Hagalundsgatan 40, P.O. Box 3003, S-171 03 Solna, Stockholm,
    Sweden

TANDEM COMPUTERS INC   19333 Valco Pkwy, Cupertino, CA 95014,
  Tel: (408) 725-6000
  (Mfr multiple processor computer sys)
    Tandem Computers (Sweden) AB, S-171 48 Solna, Sweden

TECHNICON INSTRUMENTS CORP   511 Benedict Ave, Tarrytown, NY 10591-5097,
  Tel: (914) 631-8000
  (Mfr/serv automated blook anal equip, reagents & diagnostics)
    Technicon AB, P.O. Box 20, Raseborgsgatan 5, S-164 93 Kista, Stockholm, Sweden

TEKTRONIX INC   26660 SW Parkway, Wilsonville, OR 97070, Tel: (503) 627-7111
  (Mfr test & meas, visual sys & commun prdts)
    Tektronix AB, Solna (Stockholm) & Gothenburg, Sweden

TELLABS INC   4951 Indiana Ave, Lisle, IL 60532, Tel: (708) 969-8800
  (Design/mfr/svce voice/data transport & network access sys)
    Tellabs Intl. Inc. (Sweden), Birger Jarisgatan 34, S-114 29 Stockholm, Sweden

TENNECO INC   PO Box 2511, Houston, TX 77252-2511, Tel: (713) 757-2131
  (Natural gas pipelines, shipbuilding & repair, construction & farm equip, chemicals,
  packaging)
    AB Starla-Werken, P.O. Box 38, S-340 15 Vittaryd, Sweden
    Walker Sverige A/S, P.O. Box 38, Vittaryd, Sweden

THOMAS & BETTS CORP   1555 Lynnfield Rd, Memphis, TN 38119,
  Tel: (901) 682-7766
  (Mfr elect/electr connectors & accessories)
    T & B AB, Kanalvagen 1, S-194 61 Upplands, Vasky, Sweden

TOPFLIGHT CORP   160 E 9th Ave, York, PA 17404, Tel: (717) 843-9901
  (Commercial printing, service paper)
    Topflight AB, Box 113, S-265 22 Astorp, Sweden

TRANS WORLD AIRLINES INC   505 N 6th St, St Louis, MO 63101,
  Tel: (314) 589-3000
  (Air transportation)
    Trans World Airlines, Kungsgatan 4A, Stockholm, Sweden

TRANTER INC   1054 Claussen Rd, #314, Augusta, GA 30907, Tel: (706) 738-7900
  (Mfr heat exchangers)
    ReHeat AB, P.O. Box 3546, S-103 03 Taby, Sweden
    ReHeat AB, Regementsgatan 32, S-462 32 Vanersborg, Sweden
    SWEP International AB, P.O. Box 105, S-261 22 Landskrona, Sweden

TRINOVA CORP   3000 Strayer, PO Box 50, Maumee, OH 43537-0050,
  Tel: (419) 867-2200
  (Mfr engr components & sys for ind)
    Vickers Systems AB, P.O. Box 65, Fagerstagatan 19, S-163 91 Spaanga, Sweden

UNION CAMP CORP   1600 Valley Rd, Wayne, NJ 07470, Tel: (201) 628-2000
  (Mfr paper, packaging, chems, wood prdts)
    Bush Boake Allen Scandinavia AB, P.O. Box 107, S-289 00 Knislinge, Sweden

UNION CARBIDE CORP   39 Old Ridgebury Rd, Danbury, CT 06817,
  Tel: (203) 794-2000
  (Mfr industrial chemicals, plastics, resins)
    Union Carbide Norden AB, Vaestmannagatan 11, S-111 24 Stockholm, Sweden

UNISYS CORP   PO Box 500, Blue Bell, PA 19424, Tel: (215) 986-4011
  (Mfg/mktg/serv electr info sys)
    Unisys AB, Vallgatan 7, S-171 91 Solna, Sweden

UNITED AIRLINES INC   PO Box 66100, Chicago, IL 60666, Tel: (708) 952-4000
  (Air transp)
    United Airlines, P.O. Box 84, S-139 00 Stockholm, Sweden

UNITED TECHNOLOGIES CORP   United Technologies Bldg, Hartford, CT 06101,
  Tel: (203) 728-7000
  (Mfr aircraft engines, elevators, A/C, auto equip, space & military electr, rocket
  propulsion sys)
    Otis Hissakiebolag, Dobelnsgatan 89-95, P.O. Box 19002, S-104 32 Stockholm, Sweden

UOP INC   Ten UOP Plaza, Des Plaines, IL 60016, Tel: (708) 391-2000
  (Diversified research, development & mfr of ind prdts & sys mgmt studies & serv)
    Bostrona Div., UOP Ltd., Sodertalje, Sweden

VARIAN ASSOCIATES INC   3100 Hansen Way, Palo Alto, CA 94304-1030,
  Tel: (415) 493-4000
  (Mfr microwave tubes & devices, analytical instru, semiconductor process & med equip,
  vacuum sys)
    Varian AB, Huvadstagatan 1, P.O. Box 1099, S-171 22 Solna, Sweden

VENDO CO   7209 N Ingram, Pinedale, CA 93650, Tel: (209) 439-1770
  (Mfr coin-op automatic vending machs)
    Vendo AB, Pyramidvagen 9A, S-171 36 Solna, Stockholm, Sweden

VOLT INFORMATION SCIENCES INC   1221 Sixth Ave, 47th fl, New York,
  NY 10020-1001, Tel: (212) 704-2400
  (Computerized publishing, telecommunications & computer systems & services)
    Volt Autologic AB, Bergkallavagen 34, S-191 79 Sollentuna, Sweden

WARD HOWELL INTL INC   99 Park Ave, New York, NY 10016-1699,
  Tel: (212) 697-3730
  (Executive recruiting)
    SIMS Ward Howell Intl., Norra Skeppsbron 5-B, S-803 10 Gavle, Sweden
    SIMS Ward Howell Intl., Forsta Langgatan 30, S-413 27 Gothenburg, Sweden
    SIMS Ward Howell Intl., Hamngatan 4, S-211 21 Malmo, Sweden
    SIMS Ward Howell Intl., Soft Center, S-372 25 Ronneby, Sweden
    SIMS Ward Howell Intl., Nybrogatan 34, P.O. Box 5104, S-102 43 Stockholm, Sweden

WARNER ELECTRIC BRAKE & CLUTCH CO   449 Gardner St, South Beloit, IL 61080,
    Tel: (815) 389-3771
    (Automotive & ind brakes & clutches)
        Warner Electric AB, Lillasallskapets Vag 86, P.O. Box 2086, S-127 02 Skarholmen,
        Sweden

WATERS CHROMATOGRAPHY DIV   34 Maple St, Milford, MA 01757,
    Tel: (617) 478-2000
    (Mfr/distr liquid chromatographic instru/accessories/tech)
        Millipore AB, P.O. Box 233, S-421 23 Vastra Frolunda, Sweden
        Waters Associates AB, P.O. Box 24, S-433 21 Partille, Sweden

WHIRLPOOL CORP   2000 N M-63, Benton Harbor, MI 49022-2692,
    Tel: (616) 923-5000
    (Mfr/mkt home appliances)
        Whirlpool Europe BV, Norrkoping, Sweden

WINCHESTER ELECTRONICS   400 Park Rd, Watertown, CT 06795-0500,
    Tel: (203) 945-5000
    (Mfr elec & electr connectors, PCB assemblies & hardware)
        Litton Precision Products Intl. Inc., Heliosvagen 1C, Box 92146,
        S-120 08 Stockholm, Sweden

WMX TECHNOLOGIES INC   3003 Butterfield Rd, Oak Brook, IL 60563,
    Tel: (708) 572-8800
    (Environmental services)
        WMI Sellbergs AB, P.O. Box 19605, Tulegatan 44, S-104 32 Stockholm, Sweden

WORLD COURIER INC   46 Trinity Pl, New York, NY 10006, Tel: (718) 978-9400
    (Intl courier serv)
        World Courier Sweden AB, P.O. Box 4, Arlanda, Stockholm, Sweden

WM WRIGLEY JR CO   410 N Michigan Ave, Chicago, IL 60611-4287,
    Tel: (312) 644-2121
    (Mfr chewing gum)
        Wrigley Scandinavia AB, P.O. Box 3024, S-183 03 Taby, Sweden
        Wrigley Scandinavia AB, Stockholm, Sweden

XEROX CORP   800 Long Ridge Rd, PO Box 1600, Stamford, CT 06904,
    Tel: (203) 968-3000
    (Mfr document processing equip, sys & supplies)
        Xerox Corp., Stockholm, Sweden

YOUNG & RUBICAM INC   285 Madison Ave, New York, NY 10017, Tel: (212) 210-3000
    (Advertising, public relations, direct marketing & sales promotion, corp & product ID
    management)
        Hall & Cederquist/Young & Rubicam, Kaptensgatan 6, S-114 84 Stockholm, Sweden

SWITZERLAND

3COM CORP   5400 Bayfront Plaza, Santa Clara, CA 95052-8145,
  Tel: (408) 764-5000
  (Devel/mfr computer networking prdts & sys)
    3Com GmbH, Switzerland

3M   3M Center, St Paul, MN 55144-1000, Tel: (612) 733-1110
  (Mfr diversified prdts for industry, health care, imaging, commun, transport, safety,
  consumer, etc)
    3M (East) AG, Grundstrasse 14, CH-6343 Rotkreuz, Switzerland
    3M (Schweiz) AG, Eggstrasse 93, CH-8803 Ruschlikon, Switzerland

AAF INTL   215 Central Ave, PO Box 35690, Louisville, KY 40232-5690,
  Tel: (502) 637-0011
  (Mfr air filtration/pollution control & noise control equip)
    Lufttechnik & Metallbau, Zentralstrasse 74, CH-5430 Wettingen 1, Switzerland

ACUFF-ROSE PUBLICATION INC   65 Music Square W, Nashville, TN 37203,
  Tel: (615) 321-5000
  (Music publisher)
    Acuff Rose, Verlag AG, P.O. Box 377, Badenerstr. 555, CH-8040, Zurich, Switzerland

AIR EXPRESS INTL CORP   120 Tokeneke Rd, PO Box 1231, Darien, CT 06820,
  Tel: (203) 655-7900
  (Air frt forwarder)
    Basel Warehouse & Forwarding Co. Ltd., P.O. Box 218, CH-8058 Zurich Airport,
    Switzerland

ALBANY INTL CORP   PO Box 1907, Albany, NY 12201, Tel: (518) 445-2200
  (Paper mach clothing, engineered fabrics, plastic prdts, filtration media)
    Albany International European Group Headquarters, P.O. Box 308, CH-8034 Zurich,
    Switzerland

ALLEN-BRADLEY CO   PO Box 2086, Milwaukee, WI 53201, Tel: (414) 382-2000
  (Mfr eletrical controls & info devices)
    Allen-Bradley AG, Lohwisstrasse 50, CH-8123 Ebmatingen, Switzerland

AM INTL INC   9399 W Higgins Rd, Rosemont, IL 60618, Tel: (708) 292-0600
  (Mfr/sale/serv printing & print prod equip, mailroom/bindery sys, svces & supplies
  for graphics ind)
    AM Intl. AG, Hinterbergstrasse 11, CH-6330 Cham, Switzerland

AMDAHL CORP   1250 E Arques Ave, PO Box 3470, Sunnyvale, CA 94088-3470,
  Tel: (408) 746-6000
  (Devel/mfr large scale computers, software, data storage prdts, info-technology

(cont)

solutions & support)
  Amdahl (Schweiz) AG, Baumackerstrassse 46, CH-8050 Zurich, Switzerland

AMERICAN AIRLINES INC   PO Box 619616, Dallas-Ft Worth Arpt, TX 75261-9616,
  Tel: (817) 355-1234
  (Air transp)
  American Airlines Inc., Pelikanstr. 37, CH-8801 Zurich, Switzerland

AMERICAN OPTICAL CORP   14 Mechanic St, Southbridge, MA 01550,
  Tel: (508) 765-9711
  (Mfr opthalmic lenses & frames, custom molded prdts, specialty lenses)
  American Optical Co. Intl. AG, P.O. Box 2150, CH-4002 Basel, Switzerland

AMICON INC   72 Cherry Hill Dr, Beverly, MA 01915, Tel: (508) 777-3622
  (Mfr/sale/svce bioseparation, membrane ultrafiltration, chromatography)
  Grace AG, Ameicon Div., Hertistrasse 29, Postfach, CH-8304 Wallisellen, Switzerland

AMOCO CHEMICAL CO   200 E Randolph Dr, Chicago, IL 60601, Tel: (312) 856-3200
  (Mfr/sale petrol based chems, plastics, chem/plastic prdts)
  Amoco Chemical (Europe) SA, Switzerland

AMP INC   PO Box 3608, Harrisburg, PA 17105-3608, Tel: (717) 564-0100
  (Devel/mfr electronic & electrical connection prdts & sys)
  AMP (Schweiz) AG, Amperestrasse 3, CH-9323 Steinach, Switzerland

AMPCO METAL INC   1745 S 38th St, PO Box 2004, Milwaukee, WI 53201,
  Tel: (414) 645-3750
  (Mfr/distr/sale cast & wrought copper-based alloys)
  Ampco Metal SA, 9 Route de Chesalles, CH-1723 Marly, Switzerland

AMPEX SYSTEMS CORP   401 Broadway, Redwood City, CA 94063-3199,
  Tel: (415) 367-2011
  (Mfr hi-perf helical scanning recording sys & associated tape media)
  Ampex World Operations SA, 15 Route des Arsenaux, CH-1701 Fribourg, Switzerland

AMWAY CORP   7575 E Fulton Rd, Ada, MI 49355, Tel: (616) 676-6000
  (Mfr/sale home care, personal care, nutrition & houseware prdts)
  Amway (Schweiz) AG, Industriestrasse 444, CH-4703 Kestenholz, Switzerland

ANALOG DEVICES INC   1 Technology Way, Box 9106, Norwood, MA 02062,
  Tel: (617) 329-4700
  (Mfr integrated circuits & related devices)
  Analog Devices SA, 9 Rue de Bern, CH-1201 Geneva, Switzerland

ANDREW CORP   10500 W 153rd St, Orlando Park, IL 60462, Tel: (708) 349-3300
  (Mfr antenna sys, coaxial cable, electronic commun & network connectivity sys)
  Andrew Kommunikationssysteme AG, Backliwis 2B, CH-8184 Bachenbulach (Zurich),
    Switzerland

ANIXTER BROS INC   4711 Golf Rd, Skokie, IL 60076, Tel: (708) 677-2600
  (Dist wiring sys/prdts for voice, video, data & power applications)
  Anixter Switzerland, La Foge En La Ternaz, P.O. Box 115, CH-1815 Clarens,
    Switzerland

ARMSTRONG WORLD INDUSTRIES INC   PO Box 3001, Lancaster, PA 17604,
  Tel: (717) 397-0611
  (Mfr/mkt interior furnishings & spec prdts for bldg, auto & textile inds)
    Armstrong World Industries (Schweiz) AG, Pfaffnau,
      Switzerland (all inquiries to U.S. address)
    ISO Holding AG, Schwyz, Switzerland (all inquiries to U.S. address)

ASARCO INC   180 Maiden Lane, New York, NY 10038, Tel: (212) 510-2000
  (Nonferrous metals, specialty chems, minerals, mfr industrial prdts, environmental
  services)
    Enthone-Omi Inc., Switzerland

ASHLAND OIL INC   1000 Ashland Dr, Russell, KY 41169, Tel: (606) 329-3333
  (Petroleum exploration, refining & transportation; mfr chemicals, oils & lubricants)
    Ashland-Suedchemie Gremolith AG, CH-9602 Bazenheid, Switzerland

ASSOCIATED PRESS INC   50 Rockefeller Plaza, New York, NY 10020-1605,
  Tel: (212) 621-1500
  (News gathering agency)
    The Associated Press, 33 Chemin de Grange Canal, CH-1211 Geneva, Switzerland

AST RESEARCH INC   16215 Alton Parkway, PO Box 19658, Irvine, CA 92713-9658,
  Tel: (714) 727-4141
  (Design/devel/mfr hi-perf desktop, server & notebook computers)
    AST Switzerland, 42 route de Satigny, P.O. Box 469, CH-1214 Vernier (Geneva),
      Switzerland
    AST Switzerland, P.O. Box 23, Alte Obfelderstr. 55, CH-8910 Affoltern a/A (Zurich),
      Switzerland

AUGAT INC   89 Forbes Blvd, Mansfield, MA 02048, Tel: (508) 543-4300
  (Interconnection prdts)
    Augat AG, Aegeristr. 58, CH-6300 Zug, Switzerland
    Augat Electroform, Via Prado 110, CH-6934 Bioggio, Switzerland

AUTO-TROL TECHNOLOGY CORP   12500 N Washington St, Denver, CO 80241-2400,
  Tel: (303) 452-4919
  (Mfr/sale/serv systems integration, CAD/CAM/CAE software)
    Auto-trol Switzerland, Kanalstr. 21, CH-8152 Glattbrugg/Zurich, Switzerland

AUTODESK INC   2320 Marinship Way, Sausalito, CA 94965, Tel: (415) 332-2344
  (Devel/mkt/support computer-aided design, engineering, scientific & multimedia
  software prdts)
    Autodesk (Europe) SA, 20 route de Pre-Bois, P.O. Box 766,
      CH-1215 Geneva 15 Airport, Switzerland
    Autodesk AG, Zurlindenstrasse 29, CH-4133 Pratteln, Switzerland

AVERY DENNISON CORP   150 N Orange Grove Blvd, Pasadena, CA 91103,
  Tel: (818) 304-2000
  (Mfr pressure-sensitive adhesives & materials, office prdts, labels, tags, retail
  sys, spec chems)
    Fasson Vertriebs AG, Stettbachstrasse 8, CH-8500 Dubendorf, Switzerland

BAIN & CO INC   2 Copley Place, Boston, MA 02117-0897, Tel: (617) 572-2000
  (Strategic management consulting services)
    Bain & Co. Switzerland Inc., Rue du Parc 4, CH-1207 Geneva, Switzerland

BALTIMORE AIRCOIL CO INC   7595 Montevideo Rd, Jessup, MD 20794,
Tel: (410) 799-6200
(Mfr evaporative cooling & heat transfer equip for A/C, refrig & industrial process cooling)
    Baltimore Aircoil Italy SRL, Fermo Posta 34, CH-7744 Compocolongo, Switzerland

BANDAG INC   2905 NW 61, Muscatine, IA 52761, Tel: (319) 262-1400
(Mfr/sale retread tires)
    Bandag AG, Lachan, Switzerland
    VV-System AG, Opfikon, Switzerland

BANKAMERICA CORP   555 California St, San Francisco, CA 94104,
Tel: (415) 622-3456
(Financial services)
    Bank of America NT & SA, Giesshubelstrasse 45, CH-8027 Zurich, Switzerland

BANKERS TRUST CO   280 Park Ave, New York, NY 10017, Tel: (212) 250-2500
(Banking)
    Bankers Trust AG, Dreikonigstr. 6, CH-8022 Zurich, Switzerland

BATTELLE MEMORIAL INSTITUTE   505 King Ave, Columbus, OH 43201-2693,
Tel: (614) 424-6424
(Tech devel, commercialization & mgmt)
    Battelle Europe, 7 Route de Drize, CH-1227 Carouge-Geneva, Switzerland

BATTEN BARTON DURSTINE & OSBORN INC   1285 Ave of the Americas, New York,
NY 10019, Tel: (212) 459-5000
(Advertising agency)
    BBDO GmbH, Mueble Bachstr. 164, CH-8034 Zurich, Switzerland

BAUSCH & LOMB INC   1 Chase Square, Rochester, NY 14601, Tel: (716) 338-6000
(Mfr vision care prdts & accessories)
    Bausch & Lomb AG, Bern, Switzerland
    Bausch & Lomb Fribourg SA, Lausanne, Switzerland

BAXTER HEALTHCARE CORP   1 Baxter Pky, Deerfield, IL 60015,
Tel: (708) 948-2000
(Mfr disposable medical prdts)
    Baxter AG, Industriestr. 31, CH-8305 Dietikon, Switzerland
    Baxter Dade AG, Bonnstrasse, CH-3186 Duedingen, Switzerland
    Edwards AG/Xenomedica, Spierstrasse 5, CH-6048 Horw, Switzerland

BECHTEL GROUP INC   50 Beale St, PO Box 3965, San Francisco, CA 94119,
Tel: (415) 768-1234
(Engineering & constr)
    Bechtel Intl., Aeschenvorstadt 4, CH-4000 Basel, Switzerland

BECKMAN INSTRUMENTS INC   2500 Harbor Blvd, Fullerton, CA 92634,
Tel: (714) 871-4848
(Devel/mfr/mkt automated systems & supplies for biological analysis)
    Beckman Eurocenter SA, 22 Rue Juste Olivier, P.O. Box 301, CH-1260 Nyon, Switzerland
    Beckman Instruments Intl. SA, 22 Rue Juste Olivier, CH-1260 Nyon, Switzerland

BIJUR LUBRICATING CORP   50 Kocher Dr, Bennington, VT 05201-1994,
Tel: (802) 447-2174
(Design/mfr centralized lubrication equip)
  Bijur Products Inc., P.O. Box 56, Erlenstrasse 2a, CH-2555 Brugg/Bienne, Switzerland

SAMUEL BINGHAM CO   1555 N Mittel Blvd, #T, Wood Dale, IL 60191-1046,
Tel: (708) 238-4000
(Print & industrial rollers, inks)
  Huber & Suhner AG, CH-8330 Pfaffikon/Schweiz, Switzerland

BIO-RAD LABORATORIES INC   1000 Alfred Nobel Dr, Hercules, CA 94547,
Tel: (510) 724-7000
(Mfr life science research prdts, clinical diagnostics, analytical instruments)
  Bio-Rad Lab AG, Zurich, Switzerland

BLACK & DECKER CORP   701 E Joppa Road, Towson, MD 21286, Tel: (410) 716-3900
(Mfr power tools & accessories, security hardware, small appliances, fasteners, info
sys & servs)
  Black & Decker Corp., all mail to U.S. address

BLACK BOX CORP   1000 Park Dr, Lawrence, PA 15055, Tel: (412) 746-5500
(Direct marketer & tech service provider of commun, networking & related computer
connectivity prdts)
  Black Box (Schweiz) AG, Talstrasse 1, CH-8852 Altendorf, Switzerland

BOOLE & BABBAGE INC   510 Oakmead Pkwy, Sunnyvale, CA 94086,
Tel: (408) 735-9550
(Devel/support enterprise automation & systems mgmt software)
  Boole & Babbage (Switzerland) AG, Zurcherstrasse 200, CH-8406 Winterthur,
  Switzerland

BOSE CORP   The Mountain, Framingham, MA 01701-9168, Tel: (508) 879-7330
(Mfr audio equip)
  Bose AG, Runenbergerstrasse 13A, CH-4460 Gelterkinden, Switzerland

BOSTITCH DIV   815 Briggs St, East Greenwich, RI 02818, Tel: (401) 884-2500
(Stapling machs & supplies, wire)
  Bostitch AG, Hardturmstr. 169, CH-8037 Zurich, Switzerland

BOURNS INC   1200 Columbia Ave, Riverside, CA 92507, Tel: (909) 781-5500
(Mfr resistive com & networks, precision potentiometers, panel controls, switches,
transducers)
  Bourns AG, Zugerstr. 74, CH-6340 Baar, Switzerland

BOYDEN CONSULTING CORP   375 Park Ave, #1008, New York, NY 10152,
Tel: (212) 980-6480
(Executive search)
  Boyden Intl. SA, 4 Rue de la Scie, CH-1207 Geneva, Switzerland

BRANSON ULTRASONICS CORP   41 Eagle Rd, Danbury, CT 06813-1961,
Tel: (203) 796-0400
(Mfr plastics assembly equip, ultrasonic cleaning equip)
  Branson Ultrasonic SA, 9 Chemin du Faubourg-de-Cruseilles, CH-1227 Carouge, Geneva,
  Switzerland

BROWN & SHARPE MFG CO   Precision Park, 200 Frenchtown Rd, North Kingstown, RI 02852-1700, Tel: (401) 886-2000
(Mfr/sale/svce metrology equip & precision tools)
  P. Roch Ltd., c/o Tesa SA, Bugnon 38, CH-1020 Renens, Switzerland
  Tesa S.A., Bugnon 38, CH-1020 Renens, Switzerland

BROWN BROTHERS HARRIMAN & CO   59 Wall St, New York, NY 10005,
Tel: (212) 483-1818
(Financial services)
  Brown Brothers Harriman Services AG, Stockerstr. 38, CH-8002 Zurich, Switzerland

BRUNSWICK CORP   1 N Field Court, Lake Forest, IL 60045-4811,
Tel: (708) 735-4700
(Mfr recreational boats, marine engines, bowling centers & equip, fishing equip, defense/aerospace)
  Brunswick AG Maschinen Fabrik, Ifnagstr. 12, P.O. Box 220, CH-8603 Schwerzenbach, Switzerland

LEO BURNETT CO INC   35 West Wacker Dr, Chicago, IL 60601, Tel: (312) 220-5959
(Advertising agency)
  Marsden Hartmann & Leo Burnett Wergeagentur AG, BSW, Vorhaldenstrasse 10, CH-8049 Zurich, Switzerland
  Win Werbeagentur AG, BSW, Wehntalerstrasse 276, CH-8046 Zurich, Switzerland

BURR-BROWN RESEARCH CORP   PO Box 11400, Tucson, AZ 85734, Tel: (602) 746-1111
(Electronic components & sys modules)
  Burr-Brown Intl. AG, Weingartenstr. 9, CH-8033 Rueschlikon/Zurich, Switzerland

BURSON-MARSTELLER   230 Park Ave, New York, NY 10003-1566, Tel: (212) 614-4000
(Public relations/public affairs consultants)
  Burson-Marsteller, 2 Rue Thalberg, CH-1201 Geneva, Switzerland

BUTLER AUTOMATIC INC   480 Neponset St, Canton, MA 02021, Tel: (617) 828-5450
(Mfr web press equip)
  Butler Automatica Inc., 6 Chemin de la Graviere, CH-1227 Acacias, Geneva, Switzerland

CABOT CORP   75 State St, Boston, MA 02109-1807, Tel: (617) 890-0200
(Mfr carbon blacks, plastics; oil & gas, info sys)
  Nickel Contor AF (Hitec Div.), Gotthardstr. 21, CH-8022 Zurich, Switzerland

CALBIOCHEM-NOVABIOCHEM CORP   PO Box 12087, La Jolla, CA 92039,
Tel: (619) 450-9600
(Mfr biochems, immunochems, reagents)
  Calbiochem-Novabiochem AG, Weidenmattweg 4, CH-4880 Laufelfingen, Switzerland
  Calbiochem-Novabiochem AG East, Cysatstrasse 23A, CH-6000 Lucerne 5, Switzerland

CALCOMP INC   2411 W La Palma Ave, Anaheim, CA 92801, Tel: (714) 821-2000
(Mfr computer graphics peripherals)
  CalComp Schweiz, Wehntalerstrasse 6, CH-8154 Oberglatt, Switzerland

CAMP INTL INC   PO Box 89, Jackson, MI 49204, Tel: (517) 787-1600
(Mfr orthotics & prosthetics)
  Scharer AG, CH-6014 Littau, Luzern, Switzerland

CANBERRA INDUSTRIES INC   One State St, Meriden, CT 06450, Tel: (203) 238-2351
(Mfr instru for nuclear research)
  Canberra-Packard AG, Renggerstr. 3, CH-3038 Zurich, Switzerland

THE CAPITAL GROUP COS INC   333 S Hope, Los Angeles, CA 90071,
  Tel: (213) 486-8200
(Investment mgmt)
  Capital Intl. SA, 3 Place des Bergues, CH-1201 Geneva, Switzerland

CARGILL   PO Box 9300, Minneapolis, MN 55440, Tel: (612) 475-7575
(Food prdts, feeds, animal prdts)
  Cargill Intl. SA, P.O. Box 383, CH-1211 Geneva 12, Switzerland

CARRIER CORP   One Carrier Place, Farmington, CT 06034-4015,
  Tel: (203) 674-3000
(Mfr/distr/svce A/C, heating & refrigeration equip)
  Blocair Vente SA, Sinn, Switzerland
  Winner Airconditioning SA, 93 Rue de Servette, CH-1202 Geneva, Switzerland

CAT PUMPS   1681 94th Lane NE, Minneapolis, MN 55449-4324, Tel: (612) 780-5440
(Mfr/distr pumps)
  Cat Pumps AG, Lorentohoehe 5, CH-6300 Zug, Switzerland

CATERPILLAR INC   100 N E Adams St, Peoria, IL 61629, Tel: (309) 675-1000
(Mfr earth/material-handling & constr mach & equip, engines, generators)
  Caterpillar Overseas SA, YA 50.76 Route de Frontenex, P.O. Box 456,
    CH-1211 Geneva 6, Switzerland

CHASE MANHATTAN BANK N A   1 Chase Manhattan Plaza, New York, NY 10081,
  Tel: (212) 552-2222
(Intl banking)
  Chase Manhattan Bank (Switzerland), 63 Rue du Rhone, CH-1204 Geneva, Switzerland

CHEMICAL BANK   270 Park Ave, New York, NY 10017-2070, Tel: (212) 270-6000
(Banking & financial services)
  Chemical Bank, Freigutstrasse 16, P.O. Box 1031, CH-8039 Zurich, Switzerland

CHESTERTON BINSWANGER INTL   Two Logan Sq, 4th fl, Philadelphia,
  PA 19103-2759, Tel: (215) 448-6000
(Real estate & related svces)
  Blumenauer Immobilien, Im Hagenbrunneli 25, CH-8046 Zurich, Switzerland

CHEVRON CHEMICAL CO   PO Box 5047, San Ramon, CA 94583-0947,
  Tel: (510) 842-5500
(Chemicals)
  Chevron Chemical Intl. Sales Inc., 12 rue Le Corbusier, CH-1208 Geneva, Switzerland

CHIRON CORP   4560 Horton St, Emeryville, CA 94608-2916, Tel: (510) 601-2412
(Research/mfg/mktg therapeutics, vaccines, diagnostics, ophthalmics)
  Ciba Corning Diagnostics AG, Neue Winterthurestrasse 15, CH-8305 Dietlikon,
    Switzerland

CIGNA CORP   One Liberty Place, Philadelphia, PA 19192, Tel: (215) 523-4000
(Ins, invest, health care & other fin servs)
  Insurance Co. of North America, Hohlstrasse 190, CH-8004 Zurich, Switzerland

CINCOM SYSTEMS INC   2300 Montana Ave, Cincinnati, OH 45211,
Tel: (513) 662-2300
(Devel/distr computer software)
  Cincom Systems Inc., Geneva, Switzerland
  Cincom Systems Inc., Zurich, Switzerland

CITICORP   399 Park Ave, New York, NY 10043, Tel: (212) 559-1000
(Banking & financial services)
  Citibank (Switzerland), Switzerland

THE COCA-COLA CO   PO Drawer 1734, Atlanta, GA 30301, Tel: (404) 676-2121
(Mfr/mkt/distr soft drinks, syrups & concentrates, juice & juice-drink prdts)
  Refresca AG, all mail to U.S. address

COLGATE-PALMOLIVE CO   300 Park Ave, New York, NY 10022, Tel: (212) 310-2000
(Mfr pharms, cosmetics, toiletries, detergents)
  Colgate-Palmolive AG, Wengistrasse 30, CH-8022 Zurich, Switzerland

COLUMBIA PICTURES INDUSTRIES INC   711 Fifth Ave, New York, NY 10022,
Tel: (212) 751-4400
(Producer & distributor of motion pictures)
  Twentieth Century-Fox Film Corp., P.O. Box 121, CH-1211 Geneva 8, Switzerland

COMDISCO INC   6111 N River Rd, Rosemont, IL 60018, Tel: (708) 698-3000
(Hi-tech asset & facility mgmt, equip leasing)
  Comdisco Switzerland SA, Zurich, Switzerland

COMMERCIAL CREDIT LOANS INC   300 St Paul Place, Baltimore, MD 21202,
Tel: (301) 332-3000
(Leasing of capital goods)
  Commercial Credit Leasing Services (Switzerland), Militarstr. 36, P.O. Box 8021,
    Zurich, Switzerland

COMMERCIAL METALS CO   PO Box 1046, Dallas, TX 75221, Tel: (214) 689-4300
(Metal collecting/processing, steel mills, metal trading)
  CMC Trading AG, Postrasse 4, CH-6301 Zug, Switzerland

COMPUTER ASSOCIATES INTL INC   One Computer Associates Plaza, Islandia,
NY 11788, Tel: (516) 342-5224
(Devel/mkt/mgt info mgt & bus applications software)
  Computer Associates AG, Industriestr. 30, CH-8302 Kloten, Switzerland

CONOCO INC   600 N Dairy Ashford Rd, Houston, TX 77079, Tel: (713) 293-1000
(Oil, gas, coal, chems, minerals)
  Conoco AG, P.O. Box230, CH-6300 Zug, Switzerland

COOK INDUSTRIES INC   855 Ridge Lake Blvd, Memphis, TN 38117,
Tel: (901) 761-3700
(Ins broker & pest control)
  Cook Transportation System Inc., Switzerland

COOPER INDUSTRIES INC   1001 Fannin St, PO Box 4446, Houston, TX 77210-4446,
Tel: (713) 739-5400
(Mfr/distr electrical prdts, tools & hardware, automotive prdts)
  Cooper Hand Tools Div., Yverdon, Switzerland

CPC INTERNATIONAL INC   PO Box 8000, Englewood Cliffs, NJ 07632,
Tel: (201) 894-4000
(Consumer foods, corn refining)
   CPC Export, Steinackerweg 8, CH-8047 Zurich, Switzerland
   Knorr-Nahrmittel AG, Bahnhofstrasse, CH-8240 Thayngen, Switzerland

CRAY RESEARCH INC   655 Lone Oak Dr, Eagan, MN 55121, Tel: (612) 452-6650
(Supercomputer systems & services)
   Cray Research (Suisse) SA, Route de Renins 1, CH-1030 Bussigny-Pres-Lausanne,
   Switzerland

CULLIGAN INTL CO   One Culligan Parkway, Northbrook, IL 60062,
Tel: (708) 205-6000
(Water treatment prdts & serv)
   Culligan Schweiz AG, c/o Continental Revisions und Truehand AG, Dorfstrasse 67,
   CH-8302 Zurich, Switzerland

D'ARCY MASIUS BENTON & BOWLES INC (DMB&B)   1675 Broadway, New York,
NY 10019, Tel: (212) 468-3622
(Advertising & communications)
   Heinz Heimann SA, 3 Chemin de Mancy, CH-1222 Geneve-Vesenaz, Switzerland

DANA CORP   PO Box 1000, Toledo, OH 43697, Tel: (419) 535-4500
(Engineer/mfr/mkt prdts & sys for vehicular, ind & mobile off-highway mkt & related
aftermarkets)
   Warner Electric Inc., P.O. Box 1545, CH-1001 Lausanne, Switzerland

DATA GENERAL CORP   4400 Computer Dr, Westboro, MA 01580, Tel: (617) 366-8911
(Design, mfr gen purpose computer sys & peripheral prdts & servs)
   Data General AG, Foerrlibuckstr. 110, P.O. Box 8037, Zurich, Switzerland

DATAEASE INTL INC   7 Cambridge Dr, Trumbull, CT 06611, Tel: (203) 374-8000
(Mfr applications devel software)
   Markt & Technik Vertriess AG, Kollerstrasse 37, CH-6300 Zug, Switzerland

DDB NEEDHAM WORLDWIDE INC   437 Madison Ave, New York, NY 10022,
Tel: (212) 415-2000
(Advertising)
   DDB Needham Worldwide AG, Kohlrainstrasse 10, CH-8700 Kuesnacht-Zurich, Switzerland

DEAN WITTER REYNOLDS INC   2 World Trade Center, New York, NY 10048,
Tel: (212) 392-2222
(Securities & commodities brokerage, investment banking, money mgmt, personal trusts)
   Dean Witter (Lausanne) SA, Ave. de la Gare 10, CH-1003 Lausanne, Switzerland
   Dean Witter Reynolds (Geneva) SA, Rue Versonnex 7, CH-1207 Geneva, Switzerland

DENTSPLY INTL INC   PO Box 872, York, PA 17405, Tel: (717) 845-7511
(Mfr dental, medical & ind supplies & equip)
   DeTrey Div., Dentsply AG, Weinreben 9, CH-6300 Zug, Switzerland

DETROIT DIESEL CORP   13400 Outer Drive West, Detroit, MI 48239,
Tel: (313) 592-5000
(Mfr diesel & aircraft engines, heavy-duty transmissions)
   Detroit Diesel (Europe) SA, Schaftenholzweig 54, CH-2557 Studen (Biel-Bienne),
   Switzerland
   Detroit Diesel (Suisse) SA, Schaftenholzweig 54, CH-2557 Studen (Biel-Bienne),
   Switzerland

THE DEXTER CORP   1 Elm Street, Windsor Locks, CT 06096, Tel: (203) 627-9051
  (Mfr nonwovens, polymer prdts, magnetic materials, biotechnology)
    Dexter Packaging Products, Lack-und Farbenfabrik, CH-8267 Gruningen, Switzerland

DIBRELL BROS INC   512 Bridge St, Danville, VA 24543, Tel: (804) 792-7511
  (Sale leaf tobacco, cut flowers)
    Dibrell Bros. Intl. S.A., 9 Rue de la Gabelle, CH-1227 Carouge, Geneva, Switzerland

DICTAPHONE CORP   3191 Broadbridge Ave, Stratford, CT 06497-2559,
  Tel: (203) 381-7000
  (Mfr/sale dictation, tel answering & multi-channel voice commun recording sys)
    Dictaphone Intl. AG, Wuerenloserstr. 2, Killwangen, Switzerland

DIGITAL EQUIPMENT CORP   146 Main St, Maynard, MA 01754-2571,
  Tel: (508) 493-5111
  (Networked computer systems & services)
    Digital Equipment Corp. Intl. (Europe), 12 Ave. des Morgines, Carte Postale 176,
      CH-1213 Petit Lancy 1, Geneva, Switzerland
    Digital Equipment Intl. Ltd., Grand Places 1, CH-1701 Fribourg, Switzerland

DIONEX CORP   1228 Tital Way, PO Box 3603, Sunnyvale, CA 94088-3603,
  Tel: (408) 737-0700
  (Devel/mfr/mktg/svce chromatography sys & relted prdts)
    Dionex (Switzerland) AG, Solothurnerstrasse 259, CH-4600 Olten, Switzerland

DOMINICK & DOMINICK INC   90 Broad St, New York, NY 10090, Tel: (212) 558-8800
  (Brokers)
    Dominick & Dominick Inc., P.O. Box 47, CH-4010 Basel, Switzerland

DONALDSON LUFKIN & JENRETTE INC   140 Broadway, New York, NY 10005,
  Tel: (212) 504-3000
  (Investment mgmt)
    Donaldson Lufkin & Jenrette, Beethovenstr. 5, CH-8002 Zurich, Switzerland

THE DOW CHEMICAL CO   2030 Dow Center, Midland, MI 48674, Tel: (517) 636-1000
  (Mfr chems, plastics, pharms, agric prdts, consumer prdts)
    Dow Chemical Europe SA, Bachtobelstr. 3, CH-8810 Horgen, Switzerland
    Dow Chemical Europe SA, 17B Ancienne Route, CH-1218 Grand Saconnex, Geneva,
      Switzerland
    Dow Chemical Mideast/Africa, P.O. Box 196, Geneva, Switzerland

DRAKE BEAM MORIN INC   100 Park Ave, New York, NY 10017, Tel: (212) 692-7700
  (Human resource mgmt consulting & training)
    Drake Beam Morin, 94 rue de Lausanne, CH-1202 Geneva, Switzerland
    Drake Beam Morin, also in Basel, Berne, Geneva, Lausanne, Lugano & Zurich,
      Switzerland

DRESSER INDUSTRIES INC   PO Box 718, Dallas, TX 75221-0718,
  Tel: (214) 740-6000
  (Diversified supplier of equip & tech serv to energy & natural resource ind)
    Dresser AG, Baarerstrassse 10, CH-6300 Zug, Switzerland

E I DU PONT DE NEMOURS & CO   1007 Market St, Wilmington, DE 19898,
  Tel: (302) 774-1000
  (Mfr/sale diversified chems, plastics, specialty prdts & fibers)

Du Pont de Nemours International SA, 50-52 Route de 5 Acacias, P.O. Box 1211,
   Geneva, Switzerland

EASTMAN KODAK CO   343 State St, Rochester, NY 14650, Tel: (716) 724-4000
   (Devel/mfr photo & chem prdts, info mgmt/video/copier sys, fibers/plastics for
   various ind)
      Eastman Chemical Intl. AG, P.O. Box 3263, Hertizentrum 6, CH-6300 Zug 3, Switzerland
      Kodak SA, Case Postale, CH-1001 Lausanne, Switzerland
      Kodak SA, also in Renens & Zurich, Switzerland

EBASCO SERVICES INC   2 World Trade Center, New York, NY 10048-0752,
   Tel: (212) 839-1000
   (Engineering, constr)
      Ebasco Energy AG, c/o Hunter & Partner AG, Unter Alstadt 2F, CH-6300 Zug,
         Switzerland

EG&G INC   45 William St, Wellesley, MA 02181-4078, Tel: (617) 237-5100
   (Diversified R/D, mfg & services)
      EG&G Berthold AG, Adlikerstr. 236, CH-8105 Regensdorf, Switzerland

EMERY WORLDWIDE   One Lagoon Dr, #400, Redwood City, CA 94065,
   Tel: (800) 227-1981
   (Freight transport, global logistics, air cargo)
      Emery Worldwide, P.O. Box 103-8058 Zurich Airport, Zurich, Switzerland

ENSEARCH INTL DEVELOPMENT INC   300 South St Paul, Dallas, TX 75201,
   Tel: (214) 651-8700
   (Div energy operations)
      Losinger Ltd., Konizstr. 74, Bern, Switzerland

ENTERPRISES INTL INC   P.O. Box 293, Hoquiam, WA 98550, Tel: (360) 533-6222
   (Mfr/sale/svce capital equip for pulp, paper & newsprint ind)
      Lamb AG, Landstrasse 15, Postfach 68, CH-5430 Wettingen 3, Switzerland

ESSEX SPECIALTY PRODUCTS INC   1250 Harmon Rd, Auburn Hills, MI 48326,
   Tel: (810) 391-6300
   (Mfr adhesives, sealants, structural reinforcement composites)
      Gurit-Essex AG, Wolleraustrasse 15/17, CH-8807 Freienbach, Switzerland

ESTEE LAUDER INTL INC   767 Fifth Ave, New York, NY 10019, Tel: (212) 572-4600
   (Cosmetics)
      Estee Lauder AG, Genferstr. 35, CH-8002 Zurich, Switzerland

FARMLAND INDUSTRIES INC   PO Box 7305, Kansas City, MO 64116,
   Tel: (816) 459-6000
   (Food production & marketing)
      Tradigrain Inc., Geneva, Switzerland

FEDERAL EXPRESS CORP   PO Box 727, Memphis, TN 38194, Tel: (901) 369-3600
   (Package express delivery service)
      Federal Express (Switzerland) Ltd., Basel Mulhouse Airport, P.O. Box 115,
         CH-4030 Basel-Flughafen, Switzerland

FEDERAL-MOGUL CORP   PO Box 1966, Detroit, MI 48235, Tel: (810) 354-7700
   (Mfr/distr precision parts for automobiles, trucks, & farm/construction vehicles)
      Federal-Mogul SA, Switzerland

FIDUCIARY TRUST CO OF NY   2 World Trade Center, 94th fl, New York, NY 10048,
  Tel: (212) 466-4100
  (Banking)
    Fiduciary Trust (Intl.) SA, 7 Rue du Rhone, CH-1204 Geneva, Switzerland

FILON DIVISION   12333 S Van Ness Ave, Hawthorne, CA 90250,
  Tel: (213) 757-5141
  (Mfr fiberglass reinforced plastic coml/ind panels)
    Filon AG, Narzissenstr. 5, Postfach 109, CH-8033 Zurich, Switzerland

FIRST NATIONAL BANK OF BOSTON   100 Federal St, Boston, MA 02110,
  Tel: (617) 434-2200
  (Commercial banking)
    Boston Investment & Financial Servlces SA, 7 Rue des Alpes, P.O. Box 476,
      CH-1211 Geneva, Switzerland
    Factors AG, P.O. Box 8026, Zurich, Switzerland
    Factors AG, Backerstr. 40, CH-8004 Zurich, Switzerland

FIRST NATIONAL BANK OF CHICAGO   One First National Plaza, Chicago, IL 60670,
  Tel: (312) 732-4000
  (Financial services)
    The First National Bank of Chicago, 6 Place des Eaux Vives, P.O. Box 102,
      CH-1211 Geneva 6, Switzerland

FISHER CONTROLS INTL INC   8000 Maryland Ave, Clayton, MO 63105,
  Tel: (314) 746-9900
  (Mfr ind process control equip)
    Fisher Controls AG, P.O. Box 261, CH-8032 Zurich, Switzerland

FISHER SCIENTIFIC INC   Liberty Lane, Hampton, NH 03842, Tel: (603) 929-2650
  (Mfr sci instru & apparatus, chems, reagents)
    Fisher Scientific, Hottingstr. 14, CH-8032 Zurich, Switzerland

FMC CORP   200 E Randolph Dr, Chicago, IL 60601, Tel: (312) 861-6000
  (Produces chems & precious metals, mfr machinery, equip & sys for ind, agric & govt)
    FMC Holding AG, Switzerland
    FMC Intl. AG, Switzerland

FOOTE CONE & BELDING COMMUNICATIONS INC   101 E Erie St, Chicago,
  IL 60611-2897, Tel: (312) 751-7000
  (Advertising agency)
    BEP Publicis-FCB, 9 Chemin des Delices, CH-1006 Lausanne, Switzerland
    Farner Publicis-FCB, Thearterstrasse 8, CH-8001 Zurich, Switzerland

FORD MOTOR CO   The American Road, Dearborn, MI 48121, Tel: (313) 322-3000
  (Mfr motor vehicles)
    Ford Motor Co. (Switzerland) SA, Kurvenstr. 35, CH-8021 Zurich, Switzerland

FRANK RUSSELL CO   909 A St, PO Box 1616, Tacoma, WA 98401-1616,
  Tel: (206) 572-9500
  (Investment mgmt consulting)
    Frank Russell AG, Seestrasse 131, CH-8002 Zurich, Switzerland

THE FRANKLIN MINT   Franklin Center, PA 19091, Tel: (610) 459-6000
  (Creation/mfr/mktg collectibles & luxury items)
    Franklin Mint AG, Baarerstr. 10, CH-6300 Zug, Switzerland

GAF CORP   1361 Alps Rd, Wayne, NJ 07470, Tel: (201) 628-3000
(Chems, bldg materials, commun)
   GAF (Switzerland) AG, Gubelstr. 11, CH-6300 Zug, Switzerland

GANNETT CO INC   1100 Wilson Blvd, Arlington, VA 22234, Tel: (703) 284-6000
(Newspaper pub, opinion research, broadcasting)
   USA Today Intl., Zurich, Switzerland

GENERAL BINDING CORP   One GBC Plaza, Northbrook, IL 60062,
   Tel: (708) 272-3700
(Binding & laminating equip & associated supplies)
   GBC (Schweiz) AG, Churerstr. 162, CH-8808 Pfaeffikon, Switzerland

GENERAL ELECTRIC CO   3135 Easton Tpk, Fairfield, CT 06431,
   Tel: (203) 373-2211
(Diversified manufacturing, technology & services)
   General Electric Co.,
      all mail to U.S. address; phone (800) 626-2004 or (518) 438-6500

GENERAL MILLS INC   1 General Mills Blvd, PO Box 1113, Minneapolis, MN 55440,
   Tel: (612) 540-2311
(Mfr consumer foods)
   CPW, S.A., Ave. de la Gottaz 36, Case Postale 2184, CH-1110 Morges 2, Switzerland
   Cereal Partners Worldwide, Ave. de la Gottaz 36, Case Postale 2184,
      CH-1110 Morges 2, Switzerland

GENERAL MOTORS ACCEPTANCE CORP   3044 West Grand Blvd, Detroit, MI 48202,
   Tel: (313) 556-5000
(Automobile financing)
   GMAC, Kanalstrasse 4, CH-8152 Zurich, Switzerland
   GMAC Suisse SA, Sageweg 7, CH-2557 Studen, Switzerland

GENERAL MOTORS CORP   3044 W Grand Blvd, Detroit, MI 48202-3091,
   Tel: (313) 556-5000
(Mfr full line vehicles, automotive electronics, coml technologies, telecom, space,
finance)
   General Motors Suisse SA, Salzhausstr. 21, CH-2501 Bienne, Switzerland

GENERAL REINSURANCE CORP   PO Box 10350, Stamford, CT 06904-2350,
   Tel: (203) 328-5000
(Reinsurance)
   General Reinsurance Corp. (Europe), Bellerivestr. 29a, P.O. Box 483,
      CH-8034 Zurich, Switzerland

GENRAD INC   300 Baker Ave, Concord, MA 01742, Tel: (508) 369-4400
(Mfr automatic test equip)
   GenRad (Schweiz) AG, Drahtzugstr. 18, CH-8032 Zurich, Switzerland

THE GILLETTE CO   Prudential Tower, Boston, MA 02199, Tel: (617) 421-7000
(Devel/mfr personal care/use prdts: blades & razors, toiletries, cosmetics,
stationery)
   Anant SA, Geneva, Switzerland
   Braun Electric Intl. SA, Baden, Switzerland
   Gillette (Switzerland) AG, Schlieren, Switzerland
   Jafra Cosmetics AG, Cham, Switzerland

THE GOODYEAR TIRE & RUBBER CO   1144 E Market St, Akron, OH 44316,
  Tel: (216) 796-2121
  (Mfr tires, automotive belts & hose, conveyor belts, chemicals; oil pipeline
  transmission)
      Goodyear (Suisse) SA, Industriegebiet Volketswil, CH-8604 Hegnau, Zurich,
        Switzerland

W R GRACE & CO   One Town Center Rd, Boca Raton, FL 33486-1010,
  Tel: (407) 362-2000
  (Mfr spec chems & materials: packaging, health care, catalysts, construction, water
  treatment/process)
      Grace AG, Hertistrasse 29, CH-8304 Wallisellen, Switzerland
      Grace Europe Inc., Ave. Montchoisi 35, CH-1006 Lausanne, Switzerland

GREAT LAKES CHEMICAL CORP   One Great Lakes Blvd, W Lafayette, IN 47906,
  Tel: (317) 497-6100
  (Mfr bromine & derivatives, furfural & derivatives)
      Great Lakes Chemical (Europe) Ltd., Frauenfeld, Switzerland

GREY ADVERTISING INC   777 Third Ave, New York, NY 10017, Tel: (212) 546-2000
  (Advertising)
      Grey Geneva, Rue de la Terrassiere 8, CH-1207 Geneva, Switzerland
      Walther Gesses Grey, Seestrasse 81, CH-8803 Ruschlikon, Zurich, Switerland

GTE CORP   One Stamford Forum, Stamford, CT 06904, Tel: (203) 965-2000
  (Electr prdts, telecom sys, publ & commun)
      GTE Sylvania SA, P.O. Box 310, 21 Rue du Rhone, CH-1211 Geneva 3, Switzerland
      General Telephone & Electronics Intl. SA, P.O. Box 310, Geneva, Switzerland

GULTON INDUSTRIES INC   212 Durham Ave, Metuchen, NJ 08840,
  Tel: (908) 548-6500
  (Electr instru & controls, commun equip)
      Electro-Voice SA, Romerstr. 3, CH-2560 Nidau, Switzerland

FRANK B HALL & CO INC   549 Pleasantville Rd, Briarcliff Manor, NY 10510,
  Tel: (914) 769-9200
  (Insurance)
      Joose & Preuss AG, Glattalstr. 18, CH-8052 Zurich, Switzerland

THE HARPER GROUP   260 Townsend St, PO Box 77933, San Francisco,
  CA 94107-1719, Tel: (415) 978-0600
  (Ocean/air freight fwdg, customs brokerage, packing & whse, logistics mgt, ins)
      Circle Freight Intl. Schweiz AG, Frachthof West, CH-8058 Zurich Airport, Switzerland
      Circle Freight Intl. Schweiz AG, also in Basel & Geneva, Switzerland

HEIN-WERNER CORP   PO Box 1606, Waukesha, WI 53187-1606, Tel: (414) 542-6611
  (Mfr auto body repair equip, engine rebuilding & brake repair equip, hydraulic
  cylinders)
      Hein-Werner (Europe) SA, 2 Promenade des Artisans, P.O. Box 114,
        CH-1217 Geneva/Meyrin, Switzerland

H J HEINZ CO   PO Box 57, Pittsburgh, PA 15230-0057, Tel: (412) 456-5700
  (Processed food prdts & nutritional services)
      Weight Watchers Intl. Inc., Geneva, Switzerland

HEWLETT-PACKARD CO   3000 Hanover St, Palo Alto, CA 94304-0890,
  Tel: (415) 857-1501
  (Mfr computing, communications & measurement prdts & services)
    Hewlett-Packard (Schweiz) AG, In der Luberzen 29, CH-8902 Urdorf/Zurich, Switzerland

HOLIDAY INNS INC   3742 Lamar Ave, Memphis, TN 38195, Tel: (901) 362-4001
  (Hotels, restaurants, casinos)
    Holiday Inn & Movenpick, Walter-Mittelholzer-Strasse 8, CH-8152 Glattbrugg-Opfikon,
      Switzerland
    Holiday Inn & Movenpick, CH-8105 Regensdorf, Switzerland
    Movenpick Hotel-Projektierungs-und Management AG, Congress Center Zurich,
      Zurichstr. 108, CH-8134 Akliswil, Switzerland

HONEYWELL INC   PO Box 524, Minneapolis, MN 55440-0524, Tel: (612) 951-1000
  (Devel/mfr controls for home & building, industry, space & aviation)
    Honeywell AG, Hertistrasse 2, CH-8304 Wallisellen, Switzerland

HORWATH INTL   415 Madison Ave, New York, NY 10017, Tel: (212) 838-5566
  (Public accountants & auditors)
    Alfa Treuhand & Revisions AG, Teufenerstrasse 12, CH-9000 St. Gallen, Switzerland
    Curator & Horwath, Freigutstrasse 27, CH-8039 Zurich, Switzerland
    Horwath Fiduciare & Revision SA, 15 rue du Jeu-de-L'Arc, CH-1211 Geneva, Switzerland

HOUGHTON INTL INC   PO Box 930, Valley Forge, PA 19482-0930,
  Tel: (610) 666-4000
  (Mfr spec chems, hydraulic fluids, lubricants)
    Houghton (Switzerland) AG, Wolfhaldenstrasse 13, CH-9500 Wil, Switzerland

HYATT INTL CORP   200 West Madison, Chicago, IL 60606, Tel: (312) 750-1234
  (Intl hotel mgmt)
    Hyatt Intl. Hotels, Montreux, Switzerland

IBM CORP   Old Orchard Rd, Armonk, NY 10504, Tel: (914) 765-1900
  (Information products, technology & services)
    IBM Switzerland, General Guisan Quai 26, CH-8022 Zurich, Switzerland

ICC INDUSTRIES INC   720 Fifth Ave, New York, NY 10019, Tel: (212) 397-3300
  (Chems & plastics)
    ICC Handels AG, Chamerstr. 12C, Zug, Switzerland

IMO INDUSTRIES INC   1009 Lenox Dr, Bldg 4 West, Lawrenceville,
  NJ 08648-0550, Tel: (609) 896-7600
  (Mfr/support mech & electr controls, engineered power prdts)
    IMO-Pumpen AG, Schurlistrasse 8, P.O. Box 259, CH-8344 Baretswil/ZH, Switzerland
    WEKA AG, Schurlistrasse 8, CH-8344 Baretswil/ZH, Switzerland

IMS INTERNATIONAL INC   100 Campus Rd, Totowa, NJ 07512, Tel: (201) 790-0700
  (Market research reports)
    IMS AG, Gartenstr. 2, CH-6300 Zug, Switzerland

INFORMATION BUILDERS INC   1250 Broadway, New York, NY 10001,
  Tel: (212) 736-4433
  (Devel/mfr/serv computer software)
    Information Builders Switzerland AG, Industriestrasse 19, CH-8304 Wallisellen,
      Switzerland

INGERSOLL-RAND CO   200 Chestnut Ridge Rd, Woodcliff Lake, NJ 07675,
Tel: (201) 573-0123
(Mfr compressors, rock drills, pumps, air tools, door hardware, ball bearings)
    Ingersoll-Rand SA, Route des Arsenaux 9, P.O. Box 146, CH-1705 Fribourg, Switzerland

INTERFLORA INC   29200 Northwestern Hwy, Southfield, MI 48034,
Tel: (313) 355-9300
(Intl flowers by wire)
    Fleurop-Interflora, Dubsstrasse 36, CH-8003 Zurich, Switzerland

INTERGRAPH CORP   Huntsville, AL 35894-0001, Tel: (205) 730-2000
(Devel/mfr interactive computer graphic systems)
    Intergraph (Switzerland) AG, Thurgauerstrasse 40, CH-8050 Zurich, Switzerland

INTERMEC CORP   6001 36th Ave West, PO Box 4280, Everett, WA 98203-9280,
Tel: (206) 348-2600
(Mfr/distr automated data collection sys)
    Intermec Strichcode AG, Bucharindelstrasse 13, Postfach 1304, CH-8620 Wetzikon,
    Switzerland

INTERNATIONAL FLAVORS & FRAGRANCES INC   521 W 57th St, New York, NY 10019,
Tel: (212) 765-5500
(Create/mfr flavors, fragrances & aroma chems)
    IFF Schweiz AG, P.O. Box 273, Europa Strasse 15, CH-5734 Reinach, Switzerland

INTERNATIONAL PAPER   2 Manhattanville Rd, Purchase, NY 10577,
Tel: (914) 397-1500
(Mfr/distr container board, paper, wood prdts)
    Ilford AG, Industriestrasse 15, CH-1700 Fribourg 5, Switzerland
    Ilford Anitec AG, Industriestrasse 15, P.O. Box 126, CH-1700 Fribourg 5, Switzerland
    International Paper Co., Talacker 41, P.O. Box 8039, Zurich, Switzerland

ITT CORP   1330 Ave of the Americas, New York, NY 10019-5490,
Tel: (212) 258-1000
(Design/mfr communications & electronic equip, hotels, insurance)
    Standard Telephone & Radio, 75 Fresenbergstr., CH-8055 Zurich, Switzerland

ITT SHERATON CORP   60 State St, Boston, MA 02108, Tel: (617) 367-3600
(Hotel operations)
    Atlantis Sheraton Hotel, Doltschiweg 234, CH-8055 Zurich, Switzerland

JOHNSON & JOHNSON   One Johnson & Johnson Plaza, New Brunswick, NJ 08933,
Tel: (908) 524-0400
(R&D/mfr/sale health care prdts)
    Janssen-Cilag, Sihlbruggstrasse 111, CH-6341 Baar, Switzerland
    Johnson & Johnson AG, Rotzenbuehlstrasse 55, CH-8957 Spreitenbach, Switzerland

S C JOHNSON & SON INC   1525 Howe St, Racine, WI 53403, Tel: (414) 631-2000
(Home, auto, commercial & personal care prdts, specialty chems)
    Johnson's Wax AG, CH-8104 Weiningen, Zurich, Switzerland

JOHNSON CONTROLS INC   5757 N Green Bay Ave, PO Box 591, Milwaukee,
WI 53201-0591, Tel: (414) 228-1200
(Mfr facility mgmt & control sys, auto seating, batteries & plastics)
    Johnson Controls SA, 38 Ch. du Grand-Puits, CH-1217 Meyrin 2, Switzerland

KEITHLEY INSTRUMENTS INC   28775 Aurora Rd, Cleveland, OH 44139,
  Tel: (216) 248-0400
  (Mfr electr test/meas instru, PC-based data acquisition hdwe/software)
    Keithley Instruments SA, Kreisbacherstr. 4, CH-8600 Dobendorf, Switzerland

KELLY SERVICES   999 W Big Beaver Rd, Troy, MI 48084, Tel: (810) 244-4313
  (Temporary help placement)
    O.K. Personnel Holding SA, 36 branches throughout Switzerland
    O.K. Personnel Service Holding SA (HQ), Rue des Moulins 51, CH-2000 Neuchatel,
    Switzerland

KENT-MOORE DIV   28635 Mound Rd, Warren, MI 48092, Tel: (313) 574-2332
  (Mfr service equip for auto, constr, recreational, military & agric vehicles)
    Kent Moore (Europe) AG, Oberneuhofstr. 1, P.O. Box 64, CH-6340, Baar, Switzerland

KEPNER-TREGOE INC   PO Box 704, Princeton, NJ 08542-0740, Tel: (609) 921-2806
  (Mgmt consulting & training)
    Kepner-Tregoe SA, Rue de la Porcelaine 13, P.O. Box 90, CH-1260 Nyon 1, Switzerland

KIDDER PEABODY GROUP INC   10 Hanover Sq, New York, NY 10005,
  Tel: (212) 510-3000
  (Investment banking)
    Kidder, Peabody (Suisse) SA, 13-15 Cours de Rive, CH-1211 Geneva 3, Switzerland
    Kidder, Peabody (Suisse) SA, Talacker 41, CH-8001 Zurich, Switzerland
    Kidder, Peabody Finance SA, 13-15 Cours de Rive, CH-1211 Geneva 3, Switzerland
    Kidder, Peabody Services SA, 13-15 Cours de Rive, CH-1211 Geneva 3, Switzerland

KINETICSYSTEMS CORP   900 N State St, Lockport, IL 60441, Tel: (815) 838-0005
  (Mfr electr data acquisition & process control sys)
    Kinetic Systems Intl. SA, 3 Taverney, Le Grand Saconnex, CH-1218 Geneva, Switzerland

LESTER B KNIGHT & ASSOC INC   549 W Randolph St, Chicago, IL 60661,
  Tel: (312) 346-2300
  (Architecture, engineering, planning, operations & mgmt consulting)
    Knight Wendling AG, Forrlibuckstrasse 66, Postfach 490, CH-8037 Zurich, Switzerland

KNIGHT-RIDDER INC   One Herald Plaza, Miami, FL 33132, Tel: (303) 376-3800
  (Newspaper publishing, business info services)
    Knight-Ridder Information Inc., Laupenstrasse 18A, CH-3008 Berne, Switzerland

KNOGO CORP   350 Wireless Blvd, Hauppauge, NY 11788-3907, Tel: (516) 232-2100
  (Mfr electr article surveillance sys)
    Knogo Suisse SA, Route de Denges, CH-1027 Lonay, Switzerland

THE KNOLL GROUP   105 Wooster St, New York, NY 10021, Tel: (212) 343-4000
  (Mfr/sale office furnishings)
    Schwerz AG, Bernerstr. Nord 208, CH-8064 Zurich, Switzerland

KOLLMORGEN CORP   1601 Trapelo Rd, Waltham, MA 02154, Tel: (617) 890-5655
  (Mfr printed circuits, elec motors & controls, electro-optical instru)
    Kollmorgen AG, P.O. Box 78, CH-6300 Zug 2, Switzerland

KORN/FERRY INTL   1800 Century Park East, Los Angeles, CA 90067,
  Tel: (310) 552-1834
  (Executive search)
    Korn/Ferry Intl. SA, 61 Rue du Rhone, CH-1204 Geneva, Switzerland
    Korn/Ferry Intl. SA, C.F. Meyer-Strasse 14, CH-8002 Zurich, Switzerland

KOSS CORP   4129 N Port Washington Rd, Milwaukee, WI 53212-1052,
 Tel: (414) 964-5000
 (Mfr stereophones & access, loudspeakers, portable listening prdts)
  Koss Europe, Centro Commerciale, CH-6855 Stabio, Switzerland

KRATOS ANALYTICAL   535 E Crescent Ave, Ramsey, NJ 07466, Tel: (201) 825-7500
 (Mfr liq chromatography, mass spectrometry & surface analysis instru)
  Kratos Analytical AG, Ruechligweg 101, CH-4125 Riehen, Switzerland

KULICKE & SOFFA INDUSTRIES INC   2101 Blair Mill Rd, Willow Grove, PA 19090,
 Tel: (215) 784-6000
 (Semiconductor assembly systems & services)
  Kulicke & Soffa AG, Baarerstrasse 8, CH-6301 Zug, Switzerland

KURT SALMON ASSOCIATES INC   1355 Peachtree St NE, Atlanta, GA 30309,
 Tel: (404) 892-0321
 (Management consulting: consumer products, retailing)
  Kurt Salmon Associates AG, Tirolerweg 6, CH-6300 Zug, Switzerland

LEARONAL INC   272 Buffalo Ave, Freeport, NY 11520, Tel: (516) 868-8800
 (Mfr chem specialties)
  LeaRonal AG, Grossmatte 4, CH-6014 Littau/Lucerne, Switzerland

LEVI STRAUSS & CO   1155 Battery, San Francisco, CA 94111, Tel: (415) 544-6000
 (Mfr casual wearing apparel)
  Levi Strauss (Suisse) SA, Route de la Pierre, CH-1024 Ecublens Vaud, Switzerland

ELI LILLY & CO   Lilly Corporate Center, Indianapolis, IN 46285,
 Tel: (317) 276-2000
 (Mfr pharmaceuticals, animal health prdts)
  Eli Lilly Export SA, Air Center, Chemin des Coquelicots 16, CH-1214 Vernier/Geneva,
  Switzerland

LINTAS:WORLDWIDE   1 Dag Hammarskjold Plaza, New York, NY 10017,
 Tel: (212) 605-8000
 (Advertising agency)
  Lintas:Zurich, Werbeagentur BSR, Baumgasse 2, CH-8031 Zurich, Switzerland

ARTHUR D LITTLE INC   25 Acorn Park, Cambridge, MA 02140-2390,
 Tel: (617) 498-5000
 (Mgmt, environ, health & safety consulting; tech & prdt development)
  Arthur D. Little AG, Seestrasse 185, CH-8800 Thalwil/Zurich, Switzerland

LITTON INDUSTRIES INC   21240 Burbank Blvd, Woodland Hills, CA 91367,
 Tel: (818) 598-5000
 (Elec sys, ind automation, resource explor)
  Litton International SA, Gubelstr. 28, CH-8050 Zurich, Switzerland
  Litton Precision Products Intl. Inc., Gubelstr. 28, CH-8050 Zurich, Switzerland
  Litton World Trade Corp., Gubelstr. 28, CH-8050 Zurich, Switzerland

LOCKHEED MARTIN CORP   6801 Rockledge Dr, Bethesda, MD 20817,
 Tel: (301) 897-6000
 (Design/mfr/mgmt sys in fields of space, defense, energy, electronics, materials,
 info & tech svces)
  Lockheed Martin Intl. SA, 1 Place Longemalle, CH-1204 Geneva, Switzerland

LOUIS ALLIS CO   PO Box 2020, Milwaukee, WI 53201, Tel: (414) 481-6000
  (Elec motors, adjustable speed drives, generators, compressors)
    Litton Precision Products Intl. Inc., Gubelstr. 28, P.O. Box 110, CH-8050 Zurich,
    Switzerland

THE LUBRIZOL CORP   29400 Lakeland Blvd, Wickliffe, OH 44092-2298,
  Tel: (216) 943-4200
  (Mfr chem additives for lubricants & fuels)
    Lubrizol AG, CH-6702 Claro, Switzerland

MANPOWER INTL INC   5301 N Ironwood Rd, PO Box 2053, Milwaukee,
  WI 53201-2053, Tel: (414) 961-1000
  (Temporary help service)
    Manpower SA, 4 Rue Winkelried, CH-1201 Geneva, Switzerland

MARSTELLER INTL   1 E Wacker Dr, Chicago, IL 60601, Tel: (312) 329-1100
  (Advertising, marketing research, sales promotion)
    Marsteller Intl. SA, 2 Rue Thalberg, CH-1201 Geneva, Switzerland

MATTEL INC   333 Continental Blvd, El Segundo, CA 90245, Tel: (310) 252-2000
  (Mfr toys, dolls, games, crafts & hobbies)
    Mattel AG, Monbijoustr. 68, CH-3007 Bern, Switzerland

MEAD CORP   Courthouse Plaza, NE, Dayton, OH 45463, Tel: (513) 222-6323
  (Mfr paper, packaging, pulp, lumber & other wood prdts, school & office prdts; electr
  pub, distri)
    Mead Management Services SA, Gaullusstr. 4, 8006 CH-Zurich, Switzerland

MEDTRONIC INC   7000 Central Ave, NE, Minneapolis, MN 55432,
  Tel: (612) 574-4000
  (Mfr/sale/svce therapeutic medical devices)
    Meditronic (Schweiz) AG, Postfach 709, Bahnhofstrasse 60, CH-8600 Dubendorf 1,
    Switzerland

MEMOREX CORP   San Thomas at Central Expressway, Santa Clara, CA 95052,
  Tel: (408) 987-1000
  (Magnetic recording tapes, etc)
    Memorex AG, Beckenhofstr. 6, CH-8035 Zurich, Switzerland

MERCK SHARP & DOHME INTL   PO Box 2000, Rahway, NJ 07065, Tel: (201) 574-4000
  (Pharms, chems & biologicals)
    Merck, Sharp & Dohme AG, Utoquai 55, CH-8008 Zurich, Switzerland

MERISEL INC   200 Continental Blvd, El Segundo, CA 90245, Tel: (310) 615-3080
  (Distr software & hardware)
    Euro Software Services, Chemins des Rosiers, CH-1260 Nyon, Switzerland

MERRILL LYNCH   World Financial Center, New York, NY 10281-1323,
  Tel: (212) 449-1000
  (Security brokers & dealers, investment & business services)
    Merrill Lynch Bank Suisse SA, Rue Munier-Romilly 7, CH-1206 Geneva, Switzerland

METALLURG INC   25 E 39th St, New York, NY 10016, Tel: (212) 686-4010
  (Mfr ferrous & nonferrous alloys & metals)
    Ferrolegeringar AG, P.O. Box 131, CH-8034 Zurich, Switzerland

MICROSOFT CORP   One Microsoft Way, Redmond, WA 98052-6399,
  Tel: (206) 882-8080
  (Computer software, peripherals & services)
    Microsoft Switzerland AG, Alte Winterthurerstr. 14A, CH-8304 Wallisellen,
      Switzerland

MILLIPORE CORP   Ashley Rd, Bedford, MA 01730, Tel: (617) 275-9205
  (Mfr precision filters, hi-performance liquid chromatography instru)
    Millipore AG, Chriesbaumstrasse 6, CH-8604 Volketswil, Switzerland

MOBIL CORP   3225 Gallows Rd, Fairfax, VA 22037-0001, Tel: (703) 846-3000
  (Petroleum explor & refining, mfr petrol prdts, chems, petrochems)
    Mobil Oil Switzerland, Picassoplatz 4, CH-4010 Basel, Switzerland

MOORE SPECIAL TOOL CO INC   800 Union Ave, PO Box 4088, Bridgeport,
  CT 06607-0088, Tel: (203) 366-3224
  (Mfr precision jig borers/grinders, coordinate meas machines, aspheric generataors)
    Moore Special Tool AG, Hohlstrasse 608, CH-8048 Zurich, Switzerland

MOTOROLA INC   1303 E Algonquin Rd, Schaumburg, IL 60196, Tel: (708) 576-5000
  (Mfr commun equip, semiconductors, cellular phones)
    Motorola Suisse SA, 16 Chemin de la Voie-Creuse, CH-1121 Geneva 20, Switzerland

MacDERMID INC   245 Freight St, Waterbury, CT 06702, Tel: (203) 575-5700
  (Chem processing for metal ind, plastics, electronics cleaners, strippers)
    MacDermid Suisse Trading, 1a rue de la Bergere, CH-1217 Meyrin, Switzerland

THE MacNEAL-SCHWENDLER CORP   815 Colorado Blvd, Los Angeles, CA 90041,
  Tel: (213) 258-9111
  (Devel/mfr computer-aided engineering software)
    MacNeal-Schwendler GmbH, Route Andre Piller 21, CH-1762 Givisiez, Switzerland

McCANN-ERICKSON WORLDWIDE   750 Third Ave, New York, NY 10017,
  Tel: (212) 697-6000
  (Advertising)
    McCann-Erickson SA, 15 Passage Malbuisson, P.O. Box Q96, CH-1211 Geneva 11,
      Switzerland
    McCann-Erickson SA, Registrasse 9, P.O. Box 295, CH-8033 Zurich, Switzerland

McCORMICK & CO INC   18 Loveton Circle, Sparks, MD 21152-6000,
  Tel: (410) 771-7301
  (Mfr/dist/sale seasonings, flavorings, specialty foods)
    McCormick SA, Postfach 541, CH-8105 Regensdorf, Switzerland

McKINSEY & CO INC   55 E 52nd St, New York, NY 10022, Tel: (212) 446-7000
  (Mgmt consultants)
    McKinsey & Co., Zolickerstr. 225, CH-8008 Zurich, Switzerland

NATIONAL CAR RENTAL SYSTEM INC   7700 France Ave S, Minneapolis, MN 55435,
  Tel: (612) 830-2121
  (Car rental)
    Europe Car AG, Babenerstr. 812, CH-8040 Zurich, Switzerland

NATIONAL CHEMSEARCH CORP   2727 Chemsearch Blvd, Irving, TX 75061,
  Tel: (214) 438-0211
  (Commercial chem prdts)

National Chemsearch (Switz.) AG, Lubernstr. 49, P.O. Box 62, CH-6300 Zug 2,
   Switzerland

NATIONAL ENGINEERING CO   751 Shoreline Dr, Aurora, IL 60504,
  Tel: (708) 978-0044
  (Mfr/serv foundry equip)
     National Engineering Co. - Zug, Baarerstrasse 77, CH-6300 Zug, Switzerland

NATIONAL SERVICE INDUSTRIES INC   1420 Peachtree St NE, Atlanta, GA 30309,
  Tel: (404) 853-1000
  (Mfr lighting equip, spec chems; textile rental)
     Zep Europe, Bern, Switzerland

NATIONAL STARCH & CHEMICAL CO   10 Finderne Ave, Bridgewater, NJ 08807-3300,
  Tel: (908) 685-5000
  (Mfr adhesives & sealants, resins & spec chems, electr materials & adhesives, food
  prdts, ind starch)
     Elotex AG, Sempach Station, Switzerland
     National Starch & Chemical AG, Affoltern a.A, Switzerland

A C NIELSEN CO   Nielsen Plaza, Northbrook, IL 60062-6288, Tel: (708) 498-6300
  (Market research)
     A.C. Nielsen SA, P.O. Box 3967, CH-6002 Lucerne, Switzerland

NORDSON CORP   28601 Clemens Rd, Westlake, OH 44145, Tel: (216) 892-1580
  (Mfr ind application equip & packaging mach)
     Nordson (Schweiz) AG, Pumpwerkstr. 25, CH-4142 Muenchenstein 2, Switzerland

NORTHERN TELECOM SYSTEMS CORP   PO Box 1222, Minneapolis, MN 55440,
  Tel: (612) 932-8000
  (Remote information processing sys)
     Data 100 AG, Baunatkerstr. 46, CH-8050 Zurich, Switzerland

NYNEX CORP   1095 Ave of the Americas, New York, NY 10036, Tel: (212) 370-7400
  (Telecom & info servs)
     NYNEX International Co., 6 Avenue Jules-Crosnier, CH-1206 Geneva, Switzerland

OCCIDENTAL PETROLEUM CORP   10889 Wilshire Blvd, Los Angeles, CA 90024,
  Tel: (213) 879-1700
  (Petroleum & petroleum prdts, chems, plastics)
     Occidental Chemical (Europe) SA, Seestr. 50, CH-8802 Kilchberg-Zurich, Switzerland

OCEANEERING INTL INC   PO Box 218130, Houston, TX 77218-8130,
  Tel: (713) 578-8868
  (Underwater serv to offshore oil & gas ind)
     Oceaneering Intl. Inc., Operational base in Zug

OIL-DRI CORP OF AMERICA   520 N Michigan Ave, Chicago, IL 60611,
  Tel: (312) 321-1515
  (Oil & grease absorbants, soil conditioners, etc)
     Oil-Dri SA, Place du Four, P.O. Box 47, CH-1296 Coppet, Switzerland

ORACLE CORP   500 Oracle Parkway, Redwood Shores, CA 94065,
  Tel: (415) 506-7000
  (Develop/mfr software)
     Oracle Software (Schweiz), Riedstrasse 10, Ch-8953 Dietikon, Switzerland

OSMONICS INC   5951 Clearwater Dr, Minnetonka, MN 55343-8995,
   Tel: (612) 933-2277
   (Mfr fluid filtration & separation equip & components)
      Osmonics Europa SA, LeSaut, CH-2042 Valangin (Neuchatel) Switzerland

OTIS ELEVATOR CO   10 Farm Springs, Farmington, CT 06032, Tel: (860) 676-6528
   (Mfr elevators & escalators)
      Otis, Route du Petit Moncor 17/19, P.O. Box 1047, CH-1701 Fribourg/Moncor,
         Switzerland

OWENS-ILLINOIS INC   1 Seagate, Toledo, OH 43666, Tel: (419) 247-5000
   (Glass & plastic containers, house- hold & ind prdts, packaging)
      Owens Illinois Intl. SA, 48 Route des Acacias, CH-1227 Carouge, Geneva, Switzerland

PAINEWEBBER GROUP INC   1285 Ave of the Americas, New York, NY 10019,
   Tel: (212) 713-2000
   (Stock brokerage serv & invest)
      PaineWebber Intl., 2 Rue Vallin, CH-1201 Geneva, Switzerland
      PaineWebber Intl., Holbeinstrasse 30, CH-8008 Zurich, Switzerland
      PaineWebber Intl., Palazzo Riforma, Crocicchio Cortogna 6, CH-6901 Lugano,
         Switzerland

PEAVEY CO/CONAGRA TRADING COS   730 Second Ave, Minneapolis, MN 55402,
   Tel: (612) 370-7500
   (Flour, feeds, seeds)
      Conagra Trading Co. SA, Geneva, Switzerland

THE PERKIN-ELMER CORP   761 Main Ave, Norwalk, CT 06859-0001,
   Tel: (203) 762-1000
   (Mfr analytical instrumentation sys, high performance thermal spray coatings)
      Perkin-Elmer AG, Grundstrasse 10, CH-6343 Rotkreuz, Switzerland

PFIZER INC   235 E 42nd St, New York, NY 10017-5755, Tel: (212) 573-2323
   (Mfr healthcare products)
      AMS Medinvent SA, Switzerland
      Jaquet Orthopedie SA, Switzerland
      Nilo Holdings SA, Switzerland
      Pfizer AG, Switzerland
      Schneider (Europe) AB, Switzerland

PHILIP MORRIS COS INC   120 Park Ave, New York, NY 10017, Tel: (212) 880-5000
   (Mfr cigarettes, food prdts, beer)
      Kraft Jacobs Suchard, Klausstrasse 4, P.O. Box 147, CH-8034 Zurich, Switzerland
      Philip Morris EFTA, Ave. de Cour 107, CH-1001 Lausanne, Switzerland
      Philip Morris European Union, Brillancourt 4, CH-1001 Lausanne, Switzerland

PHILIPP BROTHERS CHEMICALS INC   1 Parker Plaza, Fort Lee, NJ 07029,
   Tel: (201) 944-6020
   (Mfr ind & agric chems)
      Philipp Bros. Green AG, Grienbachstr. 11, CH-6301 Zug, Switzerland

PHILLIPS PETROLEUM CO   Phillips Bldg, Bartlesville, OK 74004,
   Tel: (918) 661-6600
   (Crude oil, natural gas, liquefied petroleum gas, gasoline & petro-chems)
      Phillips Petroleum Intl., Dienerstr. 15, CH-8004 Zurich, Switzerland

PICTURETEL CORP 222 Rosewood Dr, Danvers, MA 01923, Tel: (508) 762-5000
(Mfr video conferencing systems, network bridging & multiplexing prdts, system
peripherals)
PictureTel AG, Lowenstrasse 17, CH-8001 Zurich, Switzerland

PITNEY BOWES INC Wheeler Dr, Stamford, CT 06926-0700, Tel: (203) 356-5000
(Mfr postage meters, mailroom equip, copiers, bus supplies; bus servs)
Pitney Bowes AG, Vogelsangstrasse 17, CH-8307 Effretikon, Switzerland

PLANTRONICS 337 Encinal St, Santa Cruz, CA 95060, Tel: (408) 426-6060
(Mfr commun equip, elect & electr appliances & apparatus)
Plantronics AG, Alte Steinhauserstr. 19, CH-6330 Zug, Switzerland

PLAYSKOOL INC 1027 Newport Ave, PO Box 1059, Pawtucket, RI 02862,
Tel: (401) 727-5000
(Mfr wooden/plastic preschool & riding toys)
Playskool AG, Alte Bremgartenstr. 2, CH-8968 Mutschellen, Zurich, Switzerland

POLAROID CORP 549 Technology Sq, Cambridge, MA 02139, Tel: (617) 386-2000
(Photographic equip & supplies, optical prdts)
Polaroid AG, Hardturmstr. 175, CH-8037 Zurich, Switzerland

PREMARK INTL INC 1717 Deerfield Rd, Deerfield, IL 60015, Tel: (708) 405-6000
(Mfr/sale diversified consumer & coml prdts)
Dart (Suisse) SA, 1 Chemin de Pre-Fleuri, CH-1260 Nyon (VD), Switzerland

PROCTER & GAMBLE CO One Procter & Gamble Plaza, Cincinnati, OH 45202,
Tel: (513) 983-1100
(Personal care, food, laundry, cleaning & ind prdts)
Procter & Gamble AG, 80 Rue de Lausanne, CH-1211 Geneva 2, Switzerland

PUROLATOR COURIER CORP 3240 Hillview Ave, Palo Alto, CA 94304,
Tel: (415) 494-2900
(Time-sensitive package delivery)
Kurier AG, Zurich, Switzerland

QMS INC One Magnum Pass, Mobile, AL 36618, Tel: (205) 633-4300
(Mfr monochrome & color computer printers)
QMS Inc., Winterthur, Switzerland

RADISSON HOTELS INTL Carlson Pkwy, PO Box 59159, Minneapolis,
MN 55459-8204, Tel: (612) 540-5526
(Hotels)
Radisson Hotels Intl.,
10 locations throughout Switzerland (inquiries to U.S. address)

RANSBURG CORP 3939 W 56th St, Indianapolis, IN 46208, Tel: (317) 298-5000
(Mfr electrostatic coating sys)
Ransburg-Gema AG, Movenstr. 17, CH-9016 St. Gallen, Switzerland

RAYCHEM CORP 300 Constitution Dr, Menlo Park, CA 94025, Tel: (415) 361-3333
(Devel/mfr/mkt materials science products for electronics, telecommunications &
industry)
Raychem AG, Oberneuhofstrasse 8, Postfach 229, CH-6341 Baar, Switzerland

RAYTHEON CO 141 Spring St, Lexington, MA 02173, Tel: (617) 862-6600
(Mfr divers electronics, appliances, aviation, energy & environ prdts; publishing, ind & constr servs)
Tag Semiconductors Ltd., Hohlstr. 610, CH-8048 Zurich, Switzerland

READER'S DIGEST ASSOCIATION INC PO Box 235, Pleasantville, NY 10570,
Tel: (914) 238-1000
(Publisher magazines & books, direct mail marketer)
Das Beste aus Reader's Digest AG, Raffelstr. 11, Gallushof, CH-8021 Zurich, Switzerland

RED WING SHOE CO INC 314 Main St, Red Wing, MN 55066, Tel: (612) 388-8211
(Leather tanning & finishing, mfr footwear, retail shoe stores)
Red Wing SA, Rue de Daillettes 21, CH-1700 Fribourg, Switzerland

REFAC TECHNOLOGY DEVELOPMENT CORP 122 E 42nd St, #4000, New York, NY 10168,
Tel: (212) 687-4741
(Consult, intl tech transfer, foreign trade, power supplies)
Refac Technology Dev. Corp., 35 Route des Jeunes, CH-1211 Geneva 26, Switzerland

RELIANCE ELECTRIC CO 24701 Euclid Ave, Cleveland, OH 44117,
Tel: (216) 266-7000
(Equip & sys for ind automation, telecom equip)
Reliance Electric AG, CH-6036 Dierikon, Lucerne, Switzerland

RENA-WARE DISTRIBUTORS INC 8383 158th Ave NE, Redmond, WA 98052,
Tel: (206) 881-6171
(Cookware & china)
Rena-Ware GmbH, Seftigenstr. 300B, P.O. Box 19, CH-3084 Wabern/Bern, Switzerland

REYNOLDS INTERNATIONAL INC 6601 W Broad St, PO Box 27002, Richmond,
VA 23261, Tel: (804) 281-2000
(Mfr aluminum primary & fabricated prdts, plastic & paper packaging & foodservice prdts; gold mining)
Reynolds (Europe) Ltd., 34 Ave. du Tribunal Federal, CH-1005 Lausanne, Switzerland

RHONE-POULENC RORER INC PO Box 1200, Collegeville, PA 19426-0107,
Tel: (215) 454-8000
(R&D/mfr human pharmaceuticals)
Chemical & Pharmaceutical Products SA, Lausanne, Switzerland

RIDGE TOOL CO 400 Clark St, Elyria, OH 44035, Tel: (216) 323-5581
(Hand & power tools for working pipe, drain cleaning equip, etc)
Ridgid Werkzeuge, Baar-Inwil, Zurich, Switzerland

RIGHT ASSOCIATES 1818 Market St, 14th Fl, Philadelphia, PA 19103-3614,
Tel: (215) 988-1588
(Outplacement & human resources consult servs)
Right Associates, 64 Rue de Monthoux, P.O. Box 2245, CH-1211 Geneva 1, Switzerland

RJR NABISCO INC 1301 Ave of the Americas, New York, NY 10019,
Tel: (212) 258-5600
(Mfr consumer packaged food prdts & tobacco prdts)
R.J. Reynolds Finance SA, Chemin Rieu 12-14, Geneva, Switzerland
R.J. Reynolds Tobacco AG, Baslerstrasse 65, CH-6252 Luzern, Switzerland
R.J. Reynolds Tobacco Intl. SA, Chemin Rieu 12-14, Geneva, Switzerland

A H ROBINS CO INC   1407 Cummings Dr, PO Box 26609, Richmond, VA 23261-6609,
  Tel: (804) 257-2000
  (Mfr ethical pharms & consumer prdts)
    Diffucap SA, Stabio, Switzerland

ROCKWELL INTL CORP   2201 Seal Beach Blvd, PO Box 4250, Seal Beach,
  CA 90740-8250, Tel: (310) 797-3311
  (Prdts & serv for aerospace, automotive, electronics, graphics & automation inds)
    Allen-Bradley AG, Lohwisstrasse 50, CH-8123 Ebmatingen, Switzerland

ROWE INTL INC   75 Troy Hill Rd, Whippany, NJ 07981, Tel: (201) 887-0400
  (Vending machs, background music sys & jukeboxes, bill & coin changers)
    Rowe (Europe) SA, 25 Route des Acacias, CH-1211 Geneva 24, Switzerland

SARGENT & GREENLEAF INC   1 Security Dr, Nicholasville, KY 40356-0569,
  Tel: (606) 885-9411
  (Mfr hi-security locking mechanisms)
    Sargent & Greenleaf SA, Ch. du Croset 9, CH-1024 Ecublens, Switzerland

SCANTRON CORP   1361 Valencia Ave, Tustin, CA 92680-6463, Tel: (714) 259-8887
  (Design/mfr optical mark readers, test scoring & data entry equip, scannable forms,
  computer prdts)
    Datascan SA, CH-2613 Villeret, Switzerland

SCHENECTADY INTERNATIONAL INC   PO Box 1046, Schenectady, NY 12301,
  Tel: (518) 370-4200
  (Mfr elec insulating varnishes, enamels, phenolic resins, alkylphenols)
    Schenectady Pratteln AG, Kasteliweg 7, CH-4233 Pratteln, Switzerland

A SCHULMAN INC   3550 W Market St, Akron, OH 44333, Tel: (216) 666-3751
  (Mfr/sale plastic resins & compounds)
    A. Schulman AG, Kernstrasse 10, CH-8004 Zurich, Switzerland

SEA-LAND SERVICE INC   150 Allen Rd, Liberty Corner, NJ 07920,
  Tel: (201) 558-6000
  (Container transport)
    Sea-Land Service, CH-4002 Basel, Switzerland

G D SEARLE & CO   5200 Old Orchard Rd, Skokie, IL 60077, Tel: (708) 982-7000
  (Mfr pharms, health care & optical prdts, specialty chems)
    Searle SA (Suisse), Chemin des Muriers, CH-1170 Aubonne, Switzerland

SENSORMATIC ELECTRONICS CORP   500 NW 12th Ave, Deerfield Beach, FL 33341,
  Tel: (305) 427-9700
  (Electronic article surveillance equip)
    Senelco AG, Im Glockenacker 22, CH-8053 Zurich, Switzerland

SERVCO CORP OF AMERICA   111 New South Rd, Hicksville, NY 11802,
  Tel: (516) 938-9700
  (Electronic equip)
    Servo Corp. of America, Chemin du Cap 1-3, CH-1006 Lausanne, Switzerland

SHIPLEY CO INC   455 Forest St, Marlborough, MA 01752, Tel: (508) 481-7950
  (Mfr chems for printed circuit boards & microelectronic mfg)
    Shipley AG, Gewerbestrasse 13, CH-3421 Lyssach, Switzerland

SIGNETICS CORP   PO Box 3409, Sunnyvale, CA 94088-3409, Tel: (408) 991-2000
  (Solid state circuits)
    Pilips AG, Zurich, Switzerland

SILICON GRAPHICS INC   PO Box 7311, Mountain View, CA 94039-7311,
  Tel: (415) 960-1980
  (Design/mfr computer graphic sys)
    Silicon Graphics SA, Ave. Louis Casai 18, CH-1209 Geneva, Switzerland

SKIL CORP   4801 W Peterson Ave, Chicago, IL 60646, Tel: (312) 286-7330
  (Portable electric power tools)
    Skil AG, Baarerstr. 86, CH-6300 Zug 2, Switzerland

SLOAN CO   7704 San Fernando Rd, Sun Valley, CA 91352, Tel: (213) 875-1123
  (Mfr indicator lights)
    Sloan AG, Birmannsgasse 8, CH-4009 Basel, Switzerland

SOCOTAB LEAF TOBACCO CO INC   122 E 42 St, New York, NY 10168,
  Tel: (212) 687-2590
  (Tobacco dealer)
    Frana SA Geneve, Rue du Leman 6, CH-1201 Geneva, Switzerland

SPECTRA-PHYSICS ANALYTICAL INC   45757 Northport Loop W, Fremont, CA 94537,
  Tel: (510) 657-1100
  (Mfr liquid chromatography equip)
    Spectra-Physics AG, Hegenheimermattweg 65, CH-4123 Allschwil/BL, Switzerland

SPINLAB INC   456 Troy Circle, Knoxville, TN 37950, Tel: (615) 588-9716
  (Textile fiber testers)
    Spinlab AG, Rautistr. 58, P.O. Box 180, CH-8048 Zurich, Switzerland

SPRAYING SYSTEMS CO   PO Box 7900, Wheaton, IL 60188, Tel: (708) 665-5000
  (Fabricated metal prdts)
    Spraying Systems AG, Schuetzenstr. 29, CH-8808 Pfaffikon, Switzerland

SPX CORP   700 Terrace Point Dr, PO Box 3301, Muskegon, MI 49443-3301,
  Tel: (616) 724-5000
  (Mfr spec service tools, engine & drive-train parts)
    Euroline (SPX Europe AG), Oberneuhofstrasse 1, Postfach 64, CH-6340 Baar,
      Switzerland
    Robinair Europe, c/o SPX (Europe) AG, Oberneuhofstrasse 1, Postfach 64,
      CH-6340 Baar, Switzerland
    SPX Europe, Oberneuhofstr. 1, P.O. Box 64, CH-6340 Baar, Switzerland

SRI INTL   333 Ravenswood Ave, Menlo Park, CA 94025-3493, Tel: (415) 326-6200
  (Intl consulting & research)
    SRI-Zurich, Pelikanstr. 37, CH-8001 Zurich, Switzerland

STANDARD COMMERCIAL CORP   PO Box 450, Wilson, NC 27893, Tel: (919) 291-5507
  (Leaf tobacco dealers/processors, wool processors)
    Pierer Freres & Cie. SA, Geneva, Switzerland

STEINER CO   1 E Superior St, Chicago, IL 60611, Tel: (312) 642-1242
  (Soap & towel dispensers)
    Steiner Co., Avenue Jurigoz 5, P.O. Box 10011, CH-1000 Lausanne 19, Switzerland

STEINER CORP   505 E South Temple St, Salt Lake City, UT 84102,
  Tel: (801) 328-8831
  (Linen supply service)
    Steiner, P.O. Box, CH-1000 Lausanne 19, Switzerland

STORAGE TECHNOLOGY CORP   2270 S 88th St, Louisville, CO 80028-0001,
  Tel: (303) 673-5151
  (Mfr/mkt/serv info storage & retrieval sys)
    Storage Technology Switzerland AG, Wallisellerstrasse 114, CH-8152 Opfikon/Zurich,
    Switzerland

SUDLER & HENNESSEY   1633 Broadway, New York, NY 10019, Tel: (212) 969-5800
  (Healthcare prdts advertising)
    Sudler & Hennessey, Muhlebachstrasse 20, CH-8008 Zurich, Switzerland

SUNDSTRAND CORP   PO Box 7003, Rockford, IL 61125-7003, Tel: (815) 226-6000
  (Design/mfr proprietary technology based comps & sub-sys for aerospace & ind)
    Sundstrand Intl. Corp. SA, 8 Place de la Gare, CH-1700 Fribourg, Switzerland

SUNKIST GROWERS INC   14130 Riverside Dr, Van Nuys, CA 91423,
  Tel: (818) 423-4800
  (Fruits & vegetables)
    Sunkist (Europe) SA, Rue du Valentin 29, CH-1004 Lausanne, Switzerland

SYBRON INTL CORP   411 E Wisconsin Ave, Milwaukee, WI 53202,
  Tel: (414) 274-6600
  (Mfr prdts for laboratories, professional orthodontic & dental mkts)
    Erie Electroverre SA, Route de Fribourg 22, P.O. Box 192, CH-1680 Romont (Fr),
    Switzerland
    Ormco (Europe) AG, Thurgauerstrasse 40, CH-8050 Zurich, Switzerland

TANDEM COMPUTERS INC   19333 Valco Pkwy, Cupertino, CA 95014,
  Tel: (408) 725-6000
  (Mfr multiple processor computer sys)
    Tandem Computers AG, Sweirstr. 138, CH-8003 Zurich, Switzerland

TECHNICON INSTRUMENTS CORP   511 Benedict Ave, Tarrytown, NY 10591-5097,
  Tel: (914) 631-8000
  (Mfr/serv automated blook anal equip, reagents & diagnostics)
    Bayer (Schweiz) AG, Letzigraben 176, CH-8047 Zurich, Switzerland

TEEPAK INC   3 Westbrook Corp Center, Westchester, IL 60154,
  Tel: (708) 409-3000
  (Mfr cellulose, fibrous, collegen sausage casings & plastic packaging)
    Tee-Pak Inc., Weinbergstrasse 72, CH-8006 Zurich, Switzerland

TEKTRONIX INC   26660 SW Parkway, Wilsonville, OR 97070, Tel: (503) 627-7111
  (Mfr test & meas, visual sys & commun prdts)
    Tektronix Intl. AG, Zug, Switzerland

THERMO ELECTRIC CO   109 Fifth St, Saddle Brook, NJ 07662, Tel: (201) 843-5800
  (Mfr temp/meas control prdts)
    Thermo Electric Co., Lenzgasse 36, CH-4025 Basel, Switzerland

TIFFANY & CO   727 Fifth Ave, New York, NY 10022, Tel: (212) 755-8000
  (Mfr/retail fine jewelry, silverware, china, crystal, leather goods, etc)
    Tiffany & Co. Zurich, Bahnhofstrasse 24, CH-8022 Zurich, Switzerland

TOPFLIGHT CORP   160 E 9th Ave, York, PA 17404, Tel: (717) 843-9901
  (Commercial printing, service paper)
    Tovenca AG, Lohwiesstrasse 52, CH-8123 Ebmatingen, Switzerland

TOWERS PERRIN   245 Park Ave, New York, NY 10167, Tel: (212) 309-3400
  (Management consultants)
    Tillinghast, P.O. Box 633, CH-1215 Geneva 15, Switzerland
    Towers, Perrin, Forster & Crosby, ICC Bldg. C, 20 Route de Pre'Bois, P.O. Box 633,
    CH-1215 Geneva 15, Switzerland

TOYS R US INC   461 From Rd, Paramus, NJ 07652, Tel: (201) 262-7800
  (Retail stores: toys & games, sporting goods, computer software, books, records)
    Tru Toys R Us AB, Forchstrasse 456, CH-7802 Zurich, Switzerland

TRACOR INC   6500 Tracor Lane, Austin, TX 78725-2000, Tel: (512) 926-2800
  (Time & frequency prdts, gas & liquid chromatographs, eng serv, ship repair)
    Olvis AG, Rebgasse 40, CH-2540 Grenchen, Switzerland

TRANE CO   3600 Pammel Creek Rd, La Crosse, WI 54601, Tel: (608) 787-2000
  (Mfr/distr/svce A/C sys & equip)
    Trane (Schweiz) AG, Badenerstrasse 13C, CH-8953 Dietikon, Switzerland
    Trane (Suisse) SA, Succursale de Geneve, Rue Eugene Marziano 17A,
    CH-1227 Geneva-Acacias, Switzerland
    Trane (Svizzera) SA, Via Stazio 10, CH-6900 Lugano, Switzerland

TRANS WORLD AIRLINES INC   505 N 6th St, St Louis, MO 63101,
  Tel: (314) 589-3000
  (Air transportation)
    Trans World Airlines, Talacker 35, Zurich, Switzerland

TRANTER INC   1054 Claussen Rd, #314, Augusta, GA 30907, Tel: (706) 738-7900
  (Mfr heat exchangers)
    SWEP AG, Postfach 76, CH-1734 Tentlingen, Switzerland

TRW INC   1900 Richmond Rd, Cleveland, OH 44124, Tel: (216) 291-7000
  (Electr & energy-related prdts, automotive & aerospace prdts, tools & fasteners)
    TRW Intl. SA, Rue de Lyon 75, CH-1211 Geneva 13, Switzerland
    TRW Intl. SA, Letzlgraben 89, CH-8003 Zurich, Switzerland

U S SURGICAL CORP   150 Glover Ave, Norwalk, CT 06856, Tel: (203) 845-1000
  (Mfr/devel/mkt surgical staplers, laparoscopic instru & sutures)
    Auto Suture (Schweiz) AG, all mail to U.S. address
    USSC AG, all mail to U.S. address
    USSC Medical AG, all mail to U.S. address

U S TRUST CO OF NEW YORK   114 W 47th St, New York, NY 10036,
  Tel: (212) 852-1000
  (Invest, mgmt & commercial banking)
    Financiere UST SA, 7 Avenue Krieg, CH-1211 Geneva 17, Switzerland

UNION CARBIDE CORP   39 Old Ridgebury Rd, Danbury, CT 06817,
  Tel: (203) 794-2000
  (Mfr industrial chemicals, plastics, resins)
    Union Carbide (Europe) SA, Rue Pre-Bouvier 7, CH-1217 Meyrin, Geneva, Switzerland
    Union Carbide Chemicals & Plastics (Europe) SA, 21 Ave. Choiseul, CH-1290 Versoix,
    Switzerland

UNISYS CORP PO Box 500, Blue Bell, PA 19424, Tel: (215) 986-4011
  (Mfg/mktg/serv electr info sys)
    Sperry Finanz AG, Bahnhofstrasse 27, CH-6300 Zug, Switzerland
    Sperry Intl. Marketing AG, Hardturmstrasse 161, CH-8002 Zurich, Switzerland
    Sperry Overseas Corp., Bahnhofstrasse 27, CH-6300 Zug, Switzerland
    Sperry Rand Intl. Corp., Bahnhofstrasse 27, CH-6300 Zug, Switzerland
    Unisys Investments AG, Bahnhofstrasse 27, CH-6300 Zug, Switzerland
    Unisys Schweiz AG, Zuercherstrasse 59, CH-8800 Zurich, Switzerland

UNITED TECHNOLOGIES CORP United Technologies Bldg, Hartford, CT 06101,
  Tel: (203) 728-7000
  (Mfr aircraft engines, elevators, A/C, auto equip, space & military electr, rocket
  propulsion sys)
    Ascenseurs Gendre Otis SA, 17-19 Route du Petit Moncor, P.O. Box 1047,
      CH-1701 Fribourg/Moncor, Switzerlan
    Carrier Industrial Refrigeration Group, c/o Elliott Turbomachinery S.A.,
      Winterthurerstr. 92, CH-80006 Zurich, Switzerland
    Carrier Intl. SA, Hofwiesenstr. 379, CH-8050 Zurich, Switzerland

UNITEK CORP/3M 2724 S Peck Rd, Monrovia, CA 91016-7118, Tel: (818) 574-4000
  (Mfr orthodontic prdts)
    Inter-Unitek AG, Florastr. 28, CH-8008 Zurich, Switzerland

UNIVERSAL CORP PO Box 25099, Richmond, VA 23260, Tel: (804) 359-9311
  (Holding co: tobacco, commodities)
    Continental Tobacco SA, Switzerland

UPJOHN CO 7000 Portage Rd, Kalamazoo, MI 49001, Tel: (616) 323-4000
  (Mfr pharms, agric prdts, ind chems)
    Upjohn SA, P.O. Box 208, Blumlisalpstr. 56, CH-8006 Zurich, Switzerland

URSCHEL LABORATORIES INC 2503 Calumet Ave, PO Box 2200, Valparaiso,
  IN 46384-2200, Tel: (219) 464-4811
  (Design/mfr precision food processing equip)
    Urschell Intl. Ltd., Steineggstr. 32, CH-8852 Altendorf, Switzerland

USF&G FINANCIAL SERVICES CORP 100 Light St, Baltimore, MD 21202,
  Tel: (301) 547-3000
  (Investment mgt, real estate, computer leasing, fin prdt mktg & admin, strategic
  consult)
    Megatron Inc., Dufourstrasse 119, CH-8008 Zurich, Switzerland
    Orbat AG, Splugenstrasse 6, CH-8002 Zurich, Switzerland

VALENITE INC PO Box 9636, Madison Heights, MI 48071-9636,
  Tel: (810) 589-1000
  (Cemented carbide, high speed steel, ceramic & diamond cutting tool prdts, etc)
    Valenite-Modco GmbH, Murgenthalstr. 15, CH-4900 Langenthal, Switzerland

VARIAN ASSOCIATES INC 3100 Hansen Way, Palo Alto, CA 94304-1030,
  Tel: (415) 493-4000
  (Mfr microwave tubes & devices, analytical instru, semiconductor process & med equip,
  vacuum sys)
    Varian AG, Kollerstrasse 38, CH-6300 Zug, Switzerland

VIACOM INC 200 Elm St, Dedham, MA 02026, Tel: (617) 461-1600
  (Communications, publishing, entertainment)
    Viacom SA, Chamerstr. 18, CH-6300 Zug, Switzerland

WANG LABORATORIES INC   1 Industrial Ave, Lowell, MA 01851,
   Tel: (508) 459-5000
   (Mfr computer info processing sys)
      Wang SA/AG, Talackustr. 7, CH-8152 Glallbrugy, Switzerland

WARD HOWELL INTL INC   99 Park Ave, New York, NY 10016-1699,
   Tel: (212) 697-3730
   (Executive recruiting)
      Ward Howell, Enderlin & Partner AG, Holbeinstrasse 34, CH-8008 Zurich, Switzerland

WARNER ELECTRIC BRAKE & CLUTCH CO   449 Gardner St, South Beloit, IL 61080,
   Tel: (815) 389-3771
   (Automotive & ind brakes & clutches)
      Warner Electric SA, Avenue d'Ouchy 14, CH-1001 Lausanne, Switzerland

WATERS CHROMATOGRAPHY DIV   34 Maple St, Milford, MA 01757,
   Tel: (617) 478-2000
   (Mfr/distr liquid chromatographic instru/accessories/tech)
      Brechbuhler AG, Steinwiesenstr. 3, CH-8952 Schlieren/ZH, Switzerland

WERTHEIM SCHRODER & CO INC   787 Seventh Ave, New York, NY 10019,
   Tel: (212) 492-6000
   (Investment banking, security brokers)
      Wertheim and Co. Inc., 16 Ave. Eugene Pittard, CH-1206 Geneva, Switzerland

WESTERN TEMPORARY SERVICES INC   301 Lennon Lane, Walnut Creek, CA 94598,
   Tel: (510) 930-5300
   (Secretarial & clerical temporary service)
      Western Temporary Services, Marketgasse 56, CH-3011 Bern, Switzerland

WHEELABRATOR CLEAN WATER INC, HPD DIV   55 Shuman Blvd, Naperville, IL 60563,
   Tel: (708) 357-7330
   (Technical design & service process systems)
      HPD Evatherm AG, Wehrlistrasse 3, CH-5610 Wohlen, Switzerland

WINCHESTER ELECTRONICS   400 Park Rd, Watertown, CT 06795-0500,
   Tel: (203) 945-5000
   (Mfr elec & electr connectors, PCB assemblies & hardware)
      Litton Precision Products Intl. Inc., Gubelstrasse 28, CH-8050 Zurich, Switzerland

HARRY WINSTON INC   718 Fifth Ave, New York, NY 10019, Tel: (212) 245-2000
   (Diamonds, lapidary work)
      Harry Winston SA of New York, 24 Quai General-Guisan, Geneva, Switzerland

WORLD COURIER INC   46 Trinity Pl, New York, NY 10006, Tel: (718) 978-9400
   (Intl courier serv)
      World Courier (Switz) AG, Thurgauerstr. 74, Zurich, Switzerland
      World Courier (Switz.) SA, 4 Rue de la Maladiere, CH-1211 Geneva 9, Switzerland

XEROX CORP   800 Long Ridge Rd, PO Box 1600, Stamford, CT 06904,
   Tel: (203) 968-3000
   (Mfr document processing equip, sys & supplies)
      Xerox Corp., Zurich, Switzerland

YATES INDUSTRIES INC   U S Hwy 130, Bordentown, NJ 08505, Tel: (609) 298-4800
(Electro-deposited copper foil)
    Yates Trading AG, P.O. Box 105A, Zug, Switzerland

YOUNG & RUBICAM INC   285 Madison Ave, New York, NY 10017, Tel: (212) 210-3000
(Advertising, public relations, direct marketing & sales promotion, corp & product ID
management)
    Young & Rubicam Business Communications, Rue Thalberg 2, CH-1201 Geneva, Switzerland

ZIPPERTUBING CO   13000 S Broadway, PO Box 61129, Los Angeles, CA 90061,
Tel: (310) 527-0488
(Mfr zip-on plastic tubing, wire markers, pipe insulation, EMI shielding)
    Ticon AG, Engelgasse 7, CH-9630 Wattwil, Switzerland

SYRIA

BAKER OIL TOOLS   PO Box 40129, Houston, TX 77240-0129, Tel: (713) 466-1322
(Mfr/serv oil/gas well completions equip)
    Electra Trading Co., c/o Moukhtar Kilarji, P.O. Box 2537, Damascus, Syria

ITT SHERATON CORP   60 State St, Boston, MA 02108, Tel: (617) 367-3600
(Hotel operations)
    Damascus Sheraton Hotel, Omayad Sq., P.O. Box 4795, Damascus, Syria

THE KULJIAN CO   3624 Science Center, Philadelphia, PA 19104,
Tel: (215) 243-1900
(Studies, design, engineeering, constr mgmt, site supervision)
    Kuljian Corp., P.O. Box 3107, Damascus, Syria

MARATHON OIL CO   539 S Main St, Findlay, OH 45840, Tel: (419) 422-2121
(Petroleum explor & prod)
    Marathon Petroleum Ltd., P.O. Box 7577, Damascus, Syria

WEATHERFORD INTL INC   1360 Post Oak Blvd, PO Box 27608, Houston,
TX 77227-7608, Tel: (713) 439-9400
(Oilfield servs, prdts & equip; mfr marine cranes)
    Weatherford Intl. Inc., c/o Al-Diaa Trading, 42 Foud Salem, Hou Boubi Thani,
    P.O. Box 415, Damascus, Syria

WESTERN ATLAS INTL INC   10205 Westheimer, PO Box 1407, Houston,
TX 77251-1407, Tel: (713) 266-5700
(Full service to the oil industry)
    Western Atlas Logging Services, P.O. Box 32124, Eastern Mezzeh Ext. 252/A,
    Shirazi Bldg., Damascus, Syria

TAIWAN

3COM CORP   5400 Bayfront Plaza, Santa Clara, CA 95052-8145,
  Tel: (408) 764-5000
  (Devel/mfr computer networking prdts & sys)
    3Com Asia Ltd., Taiwan

3M   3M Center, St Paul, MN 55144-1000, Tel: (612) 733-1110
  (Mfr diversified prdts for industry, health care, imaging, commun, transport, safety,
  consumer, etc)
    3M Taiwan Ltd., Lotus Bldg. 13/F, 136 Section 3, Jen Ai Rd., Taipei 10628, Taiwan

ACTION OVERSEAS BUYING LTD   460 Nixon Rd, Allegheny Ind Park, Cheswick,
  PA 15024, Tel: (412) 782-4800
  (Distr/sale housewares, hardware, giftware, light bulbs & crystal)
    Action Overseas Buying Ltd., 5th Floor, 41-2 Hsin Yi Rd., Section 3, Taipei 106,
      Taiwan

AFLAC INC   1932 Wynnton Rd, Columbus, GA 31999, Tel: (706) 323-3431
  (Insurance, TV broadcasting)
    AFLAC Taiwan, 66 Sung-Chiang Rd. 6/F, Taipei, Taiwan

AIR EXPRESS INTL CORP   120 Tokeneke Rd, PO Box 1231, Darien, CT 06820,
  Tel: (203) 655-7900
  (Air frt forwarder)
    Air Express Intl., c/o Morrison Express Corp. Ltd., 25 Jen Al Rd., Section 4,
      Taipei, Taiwan

AIR PRODUCTS & CHEMICALS INC   7201 Hamilton Blvd, Allentown, PA 18195-1501,
  Tel: (215) 481-4911
  (Mfr ind gases & related equip, spec chems, environmental/energy sys)
    San Fu Chemical Co. Ltd., 5th Floor, Shankong Bldg. 21, Sec. 2,
      Chung Shan North Rd., Taipei, Taiwan

AIRBORNE EXPRESS   3101 Western Ave, PO Box 662, Seattle, WA 98111,
  Tel: (206) 285-4600
  (Air transp serv)
    Airborne Express, Room 1001, Intl. Trade Bldg., Keelung Rd., Section 1, Taipei,
      Taiwan
    Airborne Express, Room 309, Industrial East 6 Rd., Science-Based Ind. Park,
      Hsinchu, Taiwan
    Airborne Express, Room 5, Mariners Assurance Bldg., Chung Shan 2nd Rd., Kaohsiung,
      Taiwan
    Airborne Express, 3rd Floor, 3 Pei Huan Rd., Tanzu Hsiang, Taichung Hsien, Taiwan

THE ALLEN GROUP INC 25101 Chagrin Blvd, Beachwood, OH 44122,
Tel: (216) 765-5800
(Mfr communications equip, automotive bodies & parts, electronic components)
Orion Taiwan Ltd., 26 Chung Shan N. Rd., Sector 3, Taipei, Taiwan

ALLEN-BRADLEY CO PO Box 2086, Milwaukee, WI 53201, Tel: (414) 382-2000
(Mfr eletrical controls & info devices)
Allen-Bradley Div., Rockwell Intl. Taiwan Co. Ltd., 7-1 Floor, Ta-Nan Rd.,
Shih-Lin District, Taipei 11150, Taiwan

AMERICAN AIRLINES INC PO Box 619616, Dallas-Ft Worth Arpt, TX 75261-9616,
Tel: (817) 355-1234
(Air transp)
China Express Ltd., 68 Chung Shan N. Rd., Section 2, Taipei, Taiwan
China Express Ltd., 5 Chung Hwa Shan Rd., Kaoshiung, Taiwan

AMERICAN APPRAISAL ASSOCS INC 411 E Wisconsin Ave, Milwaukee, WI 53202,
Tel: (414) 271-7240
(Valuation consulting serv)
American Appraisal Taiwan ltd., Morrison Plaza, 12/F, 25 Jen Ai Rd., Sec. 4,
Taipei, Taiwan

AMERICAN EXPRESS CO World Financial Center, New York, NY 10285-4765,
Tel: (212) 640-2000
(Travel, travelers cheques, charge card & financial services)
merican Express Intl. (Taiwan) Inc.

AMERICAN INTL GROUP INC 70 Pine St, New York, NY 10270, Tel: (212) 770-7000
(Insurance, financial services)
Nan Shan Life Insurance Co. Ltd., 302 Min Chuan East Rd., Chungstan, Taipei, Taiwan

AMERICAN PRESIDENT LINES LTD 1111 Broadway, Oakland, CA 94607,
Tel: (415) 272-8000
(Intermodal shipping serv)
American President Lines Ltd., 5th Floor, Tun Hua South Rd 473, 5/F,
P.O. Box 108143, Taipei 10648, Taiwan

AMERICAN TOOL COMPANIES INC 8400 LakeView Pkwy, #400, Kenosha, WI 53142,
Tel: (800) 866-5740
(Mfr hand tools, cutting tools, power tool accessories)
American Tool Companies Inc., 6th Floor, 122 Chung Cheng Rd., Section 2, Tien Mou,
Taipei 111, Taiwan

AMOCO CHEMICAL CO 200 E Randolph Dr, Chicago, IL 60601, Tel: (312) 856-3200
(Mfr/sale petrol based chems, plastics, chem/plastic prdts)
China American Petrochemical Co. Ltd., Taiwan

AMP INC PO Box 3608, Harrisburg, PA 17105-3608, Tel: (717) 564-0100
(Devel/mfr electronic & electrical connection prdts & sys)
AMP Taiwan BV, Room 1404, 136 Jen Ai Rd., Section 3, Taipei, Taiwan

AMWAY CORP 7575 E Fulton Rd, Ada, MI 49355, Tel: (616) 676-6000
(Mfr/sale home care, personal care, nutrition & houseware prdts)
Amway (Taiwan) Ltd., 8th Floor, Central Commercial Bldg., 18 Nanking E Rd.,
Section 4, Taipei, Taiwan

ANIXTER BROS INC   4711 Golf Rd, Skokie, IL 60076, Tel: (708) 677-2600
  (Dist wiring sys/prdts for voice, video, data & power applications)
    Asiacom, 10th Floor, 598 Min Sheng E. Rd., Taipei, Taiwan

ARBOR ACRES FARM INC   439 Marlborough Rd, Glastonbury, CT 06033,
  Tel: (860) 633-4681
  (Producers of male & female broiler breeders, commercial egg layers)
    Arbor Acres (Taiwan) Co. Ltd., 8th Floor, Cathay Sung Chiang Bldg.,
      129 Sung Chiang Rd., Taipei, Taiwan

ARGOSY INTL (USA) INC   225 W 34th St, New York, NY 10122, Tel: (212) 268-0003
  (Mfr/distr construction materials, chemicals)
    Argosy Taiwan, 17 Lane 407, Chi Lin Rd., Taipei, Taiwan

ASARCO INC   180 Maiden Lane, New York, NY 10038, Tel: (212) 510-2000
  (Nonferrous metals, specialty chems, minerals, mfr industrial prdts, environmental
  services)
    Enthone-Omi Inc., Taiwan

ASSOCIATED MERCHANDISING CORP   1440 Broadway, New York, NY 10018,
  Tel: (212) 536-4000
  (Retail service organization)
    Associated Merchandising Corp., P.O. Box 67-133, Taipei 10404, Taiwan

AST RESEARCH INC   16215 Alton Parkway, PO Box 19658, Irvine, CA 92713-9658,
  Tel: (714) 727-4141
  (Design/devel/mfr hi-perf desktop, server & notebook computers)
    AST Taiwan Mfg., 46 Park Ave. 2, Science-Based Industrial Park, Hsin-chu, Taiwan
    AST Taiwan Sales, Room B, 16/F, Section 2, 216 Cathay Taipei Intl. Bldg.,
      Tun Hua South Rd., Taipei, Taiwan

AT&T INTERNATIONAL   412 Mt Kemble Ave, Morristown, NJ 07962-1995,
  Tel: (810) 262-6646
  (Telecommunications)
    AT&T Taiwan Inc., 4/16/19th Floors, Hung Tai Century Tower, 156 Min Sheng E. Rd.,
      Sec. 3, Taipei, Taiwan

ATLANTIC GULF COMMUNITIES CORP   2601 S Bayshore Dr, Miami, FL 33133-5461,
  Tel: (305) 859-4500
  (Real estate development)
    Atlantic Gulf Communities Service Corp., Suite 2106, 21/F, 333 Keelung Rd., Sec. 1,
      Taipei, Taiwan

THE BANK OF CALIFORNIA NA   400 California St, San Francisco, CA 94104,
  Tel: (415) 765-0400
  (Banking)
    Bank of California NA, 7th Floor, Commercial Bank Bldg., 8 Hsiang Yang Rd., Taipei,
      Taiwan

THE BANK OF NEW YORK   48 Wall St, New York, NY 10286, Tel: (212) 495-1784
  (Banking)
    The Bank of New York, 245 Tun Hwa South Rd., Section 1, 4th fl., P.O. Box 58040,
      Taipei 106, Taiwan

BANKAMERICA CORP   555 California St, San Francisco, CA 94104,
Tel: (415) 622-3456
(Financial services)
  Bank of America NT & SA, Bank Tower 2/F, 205 Tun Hwa North Rd., Taipei 105, Taiwan

BANKERS TRUST CO   280 Park Ave, New York, NY 10017, Tel: (212) 250-2500
(Banking)
  Bankers Trust Co., 8th Floor, Enterprise Bldg., 46 Kuan Chien Rd., Taipei 100,
    Taiwan
  Bankers Trust Co., 8th Floor, Bank Tower, 205 Tun Hua North Rd., Taipei 100, Taiwan

BAUSCH & LOMB INC   1 Chase Square, Rochester, NY 14601, Tel: (716) 338-6000
(Mfr vision care prdts & accessories)
  B&L Lord Co. Ltd., Taipei, Taiwan
  Bausch & Lomb Taiwan Ltd., Taipei, Taiwan

BAXTER HEALTHCARE CORP   1 Baxter Pky, Deerfield, IL 60015,
Tel: (708) 948-2000
(Mfr disposable medical prdts)
  Baxter Healthcare Ltd., 62-3/F Tun-Hua N. Rd., Taipei 10590, Taiwan

BDM INTL INC   7915 Jones Branch Dr, McLean, VA 22102, Tel: (703) 848-5000
(Professional & technical services)
  The BDM Corp., No. 3, Sect. 3, Chung Shan N. Rd., Taipei, Taiwan

BECKMAN INSTRUMENTS INC   2500 Harbor Blvd, Fullerton, CA 92634,
Tel: (714) 871-4848
(Devel/mfr/mkt automated systems & supplies for biological analysis)
  Beckman Instruments (Taiwan) Inc., 8th fl., 216 Tun Hwa South Rd., Section 2,
    Taipei 101, Taiwan

BENTLY NEVADA CORP   PO Box 157, Minden, NV 89423, Tel: (702) 782-3611
(Electronic monitoring system)
  Lumax Intl. Corp. Ltd., P.O. Box 81-228, Taipei, Taiwan

BORDEN INC   180 E Broad St, Columbus, OH 43215-3799, Tel: (614) 225-4000
(Mfr foods, snacks & beverages, adhesives)
  Borden Inc., all mail to U.S. address

BOURNS INC   1200 Columbia Ave, Riverside, CA 92507, Tel: (909) 781-5500
(Mfr resistive com & networks, precision potentiometers, panel controls, switches,
transducers)
  Bourns Electrtonics (Taiwan) Ltd., 1 Kung 6th Rd., Lin-Kou Shiang, Taipei Hsien,
    Taiwan

BOYDEN CONSULTING CORP   375 Park Ave, #1008, New York, NY 10152,
Tel: (212) 980-6480
(Executive search)
  Investec/Boyden Ltd., 14th Floor, Ever Spring Bldg., 147 Chien Kuo North Rd.,
    Section 2, Taipei, Taiwan

BRANSON ULTRASONICS CORP   41 Eagle Rd, Danbury, CT 06813-1961,
Tel: (203) 796-0400
(Mfr plastics assembly equip, ultrasonic cleaning equip)
  Branson Ultrasonics-Taiwan, Rm. 609, Chung-Hsiao Bldg., Wu-Ku Ind. Pk.,
    Wu-Chuan First Rd., Hsin-Chuang City, Taipei 242, Taiwan

BROWN GROUP INC   8300 Maryland Ave, St Louis, MO 63105, Tel: (314) 854-4000
  (Mfr/sale footwear)
    Pagoda Intl. Footwear Ltd., 2-6/F, 126 Wen Hsin Rd., Sec 3, Taichung, Taiwan
    Pagoda Trading, Goldstone Bldg, 4/F 380, Lin Shen N. Rd., Taipei 10454, Taiwan

BURLINGTON AIR EXPRESS   18200 Van Karman Ave, Irvine, CA 92715,
  Tel: (714) 752-4000
  (Air freight)
    Burlington Air Express (Taiwan) Ltd., 5th Floor, 778 Pa Teh Rd., Section 4, Taipei,
    Taiwan

LEO BURNETT CO INC   35 West Wacker Dr, Chicago, IL 60601, Tel: (312) 220-5959
  (Advertising agency)
    Leo Burnett Co. Inc., 7th Floor, Chung Hsin Textile Bldg.,
    123 Chung Hsiao East Rd., Section 2, Taipei, Taiwan

BURNS & ROE INC   800 Kinderkamack Rd, Oradell, NJ 07649, Tel: (201) 986-4800
  (Engineering, construction)
    Lin & Roe Co. Ltd., 155 Sin-yi Rd., Section 4, Taipei, Taiwan

CALTEX PETROLEUM CORP   PO Box 619500, Dallas, TX 75261, Tel: (214) 830-1000
  (Petroleum prdts)
    Caltex (Asia) Ltd., 12th Floor, 24 Chi Lin Rd., Taipei 10424, Taiwan

CARBOLINE CO   350 Hanley Industrial Ct, St Louis, MO 63144,
  Tel: (314) 644-1000
  (Mfr coatings, sealants)
    Central Paints Industrial Inc., 1-3 San Hsia San Ton Lee, Sub Ward Da Lun,
    Chung Li City, Taiwan

CARGILL   PO Box 9300, Minneapolis, MN 55440, Tel: (612) 475-7575
  (Food prdts, feeds, animal prdts)
    Cargill Taiwan Corp., 3rd Floor, 9 Chin Tao East Rd., Taipei 10022, Taiwan

CARPENTER TECHNOLOGY CORP   101 W Bern St, PO Box 14662, Reading,
  PA 19612-4662, Tel: (610) 208-2000
  (Mfr specialty steels & structural ceramics for casting ind)
    Walsin-CarTech (JV - early 1994), 3-10 Shi Jou Liau, Chin Shuei Li, Yenshui Chen,
    Tainan, Taiwan

CARRIER CORP   One Carrier Place, Farmington, CT 06034-4015,
  Tel: (203) 674-3000
  (Mfr/distr/svce A/C, heating & refrigeration equip)
    Carrican Enterprises, Taipei, Taiwan
    Carrier Taiwan Co. Ltd., P.O. Box 1-143, Taipei, Taiwan

CDM INTL INC   Ten Cambridge Center, Cambridge, MA 02142, Tel: (617) 252-8000
  (Consulting engineers)
    Camp Dresser & McKee Inc., 6/F, 32 Jen-Ai Rd., Section 3, Taipei, Taiwan

CHASE MANHATTAN BANK N A   1 Chase Manhattan Plaza, New York, NY 10081,
  Tel: (212) 552-2222
  (Intl banking)
    Chase Manhattan Bank N.A., P.O. Box 3996, 72 Nanking E. Rd., Section 2, Taipei 104,
    Taiwan

CHEMICAL BANK   270 Park Ave, New York, NY 10017-2070, Tel: (212) 270-6000
  (Banking & financial services)
    Chemical Bank, Taipei Financial Center 10/F, 62 Tun Hwa N. Rd., Taipei, Taiwan

THE CHUBB CORP   15 Mountain View Rd, Warren, NJ 07060, Tel: (908) 580-2000
  (Holding co: property/casualty ins)
    Federal Insurance Co., Taiwan

CIGNA CORP   One Liberty Place, Philadelphia, PA 19192, Tel: (215) 523-4000
  (Ins, invest, health care & other fin servs)
    Connecticut General Life Insurance Co., Room 2005, Intl. Trade Bldg.,
      333 Keelung Rd., Section 1, Taipei, Taiwan
    Insurance Co. of North America, Room 2005, Intl. Trade Bldg., 333 Keelung Rd.,
      Section 1, Taipei, Taiwan

CITICORP   399 Park Ave, New York, NY 10043, Tel: (212) 559-1000
  (Banking & financial services)
    Citibank NA, Taiwan

CLINTON ELECTRONICS CORP   6701 Clinton Road, Rockford, IL 61111,
  Tel: (815) 633-1444
  (Cathode ray tubes)
    Clinton Taiwan Corp., 4th Floor, 43 Kuan Chien Rd., Taipei, Taiwan

THE COCA-COLA CO   PO Drawer 1734, Atlanta, GA 30301, Tel: (404) 676-2121
  (Mfr/mkt/distr soft drinks, syrups & concentrates, juice & juice-drink prdts)
    Taiwan Bottling Co., all mail to U.S. address

COILCRAFT INC   1102 Silver Lake Rd, Cary, IL 60013, Tel: (708) 639-2361
  (Leaded & surface-mount coils & transformers)
    Coilcraft Taiwan, P.O. Box 218, Tu-cheng, Taipei, Taiwan

COLUMBIA PICTURES INDUSTRIES INC   711 Fifth Ave, New York, NY 10022,
  Tel: (212) 751-4400
  (Producer & distributor of motion pictures)
    Columbia Films of China Ltd., 3rd Floor, 20 Hsi-Ning S. Rd., Taipei 100, Taiwan

COMBUSTION ENGINEERING INC   900 Long Ridge Road, Stamford, CT 06902,
  Tel: (203) 329-8771
  (Tech constr)
    Wayne Hoh Corp., Je Ai Rd., Section 4 #33, P.O. Box 24-77, Taipei, Taiwan

COMPUTER ASSOCIATES INTL INC   One Computer Associates Plaza, Islandia,
  NY 11788, Tel: (516) 342-5224
  (Devel/mkt/mgt info mgt & bus applications software)
    Computer Associates Taiwan Ltd., 170 Tun Hua North Rd., Room C, 4th Fl., Taipei,
      Taiwan

CONAIR CORP   150 Milford Rd, E Windsor, NJ 08520, Tel: (609) 426-1300
  (Mfr personal care & household appliances)
    Tatung/Conair, 22 Chung Shan North Rd., Section 3, Taipei, Taiwan

COOPER INDUSTRIES INC   1001 Fannin St, PO Box 4446, Houston, TX 77210-4446,
  Tel: (713) 739-5400
  (Mfr/distr electrical prdts, tools & hardware, automotive prdts)
    Cooper Automotive, Hsinchu, Taiwan
    Cooper Power Systems Div., Taoyuan, Taiwan

CORESTATES FINANCIAL CORP   1500 Market St, Philadelphia, PA 19101,
  Tel: (215) 973-3100
  (Banking)
    Corestates Bank, 44 Chung Shan North Rd. 17/F, Sec. 2, Taipei, Taiwan

CPC INTERNATIONAL INC   PO Box 8000, Englewood Cliffs, NJ 07632,
  Tel: (201) 894-4000
  (Consumer foods, corn refining)
    CPC/AJI (Taiwan) Ltd., P.O. Box 45-97, Taipei, Taiwan

CRAY RESEARCH INC   655 Lone Oak Dr, Eagan, MN 55121, Tel: (612) 452-6650
  (Supercomputer systems & services)
    Cray Asia/Pacific Inc., 8F-1, 37 Ming Chuan East Rd., Sec. 3, Taipei 104, Taiwan

CRSS INTL INC   1177 W Loop So, PO Box 22427, Houston, TX 77227-2427,
  Tel: (713) 552-2000
  (Consulting, architecture, engineering, construction mgmt)
    CRSS Intl. (Taiwan), 9/F, Kuan Fu Bldg., 310 Chung Hsio E. Rd., Sec. 4, Taipei,
      Taiwan

CTS CORP   905 N West Blvd, Elkhart, IN 46514, Tel: (215) 293-7511
  (Mfr electr components)
    CTS Components Taiwan Ltd., 7 Central 6th Rd., Kaohsiung Export Processing Zone,
      P.O. Box 26-20, Kaohsiung, Taiwan

D-M-E COMPANY   29111 Stephenson Highway, Madison Heights, MI 48071,
  Tel: (313) 398-6000
  (Basic tooling for plastic molding & die casting)
    FKL Taiwan Steel Co., 72 Wuu-Chueng 7th Rd., Wuu-Guu Industrial Park, Taipei, Taiwan

LEO A DALY   8600 Indian Hills Dr, Omaha, NE 68114, Tel: (402) 391-8111
  (Planning, arch, engr & interior design servs)
    Leo A. Daly, 7th Floor, 367 Fu Hsing N Rd., Taipei 104, Taiwan

DANA CORP   PO Box 1000, Toledo, OH 43697, Tel: (419) 535-4500
  (Engineer/mfr/mkt prdts & sys for vehicular, ind & mobile off-highway mkt & related
  aftermarkets)
    ROC-Spicer Ltd., 822 Kuang Fu Rd., Pai-Lu Tsun, Pa-Teh Hsiang, Tao-Yuan, Taiwan
    Societe de Vente Warner Electric SA, 2/F, No. 2, Fuhsing North Rd., Taipei, Taiwan
    Taiway Ltd., 14 Kwang Fu Rd., Enlarging Industrial District, Hukou, Hsinchu, Taiwan

DANIEL MANN JOHNSON & MENDENHALL   3250 Wilshire Blvd, Los Angeles, CA 90010,
  Tel: (213) 381-3663
  (Architects & engineers)
    DMJM, c/o Sinotech Engineering Consultants, 171 Nanking East Rd. 1/F, Sec. 5,
      Taipei 10572, Taiwan

DDB NEEDHAM WORLDWIDE INC   437 Madison Ave, New York, NY 10022,
  Tel: (212) 415-2000
  (Advertising)
    DDB Needham Worldwide Inc., 12th Floor, Quanta Place, 678 Tun Hwa South Rd.,
      Taipei, Taiwan

DIGITAL EQUIPMENT CORP   146 Main St, Maynard, MA 01754-2571,
   Tel: (508) 493-5111
   (Networked computer systems & services)
     Digital Equipment (Taiwan) Ltd., 180 Nanking E Rd., Section 4, Taipei, Taiwan

THE DOW CHEMICAL CO   2030 Dow Center, Midland, MI 48674, Tel: (517) 636-1000
   (Mfr chems, plastics, pharms, agric prdts, consumer prdts)
     Dow Chemical Pacific Ltd., Room 1007, Chia Hsin Bldg., 96 Chung Shan N. Rd.,
       Section 2, Taipei, Taiwan

DOW CORNING CORP   2220 W Salzburg Rd, PO Box 1767, Midland, MI 48640,
   Tel: (517) 496-4000
   (Silicones, silicon chems, solid lubricants)
     Asia Silicones Ltd., 11th Floor, Formosa Plastics Bldg., 201 Tun Hwa N. Rd.,
       Taipei, Taiwan

E I DU PONT DE NEMOURS & CO   1007 Market St, Wilmington, DE 19898,
   Tel: (302) 774-1000
   (Mfr/sale diversified chems, plastics, specialty prdts & fibers)
     DuPont Far East Inc., 6th Floor, Intl. Bldg., 8 Tun Hua N. Rd., Taipei, Taiwan
     DuPont Taiwan Ltd., 6th Floor, Intl. Bldg., 8 Tun Hua N. Rd., Taipei, Taiwan

E-SYSTEMS INC   PO Box 660248, Dallas, TX 75266-0248, Tel: (214) 661-1000
   (Dev & mfr high-tech defense electronic sys & prdts; aircraft modification & maint)
     Air Asia Co. Ltd., Taiwan Airfield, Taipei 700, Taiwan

THE EASTERN CO   112 Bridge St, Naugatuck, CT 06770, Tel: (203) 729-2255
   (Mfr locks & security hardware)
     World Lock Co. Ltd., No. 135, Section 1, Nan Kan Rd., Lu Chu Hsiang, Taoyuan Hsien,
       Taiwan

EASTMAN KODAK CO   343 State St, Rochester, NY 14650, Tel: (716) 724-4000
   (Devel/mfr photo & chem prdts, info mgmt/video/copier sys, fibers/plastics for
   various ind)
     Kodak Taiwan Ltd., P.O. Box 200, 35 Chung Yang South Rd., Section 2, Taipei, Taiwan

EBASCO SERVICES INC   2 World Trade Center, New York, NY 10048-0752,
   Tel: (212) 839-1000
   (Engineering, constr)
     Ebasco-CTCI Corp., 19th Fl., 77 Tun Hwa S. Rd., Taipei, Taiwan

EFCO   1800 NE Broadway Ave, Des Moines, IA 50316-0386, Tel: (515) 266-1141
   (Mfr systems for concrete construction)
     EFCO, 143 Nanking E. Rd. 9F-1, Sec. 4, Unit B, Taipei, Taiwan

EG&G INC   45 William St, Wellesley, MA 02181-4078, Tel: (617) 237-5100
   (Diversified R/D, mfg & services)
     EG&G Inc., 5/F No. 16-4 Tien Mou West Rd., Taipei, Taiwan

ELECTROGLAS INC   2901 Coronado Dr, Santa Clara, CA 95054, Tel: (408) 727-6500
   (Mfr semi-conductor test equip, automatic wafer probers)
     Electroglas Intl. Inc., 2F-4, 105 Dong Nan St., Hsin Chu City, Taiwan

EMERSON RADIO CORP   1 Emerson Lane, N Bergen, NJ 07047, Tel: (201) 854-6600
   (Consumer electronics, radios, TV & VCR, tape recorders & players, computer prdts)
     Emerson Radio/Taiwan, Room 13-4, 112 Chung Shan N., Section 2, Taipei, Taiwan

EXPEDITORS INTL OF WASHINGTON INC   PO Box 69620, Seattle, WA 98168-9620,
Tel: (206) 246-3711
(Air/ocean freight forwarding, customs brokerage, intl logistics solutions)
  EI Freight (Taiwan) Ltd., Central Finance Bldg. 11/F, 181 Fu-Hsing North Rd.,
    Taipei, Taiwan
  EI Freight (Taiwan) Ltd., other locations throughout Taiwan

FAIRCHILD SEMICONDUCTOR DIV   PO Box 58090, Santa Clara, CA 95052-8090,
Tel: (408) 743-3355
(Mfr semiconductor components)
  Fairchild Semiconductor (Taiwan) Ltd., Room 502, 47 Chungshan N. Rd., Section 3,
    Taipei, Taiwan

FERRO CORPORATION   1000 Lakeside Ave, Cleveland, OH 44114,
Tel: (216) 641-8580
(Mfr chems, coatings, plastics, colors, refractories)
  Ferro Industrial Prdts. Ltd., Hsin Wu, P.O. Box 19, Taoyuan 327, Taiwan

FIRST CHICAGO CORP   One First National Plaza, Chicago, IL 60670,
Tel: (312) 732-4000
(Banking)
  First Chicago Corp., Taipei, Taiwan

FIRST NATIONAL BANK OF BOSTON   100 Federal St, Boston, MA 02110,
Tel: (617) 434-2200
(Commercial banking)
  First Natl. Bank of Boston, 5th Floor, United Commercial Bldg., 137 Nanking E. Rd.,
    Section 2, Taipei, Taiwan

FISCHBACH & MOORE INTL CORP   2525 Walnut Hill Lane, Dallas, TX 75229,
Tel: (214) 484-4586
(General, mechanical & electrical construction)
  Fischbach & Moore Intl. Corp., 5th Fl., Min Hwa Bldg., 150 Fu Hsing N. Rd., Taipei,
    Taiwan

FLOW INTL CORP   23500 64th Ave S, PO Box 97040, Kent, WA 98064-9740,
Tel: (206) 850-3500
(Mfr high-pressure waterjet cutting/cleaning equip, powered scaffolding; concrete
cleaning/removal)
  Flow Asia Corp., 2 Technology 3rd Rd., Science-Based Ind. Park, Hsin Chu, Taiwan

FORD MOTOR CO   The American Road, Dearborn, MI 48121, Tel: (313) 322-3000
(Mfr motor vehicles)
  Ford Lio Ho Motor Co. Ltd., Room 902, Bank Tower, 205 Tuan Hua N. Rd., Taipei,
    Taiwan

FOUR WINDS INTL GROUP   1500 SW First Ave, #850, Portland, OR 97201,
Tel: (503) 241-2732
(Transp of household goods & general cargo, third party logistics)
  Four Winds Taiwan, 100 (7F-2) Lin Shen North Rd., Taipei, Taiwan

THE FRANKLIN MINT   Franklin Center, PA 19091, Tel: (610) 459-6000
(Creation/mfr/mktg collectibles & luxury items)
  Franklin Mint Far East Trading Ltd., 9th Floor, 33 Chien Kua North Rd., Section 2,
    Taipei 10433, Taiwan

FRITZ COMPANIES INC   706 Mission St, San Francisco, CA 94103,
  Tel: (415) 904-8360
  (Integrated transportation, sourcing, distribution & customs brokerage services)
    Fritz Air Freignt Taiwan Ltd., 140 Roosevelt Rd. 9/F, Section 2, Taipei, Taiwan
    Fritz Project Forwarding (Asia) Ltd., 136 Roosevelt Rd. 11/F, Section 2, Taipei,
    Taiwan
    Fritz Transportation Intl., 140 Roosevelt Rd. 9/F, Section 2, Taipei, Taiwan

H B FULLER CO   2400 Energy Park Dr, St Paul, MN 55108, Tel: (612) 645-3401
  (Mfr/distr adhesives, sealants, coatings, paints, waxes, sanitation chems)
    H.B. Fuller Taiwan Co. Ltd., 79 Koung-Fu Rd., Hu-Kou, Hsin Chu, Taiwan

GENERAL ELECTRIC CO   3135 Easton Tpk, Fairfield, CT 06431,
  Tel: (203) 373-2211
  (Diversified manufacturing, technology & services)
    General Electric Co.,
      all mail to U.S. address; phone (800) 626-2004 or (518) 438-6500

GENERAL INSTRUMENT CORP   181 W Madison, Chicago, IL 60602,
  Tel: (312) 541-5000
  (Mfr broadband communications & power rectifying components)
    General Instrument of Taiwan Ltd., 233 Pao Chiao Rd., Hsin Tien, Taipei, Taiwan

GENERAL MOTORS ACCEPTANCE CORP   3044 West Grand Blvd, Detroit, MI 48202,
  Tel: (313) 556-5000
  (Automobile financing)
    General Motors Taiwan Credit Sales, 4/1F, 76 Tun Hua S. Rd., Sec. 2, Taipei, Taiwan

GETZ BROS & CO INC   150 Post St, #500, San Francisco, CA 94108,
  Tel: (415) 772-5500
  (Divers mfg, mktg/distr serv, travel serv)
    Getz Bros. & Co. Inc., P.O. Box 24-544, Taipei 104, Taiwan

GIBBS & HILL INC   11 Penn Plaza, New York, NY 10001, Tel: (212) 216-6000
  (Consulting engineers)
    Gibsin Engineers Ltd., P.O. Box 68-3161, Taipei, Taiwan

THE GILLETTE CO   Prudential Tower, Boston, MA 02199, Tel: (617) 421-7000
  (Devel/mfr personal care/use prdts: blades & razors, toiletries, cosmetics,
  stationery)
    Colton Taiwan Ltd., Taipei, Taiwan

THE GOODYEAR TIRE & RUBBER CO   1144 E Market St, Akron, OH 44316,
  Tel: (216) 796-2121
  (Mfr tires, automotive belts & hose, conveyor belts, chemicals; oil pipeline
  transmission)
    Goodyear Taiwan Ltd., 4th Floor, Tai-Fong Bldg., 71 Nanking E. Rd., Section 2,
    Taipei, Taiwan,

GREY ADVERTISING INC   777 Third Ave, New York, NY 10017, Tel: (212) 546-2000
  (Advertising)
    Hwa Wei & Grey, 12th Floor, #180, Sec. 4, Nanking E. Rd., Taipei, Taiwan

GRIFFITH LABORATORIES INC   I Griffith Center, Alsip, IL 60658,
  Tel: (708) 371-0900
  (Ind food ingredients & equip)

(cont)

Griffith Laboratories Ltd., 10th Floor, Worldwide House, 683 Ming Sheng E. Rd., Taipei, Taiwan

GTE CORP   One Stamford Forum, Stamford, CT 06904, Tel: (203) 965-2000
(Electr prdts, telecom sys, publ & commun)
GTE Taiwan Telecommunications Ltd., 21-6 Tun Hua S. Rd., Taipei, Taiwan

GTE SYLVANIA INC   One Stamford Forum, Stamford, CT 06904, Tel: (203) 357-2000
(Lamps & specialized lighting prdts)
Union Electronics Inc., 12th Floor, 15 Lane 135, Fu Shin S. Rd., Section 1, Taipei, Taiwan

HAMBRECHT & QUIST   One Bush St, San Francisco, CA 94104, Tel: (415) 576-3300
(Invest banking & venture capital serv)
H&Q Taiwan Co. Ltd., 32nd Floor, Intl. Trade Bldg., 333 Keelung Rd., Section 1, Taipei 10548, Taiwan

THE HARPER GROUP   260 Townsend St, PO Box 77933, San Francisco,
CA 94107-1719, Tel: (415) 978-0600
(Ocean/air freight fwdg, customs brokerage, packing & whse, logistics mgt, ins)
Circle Airfreight Intl. (Taiwan) Ltd., No. 25, 10/F, Section 1, Chang-An East Rd., Taipei, Taiwan
Sekin Transport Intl. (Taiwan) Ltd., No. 58, 4/F, Ming Sheng East Rd., Section 1, Taipei, Taiwan
United Intermodal Line Consolidation Services, No. 25, 10/F, Section 1, Chang-An East Rd., Taipei, Taiwan

H J HEINZ CO   PO Box 57, Pittsburgh, PA 15230-0057, Tel: (412) 456-5700
(Processed food prdts & nutritional services)
Star-Kist Foods Inc., Kaohsiung, Taiwan

HERCULES INC   Hercules Plaza, Wilmington, DE 19894-0001, Tel: (302) 594-5000
(Mfr spec chems, plastics, film & fibers, coatings, resins, food ingredients)
Taiwan Hercules Chemicals Inc., 6th Floor, Universal Enterprise Center, 624 Min Chuan East Rd., Taipei 104, Taiwan

HEWLETT-PACKARD CO   3000 Hanover St, Palo Alto, CA 94304-0890,
Tel: (415) 857-1501
(Mfr computing, communications & measurement prdts & services)
Hewlett-Packard Taiwan Ltd., 8th Floor, 337 Fu Hsing N. Rd., Taipei, Taiwan

HOLIDAY INNS INC   3742 Lamar Ave, Memphis, TN 38195, Tel: (901) 362-4001
(Hotels, restaurants, casinos)
Holiday Inn, 269 Dah Shing Rd., Taoyuan, Taiwan
Holiday Inn, 279 Liu-Ho, Kaohsiung Airport, Kaohsiung, Taiwan

HONEYWELL INC   PO Box 524, Minneapolis, MN 55440-0524, Tel: (612) 951-1000
(Devel/mfr controls for home & building, industry, space & aviation)
Honeywell Taiwan Ltd., 11th Floor, 4, Sec. 3, Ming-Sheng East Rd., Taipai, Taiwan

HOUGHTON INTL INC   PO Box 930, Valley Forge, PA 19482-0930,
Tel: (610) 666-4000
(Mfr spec chems, hydraulic fluids, lubricants)
Houghton Oil & Chemicals Far East Co. Ltd., 9th Floor, Lan Tsin Mansion, No. 314, Sec. 1, Tun Hua S. Road., Taipei, Taiwan

HUCK INTL INC   6 Thomas, PO Box 19590, Irvine, CA 92713, Tel: (714) 855-9000
  (Mfr advanced fastening sys)
    Huck Technologies Co. Ltd., 2/F, 119 Chung Cheng Rd., Section 1, Taipei, Taiwan

HUGHES AIRCRAFT CO   PO Box 80028, Los Angeles, CA 90080-0028,
  Tel: (310) 568-6904
  (Mfr electronics equip & sys)
    Hughes Aircraft Intl. Service Co., Room 701, Bank Tower, 205 Tun Hwa N. Rd.,
    Taipei 10592, Taiwan

HYATT INTL CORP   200 West Madison, Chicago, IL 60606, Tel: (312) 750-1234
  (Intl hotel mgmt)
    Hyatt Intl. Hotels, Taipei, Taiwan

IBM CORP   Old Orchard Rd, Armonk, NY 10504, Tel: (914) 765-1900
  (Information products, technology & services)
    IBM Taiwan Corp., Taipei, Taiwan

ICF KAISER INTL INC   9300 Lee Hwy, Fairfax, VA 22031, Tel: (703) 934-3600
  (Engineering, construction & consulting services)
    Kaiser Engineers, F/10, 44 Lane 11, Kuan-Fu North Rd., Taipei, Taiwan

ILLINOIS TOOL WORKS INC   3600 W Lake Ave, Glenview, IL 60025,
  Tel: (708) 724-7500
  (Mfr gears, tools, fasteners, sealants, plastic & metal components for ind, med, etc.)
    ITW Paktron Ltd., B8-53 Kaohsiung Export Processing Zone, Kaohsiung, Taiwan

INDUCTOTHERM CORP   10 Indel Ave, Rancocas, NJ 08073-0157, Tel: (609) 267-9000
  (Mfr induction melting furnaces)
    Inductotherm Taiwan Ltd., 695 Kao Shih Rd., Yang Mei, Tac Yuan, Hsien, Taiwan

INGERSOLL-RAND CO   200 Chestnut Ridge Rd, Woodcliff Lake, NJ 07675,
  Tel: (201) 573-0123
  (Mfr compressors, rock drills, pumps, air tools, door hardware, ball bearings)
    Ingersoll-Rand (Taiwan), Suite 700 205, Sec. 1, Tun Hwa South Rd., Taipei 106,
    Taiwan

INTERGRAPH CORP   Huntsville, AL 35894-0001, Tel: (205) 730-2000
  (Devel/mfr interactive computer graphic systems)
    Intergraph Corp. Taiwan, 21st Century Bldg. 207, 11/F, Tung Hwa North Rd.,
    Taipei 10592, Taiwan

INTERMEC CORP   6001 36th Ave West, PO Box 4280, Everett, WA 98203-9280,
  Tel: (206) 348-2600
  (Mfr/distr automated data collection sys)
    CCT Associates Inc., P.O. Box 32-079, Taipei, Taiwan

INTERNATIONAL DATA APPLICATIONS INC   475 Virginia Drive, Fort Washington,
  PA 19034, Tel: (215) 643-5000
  (Computer software consulting serv, etc)
    Intl. Data Applications Inc., 4th Floor, 128 Nanking Rd., Section 1, Taipei, Taiwan

INTERNATIONAL PAPER   2 Manhattanville Rd, Purchase, NY 10577,
  Tel: (914) 397-1500
  (Mfr/distr container board, paper, wood prdts)
    International Paper Taiwan Ltd., 7th Fl., Walsin Fin. Bldg., 675 Min Sheng E. Rd.,
    Taipei 10446, Taiwan

(cont)

Intl. Paper (Far East), 7th Fl., Walsin Fin. Bldg., 675 Ming Sheng E. Rd.,
Taipei 10446, Taiwan

ITT CORP   1330 Ave of the Americas, New York, NY 10019-5490,
Tel: (212) 258-1000
(Design/mfr communications & electronic equip, hotels, insurance)
Taiwan Intl. Standard Electronics Ltd., 10th Floor, 261 Nanking E. Rd., Section 3,
Taipei, Taiwan

ITT SHERATON CORP   60 State St, Boston, MA 02108, Tel: (617) 367-3600
(Hotel operations)
Lai Lai Sheraton Hotel Taipei, 12 Chung Hsiao E. Rd., Section 1, Taipei, Taiwan

JASON INC   411 E Wisconsin Ave, Milwaukee, WI 53202, Tel: (414) 277-9300
(Mfr auto trim, finishing products)
Hsin-feng Chemical Corp. (JV), 57 Ho-Pin Rd., Lu Chou Hsiang, Taipei, Taiwan

JCPENNEY PURCHASING CORP   PO Box 10001, Dallas, TX 75301-0001,
Tel: (214) 431-5380
(Department stores)
JCPenney Purchasing Corp., Suite 306, Worldwide House, 129 Min Sheng E. Rd.,
Sec. 3, Taipei 10445, Taiwan

JOHNSON & HIGGINS   125 Broad St, New York, NY 10004-2424, Tel: (212) 574-7000
(Ins brokerage, employee benefit conslt, risk mgmt, human resource conslt, ins/reins
servs)
Johnson & Higgins Inc., Chung Shan Bldg., 2 Min Tsu E. Rd., P.O. Box 68159,
Taipei 104, Taiwan

JOHNSON & JOHNSON   One Johnson & Johnson Plaza, New Brunswick, NJ 08933,
Tel: (908) 524-0400
(R&D/mfr/sale health care prdts)
Janssen Taiwan, c/o Johnson & Johnson Taiwan Ltd., P.O. Box 96688, Taipei, Taiwan
Johnson & Johnson Taiwan Ltd., P.O. Box 96855, Taipei, Taiwan

S C JOHNSON & SON INC   1525 Howe St, Racine, WI 53403, Tel: (414) 631-2000
(Home, auto, commercial & personal care prdts, specialty chems)
S.C. Johnson & Son (Taiwan) Ltd., P.O. Box 68-852, Taipei, Taiwan

JOY ENVIRONMENTAL TECHNOLOGIES INC   10700 North Freeway, Houston, TX 77037,
Tel: (713) 878-1000
(Design/eng air pollution control & material handling sys)
Joy Environmental Technologies Inc., 7-4 Fl., CTCI Tower, 77 Tung Hwa S. Rd.,
Taipei, Taiwan

K-SWISS INC   20664 Bahama St, Chatsworth, CA 91311, Tel: (818) 998-3388
(Mfr casual & athletic shoes, socks, leisure apparel)
K-Swiss Intl. Ltd., Fl, 17-1, #367 Taichung-Kan Rd., Section 1, Taichung, Taiwan

KEY TRONIC CORP   PO Box 14687, Spokane, WA 92214, Tel: (509) 928-8000
(Computers & peripherals)
Key Tronic Taiwan Corp, Science-Based Industrial Park, Hsin-chu, Taiway

KEYSTONE INTL INC   PO Box 40010, Houston, TX 77040, Tel: (713) 466-1176
(Mfr butterfly valves, actuators & control accessories)
Keystone Valve, Taiwan

KIMBERLY-CLARK CORP   PO Box 619100, Dallas, TX 75261, Tel: (214) 281-1200
(Mfr fiber-based prdts for personal care, lumber & paper prdts)
   Taiwan Kimberly-Clark Paper Corp., Taiwan

KNOWLES ELECTRONICS INC   3100 N Mannheim Rd, Franklin Park, IL 60131,
   Tel: (708) 455-3600
   (Microphones & loudspeakers)
      Knowles Electronics Taiwan Ltd., 245 Pei-Shin Rd., Section 1, Hsin Tien, Taipei,
      Taiwan

KOPPERS CO INC   Koppers Bldg, 437 Seventh Ave, Pittsburgh, PA 15219,
   Tel: (412) 227-2000
   (Constr materiald & serv; chem & bldg prdts)
      Koppers Co. Inc., 28 Nan Yang St, Taipei, Taiwan

L&F PRODUCTS   225 Summit Ave, Montvale, NJ 07645-1575, Tel: (201) 573-5700
   (Mfr household, personal care, woodworking & ind prdts)
      L&F Products Taiwan, Room 507-508, 5th Fl., 148 Chung Hsiao E. Rd., Sec. 4, Taipei,
      Taiwan

LEARONAL INC   272 Buffalo Ave, Freeport, NY 11520, Tel: (516) 868-8800
   (Mfr chem specialties)
      LeaRonal (SE Asia) Ltd., Taiwan Branch, 722 Kuang Fu Rd., Pa Te Hsiang,
      Taoyuan Hsien, Taiwan

LEASEWAY INTL CORP   3700 Park East Dr, Beechwood, OH 44122,
   Tel: (216) 765-5500
   (Trucking, warehousing, leasing)
      Orient Star Shipping Agency Co. Ltd., P.O. Box 81-41, Taipei, Taiwan

ELI LILLY & CO   Lilly Corporate Center, Indianapolis, IN 46285,
   Tel: (317) 276-2000
   (Mfr pharmaceuticals, animal health prdts)
      Eli Lilly & Co. (Taiwan) Inc., 11th Fl., 365 Fu-Hsing N. Rd., Taipei 10483, Taiwan

LILLY INDUSTRIES INC   733 S West St, Indianapolis, IN 46225,
   Tel: (317) 687-6700
   (Mfr industrial finishes, coatings & fillers)
      Lilly Industries Inc. Far East, 1 Kung Yeh First Rd., Zenwu Village,
      Kaohsiung Hsien, Taiwan

LOCKHEED MARTIN CORP   6801 Rockledge Dr, Bethesda, MD 20817,
   Tel: (301) 897-6000
   (Design/mfr/mgmt sys in fields of space, defense, energy, electronics, materials,
   info & tech svces)
      Lockheed Martin Intl. Ltd., Suite 908, 205 Tun Hwa N. Td., Taipei, Taiwan

LOCTITE CORP   10 Columbus Blvd, Hartford, CT 06106, Tel: (203) 520-5000
   (Mfr/sale ind adhesives & sealants)
      Loctite (Taiwan) Co. Ltd., 2/F, 87 Lane 155, Tun Hwa North Rd., Taipei, Taiwan

MANPOWER INTL INC   5301 N Ironwood Rd, PO Box 2053, Milwaukee,
   WI 53201-2053, Tel: (414) 961-1000
   (Temporary help service)
      Manpower Temporary Services, 11th Floor, Formosa Plastic Bldg.,
      201/30 Tun Hua N. Rd., Taipei, Taiwan

MATTEL INC   333 Continental Blvd, El Segundo, CA 90245, Tel: (310) 252-2000
  (Mfr toys, dolls, games, crafts & hobbies)
    Mattel Molds Ltd., 214 Tai Lin Rd., Section 2, Taishan Hsiang, Taipei, Taiwan

MAXTOR CORP   211 River Oaks Pkwy, San Jose, CA 95134, Tel: (408) 432-1700
  (Design/mfr magnetic storage prdts)
    Maxtor Asia Pacific Ltd., Taipei, Taiwan

MAY DEPARTMENT STORES CO   611 Olive St, St Louis, MO 63101-1799,
  Tel: (314) 342-3300
  (Retail dept stores)
    Volume Shoe Intl. Corp., 3rd Floor, Lotus Bldg., 136 Jen Ai Rd., Section 3,
      Taipei 10628, Taiwan

THE MENTHOLATUM CO INC   1360 Niagara St, Buffalo, NY 14213,
  Tel: (716) 882-7660
  (Mfr/distr proprietary medicines, drugs, OTC's)
    Mentholatum Taiwan Ltd., 5th fl., 45 Section 1, Hankow St., Taipei, Taiwan

METROPOLITAN LIFE INSURANCE CO   1 Madison Ave, New York, NY 10010-3690,
  Tel: (212) 578-2211
  (Insurance & retirement savings prdts & services)
    Metropolitan Insurance & Annuity Co., 85 Jen Ai Rd., 4th Floor, Sec. 4,
      Taipei 10649, Taiwan

MICROSOFT CORP   One Microsoft Way, Redmond, WA 98052-6399,
  Tel: (206) 882-8080
  (Computer software, peripherals & services)
    Microsoft Taiwan TC, 6 Min Chuan Rd. 10/F, Section 3, Taipei, Taiwan

MOBIL CORP   3225 Gallows Rd, Fairfax, VA 22037-0001, Tel: (703) 846-3000
  (Petroleum explor & refining, mfr petrol prdts, chems, petrochems)
    Mobil Petroleum Co. Inc., Room 1, 6th Floor, Metropolitan Bank Bldg.,
      Chung Hsiao E. Rd., Sec. 4, Taipei, Taiwan
    Taita Chemical Co., P.O. Box 36-173, Taipei, Taiwan

MOEN INC   377 Woodland Ave, Elyria, OH 44036, Tel: (216) 323-3341
  (Mfr/serv plumbing prdts)
    Hostan Co. Ltd., 2nd Floor, 26 Nanking East Rd., Section 3, Taipei 10411, Taiwan

MOLEX INC   2222 Wellington Ct, Lisle, IL 60532, Tel: (708) 969-4550
  (Mfr electronic, electrical & fiber optic interconnection prdts & sys, switches,
  application tooling)
    Molex Inc., Taipei, Taiwan

MONMOUTH PLASTICS INC   PO Box 921, Asbury Park, NJ 07712, Tel: (201) 775-5100
  (Flame retardant concentrates, thermoplastic sys, spec formulations)
    Deco Corp., BM702 Hueifong Bldg., 25 Chungshrio Rd., Section 3, Taipei, Taiwan

MORRISON KNUDSEN CORP   1 Morrison Knudsen Plaza, PO Box 73, Boise, ID 83729,
  Tel: (208) 386-5000
  (Design/construction for environmental, industrial, process, power & transportation
  mkts)
    MKI Taipei, Tun Nan Commercial Bldg., Room A-1, 5/F, 333 Tun Twa S. Rd., Sec. 2,
      Taipei, Taiwan

MORTON INTERNATIONAL INC   100 N Riverside Plaza, Chicago, IL 60606-1596,
Tel: (312) 807-2000
(Mfr adhesives, coatings, finishes, spec chems, advanced & electr materials, salt, airbags)
Morton Intl. Inc., 1st Floor, No. 31, Lane 313, Fu Hsin N. Rd., Taipei, Taiwan

MOTOROLA INC   1303 E Algonquin Rd, Schaumburg, IL 60196, Tel: (708) 576-5000
(Mfr commun equip, semiconductors, cellular phones)
Motorola Electronics Taiwan Ltd., 516 Ching Hua Rd., Section 1, Chungli, Taoyuan, Taiwan

MacDERMID INC   245 Freight St, Waterbury, CT 06702, Tel: (203) 575-5700
(Chem processing for metal ind, plastics, electronics cleaners, strippers)
MacDermid Taiwan Ltd., 77 Kuang Fu N. Rd., Hsin-Chu Enlarged Industrial Park, Hsin-Chu, Taiwan

THE MacNEAL-SCHWENDLER CORP   815 Colorado Blvd, Los Angeles, CA 90041,
Tel: (213) 258-9111
(Devel/mfr computer-aided engineering software)
The MacNeal-Schwendler Co. Ltd., 12/F-6, 391 Hsin-Yi Hotel, Sec. 4, Taipei, Taiwan

McCANN-ERICKSON WORLDWIDE   750 Third Ave, New York, NY 10017,
Tel: (212) 697-6000
(Advertising)
McCann-Erickson Taiwan Co., 120 Chian-kuo, North Rd., Section 2, Taipei 10433, Taiwan

NALCO CHEMICAL CO   One Nalco Center, Naperville, IL 60563-1198,
Tel: (708) 305-1000
(Chems for water & waste water treatment, oil prod & refining, ind processes; water/energy mgmt serv)
Taiwan Nalco Chemical Co. Ltd., P.O. Box 46-494, Taipei, Taiwan

NATIONAL STARCH & CHEMICAL CO   10 Finderne Ave, Bridgewater, NJ 08807-3300,
Tel: (908) 685-5000
(Mfr adhesives & sealants, resins & spec chems, electr materials & adhesives, food prdts, ind starch)
National Starch & Chemical (Taiwan) Ltd., Chung Li, Taiwan

A C NIELSEN CO   Nielsen Plaza, Northbrook, IL 60062-6288, Tel: (708) 498-6300
(Market research)
The D&B Cos. of Canada Ltd., 8/F-2 Empire Bldg., 87 Sung Chiang Rd., Taipei 10428, Taiwan

NORWEST BANK MINNESOTA NA   Norwest Center, 6th & Marquette, Minneapolis,
MN 55479-0095, Tel: (612) 667-8110
(Banking)
Norwest Bank Minnesota NA, 10/F, 129 Min Sheng E. Rd., Sec. 3, Taipei 10446, Taiwan

NOVELLUS SYSTEMS INC   81 Vista Montana, San Jose, CA 95134,
Tel: (408) 943-9700
(Mfr advanced processing systems used in fabrication of integrated circuits)
Novellus Systems, Taiwan

OLIN CORP   120 Long Ridge Rd, PO Box 1355, Stamford, CT 06904-1355,
Tel: (203) 356-2000
(Mfr chems, metals, applied physics in elect, defense, aerospace inds)
  Olin Taiwan, 7/F-2, 137 Fu Hsing S. Rd., Sec. 1, Taipei 10639, Taiwan

OTIS ELEVATOR CO   10 Farm Springs, Farmington, CT 06032, Tel: (860) 676-6528
(Mfr elevators & escalators)
  Tatung Otis Elevator Co., 6/F, 22 Chungshan North Rd., Sec. 3, Taipei, Taiwan

OUTDOOR TECHNOLOGIES GROUP   One Berkley Dr, Spirit Lake, IA 51360,
Tel: (712) 336-1520
(Mfr fishing rods, reels, lines & tackle, outdoor & marine prdts, soft & hard baits)
  Outdoor Technologies Intl. (OTI), 5 360 Lane, Chun Shang Rd., Sheng-Kang Hsiang,
   Taichung, Hsien, Taiwan

PANDUIT CORP   17301 Ridgeland Ave, Tinley Park, IL 60477-0981,
Tel: (708) 532-1800
(Mfr elec/electr wiring comps)
  Panduit Intl. Corp. (Taiwan), Rm. 901, 20 Nan King E. Rd., Sec. 2, Taipei, Taiwan

PARSONS DE LEUW INC   1133 15th St NW, Washington, DC 20005,
Tel: (202) 775-3300
(Consulting engineers)
  De Leuw Cather Intl. Ltd., 11th Floor, 111 Min-Sheng First Rd., Kaohsiung, Taiwan
  De Leuw, Cather Intl. Ltd., 6th Floor, 118-1 Chung Cheng Rd., Shihlin, Taipei,
   Taiwan

PARSONS ENGINEERING SCIENCE INC   100 W Walnut St, Pasadena, CA 91124,
Tel: (818) 440-6000
(Environmental engineering)
  Parsons Engineering Science Inc., c/o UEPPEG, 2 Tso-Nan Rd., Nan-Tsi Dist.,
   Kaohsiung 81126, Taiwan

PFIZER INC   235 E 42nd St, New York, NY 10017-5755, Tel: (212) 573-2323
(Mfr healthcare products)
  Pfizer Ltd., Taiwan
  Pfizer Trading Corp., Taiwan

PILLAR INDUSTRIES   N92 W15800 Megal Dr, Menomonee Falls, WI 53051,
Tel: (414) 255-6470
(Mfr induction heating & melting equip)
  Pillar Far East, 20 Bideford Rd. #12-01/02 Wellington Bldg., Singapore 0922

MAURICE PINCOFFS CO INC   2040 North Loop West, #200, Houston, TX 77018,
Tel: (713) 681-5461
(Intl marketing & distr)
  Maurice Pincoffs Taipei, 4th Floor, 34 Cheng Kung Rd., Section 4, Nei Hu, Taipei,
   Taiwan

PINKERTON SECURITY & INVESTIGATION SERVICES   6727 Odessa Ave, Van Nuys,
CA 91406-5796, Tel: (818) 373-8800
(Security & investigation services)
  Pinkerton Consulting & Investigation Services, Unit A-2, 12th Floor,
   Union Commercial Bldg., 137 Nanking E. Rd., Sec. 2, Taipei, Taiwan

PPG INDUSTRIES   One PPG Place, Pittsburgh, PA 15272, Tel: (412) 434-3131
  (Mfr flat glass, fiber glass, chems, coatings)
    PFG Fiber Glass Corp., Room 216, 5th Fl., 201 Tung Hwa North Rd., Taipei 10591,
      Taiwan
    PPG Industries Taiwan Ltd., 131 Min Sheng East Rd., Section 3, Suite 601,
      Taipei 105, Taiwan
    Taiwan Chlorine Industries Ltd., 131 Min Sheng East Rd., Section 3, Suite 603,
      Taipei 105, Taiwan

PROCTER & GAMBLE CO   One Procter & Gamble Plaza, Cincinnati, OH 45202,
  Tel: (513) 983-1100
  (Personal care, food, laundry, cleaning & ind prdts)
    Modern Home Products Ltd., Taipei, Taiwan

RAYCHEM CORP   300 Constitution Dr, Menlo Park, CA 94025, Tel: (415) 361-3333
  (Devel/mfr/mkt materials science products for electronics, telecommunications &
  industry)
    Raychem Taiwan Ltd., 542-4 Chung Cheng Rd. 4/F, Far East Industrial Zone,
      Hsintien 231, Taipei, Taiwan

REFAC TECHNOLOGY DEVELOPMENT CORP   122 E 42nd St, #4000, New York, NY 10168,
  Tel: (212) 687-4741
  (Consult, intl tech transfer, foreign trade, power supplies)
    Certified Electronics Ltd., 237 Nanking E. Rd., Section 5, Taipei, Taiwan

A H ROBINS CO INC   1407 Cummings Dr, PO Box 26609, Richmond, VA 23261-6609,
  Tel: (804) 257-2000
  (Mfr ethical pharms & consumer prdts)
    A.H. Robins Intl. Co., Taipei, Taiwan

THE ROCKPORT CO   220 Donald J Lynch Blvd, Marlboro, MA 01752,
  Tel: (508) 485-2090
  (Mfr/imp dress & casual footwear)
    Highland Import Corp., 10/F Sunluck Bldg., 271 Chung Chen Rd., Taichung, Taiwan

ROCKWELL INTL CORP   2201 Seal Beach Blvd, PO Box 4250, Seal Beach,
  CA 90740-8250, Tel: (310) 797-3311
  (Prdts & serv for aerospace, automotive, electronics, graphics & automation inds)
    Allen-Bradley Taiwan, Room 7, First Floor, 361 Ta-Nan Rd., Shih-Lin District,
      Taipei 11150, Taiwan
    Rockwell Intl. Taiwan Co. Ltd., Room 2808, Intl. Trade Bldg., 333 Keelung Rd.,
      Sec. 1, Taipei 10548, Taiwan

ROHM AND HAAS CO   100 Independence Mall West, Philadelphia, PA 19106,
  Tel: (215) 592-3000
  (Mfr ind & agric chems, plastics)
    Rohm and Haas Asia Inc., 4th Floor, 102 Tun Hwa North Rd., Taipei 10590, Taiwan

RUSSIN & VECCHI   1140 Connecticut Ave, #250, Washington, DC 20036,
  Tel: (202) 223-4793
  (Lawyers)
    Russin & Vecchi, 9th Floor, Bank Tower, 205 Tun Hwa N Rd., Taipei, Taiwan,

SEA-LAND SERVICE INC   150 Allen Rd, Liberty Corner, NJ 07920,
  Tel: (201) 558-6000
  (Container transport)

(cont)

Sea-Land Service Inc., 9th Floor, No. 2, Section 2, Nanking E. Rd., Taipei, Taiwan
Sea-Land Service Inc., other locations in Taiwan

SEALED AIR CORP   Park 80 Plaza E, Saddle Brook, NJ 07662-5291,
Tel: (201) 791-7600
(Mfr protective packaging prdts)
Sealed Air (Taiwan) Ltd., 20 Lane 238, Tun Hwa N. Rd., Taipei, Taiwan

SHEARMAN & STERLING   599 Lexington Ave, New York, NY 10022-6069,
Tel: (212) 848-4000
(Lawyers)
Shearman & Sterling, 7th Fl., Hung Kuo Bldg., 167 Tun Hwa North Rd., Taipei, Taiwan

SIGNODE PACKAGING SYSTEMS   3600 W Lake Ave, Glenview, IL 60025,
Tel: (708) 724-6100
(Mfr packaging systems)
Signode Intl. Trading Corp., 80-8 Taichung Kang Rd. 10/F-1, Sec. 2, Taichung 407,
Taiwan

SNAP-ON TOOLS CORP   2801 80th St, Kenosha, WI 53141-1410, Tel: (414) 656-5200
(Mfr automotive & ind maint serv tools)
Snap-On Tools Worldwide Inc., 824 Min Sheng Rd., Tao Yuan 33014, Taiwan

SONOCO PRODUCTS CO   North Second St, PO Box 160, Hartsville, SC 29550,
Tel: (803) 383-7000
(Mfr packaging for consumer & ind mkt)
Cosmos-Shows Products Co. Ltd., 125 Shin-Sheng South Rd., Section 1, Taipei, Taiwan
Sonoco Taiwan Ltd., 5th Floor, Min Hwa Bldg., 150 Fu Hsing N. Rd., Taipei, Taiwan

THE STANLEY WORKS   1000 Stanley Dr, PO Box 7000, New Britain, CT 06050,
Tel: (203) 225-5111
(Mfr hand tools & hardware)
Stanley Works (Hong Kong) Ltd., P.O. Box 58-978, 76 Chung Hsiaso E. Rd., Taipei,
Taiwan

STATE STREET BANK & TRUST CO   225 Franklin St, Boston, MA 02101,
Tel: (617) 786-3000
(Banking & financial services)
State Street Bank & Trust Co., Bank Tower #607, 6/F, 205 Tun Hwa N. Rd., Taipei,
Taiwan

STIEFEL LABORATORIES INC   255 Alhambra Circle, Coral Gables, FL 33134,
Tel: (305) 443-3807
(Mfr pharmaceuticals, dermatological specialties)
Stiefel Laboratories Taiwan Inc., 6th Floor, No. 4, Lane 345, Lung Chiang Rd.,
Taipei, Taiwan

STOKES DIV   5500 Tabor Rd, Philadelphia, PA 19120, Tel: (215) 289-5671
(Vacuum pumps & components, vacuum dryers, oil-upgrading equip)
Tonk Hsing Enterprise Co. Ltd., 85 Yenping Rd. S., Taipei, Taiwan

STONE & WEBSTER ENGINEERING CORP   245 Summer St, Boston, MA 02210-2288,
Tel: (617) 589-5111
(Engineering, constr & environmental & mgmt services)
Stone & Webster Taiwan Corp., TFIT Tower 8/F, 85 Jen-Al Rd., Section 4, Taipei 106,
Taiwan

STV GROUP   11 Robinson St, PO Box 459, Pottstown, PA 19464-0459,
  Tel: (215) 326-4600
  (Engineering, architectural, planning, environmental & construction mgmt services)
    STV Inc., 85 Chung-Hsino East Rd. 12F, Section 1, Taipei, Taiwan

SULLAIR CORP   3700 E Michigan Blvd, Michigan City, IN 46360,
  Tel: (219) 879-5451
  (Refrigeration sys, vacuum pumps, generators, etc)
    Sullair Taiwan Ltd., 4th Floor, 261 Nanking E. Rd., Section 3, Taipei, Taiwan

SUMMIT INDUSTRIAL CORP   600 Third Ave, New York, NY 10016,
  Tel: (212) 490-1100
  (Pharms, agric chem prdts)
    Summit Engineering Co. Ltd., 3rd Floor, 25 Jen Ai Rd., Section 4, Taipei, Taiwan
    Summit Industrial Corp., 20-9C Pa Teh Rd., Section 3, Taipei, Taiwan
    Summit Taiwan Corp., 3rd Floor, 25 Jen Ai Rd., Section 4, Taipei, Taiwan

TANDY CORP   1800 One Tandy Center, Fort Worth, TX 76102, Tel: (817) 390-3700
  (Electronic & acoustic equip)
    A&A Intl., Shen Hsing Tandy Bldg., 148 Sung Chiang Rd., Taipei, Taiwan
    TC Electronics (Taiwan) Corp., 1-6 W. Third St., Nantze, EPZ, Koahsiung, Taiwan

TEKTRONIX INC   26660 SW Parkway, Wilsonville, OR 97070, Tel: (503) 627-7111
  (Mfr test & meas, visual sys & commun prdts)
    Tektronix Taiwan Ltd., Taipei & Kaohsiung, Taiwan

TELEDYNE INC   2049 Century Park East, Los Angeles, CA 90067-3101,
  Tel: (310) 277-3311
  (Divers mfg: aviation & electronics, specialty metals, industrial & consumer prdts)
    Teledyne Taiwan, Formosa Plastic Bldg. "B" 10/F, 201 Tun Hwa N. Rd., Taipei 10591,
    Taiwan

TERADYNE INC   321 Harrison Ave, Boston, MA 02118, Tel: (617) 482-2700
  (Mfr electronic test equip & blackplane connection sys)
    Teradyne Taiwan Ltd., 6 Ta Hsin Rd., Taoyuan, Taiwan

TEXAS INSTRUMENTS INC   13500 N Central Expwy, Dallas, TX 75265,
  Tel: (214) 995-2011
  (Mfr semiconductor devices, electr/electro-mech sys, instr & controls)
    Texas Instruments Taiwan Ltd., 142 Hsin Nan Rd., Section 1, Chung Ho City, Taipei,
    Taiwan

TIFFANY & CO   727 Fifth Ave, New York, NY 10022, Tel: (212) 755-8000
  (Mfr/retail fine jewelry, silverware, china, crystal, leather goods, etc)
    Tiffany & Co. Taipei, Taipei Regent Hotel, Chung Shan North Rd., Taipei, Taiwan

TRANE CO   3600 Pammel Creek Rd, La Crosse, WI 54601, Tel: (608) 787-2000
  (Mfr/distr/svce A/C sys & equip)
    Taipei Sales & Service, Chia Hsin Bldg. 2, Room N-612, 9 Lane 3,
    Min Sheng West Rd., Taipei, Taiwan

TRW INC   1900 Richmond Rd, Cleveland, OH 44124, Tel: (216) 291-7000
  (Electr & energy-related prdts, automotive & aerospace prdts, tools & fasteners)
    TRW Electronics Components Co., 121 Chung Shan Rd., Section 2, Shulin,
    Taipei Hsien, Taiwan

U S SUMMIT CORP   600 Third Ave, New York, NY 10016, Tel: (212) 490-1100
(Mktg/distrib pharms, chems)
    U.S. Summit Corp., 8th Floor, Tai Tze Bldg., 20/1 Pade Rd., Section 3, Taipei,
     Taiwan

U S WHEAT ASSOCIATES   1200 NW Front Ave, #600, Portland, OR 97209,
Tel: (503) 223-8123
(Market development for wheat prdts)
   U.S. Wheat Associates Inc., all mail to P.O. Box 1612, Washington, DC 20013

UNION CARBIDE CORP   39 Old Ridgebury Rd, Danbury, CT 06817,
Tel: (203) 794-2000
(Mfr industrial chemicals, plastics, resins)
   Union Carbide Formosa Co. Ltd., P.O. Box 17-94, Taipei, Taiwan

UNISYS CORP   PO Box 500, Blue Bell, PA 19424, Tel: (215) 986-4011
(Mfg/mktg/serv electr info sys)
   Unisys (Taiwan) Ltd., 1035 Tun Hua S Rd., Tun Nan Commercial Bldg., Taipei, Taiwan

UNITED CALIFORNIA BANK   PO Box 54191, Los Angeles, CA 90054,
Tel: (213) 624-0111
(Banking)
   United California Bank, P.O. Box 59584, 221 Nanking E. Rd., Section 3, Taipei,
     Taiwan

UPJOHN CO   7000 Portage Rd, Kalamazoo, MI 49001, Tel: (616) 323-4000
(Mfr pharms, agric prdts, ind chems)
   Upjohn Intl. Inc., Room N-811, Chia Hsin Bldg., 9 Lane 3, Min Shen W. Rd., Taipei,
     Taiwan

UPLAND INDUSTRIES INC   3575 Hempland Rd, Lancaster, PA 17604,
Tel: (215) 874-4261
(Hand tools, casting, etc)
   Taiwan Upland Industries, 249 Chia Hou Rd., Wal Pu, Tachia, Taichung Hsien, Taiwan

VALENITE INC   PO Box 9636, Madison Heights, MI 48071-9636,
Tel: (810) 589-1000
(Cemented carbide, high speed steel, ceramic & diamond cutting tool prdts, etc)
   Valenite-Modco Intl. Inc., 3/F-4, 35 Nan Hua 1st St., Lu Chu, Tao-Yuan, Taiwan

WARD HOWELL INTL INC   99 Park Ave, New York, NY 10016-1699,
Tel: (212) 697-3730
(Executive recruiting)
   Traub, Au & Associates Ltd., 207 Tun Hwa N. Rd. #504, Taipei, Taiwan

WARNER-LAMBERT CO   201 Tabor Road, Morris Plains, NJ 07950,
Tel: (201) 540-2000
(Mfr ethical & proprietary pharms, confectionary & consumer prdts)
   Warner-Lambert Ltd./Parke-Davis Corp., 18th Floor, No. 65, 681 Tun Hwa South Rd.,
     Taipei 10661, Taiwan

WATLOW ELECTRIC MFG CO   12001 Lackland Rd, St Louis, MO 63146-4039,
Tel: (314) 878-4600
(Mfr elec heating units, electr controls, thermocouple wire, metal-sheathed cable,
infrared sensors)
   Watlow Taiwan Inc., 10F-1, 189 Chi-Shen 2nd Rd., Koahsiung, Taiwan

WAXMAN INDUSTRIES INC   24460 Aurora Rd, Bedford Heights, OH 44146,
  Tel: (216) 439-1830
  (Assemble/distr plumbing, electrical & hardware prdts)
    TWI Intl. Taiwan Inc., 10 7th Rd. Industrial Pk., Taichung 40707, Taiwan

WESTERN DIGITAL CORP   8105 Irvine Center Dr, Irvine, CA 92718,
  Tel: (714) 932-5000
  (Mfr hard disk drives, video graphics boards, VLSI)
    Western Digital Taiwan Ltd., 205 Tun Hwa North Rd. #1103, Taipei, Taiwan

WHIRLPOOL CORP   2000 N M-63, Benton Harbor, MI 49022-2692,
  Tel: (616) 923-5000
  (Mfr/mkt home appliances)
    Great Teco Whirlpool Ltd., Taipei, Taiwan

WILBUR-ELLIS CO   320 California St, #200, San Francisco, CA 94104,
  Tel: (415) 772-4000
  (Intl merchants & distributors)
    Connell Bros. Co. (Taiwan) Ltd., 4/F, 86 Yenping Rd. South, Taipei, Taiwan

WM WRIGLEY JR CO   410 N Michigan Ave, Chicago, IL 60611-4287,
  Tel: (312) 644-2121
  (Mfr chewing gum)
    Wrigley Taiwan Ltd., P.O. Box 10436, Taipei, Taiwan

XEROX CORP   800 Long Ridge Rd, PO Box 1600, Stamford, CT 06904,
  Tel: (203) 968-3000
  (Mfr document processing equip, sys & supplies)
    Xerox Corp., Taipei, Taiwan

YORK INTERNATIONAL CORP   PO Box 1592, York, PA 17405-1592,
  Tel: (717) 771-7890
  (Mfr A/C, heating & refrig sys & equip)
    Taiwan-York Service Co. Inc., 996 Cheng-Te Rd., Taipei 11148, Taiwan

ZYCAD CORP   47100 Bayside Pkwy, Fremont, CA 94538-9942, Tel: (510) 623-4400
  (Design/devel/mfr/mkt logic & fault simulation acceleration prdts; system engineering
  services)
    Zycad Corp., Floor 13-2, 295 Kuang Fu Rd., Sec. 2, Hsin Chu, Taiwan

TANZANIA

BECHTEL GROUP INC   50 Beale St, PO Box 3965, San Francisco, CA 94119,
  Tel: (415) 768-1234
  (Engineering & constr)
    Bechtel Intl. Corp., P.O. Box 2157, Dar es Salaam, Tanzania

LOUIS BERGER INTL INC   100 Halsted St, East Orange, NJ 07019,
Tel: (201) 678-1960
(Consulting engineers, architects, economists & planners)
  Louis Berger Intl. Inc., P.O. Box 33060, Dar es Salaam, Tanzania

CALTEX PETROLEUM CORP   PO Box 619500, Dallas, TX 75261, Tel: (214) 830-1000
(Petroleum prdts)
  Caltex Oil (Tanzania) Ltd., 4 Mafuta St., Kurasini, Dar es Salaam, Tanzania

THE KULJIAN CO   3624 Science Center, Philadelphia, PA 19104,
Tel: (215) 243-1900
(Studies, design, engineeering, constr mgmt, site supervision)
  Kuljian Corp., P.O. Box 4123, Dar es Salaam, Tanzania

PAPER CORP OF U S   PO BOX 951, Valley Forge, PA 19487, Tel: (215) 296-8000
(Paper & allied prdts)
  Wiggins Teape Overseas Sales Ltd., P.O. Box 171, Dar es Salaam, Tanzania

PARSONS DE LEUW INC   1133 15th St NW, Washington, DC 20005,
Tel: (202) 775-3300
(Consulting engineers)
  De Leuw Cather Intl. Ltd., M-Konsult Ltd., P.O. Box 2711, Dar es Salaam, Tanzania

PFIZER INC   235 E 42nd St, New York, NY 10017-5755, Tel: (212) 573-2323
(Mfr healthcare products)
  Pfizer Ltd., Tanzania

THAILAND

3M   3M Center, St Paul, MN 55144-1000, Tel: (612) 733-1110
(Mfr diversified prdts for industry, health care, imaging, commun, transport, safety, consumer, etc)
  3M Thailand Ltd., Serm-mit Tower 12/F, 159 Asoke Rd., Sukhumvit 21, Bangkok 10110, Thailand

ADVANCED MICRO DEVICES INC   PO Box 3453, Sunnyvale, CA 94088-3000,
Tel: (408) 732-2400
(Mfr integrated circuits for commun & computation ind)
  Advanced Micro Devices Ltd., 299/50/60 Changwattna Rd., Jweng Tung Seegun, Khet Bang Ken, Bangkok 10210, Thailand

AERONAUTICAL INSTRUMENTS & RADIO CO   234 Garibaldi Ave, Lodi, NJ 07644,
Tel: (201) 473-0034
(Mfr aeronautical instru)
  Bongkote Co. Ltd., 1-2 Uipavadeerungsit Rd., Bangkok, Thailand

AIR EXPRESS INTL CORP 120 Tokeneke Rd, PO Box 1231, Darien, CT 06820,
Tel: (203) 655-7900
(Air frt forwarder)
Air Express Intl., c/o Commercial Transport Intl. Co. Ltd., Thavich Bldg.,
61 Kasemras Rd., Bangkok, Thailand

ALLEN-BRADLEY CO PO Box 2086, Milwaukee, WI 53201, Tel: (414) 382-2000
(Mfr eletrical controls & info devices)
Allen-Bradley Thai Co. Ltd., 92/166 Muang Ake 3, Luk Hok, Ampur Muang,
Pathumthani 12000, Thailand

AMDAHL CORP 1250 E Arques Ave, PO Box 3470, Sunnyvale, CA 94088-3470,
Tel: (408) 746-6000
(Devel/mfr large scale computers, software, data storage prdts, info-technology
solutions & support)
Amdahl Pacific Basin Operations Inc., 35/F, 193-195 Ratchadapisek Rd., Klongtoey,
Bangkok 10110, Thailand

AMERICAN AIRLINES INC PO Box 619616, Dallas-Ft Worth Arpt, TX 75261-9616,
Tel: (817) 355-1234
(Air transp)
Pacific Leisure, 518-2 Ploenchit Rd., Bangkok, Thailand

AMERICAN APPRAISAL ASSOCS INC 411 E Wisconsin Ave, Milwaukee, WI 53202,
Tel: (414) 271-7240
(Valuation consulting serv)
Asian Appraisal Thailand Ltd., Room 313-319, 31/F, Thai CC Tower,
889 S. Sathorn Rd., Bangkok 10120, Thailand

AMERICAN EXPRESS CO World Financial Center, New York, NY 10285-4765,
Tel: (212) 640-2000
(Travel, travelers cheques, charge card & financial services)
American Express (Thai) Co. Ltd., all inquiries to U.S. address

AMERICAN PRESIDENT LINES LTD 1111 Broadway, Oakland, CA 94607,
Tel: (415) 272-8000
(Intermodal shipping serv)
American President Lines Ltd., Panjabhum Bldg. 11/F, 127 South Sathorn Rd.,
Yannawa Bangkok 10120, Thailand

AMERICAN STANDARD INC 1 Centennial Ave, Piscataway, NJ 08855,
Tel: (908) 980-3000
(Mfr heating & sanitary equip)
American Standard Sanitaryware (Thailand) Ltd., 392 Sukhumvit Rd., Bangkok, Thailand

AMP INC PO Box 3608, Harrisburg, PA 17105-3608, Tel: (717) 564-0100
(Devel/mfr electronic & electrical connection prdts & sys)
AMP (Thailand) Ltd., Bangkok, Thailand

AMWAY CORP 7575 E Fulton Rd, Ada, MI 49355, Tel: (616) 676-6000
(Mfr/sale home care, personal care, nutrition & houseware prdts)
Amway (Thailand) Ltd., 52/182 Ramkhamhaeng Rd., Bangkapi, Bangkok 10240, Thailand

ARBOR ACRES FARM INC 439 Marlborough Rd, Glastonbury, CT 06033,
Tel: (860) 633-4681
(Producers of male & female broiler breeders, commercial egg layers)

(cont)

Arbor Acres (Thailand) Co. Ltd., 2387 New Petchburi Rd., Bangkapi, Huay-Kwang, Bangkok, Thailand

ARMSTRONG WORLD INDUSTRIES INC   PO Box 3001, Lancaster, PA 17604,
Tel: (717) 397-0611
(Mfr/mkt interior furnishings & spec prdts for bldg, auto & textile inds)
Armstrong World Industries (Thailand) Ltd., Bangkok,
Thailand (all inquiries to U.S. address)

AT&T INTERNATIONAL   412 Mt Kemble Ave, Morristown, NJ 07962-1995,
Tel: (810) 262-6646
(Telecommunications)
AT&T Thailand Inc., Silom Complex Bldg. 20th & 25th Floors, 191 Silom Rd.,
Bangkok 10500, Thailand

AVIS INC   900 Old Country Rd, Garden City, NY 11530, Tel: (516) 222-3000
(Car rental serv)
Avis Rent Office, 1 North Sathorn Rd., Bangkok, Thailand

AVON PRODUCTS INC   9 W 57th St, New York, NY 10019, Tel: (212) 546-6015
(Mfr/distr beauty & related prdts, fashion jewelry, gifts & collectibles)
Avon Cosmetics (Thailand) Ltd., Bangkok, Thailand

THE BANK OF CALIFORNIA NA   400 California St, San Francisco, CA 94104,
Tel: (415) 765-0400
(Banking)
Bank of California, 699 Silom Rd., Bangkok, Thailand

BANKAMERICA CORP   555 California St, San Francisco, CA 94104,
Tel: (415) 622-3456
(Financial services)
Bank of America NT & SA, BofA Bldg, 2/2 Wireless Rd., GPO Box 158, Bangkok 10330,
Thailand

BANKERS TRUST CO   280 Park Ave, New York, NY 10017, Tel: (212) 250-2500
(Banking)
Thai Investment & Securities Co. Ltd. (TISCO), Boonmitr Bldg., 138 Silom Rd.,
Bangkok, Thailand

LOUIS BERGER INTL INC   100 Halsted St, East Orange, NJ 07019,
Tel: (201) 678-1960
(Consulting engineers, architects, economists & planners)
Louis Berger Intl. Inc., P.O. Box 11-1369, Bangkok, Thailand

BLACK & VEATCH INTL   8400 Ward Pkwy, PO Box 8405, Kansas City, MO 64114,
Tel: (913) 339-2000
(Engineering/architectural servs)
Black & Veatch Intl./Sindhu Pulsirivong Consultants, SPC Bldg. 1 Soi Chaemchan,
Sukhumvit 55, Bangkok 10110, Thailand

BOYDEN CONSULTING CORP   375 Park Ave, #1008, New York, NY 10152,
Tel: (212) 980-6480
(Executive search)
Boyden Assocs., CSN & Assocs. Co. Ltd., 142-21 Soi Suksavittaya, N. Sathord Rd.,
Bangkok 10500, Thailand

BRANSON ULTRASONICS CORP   41 Eagle Rd, Danbury, CT   06813-1961,
   Tel: (203) 796-0400
   (Mfr plastics assembly equip, ultrasonic cleaning equip)
      Branson Ultrasonics-Thailand, 10/150 SOI St. Louis 3, Chan Sapan 3 Rd.,
      Bangkok 10120, Thailand

BROWN & ROOT INC   4100 Clinton Dr, Houston, TX   77020-6299,
   Tel: (713) 676-3011
   (Engr, constr & maintenance)
      Siam Broan & Root Ltd., c/o Loxley (Bangkok), GPO Box 214, Bangkok 10501, Thailand

LEO BURNETT CO INC   35 West Wacker Dr, Chicago, IL   60601, Tel: (312) 220-5959
   (Advertising agency)
      Leo Burnett Ltd., USOM Bldg. 2/F, 37 Soi Somprasong 3, Petchburi Rd.,
      Bangkok 10400, Thailand

BURSON-MARSTELLER   230 Park Ave, New York, NY   10003-1566, Tel: (212) 614-4000
   (Public relations/public affairs consultants)
      Burson Marsteller, 133-19 Rajprosong, Bangkok 10500, Thailand

CALTEX PETROLEUM CORP   PO Box 619500, Dallas, TX   75261, Tel: (214) 830-1000
   (Petroleum prdts)
      Caltex Oil (Thailand) Ltd., Thai Life Insurance Bldg., 123 Rachadaphisek Rd.,
      Huay Kwang, Bangkok 10310, Thailand

CARBOLINE CO   350 Hanley Industrial Ct, St Louis, MO   63144,
   Tel: (314) 644-1000
   (Mfr coatings, sealants)
      CarboThai Co. Ltd., 2222/5 Moo4 Samyhakpoochaosamingprai, Sukhumvit Rd.,
      Samut Prakarn 10720, Thailand

CARGILL   PO Box 9300, Minneapolis, MN   55440, Tel: (612) 475-7575
   (Food prdts, feeds, animal prdts)
      Cargill Ltd., 18/F Sintorn III Bldg., 130-132 Wireless Rd., Lumpini, Patumwan,
      Bangkok 10330, Thailand

CARRIER CORP   One Carrier Place, Farmington, CT   06034-4015,
   Tel: (203) 674-3000
   (Mfr/distr/svce A/C, heating & refrigeration equip)
      Grimm-Carrier Ltd., 239-2 Sarasin Rd., Kwaeng Lumpini, Pathumwan District, Bangkok,
      Thailand

CDM INTL INC   Ten Cambridge Center, Cambridge, MA   02142, Tel: (617) 252-8000
   (Consulting engineers)
      Camp Dresser & McKee Intl. Inc., 994 Soi Thonglor (55), Sukhumvit Rd.,
      Bangkok 10110, Thailand

CHEMICAL BANK   270 Park Ave, New York, NY   10017-2070, Tel: (212) 270-6000
   (Banking & financial services)
      Chemical Bank, Bangkok Bank Bldg. #1602/4, 333 Silom Rd., Bangkok 10500, Thailand

CHESTERTON BINSWANGER INTL   Two Logan Sq, 4th fl, Philadelphia,
   PA 19103-2759, Tel: (215) 448-6000
   (Real estate & related svces)
      Chesterton Thai Property Consultants Ltd., 8th fl., SG Tower,
      161/1 Soi Mahadlek Luang 3, Rajdamri Rd., Bangkok 10330, Thailand

CHEVRON CORP   225 Bush St, San Francisco, CA 94104, Tel: (415) 894-7700
  (Oil & gas exploration, production, refining, products; oilfield & financial services)
    Chevron Corp., all mail to U.S. address

CIGNA CORP   One Liberty Place, Philadelphia, PA 19192, Tel: (215) 523-4000
  (Ins, invest, health care & other fin servs)
    Cigna Property & Casualty Insurance Co., Sinthon Bldg. 12/F, 132 Wireless Rd.,
      Bangkok 10330, Thailand
    Cigna Thai Co. Ltd., Sinthon Bldg. 12/F, 132 Wireless Rd., Bangkok 10500, Thailand

CITICORP   399 Park Ave, New York, NY 10043, Tel: (212) 559-1000
  (Banking & financial services)
    Citibank, Thailand

THE COCA-COLA CO   PO Drawer 1734, Atlanta, GA 30301, Tel: (404) 676-2121
  (Mfr/mkt/distr soft drinks, syrups & concentrates, juice & juice-drink prdts)
    Thai Pure Drinks Ltd., all mail to U.S. address

COLGATE-PALMOLIVE CO   300 Park Ave, New York, NY 10022, Tel: (212) 310-2000
  (Mfr pharms, cosmetics, toiletries, detergents)
    Colgate-Palmolive (Thailand) Ltd., 19 Yaek Soonthomkosa Rd., Klong Roey, Bangkok,
      Thailand

COLUMBIA PICTURES INDUSTRIES INC   711 Fifth Ave, New York, NY 10022,
  Tel: (212) 751-4400
  (Producer & distributor of motion pictures)
    Columbia Films of Thailand Ltd., P.O. Box 644, Bangkok, Thailand

CORESTATES FINANCIAL CORP   1500 Market St, Philadelphia, PA 19101,
  Tel: (215) 973-3100
  (Banking)
    Corestates Bank, 139 Sethiwan Tower 18/F, Pan Rd., Silom, Bangkok 10500, Thailand

COUDERT BROTHERS   1114 Ave of the Americas, New York, NY 10036-7794,
  Tel: (212) 626-4400
  (Lawyers)
    Coudert Brothers, c/o Chandler & Thong-Ek Ltd., Sutheast Insurance Bldg. 10/F,
      315 Silom Rd., Bangkok 10500, Thailand

CPC INTERNATIONAL INC   PO Box 8000, Englewood Cliffs, NJ 07632,
  Tel: (201) 894-4000
  (Consumer foods, corn refining)
    Asia Modified Starch Co. Ltd., 183 Rajadmnri Rd., Limpini Pathumwan, Bangkok 10550,
      Thailand
    CPC/AJI (Thailand) Ltd., P.O. Box 10-112 Phetchaburi Tat Jai, Bangkok 10311,
      Thailand

CROWN CORK & SEAL CO INC   9300 Ashton Rd, Philadelphia, PA 19136,
  Tel: (215) 698-5100
  (Mfr cans, bottle caps; filling & packaging mach)
    Thailand Crown Cork & Seal Co. Ltd., 903 Kasemkij Blvd., 120 Silom Rd., Bangkok,
      Thailand

D'ARCY MASIUS BENTON & BOWLES INC (DMB&B)   1675 Broadway, New York,
  NY 10019, Tel: (212) 468-3622
  (Advertising & communications)

Synergie, Tokyu, DMB&B Ltd., 602 Central Plaza Office Tower, 1963 Phaholyothin Rd., Laryao, Bangkok 10900, Thailand

DANA CORP PO Box 1000, Toledo, OH 43697, Tel: (419) 535-4500
(Engineer/mfr/mkt prdts & sys for vehicular, ind & mobile off-highway mkt & related aftermarkets)
Warner Electric Thailand, 50 Soi Patanawes, Sukhumvit 71, Kiongton, Bangkok 10110, Thailand

DANIEL MANN JOHNSON & MENDENHALL 3250 Wilshire Blvd, Los Angeles, CA 90010, Tel: (213) 381-3663
(Architects & engineers)
DMJM Intl., 183/41 Sailom Condotel, Wiphawadi Rangsit Rd., Don Muang, Bangkok 10210, Thailand

DDB NEEDHAM WORLDWIDE INC 437 Madison Ave, New York, NY 10022, Tel: (212) 415-2000
(Advertising)
DDB Needham Worldwide Ltd., 511 Sri Ayudhaya Rd., Phyathai, Bangkok 10400, Thailand
Far East Advertising Co. Ltd., 465/1 Sri Ayudhaya Rd., Phyathai, Bangkok 10400, Thailand

DEKALB PLANT GENETICS 3100 Sycamore Rd, DeKalb, IL 60115, Tel: (815) 753-7333
(Devel/produce hybrid corn, sorghum, sunflowers, sudax, varietal soybeans, alfalfa)
Charoen Seeds Co. Ltd., 26/4-5 Soi Yenchit Chan Rd., Bangkok 10120, Thailand

DIGITAL EQUIPMENT CORP 146 Main St, Maynard, MA 01754-2571, Tel: (508) 493-5111
(Networked computer systems & services)
Digital Equipment Thailand Ltd.,

THE DOW CHEMICAL CO 2030 Dow Center, Midland, MI 48674, Tel: (517) 636-1000
(Mfr chems, plastics, pharms, agric prdts, consumer prdts)
Dow Chemical Pacific Ltd., Silom Bldg., 197/1 Silom Rd., Bangkok, Thailand

E I DU PONT DE NEMOURS & CO 1007 Market St, Wilmington, DE 19898, Tel: (302) 774-1000
(Mfr/sale diversified chems, plastics, specialty prdts & fibers)
Du Pont Far East Inc., Siboonruang 11 Bldg., 1/7 Convent Rd., Bangkok, Thailand

EASTMAN KODAK CO 343 State St, Rochester, NY 14650, Tel: (716) 724-4000
(Devel/mfr photo & chem prdts, info mgmt/video/copier sys, fibers/plastics for various ind)
Kodak (Thailand) Ltd., P.O. Box 2496, Bangkok 10501, Thailand

EATON CORP 1111 Superior Ave, Cleveland, OH 44114, Tel: (216) 523-5000
(Advanced tech prdts for transp & ind mkts)
Cutler Hammer Inc., 321 Soi Helanut Ekami Rd., Sukheimuit, Thailand

EXPEDITORS INTL OF WASHINGTON INC PO Box 69620, Seattle, WA 98168-9620, Tel: (206) 246-3711
(Air/ocean freight forwarding, customs brokerage, intl logistics solutions)
EI Freight Forwarding (Thailand) Ltd., 889 Rm. 226, 26th Fl., Thai C C Tower, Sathorn Thai Rd., Yannawa, Bangkok 10120, Thailand
Expeditors Cargo Management Systems, 3656/32 10th Fl. Green Tower, Rama IV Rd., Klongtoey, Bangkok 10110, Thailand

EXXON CORP   225 E John W Carpenter Freeway, Irving, TX 75062-2298,
Tel: (214) 444-1000
(Petroleum explor, prod, refining; mfr petrol & chem prdts; coal & minerals)
Esso Standard Thailand Ltd., 1016 Rama IV Rd., Khwaeng Silom, Khet Bangrak,
Bangkok, Thailand

FELTON INTERNATIONAL INC   599 Johnson Ave, Brooklyn, NY 11237,
Tel: (212) 497-4664
(Essential oils & extracts, perfumes & flavor material, aromatic chems)
Felton Intl. (Thailand) Ltd., Chokchai Intl. Bldg., 690 Sukhumvit Rd., Bangkok,
Thailand

FISCHBACH & MOORE INTL CORP   2525 Walnut Hill Lane, Dallas, TX 75229,
Tel: (214) 484-4586
(General, mechanical & electrical construction)
Fischbach & Moore Intl. Corp., 116 Wireless Rd., Patumwan County, Bangkok, Thailand

FLORASYNTH INC   300 North St, Teterboro, NJ 07608, Tel: (201) 288-3200
(Mfr fragrances & flavors)
Florasynth (Thailand) Co. Ltd., 4/F WENCO Bldg., 2083 New Petchburi Rd.,
Bangkok 10310, Thailand

FLUOR DANIEL INC   3333 Michelson Dr, Irvine, CA 92730, Tel: (714) 975-2000
(Engineering, construction, maintenance & technical services)
Fluor Daniel Thailand Ltd., B.B. Bldg #2108, 54 Akoke Rd., Sukhumvit 21,
Bangkok 10110, Thailand

FMC CORP   200 E Randolph Dr, Chicago, IL 60601, Tel: (312) 861-6000
(Produces chems & precious metals, mfr machinery, equip & sys for ind, agric & govt)
FMC (Thailand) Ltd., Thailand
Thai Peroxide Co. Ltd., Thailand

FOOTE CONE & BELDING COMMUNICATIONS INC   101 E Erie St, Chicago,
IL 60611-2897, Tel: (312) 751-7000
(Advertising agency)
Prakit/FCB, 131/27-28 Sukhumvit 9, Bangkok 10110, Thailand

FOUR WINDS INTL GROUP   1500 SW First Ave, #850, Portland, OR 97201,
Tel: (503) 241-2732
(Transp of household goods & general cargo, third party logistics)
Four Winds Thai Intl., 279 Soi Navasari, Ramkhamhaeng 21 Rd., Hua Mark,
Bangkok 10310, Thailand

THE FRANKLIN MINT   Franklin Center, PA 19091, Tel: (610) 459-6000
(Creation/mfr/mktg collectibles & luxury items)
Franklin Mint Far East Trading Ltd., KCC Bldg., 5/F, 2 Silom Rd., Bangrak,
Bangkok 10500, Thailand

FRITZ COMPANIES INC   706 Mission St, San Francisco, CA 94103,
Tel: (415) 904-8360
(Integrated transportation, sourcing, distribution & customs brokerage services)
Fritz Air Freight Thailand, 1888/8 New Petchauri Rd., Klong Bangkapi Bridge,
Bangkok 10310, Thailand
Fritz Transportation Intl. (Thailand), 1888/8 New Petchauri Rd.,
Klong Bangkapi Bridge, Bangkok 10310, Thailand

GEMRUSA INC   135 E 50th St, #3E, New York, NY 10022, Tel: (212) 921-9888
  (Whl jewelry, trading commodities)
    Gemrusa (Thai) Ltd., CS Bldg., 35 Surasak Rd. #302, Bangkok, Thailand

GENERAL ELECTRIC CO   3135 Easton Tpk, Fairfield, CT 06431,
  Tel: (203) 373-2211
  (Diversified manufacturing, technology & services)
    General Electric Co.,
      all mail to U.S. address; phone (800) 626-2004 or (518) 438-6500

GETZ BROS & CO INC   150 Post St, #500, San Francisco, CA 94108,
  Tel: (415) 772-5500
  (Divers mfg, mktg/distr serv, travel serv)
    Louis T. Leonowens (Thai) Ltd., 723 Siphya Rd., GPO Box 791, Bangkok 10500, Thailand

THE GILLETTE CO   Prudential Tower, Boston, MA 02199, Tel: (617) 421-7000
  (Devel/mfr personal care/use prdts: blades & razors, toiletries, cosmetics,
  stationery)
    Gillette (Thailand) Ltd., Bangkok, Thailand
    Oral-B Laboratories Thailand Ltd., Bangkok, Thailand

THE GOODYEAR TIRE & RUBBER CO   1144 E Market St, Akron, OH 44316,
  Tel: (216) 796-2121
  (Mfr tires, automotive belts & hose, conveyor belts, chemicals; oil pipeline
  transmission)
    Goodyear (Thailand) Ltd., Sirinee Bldg., 518/4 Ploenchit Rd., Bangkok 10330,
      Thailand

GREY ADVERTISING INC   777 Third Ave, New York, NY 10017, Tel: (212) 546-2000
  (Advertising)
    Grey (Thailand) Ltd., Park Ave. Home Office 11, 5th Fl., 446/54-58 Sukhumvit 71,
      Klongton, Bangkok 10110, Thailand

GRIFFITH LABORATORIES INC   I Griffith Center, Alsip, IL 60658,
  Tel: (708) 371-0900
  (Ind food ingredients & equip)
    Griffith Labs Inc., 482 MOI 19 SOI Pookmitr, Rod Rang Kao Rd., Samrong Tai,
      Phrapradaeng, Sumutrakarn, Thailand

GTE CORP   One Stamford Forum, Stamford, CT 06904, Tel: (203) 965-2000
  (Electr prdts, telecom sys, publ & commun)
    Asia Lamp Industry Co. Ltd., Bangkok, Thailand

FRANK B HALL & CO INC   549 Pleasantville Rd, Briarcliff Manor, NY 10510,
  Tel: (914) 769-9200
  (Insurance)
    Leslie-Hall PBCO Ltd., P.O. Box 11-1255, 17 Sukhumvit 4, Nana Tai, Bangkok, Thailand

THE HARPER GROUP   260 Townsend St, PO Box 77933, San Francisco,
  CA 94107-1719, Tel: (415) 978-0600
  (Ocean/air freight fwdg, customs brokerage, packing & whse, logistics mgt, ins)
    Circle Freight Intl. (Thailand) Ltd., 301-302 Ruamrudee 3 Bldg.,
      51/2 Soi Ruamrudee, Ploenchit Rd., Pathumwan, Bangkok 10330, Thailand

H J HEINZ CO   PO Box 57, Pittsburgh, PA 15230-0057, Tel: (412) 456-5700
  (Processed food prdts & nutritional services)
    Heinz Win Chance Ltd., Bangkok, Thailand

HEWLETT-PACKARD CO   3000 Hanover St, Palo Alto, CA 94304-0890,
  Tel: (415) 857-1501
  (Mfr computing, communications & measurement prdts & services)
    Hewlett-Packard (Thailand) Ltd., Pacific Place 11/F, 140 Sukhumvit Rd.,
      Bangkok 10110, Thailand

HOLIDAY INNS INC   3742 Lamar Ave, Memphis, TN 38195, Tel: (901) 362-4001
  (Hotels, restaurants, casinos)
    Holiday Inn Pattaya, Bangkok, Thailand

HONEYWELL INC   PO Box 524, Minneapolis, MN 55440-0524, Tel: (612) 951-1000
  (Devel/mfr controls for home & building, industry, space & aviation)
    Honeywell Systems (Thailand) Ltd., Times Square Bldg. #15-02,
      246 Sukhumvit Rd. (bet. SOI 12-14), Klongtoey, Bangkok 10110, Thailand

HORWATH INTL   415 Madison Ave, New York, NY 10017, Tel: (212) 838-5566
  (Public accountants & auditors)
    Bunohikij & Horwath, 11th Fl., Modern Town Bldg., 87 Sukhumvit 63 (Ekamai) Rd.,
      Bangkok 10110, Thailand

HYATT INTL CORP   200 West Madison, Chicago, IL 60606, Tel: (312) 750-1234
  (Intl hotel mgmt)
    Hyatt Intl. Hotels, Bangkok, Thailand

IBM CORP   Old Orchard Rd, Armonk, NY 10504, Tel: (914) 765-1900
  (Information products, technology & services)
    IBM Thailand Co. Ltd., Bangkok, Thailand

ITT CORP   1330 Ave of the Americas, New York, NY 10019-5490,
  Tel: (212) 258-1000
  (Design/mfr communications & electronic equip, hotels, insurance)
    ITT Far East & Pacific, Shell Bldg., 140 Wireless Rd., Bangkok, Thailand
    ITT Thailand Ltd., 233 Poochao Samingprai Rd., Samutprakam, Thailand

ITT SHERATON CORP   60 State St, Boston, MA 02108, Tel: (617) 367-3600
  (Hotel operations)
    Royal Orchid Sheraton Hotel & Towers, 2 Capt. Bush Lane, Siphya Rd., Bangkok,
      Thailand

JCPENNEY PURCHASING CORP   PO Box 10001, Dallas, TX 75301-0001,
  Tel: (214) 431-5380
  (Department stores)
    JCPenney Purchasing Corp., Kongboonma Bldg. 8/F, 699 Silom Rd., Bangkok 10500,
      Thailand

JETWAY SYSTEMS   1805 W 2550 South, Ogden, UT 84401, Tel: (801) 627-6600
  (Mfr aircraft loading bridges & ground support equip)
    Jetway Systems Bangkok Office, 201/698 MU 7 Mahanakornnives, Vibhavadi Rangsit Rd.,
      Bangkhen, Bangkok 10210, Thailand

JOHNSON & HIGGINS   125 Broad St, New York, NY 10004-2424, Tel: (212) 574-7000
  (Ins brokerage, employee benefit conslt, risk mgmt, human resource conslt, ins/reins
    servs)
    Johnson & Higgins/PB Co. Ltd., Bangkok, Thailand

JOHNSON & JOHNSON   One Johnson & Johnson Plaza, New Brunswick, NJ 08933,
  Tel: (908) 524-0400
  (R&D/mfr/sale health care prdts)
    Janssen Pharmaceutica Ltd., P.O. Box 31, Pratanum 10409, Thailand
    Johnson & Johnson (Thailand) Ltd., P.O. Box 1, Lat Krabang, Bangkok 10520, Thailand

THE KENDALL CO   15 Hampshire St, Mansfield, MA 02048, Tel: (508) 261-8000
  (Mfr medical disposable prdts, home health care prdts, spec adhesive prdts)
    Kendall-Gammatron Ltd., P.O. Box 9, Sampron, Nakorn Prathom 73110, Thailand

KEPNER-TREGOE INC   PO Box 704, Princeton, NJ 08542-0740, Tel: (609) 921-2806
  (Mgmt consulting & training)
    Kepner-Tregoe (Thailand) Ltd., Land & Tower Bldg. 10/F, 230 Rajehadaphisaek Rd.,
      Huaykwang, Bangkok 10310, Thailand

KEYSTONE INTL INC   PO Box 40010, Houston, TX 77040, Tel: (713) 466-1176
  (Mfr butterfly valves, actuators & control accessories)
    Keystone Valve, Thailand

KIMBERLY-CLARK CORP   PO Box 619100, Dallas, TX 75261, Tel: (214) 281-1200
  (Mfr fiber-based prdts for personal care, lumber & paper prdts)
    Kimberly-Clark Thailand Ltd., Bangkok, Thailand
    Kimberly-Clark Trading Ltd., Thailand
    Thai-Kimberly-Clark Co. Ltd., Thailand

KORN/FERRY INTL   1800 Century Park East, Los Angeles, CA 90067,
  Tel: (310) 552-1834
  (Executive search)
    Korn/Ferry Intl., Rajapark Bldg. 12/F, 163 Soi Asoke (21) Sukhumvit Rd.,
      Bangkok 10110, Thailand

L&F PRODUCTS   225 Summit Ave, Montvale, NJ 07645-1575, Tel: (201) 573-5700
  (Mfr household, personal care, woodworking & ind prdts)
    L&F Products/Sterling Drug, 1474 Grand Amrin Tower, New Petchburi Rd., Rachtavee,
      Bangkok 10310, Thailand

ELI LILLY & CO   Lilly Corporate Center, Indianapolis, IN 46285,
  Tel: (317) 276-2000
  (Mfr pharmaceuticals, animal health prdts)
    Eli Lilly Asia Inc., Grand Amarin Tower 14/F, 1550 New Petchburi Rd., Makasan,
      Rachtavee, Bangkok 10310, Thailand

LINTAS:WORLDWIDE   1 Dag Hammarskjold Plaza, New York, NY 10017,
  Tel: (212) 605-8000
  (Advertising agency)
    Lintas:Bangkok, Sathorn Thani Bldg. 6/F, N. Sathorn Rd., Bangkok 10500, Thailand

LOCTITE CORP   10 Columbus Blvd, Hartford, CT 06106, Tel: (203) 520-5000
  (Mfr/sale ind adhesives & sealants)
    Loctite (Thailand) Ltd., TVO Bldg. 4/F, 149 Ratchadapisek (Thapra-Taksin) Rd.,
      Bukkhalo, Thonburi, Bangkok 10600, Thailand

MAGNETEK UNIVERSAL ELECTRIC   300 E Main St, Owosso, MI 48867,
  Tel: (517) 723-7866
  (Mfr fractional horsepower elect motors)
    Kulthorn Universal Electric Co. Ltd., 17-13 Larn Luang Rd., P.O. Box 2790,
      Bangkok 10100, Thailand

MARATHON LE TOURNEAU CO   PO Box 2307, Longview, TX 75606, Tel: (903) 237-7000
 (Mfr heavy constr, mining mach & equip)
   C&S Engineering Supply Ltd., 24 Vibhavadivengsh Rd., Bangkok 10900, Thailand

MARY KAY COSMETICS INC   8787 Stemmons Fwy, Dallas, TX 75247,
 Tel: (214) 630-8787
 (Cosmetics & toiletries)
   Mary Kay (Thailand) Ltd., 984 Klongton Center, Sukhumvit 71, Bangkok, Thailand

MAY DEPARTMENT STORES CO   611 Olive St, St Louis, MO 63101-1799,
 Tel: (314) 342-3300
 (Retail dept stores)
   Alpha Merchandising Service Ltd., A.I. Tower 15/F, 181-19 Suriwongse Rd.,
     Bangkok 1500, Thailand

MICROPOLIS CORP   21211 Nordhoff St, Chatsworth, CA 91311, Tel: (818) 709-3300
 (Mfr computer disk drives)
   Micropolis Corp. Thailand Ltd., 733-3-6 Phaholyothin Rd., Lumlookkar,
     Pathumthaim 12130, Thailand

MICROSOFT CORP   One Microsoft Way, Redmond, WA 98052-6399,
 Tel: (206) 882-8080
 (Computer software, peripherals & services)
   Microsoft Thailand, Thailand

MILCHEM INC   3900 Essex Lane, PO Box 22111, Houston, TX 77027,
 Tel: (214) 439-8000
 (Gas & oil well drilling fluids & chem additives)
   Milchem Drilling Fluids Inc., 629 President Hotel, 125/6 Gaysorn Rd., Bangkok,
     Thailand

MOBIL CORP   3225 Gallows Rd, Fairfax, VA 22037-0001, Tel: (703) 846-3000
 (Petroleum explor & refining, mfr petrol prdts, chems, petrochems)
   Mobil Oil Thailand Ltd., GPO Box 1698, Bangkok 10501, Thailand

MOLEX INC   2222 Wellington Ct, Lisle, IL 60532, Tel: (708) 969-4550
 (Mfr electronic, electrical & fiber optic interconnection prdts & sys, switches,
 application tooling)
   Molex Inc., Bangkok, Thailand

MULLER & PHIPPS INTL CORP   Box 3994, San Francisco, CA 94119,
 Tel: (415) 772-5650
 (General merchandise)
   Muller & Phipps (Thai) Ltd., P.O. Box 392, Bangkok, Thailand

McCANN-ERICKSON WORLDWIDE   750 Third Ave, New York, NY 10017,
 Tel: (212) 697-6000
 (Advertising)
   McCann-Erickson (Thailand) Ltd., Kian Gwan Bldg. 11/F, 140 Wireless Rd.,
     GPO Box 2555, Bangkok 10501, Thailand

NATIONAL STARCH & CHEMICAL CO   10 Finderne Ave, Bridgewater, NJ 08807-3300,
 Tel: (908) 685-5000
 (Mfr adhesives & sealants, resins & spec chems, electr materials & adhesives, food
 prdts, ind starch)

National Adhesives Co., Bangkok, Thailand
National Starch & Chemical (Thailand) Ltd., Samutprakarn, Thailand

OCEANEERING INTL INC   PO Box 218130, Houston, TX 77218-8130,
  Tel: (713) 578-8868
  (Underwater serv to offshore oil & gas ind)
    Oceaneering Intl. Inc., Operational base in Bangkok

OSMONICS INC   5951 Clearwater Dr, Minnetonka, MN 55343-8995,
  Tel: (612) 933-2277
  (Mfr fluid filtration & separation equip & components)
    Osmonics Asia/Pacific Ltd., 1044/8 SOI Sukhumvit 44/2, Sukhumvit Rd., Prakanong,
    Bangkok 10110, Thailand

OTIS ELEVATOR CO   10 Farm Springs, Farmington, CT 06032, Tel: (860) 676-6528
  (Mfr elevators & escalators)
    Otis Elevator Co. (Thailand) Ltd., P.O. Box 1177, Bangkok 10501, Thailand

PACIFIC TELESIS GROUP   130 Kearney St, San Francisco, CA 94108,
  Tel: (415) 394-3000
  (Telecommun & info sys)
    Pacific Telesis (Thailand) Ltd., Regent House, 183 Rajdamri Rd., Bangkok 10500,
    Thailand

PANDUIT CORP   17301 Ridgeland Ave, Tinley Park, IL 60477-0981,
  Tel: (708) 532-1800
  (Mfr elec/electr wiring comps)
    Panduit Trading Pte. Ltd., 3B/17 Suparkan Bldg., 723 Charoen Nakom Rd., Klong,
    Sarn, Bangkok 10600, Thailand

PARSONS DE LEUW INC   1133 15th St NW, Washington, DC 20005,
  Tel: (202) 775-3300
  (Consulting engineers)
    De Leuw, Cather Intl. Ltd., 198/5 Rama VI Rd., Bangkok 10400, Thailand

PFIZER INC   235 E 42nd St, New York, NY 10017-5755, Tel: (212) 573-2323
  (Mfr healthcare products)
    Pfizer Ltd., Thailand

PHELPS DODGE CORP   2600 N Central Ave, Phoenix, AZ 85004-3014,
  Tel: (602) 234-8100
  (Copper, minerals, metals & spec engineered prdts for trans & elect mkts)
    Phelps Dodge Thailand Ltd., P.O. Box 11-58, Bangkok, Thailand

PINKERTON SECURITY & INVESTIGATION SERVICES   6727 Odessa Ave, Van Nuys,
  CA 91406-5796, Tel: (818) 373-8800
  (Security & investigation services)
    Pinkerton Consulting & Investigation Services, 3rd Floor, Sarasin Bldg.,
    14 Surasak Rd., Bangkok 10500, Thailand

PIONEER HI-BRED INTL INC   700 Capital Sq, 400 Locust St, Des Moines,
  IA 50309, Tel: (515) 245-3500
  (Agricultural chemicals, farm supplies, biological prdts, research)
    Pioneer Overseas Corp. (Thailand) Ltd., P.O. Box 16, Praputhabat, Saraburi 18120,
    Thailand

PREMARK INTL INC   1717 Deerfield Rd, Deerfield, IL 60015, Tel: (708) 405-6000
(Mfr/sale diversified consumer & coml prdts)
  Tupperware (Thailand) Ltd., Sivanart Bldg. 2/F, 43-18 Ladprao Rd., Wangthongland,
  Bangkapi, Bangkok, Thailand

RADISSON HOTELS INTL   Carlson Pkwy, PO Box 59159, Minneapolis,
  MN 55459-8204, Tel: (612) 540-5526
(Hotels)
  Colony Kamala Beach Resort, Phuket, Thailand

RAYCHEM CORP   300 Constitution Dr, Menlo Park, CA 94025, Tel: (415) 361-3333
(Devel/mfr/mkt materials science products for electronics, telecommunications &
industry)
  Raychem Thai Ltd., Vanissa Bldg. 3/F, 29 Chidlom Rd., Bangkok 10330, Thailand

ROHM AND HAAS CO   100 Independence Mall West, Philadelphia, PA 19106,
  Tel: (215) 592-3000
(Mfr ind & agric chems, plastics)
  Rohm and Haas Southeast Asia Inc., Suite 99/47, 14/F Bldg. One, 99 Wireless Rd.,
  Bangkok 10330, Thailand

RUSSIN & VECCHI   1140 Connecticut Ave, #250, Washington, DC 20036,
  Tel: (202) 223-4793
(Lawyers)
  Russin & Vecchi, Bangkok Bank Bldg. 18/F, 333 Silom Rd., Bangkok 10500, Thailand

SCI SYSTEMS INC   PO Box 1000, Huntsville, AL 35807, Tel: (205) 882-4800
(R/D & mfr electronics systems for commerce, industry, aerospace, etc)
  SCI Thailand Ltd., 90 Taiwan Rd., Banmai 12000, Thailand

SEA-LAND SERVICE INC   150 Allen Rd, Liberty Corner, NJ 07920,
  Tel: (201) 558-6000
(Container transport)
  Sea-Land Service Inc., Tavich Bldg. 5/F, 61 Kasemrat Rd., Klong Toey, Bangkok,
  Thailand
  Sea-Land Service Inc., c/o Commercial Transport Intl., International Airport,
  Bangkok, Thailand

G D SEARLE & CO   5200 Old Orchard Rd, Skokie, IL 60077, Tel: (708) 982-7000
(Mfr pharms, health care & optical prdts, specialty chems)
  G.D. Searle Thailand Ltd., The Ararin Tower 12/F, 500 Ploenchitr Rd.,
  Bangkok 10330, Thailand

SIGNETICS CORP   PO Box 3409, Sunnyvale, CA 94088-3409, Tel: (408) 991-2000
(Solid state circuits)
  Signetics (Thailand) Co. Ltd., 303 Choergwatar Rd., Bangkok, Thailand

WILBUR SMITH ASSOCS   NationsBank Tower, PO Box 92, Columbia, SC 29202,
  Tel: (803) 708-4500
(Consulting engineers)
  Wilbur Smith Associates Inc., 703 Golden Pavilion Bldg.,
    153-3 Soi Mahadlek Luang 1, Rajdamri Rd., Lumpini, Bangkok 10330, Thailan

A E STALEY MFG CO   2200 E Eldorado St, Decatur, IL 62525, Tel: (217) 423-4411
(Mfr corn prdts, food & ind starches, corn sweeteners)
   Tapioca Development Corp. Ltd., Thai Wah Tower 21-22/F, 21 South Sathorn Rd.,
   Yannawa, Bangkok 10120, Thailand

STANDARD COMMERCIAL CORP   PO Box 450, Wilson, NC 27893, Tel: (919) 291-5507
(Leaf tobacco dealers/processors, wool processors)
   Siam Tobacco Export Corp. Ltd., Chiengmai, Thailand

STIEFEL LABORATORIES INC   255 Alhambra Circle, Coral Gables, FL 33134,
   Tel: (305) 443-3807
(Mfr pharmaceuticals, dermatological specialties)
   Stiefel Laboratories (Thailand) Ltd., 2488/2 Soi Udomsub, Krungthep-Nont Rd.,
   Bangsue, Bangkok 10800, Thailand

STONE & WEBSTER ENGINEERING CORP   245 Summer St, Boston, MA 02210-2288,
   Tel: (617) 589-5111
(Engineering, constr & environmental & mgmt services)
   Stone & Webster Thailand Corp., Diethelm Tower A #1202, 93/1 Wireless Rd.,
   Bangkok 10330, Thailand

TENNESSEE ASSOCIATES INTL   223 Associates Blvd, PO Box 710, Alcoa,
   TN 37701-0710, Tel: (423) 982-9514
(Mgt consulting servs)
   Tennessee Associates Intl. Asia Ltd., 10 Soi Supakorn, Larn Luang 5, Pomprab,
   Bangkok 10100, Thailand

TRANE CO   3600 Pammel Creek Rd, La Crosse, WI 54601, Tel: (608) 787-2000
(Mfr/distr/svce A/C sys & equip)
   Jardine Trane Air Conditioning, 1032/1-5 Rama 4 Rd., Bangkok 10120, Thailand

U S SUMMIT CORP   600 Third Ave, New York, NY 10016, Tel: (212) 490-1100
(Mktg/distrib pharms, chems)
   U.S. Summit Corp. (Overseas), P.O. Box 1403, Bangkok, Thailand

UNION CARBIDE CORP   39 Old Ridgebury Rd, Danbury, CT 06817,
   Tel: (203) 794-2000
(Mfr industrial chemicals, plastics, resins)
   Union Carbide Thailand Ltd., GPO Box 1254, Bangkok 10501, Thailand

UNION OIL INTL DIV   Union Oil Center, PO Box 7600, Los Angeles, CA 90017,
   Tel: (213) 977-7600
(Petroleum prdts, petrochems)
   Union Oil Co. of Thailand, Thai Military Bank Bldg., 34 Phyathai Rd., Bangkok 4,
   Thailand

UNITED AIRLINES INC   PO Box 66100, Chicago, IL 60666, Tel: (708) 952-4000
(Air transp)
   United Airlines, Regent House Bldg. 9/F, 183 Rajdamri Rd., Bangkok 10500, Thailand

UNITED CALIFORNIA BANK   PO Box 54191, Los Angeles, CA 90054,
   Tel: (213) 624-0111
(Banking)
   United California Bank, Cathay Trust Bldg., 1016 Rama IV Rd., Bangkok, Thailand

UNIVERSAL CORP   PO Box 25099, Richmond, VA 23260, Tel: (804) 359-9311
   (Holding co: tobacco, commodities)
     Thai-Am Tobacco Ltd., P.O. Box 105, Chengmai, Thailand

UNOCAL CORP   PO Box 7600, Los Angeles, CA 90051, Tel: (213) 977-7600
   (Fully integrated high-tech energy resources devel)
     Unocal Thailand Ltd., Central Plaza Office Bldg., 1693 Phaholyothin Rd.,
       Bangkok 10900, Thailand

UPJOHN CO   7000 Portage Rd, Kalamazoo, MI 49001, Tel: (616) 323-4000
   (Mfr pharms, agric prdts, ind chems)
     Upjohn Co. Ltd., P.O. Box 224, Bangkok, Thailand

WACKENHUT CORP   1500 San Remo Ave, Coral Gables, FL 33146,
   Tel: (305) 666-5656
   (Security systems & services)
     Wackenhut Thailand Co. Ltd., 952 Sukhumvit 71 Klong-Ton, Klong-Toey, Bangkok 10110,
       Thailand

WARNER-LAMBERT CO   201 Tabor Road, Morris Plains, NJ 07950,
   Tel: (201) 540-2000
   (Mfr ethical & proprietary pharms, confectionary & consumer prdts)
     Warner-Lambert (Thailand) Ltd., GPO Box 1448, Bangkok, Thailand

WEATHERFORD INTL INC   1360 Post Oak Blvd, PO Box 27608, Houston,
   TX 77227-7608, Tel: (713) 439-9400
   (Oilfield servs, prdts & equip; mfr marine cranes)
     Weatherford Inc., Room B, 6th Floor, Anekvanich Bldg., 158-5 Sukhumvit 55,
       Prakhanong, Bangkok 10110, Thailand

WILBUR-ELLIS CO   320 California St, #200, San Francisco, CA 94104,
   Tel: (415) 772-4000
   (Intl merchants & distributors)
     Connell Bros. Co. (Thailand) Ltd., Central Plaza Office Bldg. 9/F,
       1693 Phaholyothin Rd., Bangkok 10900, Thailand

XEROX CORP   800 Long Ridge Rd, PO Box 1600, Stamford, CT 06904,
   Tel: (203) 968-3000
   (Mfr document processing equip, sys & supplies)
     Xerox Corp., Bangkok, Thailand

ZEMEX CORP   1 West Pack Sq, Asheville, NC 28801, Tel: (704) 255-4900
   (Tin mining, industrial minerals & metal powders)
     Sierra Mining Co. Ltd., 119 Mahaesak Rd., Bangkok 10500, Thailand

TRINIDAD & TOBAGO

3M   3M Center, St Paul, MN 55144-1000, Tel: (612) 733-1110
(Mfr diversified prdts for industry, health care, imaging, commun, transport, safety, consumer, etc)
   3M Interamerica Inc., I Jamingham Ave., Belmont, Port of Spain, Trinidad & Tobago

ALCOA STEAMSHIP CO INC   1501 Alcoa Bldg, Pittsburgh, PA 15219,
Tel: (412) 553-4545
(Ship owners/operators)
   Alcoa Steamship Co. Inc., P.O. Box 609, Port of Spain, Trinidad & Tobago

BAKER OIL TOOLS   PO Box 40129, Houston, TX 77240-0129, Tel: (713) 466-1322
(Mfr/serv oil/gas well completions equip)
   Baker Transworld Inc., Prince Charles St., Cross Crossing, San Fernando,
      Trinidad & Tobago

BECHTEL GROUP INC   50 Beale St, PO Box 3965, San Francisco, CA 94119,
Tel: (415) 768-1234
(Engineering & constr)
   Caribbean Bechtel Ltd., Port of Spain, Trinidad & Tobago

SAMUEL BINGHAM CO   1555 N Mittel Blvd, #T, Wood Dale, IL 60191-1046,
Tel: (708) 238-4000
(Print & industrial rollers, inks)
   Coates Brothers (Caribbean) Ltd., P.O. Box 445, Port of Spain, Trinidad & Tobago

CARBOLINE CO   350 Hanley Industrial Ct, St Louis, MO 63144,
Tel: (314) 644-1000
(Mfr coatings, sealants)
   Berger Paints Trinidad Ltd., P.O. Box 546, 11 Concessions Rd., Sea Lots,
      Port of Spain, Trinidad & Tobago

CH2M HILL INC   PO Box 428, Corvallis, OR 97339, Tel: (503) 752-4271
(Consulting engrs, planners, economists, scientists)
   Trintoplan-CH2M, P.O. Box 1262, Port of Spain, Trinidad & Tobago

CHASE MANHATTAN BANK N A   1 Chase Manhattan Plaza, New York, NY 10081,
Tel: (212) 552-2222
(Intl banking)
   Chase Manhattan Bank N.A., 53 Independence Sq., Port of Spain, Trinidad & Tobago

CHEVRON CORP   225 Bush St, San Francisco, CA 94104, Tel: (415) 894-7700
(Oil & gas exploration, production, refining, products; oilfield & financial services)
   Chevron Corp., all mail to U.S. address

CITICORP   399 Park Ave, New York, NY 10043, Tel: (212) 559-1000
  (Banking & financial services)
    Citibank NA, Trinidad & Tobago

COLGATE-PALMOLIVE CO   300 Park Ave, New York, NY 10022, Tel: (212) 310-2000
  (Mfr pharms, cosmetics, toiletries, detergents)
    Colgate-Palmolive Co. Inc., El Socorro Ext. Rd., San Juan, Trinidad & Tobago

COLUMBIA PICTURES INDUSTRIES INC   711 Fifth Ave, New York, NY 10022,
  Tel: (212) 751-4400
  (Producer & distributor of motion pictures)
    Morgan Films Ltd., Deluxe Theatre, 9-11 Keate St., Port of Spain, Trinidad & Tobago

CUNA MUTUAL INSURANCE SOCIETY   5910 Mineral Point Road, PO Box 391, Madison,
  WI 53701, Tel: (608) 238-5851
  (Insurance)
    Cuna Mutual Insurance, 10 Victoria Ave., P.O. Box 193, Port of Spain,
      Trinidad & Tobado

FOOTE CONE & BELDING COMMUNICATIONS INC   101 E Erie St, Chicago,
  IL 60611-2897, Tel: (312) 751-7000
  (Advertising agency)
    Hernandez/FCB, Long Circular Mall, Level 4, St. James, Port of Spain,
      Trinidad & Tobago

GLOBAL MARINE INC   777 N Eldridge, Houston, TX 77079, Tel: (713) 596-5100
  (Offshore contract drilling, turnkey drilling, oil & gas explor & prod)
    Global Marine Inc., Port of Spain, Trinidad

FRANK B HALL & CO INC   549 Pleasantville Rd, Briarcliff Manor, NY 10510,
  Tel: (914) 769-9200
  (Insurance)
    Agostina Insurance Brokers Ltd., P.O. Box 950, Port of Spain, Trinidad & Tobago

HELMERICH & PAYNE INC   1579 E 21st St, Tulsa, OK 74114, Tel: (918) 742-5531
  (Oil/gas exploration & drilling, real estate, mfr gas odorants)
    Helmerich & Payne Finco, 21 Scott St., Gooding Village, San Fernando,
      Trinidad & Tobago

HOLIDAY INNS INC   3742 Lamar Ave, Memphis, TN 38195, Tel: (901) 362-4001
  (Hotels, restaurants, casinos)
    Holiday Inn, P.O. Box 1017, Dwin at Wrightson Rd. & London St., Port of Spain,
      Trinidad & Tobago

JOHNSON & JOHNSON   One Johnson & Johnson Plaza, New Brunswick, NJ 08933,
  Tel: (908) 524-0400
  (R&D/mfr/sale health care prdts)
    Johnson & Johnson (Trinidad) Ltd., P.O. Box 1140, Port of Spain, Trinidad & Tobago

MOBIL CORP   3225 Gallows Rd, Fairfax, VA 22037-0001, Tel: (703) 846-3000
  (Petroleum explor & refining, mfr petrol prdts, chems, petrochems)
    Mobil Corp., 5 Queens Park East, P.O. Box 498, Port of Spain, Trinidad & Tobago

MYERS INTL INC   1293 South Main St, Akron, OH 44301, Tel: (216) 253-5592
  (Mfr tire retreading & maintenance equip & supplies)
    Equipment & Supply (WI) Ltd., 192 Southern Main Rd., La Romain, Trinidad & Tobago

McCANN-ERICKSON WORLDWIDE   750 Third Ave, New York, NY 10017,
  Tel: (212) 697-6000
  (Advertising)
    McCann-Erickson Ltd., 81-83 Abercromby St., P.O. Box 38, Port of Spain,
      Trinidad & Tobago

OCCIDENTAL PETROLEUM CORP   10889 Wilshire Blvd, Los Angeles, CA 90024,
  Tel: (213) 879-1700
  (Petroleum & petroleum prdts, chems, plastics)
    Occidental of Trinidad Inc., 22 Queen's Park West, Port of Spain, Trinidad & Tobago

OCEANEERING INTL INC   PO Box 218130, Houston, TX 77218-8130,
  Tel: (713) 578-8868
  (Underwater serv to offshore oil & gas ind)
    Oceaneering Intl. Inc., Operational base in Port of Spain

PETROLEUM HELICOPTERS INC   5728 Jefferson Hwy, Box 23502, Harahan, LA 70183,
  Tel: (504) 733-6790
  (Aerial transp, helicopter charter)
    Transnational Transit Ltd., Camden Field, Couva, Trinidad & Tobago

PETROLITE CORP   369 Marshall Ave, St Louis, MO 63119-1897,
  Tel: (314) 961-3500
  (Mfr/prod spec chem treating programs, performance-enhancing additives & related
  equip & svces)
    Petrolite Trinidad Inc., Isthmus Rd., Galeota Point, Trinidad & Tobago

RJR NABISCO INC   1301 Ave of the Americas, New York, NY 10019,
  Tel: (212) 258-5600
  (Mfr consumer packaged food prdts & tobacco prdts)
    Pan American Standard Brands Inc., Streatham Lodge, Macoya Rd., Tunapuna,
      Trinidad & Tobago

SEA-LAND SERVICE INC   150 Allen Rd, Liberty Corner, NJ 07920,
  Tel: (201) 558-6000
  (Container transport)
    Sea-Land Service Inc., Salvatori Bldg., Independence Sq., P.O. Box 857,
      Port of Spain, Trinidad & Tobago

TIDEWATER INC   Tidewater Place, 1440 Canal St, New Orleans, LA 70112,
  Tel: (504) 568-1010
  (Marine serv & equip to companies engaged in explor, development & prod of oil, gas &
  minerals)
    Tidewater Marine Ltd., Tidewater Bldg., Isthmus Rd., Galeota, Guayaguayare,
      Trinidad & Tobago

WACKENHUT CORP   1500 San Remo Ave, Coral Gables, FL 33146,
  Tel: (305) 666-5656
  (Security systems & services)
    Guardia Wackenhut Ltd., 35 French St., Woodbrook, Port of Spain, Trinidad & Tobago

TUNISIA

AIR EXPRESS INTL CORP   120 Tokeneke Rd, PO Box 1231, Darien, CT 06820,
Tel: (203) 655-7900
(Air frt forwarder)
   Air Express Intl., c/o A.A.C.C., 5 Rue Champlain, Boite Postale 585, Tunis, Tunisia

BANKERS TRUST CO   280 Park Ave, New York, NY 10017, Tel: (212) 250-2500
(Banking)
   Bankers Trust Co., 4 Rue As-Sahab Ibn-Abbad, Tunis, Tunisia
   Bankers Trust Co., Banque de Tunisia, 3 Ave. de France, Tunis, Tunisia

CHASE MANHATTAN BANK N A   1 Chase Manhattan Plaza, New York, NY 10081,
Tel: (212) 552-2222
(Intl banking)
   Chase Manhattan Bank NA, Immeuble Saadi, 3 Rue de Guinee, Nouvelle, Arianna Tunis,
   Tunisia

CITICORP   399 Park Ave, New York, NY 10043, Tel: (212) 559-1000
(Banking & financial services)
   Citibank, Tunisia

COMBUSTION ENGINEERING INC   900 Long Ridge Road, Stamford, CT 06902,
Tel: (203) 329-8771
(Tech constr)
   C-E Soccursale en Tunisia, Route Si Di Mansour 283, Boite Postale 635, Sfax, Tunisia
   Gray Tool Intl. Inc., c/o Starep, Immeuble Saadi, Boite Postale 232, Tunis, Tunisia

CONOCO INC   600 N Dairy Ashford Rd, Houston, TX 77079, Tel: (713) 293-1000
(Oil, gas, coal, chems, minerals)
   Continental Oil Co., 100 Ave. de Lesseps, Tunis, Tunisia

DRESSER INDUSTRIES INC   PO Box 718, Dallas, TX 75221-0718,
Tel: (214) 740-6000
(Diversified supplier of equip & tech serv to energy & natural resource ind)
   Dresser Europe SA, Villa Rajeb Turki, Route de Teniour Km. 15, Sfax, Tunisia

FREEPORT-McMORAN INC   1615 Poydras St, New Orleans, LA 70112,
Tel: (504) 582-4000
(Natural resources exploration & processing)
   N.P.K. Engrais, 20 Rue du Dr. Burnet, Tunis, Tunisia

GENERAL MOTORS CORP   3044 W Grand Blvd, Detroit, MI 48202-3091,
Tel: (313) 556-5000
(Mfr full line vehicles, automotive electronics, coml technologies, telecom, space,

finance)
Industries Mecaniques Maghrebines SA, Tunis, Tunisia

IMCO SERVICES   5950 N Course Dr, Houston, TX 70072, Tel: (713) 561-1300
(Drilling fluids)
Halliburton Ltd., Imco Svcs. Div., Tunisia, 4 Rue de Kenya, Tunis, Tunisia

ITT CORP   1330 Ave of the Americas, New York, NY 10019-5490,
Tel: (212) 258-1000
(Design/mfr communications & electronic equip, hotels, insurance)
Intl. Telephone & Telegraph Corp., 17 Rue Es-Sadikia, Tunis, Tunisia

ITT SHERATON CORP   60 State St, Boston, MA 02108, Tel: (617) 367-3600
(Hotel operations)
Hammamet Sheraton Hotel, Ave. Moncef Bey, Hammamet, Tunisia

MARATHON OIL CO   539 S Main St, Findlay, OH 45840, Tel: (419) 422-2121
(Petroleum explor & prod)
Marathon Petroleum Tunisia Ltd., Boite Postale 71, Tunis, Tunisia

MURACHANIAN EXPORT CO   Armstrong Rd, Garden City Park, NY 11530,
Tel: (516) 248-3830
(Reconditioned used clothing)
Societe Tuniso-Americaine pour l'Exportation, 6 Rue de Mauritanie, Tunis, Tunisia

OCCIDENTAL PETROLEUM CORP   10889 Wilshire Blvd, Los Angeles, CA 90024,
Tel: (213) 879-1700
(Petroleum & petroleum prdts, chems, plastics)
Occidental of Tunisia Inc., 9 Ave. de Mutuelleville, Tunis Belvedere 1002, Tunisia

READING & BATES CORP   901 Threadneedle, #200, Houston, TX 77079,
Tel: (713) 496-5000
(Offshore contract drilling)
Reading & Bates BV, Route Mharza Km. 0.5, Cite Ezzahra, Ville Chaabane, Sfax,
Tunisia

SAMEDAN OIL CORP   PO Box 909, Ardmore, OK 73402, Tel: (405) 223-4110
(Gas & oil exploration & production)
Samedan of Tunisia Inc., Immeuble Dhamen/Astree, 43 Ave. Khereddine Pacha,
1080 Tunis, Tunisia

WEATHERFORD INTL INC   1360 Post Oak Blvd, PO Box 27608, Houston,
TX 77227-7608, Tel: (713) 439-9400
(Oilfield servs, prdts & equip; mfr marine cranes)
Weatherford Oil Tool GmbH, Cite Pace - El Bustan, Sfax, Tunisia

TURKEY

3M   3M Center, St Paul, MN 55144-1000, Tel: (612) 733-1110
(Mfr diversified prdts for industry, health care, imaging, commun, transport, safety, consumer, etc)
   3M Sanayii ve Ticaret AS, Buyukdere Cad. Ucyol Mevkii, Noramin is Merkezi 414-416, Maslak, 80670 Istanbul, Turkey

AAF-McQUAY INC   111 S Calvert St, #2800, Baltimore, MD 21202,
Tel: (410) 528-2755
(Mfr air quality control prdts: heating, ventilating, air-conditioning & filtration prdts & services)
   AAF Hava Filtreleri Ve Cicaret, Istanbul, Turkey

ALTHEIMER & GRAY   10 S Wacker Dr, #4000, Chicago, IL 60606-7482,
Tel: (312) 715-4000
(Lawyers)
   Altheimer & Gray, Tesvikiye Cad. 107, Tesvikiye Palas 7, Tesvikiye 80200 Istanbul, Turkey

THE AMERICAN TOBACCO CO   PO Box 10380, Stamford, CT 06904,
Tel: (203) 325-4900
(Tobacco prdts)
   American Tobacco Co. of the Orient, Posta Kutusu 222, Izmir, Turkey

AMP INC   PO Box 3608, Harrisburg, PA 17105-3608, Tel: (717) 564-0100
(Devel/mfr electronic & electrical connection prdts & sys)
   AMP Turkey, Istanbul, Turkey

ASSOCIATED MERCHANDISING CORP   1440 Broadway, New York, NY 10018,
Tel: (212) 536-4000
(Retail service organization)
   Associated Merchandising Corp., Kore Sehitleri Caddesi,
      Yuzbasi Kaya Aldogan Sokak 7, Daire 5, Zincirlikuyu, Istanbul, Turkey

ASSOCIATED PRESS INC   50 Rockefeller Plaza, New York, NY 10020-1605,
Tel: (212) 621-1500
(News gathering agency)
   Associated Press, Cesme Han, Catalcesme Sokak 5, Cagaloglu, P.O. Box 724, Istanbul, Turkey

AYDIN CORP   700 Dresher Rd, PO Box 349, Horsham, PA 19044,
Tel: (215) 657-7510
(Mfr wireless communications equip)
   Aydin Yazilim Ve Electronik Sanayi AS, Mustafa Kemal Mahallesi 19 uncu Sokak,
      Eskisehir Yolu Km. 7, 06520 Ankara, Turkey

BECHTEL GROUP INC   50 Beale St, PO Box 3965, San Francisco, CA 94119,
  Tel: (415) 768-1234
  (Engineering & constr)
    Gizbili Consulting Engineers, Necatibey Caddesi, Sezenler Sokak 2/21, Yenisehir,
    Ankara, Turkey

LOUIS BERGER INTL INC   100 Halsted St, East Orange, NJ 07019,
  Tel: (201) 678-1960
  (Consulting engineers, architects, economists & planners)
    Ankara Metro Consultants, 1 Cadde 9 Sokak #2, Balgat, Ankara 06520, Turkey

SAMUEL BINGHAM CO   1555 N Mittel Blvd, #T, Wood Dale, IL 60191-1046,
  Tel: (708) 238-4000
  (Print & industrial rollers, inks)
    Dokloroglu, Ebussuud Cad. Hak Han Kat, 2 Sirkeci , Istanbul, Turkey

BLACK & VEATCH INTL   8400 Ward Pkwy, PO Box 8405, Kansas City, MO 64114,
  Tel: (913) 339-2000
  (Engineering/architectural servs)
    Black & Veatch Intl., Ordu Caddesi 104/Kat 4, Room 406, Yesilyurt, 35370 Ismir,
    Turkey

BRANSON ULTRASONICS CORP   41 Eagle Rd, Danbury, CT 06813-1961,
  Tel: (203) 796-0400
  (Mfr plastics assembly equip, ultrasonic cleaning equip)
    Intersonik Co. Ltd., Canayakin Sitesi, Haltepe Caddesi-Topkapi, 34020 Istanbul,
    Turkey

BROWN & ROOT INC   4100 Clinton Dr, Houston, TX 77020-6299,
  Tel: (713) 676-3011
  (Engr, constr & maintenance)
    Brown & Root Intl. Eastern Inc., Sakir Kesebir Sokak, Plaza 3 Is Hani, Daire 1,
    Balmumcu 80070, Istanbul, Turkey

LEO BURNETT CO INC   35 West Wacker Dr, Chicago, IL 60601, Tel: (312) 220-5959
  (Advertising agency)
    MarKom/Leo Burnett AS, Ergenekon Cad., Bilezikci Sokak 25, Kurtulus, Istanbul,
    Turkey

CARL BYOIR & ASSOCIATES INC   420 Lexington Ave, New York, NY 10017,
  Tel: (212) 210-6000
  (Public relations, intl commun)
    Basin Organizasyon Advertising Agency AS, 59/4 Siraselvilek Taksim, Istanbul, Turkey

CDM INTL INC   Ten Cambridge Center, Cambridge, MA 02142, Tel: (617) 252-8000
  (Consulting engineers)
    Camp Dresser & McKee Intl. Inc., c/o IMC, Kasap Sokak 22, Hilm Hak Han, Kat 6,
    Esentepe, Istanbul, Turkey

CHEMICAL BANK   270 Park Ave, New York, NY 10017-2070, Tel: (212) 270-6000
  (Banking & financial services)
    Chemical Bank AS, Cumhuriyet Bulvari 63/3, 35210 Izmir, Turkey
    Chemical Finans AS, Abdi Ipekci Cad. 63, Polat Palas, Macka, Istanbul, Turkey

CIGNA CORP   One Liberty Place, Philadelphia, PA 19192, Tel: (215) 523-4000
  (Ins, invest, health care & other fin servs)
    Cigna-Sabanci Sigorta AS, Barbados Bulvari #19, Besiktas, 80690 Istanbul, Turkey

CITICORP   399 Park Ave, New York, NY   10043, Tel: (212) 559-1000
(Banking & financial services)
   Citibank, Turkey

CLARK OIL & REFINING CORP   8530 W National Ave, Milwaukee, WI   53227,
Tel: (414) 321-5100
(Petrochems)
   Clark Middle East Oil Corp., Kumrular Sokak 6/6, Yenisehir, Ankara, Turkey

THE COCA-COLA CO   PO Drawer 1734, Atlanta, GA   30301, Tel: (404) 676-2121
(Mfr/mkt/distr soft drinks, syrups & concentrates, juice & juice-drink prdts)
   ANSAN, all mail to U.S. address
   MAKSAN, all mail to U.S. address

COMBUSTION ENGINEERING INC   900 Long Ridge Road, Stamford, CT   06902,
Tel: (203) 329-8771
(Tech constr)
   Combustion Engineering Overseas Inc., Anbarli Santiyesi, Soguksu, Cekmece,
      Istanbul, Turkey

COMPUTER ASSOCIATES INTL INC   One Computer Associates Plaza, Islandia,
NY   11788, Tel: (516) 342-5224
(Devel/mkt/mgt info mgt & bus applications software)
   Computer Associates Ltd. Sti., Iran Cad. 45/10, Cankaya, Ankara 06700, Turkey

COULTER CORP   PO Box 169015, Miami, FL   33116-9015, Tel: (305) 885-0131
(Mfr blood analysis sys, flow cytometers, chem sys, scientific sys & reagents)
   Coulter Electronics Ltd., E-5 Yanyol Fatih Cad. 1/B, 81410 Soganlik Kartal,
      Istanbul, Turkey

CPC INTERNATIONAL INC   PO Box 8000, Englewood Cliffs, NJ   07632,
Tel: (201) 894-4000
(Consumer foods, corn refining)
   Besan-Besin Sanayi ve Ticaret AS, Perihan Sokak 126, A.E.A. Is Hani Kat 4,
      80260 Sisli, Istanbul, Turkey

CRAY RESEARCH INC   655 Lone Oak Dr, Eagan, MN   55121, Tel: (612) 452-6650
(Supercomputer systems & services)
   Cray Research Supercomputer Trade & Services AS, c/o Franko & Azizoglu,
      Musterek Hukak Burosu, Valikonagi Cad. 33/6 Harbiye, 80220 Istanbul, Turkey

D'ARCY MASIUS BENTON & BOWLES INC (DMB&B)   1675 Broadway, New York,
NY   10019, Tel: (212) 468-3622
(Advertising & communications)
   PENAJANS/DMB&B Ticaret AS, Tesvikiye Cad. 105, 80200 Tesvikiye, Istanbul, Turkey

DANIEL MANN JOHNSON & MENDENHALL   3250 Wilshire Blvd, Los Angeles, CA   90010,
Tel: (213) 381-3663
(Architects & engineers)
   DMJM/Ankara Metro Consultants, c/o Yapi Teknik, Muhedislik Musavirlik Ltd. Sti.,
      1 Cadde, 9 Sokak 2, 06520 Balgat-Ankara, Turkey

DIGITAL EQUIPMENT CORP   146 Main St, Maynard, MA   01754-2571,
Tel: (508) 493-5111
(Networked computer systems & services)
   Digital Equipment Turkiye AS, 78080 Buyukdere Caddesi, Istanbul, Turkey

EASTMAN KODAK CO   343 State St, Rochester, NY 14650, Tel: (716) 724-4000
  (Devel/mfr photo & chem prdts, info mgmt/video/copier sys, fibers/plastics for
  various ind)
    Kodak (Near East) Inc., Buyukdere Cad. 80/6, Gayrettepe 80290, Istanbul, Turkey

EXPEDITORS INTL OF WASHINGTON INC   PO Box 69620, Seattle, WA 98168-9620,
  Tel: (206) 246-3711
  (Air/ocean freight forwarding, customs brokerage, intl logistics solutions)
    Turnak Intl. Forwarding & Trading Co. Ltd., Sehit Fethi Bey Cad.,
      Yunculer Ishani 77/5, 35210 Pasaport-Izmir, Turkey

FIRST NATIONAL BANK OF BOSTON   100 Federal St, Boston, MA 02110,
  Tel: (617) 434-2200
  (Commercial banking)
    Bank of Boston Istanbul, Yildiz Posta Cadessi 17, Esentepe, Istanbul, Turkey

FMC CORP   200 E Randolph Dr, Chicago, IL 60601, Tel: (312) 861-6000
  (Produces chems & precious metals, mfr machinery, equip & sys for ind, agric & govt)
    FMC Nurol Savunma Sanayii AS, Turkey

FOOTE CONE & BELDING COMMUNICATIONS INC   101 E Erie St, Chicago,
  IL 60611-2897, Tel: (312) 751-7000
  (Advertising agency)
    Yaratim/FCB, Buyukdere Caddesi 15/A, Hur Han Kat 8, 80260 Sisli, Istanbul, Turkey

FOREST OIL CORP   950 17th St, #1500, Denver, CO 80202, Tel: (303) 592-2400
  (Crude oil & natural gas)
    Forest Oil of Turkey Ltd., Istanbul, Turkey (all mail to U.S. address)

FOSTER WHEELER CORP   Perryville Corporate Park, Clinton, NJ 08809-4000,
  Tel: (908) 730-4000
  (Engr, constr, mfg)
    Bimas Birlesik Insaat Ve Muhendislik AS, P.K. 20 Besiktas, Istanbul, Turkey

GENERAL ELECTRIC CO   3135 Easton Tpk, Fairfield, CT 06431,
  Tel: (203) 373-2211
  (Diversified manufacturing, technology & services)
    General Electric Co.,
      all mail to U.S. address; phone (800) 626-2004 or (518) 438-6500

THE GILLETTE CO   Prudential Tower, Boston, MA 02199, Tel: (617) 421-7000
  (Devel/mfr personal care/use prdts: blades & razors, toiletries, cosmetics,
  stationery)
    Gillette Sanayi ve Ticaret AS, Istanbul, Turkey
    Kromatik Celik ve Plastik Sanayi AS, Istanbul, Turkey
    Permatik Celik ve Plastic Sanayi AS, Istanbul, Turkey

THE GOODYEAR TIRE & RUBBER CO   1144 E Market St, Akron, OH 44316,
  Tel: (216) 796-2121
  (Mfr tires, automotive belts & hose, conveyor belts, chemicals; oil pipeline
  transmission)
    Goodyear Lastikleri TAS, Buyukdere Caddesi 41, Maslak Meydani, 80670 Levent,
      Istanbul, Turkey

GREY ADVERTISING INC   777 Third Ave, New York, NY 10017, Tel: (212) 546-2000
  (Advertising)
    Ajans Grey, Mete Cad. Suren Apt. #14, Kat 5 Daire 13, 80090 Istanbul, Turkey
    Cenajans Grey, Osmali Sokak 19, 80090 Taksim, Istanbul, Turkey

HEWLETT-PACKARD CO   3000 Hanover St, Palo Alto, CA 94304-0890,
  Tel: (415) 857-1501
  (Mfr computing, communications & measurement prdts & services)
    Hewlett-Packard Bilgisayar ve Olcum Sistemleri AS, 19 Mayis caddesi Nova,
      Baran Plaza, Kat. 12, 80220 Kisli, Istanbul, Turkey

HONEYWELL INC   PO Box 524, Minneapolis, MN 55440-0524, Tel: (612) 951-1000
  (Devel/mfr controls for home & building, industry, space & aviation)
    Honeywell AS, Emirhan Cad 145, Barbaros Plaza C/18, Dikilitas 80700, Istanbul,
      Turkey

HORWATH INTL   415 Madison Ave, New York, NY 10017, Tel: (212) 838-5566
  (Public accountants & auditors)
    Er-Genc Denetim ve Yeminli, Mali Mosavirlik AS, Nazmiye Hak Apt. #6, Kat 3 Daire 6,
      Esentepe, Istanbul, Turkey

HYATT INTL CORP   200 West Madison, Chicago, IL 60606, Tel: (312) 750-1234
  (Intl hotel mgmt)
    Hyatt Intl. Hotels, Istanbul, Turkey

IBM CORP   Old Orchard Rd, Armonk, NY 10504, Tel: (914) 765-1900
  (Information products, technology & services)
    IBM Turk Ltd., Sirketi, Turkey

ICC INDUSTRIES INC   720 Fifth Ave, New York, NY 10019, Tel: (212) 397-3300
  (Chems & plastics)
    ICC (Intl. Chemical Corp.), A. Hamit Caddesi 4/5, Taksim, Istanbul, Turkey

INDUCTOTHERM CORP   10 Indel Ave, Rancocas, NJ 08073-0157, Tel: (609) 267-9000
  (Mfr induction melting furnaces)
    Inductotherm Ocaklari Sanayi AS, Sultan Orhan Mahalless, 1 Kurucesme Mevkii,
      Yan Yol, 41400 Gebze, Kocaeli, Turkey

INTERGRAPH CORP   Huntsville, AL 35894-0001, Tel: (205) 730-2000
  (Devel/mfr interactive computer graphic systems)
    Intergraph Computer Services Industry & Trade, Zeytinoglu Cad., Yonca Sok.,
      Metropol Apt. D.3, Akadlar-Etiler, Istanbul, Turkey

INTERMEC CORP   6001 36th Ave West, PO Box 4280, Everett, WA 98203-9280,
  Tel: (206) 348-2600
  (Mfr/distr automated data collection sys)
    Porcan AS, Kucukyali, Akguvercin Sok. #9, 81580 Istanbul, Turkey

ITT CORP   1330 Ave of the Americas, New York, NY 10019-5490,
  Tel: (212) 258-1000
  (Design/mfr communications & electronic equip, hotels, insurance)
    ITT Standard SA, Ziya Gokalp Caddesi 16/10, Yenisehir, Turkey

ITT SHERATON CORP   60 State St, Boston, MA 02108, Tel: (617) 367-3600
  (Hotel operations)
    Istanbul Sheraton Hotel & Towers, Tasmin Park, Istanbul, Turkey
    Sheraton Voyager Antalya Hotel, 100 Yil Bulvari, 07050 Antalya, Turkey

JOHNSON & JOHNSON   One Johnson & Johnson Plaza, New Brunswick, NJ 08933,
  Tel: (908) 524-0400
  (R&D/mfr/sale health care prdts)
    Johnson & Johnson Ltd., Ebulula Caddesi 23, 1 Levent, 80620 Istanbul, Turkey

LINTAS:WORLDWIDE   1 Dag Hammarskjold Plaza, New York, NY 10017,
  Tel: (212) 605-8000
  (Advertising agency)
    Grafika:Lintas, Maslak Is Merkezi, Buyukdere Cad., Maslak Meydani 41/Levent,
      80670 Istanbul, Turkey

LOCTITE CORP   10 Columbus Blvd, Hartford, CT 06106, Tel: (203) 520-5000
  (Mfr/sale ind adhesives & sealants)
    Loctite Yapistiricilar AS, Buyukdere Cad. Kircicegi Sok, B2 Blok D.8,
      80620 Levent-Istanbul, Turkey

MARATHON LE TOURNEAU CO   PO Box 2307, Longview, TX 75606, Tel: (903) 237-7000
  (Mfr heavy constr, mining mach & equip)
    Temsa, Sehit Ersan Caddesi 32-9, Cankaya, Ankara, Turkey

THE MEARL CORP   320 Old Briarcliff Rd, Briarcliff Manor, NY 10510,
  Tel: (914) 923-8500
  (Mfr pearlescent luster pigments, mica, decorative iridescent film)
    Mearl Intl. Turkey, Celal Altinay Cad. 205, Memur Evleri, Seyrantepe, Istanbul,
      Turkey

METALLURG INC   25 E 39th St, New York, NY 10016, Tel: (212) 686-4010
  (Mfr ferrous & nonferrous alloys & metals)
    Turk Maadin Sirketi AS, PK 33, 80002 Karakoy, Anatolia, Turkey

MICROSOFT CORP   One Microsoft Way, Redmond, WA 98052-6399,
  Tel: (206) 882-8080
  (Computer software, peripherals & services)
    Microsoft Turkey, Istanbul, Turkey

MOBIL CORP   3225 Gallows Rd, Fairfax, VA 22037-0001, Tel: (703) 846-3000
  (Petroleum explor & refining, mfr petrol prdts, chems, petrochems)
    Mobil Oil Turk AS, Cumhuriyet Caddesi 26, Pegasus Evi, Harbiye, Istanbul 80200,
      Turkey

McCANN-ERICKSON WORLDWIDE   750 Third Ave, New York, NY 10017,
  Tel: (212) 697-6000
  (Advertising)
    Pars-McCann Reklamcilik AS, Buyukdere Caddesi, Exca Sokak 6, Gultepe 80498,
      Istanbul, Turkey

OTIS ELEVATOR CO   10 Farm Springs, Farmington, CT 06032, Tel: (860) 676-6528
  (Mfr elevators & escalators)
    Buga Otis Asansor Sanayi ve Ticaret AS, Meclisi Mebusan Cad. 167,
      Tutun Han Kat. 3-5, 80040 Kabatas, Istanbul, Turkey

PARSONS BRINKERHOFF QUADE & DOUGLAS   1 Penn Plaza, New York, NY 10119,
Tel: (212) 465-5000
(Engineering consultants, planners, architects)
  Parsons, Brinckerhoff-Gama of Turkey, Mithat Pasa Caddesi 50, Yenisehir, Ankara,
    Turkey

PEPSICO INC   700 Anderson Hill Rd, Purchase, NY 10577-1444,
Tel: (914) 253-2000
(Beverages, snack foods, restaurants)
  Pepsi-Cola Mamulleri Ltd. Sirketi, Turkey
  Pizza Gida Isletmeleri, Turkey

PFIZER INC   235 E 42nd St, New York, NY 10017-5755, Tel: (212) 573-2323
(Mfr healthcare products)
  Pfizer Ilaclari AS, Turkey

RADISSON HOTELS INTL   Carlson Pkwy, PO Box 59159, Minneapolis,
MN 55459-8204, Tel: (612) 540-5526
(Hotels)
  Movenpick Hotel, Buyukdere Caddesi 49, Ucyol Mevkii Maslak, 80670 Istanbul, Turkey

RAYCHEM CORP   300 Constitution Dr, Menlo Park, CA 94025, Tel: (415) 361-3333
(Devel/mfr/mkt materials science products for electronics, telecommunications &
industry)
  Raychem Corp., Buyukdere Cad. Arzu #99/3, 80300 Gayrettepe, Istanbul, Turkey

SIGNETICS CORP   PO Box 3409, Sunnyvale, CA 94088-3409, Tel: (408) 991-2000
(Solid state circuits)
  Turk Philips Ticaret AS, Istanbul, Turkey

SOCOTAB LEAF TOBACCO CO INC   122 E 42 St, New York, NY 10168,
Tel: (212) 687-2590
(Tobacco dealer)
  Socotab Leaf Tobacco Co., 1600 Sokak 17, Bayrakli, Izmir, Turkey

STANDARD COMMERCIAL CORP   PO Box 450, Wilson, NC 27893, Tel: (919) 291-5507
(Leaf tobacco dealers/processors, wool processors)
  Spierer Tutun Ihracat Sarayi Ticaret AS, Gaziler Caddesi 151, P.O. Box 50, Izmir,
    Turkey

TRANE CO   3600 Pammel Creek Rd, La Crosse, WI 54601, Tel: (608) 787-2000
(Mfr/distr/svce A/C sys & equip)
  Trane Klima Ticaret AS, Kore Sehitleri Cad. 30/n Zincirli Kuyu, 80300 Istanbul,
    Turkey

UNION CARBIDE CORP   39 Old Ridgebury Rd, Danbury, CT 06817,
Tel: (203) 794-2000
(Mfr industrial chemicals, plastics, resins)
  Union Carbide Turkey Inc., Bagat Cad. 347/9, 81060 Erenkoy-Istanbul, Turkey

WEATHERFORD INTL INC   1360 Post Oak Blvd, PO Box 27608, Houston,
TX 77227-7608, Tel: (713) 439-9400
(Oilfield servs, prdts & equip; mfr marine cranes)
  Weatherford Intl. Inc., Korglu Caddesi 45/3, GOP, Ankara, Turkey

XEROX CORP   800 Long Ridge Rd, PO Box 1600, Stamford, CT 06904,
  Tel: (203) 968-3000
  (Mfr document processing equip, sys & supplies)
    Xerox Corp., Istanbul, Turkey

UGANDA

AMERICAN INTL GROUP INC   70 Pine St, New York, NY 10270, Tel: (212) 770-7000
  (Insurance, financial services)
    The Uganda American Insurance Co. Ltd., P.O. Box 7077, Kampala, Uganda

LOUIS BERGER INTL INC   100 Halsted St, East Orange, NJ 07019,
  Tel: (201) 678-1960
  (Consulting engineers, architects, economists & planners)
    Louis Berger Intl. Inc., c/o Sunshine Projects Ltd., P.O. Box 9073, Baumann House,
      Parliament Ave., Kampala, Uganda

CALTEX PETROLEUM CORP   PO Box 619500, Dallas, TX 75261, Tel: (214) 830-1000
  (Petroleum prdts)
    Caltex Oil (Uganda) Ltd., Plot 7, Seventh St., Box 7095, Kampala, Uganda

ITT SHERATON CORP   60 State St, Boston, MA 02108, Tel: (617) 367-3600
  (Hotel operations)
    Kampala Sheraton Hotel, Terman Ave., P.O. Box 7041, Kampala, Uganda

PFIZER INC   235 E 42nd St, New York, NY 10017-5755, Tel: (212) 573-2323
  (Mfr healthcare products)
    Pfizer Ltd., Uganda

XEROX CORP   800 Long Ridge Rd, PO Box 1600, Stamford, CT 06904,
  Tel: (203) 968-3000
  (Mfr document processing equip, sys & supplies)
    Xerox Corp., Kampala, Uganda

UKRAINE

ALTHEIMER & GRAY   10 S Wacker Dr, #4000, Chicago, IL 60606-7482,
  Tel: (312) 715-4000
  (Lawyers)
    Altheimer & Gray, Kontraktova Ploscha 4, Bldg. 3 Room 304, 254145 Kiev, Ukraine

DATAEASE INTL INC   7 Cambridge Dr, Trumbull, CT 06611, Tel: (203) 374-8000
  (Mfr applications devel software)
    NPO Gorsistemotekhnika, 23-B Krasnoarmejskaja Str, Kiev 252004, Ukraine

FMC CORP   200 E Randolph Dr, Chicago, IL 60601, Tel: (312) 861-6000
  (Produces chems & precious metals, mfr machinery, equip & sys for ind, agric & govt)
    FMC Intl. AG, Ukraine

HONEYWELL INC   PO Box 524, Minneapolis, MN 55440-0524, Tel: (612) 951-1000
  (Devel/mfr controls for home & building, industry, space & aviation)
    Honeywell, Reytarskaya 8, Kiev, Ukraine

ORION MARINE CORP   79 W Monroe #1105, Chicago, IL 60603, Tel: (312) 263-5153
  (Ocean transportation)
    Inflot Shipping Agency, 1 Place Vakulenchuka, Odessa 266004, Ukraine

OTIS ELEVATOR CO   10 Farm Springs, Farmington, CT 06032, Tel: (860) 676-6528
  (Mfr elevators & escalators)
    UKR OTIS (JV), Kievlift 4, ulitsa Vladimirskaya 41, Kiev 252034, Ukraine

RJR NABISCO INC   1301 Ave of the Americas, New York, NY 10019,
  Tel: (212) 258-5600
  (Mfr consumer packaged food prdts & tobacco prdts)
    Kremenchug Tobacco Factory, Kremenchug, Ukraine
    Lviv Tobacco Factory, Vinniki, Ukraine

U S FUR EXCHANGE   515 Lake St S, Kirkland, WA 98033, Tel: (206) 828-6774
  (Fur auctioning, distr & sale)
    Palms & Co. Inc., Ulitsa Arsenalnaya 9-11, Kiev 252011, Ukraine
    Ukrainian Venture Capital Fund of America, 3 Lipskaya Ulitsa, Kiev 25201, Ukraine

XEROX CORP   800 Long Ridge Rd, PO Box 1600, Stamford, CT 06904,
  Tel: (203) 968-3000
  (Mfr document processing equip, sys & supplies)
    Xerox Corp., Kiev, Ukraine

UNITED ARAB EMIRATES

3COM CORP   5400 Bayfront Plaza, Santa Clara, CA 95052-8145,
  Tel: (408) 764-5000
  (Devel/mfr computer networking prdts & sys)
    3Com Middle East, Dubai, United Arab Emirates

3M   3M Center, St Paul, MN 55144-1000, Tel: (612) 733-1110
  (Mfr diversified prdts for industry, health care, imaging, commun, transport, safety,
  consumer, etc)
    3M Gulf Ltd., 4th Floor, Entrance 4, Hamarain Center, Muraghabat Roundabout, Deira,
    Dubai, United Arab Emirates

A-Z INTL TOOL CO   PO Box 7108, Houston, TX 77248-7108, Tel: (713) 880-8888
  (Mfr oil field, milling & casing cutting tools)
    Grant Oil Tool Co., P.O. Box 4352, Abu Dhabi, United Arab Emirates

ALLEN-BRADLEY CO   PO Box 2086, Milwaukee, WI 53201, Tel: (414) 382-2000
  (Mfr eletrical controls & info devices)
    Allen-Bradley Middle East, P.O. Box 51022, Dubai, United Arab Emirates

AMERICAN BUREAU OF SHIPPING   2 World Trade Center, 106th Fl, New York,
  NY 10048, Tel: (212) 839-5000
  (Classification/certification of ships & offshore structures, devel & tech assistance)
    ABS Europe, P.O. Box 24860, Dubai, United Arab Emirates

AST RESEARCH INC   16215 Alton Parkway, PO Box 19658, Irvine, CA 92713-9658,
  Tel: (714) 727-4141
  (Design/devel/mfr hi-perf desktop, server & notebook computers)
    AST Middle East, P.O. Box 16972, RA 5/34B-R-7, Jebel Ali Free Zone, Dubai,
    United Arab Emirates

ATWOOD OCEANICS INTL   PO Box 218350, Houston, TX 77218, Tel: (713) 492-2929
  (Offshore drilling for gas/oil)
    Atwood Oceanics Intl. SA, P.O. Box 5019, Dubai, United Arab Emirates

BAKER OIL TOOLS   PO Box 40129, Houston, TX 77240-0129, Tel: (713) 466-1322
  (Mfr/serv oil/gas well completions equip)
    Baker Eastern SA, Baker Oil Tools Div., P.O. Box 7621, Abu Dhabi,
    United Arab Emirates

BECHTEL GROUP INC   50 Beale St, PO Box 3965, San Francisco, CA 94119,
  Tel: (415) 768-1234
  (Engineering & constr)
    Bechtel Intl. Corp., P.O. Box 1896, Sharjah, United Arab Emirates
    Intl. Bechtel Inc., P.O. Box 2661, Abu Dhabi, United Arab Emirates

BENTLY NEVADA CORP   PO Box 157, Minden, NV 89423, Tel: (702) 782-3611
(Electronic monitoring system)
   National Engineering Services & Trading Corp., Al Salam St., P.O. Box, 1392,
   Abu Dhabi, United Arab Emirates

BROWN & ROOT INC   4100 Clinton Dr, Houston, TX 77020-6299,
Tel: (713) 676-3011
(Engr, constr & maintenance)
   Brown & Root Intl. Ltd., P.O. Box 6588, Abu Dhabi, United Arab Emirates

LEO BURNETT CO INC   35 West Wacker Dr, Chicago, IL 60601, Tel: (312) 220-5959
(Advertising agency)
   Radius Advertising, P.O. Box 7534, Dubai, United Arab Emirates

BUTTES GAS & OIL CO   3040 Post Oak Blvd, Houston, TX 77056,
Tel: (713) 627-9277
(Natural gas, crude oil)
   Crescent Petroleum Co., P.O. Box 211, Sharjah, United Arab Emirates

CALTEX PETROLEUM CORP   PO Box 619500, Dallas, TX 75261, Tel: (214) 830-1000
(Petroleum prdts)
   Caltex Alkhalij, P.O. Box 2155, Dubai, United Arab Emirates

CAMCO INC   7010 Ardmore St, Houston, TX 77021, Tel: (713) 747-4000
(Oil field equip)
   Camco Ltd., P.O. Box 1882, Dubai, United Arab Emirates

CARBOLINE CO   350 Hanley Industrial Ct, St Louis, MO 63144,
Tel: (314) 644-1000
(Mfr coatings, sealants)
   Carboline Dubai Corp., P.O. Box 3034, Dubai, United Arab Emirates

CARRIER CORP   One Carrier Place, Farmington, CT 06034-4015,
Tel: (203) 674-3000
(Mfr/distr/svce A/C, heating & refrigeration equip)
   UTS Carrier, P.O. Box 3977, Electra St., Abu Dhabi, United Arab Emirates

CBI INDUSTRIES INC   800 Jorie Blvd, Oak Brook, IL 60521, Tel: (708) 654-7000
(Holding co: metal plate fabricating, constr, oil & gas drilling)
   CBI Eastern Anstalt, P.O. Box 2750, Dubai, United Arab Emirates

CHADBOURNE & PARKE   30 Rockefeller Plaza, New York, NY 10112-0127,
Tel: (212) 408-5100
(Lawyers)
   Chadbourne & Parke, Dubai World Trade Centre, P.O. Box 9329, Dubai,
      United Arab Emirates

CHASE MANHATTAN BANK N A   1 Chase Manhattan Plaza, New York, NY 10081,
Tel: (212) 552-2222
(Intl banking)
   Chase Manhattan Bank NA, P.O. Box 3491, Abu Dhabi, United Arab Emirates

CHESTERTON BINSWANGER INTL   Two Logan Sq, 4th fl, Philadelphia,
PA 19103-2759, Tel: (215) 448-6000
(Real estate & related svces)

Dabbagh Group Holding Co. Ltd., Danah Bldg. #201, Al Maktoum St., Dubai,
  United Arab Emirates

CITICORP   399 Park Ave, New York, NY 10043, Tel: (212) 559-1000
  (Banking & financial services)
    Citibank NA, United Arab Emirates

THE COLEMAN CO INC   1526 Cole Blvd, #300, Golden, CO 80401,
  Tel: (303) 202-2470
  (Mfr/distr/sales camping & outdoor recreation prdts)
    Coleman Dubai Ltd., PO Box 17189, Jebel Ali Free Zone, Roundabout 8,
      Warehouse CA-1, Dubai, UAE

COMBUSTION ENGINEERING INC   900 Long Ridge Road, Stamford, CT 06902,
  Tel: (203) 329-8771
  (Tech constr)
    Combustion Engineering Inc., c/o Abdul Jalil Industrial Development, P.O. Box 279,
      Abu Dhabi, United Arab Emirates
    Crest Engineering Overseas Inc., P.O. Box 7444, Abu Dhabi, United Arab Emirates
    Gray Tool Intl. Inc., c/o Emirates Consulting Agency, P.O. Box 3702, Abu Dhabi,
      United Arab Emirates
    Gray Tool Intl. Inc., c/o Emirates Consulting Agency, P.O. Box 980, Dubai,
      United Arab Emirates
    Vetco Offshore, c/o Yusef Bin Ahmed Kanoo, P.O. Box 290, Dubai, United Arab Emirates

CONOCO INC   600 N Dairy Ashford Rd, Houston, TX 77079, Tel: (713) 293-1000
  (Oil, gas, coal, chems, minerals)
    Dubai Petroleum Co., P.O. Box 2222, Dubai, United Arab Emirates

CORE LABORATORIES   10205 Westheimer, Houston, TX 77042, Tel: (713) 972-6311
  (Petroleum testing/analysis, analytical chem, lab & octane analysis instrumentation)
    Core Laboratories Inc., P.O. Box 49, Abu Dhabi, United Arab Emirates

COULTER CORP   PO Box 169015, Miami, FL 33116-9015, Tel: (305) 885-0131
  (Mfr blood analysis sys, flow cytometers, chem sys, scientific sys & reagents)
    Coulter Electronics Dubai Ltd., P.O. Box 2098, Shiekh Hamdan St., Abu Dhabi,
      United Arab Emirates

CRSS INTL INC   1177 W Loop So, PO Box 22427, Houston, TX 77227-2427,
  Tel: (713) 552-2000
  (Consulting, architecture, engineering, construction mgmt)
    CRSS Intl. Inc., P.O. Box 44482, Abu Dhabi, United Arab Emirates

D'ARCY MASIUS BENTON & BOWLES INC (DMB&B)   1675 Broadway, New York,
  NY 10019, Tel: (212) 468-3622
  (Advertising & communications)
    Tamra DMB&B, P.O. Box 2642, 3/F Chamber of Commerce Bldg., Dubai,
      United Arab Emirates

DAMES & MOORE   911 Wilshire Blvd, Los Angeles, CA 90017, Tel: (213) 683-1560
  (Engineering, environmental & construction mgmt services)
    Dames & Moore, P.O. Box 43855, Abu Dhabi, United Arab Emirates

DRILCO DIV   16740 Hardy Rd, PO Box 60068, Houston, TX 77205,
  Tel: (713) 443-3370
  (Oil well down-hole drilling tools)
    Drilco Div., c/o Smith Intl. Gulf., P.O. Box 4983, Dubai, United Arab Emirates

EASTMAN KODAK CO　　343 State St, Rochester, NY　14650, Tel: (716) 724-4000
(Devel/mfr photo & chem prdts, info mgmt/video/copier sys, fibers/plastics for various ind)
　　Kodak Near East Inc., P.O. Box 11460, Dubai, United Arab Emirates

EATON CORP/CUTLER HAMMER　　4201 North 27th St, Milwaukee, WI　53216,
　Tel: (414) 449-6000
(Electric control apparatus, mfr of advanced technologic prdts)
　　Cutler-Hammer Products, P.O. Box 50048, Dubai, United Arab Emirates

EXPEDITORS INTL OF WASHINGTON INC　　PO Box 69620, Seattle, WA　98168-9620,
　Tel: (206) 246-3711
(Air/ocean freight forwarding, customs brokerage, intl logistics solutions)
　　Expeditors Intl. Forwarding & Clearing, P.O. Box 60844, Dubai, United Arab Emirates
　　Expeditors Intl. Service Center, P.O. Box 44256, Abu Dhabi, United Arab Emirates

FMC CORP　　200 E Randolph Dr, Chicago, IL　60601, Tel: (312) 861-6000
(Produces chems & precious metals, mfr machinery, equip & sys for ind, agric & govt)
　　FMC Intl. AG (Dubai), United Arab Emirates
　　FMC Intl. SA, Al Moosa Tower 17th fl., Box 3228, Dubai, United Arab Emirates
　　FMC Intl. SA (Abu Dhabi), United Arab Emirates

GENERAL ELECTRIC CO　　3135 Easton Tpk, Fairfield, CT　06431,
　Tel: (203) 373-2211
(Diversified manufacturing, technology & services)
　　General Electric Co.,
　　　all mail to U.S. address; phone (800) 626-2004 or (518) 438-6500

GLOBAL MARINE INC　　777 N Eldridge, Houston, TX　77079, Tel: (713) 596-5100
(Offshore contract drilling, turnkey drilling, oil & gas explor & prod)
　　Global Marine Inc., Dubai, United Arab Emirates

GREY ADVERTISING INC　　777 Third Ave, New York, NY　10017, Tel: (212) 546-2000
(Advertising)
　　CSS & Grey, City Tower 12/F, Dubai-Abu Dhabi Rd., Dubai, United Arab Emirates

FRANK B HALL & CO INC　　549 Pleasantville Rd, Briarcliff Manor, NY　10510,
　Tel: (914) 769-9200
(Insurance)
　　Frank B. Hall & Co. Middle East, Seif A. Al-Ashram Bldg., Abu-Baker, Al-Siddik St.,
　　　P.O. Box 10764, Dubai, United Arab Emirates

HALLIBURTON CO　　500 N Akard St, #3600, Dallas, TX　75201-3391,
　Tel: (214) 978-2600
(Energy, construction, insurance)
　　Halliburton Ltd., Al Moosa Tower 11/F, Dubai/Abu Dhabi Hwy., Dubai,
　　　United Arab Emirates

HOLIDAY INNS INC　　3742 Lamar Ave, Memphis, TN　38195, Tel: (901) 362-4001
(Hotels, restaurants, casinos)
　　Holiday Inn, P.O. Box 3541, Abu Dhabi, United Arab Emirates
　　Holiday Inn, P.O. Box 10444, Khor Fakkan, United Arab Emirates
　　Holiday Inn, P.O. Box 5802, Sharjah, United Arab Emirates

HONEYWELL INC   PO Box 524, Minneapolis, MN 55440-0524, Tel: (612) 951-1000
  (Devel/mfr controls for home & building, industry, space & aviation)
    Honeywell Middle East Ltd., Dr. Jaffar Bldg., King Faisal Rd. 11, Sharjah,
      United Arab Emirates
    Honeywell Middle East Ltd., Sheikh Faisal Bldg., Khalifa St., Abu Dhabi,
      United Arab Emirates

HORWATH INTL   415 Madison Ave, New York, NY 10017, Tel: (212) 838-5566
  (Public accountants & auditors)
    Horwath Abou Chakra Co., Al-Cornich Pearl Gulf Tower, 5th Fl., Sharjah,
      United Arab Emirates

HUGHES TOOL CO   PO Box 2539, Houston, TX 77001, Tel: (713) 924-2222
  (Equip & serv to oil & gas explor & prod ind)
    BJ-Hughes Ltd., P.O. Box 4352, Abu Dhabi, United Arab Emirates

HYATT INTL CORP   200 West Madison, Chicago, IL 60606, Tel: (312) 750-1234
  (Intl hotel mgmt)
    Hyatt Intl. Hotels, Dubai, United Arab Emirates

IMCO SERVICES   5950 N Course Dr, Houston, TX 70072, Tel: (713) 561-1300
  (Drilling fluids)
    Imco Services, P.O. Box 4076, Abu Dhabi, United Arab Emirates
    Imco Services, Div. of Halliburton Ltd., P.O. Box 11628, Jumariah, Dubai,
      United Arab Emirates

IMS INTERNATIONAL INC   100 Campus Rd, Totowa, NJ 07512, Tel: (201) 790-0700
  (Market research reports)
    Delfzee Dubai Petroleum NV, c/o IMS, P.O. Box 1882, Dubai, United Arab Emirates

INTERGRAPH CORP   Huntsville, AL 35894-0001, Tel: (205) 730-2000
  (Devel/mfr interactive computer graphic systems)
    Intergraph Middle East Ltd., P.O. Box 45805, Abu Dhabi, United Arab Emirates

ITT SHERATON CORP   60 State St, Boston, MA 02108, Tel: (617) 367-3600
  (Hotel operations)
    Dubai Sheraton Hotel, P.O. Box 4250, Dubai, United Arab Emirates

JOHNSON & JOHNSON   One Johnson & Johnson Plaza, New Brunswick, NJ 08933,
  Tel: (908) 524-0400
  (R&D/mfr/sale health care prdts)
    Janssen Pharmaceutica/Mid East & West Asia, P.O. Box 6391, Dubai,
      United Arab Emirates

THE M W KELLOGG CO   601 Jefferson Ave, Houston, TX 77002, Tel: (713) 753-2000
  (Design, engr, procurement & constr for process & energy ind)
    Kellogg Construction Ltd., P.O. Box 26391, Abu Dhabi, United Arab Emirates

THE KENDALL CO   15 Hampshire St, Mansfield, MA 02048, Tel: (508) 261-8000
  (Mfr medical disposable prdts, home health care prdts, spec adhesive prdts)
    The Kendall Co., P.O. Box 52176, Dubai, United Arab Emirates

KEYSTONE INTL INC   PO Box 40010, Houston, TX 77040, Tel: (713) 466-1176
  (Mfr butterfly valves, actuators & control accessories)
    Keystone Abu Dhabi, United Arab Emirates
    Keystone Valve, United Arab Emirates

ARTHUR D LITTLE INC   25 Acorn Park, Cambridge, MA 02140-2390,
Tel: (617) 498-5000
(Mgmt, environ, health & safety consulting; tech & prdt development)
    Arthur D. Little Intl. Inc., P.O. Box 5771, Abu Dhabi, United Arab Emirates

LOCKHEED MARTIN CORP   6801 Rockledge Dr, Bethesda, MD 20817,
Tel: (301) 897-6000
(Design/mfr/mgmt sys in fields of space, defense, energy, electronics, materials,
info & tech svces)
    Lockheed Martin Intl. SA, Blue Tower Office Bldg. #12A01, Khalifa St.,
    P.O. Box 47796, Abu Dhabi, United Arab Emirates

MICROSOFT CORP   One Microsoft Way, Redmond, WA 98052-6399,
Tel: (206) 882-8080
(Computer software, peripherals & services)
    Microsoft Middle East, Dubai World Trade Center, 7-27 Dubai, United Arab Emirates

MILCHEM INC   3900 Essex Lane, PO Box 22111, Houston, TX 77027,
Tel: (214) 439-8000
(Gas & oil well drilling fluids & chem additives)
    Milchem Intl Ltd., P.O. Box 6746, Arenco A Bldg., Zabeel Rd., Dubai,
    United Arab Emirates

MINE SAFETY APPLIANCES CO   PO Box 426, Pittsburgh, PA 15230,
Tel: (421) 273 5000
(Safety equip, ind filters)
    MSA Middle East, P.O. Box 6338, 13/F Bin Hamoodah Bldg., Khalifa St., Dhabi,
    United Arab Emirates

MOBIL CORP   3225 Gallows Rd, Fairfax, VA 22037-0001, Tel: (703) 846-3000
(Petroleum explor & refining, mfr petrol prdts, chems, petrochems)
    Mobil Abu Dhabi Inc., P.O. Box 7695, Abu Dhabi, United Arab Emirates

NATIONAL CAR RENTAL SYSTEM INC   7700 France Ave S, Minneapolis, MN 55435,
Tel: (612) 830-2121
(Car rental)
    National Car Rental System, P.O. Box 4399, Abu Dhabi, United Arab Emirates

OCCIDENTAL PETROLEUM CORP   10889 Wilshire Blvd, Los Angeles, CA 90024,
Tel: (213) 879-1700
(Petroleum & petroleum prdts, chems, plastics)
    Occidental of Abu Dhabi Ltd., c/o Ali Ghosheh, P.O. Box 767, Abu Dhabi,
    United Arab Emirates

OCEANEERING INTL INC   PO Box 218130, Houston, TX 77218-8130,
Tel: (713) 578-8868
(Underwater serv to offshore oil & gas ind)
    Oceaneering Intl. Inc., Operational bases in Abu Dhabi, Dubai & Sharjah

OTIS ENGINEERING CORP   PO Box 819052, Dallas, TX 75381-9052,
Tel: (214) 418-3932
(Mfr oil/gas field equip; service well completion & maint)
    Otis Intl Ltd, P.O. Box 10122, Dubai, United Arab Emirates

PANDUIT CORP   17301 Ridgeland Ave, Tinley Park, IL   60477-0981,
   Tel: (708) 532-1800
   (Mfr elec/electr wiring comps)
     Panduit Middle East, P.O. Box 17021, Jebel Ali, Dubai, United Arab Emirates

PARKER HANNIFIN CORP   17325 Euclid Ave, Cleveland, OH   44112,
   Tel: (216) 531-3000
   (Mfr motion-control prdts)
     Parker Hannifin Corp., P.O. Box 46451, Abu Dhabi, United Arab Emirates

PARSONS DE LEUW INC   1133 15th St NW, Washington, DC   20005,
   Tel: (202) 775-3300
   (Consulting engineers)
     De Leuw Cather Intl. Ltd., P.O. Box 46736, Abu Dhabi, United Arab Emirates

PARSONS ENGINEERING SCIENCE INC   100 W Walnut St, Pasadena, CA   91124,
   Tel: (818) 440-6000
   (Environmental engineering)
     Parsons Engineering Science Inc., P.O. Box 4671, Abu Dhabi, United Arab Emirates
     Parsons Engineering Science Inc., P.O. Box 9123, Dubai, United Arab Emirates

PHILLIPS PETROLEUM CO   Phillips Bldg, Bartlesville, OK   74004,
   Tel: (918) 661-6600
   (Crude oil, natural gas, liquefied petroleum gas, gasoline & petro-chems)
     Phillips Petroleum Co., P.O. Box 6, Abu Dhabi, United Arab Emirates

RAIN BIRD SPRINKLER MFG CORP   7045 N Grand Ave, Glendora, CA   91740,
   Tel: (213) 963-9311
   (Lawn sprinklers, irrigation equip)
     Rain Bird Middle East Ltd., P.O. Box 6630, Sharjah, United Arab Emirates

READING & BATES CORP   901 Threadneedle, #200, Houston, TX   77079,
   Tel: (713) 496-5000
   (Offshore contract drilling)
     Reading & Bates Drilling Co., P.O. Box 45108, Al-Aweidha Bldg. 12/F, Liwa St.,
     Abu Dhabi, United Arab Emirates

ROCKWELL INTL CORP   2201 Seal Beach Blvd, PO Box 4250, Seal Beach,
   CA 90740-8250, Tel: (310) 797-3311
   (Prdts & serv for aerospace, automotive, electronics, graphics & automation inds)
     Allen-Bradley Co., P.O. Box 51022, Dubai, United Arab Emirates

SEA-LAND SERVICE INC   150 Allen Rd, Liberty Corner, NJ   07920,
   Tel: (201) 558-6000
   (Container transport)
     Sea-Land Service Inc., P.O. Box 1721, Dubai, United Arab Emirates
     United Shipping Co., P.O. Box 11328, Dubai, United Arab Emirates

SHEARMAN & STERLING   599 Lexington Ave, New York, NY   10022-6069,
   Tel: (212) 848-4000
   (Lawyers)
     Shearman & Sterling, P.O. Box 2948, Abu Dhabi, United Arab Emirates

SMITH INTL INC   16740 Hardy St, Houston, TX   77032, Tel: (713) 443-3370
   (Mfr/serv downhole drilling equip)
     Smith Intl. Gulf Services Ltd., P.O. Box 4983, Dubai, United Arab Emirates

SONAT OFFSHORE DRILLING INC   PO Box 2765, Houston, TX 77252-2765,
   Tel: (713) 871-7500
   (Offshore oil well drilling)
    Mazroui-Sonat Drilling, P.O. Box 890, Abu Dhabi, United Arab Emirates

SPERRY-SUN INC   104 Industrial Blvd, Sugar Land, TX 77478,
   Tel: (713) 491-2280
   (Oilfield serv)
    Sperry-Sun Well Surveying Co., P.O. Box 3101, Dubai, United Arab Emirates

STATE STREET BANK & TRUST CO   225 Franklin St, Boston, MA 02101,
   Tel: (617) 786-3000
   (Banking & financial services)
    State Street Global Advisors/Middle East, P.O. Box 26838, City Tower 2, Suite 1702,
    Sheikh Zayed Rd., Dubai, United Arab Emirates

TELLABS INC   4951 Indiana Ave, Lisle, IL 60532, Tel: (708) 969-8800
   (Design/mfr/svce voice/data transport & network access sys)
    Tellabs Intl. Inc. (Middle East), Al Khaleej Bldg. #308, Zaabeel Rd., Dubai,
    United Arab Emirates

TIDEWATER INC   Tidewater Place, 1440 Canal St, New Orleans, LA 70112,
   Tel: (504) 568-1010
   (Marine serv & equip to companies engaged in explor, development & prod of oil, gas &
   minerals)
    Tidex Intl. Inc., P.O. Box 3640, Dubai, United Arab Emirates

TRANE CO   3600 Pammel Creek Rd, La Crosse, WI 54601, Tel: (608) 787-2000
   (Mfr/distr/svce A/C sys & equip)
    Trane SA, P.O. Box 5810, Sharjah, United Arab Emirates

TRW INC   1900 Richmond Rd, Cleveland, OH 44124, Tel: (216) 291-7000
   (Electr & energy-related prdts, automotive & aerospace prdts, tools & fasteners)
    Reda Ras al Khaimah Ltd., P.O. Box 518, Ras al Khaimah, United Arab Emirates

U S INDUSTRIES INC   PO Box 629, Evansville, IN 47704, Tel: (812) 425-2428
   (Diversified prdts & sys for industry, agribusiness & retail markets)
    Axelson Inc., P.O. Box 5784, Sharjah, United Arab Emirates

UNION CARBIDE CORP   39 Old Ridgebury Rd, Danbury, CT 06817,
   Tel: (203) 794-2000
   (Mfr industrial chemicals, plastics, resins)
    Union Carbide Europe SA, P.O. Box 16943 Jebel Ali, Dubai, United Arab Emirates

VAREL MFG CO   9230 Denton Rd, PO Box 540157, Dallas, TX 75354-0157,
   Tel: (214) 351-6486
   (Mfr oil, mining, geophysical, water-well & constr equip)
    Varel Middle East, P.O. Box 6802, Dubai, United Arab Emirates

WEATHERFORD INTL INC   1360 Post Oak Blvd, PO Box 27608, Houston,
   TX 77227-7608, Tel: (713) 439-9400
   (Oilfield servs, prdts & equip; mfr marine cranes)
    Weatherford Oil Tool Middle East Ltd., P.O. Box 4627, Dubai, United Arab Emirates

WESTERN ATLAS INTL INC   10205 Westheimer, PO Box 1407, Houston,
  TX 77251-1407, Tel: (713) 266-5700
  (Full service to the oil industry)
    Western Atlas Logging Services, P.O. Box 8786, Mussafah, Abu Dhabi,
      United Arab Emirates
    Western Geophysical, P.O. Box 44610, Abu Dhabi, United Arab Emirates

WESTERN OCEANIC INC   515 Post Oak Blvd, Houston, TX 77027,
  Tel: (713) 629-2700
  (Oil explor, drilling)
    Western Oceanic Intl. Inc., P.O. Box 3538, Abu Dhabi, United Arab Emirates

YORK INTERNATIONAL CORP   PO Box 1592, York, PA 17405-1592,
  Tel: (717) 771-7890
  (Mfr A/C, heating & refrig sys & equip)
    York Air Conditioning & Refrigeration Inc., P.O. Box 16778, Jebil Ali Port,
      Jebil Ali, United Arab Emirates

URUGUAY

3M   3M Center, St Paul, MN 55144-1000, Tel: (612) 733-1110
  (Mfr diversified prdts for industry, health care, imaging, commun, transport, safety,
  consumer, etc)
    3M Uruguay, Casilla de Correo 239, Cno. Carrasco 4683, 12100 Montevideo, Uruguay

ASSOCIATED MERCHANDISING CORP   1440 Broadway, New York, NY 10018,
  Tel: (212) 536-4000
  (Retail service organization)
    Associated Merchandising Corp., Av. Libertador Lavalleja 1513, 11100 Montevideo,
      Uruguay

ASSOCIATED PRESS INC   50 Rockefeller Plaza, New York, NY 10020-1605,
  Tel: (212) 621-1500
  (News gathering agency)
    Associated Press, Calle Cuareim 1287, Montevideo, Uruguay

AVIS INC   900 Old Country Rd, Garden City, NY 11530, Tel: (516) 222-3000
  (Car rental serv)
    Avis Rent Office, Rambia Rep. de Mexico 63333/37, Montevideo, Uruguay

AVON PRODUCTS INC   9 W 57th St, New York, NY 10019, Tel: (212) 546-6015
  (Mfr/distr beauty & related prdts, fashion jewelry, gifts & collectibles)
    Avon Cosmetics SA, Montevideo, Uruguay

THE BANK OF NEW YORK   48 Wall St, New York, NY 10286, Tel: (212) 495-1784
  (Banking)
    Compania Dowson, 25 de Mayo 455, Piso 4, Montevideo, Uruguay

BANKAMERICA CORP   555 California St, San Francisco, CA 94104,
Tel: (415) 622-3456
(Financial services)
  Bank of America NT & SA, P.O. Box 25671, Dubai, United Arab Emirates

LOUIS BERGER INTL INC   100 Halsted St, East Orange, NJ 07019,
Tel: (201) 678-1960
(Consulting engineers, architects, economists & planners)
  Louis Berger Intl. Inc., Brandzen 1961, Oficina 502, Montevideo, Uruguay

BORDEN INC   180 E Broad St, Columbus, OH 43215-3799, Tel: (614) 225-4000
(Mfr foods, snacks & beverages, adhesives)
  Borden Inc., all mail to U.S. address

CITICORP   399 Park Ave, New York, NY 10043, Tel: (212) 559-1000
(Banking & financial services)
  Citibank NA, Uruguay

THE CLOROX CO   1221 Broadway, PO Box 24305, Oakland, CA 94623-1305,
Tel: (510) 271-7000
(Mfr domestic consumer packaged prdts)
  Clorox Uruguay SA, Uruguay

THE COCA-COLA CO   PO Drawer 1734, Atlanta, GA 30301, Tel: (404) 676-2121
(Mfr/mkt/distr soft drinks, syrups & concentrates, juice & juice-drink prdts)
  Montivedeo Refrescos, all mail to U.S. address

COLGATE-PALMOLIVE CO   300 Park Ave, New York, NY 10022, Tel: (212) 310-2000
(Mfr pharms, cosmetics, toiletries, detergents)
  Colgate-Palmolive Inc., Camino Colman 5360, Casilla de Correo 828,
    12400 Montevideo, Uruguay

COLUMBIA PICTURES INDUSTRIES INC   711 Fifth Ave, New York, NY 10022,
Tel: (212) 751-4400
(Producer & distributor of motion pictures)
  Cinema Intl. Corp. Ltd., San Jose 1211, Montevideo, Uruguay
  Columbia Pictures of Uruguay Inc., Calle Canelones 1273, Montevideo, Uruguay

CPC INTERNATIONAL INC   PO Box 8000, Englewood Cliffs, NJ 07632,
Tel: (201) 894-4000
(Consumer foods, corn refining)
  Agroindustrias La Sierra SA, Las Heras 1964, Casilla de Correo 6403,
    11600 Montevideo, Uruguay
  Industrializadora de Maiz SA (IMSA), Casilla de Correo 1396, Yaguaron 1231,
    Montevideo, Uruguay

DRAKE BEAM MORIN INC   100 Park Ave, New York, NY 10017, Tel: (212) 692-7700
(Human resource mgmt consulting & training)
  DBM Uruguay, Rio Branco 1208, Montevideo, Uruguay

EASTMAN KODAK CO   343 State St, Rochester, NY 14650, Tel: (716) 724-4000
(Devel/mfr photo & chem prdts, info mgmt/video/copier sys, fibers/plastics for
various ind)
  Kodak Uruguaya Ltd., Casilla de Correo 806, Calle Yi 1532, Montevideo, Uruguay

FEDERAL-MOGUL CORP   PO Box 1966, Detroit, MI 48235, Tel: (810) 354-7700
  (Mfr/distr precision parts for automobiles, trucks, & farm/constrution vehicles)
    Federal-Mogul Uruguay, Uruguay

FIRST NATIONAL BANK OF BOSTON   100 Federal St, Boston, MA 02110,
  Tel: (617) 434-2200
  (Commercial banking)
    Boston Investment & Financial Services SA, Calle Cerrito 461,
      Casilla de Correo 6711, Montevideo, Uruguay
    First Natl. Bank of Boston, Zabala 1463, Casilla de Correo 90, Montevideo, Uruguay

FMC CORP   200 E Randolph Dr, Chicago, IL 60601, Tel: (312) 861-6000
  (Produces chems & precious metals, mfr machinery, equip & sys for ind, agric & govt)
    Lanfor Investments SA, Uruguay

GENERAL MOTORS CORP   3044 W Grand Blvd, Detroit, MI 48202-3091,
  Tel: (313) 556-5000
  (Mfr full line vehicles, automotive electronics, coml technologies, telecom, space,
  finance)
    General Motors Uruguaya SA, Avenida Sayago 1385, Montevideo, Uruguay

THE GILLETTE CO   Prudential Tower, Boston, MA 02199, Tel: (617) 421-7000
  (Devel/mfr personal care/use prdts: blades & razors, toiletries, cosmetics,
  stationery)
    Davina SA, Montevideo, Uruguay

GOLD STANDARD INC   712 Kearns Bldg, Salt Lake City, UT 84101,
  Tel: (801) 328-4452
  (Gold mining exploration)
    Goldol SA, Guayabo 1729, P. 4 Esc 402, Montevideo, Uruguay
    Tormin SA, Guayabo 1729, P. 4 Esc. 402, Montevideo, Uruguay

GREY ADVERTISING INC   777 Third Ave, New York, NY 10017, Tel: (212) 546-2000
  (Advertising)
    Grey Uruguay, Blvd. Antigas 1913, Montevideo, Uruguay

JOHNSON & JOHNSON   One Johnson & Johnson Plaza, New Brunswick, NJ 08933,
  Tel: (908) 524-0400
  (R&D/mfr/sale health care prdts)
    Johnson & Johnson de Uruguay SA, Casilla de Correo 273, Montevideo, Uruguay

THE KNOLL GROUP   105 Wooster St, New York, NY 10021, Tel: (212) 343-4000
  (Mfr/sale office furnishings)
    Mobil Ltd., San Jose 1028, Montevideo, Uruguay

LOS PINOS II CORP   1111 Park Centre Blvd #245, Miami, FL 33169,
  Tel: (305) 625-1151
  (On-line service internet provider)
    Los Pinos II Uruguay, Agraciada 3064, Off. 601, Montevideo, Uruguay

MANPOWER INTL INC   5301 N Ironwood Rd, PO Box 2053, Milwaukee,
  WI 53201-2053, Tel: (414) 961-1000
  (Temporary help service)
    Manpower, Blvd. Artigas 2003, 11800 Montivideo, Uruguay

McCANN-ERICKSON WORLDWIDE   750 Third Ave, New York, NY 10017,
  Tel: (212) 697-6000
  (Advertising)
    McCann-Erickson Corp. SA, 18 de Julio 1474, Piso 12, Montevideo, Uruguay

OTIS ELEVATOR CO   10 Farm Springs, Farmington, CT 06032, Tel: (860) 676-6528
  (Mfr elevators & escalators)
    Ascensores Otis de Uruguay SA, Colonia 1972, 11200 Montevideo, Uruguay

REPUBLIC NEW YORK CORP   452 Fifth Ave, New York, NY 10018,
  Tel: (212) 525-6901
  (Banking)
    Republic National Bank of New York (Uruguay) SA, Montevideo & Punta del Este,
      Uruguay

RJR NABISCO INC   1301 Ave of the Americas, New York, NY 10019,
  Tel: (212) 258-5600
  (Mfr consumer packaged food prdts & tobacco prdts)
    Fleischmann Uruguaya Inc., Juan Paullier 2373, Montevideo, Uruguay

TEXACO INC   2000 Westchester Ave, White Plains, NY 10650, Tel: (914) 253-4000
  (Explor/mktg crude oil, mfr petro chems & prdts)
    Texaco Uruguay SA, Casilla de Correo 723, Calle Solis 1480, Montevideo, Uruguay

VOLT INFORMATION SCIENCES INC   1221 Sixth Ave, 47th fl, New York,
  NY 10020-1001, Tel: (212) 704-2400
  (Computerized publishing, telecommunications & computer systems & services)
    Volt Autologic Directories SA, Cebollati 1470, 11245 Montevideo, Uruguay

WACKENHUT CORP   1500 San Remo Ave, Coral Gables, FL 33146,
  Tel: (305) 666-5656
  (Security systems & services)
    Wackenhut Uruguay SA, Domingo Aramburu 212/23, Montevideo, Uruguay

WARNER-LAMBERT CO   201 Tabor Road, Morris Plains, NJ 07950,
  Tel: (201) 540-2000
  (Mfr ethical & proprietary pharms, confectionary & consumer prdts)
    Warner-Lambert Ltd., Casilla de Correo 1430, Montevideo, Uruguay

WORLD COURIER INC   46 Trinity Pl, New York, NY 10006, Tel: (718) 978-9400
  (Intl courier serv)
    World Courier Inc., Montevideo, Uruguay

XEROX CORP   800 Long Ridge Rd, PO Box 1600, Stamford, CT 06904,
  Tel: (203) 968-3000
  (Mfr document processing equip, sys & supplies)
    Xerox Corp., Montevideo, Uruguay

VENEZUELA

3COM CORP   5400 Bayfront Plaza, Santa Clara, CA 95052-8145,
  Tel: (408) 764-5000
  (Devel/mfr computer networking prdts & sys)
    3Com Northern Latin America, Venezuela

3M   3M Center, St Paul, MN 55144-1000, Tel: (612) 733-1110
  (Mfr diversified prdts for industry, health care, imaging, commun, transport, safety,
  consumer, etc)
    3M Manufacturera Venezuela SA, Puente Brion a Luis Razetti, Edif. 3M,
    La Candelaria, Caracas 1010A, a Venezuela

AAF-McQUAY INC   111 S Calvert St, #2800, Baltimore, MD 21202,
  Tel: (410) 528-2755
  (Mfr air quality control prdts: heating, ventilating, air-conditioning & filtration
  prdts & services)
    Purificacion de Aire Venezolana CA, Edificio San Remo, Avda. San Sebastian,
    Caracas 1081, Venezuela

ACCO INTL INC   770 S Acco Plaza, Wheeling, IL 60090, Tel: (708) 541-9500
  (Paper fasteners & clips, metal fasteners, binders, staplers)
    CA Acco Mfg., Apartado 30056, Caracas 103, Venezuela

ADC TELECOMMUNICATIONS INC   4900 W 78th St, Minneapolis, MN 55435,
  Tel: (612) 835-6800
  (Mfr telecom equip)
    ADC Venezuela, Edif. EXA, Av. Libertador con Av. Venezuela, El Rosal, Caracas 1060,
    Venezuela

AIR EXPRESS INTL CORP   120 Tokeneke Rd, PO Box 1231, Darien, CT 06820,
  Tel: (203) 655-7900
  (Air frt forwarder)
    Air Express Intl., c/o Taurel & Cia., Sucrs. C.A. Cujia Romualda 69, Apartado 1592,
    Carmelitas, Caracas, Venezuela

ALBERTO-CULVER CO   2525 Armitage Ave, Melrose Park, IL 60160,
  Tel: (708) 450-3000
  (Mfr/mktg personal care & beauty prdts, household & grocery prdts, institutional food
  prdts)
    Alberto-Culver de Venezuela, Apartado 423, Caracas 1010-A, Venezuela

ALLEN-BRADLEY CO   PO Box 2086, Milwaukee, WI 53201, Tel: (414) 382-2000
  (Mfr eletrical controls & info devices)
    Allen-Bradley de Venezuela CA, Av. Gonzalez Rincones, Galpon Allen-Bradley,
    Z.I. La Trinidad, Urb. La Trinidad, Caracas, Venezuela

ALLIED AFTERMARKET DIV   105 Pawtucket Ave, East Providence, RI   02916,
  Tel: (401) 434-7000
  (Mfr spark plugs, filters, brakes)
    Covefilca, Apartado 1267, Caracas 1010A, Venezuela

AMERICAN & EFIRD INC   PO Box 507, Mt Holly, NC   28120, Tel: (704) 827-4311
  (Mfr ind thread, yarn & consumer sewing prdts)
    Hilos Magic H.M. de Venezuela CA, Torre Credival, Piso 12,
      Segunda Avenida Campo Alegre, Francisco de Miranda, Caracas 1060, Venezuela

AMERICAN AIRLINES INC   PO Box 619616, Dallas-Ft Worth Arpt, TX   75261-9616,
  Tel: (817) 355-1234
  (Air transp)
    American Airlines Inc., Torre Lincoln, Piso 13, Oficina K, Apartado 1613, Caracas,
    Venezuela

AMERICAN BROADCASTING COS INC   77 W 66th St, New York, NY   10023,
  Tel: (212) 456-7777
  (Radio/TV prod & broadcast)
    Venezolana de Television SA, Av. La Salle, La Colina, Caracas, Venezuela

AMERICAN CHICLE CO   201 Tabor Rd, Morris Plains, NJ   07950,
  Tel: (201) 540-2000
  (Chewing gum)
    Chicle Adams Inc., Calle Luis de Camoens, La Trinidad, Baruta, Edo. Miranda,
    Venezuela

ARBOR ACRES FARM INC   439 Marlborough Rd, Glastonbury, CT   06033,
  Tel: (860) 633-4681
  (Producers of male & female broiler breeders, commercial egg layers)
    DIACA CA, Arbor Acres de Venezuela, Apartado 359, Valencia, Venezuela
    Las Clavellinas CA, Agricola Las Clavellinas, Apartado 83, Valencia, Carabobo,
    Venezuela

ARO INTL CORP   One Aro Center, Bryan, OH   43506, Tel: (419) 636-4242
  (Mfr portable air tools, drills, motors, fluid handling pumps)
    Aro de Venezuela CA, Apartado 60207, Caracas 1060, Venezuela

ASSOCIATED PRESS INC   50 Rockefeller Plaza, New York, NY   10020-1605,
  Tel: (212) 621-1500
  (News gathering agency)
    Associated Press, Edif. El Nacional, Puerto Escondido a Puente Nuevo, Caracas,
    Venezuela

GUY F ATKINSON CO OF CA INC   1001 Bayhill Dr, San Bruno, CA   94066,
  Tel: (415) 876-1000
  (Construction)
    Atkinson Intl. Venezuela, Av. Urdaneta, Centro Financiero Latino, Piso 17,
    Caracas 60079, Venezuela

AVIS INC   900 Old Country Rd, Garden City, NY   11530, Tel: (516) 222-3000
  (Car rental serv)
    Fiesta Car Rentals de Venezuela, Av. Esabana Grande, Cassanova, Caracas, Venezuela

AVON PRODUCTS INC   9 W 57th St, New York, NY 10019, Tel: (212) 546-6015
(Mfr/distr beauty & related prdts, fashion jewelry, gifts & collectibles)
   Avon Cosmeticos de Venezuela CA, Apartado 60404, Caracas, Venezuela

J T BAKER INC   222 Red School Lane, Phillipsburg, NJ 08865,
Tel: (201) 859-2151
(Mfr/sale/serv lab & process chems)
   J.T. Baker Inc., Apartado 61160, Caracas 1060, Venezuela

BAKER OIL TOOLS   PO Box 40129, Houston, TX 77240-0129, Tel: (713) 466-1322
(Mfr/serv oil/gas well completions equip)
   Baker Hughes de Venezuela SA, Av. 66 #146-178, Zona Industrial, Planta Maracaibo,
   Venezuela

THE BANK OF NEW YORK   48 Wall St, New York, NY 10286, Tel: (212) 495-1784
(Banking)
   BK Investments, Edificio Polar, Mezzanina 2, Plaza Venezuela, Caracas 1050,
   Venezuela

BANKAMERICA CORP   555 California St, San Francisco, CA 94104,
Tel: (415) 622-3456
(Financial services)
   Bank of America NT & SA, Edif. Torre Cavendes, Piso 2, Av. Francisco de Miranda,
   Los Palos Grandes Caracas 1010-A, Venezuela

BANKERS TRUST CO   280 Park Ave, New York, NY 10017, Tel: (212) 250-2500
(Banking)
   Bankers Trust Co., Apartado 61028, Chacao, Caracas 106, Venezuela

BAUSCH & LOMB INC   1 Chase Square, Rochester, NY 14601, Tel: (716) 338-6000
(Mfr vision care prdts & accessories)
   B&L Venezuela CA, Caracas, Venezuela

BAXTER HEALTHCARE CORP   1 Baxter Pky, Deerfield, IL 60015,
Tel: (708) 948-2000
(Mfr disposable medical prdts)
   Baxter de Venezuela CA, Apartado de Correos 68739, Caracas 1062-A, Venezuela

BENTLY NEVADA CORP   PO Box 157, Minden, NV 89423, Tel: (702) 782-3611
(Electronic monitoring system)
   Venmanser CA, Apartado 3495, Caracas 1010A, Venezuela

BESSEMER SECURITIES INC   630 Fifth Ave, New York, NY 10022,
Tel: (212) 708-9100
(Consumer goods retail financing)
   Continental de Creditos Mercantiles CA (CREMERCA), Edif. Icauca, Punceres a Pelota,
   Av. Urdaneta, Caracas, Venezuela

SAMUEL BINGHAM CO   1555 N Mittel Blvd, #T, Wood Dale, IL 60191-1046,
Tel: (708) 238-4000
(Print & industrial rollers, inks)
   Argomin CA, Apartado 76300, Caracas 1070A, Venezuela
   Argomin CA, Apartado Postal 76300, Caracas 1070-A, Venezuela

BLACK & DECKER CORP   701 E Joppa Road, Towson, MD 21286, Tel: (410) 716-3900
  (Mfr power tools & accessories, security hardware, small appliances, fasteners, info
  sys & servs)
     Black & Decker Corp., all mail to U.S. address

BOZELL JACOBS KENYON & ECKHARDT INC   40 West 23rd St, New York, NY 10010,
  Tel: (212) 727-5000
  (Advertising agency)
     LPE Novas-Criswell Venezuela CA, Edif. Atlantic, Av. Andres Bello,
       Los Palos Grandes, Caracas, Venezuela

BRANSON ULTRASONICS CORP   41 Eagle Rd, Danbury, CT 06813-1961,
  Tel: (203) 796-0400
  (Mfr plastics assembly equip, ultrasonic cleaning equip)
     Ferrostaal de Venezuela SA, Edif. la Piramiae, Piso 3, Prados del Este,
       Apdo. 80635, Caracas 1080-A, Venezuela

BROCKWAY INC (NY)   McCullough Ave, Brockway, PA 15824, Tel: (814) 268-3015
  (Glass, plastics, metal packaging)
     Productos de Vidrio SA, Apartado 60369, Chacao, Caracas, Venezuela

BROWN & ROOT INC   4100 Clinton Dr, Houston, TX 77020-6299,
  Tel: (713) 676-3011
  (Engr, constr & maintenance)
     Brown & Root Constructores Petroleros de Venezuela CA, Bulevar de Sabana Grance,
       Edificio Mecy's, 4 Piso, Caracas, Venezuela

CARL BYOIR & ASSOCIATES INC   420 Lexington Ave, New York, NY 10017,
  Tel: (212) 210-6000
  (Public relations, intl commun)
     Asesorac CA, Edif. El Candil Esq. Candilito, Av. Urdaneta, Caracas, Venezuela

CALGON CORP   PO Box 1346, Pittsburgh, PA 15230, Tel: (412) 777-8000
  (Mfr. cosmetic, personal care & water treatment prdts)
     Calgon Interamerican Corp., Apartado 68213, Caracas, Venezuela

CAMCO INC   7010 Ardmore St, Houston, TX 77021, Tel: (713) 747-4000
  (Oil field equip)
     Camco Wire Line CA, Carretera Nacional, Las Morochas, Edo. Zulia, Venezuela

CARBOLINE CO   350 Hanley Industrial Ct, St Louis, MO 63144,
  Tel: (314) 644-1000
  (Mfr coatings, sealants)
     Carboline de Venezuela, Calle Lecuna 12, Boleita Sur, Caracas, Venezuela

CARGILL   PO Box 9300, Minneapolis, MN 55440, Tel: (612) 475-7575
  (Food prdts, feeds, animal prdts)
     Cargill de Venezuela CA, Carretera a Perija Km 3.5, Maracaibo, Estado Zulia,
       Venezuela

CARRIER CORP   One Carrier Place, Farmington, CT 06034-4015,
  Tel: (203) 674-3000
  (Mfr/distr/svce A/C, heating & refrigeration equip)
     Carrier Aire Acondicionado de Venezuela SA, CCCT, Torre C, Piso 6, Ofic. 604-C,
       Caracas 1064, Venezuela

CBI INDUSTRIES INC   800 Jorie Blvd, Oak Brook, IL 60521, Tel: (708) 654-7000
(Holding co: metal plate fabricating, constr, oil & gas drilling)
   CBI de Venezuela CA, Circunvalacion No. 2 y Avda. 19C, Apartado 518, Maracaibo,
   Venezuela
   CBI de Venezuela SA, 2 Transversal, Edif. Rosa Blanca, La Campina, Caracas,
   Venezuela

CENTRAL NATIONAL-GOTTESMAN INC   3 Manhattanville Rd, Purchase,
NY 10577-2110, Tel: (914) 696-9000
(Worldwide sales pulp & paper prdts)
   Central National de Venezuela (CNV) CA, Torre Humboldt - Piso 16, Av. Rio Caura,
   Urban. Prados del Este, Caracas, Venezuela

CHAMPION SPARK PLUG CO   PO Box 910, Toledo, OH 43661-0001,
Tel: (419) 535-2567
(Mfr spark plugs, wiper blades & related prdts)
   Bujias-Champino de Venezuela SA, Apartado 113 y 546, Valencia, Edo. Carabobo,
   Venezuela

CHASE MANHATTAN BANK N A   1 Chase Manhattan Plaza, New York, NY 10081,
Tel: (212) 552-2222
(Intl banking)
   Chase Manhattan Bank N.A., Torre Phelps, Piso 26, Plaza Venezuela, Apartado 6559,
   Caracas, Venezuela

CHINET CO   101 Merritt 7, Norwalk, CT 06851, Tel: (203) 846-1499
(Mfr molded containers)
   Molanca (Moldeados Andinos CA), Zona Industrial Municipal Sur,
   Avda. Domingo Olavarria, Valencia, Venezuela

CIGNA CORP   One Liberty Place, Philadelphia, PA 19192, Tel: (215) 523-4000
(Ins, invest, health care & other fin servs)
   Cigna de Venezuela Intermediarios de Reaseguros SA, Torre Banco de Lara, Piso 11,
   Av. Principal La Castella, Caracas 1062, Venezuela
   Inversiones La Libertad CA, Edif. Centro la Paz, Piso 7, Av. Fco. de Miranda,
   Caracas 1071, Venezuela

CITICORP   399 Park Ave, New York, NY 10043, Tel: (212) 559-1000
(Banking & financial services)
   Citibank NA, Venezuela

THE CLOROX CO   1221 Broadway, PO Box 24305, Oakland, CA 94623-1305,
Tel: (510) 271-7000
(Mfr domestic consumer packaged prdts)
   Corporacion Clorox de Venezuela SA, Caracas, Venezuela

COLGATE-PALMOLIVE CO   300 Park Ave, New York, NY 10022, Tel: (212) 310-2000
(Mfr pharms, cosmetics, toiletries, detergents)
   Colgate-Palmolive CA, Av. Dugo Cisneros, Edif. Centro Colgate, Torre Norte,
   Caracas 1071, Venezuela

COLUMBIA PICTURES INDUSTRIES INC   711 Fifth Ave, New York, NY 10022,
Tel: (212) 751-4400
(Producer & distributor of motion pictures)
   Columbia Pictures de Venezuela Inc., Apartado 5648, Carmelitas, Caracas, Venezuela

COMBUSTION ENGINEERING INC   900 Long Ridge Road, Stamford, CT 06902,
Tel: (203) 329-8771
(Tech constr)
  Crest Venezuela Inc., Maracaibo, Edo. Zulia, Apartado 2331, Venezuela
  Gray Tool Co. de Venezuela CA, Apartado 1994, Maracaibo, Venezuela
  Lumus Company Venezuela CA, Av. Francisco de Miranda, Los Palos Grandes, Caracas,
  Venezuela

CONTINENTAL BANK NA   231 S LaSalle St, Chicago, IL 60697, Tel: (312) 828-2345
(Coml banking servs)
  Continental Bank Corp., Torre Clemente, Piso 5, Av. Venezuela, Caracas 1010A,
  Venezuela

CONTINENTAL CAN CO   PO Box 5410, Stamford, CT 06856, Tel: (203) 357-8110
(Packaging prdts & mach, metal, plastic & paper containers)
  Dominguez & Cia. Caracas SA, Apartado 3986, Caracas 1062A, Venezuela

COOK & CO   Omulgee St, Lumber City, GA 31549, Tel: (912) 363-4371
(Forestry; mfr steel, tire cord)
  Real Intl. CA, c/o Tamayo & Cia., Edif. Tamayo, Avda. Nueva Granada, Caracas,
  Venezuela

COOPER INDUSTRIES INC   1001 Fannin St, PO Box 4446, Houston, TX 77210-4446,
Tel: (713) 739-5400
(Mfr/distr electrical prdts, tools & hardware, automotive prdts)
  Cooper Automotive, Valencia, Carabobo, Venezuela

CORE LABORATORIES   10205 Westheimer, Houston, TX 77042, Tel: (713) 972-6311
(Petroleum testing/analysis, analytical chem, lab & octane analysis instrumentation)
  Core Laboratories, Calle 25, Carretera Via El Mojan, Parcelamiento Buena Vista,
  Apartado 116, Maracaibo, Venezuela

COULTER CORP   PO Box 169015, Miami, FL 33116-9015, Tel: (305) 885-0131
(Mfr blood analysis sys, flow cytometers, chem sys, scientific sys & reagents)
  Coulter Electronics SA, Avda. Rafael Seijas, Quinta 1, San Bernardino,
  Caracas 1011, Venezuela

CPC INTERNATIONAL INC   PO Box 8000, Englewood Cliffs, NJ 07632,
Tel: (201) 894-4000
(Consumer foods, corn refining)
  Alfonzo Rivas & Cia. CA, Apartado 122, Av. Veracruz con Calle Cali, Caracas 1061,
  Venezuela
  Aliven SA, Apartado 60306, Edif. Centro Altamira, Av. San Juan Bosco, Caracas 1010,
  Venezuela

CUMMINS SALES & SERVICE INC   600 Watson Rd, Arlington, TX 76010,
Tel: (817) 275-3361
(Sales, service of diesel engines)
  Cummins Sales & Service de Venezuela SA, Edif. Nuevo, La Quebradita, San Martin,
  Caracas, Venezuela

D'ARCY MASIUS BENTON & BOWLES INC (DMB&B)   1675 Broadway, New York,
NY 10019, Tel: (212) 468-3622
(Advertising & communications)
  DMB&B de Venezuela CA, Edif. Av. Don Diego Cisneros, Centro Colgate, 2 piso,
  Torre Sur, Los Ruices, Caracas, Venezuela

D-M-E COMPANY   29111 Stephenson Highway, Madison Heights, MI   48071,
Tel: (313) 398-6000
(Basic tooling for plastic molding & die casting)
  Productos Humar CA, Apartado 60900, Caracas 1060A, Venezuela

DANA CORP   PO Box 1000, Toledo, OH   43697, Tel: (419) 535-4500
(Engineer/mfr/mkt prdts & sys for vehicular, ind & mobile off-highway mkt & related
aftermarkets)
  Metalmechanica Consolidada CA, Apartado 766, Avda. Irribaren Borges,
    Zona Industrial Sur, Valencia, Venezuela

DATA GENERAL CORP   4400 Computer Dr, Westboro, MA   01580, Tel: (617) 366-8911
(Design, mfr gen purpose computer sys & peripheral prdts & servs)
  Data General CA, Multicentro Empresarial del Este, Edif. Libertador,
    Av. Libertador, Chacao, Venezuela

DATAEASE INTL INC   7 Cambridge Dr, Trumbull, CT   06611, Tel: (203) 374-8000
(Mfr applications devel software)
  SIDIF, Av. Libertador, Cen. Comercial los Cedros, La Florida, Caracas 1050,
    Venezuela

DELTA DRILLING CO   PO Box 2012, Tyler, TX   75710, Tel: (214) 595-1911
(Oil & gas explor & contract drilling)
  Perforaciones Delta CA, Apartado 9138, Caracas, Venezuela

THE DEXTER CORP   1 Elm Street, Windsor Locks, CT   06096, Tel: (203) 627-9051
(Mfr nonwovens, polymer prdts, magnetic materials, biotechnology)
  Midland Dexter of Venezuela SA (Midevensa), Apartado 75005, Caracas 1070-A,
    Venezuela

THE DOW CHEMICAL CO   2030 Dow Center, Midland, MI   48674, Tel: (517) 636-1000
(Mfr chems, plastics, pharms, agric prdts, consumer prdts)
  Dow Quimica de Venezuela CA, Edif. Citibank, Caracas, Venezuela

DOW CORNING CORP   2220 W Salzburg Rd, PO Box 1767, Midland, MI   48640,
Tel: (517) 496-4000
(Silicones, silicon chems, solid lubricants)
  Dow Corning, Calle Nueva York, Edif. Feran, Ofic. 32, Piso 3,
    Las Mercedes-Caracas 1060, Venezuela
  Dow Corning, Apartado 70458, Caracas 1071A, Venezuela

DRAKE BEAM MORIN INC   100 Park Ave, New York, NY   10017, Tel: (212) 692-7700
(Human resource mgmt consulting & training)
  DBM Venezuela, Av. Venezuela, Edif. Venezuela PH3, El Rosal, Caracas 1060, Venezuela

DRAVO CORP   1 Oliver Plaza, Pittsburgh, PA   15222, Tel: (412) 777-5000
(Material handling equip, process plants)
  Dravo Corp. Regional, Apartado 70612, Los Ruices, Caracas 107, Venezuela

E I DU PONT DE NEMOURS & CO   1007 Market St, Wilmington, DE   19898,
Tel: (302) 774-1000
(Mfr/sale diversified chems, plastics, specialty prdts & fibers)
  DuPont de Venezuela CA, Edif. La Estancia, Ciudad Comercial Tamanaco, Caracas,
    Venezuela

EASTMAN KODAK CO   343 State St, Rochester, NY 14650, Tel: (716) 724-4000
  (Devel/mfr photo & chem prdts, info mgmt/video/copier sys, fibers/plastics for various ind)
    Kodak Venezuela SA, Av. La Guairita la Trinidad, Apartado 80658, Caracas 1080-A, Venezuela

EATON CORP   1111 Superior Ave, Cleveland, OH 44114, Tel: (216) 523-5000
  (Advanced tech prdts for transp & ind mkts)
    Ejevan SA, Valencia, Venezuela

ECOLOGY AND ENVIRONMENT INC   368 Pleasant View Dr, East Amherst,
  NY 14086-1397, Tel: (716) 684-8060
  (Environmental, scientific & engineering consulting)
    Ecology and Environment SA, CCCT - Torre A, Piso 6, 608 Chuao, Caracas, Venezuela

EFCO   1800 NE Broadway Ave, Des Moines, IA 50316-0386, Tel: (515) 266-1141
  (Mfr systems for concrete construction)
    EFCO SA, Urbanizacion Industrial Castallito, Calle 103, Parcela P-6 Valencia, Carabobo, Venezuela

EG&G INC   45 William St, Wellesley, MA 02181-4078, Tel: (617) 237-5100
  (Diversified R/D, mfg & services)
    EG&G Sealol SA, Km 8.5 Carretera via a Perija, Zona Industrial, Apartado 818, Maracaibo 4001-A, Venezuela

EXQUISITE FORM INDUSTRIES INC   3010 Westchester Ave, Purchase, NY 10577,
  Tel: (914) 251-1001
  (Mfr foundation garments)
    Exquisite Form Brassiere de Venezuela SA, Edif. Centro Industrial 1, Los Cortijos de Lourdes, Caracas, Venezuela

FAHNESTOCK & CO   110 Wall St, New York, NY 10005, Tel: (212) 668-8000
  (Security brokers, dealers)
    Fahnestock CA, Edif. Seguros, Venezuela

FEDERAL-MOGUL CORP   PO Box 1966, Detroit, MI 48235, Tel: (810) 354-7700
  (Mfr/distr precision parts for automobiles, trucks, & farm/constrution vehicles)
    Federal-Mogul de Venezuela CA, Venezuela

FELTON INTERNATIONAL INC   599 Johnson Ave, Brooklyn, NY 11237,
  Tel: (212) 497-4664
  (Essential oils & extracts, perfumes & flavor material, aromatic chems)
    Felton Intl., Apartado 66190, Caracas 1061A, Venezuela

FERRO CORPORATION   1000 Lakeside Ave, Cleveland, OH 44114,
  Tel: (216) 641-8580
  (Mfr chems, coatings, plastics, colors, refractories)
    Ferro de Venezuela CA, Apartado 304, Valencia 2001A, Edo. Carabobo, Venezuela

FIRST NATIONAL BANK OF BOSTON   100 Federal St, Boston, MA 02110,
  Tel: (617) 434-2200
  (Commercial banking)
    Bank of Boston, Torre la Previsora, Apartado 51973, Caracas 105, Venezuela

FLUOR DANIEL INC   3333 Michelson Dr, Irvine, CA 92730, Tel: (714) 975-2000
  (Engineering, construction, maintenance & technical services)
    Tecnofluor, Avda. Sur 11 #33, Monroy a Puenta Victoria, Caracas 1050-A, Venezuela

FMC CORP   200 E Randolph Dr, Chicago, IL 60601, Tel: (312) 861-6000
  (Produces chems & precious metals, mfr machinery, equip & sys for ind, agric & govt)
    FMC Wellhead de Venezuela SA, Venezuela
    Tripoliven CA, Venezuela

FOOTE CONE & BELDING COMMUNICATIONS INC   101 E Erie St, Chicago,
  IL 60611-2897, Tel: (312) 751-7000
  (Advertising agency)
    FCB/Sibone/Blanco Uribe, Av. Venezuela, Edf. Cremerca, Pisos 8 y 9, El Rosal,
      Caracas 1060, Venezuela

FORD MOTOR CO   The American Road, Dearborn, MI 48121, Tel: (313) 322-3000
  (Mfr motor vehicles)
    Ford Motor de Venezuela SA, Apartado 61131 del Este, Caracas, Venezuela

FOSTER WHEELER CORP   Perryville Corporate Park, Clinton, NJ 08809-4000,
  Tel: (908) 730-4000
  (Engr, constr, mfg)
    Foster Wheeler Venezolana CA, Apartado 6664 Carmelita, Caracas 1010, Venezuela

FRITZ COMPANIES INC   706 Mission St, San Francisco, CA 94103,
  Tel: (415) 904-8360
  (Integrated transportation, sourcing, distribution & customs brokerage services)
    Fritz Venezuela Transportistas Intl. SA, Edif. Helena, Piso 5, Ofic. 54,
      Av. Luis Roche Urb. Altamara, Caracas, Venezuela

GENERAL ELECTRIC CO   3135 Easton Tpk, Fairfield, CT 06431,
  Tel: (203) 373-2211
  (Diversified manufacturing, technology & services)
    General Electric Venezuela,
      all mail to U.S. address; phone (800) 626-2004 or (518) 438-6500

GENERAL MOTORS ACCEPTANCE CORP   3044 West Grand Blvd, Detroit, MI 48202,
  Tel: (313) 556-5000
  (Automobile financing)
    Gemacven SA, Apartado 50981, Caracas 1050A, Venezuela

GENERAL MOTORS CORP   3044 W Grand Blvd, Detroit, MI 48202-3091,
  Tel: (313) 556-5000
  (Mfr full line vehicles, automotive electronics, coml technologies, telecom, space,
  finance)
    Compresores Delfa CA, Caracas, Venezuela
    Constructora Venezolana de Vehiculos CA, Caracas, Venezuela
    General Motors de Venezuela CA, Apartado 666, Caracas 1100, Venezuela

THE GILLETTE CO   Prudential Tower, Boston, MA 02199, Tel: (617) 421-7000
  (Devel/mfr personal care/use prdts: blades & razors, toiletries, cosmetics,
  stationery)
    Caracas Propiedades CA, Los Teques, Venezuela
    Compania Gillette de Venezuela SA, Caracas, Venezuela
    Jafra Cosmetics CA, Caracas, Venezuela
    Oral-B Productos SA, Caracas, Venezuela
    Representaciones Gedeve SA, Caracas, Venezuela

THE GOODYEAR TIRE & RUBBER CO   1144 E Market St, Akron, OH 44316,
  Tel: (216) 796-2121
  (Mfr tires, automotive belts & hose, conveyor belts, chemicals; oil pipeline
  transmission)
    Compania Anonima Goodyear de Venezuela, Apartado 186, Edo. Carabobo, Valencia,
      Venezuela

W R GRACE & CO   One Town Center Rd, Boca Raton, FL 33486-1010,
  Tel: (407) 362-2000
  (Mfr spec chems & materials: packaging, health care, catalysts, construction, water
  treatment/process)
    Grace Venezuela SA, Apartado 61136, Chacao, Caracas 1060, Venezuela

GRANT THORNTON INTL   Prudential Plaza, Chicago, IL 60601, Tel: (312) 856-0001
  (Intl accountants)
    Grant Thornton Intl., Edif. Torre Lincoln, Av. A. Lincoln Esq., Apartado 51470,
      Caracas, Venezuela

GREY ADVERTISING INC   777 Third Ave, New York, NY 10017, Tel: (212) 546-2000
  (Advertising)
    Fischer-Grey, Av. Diego Cisneros, Edif. Oficentro Los Ruices, Piso 2,
      Urb. Los Ruices, Caracas 1070, Venezuela

GTE DIRECTORIES CORP   West Airport Dr, DFW Airport, TX 75261-9810,
  Tel: (214) 453-7000
  (Pub telephone directories)
    GTE Directories Corp./Mellers SA, Av. Juan B. Justo 4715, 1416 Buenos Aires,
      Venezuela

FRANK B HALL & CO INC   549 Pleasantville Rd, Briarcliff Manor, NY 10510,
  Tel: (914) 769-9200
  (Insurance)
    Ronto-Aralca y Asociados CA, Apartado 75918, Caracas 107, Venezuela

THE HARPER GROUP   260 Townsend St, PO Box 77933, San Francisco,
  CA 94107-1719, Tel: (415) 978-0600
  (Ocean/air freight fwdg, customs brokerage, packing & whse, logistics mgt, ins)
    Adelcomar, Calle 69-A #17-64, Maracaibo, Venezuela
    Circle Freight Venezuela SA, Edificio Centro Parima, Piso 8, Avda. Libertador,
      Chacao, Caracas, Venezuela

H J HEINZ CO   PO Box 57, Pittsburgh, PA 15230-0057, Tel: (412) 456-5700
  (Processed food prdts & nutritional services)
    Alimentos Heinz CA, Caracas, Venezuela

HELMERICH & PAYNE INC   1579 E 21st St, Tulsa, OK 74114, Tel: (918) 742-5531
  (Oil/gas exploration & drilling, real estate, mfr gas odorants)
    Helmerich & Payne de Venezuela CA, Apartado 6, Anaco, Venezuela

HEWLETT-PACKARD CO   3000 Hanover St, Palo Alto, CA 94304-0890,
  Tel: (415) 857-1501
  (Mfr computing, communications & measurement prdts & services)
    Hewlett-Packard de Venezuela CA, 3ra Transversal, Los Ruices Norte, Edif. Segre,
      Pisos 1-3, Caracas 1071, Venezuela

HOLIDAY INNS INC   3742 Lamar Ave, Memphis, TN 38195, Tel: (901) 362-4001
(Hotels, restaurants, casinos)
    Holiday Inn, Carrevali Airport, Merida, Venezuela
    Holiday Inn. HICAR, Av. Principal Las Mercedes, Maiquetia Intl. Airport, Caracas,
    Venezuela

HONEYWELL INC   PO Box 524, Minneapolis, MN 55440-0524, Tel: (612) 951-1000
(Devel/mfr controls for home & building, industry, space & aviation)
    Honeywell CA, Avda. Principal los Cortijos de Lourdes, Edif. Honeywell,
    Caracas 1071, Venezuela

HORWATH INTL   415 Madison Ave, New York, NY 10017, Tel: (212) 838-5566
(Public accountants & auditors)
    Fernandez Machado y Asociados, Edidicio Dilcan, Piso 6, Ofic. 6-A, Esq. Candilito,
    Av. Urdaneta, Caracas 1011, Venezuela

J M HUBER CORP   PO Box 277, Rumson, NJ 07760, Tel: (201) 291-1880
(Inks, crude oil, gas, carbon black, kaolin clay, rubber & paper pigments, timber &
minerals)
    J.M. Huber de Venezuela CA, Calle 3, Urb. Industrial, Carapa, Caracas, Venezuela

HUGHES TOOL CO   PO Box 2539, Houston, TX 77001, Tel: (713) 924-2222
(Equip & serv to oil & gas explor & prod ind)
    Hughes Tool Co. SA, Av. 66 62609, Zona Ind. Maracaibo, Apartado 1346, Maracaibo,
    Venezuela
    Hughes-Pacemaicer Service CA, Apartado 434, El Tigre, Anzoategoi, Venezuela

IBM CORP   Old Orchard Rd, Armonk, NY 10504, Tel: (914) 765-1900
(Information products, technology & services)
    IBM de Venezuela SA, Caracas, Venezuela

ILLINOIS TOOL WORKS INC   3600 W Lake Ave, Glenview, IL 60025,
Tel: (708) 724-7500
(Mfr gears, tools, fasteners, sealants, plastic & metal components for ind, med, etc.)
    Miltipak de Venezuela CA, Caracas, Venezuela

IMCO SERVICES   5950 N Course Dr, Houston, TX 70072, Tel: (713) 561-1300
(Drilling fluids)
    Imco Services Div. Cia. Halliburton de Cementation y Fomento, Centro,
    Comercial Socuy, Av. 4 con Calle 67, Apartado 698, Maracaibo, Zulia 4002,
    Venezuela

INTERGRAPH CORP   Huntsville, AL 35894-0001, Tel: (205) 730-2000
(Devel/mfr interactive computer graphic systems)
    Intergraph Servicios de Venezuela CA, CCC Tamanaco, Torre C, Piso 11,
    Ofic. C-1102/Chuao, Caracas 1064-A, Venezuela

INTERNATIONAL FLAVORS & FRAGRANCES INC   521 W 57th St, New York, NY 10019,
Tel: (212) 765-5500
(Create/mfr flavors, fragrances & aroma chems)
    Intl. Flavors & Fragrances de Venezuela SA, Apartado 70268, Caracas 1071A, Venezuela

INTERNATIONAL MULTIFOODS CORP   Box 2942, Minneapolis, MN 55402,
Tel: (612) 340-3300
(Food serv, grain & feed, food prdts)
    Molinos Nacionales CA (MONACA), Apartado 70384, Caracas 1071A, Venezuela

INTERNATIONAL PAPER   2 Manhattanville Rd, Purchase, NY 10577,
  Tel: (914) 397-1500
  (Mfr/distr container board, paper, wood prdts)
    Corporacion Forestal de Venezuela, c/o Manufacturas de Papel C.A., Apartado 2046,
      Carmelitas, Caracas, Venezuela

ITT SHERATON CORP   60 State St, Boston, MA 02108, Tel: (617) 367-3600
  (Hotel operations)
    Sheraton Macuto Resort, Apartado 65, La Guaira, Venezuela

JOHNSON & HIGGINS   125 Broad St, New York, NY 10004-2424, Tel: (212) 574-7000
  (Ins brokerage, employee benefit conslt, risk mgmt, human resource conslt, ins/reins
  servs)
    Johnson & Higgins de Venezuela CA, Edif. Banco Exterior, Apartado 14139, Caracas,
      Venezuela
    Johnson & Higgins de Venezuela CA, also in Barquisimeto, Maracaibo,
      Puerto La Cruz & Valencia, Venezuela

JOHNSON & JOHNSON   One Johnson & Johnson Plaza, New Brunswick, NJ 08933,
  Tel: (908) 524-0400
  (R&D/mfr/sale health care prdts)
    Johnson & Johnson de Venezuela SA, Caracas, Venezuela

S C JOHNSON & SON INC   1525 Howe St, Racine, WI 53403, Tel: (414) 631-2000
  (Home, auto, commercial & personal care prdts, specialty chems)
    S.C. Johnson & Son de Venezuela CA, Apartado 40041, Los Ruices, Caracas 1071,
      Venezuela

KELLOGG CO   One Kellogg Sq, PO Box 3599, Battle Creek, MI 49016-3599,
  Tel: (616) 961-2000
  (Mfr ready-to-eat cereals, convenience foods)
    Alimentos Kellogg SA, Maracay, Edo. Aragua,
      Venezuela (all inquiries to U.S. address)

KELSEY-HAYES CO   38481 Huron River Dr, Romulus, MI 48174, Tel: (313) 941-2000
  (Automotive & aircraft parts)
    Ruedas de Venezuela SA, Zona Industrial, 1-A Victoria, Edo. Aragua, Caracas,
      Venezuela

THE KENDALL CO   15 Hampshire St, Mansfield, MA 02048, Tel: (508) 261-8000
  (Mfr medical disposable prdts, home health care prdts, spec adhesive prdts)
    Kendall de Venezuela CA, Calle Madrid con Caroni, Edif. Centro Caroni, Piso B,
      Urb. Las Mercedes, Caracas, Venezuela

KORN/FERRY INTL   1800 Century Park East, Los Angeles, CA 90067,
  Tel: (310) 552-1834
  (Executive search)
    Korn/Ferry Intl. de Venezuela CA, Multicentro Empres. del Este,
      Torre Miranda Nuc. B, P/15 #153, Av. Chacao, Caracas 1060, Venezuela

KRAFT INC   Kraft Court, Glenview, IL 60025, Tel: (708) 998-2000
  (Dairy prdts, processed food, chems)
    Alimentos Kraft de Venezuela CA, Apartado 450, Valencia, Venezuela

THE KULJIAN CO   3624 Science Center, Philadelphia, PA 19104,
  Tel: (215) 243-1900
  (Studies, design, engineeering, constr mgmt, site supervision)
    Development Consultants Intl., Apartado 123, Puerto Ordaz, Edo. Bolivar, Venezuela

LANMAN & KEMP-BARCLAY & CO INC   25 Woodland Ave, Westwood, NJ 07675,
  Tel: (201) 666-4990
  (Mfr pharms, toiletries)
    Lanman & Kemp-Barclay & Co. de Venezuela SA, Apartado 694, Caracas, Venezuela

ELI LILLY & CO   Lilly Corporate Center, Indianapolis, IN 46285,
  Tel: (317) 276-2000
  (Mfr pharmaceuticals, animal health prdts)
    Eli Lilly y Compania de Venezuela SA, Edificio Torre Uno, Piso 3,
      Urb. Las Mercedes, Caracas, Venezuela

THE LINCOLN ELECTRIC CO   22801 St Clair Ave, Cleveland, OH 44117-1199,
  Tel: (216) 481-8100
  (Mfr arc welding & welding related prtds, oxy-fuel & thermal cutting equip, integral
  AC motors)
    Industrias Soldarco SA, Av. Henry Ford, Centro Civico Romulo Betancourt,
      Edif. Orion, ZI Municipal Sur, Valencia, Venezuela

LINTAS:WORLDWIDE   1 Dag Hammarskjold Plaza, New York, NY 10017,
  Tel: (212) 605-8000
  (Advertising agency)
    Franklin Whaite & Asociados SA, Av. Francisco de Miranda, Edif. Seguros, Adriatica,
      Altamira 1062, Caracas, Venezuela

LIQUID CARBONIC INDUSTRIES CORP   810 Jorie Blvd, Oak Brook, IL 60521,
  Tel: (708) 572-7500
  (Mfr compressed gasses)
    Liquid Carbonic Venezolana SA, Edif. Centro Empres'l Parque del Este,
      Av. F. de Miranda, Sec. La Carlota, Caracas, Venezuela

ARTHUR D LITTLE INC   25 Acorn Park, Cambridge, MA 02140-2390,
  Tel: (617) 498-5000
  (Mgmt, environ, health & safety consulting; tech & prdt development)
    Arthur D. Little de Venezuela CA, Edif. Banco de Lara-PH1,
      Av. Principal de La Castellana, La Castellana Caracas, DF, Venezuela

LOCTITE CORP   10 Columbus Blvd, Hartford, CT 06106, Tel: (203) 520-5000
  (Mfr/sale ind adhesives & sealants)
    Loctite de Venezuela CA, Apartado 206, Caracas 1010-A, Venezuela

THE LUBRIZOL CORP   29400 Lakeland Blvd, Wickliffe, OH 44092-2298,
  Tel: (216) 943-4200
  (Mfr chem additives for lubricants & fuels)
    CA Lubricantes Quimicos LQ, Venezuela
    Lubrizol de Venezuela CA, Venezuela

LUFKIN RULE CO   PO Box 728, Apex, NC 27502, Tel: (919) 362-7510
  (Mfr measuring tapes & rules, hand tools)
    Lufkin Foundry & Machine So., Anaco, Edo. Anzoategui, Venezuela

MANPOWER INTL INC   5301 N Ironwood Rd, PO Box 2053, Milwaukee,
  WI 53201-2053, Tel: (414) 961-1000
  (Temporary help service)
    Manpower de Venezuela CA, Av. Francisco de Miranda - Torre Delta, La Castellana,
    Caracas, Venezuela

MARATHON LE TOURNEAU CO   PO Box 2307, Longview, TX 75606, Tel: (903) 237-7000
  (Mfr heavy constr, mining mach & equip)
    V.K. International Commerce CA, Torre Europa, Avenida Francisco de Miranda,
    Campo Alegre, Caracas 1050, Venezuela

MARSH & McLENNAN COS INC   1166 Ave of the Americas, New York, NY 10036-1011,
  Tel: (212) 345-5000
  (Insurance)
    Lansing Cox y Asociadas CA, Edif. Panaven, 3-A Transversal y Av. San Juan Bosco,
    Altamira, Caracas, Venezuela

MCI INTERNATIONAL   2 International Dr, Rye Brook, NY 10573,
  Tel: (914) 937-3444
  (Telecommunications)
    MCI Intl. de Venezuela SA, Avda. Liberatador, Edif. Exa, Penthouse 9-10-11,
    El Rosal, Caracas, Venezuela

MEASUREX CORP   One Results Way, Cupertino, CA 95014-5991, Tel: (408) 255-1500
  (Mfr computer integrated mfg sys)
    Measures (Venezuela), Av. 19 de Abril, Edif. Torre Cosmopoliton, Piso 13,
    Ofic. 133, Maracay, Venezuela

MEMOREX CORP   San Thomas at Central Expressway, Santa Clara, CA 95052,
  Tel: (408) 987-1000
  (Magnetic recording tapes, etc)
    Memorex Inter-America CA, Av. Principal de Chuao, Residencias Don Julian, 5 Piso,
    Apartado 51523, Caracas, Venezuela

MERCK SHARP & DOHME INTL   PO Box 2000, Rahway, NJ 07065, Tel: (201) 574-4000
  (Pharms, chems & biologicals)
    Merck, Sharp & Dohme de Venezuela CA, Edif. Merck, Sharp & Dohme,
      Av. Principal de los Ruices, Los Dos Caminos, Caracas, Venezuela

MICROSOFT CORP   One Microsoft Way, Redmond, WA 98052-6399,
  Tel: (206) 882-8080
  (Computer software, peripherals & services)
    Microsoft Venezuela, Centro Profesional Eurobuilding, Piso 7, Of. 7-E,
      Calle La Guairita, Chuao, Caracas, Venezuela

MOBIL CORP   3225 Gallows Rd, Fairfax, VA 22037-0001, Tel: (703) 846-3000
  (Petroleum explor & refining, mfr petrol prdts, chems, petrochems)
    Mobil Oil Co. de Venezuela, Apartado 60167, Caracas 106, Venezuela
    Mobil de Desarrollo CA, Edif. Sucre, La Floresta, Caracas 106, Venezuela

MONROE SYSTEMS FOR BUSINESS INC   1000 American Rd, Morris Plains, NJ 07950,
  Tel: (201) 993-2000
  (Mfr business machines, calculators, copiers, faxes, shredders & supplies)
    C.A. Monroe Sistemas Empresariales, Av. Galipan 29 y 31,
      a Media Cuadra de la Av. Panteon, San Bernardino, Caracas, Venezuela

MORGAN GUARANTY TRUST CO   23 Wall St, New York, NY 10260, Tel: (212) 483-2323
(Banking)
  Morgan Guaranty Trust Co., Edif. Centro Altamira, Piso 5, Av. San Juan Bosco,
    Altamira 106, Caracas, Venezuela

MYERS INTL INC   1293 South Main St, Akron, OH 44301, Tel: (216) 253-5592
(Mfr tire retreading & maintenance equip & supplies)
  Ventisuco CA, Apartado 70171, Caracas, Venezuela

McCANN-ERICKSON WORLDWIDE   750 Third Ave, New York, NY 10017,
  Tel: (212) 697-6000
(Advertising)
  ABC/McCann Publicidad SA, Torre la Primera, Av. Francisco de Miranda,
    Apartado 50163, Caracas, Venezuela

McCORMICK & CO INC   18 Loveton Circle, Sparks, MD 21152-6000,
  Tel: (410) 771-7301
(Mfr/dist/sale seasonings, flavorings, specialty foods)
  McCormick de Venezuela CA, Apartado 75, 093, Av. Chicago & Trieste, California Sur,
    Caracas 1070-A, Venezuela

McKESSON CORP   One Post St, San Francisco, CA 94104-5296, Tel: (415) 983-8300
(Mfr drugs, car-care prdts, toiletries)
  Laboratorios Calox, Apartado 62483, Caracas, Venezuela

NABORS INDUSTRIES INC   515 W Greens Rd, #1200, Houston, TX 77067,
  Tel: (713) 874-0035
(Oil & gas drilling, petrol prdts)
  Loffland Brothers de Venezuela CA, Avda. 28 - 17 C-105, Maracaibo, Venezuela

NALCO CHEMICAL CO   One Nalco Center, Naperville, IL 60563-1198,
  Tel: (708) 305-1000
(Chems for water & waste water treatment, oil prod & refining, ind processes;
water/energy mgmt serv)
  Nalco de Venezuela CA, Apartado 62176, Chacao, Caracas, Venezuela

NATIONAL CAR RENTAL SYSTEM INC   7700 France Ave S, Minneapolis, MN 55435,
  Tel: (612) 830-2121
(Car rental)
  Natl. Car Rental System Inc., Apartado 51959, Caracas 105, Venezuela

NATIONAL CHEMSEARCH CORP   2727 Chemsearch Blvd, Irving, TX 75061,
  Tel: (214) 438-0211
(Commercial chem prdts)
  Natl. Chemsearch SA, Quinta Maria, Este 10 bis 74, El Conde, Caracas, Venezuela

NATIONAL STARCH & CHEMICAL CO   10 Finderne Ave, Bridgewater, NJ 08807-3300,
  Tel: (908) 685-5000
(Mfr adhesives & sealants, resins & spec chems, electr materials & adhesives, food
prdts, ind starch)
  National Starch & Chemical CA, Caracas, Venezuela

NOBLE DRILLING CORP   10370 Richmond Ave, #400, Houston, TX 77042,
  Tel: (713) 974-3131
(Drilling contractor, engineering services)
  Noble Drilling de Venezuela SA, Carretera L. Frente al Callejon 7,
    Edif. San Martin de Loba, Las Morochas, Edo. Zulia, Venezuela

NORTON CO   1 New Bond St, Worcester, MA 01606, Tel: (508) 795-5000
(Abrasives, drill bits, constr & safety prdts, plastics)
   Christensen Diamond Products de Venezuela CA, Apartado 463, Maracaibo, Venezuela

OCCIDENTAL PETROLEUM CORP   10889 Wilshire Blvd, Los Angeles, CA 90024,
Tel: (213) 879-1700
(Petroleum & petroleum prdts, chems, plastics)
   Occidental de Hidrocarburos Inc., Centro Plaza, Av. Francisco Miranda, Torre A,
   Los Palos, Grandes, Caracas 1206, Venezuela
   Plasticos y Derivados CA (PLAYDECA), Final Calle Faez, Baruta, Edo. Miranda,
   Caracas 1060A, Venezuela

OLIN CORP   120 Long Ridge Rd, PO Box 1355, Stamford, CT 06904-1355,
Tel: (203) 356-2000
(Mfr chems, metals, applied physics in elect, defense, aerospace inds)
   Olin Quimica SA, Edif. Galipan, Piso 2, Entr. C, Av. Francisco Miranda,
   Apartado 3781, Caracas, Venezuela

ORACLE CORP   500 Oracle Parkway, Redwood Shores, CA 94065,
Tel: (415) 506-7000
(Develop/mfr software)
   Oracle Venezuela, Av. Francisco de Miranda, Centro Plaza Torre A, Piso 18,
   Los Palos Grandes, Caracas 1060, Venezuela

OSCAR MAYER & CO   PO Box 7188, Madison, WI 53707, Tel: (608) 241-3311
(Meat & food prdts)
   Ven Packers Inc., Apartado 62296, Caracas, Venezuela
   Venezolana Empacadora CA, Apartado del Este 11446, Caracas, Venezuela

OWENS-ILLINOIS INC   1 Seagate, Toledo, OH 43666, Tel: (419) 247-5000
(Glass & plastic containers, house- hold & ind prdts, packaging)
   Manufacturera de Vidrio Plano CA, Zona Industrial, La Victoria, Edo. Aragua,
   Venezuela

PARKER HANNIFIN CORP   17325 Euclid Ave, Cleveland, OH 44112,
Tel: (216) 531-3000
(Mfr motion-control prdts)
   Parker Connector Plant, Calle Neveri, Parc. 279-01, Zona Ind. Unare 2,
   Galpon Parker, Puerto Ordaz, Edo. Bolivar, Venezuela
   Parker Hannifin de Venezuela SA, Edif. Draza PB,
   Esq. Calle Miraima con Av. Principal de Voleita Norte, Caracas, Venezuela

THE PARSONS CORP   100 W Walnut St, Pasadena, CA 91124, Tel: (818) 440-2000
(Engineering & construction)
   Proyeparsons CA, Torre La Noria, Paseo Enrique Eraseo, Las Mercedes,
   Apartado 60632, Caracas 1060, Venezuela

PET INC   400 S 4th St, St Louis, MO 63102, Tel: (314) 622-7700
(Mfr packaged foods)
   Diablitos Venezolanos CA, Torre Clement, Piso 1, Av. Venezuela, El Rosal,
   Caracas 1050, Venezuela

PFIZER INC   235 E 42nd St, New York, NY 10017-5755, Tel: (212) 573-2323
(Mfr healthcare products)
   Laboratorios Pfizer de Venezuela SA, Venezuela

Pfizer Bioquimicos SA, Venezuela
Pfizer SA, Venezuela

PHELPS DODGE CORP   2600 N Central Ave, Phoenix, AZ 85004-3014,
Tel: (602) 234-8100
(Copper, minerals, metals & spec engineered prdts for trans & elect mkts)
  Alambres y Cables Venezolanos CA (ALCAVE), Apartado 62107 (Chaco), Caracas 1060-A,
  Venezuela

PHILLIPS PETROLEUM CO   Phillips Bldg, Bartlesville, OK 74004,
Tel: (918) 661-6600
(Crude oil, natural gas, liquefied petroleum gas, gasoline & petro-chems)
  CA Venezolana Internacional de Productos Quimicos, Apartado del Este 5522, Caracas,
  Venezuela
  Venezoil CA, Apartado 1031, Caracas, Venezuela

PIONEER HI-BRED INTL INC   700 Capital Sq, 400 Locust St, Des Moines,
IA 50309, Tel: (515) 245-3500
(Agricultural chemicals, farm supplies, biological prdts, research)
  Hibreven Hibridos Venezolanos CA, Con Calle Tamanco, Estado, Aragua, Venezuela

PPG INDUSTRIES   One PPG Place, Pittsburgh, PA 15272, Tel: (412) 434-3131
(Mfr flat glass, fiber glass, chems, coatings)
  Inveca-Pittsburgh CA, Calle A, Jrb. Industrial Tejerias, Argua, Venezuela
  VFG-Sudamtex CA, Av. 3, Zona Industrial Los Montones, Estado Anzoategui, Barcelona,
  Venezuela

PRECISION VALVE CORP   PO Box 309, Yonkers, NY 10702, Tel: (914) 969-6500
(Mfr aerosol valves)
  Prevalco CA, Apartado 67313, Plaza las Americas, Caracas 1061, Venezuela

PREMARK INTL INC   1717 Deerfield Rd, Deerfield, IL 60015, Tel: (708) 405-6000
(Mfr/sale diversified consumer & coml prdts)
  Dart Venezuela CA, Apartado 61836, Chacao, Caracas 1060A, Venezuela

PROCTER & GAMBLE CO   One Procter & Gamble Plaza, Cincinnati, OH 45202,
Tel: (513) 983-1100
(Personal care, food, laundry, cleaning & ind prdts)
  Mavesa SA, Av. Principal los Cortijos de Lourdes, Caracas, Venezuela
  Procter & Gamble de Venezuela SA, Edif. Torre del Este, Av. Francisco de Miranda,
  Chacao, Caracas, Venezuela

PROCTER & GAMBLE PHARMACEUTICALS   17 Eaton Ave, Norwich, NY 13815-1799,
Tel: (607) 335-2111
(Devel/mfr pharms, chems, health prdts)
  Norwich de Venezuela, Av. Romulo Gallegos 402, 40 Piso B, Urb. Dos Caminos,
  Caracas 118, Venezuela

THE PROTANE CORP   1400 Smith St, Houston, TX 77210, Tel: (713) 853-7047
(Holding co: foreign invest in LPG ind & distribution)
  Industrias Ventane SA, Apartado 61332, Caracas, Venezuela

QUAKER CHEMICAL CORP   Elm & Lee Sts, Conshohocken, PA 19428-0809,
Tel: (610) 832-4000
(Mfr chem specialties; total fluid mgmt services)
  Kelko Quaker Chemical SA, Av. F. de Miranda, Edif. Parque Cristal p.7, Torre Este,
  Los Palos Grandes, Caracas 1060A, Venezuela

THE QUAKER OATS CO   321 N Clark St, PO Box 049001, Chicago, IL 60604-9001,
  Tel: (312) 222-7111
  (Mfr foods & beverages)
    Productos Quaker CA, Centro Plaza, Torre C-Piso 16, La. Transversal,
    Los Palos Grandes, Caracas, Venezuela

RAYCHEM CORP   300 Constitution Dr, Menlo Park, CA 94025, Tel: (415) 361-3333
  (Devel/mfr/mkt materials science products for electronics, telecommunications &
  industry)
    Raychem de Venezuela CA, Edificio Segre II, Piso 2, Calle 6, La Urbina, Caracas,
    Venezuela

REVLON INC   625 Madison Ave, New York, NY 10022, Tel: (212) 527-4000
  (Mfr cosmetics, fragrances, toiletries, beauty care prdts)
    Revlon Overseas Corp., Apartado 5733, Caracas, Venezuela

RJR NABISCO INC   1301 Ave of the Americas, New York, NY 10019,
  Tel: (212) 258-5600
  (Mfr consumer packaged food prdts & tobacco prdts)
    Royal Productos Alimenticios CA, Edif. Sturgis, Av. Chicago, Caracas 1070, Venezuela

A H ROBINS CO INC   1407 Cummings Dr, PO Box 26609, Richmond, VA 23261-6609,
  Tel: (804) 257-2000
  (Mfr ethical pharms & consumer prdts)
    Laboratorios Ergos SA, 2 Transversal 8, Urb. Buena Vista, Apartado del Este 60590,
    Caracas, Venezuela

ROCKWELL INTL CORP   2201 Seal Beach Blvd, PO Box 4250, Seal Beach,
  CA 90740-8250, Tel: (310) 797-3311
  (Prdts & serv for aerospace, automotive, electronics, graphics & automation inds)
    Allen-Bradley de Venezuela CA, Avda. Gonzalez Rincones,
    La Trinidad (Zona Industrial) 23-06, Caracas 1080, Venezuela

R P SCHERER CORP   2075 W Big Beaver Rd, Troy, MI 48084, Tel: (810) 649-0900
  (Mfr soft gelatin & two-piece hard shell capsules)
    R.P. Scherer de Venezuela CA, Edif. R. P. Scherer, lra. Transv. Urb. Artigas,
    Caracas 1060, Venezuela

SCIENTIFIC SOFTWARE INTERCOMP INC   1801 California St, Denver, CO 80202,
  Tel: (303) 292-1111
  (Computer services to oil/gas industry)
    Scientific Software de Sud America, Caracas, Venezuela

G D SEARLE & CO   5200 Old Orchard Rd, Skokie, IL 60077, Tel: (708) 982-7000
  (Mfr pharms, health care & optical prdts, specialty chems)
    Serale de Venezuela CA, Zona Industrial del Este, Manzana M, Urb. Maturin,
    Maturin Guarenas, Edo. de Miranda, Venezuela

SEARS ROEBUCK & CO   Sears Tower, Chicago, IL 60684, Tel: (312) 875-2500
  (Diversified general merchandise)
    Sears, Roebuck de Venezuela SA, Edif. Sears, Av. Principal Colinas de Bello Monte,
    Caracas, Venezuela
    Sears, Roebuck de Venezuela SA, Apartado 1509, Caracas, Venezuela

SEARS WORLD TRADE   633 Pennsylvania Ave, NW, Washington, DC 20004,
Tel: (202) 626-1600
(Consumer & light ind goods, processed foods)
   Searle Venezuela CA, Apartado 75737, Caracas 107, Venezuela

SMITH INTL INC   16740 Hardy St, Houston, TX 77032, Tel: (713) 443-3370
(Mfr/serv downhole drilling equip)
   Smith Internacional de Venezuela CA, Carretera Via Los Pilones Km. 1, Anco,
      Edo. Anzoatequi, Venezuela

SONOCO PRODUCTS CO   North Second St, PO Box 160, Hartsville, SC 29550,
Tel: (803) 383-7000
(Mfr packaging for consumer & ind mkt)
   Sonoco de Venezuela CA, Apartado de Correos 1250, Maracay (Edo. Aragua), Venezuela

STEWART & STEVENSON SERVICES INC   2707 N Loop W, Houston, TX 77008,
Tel: (713) 868-7700
(Design/mfr customized diesel & turbine power sys)
   Stewart & Stevenson de Venezuela SA, Km. 4.5 Carretera Canada, Apartado 1087,
      Maracaibo, Venezuela

STIEFEL LABORATORIES INC   255 Alhambra Circle, Coral Gables, FL 33134,
Tel: (305) 443-3807
(Mfr pharmaceuticals, dermatological specialties)
   Laboratorios Stiefel de Venezuela SA, Urban. Industrial Guayabal,
      Edif. Ind. Andrade Pools, piso 3, Guarenas, Edo Miranda, Venezuela

STOKES DIV   5500 Tabor Rd, Philadelphia, PA 19120, Tel: (215) 289-5671
(Vacuum pumps & components, vacuum dryers, oil-upgrading equip)
   Pennwalt Inter-Americana SA, Apartado 5004, Caracas 1010, Venezuela

TENNESSEE ASSOCIATES INTL   223 Associates Blvd, PO Box 710, Alcoa,
TN 37701-0710, Tel: (423) 982-9514
(Mgt consulting servs)
   Tennessee Associates de Venezuela CA, Av. Casanova 2nd a Calle de Bella Monte,
      Edif. La Paz, Off. G2, Caracas 1060, Venezuela

TIDEWATER INC   Tidewater Place, 1440 Canal St, New Orleans, LA 70112,
Tel: (504) 568-1010
(Marine serv & equip to companies engaged in explor, development & prod of oil, gas &
minerals)
   Tidewater Marine Service, Edif. Semarca, Av. Principal de la Ensenada,
      Dtto. Urdaneta, Estado Zulia, Maracaibo, Venezuela

TOPFLIGHT CORP   160 E 9th Ave, York, PA 17404, Tel: (717) 843-9901
(Commercial printing, service paper)
   Topflight de Venezuela CA (Tovenca), Calle Luis Camoens Edif. Industrial, Caracas,
      Venezuela

TOWERS PERRIN   245 Park Ave, New York, NY 10167, Tel: (212) 309-3400
(Management consultants)
   Towers, Perrin, Forster & Crosby, Apartado 50247, Caracas 1050A, Venezuela

TRANE CO   3600 Pammel Creek Rd, La Crosse, WI 54601, Tel: (608) 787-2000
(Mfr/distr/svce A/C sys & equip)
   Trane Caracas, Andre Narce, Apartado 62015, Chacao, Caracas 1060A, Venezuela

U S LIFE INSURANCE CO   125 Maiden Lane, New York, NY 10038,
Tel: (212) 425-8010
(Insurance)
   Seguros Venezuela CA, Edif. Luz Electrica, Av. Urdaneta, Caracas, Venezuela

UNION CARBIDE CORP   39 Old Ridgebury Rd, Danbury, CT 06817,
Tel: (203) 794-2000
(Mfr industrial chemicals, plastics, resins)
   Union Carbide Commercial CA, Apartado 60552, Caracas 1060A, Venezuela

UNISYS CORP   PO Box 500, Blue Bell, PA 19424, Tel: (215) 986-4011
(Mfg/mktg/serv electr info sys)
   Sperry CA, Av. 2 con 41a Transversal, Edif. Los Cortijos de Lourdes, Caracas 1071,
   Venezuela
   Unisys de Venezuela CA, Avda. Principal y Diego Cisnero, Edif. Centro Empresarial,
   Caracas 1071, Venezuela

UNITED TECHNOLOGIES CORP   United Technologies Bldg, Hartford, CT 06101,
Tel: (203) 728-7000
(Mfr aircraft engines, elevators, A/C, auto equip, space & military electr, rocket
propulsion sys)
   Ascensores Otis de Venezuela CA, Edif. Mene Grande, Piso 3,
      Av. Francisco de Miranda, Los Palos Grandes, Caracas 106, Venezuela

UPJOHN CO   7000 Portage Rd, Kalamazoo, MI 49001, Tel: (616) 323-4000
(Mfr pharms, agric prdts, ind chems)
   Laboratorios Upjohn CA, Edif. Ofinca, Calle Los Laboratorios, Los Ruices, Caracas,
   Venezuela

WACKENHUT CORP   1500 San Remo Ave, Coral Gables, FL 33146,
Tel: (305) 666-5656
(Security systems & services)
   Wackenhut de Venezuela SA, c/Serenos Victoria CA, Calle la Industria, Edif. Mijal,
      Urb. Palo Verde, Petare, Caracas, Venezuela

WARD HOWELL INTL INC   99 Park Ave, New York, NY 10016-1699,
Tel: (212) 697-3730
(Executive recruiting)
   Ward Howell Intl. Ponsowy, Tejeiro & Asociados, Apartado Postal 61650,
      Caracas 1060-A, Venezuela

WARNER-LAMBERT CO   201 Tabor Road, Morris Plains, NJ 07950,
Tel: (201) 540-2000
(Mfr ethical & proprietary pharms, confectionary & consumer prdts)
   Laboratorios Substancia CA, Apartado 5828, Caracas 1010A, Venezuela

WEATHERFORD INTL INC   1360 Post Oak Blvd, PO Box 27608, Houston,
TX 77227-7608, Tel: (713) 439-9400
(Oilfield servs, prdts & equip; mfr marine cranes)
   Weatherford Intl. Inc., c/o Servicios Technicos Oilwell SA,
      Av. Jose A. Anzoategui Km. 100, Anaco, Venezuela

THE WEST CO   101 Gordon Dr, PO Box 645, Lionville, PA 19341-0645,
Tel: (610) 594-2900
(Mfr prdts for filling, sealing, dispensing & delivering needs of health care &

consumer prdts mkts)
   The West Co., Caracas, Venezuela

WESTERN ATLAS INTL INC   10205 Westheimer, PO Box 1407, Houston,
  TX 77251-1407, Tel: (713) 266-5700
  (Full service to the oil industry)
    Western Atlas Logging Services, Edif. Multicentro Los Palos Grandes,
      Avda. A. Bello Cruce con Primera Transv., Caracas, Venezuela
    Western Atlas Logging Services, Avda. Penalver, Campo Dresser Atlas,
      352092 El Tigre, Edo. Anzoatequi, Venezuela
    Western Atlas Logging Services, Avda. Intercommunal, Via Terminales Maracaibo,
      Las Morochas, Edo. Zulia, Venezuela
    Western Geophysical, Edif. Seguros Venezuela, Piso 5, Av. Francisco de Miranda,
      Chacaito, Caracas, Venezuela

WIX FILTRATION PRODUCTS   1301 E Ozark Ave, Gastonia, NC 28052,
  Tel: (704) 864-6711
  (Mfr oil, air & water filters)
    CA Danaven, Aptdo. 766, Avda. Irribaren Borges, Zona Industrial Sur, Valencia,
    Venezuela

WORLD COURIER INC   46 Trinity Pl, New York, NY 10006, Tel: (718) 978-9400
  (Intl courier serv)
    World Courier de Venezuela, Transportes Urgentes Transur, Av. el Bosque,
      Qtz. Los Indra 7-13, La Florida, Caracas, Venezuela

XEROX CORP   800 Long Ridge Rd, PO Box 1600, Stamford, CT 06904,
  Tel: (203) 968-3000
  (Mfr document processing equip, sys & supplies)
    Xerox Corp., Caracas, Venezuela

YORK INTERNATIONAL CORP   PO Box 1592, York, PA 17405-1592,
  Tel: (717) 771-7890
  (Mfr A/C, heating & refrig sys & equip)
    Yorkven SA, Apartado 88190, Caracas 1084A, Venezuela

VIETNAM

3M   3M Center, St Paul, MN 55144-1000, Tel: (612) 733-1110
  (Mfr diversified prdts for industry, health care, imaging, commun, transport, safety,
  consumer, etc)
    3M, Han Nam Bldg. Unit 2B1, 65 Nguyen Du St., District 1, Ho Chi Minh City, Vietnam

BANKAMERICA CORP   555 California St, San Francisco, CA 94104,
  Tel: (415) 622-3456
  (Financial services)
    Bank of America NT & SA, 27 Ly Thuong Kiet St., Hoan Kiem District, Hanoi, Vietnam

CARRIER CORP   One Carrier Place, Farmington, CT 06034-4015,
  Tel: (203) 674-3000
  (Mfr/distr/svce A/C, heating & refrigeration equip)
    Carrier Intl. Corp., 25 Ly Thuong Kiet, Hanoi, Vietnam

CITICORP   399 Park Ave, New York, NY 10043, Tel: (212) 559-1000
  (Banking & financial services)
    Citibank, Vietnam

CPC INTERNATIONAL INC   PO Box 8000, Englewood Cliffs, NJ 07632,
  Tel: (201) 894-4000
  (Consumer foods, corn refining)
    CPC Asia Ltd., TECASIN Business Centre, 243-243B Hoang Van Thu St.,
      District Tan Binh, Ho Chi Minh City, Vietnam

DANIEL MANN JOHNSON & MENDENHALL   3250 Wilshire Blvd, Los Angeles, CA 90010,
  Tel: (213) 381-3663
  (Architects & engineers)
    DMJM, B3/105B Ngoc Khanh St., Hanoi, Vietnam
    DMJM, c/o Transport Engineering Design Inc., 278 Ton Duc Thang St., Hanoi, Vietnam

FORD MOTOR CO   The American Road, Dearborn, MI 48121, Tel: (313) 322-3000
  (Mfr motor vehicles)
    Ford Motor Co./Song Cong Diesel, Hai Hung Province, Vietnam

GEMRUSA INC   135 E 50th St, #3E, New York, NY 10022, Tel: (212) 921-9888
  (Whl jewelry, trading commodities)
    Gemrusa Inc., 2 Phung Khac Khan, Ho Chi Minh City, Vietnam

GREY ADVERTISING INC   777 Third Ave, New York, NY 10017, Tel: (212) 546-2000
  (Advertising)
    Grey Vietnam, 78A Nguyen Van Troi St., Phu Nhuan District, Ho Chi Minh City, Vietnam

PARSONS ENGINEERING SCIENCE INC   100 W Walnut St, Pasadena, CA 91124,
  Tel: (818) 440-6000
  (Environmental engineering)
    Parsons Engineering Science Inc., c/o ENCO, 244 Dien Bien Phu St., District 3,
      Ho Chi Minh City, Vietnam

PHAM BROTHERS & CO   3759 Longchamp Circle, Tallahassee, FL 32308,
  Tel: (904) 668-7824
  (Business consulting)
    Pham Brothers & Co., 161A Tran Hung Dao, Q.1, Ho Chi Minh City, Vietnam

VINA USA INC   150 Fifth Ave, #524, New York, NY 10011, Tel: (212) 674-2763
  (Financial services)
    VINA U.S.A. Inc., 91 Nguyen Du, District 1, Ho Chi Minh City, Vietnam

WALES

ADVANCE MACHINE CO   14600 21st Ave N, Plymouth, MN 55447, Tel: (612) 473-2235
   (Ind floor cleaning equip)
     Advance Machine Co. Ltd., The Industrial Estate Llantrisant, Pontyclun,
       Mid Glamorgan CF7 8YZ, Wales

ALBERTO-CULVER CO   2525 Armitage Ave, Melrose Park, IL 60160,
   Tel: (708) 450-3000
   (Mfr/mktg personal care & beauty prdts, household & grocery prdts, institutional food
   prdts)
     Alberto-Culver Co. (UK) Ltd., Alberto Rd., Valley Way, Enterprise Park,
       Swansea SA6 8RG, Wales

ALLIED AFTERMARKET DIV   105 Pawtucket Ave, East Providence, RI 02916,
   Tel: (401) 434-7000
   (Mfr spark plugs, filters, brakes)
     Fram Europe Ltd., Llantrisant, Pontyclun, Glamorgan, Wales

AVERY DENNISON CORP   150 N Orange Grove Blvd, Pasadena, CA 91103,
   Tel: (818) 304-2000
   (Mfr pressure-sensitive adhesives & materials, office prdts, labels, tags, retail
   sys, spec chems)
     Metallised Films & Paper Ltd., Gilchrist Thomas Ind. Estate. Blaenavon,
       Gwent NP4 9RL, Wales

BLACK & VEATCH INTL   8400 Ward Pkwy, PO Box 8405, Kansas City, MO 64114,
   Tel: (913) 339-2000
   (Engineering/architectural servs)
     Binnie Black & Veatch, Pembroke House, Charter Court, Phoenix Way,
       Swansea Enterprise Park, Swansea SA7 9EH, Wales

BORG-WARNER AUTOMOTIVE INC   200 S Michigan Ave, Chicago, IL 60604,
   Tel: (312) 322-8500
   (Mfr automotive components; provider of security services)
     Borg-Warner Automotive GmbH, Kenfig Industrial Estate, Margam, Port Talbot,
       West Glamorgan SA13 2PG, Wales

CORNING INC   One Riverfront Plaza, Corning, NY 14831, Tel: (607) 974-9000
   (Mfr glass & specialty materials, consumer prdts; communications, lab services)
     Optical Fibres, Clywd, Wales

CURTISS-WRIGHT CORP   1200 Wall St W, Lyndhurst, NJ 07071, Tel: (201) 896-8400
   (Mfr precision components & sys, engineered svces to aerospace, flow control & marine
   ind)
     Metal Improvement Co. Inc., Parkway, Deeside Industrial Park, Deeside,
       Clwyd CH5 2NS, Wales

THE DEXTER CORP   1 Elm Street, Windsor Locks, CT   06096, Tel: (203) 627-9051
  (Mfr nonwovens, polymer prdts, magnetic materials, biotechnology)
    Dexter Packaging Products, Parkway, Deeside Industrial Park, Deeside,
      Clwyd CH5 2NN, Wales

ERIEZ MAGNETICS   PO Box 10652, Erie, PA   16514, Tel: (814) 833-9881
  (Mfr magnets, vibratory feeders, metal detectors, screeners/sizers, mining equip,
  current separators)
    Eriez Magnetics UK Ltd., Bedwas House Industrial Estate, Bedwas, Newport,
      Gwent NP1 8YG, Wales

HARMAN INTL INDUSTRIES INC   1101 Pennsylvania Ave NW, Washington, DC 20004,
  Tel: (202) 393-1101
  (Mfr audio & video equipment)
    Electro Acoustic Inds. Ltd., Bennett St., Bridgend Ind. Estate, Bridgend,
      Mid Glamorgan CF31 3SH, Wales

THE HARPER GROUP   260 Townsend St, PO Box 77933, San Francisco,
  CA 94107-1719, Tel: (415) 978-0600
  (Ocean/air freight fwdg, customs brokerage, packing & whse, logistics mgt, ins)
    Harper Freight Intl. (UK) Ltd., Cargo Terminal, Cardiff-Wales Airport,
      South Glamorgan CF6 9BD, Wales

HECKETT   PO Box 1071, Butler, PA   16001-1071, Tel: (412) 283-5741
  (Metal reclamation, steel mill services)
    Heckett, Llanwern Works, Llanwern, Newport, Gwent NP9 0XQ, Wales

H J HEINZ CO   PO Box 57, Pittsburgh, PA   15230-0057, Tel: (412) 456-5700
  (Processed food prdts & nutritional services)
    H.J. Heinz Co. Ltd., Deeside, Wales

JAMES RIVER CORP   PO Box 2218, Richmond, VA   23217, Tel: (804) 644-5411
  (Mfr paper & paper-related prdts)
    Dixie Benders Ltd., Wrexham, Wales

KAISER ALUMINUM & CHEMICAL CORP   6177 Sunol Blvd, Pleasanton, CA   94566,
  Tel: (510) 462-1122
  (Mfr aluminum & aluminum prdts, chems)
    Anglesey Aluminum Ltd., P.O. Box 4, Penrhos Works, Holyhead, Anglesey, Wales

KELLY SERVICES   999 W Big Beaver Rd, Troy, MI   48084, Tel: (810) 244-4313
  (Temporary help placement)
    Kelly Services (UK) Ltd., Wales

KYSOR INDUSTRIAL CORP   One Madison Ave, Cadillac, MI   49601-9785,
  Tel: (616) 779-2200
  (Mfr commercial refrigeration, commercial vehicle components)
    Kysor/Europe, Dyffryr Ind. Estate, Yotrad Myrach, Hingaed, Mid-Glamorgan CF8 7YH,
      Wales

METAL IMPROVEMENT CO   10 Forest Ave, Paramus, NJ   07652, Tel: (201) 843-7800
  (Mfr shot peening)
    Metal Improvement Co., Deeside Ind. Park, Clwyd CH5 2NS, Deeside, Wales

MONSANTO CO   800 N Lindbergh Blvd, St Louis, MO 63167, Tel: (314) 694-1000
(Mfr agric & food prdts, chems, plastics, fibers, pharms, process control equip,
performance material)
   Monsanto Co. Chemical Group, Ruabon, Wales

McCANN-ERICKSON WORLDWIDE   750 Third Ave, New York, NY 10017,
Tel: (212) 697-6000
(Advertising)
   McCann-Erickson Wales Ltd., Avon House, Stanwell Rd., Penarth,
   So. Glamorgan CR6 2XY, Wales

PENTAIR INC   1700 West Hwy 36, St Paul, MN 55113, Tel: (612) 636-7920
(Diversified mfg)
   Hoffman UK Ltd., P.O. Box 14, Llartarnam Park, Cwmbran, Gwent NP44 3XN, Wales

PORTEC INC   122 W 22nd St, #100, Oak Brook, IL 60521-1553,
Tel: (708) 573-4619
(Mfr engineered prdts for constr equip, material handling & railroad track components)
   Portec (UK) Ltd., Vauxhall Industrial Estate, Ruabon, Wrexham, Clwyd LL14 6UY, Wales

PRESTOLITE ELECTRIC INC   2100 Commonwealth, Ann Arbor, MI 48105,
Tel: (313) 913-6600
(Mfr alternators, DC motors, relays, switches)
   Prestolite Electric Ltd., Ipswich Rd., Cardiff CF3 7YP, Wales

ROCKWELL INTL CORP   2201 Seal Beach Blvd, PO Box 4250, Seal Beach,
CA 90740-8250, Tel: (310) 797-3311
(Prdts & serv for aerospace, automotive, electronics, graphics & automation inds)
   ROR Rockwell Ltd., Rackery Lane, Llay, Wrexham, Clwyd LL12 0PB, Wales

A SCHULMAN INC   3550 W Market St, Akron, OH 44333, Tel: (216) 666-3751
(Mfr/sale plastic resins & compounds)
   A. Schulman Inc. Ltd., Croespenmaen Ind. Estate, Crumlin, Newport, Gwent NP1 4AG,
   Wales

SEQUA CORP   200 Park Ave, New York, NY 10166, Tel: (212) 986-5500
(Mfr aerospace prdts & sys, machinery & metal coatings, spec chems, automotive prdts)
   Warwick Intl. Group Ltd., Mostyn Dock, Mostyn, Holywell, Clwyd CH8 9HE, Wales

SIGNODE PACKAGING SYSTEMS   3600 W Lake Ave, Glenview, IL 60025,
Tel: (708) 724-6100
(Mfr packaging systems)
   Signode Pan-European Container Industry Systems, Queensway, Fforestfach,
   Swansea SA5 4ED, Wales

SILICONIX INC   2201 Laurelwood Dr, Santa Clara, CA 95054, Tel: (408) 988-8000
(Semiconductor components)
   Siliconix Ltd., Morristown, Swansea SA6 6NE, Wales

TECH/OPS SEVCON INC   1 Beacon St, Boston, MA 02108, Tel: (617) 523-2030
(Mfr solid state controllers for elec powered vehicles)
   ICW Ltd., Miners Rd., Llay Industrial Estate, Wrexham, Clwyd LL12 0PJ, Wales

TRINOVA CORP   3000 Strayer, PO Box 50, Maumee, OH 43537-0050,
Tel: (419) 867-2200
(Mfr engr components & sys for ind)

(cont)

Aeroquip Ltd., P.O. Box 725, Ty Glas Industrial Estate, Malvern Dr.,
Cardiff CF4 5ZR, Wales

WALL COLMONOY CORP   30261 Stephenson Hwy, Madison Hghts, MI 48071,
Tel: (810) 585-6400
(Mfr hard-surfacing & brazing alloys, equip & services)
Wall Colmonoy Ltd., Pontardawe, Swansea, W. Glamorgan SA8 4HL, Wales

WOODHEAD INDUSTRIES INC   2150 E Lake Cook Rd, #400, Buffalo Grove, IL 60089,
Tel: (708) 465-8300
(Devel/mfr/sale/distr elect/electr, fiber optic & ergonomic special-function,
non-commodity prdts)
Aero-Motive (UK) Ltd., Factory 9, Rassau Industrial Estate, Ebbw Vale,
Gwent NP3 5SD, Wales

YEMEN

CHEVRON CORP   225 Bush St, San Francisco, CA 94104, Tel: (415) 894-7700
(Oil & gas exploration, production, refining, products; oilfield & financial services)
Chevron Corp., all mail to U.S. address

THE CLOROX CO   1221 Broadway, PO Box 24305, Oakland, CA 94623-1305,
Tel: (510) 271-7000
(Mfr domestic consumer packaged prdts)
United Cleaning Products Mfg. Co. Ltd., Sana'a, Yemen

GLOBAL INTERNATIONAL   1304 Willow St, Martinez, CA 94553, Tel: (510) 229-9330
(International moving & forwarding)
Yemen Kuwait Forwarding Co. Inc., P.O. Box 11145, San'a, Yemen

ITT SHERATON CORP   60 State St, Boston, MA 02108, Tel: (617) 367-3600
(Hotel operations)
San'a Sheraton Hotel, Green Hill, Ring Rd., P.O. Box 2467, San'a, Yemen

PARKER DRILLING CO   8 E Third St, Tulsa, OK 74103-3637, Tel: (918) 585-8221
(Drilling contractor)
Parker Drilling Co. Kuwait Ltd., P.O. Box 19299, San'a Yemen

RADISSON HOTELS INTL   Carlson Pkwy, PO Box 59159, Minneapolis,
MN 55459-8204, Tel: (612) 540-5526
(Hotels)
Movenpick Hotel, Khormaksar, P.O. Box 6111, Aden, Yemen

WESTERN ATLAS INTL INC   10205 Westheimer, PO Box 1407, Houston,
  TX 77251-1407, Tel: (713) 266-5700
  (Full service to the oil industry)
    Western Geophysical, 34 Khartoum St. (Mujahid), P.O. Box 19451, Sana'a, Yemen

YUGOSLAVIA

ADAMAS CARBIDE CORP   Market & Passaic St, Kenilworth, NJ 07033,
  Tel: (201) 241-1000
  (Metal prdts)
    Adamas Carbide Corp., Futoski Put 8, 21000 Novi Sad, Yugoslavia

BANKERS TRUST CO   280 Park Ave, New York, NY 10017, Tel: (212) 250-2500
  (Banking)
    Bankers Trust Co. Intl., Terazije 3, 11000 Belgrade, Yugoslavia

CPC INTERNATIONAL INC   PO Box 8000, Englewood Cliffs, NJ 07632,
  Tel: (201) 894-4000
  (Consumer foods, corn refining)
    IPOK, Pancevacka 70, YU-23103 Zrenjanin, Yugoslavia

GENERAL ELECTRIC CO   3135 Easton Tpk, Fairfield, CT 06431,
  Tel: (203) 373-2211
  (Diversified manufacturing, technology & services)
    GE Technical Services Co.,
      all mail to U.S. address; phone (800) 626-2004 or (518) 438-6500

GENERAL MOTORS CORP   3044 W Grand Blvd, Detroit, MI 48202-3091,
  Tel: (313) 556-5000
  (Mfr full line vehicles, automotive electronics, coml technologies, telecom, space,
  finance)
    Industria Delova Automobila, Kikinda, Yugoslavia

HYATT INTL CORP   200 West Madison, Chicago, IL 60606, Tel: (312) 750-1234
  (Intl hotel mgmt)
    Hyatt Intl. Hotels, Belgrade, Yugoslavia

INTERMEC CORP   6001 36th Ave West, PO Box 4280, Everett, WA 98203-9280,
  Tel: (206) 348-2600
  (Mfr/distr automated data collection sys)
    ID Sistemi, S.C. Zvezdara, Vjekoslava Kovaca 11, 10050 Belgrade, Yugoslavia

MARATHON LE TOURNEAU CO   PO Box 2307, Longview, TX 75606, Tel: (903) 237-7000
  (Mfr heavy constr, mining mach & equip)
    Jugotechna, Kolarceva Str. 7, 1100 Belgrade, Yugoslavia

SEA-LAND SERVICE INC   150 Allen Rd, Liberty Corner, NJ 07920,
Tel: (201) 558-6000
(Container transport)
Sea-Land Service, P.O. Box 298, Knez Mihajlova, 11001 Belgrade, Yugoslavia

SPI PHARMACEUTICALS INC   ICN Plaza, 3300 Hyland Ave, Costa Mesa, CA 92626,
Tel: (714) 545-0100
(Mfr pharms, biochems, radioactive materials)
Galenika, Batajnicki put 66, 11080 Zemur, Belgrade, Yugoslavia

THE WEST CO   101 Gordon Dr, PO Box 645, Lionville, PA 19341-0645,
Tel: (610) 594-2900
(Mfr prdts for filling, sealing, dispensing & delivering needs of health care &
consumer prdts mkts)
The West Co., Kovin, Yugoslavia

XEROX CORP   800 Long Ridge Rd, PO Box 1600, Stamford, CT 06904,
Tel: (203) 968-3000
(Mfr document processing equip, sys & supplies)
Xerox Corp., Belgrade, Yugoslavia

ZAIRE

CITICORP   399 Park Ave, New York, NY 10043, Tel: (212) 559-1000
(Banking & financial services)
Citibank NA, Zaire

CROWN CORK & SEAL CO INC   9300 Ashton Rd, Philadelphia, PA 19136,
Tel: (215) 698-5100
(Mfr cans, bottle caps; filling & packaging mach)
Crown Cork Co., Boite Postale 2684, Lubumbashi, Zaire

GENERAL MOTORS CORP   3044 W Grand Blvd, Detroit, MI 48202-3091,
Tel: (313) 556-5000
(Mfr full line vehicles, automotive electronics, coml technologies, telecom, space,
finance)
General Motors Zaire SARL, Boite Postale 11199, Kinshasa, Zaire

ITT CORP   1330 Ave of the Americas, New York, NY 10019-5490,
Tel: (212) 258-1000
(Design/mfr communications & electronic equip, hotels, insurance)
ITT Bell Telephone Co., Boite Postale 11210, Kin 1, Kinshasa, Zaire

ITT SHERATON CORP   60 State St, Boston, MA 02108, Tel: (617) 367-3600
(Hotel operations)
Karavia Sheraton, Boite Postale 4701, Lumbumbashi, Zaire

MOBIL CORP   3225 Gallows Rd, Fairfax, VA 22037-0001, Tel: (703) 846-3000
(Petroleum explor & refining, mfr petrol prdts, chems, petrochems)
   Zaire Mobil Oil, 3900 PC Ave. de la Republic du Tchad, Face Au Memling,
      Boite Postale 2400, Kinshasa, Zaire

PLUSWOOD INC   PO Box 2248, Oshkosh, WI 54903, Tel: (414) 235-0440
(Hardwood plywood paneling, etc)
   Pluswood Inc., Kinshasa, Zaire

UPJOHN CO   7000 Portage Rd, Kalamazoo, MI 49001, Tel: (616) 323-4000
(Mfr pharms, agric prdts, ind chems)
   Upjohn Intl. Co., 483 Ave. Zinnias Limite, Boite Postale 894, Kinshasa, Zaire

ZAMBIA

AIR EXPRESS INTL CORP   120 Tokeneke Rd, PO Box 1231, Darien, CT 06820,
   Tel: (203) 655-7900
   (Air frt forwarder)
      Air Express Intl., Interchem Bldg., Plot 2401, Kabelenga Road, Lusaka, Zambia

ARBOR ACRES FARM INC   439 Marlborough Rd, Glastonbury, CT 06033,
   Tel: (860) 633-4681
   (Producers of male & female broiler breeders, commercial egg layers)
      Hybrid Poultry Farm Ltd., P.O. Box CH 97, Chelston, Lusaka, Zambia

BECHTEL GROUP INC   50 Beale St, PO Box 3965, San Francisco, CA 94119,
   Tel: (415) 768-1234
   (Engineering & constr)
      Bechtel Intl. Corp., P.O. Box RW 198, Lusaka, Zambia

SAMUEL BINGHAM CO   1555 N Mittel Blvd, #T, Wood Dale, IL 60191-1046,
   Tel: (708) 238-4000
   (Print & industrial rollers, inks)
      Coates Brothers (Zambia) Ltd., P.O. Box 230025, Ulengo Rd., Ndola, Zambia

BURLINGTON AIR EXPRESS   18200 Van Karman Ave, Irvine, CA 92715,
   Tel: (714) 752-4000
   (Air freight)
      Burlington Air Express Zambia, Longolongo Rd., P.O. Box 35063, Lusaka, Zambia

CALTEX PETROLEUM CORP   PO Box 619500, Dallas, TX 75261, Tel: (214) 830-1000
   (Petroleum prdts)
      Caltex Oil Zambia Ltd., 1711 Mungwi Rd., Lusaka, Zambia

CITICORP   399 Park Ave, New York, NY 10043, Tel: (212) 559-1000
   (Banking & financial services)
      Citibank, Zambia

THE COCA-COLA CO   PO Drawer 1734, Atlanta, GA 30301, Tel: (404) 676-2121
  (Mfr/mkt/distr soft drinks, syrups & concentrates, juice & juice-drink prdts)
    Zambia Bottlers Ltd., all mail to U.S. address

COLGATE-PALMOLIVE CO   300 Park Ave, New York, NY 10022, Tel: (212) 310-2000
  (Mfr pharms, cosmetics, toiletries, detergents)
    Colgate-Palmolive Ltd., P.O. Box 2071, Ndola, Zambia

CROWN CORK & SEAL CO INC   9300 Ashton Rd, Philadelphia, PA 19136,
  Tel: (215) 698-5100
  (Mfr cans, bottle caps; filling & packaging mach)
    Crown Cork Co. Ltd., P.O. Box 1564, Ndola, Zambia

EATON CORP   1111 Superior Ave, Cleveland, OH 44114, Tel: (216) 523-5000
  (Advanced tech prdts for transp & ind mkts)
    Cutler Hammer Ltd., P.O. Box 1779, Kitwe, Zambia

FOUR WINDS INTL GROUP   1500 SW First Ave, #850, Portland, OR 97201,
  Tel: (503) 241-2732
  (Transp of household goods & general cargo, third party logistics)
    Four Winds Zambia, Zega Terminal, Plot 197M, Lusaka Intl. Airport, Lusaka, Zambia

ITT CORP   1330 Ave of the Americas, New York, NY 10019-5490,
  Tel: (212) 258-1000
  (Design/mfr communications & electronic equip, hotels, insurance)
    ITT Zambia Ltd., P.O. Box 2420, Lusaka, Zambia

JOHNSON & JOHNSON   One Johnson & Johnson Plaza, New Brunswick, NJ 08933,
  Tel: (908) 524-0400
  (R&D/mfr/sale health care prdts)
    Johnson & Johnson Ltd., P.O. Box 71810, Ndola, Zambia

MINE SAFETY APPLIANCES CO   PO Box 426, Pittsburgh, PA 15230,
  Tel: (421) 273 5000
  (Safety equip, ind filters)
    Mine Safety Appliances Zambia Ltd., P.O. Box 70027, Ndola, Zambia

MOBIL CORP   3225 Gallows Rd, Fairfax, VA 22037-0001, Tel: (703) 846-3000
  (Petroleum explor & refining, mfr petrol prdts, chems, petrochems)
    Mobil Oil Zambia Ltd., P.O. Box 70222, Mobil House, Bwana Mkubwa, Ndola, Zambia

PFIZER INC   235 E 42nd St, New York, NY 10017-5755, Tel: (212) 573-2323
  (Mfr healthcare products)
    Pfizer Ltd., Zambia

PHELPS DODGE CORP   2600 N Central Ave, Phoenix, AZ 85004-3014,
  Tel: (602) 234-8100
  (Copper, minerals, metals & spec engineered prdts for trans & elect mkts)
    Metal Fabricators of Zambia Ltd., P.O. Box 90295, Luanshya, Zambia

STANLEY CONSULTANTS INC   225 Iowa Ave, Muscatine, IA 52761,
  Tel: (319) 264-6600
  (Engineering, architectural, planning & management services)
    Sheladia/Stanley/Burrow, P.O. Box 31923, Kalima Tower 10/F, Katunjila Rd., Lusaka,
    Zambia

ZIMBABWE

3M   3M Center, St Paul, MN 55144-1000, Tel: (612) 733-1110
(Mfr diversified prdts for industry, health care, imaging, commun, transport, safety, consumer, etc)
  3M Zimbabwe (Pvt.) Ltd., 23 George Dr., Beverly East, Amby, Msasa, Harare, Zimbabwe

AIR EXPRESS INTL CORP   120 Tokeneke Rd, PO Box 1231, Darien, CT 06820,
  Tel: (203) 655-7900
  (Air frt forwarder)
  Air Express Intl., Cargo Agents Bldg., Harare Airport, Harare, Zimbabwe

AMERICAN OPTICAL CORP   14 Mechanic St, Southbridge, MA 01550,
  Tel: (508) 765-9711
  (Mfr opthalmic lenses & frames, custom molded prdts, specialty lenses)
    M. Wiseman & Co. (Zimbabwe) Ltd., Khatri Bldg., Cor. Speke Ave. & 4th St.,
    P.O. Box 2335, Harare, Zimbabwe

ARBOR ACRES FARM INC   439 Marlborough Rd, Glastonbury, CT 06033,
  Tel: (860) 633-4681
  (Producers of male & female broiler breeders, commercial egg layers)
    Arbor Acres Ltd., P.O. Box W99, Waterfalls, Harare, Zimbabwe

CALTEX PETROLEUM CORP   PO Box 619500, Dallas, TX 75261, Tel: (214) 830-1000
  (Petroleum prdts)
    Caltex Oil Zimbabwe (Pvt.) Ltd., Southampton House, 1st St. & Union Ave., Harare,
    Zimbabwe

CHINET CO   101 Merritt 7, Norwalk, CT 06851, Tel: (203) 846-1499
  (Mfr molded containers)
    Van Leer Zimbabwe Pvt. Ltd., P.O. Box ST 193, Southerton, Harare, Zimbabwe

COLUMBUS McKINNON CORP   140 John James Audubon Pkwy, Amherst, NY 14228-1197,
  Tel: (716) 696-3212
  (Mfr chains, forgings, hoists, tire shredders, manipulators)
    Columbus McKinnon (Pvt.) Ltd., 7029 Plymouth Rd., P.O. Box ST 399, Southerton,
    Harare, Zimbabwe

CROWN CORK & SEAL CO INC   9300 Ashton Rd, Philadelphia, PA 19136,
  Tel: (215) 698-5100
  (Mfr cans, bottle caps; filling & packaging mach)
    Crown Cork Co. Ltd., P.O. Box 3629, Harare, Zimbabwe

CUMMINS ENGINE CO INC   PO Box 3005, Columbus, IN 47202, Tel: (812) 377-5000
  (Mfr diesel engines)
    Cummins Diesel Intl. Ltd., P.O. Box 8440, Causeway, Harare, Zimbabwe

DATAEASE INTL INC   7 Cambridge Dr, Trumbull, CT   06611, Tel: (203) 374-8000
(Mfr applications devel software)
     Compuserve Pvt. Ltd., Pegasus House 5/F, Samora Machel Ave., Harare, Zimbabwe

EASTMAN KODAK CO   343 State St, Rochester, NY   14650, Tel: (716) 724-4000
(Devel/mfr photo & chem prdts, info mgmt/video/copier sys, fibers/plastics for various ind)
     Kodak (Zimbabwe) Ltd., P.O. Box 2170, Kodak House, 86 Samora Machel Ave., Harare, Zimbabwe

THE GILLETTE CO   Prudential Tower, Boston, MA   02199, Tel: (617) 421-7000
(Devel/mfr personal care/use prdts: blades & razors, toiletries, cosmetics, stationery)
     Gillette Central Africa (Pvt.) Ltd., Bulawayo, Zimbabwe

H J HEINZ CO   PO Box 57, Pittsburgh, PA   15230-0057, Tel: (412) 456-5700
(Processed food prdts & nutritional services)
     Chegutu Canners (Pvt.) Ltd., Chegutu, Zimbabwe
     Olivine Industries (Pvt.) Ltd., Harare, Zimbabwe

ITT SHERATON CORP   60 State St, Boston, MA   02108, Tel: (617) 367-3600
(Hotel operations)
     Harare Sheraton Hotel, P.O. Box 3033, Harare, Zimbabwe

JOHNSON & JOHNSON   One Johnson & Johnson Plaza, New Brunswick, NJ   08933, Tel: (908) 524-0400
(R&D/mfr/sale health care prdts)
     Johnson & Johnson (Pvt.) Ltd., P.O. Box 3355, Harare, Zimbabwe

LINTAS:WORLDWIDE   1 Dag Hammarskjold Plaza, New York, NY   10017, Tel: (212) 605-8000
(Advertising agency)
     Lintas:Zimbabwe, Lintas House, 46 Union Ave., Harare, Zimbabwe

MINE SAFETY APPLIANCES CO   PO Box 426, Pittsburgh, PA   15230, Tel: (421) 273 5000
(Safety equip, ind filters)
     MSA Zimbabwe (Pvt.) Ltd., P.O. Box AY 280, Amby, Harare, Zimbabwe

NATIONAL CAR RENTAL SYSTEM INC   7700 France Ave S, Minneapolis, MN   55435, Tel: (612) 830-2121
(Car rental)
     National Car Rental, Mayco House, 10th & Fife Ave., Airport Arrival Hall, Bulawayo, Zimbabwe
     National Car Rental, other locations in Zimbabwe

OTIS ELEVATOR CO   10 Farm Springs, Farmington, CT   06032, Tel: (860) 676-6528
(Mfr elevators & escalators)
     Otis Elevator Co. (Zimbabwe) Pvt. Ltd., 16 South Ave., P.O. Box 3890, Harare, Zimbabwe

PFIZER INC   235 E 42nd St, New York, NY   10017-5755, Tel: (212) 573-2323
(Mfr healthcare products)
     Pfizer (Pvt.) Ltd., Zimbabwe

STANDARD COMMERCIAL CORP   PO Box 450, Wilson, NC 27893, Tel: (919) 291-5507
(Leaf tobacco dealers/processors, wool processors)
  Tobacco Processors (Pvt.) Ltd., Harare, Zimbabwe
  Trans-Continental Leaf Tobacco Co. (Central Africa) Ltd., Harare, Zimbabwe

UNION CAMP CORP   1600 Valley Rd, Wayne, NJ 07470, Tel: (201) 628-2000
(Mfr paper, packaging, chems, wood prdts)
  Bush Boake Allen Zimbabwe (Pvt.) Ltd., 11 Coventry St., Belmont, Bulawayo, Zimbabwe

UNION CARBIDE CORP   39 Old Ridgebury Rd, Danbury, CT 06817,
Tel: (203) 794-2000
(Mfr industrial chemicals, plastics, resins)
  UC Management Services (Pvt.) Ltd., Level 6, Pegasus House, Samora Machel Ave.,
    Harare, Zimbabwe

UNIVERSAL CORP   PO Box 25099, Richmond, VA 23260, Tel: (804) 359-9311
(Holding co: tobacco, commodities)
  Zimleaf Holdings Ltd., P.O. Box 1597, Harare, Zimbabwe